Published by Collins
An imprint of HarperCollins Publishers
Westerhill Road
Bishopbriggs
Glasgow G64 2QT

Seventh edition 2016

ISBN 978-0-00-814179-0

10 9 8 7 6 5 4 3

© HarperCollins Publishers 2009, 2012, 2016

Collins® is a registered trademark
of HarperCollins Publishers Limited

www.collinsdictionary.com
www.collins.co.uk/languagesupport

Typeset by Davidson Publishing
Solutions, Glasgow

Printed in Italy by Grafica Veneta S.p.A.

Entered words that we have reason to
believe constitute trademarks have
been designated as such. However,
neither the presence nor absence of
such designation should be regarded
as affecting the legal status of any
trademark.

The contents of this publication
are believed correct at the time of
printing. Nevertheless the Publisher
can accept no responsibility for errors
or omissions, changes in the detail
given or for any expense or loss
thereby caused.

HarperCollins does not warrant
that any website mentioned in this
title will be provided uninterrupted,
that any website will be error free,
that defects will be corrected, or that
the website or the server that makes
it available are free of viruses or bugs.
For full terms and conditions please
refer to the site terms provided on
the website.

A catalogue record for this book is
available from the British Library.

If you would like to comment on any
aspect of this book, please contact us
at the given address or online.
E-mail: dictionaries@harpercollins.co.uk
 facebook.com/collinsdictionary
 @collinsdict

Acknowledgements

We would like to thank those authors
and publishers who kindly gave
permission for copyright material to be
used in the Collins Corpus. We would
also like to thank Times Newspapers
Ltd for providing valuable data.

Editors: Ian Brookes, Mary O'Neill
For the publisher: Gerry Breslin,
Hannah Dove, Kerry Ferguson

Contents

How to use this Dictionary and Thesaurus

Main entry words from the Dictionary with a corresponding
entry in the Thesaurus are marked with a ❶.

The thesaurus gives the main entry word in bold black, followed
by its part of speech and a list of synonyms. Key synonyms are
preceded by an **=** symbol and highlighted in bold. Antonyms
are preceded by a **≠** symbol and are highlighted in bold.

Synonyms belonging to different meanings of the word are
separated by a semicolon, and a change in part of speech is
indicated by an arrow, eg

> **account** *n* = **description**, report, story,
>   statement, version; = **importance**,
>   standing, concern/value, note
>   ▷ *v* = **consider**, rate, value, judge,
>   estimate

Abbreviations

abbrev	abbreviation	Lit	Literary
adj	adjective	masc	masculine
adv	adverb	Maths	Mathematics
Afr	African	Med	Medicine
Anat	Anatomy	Mil	Military
arch	Archaic	Mus	Music
Aust	Australian	Myth	Mythology
Bot	Botany	n	noun
Brit	Britain, British	N	North(ern)
Canad	Canadian	Naut	Nautical
cap.	capital	NZ	New Zealand
Chem	Chemistry	obs	Obsolete
comb.	combining	offens	Offensive
conj	conjuction	oft.	often
Comp	Computers	orig.	originally
dial	Dialect	Pathol	Pathology
E	East(ern)	pert.	pertaining
Eng	England, English	Photog	Photography
e.g.	for example	pl	plural
esp.	especially	Poet	Poetic
etc.	et cetera	prep	preposition
fem	feminine	pron	pronoun
fig	Figurative	S Afr	South African
foll.	followed	S	South(ern)
Fr	French	Scot	Scottish
Geog	Geography	sing.	singular
Hist	History	Sl	slang
Inf	Informal	US	United States
interj	interjection	usu.	usually
kg	kilogram(s)	v	verb
km	kilometre(s)	Vulg	Vulgar
Lat	Latin	W	West(ern)
lb(s)	pound(s)		

a

a, an *adj* **1** the indefinite article meaning one **2** *an* is used before vowels

AA 1 Alcoholics Anonymous **2** Automobile Association

aardvark *n* S Afr. anteater

aback *adv* **taken aback** startled

abandon ❶ *v* **1** desert **2** give up ▷ *n* **3** freedom from inhibitions etc. **abandoned** *adj* **1** deserted **2** uninhibited **3** wicked

abase *v* humiliate, degrade

abashed *adj* ashamed

abate *v* make or become less

abattoir *n* slaughterhouse

abbey ❶ *n* **1** community of monks or nuns **2** abbey church **abbot** *n* head of monastery

abbreviate *v* shorten **abbreviation** *n* shortened word or phrase

abdicate *v* give up (throne etc.)

abdomen *n* belly **abdominal** *adj*

abduct ❶ *v* carry off, kidnap

aberration *n* **1** deviation from normal **2** lapse

abet *v* **abetting, abetted** help, esp. in doing wrong

abeyance *n* **in abeyance** not in use

abhor *v* **-horring, -horred** loathe **abhorrence** *n* **abhorrent** *adj*

abide ❶ *v* **1** endure **2** *(Obs)* reside **abide by** obey

ability ❶ *n, pl* **-ties** competence, power

abject *adj* **1** wretched **2** servile

ablaze *adj* burning

able ❶ *adj* capable, competent, or talented **ably** *adv*

abnormal ❶ *adj* **1** not usual or typical **2** odd **abnormally** *adv* **abnormality** *n*

aboard *adv* on, onto ship, train, or aircraft

————— THESAURUS —————

abandon *v* = **leave**, strand, ditch, forsake, run out on; = **stop**, give up, halt, pack in *(Brit Inf)*, discontinue **≠ continue** ▷ *n* = **recklessness**, wildness **≠ restraint**

abbey *n* = **monastery**, convent, priory, nunnery, friary

abduct *v* = **kidnap**, seize, carry off, snatch *(Sl)*

abide *v* = **tolerate**, suffer, accept, bear, endure

ability *n* = **capability**, potential, competence, proficiency **≠ inability**; = **skill**, talent, expertise, competence, aptitude

able *adj* = **capable**, qualified, efficient, accomplished, competent **≠ incapable**

abnormal *adj* = **unusual**, different, odd, strange, extraordinary **≠ normal**

abolish ❶ v do away with
abolition n
Aborigine n original inhabitant of
Australia
abort ❶ v 1 terminate (a
pregnancy) prematurely 2 end
prematurely and unsuccessfully
abortion n **abortive** adj
unsuccessful
abound ❶ v be plentiful
about ❶ adv 1 on all sides
2 nearly 3 astir ▷ prep 4 round
5 near 6 concerning **about-turn**
n turn to the opposite direction
above ❶ adv 1 higher up ▷ prep
2 over 3 higher than, more than
4 beyond
abrasion n 1 place scraped (e.g.
on skin) 2 a wearing down
abrasive n 1 substance for
grinding, polishing etc. ▷ adj
2 causing abrasion 3 grating

abreast adv side by side
abridge v shorten
abroad ❶ adv 1 to or in a foreign
country 2 at large
abrupt ❶ adj 1 sudden 2 blunt
3 steep **abruptly** adv
abscess n gathering of pus
abscond v leave secretly
absent ❶ adj 1 away 2 missing
▷ v 3 keep away **absence** n
absentee n one who stays away
absently adv
absolute ❶ adj 1 complete
2 unrestricted 3 pure **absolutely**
adv 1 completely ▷ interj
2 certainly
absolve v free from, pardon
absorb ❶ v 1 suck up 2 engross
3 take in **absorption** n
absorbent adj
abstain v refrain **abstention** n
abstinence n

————————————————— THESAURUS —————————————————

abolish v = **do away with**, end,
destroy, eliminate, cancel
≠ establish
abort v = **terminate** (a pregnancy),
miscarry; = **stop**, end, finish, check,
arrest
abound v = **be plentiful**, thrive,
flourish, be numerous, proliferate
about prep = **regarding**, on,
concerning, dealing with, referring
to; = **near**, around, close to, nearby,
beside ▷ adv = **approximately**,
around, almost, nearly,
approaching
above prep = **over**, upon, beyond,
on top of, exceeding **≠ under**;
= **senior to**, over, ahead of, in
charge of, higher than

abroad adv = **overseas**, out of the
country, in foreign lands,
everywhere, here and there
abrupt adj = **sudden**, unexpected,
rapid, surprising, quick **≠ slow**;
= **curt**, brief, short, rude, impatient
≠ polite
absent adj = **away**, missing, gone,
elsewhere, unavailable **≠ present**;
= **absent-minded**, blank, vague,
distracted, vacant **≠ alert**
absolute adj = **complete**, total,
perfect, pure, sheer; = **supreme**,
sovereign, unlimited, ultimate,
full
absorb v = **soak up**, suck up,
receive, digest, imbibe; = **engross**,
involve, engage, fascinate, rivet

abstemious *adj* sparing in eating and drinking

abstract ❶ *adj* **1** existing only in the mind **2** not concrete ▷ *n* **3** summary ▷ *v* **4** remove **5** summarize **abstracted** *adj* preoccupied **abstraction** *n*

abstruse *adj* hard to understand

absurd ❶ *adj* ridiculous **absurdity** *n*

abundant ❶ *adj* plentiful **abundantly** *adv* **abundance** *n* great amount

abuse ❶ *v* **1** misuse **2** address rudely ▷ *n* **3** wrong treatment **4** insulting comments **abusive** *adj* **abusively** *adv*

abut *v* **abutting, abutted** adjoin

abysmal *adj* **1** immeasurable, very great **2** (*Inf*) extremely bad **abysmally** *adv*

abyss *n* very deep gulf or pit

AC alternating current

acacia *n* gum-yielding tree or shrub

academy *n, pl* **-mies 1** society to advance arts or sciences **2** institution for specialized training **3** (*Scot*) secondary school **academic** *adj* **1** of a place of learning **2** theoretical ▷ *n* **3** member of college or university

accede *v* **1** agree **2** attain (office etc.)

accelerate ❶ *v* (cause to) increase speed **acceleration** *n* **accelerator** *n* mechanism to increase speed

accent ❶ *n* **1** stress or pitch in speaking **2** mark to show this **3** style of pronunciation ▷ *v* **4** emphasize

accentuate *v* stress, emphasize

accept ❶ *v* **1** take, receive **2** admit, believe **3** agree to **acceptable** *adj* **acceptance** *n*

access ❶ *n* **1** right or means of entry ▷ *v* **2** (*Comp*) obtain (data) **accessible** *adj* easy to approach **accessibility** *n*

—— THESAURUS ——

abstract *adj* = **theoretical**, general, academic, speculative, indefinite ≠ **actual** ▷ *n* = **summary**, résumé, outline, digest, epitome ≠ **expansion** ▷ *v* = **extract**, draw, pull, remove, separate ≠ **add**

absurd *adj* = **ridiculous**, crazy (*Inf*), silly, foolish, ludicrous ≠ **sensible**

abundant *adj* = **plentiful**, full, rich, liberal, generous ≠ **scarce**

abuse *n* = **maltreatment**, damage, injury, hurt, harm; = **insults**, blame, slights,

put-downs, censure; = **misuse**, misapplication ▷ *v* = **ill-treat**, damage, hurt, injure, harm ≠ **care for**; = **insult**, offend, curse, put down, malign ≠ **praise**

accelerate *v* = **increase**, grow, advance, extend, expand ≠ **fall**

accent *n* = **pronunciation**, tone, articulation, inflection, brogue ▷ *v* = **emphasize**, stress, highlight, underline, underscore

accept *v* = **receive**, take, gain, pick up, secure

access *n* = **admission**, entry, passage

accession n 1 attaining of office, right etc. 2 addition

accessory ❶ n, pl -ries 1 supplementary part of car, woman's dress etc. 2 person assisting crime

accident ❶ n 1 event happening by chance 2 mishap, esp. causing injury **accidental** adj **accidentally** adv

acclaim ❶ v 1 applaud, praise ▷ n 2 applause **acclamation** n

acclimatize v accustom to new climate or environment

accolade n 1 public approval 2 honour 3 token of knighthood

accommodate ❶ v 1 supply, esp. with lodging 2 oblige 3 adapt **accommodating** adj obliging **accommodation** n lodgings

accompany ❶ v -nying, -nied 1 go with 2 supplement 3 occur with 4 play music to support a soloist **accompaniment** n

accomplice n one assisting another in crime

accomplish v 1 carry out 2 finish **accomplished** adj 1 complete 2 proficient

accord ❶ n 1 agreement, harmony ▷ v 2 (cause to) be in accord with 3 grant **according to** 1 as stated by 2 in conformity with **accordingly** adv 1 as the circumstances suggest 2 therefore

accordion n musical instrument with bellows and reeds

accost v approach and speak to

account ❶ n 1 report 2 importance 3 statement of moneys received, paid, or owed 4 person's money held in bank ▷ v 5 regard as 6 give reason, answer (for) **accountable** adj responsible **accountancy** n keeping, preparation of business accounts **accountant** n **accounting** n

accoutrements pl n 1 equipment, esp. military 2 trappings

accredited adj authorized, officially recognized

─────────────── THESAURUS ───────────────

accessory n = **extra**, addition, supplement, attachment, adjunct; = **accomplice**, partner, ally, associate (in crime), assistant

accident n = **crash**, smash, wreck, collision; = **misfortune**, disaster, tragedy, setback, calamity

acclaim v = **praise**, celebrate, honour, cheer, admire ▷ n = **praise**, honour, celebration, approval, tribute ≠ **criticism**

accommodate v = **house**, put up, take in, lodge, shelter; = **help**, support, aid, assist, cooperate

with; = **adapt**, fit, settle, alter, adjust

accompany v = **go with**, lead, partner, guide, attend; = **occur with**, belong to, come with, supplement, go together with

accord n = **treaty**, contract, agreement, arrangement, settlement

account n = **description**, report, story, statement, version; = **importance**, standing, concern/ value, note ▷ v = **consider**, rate, value, judge, estimate

a

accrue v -cruing, -crued 1 be added 2 result
accumulate ❶ v 1 gather 2 collect **accumulation** n
accurate ❶ adj exact, correct **accurately** adv **accuracy** n
accursed adj 1 under a curse 2 detestable
accuse ❶ v 1 charge with wrongdoing 2 blame **accusation** n
accustom ❶ v make used to, familiarize **accustomed** adj 1 usual 2 used (to) 3 in the habit (of)
ace ❶ n 1 one at dice, cards, dominoes 2 (Tennis) winning serve 3 (Inf) expert
acetylene n colourless, flammable gas
ache ❶ n 1 continuous pain ▷ v 2 to be in pain **aching** adj
achieve ❶ v accomplish, gain

achievement n
acid ❶ adj 1 sharp, sour ▷ n 2 (Chem) compound which combines with bases to form salts **acidic** adj **acidity** n
acknowledge ❶ v 1 admit, recognize 2 say one has received **acknowledgment, acknowledgement** n
acme n highest point
acne n pimply skin disease
acorn n fruit of the oak tree
acoustic adj of sound and hearing **acoustics** pl n 1 science of sounds 2 features of room or building as regards sounds heard in it
acquaint v make familiar, inform **acquaintance** n 1 person known 2 personal knowledge
acquiesce v agree, consent **acquiescence** n
acquire ❶ v gain, get **acquisition** n 1 act of getting 2 material gain

——— THESAURUS ———

accumulate v = build up, increase, be stored, collect, gather ≠ disperse
accurate adj = precise, close, correct, careful, strict ≠ inaccurate
accuse v = charge with, indict for, impeach for, censure with, incriminate for ≠ absolve
accustom v = familiarize, train, discipline, adapt, instruct
ace n (Cards, dice, etc.) = one, single point; (Inf) = expert, star, champion, authority, professional ▷ adj (Inf) = great, brilliant, fine, wonderful, excellent

ache v = hurt, suffer, burn, pain, smart ▷ n = pain, discomfort, suffering, hurt, throbbing (Inf)
achieve v = accomplish, fulfil, complete, gain, perform
acid adj = sour, tart, pungent, acerbic, acrid ≠ sweet; = sharp, cutting, biting, bitter, harsh ≠ kindly
acknowledge v = admit, own up, allow, accept, reveal ≠ deny; = greet, address, notice, recognize, salute ≠ snub; = reply to, answer, notice, recognize, respond to ≠ ignore
acquire v = get, win, buy, receive, gain ≠ lose

acquit ❶ v -quitting, -quitted
1 declare innocent **2** settle (a debt)
3 behave (oneself) **acquittal** n
acre n measure of land, 4840
square yards
acrid adj pungent, sharp
acrobat n one skilled in gymnastic
feats, esp. in circus etc. **acrobatic**
adj **acrobatics** pl n
acronym n word formed from
initial letters of other words
across adv/prep **1** crosswise
2 from side to side **3** on or to the
other side
acrylic n synthetic fibre
ACT Australian Capital Territory
act ❶ n **1** thing done, deed
2 doing **3** law or decree **4** section
of a play ▷ v **5** perform, as in a
play **6** exert force, work, as
mechanism **7** behave **acting**
adj temporary **action** n
1 operation **2** deed **3** gesture
4 expenditure of energy **5** battle
6 lawsuit **active** adj **1** in
operation **2** busy, occupied
3 brisk, energetic **activate** v
actively adv **activity** n **actor,**

actress n one who acts in a play,
film etc.
actual ❶ adj **1** existing in the
present **2** real **actuality** n
actually adv really, indeed
actuary n, pl -aries expert in
insurance statistics
actuate v activate
acumen n keen discernment
acupuncture n medical
treatment by insertion of needles
into the body
acute ❶ adj **1** shrewd **2** sharp
3 severe ▷ n **4** accent (´) over
letter **acutely** adv
AD anno Domini
ad n abbrev. of ADVERTISEMENT
adage n proverb
adagio adj/n, pl -gios (Mus) slow
(passage)
adamant ❶ adj unyielding
Adam's apple projecting part at
front of throat
adapt ❶ v **1** alter for new use
2 modify **3** change **adaptable** adj
adaptation n **adaptor, -er** n
device for connecting two electrical
appliances to a single socket

THESAURUS

acquit v = **clear**, free, release,
excuse, discharge ≠ **find guilty**
act v = **do something**, perform,
function, pretend to be,
impersonate; = **perform**, mimic
▷ n = **deed**, action, performance,
achievement, undertaking;
= **pretence**, show, front,
performance, display; = **law**, bill,
measure, resolution, decree;
= **performance**, show, turn,
production, routine

actual adj = **real**, substantial,
concrete, definite, tangible
≠ **theoretical**
acute adj = **serious**, important,
dangerous, critical, crucial;
= **sharp**, shooting, powerful,
violent, severe
adamant adj = **determined**, firm,
fixed, stubborn, uncompromising
≠ **flexible**
adapt v = **adjust**, change, alter,
modify, accommodate

add ❶ v 1 join 2 increase by 3 say further **addition** n **additional** adj **additionally** adv **additive** n something added, esp. to foodstuffs
addendum n, pl **-da** thing to be added
adder n small poisonous snake
addict ❶ n one who has become dependent on something **addicted** adj **addiction** n
address ❶ n 1 direction on letter 2 place where one lives 3 speech ▷ v 4 mark destination 5 speak to 6 direct
adenoids pl n tissue at back of nose
adept ❶ adj 1 skilled ▷ n 2 expert
adequate ❶ adj 1 sufficient, suitable 2 not outstanding **adequacy** n **adequately** adv
adhere v 1 stick to 2 be firm in opinion etc. **adherence** n **adherent** n **adhesion** n **adhesive** adj/n
ad hoc adj/adv for a particular occasion only

adieu interj farewell
adjacent ❶ adj lying near, next (to)
adjective n word which qualifies a noun
adjoin ❶ v 1 be next to 2 join
adjourn ❶ v 1 close (meeting etc.) temporarily 2 (Inf) move elsewhere **adjournment** n
adjudge v 1 declare 2 decide
adjudicate v 1 judge 2 sit in judgment **adjudication** n **adjudicator** n
adjunct n person or thing added or subordinate
adjure v earnestly entreat
adjust ❶ v 1 adapt 2 alter slightly, regulate **adjustable** adj **adjustment** n
adjutant n military officer who assists superiors
ad-lib v **-libbing, -libbed** 1 improvise ▷ n 2 improvised remark
administer ❶ v 1 manage 2 dispense, as justice etc.

— THESAURUS —

add v = **count up**, total, reckon, compute, add up ≠ **take away**; = **include**, attach, supplement, adjoin, augment
addict n = **junkie** (Inf), freak (Inf), fiend (Inf); = **fan**, lover, nut (Sl), follower, enthusiast
address n = **location**, home, place, house, point; = **speech**, talk, lecture, discourse, sermon ▷ v = **speak to**, talk to, greet, hail, approach
adept adj = **skilful**, able, skilled, expert, practised ≠ **unskilled** ▷ n = **expert**, master, genius, hotshot (Inf), dab hand (Brit Inf)

adequate adj = **sufficient**, enough ≠ **insufficient**
adjacent adj = **adjoining**, neighbouring, nearby ≠ **far away**
adjoin v = **connect with** or **to**, join, link with, touch on, border on
adjourn v = **postpone**, delay, suspend, interrupt, put off ≠ **continue**
adjust v = **adapt**, change, alter, accustom, conform; = **change**, reform, alter, adapt, revise
administer v = **manage**, run, control, direct, handle; = **dispense**, give, share, provide, apply

administrate v manage (an organization) **administration** n 1 management, supervision 2 governing body **administrative** adj **administrator** n

admiral n naval officer of highest rank

admire ❶ v regard with approval, respect, or wonder **admirable** adj **admirably** adv **admiration** n **admirer** n **admiring** adj

admit ❶ v -mitting, -mitted 1 confess 2 accept as true 3 allow 4 let in **admissible** adj **admission** n 1 permission to enter 2 entrance fee 3 confession **admittance** n permission to enter **admittedly** adv

admonish v 1 reprove 2 exhort **admonition** n

ad nauseam (Lat) to a boring or disgusting extent

ado n fuss

adolescence ❶ n period of life just before maturity **adolescent** n/adj young (person)

adopt ❶ v 1 take as one's child 2 take up, as principle, resolution **adoption** n

adore ❶ v 1 love intensely 2 worship **adorable** adj **adoration** n **adoring** adj

adorn ❶ v decorate

adrenal adj near the kidney **adrenalin** n hormone secreted by adrenal glands

adrift ❶ adj/adv 1 drifting 2 (Inf) detached 3 (Inf) off course

adroit adj 1 skilful 2 clever **adroitly** adv

adulation n flattery

adult ❶ adj 1 grown-up 2 mature ▷ n 3 mature person, animal or plant

adulterate v make impure by addition **adulteration** n

adultery n, pl -teries sexual unfaithfulness of a husband or wife **adulterer** n **adulterous** adj

advance ❶ v 1 bring forward 2 suggest 3 lend (money) 4 go forward 5 improve in position or

———————— THESAURUS ————————

admire v = **respect**, value, prize, honoured, praise ≠ **despise**

admit v = **confess**, confide, own up, come clean (Inf); = **allow**, agree, accept, reveal, grant ≠ **deny**; = **let in**, allow, receive, accept, introduce ≠ **keep out**

adolescence n = **teens**, youth, minority, boyhood, girlhood

adopt v = **take in**, raise, nurse, mother, rear ≠ **abandon**

adore v = **love**, honour, admire, worship, esteem ≠ **hate**

adorn v = **decorate**, array,

embellish, festoon

adrift adj = **drifting**, afloat, unmoored, unanchored; = **aimless**, goalless, directionless, purposeless

adult n = **grown-up**, mature person, person of mature age, grown or grown-up person, man or woman ▷ adj = **fully grown**, mature, grown-up, of age, ripe

advance v = **progress**, proceed, come forward, make inroads, make headway ≠ **retreat**; = **accelerate**, speed, promote, hasten, bring forward; = **improve**, rise, develop, value ▷ n **6** progress **7** movement forward **8** improvement **9** a loan ▷ adj **10** ahead in time or position **advanced** adj **1** at a late stage **2** not elementary **3** ahead of the times **advancement** n

advantage ⊕ n more favourable position or state **advantageous** adj

advent n **1** arrival, coming **2** (with cap.) the four weeks before Christmas

adventure ⊕ n exciting undertaking or happening **adventurous** adj

adverb n word added to verb etc. to modify meaning

adverse ⊕ adj **1** hostile **2** unfavourable **adversary** n enemy **adversely** adv **adversity** n distress, misfortune

advert ⊕ n (Inf) advertisement

advertise ⊕ v **1** publicize **2** give notice of, esp. in newspapers etc. **3** make public request (for) **advertisement** n **advertising** adj/n

advice ⊕ n **1** counsel **2** notification

advocate ⊕ n **1** one who pleads the cause of another, esp. in court of law **2** (Scot) barrister ▷ v **3** recommend **advocacy** n

aeon n long period of time

aerate v **1** charge liquid with gas **2** expose to air

aerial adj **1** operating in the air **2** pertaining to aircraft ▷ n **3** part of radio etc. receiving or sending radio waves

aerobatics pl n stunt flying

aerobics pl n exercise system designed to increase oxygen in the blood **aerobic** adj

aerodrome n airfield

aerodynamics pl n study of air flow, esp. round moving solid bodies **aerodynamic** adj

a

THESAURUS

pick up, progress; **= suggest**, offer, present, propose, advocate **≠ withhold** ▷ n **= down payment**, credit, loan, fee, deposit; **= attack**, charge, strike, assault, raid; **= improvement**, development, gain, growth, breakthrough ▷ adj **= prior**, early, beforehand

advantage n **= benefit**, help, profit, favour **≠ disadvantage**; **= lead**, sway, dominance, precedence

adventure n **= venture**, experience, incident, enterprise, undertaking

adverse adj **= unfavourable**, hostile, unlucky, opposing, hostile

advert n (Brit Inf) **= advertisement**, notice, commercial, ad (Inf), announcement

advertise v **= publicize**, promote, plug (Inf), announce, inform

advice n **= guidance**, help, opinion, direction, suggestion

advocate v **= recommend**, support, champion, encourage, propose **≠ oppose** ▷ n **= supporter**, spokesman, champion, defender, campaigner; (Law) **= lawyer**, attorney, solicitor, counsel, barrister

aeronautics *pl n* science of air navigation and flying in general **aeronautical** *adj*

aeroplane *n* heavier-than-air flying machine

aerosol *n* (substance dispensed from) pressurized can

aerospace *n* earth's atmosphere and space beyond

aesthetic *adj* relating to principles of beauty **aesthetics** *pl n* study of beauty **aesthetically** *adv* **aesthete** *n*

afar *adv* from, at, or to, a great distance

affable *adj* polite and friendly

affair ❶ *n* **1** thing done or attended to **2** business **3** happening **4** sexual liaison ▷ *pl* **5** personal or business interests **6** matters of public interest

affect ❶ *v* **1** act on **2** move feelings **3** make show of **affectation** *n* show, pretence **affected** *adj* **1** making a pretence

2 moved **3** acted upon **affection** *n* fondness, love **affectionate** *adj* **affectionately** *adv*

affidavit *n* written statement on oath

affiliate ❶ *v/n* (join as an) associate **affiliation** *n*

affinity ❶ *n*, *pl* **-ties 1** natural liking **2** resemblance **3** chemical attraction

affirm ❶ *v* **1** assert positively **2** make solemn declaration **affirmation** *n* **affirmative** *adj/n* positive (statement)

affix *v* fasten (to)

afflict ❶ *v* cause to suffer **affliction** *n*

affluent ❶ *adj* wealthy **affluence** *n*

afford ❶ *v* **1** to be able to (buy, do) **2** provide **affordable** *adj*

affront *v/n* insult

afield *adv* **far afield** far away

aflame *adv/adj* burning

afloat *adv* **1** floating **2** at sea

afoot *adv* **1** astir **2** on foot

━━━━━━━━ THESAURUS ━━━━━━━━

affair *n* = **matter**, business, happening, event, activity; = **relationship**, romance, intrigue, fling, liaison

affect *v* = **influence**, concern, alter, change, manipulate; = **emotionally move**, touch, upset, overcome, stir

affiliate *v* = **associate**, unite, join, link, ally

affinity *n* = **attraction**, liking, leaning, sympathy, inclination ≠ **hostility**; = **similarity**, relationship, connection,

correspondence, analogy ≠ **difference**

affirm *v* = **declare**, state, maintain, swear, assert ≠ **deny**; = **confirm**, prove, endorse, ratify, verify ≠ **refute**

afflict *v* = **torment**, trouble, pain, hurt, distress

affluent *adj* = **wealthy**, rich, prosperous, loaded (*Sl*), well-off ≠ **poor**

afford *v* = **have the money for**, manage, bear, pay for, spare; = **bear**, stand, sustain, allow yourself

aforesaid, aforementioned
adj previously mentioned

afraid ❶ *adj* 1 frightened
2 regretful

afresh *adv* again, anew

African *adj* of Africa **African
violet** house plant with pink or
purple flowers

aft *adv* towards stern of ship

after ❶ *adv* 1 later 2 behind
▷ *prep* 3 behind 4 later than 5 on
the model of 6 pursuing ▷ *conj*
7 later than **afters** *pl n* dessert

afterbirth *n* membrane expelled
after a birth

aftermath ❶ *n* result, consequence

afternoon *n* time from noon to
evening

aftershave *n* lotion applied to
face after shaving

afterwards, afterward *adv*
later

again ❶ *adv* 1 once more 2 in

addition

against ❶ *prep* 1 in opposition to
2 in contact with 3 opposite

agape *adj/adv* open-mouthed

agate *n* semiprecious quartz

age ❶ *n* 1 length of time person or
thing has existed 2 time of life
3 period of history 4 long time
5 maturity, old age ▷ *v* 6 make or
grow old **aged** *adj* 1 old ▷ *pl n*
2 old people **ageing** *n/adj*

agenda ❶ *pl n* list of things to be
attended to

agent ❶ *n* 1 one authorized to act
for another 2 person or thing
producing effect **agency** *n*
1 organization providing service
2 business, premises of agent

aggrandize *v* make greater in
size, power, or rank

aggravate ❶ *v* 1 make worse or
more severe 2 (*Inf*) annoy
aggravation *n*

—— THESAURUS ——

afraid *adj* = **scared**, frightened,
nervous, terrified, shaken
≠ **unafraid**; = **reluctant**, frightened,
scared, unwilling, hesitant

after *adv* = **following**; later, next,
succeeding, afterwards

aftermath *n* = **effects**, results,
wake, consequences, outcome

again *adv* = **once more**, another
time, anew, afresh; = **also**, in
addition, moreover, besides,
furthermore

against *prep* = **beside**, on, up
against, in contact with, abutting;
= **opposed to**, anti (*Inf*), hostile to,
in opposition to, averse to; = **in
opposition to**, resisting, versus,

counter to, in the opposite direction
of

age *n* = **years**, days, generation,
lifetime, length of existence; = **old
age**, experience, maturity,
seniority, majority ≠ **youth**

agenda *n* = **programme**, list, plan,
schedule, diary

agent *n* = **representative**, rep
(*Inf*), negotiator, envoy, surrogate;
= **author**, worker, vehicle,
instrument, operator

aggravate *v* = **make worse**,
exaggerate, intensify, worsen,
exacerbate ≠ **improve**; (*Inf*) =
annoy, bother, provoke, irritate,
nettle ≠ **please**

aggregate ❶ v 1 gather into mass ▷ adj 2 gathered thus ▷ n 3 mass, sum total 4 gravel etc. for concrete

aggression ❶ n 1 unprovoked attack 2 hostile activity **aggressive** adj **aggressively** adv

aggrieved adj upset, angry

aghast adj appalled

agile adj 1 nimble 2 quick **agility** n

agitate ❶ v 1 stir, shake up 2 trouble 3 stir up public opinion (for or against) **agitation** n **agitator** n

aglow adj glowing

AGM Annual General Meeting

agnostic n one who believes that we cannot know whether God exists

ago adv in the past

agog adj/adv eager, astir

agony ❶ n, pl **-nies** extreme suffering **agonize** v 1 suffer agony 2 worry greatly **agonizing** adj

agoraphobia n fear of open spaces **agoraphobic** adj/n

agree ❶ v **agreeing, agreed** 1 be of same opinion 2 consent 3 harmonize 4 approve **agreeable** adj 1 willing 2 pleasant **agreeably** adv **agreement** n

agriculture ❶ n (science of) farming **agricultural** adj

aground adv (of boat) touching bottom

ahead ❶ adv 1 in front 2 onwards

ahoy interj ship's hailing cry

aid ❶ v/n help, support

aide ❶ n assistant

AIDS n disease that destroys the body's immune system

ail v 1 trouble 2 be ill **ailing** adj **ailment** n illness

aim ❶ v 1 direct (weapon etc.) 2 intend ▷ n 3 aiming 4 intention **aimless** n without purpose **aimlessly** adv

ain't (Nonstandard) 1 am not

THESAURUS

aggregate n = **total**, body, whole, amount, collection ▷ v = **combine**, mix, collect, assemble, heap

aggression n = **hostility**, malice, antagonism, antipathy, aggressiveness; = **attack**, campaign, injury, assault, raid

agitate v = **stir**, beat, shake, disturb, toss; = **upset**, worry, trouble, excite, distract ≠ **calm**

agony n = **suffering**, pain, distress, misery, torture

agree v = **concur**, be as one, sympathize, assent, see eye to eye

≠ **disagree**; = **correspond**, match, coincide, tally, conform

agriculture n = **farming**, culture, cultivation, husbandry, tillage

ahead adv = **in front**, in advance, towards the front, frontwards

aid n = **help**, backing, support, benefit, favour ≠ **hindrance** ▷ v = **help**, support, serve, sustain, assist ≠ **hinder**

aide n = **assistant**, supporter, attendant, helper, right-hand man

aim v = **try for**, seek, work for, plan for, strive ▷ n = **intention**, point, plan, goal, design

2 is not **3** are not **4** has not **5** have not

air ❶ *n* **1** (gases of) earth's atmosphere **2** breeze **3** tune **4** manner ▷ *pl* **5** affected manners ▷ *v* **6** expose to air **7** communicate, make known **airless** *adj* stuffy **airy** *adj* **1** well-ventilated **2** jaunty, nonchalant **air bed** inflatable mattress **air conditioning** control of temperature and humidity in building **aircraft** *n* **1** flying machines generally **2** aeroplane **airfield** *n* landing and taking-off area for aircraft **air force** armed force using aircraft **air gun** gun discharged by compressed air **airline** *n* company operating aircraft **airliner** *n* large passenger aircraft **air mail** mail sent by aircraft **airman** *n* member of air force **airplay** *n* performances of a record on radio **airport** *n* station for civilian aircraft **air raid** attack by aircraft **airship** *n* lighter-than-air flying machine with means of propulsion **airstrip** *n* strip of ground where aircraft can take off and land **airtight** *adj* not allowing passage of air **airworthy** *adj* fit to fly

aisle ❶ *n* passage between rows of seats

ajar *adv* partly open

akimbo *adv* with hands on hips

akin *adj* **1** related by blood **2** alike

alabaster *n* white, decorative stone

à la carte (*Fr*) selected freely from the menu

alacrity *n* eager willingness

alarm ❶ *n* **1** fright **2** apprehension **3** danger signal ▷ *v* **4** frighten **5** alert **alarming** *adj*

alas *interj* cry of grief

albatross *n* large sea bird

albino *n, pl* **-nos** individual lacking pigmentation

album *n* **1** book for photographs, stamps etc. **2** collection of items in book or record form

alchemy *n* medieval form of chemistry **alchemist** *n*

alcohol *n* **1** intoxicating fermented liquor **2** class of organic chemical substances **alcoholic** *adj* **1** of alcohol ▷ *n* **2** person addicted to alcoholic drink **alcoholism** *n*

alcove *n* recess

alder *n* tree related to the birch

alderman *n* formerly, senior local councillor

ale *n* kind of beer

— THESAURUS —

air *n* = **wind**, breeze, draught, gust, zephyr; = **atmosphere**, sky, heavens, aerosphere; = **tune**, song, theme, melody, strain; = **manner**, appearance, look, aspect, atmosphere ▷ *v* = **publicize**, reveal, exhibit, voice, express; = **ventilate**, expose, freshen, aerate

aisle *n* = **passageway**, path, lane, passage, corridor

alarm *n* = **fear**, panic, anxiety, fright, apprehension ≠ **calmness**; = **danger signal**, warning, bell, alert, siren ▷ *v* = **frighten**, scare, panic, distress, startle ≠ **calm**

alert ❶ adj 1 watchful 2 brisk ▷ n
3 warning ▷ v 4 warn 5 draw
attention to **alertness** n
alfresco adv/adj in the open air
algae pl n various water
plants
algebra n method of calculating,
using symbols to represent
quantities
Algonquin, Algonkin n 1 a
member of a North American
Indian people formerly living along
the St Lawrence and Ottawa Rivers
in Canada 2 the language of this
people, a dialect of Ojibwa
alias adv 1 otherwise ▷ n
2 assumed name
alibi n plea of being elsewhere at
time of crime
alien ❶ adj 1 foreign 2 different in
nature 3 repugnant (to) ▷ n
4 foreigner **alienate** v 1 estrange
2 transfer **alienation** n

alight¹ ❶ v 1 get down 2 land
alight² ❶ adj 1 burning 2 lit up
align ❶ v 1 bring into line or
agreement 2 ally, side (with)
alignment n
alike ❶ adj/adv similar(ly)
alimony n allowance paid to
separated or divorced spouse
alive ❶ adj 1 living 2 active
3 aware 4 swarming
alkali n substance which
combines with acid and
neutralizes it, forming a salt
alkaline adj
all ❶ adj 1 the whole of, every one
of ▷ adv 2 entirely ▷ n 3 the
whole 4 everything, everyone **all
right** adj 1 adequate, satisfactory
2 unharmed ▷ interj 3 expression
of approval
allay v relieve, soothe
allege ❶ v state without proof
allegation n **allegedly** adv

———————————————— THESAURUS ————————————————

alert adj = **attentive**, awake,
vigilant, watchful, on the lookout
≠ **careless** ▷ n = **warning**, signal,
alarm, siren ≠ **all clear** ▷ v
= **warn**, signal, inform, alarm,
notify ≠ **lull**
alien adj = **foreign**, strange,
imported, unknown, exotic ▷ n
= **foreigner**, incomer, immigrant,
stranger, outsider ≠ **citizen**
alight¹ v = **get off**, descend, get
down, disembark, dismount;
= **land**, light, settle, come down,
descend ≠ **take off**
alight² adj = **lit up**, bright, brilliant,
shining, illuminated
align v = **ally**, side, join, associate,

affiliate; = **line up**, order, range,
regulate, straighten
alike adj = **similar**, close, the same,
parallel, resembling ≠ **different**
▷ adv = **similarly**, identically,
equally, uniformly, correspondingly
≠ **differently**
alive adj = **living**, breathing,
animate, subsisting, existing
≠ **dead**; = **in existence**, existing,
functioning, active, operative
≠ **inoperative**
all adj = **complete**, greatest, full,
total, perfect ▷ adv = **completely**,
totally, fully, entirely, absolutely
allege v = **claim**, charge, challenge,
state, maintain ≠ **deny**

allegiance ⊕ n loyalty, esp. to one's country

allegory n, pl **-ries** symbolic story, poem **allegorical** adj

allegro adv/adj/n, pl **-gros** (Mus) fast (passage)

allergy ⊕ n, pl **-gies** abnormal sensitivity to a specific substance **allergic** adj

alleviate ⊕ v ease, lessen

alley ⊕ n **1** narrow street **2** enclosure for skittles

alliance ⊕ n union, e.g. by treaty, agreement, or marriage

alligator n animal of crocodile family found in America

alliteration n beginning of successive words with same sound

allocate ⊕ v assign as a share **allocation** n

allot v **-lotting, -lotted** allocate **allotment** n **1** distribution **2** portion of land rented for cultivation **3** portion allotted

allow ⊕ v **1** permit **2** set aside **3** acknowledge **allowable** adj **allowance** n

alloy n metallic mixture

allude v refer (to) **allusion** n

allure v **1** entice ▷ n **2** attractiveness **alluring** adj

ally ⊕ v, pl **-lies 1** join by treaty, friendship etc. ▷ n **2** friend **allied** adj

almanac n calendar of tides, events etc.

almighty adj **1** all-powerful **2** (Inf) very great

almond n **1** tree of peach family **2** its edible seed

almost ⊕ adv very nearly

alms pl n gifts to the poor

aloft adv **1** on high **2** overhead

alone ⊕ adj/adv **1** by oneself, by itself **2** without equal, unique

along adv **1** lengthwise **2** together (with) **3** forward ▷ prep **4** over the length of **alongside** adv/prep beside

aloof adj **1** indifferent **2** at a distance

THESAURUS

allegiance n = **loyalty**, devotion, fidelity, obedience, constancy ≠ **disloyalty**

allergy n = **sensitivity**, reaction, susceptibility, antipathy, hypersensitivity

alleviate v = **ease**, reduce, relieve, moderate, soothe

alley n = **passage**, walk, lane, pathway, alleyway

alliance n = **union**, league, association, agreement, marriage ≠ **division**

allocate v = **assign**, grant, distribute, designate, set aside

allow v = **permit**, approve, enable, sanction, endure ≠ **prohibit**; = **let**, permit, sanction, authorize, license ≠ **forbid**; = **give**, provide, grant, spare, devote

ally n = **partner**, friend, colleague, associate, mate ≠ **opponent**

almost adv = **nearly**, about, close to, virtually, practically

alone adj = **solitary**, isolated, separate, apart, by yourself ≠ **accompanied**

aloud ⊕ *adv* 1 loudly 2 audibly
alphabet *n* set of letters used in writing a language
already ⊕ *adv* 1 previously 2 sooner than expected
Alsatian *n* large wolflike dog
also ⊕ *adv* besides, moreover
also-ran *n* loser in a contest
altar *n* 1 Communion table 2 sacrificial table
alter ⊕ *v* change, make or become different **alterable** *adj* **alteration** *n*
altercation *n* quarrel
alternate ⊕ *v* 1 (cause to) occur by turns ▷ *adj* 2 in turn 3 every second **alternately** *adv*
alternative *n* 1 one of two choices ▷ *adj* 2 replacing **alternatively** *adv*
although ⊕ *conj* despite the fact that
altitude *n* height, elevation
alto *n, pl* **-tos** (*Mus*) 1 male singing voice or instrument above tenor 2 contralto
altogether ⊕ *adv* 1 entirely 2 in total
altruism *n* unselfish concern for others
aluminium *n* light nonrusting silvery metal
always ⊕ *adv* 1 at all times 2 for ever
am first person sing. of BE
a.m. before noon
amalgamate *v* mix, (cause to) combine **amalgamation** *n*
amass ⊕ *v* collect in quantity
amateur ⊕ *n* 1 one who does something for interest not money 2 unskilled practitioner **amateurish** *adj*
amaut, amowt *n* (*Canad*) a hood on an Eskimo woman's parka for carrying a child
amaze ⊕ *v* surprise greatly, astound **amazing** *adj*

——————— THESAURUS ———————

aloud *adv* = **out loud**, clearly, plainly, distinctly, audibly
already *adv* = **before now**, before, previously, at present, by now
also *adv* = **and**, too, further, in addition, as well
alter *v* = **modify**, change, reform, vary, transform
alternate *v* = **interchange**, change, fluctuate, take turns, oscillate ▷ *adj* = **alternating**, interchanging, every other, rotating, every second
although *conj* = **though**, while, even if, even though, whilst
altogether *adv* = **absolutely**, quite, completely, totally, perfectly; = **completely**, fully, entirely, thoroughly, wholly ≠ **partially**; = **on the whole**, generally, mostly, in general, collectively
always *adv* = **habitually**, regularly, every time, consistently, invariably ≠ **seldom**; = **forever**, for keeps, eternally, for all time, evermore
amass *v* = **collect**, gather, assemble, compile, accumulate
amateur *n* = **nonprofessional**, outsider, layman, dilettante, layperson
amaze *v* = **astonish**, surprise, shock, stun, alarm

amazement *n*

ambassador ⊙ *n* senior diplomatic representative overseas

amber *n* yellow fossil resin

ambidextrous *adj* able to use both hands with equal ease

ambience *n* atmosphere of a place

ambiguous ⊙ *adj* 1 having more than one meaning 2 obscure **ambiguity** *n*

ambition ⊙ *n* 1 desire for success 2 goal, aim **ambitious** *adj*

ambivalence *n* simultaneous existence of conflicting emotions

amble *v/n* (move at an) easy pace

ambulance *n* conveyance for sick or injured people

ambush ⊙ *v/n* attack from hiding

ameliorate *v* improve

amen *interj* so be it

amenable *adj* 1 easily controlled 2 answerable

amend ⊙ *v* 1 correct 2 alter **amendment** *n*

amenity ⊙ *n, pl* **-ties** (*oft. pl*) useful or pleasant facility or service

amiable *adj* friendly, kindly

amicable *adj* friendly **amicably** *adv*

amid, amidst ⊙ *prep* among

amiss *adj* 1 wrong ▷ *adv* 2 faultily

ammonia *n* pungent alkaline gas

ammunition ⊙ *n* 1 projectiles that can be discharged from weapon 2 facts that can be used in argument

amnesia *n* loss of memory

amnesty ⊙ *n, pl* **-ties** general pardon

amoeba *n, pl* **-bae, -bas** microscopic single-celled animal

amok *adv* **run amok** run about in a violent frenzy

among, amongst ⊙ *prep* 1 in the midst of 2 of the number of 3 between 4 with one another

amoral *adj* having no moral standards

amorous *adj* inclined to love

amorphous *adj* without distinct shape

a

THESAURUS

---

ambassador *n* = **representative**, minister, agent, deputy, diplomat

ambiguous *adj* = **unclear**, obscure, vague, dubious, enigmatic ≠ **clear**

ambition *n* = **goal**, hope, dream, target, aim; = **enterprise**, longing, drive, spirit, desire

ambush *v* = **trap**, attack, surprise, deceive, dupe ▷ *n* = **trap**, snare, lure, waylaying

amend *v* = **change**, improve, reform, fix, correct

amenity *n* = **facility**, service, advantage, comfort, convenience

amid, amidst *prep* = **during**, among, at a time of, in an atmosphere of

ammunition *n* = **munitions**, rounds, shot, shells, powder

amnesty *n* = **general pardon**, mercy, pardoning, immunity, forgiveness

among, amongst *prep* = **in the midst of**, with, together with, in the middle of, amid; = **in the group of**, one of, part of, included in, in the company of; = **between**, to

amount ❶ v **1** come, be equal (to) ▷ n **2** quantity **3** sum total

amp n **1** ampere **2** (Inf) amplifier

ampere n unit of electric current

ampersand n sign (&) meaning and

amphetamine n synthetic medicinal stimulant

amphibian n **1** animal that lives first in water then on land **2** vehicle, plane adapted to land and water **amphibious** adj

amphitheatre n arena surrounded by rising tiers of seats

ample ❶ adj **1** big enough **2** large, spacious **amply** adv

amplify v **-fying, -fied 1** increase **2** make bigger, louder etc. **amplification** n **amplifier** n

amplitude n spaciousness, width

amputate v cut off (limb etc.) **amputation** n

amulet n thing worn as a charm against evil

amuse ❶ v **1** entertain **2** cause to laugh or smile **amusing** adj **amusement** n

an see A

anachronism n something put in wrong historical period

anaconda n large snake which kills by constriction

anaemia n deficiency of red blood cells **anaemic** adj pale, sickly

anaesthetic ❶ n/adj (drug) causing loss of sensation **anaesthetist** n **anaesthetize** v

anagram n word(s) whose letters can be rearranged to make new word(s)

anal see ANUS

analgesic adj/n (drug) relieving pain

analogy ❶ n, pl **-gies** likeness in certain respects **analogous** adj similar

analysis ❶ n, pl **-ses 1** separation into elements or components **2** evaluation, study **analyse** v **1** examine critically **2** determine constituent parts **analyst** n **analytical** adj

anarchy ❶ n **1** absence of government and law **2** disorder **anarchic** adj **anarchist** n one who opposes all forms of government

anathema n **1** anything detested **2** curse of excommunication or denunciation

————————————— THESAURUS —————

amount n = **quantity**, measure, size, supply, mass

ample adj = **plenty of**, generous, lavish, abundant, plentiful ≠ **insufficient**

amuse v = **entertain**, please, delight, charm, cheer ≠ **bore**

anaesthetic n = **painkiller**, narcotic, sedative, opiate, anodyne ▷ adj = **pain-killing**, dulling, numbing, sedative, deadening

analogy n = **similarity**, relation, comparison, parallel, correspondence

analysis n = **examination**, test, inquiry, investigation, interpretation

anarchy n = **lawlessness**, revolution, riot, disorder, confusion ≠ **order**

anatomy ⊙ *n, pl* **-mies** 1 (study of) bodily structure 2 detailed analysis **anatomical** *adj* **anatomist** *n*

ancestor ⊙ *n* 1 person from whom another is descended 2 forerunner **ancestral** *adj* **ancestry** *n*

anchor *n* 1 heavy implement dropped to stop vessel drifting 2 any similar device ▷ *v* 3 secure with anchor **anchorage** *n* act, place of anchoring

anchovy *n, pl* **-vies** small savoury fish of herring family

ancient ⊙ *adj* 1 belonging to former age 2 very old

ancillary *adj* subordinate, auxiliary

and ⊙ *conj* word used to join words and sentences, introduce a consequence etc.

andante *adv/adj/n (Mus)* moderately slow (passage)

androgynous *adj* having male and female characteristics

android *n* robot resembling a human

anecdote ⊙ *n* short account of a single incident **anecdotal** *adj*

anemone *n* flower related to buttercup

anew *adv* afresh, again

angel ⊙ *n* 1 divine messenger 2 guardian spirit 3 very kind person **angelic** *adj*

anger ⊙ *n* 1 extreme annoyance 2 wrath ▷ *v* 3 make angry **angry** *adj* **angrily** *adv*

angina *n* severe pain accompanying heart disease

angle ⊙ *n* 1 meeting of two lines or surfaces 2 point of view ▷ *v* 3 bend at an angle 4 fish **angler** *n* one who fishes for sport **angling** *n*

Anglican *adj/n* (member) of the Church of England

Anglo- *comb. form* English or British, as in *Anglo-Scottish, Anglo-American*

angora *n* 1 goat with long white silky hair 2 cloth or wool of this

anguish ⊙ *n* great mental or bodily pain **anguished** *adj*

── THESAURUS ──

anatomy *n* = **structure**, build, make-up, frame, framework; = **examination**, study, division, inquiry, investigation

ancestor *n* = **forefather**, predecessor, precursor, forerunner, forebear ≠ **descendant**

ancient *adj* = **classical**, old, former, past, bygone

and *conj* = **also**, including, along with, together with, in addition to

anecdote *n* = **story**, tale, sketch, short story, yarn

angel *n* = **divine messenger**, cherub, archangel, seraph; (Inf) = **dear**, beauty, saint, treasure, darling

anger *n* = **rage**, outrage, temper, fury, resentment ≠ **calmness** ▷ *v* = **enrage**, outrage, annoy, infuriate, incense ≠ **soothe**

angle *n* = **gradient**, bank, slope, incline, inclination; = **intersection**, point, edge, corner, bend; = **point of view**, position, approach, direction, aspect

anguish *n* = **suffering**, pain, distress, grief, misery

angular adj 1 (of people) bony 2 having angles 3 measured by an angle

animal ● n 1 living creature that can move at will 2 beast ▷ adj 3 of animals 4 sensual

animate ● v 1 give life to 2 enliven 3 inspire 4 actuate 5 make cartoon film of **animated** adj **animation** n **animator** n

animosity n, pl -ties hostility, enmity

animus n 1 hatred 2 animosity

aniseed n liquorice-flavoured seed of plant

ankle n joint between foot and leg

annals pl n yearly records

annex v 1 append, attach 2 take possession of **annexation** n

annexe n 1 extension to a building 2 nearby building used as an extension

annihilate v reduce to nothing, destroy utterly **annihilation** n

anniversary n, pl -ries 1 yearly return of a date 2 celebration of this

anno Domini (Lat) in the year of our Lord

annotate v make notes upon **annotation** n

announce ● v make known, proclaim **announcement** n **announcer** n

annoy ● v 1 vex 2 irritate **annoyance** n

annual ● adj 1 yearly ▷ n 2 plant which completes its life cycle in a year 3 book published each year **annually** adv

annul v -nulling, -nulled make void, cancel **annulment** n

anodyne n 1 thing that relieves pain or distress ▷ adj 2 relieving pain or distress

anoint v 1 smear with oil or ointment 2 consecrate with oil

anomaly ● n, pl -lies irregular or abnormal thing **anomalous** adj

anon. anonymous

anonymous ● adj without (author's) name **anonymously** adv **anonymity** n

anorak n waterproof hooded jacket

anorexia n loss of appetite **anorexic** adj/n

———— THESAURUS ————

animal n = **creature**, beast, brute ▷ adj = **physical**, gross, bodily, sensual, carnal

animate adj = **living**, live, moving, alive, breathing ▷ v = **enliven**, excite, inspire, move, fire ≠ **inhibit**

announce v = **make known**, tell, report, reveal, declare, post, tweet ≠ **keep secret**

annoy v = **irritate**, trouble, anger, bother, disturb ≠ **soothe**

annual adj = **once a year**, yearly; = **yearlong**, yearly

anomaly n = **irregularity**, exception, abnormality, inconsistency, eccentricity

anonymous adj = **unnamed**, unknown, unidentified, nameless, unacknowledged ≠ **identified**; = **unsigned**, uncredited, unattributed ≠ **signed**; impersonal, faceless

another pron/adj **1** one other **2** a different one **3** one more

answer ❶ v **1** reply (to) **2** be accountable (for, to) **3** match **4** suit ▷ n **5** reply **6** solution **answerable** adj

ant n small social insect **anteater** n animal which feeds on ants

antagonist n opponent **antagonism** n **antagonistic** adj **antagonize** v arouse hostility in

Antarctic adj/n (of) south polar regions

ante- comb. form before, as in antechamber

antecedent adj/n (thing) going before

antelope n deerlike animal

antenatal adj of care etc. during pregnancy

antenna n **1** insect's feeler **2** aerial

anterior adj **1** to the front **2** before

anthem ❶ n **1** song of loyalty **2** sacred choral piece

anther n pollen sac of flower

anthology ❶ n, pl **-gies** collection of poems

anthracite n slow-burning coal

anthrax n infectious disease of cattle and sheep

anthropoid adj/n manlike (ape)

anthropology n study of origins, development of human race

anti- comb. form against, as in anti-aircraft

antibiotic n/adj (of) substance used against bacterial infection

antibody n, pl **-bodies** substance which counteracts bacteria

anticipate ❶ v **1** expect **2** look forward to **3** foresee **anticipation** n

anticlimax n sudden descent to the trivial or ludicrous

anticlockwise adv/adj in the opposite direction to the rotation of the hands of a clock

antics ❶ pl n absurd behaviour

anticyclone n high-pressure area and associated winds

antidote n counteracting remedy

antifreeze n liquid added to water to prevent freezing

antihistamine n drug used esp. to treat allergies

antimony n brittle, bluish-white metal

antipathy n dislike, aversion

antiperspirant n substance used to reduce sweating

─────── THESAURUS ───────

answer v = **reply**, explain, respond, resolve, react ≠ **ask** ▷ n = **reply**, response, reaction, explanation, comeback ≠ **question**; = **solution**, resolution, explanation; = **remedy**, solution

anthem n = **song of praise**, carol, chant, hymn, psalm

anthology n = **collection**, selection, treasury, compilation, compendium

anticipate v = **expect**, predict, prepare for, hope for, envisage; = **await**, look forward to, count the hours until

antics pl n = **clowning**, tricks, mischief, pranks, escapades

antipodes *pl n* regions on opposite side of the globe **antipodean** *adj*

antique ❶ *n* **1** object valued because of its age ▷ *adj* **2** ancient **3** old-fashioned **antiquarian** *n* collector of antiques **antiquated** *adj* out-of-date **antiquity** *n* **1** great age **2** former times

antiseptic *n/adj* **1** (substance) preventing infection ▷ *adj* **2** free from infection

antisocial *adj* **1** avoiding company **2** (of behaviour) harmful to society

antithesis *n, pl* **-ses 1** direct opposite **2** contrast

antler *n* branching horn of certain deer

antonym *n* word of opposite meaning to another

anus *n* open end of rectum **anal** *adj*

anvil *n* heavy iron block on which a smith hammers metal

anxious ❶ *adj* **1** uneasy **2** concerned **anxiety** *n* **anxiously** *adv*

any *adj/pron* **1** one indefinitely **2** some **3** every **anybody** *n* **anyhow** *adv* **anyone** *n* **anything** *n* **anyway** *adv* **anywhere** *adv*

aorta *n* main artery carrying blood from the heart

apace *adv* swiftly

apart ❶ *adv* **1** separately, aside **2** in pieces

apartheid *n* (esp. formerly in S Africa) official policy of segregation

apartment ❶ *n* **1** room **2** flat

apathy ❶ *n* **1** indifference **2** lack of emotion **apathetic** *adj*

ape *n* **1** tailless monkey **2** imitator ▷ *v* **3** imitate

aperitif *n* alcoholic appetizer

aperture *n* opening, hole

apex *n* **1** top, peak **2** vertex

aphid, aphis *n* small insect which sucks the sap from plants

aphorism *n* maxim, clever saying

aphrodisiac *adj/n* (substance) exciting sexual desire

apiece ❶ *adv* for each

aplomb *n* assurance

apocalypse *n* prophetic

———— THESAURUS ————

antique *n* = **period piece**, relic, bygone, heirloom, collector's item ▷ *adj* = **vintage**, classic, antiquarian, olden; = **old-fashioned**, outdated, obsolete, archaic

anxious *adj* = **eager**, keen, intent, yearning, impatient ≠ **reluctant**; = **uneasy**, concerned, worried, troubled, nervous ≠ **confident**

apart *adv* = **to pieces**, to bits, asunder; = **away from each other**, distant from each other

apartment *n* (US) = **flat**, room, suite, penthouse, crib; = **rooms**, quarters, accommodation, living quarters

apathy *n* = **lack of interest**, indifference, inertia, coolness, passivity ≠ **interest**

apiece *adv* = **each**, individually, separately, for each, to each ≠ **all together**

a

revelation, esp. of the end of the world **apocalyptic** adj

apocryphal adj of questionable authenticity

apology ❶ n, pl **-gies 1** expression of regret for a fault **2** poor substitute (for) **apologetic** adj **apologetically** adv **apologize** v

apoplexy n paralysis caused by broken or blocked blood vessel in the brain **apoplectic** adj **1** of apoplexy **2** (Inf) furious

Apostle n **1** one of the first disciples of Jesus **2** (without cap.) enthusiastic supporter of a cause

apostrophe n mark (') showing omission of letter(s)

app n computer program designed for a particular purpose

appal ❶ v **-palling, -palled** dismay, terrify **appalling** adj (Inf) terrible

apparatus ❶ n equipment for performing experiment, operation etc.

apparel n clothing

apparent ❶ adj **1** seeming **2** obvious **3** acknowledged **apparently** adv

apparition n ghost

appeal ❶ v **1** make earnest request **2** be attractive **3** apply to higher court ▷ n **4** request **5** attractiveness **appealing** adj

appear ❶ v **1** become visible or present **2** seem, be plain **3** be seen in public **4** perform **appearance** n **1** an appearing **2** aspect **3** pretence

appease ❶ v pacify, satisfy **appeasement** n

append v join on, add

appendicitis n inflammation of the appendix

appendix ❶ n, pl **-dices, -dixes 1** supplement **2** (Anat) small worm-shaped part of the intestine

appertain v belong, relate to

appetite ❶ n desire, inclination, esp. for food **appetizer** n

apology n = **regret**, explanation, excuse, confession; = **mockery of**, excuse for, imitation of, caricature of, travesty of

appal v = **horrify**, shock, alarm, frighten, outrage

apparatus n = **organization**, system, network, structure, bureaucracy

apparent adj = **seeming**, outward, superficial, ostensible ≠ **actual**; = **obvious**, marked, visible, evident, distinct ≠ **unclear**

appeal v = **plead**, ask, request, pray, beg ≠ **refuse** ▷ n = **plea**, call, application, request, prayer

≠ **refusal**; = **attraction**, charm, fascination, beauty, allure ≠ **repulsiveness**

appear v = **look (like** or **as if)**, seem, occur, look to be, come across as; = **come into view**, emerge, occur, surface, come out ≠ **disappear**

appease v = **pacify**, satisfy, calm, soothe, quiet ≠ **anger**; = **ease**, calm, relieve, soothe, alleviate

appendix n = **supplement**, postscript, adjunct, appendage, addendum

appetite n = **desire**, liking, longing, demand, taste ≠ **distaste**

something stimulating appetite **appetizing** adj

applaud ❶ v 1 praise by clapping 2 praise loudly **applause** n

apple n 1 round, firm fleshy fruit 2 tree bearing it

appliance ❶ n piece of equipment, esp. electrical

apply ❶ v -plying, -plied 1 utilize 2 lay or place on 3 devote 4 have reference (to) 5 make request (to) **applicable** adj relevant **applicant** n **application** n 1 request for a job etc. 2 diligence 3 use, function **applied** adj put to practical use

appoint ❶ v 1 assign to a job or position 2 fix, equip **appointment** n 1 engagement to meet 2 (selection for a) job

apportion v divide out in shares

apposite adj appropriate

appraise v estimate value of **appraisal** n

appreciate ❶ v 1 value at true worth 2 be grateful for 3 understand 4 rise in value **appreciable** adj noticeable **appreciably** adv **appreciation** n **appreciative** adj

apprehend v 1 arrest 2 understand 3 dread **apprehension** n anxiety **apprehensive** adj

apprentice ❶ n 1 person learning a trade 2 novice

apprise v inform

approach ❶ v 1 draw near (to) 2 set about 3 address request to 4 approximate to ▷ n 5 a drawing near 6 means of reaching or doing 7 approximation **approachable** adj

approbation n approval

appropriate ❶ adj 1 suitable, fitting ▷ v 2 take for oneself 3 allocate **appropriately** adv

———————— THESAURUS ————

applaud v = **clap**, encourage, praise, cheer, acclaim ≠ **boo**; = **praise**, celebrate, approve, acclaim, compliment ≠ **criticize**

appliance n = **device**, machine, tool, instrument, implement

apply v = **request**, appeal, put in, petition, inquire; = **be relevant**, relate, refer, be fitting, be appropriate; = **use**, exercise, carry out, employ, implement; = **put on**, work in, cover with, lay on, paint on

appoint v = **assign**, name, choose, commission, select ≠ **fire**; = **decide**, set, choose, establish, fix ≠ **cancel**

appreciate v = **enjoy**, like, value,

respect, prize ≠ **scorn**; = **be aware of**, understand, realize, recognize, perceive ≠ **be unaware of**; = **be grateful**, be obliged, be thankful, give thanks, be indebted ≠ **be ungrateful for**; = **increase**, rise, grow, gain, improve ≠ **fall**

apprentice n = **trainee**, student, pupil, novice, beginner ≠ **master**

approach v = **move towards**, reach, near, come close, come near; = **make a proposal to**, speak to, apply to, appeal to, proposition; = **set about**, tackle, undertake, embark on, get down to ▷ n = **advance**, coming, nearing, appearance, arrival; = **access**, way,

approve ❶ *v* **1** think well of, commend **2** authorize **approval** *n*

approx. approximate(ly)

approximate *adj* **1** nearly correct **2** inexact ▷ *v* **3** come or bring close **4** be almost the same as **approximately** *adv* **approximation** *n*

Apr. April

après-ski *n* social activities after skiing

apricot *n* orange-coloured fruit related to plum

April *n* fourth month

apron *n* **1** covering worn in front to protect clothes **2** in theatre, strip of stage before curtain **3** on airfield, tarmac area where aircraft stand, are loaded etc.

apropos *adv* **1** with reference to ▷ *adj* **2** appropriate

apt ❶ *adj* **1** suitable **2** likely **3** quick-witted **aptitude** *n* **aptly** *adv*

aqualung *n* breathing apparatus used in underwater swimming

aquamarine *n* **1** precious stone ▷ *adj* **2** greenish-blue

aquarium *n, pl* **aquariums, aquaria** tank for water animals or plants

aquatic *adj* living, growing, done in or on water

aqueduct *n* artificial channel for water, esp. one like a bridge

aquiline *adj* like an eagle

arable *adj* suitable for growing crops

arbiter *n* judge, umpire **arbitrary** *adj* **1** despotic **2** random **arbitrate** *v* settle (dispute) impartially **arbitration** *n* **arbitrator** *n*

arboreal *adj* of or living in trees

arc ❶ *n* part of circumference of circle or similar curve

arcade ❶ *n* **1** row of arches on pillars **2** covered walk or avenue

arcane *adj* secret

arch¹ ❶ *n* **1** curved structure spanning an opening **2** a curved shape **3** curved part of the sole of the foot ▷ *v* **4** form, make into, an arch

— THESAURUS —

drive, road, passage; *often plural* = **proposal**, offer, appeal, advance, application

appropriate *adj* = **suitable**, fitting, relevant, to the point, apt ≠ **unsuitable** ▷ *v* = **seize**, claim, acquire, confiscate, usurp ≠ **relinquish**; = **allocate**, allow, budget, devote, assign ≠ **withhold**

approve *v* = **agree to**, allow, pass, recommend, permit ≠ **veto**

apt *adj* = **appropriate**, fitting,

suitable, relevant, to the point ≠ **inappropriate**; = **inclined**, likely, ready, disposed, prone; = **gifted**, skilled, quick, talented, sharp ≠ **slow**

arc *n* = **curve**, bend, bow, arch, crescent

arcade *n* = **gallery**, cloister, portico, colonnade

arch¹ *n* = **archway**, curve, dome, span/vault; = **curve**, bend, bow, crook, arc ▷ *v* = **curve**, bridge, bend, bow, span

arch² ❶ *adj* knowingly playful

arch- *comb. form* chief, as in *archangel, archenemy*

archaeology *n* study of ancient times from remains **archaeologist** *n*

archaic *adj* old, primitive **archaism** *n* word no longer in use

archbishop *n* chief bishop

archetype *n* 1 prototype 2 perfect specimen **archetypal** *adj*

archipelago *n, pl* **-gos** group of islands

architect ❶ *n* 1 person qualified to design buildings 2 contriver **architecture** *n*

Arctic ❶ *adj* 1 of north polar region 2 *(without cap.)* very cold ▷ *n* 3 north polar region

ardent ❶ *adj* 1 intensely enthusiastic 2 passionate **ardently** *adv*

arduous *adj* hard to accomplish

are pres. tense of BE *(used with you, we and they)*

area ❶ *n* 1 surface extent

2 two-dimensional expanse enclosed by boundary 3 region 4 part 5 field of activity

arena ❶ *n* 1 space in middle of amphitheatre or stadium 2 sphere, territory

argon *n* gas found in the air

argue ❶ *v* **-guing, -gued** 1 quarrel, offer reasons (for) 2 debate **arguable** *adj* **arguably** *adv* **argument** *n* **argumentative** *adj*

aria *n* song in opera etc.

arid *adj* 1 dry 2 dull

arise ❶ *v* **arising, arose, arisen** 1 get up 2 rise (up) 3 come about

aristocracy *n, pl* **-cies** upper classes **aristocrat** *n* **aristocratic** *adj*

arithmetic *n* science of numbers

ark *n* Noah's vessel

arm¹ ❶ *n* 1 upper limb from shoulder to wrist 2 anything similar, as branch of sea, supporting rail of chair etc. 3 sleeve **armful** *n* **armhole** *n* **armpit** *n* hollow under arm at shoulder

——————————————— THESAURUS ———————————————

arch² *adj* = **playful**, sly, mischievous, saucy, pert

architect *n* = **designer**, planner, draughtsman, master builder, father

Arctic *adj* = **polar**, far-northern, hyperborean

ardent *adj* = **enthusiastic**, keen, eager, avid, zealous ≠ **indifferent**; = **passionate**, intense, impassioned, lusty, amorous ≠ **cold**

area *n* = **region**, quarter, district, zone, neighbourhood; = **part**,

section, sector, portion, reach

arena *n* = **ring**, ground, field, theatre, bowl

argue *v* = **quarrel**, fight, row, clash, dispute; = **discuss**, debate, dispute; = **claim**, reason, challenge, insist, maintain

arise *v* = **happen**, start, begin, follow, result; *(Old-fashioned)* = **get to your feet**, get up, rise, stand up, spring up

arm¹ *n* = **upper limb**, limb, appendage, part, office

arm² ❶ v 1 supply with weapons
2 take up arms ▷ pl n 3 weapons
4 war 5 heraldic emblem

armada n large fleet

armadillo n, pl **-los** S Amer.
animal protected by bony plates

armistice n truce

armour ❶ n 1 defensive covering
2 plating of tanks, warships etc.
3 armoured fighting vehicles
armoury n

army ❶ n, pl **armies** 1 military
land force 2 great number

aroma ❶ n sweet smell **aromatic**
adj

around ❶ prep/adv 1 on all sides
(of) 2 somewhere in or near
3 approximately 4 in a circle

5 here and there

arouse ❶ v awaken, stimulate

arraign v accuse, indict

arrange ❶ v 1 set in proper
order 2 make agreement
3 plan 4 adapt music
arrangement n

array ❶ n 1 order, esp. military
2 dress 3 imposing show ▷ v 4 set
out 5 dress richly

arrears pl n money owed

arrest ❶ v 1 detain by legal
authority 2 stop 3 catch attention
▷ n 4 seizure by warrant
arresting adj striking

arrive ❶ v 1 reach destination
2 reach, attain 3 (Inf) succeed
arrival n

— THESAURUS —

arm² v = **equip**, provide, supply,
array, furnish

armour n = **protection**, covering,
shield, sheathing, armour plate

army n = **soldiers**, military, troops,
armed force, legions; = **vast
number**, host, gang, mob, flock

aroma n = **scent**, smell, perfume,
fragrance, bouquet

around prep = **surrounding**,
about, enclosing, encompassing,
framing; = **approximately**, about,
nearly, close to, roughly ▷ adv
= **everywhere**, about, throughout,
all over, here and there; = **near**,
close, nearby, at hand, close at hand

arouse v = **stimulate**, encourage,
inspire, prompt, spur ≠ **quell**;
= **awaken**, wake up, rouse, waken

arrange v = **plan**, agree, prepare,
determine, organize; = **put in
order**, group, order, sort, position

≠ **disorganize**; = **adapt**, score,
orchestrate, harmonize, instrument

array n = **arrangement**, show,
supply, display, collection; (Poet)
= **clothing**, dress, clothes,
garments, apparel ▷ v = **arrange**,
show, group, present, range;
= **dress**, clothe, deck, decorate,
adorn

arrest v = **capture**, catch, nick (Sl,
chiefly Brit), seize, detain ≠ **release**;
= **stop**, end, limit, block, slow
≠ **speed up**; = **fascinate**, hold,
occupy, engage, grip ▷ n
= **capture**, bust (Inf), detention,
seizure ≠ **release**; = **stoppage**,
suppression, obstruction, blockage,
hindrance ≠ **acceleration**

arrive v = **come**, appear, turn up,
show up (Inf), draw near ≠ **depart**;
(Inf) = **succeed**, make it (Inf),
triumph, do well, thrive

arrow ❶ *n* shaft shot from bow
arsenal ❶ *n* stores for guns etc.
arsenic *n* soft, grey, very poisonous metallic element
arson *n* crime of intentionally setting property on fire
art ❶ *n* **1** human skill as opposed to nature **2** creative skill in painting, poetry, music etc. **3** any of the works produced thus **4** craft **5** knack ▷ *pl* **6** branches of learning other than science **7** wiles **artful** *adj* wily **artfully** *adv*
artist *n* one who practises fine art, esp. painting **artiste** *n* professional entertainer **artistic** *adj* **artistry** *n* **artless** *adj* natural, frank **arty** *adj* **artier, artiest** ostentatiously artistic
artefact *n* something made by man
artery *n, pl* **-teries 1** tube carrying blood from heart **2** any main channel of communications
arthritis *n* painful inflammation of joint(s) **arthritic** *adj/n*
artichoke *n* thistle-like plant with edible flower
article ❶ *n* **1** item, object **2** short written piece **3** *(Grammar)* words the, a, an **4** clause in a contract **articled** *adj* bound as an apprentice
articulate ❶ *adj* **1** fluent **2** clear, distinct ▷ *v* **3** utter distinctly **articulated** *adj* jointed
artifice *n* contrivance, trick **artificial** *adj* **1** synthetic **2** insincere **artificially** *adv*
artillery ❶ *n* **1** large guns on wheels **2** troops who use them
artisan *n* craftsman
as ❶ *adv/conj* **1** denoting: comparison **2** similarity **3** equality **4** identity **5** concurrence **6** reason
asbestos *n* fibrous mineral which does not burn
ascend *v* **1** go, come up **2** climb **ascendancy** *n* dominance **ascent** *n*
ascertain *v* find out
ascetic *n/adj* (person) practising severe self-denial
ascribe *v* attribute, assign

—————————————— THESAURUS ——————————————

arrow *n* = **dart**, flight, bolt, shaft *(Archaic)*, quarrel; = **pointer**, indicator, marker
arsenal *n* = **armoury**, supply, store, stockpile, storehouse
art *n* = **artwork**, style of art, fine art, creativity
article *n* = **feature**, story, paper, piece, item; = **thing**, piece, unit, item, object; = **clause**, point, part, section, item
articulate *adj* = **expressive**, clear, coherent, fluent, eloquent
≠ incoherent ▷ *v* = **express**, say, state, word, declare
artillery *n* = **big guns**, battery, cannon, ordnance, gunnery
as *conj* = **when**, while, just as, at the time that, during the time that ▷ *prep* = **in the role of**, being, under the name of, in the character of ▷ *conj* = **in the way that**, like, in the manner that; = **since**, because, seeing that, considering that, on account of the fact that

asexual *adj* without sex

ash¹ *n* remains of anything burnt
 ashen *adj* pale

ash² *n* **1** deciduous timber tree **2** its wood

ashamed ❶ *adj* feeling shame

ashore ❶ *adv* on shore

aside ❶ *adv* **1** to, on one side **2** privately ▷ *n* **3** words spoken so as not to be heard by all

asinine *adj* stupid, silly

ask ❶ *v* **1** make request or inquiry **2** invite **3** require

askance *adv* with mistrust

askew *adv* awry

asleep ❶ *adj/adv* sleeping

asp *n* small poisonous snake

asparagus *n* plant with edible young shoots

aspect ❶ *n* **1** appearance **2** outlook **3** side

aspen *n* type of poplar tree

aspersion *n* (*usu. pl*) malicious remark

asphalt *n* covering for road surfaces etc.

aspic *n* jelly used to coat meat, eggs, fish etc.

aspidistra *n* plant with long tapered leaves

aspire *v* have great ambition
 aspiration *n* **aspiring** *adj*

aspirin *n* (tablet of) drug used to relieve pain and fever

ass ❶ *n* **1** donkey **2** fool

assail *v* **1** attack, assault **2** criticize **assailable** *adj*
 assailant *n*

assassin ❶ *n* one who kills for money or political reasons
 assassinate *v* **assassination** *n*

assault ❶ *n/v* attack

assemble ❶ *v* **1** meet, bring together **2** put together
 assembly *n*

assent *v* **1** agree ▷ *n* **2** agreement

THESAURUS

---

ashamed *adj* = **embarrassed**, sorry, guilty, distressed, humiliated ≠ **proud**

ashore *adv* = **on land**, on the beach, on the shore, aground, to the shore

aside *adv* = **to one side**, separately, apart, beside, out of the way ▷ *n* = **interpolation**, parenthesis

ask *v* = **inquire**, question, quiz, query, interrogate ≠ **answer**; = **request**, appeal to, plead with, demand, beg; = **invite**, bid, summon

asleep *adj* = **sleeping**, napping, dormant, dozing, slumbering

aspect *n* = **feature**, side, factor, angle, characteristic; = **position/view**, situation, scene, prospect; = **appearance**, look, air, condition, quality

ass *n* = **donkey**, moke (*Sl*); = **fool**, idiot, twit (*Inf, chiefly Brit*), oaf, jackass

assassin *n* = **murderer**, killer, slayer, liquidator, executioner

assault *n* = **attack**, raid, invasion, charge, offensive ≠ **defence** ▷ *v* = **strike**, attack, beat, knock, bang

assemble *v* = **gather**, meet, collect, rally, come together ≠ **scatter**; = **bring together**, collect, gather, rally, come together

assert ❶ v declare strongly, insist upon **assertion** n **assertive** adj **assertively** adv

assess ❶ v 1 fix value or amount of 2 evaluate **assessment** n **assessor** n

asset ❶ n 1 valuable or useful person, thing ▷ pl 2 things that can be used to raise money

assiduous adj persevering **assiduously** adv

assign ❶ v 1 appoint 2 allot 3 transfer **assignation** n secret meeting **assignment** n

assimilate v 1 take in 2 incorporate 3 (cause to) become similar **assimilation** n

assist ❶ v give help to **assistance** n **assistant** n

associate ❶ v 1 link, connect 2 join 3 keep company 4 combine, unite ▷ n 5 partner 6 friend 7 subordinate member ▷ adj

8 affiliated **association** n

assonance n rhyming of vowel sounds but not consonants

assorted ❶ adj mixed **assortment** n mixture

assume ❶ v 1 take for granted 2 pretend 3 take on **assumption** n

assure ❶ v 1 tell positively, promise 2 make sure 3 insure against loss, esp. of life **assurance** n **assured** adj 1 sure 2 confident, self-possessed

aster n plant with starlike flowers

asterisk n star (°) used in printing

astern adv 1 in, behind the stern 2 backwards

asteroid n small planet

asthma n illness in which one has difficulty breathing **asthmatic** adj/n

astigmatism n inability of lens (esp. of eye) to focus properly

astir adv on the move

——————— THESAURUS ———————

assert v = **state**, argue, maintain, declare, swear ≠ **deny**; = **insist upon**, stress, defend, uphold, put forward ≠ **retract**

assess v = **judge**, estimate, analyse, evaluate, rate; = **evaluate**, rate, tax, value, estimate

asset n = **benefit**, help, service, aid, advantage ≠ **disadvantage**

assign v = **give**, set, grant, allocate, give out; = **select for**, post, commission, elect, appoint; = **attribute**, credit, put down, set down, ascribe

assist v = **help**, support, aid, cooperate with, abet

associate v = **connect**, link, ally,

identify, join ≠ **separate**; = **socialize**, mix, accompany, mingle, consort ≠ **avoid** ▷ n = **partner**, friend, ally, colleague, mate (Inf)

assorted adj = **various**, different, mixed, varied, diverse ≠ **similar**

assume v = **presume**, think, believe, expect, suppose ≠ **know**; = **take on**, accept, shoulder, take over, put on; = **simulate**, affect, adopt, put on, imitate

assure v = **convince**, encourage, persuade, satisfy, comfort; = **make certain**, ensure, confirm, guarantee, secure; = **promise to**, pledge to, vow to, guarantee to, swear to

astonish ● *v* amaze, surprise, stun **astonishment** *n*

astound *v* astonish greatly **astounding** *adj*

astral *adj* of the stars

astray *adv/adj* **1** off the right path **2** into error or sin

astride *adv* with legs apart

astringent *adj* **1** sharp **2** stopping bleeding ▷ *n* **3** astringent substance

astrology *n* foretelling of events by stars **astrologer** *n* **astrological** *adj*

astronaut *n* one trained for travel in space

astronomy *n* scientific study of heavenly bodies **astronomer** *n* **astronomical** *adj* **1** very large **2** of astronomy **astronomically** *adv*

astute ● *adj* perceptive, shrewd **astutely** *adv*

asunder *adv* **1** apart **2** in pieces

asylum ● *n* **1** refuge, place of safety **2** (*Obs*) psychiatric hospital

asymmetry *n* lack of symmetry **asymmetrical** *adj*

at *prep/adv* **1** denoting: location in space or time **2** rate **3** condition or state **4** amount **5** direction **6** cause

atheism *n* belief that there is no God **atheist** *n*

athlete *n* person trained in or good at track and field sports

atlas *n* book of maps

atmosphere ● *n* **1** gases surrounding earth etc. **2** prevailing mood **atmospheric** *adj* **atmospherics** *pl n* radio interference

atoll *n* ring-shaped coral island enclosing lagoon

atom ● *n* **1** smallest unit of matter which can enter into chemical combination **2** any very small particle **atomic** *adj* **atomizer** *n* instrument for discharging liquids in a fine spray **atomic bomb** bomb with immense power derived from nuclear fission or fusion **atomic energy** nuclear energy

atonal *adj* (of music) not in an established key

atone *v* make amends (for) **atonement** *n*

atop *prep* on top of

atrocious *adj* **1** extremely cruel **2** horrifying **3** (*Inf*) very bad **atrociously** *adv* **atrocity** *n*

atrophy *n, pl* **-phies 1** wasting away ▷ *v* **2** waste away

attach ● *v* **1** join, fasten **2** attribute **attached** *adj* (with *to*) fond of **attachment** *n*

— THESAURUS —

astonish *v* = **amaze**, surprise, stun, stagger, bewilder

astute *adj* = **intelligent**, sharp, clever, subtle, shrewd ≠ **stupid**

asylum *n* (*Old-fashioned*) = **psychiatric hospital**, hospital, institution, mental hospital, madhouse (*Inf*); = **refuge**, haven, safety, protection, preserve

atmosphere *n* = **air**, sky, heavens, aerosphere; = **feeling**, character, environment, spirit, surroundings

atom *n* = **particle**, bit, spot, trace, molecule

attach *v* = **ascribe**, connect, attribute, assign, associate

attaché n specialist attached to diplomatic mission **attaché case** flat rectangular briefcase

attack ❶ v 1 take action against 2 criticize 3 set about with vigour 4 affect adversely ▷ n 5 attacking action 6 bout **attacker** n

attain ❶ v 1 arrive at 2 achieve **attainable** adj **attainment** n

attempt ❶ v/n try

attend ❶ v 1 be present at 2 accompany 3 (with to) take care of 4 pay attention to **attendance** n 1 an attending 2 persons attending **attendant** n/adj **attention** n 1 notice 2 heed 3 care 4 courtesy **attentive** adj 1 giving attention 2 considerately helpful

attest v bear witness to

attic ❶ n space within roof

attire v/n dress, array

attitude ❶ n 1 mental view, opinion 2 posture, pose 3 disposition, behaviour

attorney n person legally appointed to act for another, esp. a lawyer

attract ❶ v 1 draw (attention etc.) 2 arouse interest of 3 cause to come closer (as magnet etc.) **attraction** n **attractive** adj

attribute ❶ v 1 regard as belonging to or produced by ▷ n 2 quality or characteristic **attributable** adj **attribution** n

attrition n wearing away

attune v 1 tune 2 adjust

atypical adj not typical

aubergine n purple fruit eaten as vegetable

auburn adj/n reddish brown

auction n 1 public sale in which goods are sold to the highest bidder ▷ v 2 sell by auction **auctioneer** n

audacious adj 1 bold 2 impudent **audaciously** adv **audacity** n

audible adj able to be heard **audibly** adv

————————— THESAURUS —————————

attack v = **assault**, strike (at), mug, ambush, tear into ≠ **defend**; = **invade**, occupy, raid, infringe, storm ▷ n = **assault**, charge, campaign, strike, raid ≠ **defence**; = **criticism**, censure, disapproval, abuse, bad press; = **bout**, fit, stroke, seizure, spasm

attain v = **obtain**, get, reach, complete, gain

attempt v = **try**, seek, aim, struggle, venture ▷ n = **try**, go (Inf), shot (Inf), effort, trial

attend v = **be present**, go to, visit, frequent, haunt ≠ **be absent**; = **pay attention**, listen, hear, mark, note ≠ **ignore**

attic n = **loft**, garret, roof space

attitude n = **opinion/view**, position, approach, mood, = **position**, bearing, pose, stance, carriage

attract v = **allure**, draw, persuade, charm, appeal to ≠ **repel**; = **pull**, draw, magnetize

attribute v = **ascribe**, credit, refer, trace, assign ▷ n = **quality**, feature, property, character, element

audience ❶ n 1 people assembled to listen or watch 2 formal interview

audit n 1 formal examination of accounts ▷ v 2 examine accounts **auditor** n

audition n 1 test of prospective performer ▷ v 2 set, perform such a test **auditorium** n place where audience sits

Aug. August

augment v increase, enlarge

augur v foretell

August n eighth month

auk n northern sea bird

aunt n 1 father's or mother's sister 2 wife of parent's sibling **auntie** n (Inf) aunt

au pair n young foreigner who receives board and lodging in return for housework etc.

aura ❶ n atmosphere considered distinctive of person or thing

aural adj of, by ear

auricle n 1 outside ear 2 an upper cavity of heart

aurora n, pl **-ras, -rae** 1 lights in the sky radiating from polar regions 2 dawn

auspices pl n patronage **auspicious** adj giving hope of future success **auspiciously** adv

austere adj 1 severe 2 without luxury **austerity** n

authentic ❶ adj genuine **authentically** adv **authenticate** v make valid **authenticity** n

author ❶ n 1 writer 2 originator

authority ❶ n, pl **-ties** 1 legal power or right 2 delegated power 3 influence 4 permission 5 expert 6 board in control **authoritarian** n/adj (person) insisting on strict obedience **authoritative** adj **authorize** v 1 empower 2 permit **authorization** n

autism n developmental condition characterized by limited ability to communicate **autistic** adj

auto- comb. form self, as in autosuggestion

autobiography n, pl **-phies** life of person written by himself **autobiographical** adj

autocrat n 1 absolute ruler 2 despotic person **autocratic** adj **autocracy** n

Autocue® n electronic television device displaying speaker's script unseen by audience

autogiro, autogyro n, pl **-ros** self-propelled aircraft with unpowered rotor

--- THESAURUS ---

audience n = **spectators**, company, crowd, gathering, gallery; = **interview**, meeting, hearing, exchange, reception

aura n = **air**, feeling, quality, atmosphere, tone

authentic adj = **real**, pure, genuine, valid, undisputed ≠ **fake**

author n = **writer**, composer, novelist, hack, creator; = **creator**, father, producer, designer, founder

authority n usually plural = **powers that be**, government, police, officials, the state; = **expert**, specialist, professional, master, guru; = **command**, power, control, rule, management (Inf)

autograph n **1** signature ▷ v **2** sign

automatic ❶ adj **1** operated or controlled mechanically **2** done without conscious thought ▷ adj/n **3** self-loading (weapon) **automatically** adv **automation** n introduction of automatic devices in industry **automaton** n **1** robot **2** person who acts mechanically

automobile n motorcar

autonomy ❶ n self-government **autonomous** adj

autopsy n, pl **-sies** postmortem

autumn n season after summer **autumnal** adj

auxiliary adj/n (person) helping, subsidiary

avail v **1** be of use, advantage ▷ n **2** benefit **available** adj **1** obtainable **2** accessible **availability** n

avalanche ❶ n **1** mass of snow, ice, sliding down mountain **2** any great quantity

avant-garde ❶ adj innovative and progressive

avarice n greed for wealth **avaricious** adj

avatar n **1** (Hinduism) appearance of a god in animal or human form **2** (Computers) graphical representation of a person in a virtual environment, such as an online role-playing game

avenge v take vengeance for

avenue ❶ n **1** wide street **2** approach **3** double row of trees

aver v **averring, averred** affirm, assert

average ❶ n **1** middle or usual value ▷ adj **2** ordinary ▷ v **3** calculate an average **4** form an average

averse adj disinclined **aversion** n (object of) dislike

avert ❶ v **1** turn away **2** ward off

aviary n, pl **aviaries** enclosure for birds

—— THESAURUS ——

automatic adj = **mechanical**, automated, mechanized, push-button, self-propelling ≠ **done by hand**; = **involuntary**, natural, unconscious, mechanical, spontaneous ≠ **conscious**

autonomy n = **independence**, freedom, sovereignty, self-determination, self-government ≠ **dependency**

avalanche n = **snow-slide**, landslide, landslip; = **large amount**, barrage, torrent, deluge, inundation

avant-garde adj = **progressive**, pioneering, experimental, innovative, unconventional ≠ **conservative**

avenue n = **street**, way, course, drive, road

average n = **standard**, normal, usual, par ▷ adj = **usual**, standard, general, normal, regular ≠ **unusual**; = **mean**, middle, medium, intermediate, median ≠ **minimum** ▷ v = **make on average**, be on average, even out to, do on average, balance out to

avert v = **ward off**, avoid, prevent, frustrate, fend off; = **turn away**, turn aside

aviation n art of flying aircraft
  aviator n
avid adj 1 keen 2 greedy (for)
  avidly adv
avocado n, pl **-dos** tropical
  pear-shaped fruit
avoid ❶ v 1 keep away from
  2 refrain from 3 not allow to
  happen **avoidable** adj **avoidance**
  n
avow v 1 declare 2 admit **avowal**
  n **avowed** adj
await ❶ v 1 wait or stay for 2 be
  in store for
awake ❶ v **awaking, awoke,**
  awoken 1 emerge or rouse from
  sleep 2 (cause to) become alert
  ▷ adj 3 not sleeping 4 alert
  awaken v awake **awakening** n

award ❶ v 1 give formally ▷ n
  2 thing awarded
aware ❶ adj informed, conscious
  awareness n
awash adv covered by water
away ❶ adv 1 absent, apart, at a
  distance, out of the way ▷ adj
  2 not present
awe ❶ n 1 dread mingled with
  reverence ▷ v 2 astonish, frighten
  awesome adj
awful ❶ adj 1 dreadful 2 (Inf) very
  great **awfully** adv 1 in an
  unpleasant way 2 (Inf) very much
awhile adv for a time
awkward ❶ adj 1 clumsy
  2 difficult 3 inconvenient
  4 embarrassed **awkwardly** adv
  awkwardness n

—————— THESAURUS ——————

avoid v = **prevent**, stop, frustrate,
hamper, foil; = **refrain from**,
bypass, dodge, eschew, escape;
= **keep away from**, dodge, shun,
evade, steer clear of
await v = **wait for**, expect, look for,
look forward to, anticipate; = **be in**
store for, wait for, be ready for, lie
in wait for, be in readiness for
awake adj = **not sleeping**,
sleepless, wide-awake, aware,
conscious ≠ **asleep** ▷ v = **wake**
up, come to, wake, stir, awaken;
= **alert**, stimulate, provoke, revive,
arouse
award n = **prize**, gift, trophy,
decoration, grant ▷ v = **present**
with, give, grant, hand out, confer
aware adj = **informed**,
enlightened, knowledgeable,
learned, expert ≠ **ignorant**

away adj = **absent**, out, gone,
elsewhere, abroad ▷ adv = **off**,
elsewhere, abroad, hence, from
here; = **aside**, out of the way, to one
side; = **at a distance**, far, apart,
remote, isolated
awe n = **wonder**, fear, respect,
reverence, horror ≠ **contempt** ▷ v
= **impress**, amaze, stun, frighten,
terrify
awful adj = **bad**, poor, terrible,
appalling, foul ≠ **wonderful**;
= **unwell**, poorly (Inf), ill, terrible, sick
awkward adj = **embarrassing**,
difficult, sensitive, delicate,
uncomfortable ≠ **comfortable**;
= **inconvenient**, difficult,
troublesome, cumbersome,
unwieldy ≠ **convenient**; = **clumsy**,
lumbering, bumbling, unwieldy,
ponderous ≠ **graceful**

awl n tool for boring wood etc.

awning n (canvas) roof to protect from weather

AWOL adj (Mil) absent without leave

awry adv 1 crookedly 2 amiss ▷ adj 3 crooked 4 wrong

axe ❶ n 1 tool for chopping 2 (Inf) dismissal from employment ▷ v 3 (Inf) dismiss from employment

axiom n accepted principle **axiomatic** adj

axis ❶ n, pl **axes** (imaginary) line round which body spins

axle n shaft on which wheels turn

aye, ay interj 1 yes ▷ n 2 affirmative answer or vote

azalea n genus of shrubby flowering plants

azure adj sky-blue

————————————————— THESAURUS —————————————

axe n = **hatchet**, chopper, tomahawk, cleaver, adze ▷ v (Inf) = **abandon**, end, eliminate, cancel, scrap

axis n = **pivot**, shaft, axle, spindle, centre line

b

b

BA Bachelor of Arts

baas n (S Afr) boss

babble v/n (make) foolish, incoherent speech

babe n baby

babiche n (Canad) thongs or lacings of rawhide

baboon n large monkey

baby ❶ n, pl **-bies** infant **baby-sitter** n one who cares for children when parents are out **baby-sit** v

bach n (NZ) small holiday cottage

bachelor n unmarried man

bacillus n, pl **-li** minute organism sometimes causing disease

back ❶ n **1** hind part of anything, e.g. human body **2** part opposite front **3** part further away or less used **4** (position of) player in ball games ▷ adj **5** situated behind **6** earlier ▷ adv **7** at, to the back **8** in, into the past **9** in return ▷ v **10** move backwards **11** support **12** put wager on **13** provide with back **14** provide with musical accompaniment **backer** n **backward** adj towards the rear **backwardness** n **backwards** adv to rear, past, worse state **backbite** v slander absent person **backbone** n **1** spinal column **2** strength of character **backcloth, backdrop** n painted cloth at back of stage **backdate** v make effective from earlier date **backfire** v **1** (of plan, scheme, etc.) fail to work **2** ignite wrongly **backgammon** n game played with draughtsmen and dice **background** n **1** space behind chief figures of picture etc. **2** past history of person **backhand** n stroke made with hand turned backwards **backlash** n sudden adverse reaction **backside** n rump **backpack** n **1** large pack carried on the back ▷ v **2** go travelling or hiking with a backpack

bacon n cured pig's flesh

bacteria ❶ pl n, sing **-rium** microscopic organisms **bacterial** adj **bacteriology** n

bad ❶ adj **worse, worst 1** faulty

THESAURUS

baby n = **child**, infant, babe, bairn (Scot.), newborn child ▷ adj = **small**, little, minute, tiny, mini

back n = **spine**, backbone, vertebrae, spinal column/vertebral column ▷ adj = **rearmost**, hind, hindmost ▷ v = **support**, help, aid, champion, defend ≠ **oppose**

bacteria pl n = **microorganisms**, viruses, bugs (Sl), germs, microbes

bad adj = **harmful**, damaging, dangerous, destructive, unhealthy

b

2 harmful **3** evil **4** severe **5** rotten **6** (Sl) very good **badly** adv

badge ❶ n distinguishing emblem

badger ❶ n **1** burrowing night animal ▷ v **2** pester, worry

badminton n game played with rackets and shuttlecocks

baffle ❶ v **1** check, frustrate, bewilder ▷ n **2** device to regulate flow of liquid etc.

bag ❶ n **1** sack **2** measure of quantity **3** woman's handbag ▷ v **4** bulge **5** sag **6** put in bag **7** kill as game, etc. **baggy** adj loose

bagatelle n **1** trifle **2** game like pinball

baggage ❶ n suitcases, luggage

bagpipes pl n musical wind instrument

bail¹ ❶ n (Law) **1** security given for person's reappearance in court ▷ v **2** (obtain) release on security

bail² n (Cricket) crosspiece on wicket

bail³, bale v empty water from boat **bail out** parachute

bailiff n land steward, agent

bait ❶ n **1** food to entice fish **2** any lure ▷ v **3** lure **4** persecute

baize n smooth woollen cloth

bake v **1** cook or harden by dry heat ▷ v **2** make bread, cakes etc. **baker** n **bakery** n, pl **-eries** **baking powder** raising agent used in cooking

bakeapple n cloudberry

bakkie n (S Afr) small truck

balalaika n Russian musical instrument, like guitar

balance ❶ n **1** pair of scales **2** equilibrium **3** surplus **4** sum due on an account **5** difference between two sums ▷ v **6** weigh **7** bring to equilibrium

━━━━━━━━━━ THESAURUS ━━━━━━━

≠ **beneficial**; = **unfavourable**, distressing, unfortunate, grim, unpleasant; = **inferior**, poor, inadequate, faulty, unsatisfactory ≠ **satisfactory**; = **incompetent**, poor, useless, incapable, unfit; = **grim**, severe, hard, tough; = **wicked**, criminal, evil, corrupt, immoral ≠ **virtuous**

badge n = **image**, brand, stamp, identification, crest

badger v = **pester**, harry, bother, bug (Inf), bully

baffle v = **puzzle**, confuse, stump, bewilder, confound ≠ **explain**

bag n = **sack**, container, sac, receptacle, land ▷ v = **catch**, kill, shoot, capture, acquire

baggage n = **luggage**, things, cases, bags, equipment

bail¹ n (Law) = **security**, bond, guarantee, pledge, warranty

bait n = **lure**, attraction, incentive, carrot (Inf), temptation ▷ v = **tease**, annoy, irritate, bother, mock

balance v = **stabilize**, level, steady ≠ **overbalance**; = **offset**, match, square, even up; = **weigh**, consider, compare, estimate, contrast; (Accounting) = **calculate**, total, determine, estimate, settle ▷ n = **equilibrium**, stability, steadiness, evenness ≠ **instability**; = **stability**, equanimity, steadiness; = **parity**, equity, fairness, impartiality, equality

b

balcony ❶ n, pl **-nies 1** platform outside window **2** upper seats in theatre

bald ❶ adj **1** hairless **2** plain **3** bare **balding** adj

bale n, v bundle or package

baleful adj menacing

balk, baulk v **1** swerve, pull up **2** thwart **3** shirk ▷ n **4** hindrance

ball[1] ❶ n **1** anything round **2** globe, sphere, esp. as used in games ▷ v **3** gather into a mass **ball bearings** steel balls used to lessen friction

ball[2] n assembly for dancing **ballroom** n

ballad n **1** narrative poem **2** simple song

ballast n heavy material put in ship to steady it

ballet n theatrical presentation of dancing and miming **ballerina** n

ballistics pl n scientific study of motion of projectiles

balloon ❶ n **1** large bag filled with air or gas ▷ v **2** puff out

ballot ❶ n **1** voting, usually by paper ▷ v **2** vote

balm n healing or soothing (ointment)

balmy adj **balmier, balmiest** (of weather) mild and pleasant

balsa n Amer. tree with light but strong wood

balsam n resinous aromatic substance

bamboo n large tropical treelike reed

bamboozle v mystify, hoax

ban ❶ v **banning, banned 1** prohibit, forbid, outlaw ▷ n **2** prohibition **3** proclamation

banal adj commonplace, trite **banality** n

banana n **1** tropical treelike plant **2** its fruit

band[1] ❶ n **1** strip used to bind **2** range of frequencies **bandage** n, v (apply) strip of cloth for binding wound

band[2] ❶ n **1** company **2** company of musicians ▷ v **3** bind together

bandanna, bandana n handkerchief

B & B bed and breakfast

bandit ❶ n **1** outlaw **2** robber

bandwagon n **jump on the bandwagon** join something that

— THESAURUS —

balcony n = **terrace**, veranda; = **upper circle**, gods, gallery

bald adj = **hairless**, depilated, baldheaded; = **plain**, direct, frank, straightforward, blunt

ball[1] n = **sphere**, drop, globe, pellet, orb

balloon v = **expand**, rise, increase, swell, blow up

ballot n = **vote**, election/voting, poll, polling

ban v = **prohibit**, bar, block, veto, forbid ≠ **permit** ▷ n = **prohibition**, restriction/veto, boycott, embargo ≠ **permission**

band[1] n = **headband**, strip, ribbon, strip, belt

band[2] n = **ensemble**, group, orchestra, combo; = **gang**, company, group, party, team

bandit n = **robber**, outlaw, raider, plunderer, mugger (Inf)

seems assured of success

bandy v **-dier, -diest** toss from one to another **bandy-legged** adj curving outwards

bane n person or thing causing misery or distress **baneful** adj

bang ❶ n **1** sudden loud noise **2** heavy blow ▷ v **3** make loud noise **4** beat **5** slam

banger n (Sl) **1** sausage **2** (Inf) old car **3** loud firework

bangle n ring worn on arm or leg

banish ❶ v **1** exile **2** drive away

banisters pl n railing on staircase

banjo n, pl **-jos, -joes** musical instrument like guitar

bank¹ ❶ n **1** mound of earth **2** edge of river etc. ▷ v **3** enclose with ridge **4** pile up

bank² ❶ n **1** establishment for keeping, lending, exchanging etc. money ▷ v **2** put in bank **3** keep with bank **banker** n **banking** n **banknote** n written promise of payment **bank on** rely on

bankrupt ❶ n **1** one who fails in

business, insolvent debtor ▷ adj **2** financially ruined ▷ v **3** make bankrupt **bankruptcy** n

banner ❶ n **1** placard **2** flag

banns pl n public declaration of intended marriage

banquet ❶ n/v feast

banshee n spirit whose wailing warns of death

bantam n **1** small chicken **2** very light boxing weight

banter v **1** make fun of ▷ n **2** light, teasing language

bar ❶ n **1** rod or block of any substance **2** obstacle **3** rail in law court **4** body of lawyers **5** counter where drinks are served **6** unit of music ▷ v **7** fasten **8** obstruct **9** exclude ▷ prep **10** except **barman** n

barachois n (in the Atlantic Provinces of Canada) a shallow lagoon formed by a sand bar

barb n **1** sharp point curving backwards **2** cutting remark **barbed** adj

— THESAURUS —

bang n = **explosion**, pop, clash, crack, blast; = **blow**, knock, stroke, punch, bump ▷ v = **resound**, boom, explode, thunder, thump ▷ adv = **exactly**, straight, square, squarely, precisely

banish v = **expel**, exile, outlaw, deport ≠ **admit**; = **get rid of**, remove

bank¹ n = **side**, edge, margin, shore, brink; = **mound**, banking, rise, hill, mass ▷ v = **tilt**, tip, pitch, heel, slope

bank² n = **financial institution**, repository, depository; = **store**,

fund, stock, source, supply ▷ v = **deposit**, keep, save

bankrupt adj = **insolvent**, broke (Inf), ruined, wiped out (Inf), impoverished ≠ **solvent**

banner n = **flag**, standard, colours, placard, pennant

banquet n = **feast**, spread (Inf), dinner, meal, revel

bar n = **public house**, pub (Inf, chiefly Brit), counter, inn, saloon; = **rod**, staff, stick, stake, rail; = **obstacle**, block, barrier, hurdle, hitch ≠ **aid** ▷ v = **lock**, block, secure, attach,

barbecue n 1 meal cooked outdoors over open fire ▷ v 2 cook thus

barber n person who shaves beards and cuts hair

barbiturate n derivative of barbituric acid used as drug

bard n poet

bare ❶ adj 1 uncovered 2 naked 3 plain 4 scanty ▷ v 5 make bare **barely** adv only just **barefaced** adj shameless

bargain ❶ n 1 something bought at favourable price 2 agreement ▷ v 3 haggle, negotiate

barge ❶ n 1 flat-bottomed freight boat ▷ v 2 (Inf) bump (into), push

baritone n 1 (singer with) second lowest adult male voice ▷ adj 2 of, for this voice

barium n white metallic element

bark¹ ❶ n/v (utter) sharp loud cry of dog etc.

bark² ❶ n outer layer of tree

barley n grain used for food and making malt

barmy adj -mier, -miest (Sl) insane

barn n building to store grain, hay etc. **barnyard** n

barnacle n shellfish which sticks to rocks and ships

barometer n instrument to measure pressure of atmosphere **barometric** adj

baron n 1 member of lowest rank of peerage 2 powerful businessman **baronial** adj

baronet n lowest British hereditary title

baroque adj extravagantly ornamented

barque n sailing ship

barracks ❶ pl n building for lodging soldiers

barrage ❶ n 1 heavy artillery fire 2 continuous heavy delivery of questions etc. 3 dam across river

barrel n 1 round wooden vessel 2 tube of gun etc.

barren ❶ adj 1 sterile 2 unprofitable

———— THESAURUS ————

bolt; = **block**, restrict, restrain, hamper, thwart; = **exclude**, ban, forbid, prohibit, keep out of ≠ **admit**

bare adj = **naked**, nude, stripped, uncovered, undressed ≠ **dressed**; = **simple**, spare, stark, austere, spartan ≠ **adorned**

bargain n = **good buy**, discount purchase, good deal, steal (Inf), snip (Inf); = **agreement**, deal (Inf), promise, contract, arrangement ▷ v = **negotiate**, deal, contract, mediate, covenant

barge n = **canal boat**, lighter, narrow boat, flatboat

bark¹ v = **yap**, bay, howl, snarl, growl ▷ n = **yap**, bay, howl, snarl, growl

bark² n = **covering**, casing, cover, skin, layer

barracks pl n = **camp**, quarters, garrison, encampment, billet

barrage n = **bombardment**, attack, bombing, assault, shelling; = **torrent**, mass, burst, stream, hail

barren adj = **desolate**, empty, desert, waste; = **unproductive**, dry, arid, unfruitful ≠ **fertile**

barricade ❶ *n* **1** improvised barrier ▷ *v* **2** block
barrier ❶ *n* fence, obstruction
barrister *n* advocate in the higher law courts
barrow *n* **1** small wheeled handcart **2** wheelbarrow
barter *v/n* (trade by) exchange of goods
base¹ ❶ *n* **1** bottom, foundation **2** starting point **3** centre of operations ▷ *v* **4** found, establish
baseless *adj* **basement** *n* lowest storey of building
base² ❶ **1** low, mean **2** despicable
baseball *n* game played with bat and ball
bash ❶ (*Inf*) ▷ *v* **1** strike violently ▷ *n* **2** blow **3** attempt
bashful *adj* shy, modest
basic ❶ *adj* **1** relating to, serving as base **2** fundamental **3** necessary
basically *adv* **basics** *pl n* fundamental principles, facts etc.
basil *n* aromatic herb
basin *n* **1** deep circular dish

2 harbour **3** land drained by river
basis ❶ *n, pl* **-ses 1** foundation **2** principal constituent
bask ❶ *v* lie in warmth and sunshine
basket *n* vessel made of woven cane, straw etc. **basketball** *n* ball game played by two teams
bass¹ ❶ *n* **1** lowest part in music **2** bass singer or voice ▷ *adj* **3** of bass
bass² *n* sea fish
bassoon *n* woodwind instrument of low tone
bastard *n* **1** child born of unmarried parents **2** (*Inf*) unpleasant person ▷ *adj* **3** illegitimate **4** spurious
bastion *n* **1** projecting part of fortification **2** defence
bat¹ *n* **1** club used to hit ball in cricket etc. ▷ *v* **2** strike with bat
bat² *n* nocturnal mouselike flying animal
batch ❶ *n* group or set of similar objects

— THESAURUS —

barricade *n* = **barrier**, wall, fence, blockade, obstruction ▷ *v* = **bar**, block, defend, secure, lock
barrier *n* = **barricade**, wall, bar, fence, boundary
base¹ *n* = **bottom**, floor, lowest part ≠ **top**; = **support**, stand, foot, rest, bed; = **foundation**, institution, organization, establishment ▷ *v* = **ground**, found, build, establish, depend; = **place**, set, post, station, establish
base² *adj* = **dishonourable**, evil, disgraceful, shameful, immoral

≠ **honourable**
bash *v* (*Inf*) = **hit**, beat, strike, knock, smash
basic *adj* = **fundamental**, main, essential, primary, vital; = **vital**, needed, important, key, necessary
basis *n* = **arrangement**, way, system, footing, agreement
bask *v* = **lie**, relax, lounge, sprawl, loaf
bass¹ *adj* = **deep**, low, resonant, sonorous, low-pitched
batch *n* = **group**, set, lot, crowd, pack

b

bated *adj* **with bated breath** anxiously

bath ❶ *n* **1** vessel or place to bathe in **2** water for bathing **3** act of bathing ▷ *v* **4** wash **bathroom** *n*

bathe ❶ *v* **1** swim **2** apply liquid **3** wash **4** immerse in water ▷ *n* **5** swim **6** wash **bather** *n*

baton ❶ *n* stick, esp. of policeman, conductor, marshal

battalion *n* military unit of three companies

batten *n* **1** strip of wood ▷ *v* **2** fasten

batter ❶ *v* **1** strike continuously ▷ *n* **2** mixture of flour, eggs, milk, used in cooking

battery ❶ *n, pl* **-teries 1** connected group of electrical cells **2** accumulator **3** number of similar things occurring together **4** (*Law*) assault by beating **5** number of guns

battle ❶ *n* **1** fight between armies ▷ *v* **2** fight **battle-axe** *n* **1** large heavy axe **2** (*Inf*) domineering woman

battlement *n* wall with openings for shooting

battleship *n* heavily armed and armoured fighting ship

batty ❶ *adj* **-tier, -tiest** (*Inf*) crazy, silly

bauble *n* showy trinket

bawdy *adj* **bawdier, bawdiest** obscene, lewd

bawl *v/n* **1** cry **2** shout

bay¹ ❶ *n* wide inlet of sea

bay² ❶ *n* **1** space between two columns **2** recess

bay³ ❶ *n/v* bark **at bay 1** cornered **2** at a distance

bayonet *n* **1** stabbing weapon fixed to rifle ▷ *v* **2** stab with this

bazaar ❶ *n* **1** market (esp. in the East) **2** sale for charity

bazooka *n* powerful rocket launcher

BBC British Broadcasting Corporation

BC before Christ

——————— THESAURUS ———————

bath *n* = **wash**, cleaning, shower, soak, cleansing ▷ *v* = **clean**, wash, shower, soak, cleanse

bathe *v* = **wash**, clean, bath, shower, soak; = **cleanse**, clean, wash, soak, rinse

baton *n* = **stick**, club, staff, pole, rod

batter *v* = **beat**, hit, strike, knock, bang

battery *n* = **artillery**, ordnance, gunnery, gun emplacement, cannonry

battle *n* = **fight**, attack, action, struggle, conflict ≠ **peace**; = **conflict**, campaign, struggle, dispute, contest ▷ *v* = **wrestle**, war, fight, argue, dispute

batty *adj* = **crazy**, odd, mad, eccentric, peculiar

bay¹ *n* = **inlet**, sound, gulf, creek, cove

bay² *n* = **recess**, opening, corner, niche, compartment

bay³ *v* = **howl**, cry, roar, bark, wail ▷ *n* = **cry**, roar, bark, howl, wail

bazaar *n* = **market**, exchange, fair, marketplace; = **fair**, fête, gala, bring-and-buy

b

be ① v, present sing 1st person **am**
2nd person **are** 3rd person **is**
present pl **are** past sing 1st person
was 2nd person **were** 3rd person
was past pl **were** present
participle **being** past participle
been 1 live 2 exist 3 have a state
or quality
beach ① n 1 shore of sea ▷ v
2 run boat on shore
beacon ① n 1 fire used to give
signal 2 lighthouse, buoy
bead ① n 1 little ball pierced for
threading 2 drop of liquid
beaded adj **beady** adj small
and glittering
beagle n small hound
beak n 1 projecting horny jaws of
bird 2 anything similar 3 (Sl)
magistrate
beaker n 1 large drinking cup
2 glass vessel used by chemists
beam ① n 1 long thick piece of
wood 2 ray of light etc. ▷ v 3 aim
light, radio waves etc. (to) 4 shine
5 smile broadly

bean n edible seed of various
leguminous plants
beanie n (Brit, Aust & NZ)
close-fitting woolen hat
bear¹ ① v **bearing, bore, borne**
1 carry 2 support 3 produce
4 endure 5 press (upon)
bearer n
bear² n heavy carnivorous
animal
beard n 1 hair on chin ▷ v
2 oppose boldly
bearing ① n 1 support for
mechanical part 2 relevance
3 behaviour 4 direction 5 relative
position
beast ① n 1 four-footed animal
2 brutal man **beastly** adj
beat ① v **beating, beat, beaten**
1 strike repeatedly 2 overcome
3 surpass 4 stir vigorously 5 flap
(wings) 6 make, wear (path)
7 throb ▷ n 8 stroke 9 pulsation
10 appointed course 11 basic
rhythmic unit of music ▷ adj 12 (Sl)
exhausted **beater** n

———————————————— THESAURUS ————————————————

be v = **be alive**, live, exist, survive,
breathe
beach n = **shore**, coast, sands,
seaside, water's edge
beacon n = **signal**, sign, beam,
flare, lighthouse
bead n = **drop**, tear, bubble, pearl,
dot
beam v = **smile**, grin; = **transmit**,
show, air, broadcast, cable ▷ n
= **ray**, flash, stream, glow, streak;
= **rafter**, support, timber, spar,
plank; = **smile**, grin
bear¹ v = **carry**, take, move, bring,

transfer ≠ **put down**; = **support**,
shoulder, sustain, endure, uphold
≠ **give up**; = **display**, have, show,
hold, carry; = **suffer**, experience, go
through, sustain, stomach
bearing n usually with **on** or **upon**
= **relevance**, relation, application,
connection, import ≠ **irrelevance**;
= **manner**, attitude, conduct,
aspect, behaviour
beast n = **animal**, creature, brute;
= **brute**, monster, savage,
barbarian, fiend
beat v = **batter**, hit, strike, knock,

beau *n, pl* **beaux, beaus** suitor
beauty ❶ *n, pl* **-ties 1** loveliness, grace **2** beautiful person or thing **beautiful** *adj* **beautifully** *adv* **beautician** *n* person who gives beauty treatments
beaver *n* **1** amphibious rodent **2** its fur ▷ *v* **3** work industriously
becalmed *adj* (of ship) motionless through lack of wind
because ❶ *adv/conj* by reason of, since
beckon ❶ *v* summon by signal
become ❶ *v* **-coming, -came, -come 1** come to be **2** suit **becoming** *adj* suitable
bed ❶ *n* **1** piece of furniture for sleeping on **2** garden plot **3** bottom of river **4** layer, stratum ▷ *v* **5** lay in a bed **6** plant **bedding** *n* **bedpan** *n* container used as lavatory by bedridden people **bedridden** *adj* confined to bed **bedroom** *n* **bedsit** *n* one-roomed flat **bedstead** *n* framework of a bed

bedevil *v* **-illing, -illed** harass or torment
bedlam *n* noisy confused scene
bedraggled *adj* messy and wet
bee *n* insect that makes honey
beech *n* European tree with smooth greyish bark and small nuts
beef *n* **1** flesh of cattle for eating **2** (*Inf*) complaint ▷ *v* **3** (*Inf*) complain **beefy** *adj* muscular **beefburger** *n* flat grilled or fried cake of minced beef
beer *n* fermented alcoholic drink made from hops and malt **beer parlour** (*Canad*) licensed place where beer is sold to the public
beet *n* any of various plants with root used for food **beetroot** *n* type of beet plant with a dark red root
beetle *n* class of insect with hard upper-wing cases
befall *v* happen (to)
befit *v* be suitable to
before ❶ *prep* **1** in front of **2** in presence of **3** in preference to **4** earlier than ▷ *adv* **5** earlier **6** in

——————— THESAURUS ———————

pound (*Inf*); **= pound**, strike, hammer, batter, thrash; **= throb**, thump, pound, quake, vibrate; **= hit**, strike, bang ▷ *n* **= throb**, pounding, pulse, thumping, vibration; **= route**, way, course, rounds, path
beauty *n* **= attractiveness**, charm, grace, glamour, elegance **≠ ugliness**; **= good-looker**, lovely (*Sl*), belle, stunner (*Inf*)
because *conj* **= since**, as, in that
beckon *v* **= gesture**, sign, wave, indicate, signal

become *v* **= come to be**, develop into, be transformed into, grow into, change into; **= suit**, fit, enhance, flatter, embellish
bed *n* **= bedstead**, couch, berth, cot, bunk; **= plot**, area, row, strip, patch; **= bottom**, ground, floor
before *prep* **= earlier than**, ahead of, prior to, in advance of **≠ after**; **= in front of**, ahead of, in advance of ▷ *adv* **= previously**, earlier, sooner, in advance, formerly **≠ after**; **= in the past**, earlier, once, previously, formerly

front ▷ *conj* **7** sooner than
beforehand *adv* previously
befriend *v* become a friend to
beg ⓥ *v* **begging, begged 1** ask
earnestly **2** ask for money or food
beggar *n*
begin ⓥ *v* **-ginning, -gan, -gun**
(cause to) start **beginner** *n*
beginning *n*
begonia *n* tropical plant
begrudge *v* grudge, envy anyone
the possession of
beguile *v* **1** charm, fascinate
2 amuse **3** deceive
behalf *n* **on behalf of** in the
interest of
behave ⓥ *v* **1** act in particular way
2 act properly **behaviour** *n*
conduct
behead *v* cut off the head of
behest *n* charge, command
behind ⓥ *prep* **1** further back or
earlier than ▷ *adv* **2** in the rear
behold *v* **-holding, -held** watch,
see

beholden *adj* bound in gratitude
beige *n* **1** undyed woollen cloth
2 its colour
being ⓥ *n* **1** existence **2** that
which exists **3** creature: present
participle of BE
belated *adj* **1** late **2** too late
belch *v* **1** expel wind by mouth
2 eject violently ▷ *n* **3** this act
beleaguered ⓥ *adj* **1** besieged
2 surrounded or beset
belfry *n, pl* **-fries** bell tower
belie *v* show to be untrue
believe *v* **1** regard as true or real
2 have faith **belief** *n* **believable**
adj **believer** *n*
belittle *v* regard, speak of, as
having little worth
bell *n* **1** hollow metal instrument
giving ringing sound when struck
2 electrical device emitting ring
belle *n* beautiful woman
bellicose *adj* warlike

───────── THESAURUS ─────────

beg *v* = **implore**, plead with,
beseech, request, petition;
= **scrounge**, bum (*Inf*), touch
(someone) for (*Sl*), cadge, sponge
on (someone) for ≠ **give**
begin *v* = **start**, commence,
proceed ≠ **stop**; = **commence**,
start, initiate, embark on, set
about
behave *v often reflexive* = **be
well-behaved**, mind your manners,
keep your nose clean, act correctly,
conduct yourself properly
≠ **misbehave**
behind *prep* = **at the rear of**, at the
back of, at the heels of; = **after**,

following ▷ *adv* = **after**, next,
following, afterwards,
subsequently ≠ **in advance of**;
= **behind schedule**, delayed,
running late, behind time
≠ **ahead**
being *n* = **individual**, creature,
human being, living thing; = **life**,
reality ≠ **nonexistence**; = **soul**,
spirit, substance, creature,
essence
beleaguered *adj* = **harassed**,
troubled, plagued, hassled (*Inf*),
badgered; = **besieged**, surrounded,
blockaded, beset, encircled
bellow *v* = **shout**, cry (out),

belligerent adj 1 hostile, aggressive 2 making war **belligerence** n

bellow ⓣ v/n 1 roar 2 shout

bellows pl n instrument for creating stream of air

belly ⓣ n, pl **-lies** 1 stomach ▷ v 2 swell out

belong v 1 be property of 2 be member of 3 have an allotted place 4 pertain to **belongings** pl n personal possessions

beloved ⓣ adj 1 much loved ▷ n 2 dear one

below ⓣ adv 1 beneath ▷ prep 2 lower than

belt ⓣ n 1 band 2 girdle 3 zone ▷ v 4 (Inf) thrash

bemoan v grieve over

bench ⓣ n 1 long seat 2 seat or body of judges etc.

bend ⓣ v **bending, bent** (cause to) form a curve

beneath ⓣ prep 1 under, lower than ▷ adv 2 below

benefit ⓣ n 1 advantage, profit 2 money paid to unemployed etc. ▷ v 3 do good to 4 receive good **benefactor** n 1 one who helps or does good to others 2 patron **beneficial** adj

benign ⓣ adj kindly, favourable

bent ⓣ adj 1 curved 2 resolved (on) 3 (Inf) corrupt 4 (Inf) deviant ▷ n 5 inclination

benzene n one of group of flammable liquids used as solvents etc.

bequeath v leave property etc. by will **bequest** n 1 bequeathing 2 legacy

berate v scold harshly

b

—— THESAURUS ——

scream, roar, yell ▷ n = **shout**, cry, scream, roar, yell

belly n = **stomach**, insides (Inf), gut, abdomen, tummy

beloved adj = **dear**, loved, valued, prized, admired

below prep = **under**, underneath, lower than ▷ adv = **lower**, down, under, beneath, underneath

belt n = **waistband**, band, sash, girdle, girth; = **conveyor belt**, band, loop, fan belt, drive belt

bench n = **seat**, stall, pew; = **worktable**, stand, table, counter, trestle table

bend v = **twist**, turn, wind, lean, hook ▷ n = **curve**, turn, corner, twist, angle

beneath prep = **under**, below, underneath, lower than ≠ **over**; = **inferior to**, below ▷ adv = **underneath**, below, in a lower place

benefit n = **good**, help, profit, favour ≠ **harm** ▷ v = **profit from**, make the most of, gain from, do well out of, reap benefits from

benign adj = **benevolent**, kind, kindly, warm, friendly ≠ **unkind**; (Medical) = **harmless**, innocent, innocuous, curable, inoffensive ≠ **malignant**

bent adj = **misshapen**, twisted, angled, bowed, curved ≠ **straight** ▷ n = **inclination**, ability, leaning, tendency, preference

beret n round, close-fitting hat

berg[1] n (S Afr) mountain

berg[2] n iceberg

berry n, pl **-ries** small juicy stoneless fruit

berm n (NZ) narrow grass strip between the road and the footpath in a residential area

berserk adj **go berserk** become violent or destructive

berth ⊕ n **1** ship's mooring place **2** place to sleep in ship ▷ v **3** moor

beryl n variety of crystalline mineral, e.g. aquamarine, emerald

beseech v **-seeching, -sought** entreat, implore

beset v surround with danger, problems

beside ⊕ prep **1** by the side of, near **2** distinct from **besides** adv/prep in addition (to)

besiege ⊕ v surround

besotted adj **1** drunk **2** foolish **3** infatuated

best ⊕ adj/adv **1** superlative of GOOD and WELL ▷ v **2** defeat **best man** groom's attendant at wedding **bestseller** n book sold in great numbers

bestial adj like a beast, brutish

bestir v rouse to activity

bestow ⊕ v give, confer

bet ⊕ v **1** agree to pay money if wrong in guessing result of contest ▷ n **2** money so risked

bête noire n particular dislike

betray ⊕ v **1** be disloyal to **2** reveal, divulge **3** show signs of **betrayal** n

better ⊕ adj/adv **1** comparative of GOOD and WELL ▷ v **2** improve

between ⊕ prep/adv **1** in the intermediate part, in space or time **2** indicating reciprocal relation or

———————————————— THESAURUS ————————————————

berth n = **bunk**, bed, hammock, billet; = **anchorage**, haven, port, harbour, dock ▷ v = **anchor**, land, dock, moor, tie up

beside prep = **next to**, near, close to, neighbouring, alongside

besiege v = **harass**, harry, plague, hound, hassle (Inf); = **surround**, enclose, blockade, encircle, hem in

best adj = **finest**, leading, supreme, principal, foremost ▷ adv = **most highly**, most fully, most deeply

bestow v = **present**, give, award, grant, commit ≠ **obtain**

bet v = **gamble**, chance, stake, venture, hazard ▷ n = **gamble**, risk, stake, venture, speculation

betray v = **be disloyal to**, double-cross (Inf), stab in the back, be unfaithful to, inform on or against; = **give away**, reveal, expose, disclose, uncover

better adv = **to a greater degree**, more completely, more thoroughly; = **in a more excellent manner**, more effectively, more attractively, more advantageously, more competently ≠ **worse** ▷ adj = **well**, stronger, recovering, cured, fully recovered ≠ **worse**; = **superior**, finer, higher-quality, surpassing, preferable ≠ **inferior**

between prep = **amidst**, among, mid, in the middle of, betwixt

comparison

bevel n 1 angled surface ▷ v 2 slope, slant

beverage ① n drink

beverage room n (Canad) tavern

bevy n, pl **bevies** flock or group

bewail v lament

beware ① v be on one's guard

bewilder ① v puzzle, confuse

bewitch v charm, fascinate

beyond ① adv 1 farther away ▷ prep 2 on the farther side of 3 out of reach of

bias ① n 1 slant 2 inclination ▷ v 3 influence, affect **biased** adj prejudiced

bib n 1 cloth put under child's chin when eating 2 top of apron

Bible n sacred writings of the Christian religion **biblical** adj

bibliography n, pl **-phies** list of books on a subject

bicentenary n 200th anniversary

biceps n two-headed muscle, esp. of upper arm

bicker v/n quarrel over petty things

bicycle n vehicle with two wheels **bicyclist** n

bid ① v **bidding, bade, bidden** 1 offer 2 say 3 command 4 invite ▷ n 5 offer, esp. of price 6 try 7 (Card games) call **bidder** n **bidding** n command

bide v 1 remain 2 dwell 3 await

bier n frame for coffin

big ① adj **bigger, biggest** of great size, height, number, power etc. **bighead** n (Inf) conceited person **big-headed** adj

bigamy n crime of marrying a person while one is still legally married to someone else **bigamist** n

bigot n person intolerant of ideas of others **bigoted** adj **bigotry** n

bike n short for BICYCLE or MOTORBIKE

bikini n woman's two-piece swimming costume

bilberry n small moorland plant with edible blue berries

bile n 1 fluid secreted by the liver

———— THESAURUS ————

beverage n = **drink**, liquid, liquor, refreshment

beware v = **be careful**, look out, watch out, be wary, be cautious

bewilder v = **confound**, confuse, puzzle, baffle, perplex

beyond prep = **after**, over, past, above

bias n = **prejudice**, leaning, tendency, inclination, favouritism ≠ **impartiality** ▷ v = **influence**, colour, weight, prejudice, distort

bid n = **attempt**, try, effort, go (Inf),

shot (Inf); = **offer**, price, amount, advance, proposal ▷ v = **make an offer**, offer, propose, submit, tender; = **wish**, say, call, tell, greet; = **tell**, ask, order, require, direct

big adj = **large**, great, huge, massive, vast ≠ **small**; = **important**, significant, urgent, far-reaching ≠ **unimportant**; = **powerful**, important, prominent, dominant, influential; = **grown-up**, adult, grown, mature, elder ≠ **young**

2 ill temper **bilious** *adj* nauseous, nauseating

bilge *n* 1 bottom of ship's hull 2 dirty water collecting there 3 (*Inf*) nonsense

bilingual *adj* speaking, or written in, two languages

bill¹ ❶ *n* 1 written account of charges 2 draft of Act of Parliament 3 poster 4 commercial document 5 (*US & Canad*) banknote ▷ *v* 6 present account of charges 7 announce by advertisement

bill² ❶ *n* bird's beak

billet *n/v* **-leting, -leted** (provide) civilian quarters for troops

billiards *n* game played on table with balls and cues

billion *n* 1 thousand million, 10^9 2 (*Obs*) million million, 10^{12}

billow *n* 1 swelling wave ▷ *v* 2 swell

biltong *n* (*S Afr*) strips of dried meat

bin *n* receptacle for corn, refuse etc.

binary *adj* 1 composed of, characterized by, two 2 dual

bind ❶ *v* **binding, bound** 1 tie fast 2 tie round 3 oblige 4 seal 5 constrain 6 bandage 7 cohere

8 put (book) into cover **binder** *n*

binding *n* 1 cover of book 2 tape for hem etc.

binge ❶ *n* (*Inf*) spree

bingo *n* game of chance in which numbers drawn are matched with those on a card

binoculars *pl n* telescope made for both eyes

bio- *comb. form* life, living, as in *biochemistry*

biodegradable *adj* capable of decomposition by natural means

biofuel *n* fuel derived from renewable biological resources

biography ❶ *n, pl* **-phies** story of one person's life **biographer** *n* **biographical** *adj*

biology *n* study of living organisms **biological** *adj* **biologist** *n*

bionic *adj* having physical functions aided by electronic equipment

biopsy *n, pl* **-sies** examination of tissue from a living body

biped *n* two-footed animal

birch *n* 1 tree with silvery bark 2 rod for punishment ▷ *v* 3 flog

bird *n* feathered animal

——————— THESAURUS ———————

bill¹ *n* = **charges**, rate, costs, score, account; = **act of parliament**, measure, proposal, piece of legislation, projected law; = **list**, listing, programme, card, schedule; = **advertisement**, notice, poster, leaflet, bulletin ▷ *v* = **charge**, debit, invoice, send a statement to, send an invoice to; = **advertise**, post, announce, promote, plug

(*Inf*)

bill² *n* = **beak**, nib, neb (*archaic or dialect*), mandible

bind *v* = **oblige**, make, force, require, engage; = **tie**, join, stick, secure, wrap ≠ **untie**

binge *n* (*Inf*) = **bout**, spell, fling, feast, stint

biography *n* = **life story**, life, record, account, profile

birdie n (Golf) score of one stroke under par

Biro® n Trademark ballpoint pen

birth ❶ n 1 bearing, or the being born, of offspring 2 parentage, origin **birthday** n **birthmark** n blemish on the skin

biscuit n dry, small, thin variety of cake

bisect v divide into two equal parts

bisexual adj sexually attracted to both men and women

bishop n 1 clergyman governing diocese 2 chess piece

bison n, pl **-son** 1 large wild ox 2 Amer. buffalo

bistro n, pl **-tros** small restaurant

bit¹ ❶ n fragment, piece

bit² n 1 biting, cutting part of tool 2 mouthpiece of horse's bridle

bit³ n (Comp) smallest unit of information

bitch n 1 female dog, fox, or wolf 2 (Offens) spiteful woman **bitchy** adj

bite ❶ v biting, bit, bitten 1 cut into, esp. with teeth 2 grip 3 rise to the bait 4 corrode ▷ n

5 act of biting 6 wound so made 7 mouthful **biting** adj 1 piercing or keen 2 sarcastic

bitter ❶ adj 1 sour tasting 2 (of person) resentful 3 sarcastic **bitterly** adv **bitterness** n

bittern n wading bird

bitumen n viscous substance occurring in asphalt, tar etc.

bivouac n 1 temporary encampment of soldiers, hikers etc. ▷ v 2 camp

bizarre ❶ adj unusual, weird

blab v **blabbing, blabbed** 1 reveal secrets 2 chatter idly

black ❶ adj 1 of the darkest colour 2 without light 3 dark 4 evil ▷ n 5 darkest colour 6 black dye, clothing etc. 7 (with cap.) person of dark-skinned race ▷ v 8 boycott in industrial dispute **blacken** v 1 make black 2 defame **blackball** v vote against, exclude **blackberry** n plant with dark juicy berries, bramble **blackbird** n common European songbird **blackboard** n dark surface for writing on with chalk **black box** Inf. name for FLIGHT RECORDER **blackhead** n

---

THESAURUS

birth n = **childbirth**, delivery, nativity, parturition ≠ **death**; = **ancestry**, stock, blood, background, breeding

bit¹ n = **piece**, scrap

bite v = **nip**, cut, tear, wound, snap ▷ n = **snack**, food, piece, taste, refreshment; = **wound**, sting, pinch, nip, prick

bitter adj = **resentful**, angry, offended, sour, sore ≠ **happy**;

= **freezing**, biting, severe, intense, raw ≠ **mild**; = **sour**, sharp, acid, harsh, tart ≠ **sweet**

bizarre adj = **strange**, unusual, extraordinary, fantastic, weird ≠ **normal**

black adj = **dark**, raven, ebony, sable, jet ≠ **light**; = **gloomy**, sad, depressing, grim, bleak ≠ **happy**; = **terrible**, bad, devastating, tragic, fatal

small dark spot on skin **blackleg** n strikebreaker **blacklist** n 1 list of people considered suspicious ▷ v 2 put on such a list **black market** illegal buying and selling of goods **black spot** dangerous place, esp. on a road

blackguard n scoundrel

blackmail ● v 1 extort money by threats ▷ n 2 extortion **blackmailer** n

blackout n 1 complete failure of electricity supply 2 state of temporary unconsciousness 3 obscuring of lights as precaution against night air attack

blacksmith n person who works in iron

bladder n membranous bag to contain liquid

blade n 1 edge, cutting part of knife or tool 2 leaf of grass etc. 3 sword

blame ● n 1 censure 2 culpability ▷ v 3 find fault with 4 censure **blameless** adj **blameworthy** adj

blanch v 1 whiten, bleach 2 turn pale

blancmange n pudding made from milk

bland ● adj 1 devoid of distinctive characteristics 2 smooth in manner **blandly** adv

blank ● adj 1 without marks or writing 2 empty 3 vacant, confused ▷ n 4 empty space 5 cartridge containing no bullet **blankly** adv

blanket ● n 1 thick bed cover 2 concealing cover ▷ v 3 cover, stifle

blare v 1 sound loudly and harshly ▷ n 2 such sound

blarney n flattering talk

blasé adj 1 indifferent through familiarity 2 bored

blaspheme v show contempt for God, esp. in speech **blasphemous** adj **blasphemy** n

blast ● n 1 explosion 2 shock wave 3 gust of wind 4 loud sound ▷ v 5 blow up 6 blight

——————— THESAURUS ———————

blackmail n = **threat**, intimidation, ransom, extortion, hush money (SI) ▷ v = **threaten**, squeeze, compel, intimidate, coerce

blame v = **hold responsible**, accuse, denounce, indict, impeach ≠ **absolve** (used in negative constructions) ▷ n = **responsibility**, liability, accountability, onus, culpability ≠ **praise**

bland adj = **dull**, boring, plain, flat, dreary ≠ **exciting**

blank adj = **unmarked**, white, clear, clean, empty ≠ **marked**; = **expressionless**, empty, vague, vacant, deadpan ≠ **expressive** ▷ n = **empty space**, space, gap

blanket n = **cover**, rug, coverlet; = **covering**, sheet, coat, layer, carpet ▷ v = **coat**, cover, hide, mask, conceal

blast n = **explosion**, crash, burst, discharge, eruption; = **gust**, rush, storm, breeze, puff; = **blare**, blow, scream, trumpet, wail ▷ v = **blow up**, bomb, destroy, burst, ruin

blatant ❶ *adj* obvious **blatantly** *adv*

blaze¹ ❶ *n* **1** strong fire or flame **2** brightness **3** outburst ▷ *v* **4** burn strongly **5** be very angry

blaze² *v* **1** establish trail ▷ *n* **2** white mark on horse's face

blazer *n* type of jacket worn esp. for sports

bleach ❶ *v* **1** make or become white ▷ *n* **2** bleaching substance

bleak ❶ *adj* **1** cold, exposed **2** dismal **bleakness** *n*

bleary *adj* **-rier, -riest** with eyes dimmed, as with tears, sleep

bleat *v* **1** cry, as sheep **2** say plaintively ▷ *n* **3** sheep's cry

bleed ❶ *v* **bleeding, bled 1** lose blood **2** draw blood from

bleep *n* short high-pitched sound **bleeper** *n*

blemish *n* **1** defect ▷ *v* **2** make defective **blemished** *adj*

blend ❶ *v* **1** mix ▷ *n* **2** mixture **blender** *n* electrical appliance for mixing food

bless ❶ *v* **1** consecrate **2** ask God's favour for **3** make happy **blessed** *adj* **blessing** *n*

blether *v* **1** speak at length, esp. foolishly ▷ *n* **2** foolish or babbling talk

blight ❶ *n* **1** plant disease **2** harmful influence ▷ *v* **3** injure

blighter *n* (*Inf*) irritating person

blind ❶ *adj* **1** unable to see **2** heedless **3** closed at one end ▷ *v* **4** deprive of sight ▷ *n* **5** window screen **6** pretext **blindly** *adv* **blindness** *n* **blindfold** *v/n* (cloth used to) cover the eyes

blatant *adj* **= obvious**, clear, plain, evident, glaring ≠ **subtle**

blaze¹ *v* **= burn**, glow, flare, be on fire, go up in flames ▷ *n* **= inferno**, fire, flames, bonfire, combustion; **= flash**, glow, glitter, flare, glare

bleach *v* **= lighten**, wash out, blanch, whiten

bleak *adj* **= dismal**, dark, depressing, grim, discouraging ≠ **cheerful**; **= exposed**, empty, bare, barren, desolate ≠ **sheltered**

bleed *v* **= lose blood**, flow, gush, spurt, shed blood; (*Inf*) **= extort**, milk, squeeze, drain, exhaust

blend *v* **= mix**, join, combine, compound, merge; **= go well**, match, fit, suit, go with ▷ *n*

= mixture, mix, combination, compound, brew

bless *v* **= sanctify**, dedicate, ordain, exalt, anoint ≠ **curse**; **= endow**, give to, provide for, grant for, favour ≠ **afflict**

blight *n* **= curse**, suffering, evil, corruption, pollution ≠ **blessing**; **= disease**, pest, fungus, mildew, infestation ▷ *v* **= frustrate**, destroy, ruin, crush, mar

blind *adj* **= sightless**, unsighted, unseeing, eyeless, visionless ≠ **sighted**; (*often with* **to**) **= unaware of**, unconscious of, ignorant of, indifferent to, insensitive to ≠ **aware**; **= unquestioning**, prejudiced, wholesale, indiscriminate, uncritical

blink ❶ v 1 wink 2 twinkle ▷ n 3 gleam **blink at** ignore **on the blink** (Inf) not working

blip n repetitive sound or visible pulse, e.g. on radar screen

bliss ❶ n perfect happiness **blissful** adj **blissfully** adv

blister ❶ n 1 bubble on skin 2 surface swelling ▷ v 3 form blisters (on) **blistering** adj 1 very hot 2 extremely harsh

blithe adj happy **blithely** adv

blitz ❶ n concentrated attack

blizzard n blinding storm of wind and snow

blob n soft mass or drop

block ❶ n 1 solid (rectangular) piece of wood, stone etc. 2 obstacle 3 pulley with frame 4 large building of offices, flats etc. ▷ v 5 obstruct, stop up 6 shape **blockage** n **blockhead** n stupid person **block letter** plain capital letter

blockade ❶ n 1 physical prevention of access, esp. to port ▷ v 2 prevent access

bloke ❶ n (Inf) fellow, chap

blood ❶ n 1 red fluid in veins 2 kindred ▷ v 3 initiate (into hunting, war etc.) **bloodless** adj **bloody** adj 1 covered in blood 2 savage 3 extreme ▷ adv 4 (Sl) extremely ▷ v 5 make bloody **blood bath** massacre **bloodhound** n large dog used for tracking **bloodshed** n slaughter **bloodshot** adj (of eyes) inflamed **bloodthirsty** adj cruel **bloody-minded** adj deliberately unhelpful

bloom ❶ n 1 flower 2 prime 3 glow ▷ v 4 be in flower 5 flourish

bloomer n (Inf) mistake

bloomers pl n wide, baggy knickers

blossom ❶ n 1 flower ▷ v

───────────────────────── THESAURUS ─────────────────────────

blink v = **flutter**, wink, bat; = **flash**, flicker, wink, shimmer, twinkle **on the blink** (Inf) = **not working (properly)**, faulty, defective, playing up, out of action

bliss n = **joy**, ecstasy, euphoria, rapture, nirvana ≠ **misery**

blister n = **sore**, boil, swelling, cyst, pimple

blitz n = **attack**, strike, assault, raid, offensive

block n = **piece**, bar, mass, brick, lump; = **obstruction**, bar, barrier, obstacle, impediment ▷ v = **obstruct**, close, stop, plug, choke ≠ **clear**

blockade n = **stoppage**, block, barrier, restriction, obstacle

bloke n (Inf) = **man**, person, individual, character (Inf), guy (Inf)

blood n = **lifeblood**, gore, vital fluid; = **family**, relations, birth, descent, extraction

bloom n = **flower**, bud, blossom; = **prime**, flower, beauty, height, peak; = **glow**, freshness, lustre, radiance ≠ **pallor** ▷ v = **flower**, blossom, open, bud ≠ **wither**; = **grow**, develop, wax

blossom n = **flower**, bloom, bud, efflorescence, floret ▷ v = **bloom**, grow, develop, mature; = **succeed**,

2 flower **3** flourish

blot n **1** spot, stain ▷ v **2** spot, stain **3** obliterate **4** soak up ink **blotter** n

blotch n **1** dark spot ▷ v **2** make spotted

blouse n light, loose upper garment

blow¹ ❶ v blowing, blew, blown **1** make a current of air **2** pant **3** drive air upon or into **4** drive by current of air **5** make sound **6** (Sl) squander ▷ n **7** blast **8** gale **blower** n **blowfly** n fly which infects food etc. **blowlamp** n small burner with very hot flame **blowout** n **1** sudden puncture in tyre **2** uncontrolled escape of oil, gas, from well **3** (Sl) large meal **blow up 1** explode **2** fill with air **3** (Inf) enlarge photograph **4** (Inf) lose one's temper

blow² ❶ n **1** stroke, knock **2** sudden misfortune

blubber v **1** weep ▷ n **2** whale fat

bludge v **1** (Aust & NZ, Inf) evade work **2** scrounge **bludger** n person who scrounges

bludgeon n **1** short thick club ▷ v **2** strike with one **3** coerce

blue ❶ adj **1** of the colour of sky **2** depressed **3** indecent ▷ n **4** colour of sky **5** dye or pigment ▷ pl **6** (Inf) depression **7** form of jazz music ▷ v **8** make blue **bluish** adj **bluebell** n wild spring flower **bluebottle** n blowfly **blueprint** n **1** copy of drawing **2** original plan

bluff¹ ❶ n **1** cliff, steep bank **2** (Canad) clump of trees ▷ adj **3** hearty **4** blunt

bluff² ❶ v/n (deceive by) pretence

blunder ❶ n/v (make) clumsy mistake

blunt ❶ adj **1** not sharp **2** (of speech) abrupt ▷ v **3** make blunt **bluntly** adv

blur ❶ v blurring, blurred **1** make, become less distinct ▷ n **2** something indistinct

---

THESAURUS

progress, thrive, flourish, prosper

blow¹ v = **move**, carry, drive, sweep, fling; = **be carried**, flutter; = **exhale**, breathe, pant, puff

blow² n = **knock**, stroke, punch, bang, sock (Sl); = **setback**, shock, disaster, reverse, disappointment

blue adj = **depressed**, low, sad, unhappy, melancholy ≠ **happy**; = **smutty**, obscene, indecent, lewd, risqué ≠ **respectable**

bluff¹ n = **precipice**, bank, peak, cliff, ridge ▷ adj = **hearty**, open, blunt, outspoken, genial ≠ **tactful**

bluff² n = **deception**, fraud, sham,

pretence, deceit ▷ v = **deceive**, trick, fool, pretend, cheat

blunder n = **mistake**, slip, fault, error, oversight ≠ **correctness** ▷ v = **make a mistake**, blow it (Sl), err, slip up (Inf), foul up ≠ **be correct**; = **stumble**, fall, reel, stagger, lurch

blunt adj = **frank**, forthright, straightforward, rude, outspoken ≠ **tactful**; = **dull**, rounded, dulled, edgeless, unsharpened ≠ **sharp** ▷ v = **dull**, weaken, soften, numb, dampen ≠ **stimulate**

blur n = **haze**, confusion, fog, obscurity, indistinctness ▷ v

blurb n statement recommending book etc.

blurt v utter suddenly

blush ❶ v 1 become red in face 2 be ashamed ▷ n 3 this effect **blusher** n cosmetic to give rosy colour to face

bluster v/n (indulge in) noisy, aggressive behaviour **blustery** adj (of wind) gusty

BO (Inf) body odour

boa n 1 large, nonpoisonous snake 2 long scarf of fur or feathers

boar n 1 male pig 2 wild pig

board ❶ n 1 broad, flat piece of wood, card etc. 2 table 3 meals 4 group of people who administer company ▷ v 5 cover with planks 6 supply food daily 7 enter ship etc. 8 take daily meals **boarder** n **boardroom** n

boast ❶ v 1 speak too much in praise of oneself 2 brag of 3 have to show ▷ n 4 thing boasted (of) **boastful** adj

boat n 1 small open vessel 2 ship ▷ v 3 sail about in boat **boater** n flat straw hat **boatswain** n ship's

officer in charge of equipment

bob ❶ v **bobbing, bobbed** 1 move up and down 2 move jerkily 3 cut (women's) hair short ▷ n 4 jerking motion 5 short hairstyle 6 weight on pendulum etc.

bobbin n reel for thread

bobble n small, tufted ball

bobby n, pl **-bies** (Inf) police officer

bobotie n (S Afr) dish of curried mince

bobsleigh n 1 sledge for racing ▷ v 2 ride on this

bode v be an omen of

bodice n upper part of woman's dress

bodkin n large blunt needle

body ❶ n, pl **bodies** 1 whole frame of man or animal 2 corpse 3 main part 4 substance 5 group regarded as single entity **bodily** adj/adv **bodyguard** n escort to protect important person **body mass index** measure used to gauge whether a person is overweight: a person's weight in kilograms divided by the square of his or her height in

= **become indistinct**, become vague, become hazy, become fuzzy

blush v = **turn red**, colour, glow, flush, redden ≠ **turn pale** ▷ n = **reddening**, colour, glow, flush, pink tinge

board n = **plank**, panel, timber, slat, piece of timber; = **council**, directors, committee, congress, advisers; = **meals**, provisions, victuals, daily meals ▷ v = **get on**, enter, mount, embark ≠ **get off**

boast v = **brag**, crow, vaunt, talk big (Sl), blow your own trumpet ≠ **cover up**; = **possess**, exhibit

bob v = **bounce**, duck, hop, wobble, oscillate

body n = **physique**, build, form, figure, shape; = **torso**, trunk; = **corpse**, dead body, remains, stiff (Sl), carcass; = **organization**, company, group, society, association; = **main part**, matter, material, mass, substance

metres **bodywork** n outer shell of motor vehicle

boffin n (Inf) scientist

bog ⊕ n wet, soft ground **boggy** adj **bog down bogging, bogged** stick as in a bog

bogan n (Aust dated & NZ, Sl) youth who dresses and behaves rebelliously

bogey, bogy ⊕ n 1 thing that causes fear 2 (Golf) score of one stroke over par

boggle v stare, be surprised

bogus ⊕ adj sham, false

bohemian n/adj (person) leading unconventional life

boil¹ ⊕ v 1 (cause to) change from liquid to gas, esp. by heating 2 cook or become cooked by boiling 3 (Inf) be hot 4 (Inf) be angry ▷ n 5 boiling state **boiler** n equipment providing hot water

boil² ⊕ n inflamed swelling on skin

boisterous adj 1 wild 2 noisy

bold ⊕ adj 1 daring, presumptuous 2 prominent **boldly** adv **boldness** n

bole n tree trunk

bolero n, pl **-ros** 1 Spanish dance 2 short loose jacket

bollard n 1 post to secure mooring lines 2 post in road as barrier

bolster ⊕ v 1 support, uphold ▷ n 2 long pillow 3 pad, support

bolt ⊕ n 1 bar or pin (esp. with thread for nut) 2 rush 3 lightning 4 roll of cloth ▷ v 5 fasten 6 swallow hastily 7 rush away

bomb ⊕ n 1 explosive projectile 2 any explosive device ▷ v 3 attack with bombs **bomber** n 1 aircraft that drops bombs 2 person who throws or plants a bomb **bombard** v 1 shell 2 attack (verbally) **bombshell** n shocking surprise

bona fide (Lat) genuine

bonanza n sudden wealth

bond ⊕ n 1 thing which binds 2 link 3 written promise ▷ v 4 bind

bondage n slavery

bone n 1 hard substance forming

— THESAURUS —

bog n = **marsh**, swamp, slough, wetlands, fen

bogey n = **bugbear**, bête noire, horror, nightmare, bugaboo

bogus adj = **fake**, false, artificial, forged, imitation ≠ **genuine**

boil¹ v = **simmer**, bubble, foam, seethe, fizz

boil² n = **pustule**, gathering, swelling, blister, carbuncle

bold adj = **fearless**, enterprising, brave, daring, heroic ≠ **timid**; = **impudent**, forward, confident, rude, cheeky ≠ **shy**

bolster v = **support**, help, boost, strengthen, reinforce

bolt n = **pin**, rod, peg, rivet; = **bar**, catch, lock, latch, fastener ▷ v = **lock**, close, bar, secure, fasten; = **dash**, fly; = **gobble**, stuff, wolf, cram, gorge

bomb n = **explosive**, mine, shell, missile, device ▷ v = **blow up**, attack, destroy, assault, shell

bond n = **tie**, union, coupling, link, association; = **fastening**, tie, chain, cord, shackle; = **agreement**, word,

skeleton **2** piece of this ▷ v **3** take out bone **bony** adj **bone-idle** adj extremely lazy

bonfire n large outdoor fire

bongo n, pl **-gos, -goes** small drum played with fingers

bonk v (Inf) **1** hit **2** have sexual intercourse (with)

bonnet n **1** hat with strings **2** cap **3** cover of motor vehicle engine

bonny adj **-nier, -niest** beautiful, handsome

bonsai n, pl **-sai** (art of growing) dwarf trees, shrubs

bonus ❶ n extra (unexpected) payment or gift

boo interj **1** expression of disapproval **2** exclamation to surprise esp. child ▷ v **3** make this sound

boob n (Sl) **1** foolish mistake **2** female breast

boogie v (Inf) dance quickly to pop music

book ❶ n **1** sheets of paper bound together **2** literary work ▷ v **3** reserve room, ticket etc. **4** charge with legal offence **5** enter name in book **booklet** n **book-keeping** n systematic

recording of business transactions

bookmaker n one who takes bets

bookworm n person devoted to reading

boom¹ ❶ n **1** sudden commercial activity **2** prosperity ▷ v **3** prosper

boom² v/n (make) deep sound

boom³ n long spar for bottom of sail

boomerang n curved wooden missile of Aust. Aborigines, which returns to the thrower

boon ❶ n something helpful, favour

boor n rude person **boorish** adj

boost ❶ n **1** encouragement **2** upward push **3** increase ▷ v **4** encourage **5** push **booster** n

boot ❶ n **1** covering for the foot and ankle **2** luggage space in car **3** (Inf) kick ▷ v **4** (Inf) kick

booth n **1** stall **2** cubicle

bootleg v **1** make, carry, sell illicit goods, esp. alcohol ▷ adj **2** produced, sold illicitly **bootlegger** n

booty n, pl **-ties** plunder, spoil

booze n/v (Inf) (consume) alcoholic drink

— THESAURUS —

promise, contract, guarantee ▷ v **= form friendships**, connect

bonus n **= extra**, prize, gift, reward, premium

book n **= work**, title, volume, publication, tract; **= notebook**, album, journal, diary, pad ▷ v **= reserve**, schedule, engage, organize, charter

boom¹ n **= expansion**, increase,

development, growth, jump ≠ **decline**

boon n **= benefit**, blessing, godsend, gift

boost v **= increase**, develop, raise, expand, add to ≠ **decrease** ▷ n **= rise**, increase, jump, addition, improvement ≠ **fall**; **= encouragement**, help

boot v **= kick**, punt, put the boot

border ① *n* **1** margin **2** frontier
3 limit **4** strip of garden ▷ *v*
5 provide with border **6** adjoin
bore¹ ① *v* **1** pierce hole ▷ *n* **2** hole
3 calibre of gun
bore² ① *v* **1** make weary by
repetition ▷ *n* **2** tiresome person
or thing **boredom** *n* **boring** *adj*
boron *n* chemical element used in
hardening steel etc.
borough *n* town
borrow ① *v* **1** obtain on loan
2 copy, steal **borrower** *n*
borstal *n* formerly, prison for
young criminals
borzoi *n* tall dog with long, silky
coat
bosom *n* human breast
boss ① *n* **1** person in charge of or
employing others ▷ *v* **2** be in
charge of **3** be domineering over
bossy *adj* **bossier, bossiest**
overbearing
botany *n* study of plants
botanical *adj* **botanist** *n*
botch *v* **1** spoil by clumsiness ▷ *n*

2 blunder
both *adj/pron* the two
bother ① *v* **1** pester **2** perplex
3 trouble ▷ *n* **4** fuss, trouble
Botox® *n* **1** drug used to treat
muscle spasms and to reduce
wrinkles ▷ *v* **2** apply Botox to (a
person or a body part)
bottle *n* **1** vessel for holding liquid
2 its contents ▷ *v* **3** put into bottle
4 restrain **bottleneck** *n* narrow
outlet which impedes smooth flow
bottom ① *n* **1** lowest part **2** bed
of sea etc. **3** buttocks ▷ *adj*
4 lowest ▷ *v* **5** put bottom to
6 base (upon) **7** get to bottom of
bottomless *adj*
bough *n* branch of tree
boulder *n* large rock
boulevard *n* broad street or
promenade
bounce ① *v* **1** (cause to) rebound
on impact ▷ *n* **2** rebounding
3 quality causing this **4** (*Inf*)
vitality **bouncer** *n* person who
removes unwanted people from

in(to) (*Sl*), drop-kick
border *n* = **frontier**, line, limit,
bounds, boundary; = **edge**, margin/
verge, rim ▷ *v* = **edge**, bound,
decorate, trim, fringe
bore¹ *v* = **drill**, mine, sink, tunnel,
pierce
bore² *v* = **tire**, fatigue, weary, wear
out, jade ≠ **excite** ▷ *n* = **nuisance**,
pain (*Inf*), yawn (*Inf*), anorak (*Inf*)
borrow *v* = **take on loan**, touch
(someone) for (*Sl*), scrounge (*Inf*),
cadge, use temporarily ≠ **lend**;
= **steal**, take, copy, adopt, pinch (*Inf*)

boss *n* = **manager**, head, leader,
director, chief
bother *v* = **trouble**, concern,
worry, alarm, disturb ▷ *n*
= **trouble**, problem, worry,
difficulty, fuss ≠ **help**
bottom *n* = **lowest part**, base,
foot, bed, floor ≠ **top**; = **underside**,
sole, underneath, lower side ▷ *adj*
= **lowest**, last ≠ **higher**
bounce *v* = **rebound**, recoil,
ricochet ▷ *n* = **springiness**, give,
spring, resilience, elasticity; (*Inf*)
= **life**, go (*Inf*), energy, zip (*Inf*),

b

nightclub etc. **bouncing** *adj* vigorous

bound¹ ⊕ *n* 1 *(usu. pl)* limit ▷ *v* 2 restrict **boundary** *n* **boundless** *adj*

bound² ⊕ *v/n* spring, leap

bound³ *adj* on a specified course

bound⁴ *adj* 1 committed 2 certain 3 tied

bounty *n, pl* **-ties** 1 liberality 2 gift 3 premium **bounteous, bountiful** *adj*

bouquet ⊕ *n* 1 bunch of flowers 2 aroma 3 compliment

bourbon *n* (*US*) whisky made from maize

bourgeois ⊕ *n/adj* middle class

bout ⊕ *n* 1 period of time spent doing something 2 contest, fight

boutique *n* small shop, esp. one selling clothes

bow¹ ⊕ *v* 1 bend body in respect, assent etc. 2 submit 3 bend downwards 4 crush ▷ *n* 5 bowing

bow² *n* 1 weapon for shooting arrows 2 implement for playing

violin etc. 3 ornamental knot 4 bend ▷ *v* 5 bend

bow³ ⊕ *n* fore end of ship

bowel *n* 1 part of intestine 2 (*oft. pl*) inside of anything

bowl¹ ⊕ *n* 1 round vessel, deep basin 2 drinking cup 3 hollow

bowl² ⊕ *n* 1 wooden ball ▷ *pl* 2 game played with such balls ▷ *v* 3 roll or throw ball in various ways **bowler** *n* **bowling** *n*

bowler *n* man's low-crowned stiff felt hat

box¹ ⊕ *n* 1 (wooden) container, usu. rectangular 2 its contents 3 any boxlike cubicle or receptacle ▷ *v* 4 put in box 5 confine **box office** place where tickets are sold

box² ⊕ *v* 1 fight with fists, esp. with padded gloves on 2 strike ▷ *n* 3 blow **boxer** *n* 1 one who boxes 2 large dog resembling bulldog **boxing** *n*

box³ ⊕ *n* evergreen shrub used for hedges

———————————— THESAURUS ————————————

vigour

bound¹ *v* = **surround**, confine, enclose, encircle, hem in; = **limit**, restrict, confine, restrain, circumscribe

bound² *n* = **leap**, bob, spring, jump, bounce

bouquet *n* = **bunch of flowers**, spray, garland, wreath, posy; = **aroma**, smell, scent, perfume, fragrance

bourgeois *adj* = **middle-class**, traditional, conventional, materialistic, hidebound

bout *n* = **period**, term, fit, spell, turn; = **fight**, match, competition, struggle, contest

bow¹ *v* = **bend**, bob, nod, stoop, droop ▷ *n* = **bending**, bob, nod, obeisance, kowtow

bowl¹ *n* = **basin**, plate, dish, vessel

bowl² *v* = **throw**, hurl, launch, cast, pitch

box¹ *n* = **container**, case, chest, trunk, pack ▷ *v* = **pack**, package, wrap, encase, bundle up

box² *v* = **fight**, spar, exchange blows

boy ⊕ *n* **1** male child **2** young man **boyish** *adj* **boyfriend** *n* woman's male companion

boycott ⊕ *v* **1** refuse to deal with or participate in ▷ *n* **2** such refusal

bra *n* woman's undergarment, supporting breasts

braaivlies, braai (*S Afr*) *n* **1 2** grill on which food is cooked over hot charcoal, usu. outdoors ▷ *v* **3 4** cook (food) on in this way

brace ⊕ *n* **1** tool for boring **2** clamp **3** pair **4** support ▷ *pl* **5** straps to hold up trousers ▷ *v* **6** steady (oneself) as before a blow **7** support **bracelet** *n* ornament for the arm **bracing** *adj* invigorating

bracken *n* large fern

bracket *n* **1** support for shelf etc. **2** group ▷ *pl* **3** marks, () used to enclose words etc. ▷ *v* **4** enclose in brackets **5** connect

brackish *adj* (of water) slightly salty

brag *v* **bragging, bragged 1** boast ▷ *n* **2** boastful talk **braggart** *n*

braid *v* **1** interweave **2** trim with braid ▷ *n* **3** anything plaited **4** ornamental tape

Braille *n* system of printing for blind, with raised dots

brain *n* **1** mass of nerve tissue in head **2** intellect ▷ *v* **3** kill by hitting on head **brainy** *adj* **brainchild** *n* creative idea of a person **brainwash** *v* force someone to change beliefs **brainwave** *n* sudden, clever idea

braise *v* stew in covered pan

brake ⊕ *n* **1** instrument for slowing motion of wheel on vehicle ▷ *v* **2** apply brake to

bramble *n* prickly shrub

bran *n* sifted husks of corn

branch ⊕ *n* **1** limb of tree **2** local office ▷ *v* **3** bear branches **4** diverge **5** spread

brand ⊕ *n* **1** trademark **2** class of goods **3** particular kind **4** mark made by hot iron **5** burning piece of wood ▷ *v* **6** burn with iron **7** mark **8** stigmatize **brand-new** *adj* absolutely new

brandish *v* flourish, wave

brandy *n, pl* **-dies** spirit distilled from wine

brash ⊕ *adj* bold, impudent

brass *n* **1** alloy of copper and zinc **2** group of brass wind instruments

boy *n* = **lad**, kid (*Inf*), youth, fellow, youngster

boycott *v* = **embargo**, reject, snub, black ≠ **support**

brace *v* = **steady**, support, secure, stabilize ▷ *n* = **support**, stay, prop, bolster, bracket

brake *n* = **control**, check, curb, restraint, constraint ▷ *v* = **slow**, decelerate, reduce speed

branch *n* = **bough**, shoot, arm, spray, limb; = **office**, department, unit, wing, chapter

brand *n* = **label**, mark, sign, stamp, symbol ▷ *v* = **stigmatize**, mark, expose, denounce, disgrace; = **mark**, burn, label, stamp, scar

brash *adj* = **bold**, rude, cocky, pushy (*Inf*), brazen ≠ **timid**

b

3 (*Inf*) money 4 (*Inf*) (army) officers ▷ *adj* 5 made of brass

brassiere *n* bra

brat *n* unruly child

bravado *n* showy display of boldness

brave ❶ *adj* 1 courageous 2 splendid ▷ *n* 3 warrior ▷ *v* 4 defy, meet boldly **bravery** *n*

bravo *interj* well done!

brawl ❶ *v/n* (take part in) noisy fight

brawn *n* 1 muscle 2 strength 3 pickled pork **brawny** *adj*

bray *n/v* (make) donkey's cry

brazen *adj* 1 of, like brass 2 shameless ▷ *v* 3 face, carry through with impudence

brazier *n* pan for burning coals

breach ❶ *n* 1 opening 2 breaking of rule etc. ▷ *v* 3 make a gap in

bread ❶ *n* 1 food made of flour baked 2 food 3 (*Sl*) money **breadwinner** *n* main earner in family

breadth ❶ *n* 1 extent across,

width 2 largeness of view, mind

break ❶ *v* **breaking, broke, broken** 1 part by force 2 shatter 3 burst, destroy 4 become broken 5 fail to observe 6 disclose 7 interrupt 8 surpass 9 weaken 10 accustom (horse) to being ridden 11 decipher (code) 12 open, appear 13 come suddenly ▷ *n* 14 fracture 15 gap 16 opening 17 separation 18 interruption 19 respite 20 interval 21 (*Inf*) opportunity **breakable** *adj* **breakage** *n* **breaker** *n* 1 one that breaks 2 wave beating on shore **breakdown** *n* 1 collapse 2 failure to function 3 analysis **breakfast** *n* first meal of the day **break-in** *n* illegal entering of building **breakneck** *adj* fast and dangerous **breakthrough** *n* important advance **breakwater** *n* barrier to break force of waves

bream *n* broad, thin fish

breast *n* 1 human chest

— THESAURUS —

brave *adj* = **courageous**, daring, bold, heroic, adventurous ≠ **timid** ▷ *v* = **confront**, face, suffer, tackle, endure ≠ **give in to**

brawl *n* = **fight**, clash, fray, skirmish, scuffle ▷ *v* = **fight**, scrap (*Inf*), wrestle, tussle, scuffle

breach *n* = **nonobservance**, abuse, violation, infringement, trespass ≠ **compliance**; = **opening**, crack, split, gap, rift

bread *n* = **food**, fare, nourishment, sustenance

breadth *n* = **width**, spread, span, latitude, broadness; = **extent**, range, scale, scope, compass

break *v* = **shatter**, separate, destroy, crack, snap ≠ **repair**; = **fracture**, crack, smash; = **burst**, tear, split; = **disobey**, breach, defy, violate, disregard ≠ **obey**; = **stop**, cut, suspend, interrupt, cut short; = **disturb**, interrupt ▷ *n* = **fracture**, opening, tear, hole, split; = **interval**, pause, interlude, intermission; = **holiday**, leave, vacation, time off, recess

2 milk-secreting gland on woman's chest **3** seat of the affections ▷ v **4** face, oppose **5** reach summit of **breaststroke** n stroke in swimming

breath ❶ n **1** air used by lungs **2** life **3** respiration **4** slight breeze **breathe** v **1** inhale and exhale (air) **2** live **3** rest **4** whisper **breather** n short rest **breathing** n **breathless** adj **breathtaking** adj causing awe or excitement

Breathalyser® n Trademark device that estimates amount of alcohol in breath **breathalyse** v

breech n **1** buttocks **2** hind part of anything **breeches** pl n trousers

breed ❶ v **breeding, bred 1** generate **2** rear **3** be produced **4** be with young ▷ n **5** offspring produced **6** race, kind **breeder** n **breeding** n result of good upbringing

breeze ❶ n gentle wind **breezy** adj **1** windy **2** lively

brethren pl n brothers

brevity n **1** conciseness of expression **2** short duration

brew ❶ v **1** prepare liquor, as beer **2** make drink, as tea **3** plot **4** be in preparation ▷ n **5** beverage produced by brewing **brewer** n **brewery** n, pl **-eries**

brier, briar n wild rose with long thorny stems

bribe ❶ n **1** anything offered or given to gain favour ▷ v **2** influence by bribe **bribery** n

bric-a-brac n small ornamental objects

brick n **1** oblong mass of hardened clay used in building ▷ v **2** build, block etc. with bricks **bricklayer** n

bride n woman about to be, or just, married **bridal** adj **bridesmaid** n

bridge¹ ❶ n **1** structure for crossing river etc. **2** something joining or supporting other parts **3** raised narrow platform on ship **4** upper part of nose ▷ v **5** make bridge over, span

bridge² n card game

bridle n **1** headgear of horse **2** curb ▷ v **3** put on bridle **4** restrain **5** show resentment

— THESAURUS —

breath n = **inhalation**, breathing, pant, gasp, gulp

breed n = **variety**, race, stock, type, species; = **kind**, sort, type, variety, brand ▷ v = **rear**, tend, keep, raise, maintain; = **reproduce**, multiply, propagate, procreate, produce offspring; = **produce**, cause, create, generate, bring about

breeze n = **light wind**, air, draught, gust, waft

brew v = **boil**, make, soak, steep, stew; = **make**, ferment ▷ n = **drink**, preparation, mixture, blend, liquor

bribe n = **inducement**, pay-off (Inf), sweetener (Sl), kickback (US), backhander (Sl) ▷ v = **buy off**, reward, pay off (Inf), corrupt, suborn

bridge¹ n = **arch**, span/viaduct, flyover, overpass

ief | 64

CTIONARY

f

brief *adj* 1 short in duration
2 concise 3 scanty ▷ *n*
4 document containing facts of
legal case 5 summary ▷ *pl*
6 underpants 7 panties ▷ *v* 8 give
instructions **briefly** *adv* **briefcase**
n flat case for carrying papers,
books etc.

brier, briar see BRIAR

brigade *n* 1 subdivision of army
2 organized band **brigadier** *n*
high-ranking army officer

brigand *n* bandit

bright *adj* 1 shining 2 full of
light 3 cheerful 4 clever **brighten**
v **brightly** *adv* **brightness** *n*

brilliant *adj* 1 shining
2 sparkling 3 splendid 4 very
clever 5 distinguished **brilliance,
brilliancy** *n*

brim *n* margin, edge, esp. of
river, cup, hat **brimful** *adj*

brine *n* 1 salt water 2 pickle

bring *v* **bringing, brought**
1 fetch 2 carry with one 3 cause to
happen

brinjal *n* (S Afr) dark purple tropical
fruit, cooked and eaten as a
vegetable

brink *n* edge of steep place

brisk *adj* active, vigorous
briskly *adv*

brisket *n* meat from breast

bristle *n* 1 short stiff hair ▷ *v*
2 stand erect 3 show temper
bristly *adj*

brittle *adj* 1 easily broken
2 curt

broach *v* 1 introduce (subject)
2 open

broad *adj* 1 wide, spacious,
open 2 obvious 3 coarse
4 general **broaden** *v* **broadly**
adv **broadcast** *v* 1 transmit by

THESAURUS

brief *adj* = **short**, quick, fleeting,
swift, short-lived ≠ **long** ▷ *v*
= **inform**, prime, prepare, advise, fill
in (*Inf*) ▷ *n* = **summary**, résumé,
outline, sketch, abstract

brigade *n* = **corps**, company, force,
unit, division

bright *adj* = **vivid**, rich, brilliant,
glowing, colourful; = **shining**,
glowing, dazzling, gleaming,
shimmering

brilliant *adj* = **intelligent**, sharp,
intellectual, clever, profound
≠ **stupid**; = **expert**, masterly,
talented, gifted, accomplished
≠ **untalented**; = **splendid**, famous,
celebrated, outstanding, superb

brim *n* = **rim**, edge, border, lip,
margin ▷ *v* = **be full**, spill, well
over, run over

bring *v* = **fetch**, take, carry, bear,
transfer; = **take**, guide, conduct,
escort

brink *n* = **edge**, limit, border, lip,
margin

brisk *adj* = **quick**, lively, energetic,
active, vigorous ≠ **slow**

bristle *n* = **hair**, spine, thorn,
whisker, barb ▷ *v* = **stand up**, rise,
stand on end; = **be angry**, rage,
seethe, flare up, bridle

brittle *adj* = **fragile**, delicate, crisp,
crumbling, frail ≠ **tough**

broad *adj* = **wide**, large, ample,
generous, expansive; = **large**, huge,
vast, extensive, ample ≠ **narrow**

radio or television **2** make widely known ▷ *n* **3** radio or television programme **broadcaster** *n* **broadcasting** *n* **broad-minded** *adj* tolerant **broadside** *n* **1** discharge of guns **2** strong (verbal) attack

brocade *n* rich woven fabric with raised design

broccoli *n* type of cabbage

brochure 🅟 *n* pamphlet

broekies *pl n (S Afr, Inf)* underpants

brogue *n* **1** stout shoe **2** dialect, esp. Irish accent

broil *v (US & Canad)* grill

broke 🅟 *adj (Inf)* having no money

broker 🅟 *n* one employed to buy and sell for others

bromide *n* chemical compound used in medicine and photography

bromine *n* liquid element used in production of chemicals

bronco *n, pl* **-cos** *(US)* wild pony

brontosaurus *n* large plant-eating dinosaur

bronze 🅟 *n* **1** alloy of copper and tin ▷ *adj* **2** made of, or coloured like, bronze ▷ *v* **3** give appearance of bronze to

brooch *n* ornamental pin

brood 🅟 *n* **1** family of young, esp. of birds ▷ *v* **2** sit, as hen on eggs **3** fret over **broody** *adj*

brook¹ 🅟 *n* small stream

brook² *v* put up with

broom *n* **1** brush for sweeping **2** yellow-flowered shrub **broomstick** *n* handle of broom

broth *n* thick soup

brothel *n* house of prostitution

brother 🅟 *n* **1** son of same parents **2** one closely united with another **brotherly** *adj* **brotherhood** *n* **1** fellowship **2** association **brother-in-law** *n, pl* **brothers-in-law 1** brother of husband or wife **2** husband of sibling

brow *n* **1** ridge over eyes **2** forehead **3** eyebrow **4** edge of hill **browbeat** *v* frighten with threats

brown 🅟 *adj* **1** of dark colour inclining to red or yellow ▷ *n* **2** the colour ▷ *v* **3** make, become brown

browse 🅟 *v* **1** look through (book etc.) in a casual manner **2** feed on shoots and leaves

---- THESAURUS ----

brochure *n* = **booklet**, advertisement, leaflet, hand-out, circular

broke *adj (Inf)* = **penniless**, short, ruined, bust *(Inf)*, bankrupt ≠ **rich**

broker *n* = **dealer**, agent, trader, supplier, merchant

bronze *adj* = **reddish-brown**, copper, tan, rust, chestnut

brood *n* = **offspring**, issue, clutch, litter, progeny ▷ *v* = **think**, obsess, muse, ponder, agonize

brook¹ *n* = **stream**, burn *(Scot. & Northern English)*, rivulet, beck, watercourse

brother *n* = **sibling**, blood brother, kin, kinsman, relation, relative

brown *adj* = **brunette**, bay, coffee, chocolate, chestnut ▷ *v* = **fry**, cook, grill, sear, sauté

browse *v* = **skim**, scan, glance at, survey, look through; = **graze**, eat,

bruise ❶ v **1** injure without breaking skin ▷ n **2** contusion, discoloration caused by blow **bruiser** n tough person

brumby n (Aust) **1** wild horse **2** unruly person

brunch n breakfast and lunch combined

brunette n **1** woman of dark complexion and hair ▷ adj **2** dark brown

brunt n chief shock of attack

brush¹ ❶ n **1** device with bristles, hairs etc. used for cleaning, painting etc. **2** act of brushing **3** brief contact **4** skirmish **5** bushy tail ▷ v **6** apply, remove, clean, with brush **7** touch lightly

brush² n thick shrubbery

brusque adj curt

Brussels sprout vegetable like a tiny cabbage

brute n **1** any animal except man **2** crude, vicious person ▷ adj **3** animal **4** sensual **5** stupid **6** physical **brutal** adj **brutality** n **brutally** adv

BSc Bachelor of Science

BST British Summer Time

bubble ❶ n **1** hollow globe of liquid, blown out with air **2** something insubstantial ▷ v **3** rise in bubbles **bubbly** adj

bubonic plague acute infectious disease characterized by swellings

buccaneer n pirate

buck n **1** male deer, or other male animal **2** act of bucking **3** (US & Aust, SI) dollar ▷ v **4** (of horse) attempt to throw rider **buckshot** n lead shot in shotgun shell

bucket n vessel, round with arched handle, for water etc. **bucketful** n

buckle ❶ n **1** metal clasp for fastening belt, strap etc. ▷ v **2** fasten with buckle **3** warp, bend

bud ❶ n **1** shoot containing unopened leaf, flower etc. ▷ v **2** begin to grow

budge ❶ v move, stir

budgerigar, budgie n small Aust. parakeet

budget ❶ n **1** annual financial statement **2** plan of systematic

───────── THESAURUS ─────────

feed, nibble

bruise n = **discoloration**, mark, injury, blemish, black mark ▷ v = **hurt**, injure, mark

brush¹ n = **broom**, sweeper, besom; = **conflict**, clash, confrontation, skirmish, tussle; = **encounter**, meeting, confrontation, rendezvous ▷ v = **clean**, wash, polish, buff; = **touch**, sweep, kiss, stroke, glance

bubble n = **air ball**, drop, bead,

blister, blob ▷ v = **boil**, seethe; = **foam**, fizz, froth, percolate, effervesce

buckle n = **fastener**, catch, clip, clasp, hasp ▷ v = **fasten**, close, secure, hook, clasp; = **distort**, bend, warp, crumple, contort

bud n = **shoot**, branch, sprout, sprig, offshoot ▷ v = **develop**, grow, shoot, sprout, burgeon

budge v = **move**, stir

budget n = **allowance**, means, funds, income, finances ▷ v

b

spending ▷ v **3** make financial plan
buff¹ ❶ n **1** leather from buffalo hide **2** light yellow colour **3** polishing pad ▷ v **4** polish
buff² ❶ n expert
buffalo n type of cattle
buffer ❶ n device to lessen impact
buffet¹ ❶ n **1** refreshment bar **2** meal at which guests serve themselves **3** sideboard
buffet² n **1** blow, slap ▷ v **2** strike with blows **3** contend against
buffoon n **1** clown **2** fool
bug ❶ n **1** any small insect **2** (Inf) disease, infection **3** concealed listening device ▷ v **4** annoy **5** listen secretly
bugbear n **1** object of needless terror **2** nuisance
bugger n (Sl) unpleasant person or thing
bugle n instrument like trumpet
build ❶ v **building, built** **1** construct by putting together

parts **2** develop ▷ n **3** make, form
builder n **building** n **building society** organization where money can be borrowed or invested
bulb ❶ n **1** modified leaf bud emitting roots from base, e.g. onion **2** globe surrounding filament of electric light **bulbous** adj
bulge ❶ n **1** swelling **2** temporary increase ▷ v **3** swell
bulk ❶ n **1** size **2** volume **3** greater part **4** cargo ▷ v **5** be of weight or importance **bulky** adj
bull n **1** male of cattle **2** male of various other animals **bulldog** n thickset breed of dog **bulldozer** n powerful tractor for excavating etc. **bullfight** n public show in which bull is killed **bullock** n castrated bull **bull's-eye** n centre of target
bullet ❶ n projectile discharged from rifle, pistol etc.
bulletin ❶ n official report

THESAURUS

= **plan**, estimate, allocate, cost, ration
buff¹ v = **polish**, smooth, brush, shine, rub
buff² n (Inf) = **expert**, fan, addict, enthusiast, admirer
buffer n = **safeguard**, screen, shield, cushion, intermediary
buffet¹ n = **snack bar**, café, cafeteria, brasserie, refreshment counter
bug n (Inf) = **illness**, disease, virus, infection, disorder ▷ v = **tap**, eavesdrop, listen in on; (Inf) = **annoy**, bother, disturb, irritate, hassle (Inf)

build v = **construct**, make, raise, put up, assemble ≠ **demolish** ▷ n = **physique**, form, body, figure, shape
bulge v = **swell out**, project, expand, stick out, protrude ▷ n = **lump**, swelling, bump, projection, hump ≠ **hollow**; = **increase**, rise, boost, surge, intensification
bulk n = **size**, volume, dimensions, magnitude, substance; = **weight**, size, mass, heaviness, poundage
bullet n = **projectile**, ball, shot, missile, slug
bulletin n = **report**, account,

bullion n gold or silver in mass
bully ● n, pl **-lies** one who hurts or intimidates weaker people ▷ v
bulrush n tall reedlike marsh plant
bulwark n 1 rampart 2 any defence
bum n (Sl) buttocks, anus
bumble v perform clumsily
bumblebee n large hairy bee
bumf, bumph n (Inf) official papers
bump ● n 1 knock 2 thud 3 swelling ▷ v 4 strike or push against **bumper** n 1 horizontal bar on motor vehicle to protect against damage ▷ adj 2 abundant
bumpkin n simple country person
bumptious adj self-assertive
bun n 1 small, round cake 2 round knot of hair
bunch ● n 1 number of things tied or growing together 2 group, party ▷ v 3 gather together
bundle ● n 1 package 2 number of things tied together ▷ v 3 tie in bundle 4 send (off) without ceremony

bung n 1 stopper for cask ▷ v 2 stop up 3 (Sl) sling
bungalow n one-storeyed house
bungle ● v/n botch
bunion n inflamed swelling on foot or toe
bunk n narrow shelflike bed
bunker n 1 large storage container for coal etc. 2 sandy hollow on golf course 3 underground defensive position
bunny n, pl **-nies** (Inf) rabbit
bunting n material for flags
bunyip n (Aust) legendary monster said to live in swamps and lakes
buoy ● n 1 floating marker anchored in sea ▷ v 2 prevent from sinking **buoyancy** n **buoyant** adj
burden ● n 1 load 2 weight, cargo 3 anything difficult to bear ▷ v 4 load, encumber **burdensome** adj
bureau ● n, pl **-reaus, -reaux** 1 writing desk 2 office

━━━━━━━━━━━━━━ THESAURUS ━━━━━━━━

statement, message, communication
bully n = **persecutor**, tough, oppressor, tormentor, bully boy ▷ v = **persecute**, intimidate, torment, oppress, pick on
bump v = **knock**, hit, strike, crash, smash; = **jerk**, shake, bounce, rattle, jog ▷ n = **knock**, blow, impact, collision, thump; = **thud**, crash, knock, bang, smack
bunch n = **group**, band, crowd, party, team; = **cluster**, clump

bundle n = **bunch**, group, collection, mass, pile ▷ v = **push**, thrust, shove, throw, rush
bungle v = **mess up**, blow (Sl), ruin, spoil, blunder ≠ **accomplish**
buoy n = **float**, guide, signal, marker, beacon
burden n = **trouble**, worry, weight, responsibility, strain; = **load**, weight, cargo, freight, consignment ▷ v = **weigh down**, worry, load, tax, bother
bureau n = **office**, department, section, branch, station

3 government department
bureaucracy n **1** government by officials **2** body of officials **bureau de change** place where foreign currencies can be exchanged **bureaucrat** n
burgeon v **1** bud **2** flourish
burglar 🟊 n one who enters building to commit crime esp. theft **burglary** n **burgle** v
burgundy n name of various wines, white and red
burlesque n/v caricature
burly adj **-lier, -liest** sturdy, stout, robust
burn 🟊 v **burning, burnt**
1 destroy or injure by fire **2** be on fire **3** be consumed by fire ▷ n **4** injury, mark caused by fire **burning** adj **1** intense **2** urgent
burnish v, n polish
burp v, n (Inf) belch
burrow 🟊 n **1** hole dug by rabbit etc. ▷ v **2** dig
bursar n official managing finances of college etc. **bursary** n

scholarship
burst 🟊 v **bursting, burst 1** break into pieces **2** break suddenly into some expression of feeling **3** shatter, break violently ▷ n **4** bursting **5** explosion **6** outbreak **7** spurt
bury 🟊 v **burying, buried 1** put underground **2** inter **3** conceal **burial** n/adj
bus n large motor vehicle for passengers
bush 🟊 n **1** shrub **2** uncleared country **bushy** adj shaggy **bushbaby** n tree-living, nocturnal Afr. animal
bushel n dry measure of eight gallons
business 🟊 n **1** occupation **2** commercial or industrial establishment **3** trade **4** responsibility **5** work **businesslike** adj **businessman** n **businesswoman** n
busker n street entertainer **busk** v

——— THESAURUS ———

burglar n = **housebreaker**, thief, robber, pilferer, filcher
burn v = **be on fire**, blaze, be ablaze, smoke, flame; = **set on fire**, light, ignite, kindle, incinerate; = **scorch**, toast, sear, char, singe
burrow n = **hole**, shelter, tunnel, den, lair ▷ v = **dig**, tunnel, excavate
burst v = **explode**, blow up, break, split, crack; = **rush**, run, break, break out, erupt ▷ n = **rush**, surge, outbreak, outburst, spate; = **explosion**, crack, blast, bang, discharge

bury v = **inter**, lay to rest, entomb, consign to the grave, inhume **≠ dig up**; = **hide**, cover, conceal, stash (Inf), secrete **≠ uncover**
bush n = **shrub**, plant, hedge, thicket, shrubbery
business n = **trade**, selling, industry, manufacturing, commerce; = **establishment**, company, firm, concern, organization; = **profession**, work, job, line, trade; = **concern**, affair

b

bust¹ ❶ *n* **1** sculpture of head and shoulders **2** woman's breasts

bust ❶ ² (*Inf*) ▷ *v* **1** burst **2** make, become bankrupt **3** raid **4** arrest ▷ *adj* **5** broken **6** bankrupt

bustle ❶ *v* **1** be noisily busy ▷ *n* **2** fuss, commotion

busy ❶ *adj* **busier, busiest** **1** actively employed **2** full of activity ▷ *v* **3** occupy **busily** *adv* **busybody** *n* nosy person

but ❶ *conj* **1** without **2** except **3** yet **4** still **5** besides ▷ *adv* **6** only

butane *n* gas used for fuel

butch *adj* (*Inf*) aggressively masculine

butcher ❶ *n* **1** one who kills animals for food, or sells meat **2** savage man ▷ *v* **3** slaughter **butchery** *n*

butler *n* chief male servant

butt¹ ❶ *n* **1** thick end **2** unused end

butt² ❶ *n* **1** target **2** object of ridicule

butt³ ❶ *v* **1** strike with head **2** interrupt ▷ *n* **3** blow made with head

butter *n* **1** fatty substance got from cream by churning ▷ *v* **2** spread with butter **3** flatter

buttercup *n* plant with glossy, yellow flowers

butterfly *n* insect with large wings

butterscotch *n* kind of hard, brittle toffee

buttock *n* (*usu. pl*) rump, protruding hind part

button *n* **1** knob, stud for fastening dress **2** knob that operates doorbell, machine etc. ▷ *v* **3** fasten with buttons **buttonhole** *n* **1** slit in garment to pass button through **2** flower worn on lapel etc. ▷ *v* **3** detain (unwilling) person in conversation

buttress *n* **1** structure to support wall **2** prop ▷ *v* **3** support

buxom *adj* full of health, plump

───────────── THESAURUS ─────────────

bust¹ *n* = **bosom**, breasts, chest, front

bust² (*Inf*) ▷ *v* = **break**, smash, split, burst, shatter; = **arrest**, catch, raid

bustle *v* = **hurry**, rush, fuss, hasten, scuttle ≠ **idle** ▷ *n* = **activity**, to-do, stir, excitement, fuss ≠ **inactivity**

busy *adj* = **active**, industrious, rushed off your feet ≠ **idle**; = **occupied with**, working, engaged in, on duty, employed in ≠ **unoccupied**

but *conj* = **however**, still, yet, nevertheless ▷ *adv* = **only**, just, simply, merely

butcher *n* = **murderer**, killer, slaughterer, slayer, destroyer ▷ *v* = **slaughter**, prepare, carve, cut up, dress; = **kill**, slaughter, massacre, destroy, cut down

butt¹ *n* = **end**, handle, shaft, stock, shank; = **stub**, tip, leftover, fag end (*Inf*)

butt² *n* = **target**, victim, dupe, laughing stock, Aunt Sally

butt³ *v* = **knock**, push, bump, thrust, ram

buy ❶ v **buying, bought 1** get by payment, purchase **2** bribe ▷ n **3** thing purchased **buyer** n

buzz v/n (make) humming sound **buzzer** n **buzzword** n fashionable word

buzzard n bird of prey

by ❶ prep **1** near **2** along **3** past **4** during **5** not later than **6** through use or agency of **7** in units of ▷ adv **8** near **9** aside **10** past **by and by** soon **by and large** on the whole

bye, bye-bye n (Sport) situation where player or team wins by default of opponent

by-election n election to fill vacant seat

bygone adj **1** past, former ▷ n **2** (oft. pl) past occurrence **3** small antique

bylaw, bye-law n law, regulation made by local authority

bypass ❶ n **1** road for diversion of traffic from overcrowded centres ▷ v **2** make detour round

byre n cowshed

byte n (Comp) sequence of bits processed as single unit of information

byway n secondary or side road

byword n well-known name or saying

——————— THESAURUS ———————

buy v = **purchase**, get, pay for, obtain, acquire ≠ **sell** ▷ n = **purchase**, deal, bargain, acquisition, steal (Inf)

by prep = **through**, through the agency of; = **via**, over, by way of; = **near**, past, along, close to, closest to ▷ adv = **nearby**, close, handy, at hand, within reach

bypass v = **get round**, avoid

C **1** (*Chem*) carbon **2** Celsius **3** Centigrade

c. circa

cab ❶ *n* **1** taxi **2** driver's compartment on lorry etc.

cabal *n* **1** small group of intriguers **2** secret plot

cabaret *n* floor show at a nightclub

cabbage *n* green vegetable

cabin ❶ *n* **1** hut, shed **2** small room, esp. in ship

cabinet ❶ *n* **1** piece of furniture with drawers or shelves **2** outer case of television, radio etc. **3** committee of politicians

cable *n* **1** strong rope **2** wires conveying electric power, television signals etc. **3** telegraph ▷ *v* **4** telegraph by cable **cable car** vehicle pulled up slope on cable

cache *n* **1** secret hiding place

2 store of food etc.

cackle *v/n* (make) chattering noise, as of hen

cacophony *n* **1** disagreeable sound **2** discord of sounds

cactus *n, pl* **-tuses, -ti** spiny succulent plant

cad *n* unchivalrous person

cadaver *n* corpse **cadaverous** *adj*

caddie, caddy *n, pl* **-dies** golfer's attendant

caddy *n, pl* **-dies** small box for tea

cadence *n* fall or modulation of voice in music or verse

cadenza *n* (*Mus*) elaborate solo passage

cadet *n* youth in training, esp. for armed forces

cadge *v* get (food, money etc.) by begging

cadmium *n* metallic element

caecum *n, pl* **-ca** part of large intestine

Caesar *n* title of Roman emperors **Caesar salad** *n* salad of lettuce, cheese, and croutons, with olive oil, garlic, and lemon juice

Caesarean section *n* surgical operation to deliver a baby

caesium *n* metallic element

café *n* small restaurant serving light refreshments **cafeteria** *n* self-service restaurant

caffeine *n* stimulating chemical found in tea and coffee

————————————————— THESAURUS —————————————————

cab *n* = **taxi**, minicab, taxicab, hackney carriage

cabin *n* = **room**, berth, quarters, compartment; = **hut**, shed, cottage, lodge, shack

cabinet *n* = **cupboard**, case, locker, dresser, closet; (*often cap.*) = **council**, committee, administration, ministry, assembly

café *n* = **snack bar**, restaurant,

caftan n see KAFTAN

cage ❶ n 1 enclosure, box with bars or wires, esp. for keeping animals or birds ▷ v put in cage, confine **cagey** adj wary

cagoule n lightweight anorak

cairn n heap of stones, esp. as monument or landmark

cajole v persuade by flattery, wheedle

cake ❶ n 1 baked, sweet, bread-like food 2 compact mass ▷ v 3 harden (as of mud)

calamine n soothing ointment

calamity n, pl **-ties** disaster **calamitous** adj

calcium n metallic element, the basis of lime

calculate ❶ v 1 estimate 2 compute 3 make reckonings **calculable** adj **calculating** adj 1 shrewd 2 scheming **calculation** n **calculator** n electronic device for making calculations

calendar n 1 table of months and days in the year 2 list of events

calf¹ n, pl **calves** n 1 young of cow and other animals 2 leather of calf's skin

calf² n fleshy back of leg below knee

calibre, US **caliber ❶** n 1 size of bore of gun 2 capacity, character **calibrate** v

calico n, pl **-coes** cotton cloth

call ❶ v 1 speak loudly to attract attention 2 summon 3 telephone 4 name 5 shout 6 pay visit ▷ n 7 shout 8 animal's cry 9 visit 10 inner urge 11 demand **caller** n **calling** n vocation, profession **call up** 1 summon to serve in army 2 imagine

calligraphy n handwriting

callous adj hardened, unfeeling

callow adj inexperienced

callus n, pl **-luses** area of hardened skin

calm ❶ adj, v 1 (make, become) still, tranquil 2 (make) composed ▷ n 3 absence of wind **calmly** adv **calmness** n

calorie n 1 unit of heat 2 unit of

--- THESAURUS ---

cafeteria, coffee shop, brasserie

cage n = **enclosure**, pen, coop, hutch, pound

cake n = **block**, bar, slab, lump, cube

calculate v = **work out**, determine, estimate, count, reckon; = **plan**, design, aim, intend, arrange

calibre, US **caliber** n = **worth**, quality, ability, talent, capacity; = **standard**, level, quality, grade

call v = **name**, entitle, dub,

designate, term; = **cry**, shout, scream, yell, whoop ≠ **whisper**; = **phone**, telephone, ring (up) (Inf, chiefly Brit), summon; = **summon**, gather, rally, assemble, muster ≠ **dismiss**; = **waken**, arouse, rouse ▷ n = **request**, order, demand, appeal, notice; (usually used in a negative construction) = **need**, cause, reason, grounds, occasion

calm adj = **cool**, relaxed, composed, sedate, collected ≠ **excited**; = **still**, quiet, smooth, mild, serene ≠ **rough** ▷ n = **peacefulness**,

energy from foods

calypso n, pl **-sos** (West Indies) improvised song

cam n device to change rotary to reciprocating motion

camaraderie n spirit of comradeship, trust

camber n curve on road surface

cambric n fine white linen or cotton cloth

camcorder n portable video camera and recorder

camel n animal of Asia and Africa, with humped back

camellia n ornamental shrub

cameo n, pl **-meos 1** medallion, brooch etc. with design in relief **2** small part in film etc.

camera n apparatus used to make photographs **cameraman** n

camisole n underbodice

camouflage ❶ n **1** disguise, means of avoiding enemy observation ▷ v **2** disguise

camp¹ ❶ n **1** (place for) tents of hikers, army etc. **2** group supporting political party etc. ▷ v **3** form or lodge in camp

camp² ❶ adj (Inf) **1** homosexual **2** consciously artificial

campaign ❶ n/v (organize) series of coordinated activities for some

purpose, e.g. political, military

camphor n solid essential oil with aromatic taste and smell

campus n, pl **-puses** grounds of university

can¹ v past **could 1** be able **2** have the power **3** be allowed

can² n **1** container, usu. metal, for liquids, foods ▷ v **2** put in can **canned** adj **1** preserved in can **2** (of music) previously recorded

Canada Day n July 1, the anniversary of the day when Canada became the first British colony to receive dominion status

Canada goose n large greyish-brown N American goose with a black neck and head and a white throat patch

Canada jay n a large common jay of North America with a grey body, and a white-and-black crestless head

canal ❶ n **1** artificial watercourse **2** duct in body

canary n, pl **-ries** yellow singing bird

canasta n card game played with two packs

cancan n high-kicking dance

──────── THESAURUS ────────

peace, serenity ▷ v = **soothe**, quiet, relax, appease, still ≠ **excite**

camouflage n = **disguise**, cover, screen, blind, mask ▷ v = **disguise**, cover, screen, hide, mask ≠ **reveal**

camp¹ n = **camp site**, tents, encampment, bivouac, camping

ground

camp² adj (Inf) = **affected**, mannered, artificial, posturing, ostentatious

campaign n = **drive**, appeal, movement, push (Inf), offensive; = **operation**, drive, attack, movement, push

cancel ❶ v -celling, -celled
1 cross out 2 annul 3 call off
cancellation n

cancer ❶ n malignant growth or
tumour **cancerous** adj

candid adj frank, impartial
candour n

candidate ❶ n 1 one who seeks
office etc. 2 person taking
examination **candidacy,
candidature** n

candle n 1 stick of wax with wick
2 light **candelabrum** n large,
branched candle holder
candlestick n

candy n, pl -dies 1 crystallized
sugar 2 (US) confectionery in
general ▷ v 3 preserve with sugar
candyfloss n fluffy mass of spun
sugar

cane n 1 stem of small palm or
large grass 2 walking stick ▷ v
3 beat with cane

canine adj 1 of or like a dog ▷ n
2 sharp pointed tooth

canister n container, usu. of
metal, for storing dry food

canker n 1 eating sore 2 thing
that destroys, corrupts

cannabis n 1 hemp plant 2 drug
derived from this

cannelloni pl n tubular pieces of

pasta filled with meat etc.

cannibal n one who eats human
flesh **cannibalism** n

cannon¹ ❶ n large gun
cannonball n heavy metal ball

cannon² n 1 billiard stroke ▷ v
2 make this stroke 3 rebound,
collide

cannot negative form of CAN¹

canny adj -nier, -niest 1 shrewd
2 cautious

canoe n 1 very light boat propelled
with paddle ▷ v 2 travel by canoe

canon ❶ n 1 law or rule, esp. of
church 2 standard 3 list of saints
canonize v enrol in list of saints

canopy ❶ n, pl -pies 1 covering
over throne, bed etc. ▷ v 2 cover
with canopy

cant n 1 hypocritical speech
2 technical jargon 3 slang, esp. of
thieves ▷ v 4 use cant

cantankerous adj quarrelsome

cantata n choral work

canteen n place in factory, school
etc. where meals are provided

canter n/v (move at) easy gallop

cantilever n beam, girder etc.
fixed at one end only

Canuck n/adj (Inf) Canadian

canvas n coarse cloth used for
sails, painting on etc.

— THESAURUS —

canal n = **waterway**, channel,
passage, conduit, duct

cancel v = **call off**, drop, forget
about

cancer n = **growth**, tumour,
malignancy, corruption, sickness

candidate n = **contender**,
competitor, applicant, nominee,

entrant

cannon¹ n = **gun**, big gun, field
gun, mortar

canon n = **rule**, standard, principle,
regulation, formula; = **list**, index,
catalogue, roll

canopy n = **awning**, covering,
shade, sunshade

canvass v **1** solicit votes, contributions etc. **2** discuss

canyon n deep gorge

cap ❶ n **1** covering for head **2** lid, top ▷ v **3** put a cap on **4** outdo

capable ❶ adj **1** able **2** competent **3** having the power **capability** n

capacity ❶ n, pl **-ties 1** power of holding **2** room **3** volume **4** function, role **5** ability

cape¹ ❶ n headland

cape² n covering for shoulders

caper n **1** skip **2** frolic **3** escapade ▷ v **4** skip, dance

capillary n, pl **-laries** small blood vessel

capital ❶ n **1** chief town **2** money **3** large-sized letter ▷ adj **4** involving or punishable by death **5** chief **6** excellent **capitalism** n economic system based on private ownership of industry **capitalist** n/adj **capitalize** v **1** convert into capital **2** turn to advantage

capitulate v surrender

capon n castrated cock fowl fattened for eating

cappuccino n, pl **-nos** coffee with steamed milk

caprice n whim, freak **capricious** adj

capsize v (of boat) overturn accidentally

capstan n machine to wind cable

capsule ❶ n case for dose of medicine

captain ❶ n **1** commander of vessel or company of soldiers **2** leader ▷ v **3** be captain of **captaincy** n

caption n heading, title of article, picture etc.

captive ❶ n **1** prisoner ▷ adj **2** taken, imprisoned **captivate** v fascinate **captivity** n

capture ❶ v **1** seize, make prisoner ▷ n **2** seizure, taking **captor** n

car ❶ n **1** road vehicle **2** passenger

———————————— THESAURUS ————————

cap v (Inf) = **beat**, top, better, exceed, eclipse

capable adj = **accomplished**, qualified, talented, gifted, efficient ≠ **incompetent**

capacity n = **ability**, facility, gift, genius, capability; = **size**, room, range, space, volume; = **function**, position, role, post, province

cape¹ n = **headland**, point, head, peninsula, promontory

capital n = **money**, funds, investment(s), cash, finances ▷ adj (Old-fashioned) = **first-rate**, fine,

excellent, superb, sterling

capsule n = **pill**, tablet, lozenge; (Botany) = **pod**, case, shell, vessel, sheath

captain n = **leader**, boss, master, skipper, head

captive adj = **confined**, caged, imprisoned, locked up, enslaved ▷ n = **prisoner**, hostage, convict, prisoner of war, detainee

capture v = **catch**, arrest, take, bag, secure ≠ **release** ▷ n = **arrest**, catching, trapping, imprisonment, seizure

car n = **vehicle**, motor, wheels (Inf),

compartment of a vehicle

carafe n glass water bottle for the table, decanter

caramel n 1 burnt sugar for cooking 2 chewy sweet

carat n 1 weight used for gold, diamonds etc. 2 measure used to state fineness of gold

caravan n 1 large vehicle for living in, pulled by car etc. 2 company of merchants travelling together

caraway n plant with spicy seeds used in cakes etc.

carbohydrate n any compound containing carbon, hydrogen and oxygen, esp. sugars and starches

carbon n nonmetallic element, substance of pure charcoal, found in all organic matter **carbonate** n salt of carbonic acid **carbon copy** 1 copy made with carbon paper 2 very similar person or thing **carbon dioxide** colourless gas exhaled in respiration **carbon-neutral** adj not affecting the overall volume of carbon dioxide in the atmosphere

carbuncle n inflamed ulcer, boil or tumour

carburettor n device for mixing petrol with air in engine

carcass, carcase n dead animal body

card n 1 thick, stiff paper 2 piece of this giving identification etc. 3 illustrated card sending greetings etc. 4 playing card ▷ pl 5 any card game **cardboard** n thin, stiff board made of paper pulp **cardsharp** n cheating card player

cardiac adj pert. to the heart **cardiograph** n instrument which records movements of the heart **cardiology** n study of heart diseases

cardigan n knitted jacket

cardinal ❶ adj 1 chief, principal ▷ n 2 rank next to the Pope in R.C. church **cardinal numbers** 1,2,3 etc.

care ❷ v 1 be anxious 2 have regard or liking (for) 3 look after 4 be disposed to ▷ n 5 attention 6 protection 7 anxiety 8 caution **careful** adj **careless** adj **carefree** adj **caretaker** n person in charge of premises

career ❸ n 1 course through life 2 profession 3 rapid motion ▷ v 4 run or move at full speed

caress v 1 fondle, embrace, treat with affection ▷ n 2 affectionate embrace or touch

caret n mark (∧) showing where to

auto (US), automobile; (US & Canad) = **(railway) carriage**, coach, cable car, dining car, sleeping car

cardinal adj = **principal**, first, leading, chief, main ≠ **secondary**

care v = **be concerned**, mind, bother, be interested, be bothered ▷ n = **custody**, keeping, control, charge, management; = **caution**, attention, pains, consideration, heed ≠ **carelessness**; = **worry**, concern, pressure, trouble, responsibility ≠ **pleasure**

career n = **occupation**, calling, employment, pursuit, vocation ▷ v = **rush**, race, speed, tear, dash

insert word etc.

cargo ❶ *n, pl* **-goes** load, freight, carried by ship, plane etc.

caribou *n, pl* **-bou** N American reindeer

caricature ❶ *n* **1** likeness exaggerated to appear ridiculous ▷ *v* **2** portray in this way

cark *v (Aust & NZ, Sl)* die

carnage ❶ *n* slaughter

carnal *adj* fleshly, sensual

carnation *n* cultivated flower

carnival ❶ *n* **1** festive occasion **2** travelling fair

carol ❶ *n/v* (sing) song or hymn of joy

carouse *v* have merry drinking spree **carousal** *n*

carousel *n* **1** (US) merry-go-round **2** rotating device for holding slides

carp¹ ❶ *v* **1** find fault **2** nag

carp² *n* freshwater fish

carpenter ❶ *n* worker in timber **carpentry** *n*

carpet *n* heavy fabric for covering floor

carriage ❶ *n* **1** railway coach **2** bearing **3** horse-drawn vehicle **carriageway** *n* part of road along which traffic passes in a single line

carrion *n* rotting dead flesh

carrot *n* **1** plant with orange-red edible root **2** inducement

carry ❶ *v* **-rying, -ried 1** convey, transport **2** capture, win **3** effect **4** behave **5** (of projectile, sound) reach **carrier** *n*

cart *n* **1** open (two-wheeled) vehicle ▷ *v* **2** carry in cart **3** carry with effort **carthorse** *n* heavily built horse **cartwheel** *n* sideways somersault

carte blanche (Fr) complete authority

cartel *n* industrial alliance for fixing prices etc.

cartilage *n* **1** firm elastic tissue in the body **2** gristle

cartography *n* map making

carton ❶ *n* cardboard or plastic container

cartoon ❶ *n* **1** drawing, esp.

————————————— THESAURUS —————————————

cargo *n* = **load**, goods, contents, shipment, freight

caricature *n* = **parody**, cartoon, distortion, satire, send-up (Brit Inf) ▷ *v* = **parody**, take off (Inf), mock, distort, ridicule

carnage *n* = **slaughter**, murder, massacre, holocaust, havoc

carnival *n* = **festival**, fair, fête, celebration, gala

carol *n* = **song**, hymn, Christmas song

carp¹ *v* = **find fault**, complain, criticize, reproach, quibble

≠ **praise**

carpenter *n* = **joiner**, cabinet-maker, woodworker

carriage *n* = **vehicle**, coach, trap, gig, cab; = **bearing**, posture, gait, deportment, air

carry *v* = **convey**, take, move, bring, bear; = **transport**, take, transfer

carton *n* = **box**, case, pack, package, container

cartoon *n* = **drawing**, parody, satire, caricature, comic strip; = **animation**, animated film,

humorous or satirical **2** sequence of drawings telling story
cartoonist n
cartridge n **1** case containing charge for gun **2** container for film etc.
carve ① v **1** cut **2** hew **3** sculpture **4** engrave **5** cut (meat) in pieces or slices **carving** n
cascade ① n waterfall
case¹ ① n **1** instance **2** circumstance **3** question at issue **4** arguments supporting particular action etc. **5** (Med) patient **6** lawsuit **in case** so as to allow for eventualities
case² ① n **1** box, sheath, covering **2** receptacle **3** box and contents ▷ v **4** put in a case
cash ① n **1** money, banknotes and coins ▷ v **2** turn into or exchange for money **cashier** n one in charge of receiving and paying of money
cashier v dismiss from office
cashmere n fine soft fabric made from goat's wool
casino n, pl **-nos** building,

institution for gambling
cask n barrel
casket n small case for jewels etc.
casserole n **1** fireproof cooking dish **2** stew
cassette n plastic container for film, magnetic tape etc.
cassock n clergyman's long tunic
cast ① v **1** throw or fling **2** shed **3** deposit (a vote) **4** allot, as parts in play **5** mould ▷ n **6** throw **7** squint **8** mould **9** that which is shed or ejected **10** set of actors **11** type or quality **castaway** n shipwrecked person **cast-iron** adj **1** made of hard, brittle type of iron **2** rigid or unchallengeable **cast-off** adj/n discarded (garment)
castanets pl n two small curved pieces of wood clicked together in hand
caste ① n **1** section of society in India **2** social rank
caster sugar, castor sugar n finely powdered sugar
castigate v rebuke severely
castle ① n fortress

animated cartoon
carve v = **sculpt**, cut, chip, whittle, chisel; = **etch**, engrave
cascade n = **waterfall**, falls, torrent, flood, shower
case¹ n = **situation**, event, circumstance(s), state, position; = **instance**, example, occasion, specimen, occurrence; (Law) = **lawsuit**, trial, suit, proceedings, dispute
case² n = **cabinet**, box, chest, holder
cash n = **money**, funds, notes,

currency, silver
cast n = **actors**, company, players, characters, troupe; = **type**, sort, kind, style, stamp ▷ v = **choose**, name, pick, select, appoint; = **bestow**, give, level, direct; = **give out**, spread, deposit, shed, distribute; = **throw**, launch, pitch, toss, thrust
caste n = **class**, order, rank, status, stratum
castle n = **fortress**, keep, palace, tower, chateau

castor n **1** bottle with perforated top **2** small swivelled wheel on table leg etc.

castor oil n vegetable medicinal oil

castrate v remove testicles **castration** n

casual ❶ adj **1** accidental **2** unforeseen **3** occasional **4** unconcerned **5** informal **casually** adv **casualty** n person killed or injured in accident, war etc.

cat ❶ n any of various feline animals, esp. small domesticated furred animal **catty** adj spiteful **catcall** n derisive cry **catkin** n drooping flower spike **catnap** v/n doze **Catseye** n glass reflector set in road to indicate traffic lanes **catwalk** n narrow platform

cataclysm n **1** (disastrous) upheaval **2** deluge

catalogue, US **catalog ❶** n **1** descriptive list ▷ v **2** make such list of

catalyst n substance causing or assisting a chemical reaction without taking part in it

catamaran n type of sailing boat with twin hulls

catapult n **1** small forked stick with sling for throwing stones **2** launching device ▷ v **3** launch with force

cataract n **1** waterfall **2** downpour **3** disease of eye

catarrh n inflammation of mucous membrane

catastrophe ❶ n great disaster **catastrophic** adj

catch ❶ v **catching, caught 1** take hold of **2** hear **3** contract disease **4** be in time for **5** detect **6** be contagious **7** get entangled **8** begin to burn ▷ n **9** seizure **10** thing that holds, stops etc. **11** what is caught **12** (Inf) snag, disadvantage **catcher** n **catching** adj **catchy** adj (of tune) easily remembered

catechism n instruction by questions and answers

category ❶ n, pl **-ries** class, order **categorize** v **categorical** adj positive

cater v provide, esp. food **caterer** n

———————— THESAURUS ————————

casual adj = **careless**, relaxed, unconcerned, blasé, offhand ≠ **serious**; = **chance**, unexpected, random, accidental, incidental ≠ **planned**; = **informal**, leisure, sporty, non-dressy ≠ **formal**

cat n = **feline**, pussy (Inf), moggy (Sl), puss (Inf), tabby

catalogue, US **catalog** n = **list**, record, schedule, index, register ▷ v = **list**, file, index, register, classify

catastrophe n = **disaster**, tragedy, calamity, cataclysm, trouble

catch v = **capture**, arrest, trap, seize, snare ≠ **free**; = **trap**, capture, snare, ensnare, entrap; = **seize**, get, grab, snatch; = **grab**, take, grip, seize, grasp ≠ **release** ▷ n = **fastener**, clip, bolt, latch, clasp; (Inf) = **drawback**, trick, trap, disadvantage, hitch ≠ **advantage**

category n = **class**, grouping,

caterpillar n hairy grub of moth or butterfly

catharsis n, pl **-ses** relief of strong suppressed emotions **cathartic** adj

cathedral n principal church of diocese

Catherine wheel n rotating firework producing sparks

catholic adj 1 universal 2 including whole body of Christians 3 (with cap.) relating to R.C. church ▷ n 4 (with cap.) adherent of R.C. church **Catholicism** n

cattle ❶ pl n pasture animals, esp. oxen, cows **cattleman** n

cauldron n large pot used for boiling

cauliflower n variety of cabbage with edible white flowering head

cause ❶ n 1 that which produces an effect 2 reason 3 motive 4 charity, movement 5 lawsuit ▷ v 6 bring about, make happen

causeway n raised path over marsh etc.

caustic adj 1 burning 2 bitter ▷ n 3 corrosive substance

cauterize v burn with caustic or hot iron

caution ❶ n 1 heedfulness, care 2 warning ▷ v 3 warn **cautionary** adj **cautious** adj

cavalcade n procession

cavalier adj 1 careless, disdainful ▷ n 2 courtly gentleman 3 (Obs) horseman 4 (with cap.) supporter of Charles I

cavalry ❶ n, pl **-ries** mounted troops

cave ❶ n 1 hollow place in the earth 2 den **cavern** n deep cave **cavernous** adj **cavity** n hollow **caveman** n prehistoric cave dweller

caviar, caviare n salted sturgeon roe

cavil v **-illing, -illed** make trifling objections

cavort v prance, frisk

CBE Commander of the British Empire

cc cubic centimetre

CD compact disc **CD-ROM** compact disc storing written information, displayed on VDU

cease ❶ v bring or come to an end

—————— THESAURUS ——————

heading, sort, department

cattle pl n = **cows**, stock, beasts, livestock, bovines

cause n = **origin**, source, spring, agent, maker ≠ **result**; = **reason**, call, need, grounds, basis; = **aim**, movement, principle, ideal, enterprise ▷ v = **produce**, create, lead to, result in, generate ≠ **prevent**

caution n = **care**, discretion, heed, prudence, vigilance ≠ **carelessness**; = **reprimand**, warning, injunction, admonition ▷ v = **warn**, urge, advise, alert, tip off

cavalry n = **horsemen**, horse, mounted troops ≠ **infantrymen**

cave n = **hollow**, cavern, grotto, den, cavity

cease v = **stop**, end, finish, come to an end ≠ **start**

ceaseless *adj* **ceasefire** *n* temporary truce
cedar *n* large evergreen tree
cede *v* yield, give up, transfer
cedilla *n* accent (,) below letter
ceilidh *n* informal social gathering for dancing
ceiling *n* inner, upper surface of a room
celebrate ❶ *v* **1** have festivities to mark (happy day, event etc.) **2** observe (birthday etc.) **3** perform (religious ceremony etc.) **4** praise publicly **celebrated** *adj* famous **celebration** *n* **celebrity** *n, pl* **-rities 1** famous person **2** fame
celery *n* vegetable with long juicy edible stalks
celestial *adj* heavenly, divine
cell ❶ *n* **1** small room in prison **2** small cavity **3** minute, basic unit of living matter **4** device converting chemical into electrical energy **cellular** *adj*
cellar *n* **1** underground room for storage **2** stock of wine
cello *n, pl* **-los** stringed instrument of violin family
Cellophane® *n* transparent wrapping

cellulose *n* fibrous carbohydrate
Celsius *adj/n* (of) scale of temperature from 0° to 100°
cement ❶ *n* **1** fine mortar **2** glue ▷ *v* **3** unite as with cement
cemetery ❶ *n, pl* **-teries** burial ground
cenotaph *n* monument to one buried elsewhere
censor ❶ *n* **1** one authorized to examine films, books etc. and suppress parts considered unacceptable ▷ *v* **2** suppress **censorious** *adj* fault-finding **censorship** *n*
censure ❶ *n/v* blame
census *n, pl* **-suses** official counting of people, things etc.
cent *n* hundredth part of dollar etc.
centaur *n* mythical creature, half man, half horse
centenary *n, pl* **-naries 1** 100 years **2** celebration of hundredth anniversary ▷ *adj* **3** pert. to a hundred
centigrade *adj/n* another name for CELSIUS
centimetre *n* hundredth part of metre
centipede *n* small segmented

celebrate *v* = **rejoice**, party, enjoy yourself, carouse, live it up (*Inf*); = **commemorate**, honour, observe, toast, drink to
cell *n* = **room**, chamber, lock-up, compartment, cavity; = **unit**, group, section, core, nucleus
cement *n* = **mortar**, plaster, paste; = **sealant**, glue, gum, adhesive ▷ *v* = **stick**, join, bond, attach, seal

cemetery *n* = **graveyard**, churchyard, burial ground, necropolis, God's acre
censor *v* = **expurgate**, cut, blue-pencil, bowdlerize
censure *v* = **criticize**, blame, condemn, denounce, rebuke ≠ **applaud** ▷ *n* = **disapproval**, criticism, blame, condemnation, rebuke ≠ **approval**

animal with many legs

centre ❶ n 1 midpoint 2 pivot 3 place for specific organization or activity **central** adj **centralize** v **centrally** adv

centurion n Roman commander of 100 men

century n, pl **-ries** 1 100 years 2 any set of 100

cereal n 1 any edible grain 2 (breakfast) food

cerebral adj pert. to brain

ceremony ❶ n, pl **-nies** 1 formal observance 2 sacred rite 3 courteous act **ceremonial** adj/n

certain ❶ adj 1 sure 2 inevitable 3 some, one 4 moderate (in quantity, degree etc.) **certainly** adv **certainty** n

certify ❶ v **-fying, -fied** 1 declare formally 2 guarantee **certificate** n written declaration

cervix n, pl **cervixes, cervices** neck, esp. of womb **cervical** adj

cessation n stop, pause

chafe v 1 make sore or worn by rubbing 2 warm 3 vex

chaff n 1 husks of corn 2 worthless matter ▷ v 3 tease

chaffinch n small songbird

chagrin n 1 vexation, disappointment ▷ v 2 embarrass

chain ❶ n 1 series of connected rings 2 thing that binds 3 connected series of things or events 4 surveyor's measure ▷ v 5 fasten with a chain 6 restrain

chair n 1 movable seat, with back, for one person 2 seat of authority ▷ v 3 preside over 4 carry in triumph **chairman** n one who presides over meeting **chairperson** n **chairwoman** n

chalet n Swiss wooden house

chalice n (Poet) cup

chalk n 1 white substance, carbonate of lime 2 crayon ▷ v 3 mark with chalk **chalky** adj

challenge ❶ v 1 call to fight or account 2 dispute 3 stimulate ▷ n 4 challenging **challenger** n

chamber ❶ n 1 (room for)

THESAURUS

centre n = **middle**, heart, focus, core, nucleus ≠ **edge**

ceremony n = **ritual**, service, rite, observance, commemoration; = **formality**, ceremonial, propriety, decorum

certain adj = **sure**, convinced, positive, confident, satisfied ≠ **unsure**; = **bound**, sure, fated, destined ≠ **unlikely**

certify v = **confirm**, declare, guarantee, assure, testify

chain n = **tether**, coupling, link, bond, shackle; = **series**, set, train, string, sequence ▷ v = **bind**, confine, restrain, handcuff, shackle

challenge n = **dare**, provocation; = **test**, trial, opposition, confrontation, ultimatum ▷ v = **dispute**, question, tackle, confront, defy

chamber n = **hall**, room; = **council**, assembly, legislature, legislative body; = **room**, bedroom, apartment, enclosure, cubicle

assembly **2** compartment **3** cavity ▷ *pl* **4** office or apartment of barrister **chambermaid** *n* woman who cleans bedrooms

chameleon *n* lizard with power of changing colour

chamois *n, pl* **-ois 1** goatlike mountain antelope **2** soft pliable leather

champ *n* **1** munch noisily **2** be impatient

champagne *n* light, sparkling white wine

champion ❶ *n* **1** one that excels all others **2** defender of a cause ▷ *v* **3** fight for **championship** *n*

chance ❶ *n* **1** unpredictable course of events **2** luck **3** opportunity **4** possibility **5** risk **6** probability ▷ *v* **7** risk **8** happen ▷ *adj* **9** casual, unexpected **chancy** *adj*

chancel *n* part of a church where altar is

chancellor *n* **1** high officer of state **2** head of university

chandelier *n* hanging frame with branches for lights

change ❶ *v* **1** alter, make or become different **2** put on (different clothes, fresh coverings) **3** put or give for another **4** exchange ▷ *n* **5** alteration **6** variety **7** coins **8** balance received on payment **changeable** *adj*

channel ❶ *n* **1** bed of stream **2** strait **3** deeper part of strait **4** groove **5** means of conveying **6** band of radio frequencies **7** television broadcasting station ▷ *v* **8** groove **9** guide

chant ❶ *n* **1** simple song or melody **2** rhythmic slogan ▷ *v* **3** utter chant **4** speak monotonously

chaos ❶ *n* disorder, confusion **chaotic** *adj*

━━━━━━━━━━ THESAURUS ━━━━━━━━━━

champion *n* = **winner**, hero, victor, conqueror, title holder; = **defender**, guardian, patron, backer, protector ▷ *v* = **support**, back, defend, promote, advocate

chance *n* = **probability**, odds, possibility, prospect, likelihood ≠ **certainty**; = **opportunity**, opening, occasion, time; = **accident**, fortune, luck, fate, destiny ≠ **design**; = **risk**, speculation, gamble, hazard ▷ *v* = **risk**, try, stake, venture, gamble

change *n* = **alteration**, innovation, transformation, modification, mutation; = **variety**,

break (*Inf*), departure, variation, novelty ≠ **monotony** ▷ *v* = **alter**, reform, transform, adjust, revise ≠ **keep**; = **shift**, vary, transform, alter, modify ≠ **stay**

channel *n* = **means**, way, course, approach, medium; = **strait**, sound, route, passage, canal; = **duct**, artery, groove, gutter, furrow ▷ *v* = **direct**, guide, conduct, transmit, convey

chant *n* = **song**, carol, chorus, melody, psalm ▷ *v* = **sing**, chorus, recite, intone, carol

chaos *n* = **disorder**, confusion, mayhem, anarchy, lawlessness ≠ **orderliness**

chap¹ ❶ n (Inf) fellow, man

chap² v (of skin) become raw and cracked

chapati, chapatti n thin unleavened bread used in Indian cookery

chapel n 1 place of worship 2 division of church with its own altar

chaplain n clergyman attached to prison, college etc.

chapter ❶ n 1 division of book 2 assembly of clergy 3 organized branch of society

char v **charring, charred** scorch

character ❶ n 1 nature 2 qualities making up individuality 3 moral qualities 4 eccentric person 5 fictional person **characteristic** adj 1 typical ▷ n 2 distinguishing feature **characterize** v 1 mark out 2 describe

charade n 1 absurd act ▷ pl 2 word-guessing game

charcoal n charred wood

charge ❶ v 1 ask as price 2 bring accusation against 3 lay task on 4 attack 5 fill (with electricity) 6 make onrush, attack ▷ n 7 price 8 accusation 9 attack 10 command 11 accumulation of electricity **chargeable** adj **charger** n 1 that which charges, esp. electrically 2 warhorse

chargé d'affaires pl **chargés d'affaires** head of small diplomatic mission

chariot n 1 two-wheeled vehicle used in ancient fighting 2 state carriage **charioteer** n

charisma ❶ n special power of individual to inspire fascination, loyalty etc. **charismatic** adj

charity ❶ n, pl **-ties** 1 giving of help, money to needy

———————— THESAURUS ————————

chap¹ n (Inf) = **fellow**, man, person, individual, character

chapter n = **section**, part, stage, division, episode; = **period**, time, stage, phase

character n = **personality**, nature, attributes, temperament, complexion; = **nature**, kind, quality, calibre; = **reputation**, honour, integrity, good name, rectitude; = **role**, part, persona; = **eccentric**, card (Inf), original, oddball (Inf)

charge v = **accuse**, indict, impeach, incriminate, arraign ≠ **acquit**; = **attack**, assault, assail ≠ **retreat**; = **rush**, storm,

stampede; = **fill**, load ▷ n = **price**, rate, cost, amount, payment; = **accusation**, allegation, indictment, imputation ≠ **acquittal**; = **care**, trust, responsibility, custody, safekeeping; = **attack**, rush, assault, onset, onslaught ≠ **retreat**

charisma n = **charm**, appeal, personality, attraction, lure

charity n = **charitable organization**, fund, movement, trust, endowment; = **donations**, help, relief, gift, contributions ≠ **meanness**; = **kindness**, humanity, goodwill, compassion, generosity ≠ **ill will**

2 organization for this **3** love, kindness **charitable** adj
charlatan n impostor
charm ❶ n **1** attractiveness **2** anything that fascinates **3** amulet **4** magic spell ▷ v **5** bewitch **6** delight **charmer** n **charming** adj
chart ❶ n **1** map of sea **2** tabulated statement ▷ v **3** map
charter ❶ n **1** document granting privileges etc. ▷ v **2** let or hire **3** establish by charter **chartered** adj officially qualified
charwoman n woman paid to clean office, house etc.
chary adj **-rier, -riest** cautious, sparing
chase ❶ v **1** hunt, pursue **2** drive from, away, into etc. ▷ n **3** pursuit, hunting
chasm n deep cleft

chassis n, pl **-sis** framework of motor vehicle
chaste adj **1** virginal **2** pure **3** modest **4** virtuous **chastity** n
chasten v **1** correct by punishment **2** subdue **chastise** v inflict punishment on
chat ❶ v **1** talk idly or familiarly ▷ n **2** such talk **chatty** adj
chateau n, pl **-teaux, -teaus** (esp. in France) castle, country house
chauffeur n paid driver of motorcar
chauvinism n irrational feeling of superiority **chauvinist** n/adj
cheap ❶ adj **1** low in price **2** of little value **3** inferior **cheaply** adv **cheapen** v **cheapskate** n (Inf) miserly person
cheat ❶ v **1** deceive **2** practise deceit to gain advantage ▷ n

———————— THESAURUS ————————

charm n = **attraction**, appeal, fascination, allure, magnetism ≠ **repulsiveness**; = **talisman**, trinket, amulet, fetish; = **spell**, magic, enchantment, sorcery ▷ v = **attract**, delight, fascinate, entrance, win over ≠ **repel**; = **persuade**, seduce, coax, beguile, sweet-talk (Inf)
chart n = **table**, diagram, blueprint, graph, plan ▷ v = **plot**, map out, delineate, sketch, draft; = **monitor**, follow, record, note, document
charter n = **document**, contract, permit, licence, deed ▷ v = **hire**, commission, employ, rent, lease; = **authorize**, permit, sanction,

entitle, license
chase v = **pursue**, follow, track, hunt, run after ▷ n = **pursuit**, race, hunt, hunting
chat v = **talk**, gossip, jaw (Sl), natter, blather ▷ n = **talk**, tête-à-tête, conversation, gossip, heart-to-heart
cheap adj = **inexpensive**, reduced, keen, reasonable, bargain ≠ **expensive**; = **inferior**, poor, worthless, second-rate, shoddy ≠ **good**; (Inf) = **despicable**, mean, contemptible ≠ **decent**
cheat v = **deceive**, trick, fool, con (Inf), mislead ▷ n = **deceiver**, sharper, shark, charlatan, trickster

3 fraud

check ❶ v **1** stop **2** control **3** examine ▷ n **4** stoppage **5** restraint **6** brief examination **7** pattern of squares **8** threat to king at chess **checkmate** n/v (make) final winning move **checkout** n counter in supermarket where customers pay **check-up** n examination (esp. medical) to see if all is in order

Cheddar n smooth hard cheese

cheek ❶ n **1** side of face below eye **2** (Inf) impudence **cheeky** adj

cheep v/n (utter) high-pitched cry, as of young bird

cheer ❶ v **1** comfort **2** gladden **3** encourage by shouts **4** shout applause ▷ n **5** shout of approval **6** happiness **7** mood **cheerful** adj **cheerless** adj **cheery** adj

cheerio interj (Inf) goodbye

cheese n food made from solidified curd of milk **cheesy** adj **cheesecake** n dessert made from biscuits and cream cheese

cheetah n large, swift, spotted feline animal

chef n head cook

chemistry n science concerned with properties of substances and their combinations and reactions **chemical** n/adj **chemically** adv

chemist n **1** dispenser of medicines **2** shop that sells medicines etc. **3** one trained in chemistry

chemotherapy n treatment of disease by chemicals

chenille n soft cord, fabric of silk or worsted

cheque n **1** written order to banker to pay money from one's account **2** printed slip of paper used for this **chequebook** n **cheque card** banker's card

chequer n **1** marking as on chessboard **2** marble, peg etc. used in games ▷ v **3** mark in squares **4** variegate **chequered** adj

cherish ❶ v treat tenderly

cherry n, pl **-ries 1** small red fruit with stone **2** tree bearing it

cherub n, pl **-ubs, -ubim 1** winged creature with human face **2** angel **cherubic** adj

chess n game played on chequered board **chessman** n piece used in chess

chest ❶ n **1** upper part of trunk of body **2** large, strong box **chest of drawers** piece of furniture

C

— THESAURUS —

check v (often with **out**) = **examine**, test, study, look at, research ≠ **overlook**; = **stop**, limit, delay, halt, restrain ≠ **further** ▷ n = **examination**, test, research, investigation, inspection

cheek n (Inf) = **impudence**, nerve, disrespect, audacity, lip (Sl)

cheer v = **applaud**, hail, acclaim, clap ≠ **boo**; = **hearten**, encourage, comfort, uplift, brighten ≠ **dishearten** ▷ n = **applause**, ovation, plaudits, acclamation

cherish v = **care for**, love, support, comfort, look after ≠ **neglect**

chest n = **breast**, front

containing drawers

chestnut n **1** tree bearing large nut in prickly husk **2** (Inf) old joke ▷ adj **3** reddish-brown

chevron n (Mil) V-shaped braid designating rank

chew 🔊 v **1** grind with teeth ▷ n **2** chewing **chewy** adj **chewing gum** flavoured gum

chianti n red Italian wine

chic 🔊 adj **1** stylish ▷ n **2** stylishness

chicane n obstacle on racing circuit **chicanery** n trickery

chick n **1** young of birds, esp. of hen **2** (Sl) girl, young woman **chickpea** n edible pealike seed

chicken n **1** domestic fowl **2** (Sl) coward ▷ adj **3** cowardly **chickenpox** n infectious disease

chicory n, pl **-ries** salad plant whose root is used instead of coffee

chide v **chiding, chided** scold

chief 🔊 n **1** head or principal person ▷ adj **2** principal, foremost **chiefly** adv **chieftain** n leader of tribe

chiffon n gauzy material

chilblain n inflamed sore on

hands, legs etc. due to cold

child 🔊 n, pl **children 1** young human being **2** offspring **childish** adj silly **childlike** adj **1** of or like a child **2** innocent **childhood** n

chill 🔊 n **1** coldness **2** cold with shivering **3** anything that discourages ▷ v **4** make, become cold **chilly** adj **1** cold **2** unfriendly

chilli, chili n small red hot-tasting seed pod

chime n **1** sound of bell ▷ v **2** ring harmoniously **3** agree **4** strike (bells)

chimney n vertical passage for smoke

chimpanzee n ape of Africa

chin n part of face below mouth **chinwag** n (Inf) chat

china 🔊 n **1** fine earthenware, porcelain **2** cups, saucers etc.

chinchilla n S Amer. rodent with soft, grey fur

chink n cleft, crack

chintz n cotton cloth printed in coloured designs

chip 🔊 n **1** splinter **2** place where piece has been broken off **3** thin strip of potato, fried **4** tiny wafer of

━━━━━━━━━━━ THESAURUS ━━━━━━━━

chew v = **munch**, bite, grind, champ, crunch

chic adj = **stylish**, smart, elegant, fashionable, trendy (Brit Inf) ≠ **unfashionable**

chief n = **head**, leader, director, manager, boss (Inf) ≠ **subordinate** ▷ adj = **primary**, highest, leading, main, prime ≠ **minor**

child n = **youngster**, baby, kid (Inf), infant, babe

chill v = **cool**, refrigerate, freeze; = **dishearten**, depress, discourage, dismay, dampen ▷ n = **coldness**, bite, nip, sharpness, coolness ▷ adj = **chilly**, biting, sharp, freezing, raw

china n = **pottery**, ceramics, ware, porcelain, crockery

chip n = **fragment**, shaving, wafer, sliver, shard ▷ v = **nick**, damage, gash

silicon forming integrated circuit ▷ v **5** chop into small pieces **6** break small pieces from **7** break off **chip in 1** interrupt **2** contribute

chipmunk n small, striped N Amer. squirrel

chiropodist n one who treats disorders of feet **chiropody** n

chirp n/v (make) short, sharp cry **chirpy** adj (Inf) happy

chisel n **1** cutting tool ▷ v **2** cut with chisel **3** (Sl) cheat

chit n informal note

chitchat n gossip

chivalry n **1** bravery and courtesy **2** medieval system of knighthood **chivalrous** adj

chlorine n nonmetallic element, yellowish-green poison gas **chloride** n bleaching agent **chlorinate** v disinfect

chloroform n volatile liquid formerly used as anaesthetic

chlorophyll n green colouring matter in plants

chock n block or wedge

chocolate n confectionery, drink made from ground cacao seeds

choice ❶ n **1** act or power of choosing **2** alternative **3** thing or person chosen ▷ adj **4** select, fine

choir n band of singers

choke ❶ v **1** hinder, stop the breathing of **2** smother, stifle

3 obstruct **4** suffer choking ▷ n **5** act, noise of choking **6** device to increase richness of petrol-air mixture **choker** n tight-fitting necklace

cholera n deadly infectious disease

choleric adj bad-tempered

cholesterol n substance found in animal tissue and fat

chook n (Aust & NZ) hen or chicken

choose ❶ v **choosing, chose, chosen 1** pick out, select **2** take by preference **3** decide, think fit **choosy** adj

chop ❶ v **chopping, chopped 1** cut with blow **2** hack ▷ n **3** cutting blow **4** cut of meat with bone **chopper** n **1** short axe **2** (Inf) helicopter **choppy** adj **-pier, -piest** (of sea) having short, broken waves

chopsticks pl n implements used by Chinese for eating food

choral adj of, for a choir

chorale n slow, stately hymn tune

chord n simultaneous sounding of musical notes

chore ❶ n (unpleasant) task

choreography n art of arranging dances, esp. ballet **choreographer** n

chorister n singer in choir

chortle v/n (make) happy chuckling sound

choice n = **range**, variety, selection, assortment; = **selection**, preference, pick ▷ adj = **best**, prime, select, excellent, exclusive

choke v = **suffocate**, stifle, smother, overpower, asphyxiate;

= **strangle**, throttle, asphyxiate

choose v = **pick**, prefer, select, elect, adopt ≠ **reject**

chop v = **cut**, fell, hack, sever, cleave

chore n = **task**, job, duty, burden,

chorus ❶ *n, pl* **-ruses 1** (music for) band of singers **2** refrain ▷ *v* **3** sing or say together

chow¹ *n* (*Inf*) food

chow² *n* thick-coated dog with curled tail, orig. from China

Christian *n/adj* (person) following, believing in Christ **christen** *v* baptize, give name to **christening** *n* **Christianity** *n*

Christmas ❶ *n* festival of birth of Christ

chromosome *n* microscopic gene-carrying body in the tissue of a cell

chronic *adj* **1** lasting a long time **2** habitual **3** (*Inf*) serious **4** (*Inf*) of bad quality

chronicle ❶ *n/v* (write) record of historical events

chrysalis *n* **1** resting state of insect **2** case enclosing it

chrysanthemum *n* garden flower of various colours

chub *n* freshwater fish

chubby *adj* **-bier, -biest** plump

chuck ❶ *v* (*Inf*) **1** throw **2** pat affectionately (under chin) **3** give up

chuckle ❶ *v/n* (make) soft laugh

chuffed *adj* (*Inf*) pleased, delighted

chum ❶ *n* (*Inf*) close friend **chummy** *adj*

chunk ❶ *n* thick, solid piece **chunky** *adj*

church *n* **1** building for Christian worship **2** (*with cap.*) whole body or sect of Christians **3** clergy

churlish *adj* rude or surly

churn ❶ *n* **1** large container for milk **2** vessel for making butter ▷ *v* **3** shake up, stir **4** (*with out*) produce rapidly

chute *n* slide for sending down parcels, coal etc.

chutney *n* pickle of fruit, spices etc.

CIA (*US*) Central Intelligence Agency

CID Criminal Investigation Department

cider *n* fermented drink made from apples

cigar *n* roll of tobacco leaves for smoking **cigarette** *n* finely-cut tobacco rolled in paper for smoking

cinch *n* (*Inf*) easy task

cinder *n* remains of burned coal

cinema ❶ *n* **1** building used for

THESAURUS

---

hassle (*Inf*)

chorus *n* = **refrain**, response, strain, burden; = **choir**, singers, ensemble, vocalists, choristers

Christmas *n* = **festive season**, Noël, Xmas (*Inf*), Yule (*Archaic*), Yuletide (*Archaic*)

chronicle *v* = **record**, tell, report, enter, relate ▷ *n* = **record**, story, history, account, register

chuck *v* (*Inf*); = **throw**, cast, pitch,

toss, hurl

chuckle *v* = **laugh**, giggle, snigger, chortle, titter

chum *n* (*Inf*) = **friend**, mate (*Inf*), pal (*Inf*), companion, comrade

chunk *n* = **piece**, block, mass, portion, lump

churn *v* = **stir up**, beat, disturb, swirl, agitate

cinema *n* = **pictures**, movies, picture-house, flicks (*Sl*); = **films**,

showing of films **2** films generally
cinnamon *n* spice from bark of
Asian tree
cipher *n* **1** secret writing
2 arithmetical symbol **3** person of
no importance
circa (*Lat*) about, approximately
circle ❶ *n* **1** perfectly round figure
2 ring **3** (*Theatre*) section of seats
above main level of auditorium
4 group, society with common
interest ▷ *v* **5** surround **6** move
round **circular** *adj* **1** round ▷ *n*
2 letter sent to several persons
circulate *v* **1** move round **2** pass
round **3** send round **circulation** *n*
1 flow of blood **2** act of moving
round **3** extent of sale of
newspaper etc.
circuit ❶ *n* **1** complete round or
course **2** area **3** path of electric
current **4** round of visitation
circuitous *adj* indirect
circumcise *v* cut off foreskin of
circumcision *n*
circumference *n* boundary line,
esp. of circle
circumflex *n* accent (^) over a
letter

circumnavigate *v* sail right
round
circumscribe *v* confine, bound,
limit
circumspect *adj* cautious
circumstance ❶ *n* **1** detail
2 event ▷ *pl* **3** state of affairs
4 condition in life, esp. financial
5 surroundings or things
accompanying an action
circumstantial *adj*
circumvent *v* outwit, evade, get
round
circus *n, pl* **-cuses** (performance
of) acrobats, clowns, performing
animals etc.
cirrhosis *n* disease of liver
cirrus *n, pl* **-ri** high wispy cloud
cistern *n* water tank
citadel *n* city fortress
cite ❶ *v* **1** quote **2** bring forward
as proof **citation** *n* **1** quoting
2 commendation for bravery etc.
citizen ❶ *n* **1** member of state,
nation etc. **2** inhabitant of city
citizenship *n*
citrus fruit lemons, oranges etc.
city ❶ *n, pl* **-ties** large town
civic ❶ *adj* pert. to city or citizen

THESAURUS
---

pictures, movies, big screen (*Inf*),
motion pictures
circle *n* = **ring**, disc, hoop, halo;
= **group**, company, set, club,
society ▷ *v* = **go round**, ring,
surround, enclose, envelop;
= **wheel**, spiral
circuit *n* = **course**, tour, track,
route, journey
circumstance *n* usually plural
= **situation**, condition,

contingency, state of affairs, lie of
the land
cite *v* = **quote**, name, advance,
mention, extract
citizen *n* = **inhabitant**,
resident, dweller, denizen,
subject
city *n* = **town**, metropolis,
municipality, conurbation
civic *adj* = **public**, municipal,
communal, local

civil ● *adj* **1** relating to citizens **2** not military **3** refined, polite **4** (*Law*) not criminal **civilian** *n* nonmilitary person **civility** *n*

civilize ● *v* **1** bring out of barbarism **2** refine **civilization** *n* **1** refinement **2** cultured society **civilized** *adj*

claim ● *v* **1** demand as right **2** assert **3** call for ▷ *n* **4** demand for thing supposed due **5** right **6** thing claimed **claimant** *n*

clairvoyance *n* power of seeing things not present to senses **clairvoyant** *n/adj*

clam *n* edible mollusc

clamber *v* to climb awkwardly

clammy *adj* **-mier, -miest** moist and sticky

clamour ● *n/v* (make) loud outcry **clamorous** *adj*

clamp ● *n* **1** tool for holding ▷ *v* **2** fasten with or as with clamp

3 (with *down*) become stricter

clan ● *n* **1** collection of families of common ancestry **2** group

clandestine *adj* **1** secret **2** sly

clang *v* **1** (cause to) make loud ringing sound ▷ *n* **2** this sound

clap ● *v* **clapping, clapped** **1** (cause to) strike with noise **2** strike (hands) together **3** applaud **4** pat **5** place or put quickly ▷ *n* **6** hard, explosive sound **7** slap

claret *n* dry red wine

clarify ● *v* **-fying, -fied** make or become clear **clarification** *n* **clarity** *n*

clarinet *n* woodwind instrument

clash ● *n* **1** loud noise **2** conflict, collision ▷ *v* **3** make clash **4** come into conflict **5** strike together

clasp ● *n* **1** hook or fastening **2** embrace ▷ *v* **3** fasten **4** embrace, grasp

class ● *n* **1** any division, order,

— THESAURUS —

civil *adj* = **civic**, political, domestic, municipal ≠ **state**; = **polite**, obliging, courteous, considerate, affable ≠ **rude**

civilize *v* = **cultivate**, educate, refine, tame, enlighten

claim *v* = **assert**, insist, maintain, allege, uphold; = **demand**, call for, ask for, insist on ▷ *n* = **assertion**, statement, allegation, declaration, pretension; = **demand**, application, request, petition, call

clamour *n* = **noise**, shouting, racket, outcry, din

clamp *n* = **vice**, press, grip, bracket, fastener ▷ *v* = **fasten**, fix, secure, brace, make fast

clan *n* = **family**, group, society, tribe, fraternity; = **group**, set, circle, gang, faction

clap *v* = **applaud**, cheer, acclaim ≠ **boo**

clarify *v* = **explain**, interpret, illuminate, clear up, simplify

clash *v* = **conflict**, grapple, wrangle, lock horns, cross swords; = **disagree**, conflict, vary, counter, differ ▷ *n* = **conflict**, fight, brush, confrontation, collision

clasp *v* = **grasp**, hold, press, grip, seize ▷ *n* = **grasp**, hold, grip, embrace, hug; = **fastening**, catch, grip, hook, pin

class *n* = **group**, set, division, rank

kind, sort **2** rank **3** group of school pupils **4** division by merit **5** quality ▷ *v* **6** assign to proper division
classy *adj (Inf)* stylish, elegant
classify *v* arrange methodically in classes **classification** *n*
classic ❶ *adj* **1** of highest rank, esp. of art **2** typical **3** famous ▷ *n* **4** (literary) work of recognized excellence ▷ *pl* **5** ancient Greek and Latin literature **classical** *adj* **1** refined, elegant **2** of ancient Greek and Latin culture
clatter *n* **1** rattling noise ▷ *v* **2** (cause to) make clatter
clause ❶ *n* **1** part of sentence **2** article in formal document
claustrophobia *n* abnormal fear of confined spaces **claustrophobic** *adj*
clavicle *n* collarbone
claw ❶ *n* **1** sharp hooked nail of animal ▷ *v* **2** tear with claws
clay *n* **1** fine-grained earth, plastic when wet, hardening when baked **2** earth **clayey** *adj*

clean ❶ *adj* **1** free from dirt **2** pure **3** guiltless **4** trim ▷ *adv* **5** so as to leave no dirt **6** entirely ▷ *v* **7** free from dirt **cleaner** *n* **cleanliness** *n* **cleanly** *adv* **cleanse** *v* make clean
clear ❶ *adj* **1** pure, bright **2** free from cloud **3** transparent **4** plain, distinct **5** without defect **6** unimpeded ▷ *adv* **7** brightly **8** wholly, quite ▷ *v* **9** make clear **10** acquit **11** pass over **12** make as profit **13** free from obstruction, difficulty **14** become clear, bright, free, transparent **clearly** *adv* **clearance** *n* **clearing** *n* land cleared of trees
cleave¹ *v* **cleaving, cleft, cleaved** (cause to) split **cleavage** *n* **cleaver** *n* short chopper
cleave² *v* **1** stick, adhere **2** be loyal
clef *n (Mus)* mark to show pitch
cleft *n* crack, fissure, chasm
clematis *n* climbing plant
clement *adj* **1** merciful **2** gentle **3** mild **clemency** *n*

— THESAURUS —

▷ *v* = **classify**, group, rate, rank, brand
classic *adj* = **typical**, standard, model, regular, usual; = **masterly**, best, finest, world-class, consummate ≠ **second-rate** ▷ *n* = **standard**, masterpiece, prototype, paradigm, exemplar
clause *n* = **section**, condition, article, chapter, passage
claw *n* = **nail**, talon ▷ *v* = **scratch**, tear, dig, rip, scrape
clean *adj* = **hygienic**, fresh, sterile, pure, purified ≠ **contaminated**;

= **spotless**, fresh, immaculate, impeccable, flawless ≠ **dirty**; = **moral**, good, pure, decent, innocent ≠ **immoral** ▷ *v* = **cleanse**, wash, scrub, rinse, launder ≠ **dirty**
clear *adj* = **comprehensible**, explicit, understandable ≠ **confused**; = **obvious**, plain, apparent, evident, distinct ≠ **ambiguous**; = **certain**, sure, convinced, positive, satisfied ≠ **confused**; = **transparent**, see-through, translucent,

clench v **1** set firmly together **2** grasp, close (fist)

clergy ⊕ n body of ministers of Christian church **clergyman** n

clerical adj **1** of clergy **2** of office work **cleric** n clergyman

clerk n **1** subordinate who keeps files etc. **2** officer in charge of records, correspondence etc.

clever ⊕ adj **1** intelligent **2** able, skilful, adroit **cleverly** adv

cliché ⊕ n stereotyped hackneyed phrase

click n/v (make) short, sharp sound

client ⊕ n customer **clientele** n clients

cliff ⊕ n steep rock face **cliffhanger** n thing which is exciting and full of suspense

climate ⊕ n condition of country with regard to weather

climatic adj

climax ⊕ n highest point, culmination **climactic** adj

climb ⊕ v go up or ascend **climber** n

clinch ⊕ v conclude (agreement)

cling ⊕ v **clinging, clung** **1** adhere **2** be firmly attached to **clingfilm** n thin polythene wrapping material

clinic n place for medical examination, advice or treatment **clinical** adj

clink n **1** sharp metallic sound ▷ v **2** (cause to) make this sound

clip¹ ⊕ v **clipping, clipped 1** cut with scissors **2** cut short ▷ n **3** (Inf) sharp blow **clipping** n thing cut out, esp. newspaper article

clip² ⊕ v (attach with) gripping device

━━━━━━━━ THESAURUS ━━━━━━━━

crystalline, glassy ≠ **opaque**; = **unobstructed**, open, free, empty, unhindered ≠ **blocked** ▷ v = **unblock**, free, loosen, extricate, open; = **remove**, clean, wipe, cleanse, tidy (up); = **brighten**, break up, lighten; = **pass over**, jump, leap, vault, miss

clergy n = **priesthood**, ministry, clerics, clergymen, churchmen

clever adj = **intelligent**, bright, talented, gifted, smart ≠ **stupid**; = **shrewd**, bright, ingenious, resourceful, canny ≠ **unimaginative**

cliché n = **platitude**, stereotype, commonplace, banality, truism

client n = **customer**, consumer, buyer, patron, shopper

cliff n = **rock face**, overhang, crag, precipice, escarpment

climate n = **weather**, temperature, environment, spirit, surroundings

climax n = **culmination**, top, summit, height, highlight

climb v = **ascend**, scale, mount, go up, clamber

clinch v = **secure**, close, confirm, conclude, seal

cling v = **clutch**, grip, embrace, grasp, hug

clip¹ v = **trim**, cut, crop, prune, shorten; (Inf) = **smack**, strike, knock, punch, thump ▷ n (Inf) = **smack**, strike, knock, punch, thump

clip² v = **attach**, fix, secure,

clipper *n* fast sailing ship

clique *n* 1 small exclusive set 2 faction, group of people

clitoris *n* part of female genitals **clitoral** *adj*

cloak ⊕ *n/v* 1 (cover with) loose outer garment 2 disguise **cloakroom** *n*

clobber *v* (*Inf*) beat, batter

clock *n* instrument for measuring time **clockwise** *adv/adj* in the direction that the hands of a clock rotate **clockwork** *n* wind-up mechanism for clocks, toys etc.

clod *n* lump of earth

clog ⊕ *v* **clogging, clogged** 1 hamper, impede, choke up ▷ *n* 2 wooden-soled shoe

cloister *n* 1 covered pillared arcade 2 monastery or convent **cloistered** *adj* secluded

clone *n* 1 cells of same genetic constitution as another, derived by asexual reproduction 2 (*Inf*) lookalike ▷ *v* 3 replicate

close¹ ⊕ *v* 1 shut 2 stop up

3 prevent access to 4 finish 5 come together 6 grapple ▷ *n* 7 end 8 shut-in place 9 precinct of cathedral **closure** *n*

close² ⊕ *adj* 1 near 2 compact 3 crowded 4 intimate 5 almost equal 6 careful, searching 7 confined 8 secret 9 unventilated 10 niggardly 11 restricted ▷ *adv* 12 nearly 13 tightly **closely** *adv* **close-up** *n* close view

closet *n* 1 small private room 2 (*US*) cupboard ▷ *adj* 3 secret ▷ *v* 4 shut away in private

clot *n* 1 mass or lump (of blood) 2 (*Inf*) fool ▷ *v* 3 (cause to) form into lumps

cloth ⊕ *n* woven fabric **clothe** *v* put clothes on **clothes** *pl n* 1 dress 2 bed coverings **clothing** *n*

cloud ⊕ *n* 1 vapour floating in air 2 state of gloom ▷ *v* 3 darken 4 become cloudy **cloudy** *adj*

clout ⊕ *n* (*Inf*) 1 blow 2 influence, power ▷ *v* 3 strike

connect, pin

cloak *n* = **cape**, coat, wrap, mantle ▷ *v* = **cover**, coat, wrap, blanket, shroud

clog *v* = **obstruct**, block, jam, hinder, impede

close¹ *v* = **shut**, lock, fasten, secure ≠ **open**; = **shut down**, finish, cease; = **wind up**, finish, shut down, terminate ▷ *n* = **end**, ending, finish, conclusion, completion

close² *adj* = **near**, neighbouring, nearby, handy, adjacent ≠ **far**;

= **intimate**, loving, familiar, thick (*Inf*), attached ≠ **distant**; = **careful**, detailed, intense, minute, thorough; = **even**, level, neck and neck, fifty-fifty (*Inf*), evenly matched; = **imminent**, near, impending, at hand, nigh ≠ **far away**

cloth *n* = **fabric**, material, textiles

cloud *n* = **mist**, haze, vapour, murk, gloom ▷ *v* = **darken**, dim, be overshadowed

clout (*Inf*) ▷ *v* = **hit**, strike, punch, slap, sock (*Sl*) ▷ *n* = **thump**, blow,

clove n pungent spice
clover n forage plant
clown ❶ n circus comic
club ❶ n 1 thick stick 2 bat
3 association 4 suit at cards ▷ v
5 strike 6 join
cluck v/n (make) noise of hen
clue ❶ n indication, esp. of solution
of mystery or puzzle **clueless** adj
stupid
clump¹ ❶ n cluster of plants
clump² ❷ v/n (move with) heavy
tread
clumsy ❶ adj **-sier, -siest**
awkward **clumsily** adv
clumsiness n
cluster ❶ n/v group, bunch
clutch ❶ v 1 grasp eagerly
2 snatch (at) ▷ n 3 grasp,
tight grip 4 device enabling
two revolving shafts to be

(dis)connected at will
clutter ❶ v 1 cause obstruction,
disorder ▷ n 2 disordered
mass
cm centimetre
Co. 1 Company 2 County
co- comb. form together, jointly, as
in coproduction
c/o 1 care of 2 carried over
coach ❶ n 1 long-distance bus
2 large four-wheeled carriage
3 railway carriage 4 tutor,
instructor ▷ v 5 instruct
coagulate v curdle, clot
coal n 1 mineral used as fuel
2 glowing ember
coalesce v unite
coalition ❶ n alliance
coarse ❶ adj 1 rough 2 unrefined
3 indecent **coarsely** adv
coarseness n

———————— THESAURUS ————————

punch, slap, sock (Sl)
clown n = **comedian**, fool, comic,
harlequin, joker ▷ v (usually with
around) = **play the fool**, mess
about, jest, act the fool
club n = **association**, company,
group, union, society; = **stick**, bat,
bludgeon, truncheon, cosh (Brit)
▷ v = **beat**, strike, hammer, batter,
bash
clue n = **indication**, lead, sign,
evidence, suggestion
clump¹ n = **cluster**, group, bunch,
bundle
clump² v = **stomp**, thump, lumber,
tramp, plod
clumsy adj = **awkward**,
lumbering, bumbling, ponderous,
ungainly ≠ **skilful**

cluster n = **gathering**, group,
collection, bunch, knot ▷ v
= **gather**, group, collect, bunch,
assemble
clutch v = **hold**, grip, embrace,
grasp, cling to
clutter n = **untidiness**, mess,
disorder, confusion, litter ≠ **order**
▷ v = **litter**, scatter, strew, mess up
≠ **tidy**
coach n = **instructor**, teacher,
trainer, tutor, handler; = **bus**,
charabanc ▷ v = **instruct**, train,
prepare, exercise, drill
coalition n = **alliance**, union,
association, combination,
merger
coarse adj = **rough**, crude,
unfinished, homespun, impure

coast ❶ n 1 sea shore ▷ v 2 move under momentum **coastal** adj **coaster** n 1 small ship 2 small mat

coat ❶ n 1 sleeved outer garment 2 animal's fur 3 covering layer ▷ v 4 cover **coating** n covering layer

coax ❶ v persuade

cob n 1 short-legged stout horse 2 male swan 3 head of corn

cobalt n 1 metallic element 2 blue pigment from it

cobber n (Aust or NZ, Inf) friend

cobble v 1 patch roughly 2 mend shoes ▷ n 3 round stone **cobbler** n

cobra n poisonous, hooded snake

cobweb n spider's web

cocaine n addictive narcotic drug used medicinally

cochineal n scarlet dye

cock n 1 male bird, esp. of domestic fowl 2 tap 3 hammer of gun ▷ v 4 draw back to firing position 5 raise, turn **cockerel** n young cock

cockatoo n crested parrot

cockie, cocky n, pl **-kies** (Aust & NZ, Inf) farmer

cockle n shellfish

cockpit n pilot's seat, compartment in small aircraft

cockroach n insect pest

cocktail n 1 mixed drink of spirits 2 appetizer

cocky adj **cockier, cockiest** conceited, pert

cocoa n 1 powdered seed of cacao tree 2 drink made from this

coconut n large, hard nut

cocoon n sheath of insect in chrysalis stage

COD cash on delivery

cod n large sea fish

coda n (Mus) final part of musical composition

code ❶ n 1 system of letters, symbols to transmit messages secretly 2 scheme of conduct 3 collection of laws 4 instructions in a computer program **codify** v

codeine n pain-killing drug

coerce v compel, force **coercion** n

coexist v exist together **coexistence** n

C of E Church of England

coffee n 1 seeds of tropical shrub 2 drink made from these

coffer n chest for valuables

coffin n box for corpse

cog n one of series of teeth on rim of wheel **cogwheel** n

cogent adj convincing

cogitate v think, reflect, ponder **cogitation** n

cognac n French brandy

≠ **smooth**; = **vulgar**, rude, indecent, improper, earthy

coast n = **shore**, border, beach, seaside, coastline ▷ v = **cruise**, sail, drift, taxi, glide

coat n = **fur**, hair, skin, hide, wool; = **layer**, covering, coating, overlay

▷ v = **cover**, spread, plaster, smear

coax v = **persuade**, cajole, talk into, wheedle, sweet-talk (Inf) ≠ **bully**

code n = **principles**, rules, manners, custom, convention; = **cipher**, cryptograph

cognizance n knowledge
cognizant adj
cohabit v live together as a couple without being married
cohere v stick together, be consistent **coherent** adj
1 capable of logical speech, thought
2 connected, making sense
cohesion n tendency to unite
cohesive adj
cohort n 1 troop 2 associate
coiffure n hairstyle
coil ❶ v 1 twist into winding shape ▷ n 2 series of rings 3 anything coiled
coin ❶ n 1 piece of money
2 money ▷ v 3 stamp 4 invent **coinage** n
coincide ❶ v happen together
coincidence n chance happening
coincidental adj
coke¹ n residue left from distillation of coal, used as fuel
coke² n 1 Coca-Cola 2 (Sl) cocaine
cola n flavoured soft drink
colander n strainer for food

cold ❶ adj 1 lacking heat
2 indifferent, unmoved
3 unfriendly ▷ n 4 lack of heat
5 illness, marked by runny nose etc.
coldly adv **cold-blooded** adj lacking pity
coleslaw n cabbage salad
colic n severe pains in the intestines
collaborate ❶ v work with another **collaboration** n **collaborator** n
collage n (artistic) composition of bits and pieces stuck together on background
collapse ❶ v 1 fall 2 fail ▷ n
3 act of collapsing 4 breakdown
collapsible adj
collar ❶ n 1 band, part of garment, worn round neck ▷ v
2 seize **collarbone** n bone joining shoulder blade to breast bone
collate v compare carefully
collateral n security pledged for loan
colleague ❶ n fellow worker

——— THESAURUS ———

coil v = **wind**, twist, curl, loop, spiral
coin n = **money**, change, cash, silver, copper ▷ v = **invent**, create, make up, forge, originate
coincide v = **occur simultaneously**, coexist, synchronize, be concurrent
cold adj = **chilly**, freezing, bleak, arctic, icy ≠ **hot**; = **distant**, reserved, indifferent, aloof, frigid ≠ **emotional** ▷ n = **coldness**, chill, frigidity, frostiness, iciness
collaborate v = **work together**,

team up, join forces, cooperate, play ball (Inf); = **conspire**, cooperate, collude, fraternize
collapse v = **fall down**, fall, give way, subside, cave in; = **fail**, fold, founder, break down, fall through ▷ n = **falling down**, ruin, falling apart, cave-in, disintegration; = **failure**, slump, breakdown, flop, downfall
collar v (Inf) = **seize**, catch, arrest, grab, capture
colleague n = **fellow worker**, partner, ally, associate, assistant

collect ⓣ v gather, bring, come together **collected** adj calm **collection** n **collective** n 1 factory, farm etc. owned by its workers ▷ adj 2 shared **collectively** adv **collector** n

college n place of higher education **collegiate** adj

collide ⓣ v crash together **collision** n

collie n breed of sheepdog

colliery n, pl **-lieries** coal mine

colloquial adj pert. to, or used in, informal conversation **colloquialism** n

collusion n secret agreement for a fraudulent purpose **collude** v

cologne n perfumed liquid

colon¹ n mark (:) indicating break in a sentence

colon² n part of large intestine

colonel n commander of regiment or battalion

colonnade n row of columns

colony ⓣ n, pl **-nies** 1 body of people who settle in new country 2 country so settled **colonial** adj

colonist n **colonize** v **colonization** n

colossal adj huge, gigantic

colour, US **color** ⓣ n 1 hue, tint 2 complexion 3 paint 4 pigment 5 (Fig) semblance, pretext 6 timbre, quality ▷ pl 7 flag 8 (Sport) distinguishing badge, symbol ▷ v 9 stain, paint 10 disguise 11 influence or distort 12 blush **colourful** adj 1 bright 2 interesting **colourless** adj **colour-blind** adj unable to distinguish between certain colours

colt n young male horse

columbine n garden flower

column ⓣ n 1 long vertical pillar 2 division of page 3 body of troops **columnist** n journalist writing regular feature

coma ⓣ n unconsciousness **comatose** adj

comb ⓣ n 1 toothed instrument for tidying hair 2 cock's crest 3 mass of honey cells ▷ v 4 use comb on 5 search

combat ⓣ v/n **-bating, -bated**

collect v = **gather**, save, assemble, heap, accumulate ≠ **scatter**; = **assemble**, meet, rally, cluster, come together ≠ **disperse**

collide v = **crash**, clash, meet head-on, come into collision; = **conflict**, clash, be incompatible, be at variance

colony n = **settlement**, territory, province, possession, dependency

colour, US **color** n = **hue**, tone, shade, tint, colourway; = **paint**, stain, dye, tint, pigment ▷ v = **blush**, flush, redden

column n = **pillar**, support, post, shaft, upright; = **line**, row, file, rank, procession

coma n = **unconsciousness**, trance, oblivion, stupor

comb v = **untangle**, arrange, groom, dress; = **search**, hunt through, rake, sift, scour

combat n = **fight**, war, action, battle, conflict ≠ **peace** ▷ v = **fight**, oppose, resist, defy,

c

fight, contest **combatant** n
combative adj
combine ⊕ v 1 join together ▷ n
2 syndicate, esp. of businesses
combination n **combine
harvester** machine to harvest and
thresh grain
combustion n process of burning
combustible adj
come ⊕ v coming, came, come
1 approach, arrive, move towards
2 reach 3 occur 4 originate (from)
5 become **comeback** n 1 (Inf)
return to active life 2 retort
comedown n 1 decline in status
2 disappointment **comeuppance**
n (Inf) deserved punishment
comedy ⊕ n, pl **-dies** 1 light,
amusing play 2 humour
comedian n entertainer who tells
jokes
comely adj **-lier, -liest**
good-looking

comet n luminous heavenly body
comfort ⊕ n 1 ease 2 (means of)
consolation ▷ v 3 soothe
4 console **comfortable** adj
1 giving comfort 2 well-off
comfortably adv **comforter** n
comic ⊕ adj 1 relating to comedy
2 funny ▷ n 3 comedian
4 magazine of strip cartoons
comical adj
comma n punctuation mark (,)
command ⊕ v 1 order 2 rule
3 compel 4 have in one's power
▷ n 5 order 6 power of controlling
7 mastery 8 post of one
commanding 9 jurisdiction
commandant n **commandeer** v
seize for military use **commander**
n **commandment** n
commando n, pl **-dos, -does**
(member of) special military unit
commemorate ⊕ v keep in
memory by ceremony

withstand ≠ **support**
combine v = **amalgamate**, mix,
blend, integrate, merge ≠ **separate**
come v = **approach**, near, advance,
move towards, draw near; = **reach**,
extend, come up to, come as far as;
= **happen**, fall, occur, take place,
come about
comedy n = **light entertainment**
≠ **tragedy**; = **humour**, fun,
joking, farce, jesting
≠ **seriousness**
comfort n = **ease**, luxury,
wellbeing, opulence;
= **consolation**, succour, help,
support, relief ≠ **annoyance** ▷ v
= **console**, reassure, soothe,

hearten, commiserate with
≠ **distress**
comic adj = **funny**, amusing, witty,
humorous, farcical ≠ **sad** ▷ n
= **comedian**, funny man, humorist,
wit, clown
command v = **order**, tell, charge,
demand, require ≠ **beg**; = **have
authority over**, lead, head,
control, rule ≠ **be subordinate to**
▷ n = **order**, demand, instruction,
requirement, decree;
= **domination**, control, rule,
mastery, power
commemorate v = **celebrate**,
remember, honour, recognize,
salute ≠ **ignore**

commemoration n
commemorative adj
commence ❶ v begin
commend ❶ v 1 praise 2 entrust
commendable adj
commendation n
commensurate adj 1 equal 2 in
proportion
comment ❶ n/v 1 remark
2 gossip 3 note **commentary** n,
pl **-taries** 1 explanatory notes
2 spoken accompaniment to film
etc. **commentate** v
commentator n
commerce n trade **commercial**
adj 1 of business, trade etc. ▷ n
2 advertisement, esp. on radio or
television
commiserate v sympathize with
commiseration n
commission ❶ n 1 authority
2 (body entrusted with) some
special duty 3 agent's payment by
percentage 4 document
appointing to officer's rank

5 committing ▷ v 6 charge with
duty 7 (Mil) confer a rank 8 give
order for **commissioner** n
commissionaire n uniformed
doorman
commit ❶ v -mitting, -mitted
1 give in charge 2 be guilty of
3 pledge 4 send for trial
commitment n **committal** n
committee n body appointed,
elected for special business
commode n 1 chest of drawers
2 stool containing chamber pot
commodity n, pl **-ities** article of
trade
commodore n 1 senior naval or
air officer 2 president of yacht club
common ❶ adj 1 shared by all
2 public 3 ordinary 4 inferior ▷ n
5 land belonging to community
▷ pl 6 ordinary people 7 (with cap.)
House of Commons **commoner** n
one not of the nobility **commonly**
adv **commonplace** adj 1 ordinary
▷ n 2 trite remark

——— THESAURUS ———

commence v = **embark on**, start,
open, begin, initiate ≠ **stop**
commend v = **praise**, acclaim,
applaud, compliment, extol
≠ **criticize**; = **recommend**,
suggest, approve, advocate,
endorse
comment v = **remark**, say, note,
mention, point out ▷ n = **remark**,
statement, observation; = **note**,
explanation, illustration,
commentary, exposition
commission v = **appoint**, order,
contract, select, engage ▷ n
= **duty**, task, mission, mandate,

errand; = **fee**, cut, percentage,
royalties, rake-off (Sl);
= **committee**, board,
representatives, commissioners,
delegation
commit v = **do**, perform, carry
out, execute, enact; = **put in
custody**, confine, imprison
≠ **release**
common adj = **usual**, standard,
regular, ordinary, familiar ≠ **rare**;
= **popular**, general, accepted,
standard, routine; = **shared**,
collective; = **ordinary**, average,
typical ≠ **important**

commonwealth n 1 republic
2 (with cap.) federation of
self-governing states
commotion n stir, disturbance
commune¹ v converse intimately
communion n 1 sharing of
thoughts, feelings etc. 2 (with cap.)
(participation in) sacrament of the
Lord's Supper
commune² ❶ n group living
together and sharing property,
responsibility etc. **communal** adj
for common use
communicate ❶ v 1 impart,
convey 2 reveal ▷ v 3 give or
exchange information 4 have
connecting door **communicable**
adj **communication** n 1 giving
information 2 message 3 (usu. pl)
means of exchanging messages
communicative adj willing to talk
communiqué n official
announcement
communism ❶ n doctrine that
all means of production etc. should

be property of community
communist n/adj
community ❶ n, pl -ties 1 body
of people living in one district 2 the
public 3 joint ownership
4 similarity
commute v 1 travel daily some
distance to work 2 exchange
3 reduce (punishment)
commuter n
compact¹ ❶ adj 1 closely packed
2 solid 3 terse ▷ v 4 make,
become compact **compact disc**
small audio disc played by laser
compact² ❶ n agreement
compact³ ❶ n small case to hold
face powder etc.
companion ❶ n comrade
company ❶ n, pl -nies
1 gathering of persons
2 companionship 3 guests
4 business firm 5 division of
regiment
compare ❶ v 1 notice likenesses
and differences 2 liken 3 be like

━━━━━━━━━ THESAURUS ━━━━━━━━━

commune² n = **community**,
collective, cooperative, kibbutz
communicate v = **contact**, talk,
speak, make contact, get in contact
communism n = **socialism**,
Marxism, collectivism, Bolshevism,
state socialism
community n = **society**, people,
public, residents, commonwealth
compact¹ adj = **closely packed**,
solid, thick, dense, compressed
≠ **loose**; = **concise**, brief, to the
point, succinct, terse ≠ **lengthy**
▷ v = **pack closely**, stuff, cram,
compress, condense ≠ **loosen**

compact² n = **agreement**,
deal, understanding, contract,
bond
companion n = **friend**, partner,
ally, colleague, associate;
= **assistant**, aide, escort, attendant
company n = **business**, firm,
association, corporation,
partnership; = **group**, set,
community, band, crowd; = **troop**,
unit, squad, team;
= **companionship**, society,
presence, fellowship
compare v = **contrast**, balance,
weigh, set against, juxtapose

4 compete with **comparability** n
comparable adj **comparative**
adj 1 relative 2 (Grammar)
denoting form of adjective, adverb
meaning *more* **comparison** n act
of comparing
compartment ❶ n part divided
off
compass ❶ n 1 instrument for
showing north 2 (usu. pl)
instrument for drawing circles
3 scope ▷ v 4 surround
5 comprehend 6 attain
compassion ❶ n pity, sympathy
compassionate adj
compatible ❶ adj agreeing with
compatibility n
compatriot n fellow countryman
compel ❶ v -pelling, -pelled
force
compendium n, pl -diums, -dia
1 collection of different games
2 summary **compendious** adj

brief but inclusive
compensate ❶ v 1 make up for
2 recompense **compensation** n
compere n 1 one who introduces
cabaret, television shows etc. ▷ v
2 act as compere
compete ❶ v strive in rivalry,
contend for **competition** n
1 rivalry 2 contest **competitive**
adj **competitor** n
competent ❶ adj 1 able
2 properly qualified 3 sufficient
competence n
compile ❶ v make up from various
sources **compilation** n
complacent ❶ adj self-satisfied
complacency n
complain ❶ v 1 grumble 2 make
known a grievance 3 (with of) make
known that one is suffering from
complaint n 1 grievance 2 illness
complement ❶ n 1 something
making up a whole 2 complete

— THESAURUS —

compartment n = **section**,
carriage, berth; = **bay**, booth,
locker, niche, cubicle
compass n = **range**, field, area,
reach, scope
compassion n = **sympathy**,
understanding, pity, humanity,
mercy ≠ **indifference**
compatible adj = **consistent**, in
keeping, congruous
≠ **inappropriate**
compel v = **force**, make, railroad
(Inf), oblige, constrain
compensate v = **recompense**,
repay, refund, reimburse,
remunerate; = **make amends**,
make up for, atone, make it up to

someone, pay for
compete v = **contend**, fight, vie,
challenge, struggle
competent adj = **able**, skilled,
capable, proficient ≠ **incompetent**
compile v = **put together**, collect,
gather, organize, accumulate
complacent adj = **smug**,
self-satisfied, pleased with yourself,
resting on your laurels, contented
≠ **insecure**
complain v = **find fault**, moan,
grumble, whinge (Inf), carp
complement v = **enhance**,
complete, improve, boost, crown
▷ n = **accompaniment**,
companion, accessory, completion,

amount ▷ v **3** add to, make complete **complementary** adj

complete ❶ adj **1** perfect **2** ended **3** entire **4** thorough ▷ v **5** make whole **6** finish **completely** adv **completion** n

complex ❶ adj **1** intricate, compound, involved ▷ n **2** group of related buildings **3** obsession **complexity** n

complexion ❶ n **1** look, colour of skin, esp. of face **2** aspect, character

complicate ❶ v make involved, difficult **complication** n

complicity n partnership in wrongdoing

compliment ❶ n/v praise **complimentary** adj **1** expressing

praise **2** free of charge

comply ❶ v **-plying, -plied** do as asked **compliance** n **compliant** adj

component ❶ n part, constituent of whole

compose ❶ v **1** put in order **2** write, invent **3** make up **4** calm **composer** n one who composes, esp. music **composite** adj made up of distinct parts **composition** n **composure** n calmness

compos mentis (Lat) sane

compost n decayed vegetable matter for fertilizing soil

compound¹ ❶ n **1** substance, word, made up of parts ▷ adj **2** not simple **3** composite ▷ v **4** mix,

─────────── THESAURUS ───────────

finishing touch; = **total**, capacity, quota, aggregate, contingent

complete adj = **total**, perfect, absolute, utter, outright; = **whole**, full, entire ≠ **partial**; = **entire**, full, whole, intact, unbroken ≠ **incomplete** ▷ v = **finish**, conclude, end, close, settle ≠ **start**

complex adj = **compound**, multiple, composite, manifold, heterogeneous; = **complicated**, difficult, involved, elaborate, tangled ≠ **simple** ▷ n = **structure**, system, scheme, network, organization; (Inf) = **obsession**, preoccupation, phobia, fixation, fixed idea

complexion n = **skin**, colour, colouring, hue, skin tone; = **nature**, character, make-up

complicate v = **make difficult**,

confuse, muddle, entangle, involve ≠ **simplify**

compliment n = **praise**, honour, tribute, bouquet, flattery ≠ **criticism** ▷ v = **praise**, flatter, salute, congratulate, pay tribute to ≠ **criticize**

comply v = **obey**, follow, observe, submit to, conform to ≠ **defy**

component n = **part**, piece, unit, item, element

compose v = **put together**, make up, constitute, comprise, make ≠ **destroy**; = **create**, write, produce, invent, devise; = **arrange**, make up, construct, put together, order

compound¹ n = **combination**, mixture, blend, composite, fusion ≠ **element** ▷ v = **intensify**, add to, complicate, worsen, heighten

make up **5** make worse
6 compromise
compound² n enclosure
containing houses etc.
comprehend ⊕ v **1** understand
2 include **comprehensible** adj
comprehension n
comprehensive adj **1** taking in
much **2** pert. to education of
children of all abilities
compress ⊕ v **1** squeeze together
2 make smaller ▷ n **3** pad of lint
applied to wound, inflamed part
etc. **compressible** adj
compression n **compressor** n
comprise ⊕ v include, contain
compromise ⊕ n **1** coming to
terms by giving up part of claim ▷ v
2 settle by making concessions
3 expose to suspicion

compulsion n **1** act of compelling
2 urge **compulsive** adj
compulsory adj not optional
compunction n regret
compute ⊕ v calculate
computation n **computer** n
electronic machine for processing
information **computerize** v
comrade ⊕ n friend
con¹ ⊕ v/n (Inf) swindle
con² n vote against
concave adj rounded inwards
conceal ⊕ v hide **concealment**
n
concede ⊕ v **1** admit truth of
2 give up
conceit n vanity **conceited** adj
conceive ⊕ v **1** believe **2** become
pregnant **3** devise **conceivable**
adj

C

THESAURUS

≠ **lessen**; = **combine**, unite, mix,
blend, synthesize ≠ **divide**
comprehend v = **understand**,
see, take in, perceive, grasp
≠ **misunderstand**
compress v = **squeeze**, crush,
squash, press; = **condense**,
contract, concentrate, shorten,
abbreviate
comprise v = **be composed of**,
include, contain, consist of, take in
compromise n = **give-and-take**,
agreement, settlement,
accommodation, concession
≠ **disagreement** ▷ v = **meet**
halfway, concede, make
concessions, give and take, strike a
balance ≠ **disagree**; = **undermine**,
expose, embarrass, weaken,
prejudice ≠ **support**

compute v = **calculate**, total,
count, reckon, figure out
comrade n = **companion**, friend,
partner, ally, colleague
con¹ (Inf) ▷ v = **swindle**, trick,
cheat, rip off (SI), deceive ▷ n
= **swindle**, trick, fraud, deception,
scam (SI)
conceal v = **hide**, bury, cover,
screen, disguise ≠ **reveal**
concede v = **admit**, allow, accept,
acknowledge, own ≠ **deny**; = **give**
up, yield, hand over, surrender,
relinquish ≠ **conquer**
conceive v = **imagine**, envisage,
comprehend, visualize, think;
= **think up**, create, design, devise,
formulate; = **become pregnant**,
get pregnant, become
impregnated

concentrate ❶ v 1 focus (one's efforts etc.) 2 increase in strength 3 devote all attention ▷ n 4 concentrated substance **concentration** n

concentric adj having the same centre

concept ❶ n abstract idea **conceptual** adj

conception ❶ n 1 idea, notion 2 act of conceiving

concern ❶ v 1 relate to 2 worry 3 involve (oneself) ▷ n 4 affair 5 worry 6 business, enterprise **concerned** adj 1 worried 2 involved **concerning** prep about

concert n 1 musical entertainment 2 agreement **concerted** adj mutually planned **concertina** n musical instrument with bellows **concerto** n composition for solo instrument and orchestra

concession ❶ n 1 act of conceding 2 thing conceded

concession road n (Canad) (esp. in Ontario) one of a series of roads separating concessions in a township

conch n seashell

conciliate v win over from hostility **conciliation** n **conciliatory** adj

concise adj brief, terse

conclave n private meeting

conclude ❶ v 1 finish 2 deduce 3 settle 4 decide **conclusion** n **conclusive** adj decisive

concoct v 1 make mixture 2 contrive **concoction** n

concord n 1 agreement 2 harmony

concourse n 1 crowd 2 large, open place in public area

concrete ❶ n 1 mixture of sand, cement etc. ▷ adj 2 specific 3 actual 4 solid

— THESAURUS —

concentrate v = **focus your attention on**, focus on, pay attention to, be engrossed in, put your mind to ≠ **pay no attention to**; = **focus**, centre, converge, bring to bear

concept n = **idea**, view, image, theory, notion

conception n = **idea**, plan, design, image, concept; = **impregnation**, insemination, fertilization, germination

concern n = **anxiety**, fear, worry, distress, unease; = **worry**, care, anxiety; = **affair**, issue, matter, consideration ▷ v = **worry**, trouble,

bother, disturb, distress; = **be about**, cover, deal with, go into, relate to

concession n = **compromise**, agreement, settlement, accommodation/adjustment; = **privilege**, right, permit, licence, entitlement

conclude v = **decide**, judge, assume, gather, work out; = **come to an end**, end, close, finish, wind up ≠ **begin**; = **bring to an end**, end, close, finish, complete ≠ **begin**

concrete adj = **specific**, precise, explicit, definite, clear-cut ≠ **vague**; = **real**, material, actual, substantial, sensible ≠ **abstract**

concubine n 1 woman cohabiting with man 2 secondary wife

concur v -curring, -curred 1 agree 2 happen together **concurrent** adj **concurrently** adv

concussion n brain injury

condemn ❶ v 1 blame 2 find guilty 3 doom 4 declare unfit **condemnation** n

condense v 1 concentrate 2 turn from gas to liquid **condensation** n

condescend v 1 treat graciously one regarded as inferior 2 stoop **condescension** n

condiment n seasoning for food

condition ❶ n 1 state or circumstances 2 thing on which something else depends 3 prerequisite 4 physical fitness ▷ v 5 accustom 6 regulate 7 make fit **conditional** adj dependent on events **conditioner** n liquid to make hair or clothes feel softer

condolence n sympathy

condom n sheathlike rubber contraceptive worn by man

condone ❶ v overlook, forgive

conducive adj leading (to)

conduct ❶ n 1 behaviour 2 management ▷ v 3 guide 4 direct 5 manage 6 transmit (heat etc.) **conduction** n **conductor** n 1 person in charge of bus etc. 2 director of orchestra 3 substance capable of transmitting heat etc.

conduit n channel or pipe for water, cables etc.

cone n 1 tapering figure with circular base 2 fruit of pine, fir etc. **conical** adj

confederate n 1 ally 2 accomplice ▷ v 3 unite **confederation** n alliance of political units

confer ❶ v -ferring, -ferred 1 grant 2 talk with **conference** n meeting for consultation

confess ❶ v 1 admit 2 declare one's sins orally to priest

--- THESAURUS ---

condemn v = **denounce**, damn, criticize, disapprove, censure ≠ **approve**; = **sentence**, convict, damn, doom, pass sentence on ≠ **acquit**

condition n = **state**, order, shape, nick (Brit Inf), trim; = **situation**, state, position, status, circumstances; = **requirement**, terms, rider, restriction, qualification; = **health**, shape, fitness, trim, form ▷ v = **train**, teach, adapt, accustom

condone v = **overlook**, excuse, forgive, pardon, turn a blind eye to ≠ **condemn**

conduct v = **carry out**, run, control, manage, direct; = **accompany**, lead, escort, guide, steer ▷ n = **management**, running, control, handling, administration; = **behaviour**, ways, bearing, attitude, manners

confer v = **discuss**, talk, consult, deliberate, discourse; = **grant**, give, present, accord, award

confess v = **admit**, acknowledge, disclose, confide, own up ≠ **cover**

c

confession n **confessional** n confessor's box **confessor** n priest who hears confessions

confetti pl n bits of coloured paper thrown at weddings

confide ⊕ v 1 tell secrets 2 entrust **confidence** n 1 trust 2 assurance 3 intimacy 4 secret **confident** adj 1 certain 2 self-assured **confidential** adj 1 private 2 secret

configuration n shape

confine ⊕ v 1 keep within bounds 2 shut up **confines** pl n limits **confinement** n 1 being confined 2 childbirth

confirm ⊕ v 1 make sure 2 strengthen 3 make valid 4 admit as member of church **confirmation** n **confirmed** adj long-established

confiscate ⊕ v seize by authority **confiscation** n

conflict ⊕ n 1 struggle 2 disagreement ▷ v 3 be at odds

with 4 clash

conform ⊕ v 1 comply with accepted standards etc. 2 adapt to rule, pattern, custom etc. **conformist** n **conformity** n

confound ⊕ v 1 perplex 2 confuse **confounded** adj (Inf) damned

confront ⊕ v 1 face 2 bring face to face with **confrontation** n

confuse ⊕ v 1 bewilder 2 jumble 3 make unclear 4 mistake **confusion** n

conga n 1 dance by people in single file 2 large drum

congeal v solidify

congenial adj pleasant

congenital adj 1 existing at birth 2 dating from birth

conger n sea eel

conglomerate n 1 substance composed of smaller elements 2 business organization comprising many companies **conglomeration** n

— THESAURUS —

up; = **declare**, allow, reveal, confirm, concede

confide v = **tell**, admit, reveal, confess, whisper

confine v = **imprison**, enclose, shut up, intern, incarcerate; = **restrict**, limit

confirm v = **prove**, support, establish, back up, verify; = **ratify**, establish, sanction, endorse, authorize

confiscate v = **seize**, appropriate, impound, commandeer, sequester ≠ **give back**

conflict n = **dispute**, difference,

opposition, hostility, disagreement ≠ **agreement**; = **struggle**, battle, clash, strife ▷ v = **be incompatible**, clash, differ, disagree, collide ≠ **agree**

conform v = **fit in**, follow, adjust, adapt, comply; = **fulfil**, meet, match, suit, satisfy

confound v = **bewilder**, baffle, confuse, astound, perplex

confront v = **tackle**, deal with, cope with, meet head-on

confuse v = **mix up with**, take for, muddle with; = **bewilder**, puzzle, baffle, perplex, mystify

congratulate ❶ v express pleasure at good fortune, success etc. **congratulations** pl n

congregate v 1 assemble 2 flock together **congregation** n assembly, esp. for worship

congress ❶ n 1 formal assembly 2 legislative body

conifer n cone-bearing tree **coniferous** adj

conjecture n/v guess **conjectural** adj

conjugal adj of marriage

conjugate v (Grammar) inflect verb in its various forms **conjugation** n

conjunction n 1 union 2 simultaneous happening 3 part of speech joining words, phrases etc. **conjunctive** adj

conjunctivitis n inflammation of membrane of eye

conjure ❶ v 1 produce magic effects 2 perform tricks **conjuror, -er** n

conker n (Inf) horse chestnut

connect ❶ v 1 join together, unite 2 associate in the mind **connection, connexion** n 1 association 2 connecting thing 3 relation

connive v conspire

connoisseur n expert in fine arts

conquer ❶ v 1 overcome 2 defeat 3 be victorious **conqueror** n **conquest** n

conscience ❶ n sense of right or wrong **conscientious** adj

conscious ❶ adj 1 aware 2 awake 3 intentional **consciousness** n

conscript n 1 one compulsorily enlisted for military service ▷ v 2 enlist thus **conscription** n

consecrate v make sacred **consecration** n

consecutive ❶ adj in unbroken succession **consecutively** adv

consensus ❶ n widespread agreement

consent ❶ v 1 agree to ▷ n

─────── THESAURUS ───────

congratulate v = **compliment**, pat on the back, wish joy to

congress n = **meeting**, council, conference, assembly, convention

conjure v = **produce**, generate, bring about, give rise to, make

connect v = **link**, join, couple, attach, fasten ≠ **separate**

conquer v = **seize**, obtain, acquire, occupy, overrun; = **defeat**, overcome, overthrow, beat, master ≠ **lose to**

conscience n = **principles**, scruples, moral sense, sense of right and wrong, still small voice

conscious adj (often with of) = **aware of**, alert to, responsive to, sensible of ≠ **unaware**; = **deliberate**, knowing, studied, calculated, self-conscious ≠ **unintentional**; = **awake**, wide-awake, sentient, alive ≠ **asleep**

consecutive adj = **successive**, running, succeeding, in turn, uninterrupted

consensus n = **agreement**, general agreement, unanimity, common consent, unity

consent n = **agreement**, sanction,

2 permission **3** agreement
consequence ❶ *n* **1** result, outcome **2** importance **consequent** *adj* **consequential** *adj* important **consequently** *adv* therefore
conserve ❶ *v* **1** keep from change etc. **2** preserve ▷ *n* **3** jam **conservation** *n* protection of environment **conservationist** *n* **conservative** *adj/n* **1** (person) tending to avoid change **2** moderate (person) **conservatory** *n* greenhouse
consider ❶ *v* **1** think over **2** examine **3** make allowance for **4** be of opinion that **considerable** *adj* **1** important **2** large **considerably** *adv* **considerate** *adj* thoughtful towards others **consideration** *n* **1** act of considering **2** recompense **considering** *prep* taking into account
consign *v* **1** hand over **2** entrust **consignment** *n* goods consigned

consignor *n*
consist *v* be composed of
consistency *n* **1** agreement **2** degree of firmness **consistent** *adj* **consistently** *adv*
console¹ ❶ *v* comfort, cheer in distress **consolation** *n*
console² *n* **1** bracket **2** keyboard etc. of organ **3** cabinet for television, radio etc.
consolidate ❶ *v* **1** combine **2** make firm **consolidation** *n*
consommé *n* clear meat soup
consonant *n* **1** sound, letter other than a vowel ▷ *adj* **2** agreeing with, in accord **consonance** *n*
consort *v* **1** associate ▷ *n* **2** husband, wife, esp. of ruler **consortium** *n* association of banks, companies etc.
conspicuous ❶ *adj* noticeable
conspire ❶ *v* plot together **conspiracy** *n* **conspirator** *n*
constable *n* policeman **constabulary** *n, pl* **-laries** police force

——————— THESAURUS ———————

approval, go-ahead (*Inf*), permission ≠ **refusal** ▷ *v* = **agree**, approve, permit, concur, assent ≠ **refuse**
consequence *n* = **result**, effect, outcome, repercussion, issue; = **importance**, concern, moment, value, account
conserve *v* = **save**, husband, take care of, hoard, store up ≠ **waste**
consider *v* = **think**, see, believe, rate, judge; = **think about**, reflect on, weigh, contemplate, deliberate;

= **bear in mind**, remember, respect, think about, take into account
console¹ *v* = **comfort**, cheer, soothe, support, encourage ≠ **distress**
consolidate *v* = **strengthen**, secure, reinforce, fortify, stabilize; = **combine**, unite, join, merge, unify
conspicuous *adj* = **obvious**, clear, patent, evident, noticeable ≠ **inconspicuous**
conspire *v* = **plot**, scheme, intrigue, manoeuvre, contrive

constant ❶ *adj* **1** unchanging
2 steadfast **3** continual ▷ *n*
4 quantity that does not vary
constancy *n* loyalty **constantly**
adv

constellation *n* group of stars

consternation *n* alarm, dismay

constipation *n* difficulty in
emptying bowels **constipated** *adj*

constituent ❶ *adj* **1** making up
whole ▷ *n* **2** component part
3 elector **constituency** *n, pl* **-cies**
1 body of electors **2** parliamentary
division

constitute ❶ *v* **1** form **2** found
constitution *n* **1** composition
2 health **3** principles on which
state is governed **constitutional**
adj **1** inborn **2** statutory ▷ *n*
3 walk for good of health

constrain ❶ *v* force **constraint**
n **1** compulsion **2** restriction

construct ❶ *v* **1** build **2** put
together **construction** *n*
constructive *adj* positive

construe *v* **-struing, -strued**
interpret

consul *n* government
representative in a foreign country
consulate *n* consul's office

consult ❶ *v* seek advice,
information from **consultancy** *n*,
pl **-cies** **consultant** *n* specialist,
expert **consultation** *n*
consultative *adj*

consume ❶ *v* **1** eat or drink
2 engross **3** use up **4** destroy
consumer *n* **consumption** *n*

consummate *v/adj* **1** perfect
2 complete **consummation** *n*

cont. continued

contact ❶ *n* **1** touching **2** being
in touch **3** useful acquaintance ▷ *v*
4 get in touch with **contact lens**

— THESAURUS —

constant *adj* = **continuous**,
sustained, perpetual, interminable,
unrelenting ≠ **occasional**;
= **unchanging**, even, fixed,
permanent, stable ≠ **changing**;
= **faithful**, true, devoted, loyal,
stalwart ≠ **undependable**

constituent *n* = **voter**, elector,
member of the electorate;
= **component**, element, ingredient,
part, unit ▷ *adj* = **component**,
basic, essential, integral, elemental

constitute *v* = **represent**, be,
consist of, embody, exemplify

constrain *v* = **force**, bind, compel,
oblige, necessitate

construct *v* = **build**, make, form,
create, fashion ≠ **demolish**

consult *v* = **ask**, refer to, turn to,
take counsel, pick (someone's)
brains

consume *v* = **eat**, swallow,
devour, put away, gobble (up);
= **use up**, spend, waste, absorb,
exhaust; = **destroy**, devastate,
demolish, ravage, annihilate; *often
passive* = **obsess**, dominate, absorb,
preoccupy, eat up

contact *n* = **communication**, link,
association, connection,
correspondence; = **touch**,
contiguity; = **connection**,
colleague, associate, liaison,
acquaintance ▷ *v* = **get** *or* **be in
touch with**, call, reach, approach,
write to

lens fitting over the eyeball

contain ❶ v 1 hold 2 have room for 3 comprise 4 restrain **container** n

contaminate ❶ v pollute **contamination** n

contemplate ❶ v 1 meditate on 2 gaze upon 3 intend **contemplation** n

contemporary ❶ adj 1 existing at same time 2 modern ▷ n 3 one of same age **contemporaneous** adj

contempt ❶ n 1 scorn, disgrace 2 wilful disrespect of authority **contemptible** adj **contemptuous** adj showing contempt

contend ❶ v 1 strive, dispute 2 maintain (that) **contender** n

competitor **contention** n **contentious** adj

content[1] ❶ adj 1 satisfied 2 willing (to) ▷ v 3 satisfy ▷ n 4 satisfaction **contented** adj **contentment** n

content[2] ❶ n 1 thing contained ▷ pl 2 index of topics

contest ❶ n 1 competition ▷ v 2 dispute 3 compete for **contestant** n

context ❶ n words coming before and after a word or passage

continent[1] n large continuous mass of land **continental** adj

continent[2] adj in control of bodily functions

contingent adj 1 depending (on) ▷ n 2 group part of larger group **contingency** n, pl **-cies**

————————————— THESAURUS —————————————

contain v = **hold**, incorporate, accommodate, enclose, have capacity for; = **include**, consist of, embrace, comprise, embody; = **restrain**, control, hold in, curb, suppress

contaminate v = **pollute**, infect, stain, corrupt, taint ≠ **purify**

contemplate v = **consider**, plan, think of, intend, envisage; = **think about**, consider, ponder, reflect upon, ruminate (upon); = **look at**, examine, inspect, gaze at, eye up

contemporary adj = **modern**, recent, current, up-to-date, present-day ≠ **old-fashioned**; = **coexisting**, concurrent, contemporaneous ▷ n = **peer**, fellow, equal

contempt n = **scorn**, disdain, mockery, derision, disrespect ≠ **respect**

contend v = **argue**, hold, maintain, allege, assert; = **compete**, fight, struggle, clash, contest

content[1] adj = **satisfied**, happy, pleased, contented, comfortable

content[2] n = **subject matter**, material, theme, substance, essence; = **amount**, measure, size, load, volume

contest n = **competition**, game, match, trial, tournament ▷ v = **compete in**, take part in, fight in, go in for, contend for; = **oppose**, question, challenge, argue, debate

context n = **circumstances**,

continue ❶ v -tinuing, -tinued
1 remain 2 carry on 3 resume
4 prolong **continual** adj
continually adv **continuation** n
continuity n, pl logical sequence
continuous adj
contort v twist out of normal
shape **contortion** n
contortionist n
contour n outline, shape, esp.
mountains, coast etc.
contra- comb. form against
contraband n/adj smuggled
(goods)
contraception n prevention of
conception **contraceptive** adj/n
contract ❶ v 1 make or become
smaller 2 enter into agreement
3 incur ▷ n 4 agreement
contraction n **contractor** n one
making contract, esp. builder
contractual adj

contradict ❶ v 1 deny 2 be
inconsistent with **contradiction**
n **contradictory** adj
contraflow n flow of traffic in
opposite direction
contralto n, pl -tos lowest
female voice
contraption n 1 gadget 2 device
contrary ❶ adj 1 opposed
2 perverse ▷ n 3 the exact
opposite ▷ adv 4 in opposition
contrast ❶ v 1 bring out, show
difference ▷ n 2 striking difference
contravene v infringe
contribute ❶ v 1 give, pay to
common fund 2 help to occur
3 write for the press **contribution**
n **contributor** n
contrite adj remorseful
contrition n
contrive ❶ v 1 arrange 2 devise,
invent **contrivance** n

———— THESAURUS ————

conditions, situation, ambience
continue v = **keep on**, go on,
maintain, sustain, carry on ≠ **stop**;
= **go on**, progress, proceed, carry
on, keep going; = **resume**, return
to, take up again, proceed, carry on
≠ **stop**
contract n = **agreement**,
commitment, arrangement,
settlement, bargain ▷ v = **agree**,
negotiate, pledge, bargain,
undertake ≠ **refuse**; = **constrict**,
confine, tighten, shorten,
compress; = **tighten**, narrow,
shorten ≠ **stretch**
contradict v = **deny**, challenge,
belie, fly in the face of, be at
variance with; = **deny**, negate,

rebut, controvert ≠ **confirm**
contrary adj = **opposite**, different,
opposed, clashing, counter ≠ **in
agreement**; = **perverse**, difficult,
awkward, intractable, obstinate
≠ **cooperative** ▷ n = **opposite**,
reverse, converse, antithesis
contrast n = **difference**,
opposition, comparison,
distinction, foil ▷ v
= **differentiate**, compare, oppose,
distinguish, set in opposition;
= **differ**, be contrary, be at variance,
be dissimilar
contribute v = **give**, provide,
supply, donate, subscribe
contrive v = **devise**, plan,
fabricate, create, design;

control ❶ v 1 command
2 regulate 3 direct, check ▷ n
4 power to direct or determine
5 curb, check ▷ pl 6 instruments
to control car, aircraft etc.
controller n

controversy ❶ n, pl **-sies**
debate **controversial** adj

contusion n bruise

conundrum n riddle

conurbation n large built-up area

convalesce v recover health after
illness, operation etc.
convalescence n **convalescent**
adj/n

convection n transmission of
heat by currents

convene ❶ v call together,
assemble **convenor, -er** n
convention n 1 assembly
2 treaty 3 accepted usage
conventional adj 1 (slavishly)
observing customs of society
2 customary 3 (of weapons, war
etc.) not nuclear

convenient ❶ adj 1 handy
2 favourable to needs, comfort
convenience n 1 ease, comfort,
suitability 2 public toilet ▷ adj
3 (of food) quick to prepare
conveniently adv

convent n religious community,
esp. of nuns

convention ❶ see CONVENE

converge ❶ v tend to meet

conversant adj familiar (with),
versed in

converse¹ v 1 talk (with) ▷ n
2 talk **conversation** n
conversational adj

converse² adj 1 opposite,
reversed ▷ n 2 the opposite
conversely adv

convert ❶ v 1 apply to another
purpose 2 change 3 transform
4 cause to adopt (another) religion,
opinion ▷ n 5 converted person
conversion n **convertible** n
1 car with folding roof ▷ adj
2 capable of being converted

──────────── THESAURUS ────────────

= **manage**, succeed, arrange,
manoeuvre
control n = **power**, authority,
management, command,
guidance; = **restraint**, check,
regulation, brake, limitation ▷ v
= **have power over**, manage,
direct, handle, command; = **limit**,
restrict, curb
controversy n = **argument**,
debate, row, dispute, quarrel
convene v = **call**, gather,
assemble, summon, bring together
convenient adj = **suitable**, fit,
handy, satisfactory; = **useful**,

practical, handy, serviceable,
labour-saving ≠ **useless**; = **nearby**,
available, accessible, handy, at
hand ≠ **inaccessible**
convention n = **custom**, practice,
tradition, code, usage;
= **agreement**, contract, treaty,
bargain, pact; = **assembly**,
meeting, council, conference,
congress
converge v = **come together**,
meet, join, combine, gather
convert v = **change**, turn,
transform, alter, transpose;
= **adapt**, modify, remodel,

C

convex adj curved outwards
convey ① v 1 transport **2** impart **3** (Law) transfer **conveyance** n **conveyancer** n one skilled in legal forms of transferring property **conveyancing** n **conveyor belt** continuous moving belt
convict ① v 1 prove or declare guilty ▷ n **2** criminal serving prison sentence **conviction** n **1** verdict of guilty **2** being convinced, firm belief
convince ① v persuade by evidence or argument **convincing** adj
convivial adj sociable
convoluted adj **1** involved **2** coiled **convolution** n
convoy n **1** party (of ships etc.) travelling together for protection ▷ v **2** escort
convulse v **1** shake violently **2** affect with spasms **convulsion** n
coo n/v **cooing, cooed** (make) cry of doves
cook v **1** prepare food, esp. by heat **2** undergo cooking ▷ n **3** one who prepares food **cooker** n apparatus for cooking **cookery** n **cookie** n **1** (US) biscuit **2** data allowing user of website to be identified on future visits
cool ① adj 1 moderately cold **2** calm **3** lacking friendliness ▷ v **4** make, become cool **coolly** adv
coop[1] n/v (shut up in) cage
coop[2], **co-op** n cooperative society or shop run by one
cooperate ① v work together **cooperation** n **cooperative** adj **1** willing to cooperate **2** (of an enterprise) owned collectively ▷ n **3** collectively owned enterprise
coordinate v **1** bring into order, harmony ▷ adj **2** equal in degree, status etc. **coordination** n **coordinator** n
coot n small black water bird
cop n (Sl) policeman
cope ① v 1 deal successfully (with) **2** manage
coping n sloping top course of wall
copious adj abundant
copper[1] n **1** reddish-brown metal **2** coin

THESAURUS

---

reorganize, customize ▷ n
= **neophyte**, disciple, proselyte
convey v = **communicate**, impart, reveal, relate, disclose; = **carry**, transport, move, bring, bear
convict v = **find guilty**, sentence, condemn, imprison, pronounce guilty ▷ n = **prisoner**, criminal, lag (Sl), felon, jailbird
convince v = **assure**, persuade, satisfy, reassure
cool adj = **cold**, chilled, refreshing,
chilly, nippy ≠ **warm**;
= **calm**, collected, relaxed, composed, sedate ≠ **agitated**;
= **unfriendly**, distant, indifferent, aloof, lukewarm ≠ **friendly** ▷ v = **lose heat**, cool off ≠ **warm (up)**
cooperate v = **work together**, collaborate, coordinate, join forces, conspire ≠ **conflict**
cope v = **manage**, get by (Inf), struggle through, survive, carry on

copper² n (Inf) policeman
coppice, copse n small wood
copulate v unite sexually
copulation n
copy ❶ n, pl **copies** 1 imitation
2 single specimen of book ▷ v
3 make copy of, imitate **copyright**
n 1 legal exclusive right to print and
publish book, work of art etc. ▷ v
2 protect by copyright
coquette n flirt
coracle n small round boat
coral n hard substance made by sea
polyps
cord ❶ n 1 thin rope or thick string
2 ribbed fabric
cordial adj 1 sincere, warm ▷ n
2 fruit-flavoured drink
cordon ❶ n 1 chain of troops or
police ▷ v 2 form barrier round
cordon bleu (of cookery) of the
highest standard
corduroy n cotton fabric with
velvety, ribbed surface
core ❶ n 1 seed case of apple
2 innermost part ▷ v 3 take out
core
corgi n small Welsh dog
coriander n herb
cork n 1 bark of an evergreen
Mediterranean oak tree 2 stopper
for bottle etc. ▷ v 3 stop up with

cork **corkscrew** n tool for pulling
out corks
corm n underground stem like a
bulb
cormorant n large voracious sea
bird
corn¹ n grain, fruit of cereals **corny**
adj (Inf) trite, oversentimental
corned beef beef preserved in salt
cornflakes pl n breakfast cereal
cornflour n finely ground maize
cornflower n blue flower growing
in cornfields
corn² n horny growth on foot
cornea n, pl **-neas, -neae**
transparent membrane covering
front of eye
corner ❶ n 1 part where two sides
meet 2 remote or humble place
3 (Business) monopoly ▷ v 4 drive
into position of no escape
5 establish monopoly 6 move
round corner **cornerstone** n
indispensable part
cornet n 1 trumpet with valves
2 cone-shaped ice cream wafer
cornice n moulding below ceiling
cornucopia n horn overflowing
with fruit and flowers
corollary n, pl **-laries** 1 inference
from a preceding statement
2 deduction

——————— THESAURUS ———————

copy n = **reproduction**, duplicate,
replica, imitation, forgery
≠ original ▷ v = **reproduce**,
replicate, duplicate, transcribe,
counterfeit **≠ create**; = **imitate**,
act like, emulate, behave like,
follow
cord n = **rope**, line, string, twine

cordon n = **chain**, line, ring,
barrier, picket line
core n = **heart**, essence, nucleus,
kernel, crux
corner n = **angle**, joint, crook;
= **bend**, curve ▷ v = **trap**, catch,
run to earth; = **monopolize**, take
over, dominate, control, hog (SI)

coronary adj **1** of blood vessels surrounding heart ▷ n **2** coronary thrombosis **coronary thrombosis** disease of the heart

coronation n ceremony of crowning a sovereign

coroner n officer who holds inquests on unnatural deaths

coronet n small crown

corporal¹ adj of the body

corporal² n noncommissioned officer below sergeant

corporation ⊕ n body of persons legally authorized to act as an individual **corporate** adj

corps ⊕ n, pl **corps 1** military force **2** any organized body of persons

corpse ⊕ n dead body

corpulent adj fat **corpulence** n

corpus n, pl **corpora** main part or body of something

corpuscle n minute particle, esp. of blood

corral n (US) enclosure for cattle

correct ⊕ v **1** set right **2** indicate

errors in **3** punish ▷ adj **4** right, accurate **correctly** adv

correction n **corrective** n/adj

correlate v bring into reciprocal relation **correlation** n

correspond ⊕ v **1** be similar (to) **2** exchange letters

correspondence n

correspondent n **1** writer of letters **2** one employed by newspaper etc. to report on particular topic

corridor ⊕ n passage

corroborate v confirm

corroboree n (Aust) Aboriginal gathering or dance

corrode v eat into **corrosion** n **corrosive** adj

corrupt ⊕ adj **1** lacking integrity **2** involving bribery **3** wicked ▷ v **4** make evil **5** bribe **6** make rotten **corruption** n

corsage n (flower worn on) bodice of woman's dress

corset n close-fitting undergarment to support the body

─────── THESAURUS ───────

corporation n = **business**, company, concern, firm, society; = **town council**, council, municipal authorities, civic authorities

corps n = **team**, unit, regiment, detachment, company

corpse n = **body**, remains, carcass, cadaver, stiff (Sl)

correct adj = **accurate**, right, true, exact, precise ≠ **inaccurate**; = **right**, standard, appropriate, acceptable, proper ▷ v = **rectify**, remedy, redress, right, reform

≠ **spoil**; = **rebuke**, discipline, reprimand, chide, admonish ≠ **praise**

correspond v = **be consistent**, match, agree, accord, fit ≠ **differ**; = **communicate**, write, keep in touch, exchange letters

corridor n = **passage**, alley, aisle, hallway, passageway

corrupt adj bent (Sl), crooked (Inf), fraudulent, unscrupulous; = **depraved**, vicious, degenerate, debased, profligate; = **distorted**, doctored, altered, falsified

cortege n formal (funeral) procession

cortex n, pl **-tices** outer layer of brain etc.

cortisone n synthetic hormone used medically

cosh n **1** blunt weapon ▷ v **2** strike with one

cosine n in a right-angled triangle, ratio of adjacent side to hypotenuse

cosmetic ❶ n/adj (preparation) to improve appearance only

cosmic ❶ adj **1** relating to the universe **2** vast

cosmopolitan ❶ adj/n (person) familiar with many countries

cosmos n the universe considered as an ordered system

cosset v **cosseting, cosseted** pamper, pet

cost ❶ n **1** price **2** expenditure of time, labour etc. **3** damage ▷ v **4** have as price **5** entail payment, or loss of **costly** adj **1** valuable **2** expensive

costume ❶ n style of dress of particular place or time

cosy ❶ adj **-sier, -siest** snug, comfortable

cot n child's bed

cote n shelter for animals or birds

coterie n social clique

cottage ❶ n small house **cottage cheese** mild, soft cheese **cottage pie** dish of minced meat and potato

cotton n **1** plant with white downy fibres **2** cloth of this

couch n **1** piece of furniture for reclining on ▷ v **2** put into (words)

cougar n puma

cough ❶ v **1** expel air from lungs with sudden effort and noise ▷ n **2** act of coughing

could past tense of CAN¹

coulomb n unit of electric charge

council ❶ n **1** deliberative or administrative body **2** local governing authority of town etc. **councillor** n

————————————— THESAURUS —————————————

▷ v = **bribe**, fix (Inf), buy off, suborn, grease (someone's) palm (Sl); = **deprave**, pervert, subvert, debauch ≠ **reform**

cosmetic adj = **superficial**, surface, nonessential

cosmic adj = **extraterrestrial**, stellar

cosmopolitan adj = **sophisticated**, cultured, refined, cultivated, urbane ≠ **unsophisticated**

cost n = **price**, worth, expense, charge, damage (Inf) ▷ v = **sell at**, come to, set (someone)

back (Inf), be priced at, command a price of; = **lose**, deprive of, cheat of

costume n = **outfit**, dress, clothing, uniform, ensemble

cosy adj = **comfortable**, homely, warm, intimate, snug, sheltered, comfy (Inf)

cottage n = **cabin**, lodge, hut, shack, chalet

cough v = **clear your throat**, bark, hack ▷ n = **frog** or **tickle in your throat**, bark, hack

council n = **committee**, governing body, board

counsel ❶ n 1 advice
2 barrister(s) ▷ v 3 advise,
recommend **counsellor** n

count¹ ❶ v 1 reckon, number
2 consider to be 3 be reckoned in
4 depend (on) 5 be of importance
▷ n 6 reckoning 7 total number
8 act of counting **countless** adj
too many to be counted
countdown n counting of the
seconds before an event

count² n nobleman **countess** n
noblewoman

countenance n 1 face, its
expression ▷ v 2 support, approve

counter¹ n horizontal surface in
bank, shop etc., on which business
is transacted

counter² ❶ adv 1 in opposite
direction ▷ v 2 oppose

counter- comb. form reversed,
opposite, rival, retaliatory, as in
counterclaim, counterproductive

counteract v neutralize

counterattack v/n attack in
response to attack

counterbalance n 1 weight
balancing another ▷ v 2 act as
balance

counterfeit adj 1 sham, forged
▷ n 2 imitation, forgery ▷ v
3 imitate with intent to deceive
4 forge

counterfoil n part of cheque,
receipt etc. kept as record

countermand v cancel (previous
order)

counterpane n bed covering

counterpart ❶ n something
complementary to another

counterpoint n melody added as
accompaniment to given melody

countersign v sign document
already signed by another

countersink v enlarge top of hole
to take head of screw, bolt etc.
below surface

countertenor n male alto

country ❶ n, pl -**tries** 1 region
2 nation 3 people of nation 4 land
of birth 5 rural districts
countryman n **countryside** n

counsel n = **advice**, information,
warning, direction, suggestion;
= **legal adviser**, lawyer, attorney,
solicitor, advocate ▷ v = **advise**,
recommend, advocate, warn, urge

count¹ v (often with up) = **add (up)**,
total, reckon (up), tot up, calculate;
= **matter**, be important, carry
weight, tell, rate; = **consider**,
judge, regard, deem, think of;
= **include**, number among, take
into account or consideration ▷ n
= **calculation**, poll, reckoning,
sum, tally

counter² v = **oppose**, meet, block,
resist, parry ▷ adv = **opposite to**,
against, versus, conversely, in
defiance of ≠ **in accordance with**

counterpart n = **opposite
number**, equal, twin, equivalent,
match

country n = **nation**, state, land,
commonwealth, kingdom;
= **people**, community, nation,
society, citizens; = **countryside**,
provinces, sticks (Inf), farmland,
outback (Aust & NZ) ≠ **town**;
= **territory**, land, region, terrain

county ❶ *n, pl* **-ties** division of country

coup ❶ *n* **1** successful stroke **2** sudden/violent seizure of government

coup de grace *(Fr)* decisive action

coupé *n* sporty style of motorcar

couple ❶ *n* **1** two, pair **2** husband and wife ▷ *v* **3** connect, fasten together **4** join, associate **couplet** *n* two lines of verse **coupling** *n* connecting device

coupon ❶ *n* ticket entitling holder to discount, gift etc.

courage ❶ *n* bravery, boldness **courageous** *adj* **courageously** *adv*

courgette *n* type of small vegetable marrow

courier ❶ *n* **1** messenger **2** person who guides travellers

course ❶ *n* **1** movement in space or time **2** direction **3** sequence

4 line of action **5** series of lectures etc. **6** any of successive parts of meal **7** area where golf is played **8** racetrack ▷ *v* **9** hunt **10** run swiftly **11** (of blood) circulate

court ❶ *n* **1** space enclosed by buildings, yard **2** area for playing various games **3** royal household **4** body with judicial powers, place where it meets, one of its sittings ▷ *v* **5** woo **6** seek, invite **courtier** *n* one who frequents royal court **courtly** *adj* **1** ceremoniously polite **2** characteristic of a court **court card** king, queen or jack at cards **court martial** *pl* **courts martial** court for trying naval or military offences **courtship** *n* wooing **courtyard** *n* enclosed paved area

courtesy ❶ *n* politeness **courteous** *adj*

cousin *n* son or daughter of uncle or aunt

——————— THESAURUS ———————

county *n* = **province**, district, shire

coup *n* = **masterstroke**, feat, stunt, action, exploit

couple *n* = **pair**, two, brace, duo, twosome

coupon *n* = **slip**, ticket, certificate, token/voucher

courage *n* = **bravery**, nerve, resolution, daring, pluck ≠ **cowardice**

courier *n* = **messenger**, runner, carrier, bearer, envoy; = **guide**, representative, escort, conductor

course *n* = **route**, way, line, road, track; = **procedure**, plan, policy, programme, method; = **progression**, order, unfolding,

development, movement; = **classes**, programme, schedule, lectures, curriculum; = **racecourse**, circuit, cinder track; = **period**, time, duration, term, passing ▷ *v* = **run**, flow, stream, gush, race; = **hunt**, follow, chase, pursue

court *n* = **law court**, bar, bench, tribunal; = **palace**, hall, castle, manor; = **royal household**, train, suite, attendants, entourage ▷ *v* = **cultivate**, seek, flatter, solicit, pander to; = **invite**, seek, attract, prompt, provoke; = **woo**, go (out) with, date, take out, run after

courtesy *n* = **politeness**, good

cove ⊕ *n* small inlet of coast

coven *n* gathering of witches

covenant ⊕ *n* 1 agreement 2 compact ▷ *v* 3 agree to a covenant

cover ⊕ *v* 1 place over 2 extend, spread 3 bring upon (oneself) 4 protect 5 travel over 6 include 7 be sufficient 8 report ▷ *n* 9 covering thing 10 shelter 11 insurance **coverage** *n* **coverlet** *n* top covering of bed

covert *adj* secret, sly

covet ⊕ *v* **coveting, coveted** long to possess, esp. what belongs to another **covetous** *adj*

cow¹ *n* female of bovine and other animals **cowboy** *n* 1 ranch worker who herds cattle 2 (*Inf*) irresponsible worker

cow² *v* frighten, overawe

coward ⊕ *n* one who lacks courage **cowardice** *n* **cowardly** *adj*

cower *v* crouch in fear

cowl *n* 1 monk's hooded cloak 2 hooded top for chimney

cowslip *n* wild primrose

coxswain *n* steersman of boat

coy *adj* (pretending to be) shy, modest **coyly** *adv*

coyote *n* prairie wolf

coypu *n* aquatic rodent

crab *n* edible crustacean **crabbed** *adj* (of handwriting) hard to read **crabby** *adj* bad-tempered

crab apple wild sour apple

crack ⊕ *v* 1 split partially 2 break with sharp noise 3 break down, yield 4 (*Inf*) tell (joke) 5 solve, decipher 6 make sharp noise ▷ *n* 7 sharp explosive noise 8 split 9 flaw 10 (*Inf*) joke 11 chat 12 (*Sl*) highly addictive form of cocaine ▷ *adj* 13 (*Inf*) very skilful **cracker** *n* 1 decorated paper tube, pulled apart with a bang, containing toy etc. 2 explosive firework 3 thin dry biscuit **crackers** *adj* (*Sl*) crazy **cracking** *adj* very good **crackle** *n/v* (make) sound of repeated small cracks **crackpot** *n* (*Inf*) eccentric

— THESAURUS —

manners, civility, gallantry, graciousness

cove *n* = **bay**, sound, inlet, anchorage

covenant *n* = **promise**, contract, agreement, commitment, arrangement

cover *v* = **conceal**, hide, mask, disguise, obscure ≠ **reveal**; = **clothe**, dress, wrap, envelop ≠ **uncover**; = **overlay**, blanket; = **coat**, cake, plaster, smear, envelop ▷ *n* = **protection**, shelter, shield, defence, guard;

= **insurance**, protection, compensation, indemnity, reimbursement; = **covering**, case, top, coating, envelope; = **bedclothes**, bedding, sheets, blankets, quilt

covet *v* = **long for**, desire, envy, crave, aspire to

coward *n* = **wimp**, chicken (*Sl*), scaredy-cat (*Inf*), yellow-belly (*Sl*)

crack *v* = **break**, split, burst, snap, fracture; = **snap**, ring, crash, burst, explode; (*Inf*) = **hit**, clip (*Inf*), slap, smack, clout (*Inf*); = **break**, cleave;

person; crank

cradle ❶ *n* **1** infant's bed ▷ *v* **2** hold or rock as in a cradle **3** cherish

craft¹ ❶ *n* **1** skilled trade **2** skill, ability **3** cunning **crafty** *adj* cunning, shrewd **craftsman** *n* **craftsmanship** *n*

craft² ❶ *n* **1** vessel **2** ship

crag *n* steep rugged rock

cram ❶ *v* **cramming, crammed** **1** stuff **2** prepare quickly for examination

cramp¹ ❶ *n* painful muscular contraction

cramp² ❶ *v* hinder

cranberry *n* edible red berry

crane *n* **1** wading bird with long legs **2** machine for moving heavy weights ▷ *v* **3** stretch neck **crane fly** long-legged insect

cranium *n, pl* **-niums, -nia** skull

cranial *adj*

crank *n* **1** arm at right angles to axis, for turning main shaft **2** (*Inf*) eccentric person ▷ *v* **3** start (engine) by turning crank **cranky** *adj* eccentric

cranny *n, pl* **-nies** small opening

crash ❶ *v* **1** (cause to) make loud noise **2** (cause to) fall with crash **3** smash **4** collapse **5** cause (aircraft) to hit land or water **6** collide with **7** move noisily ▷ *n* **8** loud, violent fall or impact **9** collision **10** uncontrolled descent of aircraft **11** sudden collapse **12** bankruptcy **crash helmet** protective helmet

crass *adj* grossly stupid

crate ❶ *n* large (usu. wooden) container for packing goods

crater ❶ *n* **1** mouth of volcano **2** bowl-shaped cavity

THESAURUS

= **solve**, work out, resolve, clear up, fathom ▷ *n* = **break**, chink, gap, fracture, rift; = **split**, break, fracture; = **snap**, pop, crash, burst, explosion; (*Inf*) = **blow**, slap, smack, clout (*Inf*), cuff ▷ *adj* (*Sl*) = **first-class**, choice, excellent, ace, elite

cradle *n* = **crib**, cot, Moses basket, bassinet ▷ *v* = **hold**, support, rock, nurse, nestle

craft¹ *n* = **occupation**, work, business, trade, employment; = **skill**, art, ability, technique, know-how (*Inf*)

craft² *n* = **vessel**, boat, ship, plane, aircraft

cram *v* = **stuff**, force, jam, shove,

compress; = **pack**, fill, stuff

cramp¹ *n* = **spasm**, pain, ache, contraction, pang

cramp² *v* = **restrict**, hamper, inhibit, hinder, handicap

crash *n* = **collision**, accident, smash, wreck, prang (*Inf*); = **smash**, clash, boom, bang, thunder; = **collapse**, failure, depression, ruin, downfall ▷ *v* = **fall**, plunge, topple, lurch, hurtle; = **plunge**, hurtle; = **collapse**, fail, go under, be ruined, go bust (*Inf*)

crate *n* = **container**, case, box, packing case, tea chest

crater *n* = **hollow**, hole, depression, dip, cavity

cravat n man's neckcloth
crave ❶ v 1 have very strong desire for 2 beg **craving** n
craven adj cowardly
crawl ❶ v 1 move on hands and knees 2 move very slowly 3 ingratiate oneself 4 swim with crawl stroke 5 be overrun (with) ▷ n 6 crawling motion 7 racing stroke at swimming
crayfish n edible freshwater crustacean
crayon n stick or pencil of coloured wax etc.
craze ❶ n 1 short-lived fashion 2 strong desire 3 madness **crazed** adj **crazy** adj 1 insane 2 very foolish 3 madly eager (for)
creak n/v (make) grating noise
cream ❶ n 1 fatty part of milk 2 food like this 3 cosmetic like this 4 yellowish-white colour 5 best part ▷ v 6 take cream from 7 take best part from 8 beat to creamy

consistency **creamy** adj
crease ❶ n 1 line made by folding 2 wrinkle ▷ v 3 make, develop creases
create ❶ v 1 bring into being 2 make 3 (Inf) make a fuss **creation** n **creative** adj imaginative, inventive **creativity** n **creator** n
creature ❶ n living being
crèche n day nursery for very young children
credentials ❶ pl n 1 testimonials 2 letters of introduction
credible ❶ adj worthy of belief **credibility** n
credit ❶ n 1 commendation 2 source of honour 3 trust 4 good name 5 system of allowing customers to pay later 6 money at one's disposal in bank etc. ▷ v 7 attribute, believe 8 put on credit side of account **creditable** adj bringing honour **creditor** n one to

---

THESAURUS

crave v = **long for**, yearn for, hanker after, want, desire; (Inf) = **beg**, ask for, seek, petition, pray for
crawl v = **creep**, slither, inch, wriggle, writhe ≠ **run be crawling with something** = **be full of**, teem with, be alive with, swarm with, be overrun with
craze n = **fad**, fashion, trend, rage, enthusiasm
cream n = **lotion**, ointment, oil, essence, cosmetic; = **best**, elite, prime, pick, flower ▷ adj = **off-white**, ivory, yellowish-white
crease n = **fold**, line, ridge, groove,

corrugation ▷ v = **crumple**, rumple, fold, double up, corrugate
create v = **cause**, lead to, occasion, bring about; = **make**, produce, invent, compose, devise ≠ **destroy**
creature n = **living thing**, being, animal, beast, brute
credentials pl n = **qualifications**, ability, skill, fitness, attribute
credible adj = **believable**, possible, likely, reasonable, probable ≠ **unbelievable**; = **reliable**, honest, dependable, trustworthy, sincere ≠ **unreliable**
credit n = **praise**, honour, recognition, approval, tribute;

whom debt is due **credit crunch** period during which there is a sudden reduction in the availability of credit from banks, mortgage lenders, etc

credulous adj too easy of belief, gullible **credulity** n

creed ❶ n statement of belief

creek ❶ n narrow inlet on coast

creep ❶ v **creeping, crept**
1 move slowly, stealthily **2** crawl **3** act in servile way **4** (of flesh) feel shrinking sensation ▷ n **5** creeping **6** (Sl) repulsive person ▷ pl **7** feeling of fear or repugnance **creeper** n creeping or climbing plant **creepy** adj

creole n language developed from mixture of languages

creosote n oily liquid used for preserving wood

crepe n fabric with crimped surface

crescendo n, pl **-dos** (Mus) gradual increase of loudness

crescent ❶ n (shape of) moon seen in first or last quarter

cress n various plants with edible pungent leaves

crest ❶ n **1** tuft on bird's or animal's head **2** top of mountain, wave etc. **3** badge above shield of coat of arms **crestfallen** adj disheartened

cretin n **1** (Obs) person with disability caused by thyroid deficiency **2** (Inf) stupid person **cretinous** adj

crevasse n deep open chasm

crevice n cleft, fissure

crew ❶ n **1** ship's, aircraft's company **2** (Inf) gang

crib n **1** child's cot **2** rack for fodder **3** plagiarism ▷ v **4** copy dishonestly

cribbage n card game

crick n cramp esp. in neck

cricket¹ n chirping insect

cricket² n game played with bats, ball and wickets **cricketer** n

crime ❶ n **1** violation of law **2** wicked act **criminal** adj/n

crimson adj/n (of) rich deep red

cringe v **1** shrink, cower **2** behave

THESAURUS

= **source of satisfaction** or **pride**, asset, honour, feather in your cap; = **prestige**, reputation, standing, position, influence; = **belief**, trust, confidence, faith, reliance ▷ v = **believe**, rely on, have faith in, trust, accept

creed n = **belief**, principles, doctrine, dogma, credo

creek n = **inlet**, bay, cove, bight, firth or frith (Scot, US, Canad, Aust, & NZ); = **stream**, brook, tributary, bayou, rivulet

creep v = **sneak**, steal, tiptoe, slink,

skulk ▷ n (Sl) = **bootlicker** (Inf), sneak, sycophant, crawler (Sl), toady

crescent n = **meniscus**, sickle, new moon

crest n = **top**, summit, peak, ridge, highest point; = **tuft**, crown, comb, plume, mane; = **emblem**, badge, symbol, insignia, bearings

crew n = **(ship's) company**, hands, (ship's) complement; = **team**, squad, gang, corps, posse; (Inf) = **crowd**, set, bunch (Inf), band, pack

crime n = **offence**, violation,

obsequiously

crinkle v/n wrinkle

crinoline n hooped petticoat or skirt

cripple ❶ n 1 (Offens) disabled person ▷ v 2 disable

crisis ❶ n, pl **-ses** 1 turning point 2 time of acute danger

crisp ❶ adj 1 brittle 2 brisk 3 clear-cut 4 fresh ▷ n 5 very thin, fried slice of potato **crispy** adj **crispbread** n thin dry biscuit

crisscross v 1 go in crosswise pattern ▷ adj 2 crossing in different directions

criterion ❶ n, pl **-ria** standard of judgment

critic ❶ n 1 professional judge of any of the arts 2 person who finds fault

critical adj 1 fault-finding 2 discerning 3 skilled in judging

croak v/n (utter) deep hoarse cry

crochet n/v **-cheting, -cheted** (do) handicraft like knitting

crock n earthenware pot **crockery** n earthenware dishes etc.

crocodile n large amphibious reptile

crocus n, pl **-cuses** small bulbous plant

croft n small farm

croissant n crescent-shaped bread roll

crone n witchlike old woman

crony n, pl **-nies** intimate friend

crook ❶ n 1 hooked staff 2 (Inf) swindler, criminal **crooked** adj 1 twisted 2 deformed 3 dishonest

croon v sing in soft tone

crop ❶ n 1 produce of cultivated plants 2 harvest 3 pouch in bird's gullet 4 whip 5 short haircut ▷ v 6 cut short 7 produce crop 8 (of animals) bite, eat down **cropper** n 1 (Inf) heavy fall 2 disastrous failure **crop up** (Inf) happen unexpectedly

croquet n lawn game played with balls and hoops

croquette n fried ball of minced meat, fish etc.

cross ❶ n 1 structure or symbol of two intersecting lines or pieces

trespass, felony, misdemeanour; = **lawbreaking**, corruption, illegality, vice, misconduct

cripple v = **disable**, paralyse, lame, maim, incapacitate; = **damage**, destroy, ruin, spoil, impair ≠ **help**

crisis n = **emergency**, plight, predicament, trouble, deep water; = **critical point**, climax, height, crunch (Inf), turning point

crisp adj = **firm**, crunchy, crispy, crumbly, fresh ≠ **soft**; = **bracing**, fresh, refreshing, brisk, invigorating

≠ **warm**; = **clean**, smart, trim, neat, tidy

criterion n = **standard**, test, rule, measure, principle

critic n = **judge**, authority, expert, analyst, commentator

crook n (Inf) = **criminal**, rogue, cheat, thief, shark

crop n = **yield**, produce, gathering, fruits, harvest ▷ v = **graze**, eat, browse, feed on, nibble; = **cut**, trim, clip, prune, shear

cross v = **go across**, pass over,

2 such a structure as means of execution **3** symbol of Christian faith **4** any thing in shape of cross **5** affliction **6** hybrid ▷ *v* **7** move or go across (something) **8** intersect **9** meet and pass **10** mark with lines across **11** (with *out*) delete **12** place in form of cross **13** make sign of cross **14** breed by intermixture **15** thwart ▷ *adj* **16** angry **17** transverse **18** contrary **crossing** *n* **1** intersection of roads, rails etc. **2** part of street where pedestrians are expected to cross **cross-country** *adj/adv* by way of open fields **cross-examine** *v* examine witness already examined by other side **cross-examination** *n* **cross-eyed** *adj* having eyes turning inward **cross-ply** *adj* (of tyre) having fabric cords in outer casing running diagonally **cross-reference** *n* reference within text to another part of text **crossroads** *n* **crossword puzzle** puzzle built up of intersecting

words, indicated by clues **The Cross** cross on which Jesus Christ was executed
crosswalk *n* (Canad) place marked where pedestrians may cross a road
crotch *n* angle between legs
crotchet *n* musical note
crotchety *adj* (Inf) bad-tempered
crouch ❶ *v* **1** bend low **2** huddle down close to ground **3** stoop
croupier *n* person dealing cards, collecting money etc. at gambling table
crouton *n* piece of toasted bread served in soup
crow[1] *n* large black carrion-eating bird
crow[2] ❶ *v* **1** utter cock's cry **2** boast ▷ *n* **3** cock's cry
crowbar *n* iron bar
crowd ❶ *n* **1** throng, mass ▷ *v* **2** flock together **3** cram, pack **4** fill with people
crown ❶ *n* **1** monarch's headdress **2** royal power **3** various coins **4** top of head **5** summit, top

THESAURUS

traverse, cut across, move across; **= span**, bridge, go across, extend over; **= oppose**, intertwine, crisscross; **= oppose**, interfere with, obstruct, block, resist; **= interbreed**, mix, blend, cross-pollinate, crossbreed ▷ *n* **= trouble**, worry, trial, load, burden; **= mixture**, combination, blend, amalgam, amalgamation ▷ *adj* **= angry**, annoyed, put out, grumpy, short ≠ good-humoured
crouch *v* **= bend down**, kneel, squat, stoop, bow

crow[2] *v* **= gloat**, triumph, boast, swagger, brag
crowd *n* **= multitude**, mass, throng, army, host; **= group**, set, lot, circle, gang ▷ *v* **= flock**, mass, collect, gather, stream; **= squeeze**, pack, pile, bundle, cram
crown *n* **= coronet**, tiara, diadem, circlet; **= laurel wreath**, trophy, prize, honour, garland; **= high point**, top, tip, summit, crest ▷ *v* **= top**, cap, be on top of, surmount; **= cap**, finish, complete, perfect, round off; (Sl) **= strike**, belt (Inf),

6 perfection of thing ▷ v **7** put crown on **8** occur as culmination **9** (Inf) hit on head
crucial ① adj **1** decisive, critical **2** (Inf) very important **crucially** adv
crucible n small melting pot
crude ① adj **1** vulgar **2** in natural or raw state **3** rough **crudely** adv **crudity** n
cruel ① adj causing pain or suffering **cruelly** adv **cruelty** n
cruet n small container for salt, pepper etc.
cruise ① v **1** travel about in a ship ▷ n **2** voyage **cruiser** n **1** ship that cruises **2** warship
crumb ① n fragment of bread
crumble ① v **1** break into small fragments **2** collapse **crumbly** adj
crumpet n **1** flat, soft cake eaten

with butter **2** (Sl) sexually desirable woman or women
crumple ① v **1** (cause to) collapse **2** make or become creased
crunch ① n **1** sound made by chewing crisp food, treading on gravel etc. **2** (Inf) critical situation ▷ v **3** make crunching sound **crunchy** adj
crusade ① n **1** medieval Christian war **2** concerted action to further a cause ▷ v **3** take part in crusade **crusader** n
crush ① v **1** compress so as to break **2** break to small pieces **3** defeat utterly ▷ n **4** act of crushing **5** crowd of people etc.
crust ① n **1** hard outer part of bread **2** similar casing **crusty** adj **1** having crust **2** bad-tempered
crustacean n hard-shelled

THESAURUS

bash, hit over the head, box
crucial adj (Inf) = **vital**, important, pressing, essential, urgent
crude adj = **rough**, basic, makeshift; = **simple**, rudimentary, basic, primitive, coarse; = **vulgar**, dirty, rude, obscene, coarse ≠ **tasteful**
cruel adj = **brutal**, ruthless, callous, sadistic, inhumane ≠ **kind**
cruise n = **sail**, voyage, boat trip, sea trip ▷ v = **sail**, coast, voyage; = **travel along**, coast, drift, keep a steady pace
crumb n = **bit**, grain, fragment, shred, morsel
crumble v = **disintegrate**, collapse, deteriorate, decay, fall apart; = **crush**, fragment, pulverize,

pound, grind
crumple v = **crush**, squash, screw up, scrumple; = **crease**, wrinkle, rumple, ruffle, pucker
crunch v = **chomp**, champ, munch, chew noisily, grind ▷ n (Inf) = **critical point**, test, crisis, emergency, crux
crusade n = **campaign**, drive, movement, cause, push
crush v = **squash**, break, squeeze, compress, press; = **overcome**, overwhelm, put down, subdue, overpower; = **demoralize**, depress, devastate, discourage, humble ▷ n = **crowd**, mob, horde, throng, pack
crust n = **layer**, covering, coating, skin, surface

animal, e.g. crab, lobster

crutch n 1 staff with crosspiece to go under armpit of lame person 2 support 3 crotch

crux n, pl **cruxes** that on which a decision turns

cry ❶ v **crying, cried** 1 weep 2 utter call 3 shout 4 beg (for) 5 proclaim ▷ n 6 loud utterance 7 call of animal 8 fit of weeping

crypt n vault, esp. under church

cryptic adj secret, mysterious

crystal n 1 transparent mineral 2 very clear glass 3 cut-glass ware 4 form with symmetrically arranged plane surfaces **crystalline** adj **crystallize** v 1 form into crystals 2 become definite

cu. cubic

cub ❶ n 1 young of fox and other animals 2 (with cap.) junior Scout

cubbyhole n small enclosed space

cube n 1 solid figure with six equal square sides 2 cube-shaped block 3 product obtained by multiplying number by itself twice ▷ v 4 multiply thus **cubic** adj

cubicle n enclosed section of room

cuckoo n 1 migratory bird 2 its call

cucumber n long fleshy green fruit used in salad

cud n food which ruminant animal brings back into mouth to chew again

cuddle ❶ v 1 hug 2 lie close and snug, nestle ▷ n 3 hug **cuddly** adj

cudgel n 1 short thick stick ▷ v 2 beat with cudgel

cue¹ ❶ n 1 signal to act or speak 2 hint

cue² n long tapering rod used in billiards

cuff¹ n ending of sleeve

cuff² v 1 strike with open hand ▷ n 2 blow with hand

cuisine n 1 style of cooking 2 food cooked

cul-de-sac n street open only at one end

culinary adj of, for, suitable for, cooking or kitchen

cull v 1 select 2 take out animals from herd

culminate ❶ v 1 reach highest point 2 come to a head **culmination** n

culottes pl n women's trousers flared like skirt

culpable adj blameworthy

culprit ❶ n one guilty of offence

cult ❶ n 1 system of worship 2 devotion to some person, thing

─────── THESAURUS ───────

cry v = **weep**, sob, shed tears, blubber, snivel ≠ **laugh**; = **shout**, scream, roar, yell, howl ≠ **whisper** ▷ n = **shout**, call, scream, roar, yell; = **appeal**, plea

cub n = **young**, baby, offspring, whelp

cuddle v = **hug**, embrace, fondle, cosset

cue¹ n = **signal**, sign, hint, prompt, reminder

culminate v = **end up**, close, finish, conclude, wind up

culprit n = **offender**, criminal, felon, guilty party, wrongdoer

cult n = **sect**, faction, school,

cultivate ⓥ v 1 till and prepare (ground) 2 develop, improve 3 devote attention to **cultivated** adj cultured **cultivation** n

culture ⓝ n 1 state of manners, taste and intellectual development 2 cultivating **cultural** adj **cultured** adj

culvert n drain under road

cumbersome adj unwieldy

cummerbund n sash worn round waist

cumulative adj becoming greater by successive additions

cumulus n, pl **-li** round billowing cloud

cunning ⓐ adj 1 crafty, sly ▷ n 2 skill in deceit or evasion

cup ⓝ n 1 small drinking vessel with handle 2 various cup-shaped formations 3 cup-shaped trophy as prize ▷ v 4 shape as cup (hands etc.) **cupful** n **cupboard** n piece of furniture with door, for storage

cur n 1 dog of mixed breed 2 contemptible person

curate n parish priest's appointed assistant

curator n custodian, esp. of museum

curb ⓝ n 1 check, restraint ▷ v 2 restrain 3 apply curb to

curd n coagulated milk **curdle** v turn into curd, coagulate

cure ⓥ v 1 heal, restore to health 2 remedy 3 preserve (fish, skins etc.) ▷ n 4 remedy 5 course of medical treatment 6 restoration to health **curable** adj

curfew n 1 official regulation prohibiting movement of people, esp. at night 2 deadline for this

curio n, pl **-rios** rare or curious thing sought for collections

curious ⓐ adj 1 eager to know, inquisitive 2 puzzling, odd **curiosity** n **curiously** adv

---
THESAURUS
---

religion, clique; = **craze**, fashion, trend, fad

cultivate v = **farm**, work, plant, tend, till; = **develop**, establish, foster; = **court**, seek out, run after, dance attendance upon

culture n = **civilization**, society, customs, way of life; = **lifestyle**, habit, way of life, mores

cunning adj = **crafty**, sly, devious, artful, sharp ≠ **frank**; = **ingenious**, imaginative, sly, devious, artful ▷ n = **craftiness**, guile, trickery, deviousness, artfulness ≠ **candour**; = **skill**, subtlety, ingenuity, artifice, cleverness ≠ **clumsiness**

cup n = **mug**, goblet, chalice, teacup, beaker

curb v = **restrain**, control, check, restrict, suppress ▷ n = **restraint**, control, check, brake, limitation

cure v = **make better**, correct, heal, relieve, remedy; = **preserve**, smoke, dry, salt, pickle ▷ n = **remedy**, treatment, antidote, panacea, nostrum

curious adj = **inquisitive**, interested, questioning, searching, inquiring ≠ **uninterested**; = **strange**, unusual, bizarre, odd, novel ≠ **ordinary**

curl ❶ v **1** take, bend into spiral or curved shape ▷ n **2** spiral lock of hair **3** spiral **curly** adj

curlew n large long-billed wading bird

curmudgeon n bad-tempered person

currant n **1** dried type of grape **2** fruit of various plants allied to gooseberry

current ❶ adj **1** of immediate present **2** in general use ▷ n **3** body of water or air in motion **4** transmission of electricity **currently** adv **currency** n, pl **-cies 1** money in use **2** state of being in use

curriculum n, pl **-la, -lums** specified course of study **curriculum vitae** outline of career

curry n, pl **-ries 1** highly-flavoured, pungent condiment **2** dish flavoured with it ▷ v **3** prepare, flavour dish with curry

curse ❶ n **1** profane or obscene expression of anger etc. **2** magic spell **3** affliction ▷ v **4** utter curse, swear (at) **5** afflict

cursor n movable point showing position on computer screen

cursory adj hasty, superficial

curt adj rudely brief, abrupt

curtail ❶ v cut short

curtain ❶ n **1** hanging drapery at window etc. ▷ v **2** provide, cover with curtain

curtsy, curtsey v/n, pl **-sies, -seys** (perform) woman's bow

curve ❶ n **1** line of which no part is straight ▷ v **2** bend into curve

cushion ❶ n **1** bag filled with soft stuffing or air, to support or ease body ▷ v **2** provide, protect with cushion **3** lessen effects of

cushy adj **cushier, cushiest** (Inf) easy

custard n **1** dish made of eggs and milk **2** sweet sauce of milk and cornflour

custody ❶ n guardianship, imprisonment **custodian** n keeper, curator

curl n = **ringlet**, lock ▷ v = **twirl**, turn, bend, twist, curve

current n = **flow**, course, undertow, jet, stream; = **draught**, flow, breeze, puff ▷ adj = **present**, fashionable, up-to-date, contemporary, trendy (Brit Inf) ≠ **out-of-date**; = **prevalent**, common, accepted, popular, widespread

curse v = **swear**, cuss (Inf), blaspheme, take the Lord's name in vain; = **abuse**, damn, scold, vilify ▷ n = **oath**, obscenity, blasphemy, expletive, profanity; = **malediction**,

anathema, jinx, hoodoo (Inf), excommunication; = **affliction**, plague, scourge, trouble, torment

curtail v = **reduce**, diminish, decrease, dock, cut back

curtain n = **hanging**, drape (chiefly US), portière

curve n = **bend**, turn, loop, arc, curvature ▷ v = **bend**, turn, wind, twist, arch

cushion n = **pillow**, pad, bolster, headrest, beanbag ▷ v = **soften**, dampen, muffle, mitigate, deaden

custody n = **care**, charge,

custom ❶ n 1 habit 2 practice 3 usage 4 business patronage ▷ pl 5 taxes levied on imports
customary adj usual, habitual
customer n 1 one who enters shop to buy, esp. regularly 2 purchaser
cut ❶ v cutting, cut 1 sever, wound, divide 2 pare, detach, trim 3 intersect 4 reduce, decrease 5 abridge 6 (Inf) ignore (person) ▷ n 7 act of cutting 8 stroke 9 blow, wound 10 reduction 11 fashion, shape 12 (Inf) share
cutter n **cutting** n 1 piece cut from plant 2 article from newspaper 3 passage for railway ▷ adj 4 keen, piercing 5 hurtful
cutthroat n 1 killer ▷ adj 2 murderous 3 fiercely competitive
cute ❶ adj appealing, pretty
cuticle n dead skin, esp. at base of fingernail
cutlass n curved sword
cutlery n knives, forks etc.
cutlet n small piece of meat
cuttlefish n sea mollusc like squid
CV curriculum vitae

cyanide n extremely poisonous chemical compound
cybernetics pl n comparative study of control mechanisms of electronic and biological systems
cyclamen n plant with flowers having turned-back petals
cycle ❶ n 1 recurrent, complete series or period 2 bicycle ▷ v 3 ride bicycle **cyclical** adj **cyclist** n bicycle rider
cyclone n circular storm
cygnet n young swan
cylinder n roller-shaped body, of uniform diameter **cylindrical** adj
cymbal n one of two brass plates struck together to produce clashing sound
cynic ❶ n one who believes the worst about people or outcome of events **cynical** adj **cynicism** n being cynical
cypress n coniferous tree with very dark foliage
cyst n sac containing liquid secretion or pus **cystitis** n inflammation of bladder

---
THESAURUS
---

protection, supervision, safekeeping; = **imprisonment**, detention, confinement, incarceration
custom n = **tradition**, practice, convention, ritual, policy; = **habit**, way, practice, procedure, routine; = **customers**, business, trade, patronage
cut v = **slit**, score, slice, slash, pierce; = **chop**, split, slice, dissect; = **carve**, slice; = **sever**, cut in two; = **shape**, carve, engrave, chisel, form; = **slash**, wound; = **clip**, mow,

trim, prune, snip ▷ n = **incision**, nick, stroke, slash, slit; = **gash**, nick, wound, slash, laceration; = **reduction**, fall, lowering, slash, decrease; (Inf) = **share**, piece, slice, percentage, portion
cute adj = **appealing**, sweet, attractive, engaging, charming
cycle n = **series of events**, circle, revolution, rotation
cynic n = **sceptic**, doubter, pessimist, misanthrope, misanthropist

daily ⊕ *adj/adv* **1** (done) every day
▷ *n* **2** daily newspaper
3 charwoman
dainty *adj* **-tier, -tiest 1** delicate
2 choice **3** fastidious ▷ *n*
4 delicacy **daintiness** *n*
dairy *n, pl* **dairies** place for
processing milk and its
products
dais *n* raised platform
daisy *n, pl* **-sies** flower with yellow
centre and white petals
dale *n* valley
dally *v* **-lying, -lied 1** trifle **2** loiter
Dalmatian *n* white dog with
black spots
dam ⊕ *n/v* (barrier to) hold back
flow of waters
damage ⊕ *n* **1** injury, harm ▷ *pl*
2 compensation for injury ▷ *v*
3 harm
damask *n* **1** patterned woven
material **2** velvety red
dame ⊕ *n* (*Obs*) **1** lady **2** (with
cap.) title of lady in Order of the
British Empire **3** (*Sl*) woman
damn ⊕ *v* **1** condemn **2** curse
▷ *interj* **3** expression of annoyance
etc. **damnable** *adj* **damnation** *n*

dab ⊕ *v* **dabbing, dabbed 1** apply
with momentary pressure ▷ *n*
2 small mass
dabble *v* **1** splash about **2** be
amateur (in)
dachshund *n* short-legged
long-bodied dog
dad, daddy *n* (*Inf*) father
daddy-longlegs *n* (*Inf*) fly with
long thin legs
daffodil *n* yellow spring flower
daft ⊕ *adj* foolish, crazy
dagga *n* (*S Afr, Inf*) cannabis
dagger *n* short stabbing weapon
dahlia *n* garden plant of various
colours

——————————— THESAURUS ———————————

dab *v* = **pat**, touch, tap; = **apply**,
daub, stipple ▷ *n* = **spot**, bit, drop,
pat, smudge; = **touch**, stroke, flick
daft *adj* (*Inf, chiefly Brit*); = **stupid**,
crazy, silly, absurd, foolish
daily *adv* = **every day**, day by day,
once a day ▷ *adj* = **everyday**,
diurnal, quotidian
dam *n* = **barrier**, wall, barrage,
obstruction, embankment ▷ *v*
= **block up**, restrict, hold back,

barricade, obstruct
damage *v* = **spoil**, hurt, injure,
harm, ruin ≠ **fix** ▷ *n*
= **destruction**, harm, loss, injury,
suffering ≠ **improvement**; (*Inf*)
= **cost**, price, charge, bill, amount
dame *n* = **lady**, baroness, dowager,
grande dame (*Fr*), noblewoman
damn *v* = **criticize**, condemn,
blast, denounce, put down
≠ **praise**

DICTIONARY

damp ❶ *adj* **1** moist ▷ *n* **2** moisture ▷ *v* **3** make damp **4** deaden **dampen** *v* damp **damper** *n* **1** anything that discourages **2** plate in flue

damson *n* small dark-purple plum

dance ❶ *v* **1** move with rhythmic steps, to music **2** bob up and down **3** perform (dance) ▷ *n* **4** rhythmical movement **5** social gathering **dancer** *n*

dandelion *n* yellow-flowered wild plant

dandruff *n* dead skin in small scales among the hair

dandy *n, pl* **-dies 1** man excessively concerned with smartness of dress ▷ *adj* **2** (*Inf*) excellent

danger ❶ *n* **1** exposure to harm **2** peril **dangerous** *adj* **dangerously** *adv*

dangle ❶ *v* hang loosely

dank *adj* damp and chilly

dapper *adj* neat, spruce

dappled *adj* marked with spots

dare ❶ *v* **1** have courage (to) **2** challenge ▷ *n* **3** challenge **daring** *adj/n* **daredevil** *adj/n* reckless (person)

dark ❶ *adj* **1** without light **2** gloomy **3** deep in tint **4** unenlightened ▷ *n* **5** absence of light **darken** *v* **darkly** *adv* **darkness** *n* **dark horse** person, thing about whom little is known

darling ❶ *adj/n* beloved (person)

darn *v* mend (hole) by sewing

dart ❶ *n* **1** small pointed missile **2** darting motion **3** small seam ▷ *pl* **4** indoor game played with numbered target ▷ *v* **5** throw, go rapidly

dash ❶ *v* **1** move hastily **2** throw, strike violently **3** frustrate ▷ *n* **4** rush **5** small amount

THESAURUS

damp *adj* = **moist**, wet, soggy, humid, dank ≠ **dry** ▷ *n* = **moisture**, liquid, drizzle, dampness, wetness ≠ **dryness** ▷ *v* = **moisten**, wet, soak, dampen, moisturize

dance *v* = **prance**, trip, hop, skip, sway; = **caper**, trip, spring, jump, bound ▷ *n* = **ball**, social, hop (*Inf*), disco, knees-up (*Brit Inf*)

danger *n* = **jeopardy**, vulnerability

dangle *v* = **hang**, swing, trail, sway, flap

dare *v* = **risk doing**, venture, presume, make bold, hazard doing; = **challenge**, provoke, defy, taunt, goad

dark *adj* = **dim**, murky, shady, shadowy, grey; = **black**, brunette, ebony, dark-skinned, sable ≠ **fair**; = **evil**, foul, sinister, vile, wicked; = **secret**, hidden, mysterious, concealed; = **gloomy**, sad, grim, miserable, bleak ≠ **cheerful** ▷ *n* = **darkness**, shadows, gloom, dusk, obscurity; = **night**, twilight, evening, dusk, night-time

darling *n* = **beloved**, love, dear, dearest, angel ▷ *adj* = **beloved**, dear, treasured, precious, adored

dart *v* = **dash**, run, race, shoot, fly

dash *v* = **rush**, run, race, shoot, fly ≠ **dawdle**; = **throw**, cast, pitch, slam, toss; = **crash**, break, smash,

6 smartness **7** punctuation mark (–) showing change of subject
dashing adj lively, stylish
dashboard n instrument panel
dastardly adj mean
data ❶ pl n **1** (oft. with sing v) series of facts **2** information **database** n store of information
date¹ ❶ n **1** day of the month **2** time of occurrence **3** appointment ▷ v **4** mark with date **5** reveal age of **6** exist (from) **7** become old-fashioned **dated** adj
date² n fruit of palm
daub v paint roughly
daughter n one's female child **daughter-in-law** n, pl **daughters-in-law** wife of one's child
dawdle v idle, loiter
dawn ❶ n **1** daybreak **2** beginning ▷ v **3** begin to grow light **4** (begin to) be understood
day ❶ n **1** period of 24 hours **2** time when sun is above horizon

3 time period **daybreak** n dawn
daydream n **1** idle fancy ▷ v **2** have such fancies **daydreamer** n **daylight** n **1** natural light **2** dawn
daze ❶ v **1** stun, bewilder ▷ n **2** bewildered state **dazed** adj
dazzle ❶ v **1** blind, confuse with brightness **2** impress greatly **dazzling** adj
DC direct current
de- comb. form removal of, from, reversal of, as in delouse, desegregate
deacon n one who assists in a church
dead ❶ adj **1** no longer alive **2** obsolete **3** numb **4** lacking vigour **5** complete ▷ n **6** dead person(s) ▷ adv **7** utterly **deaden** v **deadly** adj **1** fatal **2** deathlike ▷ adv **3** as if dead **4** extremely **deadline** n limit of time allowed **deadlock** n standstill **deadpan** adj expressionless

— THESAURUS —

shatter, splinter ▷ n **= rush**, run, race, sprint, dart; **= drop**, little, bit, shot (Inf), touch ≠ **lot**; **= style**, spirit, flair, flourish, verve
data n **= information**, facts, figures, details, intelligence
date n **= time**, stage, period; **= appointment**, meeting, arrangement, commitment, engagement ▷ v **= put a date on**, assign a date to, fix the period of; **= become dated**, become old-fashioned
dawn n **= daybreak**, morning, sunrise, daylight, aurora (Poet); (Lit)

= beginning, start, birth, rise, origin ▷ v **= begin**, start, rise, develop, emerge; **= grow light**, break, brighten, lighten
day n **= daytime**, daylight
daze v **= stun**, shock, paralyse, numb, stupefy ▷ n **= shock**, confusion, distraction, trance, bewilderment
dazzle v **= impress**, amaze, overwhelm, astonish, overpower; **= blind**, confuse, daze, bedazzle
dead adj **= deceased**, departed, late, perished, extinct ≠ **alive**; **= boring**, dull, dreary, flat, plain;

DICTIONARY

deaf ❶ *adj* 1 without hearing
2 unwilling to listen **deafen** *v*
make deaf **deafness** *n*

deal¹ ❶ *v* 1 distribute 2 act
3 treat 4 do business (with, in) ▷ *n*
5 agreement 6 treatment 7 share
dealer *n*

deal² *n* (plank of) pine wood

dean *n* 1 university official 2 head
of cathedral chapter

dear ❶ *adj* 1 beloved 2 precious
3 expensive ▷ *n* 4 beloved one
dearly *adv*

dearth *n* scarcity

death ❶ *n* 1 dying 2 end of life
3 end **deathly** *adj/adv*

debacle, débâcle ❶ *n* utter
collapse, rout, disaster

debase *v* lower in value

debate ❶ *v* 1 argue, esp. formally
▷ *n* 2 formal discussion
debatable *adj* **debater** *n*

debilitate *v* weaken

debit (Finance) ▷ *n* 1 entry in
account of sum owed ▷ *v* 2 enter
as due

debonair *adj* suave, genial

debrief *v* report result of mission

debris ❶ *n* rubbish

debt ❶ *n* 1 what is owed 2 state
of owing **debtor** *n*

debunk *v* expose falseness of, esp.
by ridicule

debut ❶ *n* first appearance in
public **debutante** *n* girl making
society debut

d

THESAURUS

= **not working**, useless, inactive,
inoperative ≠ **working; = numb**,
frozen, paralysed, insensitive, inert;
= **total**, complete, absolute, utter,
outright; (Inf) = **exhausted**, tired,
worn out, spent, done in (Inf) ▷ *n*
= **middle**, heart, depth, midst
▷ *adv* (Inf) = **exactly**, completely,
totally, directly, fully

deaf *adj* = **hard of hearing**,
without hearing, stone deaf;
= **oblivious**, indifferent,
unmoved, unconcerned,
unsympathetic

deal¹ *n* (Inf) = **agreement**,
understanding, contract,
arrangement, bargain;
= **amount**, quantity, measure,
degree, mass

dear *adj* = **beloved**, close, valued,
favourite, prized ≠ **hated**; (Brit Inf)
= **expensive**, costly, high-priced,

pricey (Inf), at a premium ≠ **cheap**
▷ *n* = **darling**, love, dearest, angel,
treasure

death *n* = **dying**, demise, end,
passing, departure ≠ **birth**;
= **destruction**, finish, ruin,
undoing, extinction
≠ **beginning**

debacle, débâcle *n* = **disaster**,
catastrophe, fiasco

debate *n* = **discussion**, talk,
argument, dispute, analysis ▷ *v*
= **discuss**, question, talk about,
argue about, dispute; = **consider**,
reflect, think about, weigh,
contemplate

debris *n* = **remains**, bits, waste,
ruins, fragments

debt *n* = **debit**, commitment,
obligation, liability

debut *n* = **entrance**, beginning,
launch, coming out, introduction

Dec. December
decade n period of ten years
decaffeinated adj (of tea, coffee) with caffeine removed
decant v pour off (wine) **decanter** n stoppered bottle
decapitate v behead
decathlon n athletic contest with ten events
decay ① v 1 rot 2 decline ▷ n 3 rotting
decease n 1 death ▷ v 2 die **deceased** adj/n dead (person)
deceive ① v mislead, delude **deceit** n 1 fraud 2 duplicity **deceitful** adj
decelerate v slow down
December n twelfth month
decent ① adj 1 respectable 2 fitting 3 adequate 4 (Inf) kind **decency** n
deception ① n 1 deceiving 2 trick **deceptive** adj misleading
decibel n unit for measuring intensity of sound
decide ① v 1 (cause to) reach a

decision 2 settle (a contest or question) **decision** n judgment, conclusion or resolution
deciduous adj (of trees) losing leaves annually
decimal adj 1 relating to tenths ▷ n 2 decimal fraction **decimalization** n **decimal point** dot between unit and fraction
decimate v destroy or kill a tenth of, large proportion of
decipher v 1 make out meaning of 2 decode
deck n 1 floor, esp. one covering ship's hull 2 turntable of record player ▷ v 3 decorate **deck chair** folding canvas chair
declaim v speak rhetorically
declare ① v 1 announce formally 2 state emphatically **declaration** n
decline ① v 1 refuse 2 slope downwards 3 deteriorate 4 diminish ▷ n 5 deterioration 6 diminution 7 downward slope
decode v convert from code into

— THESAURUS —

decay v = **rot**, spoil, crumble, deteriorate, perish; = **decline**, diminish, crumble, deteriorate, fall off ≠ **grow** ▷ n = **rot**, corruption, mould, blight, decomposition; = **decline**, collapse, deterioration, failing, fading ≠ **growth**
deceive v = **take in**, trick, fool (Inf), cheat, con (Inf)
decent adj = **satisfactory**, fair, all right, reasonable, sufficient ≠ **unsatisfactory**; = **proper**, becoming, seemly, fitting, appropriate ≠ **improper** (Inf);

= **respectable**, pure, proper, modest, chaste
deception n = **trickery**, fraud, deceit, cunning, treachery ≠ **honesty**; = **trick**, lie, bluff, hoax, decoy
decide = **resolve**, answer, determine, conclude, clear up; = **settle**, determine, resolve
declare v = **state**, claim, announce, voice, express
decline v = **deteriorate**, weaken, pine, decay, worsen ≠ **improve**; = **refuse**, reject, turn down, avoid,

ordinary language **decoder** n

decompose v rot

decongestant adj/n (drug) relieving (esp. nasal) congestion

decontaminate v render harmless

decor n decorative scheme

decorate 🐧 v 1 beautify 2 paint room etc. 3 invest (with medal etc.) **decoration** n **decorative** adj **decorator** n

decorum n propriety, decency **decorous** adj

decoy n 1 bait, lure ▷ v 2 lure, be lured as with decoy

decrease 🐧 v 1 diminish, lessen ▷ n 2 diminishing

decree 🐧 n/v (give) order having the force of law

decrepit adj 1 old 2 worn out

decry v -crying, -cried disparage

dedicate 🐧 v 1 commit wholly to special purpose 2 inscribe or address 3 devote **dedicated** adj **dedication** n

deduce v draw as conclusion

deduct 🐧 v subtract **deductible** adj **deduction** n 1 deducting 2 amount subtracted 3 conclusion

deed 🐧 n 1 action 2 exploit 3 legal document

deem v judge, consider, regard

deep 🐧 adj 1 extending far down 2 at, of given depth 3 profound 4 hard to fathom 5 (of colour) dark 6 (of sound) low ▷ n 7 deep place 8 the sea ▷ adv 9 far down etc. **deeply** adv **deepen** v

deer n, pl **deer** ruminant animal typically with antlers in male

deface v spoil or mar surface

defame v speak ill of **defamation** n **defamatory** adj

default 🐧 n 1 failure to act,

d

—————— THESAURUS ——————

spurn ≠ **accept** ▷ n = **depression**, recession, slump, falling off, downturn ≠ **rise**

decorate v = **adorn**, trim, embroider, ornament, embellish; = **do up**, paper, paint, wallpaper, renovate; = **pin a medal on**, cite, confer an honour on or upon

decrease v = **drop**, decline, lessen, lower, shrink ▷ n = **lessening**, decline, reduction, loss, falling off ≠ **growth**

decree n = **law**, order, ruling, act, command ▷ v = **order**, rule, command, demand, proclaim

dedicate v = **devote**, give, apply, commit, pledge; = **offer**, address, inscribe

deduct v = **subtract**, remove, take off, take away, reduce by ≠ **add**

deed n = **action**, act, performance, achievement, exploit; (Law) = **document**, title, contract

deep adj = **big**, wide, broad, profound, yawning ≠ **shallow**; = **intense**, great, serious (Inf), acute, extreme ≠ **superficial**; = **sound**, profound, unbroken, undisturbed, untroubled; = **dark**, strong, rich, intense, vivid ≠ **light**; = **low**, booming, bass, resonant, sonorous ≠ **high** ▷ n = **middle**, heart, midst, dead

default v = **fail to pay**, dodge,

appear or pay ▷ *v* **2** fail (to pay)
defeat ❶ *v* **1** vanquish **2** thwart
▷ *n* **3** overthrow
defecate *v* empty the bowels
defect ❶ *n* **1** lack, blemish ▷ *v*
2 desert **defection** *n* **defective**
adj **defector** *n*
defend ❶ *v* **1** protect, ward off
attack **2** support by argument
defence *n* **1** protection
2 justification **3** statement by
accused person in court
defenceless *adj* **defendant** *n*
person accused in court **defender**
n **defensible** *adj* **defensive** *adj*
1 serving for defence ▷ *n*
2 attitude of defence
defer¹ ❶ *v* postpone
defer² *v* **-ferring, -ferred** submit
to opinion or judgement of another
deference *n* **1** obedience
2 respect **deferential** *adj*
deficient *adj* lacking in
something **deficiency** *n* **deficit**
n amount by which sum of money
is too small
defile *v* **1** soil **2** sully
define ❶ *v* **1** state meaning of

2 mark out **definite** *adj* **1** exact
2 clear **3** certain **definitely** *adv*
definition *n* **definitive** *adj*
conclusive
deflate *v* (cause to) collapse by
release of gas from **deflation** *n*
(*Economics*) reduction of economic
and industrial activity
deflect ❶ *v* (cause to) turn from
straight course **deflection** *n*
deform *v* **1** spoil shape of
2 disfigure **deformity** *n*
defraud *v* cheat, swindle
defrost *v* **1** make, become free of
frost, ice **2** thaw
deft *adj* skilful, adroit
defunct *adj* dead, obsolete
defuse *v* **1** remove fuse of bomb
etc. **2** remove tension
defy ❶ *v* **-fying, -fied** challenge,
resist successfully **defiance** *n*
resistance **defiant** *adj* openly and
aggressively hostile
degenerate ❶ *v* **1** deteriorate to
lower level ▷ *adj* **2** fallen away in
quality ▷ *n* **3** degenerate person
degeneration *n* **degenerative**
adj

THESAURUS

evade, neglect ▷ *n* = **failure**,
neglect, deficiency, lapse, omission
defeat *v* = **beat**, crush, overwhelm,
conquer, master ≠ **surrender**;
= **frustrate**, foil, thwart, ruin,
baffle ▷ *n* = **conquest**, beating,
overthrow, rout ≠ **victory**
defect *n* = **failing** ▷ *v* = **desert**,
rebel, quit, revolt, change sides
defend *v* = **protect**, cover, guard,
screen, preserve; = **support**,
champion, justify, endorse, uphold

defer¹ *v* = **postpone**, delay, put off,
suspend, shelve
define *v* = **mark out**, outline, limit,
bound, delineate; = **describe**,
interpret, characterize, explain,
spell out
deflect *v* = **turn aside**, bend
defy *v* = **resist**, oppose, confront,
brave, disregard
degenerate *v* = **decline**, slip, sink,
decrease, deteriorate ▷ *adj*
= **depraved**, corrupt, low,

DICTIONARY

degrade ⓥ v 1 dishonour
2 debase 3 reduce 4 decompose
chemically **degradable** adj
degradation n

degree n 1 step, stage in process
2 university rank 3 unit of
measurement

dehydrate v remove moisture
from

deify v -fying, -fied make a god of
deity n god

deign v condescend

déjà vu (Fr) feeling of having
experienced something before

dejected adj miserable
dejection n

delay ⓥ v 1 postpone 2 linger ▷ n
3 delaying

delectable adj delightful

delegate ⓥ n 1 representative
▷ v 2 send as deputy 3 entrust
delegation n

delete ⓥ v remove, erase
deletion n

deliberate ⓥ adj 1 intentional
2 well-considered 3 slow ▷ v
4 consider **deliberately** adv
deliberation n

delicate ⓥ adj 1 exquisite
2 fragile 3 requiring tact **delicacy**
n 1 elegance 2 delicious food

delicatessen n shop selling esp.
imported or unusual foods

delicious ⓥ adj delightful,
pleasing to taste

delight ⓥ v 1 please greatly
2 take great pleasure (in) ▷ n
3 great pleasure **delightful** adj
charming

delinquent n/adj (one) guilty of
delinquency **delinquency** n
(minor) offence or misdeed

delirium n 1 disorder of mind, esp.
in feverish illness 2 violent

THESAURUS

perverted, immoral
degrade v = **demean**, disgrace,
humiliate, shame, humble
≠ **ennoble**; = **demote**, lower,
downgrade ≠ **promote**

delay v = **put off**, suspend,
postpone, shelve, defer; = **hold up**,
detain, hold back, hinder, obstruct
≠ **speed (up)** ▷ n = **hold-up**, wait,
setback, interruption, stoppage

delegate n = **representative**,
agent, deputy, ambassador,
commissioner ▷ v = **entrust**,
transfer, hand over, give, pass on;
= **appoint**, commission, select,
contract, engage

delete v = **remove**, cancel, erase,
strike out, obliterate

deliberate adj = **intentional**,
meant, planned, intended,
conscious ≠ **accidental**; = **careful**,
measured, slow, cautious,
thoughtful ≠ **hurried** ▷ v
= **consider**, think, ponder, discuss,
debate

delicate adj = **fine**, elegant,
exquisite, graceful; = **subtle**, fine,
delicious, faint, refined ≠ **bright**;
= **fragile**, weak, frail, brittle,
tender; = **skilled**, precise, deft,
Victorian, proper (Inf, Inf)

delicious adj = **delectable**, tasty,
choice, savoury, dainty
≠ **unpleasant**

delight n = **pleasure**, joy,
satisfaction, happiness, ecstasy

excitement **delirious** adj
deliver ❶ v **1** carry to destination
2 hand over **3** release **4** give birth
or assist in birth (of) **5** utter
deliverance n rescue **delivery** n,
pl **-eries**
dell n wooded hollow
delta n alluvial tract at river mouth
delude v **1** deceive **2** mislead
delusion n
deluge n **1** flood, downpour ▷ v
2 flood, overwhelm
de luxe 1 rich, sumptuous
2 superior in quality
delve v **1** search intensively **2** dig
demagogue n mob leader or
agitator
demand ❶ v **1** ask as giving an
order **2** call for as due, necessary
▷ n **3** urgent request **4** call for
demanding adj requiring effort
demean v degrade, lower
demeanour n conduct, bearing
demented adj mad, crazy

dementia n mental deterioration
demerit n undesirable quality
demi- comb. form half, as in
demigod
demijohn n large bottle
demilitarize v prohibit military
presence
demise ❶ n **1** death
2 conveyance by will or lease
demobilize v **1** disband (troops)
2 discharge (soldier)
democracy ❶ n, pl **-cies**
1 government by the people or their
elected representatives **2** state so
governed **democrat** n advocate
of democracy **democratic** adj
demolish ❶ v **1** knock to pieces
2 destroy utterly **demolition** n
demon ❶ n devil, evil spirit
demonstrate ❶ v **1** show by
reasoning, prove **2** describe,
explain **3** make exhibition of
support, protest etc.
demonstrable adj

━━━━━━━━━━━━━ THESAURUS ━━━━━━━━━━━━

≠ **displeasure** ▷ v = **please**,
satisfy, thrill, charm, cheer
≠ **displease**
deliver v = **bring**, carry, bear,
transport, distribute; (sometimes
with **up**) = **hand over**, commit, give
up, yield, surrender; = **give**, read,
present, announce, declare;
= **strike**, give, deal, launch, direct;
(Dated) = **release**, free, save,
rescue, loose
demand v = **request**, ask (for),
order, expect, claim; = **challenge**,
ask, question, inquire; = **require**,
want, need, involve, call for
≠ **provide** ▷ n = **request**, order;

= **need**, want, call, market, claim
demise n = **failure**, end, fall,
defeat, collapse; (Euphemistic)
= **death**, end, dying, passing,
departure
democracy n = **self-
government**, republic,
commonwealth
demolish v = **knock down**, level,
destroy, dismantle, flatten ≠ **build**
demon n = **evil spirit**, devil, fiend,
goblin, ghoul; = **wizard**, master,
ace (Inf), fiend, beast
demonstrate v = **prove**, show,
indicate, make clear, manifest;
= **show**, express, display, indicate,

demonstration n

demonstrative adj 1 expressing feelings 2 pointing out 3 conclusive **demonstrator** n 1 one who takes part in a public demonstration 2 assistant in laboratory etc.

demoralize v 1 deprive of courage 2 undermine morally

demote v reduce in rank **demotion** n

demur v -murring, -murred 1 make difficulties, object ▷ n 2 demurring

demure adj reserved

den ① n 1 hole of wild beast 2 small room, esp. study

denigrate v belittle

denim n strong cotton fabric

denizen n inhabitant

denote v 1 stand for 2 show

denouement n unravelling of plot

denounce ① v 1 speak violently

against 2 accuse **denunciation** n

dense ① adj 1 thick, compact 2 stupid **density** n, pl -ties

dent ① n/v (make) hollow or mark by blow or pressure

dental adj of teeth or dentistry **dentist** n surgeon who attends to teeth **dentistry** n art of dentist **denture** n set of false teeth

denude v strip, make bare

deny ① v -nying, -nied 1 declare untrue 2 contradict 3 reject 4 refuse to give **denial** n

depart ① v 1 go away 2 start out 3 vary 4 die **departure** n

department ① n 1 division 2 branch **departmental** adj

depend ① v 1 (usu. with on) rely entirely 2 live 3 be contingent **dependable** adj reliable **dependant** n one who relies on another **dependent** adj depending on **dependence, dependency** n

d

───── THESAURUS ─────

exhibit; **= march**, protest, rally, object, parade

den n **= lair**, hole, shelter, cave, haunt; **= study**, retreat, sanctuary, hideaway, sanctum

denounce v **= condemn**, attack, censure, revile, vilify

dense adj **= thick**, heavy, solid, compact, condensed ≠ **thin**; **= heavy**, thick, opaque, impenetrable; **= stupid** (Inf), thick, dull, dumb (Inf), dozy (Brit Inf) ≠ **bright**

dent v **= make a dent in**, press in, gouge, hollow, push in ▷ n **= hollow**, chip, indentation,

depression, impression

deny v **= contradict**, disagree with, rebuff, negate, rebut ≠ **admit**; **= renounce**, reject, retract, repudiate, disown; **= refuse**, forbid, reject, rule out, turn down ≠ **permit**

depart v **= leave**, go, withdraw, retire, disappear ≠ **arrive**; **= deviate**, vary, differ, stray, veer

department n **= section**, office, unit, station, division

depend v **= be determined by**, be based on, be subject to, hang on, rest on; **= count on**, turn to, trust in, bank on, lean on

d

depict ❶ v 1 give picture of
2 describe **depiction** n
deplete ❶ v 1 empty 2 reduce
depletion n
deplore ❶ v 1 lament, regret
2 denounce **deplorable** adj
deploy ❶ v organize (troops) in
battle formation **deployment** n
depopulate v (cause to) be
reduced in population
depopulation n
deport ❶ v expel, banish
deportation n
deportment n behaviour
depose ❶ v 1 remove from office
2 make statement on oath
deposit ❶ v 1 set down 2 give
into safe keeping 3 let fall ▷ n
4 thing deposited 5 money given
in part payment 6 sediment
deposition n 1 statement written
and attested 2 act of deposing or
depositing **depositor** n
depository n

depot ❶ n storehouse
deprecate v express disapproval of
depreciate v 1 (cause to) fall in
value, price 2 belittle
depreciation n
depress ❶ v 1 affect with low
spirits 2 lower **depression** n
1 hollow 2 low spirits 3 low state
of trade
deprive v dispossess **deprivation**
n **deprived** adj lacking adequate
food, care, amenities etc.
depth ❶ n 1 (degree of) deepness
2 deep place 3 intensity
deregulate v remove regulations
or controls from
derelict ❶ adj 1 abandoned
2 falling into ruins **dereliction** n
1 neglect of duty 2 abandonment
deride v treat with contempt,
ridicule **derision** n **derisive** adj
derisory adj
derive v get, come from
derivation n **derivative** adj

———————————— THESAURUS ————————————

depict v = **illustrate**, portray,
picture, paint, outline; = **describe**,
present, represent, outline,
characterize
deplete v = **use up**, reduce, drain,
exhaust, consume ≠ **increase**
deplore v = **disapprove of**,
condemn, object to, denounce,
censure
deploy v = **use**, station, position,
arrange, set out
deport v = **expel**, exile, throw out,
oust, banish
depose v = **oust**, dismiss, displace,
demote, dethrone
deposit n = **down payment**,

security, stake, pledge, instalment;
= **accumulation**, mass, build-up,
layer ▷ v = **put**, place, lay, drop;
= **store**, keep, put, bank, lodge
depot n = **storehouse**, depository,
warehouse
depress v = **sadden**, upset,
distress, discourage, grieve
≠ **cheer**; = **lower**, cut, reduce,
diminish, decrease ≠ **raise**;
= **devalue**, depreciate, cheapen
depth n = **deepness**, drop,
measure, extent; = **insight**,
wisdom, penetration, profundity,
discernment ≠ **superficiality**
derelict adj = **abandoned**,

dermatitis n inflammation of skin

derogatory adj belittling

derv n diesel oil for road vehicles

descant n (Mus) decorative variation to basic melody

descend ❶ v 1 come or go down 2 spring from 3 be transmitted 4 attack **descendant** n person descended from an ancestor **descent** n

describe ❶ v give detailed account of **description** n **descriptive** adj

desecrate v 1 violate sanctity of 2 profane

desert¹ ❶ n uninhabited and barren region

desert² ❶ v 1 abandon, leave 2 run away from service **deserter** n **desertion** n

desert³ n (usu. pl) what is due as reward or punishment

deserve ❶ v show oneself worthy of

design ❶ v 1 sketch 2 plan 3 intend ▷ n 4 sketch 5 plan 6 decorative pattern 7 project **designer** n/adj

designate ❶ v 1 name, appoint ▷ adj 2 appointed but not yet installed

desire ❶ v 1 wish, long for 2 ask for ▷ n 3 longing 4 expressed wish 5 sexual appetite **desirable** n 1 worth having 2 attractive **desirability** n **desirous** adj

desist v cease, stop

desk n writing table

desolate adj 1 uninhabited 2 neglected 3 solitary 4 forlorn ▷ v 5 lay waste 6 overwhelm with grief **desolation** n

despair ❶ v 1 lose hope ▷ n 2 loss of all hope 3 cause of this

---

THESAURUS

---

deserted, ruined, neglected, discarded

descend v = **fall**, drop, sink, go down, plunge ≠ **rise**; = **go down**, come down, walk down, move down, climb down; = **slope**, dip, incline, slant

describe v = **relate**, tell, report, explain, express; = **portray**, depict

desert¹ n = **wilderness**, waste, wilds, wasteland, dry

desert² v = **abandon**, leave, quit, forsake

deserve v = **merit**, warrant, be entitled to, have a right to, rate

design v = **plan**, draw, draft, trace, outline; = **create**, plan, fashion,

propose, invent; = **intend**, mean, plan, aim, purpose ▷ n = **pattern**, form, style, shape, organization; = **plan**, drawing, model, scheme, draft; = **intention**, end, aim, goal, target

designate v = **name**, call, term, style, label; = **choose**, reserve, select, label, flag

desire n = **wish**, want, longing, hope, urge; = **lust**, passion, libido, appetite, lasciviousness ▷ v = **want**, long for, crave, hope for, ache for

despair n = **despondency**, depression, misery, gloom, desperation ▷ v = **lose hope**, give

desperate ⊙ *adj* 1 reckless from despair 2 hopelessly bad **desperately** *adv* **desperation** *n* **desperado** *n* reckless, lawless person

despise ⊙ *v* look down on as inferior **despicable** *adj* base, contemptible, vile

despite ⊙ *prep* in spite of

despoil *v* plunder, rob

despondent *adj* dejected, depressed

despot *n* tyrant, oppressor **despotic** *adj* **despotism** *n*

dessert *n* sweet course, or fruit, served at end of meal

destination ⊙ *n* place one is bound for

destitute *adj* in absolute want

destroy ⊙ *v* 1 ruin 2 put an end to 3 demolish **destroyer** *n* small, swift warship **destructible** *adj* **destruction** *n* ruin **destructive** *adj*

desultory *adj* 1 aimless 2 unmethodical

detach ⊙ *v* unfasten, separate **detachable** *adj* **detached** *adj* 1 standing apart 2 disinterested **detachment** *n* 1 aloofness 2 detaching 3 body of troops on special duty

detail ⊙ *n* 1 particular 2 small or unimportant part 3 treatment of anything item by item 4 soldier assigned for duty ▷ *v* 5 relate in full 6 appoint

detain ⊙ *v* 1 keep under restraint 2 keep waiting **detention** *n*

detect ⊙ *v* find out or discover **detection** *n* **detective** *n* policeman detecting crime **detector** *n*

deter ⊙ *v* -terring, -terred 1 discourage 2 prevent **deterrent** *adj/n*

detergent *n/adj* cleaning (substance)

───── THESAURUS ─────

up, lose heart

desperate *adj* = **grave**, pressing, serious, severe, extreme; = **last-ditch**, daring, furious, risky, frantic

despise *v* = **look down on**, loathe, scorn, detest, revile ≠ **admire**

despite *prep* = **in spite of**, in the face of, regardless of, even with, notwithstanding

destination *n* = **stop**, station, haven, resting-place, terminus

destroy *v* = **ruin**, crush, devastate, wreck, shatter

detach *v* = **separate**, remove, divide, cut off, sever ≠ **attach**

detail *n* = **point**, fact, feature, particular, respect; = **fine point**, particular, nicety, triviality; *(Mil)* = **party**, force, body, duty, squad ▷ *v* = **list**, relate, catalogue, recount, rehearse; = **appoint**, name, choose, commission, select

detain *v* = **hold**, arrest, confine, restrain, imprison; = **delay**, hold up, hamper, hinder, retard

detect *v* = **discover**, find, uncover, track down, unmask; = **notice**, see, spot, note, identify

deter *v* = **discourage**, inhibit, put off, frighten, intimidate

deteriorate ⊙ v become or make worse **deterioration** n

determine ⊙ v 1 decide 2 fix 3 be deciding factor in 4 come to an end 5 come to a decision **determination** n 1 determining 2 resolute conduct 3 resolve **determined** adj resolute

detest v hate, loathe **detestable** adj

dethrone v remove from position of authority

detonate v (cause to) explode **detonation** n **detonator** n

detour n roundabout way

detract v take away (a part) from, diminish **detractor** n

detriment n harm done, loss, damage **detrimental** adj

deuce n 1 card with two spots 2 (Tennis) forty all 3 in exclamatory phrases, the devil

devalue v **-valuing, -valued** reduce in value **devaluation** n

devastate ⊙ v 1 lay waste 2 ravage **devastated** adj

extremely shocked **devastation** n

develop ⊙ v 1 bring to maturity 2 elaborate 3 evolve 4 treat photographic film to bring out image 5 improve or change use of (land) 6 grow to maturer state **developer** n **development** n

deviate v diverge **deviant** n/adj (person) deviating from normal, esp. in sexual practices **deviation** n **devious** adj 1 deceitful 2 roundabout **deviousness** n

device ⊙ n 1 contrivance 2 scheme

devil ⊙ n 1 personified spirit of evil 2 person of great wickedness, cruelty etc. 3 (Inf) fellow 4 (Inf) something difficult or annoying **devilish** adj **devilment** n **devilry** n **devil-may-care** adj happy-go-lucky

devise ⊙ v plan

devoid ⊙ adj (usu. with of) empty

devolve v (cause to) pass on to another **devolution** n devolving

devote ⊙ v give up exclusively (to

d

THESAURUS

deteriorate v = **decline**, worsen, degenerate, slump, go downhill (Inf) ≠ **improve**

determine v = **settle**, learn, establish, discover, find out; = **decide on**, choose, elect, resolve; = **decide**, conclude, resolve, make up your mind

devastate v = **destroy**, ruin, sack, wreck, demolish

develop v = **grow**, advance, progress, mature, evolve; = **establish**, set up, promote, generate, undertake

device n = **gadget**, machine, tool, instrument, implement; = **ploy**, scheme, plan, trick, manoeuvre

devil n = **evil spirit**, demon, fiend; = **brute**, monster, beast, barbarian, fiend; = **person**, individual, soul, creature, thing; = **scamp**, rogue, rascal, scoundrel, scallywag (Inf)

devise v = **work out**, design, construct, invent, conceive

devoid adj (with of) = **lacking in**, without, free from, wanting in, bereft of

devote v = **dedicate**, give,

person, purpose etc.) **devoted** adj loving **devotee** n ardent enthusiast **devotion** n 1 deep affection 2 dedication ▷ pl 3 prayers

devour ❶ v eat greedily

devout ❶ adj deeply religious

dew n moisture from air deposited as small drops at night

dexterity n manual skill **dexterous** adj

diabetes n various disorders characterized by excretion of abnormal amount of urine **diabetic** n/adj

diabolic adj devilish **diabolical** adj (Inf) extremely bad

diadem n crown

diagnosis ❶ n, pl -ses identification of disease from symptoms **diagnose** v

diagonal adj/n (line) from corner to corner

diagram ❶ n drawing, figure, to illustrate something

dial n 1 face of clock etc. 2 plate marked with graduations on which pointer moves 3 numbered disc on front of telephone ▷ v 4 operate telephone

dialect n characteristic speech of district

dialogue ❶ n conversation

dialysis n (Med) filtering of blood through membrane to remove waste products

diameter n (length of) straight line through centre of circle **diametrically** adv completely

diamond n 1 very hard and brilliant precious stone 2 rhomboid figure 3 suit at cards

diaper (US & Canad) n towelling cloth to absorb baby's excrement

diaphragm n muscle between abdomen and chest

diarrhoea n excessive looseness of the bowels

diary ❶ n, pl -ries 1 daily record of events 2 book for this

diatribe n violently bitter verbal attack, denunciation

dice n, pl dice 1 cube with six sides marked one to six for games of chance ▷ v 2 gamble with dice 3 (Cookery) cut vegetables into small cubes

dichotomy n, pl -mies division into two parts

dictate ❶ v 1 say or read for

——————— THESAURUS ———————

commit, apply, reserve

devour v = **eat**, consume, swallow, wolf, gulp

devout adj = **religious**, godly, pious, pure, holy ≠ **irreverent**

diagnosis n = **identification**, discovery, recognition, detection

diagram n = **plan**, figure, drawing, chart, representation

dialogue n = **discussion**,

conference, exchange, debate; = **conversation**, discussion, communication, discourse

diary n = **journal**, chronicle

dictate v = **speak**, say, utter, read out ▷ n = **command**, order, decree, demand, direction; = **principle**, law, rule, standard, code

another to transcribe **2** prescribe
3 impose ▷ n **4** bidding **dictation**
n **dictator** n absolute ruler
dictatorial adj **dictatorship** n

diction n **1** choice and use of
words **2** enunciation

dictionary ⊙ n, pl **-aries** book
listing, alphabetically, words with
meanings etc.

did past tense of DO

die¹ ⊙ v **dying, died 1** cease to live
2 end **3** (Inf) look forward (to)
die-hard n/adj (person) resisting
change

die² n shaped block to form metal in
forge, press etc.

diesel adj **1** pert. to internal-
combustion engine using oil as fuel
▷ n **2** this engine **3** the fuel

diet ⊙ n **1** restricted or regulated
course of feeding **2** kind of food
lived on ▷ v **3** follow a diet, as to
lose weight **dietary** adj

differ ⊙ v **1** be unlike **2** disagree
difference n **1** unlikeness **2** point

of unlikeness **3** disagreement
4 remainder left after subtraction
different adj **differently** adv

differential adj **1** varying with
circumstances ▷ n **2** mechanism
in car etc. allowing back wheels to
revolve at different speeds .
3 difference between two rates of
pay **differentiate** v **1** serve to
distinguish between, make
different **2** discriminate

difficult ⊙ adj **1** requiring effort,
skill etc. **2** not easy **3** obscure
difficulty n **1** difficult task,
problem **2** embarrassment
3 hindrance **4** trouble

diffident adj lacking confidence

diffuse v **1** spread slowly ▷ adj
2 widely spread **3** loose, wordy
diffusion n

dig ⊙ v **digging, dug 1** work with
spade **2** turn up with spade
3 excavate **4** thrust into ▷ n
5 piece of digging **6** thrust **7** jibe
▷ pl **8** (Inf) lodgings

——————————— THESAURUS ———————————

dictionary n = **wordbook**,
vocabulary, glossary, lexicon

die¹ v = **pass away**, expire, perish,
croak (Sl), give up the ghost ≠ **live**;
= **stop**, fail, halt, break down, run
down; = **dwindle**, decline, sink,
fade, diminish ≠ **increase**

diet n = **food**, provisions, fare,
rations, nourishment; = **fast**,
regime, abstinence, regimen ▷ v
= **slim**, fast, lose weight, abstain,
eat sparingly ≠ **overindulge**

differ v = **be dissimilar**, contradict,
contrast with, vary, belie ≠ **accord**;
= **disagree**, clash, dispute, dissent

≠ **agree**

difficult adj = **hard**, tough, taxing,
demanding, challenging ≠ **easy**;
= **problematical**, involved,
complex, complicated, obscure
≠ **simple**; = **troublesome**,
demanding, perverse, fussy,
fastidious ≠ **cooperative**

dig v = **hollow out**, mine, quarry,
excavate, scoop out; = **delve**,
tunnel, burrow; = **search**, hunt,
root, delve, forage ▷ n = **cutting
remark**, crack (Sl), insult, taunt,
sneer; = **poke**, thrust, nudge, prod,
jab

digest ❶ v 1 prepare (food) in stomach etc. for assimilation 2 bring into handy form by summarizing ▷ n 3 methodical summary **digestible** adj **digestion** n **digestive** adj

digit n 1 finger or toe 2 numeral **digital** adj

dignity ❶ n, pl -ties 1 stateliness, gravity 2 worthiness **dignify** v give dignity to **dignitary** n holder of high office

digress v deviate from subject **digression** n

dike n see DYKE

dilapidated adj in ruins

dilate v widen, expand **dilation** n

dilemma ❶ n position offering choice only between unwelcome alternatives

dilettante n, pl -tantes, -tanti 1 person who enjoys fine arts as pastime 2 dabbler

diligent adj hard-working

diligently adv **diligence** n

dill n herb with medicinal seeds

dilute ❶ v reduce (liquid) in strength, esp. by adding water **dilution** n

dim ❶ adj dimmer, dimmest 1 faint, not bright 2 mentally dull 3 unfavourable ▷ v 4 make, grow dim **dimly** adv

dime n (US) 10-cent piece

dimension ❶ n measurement, size

diminish ❶ v lessen **diminutive** adj very small

diminuendo adj/adv (Mus) (of sound) dying away

dimple n small hollow in surface of skin, esp. of cheek

din ❶ n 1 continuous roar of confused noises ▷ v 2 ram (fact, opinion etc.) into

dine ❶ v eat dinner **diner** n

dinghy n, pl -ghies 1 small open boat 2 collapsible rubber boat

---

THESAURUS

digest v = **ingest**, absorb, incorporate, dissolve, assimilate; = **take in**, absorb, grasp, soak up ▷ n = **summary**, résumé, abstract, epitome, synopsis

dignity n = **decorum**, gravity, majesty, grandeur, respectability; = **self-importance**, pride, self-esteem, self-respect

dilemma n = **predicament**, problem, difficulty, spot (Inf), mess

dilute v = **water down**, thin (out), weaken, adulterate, make thinner ≠ **condense**; = **reduce**, weaken, diminish, temper, decrease ≠ **intensify**

dim adj = **poorly lit**, dark, gloomy, murky, shady; = **cloudy**, grey, gloomy, dismal, overcast ≠ **bright**; = **unclear**, obscured, faint, blurred, fuzzy ≠ **distinct** ▷ v = **turn down**, fade, dull; = **grow** or **become faint**, fade, dull, grow or become dim

dimension n = **aspect**, side, feature, angle, facet

diminish v = **decrease**, decline, lessen, shrink, dwindle ≠ **grow**

din n = **noise**, row, racket, crash, clamour ≠ **silence**

dine v = **eat**, lunch, feast, sup

dingo *n, pl* **-goes** Aust. wild dog
dingy *adj* **-gier, -giest**
  dirty-looking, dull
dinner ❶ *n* **1** chief meal of the day
  2 official banquet
dinosaur *n* extinct reptile, often of
  gigantic size
dint *n* **by dint of** by means of
diocese *n* district, jurisdiction of
  bishop
diode *n* (*Electronics*) device for
  converting alternating current to
  direct current
dip ❶ *v* **dipping, dipped 1** plunge
  or be plunged partly or for a
  moment into liquid **2** take up in
  ladle, bucket etc. **3** direct
  headlights of vehicle downwards
  4 go down **5** slope downwards ▷ *n*
  6 act of dipping **7** bathe
  8 downward slope **9** hollow
diphtheria *n* infectious
  disease causing breathing
  difficulties
diphthong *n* union of two vowel
  sounds

diploma *n* document vouching for
  person's proficiency
diplomacy ❶ *n* **1** management
  of international relations **2** tactful
  dealing **diplomat** *n*
  diplomatic *adj*
dipper *n* **1** ladle, scoop **2** bird
  (water ouzel)
dipsomania *n* uncontrollable
  craving for alcohol **dipsomaniac**
  n/adj
dire ❶ *adj* **1** terrible **2** urgent
direct ❶ *v* **1** control, manage,
  order **2** point out the way **3** aim
  ▷ *adj* **4** frank **5** straight
  6 immediate **7** lineal **direction** *n*
  1 directing **2** aim **3** instruction
  directive *adj/n* **directly** *adj*
  directness *n* **director** *n* **1** one
  who directs, esp. a film **2** member
  of board managing company
  directorial *adj* **directorship** *n*
  directory *n* book of names,
  addresses, streets etc.
dirge *n* song of mourning
dirk *n* short dagger

dinner *n* = **meal**, main meal,
  spread (*Inf*), repast
dip *v* = **plunge**, immerse, bathe,
  duck, douse; = **drop (down)**, fall,
  lower, sink, descend ▷ *n* = **plunge**,
  ducking, soaking, drenching,
  immersion; = **nod**, drop, lowering,
  slump, sag; = **hollow**, hole,
  depression, pit, basin
diplomacy *n* = **statesmanship**,
  statecraft, international
  negotiation; = **tact**, skill,
  sensitivity, craft, discretion
  ≠ **tactlessness**

dire *adj* = **desperate**, pressing,
  critical, terrible, crucial
direct *adj* = **quickest**, shortest;
  = **first-hand**, personal, immediate
  ≠ **indirect** ▷ *v* = **aim**, point,
  level, train, focus; = **guide**, show,
  lead, point the way, point in the
  direction of; = **control**, run,
  manage, lead, guide; = **order**,
  command, instruct, charge,
  demand
direction *n* = **way**, course, line,
  road, track; = **management**,
  control, charge, administration,

d

dirt ⊙ n **1** filth **2** soil **3** obscene material **dirty** adj **1** unclean **2** obscene **3** unfair **4** dishonest

dis- comb. form **1** negation, opposition, deprivation **2** in many verbs indicates undoing of the action of simple verb

disable ⊙ v **1** make unable **2** cripple, maim **disabled** adj **disability** n, pl **-ties**

disabuse v **1** undeceive, disillusion **2** free from error

disadvantage ⊙ n **1** drawback **2** hindrance ▷ v **3** handicap **disadvantaged** adj deprived, discriminated against **disadvantageous** adj

disaffected adj ill-disposed **disaffection** n

disagree ⊙ v **-greeing, -greed 1** be at variance **2** conflict **3** (of food etc.) have bad effect on **disagreeable** adj **disagreement** n

disallow v reject as invalid

disappear ⊙ v **1** cease to be visible **2** cease to exist **disappearance** n

disappoint ⊙ v fail to fulfil (hope) **disappointment** n

disarm ⊙ v **1** deprive of weapons **2** win over **disarming** adj removing hostility, suspicion **disarmament** n

disarray ⊙ v **1** throw into disorder ▷ n **2** disorderliness

disaster ⊙ n sudden or great misfortune **disastrous** adj

disband v (cause to) cease to function as a group

disbelieve v reject as false

disburse v pay out money

disc n **1** thin, flat, circular object **2** record **disc jockey** announcer playing records

discard ⊙ v **1** reject **2** cast off

discern v **1** make out **2** distinguish **discernible** adj **discerning** adj discriminating

━━━━━━━━━━━━━ THESAURUS ━━━━━━━━━━

leadership

dirt n = **filth**, muck, grime, dust, mud; = **soil**, ground, earth, clay, turf

disable v = **handicap**, cripple, damage, paralyse, impair

disadvantage n = **drawback**, trouble, handicap, nuisance, snag ≠ **advantage**

disagree v = **differ (in opinion)**, argue, clash, dispute, dissent ≠ **agree**; = **make ill**, upset, sicken, trouble, hurt

disappear v = **vanish**, recede, evanesce ≠ **appear**; = **pass**, fade

away, bolt, run away, take off (Inf)

disappoint v = **let down**, dismay, fail, disillusion, dishearten

disarm v = **demilitarize**, disband, demobilize, deactivate; = **win over**, persuade

disarray n = **confusion**, disorder, indiscipline, disunity, disorganization ≠ **order**; = **untidiness**, mess, chaos, muddle, clutter ≠ **tidiness**

disaster n = **catastrophe**, trouble, tragedy, ruin, misfortune

discard v = **get rid of**, drop, throw

discharge ⊕ v 1 release
2 dismiss 3 emit 4 perform
(duties), fulfil (obligations) 5 fire
off 6 unload 7 pay ▷ n
8 discharging 9 being discharged
disciple n follower of a teacher
discipline ⊕ n 1 training that
produces orderliness, obedience,
self-control 2 system of rules etc.
3 punishment ▷ v 4 train
5 punish **disciplinarian** n person
practising strict discipline
disciplinary adj
disclaim v deny, renounce
disclaimer n
disclose ⊕ v make known
disclosure n
disco n, pl **-cos** club etc. for
dancing to recorded music

discolour v stain
discomfit v embarrass
discomfort ⊕ n inconvenience
disconcert v ruffle, upset
disconnect v 1 break connection
2 stop supply of electricity, gas etc.
disconsolate adj very unhappy
discontent ⊕ n lack of
contentment
discontinue v bring to an end
discord n 1 strife 2 disagreement
of sounds **discordant** adj
discount ⊕ v 1 reject as
unsuitable 2 deduct from usual
price ▷ n 3 amount deducted from
cost
discourse ⊕ n 1 conversation
2 speech ▷ v 3 speak, converse
discourteous adj showing bad

d

away or out, reject, abandon
≠ **keep**
discharge v = **release**, free, clear,
liberate, pardon; = **dismiss**, sack
(Inf), fire (Inf), remove, expel;
= **carry out**, perform, fulfil,
accomplish, do; = **pay**, meet, clear,
settle, square (up); = **pour forth**,
release, leak, emit, dispense; = **fire**,
shoot, set off, explode, let off ▷ n
= **release**, liberation, clearance,
pardon, acquittal; = **dismissal**,
notice, removal, the boot (Sl),
expulsion; = **emission**, ooze,
secretion, excretion, pus; = **firing**,
report, shot, blast, burst
discipline n = **control**, authority,
regulation, supervision, orderliness;
= **punishment**, penalty, correction,
chastening, chastisement ▷ v
= **punish**, correct, reprimand,

castigate, chastise; = **train**,
educate
disclose v = **make known**,
reveal, publish, relate, broadcast
≠ **keep secret**; = **show**,
reveal, expose, unveil, uncover
≠ **hide**
discomfort n ≠ **comfort**;
= **uneasiness**, worry, anxiety,
doubt, distress ≠ **reassurance**
discontent n = **dissatisfaction**,
unhappiness, displeasure, regret,
envy
discount n = **deduction**, cut,
reduction, concession, rebate ▷ v
= **mark down**, reduce, lower;
= **disregard**, reject, ignore,
overlook, discard
discourse n = **conversation**, talk,
discussion, speech,
communication; = **speech**, essay,

d

manners; impolite

discover ❶ v 1 (be the first to) find
2 learn about for first time
discovery n, pl -eries

discredit ❶ v 1 damage
reputation of 2 cast doubt on
3 reject as untrue ▷ n 4 disgrace
5 doubt

discreet ❶ adj prudent,
circumspect

discrepancy ❶ n, pl -cies
variation, as between figures

discrete adj separate, distinct

discretion ❶ n 1 quality of being
discreet 2 freedom to act as one
chooses **discretionary** adj

discriminate ❶ v 1 show
prejudice 2 distinguish between
discriminating adj showing good
taste **discrimination** n

discursive adj rambling

discus n disc-shaped object thrown
in athletic competition

discuss ❶ v 1 exchange opinions
about 2 debate **discussion** n

disdain ❶ n/v scorn **disdainful**
adj

disease ❶ n illness

disembark v land from ship etc.

disembodied adj (of spirit)
released from bodily form

disembowel v -elling, -elled
remove the entrails of

disenchanted adj disillusioned
disenchantment n

disengage v release

disfavour n disapproval

disfigure v mar appearance of

disgrace ❶ n 1 shame, dishonour
▷ v 2 bring shame upon
disgraceful adj
disgracefully adv

— THESAURUS —

lecture, sermon, treatise
discover v = **find out**, learn,
notice, realize, recognize; = **find**,
come across, uncover, unearth,
turn up
discredit v = **disgrace**, shame,
smear, humiliate, taint ≠ **honour**;
= **dispute**, question, challenge,
deny, reject ▷ n = **disgrace**,
scandal, shame, disrepute, stigma
≠ **honour**
discreet adj = **tactful**, diplomatic,
guarded, careful, cautious
≠ **tactless**
discrepancy n = **disagreement**,
difference, variation, conflict,
contradiction
discretion n = **tact**,
consideration, caution, diplomacy,

prudence ≠ **tactlessness**;
= **choice**, will, pleasure, preference,
inclination
discriminate v = **differentiate**,
distinguish, separate, tell the
difference, draw a distinction
discuss v = **talk about**,
consider, debate, examine, argue
about
disdain n = **contempt**, scorn,
arrogance, derision, haughtiness
▷ v = **scorn**, reject, slight,
disregard, spurn
disease n = **illness**, condition,
complaint, infection, disorder
disgrace n = **shame**, degradation,
disrepute, ignominy, dishonour
≠ **honour**; = **scandal**, stain,
stigma, blot, blemish ▷ v = **shame**,

disgruntled ⊙ *adj* 1 vexed 2 put out

disguise ⊙ *v* 1 change appearance of, make unrecognizable 2 conceal ▷ *n* 3 device to conceal identity

disgust ⊙ *n/v* (affect with) violent distaste, loathing

dish ⊙ *n* 1 shallow vessel for food 2 portion or variety of food ▷ *v* 3 serve (up)

dishearten *v* weaken hope, enthusiasm etc.

dishevelled *adj* untidy

dishonest *adj* not honest or fair **dishonesty** *n*

dishonour *v* 1 treat with disrespect ▷ *n* 2 lack of respect 3 shame, disgrace **dishonourable** *adj*

disillusion *v* 1 destroy ideals of ▷ *n* 2 disenchantment

disinformation *n* false information intended to mislead

disingenuous *adj* not sincere

disinherit *v* deprive of inheritance

disintegrate ⊙ *v* fall to pieces

disinterested *adj* free from bias or partiality

disk *n* computer storage device

dislike ⊙ *v* 1 consider unpleasant or disagreeable ▷ *n* 2 feeling of not liking

dislocate *v* put out of joint **dislocation** *n*

dislodge *v* drive out from previous position

disloyal *adj* deserting one's allegiance **disloyalty** *n*

dismal ⊙ *adj* depressing

dismantle ⊙ *v* take apart

dismay ⊙ *v* 1 dishearten, daunt ▷ *n* 2 consternation

dismember *v* tear limb from limb

dismiss ⊙ *v* 1 discharge from employment 2 send away 3 reject **dismissal** *n* **dismissive** *adj* scornful

---

THESAURUS

---

humiliate, discredit, degrade, taint ≠ **honour**

disgruntled *adj* = **discontented**, dissatisfied, annoyed, irritated, put out

disguise *n* = **costume**, mask, camouflage ▷ *v* = **hide**, cover, conceal, screen, mask

disgust *n* = **loathing**, revulsion, hatred, dislike, nausea ≠ **liking** ▷ *v* = **sicken**, offend, revolt, put off, repel ≠ **delight**

dish *n* = **bowl**, plate, platter, salver; = **food**, fare, recipe,

disintegrate *v* = **break up**, crumble, fall apart, separate,

shatter

dislike *v* = **hate**, object to, loathe, despise, disapprove of ≠ **like**

dismal *adj* = **bad**, awful, dreadful, rotten *(Inf)*, terrible

dismantle *v* = **take apart**, strip, demolish, disassemble, take to pieces *or* bits

dismay *n* = **alarm**, fear, horror, anxiety, dread ▷ *v* = **alarm**, frighten, scare, panic, distress

dismiss *v* = **reject**, disregard; = **banish**, dispel, discard, set aside, cast out; = **sack**, fire *(Inf)*, remove *(Inf)*, axe *(Inf)*, discharge

d

dismount v get off horse, bicycle
disobey v refuse or fail to obey
disobedience n **disobedient** adj
disorder ❶ n 1 confusion
2 ailment **disorderly** adj
1 disorganized 2 unruly
disorientate, disorient v
cause (someone) to lose his
bearings, confuse
disorientation n
disown v refuse to acknowledge
disparage v belittle
dispassionate adj impartial
dispatch, despatch ❶ v 1 send
off promptly 2 finish off ▷ n
3 speed 4 official message
dispel ❶ v -pelling, -pelled drive
away
dispense ❶ v 1 deal out 2 make
up (medicine) 3 administer
(justice) **dispensable** adj

dispensary n, pl -saries place
where medicine is made up
dispensation n **dispense with**
1 do away with 2 manage
without
disperse ❶ v scatter **dispersal** n
displace ❶ v 1 move from its
place 2 take place of
displacement n
display ❶ v/n show
displease v 1 offend 2 annoy
displeasure n
dispose ❶ v 1 arrange
2 distribute 3 deal with
disposable adj designed to be
thrown away after use **disposal** n
disposition n 1 temperament
2 arrangement **dispose of** sell,
get rid of
disprove v show to be incorrect
dispute ❶ v 1 debate, discuss

— THESAURUS —

disorder n = **illness**, disease,
complaint, condition, sickness;
= **untidiness**, mess, confusion,
chaos, muddle; = **disturbance**, riot,
turmoil, unrest, uproar
dispatch, despatch v = **send**,
consign; = **kill**, murder, destroy,
execute, slaughter; = **carry out**,
perform, fulfil, effect, finish ▷ n
= **message**, news, report, story,
account
dispel v = **drive away**, dismiss,
eliminate, expel, disperse
dispense v = **distribute**, assign,
allocate, allot, dole out; = **prepare**,
measure, supply, mix;
= **administer**, operate, carry out,
implement, enforce
disperse v = **scatter**, spread,

distribute, strew, diffuse; = **break
up**, separate, scatter, dissolve,
disband ≠ **gather**
displace v = **replace**, succeed,
supersede, oust, usurp (Inf);
= **move**, shift, disturb, budge,
misplace
display v = **show**, present, exhibit,
put on view ≠ **conceal** ▷ n
= **proof**, exhibition, demonstration,
evidence, expression; = **exhibition**,
show, demonstration,
presentation, array
dispose v = **arrange**, put, place,
group, order
dispute n = **disagreement**,
conflict, argument, dissent,
altercation ▷ v = **contest**,
question, challenge, deny, doubt;

2 call into question **3** contest ▷ n
4 disagreement **disputable** adj

disqualify ❶ v make ineligible
disqualification n

disquiet n anxiety, uneasiness

disregard ❶ v **1** ignore ▷ n **2** lack
of attention, respect

disrepair n state of bad repair,
neglect

disrepute n bad reputation
disreputable adj

disrespect n lack of respect
disrespectful adj

disrupt ❶ v throw into disorder
disruption n **disruptive** adj

dissatisfied ❶ adj not pleased,
disappointed **dissatisfaction** n

dissect v cut up (body) for detailed
examination

dissemble v pretend, disguise

disseminate v spread abroad

dissent ❶ v **1** differ in opinion ▷ n
2 such difference **dissension** n

dissertation n written thesis

disservice n ill turn, wrong

dissident ❶ n/adj (one) not in
agreement, esp. with government

dissimilar adj not alike,
different

dissipate v **1** scatter **2** waste,
squander **dissipated** adj
dissipation n

dissociate v separate, sever

dissolute adj lax in morals

dissolution n **1** break up
2 termination

dissolve ❶ v **1** absorb or melt in
fluid **2** annul **3** disappear
4 scatter **dissolvable, dissoluble**
adj

dissuade v advise to refrain,
persuade not to

distance ❶ n **1** amount of space
between two things **2** remoteness
3 aloofness **distant** adj

distaste n dislike **distasteful** adj

distemper n **1** disease of dogs
2 paint

distend v swell out **distension** n

distil v -tilling, -tilled **1** vaporize
and recondense a liquid **2** purify
distillation n **distiller** n maker of
alcoholic drinks **distillery** n, pl
-leries

d

— THESAURUS —

= **argue**, fight, clash, disagree, fall
out (Inf)

disqualify v = **ban**, rule out,
prohibit, preclude, debar

disregard v = **ignore**, discount,
overlook, neglect, pass over ≠ **pay
attention to**

disrupt v = **interrupt**, stop, upset,
hold up, interfere with

dissatisfied adj = **discontented**,
frustrated, unhappy, disappointed,
fed up ≠ **satisfied**

dissent n = **disagreement**,

opposition, protest, resistance,
refusal ≠ **assent**

dissident n = **protester**, rebel,
dissenter, demonstrator, agitator
▷ adj = **dissenting**, disagreeing,
nonconformist, heterodox

dissolve v = **melt**, soften, thaw,
liquefy, deliquesce; = **end**, suspend,
break up, wind up, terminate

distance n = **space**, length,
extent, range, stretch; = **aloofness**,
reserve, detachment, restraint,
stiffness

distinct ❶ *adj* **1** easily seen **2** definite **3** separate **distinctly** *adv* **distinction** *n* **1** point of difference **2** act of distinguishing **3** repute, high honour **distinctive** *adj* characteristic

distinguish ❶ *v* **1** make difference in **2** recognize **3** honour **4** (usu. with *between*) draw distinction, grasp difference **distinguishable** *adj* **distinguished** *adj*

distort ❶ *v* **1** put out of shape **2** misrepresent **distortion** *n*

distract ❶ *v* **1** draw attention away **2** divert **3** perplex, drive mad **distraction** *n* **1** agitation **2** amusement

distraught ❶ *adj* frantic, distracted

distress ❶ *n* **1** trouble, pain ▷ *v* **2** afflict

distribute ❶ *v* **1** deal out **2** spread **distribution** *n* **distributor** *n*

district ❶ *n* **1** region, locality **2** portion of territory

distrust ❶ *v* **1** regard as untrustworthy ▷ *n* **2** suspicion, doubt

disturb ❶ *v* **1** intrude on **2** trouble, agitate, unsettle **disturbance** *n*

disuse *n* state of being no longer used **disused** *adj*

ditch ❶ *n* **1** long narrow hollow dug in ground for drainage etc. ▷ *v* **2** (*Inf*) abandon

dither *v* **1** be uncertain or indecisive ▷ *n* **2** this state

— THESAURUS —

distinct *adj* = **different**, individual, separate, discrete, unconnected ≠ **similar**; = **striking**, dramatic, outstanding, noticeable, well-defined

distinguish *v* = **differentiate**, determine, separate, discriminate, decide; = **characterize**, mark, separate, single out, set apart; = **make out**, recognize, perceive, know, see

distort *v* = **misrepresent**, twist, bias, disguise, pervert; = **deform**, bend, twist, warp, buckle

distract *v* = **divert**, sidetrack, draw away, turn aside, lead astray; = **amuse**, occupy, entertain, beguile, engross

distraught *adj* = **frantic**, desperate, distressed, distracted,

worked-up

distress *n* = **suffering**, pain, worry, grief, misery; = **need**, trouble, difficulties, poverty, hard times ▷ *v* = **upset**, worry, trouble, disturb, grieve

distribute *v* = **hand out**, pass round; = **circulate**, deliver, convey

district *n* = **area**, region, sector, quarter, parish

distrust *v* = **suspect**, doubt, be wary of, mistrust, disbelieve ≠ **trust** ▷ *n* = **suspicion**, question, doubt, disbelief, scepticism ≠ **trust**

disturb *v* = **interrupt**, trouble, bother, plague, disrupt; = **upset**, concern, worry, trouble, alarm ≠ **calm**; = **muddle**, disorder, mix up, mess up, jumble up

ditch *n* = **channel**, drain, trench,

DICTIONARY

ditto *n, pl* **-tos** the same
ditty *n, pl* **-ties** simple song
divan *n* bed, couch without back or head
dive ❶ *v* **diving, dived** 1 plunge under surface of water 2 descend suddenly 3 go deep down into ▷ *n* 4 act of diving 5 (*Sl*) disreputable bar or club **diver** *n*
diverge *v* 1 get farther apart 2 separate
diverse ❶ *adj* different, varied **diversify** *v* **-fying, -fied** make varied **diversity** *n, pl* **-ties**
divert ❶ *v* 1 turn aside 2 amuse **diversion** *n*
divide ❶ *v* 1 make into parts, split up 2 distribute, share 3 become separated ▷ *n* 4 watershed **dividend** *n* share of profits
divine ❶ *adj* 1 of, pert. to God

2 sacred ▷ *v* 3 guess 4 predict
divinity *n* 1 being divine 2 study of theology
division ❶ *n* 1 act of dividing 2 part of whole 3 barrier 4 section 5 difference in opinion etc. 6 (*Maths*) method of finding how many times one number is contained in another 7 army unit **divisible** *adj* **divisive** *adj* causing disagreement
divorce ❶ *n/v* 1 (make) legal dissolution of marriage 2 split **divorcée** *n* divorced person
divulge *v* reveal
DIY do-it-yourself
dizzy ❶ *adj* **-zier, -ziest** feeling dazed, unsteady **dizziness** *n*
DJ disc jockey
DNA *n abbrev.* for deoxyribonucleic acid, main constituent of the chromosomes of all organisms

THESAURUS

dyke, furrow ▷ *v* (*Sl*) = **get rid of**, dump (*Inf*), scrap, discard, dispose of
dive *v* = **plunge**, drop, duck, dip, descend ▷ *n* = **plunge**, spring, jump, leap, lunge
diverse *adj* = **various**, mixed, varied, assorted, miscellaneous; = **different**, unlike, varying, separate, distinct
divert *v* = **redirect**, switch, avert, deflect, deviate; = **distract**, sidetrack, lead astray, draw or lead away from; = **entertain**, delight, amuse, please, charm
divide *v* (*sometimes with* up) = **share**, distribute, allocate, dispense, allot; = **split**, break up, come between, estrange, cause to disagree

divine *adj* = **heavenly**, spiritual, holy, immortal, supernatural; = **sacred**, religious, holy, spiritual, blessed ▷ *v* = **guess**, suppose, perceive, discern, infer
division *n* = **separation**, dividing, splitting up, partition, cutting up; = **sharing**, distribution, assignment, rationing; = **disagreement**, split, rift, rupture, abyss ≠ unity; = **department**, group, branch
divorce *n* = **separation**, split, break-up, parting, split-up ▷ *v* = **separate**, split up, part company, dissolve your marriage
dizzy *adj* = **giddy**, faint, light-headed, swimming, reeling; = **confused**, dazzled, at sea,

do v **does, doing, did, done**
1 perform, effect, finish **2** work at
3 solve **4** suit **5** provide **6** (Sl)
cheat **7** act **8** fare **9** suffice
10 makes negative and
interrogative sentences and
expresses emphasis ▷ n **11** (Inf)
celebration **do away with**
destroy **do up 1** fasten
2 renovate

dob in v **dobbing, dobbed** (Aust &
NZ, Inf) **1** inform against
2 contribute to a fund

Doberman pinscher,
Doberman large black-and-tan
dog

docile adj willing to obey,
submissive **docility** n

dock¹ ❶ n **1** artificial enclosure for
loading or repairing ships ▷ v **2** put
or go into dock **docker** n
dockyard n

dock² ❶ n **1** solid part of tail
2 stump ▷ v **3** cut short **4** deduct
(an amount) from

dock³ n enclosure in criminal court
for prisoner

dock⁴ n coarse weed

docket n piece of paper sent with
package etc.

doctor ❶ n **1** medical practitioner
2 one holding university's highest
degree ▷ v **3** treat medically
4 repair **5** falsify (accounts etc.)

doctrine ❶ n **1** what is taught
2 belief, dogma **doctrinaire** adj
stubbornly insistent about applying
theories

document ❶ n **1** piece of paper
etc. providing information ▷ v
2 furnish with proofs

documentary adj/n, pl **-ries** (of)
type of film dealing with real life

dodder v totter, as with age

dodge ❶ v **1** (attempt to) avoid by
moving quickly **2** evade ▷ n
3 trick, act of dodging **dodgy** adj
dodgier, dodgiest (Inf)
untrustworthy

Dodgem® n car used for bumping
other cars in rink at funfair

dodo n, pl **dodos, dodoes** large
extinct bird

doe n female of deer, hare, rabbit

does third person sing. of DO

doff v take off

——————— THESAURUS ———————

bewildered, muddled
dock¹ n = **port**, haven, harbour,
pier, wharf ▷ v = **moor**, land,
anchor, put in, tie up; (of spacecraft)
= **link up**, unite, join, couple,
rendezvous

dock² v = **cut**, reduce, decrease,
diminish, lessen ≠ **increase**;
= **deduct**, subtract

doctor n = **physician**, medic (Inf),
general practitioner, medical
practitioner, G.P. ▷ v = **change**,

alter, interfere with, disguise,
pervert; = **add to**, spike, cut, mix
something with something, dilute

doctrine n = **teaching**, principle,
belief, opinion, conviction

document n = **paper**, form,
certificate, report, record ▷ v
= **support**, certify, verify, detail,
validate

dodge v = **duck**, dart, swerve,
sidestep, shoot; = **evade**, avoid,
escape, get away from, elude

dog ❶ n **1** domesticated carnivorous four-legged mammal **2** male of wolf, fox and other animals **3** person (in contempt, abuse or playfully) ▷ v **4** follow closely **dogged** adj persistent, tenacious **dog-ear** n turned-down corner of page in book **dog-end** n **1** (Inf) cigarette end **2** rejected piece of anything **dogfight** n **1** close combat between fighter aircraft **2** rough fight **dogleg** n sharp bend **dogsbody** n (Inf) one carrying out menial tasks

doggerel n trivial verse

dogma n article of belief **dogmatic** adj asserting opinions with arrogance

doily n, pl **-lies** small lacy mat to place under cake, dish etc.

doldrums pl n **1** state of depression **2** region of light winds and calms near the equator

dole n (Inf) **1** payment made to unemployed ▷ v **2** (usu. with out) distribute

doleful adj dreary, mournful

doll n child's toy image of human being

dollar n standard monetary unit of many countries, esp. USA

dollop n (Inf) semisolid lump

dolly n, pl **-lies 1** doll **2** wheeled support for film, TV camera

dolphin n sea mammal with beaklike snout

domain n **1** lands held or ruled over **2** sphere of influence

dome n **1** rounded roof **2** something of this shape

domestic ❶ adj **1** of, in the home **2** home-loving **3** (of animals) tamed **4** of, in one's own country ▷ n **5** house servant **domesticate** v tame

domicile n person's regular place of abode

dominate ❶ v **1** rule, control **2** (of heights) overlook **3** be most influential **dominance** n **dominant** adj **domination** n **domineering** adj imperious

dominion n **1** sovereignty **2** rule **3** territory of government

don¹ ❶ v **donning, donned** put on (clothes)

don² n **1** fellow or tutor of college

▷ n = **trick**, scheme, ploy, trap, device

dog n = **hound**, canine, pooch (Sl), cur, man's best friend ▷ v = **plague**, follow, trouble, haunt, hound; = **pursue**, follow, track, chase, trail

domestic adj = **home**, internal, native, indigenous; = **household**, home, family, private; = **home-loving**, homely, housewifely, stay-at-home, domesticated; = **domesticated**, trained, tame, pet, house-trained ▷ n = **servant**, help, maid, daily, char (Inf)

dominate v = **control**, rule, direct, govern, monopolize; = **tower above**, overlook, survey, stand over, loom over

don¹ v = **put on**, get into, dress in, pull on, change into

2 Spanish title, Sir
donate ❶ v give **donation** n
  donor n
done past participle of DO
donkey n ass
doodle v/n scribble
doom ❶ n **1** fate **2** ruin **3** judicial
  sentence ▷ v **4** condemn
  5 destine **doomsday** n **1** day of
  Last Judgment **2** dreaded day
door ❶ n hinged barrier to close
  entrance **doorway** n
dope ❶ n **1** narcotic drug **2** (Inf)
  stupid person ▷ v **3** drug **dopey,**
  dopy adj
dormant adj **1** not active
  2 sleeping
dormitory n, pl **-ries** sleeping
  room with many beds
dormouse n, pl **-mice** small
  hibernating mouselike rodent
dorp n (S Afr) small town
dorsal adj of, on back
dose ❶ n **1** amount (of drug etc.)
  ▷ v **2** give doses to **dosage** n
dossier n set of papers on
  particular subject

dot ❶ n **1** small spot, mark ▷ v
  2 mark with dots **3** sprinkle
dote v **dote on** love to an
  excessive degree **dotage** n
  senility
double ❶ adj **1** of two parts, layers
  etc. **2** twice as much or many
  3 designed for two users ▷ adv
  4 twice **5** to twice the amount or
  extent **6** in a pair ▷ n **7** person or
  thing exactly like another
  8 quantity twice as much as
  another **9** sharp turn **10** running
  pace ▷ v **11** make, become double
  12 increase twofold **13** fold in two
  14 turn sharply **doubly** adv
  double bass lowest member of
  violin family **double-cross** v
  betray
doubt ❶ v **1** suspect **2** hesitate to
  believe **3** call in question ▷ n
  4 (state of) uncertainty **doubtful**
  adj **doubtless** adv **1** certainly
  2 presumably
dough n **1** flour or meal kneaded
  with water **2** (Sl) money
  doughnut n sweetened and fried

——————— THESAURUS ———————

donate v = **give**, present,
  contribute, grant, subscribe
doom n = **destruction**, ruin,
  catastrophe, downfall ▷ v
  = **condemn**, sentence, consign,
  destine
door n = **opening**, entry, entrance,
  exit, doorway
dope n (Sl) = **drugs**, narcotics,
  opiates; (Inf) = **idiot**, fool, twit (Inf,
  chiefly Brit), dunce, simpleton (Inf)
  ▷ v = **drug**, knock out, sedate,
  stupefy, anaesthetize

dose n = **measure**, amount,
  allowance, portion,
  prescription
dot n = **spot**, point, mark, fleck, jot
  ▷ v = **spot**, stud, fleck, speckle
double adj = **dual**, enigmatic,
  twofold ▷ v = **multiply by two**,
  duplicate, increase twofold,
  enlarge, increase twofold ▷ n
  = **twin**, lookalike, spitting image,
  clone, replica (Inf)
doubt n = **uncertainty**, confusion,
  hesitation, suspense, indecision

piece of dough

doughty *adj* **-tier, -tiest** hardy, resolute

dour *adj* grim, severe

douse *v* **1** thrust into water **2** extinguish (light)

dove *n* bird of pigeon family **dovetail** *v* fit closely, neatly together

dowager *n* widow with title or property from husband

dowdy *adj* **-dier, -diest** shabbily dressed

dowel *n* wooden, metal peg

dowry *n, pl* **-ries** property wife brings to husband

down¹ ❶ *adv* **1** to, in, or towards, lower position **2** (of payment) on the spot ▷ *prep* **3** from higher to lower part of **4** along ▷ *adj* **5** depressed ▷ *v* **6** knock, pull, push down **7** (*Inf*) drink **downward** *adj/adv* **downwards** *adv* **downbeat** *adj* (*Inf*) gloomy **downcast** *adj* **1** dejected **2** looking down **downfall** *n* sudden loss of position **downpour** *n* heavy fall of rain **downright** *adj* **1** straightforward ▷ *adv* **2** quite, thoroughly **down-and-out** *adj/n* destitute, homeless (person)

down² *n* **1** soft underfeathers, hair **2** fluff **downy** *adj*

downs *pl n* open high land

downtown (*US, Canad and NZ*) *n* **1** the central or lower part of a city, especially the main commercial area ▷ *adv* **2** towards, to, or into this area

doyen *n* senior, respected member of group

doze *v/n* sleep, nap **dozy** *adj* **dozier, doziest**

dozen *n* (set of) twelve

drab *adj* **drabber, drabbest** dull, monotonous

draconian *adj* very harsh, cruel

draft¹ ❶ *n* **1** sketch **2** rough copy of document **3** order for money **4** detachment of troops ▷ *v* **5** make sketch of **6** make rough copy of **7** send detached party

draft² *v* (*US*) select for compulsory military service

drag ❶ *v* **dragging, dragged 1** pull along with difficulty **2** trail **3** sweep with net **4** protract **5** lag, trail **6** be tediously protracted ▷ *n* **7** check on progress **8** checked motion

dragon *n* mythical fire-breathing monster **dragonfly** *n* long-bodied insect with gauzy wings

THESAURUS

≠ certainty ▷ *v* = **be uncertain**, be sceptical, be dubious; = **waver**, hesitate, vacillate, fluctuate

down¹ *adj* = **depressed**, low, sad, unhappy, discouraged ▷ *v* (*Inf*) = **swallow**, drink (down), drain, gulp (down), put away

draft¹ *n* = **outline**, plan, sketch, version, rough; = **money order**, bill (of exchange), cheque, postal order ▷ *v* = **outline**, write, plan, produce, create

drag *v* = **pull**, draw, haul, trail, tow ▷ *n* (*Sl*) = **nuisance**, pain (*Inf*), bore, bother, pest

dragoon n 1 cavalryman ▷ v 2 coerce

drain ⊕ v 1 draw off (liquid) by pipes, ditches etc. 2 dry 3 empty, exhaust 4 flow off or away ▷ n 5 channel 6 sewer 7 depletion 8 strain **drainage** n

drake n male duck

dram n small draught of strong drink

drama ⊕ n 1 stage play 2 art or literature of plays 3 playlike series of events **dramatic** adj 1 of drama 2 striking or effective **dramatist** n writer of plays **dramatize** v adapt for acting

drape ⊕ v cover, adorn with cloth **draper** n dealer in cloth, linen etc. **drapery** n, pl **-peries**

drastic ⊕ adj 1 extreme 2 severe

draught ⊕ n 1 current of air 2 act of drawing 3 act of drinking 4 quantity drunk at once ▷ pl 5 game played on chessboard with flat round pieces ▷ adj 6 for drawing 7 drawn **draughty** adj

full of air currents **draughtsman** n one who makes drawings, plans etc. **draughtsmanship** n

draw ⊕ v **drawing, drew, drawn** 1 portray with pencil etc. 2 pull, haul 3 attract 4 come (near) 5 entice 6 take from (well, barrel etc.) 7 receive (money) 8 get by lot 9 make, admit current of air 10 (of game) tie ▷ n 11 act of drawing 12 casting of lots 13 tie **drawer** n 1 one who or that which draws 2 sliding box in table or chest **drawing** n 1 art of depicting in line 2 sketch so done **drawback** n snag **drawbridge** n hinged bridge to pull up **drawing room** living room, sitting room **draw up** 1 arrange in order 2 stop

drawl v 1 speak slowly ▷ n 2 such speech

drawn ⊕ adj haggard

dread ⊕ v 1 fear greatly ▷ n 2 awe, terror ▷ adj 3 feared, awful **dreadful** adj disagreeable, shocking or bad **dreadfully** adv

———— THESAURUS ————

drain v = **remove**, draw, empty, withdraw, tap; = **flow out**, leak, trickle, ooze, seep; = **drink up**, swallow, finish, put away, quaff ▷ n = **sewer**, channel, pipe, sink, ditch; = **reduction**, strain, drag, exhaustion, sapping

drama n = **play**, show, stage show, dramatization; = **theatre**, acting, stagecraft, dramaturgy; = **excitement**, crisis, spectacle, turmoil, histrionics

drape v = **cover**, wrap, fold, swathe

drastic adj = **extreme**, strong, radical, desperate, severe

draught n = **breeze**, current, movement, flow, puff

draw v = **sketch**, design, outline, trace, portray; = **pull**, drag, haul, tow, tug; = **extract**, take, remove; = **deduce**, make, take, derive, infer ▷ n = **tie**, deadlock, stalemate, impasse, dead heat; (Inf) = **appeal**, pull (Inf), charm, attraction, lure

drawn adj = **tense**, worn, stressed, tired, pinched

dread v = **fear**, shrink from, cringe

dream 🛈 *n* **1** vision during sleep
2 fancy, reverie, aspiration ▷ *v*
3 have dreams **4** see, imagine in
dreams **5** think of as possible
dreamer *n* **dreamy** *adj*

dreary 🛈 *adj* **drearier, dreariest**
dismal, dull **drearily** *adv*

dredge *v* **1** bring up mud etc. from
sea bottom ▷ *n* **2** scoop **dredger**
n boat with machinery for dredging

dregs *pl n* sediment, grounds

drench 🛈 *v* wet thoroughly, soak

dress 🛈 *v* **1** put on clothes **2** array
for show **3** prepare **4** put dressing
on (wound) ▷ *n* **5** one-piece
garment for woman **6** clothing
7 evening wear **dresser** *n* **1** one
who dresses **2** kitchen sideboard
dressing *n* something applied, as
sauce to food, ointment to wound
etc. **dressing-down** *n* (Inf) severe
scolding **dressing gown** robe
worn before dressing **dressy** *adj*

(of persons) stylish

dressage *n* method of training
horse

drey *n* squirrel's nest

dribble 🛈 *v* **1** flow in drops, trickle
2 run at the mouth ▷ *n* **3** trickle,
drop

drift 🛈 *v* **1** be carried as by current
of air, water ▷ *n* **2** process of being
driven by current **3** tendency
4 meaning **5** wind-heaped mass of
snow, sand etc. **drifter** *n*
driftwood *n* wood washed ashore
by sea

drill¹ 🛈 *n* **1** boring tool **2** exercise
of soldiers **3** routine teaching ▷ *v*
4 bore hole **5** exercise in routine
6 practise routine

drill² 🛈 *v/n* (machine to) sow seed
in furrows

drink 🛈 *v* **drinking, drank, drunk**
1 swallow liquid ▷ *n* **2** liquid for
drinking **3** intoxicating liquor

THESAURUS
---

at the thought of, quail from,
shudder to think about ▷ *n* = **fear**,
alarm, horror, terror, dismay

dream *n* = **vision**, illusion,
delusion, hallucination;
= **ambition**, wish, fantasy, desire,
pipe dream; = **delight**, pleasure,
joy, beauty, treasure ▷ *v* = **have
dreams**, hallucinate

dreary *adj* = **dull**, boring, tedious,
drab, tiresome ≠ **exciting**

drench *v* = **soak**, flood, wet,
drown, steep

dress *n* = **frock**, gown, robe;
= **clothing**, clothes, costume,
garments, apparel ▷ *v* = **put on
clothes**, don clothes, slip on or into

something ≠ **undress**; = **bandage**,
treat, plaster, bind up

dribble *v* = **run**, drip, trickle, drop,
leak; = **drool**, drivel, slaver, slobber

drift *v* = **float**, go (aimlessly), bob,
coast, slip; = **wander**, stroll, stray,
roam, meander ▷ *n* = **pile**, bank,
mass, heap, mound; = **meaning**,
point, gist, direction, import

drill *n* = **bit**, borer, gimlet, boring
tool; = **training**, exercise,
discipline, instruction, preparation
▷ *v* = **bore**, pierce, penetrate, sink
in, puncture; = **train**, coach, teach,
exercise, discipline

drink *v* = **swallow**, sip, suck, gulp,
sup; = **booze** (Inf), tipple, tope, hit

d

drinkable adj **drinker** n
drip ● v **dripping, dripped 1** fall
or let fall in drops ▷ n **2** (Med)
intravenous administration of
solution **3** (Inf) insipid person
dripping n **1** melted fat from
roasting meat ▷ adj **2** very wet
drip-dry adj (of fabric) drying free
of creases if hung up while wet
drive ● v **driving, drove, driven
1** urge in some direction **2** make
move and steer (vehicle, animal
etc.) **3** be conveyed in vehicle **4** hit
with force ▷ n **5** act, action of
driving **6** journey in vehicle
7 united effort, campaign **8** energy
9 forceful stroke **driver** n
drivel v **1** run at the mouth **2** talk
nonsense ▷ n **3** silly nonsense
drizzle v/n rain in fine drops
droll adj funny, odd
dromedary n, pl **-daries**
one-humped camel
drone n **1** male bee **2** lazy idler

3 deep humming ▷ v **4** hum
5 talk in monotonous tone
drool v slaver, drivel
droop v **1** hang down **2** wilt, flag
▷ n **droopy** adj
drop ● n **dropping, dropped
1** globule of liquid **2** very small
quantity **3** fall, descent **4** distance
to fall ▷ v **5** (let) fall **6** utter
casually **7** set down **8** discontinue
9 come or go casually **droplet** n
dropout n person who fails to
complete course of study or one
who rejects conventional society
droppings pl n dung of rabbits,
sheep, birds etc.
dropsy n disease causing watery
fluid to collect in the body
dross n **1** scum of molten metal
2 impurity, refuse
drought ● n long spell of dry
weather
drove ● n herd, flock, esp. in motion
drover n driver of cattle etc.

THESAURUS

the bottle (Inf) ▷ n = **glass**, cup,
draught; = **beverage**, refreshment,
potion, liquid, hooch or hootch (Inf,
chiefly US & Canad)
drip v = **drop**, splash, sprinkle,
trickle, dribble ▷ n = **drop**, bead,
trickle, dribble, droplet; (Inf)
= **weakling**, wet (Brit Inf), weed
(Inf), softie (Inf), mummy's boy
(Inf)
drive v = **operate**, manage, direct,
guide, handle; = **push**, propel;
= **thrust**, push, hammer, ram;
= **herd**, urge, impel ▷ n = **run**,
ride, trip, journey, spin (Inf);
= **initiative**, energy, enterprise,

ambition, motivation; = **campaign**,
push (Inf), crusade, action,
effort
drop v = **fall**, decline, diminish;
(often with **away**) = **decline**, fall,
sink; = **plunge**, fall, tumble,
descend, plummet ▷ n
= **decrease**, fall, cut, lowering,
decline; = **droplet**, bead, globule,
bubble, pearl; = **dash**, shot (Inf),
spot, trace, sip; = **fall**, plunge,
descent
drought n = **water shortage**,
dryness, dry spell, aridity
≠ **flood**
drove n often plural = **herd**,

drown ⊙ v 1 die or be killed by immersion in liquid 2 make sound inaudible by louder sound

drudge v 1 work at menial or distasteful tasks ▷ n 2 one who drudges **drudgery** n

drug ⊙ n 1 medical substance 2 narcotic ▷ v 3 mix drugs with 4 administer drug to

drum ⊙ n 1 percussion instrument of skin stretched over round hollow frame 2 thing shaped like drum ▷ v 3 play drum 4 tap, thump continuously **drummer** n **drum major** leader of military band **drumstick** n 1 stick for beating drum 2 lower joint of cooked fowl's leg

drunk ⊙ adj/n (person) overcome by strong drink **drunkard** n **drunken** adj **drunkenness** n

dry ⊙ adj **drier, driest** 1 without moisture 2 not yielding liquid

3 unfriendly 4 caustically witty 5 uninteresting 6 lacking sweetness ▷ v 7 remove water, moisture 8 become dry 9 evaporate **dryer, drier** n 1 person or thing that dries 2 apparatus for removing moisture **dryly, drily** adv **dry-clean** v clean clothes with solvent **dry-cleaner** n **dry-cleaning** n

dual ⊙ adj twofold

dub v **dubbing, dubbed** 1 confer knighthood on 2 give title to 3 provide film with soundtrack

dubious ⊙ adj causing doubt

duchess n duke's wife or widow

duck ⊙ n 1 common swimming bird ▷ v 2 plunge (someone) under water 3 bob down 4 (Inf) avoid **duckling** n young duck

duct n channel, tube

dud n 1 futile, worthless person or thing ▷ adj 2 worthless

d

——— THESAURUS ———

company, crowds, collection, mob
drown v = **drench**, flood, soak, steep, swamp; = **overwhelm**, overcome, wipe out, overpower, obliterate

drug n = **medication**, medicine, remedy, physic, medicament; = **dope** (Sl), narcotic (Sl), stimulant, opiate ▷ v = **knock out**, dope (Sl), numb, deaden, stupefy

drum v = **pound**, beat, tap, rap, thrash

drunk adj = **intoxicated**, plastered (Sl), drunken, merry (Brit Inf), under the influence (Inf) ▷ n = **drunkard**, alcoholic, lush (Sl), boozer (Inf),

wino (Inf)

dry adj = **dehydrated**, dried-up, arid, parched, desiccated ≠ **wet**; = **thirsty**, parched; = **sarcastic**, cynical, low-key, sly, sardonic ▷ v = **drain**, make dry

dual adj = **twofold**, double, twin, matched, paired

dubious adj = **suspect**, suspicious, crooked, dodgy (Brit, Aust, & NZ Inf), questionable ≠ **trustworthy**; = **unsure**, uncertain, suspicious, hesitating, doubtful ≠ **sure**

duck v = **bob**, drop, lower, bend, bow; (Inf) = **dodge**, avoid, escape, evade, elude; = **dunk**, wet, plunge, dip, submerge

due ① adj **1** owing **2** proper, expected **3** timed for ▷ adv **4** (with points of compass) exactly ▷ n **5** person's right **6** (usu. pl) charge, fee etc. **duly** adj **1** properly **2** punctually **due to 1** attributable to **2** caused by

duel ① n **1** arranged fight with deadly weapons, between two persons ▷ v **2** fight in duel

duet n piece of music for two performers

duffel, duffle n **1** coarse woollen cloth **2** coat of this

duffer n stupid inefficient person

dugout n **1** covered excavation to provide shelter **2** canoe of hollowed-out tree **3** (Sport) covered bench for players when not on the field

duke n peer of rank next below prince **dukedom** n

dulcet adj (of sounds) sweet, melodious

dulcimer n stringed instrument played with hammers

dull ① adj **1** stupid **2** sluggish **3** tedious **4** overcast ▷ v **5** make or become dull **dullard** n **dully** adj

dumb ① adj **1** (Offens) incapable of speech **2** silent **3** (Inf) stupid **dumbbell** n weight for exercises **dumbfound** v confound into silence

dummy ① n, pl **-mies 1** tailor's or dressmaker's model **2** imitation object **3** baby's dummy teat ▷ adj **4** sham, bogus

dump ① v **1** throw down in mass **2** deposit **3** unload ▷ n **4** rubbish heap **5** temporary depot of stores **6** (Inf) squalid place ▷ pl **7** low spirits **dumpling** n small round pudding of dough **dumpy** adj short, stout

dunce n stupid pupil

dune n sandhill

dung n excrement of animals

THESAURUS

due adj = **expected**, scheduled; = **fitting**, deserved, appropriate, justified, suitable; = **payable**, outstanding, owed, owing, unpaid ▷ adv = **directly**, dead, straight, exactly, undeviatingly ▷ n = **right(s)**, privilege, deserts, merits, comeuppance (Inf)

duel n = **single combat**, affair of honour ▷ v = **fight**, struggle, clash, compete, contest

dull adj = **boring**, tedious, dreary, flat, plain ≠ **exciting**; = **lifeless**, indifferent, apathetic, listless, unresponsive ≠ **lively**; = **cloudy**, dim, gloomy, dismal, overcast

≠ **bright**; = **blunt**, blunted, unsharpened ≠ **sharp** ▷ v = **relieve**, blunt, lessen, moderate, soften

dumb adj = **silent**, mute, speechless, tongue-tied, wordless, unable to speak ≠ **articulate**

dummy n = **model**, figure, mannequin, form, manikin; = **imitation**, copy, duplicate, sham, counterfeit ▷ adj = **imitation**, false, fake, artificial, mock

dump v = **drop**, deposit, throw down, let fall, fling down; = **get rid of**, tip, dispose of, unload, jettison

dungarees pl n overalls made of coarse cotton fabric

dungeon n underground cell for prisoners

dunk v dip bread etc. into liquid before eating it

duo n, pl **duos** pair of performers

duodenum n, pl **-na, -nums** upper part of small intestine **duodenal** adj

dupe n 1 victim of delusion or sharp practice ▷ v 2 deceive

duplex n (US & Canad) an apartment on two floors

duplicate ❶ v 1 make exact copy of ▷ adj 2 double ▷ n 3 exact copy **duplication** n **duplicator** n **duplicity** n deceitfulness, double-dealing

durable ❶ adj lasting, resisting wear **durability** n

duration ❶ n time things last

duress n compulsion

during prep throughout, in the time of, in the course of

dusk ❶ n darker stage of twilight

dusky adj

dust ❶ n 1 fine particles, powder of earth or other matter 2 ashes of the dead ▷ v 3 sprinkle with powder 4 rid of dust **duster** n cloth for removing dust **dusty** adj covered with dust **dustbin** n container for household rubbish

Dutch adj pert. to the Netherlands, its inhabitants, its language

duty ❶ n, pl **-ties** 1 moral or legal obligation 2 that which is due 3 tax on goods **duteous** adj **dutiful** adj

duvet n quilt filled with down or artificial fibre

dwarf ❶ n, pl **dwarfs, dwarves** 1 very undersized person 2 mythological, small, manlike creature ▷ adj 3 unusually small ▷ v 4 make seem small 5 make stunted

dwell ❶ v **dwelling, dwelt** 1 live, make one's home (in) 2 think, speak at length (on) **dwelling** n house

▷ n = **rubbish tip**, tip, junkyard, rubbish heap, refuse heap; (Inf) = **pigsty**, hole (Inf), slum, hovel

duplicate v = **repeat**, reproduce, copy, clone, replicate ▷ adj = **identical**, matched, matching, twin, corresponding ▷ n = **copy**, facsimile

durable adj = **hard-wearing**, strong, tough, reliable, resistant ≠ **fragile**

duration n = **length**, time, period, term, stretch

dusk n = **twilight**, evening, nightfall, sunset, dark ≠ **dawn**

dust n = **grime**, grit, powder ▷ v = **sprinkle**, cover, powder, spread, spray

duty n = **responsibility**, job, task, work, role; = **tax**, toll, levy, tariff, excise

dwarf v = **tower above** or **over**, dominate, overlook, stand over, loom over ▷ adj = **miniature**, small, baby, tiny, diminutive

dwell v (Formal, Lit) = **live**, reside, lodge, abide

dwindle ❼ v waste away

dye ❼ v 1 impregnate (cloth etc.) with colouring matter 2 colour thus ▷ n 3 colouring matter in solution

dyke, dike n 1 embankment to prevent flooding 2 ditch

d **dynamic** ❼ adj full of energy, ambition, and new ideas

dynamics pl n branch of physics dealing with force as producing or affecting motion **dynamic** adj energetic and forceful

dynamite n 1 high-explosive mixture ▷ v 2 blow up with this

dynamo n, pl **-mos** machine to convert mechanical into electrical energy, generator of electricity

dynasty ❼ n, pl **-ties** line, family of hereditary rulers

dysentery n infection of intestine causing severe diarrhoea

dysfunction n abnormal, impaired functioning

dyslexia n impaired ability to read **dyslexic** adj

dyspepsia n indigestion **dyspeptic** adj/n

dystrophy n wasting of bodily tissues, esp. muscles

─────── THESAURUS ───────

dwindle v = **lessen**, decline, fade, shrink, diminish ≠ **increase**

dye v = **colour**, stain, tint, tinge, pigment ▷ n = **colouring**, colour, pigment, stain, tint

dynamic adj = **energetic**, powerful, vital, go-ahead, lively ≠ **apathetic**

dynasty n = **empire**, house, rule, regime, sovereignty

E 1 East 2 Eastern 3 English

each ● *adj, pron* every one taken separately

eager ● *adj* 1 having a strong wish 2 keen, impatient

eagle *n* large bird of prey

ear¹ ● *n* 1 organ of hearing 2 sense of hearing 3 sensitiveness to sounds 4 attention **earache** *n* pain in ear **eardrum** *n* thin piece of skin inside the ear **earmark** *v* assign for definite purpose **earphone** *n* receiver for radio etc.

held or put in ear **earring** *n* ornament for lobe of the ear **earshot** *n* hearing distance **earwig** *n* small insect with pincer-like tail

ear² ● *n* spike, head of corn

earl *n* British nobleman

early ● *adj/adv* **-lier, -liest** 1 before expected or usual time 2 in first part, near beginning

earn ● *v* 1 obtain by work or merit 2 gain **earnings** *p, n*

earnest ● *adj* serious, sincere

earth ● *n* 1 planet we live on 2 ground 3 soil 4 electrical connection to earth ▷ *v* 5 cover, connect with earth **earthly** *adj* possible **earthy** *adj* 1 of earth 2 uninhibited **earthenware** *n* (vessels of) baked clay **earthquake** *n* convulsion of earth's surface **earthworm** *n*

ease ● *n* 1 comfort 2 freedom from constraint, awkwardness or trouble 3 idleness ▷ *v* 4 reduce burden 5 give ease to 6 slacken

each *pron* = **every one**, all, each one, each and every one, one and all

eager *adj* = **anxious**, keen, hungry, impatient, itching ≠ **unenthusiastic**

ear *n* = **sensitivity**, taste, discrimination, appreciation, observation

early *adv* = **in good time**, beforehand, ahead of schedule, in advance, with time to spare ≠ **late** ▷ *adj* = **first**, opening, initial, introductory; = **premature**, forward, advanced, untimely,

unseasonable ≠ **belated**

earn *v* = **be paid**, make, get, receive, gain; = **deserve**, win, gain, attain, justify

earnest *adj* = **serious**, grave, intense, dedicated, sincere ≠ **frivolous**; = **determined**, dogged, intent, persistent, persevering

earth *n* = **world**, planet, globe, sphere, orb; = **ground**, land, dry land, terra firma

ease *n* = **straightforwardness**, simplicity, readiness; = **comfort**, luxury, leisure, relaxation,

7 (cause to) move carefully **easily**
adv **easy** *adj* **1** not difficult **2** free
from pain, care, or anxiety
3 compliant **4** comfortable
easy-going *adj* **1** not fussy
2 indolent

easel *n* frame to support picture etc.

east *n* **1** part of horizon where sun
rises **2** eastern lands, orient ▷ *adj*
3 on, in, or near, east **4** coming
from east ▷ *adv* **5** from, or to, east
easterly *adj/adv* **eastern** *adj*
eastward *adj/adv* **eastwards** *adv*

Easter *n* festival of the
Resurrection of Christ

easy ❶ *adj* **easier, easiest** see
EASE

eat ❶ *v* **eating, ate, eaten**
1 chew and swallow **2** destroy
3 gnaw **4** wear away **eatable** *adj*

eau de Cologne (Fr) light
perfume

eaves *pl n* overhanging edges of
roof **eavesdrop** *v* listen secretly

ebb ❶ *v* **1** flow back **2** decay ▷ *n*
3 flowing back of tide **4** decline,
decay

ebony *adj/n, pl* **-onies** (made of)
hard black wood

ebullient *adj* exuberant
ebullience *n*

eccentric ❶ *adj* **1** odd,
unconventional **2** irregular **3** not
placed centrally ▷ *n* **4** odd,
unconventional person
eccentricity *n*

echo ❶ *n, pl* **-oes 1** repetition of
sounds by reflection **2** imitation
▷ *v* **3** repeat as echo **4** imitate
5 resound **6** be repeated

éclair *n* finger-shaped iced cake
filled with cream

eclectic *adj* selecting from various
sources

eclipse ❶ *n* **1** blotting out of sun,
moon etc. by another heavenly

━━━━━━━━━━ THESAURUS ━━━━━━━━━━

prosperity **≠ hardship**; **= peace of
mind**, peace, content, quiet,
comfort **≠ agitation** ▷ *v* **= relieve**,
calm, soothe, lessen, alleviate
≠ aggravate; **= reduce**, diminish,
lessen, slacken; **= move carefully**,
edge, slip, inch, slide
easy *adj* **= simple**, straightforward,
no trouble, not difficult, effortless
≠ hard; **= untroubled**, relaxed,
peaceful, serene, tranquil;
= carefree, comfortable, leisurely,
trouble-free, untroubled **≠ difficult**
eat *v* **= consume**, swallow, chew,
scoff (Sl), devour; **= have a meal**,
lunch, breakfast, dine, snack
ebb *v* **= flow back**, go out,

withdraw, retreat, wane;
= decline, flag, diminish,
decrease, dwindle ▷ *n* **= flowing
back**, going out, withdrawal,
retreat, wane
eccentric *adj* **= odd**, strange,
peculiar, irregular, quirky **≠ normal**
▷ *n* **= crank** (Inf), character (Inf),
oddball (Inf), nonconformist,
weirdo or weirdie (Inf)
echo *n* **= reverberation**, ringing,
repetition, answer, resonance;
= copy, reflection, clone,
reproduction, imitation ▷ *v*
= reverberate, repeat, resound,
ring, resonate; **= recall**, reflect,
copy, mirror, resemble

body **2** obscurity ▷ v **3** obscure
4 surpass
economy ❶ n, pl **-mies 1** careful
management of resources to avoid
unnecessary expenditure **2** system
of interrelationship of money,
industry and employment
economic adj **economical** adj
frugal **economics** pl n **1** study of
economies of nations **2** (used as pl)
financial aspects **economist** n
economize v
ecstasy ❶ n exalted state of
feeling **ecstatic** adj
eczema n skin disease
eddy n, pl **eddies 1** small whirl in
water, smoke etc. ▷ v **2** move in
whirls
edge ❶ n **1** border, boundary
2 cutting side of blade **3** sharpness
4 advantage ▷ v **5** sharpen **6** give
edge or border to **7** move gradually
edgy adj irritable **on edge**
1 nervy **2** excited
edible adj eatable
edict n order, decree

edifice n building
edify v **-fying, -fied** improve
morally, instruct
edit ❶ v prepare book, film, tape
etc. **edition** n **1** form in which
something is published **2** number
of copies **editor** n **editorial** adj/n
article stating opinion of
newspaper etc.
educate ❶ v **1** provide schooling
for, teach **2** train **education** n
educational adj
eel n snakelike fish
eerie ❶ adj **eerier, eeriest** weird,
uncanny
efface v wipe or rub out
effect ❶ n **1** result **2** impression
3 condition of being operative ▷ pl
4 property **5** lighting, sounds etc.
▷ v **6** bring about **effective** adj
1 useful **2** in force **effectual** adj
effeminate adj womanish,
unmanly
efficient ❶ adj capable,
competent **efficiency** n
effigy n, pl **-gies** image, likeness

e

— THESAURUS —

eclipse n = **obscuring**, covering,
blocking, shading, dimming ▷ v
= **surpass**, exceed, overshadow,
excel, transcend
economy n = **financial system**,
financial state
ecstasy n = **rapture**, delight, joy,
bliss, euphoria ≠ **agony**
edge n = **border**, side, limit,
outline, boundary ▷ v = **inch**, ease,
creep, slink, steal; = **border**, fringe,
hem, pipe
edit v = **revise**, improve, correct,
polish, adapt

educate v = **teach**, school, train,
develop, improve
eerie adj = **uncanny**, strange,
frightening, ghostly, weird
effect n = **result**, consequence,
conclusion, outcome, event;
= **impression**, feeling, impact,
influence; = **purpose**, impression,
sense, intent, essence ▷ v = **bring
about**, produce, complete, achieve,
perform
efficient adj = **effective**,
successful, structured, productive,
systematic ≠ **inefficient**

effluent *n* liquid discharged as waste

effort ❶ *n* exertion, endeavour, attempt or something achieved **effortless** *adj*

effrontery *n* impudence

e.g. for example

egalitarian *adj* believing that all people should be equal

egg¹ *n* oval or round object from which young emerge

egg² *v* **egg on** urge

ego *n, pl* **egos** the self **egotism, egoism** *n* **1** selfishness **2** self-conceit **egotist, egoist** *n* **egotistic, -ical** *adj* **egocentric** *adj* self-centred

egregious *adj* blatant

eider *n* Arctic duck **eiderdown** *n* **1** its breast feathers **2** quilt

eight *adj/n* cardinal number one above seven **eighteen** *adj/n* eight more than ten **eighteenth** *adj/n* **eighth** *adj/n* **eightieth** *adj/n* **eighty** *adj/n* ten times eight

either *adj/n* **1** one or the other **2** one of two **3** each ▷ *adv/conj* **4** bringing in first of alternatives

ejaculate *v* **1** eject (semen) **2** exclaim **ejaculation** *n*

eject ❶ *v* **1** throw out **2** expel

ejection *n* **ejector** *n*

eke out make (supply) last

elaborate ❶ *adj* **1** detailed **2** complicated ▷ *v* **3** expand (upon) **4** work out in detail **elaboration** *n*

élan *n* style and vigour

elapse *v* (of time) pass

elastic ❶ *adj* **1** springy **2** flexible ▷ *n* **3** tape containing strands of rubber **elasticity** *n*

elbow ❶ *n* **1** joint between fore and upper parts of arm **2** part of sleeve covering this ▷ *v* **3** shove with elbow **elbowroom** *n* room to move

elder¹ ❶ *adj* **1** older, senior ▷ *n* **2** person of greater age **3** official of certain churches **elderly** *adj* **eldest** *adj* oldest

elder² ❶ *n* tree with black berries

elect ❶ *v* **1** choose by vote **2** choose ▷ *adj* **3** appointed but not yet in office **4** chosen **election** *n* **elective** *adj* appointed by election **elector** *n* **electoral** *adj* **electorate** *n* body of electors

electricity *n* **1** form of energy **2** electric current **electric** *adj* of, transmitting or powered by electricity **electrical** *adj*

— THESAURUS —

effort *n* = **attempt**, try, endeavour, shot (*Inf*), bid; = **exertion**, work, trouble, energy, struggle

eject *v* = **throw out**, remove, turn out, expel, oust

elaborate *adj* = **complicated**, detailed, studied, complex, precise ▷ *v* = **develop**, flesh out

elastic *adj* = **flexible**, supple,

rubbery, pliable, plastic ≠ **rigid**; = **adaptable**, yielding, variable, flexible, accommodating ≠ **inflexible**

elbow *n* = **joint**, angle, curve

elder *adj* = **older**, first, senior, first-born ▷ *n* = **older person**, senior, leader

elect *v* = **vote for**, choose, pick,

electrician n one trained in installation etc. of electrical devices **electrify** v **electrification** n

electro- comb. form by, caused by electricity, as in electrotherapy

electrocute v kill by electricity **electrocution** n

electrode n conductor of electric current

electron n one of fundamental components of atom, charged with negative electricity **electronics** pl n technology of electronic devices and circuits

electronic adj 1 (of a device) dependent on the action of electrons 2 (of a process) using electronic devices

elegant ① adj 1 graceful, tasteful 2 refined **elegance** n

elegy n, pl **-egies** lament for the dead in poem **elegiac** adj

element ① n 1 substance which cannot be separated by ordinary chemical techniques 2 component part 3 trace 4 heating wire in electric kettle etc. 5 proper sphere ▷ pl 6 powers of atmosphere 7 rudiments **elemental** adj

elementary adj rudimentary, simple

elephant n huge animal with ivory tusks and long trunk

elevate ① v raise, exalt **elevation** n 1 raising 2 height, esp. above sea level 3 drawing of one side of building etc. **elevator** n (US) lift

eleven adj/n number next above 10 **eleventh** adj

elf n, pl **elves** fairy **elfin, elvish** adj

elicit ① v draw out

eligible ① adj 1 qualified 2 desirable **eligibility** n

eliminate ① v remove, get rid of, set aside **elimination** n

elite ① n the pick or best part of society

elixir n remedy

elk n large deer

ellipse n oval **elliptical** adj

elm n tree with serrated leaves

elocution n art of public speaking

elongate v lengthen

elope v run away from home with lover **elopement** n

eloquence n fluent, powerful use of language **eloquent** adj **eloquently** adv

——— THESAURUS ———

determine, select

elegant adj = **stylish**, fine, sophisticated, delicate, handsome ≠ **inelegant**

element n = **component**, part, unit, section, factor

elevate v = **promote**, raise, advance, upgrade, exalt; = **increase**, lift, raise, step up, intensify

elicit v = **bring about**, cause, derive, bring out, evoke; = **obtain**, extract, exact, evoke, wrest

eligible adj = **entitled**, fit, qualified, suitable ≠ **ineligible**

eliminate v = **remove**, end, stop, withdraw, get rid of (Sl)

elite n = **aristocracy**, best, pick, cream, upper class ≠ **rabble**

else *adv* **1** besides, instead **2** otherwise **elsewhere** *adv* in or to some other place

elucidate *v* explain

elude ● *v* **1** escape **2** baffle **elusive** *adj* difficult to catch

emaciated *adj* abnormally thin

emanate ● *v* issue, proceed from **emanation** *n*

emancipate *v* set free **emancipation** *n*

emasculate *v* **1** castrate **2** enfeeble, weaken **emasculation** *n*

embalm *v* preserve corpse

embankment *n* artificial mound carrying road, railway, or to dam water

embargo ● *n, pl* **-goes 1** order stopping movement of ships **2** ban ▷ *v* **3** put under embargo **4** requisition

embark ● *v* **1** board ship, aircraft etc. **2** (with *on*) commence new project etc.

embarrass ● *v* **1** disconcert **2** abash **3** confuse **embarrassment** *n*

embassy *n, pl* **-sies** office or official residence of ambassador

embattled *adj* having many difficulties

embed *v* **-bedding, -bedded** fix fast (in)

embellish *v* adorn, enrich **embellishment** *n*

ember *n* glowing cinder

embezzle *v* misappropriate (money in trust etc.) **embezzlement** *n* **embezzler** *n*

emblem *n* **1** symbol **2** badge **emblematic** *adj*

embody ● *v* **-bodying, -bodied** represent, include, be expression of **embodiment** *n*

embolism *n* (*Med*) obstruction of artery

embrace ● *v* **1** clasp in arms, hug **2** accept **3** comprise ▷ *n* **4** hug

embrocation *n* lotion for rubbing limbs etc. to relieve pain

embroider *v* ornament with needlework **embroidery** *n*

embroil ● *v* involve (someone) in problems

—— THESAURUS ——

elude *v* = **evade**, escape, lose, avoid, flee; = **baffle,** frustrate, puzzle, stump

emanate *v* = **flow**, emerge, spring, proceed, arise

embargo *n* = **ban**, bar, restriction, boycott, restraint ▷ *v* = **block**, stop, bar, ban, restrict

embark *v* = **go aboard**, climb aboard, board ship, step aboard, go on board ≠ **get off**

embarrass *v* = **shame**, distress,

show up (*Inf*), humiliate, disconcert

embody *v* = **personify**, represent, stand for, manifest, exemplify; = **incorporate**, include, contain, combine, collect

embrace *v* = **hug**, hold, cuddle, seize, squeeze; = **accept**, support, welcome, adopt, take up; = **include**, involve, cover, contain, take in ▷ *n* = **hug**, hold, cuddle, squeeze, clinch (*Sl*)

embroil *v* = **involve**, mix up,

embryo ❶ *n, pl* **-bryos**
undeveloped offspring, germ
embryonic *adj*

emend *v* to remove errors from,
correct **emendation** *n*

emerald *n* bright green gem

emerge ❶ *v* **1** come up, out **2** rise
to notice **emergence** *n*

emergency ❶ *n, pl* **-cies** sudden
unforeseen event needing prompt
action

emery *n* hard mineral used for
polishing

emigrate ❶ *v* go and settle in
another country **emigrant** *n*
emigration *n*

eminent ❶ *adj* distinguished
eminently *adv* **eminence** *n*

emissary *n, pl* **-saries** agent,
representative sent on mission

emit ❶ *v* **emitting, emitted** give
out, put forth **emission** *n*

emoji *n* image used in electronic
messages

emollient *adj* **1** softening,
soothing ▷ *n* **2** ointment

emotion ❶ *n* excited state of
feeling, as joy, fear etc. **emotional**
adj **emotive** *adj* arousing emotion

empathy *n* understanding of
another's feelings

emperor *n* ruler of an empire

emphasis ❶ *n, pl* **-ses**
1 importance attached **2** stress on
words **emphasize** *v* **emphatic**
adj forceful

emphysema *n* disease of lungs,
causing breathlessness

empire ❶ *n* group of states under
supreme leader

empirical, empiric ❶ *adj* relying
on experiment or experience

emplacement *n* position for gun

employ ❶ *v* **1** provide work for in
return for money **2** keep busy
3 use **employee** *n* **employer** *n*
employment *n* **1** employing,
being employed **2** work

e

— THESAURUS —

implicate, entangle, mire
embryo *n* = **foetus**, unborn child,
fertilized egg
emerge *v* = **come out**, appear,
surface, rise, arise ≠ **withdraw**;
= **become apparent**, come out,
become known, come to light, crop
up
emergency *n* = **crisis**, danger,
difficulty, accident, disaster
emigrate *v* = **move abroad**,
move, relocate, migrate, resettle
eminent *adj* = **prominent**, noted,
respected, famous, celebrated
≠ **unknown**
emit *v* = **give off**, release, leak,

transmit, discharge ≠ **absorb**
emotion *n* = **feeling**, spirit, soul,
passion, excitement
emphasis *n* = **importance**,
attention, weight, significance,
stress; = **stress**, accent, force,
weight
empire *n* = **kingdom**, territory,
province, federation, commonwealth
empirical, empiric *adj*
= **first-hand**, direct, observed,
practical, actual ≠ **hypothetical**
employ *v* = **hire**, commission,
appoint, take on, retain; = **use**,
apply, exercise, exert, make use of;
= **spend**, fill, occupy, involve, engage

3 occupation; job
empower ❶ *v* authorize
empty ❶ *adj* **-tier, -tiest**
1 containing nothing **2** unoccupied
3 senseless ▷ *v* **4** make, become devoid of content **5** discharge (contents) into **empties** *pl n* empty bottles etc. **emptiness** *n*
emu *n* large Aust. flightless bird
emulate ❶ *v* **1** strive to equal or excel **2** imitate **emulation** *n*
emulsion *n* **1** light-sensitive coating of film **2** liquid with oily particles in suspension **3** paint in this form **emulsifier** *n*
enable ❶ *v* make able
enact ❶ *v* **1** make law **2** act part
enamel *n* **1** glasslike coating applied to metal etc. **2** coating of teeth **3** any hard coating ▷ *v* **4** cover with this

encapsulate *v* **1** summarize **2** enclose
enchant ❶ *v* bewitch, delight **enchantment** *n*
encircle *v* **1** surround **2** enfold
enclave *n* part of country entirely surrounded by foreign territory
enclose, inclose ❶ *v* **1** shut in **2** surround **3** place in with letter **enclosure** *n*
encompass ❶ *v* surround, contain
encore *interj* **1** again ▷ *n* **2** (call for) repetition of song etc.
encounter ❶ *v* **1** meet unexpectedly **2** meet in conflict ▷ *n* **3** encountering
encourage ❶ *v* **1** inspire with hope **2** embolden **encouragement** *n*
encroach *v* intrude (on)

empower *v* = **authorize**, allow, commission, qualify, permit
empty *adj* = **bare**, clear, abandoned, deserted, vacant ≠ **full**; = **meaningless**, cheap, hollow, vain, idle; = **worthless**, meaningless, hollow, pointless, futile ≠ **meaningful** ▷ *v* = **clear**, drain/void, unload, pour out ≠ **fill**
emulate *v* = **imitate**, follow, copy, mirror, echo
enable *v* = **allow**, permit, empower, give someone the opportunity, give someone the means ≠ **prevent**
enact *v* = **establish**, order, command, approve, sanction; = **perform**, play, present, stage, represent

enchant *v* = **fascinate**, delight, charm, entrance, dazzle
enclose, inclose *v* = **surround**, circle, bound, fence, confine; = **send with**, include, put in, insert
encompass *v* = **include**, hold, cover, admit, deal with; = **surround**, circle, enclose, close in, envelop
encounter *v* = **experience**, meet, face, suffer, have; = **meet**, confront, come across, bump into (*Inf*), run across ▷ *n* = **meeting**, brush, confrontation, rendezvous, chance meeting; = **battle**, conflict, clash, contest, run-in (*Inf*)
encourage *v* = **inspire**, comfort, cheer, reassure, console

encroachment n

encrust v cover with layer

encumber v 1 hamper 2 burden
encumbrance n

encyclopedia, encyclopaedia
n book, set of books of information
on one or all subjects
encyclopedic, -paedic adj

end ❶ n 1 limit 2 extremity
3 conclusion 4 fragment 5 latter
part 6 death 7 event 8 aim ▷ v
9 put an end to 10 come to an end,
finish **ending** n **endless** adj

endanger ❶ v put in danger

endear v make beloved
endearment n loving word

endeavour ❶ v 1 try, strive after
▷ n 2 attempt

endorse ❶ v 1 sanction
2 confirm 3 sign back of 4 record
conviction on driving licence
endorsement n

endow ❶ v 1 provide permanent
income for 2 furnish (with)
endowment n

endure ❶ v 1 undergo 2 tolerate,
bear 3 last **endurable** adj
endurance n

enema n medicine, liquid injected
into rectum

enemy ❶ n, pl **-mies** 1 hostile
person 2 opponent 3 armed foe

energy ❶ n, pl **-gies** 1 vigour,
force, activity 2 source of power, as
oil, coal etc. 3 capacity of machine,
battery etc. for work **energetic**
adj **energize** v

enervate v weaken

enfeeble v weaken

enfold v cover by wrapping
something around

enforce ❶ v 1 compel obedience
to 2 impose (action) upon
enforceable adj **enforcement** n

enfranchise v 1 give right of
voting to 2 give parliamentary

e

THESAURUS

≠ **discourage**; = **urge**, persuade,
prompt, spur, coax ≠ **dissuade**
end n = **close**, ending, finish, expiry,
expiration ≠ **beginning**;
= **conclusion**, ending, climax,
completion, finale ≠ **start**;
= **finish**, close, stop, resolution,
conclusion; = **extremity**, limit,
edge, border, extent; = **tip**, point,
head, peak, extremity ▷ v
= **stop**, finish, halt, cease, wind up
≠ **start**
endanger v = **put at risk**, risk,
threaten, compromise, jeopardize
≠ **save**
endeavour v = **try**, labour,
attempt, aim, struggle ▷ n

= **attempt**, try, effort, trial, bid
endorse v = **approve**, back,
support, champion, promote;
= **sign**, initial, countersign, sign on
the back of
endow v = **provide**, favour, grace,
bless, supply
endure v = **experience**, suffer,
bear, meet, encounter; = **last**,
continue, remain, stay, stand
enemy n = **foe**, rival, opponent,
the opposition, competitor
≠ **friend**
energy n = **strength**, might,
stamina, forcefulness
enforce v = **carry out**, apply,
implement, fulfil, execute

representation to **3** set free
engage ❶ v **1** participate
2 involve **3** employ **4** bring into
operation **5** begin conflict
engaged adj **1** pledged to be
married **2** in use **engagement** n
1 appointment **2** pledge of
marriage **engaging** adj charming
engender v give rise to
engine ❶ n **1** any machine to
convert energy into mechanical
work **2** railway locomotive
engineer n **1** one who is in charge
of engines, machinery etc. **2** one
who originates, organizes ▷ v
3 construct as engineer **4** contrive
engineering n
engrave v **1** cut in lines on metal
for printing **2** carve, incise
3 impress deeply **engraving** n
engross v **1** absorb (attention)
2 occupy wholly

engulf ❶ v swallow up
enhance ❶ v intensify value or
attractiveness of
enhancement n
enigma n puzzling thing or person
enigmatic adj
enjoy ❶ v **1** delight in **2** have
benefit of **enjoy oneself** be happy
enjoyable adj **enjoyment** n
enlarge ❶ v **1** make bigger
2 grow bigger **3** talk in greater
detail **enlargement** n
enlighten ❶ v give information to
enlightenment n
enlist ❶ v engage as soldier or
helper
enliven v animate
enmity n, pl **-ties** ill will, hostility
enormous ❶ adj very big, vast
enormity n, pl **-ties** gross offence
enough ❶ adj/n/adv as much as
need be

————————————————— THESAURUS —————————————————

engage v (with **in**) = **participate
in**, join in, take part in, undertake,
embark on; = **captivate**, catch,
arrest, fix, capture; = **occupy**,
involve, draw, grip, absorb;
= **employ**, appoint, take on, hire,
retain ≠ **dismiss**; = **set going**,
apply, trigger, activate,
switch on
engine n = **machine**, motor,
mechanism, generator, dynamo
engineer v = **design**, plan, create,
construct, devise
engulf v = **immerse**, swamp,
submerge, overrun, inundate
enhance v = **improve**, better,
increase, lift, boost ≠ **reduce**
enjoy v = **take pleasure in** or

from, like, love, appreciate, relish
≠ **hate**; = **have**, use, own,
experience, possess
enlarge v = **expand**, increase,
extend, add to, build up ≠ **reduce**;
= **grow**, increase, extend, expand,
swell
enlighten v = **inform**, tell, teach,
advise, counsel
enlist v = **join up**, join, enter (into),
register, volunteer; = **recruit**, take
on, hire, sign up, call up
enormous adj = **huge**, massive,
vast, extensive, tremendous
≠ **tiny**
enough adv = **sufficiently**, amply,
reasonably, adequately,
satisfactorily

enquire see INQUIRE
enrich ⊕ v 1 make rich 2 add to
enrol ⊕ v -rolling, -rolled 1 write name of on roll 2 enlist 3 become member
en route ⊕ (Fr) on the way
ensemble ⊕ n 1 all parts taken together 2 woman's complete outfit 3 (Mus) group of soloists performing together
enshrine v preserve with sacred affection
ensign n 1 naval or military flag 2 badge
enslave v make into slave
ensnare v 1 trap 2 entangle
ensue ⊕ v follow, happen after
ensure ⊕ v make certain

entail ⊕ v necessitate
entangle v 1 ensnare 2 perplex
entente n friendly understanding between nations
enter ⊕ v 1 go, come into 2 penetrate 3 join 4 write in 5 begin **entrance** n 1 going, coming in 2 door, passage 3 right to enter 4 fee **entrant** n one who enters **entry** n, pl -tries
enterprise ⊕ n 1 bold undertaking 2 bold spirit 3 business **enterprising** adj
entertain ⊕ v 1 amuse, receive as guest 2 consider **entertainer** n **entertainment** n
enthral v -thralling, -thralled captivate

——————— THESAURUS ———————

enrich v = **enhance**, develop, improve, boost, supplement; = **make rich**, make wealthy, make affluent, make prosperous, make well-off
enrol v = **enlist**, register, be accepted, be admitted, join up
en route adv = **on** or **along the way**, travelling, on the road, in transit, on the journey
ensemble n = **group**, company, band, troupe, cast; = **collection**, set, body, whole, total; = **outfit**, suit, get-up (Inf), costume
ensue v = **follow**, result, develop, proceed, arise ≠ **come first**
ensure v = **make certain**, guarantee, secure, make sure, confirm; = **protect**, defend, secure, safeguard, guard
entail v = **involve**, require, produce, demand, call for

enter v = **come** or **go in** or **into**, arrive, set foot in somewhere, cross the threshold of somewhere, make an entrance ≠ **exit**; = **penetrate**, get in, pierce, pass into, perforate; = **join**, start work at, begin work at, enrol in, enlist in ≠ **leave**; = **participate in**, join (in), be involved in, get involved in, play a part in
enterprise n = **firm**, company, business, concern, operation; = **venture**, operation, project, adventure, undertaking; = **initiative**, energy, daring, enthusiasm, imagination
entertain v = **amuse**, interest, please, delight, charm; = **show hospitality to**, receive, accommodate, treat, put up; = **consider**, imagine, think about, contemplate, conceive of

enthusiasm ❶ n ardent
eagerness **enthuse** v **enthusiast**
n **enthusiastic** adj
entice ❶ v allure, attract
entire ❶ adj whole, complete
entirely adv **entirety** n
entitle ❶ v 1 qualify 2 name
entitlement n
entity ❶ n, pl **-ties** 1 thing's being
or existence 2 reality
entomology n study of insects
entourage n group of people
assisting important person
entrails pl n intestines
entrance¹ ❶ see ENTER
entrance² ❶ v delight
entreat v 1 ask earnestly 2 beg,
implore **entreaty** n, pl **-ties**
entrench v establish firmly
entrepreneur ❶ n businessman

who attempts to profit by risk and
initiative
entrust, intrust ❶ v commit,
charge with
entwine v plait, interweave
enumerate v mention one by one
enunciate v state clearly
envelop v **enveloping,
enveloped** wrap up, surround
envelope ❶ n cover of letter
environment ❶ n
1 surroundings 2 conditions of life
or growth **environmental** adj
environs pl n outskirts
envisage ❶ v visualize
envoy ❶ n diplomat
envy ❶ v 1 grudge another's good
fortune ▷ n 2 (object of) this
feeling **enviable** adj **envious** adj
enzyme n any of group of proteins

enthusiasm n = **keenness**,
interest, passion, motivation, relish
entice v = **lure**, attract, invite,
persuade, tempt
entire adj = **whole**, full, complete,
total, gross
entitle v = **give the right to**,
allow, enable, permit, sanction;
= **call**, name, title, term, label
entity n = **thing**, being, individual,
object, substance
entrance¹ n = **way in**, opening,
door, approach, access ≠ **exit**;
= **appearance**, coming in, entry,
arrival, introduction ≠ **exit**;
= **admission**, access, entry, entrée,
admittance
entrance² v = **enchant**, delight,
charm, fascinate, dazzle ≠ **bore**;
= **mesmerize**, bewitch, hypnotize,

put a spell on, cast a spell on
entrepreneur n = **businessman**
or **businesswoman**, tycoon,
executive, industrialist, speculator
entrust, intrust v = **give
custody of**, deliver, commit,
delegate, hand over
envelope n = **wrapping**, casing,
case, covering, cover
environment n = **surroundings**,
setting, conditions, situation,
medium
envisage v = **imagine**,
contemplate, conceive (of),
visualize, picture
envoy n = **ambassador**, diplomat,
emissary; = **messenger**, agent,
representative, delegate, courier
envy n = **covetousness**,
resentment, jealousy, bitterness,

produced by living cells and acting as catalysts

epaulette *n* shoulder ornament on uniform

ephemeral *adj* short-lived

epic *n* **1** long poem telling of achievements of hero ▷ *adj* **2** on grand scale

epicentre *n* point immediately above origin of earthquake

epicure *n* one delighting in eating and drinking **epicurean** *adj/n*

epidemic ❶ *adj* **1** (esp. of disease) prevalent and spreading rapidly ▷ *n* **2** serious outbreak

epidermis *n* outer skin

epidural *n* spinal anaesthetic

epigram *n* witty saying

epigraph *n* **1** quotation at start of book **2** inscription

epilepsy *n* disorder of nervous system causing fits **epileptic** *n/adj*

epilogue *n* closing speech

episcopal *adj* of, ruled by bishop

episode ❶ *n* **1** incident **2** section of (serialized) book etc.

episodic *adj*

epistle *n* letter

epitaph *n* inscription on tomb

epithet *n* descriptive word

epitome *n* typical example **epitomize** *v*

epoch *n* period, era

equable *adj* even-tempered, placid

equal ❶ *adj* **1** the same in number, size, merit etc. **2** fit ▷ *n* **3** one equal to another ▷ *v* **4** be equal to **equally** *adv* **equality** *n* **equalize** *v*

equanimity *n* composure

equate ❶ *v* make equal **equation** *n* equating of two mathematical expressions

equator *n* imaginary circle round earth equidistant from the poles

equestrian *adj* of horse-riding

equilateral *adj* having equal sides

equilibrium ❶ *n, pl* **-ria** state of steadiness

equinox *n* time when sun crosses equator and day and night are equal

equip ❶ *v* **equipping, equipped** supply, fit out **equipment** *n*

THESAURUS

---

resentfulness ▷ *v* = **be jealous (of)**, resent, begrudge, be envious (of)

epidemic *n* = **outbreak**, plague, growth, spread, scourge; = **spate**, plague, outbreak, wave, rash

episode *n* = **event**, experience, happening, matter, affair; = **instalment**, part, act, scene, section

equal *adj* = **identical**, the same, matching, equivalent, uniform ≠ **unequal**; = **fair**, just, impartial, egalitarian, unbiased ≠ **unfair**;

= **even**, balanced, fifty-fifty (*Inf*), evenly matched ≠ **uneven** ▷ *n* = **match**, equivalent, twin, counterpart ▷ *v* = **amount to**, make, come to, total, level ≠ **be unequal to**

equate *v* = **identify**, associate, connect, compare, relate

equilibrium *n* = **stability**, balance, symmetry, steadiness, evenness

equip *v* = **supply**, provide for, stock, arm, array

equivalent ❶ adj equal in value
equivocal adj of double or
doubtful meaning **equivocate** v
era ❶ n period of time
eradicate ❶ v wipe out
erase ❶ v 1 rub out 2 remove
ere prep/conj (Poet) before
erect ❶ adj 1 upright ▷ v 2 set up
3 build **erection** n
ermine n stoat in northern regions
erode ❶ v 1 wear away 2 eat into
erosion n
erotic ❶ adj of sexual pleasure
err v 1 make mistakes 2 be wrong
3 sin **erratic** adj irregular
erratum n, pl **-ta** error, esp. in
printing **erroneous** adj wrong
error n mistake
errand n short journey for simple
business
errant adj wandering
erstwhile adj former

erudite adj learned
erupt ❶ v burst out **eruption** n
escalate ❶ v increase, be
increased, in extent, intensity etc.
escalation n
escalator n moving staircase
escape ❶ v 1 get free 2 get off
safely 3 find way out 4 elude
5 leak ▷ n 6 escaping **escapade**
n wild adventure **escapism** n
taking refuge in fantasy
escarpment n steep hillside
eschew v avoid, shun
escort ❶ n 1 person
accompanying another to guard,
guide etc. ▷ v 2 accompany
Eskimo n (Offens) 1 a member of a
group of peoples inhabiting N Canada,
Greenland, Alaska, and E Siberia,
having a material culture adapted
to an extremely cold climate 2 the
language of these peoples

— THESAURUS —

equivalent adj = **equal**, same,
comparable, parallel, identical
≠ **different**
era n = **age**, time, period, date,
generation
eradicate v = **wipe out**, eliminate,
remove, destroy, get rid of
erase v = **delete**, cancel out, wipe
out, remove, eradicate; = **rub out**,
remove, wipe out, delete
erect v = **build**, raise, set up,
construct, put up ≠ **demolish**;
= **found**, establish, form, create, set
up ▷ adj = **upright**, straight, stiff,
vertical, elevated ≠ **bent**
erode v = **disintegrate**, crumble,
deteriorate, corrode, break up
erotic adj = **sexual**, sexy (Inf),

crude, explicit, sensual
erupt v = **explode**, blow up, emit
lava; = **discharge**, expel, emit,
eject, spout
escalate v = **grow**, increase,
extend, intensify, expand
≠ **decrease**
escape v = **get away**, flee, take off,
fly, bolt; = **avoid**, miss, evade,
dodge, shun; = **leak out**, flow out,
gush out, emanate, seep out ▷ n
= **getaway**, break, flight,
break-out; = **avoidance**, evasion,
circumvention
escort n = **guard**, bodyguard,
train, convoy, entourage;
= **companion**, partner,
attendant, guide, beau ▷ v

esoteric *adj* obscure
ESP extrasensory perception
especial *adj* 1 pre-eminent
2 particular **especially** *adv*
espionage ❼ *n* spying
esplanade *n* promenade
espouse *v* 1 support 2 (*Obs*)
marry **espousal** *n*
espy *v* **espying, espied** catch
sight of
Esq. Esquire, title used on letters
essay ❼ *n* 1 prose composition
2 attempt ▷ *v* 3 try
essence ❼ *n* 1 all that makes
thing what it is 2 extract got by
distillation **essential** *adj* 1 vitally
important 2 basic ▷ *n* 3 essential
thing
establish ❼ *v* 1 set up 2 settle
3 prove **establishment** *n*
estate ❼ *n* 1 landed property

2 person's property 3 area of
property development **estate
agent** one who values, leases and
sells property
esteem ❼ *v/n* regard, respect
ester *n* (*Chem*) organic compound
estimate ❼ *v/n* (form)
approximate idea of (amounts,
measurements etc.) **estimable**
adj worthy of regard **estimation**
n opinion
estranged *adj* no longer living
with one's spouse
estuary ❼ *n*, *pl* **-aries** mouth of
river
etc. et cetera
et cetera (*Lat*) and the rest, and
others, and so on
etch ❼ *v* make engraving on metal
plate with acids etc. **etching** *n*
eternal ❼ *adj* everlasting

THESAURUS

= **accompany**, lead, partner,
conduct, guide
espionage *n* = **spying**, intelligence,
surveillance, counter-intelligence,
undercover work
essay *n* = **composition**, study,
paper, article, piece ▷ *v* (*Formal*)
= **attempt**, try, undertake,
endeavour
essence *n* = **fundamental
nature**, nature, being, heart,
spirit; = **concentrate**, spirits,
extract, tincture, distillate
establish *v* = **set up**, found,
create, institute, constitute;
= **prove**, confirm, demonstrate,
certify, verify
estate *n* = **lands**, property, area,
grounds, domain; = **area**, centre,

park, development, site
esteem *n* = **respect**, regard,
honour, admiration, reverence ▷ *v*
= **respect**, admire, think highly of,
love, value
estimate *v* = **calculate roughly**,
value, guess, judge, reckon;
= **think**, believe, consider, rate,
judge ▷ *n* = **approximate
calculation**, guess, assessment,
judgment, valuation;
= **assessment**, opinion, belief,
appraisal, evaluation
estuary *n* = **inlet**, mouth, creek,
firth, fjord
etch *v* = **engrave**, cut, impress,
stamp, carve
eternal *adj* = **interminable**,
endless, infinite, continual,

eternity n
ether n 1 colourless liquid used as anaesthetic 2 clear sky **ethereal** adj 1 airy 2 heavenly
ethnic, ethnical ❶ adj of race or relating to classification of humans into different groups
ethos n distinctive spirit of people, culture etc.
etiquette n conventional code of conduct
étude n short musical composition, exercise
etymology n, pl -gies tracing, account of word's origin, development
eucalyptus, eucalypt n Aust. tree, providing timber and gum
Eucharist n Christian sacrament of the Lord's Supper
eugenics pl n science of improving the human race by selective breeding
eulogy n, pl -gies praise **eulogize** v
eunuch n castrated man

euphemism n substitution of mild term for offensive one **euphemistic** adj
euphoria ❶ n sense of elation **euphoric** adj
eureka interj exclamation of triumph
euthanasia n painless putting to death to relieve suffering
evacuate ❶ v 1 empty 2 withdraw from **evacuation** n **evacuee** n
evade ❶ v 1 avoid 2 elude **evasion** n **evasive** adj
evaluate ❶ v find or judge value of **evaluation** n
evangelical adj of, or according to, gospel teaching **evangelism** n **evangelist** n
evaporate ❶ v turn into vapour **evaporation** n
eve ❶ n 1 evening before 2 time just before **evensong** n evening service
even ❶ adj 1 flat, smooth 2 uniform, equal 3 divisible by two

— THESAURUS —

immortal ≠ **occasional**
ethnic, ethnical adj = **cultural**, national, traditional, native, folk
euphoria n = **elation**, joy, ecstasy, rapture, exhilaration ≠ **despondency**
evacuate v = **remove**, clear, withdraw, expel, move out
evade v = **avoid**, escape, dodge, get away from, elude ≠ **face**; = **avoid answering**, parry, fend off, fudge, hedge
evaluate v = **assess**, rate, judge, estimate, reckon

evaporate v = **disappear**, vaporize, dematerialize, vanish, dissolve; = **dry up**, dry, dehydrate, vaporize, desiccate
eve n = **night before**, day before, vigil; = **brink**, point, edge, verge, threshold
even adj = **regular**, stable, constant, steady, smooth ≠ **variable**; = **level**, straight, flat, smooth, true ≠ **uneven**; = **equal**, like, matching, similar, identical ≠ **unequal**; = **equally matched**, level, tied, on a par, neck and neck

4 impartial ▷ v **5** smooth
6 equalize ▷ adv **7** equally
8 simply **9** notwithstanding
evening 𝟏 n close of day
event 𝟏 n **1** happening **2** notable
occurrence **3** result **4** any one
contest in sporting programme
eventful adj full of exciting events
eventual adj resulting in the end
eventuality n possible event
ever 𝟏 adv **1** always **2** at any time
evergreen n/adj (tree or shrub)
bearing foliage throughout the year
evermore adv for all time to come
every adj **1** each of all **2** all
possible **everybody** n **everyday**
adj usual, ordinary **everyone** n
everything n **everywhere** adv in
all places
evict v expel by legal process, turn
out **eviction** n
evidence 𝟏 n **1** ground of belief
2 sign **3** testimony ▷ v **4** indicate,

prove **evident** adj plain, obvious
evil 𝟏 adj/n (what is) bad or
harmful
evoke 𝟏 v **1** call to mind
2 bring about **evocation** n
evocative adj
evolve 𝟏 v **1** (cause to) develop
gradually **2** undergo slow changes
evolution n development of
species from earlier forms
ewe n female sheep
ex- comb. form **1** out from, from, out
of, formerly, as in exclaim, exodus
exacerbate v aggravate, make
worse
exact 𝟏 adj **1** precise, strictly
correct ▷ v **2** demand, extort
exacting adj making rigorous
demands **exactly** adv
exaggerate 𝟏 v magnify beyond
truth, overstate **exaggeration** n
exalt v **1** raise up **2** praise
exam n examination

e

THESAURUS

≠ ill-matched
evening n = **dusk**, night, sunset,
twilight, sundown
event n = **incident**, happening,
experience, affair, occasion;
= **competition**, game,
tournament, contest, bout
ever adv = **at any time**, at all, in
any case, at any point, by any
chance; = **always**, for ever, at all
times, evermore
evidence n = **proof**, grounds,
demonstration, confirmation/
verification; = **sign(s)**, suggestion,
trace, indication ▷ v = **show**,
prove, reveal, display, indicate
evil n = **wickedness**, bad, vice, sin,

wrongdoing; = **harm**, suffering,
hurt, woe ▷ adj = **wicked**, bad,
malicious, immoral, sinful;
= **harmful**, disastrous, destructive,
dire, catastrophic; = **demonic**,
satanic, diabolical, hellish, devilish
evoke v = **arouse**, cause, induce,
awaken, give rise to ≠ suppress
evolve v = **develop**,
metamorphose, adapt yourself
exact adj = **accurate**, correct, true,
right, specific ≠ approximate ▷ v
= **demand**, claim, force, command,
extract
exaggerate v = **overstate**,
enlarge, embroider, amplify,
embellish

e

examine ⊕ v **1** investigate **2** look at closely **3** ask questions of **4** test knowledge of **examination** n **examiner** n

example ⊕ n **1** specimen **2** model

exasperate v irritate **exasperation** n

excavate v **1** hollow out **2** dig **3** unearth **excavator** n

exceed ⊕ v **1** be greater than **2** go beyond **exceedingly** adv very

excel ⊕ v **-celling, -celled 1** surpass **2** be very good **excellence** n **excellent** adj very good

except, except for ⊕ prep **1** not including ▷ v **2** exclude **exception** n **1** thing not included in a rule **2** objection **exceptional** adj above average

excerpt ⊕ n passage from book etc.

excess ⊕ n **1** too great amount

2 intemperance **excessive** adj

exchange ⊕ v **1** give (something) in return for something else **2** barter ▷ n **3** giving one thing and receiving another **4** thing given **5** building where merchants meet for business **6** central telephone office **exchangeable** adj

excise¹ n duty charged on home goods

excise² v cut away

excite ⊕ v **1** arouse to strong emotion, stimulate **2** set in motion **excitable** adj **excitement** n **exciting** adj

exclaim ⊕ v speak suddenly, cry out **exclamation** n **exclamation mark** punctuation mark (!), used after exclamations

exclude ⊕ v **1** shut out **2** debar from **3** reject, not consider **exclusion** n **exclusive** adj **1** excluding **2** select

— THESAURUS —

examine v = **inspect**, study, survey, investigate, explore; = **test**, question, assess, quiz, evaluate; = **question**, quiz, interrogate, cross-examine, grill (Inf)

example n = **instance**, specimen, case, sample, illustration

exceed v = **surpass**, better, pass, eclipse, beat; = **go over the limit of**, go beyond, overstep

excel v = **be superior**, eclipse, beat, surpass, transcend

except, except for prep = **apart from**, but for, saving, barring, excepting ▷ v = **exclude**, leave out, omit, disregard, pass over

excerpt n = **extract**, part, piece,

section, selection

excess n = **surfeit**, surplus, overload, glut, superabundance ≠ **shortage**; = **overindulgence**, extravagance, profligacy, debauchery, dissipation ≠ **moderation**

exchange v = **interchange**, change, trade, switch, swap ▷ n = **conversation**, talk, word, discussion, chat

excite v = **thrill**, inspire, stir, provoke, animate; = **arouse**, provoke, rouse, stir up

exclaim v = **cry out**, declare, shout, proclaim, yell

exclude v = **keep out**, bar, ban,

exclusiveness, exclusivity n
excommunicate v cut off from
sacraments of the Church
excommunication n
excrement n waste matter from
bowels **excrete** v discharge from
the system **excretion** n
excretory adj
excruciating adj unbearably
painful
excursion ⊕ n trip for pleasure
excuse ⊕ v 1 overlook 2 try to
clear from blame 3 gain
exemption 4 set free ▷ n 5 that
which serves to excuse 6 apology
excusable adj
execrable adj hatefully bad
execute ⊕ v 1 inflict capital
punishment on, kill 2 carry out,
perform 3 make **execution** n
executioner n **executive** n/adj
1 (of) person in administrative

position 2 (of) branch of
government enforcing laws
executor n person appointed to
carry out provisions of a will
exemplify ⊕ v -fying, -fied
serve as example of
exempt ⊕ v 1 free from 2 excuse
▷ adj 3 freed from, not liable for
exemption n
exercise ⊕ n 1 use of limbs for
health 2 practice 3 task 4 use
▷ v 5 use 6 carry out 7 take
exercise
exert ⊕ v make effort **exertion** n
exhale v breathe out
exhaust ⊕ v 1 tire out 2 use up
3 empty ▷ n 4 waste gases from
engine 5 passage for this
exhaustible adj **exhaustion** n
state of extreme fatigue
exhaustive adj comprehensive
exhibit ⊕ v 1 show, display ▷ n

e

—————— THESAURUS ——————

refuse, forbid ≠ **let in**; = **omit**,
reject, eliminate, rule out, miss out
≠ **include**
excursion n = **trip**, tour, journey,
outing, expedition
excuse n = **justification**, reason,
explanation, defence, grounds
≠ **accusation** ▷ v = **justify**,
explain, defend, vindicate, mitigate
≠ **blame**; = **forgive**, pardon,
overlook, tolerate, acquit; = **free**,
relieve, exempt, release, spare
≠ **convict**
execute v = **put to death**, kill,
shoot, hang, behead; = **carry out**,
effect, implement, accomplish,
discharge
exemplify v = **show**, represent,

display, demonstrate, illustrate
exempt adj = **immune**, free,
excepted, excused, released
≠ **liable** ▷ v = **grant immunity**,
free, excuse, release, spare
exercise v = **put to use**, use,
apply, employ, exert; = **train**, work
out, practise, keep fit, do exercises
▷ n = **use**, practice, application,
operation, discharge; = **exertion**,
training, activity, work, labour
exert v = **apply**, use, exercise,
employ, wield
exhaust v = **tire out**, fatigue,
drain, weaken, weary; = **use up**,
spend, consume, waste, go through
exhibit v = **show**, reveal, display,
demonstrate, express; = **display**,

e

2 thing shown **exhibition** *n*
1 display **2** public show
exhibitionist *n* one with
compulsive desire to attract
attention **exhibitor** *n*
exhilarate *v* enliven, gladden
exhilaration *n*
exhort *v* urge
exhume *v* dig up (corpse etc.)
exigency *n, pl* **-cies** urgent need
exile ❶ *n* **1** banishment, expulsion
from one's own country **2** one
banished ▷ *v* **3** banish
exist ❶ *v* be, have being, live
existence *n* **existent** *adj*
exit ❶ *n* **1** way out **2** going out ▷ *v*
3 go out
exodus ❶ *n* departure
exonerate *v* free, declare free,
from blame
exorbitant *adj* excessive
exorcize *v* cast out (evil spirits) by

invocation **exorcism** *n* **exorcist** *n*
exotic ❶ *adj* **1** foreign **2** unusual
expand ❶ *v* increase, spread out
expandable *adj* **expanse** *n* wide
space **expansion** *n* **expansive**
adj **1** extensive **2** friendly
expatiate *v* speak or write at
great length (on)
expatriate ❶ *adj/n* (one) living in
exile
expect ❶ *v* **1** regard as probable
2 look forward to **expectant** *adj*
expectation *n*
expedient *adj* **1** fitting **2** politic
3 convenient ▷ *n* **4** something
suitable, useful **expediency** *n*
expedite *v* help on, hasten
expedition *n* **1** journey for
definite purpose **2** people,
equipment comprising
expedition
expel ❶ *v* **-pelling, -pelled 1** drive

— THESAURUS —

show, set out, parade, unveil
exile *n* = **banishment**, expulsion,
deportation, eviction, expatriation;
= **expatriate**, refugee, outcast,
émigré, deportee ▷ *v* = **banish**,
expel, throw out, deport, drive out
exist *v* = **live**, be present, survive,
endure, be in existence; = **occur**, be
present; = **survive**, stay alive, make
ends meet, subsist, eke out a living
exit *n* = **way out**, door, gate, outlet,
doorway ≠ **entry**; = **departure**,
withdrawal, retreat, farewell, going
▷ *v* = **depart**, leave, go out,
withdraw, retire ≠ **enter**
exodus *n* = **departure**,
withdrawal, retreat, leaving, flight
exotic *adj* = **unusual**, striking,

strange, fascinating, mysterious
≠ **ordinary**; = **foreign**, alien,
tropical, external, naturalized
expand *v* = **get bigger**, increase,
grow, extend, swell ≠ **contract**;
= **make bigger**, increase, develop,
extend, widen ≠ **reduce**; = **spread
(out)**, unfold, unravel,
diffuse
expatriate *n* = **exile**, refugee,
emigrant, émigré ▷ *adj* = **exiled**,
refugee, banished, emigrant,
émigré
expect *v* = **think**, believe, suppose,
assume, trust; = **anticipate**, look
forward to, predict, envisage, await
expel *v* = **throw out**, exclude, ban,
dismiss, kick out (*Inf*) ≠ **let in**;

out **2** exclude **expulsion** n
expend v **1** spend, pay out **2** use up **expendable** adj likely to be used up **expenditure** n **expense** n **1** cost ▷ pl **2** charges incurred **expensive** adj
experience ❶ n **1** observation of facts as source of knowledge **2** being affected by event **3** the event **4** knowledge, skill gained ▷ v **5** undergo, suffer, meet with **experienced** adj
experiment ❶ n/v test to discover or prove something **experimental** adj
expert ❶ n/adj (one) skilful, knowledgeable, in something **expertise** n
expiate v make amends for
expire ❶ v **1** come to an end **2** die

3 breathe out **expiry** n end
explain ❶ v **1** make clear, intelligible **2** account for **explanation** n **explanatory** adj
expletive n **1** exclamation **2** oath
explicable adj explainable
explicit ❶ adj clearly stated
explode ❶ v **1** (make) burst violently **2** (of population) increase rapidly **3** discredit **explosion** n **explosive** adj/n
exploit ❶ n **1** brilliant feat, deed ▷ v **2** turn to advantage **3** make use of for one's own ends **exploitation** n
explore ❶ v **1** investigate **2** examine (country etc.) by going through it **exploration** n **exploratory** adj **explorer** n

e

————— THESAURUS —————

= **banish**, exile, deport, evict, force to leave ≠ **take in**
experience n = **knowledge**, practice, skill, contact, expertise; = **event**, affair, incident, happening, encounter ▷ v = **undergo**, feel, face, taste, go through
experiment n = **test**, trial, investigation, examination, procedure; = **research**, investigation, analysis, observation, research and development ▷ v = **test**, investigate, trial, research, try
expert n = **specialist**, authority, professional, master, genius ≠ **amateur** ▷ adj = **skilful**, experienced, professional, masterly, qualified ≠ **unskilled**
expire v = **become invalid**, end,

finish, conclude, close; = **die**, depart, perish, kick the bucket (Inf), depart this life
explain v = **make clear** or **plain**, describe, teach, define, resolve; = **account for**, excuse, justify, give a reason for
explicit adj = **clear**, obvious, specific, direct, precise ≠ **vague**
explode v = **blow up**, erupt, burst, go off, shatter; = **detonate**, set off, discharge, let off
exploit v = **take advantage of**, abuse, use, manipulate, milk; = **make the best use of**, use, make use of, utilize, cash in on (Inf) ▷ n = **feat**, act, achievement, enterprise, adventure
explore v = **travel around**, tour, survey, scout, reconnoitre;

exponent see EXPOUND

export v **1** send (goods) out of the country ▷ n **2** exporting **3** product sold abroad

expose ⊕ v **1** display **2** reveal (scandalous) truth **3** leave unprotected **exposure** n

exposé n bringing of scandal, crime etc, to public notice

expound v explain, interpret **exponent** n **1** one who expounds or promotes (idea, cause etc.) **2** performer **exposition** n **1** explanation **2** exhibition of goods etc.

express ⊕ v **1** put into words **2** make known or understood ▷ adj **3** definitely stated **4** specially designed **5** speedy ▷ adv **6** with speed ▷ n **7** express train **8** rapid parcel delivery service **expression** n **1** expressing **2** word, phrase **3** look **expressive** adj

expropriate v dispossess

expunge v delete, blot out

expurgate v remove objectionable parts (from book etc.)

exquisite ⊕ adj of extreme beauty or delicacy

extend ⊕ v **1** stretch out **2** prolong **3** widen **4** accord, grant **5** reach **6** cover area **7** have range or scope **extension** n **1** extending **2** additional part **extensive** adj wide **extent** n **1** space **2** scope **3** size

extenuate v **1** make less blameworthy **2** lessen **3** mitigate

exterior ⊕ n **1** outside ▷ adj **2** outer, external

exterminate v destroy completely **extermination** n

external ⊕ adj outside, outward **externally** adv

extinct ⊕ adj **1** having died out **2** quenched **extinction** n

extinguish v **1** put out, quench

━━━━━━━━━━━━ THESAURUS ━━━━━━━━━━━━

= **investigate**, consider, research, survey, search

expose v = **uncover**, show, reveal, display, exhibit ≠ **hide**; = **make vulnerable**, subject, endanger, leave open, jeopardize

express v = **state**, communicate, convey, articulate, say; = **show**, indicate, exhibit, demonstrate, reveal ▷ adj = **explicit**, clear, plain, distinct, definite; = **specific**, exclusive, particular, sole, special; = **fast**, direct, rapid, priority, prompt

exquisite adj = **beautiful**, elegant, graceful, pleasing, attractive ≠ **unattractive**; = **fine**, beautiful,

lovely, elegant, precious

extend v = **spread out**, reach, stretch; = **stretch**, stretch out, spread out, straighten out; = **last**, continue, go on, stretch, carry on; = **protrude**, project, stand out, bulge, stick out

exterior n = **outside**, face, surface, covering, skin ▷ adj = **outer**, outside, external, surface, outward ≠ **inner**

external adj = **outer**, outside, surface, outward, exterior ≠ **internal**

extinct adj = **dead**, lost, gone, vanished, defunct ≠ **living**

2 wipe out; destroy

extol v -tolling, -tolled praise highly

extort v get by force or threats **extortion** n **extortionate** adj excessive

extra ❶ adj 1 additional 2 more than usual ▷ adv 3 additionally 4 more than usually ▷ n 5 extra person or thing 6 something charged as additional

extra- comb. form 1 beyond, as in extramural

extract ❶ v 1 take out, esp. by force 2 get by distillation etc. 3 derive 4 quote ▷ n 5 passage from book, film etc. 6 concentrated solution **extraction** n 1 extracting 2 ancestry

extramural adj outside normal courses etc. of university or college

extraneous adj 1 not essential 2 added from without

extraordinary ❶ adj very unusual **extraordinarily** adv

extrapolate v make inference from known facts

extrasensory adj of perception apparently gained without use of known senses

extravagant ❶ adj 1 wasteful 2 exorbitant **extravagance** n **extravaganza** n elaborate entertainment

extreme ❶ adj 1 of high or highest degree 2 severe 3 going beyond moderation 4 outermost ▷ n 5 utmost degree 6 thing at either end **extremely** adv **extremist** n/adj (one) favouring immoderate methods **extremity** n, pl -ties 1 end ▷ pl 2 hands and feet

extricate v disentangle

extrovert n lively, outgoing person

extrude v squeeze, force out

exuberant adj high-spirited **exuberance** n

exude v 1 ooze out 2 give off

exult v rejoice, triumph **exultant**

THESAURUS

extra adj = **additional**, more, added, further, supplementary ≠ **vital**; = **surplus**, excess, spare, redundant, unused ▷ n = **addition**, bonus, supplement, accessory ≠ **necessity** ▷ adv = **in addition**, additionally, over and above

extract v = **take out**, draw, pull, remove, withdraw; = **pull out**, remove, take out, draw, uproot ▷ n = **passage**, selection, excerpt, cutting, clipping; = **essence**, solution, concentrate, juice,

distillation

extraordinary adj = **remarkable**, outstanding, amazing, fantastic, astonishing ≠ **unremarkable**

extravagant adj = **wasteful**, lavish, prodigal, profligate, spendthrift ≠ **economical**; = **excessive**, outrageous, over the top (sl), unreasonable, preposterous ≠ **moderate**

extreme adj = **great**, highest, supreme, acute, severe ≠ **mild**; = **severe**, radical, strict, harsh,

adj **exultation** *n*

eye ❶ *n* **1** organ of sight **2** look, glance **3** attention **4** aperture **5** thing resembling eye ▷ *v* **6** look at **7** observe **eyebrow** *n* fringe of hair above eye **eyelash** *n* hair fringing eyelid **eyelet** *n* small hole

eyelid *n* **eye shadow** coloured cosmetic worn on upper eyelids **eyesore** *n* ugly object **eyetooth** *n* canine tooth **eyewitness** *n* one who was present at an event

eyrie *n* nest of bird of prey, esp. eagle

——————————————— THESAURUS ———————

e

rigid; = **radical**, excessive, fanatical, immoderate ≠ **moderate**; = **farthest**, furthest, far, remotest, far-off ≠ **nearest** ▷ *n* = **limit**, end, edge, opposite, pole

eye *n* = **eyeball**, optic (*Inf*), organ of vision, organ of sight; (*often plural*) = **eyesight**, sight, vision, perception, ability to see ▷ *v* = **look at**, view, study, watch, survey

F Fahrenheit

fable n short story with moral
fabulous adj 1 amazing 2 (Inf)
extremely good

fabric ● n 1 cloth 2 structure
fabricate v 1 construct 2 invent
(lie etc.)

face ● n 1 front of head
2 distorted expression 3 outward
appearance 4 chief side of
anything 5 dignity ▷ v 6 look or
front towards 7 meet (boldly)
8 give a covering surface 9 turn
faceless adj anonymous **face-lift**

n operation to remove wrinkles
face-saving adj maintaining
dignity **facet** n 1 one side of cut
gem 2 one aspect **face value**
apparent worth **facial** n
1 cosmetic treatment for face ▷ adj
2 of face

facetious adj given to joking

facia pl **-ciae** see FASCIA

facile adj 1 easy 2 superficial
facilitate v make easy **facility** n
1 easiness 2 dexterity ▷ pl
3 opportunities, good conditions
4 means, equipment for doing
something

facsimile n exact copy

fact ● n 1 thing known to be true
2 reality **factual** adj

faction ● n 1 (dissenting)
minority group 2 dissension

factor ● n 1 something
contributing to a result 2 one of
numbers which multiplied
together give a given number
3 agent

factory ● n, pl **-ries** building
where things are manufactured

THESAURUS

fabric n = **cloth**, material, stuff,
textile, web; = **framework**,
structure, make-up, organization,
frame

face n = **countenance**, features,
profile, mug (Sl), visage;
= **expression**, look, air,
appearance, aspect; = **side**, front,
outside, surface, exterior ▷ v
= **look onto**, overlook, be opposite,
look out on, front onto; = **confront**,
meet, encounter, deal with,
oppose; (often with **up to**) = **accept**,

deal with, tackle, acknowledge,
cope with

fact n = **truth**, reality, certainty,
verity ≠ fiction; = **event**,
happening, act, performance,
incident

faction n = **group**, set, party,
gang, bloc; = **dissension**, division,
conflict, rebellion, disagreement
≠ agreement

factor n = **element**, part, cause,
influence, item

factory n = **works**, plant, mill,

faculty ❶ n, pl **-ties 1** inherent power **2** ability **3** aptitude **4** department of university

fad ❶ n short-lived fashion

fade ❶ v **1** lose colour, strength **2** cause to fade

faeces pl n excrement

fag n (Inf) **1** boring task **2** (Sl) cigarette ▷ v (Inf) **3** tire

faggot n **1** ball of chopped liver **2** bundle of sticks

Fahrenheit adj measured by thermometric scale with freezing point of water 32°, boiling point 212°

fail ❶ v **1** be unsuccessful **2** stop working **3** (judge to) be below the required standard **4** disappoint, give no help to **5** be insufficient **6** become bankrupt **7** neglect, forget to do **failing** n **1** deficiency

2 fault ▷ prep **3** in default of **failure** n **without fail** certainly

faint ❶ adj **1** feeble, dim, pale **2** weak **3** dizzy ▷ v **4** lose consciousness temporarily

fair¹ ❶ adj **1** just **2** according to rules **3** blond **4** beautiful **5** of moderate quality or amount **6** favourable ▷ adv **7** honestly **fairly** adv **fairness** n **fairway** n smooth area on golf course between tee and green

fair² ❶ n **1** travelling entertainment with sideshows etc. **2** trade exhibition **fairground** n

fairy ❶ n, pl **fairies 1** imaginary small creature with powers of magic ▷ adj **2** of fairies **3** delicate, imaginary

━━━━━━━━━━━ THESAURUS ━━━━━━

workshop, assembly line

faculty n = **ability**, power, skill, facility, capacity ≠ **failing**; = **department**, school, staff, teachers, professors

fad n = **craze**, fashion, trend, rage, vogue

fade v = **become pale**, bleach, wash out, discolour, lose colour; = **make pale**, dim, bleach, wash out, blanch

fail v = **be unsuccessful**, founder, fall, break down, flop (Inf) ≠ **succeed**; = **disappoint**, abandon, desert, neglect, omit; = **stop working**, stop, die, break down, stall; = **wither**, perish, sag, waste away, shrivel up; = **go bankrupt**, collapse, fold (Inf), close down, go under

faint adj = **dim**, low, soft, faded, distant ≠ **clear**; = **slight**, weak, feeble, unenthusiastic, remote; = **dizzy**, giddy, light-headed, weak, exhausted ≠ **energetic** ▷ v = **pass out**, black out, lose consciousness, keel over (Inf), go out

fair¹ adj = **unbiased**, impartial, even-handed, unprejudiced, just ≠ **unfair**; = **respectable**, average, reasonable, decent, acceptable; = **light**, golden, blonde, blond, yellowish; = **fine**, clear, dry, bright, pleasant; = **beautiful**, pretty, attractive, lovely, handsome ≠ **ugly**

fair² n = **carnival**, show, fête, festival, exhibition

fairy n = **sprite**, elf, brownie, pixie, puck

faith ⊙ *n* **1** trust **2** belief (without proof) **3** religion **4** loyalty
faithful *adj* constant, true
faithfully *adv* **faithless** *adj*

fake ⊙ *v* **1** touch up **2** counterfeit ▷ *n/adj* **3** fraudulent (thing or person)

falcon *n* small bird of prey

fall ⊙ *v* **falling, fell, fallen 1** drop **2** become lower **3** hang down **4** cease to stand **5** perish **6** collapse **7** be captured **8** become **9** happen ▷ *n* **10** falling **11** amount that falls **12** decrease **13** collapse **14** drop **15** cascade **16** yielding to temptation **17** (US) autumn **fallout** *n* radioactive particles spread as result of nuclear explosion

fallacy *n, pl* **-cies** incorrect

opinion or argument **fallacious** *adj* **fallible** *adj* liable to error

fallow *adj* ploughed but left without crop

false ⊙ *adj* **1** wrong **2** deceptive **3** faithless **4** artificial **falsely** *adv* **falsehood** *n* **falsify** *v* alter fraudulently

falsetto *n, pl* **-tos** forced voice above natural range

falter ⊙ *v* **1** hesitate **2** waver **3** stumble

fame ⊙ *n* renown **famed** *adj* **famous** *adj* widely known **famously** *adv* (Inf) excellently

familiar ⊙ *adj* **1** well-known **2** customary **3** intimate **4** acquainted **5** impertinent ▷ *n* **6** friend **7** demon **familiarity** *n* **familiarize** *v*

— THESAURUS —

faith *n* = **confidence**, trust, credit, conviction, assurance ≠ **distrust**; = **religion**, church, belief, persuasion, creed ≠ **agnosticism**

fake *adj* = **artificial**, false, forged, counterfeit, put-on ≠ **genuine** ▷ *n* = **forgery**, copy, fraud, reproduction, dummy ▷ *v* = **forge**, copy, reproduce, fabricate, counterfeit; = **sham**, put on, pretend, simulate, feign

fall *v* = **drop**, plunge, tumble, plummet, collapse ≠ **rise**; = **decrease**, drop, decline, go down, slump ≠ **increase**; = **be overthrown**, surrender, succumb, submit, capitulate ≠ **triumph**; = **be killed**, die, perish, meet your end ≠ **survive**; = **occur**, happen, come about, chance, take place ▷ *n*

= **drop**, slip, plunge, dive, tumble; = **decrease**, drop, lowering, decline, reduction; = **collapse**, defeat, downfall, ruin, destruction

false *adj* = **incorrect**, wrong, mistaken, misleading, faulty ≠ **correct**; = **untrue**, fraudulent, trumped up, fallacious, untruthful ≠ **true**; = **artificial**, forged, fake, reproduction, replica ≠ **real** (Inf)

falter *v* = **hesitate**, delay, waver, vacillate ≠ **persevere**; = **tumble**, totter; = **stutter**, pause, stumble, hesitate, stammer

fame *n* = **prominence**, glory, celebrity, stardom, reputation ≠ **obscurity**

familiar *adj* = **well-known**, recognized, common, ordinary, routine ≠ **unfamiliar**; = **friendly**,

family ⊙ *n, pl* **-lies 1** parents and children, relatives **2** group of allied objects
famine ⊙ *n* **1** extreme scarcity of food **2** starvation **famished** *adj* very hungry
fan¹ ⊙ *n* **1** instrument for producing current of air **2** folding object of paper etc., for cooling the face ▷ *v* **3** blow or cool with fan **4** spread out
fan² ⊙ *n* (*Inf*) devoted admirer
fanatic ⊙ *adj/n* (person) filled with abnormal enthusiasm **fanatical** *adj* **fanaticism** *n*
fancy ⊙ *adj* **-cier, -ciest 1** ornamental ▷ *n* **2** whim **3** liking **4** imagination **5** mental image ▷ *v* **6** imagine **7** be inclined to believe

8 (*Inf*) have a liking for **fancier** *n* one with special interest in something **fanciful** *adj*
fanfare *n* **1** flourish of trumpets **2** ostentatious display
fang *n* **1** snake's tooth, injecting poison **2** long, pointed tooth
fantasy, *Archaic* **phantasy** ⊙ *n, pl* **-sies 1** power of imagination **2** mental image **3** fanciful invention **fantasize** *v* **fantastic** *adj* **1** quaint, extremely fanciful, wild **2** (*Inf*) very good **3** (*Inf*) very large
far ⊙ *adv* **farther 1** at or to a great distance or a remote time **2** by very much ▷ *adj* **3** distant **3** more distant **far-fetched** *adj* incredible
farce ⊙ *n* **1** comedy of boisterous

THESAURUS

close, dear, intimate, amicable **≠ formal**; **= relaxed**, easy, friendly, comfortable, intimate; **= disrespectful**, forward, bold, intrusive, presumptuous
family *n* **= relations**, relatives, household, folk (*Inf*), kin; **= children**, kids (*Inf*), offspring, little ones; **= ancestors**, house, race, tribe, clan
famine *n* **= hunger**, want, starvation, deprivation, scarcity
fan¹ *n* **= blower**, ventilator, air conditioner ▷ *v* **= blow**, cool, refresh, air-condition/ventilate
fan² *n* **= supporter**, lover, follower, enthusiast, admirer
fanatic *n* **= extremist**, activist, militant, bigot, zealot
fancy *adj* **= elaborate**, decorative, extravagant, intricate, baroque

≠ plain ▷ *n* **= whim**, thought, idea, desire, urge; **= delusion**, dream, vision, fantasy, daydream ▷ *v* **= wish for**, want, desire, hope for, long for; (*Inf*) **= be attracted to**, find attractive, lust after, like, take to; **= suppose**, think, believe, imagine, reckon
fantasy, *Archaic* **phantasy** *n* **= daydream**, dream, wish, reverie, flight of fancy; **= imagination**, fancy, invention, creativity, originality
far *adv* **= a long way**, miles, deep, a good way, afar; **= much**, greatly, very much, extremely, significantly ▷ *adj* (*often with* **off**) **= remote**, distant, far-flung, faraway, out-of-the-way **≠ near**
farce *n* **= comedy**, satire, slapstick, burlesque, buffoonery; **= mockery**,

humour **2** absurd and futile
proceeding **farcical** *adj*
fare ❶ *n* **1** charge for transport
2 passenger **3** food ▷ *v* **4** get on
5 happen **farewell** *interj*
1 goodbye ▷ *n* **2** leave-taking
farm ❶ *n* **1** tract of land for
cultivation or rearing livestock ▷ *v*
2 cultivate (land) **3** rear livestock
(on farm) **farmer** *n* **farmhouse** *n*
farmyard *n*
fart *(Vulgar)* ▷ *n* **1** (audible)
emission of gas from anus ▷ *v*
2 break wind
farther, farthest *adv/adj*
further: comparative of FAR
farthest *adv/adj* furthest:
superlative of FAR
farthing *n* formerly, coin worth a
quarter of a penny
fascia *n, pl* **-ciae, -cias 1** flat
surface above shop window

2 dashboard
fascinate ❶ *v* attract and delight
fascination *n*
fascism *n* authoritarian political
system opposed to democracy and
liberalism **fascist** *adj/n*
fashion ❶ *n* **1** (latest) style, esp. of
dress etc. **2** manner **3** type ▷ *v*
4 shape, make **fashionable** *adj*
fast¹ ❶ *adj* **1** (capable of) moving
quickly **2** ahead of true time
3 *(Obs)* dissipated **4** firm, steady
▷ *adv* **5** rapidly **6** tightly **fast
food** food, esp. hamburgers etc.,
served very quickly
fast² ❶ *v* **1** go without food ▷ *n*
2 fasting **fasting** *n*
fasten ❶ *v* **1** attach, fix, secure
2 become joined **fastener,
fastening** *n*
fastidious *adj* hard to please
fat ❶ *n* **1** oily

THESAURUS

---

joke, nonsense, parody, shambles
fare *n* **= charge**, price, ticket price,
ticket money; **= food**, provisions,
board, rations, nourishment ▷ *v*
= get on, do, manage, make out,
prosper
farm *n* **= smallholding**, ranch
(chiefly US & Canad), farmstead,
vineyard, plantation ▷ *v*
= cultivate, work, plant, grow
crops on, keep animals on
fascinate *v* **= entrance**, absorb,
intrigue, rivet, captivate ≠ **bore**
fashion *n* **= style**, look, trend,
rage, custom; **= method**, way,
style, manner, mode ▷ *v*
= make, shape, cast, construct,
form

fast¹ *adj* **= quick**, flying, rapid, fleet,
swift ≠ **slow**; **= fixed**, firm, sound,
stuck, secure ≠ **unstable**;
= dissipated, wild, exciting, loose,
extravagant ▷ *adv* **= quickly**,
rapidly, swiftly, hastily, hurriedly
≠ **slowly**; **= firmly**, staunchly,
resolutely, steadfastly,
unwaveringly
fast² *v* **= go hungry**, abstain, go
without food, deny yourself ▷ *n*
= fasting, diet, abstinence
fasten *v* **= secure**, close, do up
fat *adj* **= overweight**, large,
heavy, plump, stout ≠ **thin**
= large, substantial, profitable
▷ *n* **= fatness**, flesh, bulk,
obesity, flab

animal substance **2** fat part ▷ *adj*
3 having too much fat **4** greasy
5 profitable **fatten** *v* **fatty** *adj*

fate ❶ *n* **1** power supposed to
predetermine events **2** destiny
3 person's appointed lot **4** death or
destruction **fatal** *adj* ending in
death **fatality** *n* death **fatally**
adv **fated** *adj* destined **fateful** *adj*

father ❶ *n* **1** male parent
2 ancestor **3** (*with cap.*) God
4 originator **5** priest ▷ *v* **6** beget
7 originate **fatherhood** *n*
father-in-law *n, pl* **fathers-in-
law** husband's or wife's father
fatherland *n* native country

fathom *n* **1** measure of six feet of
water ▷ *v* **2** sound (water)
3 understand

fatigue ❶ *v* **1** tire ▷ *n*
2 weariness **3** toil **4** weakness of
metals etc.

fatuous *adj* very silly, idiotic
faucet (*US & Canad*) *n* valve with
handle, plug etc. to regulate or stop

flow of fluid

fault ❶ *n* **1** defect **2** misdeed
3 blame ▷ *v* **4** find fault in
5 (cause to) commit fault **faultily**
adv **faultless** *adj* **faulty** *adj*

faun *n* mythological woodland
being with tail and horns

fauna *n, pl* **-nas, -nae** animals of
region collectively

faux pas *n, pl* **faux pas** social
blunder or indiscretion

favour ❶ *n* **1** goodwill **2** approval
3 especial kindness **4** partiality ▷ *v*
5 regard or treat with favour
6 oblige **7** treat with partiality
8 support **favourable** *adj*
favourite *n* **1** favoured person or
thing ▷ *adj* **2** chosen, preferred
favouritism *n* practice of showing
undue preference

fawn¹ *n* **1** young deer ▷ *adj* **2** light
yellowish brown

fawn² *v* (*oft. with on*) cringe, court
favour servilely

fax *n* **1** facsimile ▷ *v* **2** send by

─────────── **THESAURUS** ───────────

fate *n* = **destiny**, chance, fortune,
luck, the stars; = **fortune**, destiny,
lot, portion, cup

father *n* = **daddy** (*Inf*), dad (*Inf*),
male parent, pop (*US Inf*), old man
(*Brit Inf*); = **founder**, author, maker,
architect, creator; (*usually cap.*)
= **priest**, minister, vicar, parson,
pastor; (*usually plural*) = **forefather**,
predecessor, ancestor, forebear,
progenitor ▷ *v* = **sire**, parent,
conceive, bring to life, beget

fatigue *n* = **tiredness**, lethargy,
weariness, heaviness, languor
≠ **freshness** ▷ *v* = **tire**,

exhaust, weaken, weary, drain
≠ **refresh**

fault *n* = **responsibility**, liability,
guilt, accountability, culpability;
= **mistake**, slip, error, blunder,
lapse; = **failing**, weakness, defect,
deficiency, flaw ≠ **strength** ▷ *v*
= **criticize**, blame, complain,
condemn, moan about

favour *n* = **approval**, goodwill,
commendation, approbation
≠ **disapproval**; = **favouritism**,
preferential treatment ▷ *v*
= **prefer**, opt for, like better, incline
towards, choose ≠ **object to**;

telegraphic facsimile system

FBI (US) Federal Bureau of Investigation

fear ⊕ n **1** unpleasant emotion caused by coming danger ▷ v **2** be afraid **3** regard with fear **fearful** adj **fearless** adj **fearsome** adj

feasible ⊕ adj able to be done **feasibility** n

feast ⊕ n **1** banquet **2** religious anniversary ▷ v **3** eat banquet **4** entertain with feast **5** delight

feat ⊕ n notable deed

feather n **1** one of the barbed shafts which form covering of birds **2** anything resembling this ▷ v **3** provide with feathers **4** grow feathers **feathery** adj

feature ⊕ n **1** part of face **2** notable part of anything **3** main or special item ▷ v **4** portray **5** be

prominent (in) **featureless** adj without striking features

Feb. February

February n second month

feckless adj ineffectual, irresponsible

federal adj of the government of states which are united but retain internal independence **federalism** n **federalist** n **federate** v form into, become, a federation **federation** n **1** league **2** federal union

fee ⊕ n payment for services

feeble ⊕ adj **1** weak **2** not effective or convincing

feed ⊕ v feeding, fed **1** give food to **2** supply, support **3** take food ▷ n **4** feeding **5** fodder **feedback** n response **fed up** (Inf) bored, dissatisfied

---

THESAURUS

= **indulge**, reward, side with, smile upon

fear n = **dread**, horror, panic, terror, fright ▷ v = **be afraid of**, dread, shudder at, be fearful of, tremble at; = **worry**, expect

feasible adj = **practicable**, possible, reasonable, viable, workable ≠ **impracticable**

feast n = **banquet**, repast, spread (Inf), dinner, treat; = **festival**, holiday, fête, celebration, holy day; = **treat**, delight, pleasure, enjoyment, gratification ▷ v = **eat your fill**, wine and dine, overindulge, consume, indulge

feat n = **accomplishment**, act, performance, achievement, enterprise

feature n = **aspect**, quality, characteristic, property, factor; = **article**, report, story, piece, item; = **highlight**, attraction, speciality, main item ▷ v = **spotlight**, present, emphasize, play up, foreground

fee n = **charge**, price, cost, bill, payment

feeble adj = **weak**, frail, debilitated, sickly, puny ≠ **strong**; = **inadequate**, pathetic, insufficient, lame

feed v = **cater for**, provide for, nourish, provide with food, supply; = **graze**, eat, browse, pasture ▷ n = **food**, fodder, provender, pasturage; (Inf) = **meal**, spread (Inf), dinner, lunch, tea

feel ❶ v **feeling, felt 1** touch
2 experience **3** find (one's way)
cautiously **4** be sensitive to
5 show emotion (for) **6** believe,
consider ▷ n **7** feeling
8 impression perceived by feeling
9 sense of touch **feeler** n **feeling**
n **1** sense of touch **2** sensation
3 emotion **4** sympathy **5** opinion
▷ pl **6** susceptibilities **feel like**
have an inclination for
feet see FOOT
feign v pretend, sham
feint n **1** sham attack **2** pretence
▷ v **3** make feint
feisty adj **1** (Inf) lively, resilient, and
self-reliant **2** (US & Canad) frisky
3 (US & Canad) irritable
felicity n **1** great happiness **2** apt
wording **felicitations** pl n
congratulations **felicitous** adj
feline adj **1** of cats **2** catlike
fell¹ ❶ v **1** knock down **2** cut down
(tree) **feller** n
fell² n mountain, moor
fellow ❶ n (Inf) **1** man, boy
2 associate **3** counterpart
4 member (of society, college etc.)
▷ adj **5** of the same class,
associated **fellowship** n
felon n one guilty of felony **felony**

n, pl **-nies** serious crime
felt n **1** soft, matted fabric ▷ v
2 make into, or cover with, felt
3 become matted **felt-tip pen**
pen with writing point of pressed
fibres
female adj **1** of sex which bears
offspring **2** relating to this sex ▷ n
3 one of this sex
feminine ❶ adj **1** of women
2 womanly **feminism** n advocacy
of equal rights for women
feminist n/adj **femininity** n
fen n tract of marshy land
fence ❶ n **1** structure of wire,
wood etc. enclosing an area **2** (Sl)
dealer in stolen property ▷ v
3 erect fence **4** fight with swords
5 (Sl) deal in stolen property
fencing n art of swordplay
fend v **1** ward off **2** repel **3** provide
(for oneself etc.) **fender** n low
metal frame in front of fireplace
fender n (US & Canad) the part of a
car body that surrounds the wheels
fennel n fragrant plant
feral adj wild
ferment n **1** substance causing
thing to ferment **2** excitement ▷ v
3 (cause to) undergo chemical
change with effervescence and

feel v = **experience**, bear; = **touch**,
handle, manipulate, finger, stroke,
detect, discern, experience, notice
= **grope**, explore ▷ n = **texture**,
finish, touch, surface, surface
quality; = **impression**, feeling, air,
sense, quality
fell¹ v = **cut down**, cut, level,
demolish, knock down

fellow n (Old-fashioned) = **man**,
person, individual, character, guy;
(Inf); = **associate**, colleague, peer,
partner, companion
feminine adj = **womanly**, pretty,
soft, gentle, tender ≠ **masculine**
fence n = **barrier**, wall, defence,
railings, hedge ▷ v (often with **in** or
off) = **enclose**, surround, bound,

alteration of properties
fermentation *n*

fern *n* plant with feathery fronds

ferocious ❶ *adj* fierce, savage, cruel **ferocity** *n*

ferret *n* **1** tamed animal like weasel ▷ *v* **2** drive out with ferrets **3** search about

ferric, ferrous *adj* pert. to, containing, iron

ferry ❶ *n, pl* **-ries 1** boat etc. for transporting people, vehicles, across water ▷ *v* **2** carry, travel, by ferry

fertile ❶ *adj* **1** (capable of) producing offspring, bearing crops etc. **2** producing abundantly **fertility** *n* **fertilize** *v* make fertile **fertilization** *n* **fertilizer** *n*

fervent, fervid *adj* ardent, intense **fervour** *n*

fester *v* **1** (cause to) form pus **2** rankle **3** become embittered

festival ❶ *n* **1** day, period of celebration **2** organized series of events, performances etc. **festive** *adj* joyous, merry **festivity** *n, pl* **-ties 1** gaiety **2** rejoicing ▷ *pl* **3** festive proceedings

festoon *n* **1** loop of flowers,

ribbons etc. ▷ *v* **2** form, adorn with festoons

fete *n* **1** gala, bazaar etc., esp. one held out of doors ▷ *v* **2** honour with festive entertainment

fetid *adj* stinking

fetish *n* **1** object believed to have magical powers **2** object, activity, to which excessive devotion is paid

fetter *n* **1** chain for feet **2** check ▷ *pl* **3** captivity ▷ *v* **4** chain up **5** restrain

fettle *n* state of health

fetus, foetus *n, pl* **-tuses** fully developed embryo **fetal, foetal** *adj*

feud ❶ *n* **1** long bitter hostility ▷ *v* **2** carry on feud

fever ❶ *n* **1** condition of illness with high body temperature **2** intense nervous excitement **fevered** *adj* **feverish** *adj*

few *adj* **1** not many ▷ *pron* **2** small number

fez *n, pl* **fezzes** red, brimless cap with tassel

fiancé *n* person engaged to be married

fiasco ❶ *n, pl* **-cos, -coes** breakdown, total failure

protect, pen

ferocious *adj* = **fierce**, violent, savage, ravening, predatory ≠ **gentle**

ferry *n* = **ferry boat**, boat, ship, passenger boat, packet boat ▷ *v* = **transport**, bring, carry, ship, take

fertile *adj* = **productive**, rich, lush, prolific, abundant ≠ **barren**

festival *n* = **celebration**, fair,

carnival, gala, fête; = **holy day**, holiday, feast, commemoration, feast day

feud *n* = **hostility**, row, conflict, argument, disagreement ▷ *v* = **quarrel**, row, clash, dispute, fall out

fever *n* = **excitement**, frenzy, ferment, agitation, fervour

fiasco *n* = **flop**, failure, disaster,

fib *n/v* (tell) trivial lie

fibre ❶ *n* **1** filament forming part of animal or plant tissue **2** substance that can be spun **fibrous** *adj* **fibreglass** *n* material made of fine glass fibres

fickle *adj* changeable

fiction ❶ *n* literary works of the imagination **fictional** *adj* **fictitious** *adj* **1** false **2** imaginary

fiddle ❶ *n* **1** violin **2** (*Inf*) fraudulent arrangement ▷ *v* **3** play fiddle **4** fidget **5** (*Sl*) cheat **fiddling** *adj* trivial **fiddly** *adj* small, awkward to handle

fidelity ❶ *n* faithfulness

fidget *v* **1** move restlessly ▷ *n* **2** (*oft. pl*) restless mood **3** one who fidgets **fidgety** *adj*

field ❶ *n* **1** area of (farming) land **2** tract of land rich in specified product **3** players in a game or sport collectively **4** battlefield **5** sphere of knowledge ▷ *v* **6** (*Cricket*) stop and return ball **7** send player, team, on to sports field **fielder** *n* **field day** exciting occasion **fieldwork** *n* investigation made away from classroom or laboratory

fiend *n* **1** devil **2** person addicted to something **fiendish** *adj*

fierce ❶ *adj* **1** savage, wild, violent **2** intense **fiercely** *adv*

fiery ❶ *adj* **fierier, fieriest 1** consisting of, or like, fire **2** irritable **fierily** *adv*

fiesta *n* carnival

fifteen see FIVE

fig *n* **1** soft, pear-shaped fruit **2** tree bearing this

fight ❶ *v* **fighting, fought 1** struggle against or contend with in battle **2** maintain against opponent **3** settle by combat ▷ *n* **4** fighting **fighter** *n* person or

━━━━━━━ THESAURUS ━━━━━━━

mess (*Inf*), catastrophe

fibre *n* = **thread**, strand, filament, tendril, pile

fiction *n* = **tale**, story, novel, legend, myth; = **lie**, invention, fabrication, falsehood, untruth

fiddle *v* (*usually with* **with**) = **fidget**, play, finger, tamper, mess about *or* around; (*usually with* **with**) = **tinker**, adjust, interfere, mess about *or* around ▷ *n* (*Brit Inf*) = **fraud**, racket, scam (*Sl*), fix, swindle

fidelity *n* = **loyalty**, devotion, allegiance, constancy, faithfulness **≠ disloyalty**; = **accuracy**, precision, correspondence, closeness, faithfulness

≠ inaccuracy

field *n* = **meadow**, land, green, lea (*Poet*), pasture; = **speciality**, line, area, department, territory; = **line**, reach, sweep ▷ **retrieve**, return, stop, catch, pick up

fierce *adj* = **ferocious**, wild, dangerous, cruel, savage **≠ gentle**; = **intense**, strong, keen, relentless, cut-throat

fiery *adj* = **burning**, flaming, blazing, on fire, ablaze; = **excitable**, fierce, passionate, irritable, impetuous

fight *v* = **oppose**, campaign against, dispute, contest, resist; = **battle**, combat, do battle;

aircraft that fights
figment n imaginary thing
figure ❶ n 1 numerical symbol
2 amount, number 3 (bodily)
shape 4 (conspicuous)
appearance 5 space enclosed by
lines 6 diagram, illustration
▷ v 7 calculate 8 **figurative** adj
(of language) symbolic **figurine** n
statuette **figurehead** n nominal
leader
filament n 1 fine wire
2 threadlike body
filch v steal, pilfer
file¹ ❶ n 1 (box, folder etc. holding)
papers for reference 2 orderly line
▷ v 3 arrange (papers etc.) and put
them away for reference 4 march
in file **filing** n
file² ❶ n/v (use) roughened
tool for smoothing or shaping
filing n scrap of metal removed

by file
filial adj of, befitting, son or
daughter
filibuster v 1 obstruct legislation
by making long speeches ▷ n
2 filibustering
filigree n fine tracery or openwork
of metal
fill ❶ v 1 make full 2 occupy
completely 3 discharge duties of
4 stop up 5 satisfy 6 fulfil
7 become full ▷ n 8 full supply
9 as much as desired **filling** n/adj
fillet n 1 boneless slice of meat, fish
2 narrow strip ▷ v 3 cut into fillets,
bone **filleted** adj
fillip n stimulus
filly n, pl **-lies** young female horse
film ❶ n 1 sequence of images
projected on screen, creating
illusion of movement 2 sensitized
celluloid roll used in photography,

f

THESAURUS

= **engage in**, conduct, wage,
pursue, carry on ▷ n = **battle**,
campaign, movement, struggle;
= **conflict**, clash, contest,
encounter, confrontation
figure n = **digit**, character, symbol,
number, numeral; = **shape**, build,
body, frame, proportions;
= **personage**, person, individual,
character, personality; = **diagram**,
drawing, picture, illustration,
representation; = **design**, shape,
pattern ▷ v (usually with **in**)
= **feature**, act, appear, contribute
to, play a part; = **calculate**, work
out, compute, tot up, total
file¹ n = **folder**, case, portfolio,
binder; = **dossier**, record,

information, data, documents ▷ v
= **register**, record, enter, log, put on
record; = **march**, troop, parade,
walk in line, walk behind one
another
file² v = **smooth**, shape, polish, rub,
scrape
fill v = **swell**, expand, become
bloated, extend, balloon;
= **pack**, crowd, squeeze, cram,
throng; = **stock**, supply, pack, load;
= **plug**, close, stop, seal, cork;
= **saturate**, charge, pervade,
permeate, imbue
film n = **movie**, picture, flick (SI),
motion picture; = **cinema**, the
movies ▷ v = **photograph**, record,
shoot, video, videotape

cinematography **3** thin skin or layer ▷ *adj* **4** connected with cinema ▷ *v* **5** photograph with cine camera **6** make cine film of **7** cover, become covered, with film **filmy** *adj* gauzy

filth *n* **1** disgusting dirt **2** obscenity **filthiness** *n* **filthy** *adj*

fin *n* **1** propelling organ of fish **2** anything like this

final ❶ *adj* **1** at the end **2** conclusive ▷ *n* **3** game, heat, examination etc., coming at end of series **finale** *n* closing part of musical composition **finalist** *n* competitor in a final **finalize** *v* **finally** *adv*

finance ❶ *n* **1** management of money **2** money resources ▷ *v* **3** find capital for **financial** *adj* **financier** *n*

finch *n, pl* **finches** one of family of small singing birds

find ❶ *v* **finding, found 1** come across **2** experience, discover

3 *(Law)* give verdict ▷ *n* **4** (valuable) thing found **finding** *n* conclusion from investigation

fine¹ ❶ *adj* **1** of high quality **2** not rainy **3** delicate **4** subtle **5** pure **6** in small particles **7** *(Inf)* healthy, at ease **8** satisfactory **finery** *n* showy dress **finesse** *n* skilful management **fine art** art produced for its aesthetic value **fine-tune** *v* make small adjustments

fine² ❶ *n* **1** sum fixed as penalty ▷ *v* **2** punish by fine

finger ❶ *n* **1** one of the jointed branches of the hand **2** various things like this ▷ *v* **3** touch with fingers **fingerprint** *n* impression of tip of finger

finicky *adj* fussy

finish ❶ *v* **1** bring, come to an end, conclude **2** complete **3** perfect ▷ *n* **4** end **5** way in which thing is finished **6** final appearance

finite *adj* bounded, limited

fiord see FJORD

final *adj* = **last**, latest, closing, finishing, concluding ≠ **first**; = **irrevocable**, absolute, definitive, decided, settled

finance *v* = **fund**, back, support, pay for, guarantee ▷ *n* = **economics**, business, money, banking, accounts

find *v* = **discover**, uncover, spot, locate, detect ≠ **lose**; = **obtain**, get, come by ▷ *n* = **discovery**, catch, asset, bargain, acquisition

fine¹ *adj* = **excellent**, good, striking, masterly, very good ≠ **poor**;

= **satisfactory**, good, all right, suitable, acceptable; = **thin**, light, narrow, wispy, light; = **stylish**, expensive, elegant, refined, tasteful; = **exquisite**, delicate, fragile, dainty; = **minute**, exact, precise, nice

fine² *n* = **penalty**, damages, punishment, forfeit, financial penalty ▷ *v* = **penalize**, charge, punish

finger *v* = **touch**, feel, handle, play with, manipulate

finish *v* = **stop**, close, complete,

fir *n* coniferous tree

fire ❶ *n* **1** state of burning **2** mass of burning fuel **3** destructive burning **4** device for heating a room etc. **5** shooting of guns **6** ardour ▷ *v* **7** discharge (firearm) **8** (*Inf*) dismiss from employment **9** bake **10** make burn **11** inspire **12** explode **13** begin to burn **14** become excited **firearm** *n* gun, rifle, pistol etc. **fire brigade** organized body to put out fires **fire engine** vehicle with apparatus for extinguishing fires **fire escape** means, esp. stairs, for escaping from burning buildings **firefly** *n*, *pl* **-flies** beetle that glows in dark **fireguard** *n* protective grating in front of fire **fireman** *n* member of fire brigade **fireplace** *n* recess in room for fire **fire station** building housing fire-fighting vehicles and equipment **firework** *n* **1** device to give spectacular effects by explosions and coloured sparks ▷ *pl* **2** outburst of temper **firing squad** group of soldiers ordered to execute

offender

firm ❶ *adj* **1** solid, fixed, stable ▷ *v* **2** make, become firm ▷ *n* **3** commercial enterprise

first *adj* **1** earlier in time or order **2** foremost in rank or position

First Nations *pl n* (*Canad*) Canadian aboriginal communities

First Peoples *pl n* (*Canad*) a collective term for the Native Canadian peoples, the Inuit, and the Métis

fiscal *adj* of government finances

fish *n*, *pl* **fish, fishes 1** vertebrate cold-blooded animal with gills, living in water ▷ *v* **2** (attempt to) catch fish **3** try to get information indirectly **fishy** *adj* **1** of, like, or full of fish **2** (*Inf*) suspicious **fisherman** *n* **fishmonger** *n* seller of fish

fissure *n* cleft, split **fission** *n* **1** splitting **2** reproduction by division of living cells **3** splitting of atomic nucleus

fist *n* clenched hand **fisticuffs** *pl n* fighting

f

THESAURUS

---

conclude, cease ≠ **start**; = **end**, stop, conclude, wind up, terminate; = **consume**, dispose of, devour, polish off, eat; = **use up**, empty, exhaust; = **coat**, polish, stain, texture, wax ▷ *n* = **end**, close, conclusion, run-in, completion ≠ **beginning**; = **surface**, polish, shine, texture, glaze

fire *n* = **flames**, blaze, combustion, inferno, conflagration; = **passion**, energy, spirit, enthusiasm, excitement; = **bombardment**,

shooting, firing, shelling, hail ▷ *v* = **let off**, shoot, shell, set off, discharge; = **shoot**, explode, discharge, detonate, pull the trigger; (*Inf*) = **dismiss**, sack (*Inf*), get rid of, discharge, lay off

firm *adj* = **hard**, solid, dense, set, stiff ≠ **soft**; = **secure**, fixed, rooted, stable, steady ≠ **unstable**; = **strong**, close, tight, steady, unshakeable; = **determined**, resolved, definite, set on, adamant ≠ **wavering**

fit¹ ● v **fitting, fitted 1** be suited to **2** be properly adjusted **3** adjust **4** supply ▷ adj **5** well-suited **6** proper **7** in good health ▷ n **8** way anything fits **fitness** n **fitter** n **fitting** adj **1** appropriate ▷ n **2** attachment **3** action of fitting

fit² ● n **1** seizure with convulsions **2** passing state, mood **fitful** adj spasmodic

five adj/n cardinal number after four **fifth** adj ordinal number **fifteen** adj/n ten plus five **fifteenth** adj **fiftieth** adj **fifty** adj/n five tens

fix ● v **1** fasten, make firm **2** determine **3** repair **4** (Inf) influence unfairly ▷ n **5** difficult situation **6** position of ship, aircraft ascertained by radar, observation etc. **7** (Sl) dose of narcotic drug **fixation** n obsession **fixed** adj **fixture** n **1** thing fixed in position **2** (date for) sporting event

fizz ● v **1** hiss ▷ n **2** hissing noise **3** effervescent liquid **fizzy** adj

fizzle v splutter weakly **fizzle out** (Inf) fail

fjord, fiord n (esp. in Norway) long, narrow inlet of sea

flabby adj **-bier, -biest 1** limp **2** too fat **3** weak and lacking purpose **flabbiness** n

flag¹ ● n **1** banner, piece of bunting as standard or signal ▷ v **2** inform by flag signals **flagpole, flagstaff** n pole for flag **flagship** n **1** admiral's ship **2** most important item

flag² ● v lose vigour

flagon n large bottle

flagrant adj blatant

flail n **1** instrument for threshing corn by hand ▷ v **2** beat with, move as, flail

flair ● n **1** natural ability **2** elegant style

flak n **1** anti-aircraft fire **2** (Inf) adverse criticism

— THESAURUS —

fit¹ v = **adapt**, shape, arrange, alter, adjust; = **place**, insert, connect; = **suit**, meet, match, belong to, conform to ▷ adj = **appropriate**, suitable, right, becoming, seemly ≠ **inappropriate**; = **healthy**, strong, robust, sturdy, well ≠ **unfit**

fit² n = **seizure**, attack, bout, spasm, convulsion; = **bout**, burst, outbreak, outburst, spell

fix v = **place**, join, stick, attach, set; = **decide**, set, choose, establish, determine; = **arrange**, organize, sort out, see to, fix up; = **repair**,

mend, service, correct, restore; = **focus**, direct at, fasten on; (Inf) = **rig**, set up (Inf), influence, manipulate, fiddle (Inf) ▷ n (Inf) = **mess**, corner, difficulty, dilemma, embarrassment

fizz v = **bubble**, froth, fizzle, effervesce, produce bubbles

flag¹ n = **banner**, standard, colours, pennant, ensign

flag² v = **weaken**, fade, weary, falter, wilt

flair n = **ability**, feel, talent, gift, genius; = **style**, taste, dash, chic,

flake ⊕ *n* **1** small, thin piece **2** piece chipped off ▷ *v* **3** (cause to) peel off in flakes **flaky** *adj*

flambé *v* **flambéing, flambéed** cook in flaming brandy

flamboyant ⊕ *adj* showy **flamboyance** *n*

flame ⊕ *n* **1** burning gas, esp. above fire ▷ *v* **2** give out flames

flamenco *n, pl* **-cos** rhythmical Spanish dance

flamingo *n, pl* **-gos, -goes** large pink bird with long neck and legs

flammable *adj* liable to catch fire

flan *n* open sweet or savoury tart

flange *n* projecting rim

flank ⊕ *n* **1** part of side between hips and ribs **2** side of anything ▷ *v* **3** be at, move along either side of

flannel *n* **1** soft woollen fabric **2** small piece of cloth for washing face

flap ⊕ *v* **flapping, flapped** **1** move (wings, arms etc.) as bird flying ▷ *n* **2** act of flapping **3** broad piece of anything hanging

from one side **4** (*Inf*) state of panic

flapjack *n* chewy biscuit

flare ⊕ *v* **1** blaze with unsteady flame **2** spread outwards ▷ *n* **3** instance of flaring **4** signal light

flash ⊕ *n* **1** sudden burst of light or flame **2** very short time ▷ *v* **3** break into sudden flame **4** move very fast **5** (cause to) gleam **flash, flashy** *adj* showy, sham **flashback** *n* break in narrative to introduce what has taken place previously

flask *n* type of bottle

flat¹ ⊕ *adj* **flatter, flattest** **1** level **2** at full length **3** smooth **4** downright **5** dull **6** (*Mus*) below true pitch **7** (of tyre) deflated **8** (of battery) dead ▷ *n* **9** what is flat **10** (*Mus*) note half tone below natural pitch **flatly** *adv* **flatten** *v* **flatfish** *n* type of fish with broad, flat body **flat rate** the same in all cases **flat out** at, with maximum speed or effort

elegance

flake *n* = **chip**, scale, layer, peeling, shaving ▷ *v* = **chip**, peel (off), blister

flamboyant *adj* = **showy**, elaborate, extravagant, ornate, ostentatious; = **colourful**, striking, brilliant, glamorous, stylish

flame *n* = **fire**, light, spark, glow, blaze ▷ *v* = **burn**, flash, shine, glow, blaze

flank *n* = **side**, hip, thigh, loin

flap *v* = **flutter**, wave, flail ▷ *n* = **flutter**, beating, waving, shaking,

swinging; (*Inf*) = **panic**, state (*Inf*), agitation, commotion, sweat (*Inf*)

flare *n* = **flame**, burst, flash, blaze, glare ▷ *v* = **blaze**, flame, glare, flicker, burn up

flash *n* = **blaze**, burst, spark, beam, streak ▷ *v* = **blaze**, shine, beam, sparkle, flare; = **speed**, race, shoot, fly, tear; (*Inf*) = **show quickly**, display, expose, exhibit, flourish ▷ *adj* (*Inf*) = **ostentatious**, smart, trendy, showy

flat¹ *adj* = **even**, level, levelled, smooth, horizontal ≠ **uneven**;

f

flat² ❶ n suite of rooms in larger building

flatter ❶ v **1** praise insincerely **2** gratify **flatterer** n **flattery** n

flattie n (NZ & S Afr, Inf) flat tyre

flatulent adj suffering from, generating (excess) gases from intestines **flatulence** n

flaunt v show off

flavour ❶ n **1** distinctive taste, savour ▷ v **2** give flavour to **flavouring** n

flaw ❶ n defect, blemish **flawless** adj

flax n plant grown for its fibres, spun into linen thread **flaxen** adj **1** of flax **2** light yellow

flay v **1** strip skin off **2** criticize severely

flea n small, wingless, jumping, blood-sucking insect

fleck n/v (make) small mark(s)

flee ❶ v **fleeing, fled** run away

from (a place, danger etc.)

fleece n **1** sheep's wool ▷ v **2** rob **fleecy** adj

fleet¹ ❶ n **1** number of warships organized as unit **2** number of ships, cars etc.

fleet² adj **1** swift **2** nimble **fleeting** adj passing quickly

flesh ❶ n **1** soft part, muscular substance, between skin and bone **2** in plants, pulp **3** fat **4** sensual appetites **fleshy** adj plump, pulpy **in the flesh** in person, actually present

flex n **1** flexible insulated electric cable ▷ v **2** bend, be bent **flexible** adj **1** easily bent **2** manageable **3** adaptable **flexibility** n

flick ❶ v **1** strike lightly, jerk ▷ n **2** light blow **3** jerk ▷ pl **4** (Sl) cinema

flicker ❶ v **1** burn, shine, unsteadily ▷ n **2** unsteady light or

— THESAURUS —

= **punctured**, collapsed, burst, blown out, deflated; = **used up**, finished, empty, drained, expired; = **absolute**, firm, positive, explicit, definite **flat out** (Inf) = **at full speed**, all out, to the full, hell for leather (Inf), as hard as possible

flat² n = **apartment**, rooms, quarters, digs, suite

flatter v = **praise**, compliment, pander to, sweet-talk (Inf), wheedle; = **suit**, become, enhance, set off, embellish

flavour n = **taste**, seasoning, flavouring, savour, relish ≠ **blandness**; = **quality**, feeling, feel, style, character ▷ v = **season**,

spice, add flavour to, enrich, infuse

flaw n = **weakness**, failing, defect, weak spot, fault

flee v = **run away**, escape, bolt, fly, take off (Inf)

fleet¹ n = **navy**, task force, flotilla, armada

flesh n = **fat**, muscle, tissue, brawn; = **fatness**, fat, adipose tissue, corpulence, weight; = **physical nature**, carnality, human nature, flesh and blood, sinful nature

flick v = **jerk**, pull, tug, lurch, jolt; = **strike**, tap, remove quickly, hit, touch

flicker v = **twinkle**, flash, sparkle, flare, shimmer; = **flutter**, waver,

movement **3** slight trace

flight¹ ❶ *n* **1** act or manner of flying through air **2** group of flying birds or aircraft **3** power of flying **4** stairs between two landings **flighty** *adj* frivolous **flight recorder** electronic device in aircraft storing information about its flight

flight² ❶ *n* running away

flimsy *adj* **-sier, -siest** **1** delicate **2** weak, thin

flinch *v* draw back, wince

fling ❶ *v* **flinging, flung** **1** throw, send, move with force ▷ *n* **2** throw **3** spell of indulgence **4** vigorous dance

flint *n* hard steel-grey stone

flip ❶ *v* **flipping, flipped** **1** flick lightly **2** turn over **flippant** *adj* treating serious things lightly **flipper** *n* limb, fin for swimming

flirt ❶ *v* **1** play with another's affections ▷ *n* **2** person who flirts **flirtation** *n* **flirtatious** *adj*

flit *v* **flitting, flitted** pass lightly and rapidly

float ❶ *v* **1** rest on surface of liquid **2** be suspended freely **3** in commerce, get (company) started **4** obtain loan ▷ *n* **5** anything small that floats **6** small delivery vehicle **7** motor vehicle carrying tableau etc. **8** sum of money used to provide change **floating** *adj* moving about, changing **flotation** *n*

flock ❶ *n* **1** number of animals of one kind together **2** religious congregation ▷ *v* **3** gather in a crowd

floe *n* floating ice

flog ❶ *v* **flogging, flogged** **1** beat with whip, stick etc. **2** (*Sl*) sell

flood ❶ *n* **1** inundation, overflow of water **2** rising of tide

— THESAURUS —

quiver, vibrate ▷ *n* = **glimmer**, flash, spark, flare, gleam; = **trace**, breath, spark, glimmer, iota

flight¹ *n* = **journey**, trip, voyage; = **aviation**, flying, aeronautics, ability to fly; = **flock**, group, unit, cloud, formation

flight² *n* = **escape**, fleeing, departure, retreat, exit

fling *v* = **throw**, toss, hurl, launch, cast ▷ *n* = **binge**, good time, bash, party, spree (*Inf*)

flip *v* = **flick**, switch, snap, slick ▷ *n* = **toss**, throw, spin, snap, flick

flirt *v* = **chat up**, lead on (*Inf*), make advances at, make eyes at,

philander; (*usually with* **with**) = **toy with**, consider, entertain, play with, dabble in ▷ *n* = **tease**, philanderer, coquette, heart-breaker

float *v* = **glide**, sail, drift, move gently, bob; = **be buoyant**, hang, hover ≠ **sink**; = **launch**, offer, sell, set up, promote ≠ **dissolve**

flock *n* = **herd**, group, flight, drove, colony; = **crowd**, company, group, host, collection ▷ *v* = **stream**, crowd, mass, swarm, throng

flog *v* = **beat**, whip, lash, thrash, whack

flood *n* = **deluge**, downpour, inundation, tide, overflow;

3 outpouring ▷ v **4** inundate
5 cover, fill with water **6** arrive, move etc. in great numbers
floodlight n broad, intense beam of artificial light **floodlit** adj

floor ❶ n **1** lower surface of room **2** set of rooms on one level **3** (right to speak in) legislative hall ▷ v **4** supply with floor **5** knock down **6** confound **flooring** n material for floors

flop ❶ v **flopping, flopped** **1** bend, fall, collapse loosely **2** fall flat on water etc. **3** (Inf) fail ▷ n **4** flopping movement or sound **5** (Inf) failure **floppy** adj **floppy disk** (Comp) flexible magnetic disk that stores information

flora n plants of a region **floral** adj of flowers **florist** n dealer in flowers

floret n small flower

florid adj **1** with red, flushed complexion **2** ornate

floss n mass of fine, silky fibres

flotilla n **1** fleet of small vessels **2** group of destroyers

flotsam n floating wreckage

flounce[1] v **1** go, move abruptly and impatiently ▷ n **2** fling, jerk of body or limb

flounce[2] n ornamental gathered strip on woman's garment

flounder[1] ❶ v plunge and struggle, esp. in water or mud

flounder[2] n flatfish

flour n powder prepared by sifting and grinding wheat etc.

flourish ❶ v **1** thrive **2** brandish **3** wave about ▷ n **4** ornamental curve **5** showy gesture **6** fanfare

flow ❶ v **1** glide along as stream **2** circulate, as the blood **3** hang loose **4** be present in abundance ▷ n **5** act, instance of flowing **6** quantity that flows **7** rise of tide

flower ❶ n **1** brightly coloured part of plant from which fruit is developed **2** bloom, blossom **3** choicest part ▷ v **4** produce

——————————— THESAURUS ———————————

= **torrent**, flow, rush, stream, tide; = **series**, stream, avalanche, barrage, spate ▷ v = **immerse**, swamp, submerge, inundate, drown; = **pour over**, swamp, run over, overflow, inundate
floor v (Inf) = **disconcert**, stump, baffle, confound, throw (Inf); = **knock down**, fell, knock over, prostrate, deck (Sl)
flop v = **slump**, fall, drop, collapse, sink; = **hang down**, hang, dangle, sag, droop ▷ n (Inf) = **failure**, disaster, fiasco, debacle, washout (Inf) ≠ **success**

flounder[1] v = **falter**, struggle, stall, slow down, run into trouble
flourish v = **thrive**, increase, advance, progress, boom ≠ **fail**; = **succeed**, move ahead, go places (Inf) ▷ n = **wave**, sweep, brandish, swish, swing; = **show**, display, parade, fanfare
flow v = **run**, course, rush, sweep, move; = **pour**, move, sweep, flood, stream; = **issue**, follow, result, emerge, spring ▷ n = **stream**, current, movement, motion, course
flower n = **bloom**, blossom, efflorescence; = **elite**, best, prime,

flowers **5** come to prime condition
flowery adj **flowerbed** n ground
for growing flowers
fl. oz. fluid ounce
flu n short for INFLUENZA
fluctuate ❶ v vary, rise and fall,
undulate **fluctuation** n
flue n chimney
fluent ❶ adj speaking, writing
easily and well **fluency** n
fluff n **1** soft, feathery stuff ▷ v
2 make or become soft, light **3** (Inf)
make mistake **fluffy** adj
fluid ❶ adj **1** flowing easily
2 flexible ▷ n **3** gas or liquid **fluid
ounce** unit of capacity 1/20 of pint
fluke n stroke of luck
flummox v bewilder, perplex
flunky, flunkey pl **flunkies,
flunkeys 1** liveried manservant
2 servile person
fluoride n salt containing fluorine
fluorine n nonmetallic element,
yellowish gas

flurry ❶ n, pl **-ries 1** gust **2** bustle
3 fluttering ▷ v **4** agitate
flush¹ ❶ v **1** blush **2** flow suddenly
or violently **3** be excited **4** cleanse
(e.g. toilet) by rush of water
5 excite ▷ n **6** blush **7** rush of
water **8** excitement **9** freshness
flush² ❶ adj **1** level with
surrounding surface **2** overflowing
fluster v **1** make or become
nervous, agitated ▷ n **2** agitation
flute n **1** wind instrument with
blowhole in side **2** groove ▷ v
3 play on flute **4** make grooves in
flutter ❶ v **1** flap (as wings)
rapidly **2** quiver **3** be or make
agitated ▷ n **4** flapping movement
5 agitation **6** (Inf) modest wager
flux n **1** discharge **2** constant
succession of changes **3** substance
mixed with metal in soldering etc.
fly¹ ❶ v **flying, flew, flown** pl
flies 1 move through air on wings
or in aircraft **2** pass quickly **3** float

f

— THESAURUS —

finest, pick ▷ v = **bloom**, open,
mature, flourish, unfold;
= **blossom**, grow, develop,
progress, mature
fluctuate v = **change**, swing, vary,
alternate, waver
fluent adj = **effortless**, natural,
articulate, well-versed, voluble
fluid n = **liquid**, solution, juice,
liquor, sap ▷ adj = **liquid**, flowing,
watery, molten, melted ≠ **solid**
flurry n = **commotion**, stir, bustle,
flutter, excitement; = **gust**, shower,
gale, swirl, squall
flush¹ v = **blush**, colour, glow,
redden, turn red; (often with **out**)

= **cleanse**, wash out, rinse out,
flood, swill ▷ n = **blush**, colour,
glow, reddening, redness
flush² adj = **level**, even, true, flat,
square
flutter v = **beat**, flap, tremble,
ripple, waver ▷ n = **tremor**,
tremble, shiver, shudder,
palpitation; = **vibration**,
twitching, quiver; = **agitation**,
state (Inf), confusion, excitement,
flap (Inf)
fly¹ v = **take wing**, soar, glide, wing,
sail; = **pilot**, control, operate, steer,
manoeuvre; = **airlift**, send by plane,
take by plane, take in an aircraft;

loosely **4** run away **5** operate aircraft **6** cause to fly **7** set flying ▷ *n* **8** (zip or buttons fastening) opening in trousers **flyer, flier** *n* **1** small advertising leaflet **2** aviator **flying** *adj* hurried, brief **flying colours** conspicuous success **flying saucer** unidentified disc-shaped flying object **flying squad** special detachment of police, soldiers etc., ready to act quickly **flying start** very good start **flyover** *n* road passing over another by bridge **flywheel** *n* heavy wheel regulating speed of machine

fly² *n, pl* **flies** two-winged insect, esp. common housefly

foal *n* young of horse

foam ❶ *n* **1** collection of small bubbles on liquid **2** light cellular solid ▷ *v* **3** (cause to) produce foam **foamy** *adj*

fob *v* (with *off*) ignore, dismiss in offhand manner

focus ❶ *n, pl* **-cuses, -ci 1** point at which rays meet **2** state of optical image when it is clearly defined **3** point on which interest, activity is centred ▷ *v* **4** bring to focus **5** concentrate **focal** *adj*

fodder *n* bulk food for livestock

foe ❶ *n* enemy

fog ❶ *n* **1** thick mist ▷ *v* **2** cover in fog **3** puzzle **foggy** *adj* **foghorn** *n* large horn to warn ships

fogey, fogy *n, pl* **-geys, -gies** old-fashioned person

foible *n* minor weakness, slight peculiarity of character

foil¹ ❶ *v* **1** baffle, frustrate ▷ *n* **2** blunt sword for fencing

foil² ❶ *n* **1** metal in thin sheet **2** anything which sets off another thing to advantage

foist *v* (usu. with *on*) force, impose on

fold¹ ❶ *v* **1** double up, bend part of **2** interlace (arms) **3** clasp (in arms) **4** (*Cookery*) mix gently **5** become folded **6** admit of being folded **7** (*Inf*) fail ▷ *n* **8** folding **9** line made by folding **folder** *n* binder, file for loose papers

fold² *n* enclosure for sheep

foliage *n* leaves collectively

folio *n, pl* **-lios 1** sheet of paper folded in half to make two leaves of

---

— THESAURUS —

= **flutter**, wave, float, flap; = **display**, show, flourish, brandish; = **rush**, race, shoot, career, speed

foam *n* = **froth**, spray, bubbles, lather, suds ▷ *v* = **bubble**, boil, fizz, froth, lather

focus *v* = **concentrate**, centre, spotlight, direct, aim ▷ *n* = **centre**, focal point, central point, heart, target

foe *n* = **enemy**, rival, opponent, adversary, antagonist ≠ **friend**

fog *n* = **mist**, gloom, haze, smog, murk

foil¹ *v* = **thwart**, stop, defeat, disappoint, counter

foil² *n* = **complement**, relief, contrast, antithesis

fold¹ *v* = **bend**, crease, double over; (*Inf*) = **go bankrupt**, fail, crash, collapse, founder ▷ *n* = **crease**, gather, bend, overlap, wrinkle

book **2** book of largest common size

folk ❶ *n* **1** people in general **2** family, relative **3** race of people
folksy *adj* simple, unpretentious
folklore *n* tradition, customs, beliefs popularly held
follicle *n* small sac
follow ❶ *v* **1** go or come after **2** accompany **3** keep to **4** be a consequence of **5** take as guide **6** grasp meaning of **7** have keen interest in **follower** *n* disciple, supporter **following** *adj* **1** about to be mentioned ▷ *n* **2** body of supporters
folly ❶ *n, pl* **-lies** foolishness
foment *v* foster, stir up
fond ❶ *adj* tender, loving
fondness *n* **fond of** having liking for
fondant *n* flavoured paste of sugar and water
fondle *v* caress

font *n* bowl for baptismal water
fontanelle *n* soft, membraneous gap between bones of baby's skull
food ❶ *n* **1** solid nourishment **2** what one eats
fool¹ ❶ *n* **1** silly, empty-headed person **2** *(Hist)* jester ▷ *v* **3** delude **4** dupe **5** act as fool **foolhardy** *adj* foolishly adventurous **foolish** *adj* **1** silly, stupid **2** unwise **foolishness** *n* **foolproof** *adj* unable to fail **foolscap** *n* size of paper
fool² *n* dessert made from fruit and cream
foot *n, pl* **feet** **1** lowest part of leg, from ankle down **2** lower part of anything, base, stand **3** end of bed etc. **4** measure of twelve inches ▷ *v* **5** pay cost of **footage** *n* amount of film used **footing** *n* basis, foundation **football** *n* **1** game played with large blown-up ball **2** the ball **footballer** *n*

f

folk *n* = **people**, persons, individuals, men and women, humanity; *(usually plural)* = **family**, parents, relations, relatives, tribe
follow *v* = **accompany**, attend, escort, go behind, tag along behind; = **pursue**, track, dog, hunt, chase ≠ **avoid**; = **come after**, go after, come next ≠ **precede**; = **result**, issue, develop, spring, flow; = **obey**, observe, adhere to, stick to, heed ≠ **ignore**; = **succeed**, replace, come after, take over from, come next; = **understand**, realize, appreciate, take in, grasp
folly *n* = **foolishness**, nonsense,

madness, stupidity, indiscretion ≠ **wisdom**
fond *adj* = **loving**, caring, warm, devoted, tender ≠ **indifferent**; = **unrealistic**, empty, naive, vain, foolish ≠ **sensible**
food *n* = **nourishment**, fare, diet, rations, nutrition
fool¹ *n* = **simpleton**, idiot, mug *(Brit Sl)*, dummy *(Sl)*, git *(Brit Sl)* ≠ **genius**; = **dupe**, mug *(Brit Sl)*, sucker *(Sl)*, stooge *(Sl)*, laughing stock; = **jester**, clown, harlequin, buffoon, court jester ▷ *v* = **deceive**, mislead, delude, trick, take in

foothills pl n hills at foot of mountain **foothold** n place giving secure grip for the foot **footlights** pl n lights across front of stage

footloose adj free from ties

footman n male servant in livery

footnote n note of reference or explanation printed at foot of page

footprint n mark left by foot

footstep n 1 step in walking 2 sound made by walking

footwear n anything worn to cover feet **footwork** n skilful use of the feet in football etc.

footle v (Inf) loiter aimlessly **footling** adj trivial

for prep 1 directed to 2 because of 3 instead of 4 towards 5 on account of 6 in favour of 7 respecting 8 during 9 in search of 10 in payment of 11 in the character of 12 in spite of ▷ conj 13 because

forage n 1 food for cattle and horses ▷ v 2 collect forage 3 make roving search

foray ❶ n raid, inroad

forbear v 1 cease 2 refrain (from) 3 be patient **forbearance** n

forbid ❶ v 1 prohibit 2 refuse to allow **forbidden** adj **forbidding**

adj uninviting, threatening

force ❶ n 1 strength, power 2 compulsion 3 that which tends to produce a change in a physical system 4 body of troops, police etc. 5 group of people organized for particular task 6 validity 7 vigour ▷ v 8 compel 9 produce by effort, strength 10 break open 11 hasten maturity of **forced** adj 1 compulsory 2 unnatural **forceful** adj powerful, persuasive **forcible** adj done by force

forceps pl n surgical pincers

ford n 1 shallow place where river may be crossed ▷ v 2 cross river

fore adj 1 in front ▷ n 2 front part

forearm n 1 arm between wrist and elbow ▷ v 2 arm beforehand

forebear n ancestor

forecast ❶ v -casting, -cast 1 estimate beforehand (esp. weather) ▷ n 2 prediction

forecastle n forward raised part of ship

foreclose v take away power of redeeming (mortgage)

forecourt n open space in front of building

forefather n ancestor

foray n = **raid**, sally, incursion, inroad, attack

forbid v = **prohibit**, ban, disallow, exclude, rule out ≠ **permit**

force v = **compel**, make, drive, press, oblige; = **push**, thrust, propel; = **break open**, blast, wrench, prise, wrest ▷ n = **compulsion**, pressure, violence,

constraint, oppression; = **power**, might, pressure, energy, strength ≠ **weakness**; = **intensity**, vigour, vehemence, fierceness, emphasis; = **army**, unit, company, host, troop

forecast n = **prediction**, prognosis, guess, prophecy, conjecture ▷ v = **predict**, anticipate, foresee, foretell, divine

DICTIONARY

forefinger *n* finger next to thumb
forefront ❶ *n* most active prominent position
foregoing *adj* going before, preceding **foregone** *adj* determined beforehand
foreground *n* part of view nearest observer
forehand *adj* (of stroke in racket games) made with inner side of wrist leading
forehead *n* part of face above eyebrows and between temples
foreign ❶ *adj* **1** not of, or in, one's own country **2** relating to other countries **3** strange **foreigner** *n*
foreman *n* **1** one in charge of work **2** leader of jury
foremost ❶ *adj/adv* first in time, place, importance etc.
forensic *adj* connected with a court of law **forensic medicine** application of medical knowledge in legal matters
forerunner *n* one who goes before, precursor
foresee ❶ *v* see beforehand
foreshadow *v* show, suggest beforehand

foresight *n* **1** foreseeing **2** care for future
foreskin *n* skin that covers the tip of the penis
forest *n* area with heavy growth of trees **forestry** *n*
forestall *v* prevent, guard against in advance
foretaste *n* experience of something to come
foretell *v* prophesy
forethought *n* thoughtful consideration of future events
forever, for ever ❶ *adv* **1** always **2** eternally **3** (*Inf*) for a long time
forewarn *v* warn, caution in advance
foreword *n* preface
forfeit ❶ *n* **1** thing lost by crime or fault **2** penalty, fine ▷ *adj* **3** lost by crime or fault ▷ *v* **4** lose by penalty
forge¹ *v* advance steadily
forge² ❶ *n* **1** place where metal is worked, smithy ▷ *v* **2** shape (metal) by heating and hammering **3** counterfeit **forger** *n* **forgery** *n* **1** counterfeiting **2** counterfeit thing

THESAURUS

forefront *n* = **lead**, centre, front, fore, spearhead
foreign *adj* = **alien**, exotic, unknown, strange, imported ≠ **native**; = **uncharacteristic**, inappropriate, inapposite
foremost *adj* = **leading**, best, highest, chief, prime
foresee *v* = **predict**, forecast, anticipate, envisage, prophesy
forever *adv* = **evermore**, always,

ever, for good, for keeps; = **constantly**, always, all the time, continually, endlessly
forfeit *v* = **relinquish**, lose, give up, surrender, renounce ▷ *n* = **penalty**, fine, damages, forfeiture, loss
forge² *v* = **form**, build, create, establish, set up; = **fake**, copy, reproduce, imitate, counterfeit; = **create**, make, work, found, form

forget ❶ v **-getting, -got, -gotten** lose memory of, neglect, overlook **forgetful** adj liable to forget **forget-me-not** n plant with small blue flowers

forgive ❶ v **-giving, -gave, -given** 1 cease to blame or hold resentment against 2 pardon **forgiveness** n

forgo v 1 go without 2 give up

fork ❶ n 1 pronged instrument for eating food 2 pronged tool for digging or lifting 3 division into branches ▷ v 4 branch 5 dig, lift, throw, with fork 6 make fork-shaped

forlorn adj 1 forsaken 2 desperate

form ❶ n 1 shape, visible appearance 2 structure 3 nature 4 species, kind 5 regularly drawn up document 6 condition 7 class in school 8 customary way of doing things 9 bench ▷ v 10 shape, organize 11 conceive 12 make part of 13 come into existence or shape **formation** n 1 forming 2 thing formed **formative** adj

formal ❶ adj 1 ceremonial, according to rule 2 of outward form 3 stiff **formality** n, pl **-ties** 1 observance required by custom 2 condition of being formal **formalize** v make official **formally** adv

format ❶ n size and shape of book etc.

former ❶ adj 1 earlier in time 2 of past times 3 first named ▷ pron 4 first named thing or person or fact **formerly** adv previously

Formica® n material used for heat-resistant surfaces

formidable ❶ adj 1 to be feared

━━━━━━━━━━ THESAURUS ━━━━━━

forget v = **neglect**, overlook, omit, not remember, be remiss; = **leave behind**, lose, lose sight of, mislay, ignore

forgive v = **excuse**, pardon, not hold something against, understand, acquit ≠ **blame**

fork v = **branch**, part, separate, split, divide

form n = **type**, sort, kind, variety, class; = **shape**, formation, configuration, structure, pattern; = **condition**, health, shape, nick (Inf), fitness; = **document**, paper, sheet, questionnaire, application; = **procedure**, etiquette, use, custom, convention; = **class**, year, set, rank, grade ▷ v = **arrange**, combine, line up, organize, assemble; = **make**, produce, fashion, build, create; = **constitute**, make up, compose, comprise, start; = **take shape**, grow, develop, materialize, rise; = **draw up**, devise, formulate, organize

formal adj = **serious**, stiff, detached, official, correct ≠ **informal**; = **official**, authorized, endorsed, certified, solemn; = **ceremonial**, traditional, solemn, ritualistic, dressy

format n = **arrangement**, form, style, make-up, look

former adj = **previous**, one-time, erstwhile, earlier, prior ≠ **current**

formidable adj = **impressive**,

2 overwhelming **3** likely to be difficult

formula ❶ *n, pl* **-las, -lae 1** set form of words, rule **2** (*Maths*) rule, fact expressed in symbols and figures **formulate** *v*

forsake *v* **-saking, -sook, -saken 1** abandon, desert **2** give up

forswear *v* **-swearing, -swore, -sworn 1** renounce, deny **2** perjure

fort ❶ *n* stronghold

forte¹ ❶ *n* one's strong point, that in which one excels

forte² *adv* (*Mus*) loudly

forth ❶ *adv* onwards, into view **forthcoming** *adj* **1** about to come **2** ready when wanted **3** willing to talk **forthwith** *adv* at once

forthright *adj* outspoken

fortify ❶ *v* **-fying, -fied** strengthen **fortification** *n*

fortitude ❶ *n* endurance

fortnight *n* two weeks

fortress ❶ *n* fortified place

fortuitous *adj* accidental

fortune ❶ *n* **1** good luck **2** wealth **3** chance **fortunate** *adj* **fortunately** *adv*

forty *pl* **-ties** see FOUR

forum *n* (place or medium for) meeting, discussion or debate

forward ❶ *adj* **1** lying in front of **2** onward **3** presumptuous **4** advanced **5** relating to the future ▷ *n* **6** player in various team games ▷ *adv* **7** towards the future **8** towards the front, to the front, into view ▷ *v* **9** help forward **10** send, dispatch **forwards** *adv*

fossick *v* (*Aust & NZ*) search, esp. for gold or precious stones

fossil *n* remnant or impression of animal or plant, preserved in earth

f

—— THESAURUS ——

great, powerful, tremendous, mighty; = **intimidating**, threatening, terrifying, menacing, dismaying ≠ **encouraging**

formula *n* = **method**, plan, policy, rule, principle

fort *n* = **fortress**, keep, camp, tower, castle

forte¹ *n* = **speciality**, strength, talent, strong point, métier ≠ **weak point**

forth *adv* (*Formal or Old-fashioned*) = **forward**, out, away, ahead, onward

fortify *v* = **protect**, defend, strengthen, reinforce, support; = **strengthen**, add alcohol to

fortitude *n* = **courage**, strength,

resolution, grit, bravery

fortress *n* = **castle**, fort, stronghold, citadel, redoubt

fortune *n* = **wealth**, means, property, riches, resources ≠ **poverty**; = **luck** (*Inf*), stroke of luck, serendipity, twist of fate; = **chance**, fate, destiny, providence, the stars

forward *adv* = **forth**, on, ahead, onwards ≠ **backward(s)** ▷ *adj* = **leading**, first, head, front, advance; = **future**, advanced, premature, prospective; = **presumptuous**, familiar, bold, cheeky, brash ≠ **shy** ▷ *v* = **further**, advance, promote, assist, hurry; = **send on**, send, post, pass on,

fossilize v 1 turn into fossil
2 petrify
foster ❶ v 1 promote
development of 2 bring up child,
esp. not one's own
foul ❶ adj 1 loathsome, offensive
2 stinking 3 dirty 4 unfair
5 obscene ▷ n 6 act of unfair play
7 breaking of a rule ▷ v 8 make,
become foul 9 jam 10 collide with
found¹ ❶ v 1 establish 2 lay base
of 3 base **foundation** n 1 basis
2 lowest part of building
3 founding 4 endowed institution
etc. **founder** n
found² v 1 melt and run into
mould 2 cast **foundry** n place for
casting
founder ❶ v 1 collapse 2 sink
foundling n deserted infant
fount n 1 fountain 2 source
fountain ❶ n 1 jet of water, esp.
ornamental one 2 spring
3 source

four n/adj cardinal number next
after three **fourth** adj ordinal
number **fourteen** n/adj four plus
ten **fourteenth** adj **forty** n/adj
four tens **fortieth** adj **foursome**
n group of four people
fowl n 1 domestic cock or hen
2 bird, its flesh
fox n 1 red bushy-tailed animal
2 its fur 3 cunning person ▷ v
4 perplex 5 act craftily **foxy** adj
foxglove n tall flowering plant
foxtrot n (music for) ballroom
dance
foyer ❶ n entrance hall in theatres,
hotels etc.
fracas n, pl **-cas** noisy quarrel
fraction ❶ n 1 numerical quantity
not an integer 2 fragment
fracture ❶ n 1 breakage
2 breaking of bone
▷ v 3 break
fragile ❶ adj 1 breakable
2 delicate **fragility** n

──────────────── THESAURUS ────────────────

dispatch
foster v = **bring up**, mother, raise,
nurse, look after; = **develop**,
support, further, encourage, feed
≠ **suppress**
foul adj = **dirty**, unpleasant,
stinking, filthy, grubby ≠ **clean**;
= **obscene**, crude, indecent, blue,
abusive; = **unfair**, illegal, crooked,
shady (Inf), fraudulent; = **offensive**,
bad, wrong, evil, corrupt
≠ **admirable** ▷ v = **dirty**, stain,
contaminate, pollute, taint ≠ **clean**
found¹ v = **establish**, start, set up,
begin, create
founder v = **fail**, collapse, break

down, fall through, be
unsuccessful; = **sink**, go down, be
lost, submerge, capsize
fountain n = **font**, spring,
reservoir, spout, fount; = **jet**,
stream, spray, gush; = **source**,
fount, wellspring, cause, origin
foyer n = **entrance hall**, lobby,
reception area, vestibule, anteroom
fraction n = **percentage**, share,
section, slice, portion
fracture n = **break**, split, crack ▷ v
= **break**, crack
fragile adj = **unstable**, weak,
vulnerable, delicate, uncertain;
= **fine**, weak, delicate, frail, brittle

fragrant ❶ *adj* sweet-smelling **fragrance** *n*

frail ❶ *adj* 1 fragile 2 in weak health **frailty** *n, pl* **-ties**

frame ❶ *n* 1 that in which thing is set, as square of wood round picture etc. 2 structure 3 build of body ▷ *v* 4 make 5 put into words 6 put into frame 7 bring false charge against **framework** *n* supporting structure

franc *n* monetary unit in France, Switzerland etc.

franchise *n* 1 right of voting 2 citizenship 3 privilege or right

frank ❶ *adj* 1 candid, outspoken 2 sincere ▷ *n* 3 official mark on letter either cancelling stamp or ensuring delivery without stamp ▷ *v* 4 mark letter thus

frankfurter *n* smoked sausage

frankincense *n* aromatic gum

resin burned as incense

frantic ❶ *adj* 1 distracted with rage, grief, joy etc. 2 frenzied **frantically** *adv*

fraternal *adj* of brother, brotherly **fraternity** *n* 1 brotherliness 2 brotherhood **fraternize** *v* 1 associate 2 make friends

fraud ❶ *n* 1 criminal deception 2 impostor **fraudulent** *adj*

fraught *adj* filled (with), involving

fray¹ ❶ *v* make, become ragged at edge

fray² *n* 1 fight 2 noisy quarrel

frazzle (*Inf*) ▷ *v* 1 make or become exhausted ▷ *n* 2 exhausted state

freak ❶ *n/adj* abnormal (person or thing)

freckle *n* light brown spot on skin, esp. caused by sun

free ❶ *adj* **freer, freest** 1 able to act at will, not under compulsion or

THESAURUS

≠ durable

fragrant *adj* = **aromatic**, perfumed, balmy, redolent, sweet-smelling ≠ **stinking**

frail *adj* = **feeble**, weak, puny, infirm ≠ **strong**; = **flimsy**, weak, vulnerable, delicate, fragile

frame *n* = **casing**, framework, structure, shell, construction; = **physique**, build, form, body, figure ▷ *v* = **mount**, case, enclose; = **surround**, ring, enclose, encompass, envelop; = **devise**, draft, compose, sketch, put together

frank *adj* = **candid**, open, direct, straightforward, blunt ≠ **secretive**

frantic *adj* = **frenzied**, wild, furious, distracted, distraught ≠ **calm**; = **hectic**, desperate, frenzied, fraught (*Inf*), frenetic

fraud *n* = **deception**, deceit, treachery, swindling, trickery ≠ **honesty**; = **scam**, deception

fray¹ *v* = **wear thin**, wear, rub, wear out, chafe

freak *adj* = **abnormal**, chance, unusual, exceptional, unparalleled ▷ *n* (*Inf*) = **enthusiast**, fan, nut (*Sl*), addict, buff (*Inf*); = **aberration**, eccentric, anomaly, oddity, monstrosity

free *adj* = **complimentary**, for free (*Inf*), for nothing, unpaid, for love; = **allowed**, permitted, unrestricted,

restraint **2** self-ruling **3** not restricted or affected by **4** not subject to cost or tax **5** not in use **6** (of person) not occupied **7** loose, not fixed ▷ *v* **8** set at liberty **9** remove (obstacles, pain etc.) **10** rid (of) **freedom** *n* **free-for-all** *n* brawl **freehold** *n* tenure of land without obligation of service or rent **freelance** *adj/n* (of) self-employed person **freeloader** *n* (Sl) scrounger **free-range** *adj* kept, produced in natural, nonintensive conditions **free speech** right to express opinions publicly **freewheel** *v* travel downhill on bicycle without pedalling

freeze ⊕ *v* **freezing, froze, frozen 1** change (by reduction of temperature) from liquid to solid, as water to ice **2** preserve (food etc.) by extreme cold **3** fix (prices etc.) **4** feel very cold **5** become rigid

freezer *n* insulated cabinet for long-term storage of perishable foodstuffs

freight ⊕ *n* **1** commercial transport (esp. by railway, ship) **2** cost of this **3** goods so carried ▷ *v* **4** send as or by freight **freighter** *n*

frenetic *adj* frenzied

frenzy ⊕ *n, pl* **-zies 1** violent mental derangement **2** wild excitement **frenzied** *adj*

frequent ⊕ *adj* **1** happening often **2** common **3** numerous ▷ *v* **4** go often to **frequency** *n, pl* **-cies 1** rate of occurrence **2** in radio etc., cycles per second of alternating current

fresco *n, pl* **-coes, -cos** (method of) painting on wet plaster

fresh ⊕ *adj* **1** not stale **2** new **3** additional **4** different **5** recent **6** inexperienced **7** pure **8** not pickled, frozen etc. **9** not faded

———————— THESAURUS ————————

unimpeded, clear; = **at liberty**, loose, liberated, at large, on the loose ≠ **confined**; = **independent**, unfettered, footloose = **non-working**, leisure, unemployed, idle, unoccupied; = **available**, empty, spare, vacant, unused ▷ *v* = **clear**, disengage, cut loose, release, rescue; = **release**, liberate, let out, set free, deliver ≠ **confine**

freeze *v* = **ice over** *or* **up**, harden, stiffen, solidify, become solid; = **fix**, hold, limit, hold up

freight *n* = **transportation**, traffic, delivery, carriage, shipment;

= **cargo**, goods, load, delivery, burden

frenzy *n* = **fury**, passion, rage, seizure, hysteria ≠ **calm**

frequent *adj* = **common**, repeated, usual, familiar, everyday ≠ **infrequent** ▷ *v* = **visit**, attend, haunt, be found at, patronize ≠ **keep away**

fresh *adj* = **additional**, more, new, other, added; = **natural**, unprocessed, unpreserved ≠ **preserved**; = **new**, original, novel, different, recent ≠ **old**; = **invigorating**, clean, pure, crisp, bracing ≠ **stale**; = **cool**, cold,

10 not tired 11 (of wind) strong
freshen v **freshman, fresher** n
first-year student
fret¹ ❶ v **fretting, fretted 1** be
irritated, worry ▷ n **2** irritation
fretful adj
fret² n **1** repetitive geometrical
pattern ▷ v **2** ornament with
carved pattern **fretwork** n
friable adj easily crumbled
friar n member of religious order
fricassee n dish of stewed pieces
of meat
friction ❶ n **1** rubbing
2 resistance met with by body
moving over another **3** clash of
wills etc.
Friday n sixth day of the week
fridge n (Inf) refrigerator
friend ❶ n one well known to
another and regarded with
affection and loyalty **friendly** adj
1 kind **2** favourable **friendship** n
frieze n ornamental band, strip (on
wall)
frigate n fast warship
fright ❶ n **1** sudden fear **2** shock
3 alarm **4** grotesque or ludicrous
person or thing **frighten** v cause
fear, fright in **frightening** adj

frightful adj **1** terrible, calamitous
2 shocking **3** (Inf) very great, very
large **frightfully** adv
frigid adj **1** formal **2** (sexually)
unfeeling **3** cold
frill n **1** strip of fabric gathered at
one edge **2** ruff of hair, feathers
around neck of dog, bird etc.
3 unnecessary words
4 superfluous thing **5** adornment
frilly adj
fringe ❶ n **1** ornamental edge of
hanging threads, tassels etc. **2** hair
cut in front and falling over brow
3 edge ▷ adj **4** (of theatre etc.)
unofficial
frisk v **1** move, leap, playfully
2 (Inf) search (person) **frisky** adj
frisson n shiver of excitement
fritter¹ v waste
fritter² n piece of food fried in
batter
frivolous adj **1** not serious,
unimportant **2** flippant
frivolity n
frizz v **1** crisp, curl into small curls
▷ n **2** frizzed hair **frizzy** adj
frock n **1** woman's dress **2** various
similar garments
frog n tailless amphibious animal

f

THESAURUS

refreshing, brisk, chilly; **= lively**,
keen, alert, refreshed, vigorous
≠ weary
fret¹ v **= worry**, brood, agonize,
obsess, lose sleep
friction n **= conflict**, hostility,
resentment, disagreement,
animosity; **= resistance**, rubbing,
scraping, grating, rasping
friend n **= companion**, pal, mate

(Inf), buddy (Inf), best friend **≠ foe**;
= supporter, ally, associate,
sponsor, patron
fright n **= fear**, shock, alarm,
horror, panic **≠ courage**
fringe n **= border**, edging, edge,
trimming, hem; **= edge**, limits,
border, margin, outskirts ▷ adj
= unofficial, alternative, radical,
innovative, avant-garde

developed from tadpole **frogman**
n underwater swimmer with
rubber suit

frolic *n* **-icking, -icked**
1 merrymaking ▷ *v* **2** behave
playfully

from *prep* expressing point of
departure, source, distance, cause,
change of state etc.

frond *n* plant organ consisting of
stem and foliage

front ❶ *n* **1** fore part **2** position
directly before or ahead **3** seaside
promenade **4** outward aspect
5 (*Inf*) thing serving as respectable
cover ▷ *v* **6** look, face **7** (*Inf*) be a
cover for ▷ *adj* **8** of, at the front
frontal *adj* **frontage** *n* **1** façade
of building **2** extent of front
frontier *n* part of country which
borders on another **frontispiece** *n*
illustration facing title page of book

frost ❶ *n* **1** frozen dew or mist
2 act or state of freezing ▷ *v*
3 cover, be covered with frost or
something similar in appearance
frosted *adj* (of glass) opaque
frosty *adj* **1** accompanied by frost
2 cold **3** unfriendly **frostbite** *n*
destruction of tissue by cold

froth *n* **1** collection of small

bubbles, foam ▷ *v* **2** (cause to)
foam **frothy** *adj*

frown ❶ *v* **1** wrinkle brows
2 (with *on*) disapprove of ▷ *n*
3 expression of disapproval

frugal *adj* **1** sparing **2** thrifty,
economical **3** meagre

fruit ❶ *n* **1** seed and its envelope,
esp. edible one **2** vegetable
product **3** (*usu. pl*) result, benefit
▷ *v* **4** bear fruit **fruitful** *adj*
fruition *n* **1** enjoyment
2 realization of hopes **fruitless** *adj*
fruity *adj*

frump *n* dowdy woman **frumpy**
adj

frustrate ❶ *v* **1** thwart
2 disappoint **frustration** *n*

fry¹ *v* **frying, fried 1** cook with fat
2 be cooked thus

fry² *pl n* young fishes

ft. **1** feet **2** foot

fuchsia *n* shrub with purple-red
flowers

fuddle *v* (cause to) be intoxicated,
confused

fuddy-duddy *n, pl* **-dies** (*Inf*)
(elderly) dull person

fudge¹*n* soft, variously flavoured
sweet

fudge² *v* avoid definite decision

——————————— THESAURUS ———————————

front *n* = **head**, start, lead,
forefront; = **exterior**, face, façade,
frontage; = **foreground**, fore,
forefront, nearest part; = **front
line**, trenches, vanguard, firing line;
(*Inf*) = **disguise**, cover, blind, mask,
cover-up ▷ *adj* = **foremost**, at the
front ≠ **back** ▷ *v* = **face onto**,
overlook, look out on, have a view

of, look over *or* onto

frost *n* = **hoarfrost**, freeze, rime

frown *v* = **glare**, scowl, glower,
make a face, look daggers

fruit *n* = **produce**, crop, yield,
harvest; (*often plural*) = **result**,
reward, outcome, end result, return

frustrate *v* = **thwart**, stop, check,
block, defeat ≠ **further**

fuel ❶ *n* **1** material for burning as source of heat or power ▷ *v* **2** provide with fuel

fugitive ❶ *n* **1** one who flees, esp. from arrest ▷ *adj* **2** elusive

fugue *n* musical composition in which themes are repeated in different parts

fulcrum *n, pl* **-crums, -cra** point on which a lever is placed for support

fulfil ❶ *v* **-filling, -filled** **1** satisfy **2** carry out **fulfilment** *n*

full ❶ *adj* **1** containing as much as possible **2** abundant **3** complete **4** ample **5** plump ▷ *adv* **6** very **7** quite **8** exactly **fully** *adv* **full-blooded** *adj* vigorous, enthusiastic **full-blown** *adj* fully developed **full stop** punctuation

mark (.) at end of sentence

fulminate *v* (esp. with *against*) criticize harshly

fulsome *adj* insincerely excessive

fumble ❶ *v* **1** grope about **2** handle awkwardly ▷ *n* **3** awkward attempt

fume ❶ *v* **1** be angry **2** emit smoke or vapour ▷ *n* **3** smoke **4** vapour **fumigate** *v* apply fumes or smoke to, esp. for disinfection

fun ❶ *n* anything enjoyable, amusing etc. **funny** *adj* **1** comical **2** odd **funnily** *adv* **funfair** *n* entertainment with rides and stalls

function ❶ *n* **1** work a thing is designed to do **2** (large) social event **3** duty **4** profession ▷ *v* **5** operate, work **functional** *adj*

fund ❶ *n* **1** stock or sum of money

fuel *n* = **incitement**, ammunition, provocation, incentive, power

fugitive *n* = **runaway**, refugee, deserter, escapee

fulfil *v* = **carry out**, perform, complete, achieve, accomplish ≠ **neglect**; = **achieve**, realize, satisfy, attain, consummate; = **satisfy**, please, content, cheer, refresh

full *adj* = **filled**, stocked, brimming, replete, complete; = **satiated**, having had enough, replete; = **extensive**, complete, generous, adequate, ample ≠ **incomplete**; = **comprehensive**, complete, exhaustive, all-embracing; = **rounded**, strong, rich, powerful, intense; = **plump**, rounded, voluptuous, shapely, well-rounded; = **voluminous**, large, loose, baggy,

billowing ≠ **tight**; = **rich**, strong, deep, loud, distinct ≠ **thin**

fumble *v* = **grope**, flounder, scrabble, feel around

fume *v* = **rage**, seethe, see red (*Inf*), storm, rant ▷ *pl n* = **smoke**, gas, exhaust, pollution/vapour

fun *n* = **amusement**, sport, pleasure, entertainment, recreation; = **enjoyment**, pleasure, mirth ≠ **gloom**

function *n* = **purpose**, business, job, use, role; = **reception**, party, affair, gathering, bash (*Inf*) ▷ *v* = **work**, run, operate, perform, go; = **act**, operate, perform, behave, do duty

fund *n* = **reserve**, stock, supply, store, collection ▷ *v* = **finance**, back, support, pay for, subsidize

2 supply ▷ *pl* **3** money resources ▷ *v* **4** provide or obtain funds

fundamental ❶ *adj* **1** of, affecting, or serving as, the base **2** essential, primary ▷ *n* **3** basic rule or fact **fundamentalism** *n* strict interpretation of religion **fundamentalist** *n/adj*

fundi *n* (*S Afr*) expert or boffin

funeral ❶ *n* (ceremony associated with) burial or cremation of dead **funereal** *adj* **1** like a funeral **2** dark **3** gloomy

fungus *n, pl* **-gi, -guses** plant without leaves, flowers, or roots, as mushroom, mould **fungicide** *n* substance that destroys fungi

funk *n* style of dance music **funky** *adj* **funkier, funkiest**

funnel *n* **1** cone-shaped vessel or tube **2** chimney of locomotive or ship ▷ *v* **3** (cause to) move as through funnel

fur *n* **1** soft hair of animal **2** garment of this **furry** *adj*

furious ❶ *adj* **1** extremely angry **2** violent

furl *v* roll up and bind

furlong *n* eighth of mile

furnace *n* apparatus for applying great heat to metals

furnish ❶ *v* **1** fit up house with furniture **2** supply **furnishings** *pl n* **furniture** *n*

furore ❶ *n* very angry or excited reaction to something

furrow *n* **1** trench **2** groove ▷ *v* **3** make furrows in

further, farther ❶ *adv* **1** more **2** in addition **3** at or to a greater distance or extent ▷ *adj* **4** more distant **5** additional: comparative of FAR ▷ *v* **6** promote **furthermore** *adv* besides **furthermost** *adj* **furthest** *adj/adv* superlative of FAR

furtive *adj* stealthy, sly, secret

fury ❶ *n, pl* **-ries** wild rage, violence

fuse *v* **1** blend by melting **2** melt with heat **3** (cause to) fail as a result of blown fuse ▷ *n* **4** soft wire used as safety device in electrical systems **5** device for igniting bomb etc. **fusion** *n*

— THESAURUS —

fundamental *adj* = **central**, key, basic, essential, primary ≠ **incidental**; = **basic**, essential, underlying, profound, elementary

funeral *n* = **burial**, committal, laying to rest, cremation, interment

furious *adj* = **angry**, raging, fuming, infuriated, incensed ≠ **pleased**; = **violent**, intense, fierce, savage, turbulent

furnish *v* = **decorate**, fit out, stock, equip; = **supply**, give, offer, provide, present

furore *n* = **commotion**, to-do, stir, disturbance, outcry

further, farther *adv* = **in addition**, moreover, besides, furthermore, also ▷ *adj* = **additional**, more, new, other, extra ▷ *v* = **promote**, help, develop, forward, encourage ≠ **hinder**

fury *n* = **anger**, passion, rage, madness, frenzy ≠ **calmness**; = **violence**, force, intensity, severity, ferocity ≠ **peace**

fuselage *n* body of aircraft

fuss ❶ *n* **1** needless bustle or concern **2** complaint **3** objection ▷ *v* **4** make fuss **fussy** *adj*

fusty *adj* **-tier, -tiest 1** mouldy **2** smelling of damp **3** old-fashioned

futile ❶ *adj* useless, ineffectual, trifling **futility** *n*

futon *n* Japanese padded quilt

future ❶ *n* **1** time to come **2** what will happen ▷ *adj* **3** that will be **4** of, relating to, time to come **futuristic** *adj* appearing to belong to some future time

fuzz *n* **1** fluff **2** frizzed hair **3** blur **4** (*Sl*) police **fuzzy** *adj* **fuzzier, fuzziest**

—————— THESAURUS ——————

fuss *n* = **commotion**, to-do, bother, stir, excitement; = **bother**, trouble, struggle, hassle (*Inf*), nuisance ▷ *v* = **worry**, flap (*Inf*), fret, fidget, take pains

futile *adj* = **useless**, vain, unsuccessful, pointless, worthless

≠ useful

future *n* = **time to come**, hereafter, what lies ahead; = **prospect**, expectation, outlook ▷ *adj* = **forthcoming**, coming, later, approaching, to come

≠ past

g gram

gabardine, gaberdine *n* fine twill cloth like serge

gabble *v* talk, utter inarticulately or too fast

gable *n* triangular upper part of wall at end of ridged roof

gad *v* **gadding, gadded** (esp. with *about*) go around in search of pleasure

gadget ❶ *n* small mechanical device

gaffe *n* tactless remark

gaffer *n* **1** old man **2** (*Inf*) foreman, boss

gag¹ ❶ *v* **gagging, gagged 1** stop up (person's mouth) **2** (*Sl*) retch,

choke ▷ *n* **3** cloth etc. tied across mouth

gag² *n* joke, funny story

gaggle *n* flock of geese

gain ❶ *v* **1** obtain (as profit) **2** earn **3** reach **4** increase, improve **5** get nearer ▷ *n* **6** profit **7** increase, improvement

gainsay *v* **-saying, -said** deny, contradict

gait *n* manner of walking

gala ❶ *n* **1** festive occasion **2** show **3** sporting event

galaxy *n, pl* **-axies** system of stars **galactic** *adj*

gale ❶ *n* **1** strong wind **2** (*Inf*) outburst, esp. of laughter

gall¹ ❶ *v* **1** make sore by rubbing **2** irritate

gall² *n* (*Inf*) **1** impudence **2** bitterness **gall bladder** sac for bile

gallant *adj* **1** fine, stately, brave **2** chivalrous **gallantry** *n*

galleon *n* large sailing ship

gallery *n, pl* **-ries 1** projecting upper floor in church, theatre etc. **2** place for showing works of art

galley *n* **1** one-decked vessel with

THESAURUS

gadget *n* = **device**, thing, appliance, machine, tool

gag¹ *n* = **muzzle**, tie, restraint ▷ *v* = **suppress**, silence, muffle, curb, stifle; = **retch**, heave

gain *v* = **acquire**, get, receive, pick up, secure; = **profit**, get, land, secure, collect ≠ **lose**; = **put on**, increase in, gather, build up ▷ *n* = **rise**, increase, growth, advance,

improvement; = **profit**, return, benefit, advantage, yield ≠ **loss**

gala *n* = **festival**, fête, celebration, carnival, festivity

gale *n* = **storm**, hurricane, tornado, cyclone, blast; (*Inf*) = **outburst**, scream, roar, fit, storm

gall¹ *v* = **annoy**, provoke, irritate, trouble, disturb

sails and oars **2** kitchen of ship or
aircraft
gallivant v gad about
gallon n liquid measure of eight
pints (4.55 litres)
gallop ❶ n **1** horse's fastest pace
2 ride at this pace ▷ v **3** go, ride at
gallop **4** move fast
gallows n structure for hanging
criminals
galore adv in plenty
galoshes pl n waterproof
overshoes
gambit n opening move, comment
etc. intended to secure an
advantage
gamble ❶ v **1** play games of
chance to win money **2** act on
expectation of ▷ n **3** risky
undertaking **4** bet **gambler** n
gambling n
gambol v **-bolling, -bolled** skip,
jump playfully
game¹ ❶ n **1** pastime **2** jest
3 contest for amusement
4 scheme **5** animals or birds
hunted **6** their flesh ▷ adj **7** brave

8 willing **gaming** n gambling
gamekeeper n man employed to
breed game, prevent poaching
game² adj lame
gammon n cured or smoked
ham
gamut n whole range or scale
gander n male goose
gang ❶ n **1** (criminal) group
2 organized group of workmen ▷ v
3 (esp. with up) form gang
gangling adj lanky
gangplank n portable bridge for
boarding or leaving vessel
gangrene n death or decay of
body tissue as a result of disease or
injury
gangster ❶ n member of criminal
gang
gangway n **1** bridge from ship to
shore **2** anything similar
3 passage between rows of seats
gannet n predatory sea bird
gantry n, pl **-tries** structure to
support crane, railway signals etc.
gaol n see JAIL
gap ❶ n opening, interval

gallop v = **run**, race, career, speed,
bolt
gamble n = **risk**, chance, venture,
lottery, speculation ≠ **certainty**;
= **bet**, flutter (Inf), punt (chiefly Brit),
wager ▷ v = **take a chance**,
speculate, stick your neck out (Inf);
= **risk**, chance, hazard, wager
game¹ n = **pastime**, sport, activity,
entertainment, recreation ≠ **job**;
= **match**, meeting, event,
competition, tournament;
= **amusement**, joke,

entertainment, diversion; = **wild
animals** or **birds**, prey, quarry
▷ adj = **willing**, prepared, ready,
keen, eager; = **brave**, courageous,
spirited, daring, persistent
≠ **cowardly**
gang n = **group**, crowd, pack,
company, band
gangster n = **hoodlum** (chiefly US),
crook (Inf), bandit, hood (US Sl),
robber
gap n = **opening**, space, hole,
break, crack; = **interval**, pause,

gape ① v **1** stare in wonder **2** open mouth wide **3** be, become wide open

garage n **1** (part of) building to house cars **2** refuelling and repair centre for cars

garb n/v dress

garbage n (US & Canad) rubbish

garden n **1** ground for cultivation ▷ v **2** cultivate garden **gardener** n **gardening** n

gargantuan adj immense

gargle v **1** wash throat with liquid kept moving by the breath ▷ n **2** gargling **3** preparation for this purpose

gargoyle n grotesque carving on church etc.

garish adj **1** showy **2** gaudy

garland ① n wreath of flowers as decoration

garlic n (bulb of) plant with strong smell and taste, used in cooking and seasoning

garment n article of clothing

garner v store up, collect

garnet n red semiprecious stone

garnish ① v **1** decorate (esp. food) ▷ n **2** material for this

garret n attic

garrison ① n **1** troops stationed in town, fort etc. **2** fortified place ▷ v **3** occupy with garrison

garrotte, garotte v execute by strangling

garrulous adj talkative

garter n band worn round leg to hold up sock or stocking

gas n, pl **gases, gasses 1** airlike substance **2** fossil fuel in form of gas **3** gaseous anaesthetic **4** gaseous poison or irritant **5** (Inf, US & Canad) petrol ▷ v **6** poison with gas **7** talk idly, boastfully **gaseous** adj of, like gas

gash n **1** gaping wound, slash ▷ v **2** cut deeply

gasket n seal between metal faces, esp. in engines

gasp ① v **1** catch breath as in exhaustion or surprise ▷ n **2** gasping

gastric adj of stomach

gastroenteritis n inflammation of stomach and intestines

gastronomy n art of good eating

gate ① n **1** opening in wall, fence etc. **2** barrier for closing it **3** any entrance or way out **gate-crash** v enter social function etc. uninvited

--- THESAURUS ---

interruption, respite, lull

gape v = **stare**, wonder, goggle, gawp (Brit Sl), gawk; = **open**, split, crack, yawn

garland n = **wreath**, band, bays, crown, honours

garnish n = **decoration**, embellishment, adornment, ornamentation, trimming ▷ v = **decorate**, adorn, ornament, embellish, trim ≠ **strip**

garrison n = **troops**, group, unit, section, command; = **fort**, fortress, camp, base, post ▷ v = **station**, position, post, install, assign

gasp v = **pant**, blow, puff, choke, gulp ▷ n = **pant**, puff, gulp, sharp intake of breath

gate n = **barrier**, opening, door, entrance, exit

gateway n **1** entrance with gate **2** means of access

gâteau n, pl **-teaux** elaborate, rich cake

gather ● v **1** (cause to) assemble **2** increase gradually **3** draw together **4** collect **5** learn, understand **gathering** n assembly

gaudy adj **gaudier, gaudiest** showy in tasteless way

gauge ● n **1** standard measure, as of diameter of wire etc. **2** distance between rails of railway **3** instrument for measuring ▷ v **4** measure **5** estimate

gaunt adj lean, haggard

gauntlet n (armoured) glove covering part of arm

gauze n thin transparent fabric of silk, wire etc.

gavel n auctioneer's mallet

gay ● adj **1** homosexual **2** merry **3** bright **gaiety** n **gaily** adv

gaze ● v **1** look fixedly ▷ n **2** fixed look

gazebo n, pl **-bos, -boes** summerhouse

gazelle n small graceful antelope

gazette ● n official newspaper for announcements **gazetteer** n geographical dictionary

GB Great Britain

GBH grievous bodily harm

GCE General Certificate of Education

GCSE General Certificate of Secondary Education

gear ● n **1** set of wheels working together, esp. by engaging cogs **2** equipment **3** clothing **4** (Sl) drugs ▷ v **5** adapt (one thing) so as to conform with another **gearbox** n case protecting gearing of bicycle, car etc.

geese pl of GOOSE

geezer n (Inf) (old or eccentric) man

geisha n, pl **-sha, -shas** in Japan, professional female companion for men

gel n jelly-like substance

g

gather v = **congregate**, assemble, collect, meet, mass ≠ **scatter**; = **assemble**, collect, bring together, muster, call together ≠ **disperse**; = **collect**, assemble, accumulate, mass, muster; = **pick**, harvest, pluck, reap, garner; = **build up**, rise, increase, grow, expand

gauge v = **measure**, calculate, evaluate, value, determine; = **judge**, estimate, guess, assess, evaluate ▷ n = **meter**, dial, measuring instrument

gay adj = **homosexual**, lesbian,

queer (Inf, offens); = **cheerful**, lively, sparkling, merry, upbeat (Inf) ≠ **sad**; = **colourful**, rich, bright, brilliant, vivid ≠ **drab**

gaze v = **stare**, look, view, watch, regard ▷ n = **stare**, look, fixed look

gazette n = **newspaper**, paper, journal, periodical, news-sheet

gear n = **mechanism**, works, machinery, cogs, cogwheels; = **equipment**, supplies, tackle, tools, instruments; = **clothing**, wear, dress, clothes, outfit ▷ v with **to** or **towards** = **equip**, fit, adjust,

gelatine, gelatin *n* substance prepared from animal bones etc., producing edible jelly

geld *v* castrate **gelding** *n* castrated horse

gelignite *n* powerful explosive consisting of dynamite in gelatine form

gem ⊙ *n* precious stone, esp. when cut and polished

gen *n* (*Inf*) information

gender *n* sex, male or female

gene *n* biological factor determining inherited characteristics

genealogy *n*, *pl* **-gies** study or account of descent from ancestors

general ⊙ *adj* **1** widespread **2** not particular or specific **3** usual **4** miscellaneous ▷ *n* **5** army officer of rank above colonel **generally** *adv* **generalize** *v* draw general conclusions **general practitioner** doctor serving local area

generate ⊙ *v* **1** bring into being **2** produce **generation** *n* **1** bringing into being **2** all persons born about same time **3** time

between generations (about 30 years) **generator** *n* apparatus for producing (steam, electricity etc.)

generous ⊙ *adj* **1** free in giving **2** abundant **generosity** *n*

genesis ⊙ *n*, *pl* **-eses 1** origin **2** mode of formation

genial *adj* **1** cheerful **2** mild

genie *n* in fairy tales, servant appearing by, and working, magic

genital *adj* relating to sexual organs or reproduction **genitals** *pl n* sexual organs

genius ⊙ *n* (person with) exceptional power or ability

genocide *n* murder of entire race of people

genome *n* all the genetic material within an organism

genre ⊙ *n* style of literary work

gent *n* (*Inf*) gentleman **gents** *n* men's public lavatory

genteel *adj* **1** well-bred **2** affectedly proper **gentility** *n* respectability

gentile *adj* **1** *n* **2** (person) of race other than Jewish

gentle ⊙ *adj* **1** mild, not rough or

━━━━━━━ THESAURUS ━━━━━━━

adapt

gem *n* = **precious stone**, jewel, stone; = **treasure**, prize, jewel, pearl, masterpiece

general *adj* = **widespread**, accepted, popular, public, common ≠ **individual**; = **overall**, complete, total, global, comprehensive ≠ **restricted**; = **universal**, overall, widespread, collective, across-the-board ≠ **exceptional**

generate *v* = **produce**, create, make, cause, give rise to ≠ **end**

generous *adj* = **liberal**, lavish, charitable, hospitable, bountiful ≠ **mean**; = **magnanimous**, kind, noble, good, high-minded; = **plentiful**, lavish, ample, abundant, full ≠ **meagre**

genesis *n* = **beginning**, origin, start, birth, creation ≠ **end**

genius *n* = **brilliance**, ability, talent, capacity, gift

genre *n* = **type**, group, order, sort, kind

gentle *adj* = **kind**, kindly, tender,

severe **2** moderate **3** well-born
gently adv **gentleness** n quality
of being gentle **gentleman** n
1 chivalrous well-bred man **2** man
(used as a mark of politeness)
gentry n people just below nobility
in social rank
genuine ❶ adj **1** real **2** sincere
genus n, pl **genera** class, order,
group (esp. of insects, animals etc.)
with common characteristics
geography n science of earth's
form, physical features, climate,
population etc. **geographer** n
geographical adj
geology n science of earth's crust,
rocks, strata etc. **geological** adj
geologist n
geometry n science of properties
and relations of lines, surfaces etc.
geometrical, -metric adj
geranium n plant with red, pink or
white flowers
gerbil n desert rodent of Asia and
Africa
geriatrics n science of old age and
its diseases **geriatric** adj/n old

(person), esp. a patient
germ ❶ n **1** microbe, esp. causing
disease **2** rudiment
germinate v (cause to) sprout or
begin to grow
gestation n carrying of young in
womb
gesticulate v use expressive
movements of hands and arms
when speaking
gesture ❶ n/v (make) movement
to convey meaning
get ❶ v **getting, got 1** obtain
2 catch **3** cause to go or come
4 bring into position or state
5 induce **6** be in possession of,
have (to do) **7** become
geyser n **1** hot spring throwing up
spout of water **2** water heater
ghastly ❶ adj **-lier, -liest**
1 deathlike **2** (Inf) horrible ▷ adv
3 sickly
gherkin n small pickled cucumber
ghetto n, pl **-tos, -toes** densely
populated (esp. by one racial group)
slum area **ghetto blaster** (Inf)
large portable cassette recorder

mild, humane ≠ **unkind**; = **slow**,
easy, slight, moderate, gradual;
= **moderate**, light, soft, slight, mild
≠ **violent**
genuine adj = **authentic**, real,
actual, true, valid ≠ **counterfeit**;
= **heartfelt**, sincere, honest,
earnest, real ≠ **affected**
germ n = **microbe**, virus, bug (Inf),
bacterium, bacillus; = **beginning**,
root, seed, origin, spark
gesture n = **sign**, action, signal,
motion, indication ▷ v = **signal**,

sign, wave, indicate, motion
get v = **become**, grow, turn, come
to be; = **persuade**, convince,
induce, influence, entice; (Inf)
= **annoy**, upset, anger, disturb,
trouble; = **obtain**, receive, gain,
acquire, win; = **fetch**, bring, collect;
= **understand**, follow, catch, see,
realize; = **catch**, develop, contract,
succumb to, fall victim to; = **arrest**,
catch, grab, capture, seize
ghastly adj = **horrible**, shocking,
terrible, awful, dreadful ≠ **lovely**

ghost ❶ *n* **1** dead person appearing again **2** spectre **3** faint trace **ghostly** *adj*

ghoul *n* **1** malevolent spirit **2** person with morbid interests **ghoulish** *adj*

giant ❶ *n* **1** mythical being of superhuman size **2** very tall person, plant etc. ▷ *adj* **3** huge **gigantic** *adj* enormous, huge

gibber *v* make meaningless sounds with mouth **gibberish** *n* meaningless speech or words

gibbon *n* type of ape

gibe, jibe *v/n* jeer

giblets *pl n* internal edible parts of fowl

gidday, g'day *interj* (Aust & NZ) expression of greeting

giddy *adj* **-dier, -diest 1** dizzy **2** liable to cause dizziness **3** flighty

gift ❶ *n* **1** thing given, present **2** faculty, power **gifted** *adj* talented

gig *n* performance by pop or jazz musicians

gigabyte *n* (Comp) 1024 megabytes

gigantic ❶ see GIANT

giggle ❶ *v* **1** laugh nervously, foolishly ▷ *n* **2** such a laugh

gild *v* **gilding, gilded** put thin layer of gold on **gilt** *n* thin layer of gold put on **gilt-edged** *adj*

guaranteed

gill¹ *n* (usu. pl) breathing organ in fish

gill² *n* liquid measure, quarter of pint (0.142 litres)

gimmick *n* stratagem etc., esp. designed to attract attention or publicity

gin *n* spirit flavoured with juniper berries

ginger *n* **1** plant with hot-tasting spicy root **2** the root ▷ *v* **3** stimulate **gingerbread** *n* cake flavoured with ginger

gingerly *adv* cautiously

gingham *n* cotton cloth, usu. checked

gingivitis *n* inflammation of gums

ginseng *n* plant root used as tonic

Gipsy *pl* **-sies** see GYPSY

giraffe *n* Afr. animal with very long neck

gird *v* **girding, girded 1** put belt round **2** prepare (oneself) **girder** *n* large beam

girdle *n* **1** corset **2** waistband

girl ❶ *n* **1** female child **2** young (unmarried) woman **girlfriend** *n* man's female companion

giro *n, pl* **-ros** system operated by banks and post offices for the transfer of money

girth *n* **1** measurement round thing **2** band put round horse to

——————— THESAURUS ———————

ghost *n* = **spirit**, soul, phantom, spectre, spook (Inf); = **trace**, shadow, suggestion, hint, suspicion

giant *adj* = **huge**, vast, enormous, tremendous, immense ≠ **tiny** ▷ *n* = **ogre**, monster, titan, colossus

gift *n* = **donation**, offering, present,

contribution, grant; = **talent**, ability, capacity, genius, power

gigantic *adj* = **huge**, large, giant, massive, enormous ≠ **tiny**

giggle *n* = **laugh**, chuckle, snigger, chortle, titter

girl *n* = **female child**, lass, lassie

hold saddle etc.

gist n substance, main point (of remarks etc.)

give ⊙ n **giving, gave, given** 1 make present of 2 deliver 3 assign 4 utter 5 yield, give way ▷ n 6 yielding, elasticity

glacé adj 1 crystallized 2 iced

glacier n slow-moving river of ice **glacial** adj

glad ⊙ adj **gladder, gladdest** 1 pleased 2 happy **gladden** v make glad **gladly** adv

glade n grassy space in forest

gladiator n trained fighter in Roman arena

gladiolus n, pl **-lus, -li, -luses** kind of iris, with sword-shaped leaves

glamour ⊙ n alluring charm, fascination **glamorous** adj

glance ⊙ v 1 look rapidly or briefly 2 glide off something struck ▷ n 3 brief look

gland n organ controlling different bodily functions by chemical means **glandular** adj

glare ⊙ v 1 look fiercely 2 shine intensely ▷ n 3 glaring **glaring** adj conspicuous

glass n 1 hard transparent substance 2 things made of it 3 tumbler 4 its contents ▷ pl 5 spectacles **glassy** adj 1 like glass 2 expressionless

glaucoma n eye disease

glaze ⊙ v 1 furnish with glass 2 cover with glassy substance 3 become glassy ▷ n 4 transparent coating 5 substance used for this **glazier** n one who glazes windows

gleam ⊙ n/v (give out) slight or passing beam of light

glean v 1 pick up 2 gather

glee n mirth, merriment **gleeful** adj

glen n narrow valley

glib adj **glibber, glibbest** fluent but insincere or superficial

g

——— THESAURUS ———

(Inf), miss, maiden (Archaic)

give v = **perform**, do, carry out, execute; = **communicate**, announce, transmit, pronounce, utter; = **produce**, make, cause, occasion, engender; = **present**, contribute, donate, provide, supply ≠ **take**; = **concede**, allow, grant; = **surrender**, yield, devote, hand over, relinquish

glad adj = **happy**, pleased, delighted, contented, gratified ≠ **unhappy**; (Archaic) = **pleasing**, happy, cheering, pleasant, cheerful

glamour n = **charm**, appeal, beauty, attraction, fascination

glance v = **peek**, look, view, glimpse, peep ≠ **scrutinize** ▷ n = **peek**, look, glimpse, peep, dekko (Sl) ≠ **good look**

glare v = **scowl**, frown, glower, look daggers, lour or lower; = **dazzle**, blaze, flare, flame ▷ n = **scowl**, frown, glower, dirty look, black look; = **dazzle**, glow, blaze, flame, brilliance

glaze n = **coat**, finish, polish, shine, gloss ▷ v = **coat**, polish, gloss, varnish, enamel

gleam v = **shine**, flash, glow, sparkle, glitter ▷ n = **glimmer**, flash, beam, glow, sparkle; = **trace**,

glide ● v 1 pass smoothly and continuously ▷ n 2 smooth, silent movement **glider** n aircraft without engine

glimmer v 1 shine faintly ▷ n 2 faint light

glimpse ● n 1 brief view ▷ v 2 catch glimpse of

glint v/n flash

glisten v gleam by reflecting light

glitter ● v 1 shine with bright quivering light, sparkle ▷ n 2 lustre 3 sparkle

gloat v regard with smugness or malicious satisfaction

globe ● n 1 sphere with map of earth or stars 2 ball **global** adj 1 relating to whole world 2 total, comprehensive

globule n small round drop

glockenspiel n percussion instrument played with hammers

gloom ● n 1 darkness 2 melancholy **gloomy** adj **gloomier, gloomiest**

glory ● n, pl **-ries** 1 renown 2 splendour 3 heavenly bliss ▷ v 4 take pride (in) **glorify** v 1 make glorious 2 praise **glorious** adj 1 illustrious 2 splendid 3 (Inf) delightful **gloriously** adv

gloss¹ ● n 1 surface shine, lustre ▷ v 2 put gloss on 3 (esp. with over) (try to) cover up, pass over (fault, error) **glossy** adj **-sier, -siest** smooth, shiny

gloss² ● n 1 interpretation of word 2 comment ▷ v 3 interpret 4 comment **glossary** n dictionary of special words

glove n 1 covering for the hand ▷ v 2 cover as with glove

glow ● v 1 give out light and heat without flames 2 be or look hot ▷ n 3 shining heat **glow-worm** n insect giving out light

glower v/n scowl

glucose n type of sugar found in fruit etc.

THESAURUS

suggestion, hint, flicker, glimmer

glide v = **slip**, sail, slide

glimpse n = **look**, sighting, sight, glance, peep ▷ v = **catch sight of**, spot, sight, view, spy

glitter v = **shine**, flash, sparkle, glare, gleam ▷ n = **glamour**, show, display, splendour, tinsel; = **sparkle**, flash, shine, glare, gleam

globe n = **planet**, world, earth, sphere, orb

gloom n = **darkness**, dark, shadow, shade, twilight ≠ **light**; = **depression**, sorrow, woe, melancholy, unhappiness

≠ **happiness**

glory n = **honour**, praise, fame, distinction, acclaim ≠ **shame**; = **splendour**, majesty, greatness, grandeur, nobility ▷ v = **triumph**, boast, relish, revel, exult

gloss¹ n = **shine**, gleam, sheen, polish, brightness

gloss² n = **interpretation**, comment, note, explanation, commentary ▷ v = **interpret**, explain, comment, translate, annotate

glow n = **light**, gleam, splendour, glimmer, brilliance ≠ **dullness** ▷ v

glue ⊕ *n/v* (fasten with) sticky substance **gluey** *adj*

glum *adj* **glummer, glummest** sullen, gloomy

glut *n* 1 surfeit, excessive amount ▷ *v* 2 feed, gratify to the full or to excess

glutton *n* 1 greedy person 2 one with great liking or capacity for something **gluttonous** *adj* **gluttony** *n*

glycerine, glycerin *n* colourless sweet liquid

GMT Greenwich Mean Time

gnarled *adj* knobby, twisted

gnash *v* grind (teeth) together as in anger or pain

gnat *n* small, biting fly

gnaw *v* **gnawing, gnawed** bite or chew steadily

gnome *n* legendary creature like small old man

gnu *n* oxlike antelope

go ⊕ *v* **going, went, gone** 1 move along 2 depart 3 function 4 fare 5 fail 6 elapse 7 be able to be put 8 become ▷ *n* 9 going 10 energy 11 attempt 12 turn **go-between** *n* intermediary

goad *n* 1 spiked stick for driving cattle 2 anything that urges to action ▷ *v* 3 urge on 4 torment

goal ⊕ *n* 1 end of race 2 object of effort 3 posts through which ball is to be driven in football etc. 4 the score so made

goat *n* animal with long hair, horns and beard **goatee** *n* small pointed beard

gobble¹ *v* eat hastily, noisily or greedily

gobble² *n/v* (make) cry of turkey

gobbledegook, gobbledygook *n* unintelligible language

goblet *n* drinking cup

goblin *n* (*Folklore*) small, usu. malevolent being

god *n* 1 superhuman being worshipped as having supernatural power 2 object of worship, idol 3 (*with cap.*) the Supreme Being, creator and ruler of universe **godly** *adj* devout, pious **godfather** *n* sponsor at baptism **godforsaken** *adj* desolate, dismal **godsend** *n* something unexpected but welcome

gogga *n* (*S Afr, Inf*) any small insect

goggle *v* 1 (of eyes) bulge 2 stare ▷ *pl n* 3 protective spectacles

g

= **shine**, burn, gleam, brighten, glimmer

glue *n* = **adhesive**, cement, gum, paste

go *v* = **move**, travel, advance, journey, proceed ≠ **stay**; = **leave**, withdraw, depart, move out, slope off; = **elapse**, pass, flow, fly by, expire; = **be given**, be spent, be

awarded, be allotted; = **function**, work, run, move, operate ≠ **fail**; = **match**, blend, correspond, fit, suit ▷ *n* = **attempt**, try, effort, bid, shot (*Inf*); = **turn**, shot (*Inf*), stint, fossick through (*Aust & NZ*)

goal *n* = **aim**, end, target, purpose, object

go-kart, go-cart n miniature, low-powered racing car

gold n 1 yellow precious metal 2 coins of this 3 colour of gold ▷ adj 4 of, like gold **golden** adj **golden wedding** fiftieth wedding anniversary **goldfinch** n bird with yellow feathers **goldfish** n any of various ornamental pond or aquarium fish

golf n outdoor game in which small ball is struck into holes **golfer** n

gondola n Venetian canal boat **gondolier** n rower of gondola

gong n metal plate which sounds when struck with soft mallet

good ❶ adj **better, best** 1 commendable 2 right 3 beneficial 4 well-behaved 5 virtuous 6 sound 7 valid ▷ n 8 benefit 9 wellbeing 10 profit ▷ pl 11 property 12 wares **goodly**

adj large, considerable **goodness** n **goodwill** n kindly feeling

goodbye ❶ interj/n form of address on parting

gooey adj **gooier, gooiest** (Inf) sticky, soft

goose n, pl **geese** 1 web-footed bird 2 its flesh 3 simpleton

gooseberry n 1 thorny shrub 2 its hairy fruit

gore¹ ❶ n (dried) blood from wound **gory** adj

gore² ❶ v pierce with horns

gorge ❶ n 1 ravine 2 disgust, resentment ▷ v 3 feed greedily

gorgeous ❶ adj splendid, showy

gorilla n largest anthropoid ape, found in Africa

gormless adj (Inf) stupid

gorse n prickly shrub

gosling n young goose

gospel ❶ n 1 unquestionable

──────── THESAURUS ────────

good adj = **excellent**, great, fine, pleasing, acceptable ≠ **bad**; = **proficient**, able, skilled, expert, talented ≠ **bad**; = **beneficial**, useful, helpful, favourable, wholesome ≠ **harmful**; = **honourable**, moral, worthy, ethical, upright ≠ **bad**; = **well-behaved**, polite, orderly, obedient, dutiful ≠ **naughty**; = **kind**, kindly, friendly, obliging, charitable ≠ **unkind**; = **true**, real, genuine, proper; = **full**, complete, extensive ≠ **scant** ▷ n = **benefit**, interest, gain, advantage, use ≠ **disadvantage**; = **virtue**, goodness, righteousness, worth, merit ≠ **evil**

goodbye n = **farewell**, parting, leave-taking ▷ interj = **farewell**, see you, see you later, ciao (Italian), cheerio

gore¹ n = **blood**, slaughter, bloodshed, carnage, butchery

gore² v = **pierce**, wound, transfix, impale

gorge n = **ravine**, canyon, pass, chasm, cleft ▷ v = **overeat**, devour, gobble, wolf, gulp

gorgeous adj = **magnificent**, beautiful, superb, spectacular, splendid ≠ **shabby**; = **delightful**, good, great, wonderful, excellent ≠ **awful**

gospel n = **doctrine**, news, teachings, message, revelation;

truth **2** *(with cap.)* any of first four books of New Testament

gossamer *n* filmy substance like spider's web

gossip ● *n* **1** idle (malicious) talk about other persons **2** one who talks thus ▷ *v* **3** engage in gossip

gouge *v* **1** scoop out **2** force out ▷ *n* **3** chisel with curved cutting edge

goulash *n* stew seasoned with paprika

gourd *n* **1** large fleshy fruit **2** its rind as vessel

gourmand *n* glutton

gourmet ● *n* **1** connoisseur of wine, food **2** epicure

gout *n* disease with inflammation, esp. of joints

govern ● *v* **1** rule, control **2** determine **governess** *n* woman teacher, esp. in private household **government** *n* **1** exercise of political authority in directing a people, state etc. **2** system by which community is ruled **3** governing group **4** control **governor** *n* **1** one who governs **2** chief administrator of an institution **3** member of committee responsible for an organization or institution

gown ● *n* **1** loose flowing outer garment **2** woman's (long) dress **3** official robe

GP General Practitioner

grab ● *v* **grabbing, grabbed** **1** grasp suddenly **2** snatch ▷ *n* **3** sudden clutch **4** quick attempt to seize

grace ● *n* **1** charm, elegance **2** goodwill, favour **3** sense of propriety **4** postponement granted **5** short thanksgiving for meal ▷ *v* **6** add grace to, honour **graceful** *adj* **gracious** *adj* **1** kind **2** condescending

grade ● *n* **1** step, stage **2** class

— THESAURUS —

= **truth**, fact, certainty, the last word

gossip *n* = **idle talk**, scandal, hearsay, tittle-tattle, small talk; = **busybody**, chatterbox *(Inf)*, chatterer, scandalmonger, gossipmonger ▷ *v* = **chat**, chatter, jaw *(Sl)*, blether

gourmet *n* = **connoisseur**, foodie *(Inf)*, bon vivant *(Fr)*, epicure, gastronome

govern *v* = **rule**, lead, control, command, manage; = **restrain**, control, check, master, discipline

gown *n* = **dress**, costume, garment, robe, frock

grab *v* = **snatch**, catch, seize, capture, grip

grace *n* = **elegance**, poise, ease, polish, refinement ≠ **ungainliness**; = **manners**, decency, etiquette, consideration, propriety ≠ **bad manners**; = **indulgence**, mercy, pardon, reprieve; = **benevolence**, favour, goodness, goodwill, generosity ≠ **ill will**; = **prayer**, thanks, blessing, thanksgiving, benediction ▷ *v* = **adorn**, enhance, decorate, enrich, set off; = **honour**, favour, dignify ≠ **insult**

grade *v* = **classify**, rate, order, class, group, degree

g

3 rating **4** slope ▷ v **5** arrange in classes **6** assign grade to
gradation n **1** series of steps **2** each of them
gradient n (degree of) slope
gradual ❶ adj **1** taking place by degrees **2** slow and steady **3** not steep **gradually** adv
graduate ❶ v **1** take university degree **2** divide into degrees ▷ n **3** holder of university degree **graduation** n
graffiti pl n (oft. obscene) writing, drawing on walls
graft¹ ❶ n **1** shoot of plant set in stalk of another **2** the process **3** surgical transplant of skin, tissue ▷ v **4** insert (shoot) in another stalk **5** transplant (living tissue in surgery)
graft² n (Inf) **1** hard work **2** self-advancement, profit by unfair means
grain ❶ n **1** (seed, fruit of) cereal plant **2** small hard particle **3** very small unit of weight **4** arrangement of fibres **5** any very small amount
gram, gramme n one

thousandth of a kilogram
grammar n **1** science of structure and usages of language **2** use of words **grammatical** adj
grammar school state-maintained secondary school providing academic education
gramophone n record player
gran n (Inf) grandmother
granary n, pl **-ries** storehouse for grain
grand ❶ adj **1** magnificent **2** noble **3** splendid **4** eminent **grandeur** n **1** nobility **2** magnificence **3** dignity **grandiose** adj **1** imposing **2** affectedly grand **grandchild** n child of one's child **grandson, granddaughter** n **grandparent** n parent of parent **grandfather, grandmother** n **grandstand** n structure with tiered seats for spectators
granite n hard crystalline rock
grant ❶ v **1** consent to fulfil (request) **2** permit **3** admit ▷ n **4** sum of money provided for specific purpose, esp. education **5** gift **6** allowance, concession

━━━━━━━━━━━━━━━━━━ THESAURUS ━━━━━━━━━━━━━━━━━━

gradual adj = **steady**, slow, regular, gentle, progressive **≠ sudden**
graduate v = **mark off**, grade, proportion, regulate, gauge; = **classify**, rank, grade, group, order
graft¹ n = **shoot**, bud, implant, sprout, splice ▷ v = **join**, insert, transplant, implant, splice
grain n = **seed**, kernel, grist; = **cereal**, corn; = **bit**, piece, trace,

scrap, particle; = **texture**, pattern, surface, fibre, weave
grand adj = **impressive**, great, large, magnificent, imposing **≠ unimposing**; = **ambitious**, great, grandiose
grant n = **award**, allowance, donation, endowment, gift ▷ v = **give**, allow, present, award, permit; = **accept**, allow, admit, acknowledge, concede

granule n small grain

grape n small fruit, used to make wine **grapevine** n 1 grape-bearing plant 2 (Inf) unofficial way of spreading news

grapefruit n subtropical citrus fruit

graph n drawing depicting relation of different numbers, quantities etc.

graphic ❶ adj 1 vividly descriptive 2 of writing, drawing, painting etc. ▷ pl n 3 diagrams etc. used on television, computer screen etc.

graphite n form of carbon (used in pencils)

grapple ❶ v 1 wrestle 2 struggle

grasp ❶ v 1 (try, struggle to) seize hold 2 understand ▷ n 3 grip 4 comprehension **grasping** adj greedy, avaricious

grass n 1 common type of plant with jointed stems and long narrow leaves 2 such plants grown as lawn 3 pasture 4 (Sl) marijuana 5 (Sl) informer **grassy** adj -sier, -siest **grasshopper** n jumping, chirping insect **grass roots** ordinary members of group

grate¹ n framework of metal bars for holding fuel in fireplace **grating** n framework of bars covering opening

grate² v 1 rub into small bits on rough surface 2 rub with harsh noise 3 irritate **grater** n utensil with rough surface for reducing substance to small particles **grating** adj 1 harsh 2 irritating

grateful ❶ adj 1 thankful 2 appreciative 3 pleasing **gratefully** adv **gratitude** n sense of being thankful

gratify v -fying, -fied 1 satisfy 2 please **gratification** n

gratis adv/adj free, for nothing

gratuitous adj 1 given free 2 uncalled for **gratuity** n gift of money for services rendered, tip

grave¹ ❶ n hole dug to bury corpse **graveyard** n

grave² ❶ adj 1 serious 2 solemn

grave³ n accent (`) over letter

gravel n 1 small stones 2 coarse sand **gravelly** adj

g

THESAURUS

graphic adj = **vivid**, clear, detailed, striking, explicit ≠ **vague**; = **pictorial**, visual, diagrammatic ≠ **impressionistic**

grapple v = **deal**, tackle, struggle, take on, confront; = **struggle**, fight, combat, wrestle, battle

grasp v = **grip**, hold, catch, grab, seize; = **understand**, realize, take in, get, see ▷ n = **grip**, hold, possession, embrace, clutches; = **understanding**, knowledge, grip, awareness, mastery

grateful adj = **thankful**, obliged, in (someone's) debt, indebted, appreciative

gratitude n = **thankfulness**, thanks, recognition, obligation, appreciation ≠ **ingratitude**

grave¹ n = **tomb**, vault, crypt, mausoleum, sepulchre

grave² adj = **serious**, important, critical, pressing, threatening ≠ **trifling**; = **solemn**, sober,

g

graven adj carved, engraved
gravitate v 1 move by gravity 2 tend (towards) centre of attraction 3 sink, settle down
gravity ⊕ n, pl -ties 1 force of attraction of one body for another, esp. of objects to the earth 2 heaviness 3 importance 4 seriousness
gravy n, pl -vies 1 juices from meat in cooking 2 sauce made from these
graze¹ ⊕ v feed on grass, pasture
graze² ⊕ v 1 touch lightly in passing, scratch, scrape ▷ n 2 grazing 3 abrasion
grease n 1 soft melted fat of animals 2 thick oil as lubricant ▷ v 3 apply grease to **greasy** adj **greasier, greasiest greasepaint** n theatrical make-up
great ⊕ adj 1 large 2 important 3 pre-eminent 4 (Inf) excellent ▷ comb. form 5 one degree further removed in relationship, as in

great-grandfather greatly adv
greed, greediness ⊕ n excessive consumption of, desire for, food, wealth **greedy** adj
green ⊕ adj 1 of colour between blue and yellow 2 grass-coloured 3 unripe 4 inexperienced 5 envious ▷ n 6 colour 7 area of grass, esp. for playing bowls etc. ▷ pl 8 green vegetables **greenery** n vegetation **greenfly** n aphid, small green garden pest **greengrocer** n dealer in vegetables and fruit **greenhouse** n glass building for rearing plants
greet ⊕ v 1 meet with expressions of welcome 2 salute 3 receive **greeting** n
gregarious adj sociable
gremlin n imaginary being blamed for mechanical malfunctions
grenade n bomb thrown by hand or shot from rifle **grenadier** n soldier of Grenadier Guards
grenadine n syrup made from

────────── THESAURUS ──────────

sombre, dour, unsmiling ≠ **carefree**
gravity n = **seriousness**, importance, significance, urgency, severity ≠ **triviality**; = **solemnity**, seriousness, gravitas ≠ **frivolity**
graze¹ v = **feed**, crop, browse, pasture
graze² v = **scratch**, skin, scrape, chafe, abrade; = **touch**, brush, rub, scrape, shave ▷ n = **scratch**, scrape, abrasion
great adj = **large**, big, huge, vast, enormous ≠ **small**; = **important**, serious, significant, critical, crucial

≠ **unimportant**; = **famous**, outstanding, remarkable, prominent, renowned; (Inf) = **excellent**, fine, wonderful, superb, fantastic (Inf) ≠ **poor**
greed, greediness n = **gluttony**, voracity
green adj = **verdant**, leafy, grassy; = **inexperienced**, new, raw, naive, immature; = **jealous**, grudging, resentful, envious, covetous ▷ n = **lawn**, common, turf, sward
greet v = **salute**, hail, say hello to, address, accost

pomegranate juice, for sweetening and colouring drinks

grey ❶ adj **1** between black and white **2** clouded **3** turning white **4** aged **5** intermediate, indeterminate ▷ n **6** grey colour

greyhound n swift slender dog

grid n **1** network of horizontal and vertical lines, bars etc. **2** any interconnecting system of links

griddle n flat iron plate for cooking

gridiron n frame of metal bars for grilling

grief ❶ n deep sorrow **grievance** n real or imaginary cause for complaint **grieve** v **1** feel grief **2** cause grief to **grievous** adj **1** painful, oppressive **2** very serious

grill n **1** device on cooker to radiate heat downwards **2** food cooked under grill **3** gridiron ▷ v **4** cook (food) under grill **5** subject to severe questioning

grille, grill n grating

grim ❶ adj **grimmer, grimmest 1** stern **2** relentless **3** joyless

grimace n/v (pull) wry face

grime n ingrained dirt, soot **grimy** n

grin n/v **grinning, grinned** (give) broad smile

grind ❶ v **grinding, ground 1** crush to powder **2** make sharp, smooth **3** grate ▷ n **4** (Inf) hard work **5** action of grinding

grip ❶ n **1** firm hold **2** mastery **3** handle **4** travelling bag ▷ v **5** hold tightly **6** hold attention of

gripe v (Inf) **1** complain (persistently) ▷ n **2** intestinal pain (esp. in infants) **3** (Inf) complaint

grisly adj **-lier, -liest** causing terror

grist n corn to be ground

gristle n cartilage, tough flexible tissue

grit ❶ n **1** rough particles of sand **2** courage ▷ v **3** clench (teeth)

grizzle v (Inf) whine

grizzled adj grey (haired)

grizzly n, pl **-zlies** large Amer. bear

groan ❶ v/n (make) low, deep sound of grief or pain

grocer n dealer in foodstuffs **groceries** pl n commodities sold by a grocer **grocery** n, pl **-ceries** trade, premises of grocer

g

grey adj = **dull**, dark, dim, gloomy, drab; = **boring**, dull, anonymous, faceless, colourless

grief n = **sadness**, suffering, regret, distress, misery **≠ joy**

grim adj = **terrible**, severe, harsh, forbidding, formidable

grind v = **crush**, mill, powder, grate, pulverize; = **press**, push, crush, jam, mash; = **grate**, scrape, gnash ▷ n = **hard work** (Inf),

labour, sweat (Inf), chore, toil

grip v = **grasp**, hold, catch, seize, clutch; = **engross**, fascinate, absorb, entrance, hold ▷ n = **clasp**, hold, grasp; = **control**, rule, influence, command, power

grit n = **gravel**, sand, dust, pebbles; = **courage**, spirit, resolution, determination, guts (Inf) ▷ v = **clench**, grind, grate, gnash

groan v = **moan**, cry, sigh; (Inf)

grog n spirit (esp. rum) and water
  groggy adj (Inf) shaky, weak
groin n fold where legs meet
  abdomen
groom ⊕ n 1 person caring for
  horses 2 bridegroom ▷ v 3 tend or
  look after 4 brush or clean (esp.
  horse) 5 train
groove ⊕ n 1 narrow channel
  2 routine ▷ v 3 cut groove in
grope ⊕ v feel about, search
  blindly
gross ⊕ adj 1 very fat 2 total, not
  net 3 coarse 4 flagrant ▷ n
  5 twelve dozen
grotesque ⊕ adj 1 (horribly)
  distorted 2 ugly or repulsive
grotto n, pl **-toes, -tos** cave
grotty adj **-tier, -tiest** (Inf) nasty,
  in bad condition
grouch (Inf) ▷ n 1 persistent
  grumbler 2 discontented mood
  ▷ v 3 grumble

ground ⊕ n 1 surface of earth
  2 soil, earth 3 reason 4 special
  area ▷ pl 5 dregs 6 enclosed land
  round house ▷ v 7 establish
  8 instruct 9 place on ground
  10 run ashore **grounded** adj (of
  aircraft) unable or not permitted to
  fly **grounding** n basic knowledge
  of subject **groundless** adj
  without reason **groundwork** n
  preliminary work
group ⊕ n 1 number of persons or
  things together 2 small musical
  band 3 class ▷ v 4 place, fall into
  group
grouse¹ n 1 game bird 2 its flesh
grouse² v 1 grumble, complain ▷ n
  2 complaint
grout n 1 thin fluid mortar ▷ v
  2 fill up with grout
grove ⊕ n small group of trees
grovel v **-elling, -elled** 1 abase
  oneself 2 lie face down

———————— THESAURUS ————————

= **complain**, object, moan,
grumble, gripe (Inf) ▷ n = **moan**,
cry, sigh, whine; (Inf) = **complaint**,
protest, objection, grumble, grouse
groom n = **stableman**, stableboy,
hostler or ostler (Archaic) ▷ v
= **brush**, clean, tend, rub down,
curry; = **smarten up**, clean, tidy,
preen, spruce up; = **train**, prime,
prepare, coach, ready
groove n = **indentation**, cut,
hollow, channel, trench
grope v = **feel**, search, fumble,
flounder, fish
gross adj = **flagrant**, blatant, rank,
sheer, utter ≠ **qualified**; = **vulgar**,
offensive, crude, obscene, coarse

≠ **decent**; = **fat**, overweight,
hulking, corpulent ≠ **slim**; = **total**,
whole, entire, aggregate, before tax
≠ **net**
grotesque adj = **unnatural**,
bizarre, strange, fantastic,
distorted ≠ **natural**; = **absurd**,
preposterous ≠ **natural**
ground n = **earth**, land, dry land,
terra firma ▷ v = **base**, found,
establish, set, settle; = **instruct**,
train, teach, initiate, tutor
group n = **crowd**, party, band,
pack, gang ▷ v = **arrange**, order,
sort, class, classify
grove n = **wood**, plantation,
covert, thicket, copse

g

grow ❶ v **growing, grew, grown**
1 develop naturally 2 increase
3 be produced 4 become by
degrees 5 produce by cultivation
growth n 1 growing 2 increase
3 what has grown or is growing
grown-up adj/n adult
growl v/n (make) low guttural
sound of anger
grub v 1 dig 2 root up 3 rummage
▷ n 4 short, legless larva of certain
insects 5 (Sl) food
grubby adj **-bier, -biest** dirty
grudge ❶ v 1 be unwilling to give,
allow ▷ n 2 ill will
gruel n food of oatmeal etc., boiled
in milk or water
gruelling ❶ adj exhausting
gruesome ❶ adj horrible,
grisly
gruff adj rough-voiced, surly
grumble ❶ v 1 complain
2 rumble ▷ n 3 complaint

grumpy adj **grumpier, grumpiest**
ill-tempered, surly
grunt v/n (make) sound
characteristic of pig
G-string n very small covering for
genitals
guarantee ❶ n 1 formal assurance
(esp. in writing) that product etc.
will meet certain standards ▷ v
2 give guarantee 3 secure (against
risk etc.) **guarantor** n
guard ❶ v 1 protect, defend
2 take precautions (against) ▷ n
3 person, group that protects
4 sentry 5 official in charge of train
6 protection **guarded** adj
cautious, noncommittal **guardian**
n 1 keeper, protector 2 person
having custody of infant etc.
guava n tropical tree with fruit
used to make jelly
guerrilla, guerilla ❶ n member
of irregular armed force

g

––––––––––––––––– THESAURUS –––––––––––––––––

grow v = **develop**, get bigger
≠ **shrink**; = **get bigger**, spread,
swell, stretch, expand; = **cultivate**,
produce, raise, farm, breed;
= **become**, get, turn, come to be;
= **originate**, spring, arise, stem,
issue
grudge n = **resentment**,
bitterness, grievance, dislike,
animosity ≠ **goodwill** ▷ v
= **resent**, mind, envy, covet,
begrudge ≠ **welcome**
gruelling adj = **exhausting**,
demanding, tiring, taxing, severe
≠ **easy**
gruesome adj = **horrific**,
shocking, terrible, horrible, grim

≠ **pleasant**
grumble v = **complain**, moan,
gripe (Inf), whinge (Inf), carp;
= **rumble**, growl, gurgle ▷ n
= **complaint**, protest, objection,
moan, grievance
guarantee v = **ensure**, secure,
assure, warrant, make certain ▷ n
= **promise**, pledge, assurance,
certainty, word of honour
guard v = **protect**, defend, secure,
mind, preserve ▷ n = **sentry**,
warder, warden, custodian, watch;
= **shield**, security, defence, screen,
protection
guerrilla n = **freedom fighter**,
partisan, underground fighter

guess ❶ v 1 estimate 2 conjecture 3 (US & Canad) think ▷ n 4 conclusion reached by guessing

guest ❶ n 1 one entertained at another's house 2 one living in hotel

guffaw n/v (make) burst of boisterous laughter

guide ❶ n 1 one who shows the way 2 adviser 3 book of instruction or information ▷ v 4 lead, act as guide to **guidance** n **guideline** n set principle

guild ❶ n organization for mutual help, or with common object

guile n cunning, deceit

guillotine n 1 machine for beheading 2 machine for cutting paper ▷ v 3 use guillotine on

guilt ❶ n 1 fact, state of having done wrong 2 responsibility for offence **guiltless** adj innocent **guilty** adj having committed an offence

guinea n formerly, sum of 21

shillings **guinea pig** 1 rodent originating in S Amer 2 (Inf) person or animal used in experiments

guise ❶ n external appearance, esp. one assumed

guitar n stringed instrument played by plucking or strumming **guitarist** n

gulch n (US & Canad) a narrow ravine cut by a fast stream

gulf ❶ n 1 large inlet of the sea 2 chasm 3 large gap

gull n long-winged web-footed sea bird

gullet n food passage from mouth to stomach

gullible adj easily imposed on, credulous

gully n, pl **-lies** channel or ravine worn by action of water

gulp v/n 1 swallow 2 gasp

gum[1] ❶ n 1 sticky substance issuing from certain trees

─────────────── THESAURUS ───────────────

guess v = **estimate**, predict, work out, speculate, conjecture ≠ **know**; = **suppose**, think, believe, suspect, judge ▷ n = **estimate**, speculation, judgment, hypothesis, conjecture ≠ **certainty**

guest n = **visitor**, company, caller

guide n = **handbook**, manual, guidebook, instructions, catalogue; = **directory**, street map; = **escort**, leader, usher; = **pointer**, sign, landmark, marker, beacon ▷ v = **lead**, direct, escort, conduct, accompany; = **steer**, control, manage, direct, handle

guild n = **society**, union, league, association, company

guilt n = **shame**, regret, remorse, contrition, guilty conscience ≠ **pride**; = **culpability**, blame, responsibility, misconduct, wickedness ≠ **innocence**

guise n = **form**, appearance, shape, aspect, mode; = **pretence**, disguise, aspect, semblance

gulf n = **bay**, bight, sea inlet; = **chasm**, opening, split, gap, separation

gum[1] n = **glue**, adhesive, resin, cement, paste ▷ v = **stick**, glue, affix, cement, paste

2 adhesive **3** chewing gum ▷ v
4 stick with gum **gumboots** pl n
boots of rubber **gumtree** n any
species of eucalyptus

gum² n firm flesh in which teeth
are set

gumption n **1** resourcefulness
2 shrewdness, sense

gun ❶ n **1** weapon with metal
tube from which missiles are
discharged by explosion
2 cannon, pistol etc. ▷ v **3** shoot
4 pursue vigorously **gunner** n
gunpowder n explosive
mixture of saltpetre, sulphur,
charcoal **gunshot** n **1** shot or
range of gun ▷ adj **2** caused by
missile from gun

gunge n (Inf) any sticky,
unpleasant substance

gunwale, gunnel n upper edge
of ship's side

guppy n, pl **-pies** small colourful
aquarium fish

gurgle n/v (make) bubbling noise

guru ❶ n spiritual teacher, esp. in
India

gush ❶ v **1** flow out suddenly and
copiously, spurt ▷ n **2** sudden and
copious flow

gusset n triangle or diamond-
shaped piece of material let into
garment

gust n **1** sudden blast of wind
2 burst of rain, anger, passion etc.

gusto n enjoyment, zest

gut ❶ n **1** intestines **2** material
made from guts of animals, e.g. for
violin strings etc. ▷ pl **3** (Inf)
courage ▷ v **4** remove guts from
(fish etc.) **5** remove, destroy
contents of (house)

gutter ❶ n shallow trough for
carrying off water from roof or side
of street

guttural adj harsh-sounding, as if
produced in the throat

guy¹ ❶ n **1** effigy of Guy Fawkes
burnt on Nov. 5th **2** (Inf) person
(usu. male) ▷ v **3** make fun of
4 ridicule

guy² n rope, chain to steady, secure
something, e.g. tent

guzzle v eat or drink greedily

gym n short for GYMNASIUM or
GYMNASTICS

gymkhana n competition or
display of horse riding

gymnasium n place equipped for
muscular exercises, athletic
training **gymnastics** pl n
muscular exercises **gymnast** n

gynaecology n branch of
medicine dealing with functions
and diseases of women
gynaecologist n

gypsum n chalklike mineral, used
for making plaster

——————— THESAURUS ———————

gun n = **firearm**, shooter (Sl), piece
(Sl), handgun

guru n = **authority**, expert, leader,
master, pundit

gush v = **flow**, run, rush, flood,
pour ▷ n = **stream**, flow, rush,
flood, jet

gut v = **disembowel**, clean;
= **ravage**, empty, clean out, despoil

gutter n = **drain**, channel, ditch,
trench, trough

guy¹ n (Inf) = **man**, person, fellow,

Gypsy, Gipsy ❶ *n, pl* **-sies** one of
wandering race orig. from NW
India

gyrate *v* move in circle, spiral
gyroscope *n* disc rotating on axis
that can turn in any direction

━━━━━━━━━━━━━━━━ THESAURUS ━━━━━━

lad, bloke *(Brit Inf)*
Gypsy, Gipsy *n* = **traveller**,
roamer, wanderer, Bohemian, rover

g

haberdasher *n* dealer in articles of dress, ribbons, pins, needles etc. **haberdashery** *n*

habit ❶ *n* **1** settled tendency or practice **2** customary apparel, esp. of nun or monk **habitual** *adj* **1** formed or acquired by habit **2** usual, customary

habitable *adj* fit to live in **habitat** *n* natural home (of animal etc.) **habitation** *n* abode

hack¹ ❶ *v* **1** cut, chop (at) violently **2** (*Inf*) utter harsh, dry cough ▷ *n* **3** violent blow **hacker** *n* (*Sl*) computer enthusiast who breaks into computer system of company or government

hack² ❶ *n* **1** horse for ordinary riding **2** inferior writer

hackles *pl n* hairs on back of neck of dog and other animals which are raised in anger

hackneyed *adj* (of words etc.) stale, trite because of overuse

hacksaw *n* handsaw for cutting metal

haddock *n* large, edible sea fish

haemoglobin *n* colouring and oxygen-bearing matter of red blood corpuscles

haemophilia *n* illness in which blood does not clot **haemophiliac** *n*

haemorrhage *n* profuse bleeding

haemorrhoids *pl n* swollen veins in rectum

hag *n* **1** ugly old woman **2** witch

haggard *adj* anxious, careworn

haggis *n* Scottish dish made from sheep's offal, oatmeal etc.

haggle *v* bargain over price

hail¹ ❶ *v* **1** greet **2** acclaim **3** call **4** come (from)

hail² ❶ *n* **1** (shower of) pellets of ice **2** barrage ▷ *v* **3** pour down as shower of hail **hailstone** *n*

hair ❶ *n* **1** filament growing from skin of animal, as covering of man's head **2** such filaments collectively

————— THESAURUS —————

habit *n* = **mannerism**, custom, way, practice, characteristic

hack¹ *v* = **cut**, chop, slash, mutilate, mangle

hack² *n* = **reporter**, writer, correspondent, journalist, scribbler

hail¹ *v* = **acclaim**, honour, acknowledge, cheer, applaud ≠ **condemn**; = **salute**, greet, address, welcome, say hello to ≠ **snub**; = **flag down**, summon, signal to, wave down

hail² *n* = **hailstones**, sleet, hailstorm, frozen rain; = **shower**, rain, storm, battery, volley ▷ *v* = **rain**, shower, pelt

hair *n* = **locks**, mane, tresses, shock, mop

hairy adj **hairdo** n way of dressing hair **hairdresser** n one who cuts and styles hair **hairgrip** n small, tightly bent metal hairpin **hairpin** n pin for keeping hair in place **hairpin bend** U-shaped turn of road

hale ⊙ adj robust, healthy

half ⊙ n, pl **halves** 1 either of two equal parts of thing ▷ adj 2 forming half ▷ adv 3 to the extent of half **half-baked** adj (Inf) poorly planned **half-breed, half-caste** n (Offens) person with parents of different races **half-brother, -sister** n brother, sister by one parent only **half-hearted** adj unenthusiastic **halfwit** n feeble-minded person

halibut n large edible flatfish

halitosis n bad-smelling breath

hall ⊙ n 1 (entrance) passage 2 large room or building used for esp. public assembly

hallelujah n/interj exclamation of praise to God

hallmark ⊙ n 1 mark used to indicate standard of tested gold and silver 2 mark of excellence

3 distinguishing feature

hallo interj see HELLO

hallowed adj holy

hallucinate v suffer illusions **hallucination** n **hallucinatory** adj

halo n, pl **-loes, -los** circle of light

halt ⊙ n 1 interruption or end to progress etc. (esp. as command to stop marching) ▷ v 2 (cause to) stop **halting** adj hesitant, lame

halter n 1 rope with headgear to fasten horse 2 low-cut dress style with strap passing behind neck 3 noose for hanging person

halve ⊙ v 1 cut in half 2 reduce to half 3 share

ham n 1 meat (esp. salted or smoked) from thigh of pig 2 actor adopting exaggerated style 3 amateur radio enthusiast **ham-fisted** adj clumsy

hamburger n fried cake of minced beef

hamlet n small village

hammer ⊙ n 1 tool usu. with heavy head at end of handle, for beating, driving nails etc. ▷ v 2 strike as with hammer

— THESAURUS —

hale adj = **healthy**, well, strong, sound, fit

half n = **fifty per cent**, equal part ▷ adj = **partial**, limited, moderate, halved ▷ adv = **partially**, partly, in part

hall n = **passage**, lobby, corridor, hallway, foyer; = **meeting place**, chamber, auditorium, concert hall, assembly room

hallmark n = **trademark**, sure

sign, telltale sign; (Brit) = **mark**, sign, device, stamp, seal

halt v = **stop**, break off, stand still, wait, rest ≠ **continue**; = **come to an end**, stop, cease ▷ n = **stop**, end, close, pause, standstill ≠ **continuation**

halve v = **cut in half**, reduce by fifty per cent, decrease by fifty per cent, lessen by fifty per cent

hammer v = **hit**, drive, knock,

hammock n bed of canvas etc., hung on cords

hamper[1] n large covered basket

hamper[2] ❶ v impede, obstruct

hamster n type of rodent, sometimes kept as pet

hamstring n tendon at back of knee

hand ❶ n 1 extremity of arm beyond wrist 2 side 3 style of writing 4 cards dealt to player 5 manual worker 6 help 7 pointer of dial 8 applause ▷ v 9 pass 10 deliver 11 hold out **handful** n 1 small quantity 2 (Inf) person, thing causing problems **handiness** n 1 dexterity 2 state of being near, available **handy** adj 1 convenient 2 clever with hands **handbag** n woman's bag **handbook** n small instruction book **handcuff** n 1 fetter for wrist, usu. joined in pair ▷ v 2 secure thus **handicraft** n manual occupation or skill **handiwork** n thing done by particular person **handkerchief** n small square of fabric for wiping nose etc. **hand-out** n 1 thing given free 2 written information given out at talk etc. **handwriting** n way person writes **handyman** n man employed to do various tasks

handicap ❶ n 1 something that hampers or hinders 2 race, contest in which chances are equalized 3 (Offens) any physical disability ▷ v 4 hamper, impose handicaps on

handle ❶ n 1 part of thing to hold it by ▷ v 2 touch, feel with hands 3 manage 4 deal with 5 trade **handler** n person who controls animal **handlebars** pl n curved metal bar to steer cycle

handsome ❶ adj 1 of fine appearance 2 generous 3 ample

hang ❶ v **hanging, hung** 1 suspend 2 attach, set up (wallpaper, doors etc.) 3 be suspended, cling 4 (past **hanged**) kill by suspension by neck **hanger** n frame on which clothes etc. can be hung **hangdog** adj sullen,

beat, strike

hamper[2] v = **hinder**, handicap, prevent, restrict, frustrate ≠ **help**

hand n = **palm**, fist, paw (Inf), mitt (Sl); = **worker**, employee, labourer, workman, operative; = **round of applause**, clap, ovation, big hand; = **writing**, script, handwriting, calligraphy ▷ v = **give**, pass, hand over, present to, deliver

handicap n = **disadvantage**, barrier, restriction, obstacle, limitation, drawback

≠ **advantage**; = **advantage**, head start ▷ v = **hinder**, limit, restrict, burden, hamstring ≠ **help**

handle n = **grip**, hilt, haft, stock ▷ v = **manage**, deal with, tackle, cope with; = **deal with**, manage

handsome adj = **good-looking**, attractive, gorgeous, elegant, personable ≠ **ugly**; = **generous**, large, princely, liberal, considerable ≠ **mean**

hang v = **dangle**, swing, suspend; = **execute**, lynch, string up (Inf)

dejected **hang-glider** n glider
with light frame from which pilot
hangs in harness **hangman** n
person who executes people by
hanging **hangover** n aftereffects
of too much drinking **hang-up** n
(Inf) emotional or psychological
problem
hangar n large shed for aircraft
hanker v crave
hanky, hankie n, pl **hankies**
(Inf) handkerchief
haphazard adj random, careless
hapless adj unlucky
happen ❶ v 1 come about, occur
2 chance to do **happening** n
occurrence, event
happy ❶ adj -pier, -piest 1 glad,
content 2 lucky **happily** adv
happiness n
harangue n 1 vehement speech
2 tirade ▷ v 3 address
vehemently
harass ❶ v worry, torment
harassment n
harbour ❶ n 1 shelter for ships
▷ v 2 give shelter 3 maintain

(secretly)
hard ❶ adj 1 firm, resisting
pressure 2 solid 3 difficult to do,
understand 4 unfeeling 5 heavy
▷ adv 6 vigorously 7 persistently
8 close **harden** v **hardly** adv
1 unkindly, harshly 2 scarcely, not
quite 3 only just **hardship** n 1 ill
luck 2 severe toil, suffering
3 instance of this **hard-headed**
adj shrewd **hard-hearted** adj
unfeeling **hard shoulder**
motorway verge for emergency
stops **hardware** n 1 tools,
implements 2 (Comp) mechanical
and electronic parts **hardwood** n
wood from deciduous trees
hardy ❶ adj **hardier, hardiest**
1 robust, vigorous 2 bold 3 (of
plants) able to grow in the open all
the year round
hare n animal like large rabbit
harebell n round-leaved
bell-shaped flower **harebrained**
adj rash, wild **harelip** n fissure of
upper lip
harem n 1 women's part of Muslim

———— THESAURUS ————

happen v = **occur**, take place,
come about, result, develop;
= **chance**, turn out
happy adj = **pleased**, delighted,
content, thrilled, glad; = **fortunate**,
lucky, timely, favourable, auspicious
≠ **unfortunate**
harass v = **annoy**, trouble, bother,
harry, plague
harbour n = **port**, haven, dock,
mooring, marina ▷ v = **hold**, bear,
maintain, nurse, retain; = **shelter**,
protect, hide, shield, provide

refuge
hard adj = **tough**, strong, firm,
solid, stiff ≠ **soft**; = **difficult**,
involved, complicated, puzzling,
intricate ≠ **easy**; = **exhausting**,
tough, exacting, rigorous, gruelling
≠ **easy**; = **harsh**, cold, cruel, stern,
callous ≠ **kind**; = **grim**, painful,
distressing, harsh, unpleasant
▷ adv = **intently**, closely, carefully,
sharply, keenly
hardy adj = **strong**, tough, robust,
sound, rugged ≠ **frail**

dwelling **2** one man's wives

hark v listen

harlequin n masked clown in diamond-patterned costume

harlot n whore, prostitute

harm ❶ n/v damage **harmful** adj **harmless** adj unable or unlikely to hurt

harmony ❶ n, pl **-nies 1** agreement **2** combination of notes to make chords **3** melodious sound **harmonic** adj of harmony **harmonica** n mouth organ **harmonious** adj **harmonium** n small organ **harmonize** v **1** bring into harmony **2** cause to agree **3** reconcile **4** be in harmony

harness ❶ n **1** equipment for attaching horse to cart, plough etc. ▷ v **2** put on, in harness **3** utilize energy or power of

harp n musical instrument of strings played by hand ▷ v **2** play on harp **3** dwell on continuously **harpsichord** n stringed instrument like piano

harpoon n/v (use) barbed spear for catching whales

harrier n **1** hound used in hunting hares **2** falcon

harrow n **1** implement for smoothing, levelling or stirring up soil ▷ v **2** draw harrow over **3** distress greatly **harrowing** adj distressful

harry ❶ v **-rying, -ried 1** harass **2** ravage

harsh ❶ adj **1** rough, discordant **2** severe **3** unfeeling **harshly** adv

harvest ❶ n **1** (season for) gathering grain **2** gathering **3** crop ▷ v **4** reap and gather in **harvester** n

has third person sing. of HAVE **has-been** n (Inf) one who is no longer successful

hash n **1** dish of chopped meat etc. **2** mess ▷ v **3** cut up small, chop **4** mix up

hashish n resinous extract of Indian hemp, esp. used as hallucinogen

hassle ❶ n (Inf) **1** quarrel **2** a lot of bother, trouble ▷ v **3** bother

hassock n kneeling cushion

haste n **1** speed, hurry ▷ v

h

— THESAURUS —

harm v = **injure**, hurt, wound, abuse, ill-treat ≠ **heal** ▷ n = **injury**, suffering, damage, ill, hurt

harmony n = **accord**, peace, agreement, friendship, sympathy ≠ **conflict**; = **tune**, melody, unison, tunefulness, euphony ≠ **discord**

harness v = **exploit**, control, channel, employ, utilize ▷ n = **equipment**, tackle, gear, tack

harry v = **pester**, bother, plague, harass, hassle (Inf)

harsh adj = **severe**, hard, tough, stark, austere; = **bleak**, freezing, severe, icy

harvest n = **harvesting**, picking, gathering, collecting, reaping; = **crop**, yield, year's growth, produce ▷ v = **gather**, pick, collect, bring in, pluck

hassle (Inf) ▷ n = **trouble**, problem, difficulty, bother, grief (Inf) ▷ v = **bother**, bug (Inf), annoy, hound, harass

h

2 hasten **hasten** v (cause to) hurry **hastily** adv **hasty** adj

hat n head covering usu. with brim **hat trick** set of three achievements

hatch¹ ❶ v 1 (of young birds etc.) (cause to) emerge from egg 2 contrive, devise **hatchery** n

hatch² n 1 hatchway 2 trapdoor over it 3 opening in wall, to facilitate service of meals etc. **hatchback** n car with lifting rear door **hatchway** n opening in deck of ship etc.

hatchet n small axe

hate ❶ v 1 dislike strongly 2 bear malice towards ▷ n 3 this feeling 4 that which is hated **hateful** adj detestable **hatred** n

haughty adj **-tier, -tiest** proud, arrogant **haughtily** adv

haul ❶ v 1 pull, drag with effort ▷ n 2 hauling 3 what is hauled **haulage** n **haulier** n

haunch n human hip or fleshy hindquarter of animal

haunt ❶ v 1 visit regularly 2 visit in form of ghost 3 recur to ▷ n 4 place frequently visited **haunted** adj 1 frequented by ghosts 2 worried **haunting** adj extremely beautiful or sad

have ❶ v **has, having, had** 1 hold, possess 2 be affected with 3 be obliged (to do) 4 cheat 5 obtain 6 contain 7 allow 8 cause to be done 9 give birth to 10 as auxiliary, forms perfect and other tenses

haven ❶ n place of safety

haversack n canvas bag for provisions etc. carried on back

havoc ❶ n 1 devastation, ruin 2 (Inf) confusion, chaos

hawk¹ n 1 bird of prey smaller than eagle 2 advocate of warlike policies

hawk² v offer (goods) for sale, esp. in street **hawker** n

hawthorn n thorny shrub or tree

THESAURUS

hatch¹ v = **incubate**, breed, sit on, brood, bring forth; = **devise**, design, invent, put together, conceive

hate v = **detest**, loathe, despise, dislike, abhor ≠ love; = **dislike**, detest, shrink from, recoil from, not be able to bear ≠ like ▷ n = **dislike**, hostility, hatred, loathing, animosity ≠ love

haul v = **drag**, draw, pull, heave ▷ n = **yield**, gain, spoils, catch, harvest

haunt v = **plague**, trouble, obsess, torment, possess ▷ n = **meeting**

place, hangout (Inf), rendezvous, stamping ground

have v = **own**, keep, possess, hold, retain; = **get**, obtain, take, receive, accept; = **suffer**, experience, undergo, sustain, endure; = **give birth to**, bear, deliver, bring forth, beget; = **experience**, go through, undergo, meet with, come across

haven n = **sanctuary**, shelter, retreat, asylum, refuge

havoc n (Inf) = **disorder**, confusion, chaos, disruption, mayhem

hay n grass mown and dried **hay fever** allergic reaction to pollen, dust etc. **haystack** n large pile of hay **haywire** adj **1** crazy **2** disorganized

hazard ❶ n **1** chance **2** risk, danger ▷ v **3** expose to risk **4** run risk of **hazardous** adj risky

haze ❶ n **1** mist **2** obscurity **hazy** adj **1** misty **2** vague

hazel n **1** bush bearing nuts ▷ adj **2** light brown

he pron **1** person, animal already referred to ▷ comb. form **2** male, as in *he-goat*

head ❶ n **1** upper part of body, containing mouth, sense organs and brain **2** upper part of anything **3** chief of organization, school etc. **4** chief part **5** aptitude, capacity **6** crisis **7** person, animal considered as unit ▷ adj **8** chief, principal **9** (of wind) contrary ▷ v **10** be at the top **11** lead **12** provide with head **13** hit (ball) with head **14** make for **15** form a head **heading** n title **heady** adj apt to intoxicate or excite **headache** n continuous pain in head **headland** n area of land jutting into sea **headlight** n powerful lamp on front of vehicle etc. **headline** n news summary, in large type in newspaper **headlong** adv in rush **headphones** pl n two small loudspeakers strapped against ears **headquarters** pl n centre of operations **head start** advantage **headstrong** adj self-willed **headway** n progress

heal ❶ v make or become well

health ❶ n **1** soundness of body **2** condition of body **3** toast drunk in person's honour **healthy** adj **healthier, healthiest** **health food** vegetarian food etc., eaten for dietary value

heap ❶ n **1** pile **2** great quantity ▷ v **3** pile, load with

hear ❶ v **hearing, heard**

hazard n = **danger**, risk, threat, problem, menace ▷ v = **jeopardize**, risk, endanger, threaten, expose

haze n = **mist**, cloud, fog, obscurity, vapour

head n = **skull**, crown, pate, nut (Sl), loaf (Sl); = **mind**, reasoning, understanding, thought, sense; = **top**, crown, summit, peak, crest (Inf); = **leader**, president, director, manager, chief ▷ adj = **chief**, main, leading, first, prime ▷ v = **lead**, precede, be the leader of, be or go first, be or go at the front of; = **top**, lead, crown, cap; = **be in charge of**, run, manage, lead, control

heal v (sometimes with **up**) = **mend**, get better, get well, cure, regenerate

health n = **condition**, state, shape, constitution, fettle; = **wellbeing**, strength, fitness, vigour, good condition ≠ **illness**

heap n = **pile**, lot, collection, mass, stack; often plural (Inf) = **a lot**, lots (Inf), plenty, masses, load(s) (Inf) ▷ v (sometimes with **up**) = **pile**, collect, gather, stack, accumulate

hear v = **overhear**, catch, detect;

1 perceive sound by ear **2** listen to **3** (*Law*) try (case) **4** heed **5** learn **hearing** *n* **1** ability to hear **2** earshot **3** judicial examination **hearsay** *n* rumour

hearken *v* listen

hearse *n* funeral carriage for coffin

heart ❶ *n* **1** organ which makes blood circulate **2** seat of emotions and affections **3** mind, soul, courage **4** central part **5** suit at cards **hearten** *v* make, become cheerful **heartless** *adj* unfeeling **hearty** *adj* **1** friendly **2** vigorous **3** in good health **4** satisfying **heart attack** sudden severe malfunction of heart **heartbeat** *n* single pulsation of heart **heartbreak** *n* intense grief **heartfelt** *adj* felt sincerely **heart-rending** *adj* agonizing **by heart** by memory

hearth *n* **1** part of room where fire is made **2** house

heat ❶ *n* **1** hotness **2** sensation of this **3** hot weather **4** warmth of feeling, anger etc. **5** sexual excitement in female animals

6 one of many eliminating races etc. ▷ *v* **7** make, become hot **heated** *adj* angry **heater** *n*

heath *n* tract of waste land

heathen *adj/n* **1** (one) not adhering to a religious system **2** pagan

heather *n* shrub growing on heaths and mountains

heave *v* **1** lift (and throw) with effort **2** utter (sigh) **3** swell, rise **4** feel nausea ▷ *n* **5** act of heaving

heaven ❶ *n* **1** abode of God **2** place of bliss **3** (*also pl*) sky **heavenly** *adj*

heavy ❶ *adj* **heavier, heaviest 1** weighty **2** dense **3** sluggish **4** severe **5** sorrowful **6** serious **7** dull **heavily** *adv*

heckle *v* interrupt (speaker) by questions, taunts etc.

hectare *n* one hundred ares or 10 000 square metres (2,471 acres)

hectic ❶ *adj* rushed, busy

hedge ❶ *n* **1** fence of bushes ▷ *v* **2** surround with hedge **3** be evasive **4** secure against loss

━━━━━━━━━━━━ THESAURUS ━━━━━━━━━━━━

(*Law*) = **try**, judge, examine, investigate; = **learn**, discover, find out, pick up, gather

heart *n* = **nature**, character, soul, constitution, essence; = **courage**, will, spirit, purpose, bottle (*Brit Inf*)

heat *v* (*sometimes with* **up**) = **warm (up)**, cook, boil, roast, reheat ≠ **chill** ▷ *n* = **warmth**, hotness, temperature ≠ **cold**; = **hot weather**, warmth, closeness, high temperature, heatwave

heaven *n* = **paradise**, next world, hereafter, nirvana (*Buddhism, Hinduism*), bliss; (*Inf*) = **happiness**, paradise, ecstasy, bliss, utopia

heavy *adj* = **weighty**, large, massive, hefty, bulky ≠ **light**; = **intensive**, severe, serious, concentrated, fierce

hectic *adj* = **frantic**, chaotic, heated, animated, turbulent ≠ **peaceful**

hedge *v* = **prevaricate**, evade,

hedgehog n small animal covered with spines

hedonism n pursuit of pleasure **hedonist** n

heed ⊕ v take notice of **heedless** adj careless

heel¹ ⊕ n 1 hind part of foot 2 part of shoe supporting this 3 (Sl) undesirable person ▷ v 4 supply with heel

heel² v lean to one side

hefty ⊕ adj **heftier, heftiest** 1 bulky 2 weighty 3 strong

heifer n young cow

height ⊕ n 1 measure from base to top 2 quality of being high 3 elevation 4 highest degree 5 hilltop **heighten** v 1 make higher 2 intensify

heinous adj atrocious, extremely wicked, detestable

heir ⊕ n person entitled to inherit property or rank **heirloom** n thing that has been in family for generations

helicopter n aircraft lifted by rotating blades

helium n very light, nonflammable gaseous element

helix n, pl **helices, helixes** spiral

hell ⊕ n 1 abode of the damned 2 abode of the dead generally 3 place of torture **hellish** adj **hell-bent** adj intent

hello, hallo ⊕ interj expression of greeting

helm ⊕ n tiller, wheel for turning ship's rudder

helmet n defensive or protective covering for head

help ⊕ v/n 1 aid 2 support 3 remedy **helper** n **helpful** adj **helping** n single portion of food **helpless** adj 1 incompetent 2 unaided 3 unable to help

helter-skelter adv/adj/n 1 (in) hurry and confusion ▷ n 2 high spiral slide at fairground

h

— THESAURUS —

sidestep, duck, dodge

heed v = **pay attention to**, listen to, take notice of, follow, consider ≠ **ignore**

heel¹ n (Sl) = **swine**, cad (Brit Inf), bounder (Old-fashioned Brit Sl), rotter (Sl, chiefly Brit)

hefty adj (Inf); = **big**, strong, massive, strapping, robust ≠ **small**

height n = **tallness**, stature, highness, loftiness ≠ **shortness**; = **altitude**, measurement, highness, elevation, tallness ≠ **depth**; = **peak**, top, crown, summit, crest ≠ **valley**

heir n = **successor**, beneficiary, inheritor, heiress (fem.), next in line

hell n = **the underworld**, the abyss, Hades (Greek myth), hellfire, the inferno; (Inf) = **torment**, suffering, agony, nightmare, misery

hello interj = **hi** (Inf), greetings, how do you do?, good morning, good evening

helm n = **tiller**, wheel, rudder

help v (sometimes with **out**) = **aid**, support, assist, cooperate with, abet ≠ **hinder**; = **improve**, ease, relieve, facilitate, alleviate ≠ **make worse**; = **assist**, aid, support ▷ n = **assistance**, aid, support, advice, guidance ≠ **hindrance**

hem ❶ n 1 edge of cloth, folded and sewn down ▷ v 2 sew thus 3 confine, shut in

hemisphere n 1 half sphere 2 half of the earth

hemlock n poisonous plant

hemp n 1 Indian plant 2 its fibre used for rope etc. 3 any of several narcotic drugs

hen n female of domestic fowl and others **henpecked** adj (of man) dominated by wife

hence ❶ adv 1 from this point 2 for this reason **henceforward, henceforth** adv from now onwards

henchman n trusty follower

henna n 1 flowering shrub 2 reddish dye made from it

hepatitis n inflammation of the liver

heptagon n figure with seven angles

her pron object of SHE ▷ adj of, belonging to her **hers** pron of her **herself** pron emphatic or reflexive form of SHE

herald ❶ n 1 messenger, envoy ▷ v 2 announce **heraldic** adj **heraldry** n study of (right to have) heraldic bearings

herb n plant used in cookery or medicine **herbaceous** adj 1 of, like herbs 2 perennial flowering

herbal adj **herbicide** n chemical which destroys plants **herbivore** n animal that feeds on plants **herbivorous** adj

herd ❶ n 1 company of animals feeding together ▷ v 2 crowd together 3 tend (herd) **herdsman** n

here adv 1 in this place 2 at or to this point **hereabouts** adv near here **hereafter** adv 1 in time to come ▷ n 2 future existence **hereby** adv as a result of this **herein** adv in this place **herewith** adv with this

heredity n tendency of organism to transmit its nature to its descendants **hereditary** adj descending by inheritance or heredity

heresy n, pl **-sies** unorthodox opinion or belief **heretic** n **heretical** adj

heritage ❶ n what may be or is inherited

hermaphrodite n person or animal with characteristics, or reproductive organs, of both sexes

hermetic adj sealed so as to be airtight **hermetically** adj

hermit n one living in solitude **hermitage** n hermit's dwelling

hernia n projection of organ

——————————————————— THESAURUS ———————————————————

hem n = **edge**, border, margin, trimming, fringe

hence conj = **therefore**, thus, consequently, for this reason, in consequence

herald v = **indicate**, promise, usher in, presage, portend ▷ n

= **messenger**, courier, proclaimer, announcer, crier

herd n = **flock**, crowd, collection, mass, drove

heritage n = **inheritance**, legacy, birthright, tradition, endowment

through lining

hero ❶ *n, pl* **heroes** **1** one greatly regarded for achievements or qualities **2** principal character in story **heroic** *adj* **heroism** *n*

heroin *n* highly addictive drug

heron *n* long-legged wading bird

herring *n* important food fish

hertz *n, pl* **hertz** SI unit of frequency

hesitate ❶ *v* **1** hold back **2** feel, or show indecision **3** be reluctant **hesitancy, hesitation** *n* **hesitant** *adj*

hessian *n* coarse jute cloth

heterogeneous *adj* composed of diverse elements **heterogeneity** *n*

heterosexual *n/adj* (person) sexually attracted to members of the opposite sex

hew *v* **hewing, hewed** **1** chop, cut with axe **2** carve

hexagon *n* figure with six angles **hexagonal** *adj*

hey *interj* expression of surprise or for catching attention

heyday *n* bloom, prime

hiatus *n, pl* **-tuses, -tus** break or gap

hibernate *v* pass the winter, esp. in a torpid state **hibernation** *n*

hiccup, hiccough *n/v* (have) spasm of the breathing organs with an abrupt sound

hickory *n, pl* **-ries** **1** N Amer. nut-bearing tree **2** its tough wood

hide¹ ❶ *v* **hiding, hid, hidden** **1** put, keep out of sight **2** conceal oneself

hide² ❶ *n* skin of animal **hiding** *n* (Sl) thrashing **hidebound** *adj* **1** restricted **2** narrow-minded

hideous ❶ *adj* repulsive, revolting

hierarchy ❶ *n, pl* **-chies** system of persons or things arranged in graded order **hierarchical** *adj*

hieroglyphic *adj* **1** of picture writing, as used in ancient Egypt ▷ *n* **2** symbol representing object, concept or sound

hi-fi *adj* short for HIGH-FIDELITY *n* high-fidelity equipment

high ❶ *adj* **1** tall, lofty **2** far up **3** (of sound) acute in pitch

— THESAURUS —

hero *n* = **protagonist**, leading man; = **star**, champion/victor, superstar, conqueror

hesitate *v* = **waver**, delay, pause, wait, doubt ≠ **be decisive**; = **be reluctant**, be unwilling, shrink from, think twice, scruple ≠ **be determined**

hide¹ *v* = **conceal**, stash (Inf), secrete, put out of sight ≠ **display**; = **go into hiding**, take cover, keep out of sight, hole up, lie low; = **keep secret**, suppress, withhold, keep quiet about, hush up ≠ **disclose**

hide² *n* = **skin**, leather, pelt

hideous *adj* = **ugly**, revolting, ghastly, monstrous, grotesque ≠ **beautiful**

hierarchy *n* = **grading**, ranking, social order, pecking order, class system

high *adj* = **tall**, towering, soaring, steep, elevated ≠ **short**; = **extreme**, great, acute, severe, extraordinary ≠ **low**; = **strong**, violent, extreme, blustery, squally; = **important**,

4 expensive **5** of great importance, quality, or rank **6** (*Inf*) in state of euphoria ▷ *adv* **7** at, to a height **highly** *adv* **highness** *n* **1** quality of being high **2** (*with cap.*) title of royal person **highbrow** *n/adj* intellectual **high-fidelity** *adj* of high-quality sound reproducing equipment **high-handed** *adj* domineering **highlands** *pl n* area of relatively high ground **highlight** *n* **1** outstanding feature ▷ *v* **2** emphasize **highly strung** excitable, nervous **high-rise** *adj* of building that has many storeys **high-tech** *adj* using sophisticated technology **high time** latest possible time **highwayman** *n* formerly, horseman who robbed travellers

highway *n* (*US & Canad*) main road for fast-moving traffic

hijack ❶ *v* divert or wrongfully take command of a vehicle (esp. aircraft) **hijacker** *n*

hike ❶ *v* **1** walk a long way (for pleasure) in country **2** pull (up), hitch **hiker** *n*

hill ❶ *n* **1** natural elevation, small mountain **2** mound **hillock** *n* little hill **hilly** *adj*

hilt *n* handle of sword etc.

him *pron* object of HE **himself** *pron* emphatic form of HE

hind[1] *n* female of deer

hind[2] *adj* **hinder, hindmost** at the back, posterior

hinder ❶ *v* obstruct, impede, delay **hindrance** *n*

hinge *n* **1** movable joint, as that on which door hangs ▷ *v* **2** attach with hinge **3** depend on

hint ❶ *n* **1** slight indication **2** piece of advice **3** small amount ▷ *v* **4** give hint

hinterland *n* district lying behind coast, port etc.

hip *n* **hipper, hippest 1** either side of body below waist and above thigh **2** fruit of rose

hippie *n* person who rejects conventional dress and lifestyle

hippopotamus *n*, *pl* **-muses, -mi** large Afr. animal living in rivers

hire ❶ *v* **1** obtain temporary use of by payment **2** engage for wage ▷ *n*

— THESAURUS —

chief, powerful, superior, eminent ≠ **lowly**; = **high-pitched**, piercing, shrill, penetrating, strident ≠ **deep** ▷ *adv* = **way up**, aloft, far up, to a great height

hijack *v* = **seize**, take over, commandeer, expropriate

hike *v* = **walk**, march, trek, ramble, tramp; = **hitch up**, raise, lift, pull up, jack up

hill *n* = **mount**, fell, height, mound, hilltop

hinder *v* = **obstruct**, stop, check, block, delay ≠ **help**

hint *n* = **clue**, suggestion, implication, indication, pointer; *often plural* = **advice**, help, tip(s), suggestion(s), pointer(s); = **trace**, touch, suggestion, dash, suspicion ▷ *v* (*sometimes with* **at**) = **suggest**, indicate, imply, intimate, insinuate

hire *v* = **employ**, commission, take on, engage, appoint; = **rent**, charter, lease, let, engage ▷ *n*

3 hiring or being hired **4** payment for use of thing **hire-purchase** n purchase of goods by instalments

hirsute adj hairy

his pron/adj belonging to him

hiss ❶ v **1** make sharp sound of letter s **2** express disapproval thus ▷ n **3** hissing

history ❶ n, pl **-ries 1** (record of) past events **2** study of these **historian** n **historic** adj **historical** adj

histrionic adj excessively theatrical, insincere, artificial in manner **histrionics** pl n behaviour like this

hit ❶ v **hitting, hit 1** strike with blow or missile **2** affect injuriously **3** find **4** light (upon) ▷ n **5** blow **6** success **hit man** hired assassin

hitch ❶ v **1** fasten with loop etc. **2** raise with jerk **3** be caught or fastened ▷ n **4** difficulty **5** knot **6** jerk **hitchhike** v travel by begging free rides **hitchhiker** n

hither adv to this place **hitherto** adv up to now

HIV human immunodeficiency virus

hive n structure in which bees live

hive off transfer

hives pl n eruptive skin disease

HM His (or Her) Majesty

HMS His (or Her) Majesty's Service or Ship

hoard n **1** store, esp. hidden ▷ v **2** amass and hide

hoarding n large board for displaying advertisements

hoarse adj sounding husky

hoary adj **hoarier, hoariest 1** grey with age **2** greyish-white **3** very old **hoarfrost** n frozen dew

hoax n **1** practical joke ▷ v **2** play trick upon

hob n top area of cooking stove

hobble v **1** walk lamely **2** tie legs together ▷ n **3** limping gait

hobby ❶ n, pl **-bies** favourite occupation as pastime **hobbyhorse** n **1** favourite topic **2** toy horse

hobgoblin n mischievous fairy

hobnob v **-nobbing, -nobbed 1** drink together **2** be familiar (with)

hobo n, pl **-bos** (US & Canad) shiftless, wandering person

hock[1] n backward-pointing joint on

= **rental**, hiring, rent, lease

hiss v = **whistle**, wheeze, whiz, whirr, sibilate; = **jeer**, mock, deride ▷ n = **fizz**, buzz, hissing, fizzing, sibilation

history n = **the past**, antiquity, yesterday, yesteryear, olden days; = **chronicle**, record, story, account, narrative

hit v = **strike**, beat, knock, bang, slap; = **affect**, damage, harm, ruin,

devastate; = **reach**, gain, achieve, arrive at, accomplish ▷ n = **blow**, knock, stroke, belt (Inf), rap; = **success**, winner, triumph, smash (Inf), sensation

hitch n = **problem**, catch, difficulty, hold-up, obstacle ▷ v (Inf) = **hitchhike**, thumb a lift; = **fasten**, join, attach, couple, tie

hobby n = **pastime**, relaxation, leisure pursuit, diversion, avocation

leg of horse etc.

hock² *n* dry white wine

hockey *n* **1** team game played on a field with ball and curved sticks **2** (*US & Canad*) ice hockey

hod *n* **1** small trough for carrying bricks etc. **2** coal scuttle

hoe *n* **1** tool for weeding, breaking ground etc. ▷ *v* **2** work with hoe

hog *n* **1** pig **2** greedy person ▷ *v* **3** (*Inf*) eat, use (something) selfishly

hoist ❶ *v* raise aloft, raise with tackle etc.

hold¹ ❶ *v* **holding, held 1** keep in hands **2** maintain in position **3** contain **4** occupy **5** carry on **6** detain **7** be in force **8** occur ▷ *n* **9** grasp **10** influence **holdall** *n* large travelling bag **holder** *n* **holding** *n* property **hold-up** *n* **1** armed robbery **2** delay

hold² *n* space in ship or aircraft for cargo

hole ❶ *n* **1** hollow place **2** perforation **3** opening **4** (*Inf*) unattractive place **holey** *adj*

holiday ❶ *n* day(s) of rest from work etc., esp. spent away from home

holistic *adj* considering the complete person, esp. in treatment of disease

hollow ❶ *adj* **1** having a cavity, not solid **2** empty **3** insincere ▷ *n* **4** cavity, hole, valley ▷ *v* **5** make hollow **6** excavate

holly *n* evergreen shrub with prickly leaves and red berries

hollyhock *n* tall plant bearing many large flowers

holocaust ❶ *n* great destruction of life, esp. by fire

hologram *n* three-dimensional photographic image

holster *n* leather case for pistol, hung from belt etc.

hoist *v* = **raise**, lift, erect, elevate, heave

hold¹ keep ▷ *v* = **embrace**, grasp, clutch, hug, squeeze; = **accommodate**, take, contain, seat, have a capacity for; = **occupy**, have, fill, maintain, retain; = **conduct**, convene, call, run, preside over ≠ **cancel** ▷ *n* = **grip**, grasp, clasp; = **foothold**, footing; = **control**, influence, mastery

hole *n* = **cavity**, pit, hollow, chamber, cave; = **opening**, crack, tear, gap, breach; (*Inf*) = **hovel**, dump (*Inf*), dive (*Sl*), slum

holiday *n* = **vacation**, leave, break, time off, recess

hollow *adj* = **empty**, vacant, void, unfilled ≠ **solid**; = **worthless**, useless, vain, meaningless, pointless ≠ **meaningful** ▷ *n* = **cavity**, hole, bowl, depression, pit ≠ **mound**; = **valley**, dale, glen, dell, dingle ≠ **hill** ▷ *v* (*often followed by* **out**) = **scoop out**, dig out, excavate, gouge out

holocaust *n* = **devastation**, destruction, genocide, annihilation, conflagration

holy *adj* = **sacred**, blessed, hallowed, venerable, consecrated ≠ **unsanctified**; = **devout**, godly,

holy *adj* **-lier, -liest**
1 belonging, devoted to God 2 free
from sin 3 divine 4 consecrated
holily *adv* **holiness** *n*

homage *n* tribute, respect

home *n* 1 dwelling-place
2 residence ▷ *adj* 3 of home
4 native 5 in home ▷ *adv* 6 to, at
one's home 7 to the point ▷ *v*
8 direct or be directed onto a point
or target **homeless** *adj*
homelessness *n* **homely** *adv*
1 unpretentious 2 domesticated
homeward *adj/adv* **homewards**
adv **home-made** *adj* **homesick**
adj depressed by absence from
home **homesickness** *n*
homespun *adj* 1 domestic
2 simple **homework** *n* school
work done at home

homeopathy *n* treatment of
disease by small doses of drug
that produces symptoms of the
disease in healthy people
homeopathic *adj*

homestead *n* 1 a house or estate
and the adjoining land and
buildings, esp. on a farm 2 land
assigned to a N American settler

homicide *n* 1 killing of human
being 2 killer **homicidal** *adj*

homily *n, pl* **-lies** sermon

homogeneous *adj* 1 formed of
uniform parts 2 similar
homogeneity *n* **homogenize** *v*
break up fat globules in milk and
cream to distribute them evenly

homonym *n* word of same form
as another, but of different sense

homosexual *n/adj* (person)
sexually attracted to members of
the same sex **homosexuality** *n*

hone *v* sharpen (on whetstone)

honest *adj* 1 not cheating,
lying, stealing etc. 2 genuine
honestly *adv* **honesty** *n*

honey *n* sweet fluid made by bees
honeycomb *n* 1 wax structure in
hexagonal cells ▷ *v* 2 fill with cells
or perforations **honeymoon** *n*
holiday taken by newly wedded pair
honeysuckle *n* climbing plant

honk *n* 1 call of wild goose 2 sound of
motor-horn ▷ *v* 3 make this sound

honour *n* 1 personal integrity
2 renown 3 reputation ▷ *v*

h

THESAURUS

religious, pure, righteous ≠ **sinful**

homage *n* = **respect**, honour,
worship, devotion, reverence
≠ **contempt**

home *n* = **dwelling**, house,
residence, abode, habitation;
= **birthplace**, homeland, home
town, native land ▷ *adj*
= **domestic**, local, internal, native

homicide *n* = **murder**, killing,
manslaughter, slaying, bloodshed

hone *v* = **improve**, better, enhance,

upgrade, refine

honest *adj* = **trustworthy**,
upright, ethical, honourable,
reputable ≠ **dishonest**; = **open**,
direct, frank, plain, sincere
≠ **secretive**

honour *n* = **integrity**, morality,
honesty, goodness, fairness
≠ **dishonour**; = **prestige**, credit,
reputation, glory, fame ≠ **disgrace**;
= **reputation**, standing, prestige,
image, status; = **acclaim**, praise,

4 respect highly **5** confer honour on **6** accept or pay (bill etc.) when due **honourable** adj **honorary** adj conferred for the sake of honour only

hood n **1** covering for head and neck **2** hoodlike thing **hoodwink** v deceive

hoodlum n gangster

hoof n, pl **hooves, hoofs** horny casing of foot of horse etc.

hook ❶ n **1** bent piece of metal etc., for catching hold, hanging up etc. **2** something resembling hook in shape or function ▷ v **3** grasp, catch, hold, as with hook **hooked** adj **1** shaped like hook **2** caught **3** (Sl) addicted

hooligan ❶ n violent, irresponsible (young) person **hooliganism** n

hoon n (Aust & NZ, Sl) loutish youth who drives irresponsibly

hoop ❶ n rigid circular band of metal, wood etc.

hooray interj see HURRAH

hoot n **1** owl's cry or similar sound **2** cry of derision **3** (Inf) funny person or thing ▷ v **4** utter hoot **hooter** n device (e.g. horn) to emit hooting sound

Hoover® n **1** vacuum cleaner ▷ v **2** (without cap.) vacuum

hop¹ ❶ v **hopping, hopped 1** spring on one foot ▷ n **2** leap, skip

hop² n **1** climbing plant with bitter cones used to flavour beer etc. ▷ pl **2** the cones

hope ❶ n **1** expectation of something desired **2** thing that gives, or object of, this feeling ▷ v **3** feel hope (for) **hopeful** adj **hopefully** adv **hopeless** adj

hopper n **1** one who hops **2** device for feeding material into mill

hopscotch n children's game of hopping in pattern drawn on ground

horde ❶ n large crowd

horizon ❶ n line where earth and sky seem to meet **horizontal** adj parallel with horizon, level

━━━━━━━━━━━━━━━━━━━━━ THESAURUS ━━━━━━━━━━━━━━━━━━━━━

recognition, compliments, homage ≠ **contempt** ▷ v = **acclaim**, praise, decorate, commemorate, commend; = **respect**, value, esteem, prize, appreciate ≠ **scorn**; = **fulfil**, keep, carry out, observe, discharge; = **pay**, take, accept, pass, acknowledge ≠ **refuse**

hook n = **fastener**, catch, link, peg, clasp ▷ v = **fasten**, fix, secure, clasp; = **catch**, land, trap, entrap

hooligan n = **delinquent**, vandal, ruffian, lager lout, yob or yobbo (Brit Sl)

hoop n = **ring**, band, loop, wheel, round

hop¹ v = **jump**, spring, bound, leap, skip ▷ n = **jump**, step, spring, bound, leap

hope v = **believe**, look forward to, cross your fingers ▷ n = **belief**, confidence, expectation, longing, dream ≠ **despair**

horde n = **crowd**, mob, swarm, host, band

horizon n = **skyline**, view, vista

hormone n substance secreted from gland which stimulates organs of the body

horn n 1 hard projection on heads of certain animals 2 various things made of, or resembling it 3 wind instrument 4 device (esp. in car) emitting sound **horny** adj **hornpipe** n sailor's lively dance

hornet n large insect of wasp family

horoscope n telling of person's fortune by studying positions of planets etc. at his or her birth

horrendous adj horrific

horror ❶ n 1 terror 2 loathing, fear of 3 its cause **horrible** adj 1 exciting horror, hideous, shocking 2 disagreeable **horribly** adv **horrid** adj 1 unpleasant, repulsive 2 (Inf) unkind **horrific** adj particularly horrible **horrify** v 1 cause horror (in) 2 shock

hors d'oeuvre n small dish served before main meal

horse ❶ n 1 four-footed animal used for riding 2 cavalry 3 frame for support etc. **horsy** adj 1 devoted to horses 2 like a horse **horse chestnut** tree with white or pink flowers and large nuts **horsefly** n large bloodsucking fly

horseman n rider on horse

horsepower n unit of power of engine etc. **horseradish** n plant with pungent root **horseshoe** n protective U-shaped piece of iron nailed to horse's hoof

horticulture n art or science of gardening

hose n 1 flexible tube for conveying liquid or gas 2 stockings ▷ v 3 water with hose **hosiery** n stockings

hoser n 1 (US, Sl) a person who swindles or deceives others 2 (Canad, Sl) an unsophisticated, esp. rural, person

hospice n home for care of the terminally ill

hospital n institution for care of sick **hospitalize** v send or admit to hospital

hospitality ❶ n friendly and liberal reception of strangers or guests **hospitable** adj

host¹, hostess ❶ n 1 one who entertains another 2 innkeeper 3 compere of show ▷ v 4 act as a host

host² ❶ n large number

hostage ❶ n person taken or given as pledge or security

THESAURUS

horror n = **terror**, fear, alarm, panic, dread

horse n = **nag**, mount, mare, colt, filly

hospitality n = **welcome**, warmth, kindness, friendliness, sociability

host¹, hostess n = **master of ceremonies**, proprietor, innkeeper,

landlord or landlady; = **presenter**, compere (Brit), anchorman or anchorwoman ▷ v = **present**, introduce, compere (Brit), front (Inf)

host² n = **multitude**, lot, load (Inf), wealth, array

hostage n = **captive**, prisoner, pawn

hostel n building providing accommodation at low cost for students etc.

hostile ❶ adj 1 antagonistic 2 warlike 3 of an enemy **hostility** n, pl **-ties** 1 enmity ▷ pl 2 acts of warfare

hot ❶ adj **hotter, hottest** 1 of high temperature 2 angry 3 new 4 spicy **hotly** adv **hot air** (Inf) empty talk **hotbed** n 1 bed of heated earth for young plants 2 any place encouraging growth **hot-blooded** adj excitable **hot dog** hot sausage in split bread roll **hotfoot** v/adv (go) quickly **hothead** n intemperate person **hothouse** n heated greenhouse **hotline** n direct telephone link for emergency use **hotplate** n heated plate on electric cooker **hot spot** 1 place where there is a lot of exciting activity 2 area where there is a concentration of violence or political unrest 3 (Comp) place (esp. a public building or commercial premises) offering a Wi-Fi connection

hotchpotch n 1 medley 2 dish of many ingredients

hotel n commercial establishment providing lodging and meals **hotelier** n

hound ❶ n 1 hunting dog ▷ v 2 chase, urge, pursue

hour n 1 twenty-fourth part of day 2 sixty minutes 3 appointed time ▷ pl 4 fixed periods for work etc. **hourly** adv/adj **hourglass** n timing device in which sand trickles between two glass compartments

house ❶ n 1 building for human habitation 2 legislative assembly 3 family 4 business firm ▷ v 5 give or receive shelter, lodging, or storage 6 cover or contain **housing** n 1 (providing of) houses 2 part designed to cover, protect, contain **houseboat** n boat used as home **household** n inmates of house collectively **housekeeper** n person managing affairs of household **housekeeping** n (money for) running household

---

THESAURUS

hostile adj = **antagonistic**, opposed, contrary, ill-disposed; = **unfriendly**, belligerent, antagonistic, rancorous, ill-disposed ≠ **friendly**

hot adj = **heated**, boiling, steaming, roasting, searing; = **warm**, close, stifling, humid, torrid ≠ **cold**; = **spicy**, pungent, peppery, piquant, biting ≠ **mild**; = **intense**, passionate, heated, spirited, fierce; = **new**, latest, fresh, recent, up to date ≠ **old**

hound v = **harass**, harry, bother, provoke, annoy

house n = **home**, residence, dwelling, pad (Sl), homestead; = **household**, family; = **firm**, company, business, organization, outfit (Inf); = **assembly**, parliament, Commons, legislative body ▷ v = **accommodate**, quarter, take in, put up, lodge; = **contain**, keep, hold, cover, store; = **take**, accommodate, sleep, provide shelter for, give a bed to

housewife *n* woman who runs her own household

hovel *n* lowly dwelling

hover ❶ *v* 1 hang in the air 2 loiter 3 be in state of indecision
hovercraft *n* type of craft which can travel over both land and sea on a cushion of air

how *adv* 1 in what way 2 by what means 3 in what condition 4 to what degree **however** *conj* 1 nevertheless ▷ *adv* 2 in whatever way, degree 3 all the same

howl ❶ *v/n* (utter) long loud cry **howler** *n* (*Inf*) stupid mistake

HP, h.p. hire-purchase

HQ headquarters

HRH His (*or* Her) Royal Highness

hub ❶ *n* 1 middle part of wheel 2 central point of activity

hubbub *n* confused noise

huddle ❶ *n* 1 crowded mass 2 (*Inf*) impromptu conference ▷ *v* 3 heap, crowd together 4 hunch

hue ❶ *n* colour

huff *n* 1 passing mood of anger ▷ *v* 2 make or become angry 3 blow

hug ❶ *v* **hugging, hugged** 1 clasp tightly in the arms 2 keep close to ▷ *n* 3 fond embrace

huge ❶ *adj* very big **hugely** *adv* very much

hulk *n* 1 body of abandoned vessel 2 large, unwieldy person or thing **hulking** *adj*

hull ❶ *n* 1 frame, body of ship 2 calyx of strawberry etc. ▷ *v* 3 remove shell, hull from (fruit, seeds)

hullabaloo *n, pl* **-loos** 1 uproar 2 clamour

hum ❶ *v* **humming, hummed** 1 make low continuous sound 2 sing with closed lips ▷ *n* 3 humming sound **hummingbird** *n* very small Amer. bird whose wings make humming noise

human ❶ *adj* 1 of man 2 relating to, characteristic of, man's nature

h

THESAURUS

hover *v* = **float**, fly, hang, drift, flutter; = **linger**, loiter, hang about *or* around (*Inf*); = **waver**, fluctuate, dither (*chiefly Brit*), oscillate, vacillate

howl *v* = **cry**, scream, roar, weep, yell ▷ *n* = **baying**, cry, bay, bark, barking

hub *n* = **centre**, heart, focus, core, middle

huddle *v* = **curl up**, crouch, hunch up; = **crowd**, press, gather, collect, squeeze ▷ *n* (*Inf*) = **discussion**, conference, meeting, powwow, confab (*Inf*)

hue *n* = **colour**, tone, shade, dye, tint

hug *v* = **embrace**, cuddle, squeeze, clasp, enfold ▷ *n* = **embrace**, squeeze, bear hug, clinch (*Sl*), clasp

huge *adj* = **enormous**, large, massive, vast, tremendous ≠ **tiny**

hull *n* = **framework**, casing, body, covering, frame

hum *v* = **drone**, buzz, murmur, throb, vibrate

human *adj* = **mortal**, manlike ≠ **nonhuman** ▷ *n* = **human being**, person, individual, creature, mortal ≠ **nonhuman**

humane *adj* 1 kind 2 merciful
humanism *n* belief in human
effort rather than religion
humanitarian *n* 1 philanthropist
▷ *adj* 2 philanthropic **humanity**
n 1 human nature 2 human race
3 kindliness ▷ *pl* 4 study of
literature, philosophy, the arts
humanize *v*
humble ❶ *adj* 1 lowly, modest ▷ *v*
2 humiliate **humbly** *adv*
humbug *n* 1 imposter 2 sham,
nonsense 3 sweet of boiled sugar
humdrum *adj* commonplace, dull
humid *adj* moist, damp
humidifier *n* device for increasing
amount of water vapour in air in
room etc. **humidity** *n*
humiliate ❶ *v* lower dignity of,
abase, mortify **humiliation** *n*
humility *n* 1 state of being
humble 2 meekness
hummock *n* low knoll, hillock
humour ❶ *n* 1 faculty of saying or
perceiving what excites
amusement 2 amusing speech,

writing etc. 3 state of mind, mood
▷ *v* 4 gratify, indulge **humorist** *n*
person who acts, speaks, writes
humorously **humorous** *adj*
hump *n* 1 normal or deforming
lump, esp. on back ▷ *v* 2 make
hump-shaped 3 (*Sl*) carry or
heave **humpback** *n* person with
hump
humus *n* decayed vegetable and
animal mould
hunch ❶ *n* (*Inf*) 1 intuition
2 hump ▷ *v* 3 bend into hump
hunchback *n* humpback
hundred *n/adj* cardinal number,
ten times ten **hundredth** *adj*
ordinal number **hundredweight**
n weight of 112 lbs (50.8 kg), 20th
part of ton
hunger ❶ *n/v* 1 (have) discomfort
from lack of food 2 (have) strong
desire **hungrily** *adv* **hungry** *adj*
having keen appetite
hunk ❶ *n* thick piece
hunt ❶ *v* 1 seek out to kill or capture
for sport or food 2 search (for)

humble *adj* = **modest**, meek,
unassuming, unpretentious,
self-effacing ≠ **proud**; = **lowly**,
poor, mean, simple, ordinary
≠ **distinguished**; ▷ *v* = **humiliate**,
disgrace, crush, subdue, chasten
≠ **exalt**
humiliate *v* = **embarrass**, shame,
humble, crush, put down ≠ **honour**
humour *n* = **comedy**, funniness,
fun, amusement, funny side
≠ **seriousness**; = **mood**, spirits,
temper, disposition, frame of mind
▷ *v* = **indulge**, accommodate, go

along with, flatter, gratify
≠ **oppose**
hunch *n* = **feeling**, idea,
impression, suspicion, intuition ▷ *v*
= **crouch**, bend, curve, arch, draw in
hunger *n* = **appetite**, emptiness,
hungriness, ravenousness;
= **starvation**, famine,
malnutrition, undernourishment;
= **desire**, appetite, craving, ache,
lust
hunk *n* = **lump**, piece, chunk, block,
mass
hunt *v* = **stalk**, track, chase,

▷ *n* **3** chase, search **4** (party organized for) hunting
hunter *n*

hurdle ❶ *n* **1** portable frame of bars for temporary fences or for jumping over **2** obstacle ▷ *v* **3** race over hurdles

hurdy-gurdy *n, pl* **-dies** mechanical musical instrument

hurl ❶ *v* throw violently

hurly-burly *n* loud confusion

hurrah, hurray *interj* exclamation of joy or applause

hurricane ❶ *n* very strong, violent wind or storm

hurry ❶ *v* **-rying, -ried 1** (cause to) move or act in great haste ▷ *n* **2** undue haste **3** eagerness
hurriedly *adv*

hurt ❶ *v* **hurting, hurt 1** injure, damage, give pain to **2** feel pain ▷ *n* **3** wound, injury, harm
hurtful *adj*

hurtle ❶ *v* rush violently

husband ❶ *n* **1** married man ▷ *v* **2** economize **3** use to best advantage **husbandry** *n* **1** farming **2** economy

hush ❶ *v* **1** make or be silent ▷ *n* **2** stillness **3** quietness

husk *n* **1** dry covering of certain seeds and fruits ▷ *v* **2** remove husk from **husky** *adj* **1** rough in tone **2** hoarse, throaty

husky *n* **huskier, huskiest** *pl* **huskies** Arctic sledge dog

hussy *n, pl* **-sies** cheeky young woman

hustings *pl n* political campaigning

hustle *v* **1** push about, jostle, hurry ▷ *n* **2** lively activity

hut ❶ *n* small house or shelter

hutch *n* cage for rabbits etc.

hyacinth *n* bulbous plant with bell-shaped flowers

hybrid ❶ *n* **1** offspring of two plants or animals of different species ▷ *adj* **2** crossbred

h

pursue, trail ▷ *n* = **search**, hunting, investigation, chase, pursuit

hurdle *n* = **obstacle**, difficulty, barrier, handicap, hazard; = **fence**, barrier, barricade

hurl *v* = **throw**, fling, launch, cast, pitch

hurricane *n* = **storm**, gale, tornado, cyclone, typhoon

hurry *v* = **rush**, fly, dash, scurry, scoot ≠ **dawdle** ▷ *n* = **rush**, haste, speed, urgency, flurry ≠ **slowness**

hurt *v* = **injure**, damage, wound, cut, disable ≠ **heal**; = **ache**, be sore, be painful, burn, smart; = **harm**,

injure, ill-treat, maltreat ▷ *n* = **distress**, suffering, pain, grief, misery ≠ **happiness**

hurtle *v* = **rush**, charge, race, shoot, fly

husband *n* = **partner**, spouse, mate, better half *(humorous)* ▷ *v* = **conserve**, budget, save, store, hoard ≠ **squander**

hush *v* = **quieten**, silence, mute, muzzle, shush ▷ *n* = **quiet**, silence, calm, peace, tranquillity

hut *n* = **cabin**, shack, shanty, hovel

hybrid *n* = **crossbreed**, cross, mixture, compound, composite; = **mixture**, compound, composite,

hydrangea *n* ornamental shrub

hydrant *n* water-pipe with nozzle for hose

hydraulic *adj* concerned with, operated by, pressure transmitted through liquid in pipe

hydro *adj* (*Canad*) electricity as supplied to a residence, business, institution, etc.

hydrochloric acid strong colourless acid

hydroelectric *adj* pert. to generation of electricity by use of water

hydrofoil *n* fast, light vessel with hull raised out of water at speed

hydrogen *n* colourless gas which combines with oxygen to form water **hydrogen bomb** atom bomb of enormous power **hydrogen peroxide** colourless liquid used as antiseptic and bleach

hydrophobia *n* aversion to water, esp. as symptom of rabies

hyena *n* wild animal related to dog

hygiene ❶ *n* (study of) principles and practice of health and cleanliness **hygienic** *adj*

hymen *n* membrane partly covering vagina of virgin

hymn ❶ *n* **1** song of praise, esp. to God ▷ *v* **2** praise in song

hype ❶ *n* **1** intensive publicity ▷ *v* **2** publicize

hyperbole *n* rhetorical exaggeration

hypermarket *n* huge self-service store

hypertension *n* abnormally high blood pressure

hyphen *n* short line (-) indicating that two words or syllables are to be connected **hyphenate** *v* **hyphenated** *adj*

hypnosis *n* induced state like deep sleep in which subject acts on external suggestion **hypnotic** *adj* **hypnotism** *n* **hypnotize** *v* affect with hypnosis

hypochondria *n* morbid depression without cause, about one's own health **hypochondriac** *adj/n*

hypocrisy ❶ *n, pl* **-sies** **1** assuming of false appearance of virtue **2** insincerity **hypocrite** *n* **hypocritical** *adj*

hypodermic *adj* **1** introduced, injected beneath the skin ▷ *n* **2** hypodermic syringe or needle

hypotenuse *n* side of right-angled triangle opposite the right angle

hypothermia *n* condition of having body temperature reduced to dangerously low level

———— THESAURUS ————

amalgam

hygiene *n* = **cleanliness**, sanitation, disinfection, sterility

hymn *n* = **religious song**, song of praise, carol, chant, anthem

hype *n* (*Sl*) = **publicity**, promotion, plugging (*Inf*), razzmatazz (*Sl*), brouhaha

hypocrisy *n* = **insincerity**, pretence, deception, cant, duplicity ≠ **sincerity**

hypothesis ❶ *n, pl* **-ses**
1 suggested explanation of
something 2 assumption as
basis of reasoning
hypothetical *adj*
hysterectomy *n, pl* **-mies**

surgical operation for removing
uterus
hysteria ❶ *n* 1 mental disorder
with emotional outbursts 2 fit of
crying or laughing **hysterical** *adj*
hysterics *pl n* fits of hysteria

hypothesis *n* = **theory**, premise,
proposition, assumption, thesis

hysteria *n* = **frenzy**, panic,
madness, agitation, delirium

h

I *pron* the pronoun of the first person singular

ibis *n* storklike bird

ice *n* **1** frozen water **2** ice cream ▷ *v* **3** cover, become covered with ice **4** cool with ice **5** cover with icing **icicle** *n* hanging spike of ice **icing** *n* mixture of sugar and water etc. used to decorate cakes **icy** *adj* **icier, iciest 1** covered with ice **2** cold **3** unfriendly **iceberg** *n* large floating mass of ice **ice cream** sweet creamy frozen dessert **ice hockey** team game played on ice with puck **ice skate** boot with steel blade for gliding over ice **ice-skate** *v*

icon *n* religious image **iconoclast** *n* one who attacks established ideas

idea ❶ *n* **1** notion **2** conception **3** plan, aim **ideal** *n* **1** idea of perfection **2** perfect person or thing ▷ *adj* **3** perfect **idealism** *n* tendency to seek perfection in everything **idealist** *n* **1** one who strives after the ideal **2** impractical person **idealistic** *adj* **idealization** *n* **idealize** *v* portray as ideal **ideally** *adv*

identity ❶ *n, pl* **-ties 1** individuality **2** state of being exactly alike **identical** *adj* very same **identifiable** *adj* **identification** *n* **1** recognition **2** identifying document **identify** *v* **1** establish identity of **2** associate (oneself) with **3** treat as identical

ideology *n, pl* **-gies** body of ideas, beliefs of group, nation etc. **ideological** *adj*

idiom *n* expression peculiar to a language or group **idiomatic** *adj*

idiosyncrasy *n, pl* **-sies** peculiarity of mind

idiot ❶ *n* **1** mentally deficient person **2** stupid person **idiocy** *n* **idiotic** *adj* utterly stupid

idle ❶ *adj* **1** unemployed **2** lazy **3** useless **4** groundless ▷ *v* **5** be idle **6** run slowly in neutral gear **idleness** *n* **idler** *n* **idly** *adv*

——— THESAURUS ———

idea *n* = **notion**, thought, view, teaching, opinion; = **intention**, aim, purpose, object, plan

identity *n* = **individuality**, self, character, personality, existence

idiot *n* = **fool**, moron, twit (*Inf, chiefly Brit*), chump, imbecile

idle *adj* = **unoccupied**, unemployed, redundant, inactive ≠ **occupied**; = **unused**, inactive, out of order, out of service; = **lazy**, slow, slack, sluggish, lax ≠ **busy**; = **useless**, vain, pointless, unsuccessful, ineffective ≠ **useful**

idol ❶ n 1 image worshipped as deity 2 object of excessive devotion **idolatry** n **idolize** v love or admire to excess

idyll n (poem describing) picturesque or charming scene or episode **idyllic** adj delightful

i.e. that is

if ❶ conj 1 on condition or supposition that 2 whether 3 although

igloo n, pl **-loos** domed house made of snow

ignite ❶ v (cause to) burn **ignition** n 1 act of kindling or setting on fire 2 car's electrical firing system

ignoble adj 1 mean, base 2 of low birth

ignominy n 1 public disgrace 2 shameful act **ignominious** adj

ignore ❶ v disregard, leave out of account **ignoramus** n ignorant person **ignorance** n lack of knowledge **ignorant** adj

1 lacking knowledge 2 uneducated

iguana n large tropical American lizard

ill ❶ adj 1 not in good health 2 bad, evil 3 harmful ▷ n 4 evil, harm ▷ adv 5 badly 6 hardly **illness** n
ill-advised adj imprudent
ill-disposed adj unsympathetic
ill-fated adj unfortunate
ill-gotten adj obtained dishonestly **ill-treat** v treat cruelly **ill will** hostility

illegal ❶ adj against the law

illegible adj unable to be read

illegitimate adj 1 born to unmarried parents 2 irregular **illegitimacy** n

illicit ❶ adj 1 illegal 2 prohibited, forbidden

illiterate adj 1 unable to read or write ▷ n 2 illiterate person **illiteracy** n

illogical adj not logical

illuminate ❶ v 1 light up 2 clarify 3 decorate with lights or

idol n = **hero**, pin-up, favourite, pet, darling; = **graven image**, god, deity

if conj = **provided**, assuming, given that, providing, supposing

ignite v = **catch fire**, burn, burst into flames, inflame, flare up; = **set fire to**, light, set alight, torch, kindle

ignore v = **pay no attention to**, neglect, disregard, slight, overlook ≠ **pay attention to**

ill adj = **unwell**, sick, poorly (Inf), diseased, weak ≠ **healthy**; = **harmful**, bad, damaging, evil,

foul ≠ **favourable** ▷ n = **problem**, trouble, suffering, worry, injury ▷ adv = **badly**, unfortunately, unfavourably, inauspiciously; = **hardly**, barely, scarcely, just, only just ≠ **well**

illegal adj = **unlawful**, banned, forbidden, prohibited, criminal ≠ **legal**

illicit adj = **illegal**, criminal, prohibited, unlawful, illegitimate ≠ **legal**; = **forbidden**, improper, immoral, guilty, clandestine

illuminate v = **light up**, brighten ≠ **darken**; = **explain**, interpret,

colours **illumination** n

illusion ❶ n deceptive appearance or belief **illusionist** n conjuror **illusory** adj

illustrate ❶ v 1 provide with pictures or examples 2 explain by examples **illustration** n 1 picture, diagram 2 example

illustrious adj 1 famous 2 glorious

image ❶ n 1 likeness 2 optical counterpart 3 double, copy 4 general impression 5 word picture **imagery** n images collectively

imagine ❶ v 1 picture to oneself 2 think 3 conjecture **imaginable** adj **imaginary** adj existing only in fantasy **imagination** n 1 faculty of making mental images of things not present 2 fancy **imaginative** adj

imbalance n lack of balance in emphasis or proportion

imbecile n 1 idiot ▷ adj 2 idiotic

imbibe v drink (in)

imbue v **-buing, -bued** instil, fill

imitate ❶ v 1 take as model 2 copy **imitation** n 1 act of imitating 2 copy 3 counterfeit ▷ adj 4 synthetic **imitative** adj

immaculate ❶ adj 1 spotless 2 pure

immaterial adj 1 unimportant 2 not consisting of matter

immature adj 1 not fully developed 2 lacking wisdom because of youth

immediate ❶ adj 1 occurring at once 2 closest **immediately** adv

immense ❶ adj huge, vast **immensely** adv **immensity** n

immerse ❶ v 1 submerge in liquid 2 involve 3 engross **immersion** n

immigrant n settler in foreign country

imminent ❶ adj liable to happen soon **imminence** n

━━━━━━━━━━━━━━━━━━ THESAURUS ━━━━━━━━━━━━━━━━━━

make clear, clarify, clear up ≠ **obscure**

illusion n = **delusion**, misconception, misapprehension, fancy, fallacy; = **fantasy**, vision, hallucination, trick, spectre

illustrate v = **demonstrate**, emphasize

image n = **thought**, idea, vision, concept, impression, likeness, mirror image; = **figure**, idol, icon, fetish, talisman

imagine v = **envisage**, see, picture, plan, think of; = **believe**, think, suppose, assume, suspect

imitate v = **copy**, follow, repeat,

echo, emulate

immaculate adj = **clean**, spotless, neat, spruce, squeaky-clean ≠ **dirty**; = **pure**, perfect, impeccable, flawless, faultless ≠ **corrupt**

immediate adj = **instant**, prompt, instantaneous, quick, on-the-spot ≠ **later**; = **nearest**, next, direct, close, near ≠ **far**

immense adj = **huge**, great, massive, vast, enormous ≠ **tiny**

immerse v = **engross**, involve, absorb, busy, occupy; = **plunge**, dip, submerge, sink, duck

imminent adj = **near**, coming,

immobile *adj* unable to move
immobility *n* **immobilize** *v*
immolate *v* kill, sacrifice
immoral ❶ *adj* 1 corrupt
2 promiscuous **immorality** *n*
immortal ❶ *adj* 1 deathless
2 famed for all time ▷ *n* 3 person
living forever **immortality** *n*
immortalize *v*
immune *adj* 1 protected (against a
disease etc.) 2 exempt **immunity**
n, pl **-ties immunization** *n*
process of making immune to
disease **immunize** *v*
imp *n* 1 little devil 2 mischievous
child
impact ❶ *n* 1 collision 2 profound
effect **impacted** *adj* wedged
impair ❶ *v* weaken, damage
impairment *n*
impala *n* S Afr. antelope
impale *v* pierce with sharp
instrument
impart *v* 1 communicate 2 give
impartial *adj* 1 unbiased 2 fair
impartiality *n*

impassable *adj* blocked
impasse ❶ *n* deadlock
impassioned *adj* full of feeling,
ardent
impassive *adj* 1 showing no
emotion 2 calm
impatient *adj* 1 irritable
2 restless **impatience** *n*
impeach *v* 1 charge, esp. with
treason or crime in office
2 denounce **impeachable** *adj*
impeachment *n*
impeccable ❶ *adj* faultless
impede *v* hinder **impediment** *n*
1 obstruction 2 defect
impel *v* **-pelling, -pelled** 1 induce
2 drive
impending ❶ *adj* imminent
imperative ❶ *adj* 1 necessary
2 peremptory 3 (Grammar)
expressing command ▷ *n*
4 (Grammar) imperative mood
imperfect *adj* 1 having faults
2 not complete **imperfection** *n*
imperial ❶ *adj* 1 of empire, or
emperor 2 majestic 3 denoting

close, approaching, gathering
≠ **remote**
immoral *adj* = **wicked**, bad,
wrong, corrupt, indecent ≠ **moral**
immortal *adj* = **timeless**, eternal,
everlasting, lasting, traditional
≠ **ephemeral** ▷ *n* = **hero**, genius,
great; = **god**, goddess, deity, divine
being, immortal being
impact *n* = **effect**, influence,
consequences, impression,
repercussions; = **collision**, contact,
crash, knock, stroke
impair *v* = **worsen**, reduce,

damage, injure, harm ≠ **improve**
impasse *n* = **deadlock**, stalemate,
standstill, dead end, standoff
impeccable *adj* = **faultless**,
perfect, immaculate, flawless,
squeaky-clean ≠ **flawed**
impending *adj* = **looming**,
coming, approaching, near,
forthcoming
imperative *adj* = **urgent**,
essential, pressing, vital, crucial
≠ **unnecessary**
imperial *adj* = **royal**, regal, kingly,
queenly, princely

weights and measures formerly official in Brit. **imperialism** n policy of acquiring empire

imperil v **-illing, -illed** endanger

imperious adj domineering

impersonal adj objective

impersonate v pretend to be **impersonation** n **impersonator** n

impertinent adj insolent, rude **impertinence** n

imperturbable adj calm, not excitable

impervious adj 1 impossible to penetrate 2 unaffected by

impetigo n contagious skin disease

impetuous adj rash **impetuosity** n

impetus ❶ n, pl **-tuses** 1 incentive 2 momentum

impinge v encroach (upon)

impious adj irreverent

implacable adj not to be placated

implant ❶ v insert firmly

implement ❶ n 1 tool, instrument ▷ v 2 carry out

implore v entreat earnestly

imply ❶ v **-plying, -plied** 1 hint 2 mean **implicate** v involve **implication** n something implied **implicit** adj 1 implied 2 absolute

import ❶ v 1 bring in ▷ n 2 thing imported 3 meaning **importation** n **importer** n

important ❶ adj 1 of great consequence 2 eminent, powerful **importance** n

impose v 1 place (upon) 2 take advantage (of) **imposing** adj impressive **imposition** n

impossible ❶ adj 1 not possible 2 unreasonable **impossibility** n, pl **-ties** **impossibly** adv

impotent adj 1 powerless 2 (of males) incapable of sexual intercourse **impotence** n

impound v seize legally

impoverish ❶ v make poor or weak

— THESAURUS —

impetus n = **incentive**, push, spur, motivation, impulse; = **force**, power, energy, momentum

implant v = **insert**, fix, graft; = **instil**, infuse, inculcate

implement v = **carry out**, effect, carry through, complete, apply ≠ **hinder** ▷ n = **tool**, machine, device, instrument, appliance

imply v = **suggest**, hint, insinuate, indicate, intimate; = **involve**, mean, entail, require, indicate

import v = **bring in**, buy in, ship in, introduce ▷ n (Formal) = **significance**, concern/value,

weight, consequence; = **meaning**, implication, significance, sense, intention

important adj = **significant**, critical, substantial, urgent, serious ≠ **unimportant**; = **powerful**, prominent, commanding, dominant, influential

impossible adj = **not possible**, out of the question, impracticable, unfeasible; = **unachievable**, out of the question/vain, unthinkable, inconceivable ≠ **possible**

impoverish v = **bankrupt**, ruin, beggar, break

impractical *adj* not sensible
impregnable *adj* proof against attack
impregnate *v* 1 saturate 2 make pregnant
impresario *n, pl* **-ios** 1 organizer of public entertainment 2 manager of opera, ballet etc.
impress ❶ *v* 1 affect deeply, usu. favourably 2 imprint, stamp **impression** *n* 1 effect 2 notion, belief 3 imprint 4 comic impersonation **impressionable** *adj* susceptible **impressive** *adj* making deep impression
imprint ❶ *n* 1 mark made by pressure ▷ *v* 2 stamp 3 fix in mind
imprison ❶ *v* put in prison **imprisonment** *n*
improbable ❶ *adj* unlikely
impromptu *adv/adj* 1 without preparation ▷ *n* 2 improvisation
improper ❶ *adj* 1 indecent 2 incorrect **impropriety** *n*
improve ❶ *v* make or become better **improvement** *n*

improvident *adj* thriftless
improvise ❶ *v* 1 make use of materials at hand 2 perform, speak without preparation **improvisation** *n*
impudent *adj* impertinent **impudence** *n*
impugn *v* call in question, challenge
impulse ❶ *n* 1 sudden inclination to act 2 impetus **impulsive** *adj* rash
impunity *n* **with impunity** without punishment
impure *adj* 1 having unwanted substances mixed in 2 immoral, obscene **impurity** *n*
impute *v* attribute to **imputation** *n* reproach
in *prep* 1 expresses inclusion within limits of space, time, circumstance, sphere etc. ▷ *adv* 2 in or into some state, place etc. 3 (*Inf*) in vogue etc. ▷ *adj* 4 (*Inf*) fashionable
inability *n* lack of means or skill to do something
inaccurate ❶ *adj* not correct

impress *v* = **excite**, move, strike, touch, affect
imprint *n* = **mark**, impression, stamp, indentation ▷ *v* = **engrave**, print, stamp, impress, etch
imprison *v* = **jail**, confine, detain, lock up, put away ≠ **free**
improbable *adj* = **doubtful**, unlikely, dubious, questionable, fanciful ≠ **probable**
improper *adj* = **inappropriate**, unfit, unsuitable, out of place, unwarranted ≠ **appropriate**; = **indecent**, vulgar, suggestive,

unseemly, untoward ≠ **decent**
improve *v* = **enhance**, better, add to, upgrade, touch up ≠ **worsen**; = **get better**, pick up, develop, advance, rally
improvise *v* = **devise**, contrive, concoct, throw together; = **ad-lib**, invent, busk, wing it (*Inf*), play it by ear (*Inf*)
impulse *n* = **urge**, longing, wish, notion, yearning
inaccurate *adj* = **incorrect**, wrong, mistaken, faulty, unreliable ≠ **accurate**

inaccuracy n, pl **-cies**
inadequate ❶ adj **1** not enough **2** incapable **inadequacy** n
inane adj foolish
inanimate adj lifeless
inappropriate adj not suitable
inarticulate adj unable to express oneself clearly
inaugurate v **1** initiate **2** admit to office **inaugural** adj **inauguration** n formal initiation (to office etc.)
inauspicious adj unlucky
inborn adj existing from birth
incalculable adj **1** beyond calculation **2** very great
incandescent adj **1** glowing **2** produced by glowing filament
incantation n magic spell
incapable adj helpless
incapacitate v **1** disable **2** disqualify
incarcerate v imprison
incarnate adj **1** in human form **2** typified **incarnation** n
incendiary adj **1** designed to cause fires **2** inflammatory ▷ n **3** fire-bomb
incense¹ ❶ v enrage
incense² ❶ n **1** gum, spice giving perfume when burned **2** its smoke

incentive ❶ n something that stimulates effort
inception n beginning
incessant adj unceasing
incest n sexual intercourse between close relatives
incestuous adj
inch n **1** one twelfth of a foot, or 0.0254 metre ▷ v **2** move very slowly
incident ❶ n **1** event, occurrence **2** public disturbance **incidence** n extent or frequency of occurrence
incidental adj occurring as a minor, inevitable, or chance accompaniment **incidentally** adv **1** by chance **2** by the way
incidentals pl n accompanying items
incinerate v burn up completely **incinerator** n
incipient adj beginning
incise v cut into **incision** n **incisive** adj sharp **incisor** n cutting tooth
incite v urge, stir up
inclement adj severe
incline ❶ v **1** lean, slope **2** (cause to) be disposed ▷ n **3** slope **inclination** n **1** liking, tendency **2** degree of deviation

— THESAURUS —

inadequate adj = **insufficient**, meagre, poor, lacking, scant ≠ **adequate**; = **incapable**, incompetent, faulty, deficient, unqualified ≠ **capable**
incense v = **anger**, infuriate, enrage, irritate, madden
incentive n = **inducement**, encouragement, spur, lure, bait

≠ **disincentive**
incident n = **disturbance**, scene, clash, disorder, confrontation; = **adventure**, drama, excitement, crisis, spectacle
incline v = **predispose**, influence, persuade, prejudice, sway ▷ n = **slope**, rise, dip, grade, descent

include ① v 1 have as (part of) contents 2 add in **inclusion** n **inclusive** adj including (everything)

incognito adv/adj 1 under an assumed identity ▷ n 2 assumed identity

incoherent adj 1 lacking clarity 2 inarticulate **incoherence** n

income ① n money received from salary, investments etc.

incoming ① adj 1 coming in 2 about to come into office 3 next

incomparable adj beyond comparison

incompatible ① adj inconsistent, conflicting

incompetent ① adj lacking necessary ability **incompetence** n

inconceivable adj impossible to imagine

inconclusive adj not giving a final decision

incongruous adj not appropriate **incongruity** n, pl **-ties**

inconsequential adj 1 trivial

2 haphazard

incontinent adj not able to control bladder or bowels

incontrovertible adj undeniable

inconvenience ① n trouble, difficulty **inconvenient** adj

incorporate ① v 1 include 2 form into corporation

incorrigible adj beyond correction or reform

increase ① v 1 make or become greater in size, number etc. ▷ n 2 growth, enlargement **increasingly** adv more and more

incredible ① adj 1 unbelievable 2 (Inf) amazing **incredibly** adv

incredulous adj unbelieving **incredulity** n

increment n increase

incriminate v imply guilt of

incubate v 1 provide eggs, bacteria etc. with heat for development 2 develop in this way **incubation** n **incubator** n apparatus for hatching eggs or rearing premature babies

include v = **contain**, involve, incorporate, cover, consist of ≠ **exclude**; = **add**, enter, put in, insert

income n = **revenue**, earnings, pay, returns, profits

incoming adj = **arriving**, landing, approaching, entering, returning ≠ **departing**

incompatible adj = **inconsistent**, conflicting, contradictory, incongruous, unsuited ≠ **compatible**

incompetent adj = **inept**,

useless, incapable, floundering, bungling ≠ **competent**

inconvenience n = **trouble**, difficulty, bother, fuss, disadvantage ▷ v = **trouble**, bother, disturb, upset, disrupt

incorporate v = **include**, contain, take in, embrace, integrate

increase v = **raise**, extend, boost, expand, develop ≠ **decrease** ▷ n = **growth**, rise, development, gain, expansion

incredible adj (Inf) = **amazing**, wonderful, stunning, extraordinary,

inculcate v fix in the mind

incumbent n holder of office

incur ❶ v **-curring, -curred** bring upon oneself **incursion** n invasion

indebted adj owing gratitude or money

indecent ❶ adj **1** offensive **2** unseemly

indeed ❶ adv **1** really **2** in fact ▷ interj **3** denoting surprise, doubt etc.

indefatigable adj untiring

indefensible adj not justifiable

indefinite adj without exact limits

indelible adj that cannot be blotted out **indelibly** adv

indelicate adj coarse, embarrassing

indemnity n, pl **-ties 1** compensation **2** security against loss **indemnify** v give indemnity to

indent v **1** set in (from margin etc.) **2** notch **3** order by indent ▷ n **4** notch **5** requisition **indentation** n

independent ❶ adj **1** not subject

to others **2** self-reliant **3** free **4** valid in itself **independence** n **1** being independent **2** self-reliance **3** self-support

indescribable adj beyond description

indeterminate adj uncertain

index n, pl **indices 1** alphabetical list of references **2** indicator **3** (Maths) exponent **4** forefinger ▷ v **5** provide with, insert in index

indicate ❶ v **1** point out **2** state briefly **3** signify **indication** n **indicative** adj **1** pointing to **2** (Grammar) stating fact **indicator** n

indict ❶ v accuse, esp. by legal process **indictment** n

indifferent ❶ adj **1** uninterested **2** mediocre **indifference** n

indigenous adj native

indigent adj poor, needy

indigestion n (discomfort caused by) poor digestion

indigo n **1** blue dye obtained from plant **2** the plant ▷ adj **3** deep blue

— THESAURUS —

overwhelming; = **unbelievable**, unthinkable, improbable, inconceivable, preposterous

incur v = **sustain**, experience, suffer, gain, earn

indecent adj = **obscene**, lewd, dirty, inappropriate, rude ≠ **decent**; = **unbecoming**, unsuitable, vulgar, unseemly, undignified ≠ **proper**

indeed adv = **certainly**, yes, definitely, surely, truly

independent adj = **separate**,

unattached, uncontrolled, unconstrained ≠ **controlled**; = **self-sufficient**, free, liberated, self-contained, self-reliant

indicate v = **imply**, suggest, hint, intimate, signify; = **register**, show, record, read, express

indict v = **charge**, accuse, prosecute, summon, impeach

indifferent adj = **unconcerned**, detached, cold, cool, callous ≠ **concerned**; = **mediocre**, ordinary, moderate, so-so (Inf),

indirect ❶ *adj* **1** done, caused by someone or something else **2** not by straight route

indiscreet *adj* tactless in revealing secrets **indiscretion** *n*

indiscriminate *adj* **1** lacking discrimination **2** jumbled

indispensable ❶ *adj* essential

indisposed *adj* **1** unwell **2** disinclined

indisputable *adj* without doubt

indissoluble *adj* permanent

individual ❶ *adj* **1** single **2** distinctive ▷ *n* **3** single person or thing **individuality** *n* distinctive personality **individually** *adv* singly

indoctrinate *v* implant beliefs in the mind of

indolent *adj* lazy **indolence** *n*

indoor *adj* **1** within doors **2** under cover **indoors** *adv*

indubitable *adj* beyond doubt

induce ❶ *v* **1** persuade **2** bring on **inducement** *n* incentive

induct *v* install in office **induction** *n* **1** inducting **2** general inference

from particular inferences **3** production of electric or magnetic state by proximity

indulge ❶ *v* **1** gratify **2** pamper **indulgence** *n* **1** indulging **2** extravagance **3** favour, privilege **indulgent** *adj*

industry ❶ *n, pl* **-tries** **1** manufacture, processing etc. of goods **2** branch of this **3** diligence **industrial** *adj* of industries, trades **industrialize** *v* **industrious** *adj* diligent

inedible *adj* not eatable

ineffable *adj* unutterable

ineligible *adj* not fit or qualified (for something)

inept *adj* **1** absurd **2** out of place **3** clumsy **ineptitude** *n*

inert *adj* **1** without power of motion **2** sluggish **3** unreactive **inertia** *n* **1** inactivity **2** tendency to continue at rest or in uniform motion

inescapable *adj* unavoidable

inestimable *adj* immeasurable

inevitable ❶ *adj* **1** unavoidable

passable ≠ **excellent**

indirect *adj* = **related**, secondary, subsidiary, incidental, unintended; = **circuitous**, roundabout, curving, wandering, rambling ≠ **direct**

indispensable *adj* = **essential**, necessary, needed, key, vital ≠ **dispensable**

individual *adj* = **separate**, independent, isolated, lone, solitary ≠ **collective**; = **unique**, special, fresh, novel, exclusive ≠ **conventional** ▷ *n* = **person**, being, human, unit, character

induce *v* = **cause**, produce, create, effect, lead to ≠ **prevent**; = **persuade**, encourage, influence, convince, urge ≠ **dissuade**

indulge *v* = **gratify**, satisfy, feed, give way to, yield to; = **spoil**, pamper, cosset, humour, give in to

industry *n* = **business**, production, manufacturing, trade, commerce; = **trade**, world, business, service, line

inevitable *adj* = **unavoidable**, inescapable, inexorable, sure, certain ≠ **avoidable**

2 sure to happen **inevitability** *n*
inexorable *adj* relentless
inexplicable *adj* impossible to explain
infallible *adj* not liable to fail or err
infamous ❶ *adj* **1** notorious **2** shocking **infamy** *n*
infant ❶ *n* very young child **infancy** *n* **1** babyhood **2** early stage of development **infantile** *adj* childish
infantry *n* foot soldiers
infect ❶ *v* **1** affect (with disease) **2** contaminate **infection** *n* **infectious** *adj* catching
infer *v* **-ferring, -ferred** deduce, conclude **inference** *n*
inferior ❶ *adj* **1** of poor quality **2** lower ▷ *n* **3** one lower (in rank etc.) **inferiority** *n*
infernal *adj* **1** devilish **2** hellish **3** (*Inf*) irritating, confounded
inferno *n, pl* **-nos 1** intense, raging fire **2** hell
infertile *adj* barren, not productive
infest *v* inhabit or overrun in dangerously or unpleasantly large numbers
infidelity *n, pl* **-ties**

1 unfaithfulness **2** religious disbelief **infidel** *n* unbeliever
infiltrate ❶ *v* **1** trickle through **2** gain access surreptitiously
infinite ❶ *adj* boundless **infinitely** *adv* exceedingly **infinitesimal** *adj* extremely small **infinity** *n* unlimited extent
infinitive *n* form of verb without tense, person, or number
infirm *adj* physically or mentally weak **infirmary** *n* hospital, sick quarters **infirmity** *n, pl* **-ties**
inflame ❶ *v* **1** rouse to anger, excitement **2** cause inflammation in **inflammable** *adj* **1** easily set on fire **2** excitable **inflammation** *n* painful infected swelling **inflammatory** *adj*
inflate ❶ *v* **1** blow up with air, gas **2** swell **3** raise price, esp. artificially **inflatable** *adj* **inflation** *n* increase in prices and fall in value of money
inflection, inflexion *n* **1** modification of word **2** modulation of voice
inflexible *adj* **1** incapable of being bent **2** stubborn

━━━━━━━━━━━━━━ THESAURUS ━━━━━━━━━━━━━━

infamous *adj* = **notorious**, ignominious, disreputable, ill-famed ≠ **esteemed**
infant *n* = **baby**, child, babe, toddler, tot
infect *v* = **pollute**, poison, corrupt, contaminate, taint
inferior *adj* = **lower**, minor, secondary, subsidiary, lesser ≠ **superior** (*Aust Sl*) ▷ *n* = **underling**, junior, subordinate,

lesser, menial
infiltrate *v* = **penetrate**, pervade, permeate, percolate, filter through to
infinite *adj* = **limitless**, endless, unlimited, eternal, never-ending ≠ **finite**
inflame *v* = **enrage**, stimulate, provoke, excite, anger ≠ **calm**
inflate *v* = **blow up**, pump up, swell, dilate, distend ≠ **deflate**

inflict ❶ v impose, deliver forcibly
infliction n

influence ❶ n 1 power to affect
other people, events etc. 2 person,
thing possessing such power ▷ v
3 sway 4 induce 5 affect
influential adj

influenza n contagious viral
disease

influx ❶ n 1 flowing in 2 inflow

inform ❶ v give information
(about) **informant** n one who
tells **information** n what is told,
knowledge **informative** adj
informer n

informal ❶ adj 1 relaxed and
friendly 2 appropriate for everyday
use **informally** adv **informality**
n

infrared adj below visible
spectrum

infrastructure n basic structure
or fixed capital items of an
organization or economic system

infringe v transgress, break

infuriate ❶ v enrage

infuse v 1 soak to extract flavour
etc. 2 instil **infusion** n 1 infusing
2 extract obtained

ingenious ❶ adj 1 clever at
contriving 2 cleverly contrived
ingenuity n

ingenuous adj 1 frank
2 innocent

ingot n block of cast metal, esp.
gold

ingrained adj 1 deep-rooted
2 inveterate

ingratiate v get (oneself) into
favour

ingredient ❶ n component part
of a mixture

inhabit ❶ v -habiting, -habited
dwell in **inhabitant** n

inhale ❶ v breathe in (air etc.)
inhalation n **inhaler** n container
with medical preparation inhaled to
help breathing

inherent ❶ adj existing as an
inseparable part

i

THESAURUS

embroider, embellish
inflict v = **impose**, administer,
visit, apply, deliver
influence n = **control**, power,
authority, direction, command;
= **power**, authority, pull (Inf),
importance, prestige ▷ v = **affect**,
have an effect on, have an impact
on, control, concern
influx n = **arrival**, rush, invasion,
incursion, inundation
inform v = **tell**, advise, notify,
instruct, enlighten
informal adj = **natural**, relaxed,
casual, familiar, unofficial

infuriate v = **enrage**, anger,
provoke, irritate, incense
≠ **soothe**
ingenious adj = **creative**, original,
brilliant, clever, bright
≠ **unimaginative**
ingredient n = **component**, part,
element, feature, piece
inhabit v = **live in**, occupy,
populate, reside in, dwell in
inhale v = **breathe in**, gasp, draw
in, suck in, respire ≠ **exhale**
inherent adj = **intrinsic**, natural,
essential, native, fundamental
≠ **extraneous**

inherit ❶ v **-heriting, -herited**
1 receive, succeed as heir **2** derive
from parents **inheritance** n

inhibit ❶ v **-hibiting, -hibited**
1 restrain **2** hinder **inhibition** n
repression of emotion, instinct

inhospitable adj **1** unfriendly
2 harsh

inhuman adj **1** cruel, brutal **2** not
human

inhumane adj cruel, brutal
inhumanity n

inimical adj unfavourable, hostile

inimitable adj defying imitation

iniquity n, pl **-ties 1** gross
injustice **2** sin **iniquitous** adj

initial ❶ adj **1** of, occurring at
the beginning ▷ n **2** initial letter,
esp. of person's name ▷ v **3** mark,
sign with one's initials **initially**
adv

initiate ❶ v **1** originate **2** admit
into closed society **3** instruct
initiation n **initiative** n **1** lead
2 ability to act independently

inject ❶ v **1** put (fluid, medicine
etc.) into body with syringe

2 introduce (new element)
injection n

injunction ❶ n (judicial) order

injustice ❶ n **1** want of justice
2 wrong **3** unjust act

ink n **1** fluid used for writing or
printing ▷ v **2** mark, cover with ink
inky adj

inkling n hint, vague idea

inland ❶ adj/adv **1** in, towards the
interior **2** away from the sea

inlay v **1** embed **2** decorate with
inset pattern ▷ n **3** inlaid piece or
pattern

inlet n **1** entrance **2** mouth of
creek **3** piece inserted

inmate n occupant, esp. of prison,
hospital, etc.

inmost adj most inward, deepest

inn n **1** public house providing food
and accommodation **2** hotel
innkeeper n

innards pl n (Inf) internal parts,
esp. of body

innate adj **1** inborn **2** inherent

inner ❶ adj lying within
innermost adj

inherit v = **be left**, come
into, be willed, succeed to, fall heir
to

inhibit v = **hinder**, check, frustrate,
curb, restrain ≠ **further**

initial adj = **opening**, first, earliest,
beginning, primary ≠ **final**

initiate v = **begin**, start, open,
launch, kick off (Inf); = **introduce**,
admit, enlist, enrol, launch ▷ n
= **novice**, member, pupil, convert,
amateur

inject v = **vaccinate**, administer,

inoculate; = **introduce**, bring in,
insert, instil, infuse

injunction n = **order**, ruling,
command, instruction,
mandate

injustice n = **unfairness**,
discrimination, prejudice, bias,
inequality ≠ **justice**

inland adj = **interior**, internal,
upcountry

inner adj = **inside**, internal, interior,
inward ≠ **outer**; = **central**, middle,
internal, interior, personal

innings n (Sport) **1** player's or side's turn of batting **2** turn

innocent ❶ adj **1** guiltless **2** without experience of evil ▷ n **3** innocent person **innocence** n

innocuous adj harmless

innuendo n, pl **-does** indirect accusation

innumerable adj countless

inoculate v immunize by injecting vaccine **inoculation** n

inoperable adj (Med) not able to be operated on **inoperative** adj not operative

inordinate adj excessive

inorganic adj **1** not organic **2** not containing carbon

input n material, data, current etc. fed into a system

inquest ❶ n **1** coroner's inquiry into cause of death **2** detailed inquiry

inquire, enquire ❶ v seek information **inquirer, enquirer** n **inquiry, enquiry** n **1** question **2** investigation

inquisition n **1** searching investigation (Hist) **2** (with cap.) tribunal for suppression of heresy

inquisitor n

inquisitive adj **1** curious **2** prying

insane ❶ adj **1** mentally deranged **2** crazy **insanely** adv **1** madly **2** excessively **insanity** n

insatiable adj incapable of being satisfied

inscribe v write, engrave (in or on something) **inscription** n words inscribed

inscrutable adj **1** enigmatic **2** incomprehensible

insect n small, usu. winged animal with six legs **insecticide** n preparation for killing insects

insecure ❶ adj **1** not safe or firm **2** anxious

insensible adj **1** unconscious **2** without feeling **3** not aware **insensibly** adv imperceptibly

insensitive adj unaware of other people's feelings

insert ❶ v **1** put into or between ▷ n **2** something inserted **insertion** n

inset n something extra inserted **inset** v

inshore adv/adj near shore

innocent adj = **not guilty**, in the clear, blameless, clean, honest ≠ **guilty**; = **naive**, open, trusting, simple, childlike ≠ **worldly**; = **harmless**, innocuous, inoffensive, well-meant, unobjectionable

inquest n = **inquiry**, investigation, probe, inquisition

inquire, enquire v = **ask**, question, query, quiz

insane adj = **mad**, crazy, mentally ill, crazed, demented ≠ **sane**; = **stupid**, foolish, daft (Inf), irresponsible, irrational ≠ **reasonable**

insecure worried, anxious, afraid ▷ adj = **unsafe**, exposed, vulnerable, wide-open, unprotected ≠ **safe**

insert v = **put**, place, position, slip, slide

inside ❶ n **1** inner part ▷ pl **2** (Inf) stomach, entrails ▷ adj/adv/prep **3** in, on, into the inside

insidious adj unseen but deadly

insight ❶ n discernment

insignia pl n, pl **-nias, -nia** badges, emblems

insignificant ❶ adj not important **insignificance** n

insincere adj pretending what one does not feel **insincerity** n, pl **-ties**

insinuate v **1** hint **2** introduce subtly **insinuation** n

insipid adj dull, tasteless

insist ❶ v **1** demand persistently **2** maintain **3** emphasize **insistence** n **insistent** adj

insole n inner sole of shoe or boot

insolent adj impudent **insolence** n

insoluble adj **1** incapable of being solved **2** incapable of being dissolved

insolvent adj unable to pay one's debts **insolvency** n

insomnia n inability to sleep **insomniac** adj/n

inspect ❶ v examine (closely or officially) **inspection** n **inspector** n

inspire ❶ v **1** arouse creatively **2** give rise to **inspiration** n **1** good idea **2** creative influence

install ❶ v **1** place in position **2** formally place (person) in position or rank **installation** n **1** act of installing **2** equipment installed

instalment ❶ n **1** part payment **2** one of a series of parts

instance ❶ n **1** example ▷ v **2** cite

instant ❶ n **1** moment ▷ adj **2** immediate **3** (of foods) requiring little preparation **instantaneous** adj happening in an instant **instantly** adv at once

inside n = **interior**, contents, core, nucleus ▷ adj = **inner**, internal, interior, inward ≠ **outside**; = **confidential**, private, secret, internal, exclusive ▷ adv = **indoors**, in, within, under cover

insight n = **understanding**, perception, sense, knowledge, vision

insignificant adj = **unimportant**, minor, irrelevant, petty, trivial ≠ **important**

insist v = **demand**, order, require, command, dictate; = **assert**, state, maintain, claim, declare

inspect v = **examine**, check, look at, view, survey

inspire stimulate ▷ v = **give rise to**, produce, result in, engender

install v = **set up**, put in, place, position, station; = **institute**, establish, introduce, invest, ordain

instalment n = **payment**, repayment, part payment

instance n = **example**, case, occurrence, occasion, sample ▷ v = **name**, mention, identify, point out, advance

instant n = **moment**, second, flash, split second, jiffy (Inf); = **time**, point, hour, moment, stage ▷ adj = **immediate**, prompt,

instead *adv* in place (of)

instep *n* top of foot between toes and ankle

instigate *v* incite, urge **instigation** *n* **instigator** *n*

instil *v* **-stilling, -stilled** implant

instinct *n* 1 inborn impulse 2 unconscious skill **instinctive**

institute *v* 1 establish 2 set going ▷ *n* 3 society for promoting science etc. **institution** *n* 1 setting up 2 establishment for care or education 3 established custom, law etc. **institutional** *adj* 1 of institutions 2 routine

instruct *v* 1 teach 2 inform 3 order **instruction** *n* 1 teaching, order ▷ *pl* 2 directions **instructive** *adj* informative **instructor** *n*

instrument *n* 1 thing used to make, do, measure etc. 2 mechanism for producing musical sound **instrumental** *adj* 1 acting as instrument or means 2 produced by musical instruments

insubordinate *adj* mutinous, rebellious **insubordination**

insufferable *adj* unbearable

insular *adj* 1 of an island 2 narrow-minded

insulate *v* 1 prevent or reduce transfer of electricity, heat, sound etc. 2 isolate, detach **insulation** *n* **insulator** *n*

insulin *n* hormone used in treatment of diabetes

insult *v* 1 behave rudely to 2 offend ▷ *n* 3 affront **insulting** *adj*

insuperable *adj* not able to be overcome

insurance *n* agreement to pay compensation if damage, loss or death occurs

intact *adj* 1 untouched 2 uninjured

intake *n* 1 thing, amount taken in 2 opening

integer *n* whole number

integral *adj* essential **integrate** *v* combine into one whole **integration** *n*

instantaneous, direct, quick; = **ready-made**, fast, convenience, ready-mixed, ready-cooked

instead *adv* = **rather**, alternatively, preferably, in preference, in lieu

instinct *n* = **talent**, skill, gift, capacity, bent

institute *v* = **establish**, start, found, launch, set up ≠ **end**

instruct *v* = **order**, tell, direct, charge, bid; = **teach**, school, train, coach, educate

instrument *n* = **tool**, device, implement, mechanism, appliance; = **agent**, means, medium, agency, vehicle (*SI*)

insulate *v* = **isolate**, protect, screen, defend, shelter

insult *v* = **offend**, abuse, wound, slight, put down ≠ **praise** ▷ *n* = **jibe**, slight, put-down, abuse, snub

intact *adj* = **undamaged**, whole, complete, sound, perfect ≠ **damaged**

integral *adj* = **essential**, basic, fundamental, necessary, component ≠ **inessential**

integrity ⓘ n honesty
intellect ⓘ n power of thinking
and reasoning **intellectual** adj
1 of, appealing to intellect 2 having
good intellect ▷ n 3 intellectual
person
intelligent ⓘ adj clever
intelligence n 1 intellect
2 information, esp. military
intelligent design theory that a
sentient being designed and
created the universe and all life
intelligible adj understandable
intemperate adj 1 drinking
alcohol to excess 2 immoderate
intend ⓘ v propose, mean
intense ⓘ adj 1 very strong or
acute 2 emotional **intensify** v
-fying, -fied increase **intensity** n
intensive adj
intent ⓘ n 1 purpose ▷ adj
2 concentrating (on) 3 resolved
intention n purpose, aim
intentional adj
inter ⓘ v **-terring, -terred** bury
interment n

inter- comb. form between, among,
mutually, as in interglacial,
interrelation
interact v act on each other
interaction n **interactive** adj
intercede v plead in favour of,
mediate **intercession** n
intercept ⓘ v 1 cut off 2 seize,
stop in transit **interception** n
interchange v 1 (cause to)
exchange places ▷ n 2 motorway
junction **interchangeable** adj
able to be exchanged in position or
use
intercom n internal
communication system
intercontinental adj
1 connecting continents 2 (of
missile) able to reach one continent
from another
intercourse ⓘ n 1 act of having
sex 2 communications or dealings
between individuals or groups
interest ⓘ n 1 concern, curiosity
2 thing exciting this 3 sum paid for
borrowed money 4 advantage

————————— THESAURUS —————————

integrity n = **honesty**, principle,
honour, virtue, goodness
≠ **dishonesty**; = **unity**, unification,
cohesion, coherence, wholeness
intellect n = **intelligence**, mind,
reason, understanding, sense
intelligent adj = **clever**, bright,
smart, sharp, enlightened ≠ **stupid**
intend v = **plan**, mean, aim,
propose, purpose
intense adj = **extreme**, great,
severe, fierce, deep ≠ **mild**;
= **fierce**, tough
intent adj = **absorbed**, intense,

fascinated, preoccupied, enthralled
≠ **indifferent** ▷ n = **intention**,
aim, purpose, meaning, end
≠ **chance**
inter v = **bury**, lay to rest, entomb,
consign to the grave
intercept v = **catch**, stop, block,
seize, cut off
intercourse n = **sexual
intercourse**, sex (Inf), copulation,
coitus, carnal knowledge;
= **contact**, communication,
commerce, dealings
interest n often plural = **hobby**,

5 right, share ▷ *v* **6** excite, cause to feel interest **interested** *adj* **interesting** *adj*
interface ⓘ *adj* area, surface, boundary linking two systems
interfere ⓘ *v* **1** meddle, intervene **2** clash **interference** *n* **1** act of interfering **2** *(Radio)* atmospherics
interim ⓘ *n* **1** meantime ▷ *adj* **2** temporary
interior ⓘ *adj* **1** inner **2** inland **3** indoors ▷ *n* **4** inside **5** inland region
interject *v* interpose (remark etc.) **interjection** *n* **1** exclamation **2** interjected remark
interlock *v* lock together firmly
interloper *n* intruder
interlude *n* **1** interval **2** something filling an interval
intermarry *v* **1** (of families, races, religions) become linked by marriage **2** marry within one's family **intermarriage** *n*
intermediate ⓘ *adj* **1** coming between **2** interposed

intermediary *n*
interminable *adj* endless
intermission *n* interval
intermittent *adj* occurring at intervals
intern *v* confine to special area or camp **internment** *n*
internal ⓘ *adj* **1** inward **2** interior **3** within (a country, organization)
international ⓘ *adj* **1** of relations between nations ▷ *n* **2** game or match between teams of different countries
internecine *adj* **1** mutually destructive **2** deadly
interplanetary *adj* of, linking planets
interplay *n* action and reaction of things upon each other
interpolate *v* **1** insert new matter **2** interject
interpose *v* **1** insert **2** say as interruption
interpret ⓘ *v* **1** explain **2** translate, esp. orally **3** represent **interpretation** *n* **interpreter** *n*

— THESAURUS —

activity, pursuit, entertainment, recreation; *often plural*
= advantage, good, benefit, profit; **= stake**, investment ▷ *v* **= arouse your curiosity**, fascinate, attract, grip, entertain ≠ **bore**
interface *n* **= connection**, link, boundary, border, frontier
interfere *v* **= meddle**, intervene, intrude, butt in, tamper
interim *adj* **= temporary**, provisional, makeshift, acting, caretaker
interior *n* **= inside**, centre, heart,

middle, depths ▷ *adj* **= inside**, internal, inner ≠ **exterior**; **= mental**, emotional, psychological, private, personal
intermediate *adj* **= middle**, mid, halfway, in-between *(Inf)*, midway
internal *adj* **= domestic**, home, national, local, civic; **= inner**, inside, interior ≠ **external**
international *adj* **= global**, world, worldwide, universal, cosmopolitan
interpret *v* **= take**, understand, explain, construe; **= translate**,

interrogate v question, esp. closely or officially **interrogation** n **interrogative** n word used in asking question **interrogator** n

interrupt ❶ v 1 break in (upon) 2 stop 3 block **interruption** n

intersect v 1 divide by passing across or through 2 meet and cross **intersection** n

interstellar adj between stars

interstice n slit, crevice

intertwine v twist together

interval ❶ n 1 intervening time or space 2 pause, break 3 difference (of pitch)

intervene ❶ v 1 come into a situation in order to change it 2 be, come between or among 3 occur in the meantime 4 interpose **intervention** n

interview ❶ n 1 meeting, esp. one involving questioning ▷ v 2 have interview with **interviewee** n **interviewer** n

intestate adj not having made a will

intestine n (usu. pl) lower part of alimentary canal between stomach and anus **intestinal** adj

intimate¹ ❶ adj 1 closely acquainted, familiar 2 private 3 having cosy atmosphere ▷ n 4 intimate friend **intimacy** n

intimate² ❶ v 1 announce 2 imply in indirect way **intimation** n

intimidate ❶ v frighten into submission **intimidation** n

into prep 1 expresses motion to a point within 2 indicates change of state 3 indicates coming up against, encountering 4 indicates arithmetical division

intolerable adj more than can be endured

intolerant adj narrow-minded

intone v chant **intonation** n accent

intoxicate v make drunk

intractable adj difficult

intransigent adj uncompromising

───── THESAURUS ─────

transliterate; **= explain**, make sense of, decode, decipher, elucidate

interrupt v **= intrude**, disturb, intervene, interfere (with), break in; **= suspend**, stop, end, delay, cease

interval spell, space ▷ n **= break**, interlude, intermission, rest, gap; **= delay**, gap, hold-up, stoppage

intervene v **= step in** (Inf), interfere, mediate, intrude, intercede; **= interrupt**, involve yourself

interview v **= examine**, talk to

intimate¹ adj **= close**, dear, loving, near, familiar ≠ **distant**; **= private**,

personal, confidential, special, individual ≠ **public**; **= detailed**, minute, full, deep, particular; **= cosy**, relaxed, friendly, informal, harmonious ▷ n **= friend**, close friend, crony, confidant or confidante, (constant) companion ≠ **stranger**

intimate² v **= suggest**, indicate, hint, imply, insinuate; **= announce**, state, declare, communicate, make known

intimidate v **= frighten**, pressure, threaten, scare, bully

intravenous *adj* into a vein
intrepid *adj* fearless, undaunted
intricate ❶ *adj* complex
 intricacy *n, pl* **-cies**
intrigue ❶ *n* **1** underhand plot
 2 secret love affair ▷ *v* **3** carry on
 intrigue **4** interest, puzzle
intrinsic *adj* inherent, essential
introduce ❶ *v* **1** make
 acquainted **2** present **3** bring in
 4 insert **introduction** *n*
 1 introducing **2** preliminary part of
 book etc. **introductory** *adj*
 preliminary
introvert *n* (Psychiatry) one who
 looks inward **introverted** *adj*
intrude *v* thrust (oneself) in
 intruder *n* **intrusion** *n*
 intrusive *adj*
intuition ❶ *n* spontaneous
 insight **intuitive** *adj*

Inuit *n* indigenous inhabitant of North
 America or Greenland
Inuk *n* a member of any Inuit people
Inuktitut *n* (Canad) the language
 of the Inuit
inundate *v* **1** flood **2** overwhelm
 inundation *n*
inured *adj* hardened
invade ❶ *v* **1** enter by force
 2 overrun **invader** *n* **invasion** *n*
invalid¹ ❶ *n* **1** one suffering from
 ill health ▷ *v* **2** retire because of
 illness etc.
invalid² ❶ *adj* having no legal force
 invalidate *v*
invaluable ❶ *adj* priceless
invasion ❶ see INVADE
invective *n* bitter verbal attack
inveigle *v* entice
invent ❶ *v* **1** devise, originate
 2 fabricate **invention** *n* **1** that

— THESAURUS —

intricate *adj* = **complicated**,
 involved, complex, fancy, elaborate
 ≠ **simple**
intrigue *n* = **plot**, scheme,
 conspiracy, manoeuvre, collusion;
 = **affair**, romance, intimacy, liaison,
 amour ▷ *v* = **interest**, fascinate,
 attract, rivet, titillate; = **plot**,
 scheme, manoeuvre, conspire,
 connive
introduce *v* = **bring in**, establish,
 set up, start, found; = **present**,
 acquaint, make known, familiarize,
 air; = **add**, insert, inject, throw in
 (Inf), infuse
intuition *n* = **instinct**, perception,
 insight, sixth sense
invade *v* = **attack**, storm, assault,
 capture, occupy; = **infest**, swarm,

 overrun, ravage, beset
invalid¹ *n* = **patient**, sufferer,
 convalescent, valetudinarian ▷ *adj*
 = **disabled**, ill, sick, ailing, frail
invalid² *adj* = **null and void**, void,
 worthless, inoperative ≠ **valid**;
 = **unfounded**, false, illogical,
 irrational, unsound ≠ **sound**
invaluable *adj* = **precious**,
 valuable, priceless, inestimable,
 worth your *or* its weight in gold
 ≠ **worthless**
invasion *n* = **attack**, assault,
 capture, takeover, raid;
 = **intrusion**, breach, violation,
 disturbance, disruption
invent *v* = **create**, make, produce,
 design, discover; = **make up**,
 devise, concoct, forge, fake

which is invented **2** ability to invent
inventive adj **1** resourceful
2 creative **inventor** n
inventory ⊕ n, pl **-tories**
detailed list
invert v **1** turn upside down
2 reverse **inverse** adj **1** inverted
2 opposite **inversion** n
invertebrate n/adj (animal)
without backbone
invest ⊕ v **1** lay out (money, time,
effort etc.) for profit or advantage
2 install **3** endow **investiture** n
formal installation in office or rank
investment n **1** investing
2 money invested **3** stocks and
shares bought **investor** n
investigate ⊕ v **1** inquire into
2 examine **investigation** n
investigative adj **investigator** n
inveterate adj **1** deep-rooted
2 confirmed
invidious adj likely to cause ill will
invigilate v supervise
examination candidates
invigilator n
invigorate v give vigour to
invincible adj unconquerable
inviolable adj not to be violated
inviolate adj not violated
invisible ⊕ adj not able to be seen

invite ⊕ v **1** request the company
of **2** ask courteously **3** ask for
4 attract, call forth **invitation** n
invoice n **1** list of goods or services
sold, with prices ▷ v **2** make,
present an invoice
invoke ⊕ v **1** call on **2** appeal to
3 ask earnestly for **4** summon
invocation n
involuntary adj **1** unintentional
2 instinctive
involve ⊕ v **1** include **2** entail
3 implicate (person) **4** concern
5 entangle **involved** adj
1 complicated **2** concerned (in)
inward adj **1** internal **2** situated
within **3** mental ▷ adv **4** (also
inwards) towards the inside **5** into
the mind **inwardly** adv **1** in the
mind **2** internally
iodine n nonmetallic element
found in seaweed
ion n electrically charged atom
IOU n signed paper acknowledging
debt
IP address (Comp) internet
protocol address: unique code that
identifies each computer connected
to the internet
IQ intelligence quotient
ire n anger **irascible** adj hot-tempered

——————— THESAURUS ———————

inventory n = **list**, record,
catalogue, listing, account
invest v = **spend**, expend, advance,
venture, put in; = **empower**,
provide, charge, sanction, license
investigate v = **examine**, study,
research, go into, explore
invisible adj = **unseen**,
imperceptible, indiscernible,

unseeable ≠ **visible**
invite v = **request**, look for, bid for,
appeal for; = **encourage**, attract,
cause, court, ask for (Inf)
invoke v = **apply**, use, implement,
initiate, resort to; = **call upon**,
appeal to, pray to, petition, beseech
involve v = **entail**, mean, require,
occasion, imply

irate *adj* angry

iridescent *adj* exhibiting changing colours

iris *n* **1** circular membrane of eye containing pupil **2** plant with sword-shaped leaves and showy flowers

irk *v* irritate, vex **irksome** *adj* tiresome

iron ❶ *n* **1** common metallic element **2** tool etc. of this metal **3** appliance used to smooth cloth **4** metal-headed golf club ▷ *pl* **5** fetters ▷ *adj* **6** of, like, iron **7** unyielding **8** robust ▷ *v* **9** press **ironmonger** *n* dealer in hardware

irony ❶ *n, pl* **-nies 1** use of words to mean the opposite of what is said **2** event, situation opposite of that expected **ironic, ironical** *adj* of, using, irony

irradiate *v* **1** treat with light or beams of particles **2** shine upon **irradiation** *n*

irrational ❶ *adj* not based on logic

irregular ❶ *adj* **1** not regular or even **2** unconventional **irregularity** *n, pl* **-ties**

irrelevant ❶ *adj* not connected with the matter in hand **irrelevance** *n*

irreparable *adj* not able to be repaired or remedied

irresistible ❶ *adj* **1** too strong to resist **2** enchanting, seductive

irrevocable *adj* not able to be changed

irrigate *v* water by artificial channels, pipes etc. **irrigation** *n*

irritate ❶ *v* **1** annoy **2** inflame **irritable** *adj* easily annoyed **irritant** *adj/n* (person or thing) causing irritation **irritation** *n*

is third person sing. of BE

Islam *n* Muslim faith or world **Islamic** *adj*

island ❶ *n* **1** piece of land surrounded by water **2** anything like this **islander** *n* inhabitant of island

isle *n* island **islet** *n* little island

THESAURUS

iron *adj* = **ferrous**, ferric; = **inflexible**, hard, strong, tough, rigid ≠ **weak**

irony *n* = **sarcasm**, mockery, ridicule, satire, cynicism; = **paradox**, incongruity

irrational *adj* = **illogical**, crazy, absurd, unreasonable, preposterous ≠ **rational**

irregular *adj* = **variable**, erratic, occasional, random, casual ≠ **steady**; = **uneven**, rough, ragged, crooked, jagged ≠ **even**; = **inappropriate**, unconventional, unethical, unusual, extraordinary

irrelevant *adj* = **unconnected**, unrelated, unimportant, inappropriate, peripheral ≠ **relevant**

irresistible *adj* = **overwhelming**, compelling, overpowering, urgent, compulsive

irritate *v* = **annoy**, anger, bother, needle (*Inf*), infuriate ≠ **placate**; = **inflame**, pain, rub, scratch, scrape

island *n* = **isle**, atoll, islet, ait *or* eyot (*dialect*), cay *or* key

isobar *n* line on map connecting places of equal mean barometric pressure

isolate ❶ *v* place apart or alone **isolation** *n*

isomer *n* substance with same molecules as another but different atomic arrangement

isometric *adj* **1** having equal dimensions **2** relating to muscular contraction without movement **isometrics** *pl n* system of isometric exercises

isotope *n* atom having different atomic weight from other atoms of same element

issue ❶ *n* **1** topic of discussion or dispute **2** edition of newspaper etc. **3** offspring **4** outcome ▷ *v* **5** go out **6** result in **7** arise (from)

8 give, send out **9** publish

isthmus *n, pl* **-muses** neck of land between two seas

it *pron* neuter pronoun of the third person **its** *adj* belonging to it **it's** it is **itself** *pron* emphatic form of IT

italic *adj* (of type) sloping **italics** *pl n* this type, used for emphasis etc. **italicize** *v* put in italics

itch ❶ *v/n* (feel) irritation in the skin **itchy** *adj*

item ❶ *n* **1** single thing **2** piece of information **3** entry **itemize** *v*

itinerant *adj* travelling from place to place **itinerary** *n* **1** plan of journey **2** route

ivory *n* hard white substance of the tusks of elephants etc.

ivy *n, pl* **ivies** climbing evergreen plant

───────── THESAURUS ─────────

isolate *v* = **separate**, break up, cut off, detach, split up

issue *n* = **topic**, point, matter, problem, question; = **point**, question, bone of contention; = **edition**, printing, copy, publication, number; = **children**, offspring, babies, kids (*Inf*), heirs ≠ **parent** ▷ *v* = **give out**, release,

publish, announce, deliver

itch *v* = **prickle**, tickle, tingle; = **long**, ache, crave, pine, hunger ▷ *n* = **irritation**, tingling, prickling, itchiness; = **desire**, longing, craving, passion, yen (*Inf*)

item *n* = **article**, thing, object, piece, unit; = **matter**, point, issue, case, question

jab ⊕ *v* **jabbing, jabbed 1** poke roughly **2** thrust, stab ▷ *n* **3** poke **4** (*Inf*) injection
jabber *v* **1** chatter **2** talk incoherently
jack *n* **1** device for lifting heavy weight, esp. motorcar **2** lowest court card **3** (*Bowls*) ball aimed at **4** socket and plug connection in electronic equipment **5** small flag, esp. national, at sea ▷ *v* **6** (usu. with *up*) lift with a jack
jackal *n* doglike scavenging animal of Asia and Africa
jackass *n* **1** male ass **2** blockhead
jackboot *n* large military boot
jackdaw *n* small kind of crow
jacket ⊕ *n* **1** outer garment, short coat **2** outer casing, cover

jackknife *n* **1** clasp knife ▷ *v* **2** angle sharply, esp. the parts of an articulated lorry
jackpot ⊕ *n* large prize, accumulated stake, as pool in poker
Jacuzzi® *n* bath with device that swirls water
jade *n* **1** ornamental semiprecious stone, usu. dark green **2** this colour ▷ *adj* **3** of this colour
jaded *adj* **1** tired **2** off colour
jaguar *n* large S Amer. cat
jail ⊕ *n* **1** building for confinement of criminals or suspects ▷ *v* **2** send to, confine in prison **jailer** *n*
jam ⊕ *v* **jamming, jammed 1** pack together **2** (cause to) stick and become unworkable **3** (*Radio*) block (another station) ▷ *n* **4** fruit preserved by boiling with sugar **5** crush **6** hold-up of traffic **7** awkward situation
jamb *n* side post of door, fireplace etc.
jamboree *n* large gathering or rally of Scouts
Jan. January
jangle *v* **1** (cause to) sound harshly, as bell **2** (of nerves) be irritated
janitor *n* caretaker
January *n* first month

j

jab *v* = **poke**, dig, punch, thrust, tap ▷ *n* = **poke**, dig, punch, thrust, tap
jacket *n* = **covering**, casing, case, cover, skin
jackpot *n* = **prize**, winnings, award, reward, bonanza
jail *n* = **prison**, penitentiary (*US*), confinement, dungeon, nick (*Brit Sl*)

▷ *v* = **imprison**, confine, detain, lock up, put away
jam *n* = **predicament**, tight spot, situation, trouble, hole (*Sl*) ▷ *v* = **pack**, force, press, stuff, squeeze; = **crowd**, throng, crush, mass, surge; = **congest**, block, clog, stick, stall

jar¹ ❶ *n* **1** round vessel of glass, earthenware etc. **2** (*Inf*) glass of esp. beer

jar² ❶ *v* **jarring, jarred 1** grate, jolt **2** have distressing effect on ▷ *n* **3** jarring sound **4** shock etc.

jargon ❶ *n* **1** special vocabulary for particular subject **2** pretentious language

jasmine *n* shrub with sweet-smelling flowers

jaundice *n* disease marked by yellowness of skin **jaundiced** *adj* prejudiced, bitter etc.

jaunt *n/v* (make) short pleasure excursion

jaunty *adj* **-tier, -tiest 1** sprightly **2** brisk

javelin *n* spear, esp. for throwing in sporting events

jaw ❶ *n* **1** one of bones in which teeth are set ▷ *pl* **2** mouth **3** gripping part of vice etc.

jay *n* noisy bird of brilliant plumage

jazz *n* **1** syncopated music and dance ▷ *v* **2** (with *up*) make more lively **jazzy** *adj* flashy, showy

jealous ❶ *adj* **1** envious

2 suspiciously watchful **jealousy** *n, pl* **-sies**

jeans *pl n* casual trousers, esp. of denim

Jeep® *n* light four-wheel-drive motor vehicle

jeer ❶ *v/n* scoff, taunt

jell *v* **1** congeal **2** (*Inf*) assume definite form

jelly *n, pl* **-lies 1** sweet, preserve etc. becoming softly stiff as it cools **2** anything of similar consistency **jellyfish** *n* small jelly-like sea animal

jemmy *n, pl* **-mies** short steel crowbar

jeopardy ❶ *n* danger **jeopardize** *v* endanger

jerk ❶ *n* **1** sharp push or pull **2** (*Sl*) stupid person ▷ *v* **3** move or throw with a jerk **jerky** *adj* **1** uneven **2** spasmodic

jerkin *n* sleeveless jacket

jersey *n* **1** knitted jumper **2** machine-knitted fabric

jest *n/v* joke **jester** *n* **1** joker **2** (*Hist*) professional fool at court

jet¹ ❶ *n* **1** aircraft driven by jet

THESAURUS

---

jar¹ *n* = **pot**, container, drum, vase, jug

jar² *v usually with* **on** = **irritate**, annoy, offend, nettle, irk; = **jolt**, rock, shake, bump, rattle

jargon *n* = **parlance**, idiom, usage, argot

jaw *v* (*Inf*) = **talk**, chat, gossip, chatter, spout

jealous *adj* = **suspicious**, protective, wary, doubtful, sceptical ≠ **trusting**; = **envious**,

grudging, resentful, green, green with envy ≠ **satisfied**

jeer *v* = **mock**, deride, heckle, barrack, ridicule ≠ **cheer** ▷ *n* = **mockery**, abuse, ridicule, taunt, boo ≠ **applause**

jeopardy *n* = **danger**, risk, peril, vulnerability, insecurity

jerk *v* = **jolt**, bang, bump, lurch ▷ *n* = **lurch**, movement, thrust, twitch, jolt

jet¹ *n* = **stream**, current, spring,

propulsion **2** stream of liquid, gas etc. **3** spout, nozzle ▷ *v* **4** throw out **5** shoot forth **jet lag** fatigue caused by crossing time zones in aircraft **jet propulsion** propulsion by jet of gas or liquid **jet-propelled** *adj*

jet² *n* hard black mineral **jet-black** *adj* glossy black

jetsam *n* goods thrown overboard **jettison** *v* **1** abandon **2** throw overboard

jetty *n, pl* **-ties** small pier, wharf

Jew *n* one of Hebrew religion or ancestry **Jewish** *adj*

jewel ❶ *n* **1** precious stone **2** ornament containing one **3** precious thing **jeweller** *n* dealer in jewels **jewellery** *n*

jib *n* **jibbing, jibbed 1** triangular sail set forward of mast **2** arm of crane ▷ *v* **3** (of horse, person) stop and refuse to go on

jibe see GIBE

jig *n* **1** lively dance **2** music for it **3** guide for cutting etc. ▷ *v* **4** dance jig **5** make jerky up-and-down movements **jigsaw** *n* machine fret saw **jigsaw puzzle** picture cut into pieces, which the user tries to fit together again

jilt *v* reject (lover)

jingle *n* **1** light metallic noise **2** catchy rhythmic verse, song etc.

▷ *v* **3** (cause to) make jingling sound

jingoism *n* aggressive nationalism

jinks *pl n* **high jinks** boisterous merrymaking

jinx *n* **1** force, person, thing bringing bad luck ▷ *v* **2** cause bad luck

jitters *pl n* worried nervousness, anxiety **jittery** *adj* nervous

jive *n* **1** (dance performed to) popular music, esp. of 1950s ▷ *v* **2** do this dance

job ❶ *n* **1** piece of work, task **2** post **3** (*Inf*) difficult task **jobbing** *adj* doing single, particular jobs for payment **jobless** *adj/pl n* unemployed (people)

jockey *n* **1** rider in horse races ▷ *v* **2** manoeuvre

jockstrap *n* belt with pouch to support genitals

jocular *adj* **1** joking **2** given to joking **jocularity** *n*

jodhpurs *pl n* tight-legged riding breeches

jog ❶ *v* **jogging, jogged 1** run slowly, trot, esp. for exercise **2** nudge **3** stimulate ▷ *v* **4** jogging **jogger** *n* **jogging** *n*

Johnny Canuck *n* (*Canad*) **1** an informal name for a Canadian **2** a personification of Canada

join ❶ *v* **1** fasten, unite **2** become

THESAURUS

flow, rush ▷ *v* = **fly**, wing, cruise, soar, zoom

jewel *n* = **gemstone**, gem, ornament, sparkler (*Inf*), rock (*Sl*); = **treasure**, wonder, darling, pearl, gem

job *n* = **task**, duty, work, venture, enterprise

jog *v* = **run**, trot, canter, lope; = **nudge**, push, shake, prod, stir

join *v* = **enrol in**, enter, sign up for, enlist in; = **connect**, unite, couple,

a member (of) **3** become connected **4** (with *up*) enlist **5** take part (in) ▷ *n* **6** (place of) joining **joiner** *n* maker of finished woodwork **joinery** *n* joiner's work

joint ❶ *n* **1** arrangement by which two things fit together **2** place of this **3** meat for roasting, oft. with bone **4** (*Sl*) disreputable bar or nightclub **5** (*Sl*) marijuana cigarette **6** shared ▷ *v* **7** connect by joints **8** divide at the joints **jointly** *adv* **out of joint** **1** dislocated **2** disorganized

joist *n* beam supporting floor or ceiling

joke ❶ *n* **1** thing said or done to cause laughter **2** ridiculous thing ▷ *v* **3** make jokes **joker** *n* **1** one who jokes **2** (*Sl*) fellow **3** extra card in pack **jokey** *adj*

jolly ❶ *adj* **-lier, -liest 1** jovial **2** merry ▷ *v* **3** make person, occasion happier **jollification** *n* **jollity** *n*

jolt ❶ *n/v* **1** jerk **2** jar **3** shock

joss stick incense stick

jostle *v* knock or push

jot *n* **jotting, jotted 1** small amount ▷ *v* **2** note **jotter** *n* notebook

joual *n* nonstandard Canadian French dialect, esp. as associated with ill-educated speakers

joule *n* (*Electricity*) unit of work or energy

journal ❶ *n* **1** newspaper or other periodical **2** daily record **journalism** *n* editing, writing in periodicals **journalist** *n*

journey ❶ *n* **1** going to a place, excursion **2** distance travelled ▷ *v* **3** travel

journeyman *n* qualified craftsman

jovial *adj* convivial, merry **joviality** *n*

joy ❶ *n* **1** gladness, pleasure, delight **2** cause of this **joyful** *adj* **joyous** *adj* extremely happy **joy ride** trip, esp. in stolen car **joystick** *n* **1** control column of aircraft **2** control device for video game

—————————— THESAURUS ——————————

link, combine ≠ **detach**

joint *adj* = **shared**, mutual, collective, communal, united ▷ *n* = **junction**, connection, brace, bracket, hinge

joke *n* = **jest**, gag (*Inf*), wisecrack (*Inf*), witticism, crack (*Inf*); = **laugh**, jest, jape, trick, practical joke ▷ *v* = **jest**, kid (*Inf*), mock, tease, taunt

jolly *adj* = **happy**, cheerful, merry, upbeat (*Inf*), playful ≠ **miserable**

jolt *v* = **jerk**, push, shake, knock, jar; = **surprise**, stun, disturb, stagger,

startle ▷ *n* = **jerk**, start, jump, shake, bump; = **surprise**, blow, shock, setback, bombshell

journal *n* = **magazine**, publication, gazette, periodical; = **newspaper**, paper, daily, weekly, monthly

journey *n* = **trip**, drive, tour, flight, excursion ▷ *v* = **travel**, go, move, tour, progress

joy *n* = **delight**, pleasure, satisfaction, ecstasy, enjoyment ≠ **sorrow**

JP Justice of the Peace

jubilant *adj* exultant **jubilation** *n*

jubilee ❶ *n* time of rejoicing, esp. 25th or 50th anniversary

judder *v* 1 shake, vibrate ▷ *n* 2 vibration

judge ❶ *n* 1 officer appointed to try cases in law courts 2 one who decides in a dispute, contest etc. 3 one able to form a reliable opinion ▷ *v* 4 act as judge (of, for) **judgment, judgement** *n* 1 faculty of judging 2 sentence of court 3 opinion **judgmental, judgemental** *adj*

judicial ❶ *adj* of, by a court or judge **judiciary** *n* judges collectively **judicious** *adj* well-judged, sensible

judo *n* modern sport derived from jujitsu

jug ❶ *n* 1 vessel for liquids, with handle and small spout 2 its contents

juggernaut *n* 1 large heavy lorry 2 irresistible, destructive force

juggle ❶ *v* 1 keep several objects in the air simultaneously 2 manipulate to deceive **juggler** *n*

juice ❶ *n* 1 liquid part of vegetable, fruit or meat 2 *(Inf)* electric current 3 *(Inf)* petrol **juicy** *adj* 1 succulent 2 interesting

jujitsu *n* Japanese art of wrestling and self-defence

jukebox *n* automatic, coin-operated record player

July *n* seventh month

jumble ❶ *v* 1 mix in confused heap ▷ *n* 2 confused heap or state **jumble sale** sale of miscellaneous, usu. second-hand, items

jumbo ❶ *n* *(Inf)* 1 elephant 2 anything very large

jump ❶ *v* 1 (cause to) spring, leap (over) 2 move hastily 3 pass or skip (over) 4 rise steeply 5 start (with astonishment etc.) ▷ *n* 6 act of jumping 7 obstacle to be jumped 8 distance, height jumped 9 sudden rise **jumper** *n* sweater, pullover **jumpy** *adj* nervous

jubilee *n* = **celebration**, holiday, festival, festivity

judge *n* = **magistrate**, justice, beak *(Brit Sl)*, His, Her or Your Honour; = **referee**, expert, specialist, umpire, mediator; = **critic**, assessor, arbiter ▷ *v* = **adjudicate**, referee, umpire, mediate, officiate; = **evaluate**, rate, consider, view, value

judicial *adj* = **legal**, official

jug *n* = **container**, pitcher, urn, carafe, creamer *(US & Canad)*

juggle *v* = **manipulate**, change,

alter, modify, manoeuvre

juice *n* = **liquid**, extract, fluid, liquor, sap

jumble *n* = **muddle**, mixture, mess, disorder, confusion ▷ *v* = **mix**, mistake, confuse, disorder, shuffle

jumbo *adj* = **giant**, large, huge, immense, gigantic ≠ **tiny**

jump *v* = **leap**, spring, bound, bounce, hop; = **recoil**, start, jolt, flinch, shake; = **increase**, rise, climb, escalate, advance; = **miss**, avoid, skip, omit, evade ▷ *n* = **leap**,

junction n **1** place where routes meet **2** point of connection

juncture n state of affairs

June n sixth month

jungle n **1** equatorial forest **2** tangled mass **3** condition of intense competition

junior ❶ adj **1** younger **2** of lower standing ▷ n **3** junior person

juniper n evergreen shrub

junk ❶ n useless objects **junkie** n (Sl) drug addict **junk food** food of low nutritional value **junk mail** unsolicited mail

junket n **1** flavoured curdled milk **2** excursion

junta n group holding power in country

jurisdiction ❶ n **1** authority **2** territory covered by it

jury n, pl **-ries 1** body of persons sworn to render verdict in court of law **2** judges of competition **juror** n

just ❶ adj **1** fair **2** upright, honest **3** right, equitable ▷ adv **4** exactly **5** barely **6** at this instant **7** merely **8** really **justice** n **1** moral or legal fairness **2** judge, magistrate **justice of the peace** person who can act as judge in local court **justify** v **1** prove right **2** vindicate **justifiable** adj **justification** n

jut v **jutting, jutted** project, stick out, protrude

jute n plant fibre used for rope, canvas etc.

juvenile ❶ adj **1** of, for young children **2** immature ▷ n **3** young person, child

juxtapose v put side by side **juxtaposition** n

— THESAURUS —

spring, skip, bound, hop; **= rise**, increase, upswing, advance, upsurge

junior adj **= minor**, lower, secondary, lesser, subordinate

junk n **= rubbish**, refuse, waste, scrap, litter

jurisdiction n **= authority**, power, control, rule, influence; **= range**, area, field, bounds, province

just adv **= recently**, lately, only now; **= merely**, only, simply, solely; **= barely**, hardly, by a whisker, by the skin of your teeth ▷ adj **= fair**, good, legitimate, upright, honest ≠ **unfair**; **= fitting**, due, correct, deserved, appropriate ≠ **inappropriate**

juvenile n **= child**, youth, minor, girl, boy ≠ **adult** ▷ adj **= immature**, childish, infantile, puerile, young

Kabloona *n* a person who is not of Inuit ancestry, esp. a White person

kaftan *n* woman's long, loose dress with sleeves

kak *n* (*S Afr, Sl*) **1** faeces **2** rubbish

kaleidoscope *n* **1** optical toy producing changing patterns **2** any complex pattern **kaleidoscopic** *adj*

kamik *n* (*Canad*) a traditional Inuit boot made of caribou hide or sealskin

kamikaze *n* **1** Japanese suicide pilot ▷ *adj* **2** (of action) certain to kill or injure the doer

kangaroo *n/pl* **-roos** Aust. marsupial with strong hind legs for jumping

karate *n* Japanese system of unarmed combat

karma *n* person's actions affecting fate for next incarnation

kayak *n* **1** Inuit canoe **2** any similar canoe

kebab *n* **1** dish of small pieces of meat, tomatoes etc. grilled on skewers **2** grilled minced lamb served in split slice of unleavened bread

kedgeree *n* dish of fish cooked with rice, eggs etc.

keel *n* lowest longitudinal support on which ship is built **keel over** **1** turn upside down **2** (*Inf*) collapse suddenly

keen ❶ *adj* **1** sharp **2** acute **3** eager **4** shrewd **5** (of price) competitive

keep ❶ *v* **keeping, kept 1** retain possession of, not lose **2** hold **3** (cause to) remain **4** maintain **5** remain good **6** continue ▷ *n* **7** maintenance **8** central tower of castle **keeper** *n* **keeping** *n* **1** harmony **2** care, charge **keepsake** *n* gift treasured for sake of the giver

keg *n* **1** small barrel **2** container for beer

kelp *n* large seaweed

k

THESAURUS

keen *adj* = **eager**, intense, enthusiastic, passionate, ardent ≠ **unenthusiastic**; = **sharp**, incisive, cutting, edged, razor-like ≠ **dull**; = **perceptive**, quick, sharp, acute, smart ≠ **obtuse**; = **intense**, strong, fierce, relentless, cut-throat

keep *v usually with* **from** = **prevent**, restrain, hinder, keep back; = **hold on to**, maintain, retain, save, preserve ≠ **lose**; = **store**, put, place, house, hold; = **carry**, stock, sell, supply, handle; = **support**, maintain, sustain, provide for, mind ▷ *n* = **board**, food, maintenance, living, hold

k

ken n **kenning, kenned** range of knowledge
kennel n shelter for dog
kerb n stone edging to footpath
kernel n 1 inner seed of nut or fruit stone 2 central, essential part
kerosene n (US & Canad) another name for PARAFFIN
kestrel n small falcon
ketchup n sauce of vinegar, tomatoes etc.
kettle n metal vessel with spout and handle, esp. for boiling water
  kettledrum n musical instrument made of membrane stretched over copper hemisphere
key ❶ n 1 instrument for operating lock, winding clock etc. 2 explanation, means of achieving an end etc. 3 (Mus) set of related notes 4 operating lever of typewriter, piano, organ etc. ▷ adj 5 most important **keyboard** n set of keys on piano, computer etc. **keyhole** n opening for key **keynote** n dominant idea
kg kilogram
khaki adj 1 dull, yellowish-brown ▷ n 2 khaki cloth 3 military uniform
kibbutz n/pl **kibbutzim** communal agricultural settlement in Israel

kick ❶ v 1 strike (out) with foot 2 recoil 3 resist 4 (Inf) free oneself of (habit etc.) ▷ n 5 blow with foot 6 thrill 7 strength (of flavour, alcoholic drink etc.) 8 recoil **kick off** start (a game of football) **kick out** dismiss or expel forcibly
kid ❶ n 1 young goat 2 leather of its skin 3 (Inf) child ▷ v 4 (Inf) tease, deceive 5 behave, speak in fun
kidnap ❶ v -napping, -napped seize and hold to ransom **kidnapper** n
kidney n 1 either of the pair of organs which secrete urine 2 animal kidney used as food
kill ❶ v 1 deprive of life 2 put an end to 3 pass (time) ▷ n 4 act of killing 5 animals etc. killed **killer** n **killing** adj 1 (Inf) very tiring 2 very funny
kiln furnace, oven
kilo n short for KILOGRAM
kilo- comb. form one thousand, as in kilometre, kilowatt
kilogram, kilogramme n 1000 grams
kilohertz n 1000 cycles per second
kilt n pleated tartan skirt worn orig. by Scottish Highlanders

———————————— THESAURUS ————————————

key n = **opener**, door key, latchkey ▷ adj = **essential**, leading, major, main, important ≠ **minor**
kick v = **boot**, knock, punt; (Inf) = **give up**, break, stop, abandon, quit ▷ n (Inf) = **thrill**, buzz (Sl), tingle, high (Sl)
kid n (Inf) = **child**, baby, teenager, youngster, infant, ankle-biter (Aust Sl) ▷ v (Inf) = **tease**, joke, trick, fool, pretend
kidnap v = **abduct**, capture, seize, snatch (Sl), hijack
kill v = **slay**, murder, execute, slaughter, destroy; (Inf) = **destroy**, crush, scotch, stop, halt

kimono *n, pl* **-nos** loose Japanese robe

kin, kinsfolk *n* relatives **kindred** *n* **1** relatives ▷ *adj* **2** similar **3** related **kinsman** *n*

kind ❶ *n* **1** sort, type, class ▷ *adj* **2** considerate **3** gentle **kindly** *adj* **-lier, -liest** **1** kind, genial ▷ *adv* **2** gently **kindness** *n* **kind-hearted** *adj*

kindergarten *n* class, school for children of about four to six years old

kindle *v* **1** set alight **2** arouse **3** catch fire **kindling** *n* small wood to kindle fires

kindy, kindie *n/pl* **-dies** (*Aust & NZ, Inf*) kindergarten

kinetic *adj* relating to motion

king ❶ *n* **1** male ruler **2** chess piece **3** highest court card **4** (*Draughts*) crowned piece **kingdom** *n* **1** state ruled by king **2** realm **3** sphere **kingpin** *n* (*Inf*) chief thing or person **king-size** *adj* (*Inf*) very large

kingfisher *n* small brightly-coloured bird

kink *n* **1** tight twist in rope, wire, hair etc. ▷ *v* **2** make, become kinked **kinky** *adj* **1** full of kinks **2** (*Inf*) deviant

kiosk *n* **1** small, sometimes movable booth **2** public telephone box

kip *n/v* **kipping, kipped** (*Inf*) sleep

kipper *n* smoked herring

kirk *n* in Scotland, church

kismet *n* fate, destiny

kiss ❶ *n* **1** touch or caress with lips **2** light touch ▷ *v* **3** touch with lips **kiss of life** mouth-to-mouth resuscitation

kist *n* (*S Afr*) large wooden chest

kit ❶ *n* **1** outfit, equipment **2** personal effects, esp. of traveller **3** set of pieces of equipment sold ready to be assembled ▷ *v* **4** (with *out*) provide with kit **kitbag** *n* bag for soldier's or traveller's kit

kitchen *n* room used for cooking

kite *n* **1** light papered frame flown in wind **2** large hawk

kitsch *n* vulgarized, pretentious art

kitten *n* young cat **kittenish** *adj* playful

kitty *n/pl* **-ties** **1** in some card games, pool **2** communal fund

kiwi *n* **1** NZ flightless bird **2** (*Inf*) New Zealander **kiwi fruit** edible fruit with green flesh

klaxon *n* loud horn

kleptomania *n* compulsion to steal **kleptomaniac** *n*

kloof *n* (*S Afr*) mountain pass or gorge

km kilometre

knack ❶ *n* **1** acquired facility or dexterity **2** trick **3** habit

k

kind *n* = **class**, sort, type, variety, brand

king *n* = **ruler**, monarch, sovereign, leader, lord

kiss *v* = **peck** (*Inf*), osculate, neck

(*Inf*) ▷ *n* = **peck** (*Inf*), snog, smacker (*Sl*), French kiss, osculation

kit *n* = **equipment**, materials, tackle, tools, apparatus

knack *n* = **skill**, art, ability, facility,

knacker n buyer of worn-out horses etc. for killing **knackered** adj (Sl) exhausted

knapsack n haversack

knave n 1 jack at cards 2 (Obs) rogue **knavish** adj

knead v 1 work into dough 2 massage

knee n joint between thigh and lower leg **kneecap** n bone in front of knee **kneejerk** adj (of reaction) automatic and predictable **knees-up** n (Inf) party

kneel ⊕ v **kneeling, kneeled** fall, rest on knees

knell n/v (ring) death bell

knickers ⊕ pl n woman's undergarment for lower half of body

knick-knack n trinket

knife ⊕ n, pl **knives** 1 cutting blade, esp. one in handle, used as implement or weapon ▷ v 2 cut or stab with knife

knight n 1 man of rank below baronet 2 member of medieval order of chivalry 3 piece in chess ▷ v 4 confer knighthood on **knighthood** n

knit ⊕ v **knitting, knitted** 1 form (garment etc.) by linking loops of yarn 2 draw together 3 unite **knitter** n **knitting** n 1 knitted work 2 act of knitting

knob n rounded lump **knobbly** adj

knock ⊕ v 1 strike, hit 2 (Inf) disparage 3 rap audibly 4 (of engine) make metallic noise ▷ n 5 blow, rap **knocker** n appliance for knocking on door **knock back** 1 (Inf) drink quickly 2 reject **knock-kneed** adj having incurved legs **knock out** 1 render unconscious 2 (Inf) overwhelm, amaze **knockout** n

knoll n small hill

knot ⊕ n 1 fastening of strands by looping and pulling tight 2 cluster 3 hard lump, esp. in timber 4 nautical miles per hour ▷ v 5 tie with knot, in knots **knotty** adj 1 full of knots 2 puzzling, difficult

know ⊕ v **knowing, knew, known** 1 be aware (of), have information (about) 2 be acquainted with 3 understand 4 feel certain **knowing** adj

───── THESAURUS

talent ≠ **ineptitude**
kneel v = **genuflect**, stoop
knickers pl, n = **underwear**, smalls, briefs, drawers, panties
knife n = **blade**, carver, cutter ▷ v = **cut**, wound, stab, slash, thrust
knit v = **join**, unite, link, tie, bond; = **furrow**, tighten, knot, wrinkle, crease
knock v = **bang**, strike, tap, rap, thump; = **hit**, strike, punch, belt (Inf), smack; (Inf) = **criticize**,

condemn, put down, run down, abuse ▷ n = **knocking**, pounding, beating, tap, bang; = **bang**, blow, impact, jar, collision
knot n = **connection**, tie, bond, joint, loop ▷ v = **tie**, secure, bind, loop, tether
know v = **have knowledge of**, see, understand, recognize, perceive; = **be acquainted with**, recognize, be familiar with, be friends with, be friendly with ≠ **be unfamiliar with**

shrewd **knowingly** *adv*
1 shrewdly **2** deliberately
knowledge *n* **1** knowing **2** what
one knows **3** learning
knowledgable, knowledgeable
adj well-informed
knuckle *n* bone at finger joint
knuckle down get down (to work)
knuckle-duster *n* metal appliance
on knuckles to add force to blow
knuckle under submit
KO knockout
koala *n* marsupial Aust. animal,
native bear

kohl *n* cosmetic powder
Koran *n* sacred book of Muslims
kosher *adj* **1** conforming to Jewish
dietary law **2** *(Inf)* legitimate,
authentic
kowtow *v* **1** prostrate oneself
2 be obsequious
krypton *n* rare atmospheric gas
kudos *n* **1** fame **2** credit
kugel [koog]-el *n* *(S Afr)* rich,
fashion-conscious, materialistic
young woman
kung fu *n* Chinese martial art

k

I litre

lab *n* (*Inf*) short for LABORATORY

label ❶ *n* **1** slip of paper, metal etc., giving information **2** descriptive phrase ▷ *v* **3** give label

laboratory *n, pl* **-ries** place for scientific investigations or for manufacture of chemicals

labour *n* **1** exertion of body or mind **2** workers collectively

labrador *n* breed of large, smooth-coated retriever dog

laburnum *n* tree with yellow hanging flowers

labyrinth *n* **1** maze **2** perplexity

lace ❶ *n* **1** patterned openwork fabric **2** cord, usu. one of pair, to draw edges together ▷ *v* **3** fasten with laces **4** flavour with spirit

lacy *adj* fine, like lace

lacerate *v* tear, mangle

lachrymose *adj* tearful

lack ❶ *n* **1** deficiency ▷ *v* **2** need, be short of

lackadaisical *adj* languid

lackey *n* **1** servile follower **2** footman

lacklustre *adj* lacking brilliance or vitality

laconic *adj* terse

lacquer *n* **1** hard varnish ▷ *v* **2** coat with this

lacrosse *n* ball game played with long-handled racket

lad ❶ *n* boy, young fellow

ladder *n* **1** frame with rungs, for climbing **2** line of torn stitches, esp. in stockings

laden ❶ *adj* heavily loaded

ladle *n* **1** spoon with long handle and large bowl ▷ *v* **2** serve out liquid with a ladle

lady ❶ *n, pl* **-dies 1** female counterpart of gentleman **2** polite term for a woman **3** title of some women of rank **ladybird** *n* small

━━━━━━━━━━━━━━ THESAURUS ━━━━━━━━━━━━

label *n* = **tag**, ticket, tab, marker, sticker ▷ *v* = **tag**, mark, stamp, ticket, tab

lace *n* = **netting**, net, filigree, meshwork, openwork; = **cord**, tie, string, lacing, shoelace ▷ *v* = **fasten**, tie, tie up, do up, secure; = **mix**, drug, doctor, add to, spike; = **intertwine**, interweave, entwine, twine, interlink

lack *n* = **shortage**, want, absence, deficiency, need ≠ **abundance** ▷ *v* = **miss**, want, need, require, not have ≠ **have**

lad *n* = **boy**, kid (*Inf*), guy (*Inf*), youth, fellow

laden *adj* = **loaded**, burdened, full, charged, weighed down

lady *n* = **gentlewoman**, duchess, noble, dame, baroness; = **woman**,

beetle, usu. red with black spots
ladylike *adj* gracious
lag¹ ❶ *v* go too slowly, fall behind
laggard *n* one who lags
lag² ❶ *v* wrap boiler, pipes etc. with insulating material **lagging** *n* this material
lag³ ❶ *n* (Sl) convict
lager *n* light-bodied beer
lagoon *n* saltwater lake, enclosed by atoll or sandbank
laid see LAY² **laid-back** *adj* (Inf) relaxed
lair *n* den of animal
laird *n* Scottish landowner
laissez-faire *n* principle of nonintervention
laity *n* people not belonging to clergy
lake ❶ *n* expanse of inland water
lama *n* Buddhist priest in Tibet or Mongolia
lamb *n* 1 young of the sheep 2 its meat 3 innocent or helpless creature ▷ *v* 4 give birth to lamb
lambast, lambaste *v* 1 beat, thrash 2 reprimand severely
lame ❶ *adj* 1 crippled in leg 2 limping 3 unconvincing ▷ *v* 4 cripple
lamé *n/adj* (fabric) interwoven with gold or silver thread

lament ❶ *v* 1 express sorrow (for) ▷ *n* 2 expression of grief 3 song of grief **lamentable** *adj* deplorable, disappointing **lamentation** *n*
laminate *v* 1 make (sheet of material) by bonding together two or more thin sheets 2 cover with thin sheet ▷ *n* 3 laminated sheet **lamination** *n*
lamington *n* (Aust & NZ) sponge cake coated with a sweet frosting
lamp *n* appliance (esp. electrical) that produces, light, heat etc. **lamppost** *n* post supporting lamp in street
lampoon *n/v* (make subject of) a satire
lamprey *n* fish like an eel
lance *n* 1 horseman's spear ▷ *v* 2 pierce with lance or lancet **lancet** *n* pointed two-edged surgical knife **lance corporal** lowest noncommissioned army rank
land ❶ *n* 1 solid part of earth's surface 2 ground 3 country 4 estate ▷ *v* 5 come to land 6 disembark 7 arrive on ground 8 bring to land 9 (Inf) obtain 10 catch 11 (Inf) strike **landed** *adj*

female, girl, damsel
lag¹ *v* = **hang back**, delay, trail, linger, loiter
lake *n* = **pond**, pool, reservoir, loch (Scot), lagoon
lame *adj* = **disabled**, handicapped, crippled, limping, hobbling; = **unconvincing**, poor, pathetic, inadequate, thin

lament *v* = **bemoan**, grieve, mourn, weep over, complain about ▷ *n* = **complaint**, moan, wailing, lamentation; = **dirge**, requiem, elegy, threnody
land *n* = **ground**, earth, dry land, terra firma; = **soil**, ground, earth, clay, dirt; = **countryside**, farmland; (Law) = **property**, grounds, estate,

possessing, consisting of lands
landing n **1** act of landing
2 platform between flights of stairs
landlocked adj completely
surrounded by land **landlord** n
1 person who lets land or houses
etc. **2** master or mistress of inn,
boarding house etc. **landlubber** n
person ignorant of the sea and
ships **landmark** n **1** conspicuous
object **2** event, decision etc.
considered as important stage in
development of something
landscape n **1** piece of inland
scenery **2** picture of this ▷ v
3 create, arrange garden, park etc.
landslide n **1** falling of soil, rock
etc. down mountainside
2 overwhelming election victory
lane ❶ n **1** narrow road or street
2 specified air, sea route **3** area of
road for one stream of traffic
language ❶ n **1** system of
sounds, symbols etc. for
communicating thought **2** style of
speech or expression
languish ❶ v **1** be or become
weak or faint **2** droop, pine

languid adj lacking energy,
spiritless **languor** n **1** lack of
energy **2** tender mood
languorous adj
lank adj **1** lean **2** limp **lanky** adj
lantern n transparent case for
lamp or candle
lap[1] ❶ n **1** the part between waist
and knees of a person when sitting
2 single circuit of track **3** stage or
part of journey ▷ v **4** enfold, wrap
round **5** overtake opponent to be
one or more circuits ahead
lap[2] ❶ v **1** drink by scooping up
with tongue **2** (of waves etc.) beat
softly
lapel n part of front of coat folded
back towards shoulders
lapwing n type of plover
larceny n, pl **-nies** theft
larch n deciduous conifer tree
lard n **1** prepared pig's fat ▷ v
2 insert strips of bacon in (meat)
3 intersperse
larder n storeroom for food
large ❶ adj **1** great in size, number
etc. ▷ adv **2** in a big way **largely**
adv **largesse** n **1** generosity

─────── THESAURUS ───────

real estate, realty; **= country**,
nation, region, state, district ▷ v
= arrive, dock, put down, moor,
alight; (Inf) **= gain**, get, win, secure,
acquire
lane n **= road**, street, track, path,
way
language n **= tongue**, dialect,
vernacular, patois; **= speech**,
communication, expression,
speaking, talk
languish v **= decline**, fade away,

wither away, flag, weaken
≠ flourish; (Lit) **= waste away**,
suffer, rot, be abandoned, be
neglected **≠ thrive**; often with **for**
= pine, long, desire, hunger, yearn
lap[1] n **= circuit**, tour, leg, stretch,
circle
lap[2] v **= ripple**, wash, splash, swish,
gurgle; **= drink**, sip, lick, swallow,
gulp
large adj **= big**, great, huge, heavy,
massive **≠ small**; **= massive**, great,

2 gift **at large 1** free **2** in general
large-scale *adj* wide-ranging, extensive

largo *adv/n, pl* **-gos** *(Mus)* (passage played) in slow and dignified manner

lariat *n (US & Canad)* another word for LASSO

lark¹ *n* **1** small, brown singing bird **2** skylark

lark² *n* **1** frolic, spree ▷ *v* **2** indulge in lark

larrikin *n (Aust or NZ, Old-fashioned Sl)* mischievous or unruly person

larva *n, pl* **-vae** immature insect **larval** *adj*

larynx *n, pl* **larynges** part of throat containing vocal cords **laryngitis** *n* inflammation of this

lasagne, lasagna *n* pasta formed in wide, flat sheets

lascivious *adj* lustful

laser *n* device for concentrating electromagnetic radiation in an intense, narrow beam

lash¹ 🟊 *n* **1** stroke with whip **2** flexible part of whip **3** eyelash
▷ *v* **4** strike with whip etc. **5** dash against **6** attack verbally, ridicule **7** flick, wave sharply to and fro **8** (with *out*) hit, kick

lash² 🟊 *v* fasten or bind tightly

lashings *pl n (Inf)* abundance

lass, lassie *n* girl

lassitude *n* weariness

lasso *n, pl* **-sos, -soes 1** rope with noose for catching cattle etc. ▷ *v* **2** catch with this

last¹ 🟊 *adj/adv* **1** after all others **2** most recent(ly) ▷ *adj* **3** only remaining ▷ *n* **4** last person or thing **lastly** *adv* finally **last-ditch** *adj* done as final resort **last straw** small irritation that, coming after others, is too much to bear **last word 1** final comment in argument **2** most recent or best example

last² 🟊 *v* continue, hold out

latch 🟊 *n* **1** fastening for door ▷ *v* **2** fasten with latch **3** (with *onto*) become attached to

late 🟊 *adj* **1** coming after the appointed time **2** recent **3** recently dead ▷ *adv* **4** after

big, huge, vast ≠ **small** = **plentiful**, comprehensive, lavish, bountiful, profuse

lash¹ *v* = **pound**, beat, strike, hammer, drum; = **censure**, attack, blast, put down, criticize; = **whip**, beat, thrash, birch, flog ▷ *n* = **blow**, hit, strike, stroke, stripe

lash² *v* = **fasten**, tie, secure, bind, strap

last¹ *adj* = **most recent**, latest, previous; = **hindmost**, final, at the end, remotest, furthest behind

≠ **foremost**

last² *v* = **continue**, remain, survive, carry on, endure ≠ **end**

latch *n* = **fastening**, catch, bar, lock, hook ▷ *v* = **fasten**, bar, secure, bolt, make fast

late *adj* = **overdue**, delayed, last-minute, belated, tardy ≠ **early**; = **dead**, deceased, departed, passed on, former ≠ **alive**; = **recent**, new, advanced, fresh ≠ **old** ▷ *adv* = **behind time**, belatedly, tardily, behindhand, dilatorily ≠ **early**

proper time **5** recently **6** at, till late hour **lately** *adv* not long since

latent *adj* **1** existing but not developed **2** hidden

lateral *adj* of, at, from the side

latex *n* sap or fluid of plants, esp. of rubber tree

lath *n* thin strip of wood

lathe *n* machine for turning and shaping

lather *n* **1** soapy froth **2** frothy sweat ▷ *v* **3** make frothy

Latin *n* **1** language of ancient Romans ▷ *adj* **2** of ancient Romans or their language

latitude ❶ *n* **1** angular distance in degrees N or S of equator **2** scope ▷ *pl* **3** regions

latrine *n* in army etc., lavatory

latter ❶ *adj* **1** second of two **2** later **3** more recent **latterly** *adv* **latter-day** *adj* modern

lattice *n* **1** network of strips of wood, metal etc. **2** window so made

laud *v* praise **laudable** *adj* praiseworthy

laudanum *n* sedative from opium

laugh ❶ *v/n* (make) sound of amusement, merriment or scorn **laughable** *adj* ludicrous **laughter** *n* **laughing stock** object of general derision

launch[1] ❶ *v* **1** set afloat **2** set in motion **3** begin **4** propel (missile, spacecraft) into space

launch[2] *n* large power-driven boat

laureate *adj* crowned with laurels **poet laureate** poet with appointment to Royal Household

laurel *n* **1** glossy-leaved shrub, bay tree ▷ *pl* **2** its leaves, emblem of victory or merit

lava *n* molten matter thrown out by volcano

lavatory ❶ *n, pl* **-ries** toilet, water closet

lavender *n* **1** shrub with fragrant, pale-lilac flowers **2** this colour

lavish ❶ *adj* **1** plentiful, rich **2** very generous ▷ *v* **3** spend, bestow, profusely

law ❶ *n* **1** rule binding on community **2** system of such rules

THESAURUS

latitude *n* = **scope**, liberty, freedom, play, space

latter *adj* = **last**, ending, closing, final, concluding ≠ **earlier**

laugh *v* = **chuckle**, giggle, snigger, cackle, chortle ▷ *n* = **chortle**, giggle, chuckle, snigger, guffaw; (*Inf*) = **joke**, scream (*Inf*), hoot (*Inf*), lark, prank; (*Inf*) = **clown**, character (*Inf*), scream (*Inf*), entertainer, card (*Inf*)

launch[1] *v* = **propel**, fire, dispatch, discharge, project; = **begin**, start,

open, initiate, introduce

lavatory *n* = **toilet**, bathroom, loo (*Brit Inf*), privy, cloakroom (*Brit*)

lavish *adj* = **grand**, magnificent, splendid, abundant, copious ≠ **stingy**; = **extravagant**, wild, excessive, exaggerated, wasteful ≠ **thrifty**; = **generous**, free, liberal, bountiful, open-handed ≠ **stingy** ▷ *v* = **shower**, pour, heap, deluge, dissipate ≠ **stint**

law *n* = **constitution**, code, legislation, charter; = **statute**, act,

3 legal science **4** general principle deduced from facts **lawful** adj allowed by law **lawless** adj **1** ignoring laws **2** violent **lawyer** n professional expert in law **lawsuit** n prosecution of claim in court

lawn n tended turf in garden etc.

lawyer 🄓 see LAW

lax adj **1** not strict **2** slack **laxative** adj/n (substance) having loosening effect on bowels **laxity, laxness** n

lay[1] 🄓 v **laying, laid 1** deposit, set, cause to lie **2** devise (plan) **3** attribute (blame) **4** place (bet) **5** (of animal) produce eggs **layer** n **1** single thickness as stratum or coating ▷ v **2** form layer **lay-by** n stopping place for traffic beside road **lay off** v dismiss staff during slack period **lay-off** n the act of suspending employees **layout** n arrangement

lay[2] 🄓 adj not clerical or professional **layman** n ordinary person

lay 🄓 [3] past tense of LIE **layabout** n lazy person, loafer

layette n clothes for newborn child

lazy 🄓 adj **lazier, laziest** averse to work **laze** v be lazy **lazily** adv

lbw (Cricket) leg before wicket

lead[1] 🄓 v **leading, led 1** guide, conduct **2** persuade **3** direct **4** be, go, play first **5** spend (one's life) **6** result **7** give access to ▷ n **8** that which leads or is used to lead **9** example **10** front or principal place, role etc. **11** cable bringing current to electrical instrument **leader** n **1** one who leads **2** editorial article in newspaper **leadership** n

lead[2] 🄓 n **1** soft, heavy grey metal **2** graphite in pencil **3** plummet **leaded** adj (of windows) made from small panes held together by lead strips **leaden** adj **1** sluggish **2** dull grey **3** made from lead

---

THESAURUS

---

bill, rule, order; **= principle**, code, canon, precept, axiom

lawyer n **= legal adviser**, attorney, solicitor, counsel, advocate

lay[1] v **= place**, put, set, spread, plant; **= devise**, plan, design, prepare, work out; **= produce**, bear, deposit; **= arrange**, prepare, make, organize, position; **= attribute**, assign, allocate, allot, ascribe; **= put forward**, offer, present, advance, lodge; **= bet**, stake, venture, gamble, chance

lay[2] adj **= nonclerical**, secular, non-ordained; **= nonspecialist**, amateur, unqualified, untrained, inexpert

lazy adj **= idle**, inactive, indolent, slack, negligent ≠ **industrious**; **= lethargic**, languorous, slow-moving, languid, sleepy ≠ **quick**

lead v **= go in front (of)**, head, be in front, be at the head (of), walk in front (of); **= guide**, conduct, steer, escort, precede; **= connect to**, link, open onto; **= be ahead (of)**, be first, exceed, be winning, excel; **= command**, rule, govern, preside over, head; **= live**, have, spend,

leaf ❶ *n, pl* **leaves 1** organ of photosynthesis in plants, consisting of a flat, usu. green blade on stem **2** two pages of book etc. **3** thin sheet ▷ *v* **4** turn through (pages etc.) cursorily **leaflet** *n* **1** small leaf **2** single printed and folded sheet, handbill **leafy** *adj*

league¹ ❶ *n* **1** agreement for mutual help **2** parties to it **3** federation of clubs etc. **4** (*Inf*) class, level

league² ❶ *n* former measure of distance, about 3 miles

leak ❶ *n* **1** defect that allows escape or entrance of liquid, gas, radiation etc. **2** disclosure **3** let fluid etc. in or out **4** (of fluid etc.) find its way through leak

5 (allow to) become known little by little **leakage** *n* **1** leaking **2** gradual escape or loss **leaky** *adj*

lean¹ ❶ *v* **leaning, leaned 1** rest against **2** incline **3** tend (towards) **4** rely (on) **leaning** *n* tendency **lean-to** *n* room, shed built against existing wall

lean² ❶ *adj* **1** lacking fat **2** thin **3** meagre ▷ *n* **4** lean part of meat

leap ❶ *v* **leaping, leapt 1** spring, jump **2** spring over ▷ *n* **3** jump **leapfrog** *n/v* vault over person bending down **leap year** year with extra day

learn ❶ *v* **learning, learned 1** gain skill, knowledge **2** memorize **3** find out **learned** *adj* showing much learning **learner** *n* **learning**

THESAURUS

experience, pass ▷ *n* = **first place**, winning position, primary position/ vanguard; = **advantage**, start, edge, margin, winning margin; = **example**, direction, leadership, guidance, model; = **clue**, suggestion, hint, indication, pointer; = **leading role**, principal, protagonist, title role, principal part ▷ *adj* = **main**, prime, top, leading, first

leaf *n* = **frond**, blade, cotyledon; = **page**, sheet, folio

league *n* = **association**, union, alliance, coalition, group; (*Inf*) = **class**, group, level, category, conspiring with

leak *v* = **escape**, pass, spill, release, drip; = **disclose**, tell, reveal, pass on, give away ▷ *n* = **leakage**, discharge, drip, seepage,

percolation; = **hole**, opening, crack, puncture, aperture; = **disclosure**, exposé, exposure, admission, revelation

lean¹ *v* = **bend**, tip, slope, incline, tilt; = **rest**, prop, be supported, recline, repose; = **tend**, prefer, favour, incline, be prone to

lean² *adj* = **thin**, slim, slender, skinny, angular ≠ **fat**

leap *v* = **jump**, spring, bound, bounce, hop ▷ *n* = **jump**, spring, bound, vault; = **rise**, change, increase, soaring, surge

learn *v* = **master**, grasp, pick up, take in, familiarize yourself with; = **discover**, hear, understand, find out about, become aware; = **memorize**, commit to memory, learn by heart, learn by rote, learn parrot-fashion *n* knowledge got by study

lease ① *n* **1** contract by which land or property is rented ▷ *v* **2** let, rent by lease **leasehold** *adj* held on lease

leash *n* lead for dog

least *adj* **1** smallest: superlative of LITTLE *n* **2** smallest one ▷ *adv* **3** in smallest degree

leather *n* prepared skin of animal **leathery** *adj* like leather, tough

leave¹ ① *v* **leaving, left 1** go away **2** allow to remain **3** entrust **4** bequeath

leave² ① *n* **1** permission, esp. to be absent from duty **2** period of such absence **3** formal parting

leaven *n* **1** yeast ▷ *v* **2** raise with leaven

lecherous *adj* **1** full of lust **2** lascivious **lecher** *n* lecherous man **lechery** *n*

lectern *n* reading desk

lecture ① *n* **1** instructive discourse **2** speech of reproof ▷ *v* **3** deliver discourse **4** reprove

lecturer *n*

ledge *n* **1** narrow shelf sticking out from wall, cliff etc. **2** ridge below surface of sea

ledger *n* book of debit and credit accounts

lee *n* **1** shelter **2** side, esp. of ship, away from wind **leeward** *adj/adv/n* (on, towards) lee side **leeway** *n* **1** leeward drift of ship **2** room for movement within limits

leech *n* species of bloodsucking worm

leek *n* plant like onion with long bulb and thick stem

leer *v/n* glance with malign or lascivious expression

lees ① *pl n* **1** sediment **2** dregs

left¹ ① *adj* **1** on or to the west **2** opposite to the right **3** radical, socialist ▷ *adv* **4** on or towards the left ▷ *n* **5** the left hand or part **6** (*Politics*) reforming or radical party **leftist** *n/adj* (person) of the political left

left ① ² past tense past participle of

──────── **THESAURUS** ────────

lease *v* = **hire**, rent, let, loan, charter

leave *v* = **depart from**, withdraw from, go from, escape from, quit ≠ **arrive**; = **quit**, give up, get out of, resign from, drop out of; = **give up**, abandon, dump (*Inf*), drop, surrender ≠ **stay with**; = **entrust**, commit, delegate, refer, hand over; = **bequeath**, will, transfer, endow, confer; = **forget**, leave behind, mislay ▷ *n* = **holiday**, break, vacation, time off, sabbatical; = **permission**, freedom, sanction,

liberty, concession ≠ **refusal**; = **departure**, parting, withdrawal, goodbye, farewell ≠ **arrival**

lecture *n* = **talk**, address, speech, lesson, instruction; = **telling-off** (*Inf*), rebuke, reprimand, talking-to (*Inf*), scolding ▷ *v* = **talk**, speak, teach, address, discourse; = **tell off** (*Inf*), berate, scold, reprimand, censure

lees *pl n* = **sediment**, grounds, deposit, dregs

left¹ *adj* = **left-hand**, port, larboard (*Naut*)

LEAVE¹ **leftover** n unused portion

leg ➊ n **1** one of limbs on which person or animal walks, runs, stands **2** part of garment covering leg **3** support, as leg of table **4** stage **leggings** pl n covering of leather or other material (for legs) **leggy** adj long-legged **legless** adj **1** without legs **2** (Sl) very drunk

legacy ➊ n, pl **-cies 1** bequest **2** thing handed down to successor

legal ➊ adj in accordance with law **legality** n **legalize** v make legal **legally** adv

legate n messenger, representative **legatee** n recipient of legacy **legato** adv, pl **-tos** (Mus) smoothly

legend ➊ n **1** traditional story **2** notable person or event **3** inscription **legendary** adj

legible adj readable **legibility** n

legion ➊ n **1** various military bodies **2** association of veterans **3** large number ▷ adj **4** countless **legionary** adj/n **legionnaire** n

member of legion **legionnaire's disease** serious bacterial disease similar to pneumonia

legislate v make laws **legislation** n **1** act of legislating **2** laws which are made **legislative** adj

legitimate ➊ adj **1** born in wedlock **2** lawful, regular ▷ v **3** make lawful **legitimacy** n **legitimize** v

legume n pod

leisure ➊ n spare time **leisurely** adj **1** unhurried ▷ adv **2** slowly

lekker adj (S Afr, Sl) **1** attractive or nice **2** tasty

lemming n rodent of arctic regions

lemon n **1** pale yellow fruit **2** its colour **3** (Sl) useless person or thing **lemonade** n drink made from lemon juice **lemon curd** creamy spread made of lemons, butter etc.

lemur n nocturnal animal like monkey

lend v **1** give temporary use of **2** let out at interest **3** bestow

---

THESAURUS

leg n = **limb**, member, shank, lower limb, pin (Inf); = **support**, prop, brace, upright; = **stage**, part, section, stretch, lap

legacy n = **bequest**, inheritance, gift, estate, heirloom

legal adj = **judicial**, judiciary, forensic, juridical, jurisdictive; = **lawful**, allowed, sanctioned, constitutional, valid

legend n = **myth**, story, tale, fiction, saga; = **celebrity**, star, phenomenon, genius, prodigy;

= **inscription**, title, caption, device, motto

legion n = **army**, company, force, division, troop; = **multitude**, host, mass, drove, number

legitimate adj = **lawful**, legal, genuine, authentic, authorized ≠ **unlawful**; = **reasonable**, correct, sensible, valid, warranted ≠ **unreasonable** ▷ v = **legitimize**, allow, permit, sanction, authorize

leisure n = **spare**, free, rest, ease, relaxation ≠ **work**

length ❶ n **1** measurement from end to end **2** duration **3** extent **4** piece of a certain length
lengthen v make, become, longer
lengthy adj very long
lenient adj not strict **leniency** n
lens n, pl **lenses** glass etc. shaped to converge or diverge light rays
lent see LEND
Lent n period of fasting from Ash Wednesday to Easter Eve
lentil n edible seed of leguminous plant
leopard n large, spotted, carnivorous cat
leotard n tight-fitting garment covering most of body
leper n **1** (Offens) one ill with leprosy **2** person shunned **leprosy** n ulcerous skin disease
leprechaun n mischievous Irish elf
lesbian ❶ n **1** homosexual woman ▷ adj **2** (of woman) homosexual
lesion n harmful sore on bodily organ
less ❶ adj comparative of LITTLE **1** not so much ▷ n **2** smaller part, quantity **3** a lesser amount ▷ adv **4** to a smaller extent ▷ prep **5** minus **lessen** v **1** diminish **2** reduce **lesser** adj **1** smaller **2** minor
lesson ❶ n **1** instalment of course of instruction **2** content of this **3** experience that teaches **4** portion of Scripture read in church
lest conj for fear that
let¹ ❶ v **letting, let 1** allow, enable, cause **2** rent **3** be leased **let down 1** disappoint **2** lower **3** deflate **let off 1** excuse **2** fire, explode **3** emit **let up** v diminish, stop
let² n **1** hindrance **2** in some games, minor infringement or obstruction
lethal ❶ adj deadly
lethargy n apathy, lack of energy **lethargic** adj
letter ❶ n **1** alphabetical symbol **2** written message **3** strict meaning, interpretation ▷ pl **4** literature ▷ v **5** mark with, in, letters

─── THESAURUS ───

length n = **distance**, reach, measure, extent, span; = **duration**, term, period, space, stretch; = **piece**, measure, section, segment, portion
lesbian adj = **homosexual**, gay, sapphic
less prep = **minus**, without, lacking, excepting, subtracting
lesson n = **class**, schooling, period, teaching, coaching; = **example**, warning, message, moral, deterrent
let¹ v = **allow**, permit, authorize, give the go-ahead, give permission; = **lease**, hire, rent, rent out, hire out
lethal adj = **deadly**, terminal, fatal, dangerous, devastating ≠ **harmless**
letter n = **message**, line, note, communication, dispatch; = **character**, mark, sign, symbol, education

lettuce n salad plant
leukaemia n progressive blood disease
level ❶ adj 1 horizontal 2 even, flat ▷ n 3 horizontal line or surface 4 instrument for establishing horizontal plane 5 position on scale 6 grade ▷ v 7 make, become level 8 knock down 9 aim (gun, accusation etc.) **level crossing** point where railway and road cross **level-headed** adj not apt to be carried away by emotion
lever ❶ n 1 rigid bar pivoted about a fulcrum to transfer a force with mechanical advantage 2 operating handle ▷ v 3 prise, move, with lever **leverage** n 1 action, power of lever 2 influence
leveret n young hare
leviathan n 1 sea monster 2 anything huge or formidable
levitation n raising of solid body into the air supernaturally **levitate**

v (cause to) do this
levity n, pl **-ties** (undue) frivolity
levy ❶ v **levying, levied** 1 impose (tax) 2 raise (troops) ▷ n 3 imposition or collection of taxes
lewd adj 1 lustful 2 indecent
lexicon n dictionary
liable ❶ adj 1 answerable 2 exposed (to) 3 subject (to) 4 likely (to) **liability** n 1 state of being liable 2 debt 3 hindrance, disadvantage ▷ pl 4 debts
liar ❶ n see LIE²
lib n (Inf) short for LIBERATION
libel ❶ n 1 published statement falsely damaging person's reputation ▷ v 2 defame falsely **libellous** adj defamatory
liberal ❶ adj 1 (also with cap.) of political party favouring democratic reforms and individual freedom 2 generous 3 tolerant 4 abundant ▷ n 5 one who has liberal ideas or opinions **liberality** n generosity

THESAURUS

level n = **position**, standard, degree, grade, standing ▷ adj = **equal**, balanced, at the same height; = **horizontal**, even, flat, smooth, uniform ≠ **slanted**; = **even**, tied, equal, drawn, neck and neck ▷ v = **equalize**, balance, even up; = **destroy**, devastate, demolish, flatten, knock down ≠ **build**; = **direct**, point, turn, train, aim; = **flatten**, plane, smooth, even off or out
lever n = **handle**, bar ▷ v = **prise**, force
levy n = **tax**, fee, toll, tariff, duty

▷ v = **impose**, charge, collect, demand, exact
liable adj = **likely**, tending, inclined, disposed, prone; = **vulnerable**, subject, exposed, prone, susceptible
liar n = **falsifier**, perjurer, fibber, fabricator
libel n = **defamation**, misrepresentation, denigration, smear, calumny ▷ v = **defame**, smear, slur, blacken, malign
liberal adj = **tolerant**, open-minded, permissive, indulgent, easy-going

liberalize v make (laws etc.) less restrictive **liberally** adv
liberate ⊙ v set free **liberation** n **liberator** n
libertine n **1** morally dissolute person ▷ adj **2** dissolute
liberty ⊙ n, pl **-ties** freedom **libertarian** n/adj (person) believing in freedom of thought and action **at liberty 1** free **2** having the right **take liberties** be presumptuous
libido n, pl **-dos 1** psychic energy **2** sexual drive **libidinous** adj lustful
library n, pl **-braries 1** room, building where books are kept **2** collection of books, records etc. **librarian** n keeper of library
libretto n, pl **-tos, -ti** words of opera **librettist** n
lice n pl of LOUSE
licence ⊙ n **1** permit

2 permission **3** excessive liberty **4** dissoluteness **license** v grant licence to **licensee** n holder of licence
license plate n the US and Canadian term for NUMBERPLATE
licentious adj dissolute
lichen n small flowerless plants on rocks, trees etc.
licit adj lawful
lick ⊙ v **1** pass tongue over **2** touch slightly **3** (Sl) defeat ▷ n **4** act of licking **5** small amount (esp. of paint etc.) **6** (Sl) speed **licking** n (Sl) beating
licorice n see LIQUORICE
lid n **1** movable cover **2** eyelid
lido n, pl **-dos** pleasure centre with swimming and boating
lie¹ ⊙ v **lying, lied, 1** make false statement ▷ n **2** deliberate falsehood **liar** n person who tells lies

—————— THESAURUS ——————

≠ intolerant; = **progressive**, radical, reformist, libertarian, forward-looking ≠ **conservative**; = **abundant**, generous, handsome, lavish, ample ≠ **limited**; = **generous**, kind, charitable, extravagant, open-hearted ≠ **stingy**
liberate v = **free**, release, rescue, save, deliver ≠ **imprison**
liberty n = **independence**, sovereignty, liberation, autonomy, immunity = **freedom**, liberation, emancipation, deliverance ≠ **restraint**
licence n = **certificate**, document, permit, charter, warrant;

= **permission**, the right, authority, leave, sanction ≠ **denial**; = **freedom**, creativity, latitude, independence, liberty ≠ **restraint**; = **laxity**, excess, indulgence, irresponsibility, licentiousness ≠ **moderation**
lick v = **taste**, lap, tongue; (Inf) = **beat**, defeat, overcome, rout, outstrip; (of flames) = **flicker**, touch, flick, dart, ripple ▷ n = **dab**, bit, touch, stroke; (Inf) = **pace**, rate, speed, clip (Inf)
lie¹ n = **falsehood**, deceit, fabrication, fib, fiction ▷ v = **fib**, fabricate, falsify, prevaricate, not tell the truth

lie² ⊙ *v* **lying, lay, lain 1** be horizontal, at rest **2** be situated **3** be in certain state **4** exist ▷ *n* **5** state (of affairs etc.) **lie in** remain in bed late **lie-in** *n*

lieu *n* **in lieu of** in place of

lieutenant *n* **1** deputy **2** junior army or navy officer

life ⊙ *n, pl* **lives 1** active principle of existence **2** time that it lasts **3** story of a person's life **4** way of living **5** vigour, vivacity **lifeless** *adj* **1** dead **2** insensible **3** dull **lifelike** *adj* **lifelong** *adj* lasting a lifetime **life belt, jacket** buoyant device to keep person afloat **lifeline** *n* **1** means of help **2** rope thrown to person in danger **life preserver** *n* buoyant device to keep afloat a person in danger of drowning **lifestyle** *n* particular habits, attitudes etc. of person or group **lifetime** *n* time person, animal or object lives or functions

lift ⊙ *v* **1** move upwards in position, status, mood, volume etc.

2 take up and remove **3** (*Inf*) steal **4** disappear ▷ *n* **5** cage in vertical shaft for raising and lowering people or goods **6** act of lifting **7** ride in car etc., as passenger **8** boost **liftoff** *n* moment rocket leaves the ground

ligament *n* band of tissue joining bones **ligature** *n* **1** anything which binds **2** thread for tying up artery

light¹ ⊙ *n* **1** electromagnetic radiation by which things are visible **2** source of this, lamp **3** window **4** means or act of setting fire to **5** understanding ▷ *pl* **6** traffic lights ▷ *adj* **7** bright **8** pale, not dark ▷ *v* **9** set on fire **10** give light to **11** brighten **lighten** *v* give light to **lighting** *n* apparatus for supplying artificial light **lightning** *n* visible discharge of electricity in atmosphere **lighthouse** *n* tower with a light to guide ships **light year** distance light travels in one year

---
THESAURUS
---

lie² *v* = **recline**, rest, lounge, sprawl, stretch out; = **be placed**, be, rest, exist, be situated; = **be situated**, sit, be located, be positioned, reside

life *n* = **being**, existence, vitality, sentience; = **existence**, being, lifetime, time, days; = **way of life**, situation, conduct, behaviour, life style; = **liveliness**, energy, spirit, vitality, animation; = **biography**, story, history, profile, confessions

lift *v* = **raise**, pick up, hoist, draw up, elevate ≠ **lower**; = **revoke**, end, remove, withdraw, stop ≠ **impose**;

= **disappear**, clear, vanish, disperse, dissipate ▷ *n* = **boost**, encouragement, stimulus, pick-me-up, fillip ≠ **blow**; = **elevator** (*chiefly US*), hoist, paternoster; = **ride**, run, drive, hitch (*Inf*)

light¹ *n* = **brightness**, illumination, luminosity, shining, glow ≠ **dark**; = **lamp**, torch, candle, flare, beacon; = **match**, spark, flame, lighter; = **aspect**, context, angle, point of view, interpretation ▷ *adj* = **bright**, brilliant, shining,

light² ❶ *adj* **1** of, or bearing, little weight **2** not severe **3** easy **4** trivial **5** not clumsy **6** not serious or profound **7** (industry) producing small, usu. consumer goods, using light machinery ▷ *adv* **8** in light manner ▷ *v* **9** come by chance (upon) **lighten** *v* reduce, remove (load etc.) **lightly** *adv* **lights** *pl n* lungs of animal **light-fingered** *adj* likely to steal **light-headed** *adj* dizzy, delirious **light-hearted** *adj* carefree **lightweight** *n/adj* (person) of little weight or importance

lighter *n* **1** device for lighting cigarettes etc. **2** flat-bottomed boat for unloading ships

like¹ ❶ *adj* **1** resembling **2** similar **3** characteristic of ▷ *adv* **4** in the manner of ▷ *pron* **5** similar thing **likelihood** *n* probability **likely** **1** probable **2** promising ▷ *adv* **3** probably **liken** *v* compare **likeness** *n* **1** resemblance

2 portrait **likewise** *adv* in like manner

like² ❶ *v* find agreeable, enjoy, love **likeable** *adj* **liking** *n* **1** fondness **2** inclination, taste

lilac *n* shrub bearing pale mauve or white flowers

lilt *n* rhythmical swing **lilting** *adj*

lily *n, pl* **lilies** bulbous flowering plant **lily of the valley** small garden plant with fragrant white flowers

limb ❶ *n* **1** arm or leg **2** wing **3** branch of tree

limber *adj* pliant, lithe **limber up** loosen stiff muscles by exercise

limbo¹ *n* **1** region between Heaven and Hell for the unbaptized **2** indeterminate place or state

limbo² *n* West Indian dance in which dancers lean backwards to pass under a bar

lime¹ *n* **1** calcium compound used in fertilizer, cement ▷ *v* **2** treat (land) with lime **limelight** *n* glare of publicity **limestone** *n*

THESAURUS

illuminated, luminous ≠ **dark**; = **pale**, fair, faded, blonde, blond ≠ **dark** ▷ *v* = **illuminate**, light up, brighten ≠ **darken**; = **ignite**, inflame, kindle, touch off, set alight ≠ **put out**

light² *adj* = **insubstantial**, thin, slight, portable, buoyant ≠ **heavy**; = **weak**, soft, gentle, moderate, slight ≠ **strong**; = **digestible**, modest, frugal ≠ **substantial**; = **insignificant**, small, slight, petty, trivial ≠ **serious**; = **light-hearted**, funny,

entertaining, amusing, witty ≠ **serious**; = **nimble**, graceful, deft, agile, sprightly ≠ **clumsy**

like¹ *adj* = **similar to**, same as, equivalent to, parallel to, identical to ≠ **different**

like² *v* = **enjoy**, love, delight in, go for, relish ≠ **dislike**; = **admire**, approve of, appreciate, prize, take to ≠ **dislike**; = **wish**, want, choose, prefer, desire

limb *n* = **part**, member, arm, leg, wing; = **branch**, spur, projection, offshoot, bough

sedimentary rock used in building

lime² n small acid fruit like lemon **lime-green** adj greenish-yellow

lime³ n tree

limerick n humorous verse of five lines

limit ❶ n 1 utmost extent or duration 2 boundary ▷ v 3 restrict, restrain, bound **limitation** n **limited company** one whose shareholders' liability is restricted

limousine n large, luxurious car

limp¹ ❶ v 1 walk lamely ▷ n 2 limping walk

limp² ❶ adj without firmness or stiffness

limpet n shellfish that sticks tightly to rocks

limpid adj 1 clear 2 translucent

linchpin, lynchpin n 1 pin to hold wheel on its axle 2 essential person or thing

linctus n, pl **-tuses** syrupy cough medicine

line ❶ n 1 long narrow mark 2 row 3 series, course 4 telephone connection 5 progeny 6 province of activity 7 shipping company 8 railway track 9 any class of goods 10 cord 11 approach, policy ▷ v 12 cover inside 13 mark with lines 14 bring into line **lineage** n descent from, descendants of an ancestor **lineament** n feature **linear** adj of, in lines **liner** n large ship or aircraft of passenger line **linesman** n sporting official who helps referee **line-up** n people or things assembled for particular purpose

linen adj 1 made of flax ▷ n 2 linen cloth 3 linen articles collectively

linger ❶ v 1 delay, loiter 2 remain long

lingerie n women's underwear or nightwear

linguist n one skilled in languages or language study **linguistic** adj of languages or their study **linguistics** pl n study, science of language

liniment n embrocation

lining n covering for inside of garment etc.

———— THESAURUS ————

limit n = **end**, ultimate, deadline, breaking point, extremity; = **boundary**, edge, border, frontier, perimeter ▷ v = **restrict**, control, check, bound, confine

limp¹ v = **hobble**, stagger, stumble, shuffle, hop ▷ n = **lameness**, hobble

limp² adj = **floppy**, soft, slack, drooping, flabby ≠ **stiff**

line n = **stroke**, mark, score, band, scratch; = **wrinkle**, mark, crease, furrow, crow's foot; = **row**, queue, rank, file, column; = **string**, cable, wire, rope, thread; = **trajectory**, way, course, track, channel; = **boundary**, limit, edge, border, frontier; = **occupation**, work, calling, business, job ▷ v = **border**, edge, bound, fringe; = **mark**, crease, furrow, rule, score; = **under control**, in order, in check

linger v = **stay**, remain, stop, wait, delay

DICTIONARY

link ❶ *n* **1** ring of chain
2 connection ▷ *v* **3** join with, as
with, link **4** intertwine **linkage** *n*
links *pl n* golf course
linnet *n* songbird of finch family
lino *n* short for LINOLEUM
linoleum *n* floor covering of
powdered cork, linseed oil etc.
backed with hessian
linseed *n* seed of flax plant
lint *n* soft material for dressing
wounds
lintel *n* top piece of door or window
lion *n* large animal of cat family
lip ❶ *n* **1** either edge of the mouth
2 edge or margin **3** (*Sl*) impudence
lip-reading *n* method of
understanding speech by
interpreting lip movements **lip
service** insincere tribute or respect
lipstick *n* cosmetic for colouring lips
liqueur *n* alcoholic liquor flavoured
and sweetened
liquid ❶ *adj* **1** fluid, not solid or
gaseous **2** flowing smoothly **3** (of
assets) easily converted into money
▷ *n* **4** substance in liquid form

liquefy *v* make or become liquid
liquidity *n* state of being able to
meet debts **liquidize** *v* **liquidizer**
n
liquidate *v* **1** pay (debt) **2** arrange
affairs of, and dissolve (company)
3 wipe out, kill **liquidation** *n*
1 clearing up of financial affairs
2 bankruptcy **liquidator** *n* official
appointed to liquidate business
liquor ❶ *n* alcoholic liquid
liquorice *n* black substance used
in medicine and as a sweet
lira *n, pl* **-re, -ras** monetary unit of
Italy (former) and Turkey
lisp *v/n* (speak with) faulty
pronunciation of *s* and *z*
lissom, lissome *adj* supple, agile
list¹ ❶ *n* **1** inventory, register
2 catalogue ▷ *v* **3** place on list
list² ❶ *v* **1** (of ship) lean to one side
▷ *n* **2** inclination of ship
listen ❶ *v* try to hear, attend to
listener *n*
listless *adj* indifferent, languid
litany *n, pl* **-nies** prayer with
responses

THESAURUS

link *n* = **connection**, relationship,
association, tie-up, affinity ▷ *v*
= **associate**, relate, identify,
connect, bracket; = **connect**, join,
unite, couple, tie ≠ separate
lip *n* = **edge**, rim, brim, margin,
brink; (*Sl*) = **impudence**, insolence,
impertinence, cheek (*Inf*),
effrontery
liquid *n* = **fluid**, solution, juice, sap
▷ *adj* = **fluid**, running, flowing,
melted, watery; (*of assets*)
= **convertible**, disposable,

negotiable, realizable
liquor *n* = **alcohol**, drink, spirits,
booze (*Inf*), hard stuff (*Inf*); = **juice**,
stock, liquid, extract, broth
list¹ *n* = **inventory**, record, series,
roll, index ▷ *v* = **itemize**, record,
enter, register, catalogue
list² *v* = **lean**, tip, incline, tilt, heel
over ▷ *n* = **tilt**, leaning, slant, cant
listen *v* = **hear**, attend, pay
attention, lend an ear, prick up your
ears; = **pay attention**, observe,
obey, mind, heed

literal ⬤ *adj* 1 according to the strict meaning of the words, not figurative 2 actual, true **literally** *adv*

literate ⬤ *adj* 1 able to read and write 2 educated **literacy** *n*

literature ⬤ *n* books and writings of a country, period or subject **literary** *adj*

lithe *adj* supple, pliant

lithium *n* metallic chemical element

lithography *n* method of printing using the antipathy of grease and water **lithograph** *n* 1 print so produced ▷ *v* 2 print thus

litmus *n* blue dye turned red by acids and restored to blue by alkali

litre *n* measure of volume of fluid, one cubic decimetre, about 1.75 pints

litter ⬤ *n* 1 untidy refuse 2 young of animal produced at one birth 3 kind of stretcher for wounded ▷ *v* 4 strew with litter 5 give birth to young

little ⬤ *adj* 1 small, not much 2 young ▷ *n* 3 small quantity ▷ *adv* 4 slightly

liturgy *n, pl* **-gies** prescribed form of public worship **liturgical** *adj*

live¹ ⬤ *v* 1 have life 2 pass one's life 3 continue in life 4 continue, last 5 dwell **living** *n* 1 action of being in life 2 people now alive 3 means of living 4 church benefice ▷ *adj* 5 alive **living room** room in house for relaxation and entertainment

live² ⬤ *adj* 1 living, alive, active, vital 2 flaming 3 (of electrical conductor) carrying current 4 (of broadcast) transmitted during the actual performance **liveliness** *n* **lively** *adj* brisk, active, vivid **liven** *v* (esp. with *up*) make (more) lively

livelihood ⬤ *n* means of living

— THESAURUS —

literal *adj* = **exact**, close, strict, accurate, faithful; = **actual**, real, true, simple, plain

literate *adj* = **educated**, informed, knowledgeable

literature *n* = **writings**, letters, compositions, lore, creative writing

litter *n* = **rubbish**, refuse, waste, junk, debris; = **brood**, young, offspring, progeny ▷ *v* = **clutter**, mess up, clutter up, be scattered about, disorder; = **scatter**, spread, shower, strew

little *adj* = **small**, minute, short, tiny, wee ≠ **big**; = **young**, small, junior, infant, immature ▷ *adv*

= **hardly**, barely, scarcely ≠ **much**; = **rarely**, seldom, scarcely, not often, infrequently ≠ **always** ▷ *n* = **bit**, touch, spot, trace, hint ≠ **lot**

live¹ *v* = **dwell**, board, settle, lodge, occupy; = **exist**, last, prevail, be, have being; = **survive**, get along, make a living, make ends meet, subsist; = **thrive**, flourish, prosper, have fun, enjoy yourself

live² *adj* = **living**, alive, breathing, animate; = **active**, unexploded; = **topical**, important, pressing, current, hot

livelihood *n* = **occupation**, work, employment, living, job

liver n 1 organ secreting bile
2 animal liver as food **liverish** adj
1 unwell, as from liver upset
2 touchy, irritable

livery n, pl **-eries** distinctive dress, esp. servant's

livestock n farm animals

livid adj (Inf) 1 angry, furious
2 discoloured, as by bruising

lizard n four-footed reptile

llama n woolly animal of S America

load ❶ n 1 something carried
2 quantity carried 3 burden
4 amount of power used ▷ v 5 put load on or into 6 charge (gun)
7 weigh down **loaded** adj
1 carrying a load 2 (of dice) dishonestly weighted 3 (of question) containing hidden trap or implication 4 (of weapon) charged with ammunition 5 (Sl) wealthy
6 (Sl) drunk

loaf¹ ❶ n, pl **loaves** 1 mass of baked bread 2 shaped mass of food

loaf² ❶ v idle, loiter **loafer** n idler

loam n fertile soil

loan ❶ n 1 act of lending 2 thing lent 3 money borrowed at interest ▷ v 4 lend

loath, loth adj unwilling **loathe** v feel strong disgust for **loathing** n disgust **loathsome** adj

lob n 1 in tennis etc., shot pitched high in air ▷ v 2 throw, pitch shots thus

lobby ❶ n, pl **-bies** 1 corridor into which rooms open 2 group which tries to influence legislature ▷ v
3 try to enlist support (of)

lobe n 1 soft, hanging part of ear
2 rounded segment **lobotomy** n surgical incision into lobe of brain

lobelia n garden plant with lobed flowers

lobster n shellfish with long tail and claws, turning red when boiled

local ❶ adj 1 of, existing in particular place 2 confined to particular place ▷ n 3 person from district 4 (Inf) (nearby) pub **locale** n scene of event **locality** n neighbourhood **localize** v assign, restrict to definite place **locally** adv

locate ❶ v 1 find 2 situate **location** n 1 placing 2 situation
3 site of film production away from studio

--- THESAURUS ---

load v = **fill**, stuff, pack, pile, stack; = **make ready**, charge, prime ▷ n = **cargo**, delivery, haul, shipment, batch

loaf¹ n = **lump**, block, cake, cube, slab; (Sl) = **head**, mind, sense, common sense, nous (Brit Sl)

loaf² v = **idle**, hang around, take it easy, lie around, loiter

loan n = **advance**, credit, overdraft ▷ v = **lend**, advance, let out

lobby v = **campaign**, press, pressure, push, influence ▷ n = **pressure group**, group, camp, faction, lobbyists; = **corridor**, passage, entrance, porch, hallway

local adj = **community**, regional; = **confined**, limited, restricted ▷ n = **resident**, native, inhabitant

locate v = **find**, discover, detect, come across, track down; = **place**, put, set, position, seat

loch n Scottish lake or long narrow bay

lock¹ ❶ n 1 appliance for fastening door, lid etc. 2 arrangement for moving boats from one level of canal to another 3 extent to which vehicle's front wheels will turn 4 block, jam ▷ v 5 fasten, make secure with lock 6 place in locked container 7 join firmly 8 jam 9 embrace closely **locker** n small cupboard with lock **lockjaw** n tetanus **lockout** n exclusion of workers by employers as means of coercion **locksmith** n one who makes and mends locks **lockup** n garage, storage area away from main premises

lock² n tress of hair

locket n small hinged pendant for portrait etc.

locomotive n engine for pulling carriages on railway tracks **locomotion** n action, power of moving

locum (Lat) substitute, esp. for doctor or clergyman

locus n, pl **loci** curve traced by all points satisfying specified mathematical condition

locust n destructive winged insect

lodge ❶ n 1 house, cabin used seasonally or occasionally, e.g. for hunting, skiing 2 gatekeeper's house 3 branch of Freemasons etc. ▷ v 4 house 5 deposit 6 bring (a charge etc.) 7 live in another's house at fixed charge 8 come to rest (in, on) **lodger** n **lodgings** pl n rented accommodation in another person's house

loft n space under roof **loftily** adv haughtily **lofty** adj 1 of great height 2 elevated 3 haughty

log¹ ❶ n 1 trimmed portion of felled tree 2 record of voyages of ship, aircraft etc. ▷ v 3 enter in a log 4 record 5 cut logs **logbook** n

log² n logarithm

loganberry n purplish-red fruit

logarithm n one of series of arithmetical functions tabulated for use in calculation

loggerheads pl n at **loggerheads** quarrelling, disputing

logic ❶ n 1 science of reasoning 2 reasoned thought or argument 3 coherence of various facts, events etc. **logical** adj 1 of logic 2 according to reason 3 reasonable 4 apt to reason correctly

⎯⎯⎯⎯⎯⎯⎯⎯⎯⎯ THESAURUS ⎯⎯⎯⎯⎯⎯⎯⎯⎯⎯

lock¹ v = **fasten**, close, secure, shut, bar; = **unite**, join, link, engage, clench; = **embrace**, press, grasp, clutch, hug ▷ n = **fastening**, catch, bolt, clasp, padlock

lodge n = **cabin**, shelter, cottage, hut, chalet; = **society**, group, club, section, wing ▷ v = **register**, enter, file, submit, put on record; = **stay**, room, board, reside, house; = **stick**, remain, implant, come to rest, imbed

log¹ n = **stump**, block, branch, chunk, trunk; = **record**, account, register, journal, diary ▷ v = **record**, enter, note, register, chart

logic n = **reason**, reasoning, sense, good sense

logistics pl n (with sing or pl v) the handling of supplies and personnel **logistical** adj

logo n, pl **-os** company emblem or similar device

loin n **1** part of body between ribs and hip **2** cut of meat from this ▷ pl **3** hips and lower abdomen **loincloth** n garment covering loins only

loiter v **1** dawdle, hang about **2** idle **loiterer** n

loll v **1** sit, lie lazily **2** (esp. of the tongue) hang out

lollipop n sweet on small wooden stick

lolly n, pl **-ies** (Inf) **1** lollipop or ice lolly **2** (Sl) money

lone ❶ adj solitary **loneliness** n **lonely** adj **1** sad because alone **2** unfrequented **3** solitary **loner** n one who prefers to be alone

lonesome adj (chiefly US and Canad) another word for LONELY

long¹ ❶ adj **1** having length, esp. great length, in space or time **2** extensive **3** protracted ▷ adv **4** for a long time **long-distance** adj going between places far apart **longhand** n words written in full **long-range** adj **1** into the future **2** able to travel long distances without refuelling **3** (of weapons) designed to hit distant target **long shot** competitor, undertaking, bet etc. with small chance of success **long-sighted** adj able to see distant objects in focus but not nearby ones **long-standing** adj existing for a long time **long-suffering** adj enduring trouble or unhappiness without complaint **long-winded** adj tediously loquacious

long² ❶ v have keen desire, yearn (for) **longing** n yearning

longevity n long life

longitude n distance east or west from standard meridian

longshoreman n a man employed in the loading or unloading of ships

loo n (Inf) lavatory

look ❶ v **1** direct eyes (at) **2** face **3** seem **4** search (for) **5** hope (for) **6** (with after) take care of ▷ n **7** looking **8** view **9** search **10** (oft. pl) appearance **lookalike** n person who is double of another **lookout** n **1** watchman **2** place for watching **3** prospect

lone adj = **solitary**, single, one, only, sole

long¹ adj = **elongated**, extended, stretched, expanded, extensive ≠ **short**; = **prolonged**, sustained, lengthy, lingering, protracted ≠ **brief**

long² v = **desire**, want, wish, burn, pine

look v = **see**, view, consider, watch, eye; = **search**, seek, hunt, forage; = **consider**, contemplate; = **face**, overlook; = **hope**, expect, await, anticipate, reckon on ▷ n = **glimpse**, view, glance, observation, sight; = **appearance**, bearing, air, style, aspect

loom ❶ v 1 appear dimly 2 seem ominously close

loonie n (Canad, SI) 1 a Canadian dollar coin with a loon bird on one of its faces 2 the Canadian currency

loony n/adj (SI) foolish or insane (person)

loop ❶ n 1 figure made by curved line crossing itself ▷ v 2 form loop **loophole** n means of evading rule without infringing it

loose ❶ adj 1 slack 2 not fixed or restrained 3 vague 4 dissolute ▷ v 5 free 6 unfasten 7 slacken 8 shoot, let fly **loosen** v make loose **loose-leaf** adj allowing addition or removal of pages

loot ❶ n/v plunder

lop v **lopping, lopped** 1 cut away twigs and branches 2 chop off

lope v run with long, easy strides

lopsided adj with one side lower

than the other

loquacious adj talkative

lord ❶ n 1 British nobleman 2 ruler 3 (with cap.) God ▷ v 4 domineer **lordly** adj 1 imperious 2 fit for a lord **lordship** n

lore n 1 learning 2 body of facts and traditions

lorry n, pl **-ries** motor vehicle for heavy loads, truck

lose ❶ v **losing, lost** 1 be deprived of, fail to retain or use 2 fail to get 3 (of clock etc.) run slow 4 be defeated in **loser** n **loss** n 1 act of losing 2 what is lost **lost** adj 1 unable to be found 2 unable to find one's way 3 bewildered 4 not won 5 not utilized

lot ❶ pron 1 great number ▷ n 2 collection 3 large quantity 4 share 5 fate 6 item at auction 7 object used to make decision by chance 8 area of land ▷ pl 9 (Inf)

THESAURUS

loom v = **appear**, emerge, hover, take shape, threaten

loop n = **curve**, ring, circle, twist, curl ▷ v = **twist**, turn, roll, knot, curl

loose adj = **free**, detached, insecure, unfettered, unrestricted; = **slack**, easy, relaxed, sloppy, loose-fitting ≠ **tight**; (Old-fashioned) = **promiscuous**, fast, abandoned, immoral, dissipated ≠ **chaste**; = **vague**, random, inaccurate, rambling, imprecise ≠ **precise** ▷ v = **free**, release, liberate, detach, unleash ≠ **fasten**

loot v = **plunder**, rob, raid, sack, rifle ▷ n = **plunder**, goods, prize, haul, spoils

lord n = **peer**, nobleman, count, duke, gentleman; = **ruler**, leader, chief, master, governor

lose v = **be defeated**, be beaten, lose out, come to grief; = **mislay**, drop, forget, be deprived of, lose track of; = **forfeit**, miss, yield, be deprived of, pass up (Inf)

lot n = **bunch** (Inf), group, crowd, crew, set; = **destiny**, situation, circumstances, fortune, chance

great numbers or quantity **a lot**
(*Inf*) a great deal

lotion ❶ *n* liquid for washing
wounds, improving skin etc.

lottery ❶ *n, pl* **-teries 1** method
of raising funds by selling tickets
that win prizes by chance
2 gamble

lotus *n* legendary plant whose
fruits induce forgetfulness

loud ❶ *adj* **1** strongly audible
2 noisy **3** (*Fig*) garish **loudly** *adv*
loudspeaker *n* instrument for
converting electrical signals into
sound audible at a distance

lounge ❶ *v* **1** recline, move at ease
▷ *n* **2** living room of house **3** public
room, area for sitting **lounge suit**
man's suit for daytime wear

lour see LOWER

louse *n* parasitic insect **lousy** *adj*
(*Sl*) **1** bad **2** (*Sl*) nasty **3** having lice

lout *n* crude, oafish person

louvre *n* one of set of slats slanted

to admit air but not rain

love ❶ *n* **1** warm affection
2 benevolence **3** sexual passion
4 sweetheart **5** (*Tennis*) score of
nothing ▷ *v* **6** admire passionately
7 delight in **lovable** *adj* **lovelorn**
adj pining for a lover **lovely** *adj*
beautiful, delightful **lover** *n*
loving *adj* **1** affectionate **2** tender
make love (to) have sexual
intercourse (with)

low ❶ *adj* **1** not tall, high or
elevated **2** humble **3** vulgar
4 unwell **5** below what is usual
6 not loud **lower** *v* **1** cause, allow
to move down **2** diminish, degrade
▷ *adj* **4** below **4** at an early stage,
period **lowly** *adj* modest, humble
lowbrow *n/adj* nonintellectual
(person) **lowdown** *n* (*Inf*) inside
information **low-down** *adj* (*Inf*)
mean, shabby **lower case** small
letters **low-key** *adj* not intense
lowland *n* low-lying country

—— THESAURUS ——

lotion *n* = **cream**, solution, balm,
salve, liniment

lottery *n* = **raffle**, draw, lotto
(*Brit, NZ, & S Afr*), sweepstake;
= **gamble**, chance, risk, hazard,
toss-up (*Inf*)

loud *adj* = **noisy**, booming, roaring,
thundering, forte (*Mus*) ≠ **quiet**;
= **garish**, bold, glaring, flamboyant,
brash ≠ **sombre**

lounge *v* = **relax**, loaf, sprawl, lie
about, take it easy

love *v* = **adore**, care for, treasure,
cherish, prize ≠ **hate**; = **enjoy**, like,
appreciate, relish, delight in
≠ **dislike** ▷ *n* = **passion**, affection,

warmth, attachment, intimacy
≠ **hatred**; = **liking**, taste, bent for,
weakness for, relish for; = **beloved**,
dear, dearest, lover, darling
≠ **enemy**; = **sympathy**,
understanding, pity, humanity,
warmth

low *adj* = **small**, little, short, stunted,
squat ≠ **tall**; = **inferior**, bad, poor,
inadequate, unsatisfactory; = **quiet**,
soft, gentle, whispered, muted
≠ **loud**; = **dejected**, depressed,
miserable, fed up, moody ≠ **happy**;
= **coarse**, common, rough, crude,
rude; = **ill**, weak, frail, stricken,
debilitated ≠ **strong**

lower, lour v 1 (of sky) look threatening 2 scowl

loyal 🟦 adj faithful, true to allegiance **loyalist** n **loyalty** n

lozenge n 1 small sweet or tablet of medicine 2 diamond shape

LP long-playing record

L-plate n sign on car driven by learner driver

LSD 1 lysergic acid diethylamide (hallucinogenic drug) 2 pounds, shillings, and pence

lubricate v 1 oil, grease 2 make slippery **lubricant** n substance used for this **lubrication** n

lucerne n fodder plant

lucid adj 1 clear 2 easily understood 3 sane **lucidity** n

luck 🟦 n 1 chance, whether good or bad 2 good fortune **luckily** adv fortunately **luckless** adj having bad luck **lucky** adj having good luck

lucrative 🟦 adj very profitable

ludicrous 🟦 adj ridiculous

lug¹ v drag with effort

lug² n 1 projection, serving as handle or support 2 (Inf) ear

luggage 🟦 n traveller's baggage

lugubrious adj doleful

lukewarm adj 1 tepid 2 indifferent

lull 🟦 v 1 soothe, sing to sleep 2 calm 3 subside ▷ n 4 quiet spell **lullaby** n lulling song, esp. for children

lumbago n rheumatism of the lower part of the back

lumber¹ 🟦 n 1 disused articles, useless rubbish 2 sawn timber ▷ v 3 (Inf) burden with something unpleasant **lumberjack** n (US & Canad) man who fells trees and prepares logs

lumber² 🟦 v move heavily

luminous adj 1 shedding light 2 glowing **luminary** n famous person **luminescence** n emission of light without heat

lump¹ 🟦 n 1 shapeless piece or mass 2 swelling 3 large sum ▷ v 4 throw together **lumpy** adj 1 full

THESAURUS

loyal adj = **faithful**, true, devoted, dependable, constant ≠ **disloyal**

luck n = **good fortune**, success, advantage, prosperity, blessing; = **fortune**, lot, stars, chance, accident

lucrative adj = **profitable**, rewarding, productive, fruitful, well-paid

ludicrous adj = **ridiculous**, crazy, absurd, preposterous, silly ≠ **sensible**

luggage n = **baggage**, things, cases, bags, gear

lull n = **respite**, pause, quiet, silence, calm ▷ v = **calm**, soothe, subdue, quell, allay

lumber¹ v (Brit Inf) = **burden**, land, load, saddle, encumber ▷ n (Brit) = **junk**, refuse, rubbish, trash, clutter

lumber² v = **plod**, shuffle, shamble, trudge, stump

lump¹ n = **piece**, ball, block, mass, chunk; = **swelling**, growth, bump, tumour, bulge ▷ v = **group**, throw, mass, combine, collect

of lumps **2** uneven

lump² v (Inf) tolerate

lunar adj relating to the moon

lunatic ❶ adj/n **1** foolish or irresponsible (person) **2** insane (person) **lunacy** n

lunch n **1** meal taken in middle of day ▷ v **2** eat, entertain to lunch **luncheon** n lunch **luncheon meat** tinned ground mixture of meat and cereal

lung n one of the two organs of respiration in vertebrates

lunge v **1** thrust with sword etc. ▷ n **2** thrust **3** sudden movement of body, plunge

lupin n leguminous plant with spikes of flowers

lurch ❶ n **1** sudden roll to one side ▷ v **2** stagger **leave in the lurch** leave in difficulties

lure ❶ n **1** bait **2** power to attract ▷ v **3** entice **4** attract

lurid adj **1** sensational **2** garish

lurk ❶ v lie hidden **lurking** adj (of suspicion) not definite

luscious adj **1** sweet, juicy **2** extremely attractive

lush ❶ adj **1** (of plant growth) luxuriant **2** luxurious

lust ❶ n **1** strong desire for sexual gratification **2** any strong desire ▷ v **3** have passionate desire **lustful** adj **lusty** adj vigorous, healthy

lustre n **1** gloss, sheen **2** renown **3** metallic pottery glaze **lustrous** adj shining

lute n old stringed musical instrument played like a guitar

luxury ❶ n, pl **-ries 1** possession and use of costly, choice things for enjoyment **2** enjoyable, comfortable surroundings **3** enjoyable but not essential thing **luxuriance** n abundance **luxuriant** adj **1** growing thickly **2** abundant **luxuriate** v **1** indulge in luxury **2** flourish profusely **3** take delight (in) **luxurious** adj **1** fond of luxury **2** self-indulgent **3** sumptuous

— THESAURUS —

lunatic n = **madman**, maniac, psychopath, nutcase (Sl) ▷ adj = **mad**, crazy, insane, irrational, daft

lunge v = **pounce**, charge, dive, leap, plunge ▷ n = **thrust**, charge, pounce, spring, swing

lurch v = **tilt**, roll, pitch, list, rock; = **stagger**, reel, stumble, weave, sway

lure v = **tempt**, draw, attract, invite, trick ▷ n = **temptation**, attraction, incentive, bait, carrot (Inf)

lurk v = **hide**, sneak, prowl, lie in wait, slink

lush adj = **abundant**, green, flourishing, dense, rank; = **luxurious**, grand, elaborate, lavish, extravagant

lust n = **lechery**, sensuality, lewdness, lasciviousness; = **desire**, longing, passion, appetite, craving

luxury n = **opulence**, splendour, richness, extravagance, affluence ≠ **poverty**; = **extravagance**, treat, extra, indulgence, frill ≠ **necessity**

lychee *n* Chinese fruit

Lycra® *n* fabric used for tight-fitting garments

lymph *n* colourless body fluid, mainly white blood cells **lymphatic** *adj*

lynch *v* put to death without trial

lynx *n* animal of cat family

lyre *n* instrument like harp

lyric *n* **1** songlike poem expressing personal feelings ▷ *pl* **2** words of popular song **lyrical** *adj* **1** expressed in this style **2** enthusiastic **lyricist** *n*

LANGUAGE
FOR LIFE

CONTENTS

INTRODUCTION

A dictionary can tell you what a word means and when it can be used accurately. It cannot, though, give you guidance on how to write clearly and appropriately in a variety of situations. The *Language for Life* supplement has been written to help you express yourself effectively at work and at home. It includes advice on how to structure your writing, and how to adapt tone, style and content to different forms of communication – from letters and emails to social media.

BEFORE YOU START WRITING

It is amazing how much more effective your writing will be with a bit of thinking time beforehand. There are three questions which you should be able to answer about any piece of writing, whether it's an email, text, letter or post:

- **Who am I writing to?** This will determine the style and tone that you use. If you are writing an email to a friend, for instance, then you are likely to use less formal language than if you are writing to apply for a job.

- **What do I want to say?** Make sure that all the information you want to communicate is included, and that it is set out as clearly as possible.

- **Why do I want to say it?** In other words, what do you want to happen as a result of your communication? Whether it's for a job application, to ask someone out on a date, or to offer your condolences for a bereavement, what you want to achieve should be clearly stated.

Once you've answered these questions, writing becomes much easier.

Here are some tips for making your writing successful and some common traps to avoid.

👍 Tips:

- **Use plain English.** Aim for concise, simple expression which will make your writing easy to read.

- **Plan.** Think about what you want to say, and how you want to say it. Planning will save you time and make your writing more effective. It needn't take a lot of time but, even if you're only writing a tweet or a text, it will pay dividends.

- **Vary the length of your sentences.** Short sentences are powerful. Longer sentences can express more complicated thoughts, but try to keep them to a manageable length or else they become tiring to read! Try to stick to the principle of including one main idea in a sentence, and maybe one related point.

- **Use active rather than passive verbs.** It is usually better to use active verbs because it makes your writing simpler and less stuffy to read:
  The programme was watched by an audience of 13 million people (passive)
  13 million people watched the programme (active).
  The verb 'watched' is 'active' in the second example because it is linked to the subject – '13 million people'. The sentence is shorter and clearer as a result.

- **Read your work aloud.** If the sentences work well, it will be easy to read. Check that you have commas where there are natural pauses.

- **Think about register and tone.** Are you using the right level of formality ('register')? Does your writing accurately express your attitude to the subject and the reader ('tone')? How you address a best friend will be different from how you write to a potential employer.

- **Always check your writing before sending it – and then check it again!** You'll be surprised how easy it is to overlook mistakes. Computers have introduced new errors – for instance, did you delete the original passage that you copied and pasted later in the document? If you correct one word in a sentence, make sure the rest of it still makes sense.

> *I wish people would read through what they have written before pressing 'send'. It would save me a lot of time and make their applications more successful.*
>
> (HR manager)

Traps:

- **Jargon.** Specialist words which are understood by a particular group of people, or overly technical language. Don't talk about 'interfacing' with someone, if you simply mean 'talking' to them.

- **Clichés.** Words or phrases that are used too often, and have little meaning. They will annoy your reader and distract from what you are trying to say. Examples include sayings like, '*A different kettle of fish*,' and '*At the end of the day*'.

- **Long sentences.** Avoid sentences longer than 15–20 words – they can be difficult to read, and can usually be divided into clearer statements. If your sentences work well, they will be easy to read.

- **Repeating words.** Using the same word more than once in a sentence can be clumsy, and there is usually an alternative. For instance, '*The date of the English exam is the same date as the French exam*,' sounds better as '*The English and the French exams are on the same date*.'

- **Long words.** Avoid using long or complex words for the sake of it, if they can be replaced by shorter, clearer ones. For example using 'proffer' when you mean 'give' or 'articulate' when you mean 'say'.

- **Redundancy.** Avoid using ten words where two will do: *'I am meeting Sophie later,'* is clearer than, *'Sophie and I are due to hook up together at some point in the day.'* Also avoid **tautology** – saying the same thing twice: *'10 a.m. in the morning'* is either *'10 a.m.'* or *'10 in the morning.'*

- **Ambiguity.** Many words can be understood in more than one way. So, *'Clarice was really cold'* could mean that Clarice was unfriendly or that she was shivering. Put yourself in the reader's place to make sure that the meaning of your statement is clear.

- **Causing offence.** A simple rule to follow is: *treat everyone equally in your writing, regardless of sex, age, race, sexual orientation, or physical difference.* Be aware of current customs and values, and also consider different cultures. This is especially relevant if you are communicating with people around the world.

These are only a few points to consider before you start writing, but if you refer to them regularly, they will help you express yourself clearly and consistently in all your communications.

EMAIL

Emails are an important form of written communication in many people's lives. Whether at home or at work, we spend a lot of our time sending and receiving them. Email correspondence can feel more like a conversation than an exchange of letters. The tone is generally less formal, and the time between sending your message and getting a reply can be minutes or even seconds. The fact that it is instant can be good and bad. Good because it can be a very efficient way of corresponding; bad if you write quickly and carelessly.

Addressing emails

When addressing emails, the general rule of thumb is that the fewer people you email, the better. There are three address fields to consider, and each serves a different purpose:

- **'To':** this is for the address of the main recipient, or recipients, of the information or request to do something.

- **'Cc':** if you are simply informing someone of your actions or requests, put those people in the 'Cc' ('Carbon or Courtesy Copy') field.

- **'Bcc':** if you are copying someone in but you don't want the other addressees to know you should use the 'Bcc' ('Blind Carbon or Courtesy Copy'). This is frequently used for mailing large groups, where you don't want individuals to know who else is receiving the email.

> *Bear in mind that if you send an email to one person you are 95 per cent likely to get a reply; if you send it to 10 people the response rate drops to 5 per cent.*
>
> (Linguistics professor)

Greeting and ending

Emails on work-related issues or personal business require a formal style. You can never go wrong with 'Dear Mr Blake' or 'Dear Peter'. If the contact is long-standing and you are on a familiar footing then 'Hi Peter' is acceptable. In initial exchanges of formal email you might sign off in the same way that you would in a formal letter with 'Yours sincerely' or 'Yours faithfully'. As your correspondence gets onto a slightly less formal footing then 'Kind regards' or 'Best wishes' is fine.

Subject line

You can really help your correspondents by being precise in the subject line. For example if you send out a regular set of minutes by email, don't just write 'Launch Meeting Minutes', but add the date so people can quickly find what they are looking for. If your email contains a specific question it is good practice to add 'Q:' followed by the question in the subject line.

Layout

Use a paragraph per point you wish to make, and put headings above each paragraph if there are more than three. If your email is long and will require the reader to scroll down the screen, consider writing it as a Word document and attaching it to an email – long emails are not easy to read and respond to.

Content

Always remember that with email, your writing can be forwarded to anyone with a single mouse click. Be careful that what you write is not defamatory, offensive, or detrimental to you or your business.

> *Never forward without reading the whole email: you never know what indiscretions or traps are in there. Never put anything in an email you don't want the world to know.*

(Local authority manager)

- Restrict the email to a single subject. If you want to email the same person or people about other issues, use separate emails. It makes filing and action points much easier to follow.

- Don't reply straight away to an email that irks you. You will not be able to hide your anger and will not make the situation better. Wait until you have calmed down enough to think through your response and compose a measured reply dealing with the points raised.

- Don't assume that the person you are writing to has the same cultural reference points, sense of humour, or values.

> *I know of people who communicate regularly with colleagues in Italy, where capitalization is used to show something is urgent whereas we read it as shouting.*

(Marketing executive)

9

Attachments

Email is great for sharing documents, photographs and audio-files in the form of attachments. But sending large files can cause headaches. Most email providers (and certainly most companies) allocate a storage limit to each email address; if an Inbox becomes too full, you cannot receive or send emails. So be considerate when you send anything as an attachment.

Replying

Sometimes you get an email which contains a series of questions. It is perfectly acceptable to reply to each of these questions by adding your comments (sometimes in a different colour or with your initials in square brackets before your answer) in the body of the original email. This saves you typing out the questions or writing replies that incorporate the original question. For example:

From: Asif Iqbal
To: Fiona McManus
SUBJECT: My paintings

Dear Fiona
Thank you very much for your email about the posters I sell. I've put my answers below your questions with [AI] after.

With thanks and all best wishes

Asif
Mobile: 011111 789456
www.asifiqbal.art.gallery.net

Do you have a website?
[AI] Yes. You can see all my work at www.asifiqbal.art.gallery.net
What sizes do the posters come in?
[AI] Anything from A5 to A1. I can also frame them to order – there's a selection of frames on the website.
What range of prices are there?
[AI] Prices start at $AUS 11.95 and can go up to $AUS 75.00
If you don't have a poster I want in stock, can you source it for me?
[AI] Of course, I'd be happy to help in any way. Have a look through the website and if you can't find what you want, just drop me a line and I'll do my best!

Formal email

The rules for writing formal emails are similar to those for formal letters.

- If you are communicating with someone for the first time you should adopt the structure of a formal letter.

- It is usual and proper to use a greeting of some sort when you begin your email. 'Dear' can never be misunderstood and rarely strikes the wrong note. If you are more familiar with the person you are writing to 'Hi' or 'Hello' is fine. If you're writing to close friends then use whichever greeting you are accustomed to in your social circle.

- If you are emailing someone for the first time without being invited to it is always proper to explain at the very start of the email who you are and why you are writing to them.

- Never leave the subject line blank. In most formal or professional correspondence you should aim to keep the email to one subject. Think clearly what the email is about and be as precise as you can. Keep the subject as short as possible as the recipient's inbox will often only display a limited amount of the line.

- If the email is going to be long it is polite to indicate this in the opening few sentences of the email.

- Structure your email so that each point is addressed in a separate paragraph. If you wish, it is entirely acceptable to add a heading to each paragraph. Your reader can then see at a glance the points you are covering.

- In formal emails, texting abbreviations and emoticons should be avoided.

- When you end your email use the same rules as with formal letters, using 'Yours faithfully' or 'Yours sincerely' as appropriate.

> *I avoid using multiple sub-clauses and long sentences and use lists or bullet points rather than block text.*
>
> (Marketing manager)

Informal emails

For emails to friends and family you can be more relaxed in your style and tone.

- 'Hi' or 'Hey' or other informal greetings are appropriate and you can sign off the email with 'See you' or 'lots of love' or other phrases.

- Even when you're writing to a friend remember that email can seem terse and abrupt if there is no greeting or sign-off.

- It is fine to use texting abbreviations and emoticons in informal emails – just make sure the person you're writing to understands them all!

> *I read the email back to myself as though I were reading someone else's email prior to sending.*
>
> (Course co-ordinator)

WRITING AT WORK

Email

Emails are the default means of communication for most businesses. Whenever you write an important email at work it needs to be concise, clear and well thought-out. The tone should in almost all cases be for formal.

Some research conducted recently across a wide range of professions suggested that on average people get 100 emails per day and have to respond to about 40 per cent of them. Email adds a lot of extra reading and writing to an already busy work day. So the first question you should ask is 'Is email the best way to say what I have to say?' A frequent complaint of people in business is that they are sent or copied in on emails that they really don't need to see.

> *My tip for effective communication in an organization? Don't write. Phone or speak to someone in person.*
>
> (CEO, International Management Consultancy)

Compare the two emails on the following pages which show the difference between good and bad practice in business email writing.

BAD EMAIL

Ollie
There are problems re the arrangements for the conference dinner. I met with David yesterday to finalize details and here's what we decided: The venue (Carmichael Hall) is booked for Dec 18th 7:00 – 12:00. Send out the invitations to all conference delegates the week starting November 3rd. Find out from the printers when the invitations are being returned to us and get them send out in a timely fashion to the delegates. You'll need to check against th otiginal delegate list. Hallidays need to know final numbers by Dec. 10th., latest. Call them to let them know Liaise with Sujata over the timing of the speeches and let the relevant people know when their slot is.
Can't think of anything else at the moment but it's down to you now.

- The tone is abrupt, ill-tempered and dictatorial without being helpful.

- The email is very sloppily written: there are spelling and grammatical mistakes throughout.

- Information required to carry out the actions is not provided.

- People the recipient needs to liaise with and get information from are not included in the email.

- The email generates more work for both the sender and the addressee.

- The email is one block of text which makes identifying what needs to be done laborious and time-consuming.

GOOD EMAIL

Subject: Conference dinner action points 25/10
From: "Hill, Lucy" <Lucy.Hill@bigbooks.co.uk>
To: "Ollie Walsh", "Maine, Sujata" <Sujata.Maine@bigbooks.co.uk

Hi Ollie

Thanks again for offering to help with the arrangements for the conference dinner. I do appreciate it.
David and I had a meeting yesterday to finalize the details. I've included Sujata on the email so you can liaise directly with her on a couple of the points.

Venue
The venue (Carmichael Hall) is booked for December 18th 7:00 – 12:00.
The contact there is Julia Waters.
Her number is 01354 638976.

Invitations
The invitations are currently with the printers. When they are returned to us (this Friday, 1st November) they will need checking against the original delegate list.
Sujata: could you send the list to Ollie please?
Invitations should go to all conference delegates the week starting November 3rd.

The caterers
Hallidays, the caterers, will need to know final numbers by Dec. 10th. Please call them to confirm these numbers (01354 222227).

Speeches
Finally, please could you liaise with Sujata over the timing of the speeches and let the relevant people know when their slot is? The list of speakers is on the shared drive. (K:/conference2015/speakerlist.doc)

Any questions, give me a call. I'm here all this week apart from Thursday afternoon.

Many thanks,

Lucy

- The writer includes all the people required to do something in the 'To' box.

- There is a precise 'Subject' line.

- The paragraphs are set out so that addressing each point is easy.

- All the relevant information is included (dates, contact names and numbers, and file locations).

- The tone is collaborative, helpful and professional.

> I keep all emails as brief as possible and use short sentences to get across all important points.
>
> (Food journalist)

When not to use email

Avoid the temptation to think that email can be used in all situations. For example, email isn't very good at conveying tone or emotion accurately. If you want to discuss something sensitive or personal with someone, it might be better to talk with them in person, or write them a note.

Letters at work

Formal business letters are, like memos, becoming rarer. Some professions – particularly the law – still rely on written correspondence, but for most businesses email is the default mode. When you come to write a formal letter to someone outside your organization you should observe the rules of letter writing (see pages 30–33).

> I use email for almost all written communication, but I send letters to staff over HR issues: for example, around persistent absence, capability and contract issues.
>
> (Local government manager)

A lot of letter correspondence within an organization is about HR issues – resignation letters or changes to terms and conditions, for example. These require a signature, are often 'private and confidential' and, like the work contract, may be required for future reference. For these two reasons, formal letters are the appropriate form of writing. Here is an example of a resignation letter.

Anna Wozniaki
Account Manager
Upside Down Records
Flintrock
Sussex
B45 8EP
17 June 2015

Dear Anna

Please accept this as formal notice of my resignation from the position of Account Executive, with effect from today 17th June, 2015.

In accordance with my contract of employment I am happy to continue to work until the end of my notice period which by my calculations is the 15th July.

While I believe that I am moving for good reasons, I am sorry to leave, and I thank you for your support during my time with the company, which I have found enjoyable and fulfilling.

Please let me know the arrangements for returning equipment – my company phone and laptop – and handing over outstanding work and responsibilities.

Yours sincerely

Martin Fry

Martin Fry

- The letter is polite, formal and shows that the writer wants to help to ease the process of his leaving.

- It offers no suggestions about improvements or criticisms of the company – you might be given an opportunity to do that in person at an exit interview.

PRESENTATIONS

The key to making a successful presentation is to be well-prepared. Make sure that you fill your available time, pitch the information at an appropriate level for your audience, and keep in mind the main points you want to get across.

Preparation

- Ask yourself why you are writing the presentation: is it to inform, to persuade your audience to accept your view, or to entertain? Structure your talk to fit in with your aim.

- Write the key points of your argument in a logical sequence on prompt cards. Keep the points to the minimum – just enough to remind you what you need to say.

- Rehearse until you are confident that you know exactly what you are going to say. Make sure that you can deliver the important points clearly and confidently; practice looking at an imaginary member of the audience as you speak.

> You should always aim to entertain – there's nothing worse than having to sit through a dull PowerPoint presentation where the speaker reads exactly what is on the slides.
>
> (IT Manager)

Presentation slides

There are two major mistakes that inexperienced speakers make when they use PowerPoint or other presentation slide packages:

- The speaker reads out (often word for word) what is written on the slide.

- There are too many words on the slide for the audience to read and absorb.

Remember these key points about writing presentation slides:

- Presentation slides should summarize the point you want to make so that the audience can remember what you're saying.

- You should give each slide a heading to reflect the aspect of the subject you are talking about at that time in your presentation.

- Restrict each line on the slide to very short phrases or even single words. Do not use more than five or six lines per slide.

Here are some examples of good and bad presentation slides:

GOOD PRACTICE

- Use a large, simple font.
- Write only key points on slide.
- Don't use complicated backgrounds.

BAD PRACTICE

- Use a complicated font.
- Add far too many words to the slide so that people find it really hard to take in the point of the slide and spend more time reading the slide than they do listening to you.
- Repeat exactly what you have written on the slide – it's very dull for the audience and does not reinforce your point or make it more memorable.

JOB APPLICATIONS

A covering letter and CV are usually the first things any prospective employer will see of you. If you want to get an interview for a job, it is important that these documents present you in the best possible light. The following sections deal with how to construct and write your covering letter and CV, and provide tips on how to apply for a job online.

Covering letter

The covering letter should convey confidence, enthusiasm, technical knowledge and demonstrate an understanding of what the job entails. It need not be long and it should not be a rehash of the accompanying CV. A short, clear, well-written covering letter can make all the difference between two candidates.

> *Some people think the covering letter is another CV. It's not. A covering letter is a way of introducing yourself to the employer and of providing a persuasive case for reading the CV and then getting an interview.*
>
> (HR Director)

The covering letter should alert the employer to the key points of a CV and show the match between the candidate and the job being advertised. In general it will consist of three paragraphs or so:

- **First paragraph.** Introduce yourself, say which job you are applying for and where you saw it. You can also include a general statement of why you want to apply for the job and how you feel about the company.

- **Second paragraph.** Provide information about your skills, strengths, qualifications and experience. Give specific examples of why you are the ideal candidate and don't simply restate your CV.

- **Final paragraph.** Conclude the letter expressing your desire to get the job and requesting an interview. You should also say what the best way to contact you is, and if there are any inconvenient dates. Always thank the employer for considering your application.

FAQ

Q. *Should my letter be typed or handwritten?*
A. It should be typed on A4 paper. Only the signature should be handwritten.

Q. *Is it OK to send out the same letter to all those companies I'm interested in?*
A. No. Try to avoid general letters. Find out as much as you can about the company, and tailor your letter accordingly.

Q. *Should I mention salary in my accompanying letter?*
A. It is usually best not to touch on the subject of salary at this stage, unless requested in the advertisement.

Useful phrases

First of all, identify the job you are applying for:

- I would like to inquire as to whether there are any openings for junior telesales operators in your company.

- I am writing to apply for the post of senior marketing manager.

- I would like to apply for the position of online learning coordinator, as advertised on your website.

- I am writing to apply for the above post, as advertised in the Guardian of 8 August 2015.

Next, give some examples of personal achievements:

- I have gained experience in several major aspects of publishing.

- I co-ordinated the change-over from one accounting system to another.

- I developed designs for a new range of knitwear.

- I have supervised a team of telesales operators on several projects.

- I contributed to the development of our new database software.

Then outline your personal qualities:

- I see myself as systematic and meticulous in my approach to work.

- I am a fair and broad-minded person, with an ability to get on well with people from all walks of life.

- I am hardworking and business minded, and I tend to thrive under pressure.

Explain why you want this job:

- I am now keen to find a post with more responsibility.

- I now wish to find a more permanent full-time position.

- I would like to further my career in the field of production.

- I feel that your company's activities most closely match my own values and interests.

Express your willingness to attend an interview.

Here is an example covering letter:

15 Sandybank Drive
Derby
DX27 9LC
joelmanners@email.com
01245 645201

27 July 2015

Mr H Carson
Personnel Manager
Allied Derby Building Society
HR House
Illingworth Way
DERBY
DX3 9DF

Dear Mr Carson

Customer Services Manager

I am responding to the job advertised in the *Derby Express* and on your website on the 22nd July. I feel the job is just what I have been looking for, and reading the job description, I am sure that I have the right level of experience, aptitude and training. Your company's support and promotion of ethical investment has always impressed and inspired me and I would very much like to contribute to your success. My CV is attached.

For the past three years I have been Senior Customer Services Adviser at Cathedral County Bank, leading a team of seven people. Since I took on the role our positive response rate has risen by 10 per cent and customer satisfaction in the area I look after by 15 per cent. I was voted Employee of the Month three times by my colleagues in the period. While I am very happy in my job, the opportunities for promotion are limited and I do want to take on a more responsible role in my area of expertise.

I would welcome the opportunity to discuss my application further. Email is the best way to contact me and I am available for interview at your convenience. Thank you for taking the time to read my application.

Yours sincerely

Mr Joel Manners

Mr Joel Manners

- Avoid just sending a letter or email with 'Please find my CV attached'. Remember that this application is a two-stage process to try to get an interview. Each step in the process (covering letter and CV) has to make the employer want to take the next step.

- Remember the basics:
  - Check all spelling and grammar two or three times.
  - Make sure you have spelled all names correctly.
  - Include all contact details.
  - Include any information that the job advertisement has specifically asked you to provide.

A speculative job application

- When applying for a job on a speculative basis, try to speak to the person responsible for recruitment in the appropriate department beforehand. This way, you will have a specific person to write to, as well as having established a relationship with them.

34 St Dunstan's Way
Vancouver
V6G 7D7

19 July 2015

Ms D Wallis
Youngs Accountancy and Finance
19 Lockwood Road
Vancouver
V9P 8K1

Dear Ms Wallis

post of software development co-ordinator

Thank you very much for taking the time to speak to me yesterday about the possibility of a position as software development co-ordinator with your company.

Please find attached a CV which highlights my prior professional experience, and the qualities which I feel make me suited to this position. You will see that I have a strong interest in, and knowledge of, staff management, and have gained extensive experience in handling large development projects and meeting deadlines.

I see myself as being well-organized and self-motivated, and have excellent communication skills. I am keen to develop my career with Youngs Accountancy and Finance, and so would very much appreciate the opportunity to discuss further my suitability for the post.

Please feel free to contact me, either by email: dgormanl@netserve.com, or by leaving a message on (604) 473 5522. I look forward to speaking to you soon.

Yours sincerely

D Gorman

Deborah Gorman

CV

Your CV exists to give a brief description of who you are, what you have done and what you can do.

> *What a lot of candidates forget is that the purpose of the CV is to get the interview – not the job. So they give way too much detail and don't tailor it to the role they are trying to get.*
>
> (HR Director)

- The language should always be 'active'. Avoid passive statements like 'Turnover growth of 25 per cent was achieved in the period,' say instead, 'I increased turnover for the period by 25 per cent.' Active language simplifies your statements and makes them easier to read.

- Use positive adverbs ('efficiently', 'successfully' 'effectively') so that your CV will convey a positive impression to your prospective employer.

CV structure

The most common CV format is called 'reverse chronological', meaning you start with your current job and work backwards. If your earliest jobs have little relevance to your current application, you can simply list the job title, company and the dates you worked there. Summarize your education after the employment section, and then add any additional skills and interests that may be of use to support your application.

You can see a sample CV on the next page:

Helena Shapur

12 Green Lane, Brighton, Sussex BT1 3EY
Email: h.sharpur@email.com
Mobile: 07123 456789

Personal profile

An enthusiastic, self-motivated professional, highly qualified in the field of online team management. My motivation is to use the web to help make the most of all businesses I work for. I have an in-depth understanding of a wide range of web technologies from Java to Ruby.

Career summary

2009 – present Development Team Leader, GoGetting.com

I joined the online travel company GoGetting.com as a development officer before being promoted in August 2012 to my current position. Since becoming team leader the site has had a threefold increase in unique visitors thanks to an extensive linking program I developed. As a result of the increased traffic, the company has given me extra responsibility to drive the marketing of the site with selected web partners. I manage a team of seven development officers and am in charge of a budget of £250,000.

2004 – 2009 Web Developer, Toprank Recruitment

Having learned a lot at my first company and really enjoyed the experience of working in web development, I joined this small recruitment start-up specializing in the catering trade. During the time I helped program the site's search engine and learned ASP, Java and SQL.
I was very proud to have seen one key module of the search engine's development through from design to implementation. The module generated five per cent extra revenue for the company while I was there. I learned a lot about effective teamwork in the process.

2002–2004 Junior programmer, Oakhampton Systems

This was a perfect job after graduation. I was part of a small graduate intake whose job was to develop and code account and customer databases. I went on site visits to understand what a client needed and understand the way the business works. I taught myself HTML in this period and designed the company's first website.

Education and qualifications

1998–2001 University of Windsor, BSC Computer Science (2:1)
1991 – 1998 Greenglades School, Windsor
3 A-levels: Mathematics (A), Physics (A), Chemistry (B)
10 GCSEs

Hobbies and interests

Between leaving school and starting university I worked for six months so that I could spend three months doing charity runs for Famine Relief, whom I continue to work for as a volunteer. I run long-distance competitively, enjoy cinema, computer games and chess.

References available on request

> *One of the worst mistakes a candidate can make is to send employers a 6-page 'novel' about their work experience, school qualifications and hobbies and pastimes – especially if it is written in size-9 font. Many managers skim read CVs so using short paragraphs and an almost report-like style will mean they are less likely to miss a candidate with relevant skills or experience. This is where editing down and making the CV relate to the job description/advert works to the candidate's advantage.*
>
> (HR Director)

BASIC GRADUATE CV

CV

Name	Kate Maxwell
Date of birth	29.02.92
Address	19, The Poplars, Bristol B10 2JU
Telephone	0117 123 4567
Email	katemaxwell@atlantic.net
Nationality	British

Education

2011–2015	**BA Hons in Modern Languages, University of Exeter** (final grade 2.1)
2009–2011	**Clifton Road Secondary School:** 3 'A' levels – French (A) German (A) History (B)
2004–2009	**Clifton Road Secondary School:** 8 GCSEs including Maths and English

Employment history

2011–2012	**Sales Assistant, Langs Bookshop, Bristol** I was responsible for training and supervising weekend and holiday staff.
2012–2013	**English Assistant, Lycée Benoit, Lyons** I taught conversational English to pupils aged 12–18, preparing the older students for both technical and more academic qualifications. I organized an educational trip to the UK for fourth year pupils.

Positions of responsibility held

2012–2013	**Entertainments Officer for University Student Social Society** I organized and budgeted for entertainment for a student society with over 1000 members.
2011–2014	**Captain of the university women's netball team** I was in charge of training, organizing and motivating the women's team.

Other skills

Fluent French and German
Extensive knowledge of Microsoft Word, Excel and Access
I hold a clean driving licence

References
on request

Top ten CV tips

1. Adapt your CV to the job or prospective employer.

2. You have 30–60 seconds to attract your reader's attention so lay out your CV clearly – use a plain font like Arial, Trebuchet or Times New Roman – and keep it to the point. It should not be longer than 3 sides.

3. Remember the CV is a means of getting an interview, not getting the job.

4. Avoid gimmicks like thumbnail images or pictures – they distract from the words you are writing about yourself.

5. Focus your description of your current and previous experience on achievements and the contribution you made to the organizations. If possible quantify your achievements – 'my actions led to a saving of £xx' or, 'as a result profits were up by x per cent'.

6. Give examples of your skills and qualities – don't just say 'I am a natural leader,' write a brief description of when you showed this attribute.

7. Avoid bullet points when describing your current and previous jobs. It's much better to write short paragraphs because you can give examples.

8. Format the document to make sure that the printed version reflects what you see on screen. Try not to waste paper by leaving just two or three sentences at the top of the last page.

9. Use 'active' verbs such as 'achieve', 'lead', 'manage'.

10. Finally carefully proofread your CV and, if you can, ask someone else to look at it as well.

How to send your CV

You can still post your CV if you wish but most HR professionals prefer to receive the document as an attachment to an email. This means that they can share the CV with the relevant staff or store it on their computer for future reference.

Online applications

Sometimes you will be asked to complete an application form online.
Here are some tips to do this effectively:

- As for written job applications, you should write in a formal style.

- The online system will probably dictate the particular text format (the font and size of type) – you should take this into account when you draft your answers.

- It is useful to prepare a draft of the application and then transfer the information to the online form.

- Copy and save your answers regularly into a normal document in case the system crashes or you have to break off your application and start again.

- Just because the application is automatically filed online, it does not mean you should be any less rigorous in the editing and proofreading you do. If you can print the document out before you submit it, get someone you trust to read it over to look for errors and omissions.

WRITING FORMAL LETTERS

Emails and other digital media are the prevalent forms of communication for most of us today, at work and at home, but there are still occasions when a handwritten or typed letter is more appropriate.

This section lays out the basic structure and the rules which underpin most formal letter writing. The Domestic Correspondence, Social Communication and Job Applications sections within this supplement will look more closely at situations where formal letter writing is used, and give examples of good practice.

As with any written communication, your letter should be in three discernible parts:

- **An introduction.** This is where you introduce yourself, acknowledge any previous correspondence, and briefly state the reason why you are writing. Ideally it should be no longer than a paragraph of three or four sentences.

- **The middle.** This is the section where you expand your argument, provide further details, and raise any questions you have. The middle of the letter should be a series of paragraphs set out in a logical order. Each paragraph should make a clear, separate point. If the letter is long and covers a range of subjects, it may be appropriate to divide the contents by subheadings.

- **The ending, or conclusion.** The final paragraph should set out what you would like to happen as a result of the communication, whether that be a written response, a meeting to discuss the contents of the letter, or a demand for a refund.

Here is an example of a formal letter:

55 Torrance Close
Gorton
NSW 2234

25 August 2011

Mr L Dylan
Terrigan Building Ltd
340 Shorter Street
Terrigan
NSW 2234
Dear Mr Dylan

Estimate for extension to living room, 55 Torrance Close

I am writing to thank you for the written estimate which I received this morning. I have queries about a couple of details in your letter which I would like to be resolved before we proceed any further.

First, can you say exactly when you would propose to begin work on the extension? I realize this depends, to some extent, on how quickly you can finish your current project. I need to know which week work would commence in, however, so that I can make arrangements to store the living room furniture.

Second, can you tell me when you propose to fit the additional plumbing, so that I can arrange to stay with friends while there is no running water? Also, are there any other times when you anticipate that I shall be without water or electricity?

Finally, there is no mention of additional costs for materials. Can I assume, therefore, that these are included in the estimate you have provided for the overall cost of the extension?

Assuming I receive satisfactory answers in writing to these queries, I shall be happy to accept your proposal and go ahead with the project as discussed.

Yours sincerely

Tom Peterson

Tom Peterson

Points to remember:

- **Your address.** This should be written in the top right corner of the letter. Do not write your name here, and don't put commas after each line.

- **The date.** The date should come under your address, also on the right. It is common practice to write the date as 25 August 2015, instead of 25th August 2015.

- **The recipient's address.** Write this under the date, but on the left side of the page. Again, no punctuation is required.

- **The greeting.** If you are writing to a friend then you will use, 'Dear Luke,' for instance. Otherwise it should be 'Dear Mr Dylan.' Note that if you are writing to a woman and do not know whether she prefers to be addressed as 'Dear Mrs Dylan', or 'Dear Miss Dylan', then you should use 'Dear Ms Dylan.' If you do not know the person's name then use, 'Dear Sir or Madam.'

- **Headings.** If you are using a heading, then it should summarize the subject matter of the letter, and appear between the greeting and the first paragraph. Headings should be written in bold but not capital letters.

- **The ending.** If you have used the name of the person in the greeting, then you should end with 'Yours sincerely'. Otherwise end the letter with 'Yours faithfully'. 'Yours...' should always begin with a capital letter.

- **Punctuation.** It is not necessary to include a comma after the greeting or after the ending. Don't put full stops in initials – write 'Mr L H Dylan' instead of 'Mr L.H. Dylan'.

- **Signature.** Write your signature but include your typewritten name underneath.

- **Further contact details.** If you are including your email address or telephone number as contact details, then these should be included underneath your postal address:

> 55 Torrance Close
> Gorton
> NSW 2234
> tpeterson@email.com
> (02) 4254 6398

Once you have written your letter check that:

- You have explained why you are writing in the first paragraph.

- You have made all the points that you wanted to.

- Each sentence is clear, concise and unambiguous.

- You have not included too much information, or any irrelevant details.

- Your language has been courteous and polite, even if you are writing a letter of complaint.

- Check once more for spelling mistakes – it is surprisingly easy to miss them!

DOMESTIC CORRESPONDENCE

This section tackles the range of letters and correspondence that relates to you, your home, your finances and your family. The following points about content, style and tone apply equally whether you're writing a letter, an email, filling in an online form, or if you are speaking to someone on the phone:

- Use formal language.

- Include every detail that will make the letter easier to deal with.

- Lay the letter out clearly – breaking it down so that each paragraph contains a single point.

- Be explicit about what you want to happen next and introduce a timescale where appropriate.

- What you are writing may have legal implications, so take care with the details you include and the language you use.

- Provide as many contact details as you can.

- Write 'Yours sincerely' to end the letter if you know the surname of the person you are writing to. Write 'Yours faithfully' if you do not.

> *When I'm writing to a company, I always try and find out a specific person to address the letter to – or else it can just end up getting lost in the system.*
> (Teacher)

In the following section there is a selection of letters that many of us will have to write at some point:

- Insurance claims

- Planning application objection

- Writing to your MP

- Deferring jury service

- School correspondence

- Letters of complaint

Insurance claims

Most of us find ourselves having to make a claim to an insurance company at some stage in our lives – whether it be as the result of a car accident, burglary, incident on holiday or some other regrettable occurrence.

The claim can be made verbally, online or in a written statement but whichever form it takes, it is important to consider the kind of language you use and the information that you include.

Ms C Hall
32, Lime Road
Saddleworth
Devon
SD2 8LN
christinehall@email.com
17 June 2015

Ms Ying
Claims Assessor
Admirable Insurance Company
Claims Avenue
Spottington
Hants
SP31 4AQ

My policy number: AIC008997/CH56.

Dear Ms Ying,

I am writing to make an insurance claim, resulting from an accident I was involved in on 16 June 2015. My car is covered by a comprehensive insurance policy which I took out with you some time ago. The policy number is included above.

The incident occurred at approximately 3pm at the junction of New Street and London Road in Saddleworth. The other driver, a Mr Steve Wall, turned right out of New Street and drove into the front passenger side of my vehicle, causing extensive damage to the bodywork and the headlights. I have enclosed a picture of the damage, together with a diagram showing the relative positions of the vehicles, and the direction they were travelling in at the time of the accident.

Mr Wall has admitted liability for the accident. His insurance company's details, together with his policy number, are also enclosed.

As a result of the incident, my car is not roadworthy. I need therefore, to arrange to collect a replacement car from one of your suppliers, which I am entitled to according to the terms of my policy. Can you advise me on the nearest garage and confirm my entitlement? Please let me know if there are any other details you require to process my claim, and also give me an indication of how long it will take to arrange the repair of my vehicle.

Yours sincerely

Ms C Hall

Ms C Hall

- The letter contains all the relevant information – such as dates, policy number, details of the incident – that the company is likely to require.

- In spite of the nature of the incident, the language is restrained – emotional language will not make your claim any more likely to succeed.

- The letter politely requests information from the insurance company which will move the claim on.

Opposing a planning application

Correspondence with a local authority is often in the form of a complaint or an objection. Whether you are contesting a parking fine or opposing a planning application, the information you include should be precise and accurate to back your claims.

Mr C Hopkins
75 Birchtree Row
Lessington
County Durham
D2 8LN
chopkins@email.com

1 December 2015

Mr Anderson
Director of Planning
Lime Borough Council
Acacia Road
Lessington
County Durham
D5 1AA

Dear Mr Anderson,

Planning application number LBC123456/7A
Address of proposed extension: 77 Birchtree Row, Lessington, County Durham, D2 8LN

I am writing to object to the proposal to build an extension on the above property. There are several reasons for this.

Design
The very modern design of the proposed extension is in unsympathetic contrast to the Victorian style of all the houses in the area.

Privacy
The two-storey extension will affect the privacy of my property. The plans show a window that will look directly into my garden.

Natural light

The extension will block out the natural light I get in my conservatory all-year round.

Appropriateness of use

It is clear from the plans that the owner intends to make and sell drum kits from the property. This will have a significant impact on the local noise levels – the neighbourhood at the moment is very quiet.

I am sure that other local residents will be objecting as well, and I trust you will refuse this application on the basis that it most definitely contravenes your planning regulations.

I would be grateful if you could acknowledge this letter, confirm that it has been logged as an objection to the application within the deadline set by the council, and keep me informed as to the outcome. I can be contacted at the above address or via the email address at the top of this letter.

Yours Sincerely,

Mr C Hopkins

Mr C Hopkins

- The writer has found out the deadline for his objection and complied with it.

- He has found out and addressed the criteria on which the application will be judged.

- The headings highlight the grounds on which he is basing his objection.

Writing to your MP

When writing to your MP keep the letter to a single subject and make it as concise as possible. Remember to say what you want the MP to do as a result of your letter. At all times be courteous – just because you may disagree with his views, does not mean that you should be anything other than respectful in your writing.

You can see a letter written to an MP on the next page:

Mr R Boscombe
27 Juniper Road
Flickcroft
West Midlands
reg.boscombe@email.com

15 April 2015

Derek Firbanks MP
House of Commons
Westminster
LONDON
SW1A 1AA

Dear Derek Firbanks

I am writing to draw your attention to the imminent closure of the Priory Centre on Sandhurst Road in Flickcroft. I am a parent whose child uses the premises for a theatre group on Saturday mornings. She finds the opportunity to learn about acting and to perform stimulating and great fun. The group also provides invaluable contact with other children from the area and with the community in general.

There are 120 children aged from six to 16 who attend the theatre classes every week – divided into three age bands. Last term my daughter's group staged a production dramatizing the history of the Priory Centre and its place in the local community.

The theatre group is by no means the only one affected. There are some 30 other activities put on for a huge range of people, including for elderly and disabled groups, at weekends and during the week.

The council plans to pass the plans at a meeting in three weeks' time. I, and many others, would be grateful if you could take this matter up with the leader of the council as a matter of urgency. The loss of the centre will create a huge gap in the cultural life of our community.

Please acknowledge this letter as soon as you can and let me know of your progress.

Yours sincerely,

Mr R Boscombe

Mr R Boscombe

- The letter starts with a very specific description of the problem.

- The writer includes his full address so that the MP knows the letter is from a constituent.

- The letter is about one issue which makes it easier to deal with.

- Including anecdotes or some personal detail will help the MP to remember the letter.

- The writer refers to others who are opposed to the closure. Including supporting evidence – be it a petition, or the MP's involvement with or voting record on similar issues – will help the cause.

> *When contacting your MP, a short, handwritten or printed letter is most effective. Take the time to edit your letter for brevity and clarity. Try to make a single coherent point.*
>
> (Campaigning website)

Deferring jury service

A letter requesting you to serve on a jury is a serious matter – in the UK if you ignore it you could be prosecuted. If the dates you have been called for are very disruptive to your plans, or circumstances are such that you can't attend, then you should write asking for a deferment. The grounds for deferment will be laid out in the letter you receive.

Mr J Brown
The Moorings
Chettleworth
LINCOLNSHIRE
AG7 0BC
james.brown@email.com
01285 78945613

3 February 2015

Mr R Ball
Jury Central Summoning Bureau
Derby
DA1 9IO

Dear Mr Ball

Thank you for the letter dated January 30th inviting me to serve on a jury from March 27th. I would like to ask if it would be possible to defer this until sometime next year? My wife has recently had a car accident and suffered a serious injury. I have now had to become a full-time carer for her and as a consequence cannot leave the house for an extended period.

I would be very grateful if you could agree to this request, and if you require me to provide you with any further information, please do not hesitate to contact me.

I look forward to receiving your response.

Yours sincerely,

Mr James Brown

Mr James Brown

- It is more effective to provide specific details for your request: it decreases the likelihood of having to give more information and speeds up the process.

- Do not demand that your attendance is deferred.

School correspondence

There are a few occasions when it will be necessary to write, or email, your child's school, to keep a record of important incidents during their career. Below are an example email and letter dealing with two such incidents: when your child has more than a couple of days off school, and to put on record concerns about bullying.

To: J Chalfont <jchalfont@derwentwaterschool.ed.uk
From: kevin.bond@email.net

Subject: Charlie Bond's absence 1st – 5th March

Dear Mr Chalfont

I am writing to explain why Charlie was absent from school last week (1st to 5th March). He woke up with a very sore throat on Sunday morning. We went to the doctor on Monday and Charlie was diagnosed with laryngitis. He started to feel better on Friday morning and is able to return to school today.

Charlie is worried, as the exams approach, about keeping on top of his work, so I would be very grateful if you could let him know what he has missed and help him catch up.

If you have any concerns, please do email or phone me on the number below.

Yours sincerely

Mr K Bond
kevin.bond@email.net
Tel: 01234 456789

- The letter quickly and clearly summarizes the course of events and includes evidence of the illness by referring to the doctor's diagnosis.

- The parent, having been very clear about the reason for absence, then presents their own concerns and is explicit about what they want the teacher to do. The letter is useful and effective for the parent, teacher and pupil.

Mrs J Trewin
'The Glade'
Farm Road
Kettering
XA7 2WR
janetrewin@email.com
01234 5678913

29 January 2015

Ms L Edge
Long Oak Primary School
West End Lane
Kettering
XA5 9LD

Dear Ms Edge

I am writing to follow up on our conversation on the phone two days ago. I'm afraid that Julia is still very upset when she gets home from school. The name-calling and exclusion from playground games seems to have carried on, in spite of the warning you said you gave the other children concerned. In fact, I fear that it may have made the problem worse.

As you can imagine this is causing Julia great distress and it is certainly affecting her desire to come to school and learn. I am very anxious to get this matter resolved with all possible speed, and request a meeting with you and the head of year at your earliest convenience.

Please telephone or email me as soon as you can to arrange this.

Yours sincerely

Mrs J Trewin

Mrs J Trewin

- The letter quickly summarizes the current situation to remind the teacher of the problem.

- The parent suggests a specific course of action and a timetable.

Letters of complaint

Complaining about faulty goods or services is an unpleasant but common experience. Whatever your complaint, there are several points which you should bear in mind when composing a letter or email to increase your chances of receiving a satisfactory response:

- Make sure you are complaining to the right person. It may seem obvious, but if you have paid for something in cash or by credit card, then it is the seller of the goods or services who you should address your complaint to – not the manufacturer.

- Be aware of your rights under the Sales and Supply of Goods Act, the Trades Descriptions Act and related or equivalent legislation – these decree that goods or services must be found to be 'as described' when sold.

- There are consumer watchdogs and other bodies who can help you if you are given unsatisfactory responses to your complaints. You can also write to your MP or consult a solicitor, but these should be last measures which hopefully won't be necessary.

Useful phrases

- I am writing to express my dissatisfaction with the service I received from your ...

- At the time of booking it was agreed that ...

- However, on our arrival, we discovered that ...

- I recently bought ...(include colour, model and price) in your shop in ...

- When I tried to use this item, I discovered that ...

- I have contacted you by telephone three times and each time you have promised to visit and put the faults right.

- To date these problems have not been resolved.

- Under the terms of your guarantee, I would like to request a full reimbursement of the amount paid.

- I am withholding payment of the above invoice until I have heard your response to the points outlined above.

- Under the Supply of Goods and Services Act 1982, I am entitled to expect work to be carried out using due care and skill.

- If I do not hear from you within 14 days, I will have no choice but to take the matter further.

- Because of these faults I now consider you to be in breach of contract.

Letter or email of complaint concerning faulty goods

15 High Street
Corton
LANCS
LA12 3SH
fheadley@email.com

17 August 2015

Mr D Bryant
High Fi
3 The Parade
Soulton
LANCS
LA23 8GG

Dear Mr Bryant,

I am writing to complain about the Soundalive 411 headphones which I bought from your company, High Fi in Soulton, on 14 August.

When I plugged the headphones into my iPhone and listened to music through them, the sound in the left headphone was distorted at even low levels of volume – it was clear to me that they were faulty.

I returned them to your shop, a thirty mile round trip, but the salesperson who I originally dealt with disputed my claim – stating that the item had been sold in a satisfactory state. He suggested that I take up the complaint with you, as the owner of the shop.

The Sale of Goods Act 1979 makes it clear that goods be as described, fit for purpose and of satisfactory quality. I am therefore rejecting the headphones and request that you refund the £89 I paid, as the condition of the goods I received constitutes a breach of contract. I have enclosed a copy of my receipt.

I also require you to confirm whether you will arrange for the headphones to be collected from me at the above address, or will reimburse me for the cost of returning them by post?

I expect to receive a response detailing your proposals to satisfactorily settle my claim within seven days of this date.

Yours sincerely,

F Headley

Mr F Headley

- Although the writer has being treated badly by a member of staff, the tone of the letter is formal. Emotive language is likely to produce a defensive response, whereas a detailed and factual description of the problem is more likely to succeed.

- It is quite reasonable to seek compensation for the cost of returning a faulty item.

- Don't send originals of receipts and other documentary evidence with your complaint – especially if you have paid in cash. They may be the only way you have to prove purchase should you need to take the complaint further.

Letter to a travel agency complaining about a holiday

Mrs B Pritchard
21 Churchward Close
Hintenbury
GLOS
FL34 3HQ
bpritchard@email.com

21 July 2015

Customer Services department
Sunkissed Holidays
14 The Waterglades
Hintenbury
GLOS
FL34 7HH

Dear sir or madam

I am writing to complain about the holiday I booked through your company on 5 May this year (REF: BA12303/Maga003).

The booking stated that I would have a room with a balcony with ocean views, and that I would enjoy '5 star luxury' at the Mirabelle Resort, with 'top class international cuisine', and 'a choice of four swimming pools – two of which are reserved for adult use only.' Furthermore, the booking was on an 'all-inclusive basis, guaranteeing bar snacks, soft drinks and local brands of beers, wines and spirits', as and when I requested them.

The reality of my experience was very different. On arrival at the resort, I was allocated a room at the back of the hotel, with a view over a busy street. The noise from the traffic kept me awake at night.

The 'international cuisine' turned out to be a buffet featuring the same options practically every night – mostly fried food, chips and salad.

One of the swimming pools was closed for maintenance for the duration of my stay, and there was no attempt to keep any of the three remaining pools segregated for adult use.

Finally, the availability of drinks and bar snacks was very limited – peanuts were the only snack at the poolside bar, which also only had wine stocked on two days of the fourteen I was at the hotel.

I complained about each of these issues to your firm's representative at the resort – a Mr Stephens – during my first week's holiday. He said he would 'see what he could do'. I didn't hear back from him, and he failed to turn up for the 'rep meeting' in the second week. The hotel staff were unhelpful and told me they could do nothing to rectify any of the problems.

As a result of these issues, my holiday was ruined. I am therefore writing to you seeking compensation from your firm, which has clearly failed to deliver what was contractually agreed. I request that you reply within seven days, stating your proposal to compensate me.

Yours faithfully

Mrs B Pritchard

Mrs B Pritchard

- Use the company's own description of services to compare your experience with.

- Describe each aspect of your complaint concisely; state what you have done about it, and the response that you received from the relevant authority – in this case the holiday rep and the hotel staff.

Letter of complaint to a noisy neighbour

Mr G Barton
7 Chestnut Mansions
Pibble
Cumbria
PW12 3RR
gbarton@email.com

14 October 2015

Ms R Devlin
8 Chestnut Mansions
Pibble
Cumbria
PW12 3RR

Dear Ms Devlin

I am writing to you to formally register my complaint about the excessive noise that has been generated from your flat since you moved in two months ago.

As you know, I have complained in person to you five times in the past month about extremely loud music being played after 11 pm. You have assured me that you will 'not let it happen again,' only for me and my partner to have our sleep ruined the next weekend.

We have no objection to the occasional party or celebration, but your behaviour is inconsiderate and unreasonable. The interruption to our sleep patterns is affecting our concentration at work, and therefore I am giving you notice that if this happens again, without prior notice and agreement from us, I shall instruct my solicitor to begin legal proceedings to restrain you from excessive noise pollution.

Yours sincerely

Mr G Barton

Mr G Barton

- Legal action should only be threatened after attempts to complain less formally have failed. This letter is written after five such attempts.

- Be clear about what you expect to happen as a result of your complaint – how you expect the other party to modify their behaviour in this instance.

- Also spell out what course of action you intend to take should your demands not be met. You must follow through on this course of action, if you don't get a satisfactory response, or you will not be taken seriously in the future.

SOCIAL COMMUNICATION

> *And none will hear the postman's knock*
> *Without a quickening of the heart.*
> *For who can bear to feel himself forgotten?*

(W.H. Auden)

Although seemingly belonging to a different world – predating mobile phones, texts and tablet devices, all of which convey informal messages instantly and very well – there is still a time and a place for a carefully handwritten note or card, or printed invitation.

Types of correspondence in this category include:

- Thank-you notes

- Letters of condolence

- Invitations

Here are some general points to consider when writing social communications:

Tone

Apart from invitations, the tone of most social communications is informal and friendly:

- Salutations can range from 'Dear' to 'Hi'.

- Language is usually quite conversational, with shortened sentences and contractions ('I'm', 'won't'); more emotive and less factual than in business correspondence.

- Endings are similarly warm – 'Lots of love'; 'Love'; 'Speak/write soon'; or slightly more formal such as 'Best wishes', 'Kind regards' or 'All the best' if you don't know your correspondent quite so well.

Format

Just because it is handwritten doesn't mean that a note shouldn't have a structure. It is still usual to have:

- An introductory line or paragraph, stating the purpose of the letter ('I was sorry to hear about your loss'; 'thank you for the birthday card…').

- A middle section expounding on the subject ('She was a wonderful woman…'; 'The party went really well, all things considered').

- An ending ('I shall hope to speak to you at the memorial service'; 'Let's meet up before another year goes by…").

> *One thing I can't stand? The computer-generated Christmas card – it's so impersonal – "Look, I can do a mail merge on my pc!" If you can't be bothered to handwrite a greetings card, don't bother!*
>
> (Publishing assistant)

Here are some examples of different kinds of social correspondence:

Thank-you note for a dinner party

A thank-you letter can be as varied as a formal letter: the writer's relationship with the recipient will determine the tone and language used.

Tuesday

Hi Moz,

I'm just popping this note through your letterbox to thank you so much for dinner on Saturday. Nigel and I had a wonderful evening. It was lovely to meet Sharon and Graham at last – you've talked about them so much over the years – and they were delightful company. I hope Ben has found the champagne cork (sorry about that!)

By the way, please, please send me your recipe for the chocolate mousse – it was exquisite, and Nigel talked of nothing else on Sunday.

You must come to ours for dinner soon.

Love to you both and thanks again,

Lizzie.

- Dating and address can be very informal – this is a note between friends, and knowledge of addresses and contact details can be assumed. Note that the writer uses her friend's nickname 'Moz', rather than full name. You wouldn't use this form of address if writing to a colleague, for example.

- The language is casual – contractions like 'you've' and 'I'm' are absolutely fine. "Please, please send me your recipe…' would be out of place in a formal letter, but it works here.

- In social communication you can refer to events without having to be explicit – here there was clearly an 'incident' with a champagne cork which was a shared source of humour.

Letter of condolence

46 Cork Lane
Lamington
Herts

12 May

Dear Stephen

I am writing to say how sorry I was to hear of your loss, and that I am thinking of you at this difficult time. Although I was aware that Helen was ill, I was nevertheless shocked to hear of her passing.

I know she was never happier than when she had met you, and the two of you made a lovely couple. She seemed to light up the life of everyone who met her.

I shall certainly attend the memorial service next Thursday, but if there is anything I can do in the meantime Stephen, please don't hesitate to call me. I'm sure Jo and Max are a great comfort to you at the moment.

Thinking of you all with love and affection.

Fiona

- The main point of difference with a thank-you letter, is that the writer should be acutely sensitive to the addressee's feelings, rather than trying to express their own emotions. The references made to the deceased in this letter are mainly in the context of her relationship with the bereaved partner, rather than the writer.

- A handwritten note can be more appropriate than a phone call in situations of grief and loss like this. Writing a letter also gives you more time to think about what you want to say, and how you want to say it.

- Note that the letter, although it is informal in address and tone, still has a discernible structure: the introductory sentence explains the purpose of the letter; the middle paragraph expands on the theme with the writer's memories of the deceased; and the final paragraph acknowledges the future by accepting an invitation and offering support.

> It really helped to receive letters of support from friends. Even though I didn't feel like talking to anyone at the time, it was good to know that others appreciated Jim, and that people were thinking of me and the kids.
>
> (Widow)

Invitations

Invitations are frequently made by email or by text these days, but there are occasions when a written or printed invitation is still the prevalent form of communication.

Occasions that might require an invitation include:

- Birthday parties
- Weddings
- Anniversary parties
- Christenings
- Funerals
- Housewarming parties
- Dinner parties

A wedding invitation

Boris and Isabel Andrews
request the pleasure of the company of
Phillip and Sally Bairstow
at the wedding of their daughter Florence
to James Chater
on Saturday July 18 2015
at St Bart's Church, Eggleton at 2pm.

R.S.V.P.

Isabel Andrews, The Gildings, Foxton Lane, Biblington, BB13 5TR

Tel: 01286 5543077.

- The most important feature of an invitation is that it must possess all the necessary information to allow the recipient to respond with an acceptance or a refusal. There is no point sending out wedding invitations to 400 guests without the date on them!

- Social invitations can be informal or formal. Formal invitations – to a wedding or a christening, for example – will usually be printed.

A birthday invitation

> YIKES!
> I'm (nearly) thirty!
> Help me get over it on Saturday 21 May
> at the Stag, Riddlesway, Broxton.
> There'll be drinking, dancing and a very special
> quiz – how can you refuse?
> Please RSVP as soon as possible,
> so I can sort out some eats for the night.
> See you there,
> Charlie Bright
> cbright@email.com
> 06785 4459881

- This invitation could be sent in the form of an email, handwritten note or printed card.

- The tone is humorous and the language (and punctuation) informal, which suits the occasion.

- The font is also deliberately informal.

- Note the promise of a 'very special quiz' to intrigue the reader and hopefully persuade them to attend.

- Even with this casual approach, the host has taken care to include all the information which the recipient will need to decide whether they can attend or not.

Replying to invitations

- When replying to invitations, match the style and formality of the invite.

- If you have to decline an invitation, it is good practice to sound apologetic, regretful and explain the reason why you cannot attend.

SOCIAL MEDIA

> *I use email all the time; Twitter, Facebook and blogging – weekly.*
> (Deputy director, charity)

The development of social media has significantly changed the way we communicate with each other. It differs greatly from conventional forms of communication. You are not speaking to a few specific people but with tens, hundreds or even of thousands at once. As well as words, you use pictures, clips and internet links to share information. The best way to describe what you are doing when you use social media, like Facebook, Twitter or a blog, is that you are projecting a representation of yourself to a wide audience. This makes them very powerful and positive communication tools – for everyone from teenage friends to large corporations. The downside is that you have to be careful about what information you share, and how you share it: how you represent yourself. As social media are constantly developing – in terms of their reach and the purposes for which they are being used – the ground rules for successfully using them are changeable. There are, however, definitely some fundamental 'do's' and 'don'ts', which will be considered here along with the basic mechanics. This guide focuses on Facebook and Twitter, because they are currently the most popular forms of social media. There are many others – like Instagram and Linkedin – which have different formats and purposes, but most of the observations made here will still be applicable.

Social media 'do's'

- **Decide why you're using it.** Is it to keep in touch with friends, be entertained, promote a business or service, or a mixture of all three? Blogging, Twitter and Facebook are used for all the above reasons, and they have different strengths and weaknesses.

- **Try to be consistent.** If you want to attract more followers on Twitter and other media, this is more likely to happen if people grow to trust and like your opinions or tweets.

- **Be positive.** It's a good principle to keep in mind, even if you don't always follow it. Anger and negativity do not generally translate well into social media, but a positive response to a negative issue can be effective and motivating. Consider whether you might say the same thing, or share the same information, if your audience were in the room with you. If the answer is 'no', then think twice about posting. This is true whether your audience is made up of personal or business contacts, particularly true if it contains both.

- **Be clear.** Nouns and facts work better on Facebook and Twitter than adjectives and adverbs – there is less room for misinterpretation of intention or mood if the message is clear and unambiguous. Of course, if you're casually chatting with friends on Instagram or Twitter, then it's a different matter.

- **Check your privacy settings.** This will help you avoid inadvertently sharing private information on Facebook and other media, or being embarrassed by something posted on your wall to a wider audience than you would like.

- **Reread your message, status update or tweet before you post it.** It's very easy to make mistakes in spelling or tone, especially if you're posting from a mobile phone with a very small keyboard. Consider using emoticons if you suspect your message is ambiguous.

Social media 'don'ts'

- **'Retweet' (RT) too often.** It can be off-putting to followers. Sharing a link to a video or article you've enjoyed is often welcomed, but be sparing to make a greater impact.

- **Post, or tag, pictures of friends or acquaintances on Facebook.** Unless you're sure they won't mind, keep intimate details of shared events for private Facebook messaging.

- **Be rude.** It's very tempting to react angrily to tweets or posts that we strongly disagree with – don't. Arguments can escalate very quickly in the online environment and you will almost certainly say things from behind your computer screen that you would not in real life. A well-reasoned objection, or counter argument, will have more influence than posting an abusive message but serious issues are unlikely to be resolved online. If someone you're following, or you've 'friended' on Facebook, is a continual source of annoyance, then unfollow or block them.

- **Get upset if you are 'unfollowed'.** Twitter is a more impersonal medium than Facebook, and people chop and change whom they follow with great frequency.

- **Mix up your work life and personal life.** This applies particularly on Facebook. Your work colleagues may be amused by a picture of you at last night's party but your boss, who may be a Facebook friend of one of them, might find it less amusing – especially if you call in sick the next day.

- **Post sensitive news which might be better relayed by telephone.**
  It's very easy to say things online that might be difficult to express over
  the phone, but this doesn't necessarily make it the better option.

- **Be repetitive in your posts and tweets.** Many people repeat variations on
  a theme they consider important, hoping to elicit a response, while their
  audience gets fed up with reading the same information over and over again.

- **Ramble.** On Twitter you're usually restricted to 140 characters, which is good
  practice for learning how to express yourself succinctly. Try to keep Facebook
  updates to one or two lines, if possible. If you have a lot to say, you might be
  better off sending an email, or video calling.

- **Forget to punctuate.** Just because messages are short doesn't mean that
  they will make sense without commas, full stops and other punctuation
  marks.

Glossary of social media terms

» **@.** The @ sign is used in 'tweets' directly before a username to turn it into
  a link to that person's profile: @janesmith for example.

» **# (hashtag).** Hashtags are symbols which allow tweets on a subject to
  be grouped together and located by a 'hashtag search'. For instance,
  by including the expression, '*#spaceshuttle*' in a tweet, the user makes it
  possible for other tweeters to search and locate all tweets with this
  expression in them.

» **Blocking.** Blocking is preventing someone from reading your tweets,
  or Facebook posts, by denying them access to your account.

» **Links.** Webpage references included in Facebook posts and tweets,
  which can be clicked on to take the reader to the relevant web article or
  image.

» **Retweet (RT).** Resending or forwarding someone's else tweet with or
  without a comment of your own.

» **Status update.** The space on your Facebook account where you let your
  'friends' know how you are feeling, or what you are thinking about.
  Entries should be kept short.

» **Tweeter.** A user of Twitter.

- » **Tweet(ing).** The act of posting a 'tweet' to Twitter.

- » **Tweets.** Posts on Twitter made up of 140 characters or less.

- » **Tweetup.** A physical meeting of tweeters – a 'twitter meet up'.

- » **Wall.** The personal page of your Facebook account where 'friends' can post messages, links and other material.

I use Twitter all the time and have found it very useful for work. I'm on Facebook but I never use it.

(Journalist)

Blogging

A blog – or 'weblog' – is a website where someone writes their thoughts and opinions in the form of a post. Blogs range in content from online diaries to a promotional tool for business. Mostly they are expressions of personal opinions and beliefs, and so tend to be informal and chatty in tone.

Regardless of why you are blogging, some basic rules apply:

- **Think about your reader.** Are you planning to inform them? Entertain them? Persuade them? Whether it is one of the above or all three, you will have to write accordingly, and be consistent in your approach, or the reader's interest will wane.

- **Be sincere and engaging.** A blog is usually quite conversational in style, so it may help to imagine you are chatting with the reader as you write. Share your experiences and tips, particularly if you're writing about a hobby or interest.

- **Keep posts short and interesting.** People tend to 'scan' blogs for words and images of interest – they may not be paying full attention. For this reason, try to keep sentences short and punchy. Include images and links to other web pages that reinforce your opinions or make the page look attractive. Add headings to break up the text, and keep paragraphs short.

I use Facebook to keep in touch with friends around the world, and Twitter to keep tabs on the news and celebrities. Skype is great for conference calls.

(Writer)

Emoticons and smileys

Emoticons (from 'emotion' and 'icon') and 'smileys' are typed symbols representing expressions of the human face, from happy to sad. They are used as shorthand in text messaging, email, Tweets and other real-time communications to indicate the tone of the message, when the words alone do not make this clear. For instance, 'I am going out with my parents tonight ☺', or 'I am going out with my parents tonight ☹)

These have now been supplemented and even replaced to some degree by graphical images or 'emoji', which can be selected from a menu rather than created by using keyboard characters.

There is some debate about when it is suitable to use these symbols. Some people may not appreciate them, so think of the specific individual to whom you are writing and try to assess the effect they will have on that person before you decide to include them.

In some cases, you may also find that the emoticons you type are automatically converted into images when you send a message, and this can lead to unexpectedly large phone bills.

Here is a selection of the most commonly used emoticons:

:-) or **:)**	happy
(-:	smiling back, also smiling
:-()	smiling with mouth open
8-)	smiling with glasses
D:-)	smiling with baseball cap
|-)	grin
:>	devilish grin
:^D	sounds good (agree)

:-))	cheerful
:-)))	really happy
:-D	laughing
|-D	belly laugh
:'-D	crying with laughter
xD	laughing really hard
:-&	tongue tied
;-)	winking, just kidding
;->	conspiratorial wink
>:)	evil grin
:p	tongue sticking out, playful, just kidding
<3	heart
:-°	kissing
:-X	big kiss
:-x	small kiss, peck

^5	high five
:-(	sad
:'-(	crying
:-C	very sad
:-@	screaming
:-O	shocked or surprised
:-o	wow
[:-(	frowning
:/	frustrated
:-\	sceptical
:-||	angry
>:-|	cross
:-<>	surprised
:-(*)	you make me sick
<:-]	stupid, idiot

:-S	confused
%-)	confused and happy
%-(	confused and unhappy
:-(o)	shouting
:-V	yelling
:-@	screaming
|-@!	swearing
]-()	yawning
|-i	sleeping
|-O	snoring

machine parts **2** procedures by which system functions **machinist** n **machine gun** automatic gun firing repeatedly

macho ❶ adj exhibiting exaggerated pride in masculinity **machismo** n strong, exaggerated masculinity

mackerel n edible sea fish

mackintosh n waterproof raincoat

macramé n ornamental work of knotted cord

macrocosm n **1** the universe **2** any large system

m metre

MA Master of Arts

mac n (Inf) mackintosh

macabre adj gruesome, ghastly

macaroni n pasta in thin tubes

macaroon n biscuit containing almonds

macaw n kind of parrot

mace¹ n staff of office

mace² n spice made of nutmeg shell

machete n broad, heavy knife

Machiavellian adj (politically) unprincipled, crafty

machine ❶ n **1** apparatus with several parts to apply mechanical force **2** controlling organization **3** mechanical appliance ▷ v **4** shape etc. with machine

machinery n **1** machines or

mad ❶ adj **madder, maddest** **1** suffering from mental disease, foolish **2** enthusiastic (about) **3** excited **4** (Inf) furious **madden** v make mad **madness** n

madam n polite title for a woman

madcap adj/n reckless (person)

made past tense and past participle of MAKE

Madonna n Virgin Mary

madrigal n unaccompanied part song

maelstrom n great whirlpool

maestro n, pl **-tri, -tros** **1** outstanding musician, conductor **2** master of any art

magazine ❶ n **1** periodical

m

THESAURUS

machine n = **appliance**, device, apparatus, engine, tool; = **system**, structure, organization, machinery, setup (Inf)

macho adj = **manly**, masculine, chauvinist, virile

mad adj = **insane**, crazy (Inf), nuts (Sl), raving, unstable ≠ **sane**;

= **foolish**, absurd, wild, stupid, daft (Inf) ≠ **sensible**; (Inf) = **angry**, furious, incensed, enraged, livid (Inf) ≠ **calm**; = **enthusiastic**, wild, crazy (Inf), ardent, fanatical ≠ **nonchalant**; = **frenzied**, wild, excited, frenetic, uncontrolled

magazine n = **journal**,

publication **2** appliance for
supplying cartridges to gun
3 storehouse for arms etc.

magenta *adj/n* (of) deep
purplish-red

maggot *n* grub, larva **maggoty**
adj

magic ❶ *n* **1** art of supposedly
invoking supernatural powers to
influence events etc. **2** witchcraft,
conjuring **3** fascinating quality or
power ▷ *adj* **4** of, using magic
magical *adj* **magician** *n* wizard,
conjuror

magistrate ❶ *n* civil officer
administering law **magisterial**
adj **1** of magistrate **2** authoritative

magnanimous *adj* generous, not
petty **magnanimity** *n*

magnate *n* influential person

magnesium *n* metallic element
magnesia *n* white powder used in
medicine

magnet *n* piece of iron, steel
having properties of attracting iron,
steel **magnetic** *adj* **1** of magnet

2 exerting powerful attraction
magnetism *n* **magnetize** *v*

magneto *n* apparatus for ignition
in internal-combustion engine

magnetic tape coated plastic
strip for recording sound or video
signals

magnificent ❶ *adj* **1** splendid
2 imposing **3** excellent
magnificence *n*

magnify ❶ *v* -**fying**, -**fied**
1 increase apparent size of, as with
lens **2** exaggerate **magnification**
n

magnitude ❶ *n* **1** importance
2 size

magnolia *n* tree with white,
sweet-scented flowers

magnum *n* large wine bottle

magpie *n* black-and-white bird

maharajah *n* former title of some
Indian princes

mahogany *n* tree yielding
reddish-brown wood

maiden ❶ *n* (*Lit*) **1** young
unmarried woman ▷ *adj*

———— THESAURUS ————

publication, supplement, rag (*Inf*),
issue

magic *n* = **sorcery**, wizardry,
witchcraft, enchantment, black art;
= **conjuring**, illusion, trickery,
sleight of hand, legerdemain;
= **charm**, power, glamour,
fascination, magnetism ▷ *adj*
= **miraculous**, entrancing,
charming, fascinating, marvellous

magistrate *n* = **judge**, justice,
justice of the peace, J.P.

magnificent *adj* = **splendid**,
impressive, imposing, glorious,

gorgeous ≠ **ordinary**; = **brilliant**,
fine, excellent, outstanding, superb

magnify *v* = **enlarge**, increase,
boost, expand, intensify ≠ **reduce**;
= **make worse**, exaggerate,
intensify, worsen, exacerbate

magnitude *n* = **importance**,
consequence, significance,
moment, note ≠ **unimportance**;
= **immensity**, size, extent,
enormity, volume ≠ **smallness**

maiden *n* (*Lit*) = **girl**, maid, lass,
damsel, virgin ▷ *adj* = **first**, initial,
inaugural, introductory;

2 unmarried 3 first **maid** n
1 woman servant 2 (*Lit*) maiden
maiden name woman's surname
before marriage
mail¹ ❶ n 1 letters etc. transported
and delivered by the post office
2 postal system 3 train etc.
carrying mail ▷ v 4 send by mail
mail² n armour of interlaced rings
mailbox n (*US & Canad*) 1 public
box into which letters are put for
collection and delivery 2 private
box outside house where
occupant's mail is delivered
mailman n person who collects or
delivers mail
maim v cripple, mutilate
main ❶ adj 1 chief, principal ▷ n
2 principal pipe, line carrying water
etc. 3 (*Obs*) sea **mainframe** n
1 high-speed general-purpose
computer 2 central processing
unit of computer **mainland** n
stretch of land which forms main
part of a country **mainstay** n
chief support **mainstream** n

prevailing cultural trend
maintain ❶ v 1 carry on
2 support 3 assert 4 support by
argument **maintenance** n
1 maintaining 2 means of support
3 upkeep of buildings etc.
maisonette n part of house fitted
as self-contained dwelling
maize n type of corn
majesty ❶ n, pl **-ties**
1 stateliness 2 sovereignty
majestic adj
major ❶ n 1 army officer above
captain 2 scale in music 3 (*US &
Canad*) an academic subject chosen
as a field of specialization ▷ adj
4 greater in number, extent etc.
majority n 1 greater number
2 coming of age
make ❶ v **making, made**
1 construct 2 produce 3 create
4 establish 5 appoint 6 amount
to 7 cause to do 8 reach 9 earn
10 tend 11 contribute ▷ n
12 brand, type **maker** n **making**
n **make-believe** n fantasy,

m

= **unmarried**, unwed
mail¹ n = **letters**, post,
correspondence ▷ v = **post**, send,
forward, e-mail, dispatch
main adj = **chief**, leading, head,
central, essential ≠ **minor**
maintain v = **continue**, retain,
preserve, sustain, carry on ≠ **end**;
= **assert**, state, claim, insist,
declare ≠ **disavow**; = **look after**,
care for, take care of, conserve, keep
in good condition
majesty n = **grandeur**, glory,
splendour, magnificence, nobility

≠ **triviality**
major adj = **important**, critical,
significant, great, serious; = **main**,
higher, greater, bigger, leading
≠ **minor**
make v = **produce**, cause, create,
effect, lead to; = **perform**, do,
effect, carry out, execute; = **force**,
cause, compel, drive, require;
= **create**, build, produce,
manufacture, form; = **earn**, get,
gain, net, win; = **amount to**, total,
constitute, add up to, count as ▷ n
= **brand**, sort, style, model, kind

m

pretence **make do** manage with inferior alternative **make it** (Inf) be successful **makeshift** adj serving as temporary substitute **make-up** n **1** cosmetics **2** characteristics **3** layout

mal- comb. form ill, badly, as in malformation, malfunction

maladjusted adj badly adjusted, as to society

malady n, pl **-dies** disease

malaise n vague feeling of discomfort

malapropism n ludicrous misuse of word

malaria n infectious disease transmitted by mosquitoes

malcontent adj/n discontented (person)

male ① adj **1** of sex that fertilizes female **2** of men or male animals ▷ n **3** male person or animal

malevolent adj full of ill will **malevolence** n

malice n **1** ill will **2** spite **malicious** adj spiteful

malign adj **1** causing evil ▷ v **2** slander **malignancy** n **malignant** adj **1** feeling ill will **2** (of disease) resistant to therapy

malinger v feign illness to escape duty

mall n shopping centre

mallard n wild duck

malleable adj **1** capable of being hammered into shape **2** adaptable

mallet n (wooden) hammer

malnutrition n inadequate nutrition

malodorous adj evil-smelling

malpractice n immoral, illegal or unethical conduct

malt n grain used for brewing

maltreat v treat badly

mammal n animal of type that suckles its young **mammalian** adj

mammary adj of, relating to breast

mammon n wealth regarded as source of evil

mammoth ① n **1** extinct animal like an elephant ▷ adj **2** colossal

man ① n, pl **men 1** human being **2** human race **3** adult male **4** piece used in chess etc. ▷ v **5** supply with men **manful** adj brave **manly** adj **manhandle** v treat roughly **manhole** n opening through which person may pass to a sewer etc. **mankind** n human beings **manslaughter** n unintentional homicide

mana n (NZ) authority, influence

manacle n/v fetter

manage ① v **1** be in charge of **2** succeed in doing **3** control **4** handle **manageable** adj **management** n **1** those who

─────────── THESAURUS ───────────

male adj = **masculine**, manly, macho, virile ≠ **female**

mammoth adj = **colossal**, huge, giant, massive, enormous ≠ **tiny**

man n = **male**, guy (Inf), fellow (Inf), gentleman, bloke (Brit Inf);

= **human**, human being, person, individual, soul; = **mankind**, humanity, people, human race, humankind ▷ v = **staff**, people, crew, occupy, garrison

manage v = **be in charge of**, run,

manage **2** administration
manager n **managerial** adj
mandarin n **1** small orange
2 high-ranking bureaucrat
mandate ⊙ n **1** command of, or
commission to act for, another
2 instruction from electorate to
representative or government
mandatory adj compulsory
mandible n lower jawbone
mandolin n stringed musical
instrument
mane n long hair on neck of horse,
lion etc.
manganese n metallic element
mange n skin disease of dogs etc.
mangy adj
manger n eating trough in
stable
mangle¹ n **1** machine for rolling
clothes etc. to remove water ▷ v
2 press in mangle
mangle² v mutilate
mango n, pl **-goes, -gos** tropical
fruit
mangrove n tropical tree which
grows on muddy river banks
mania n **1** madness **2** prevailing
craze **maniac** adj/n mad (person)

maniacal, manic adj affected by
mania
manicure n **1** treatment and care
of fingernails and hands ▷ v
2 treat, care for hands
manifest ⊙ adj **1** clear,
undoubted ▷ v **2** make manifest
manifestation n **manifesto** n
declaration of policy by political
party etc.
manifold adj **1** numerous and
varied ▷ n **2** in engine, pipe with
several outlets
manila, manilla n **1** fibre used
for ropes **2** tough paper
manipulate ⊙ v **1** handle
skilfully **2** manage **3** falsify
manipulation n
manna n **1** nourishment
2 unexpected gift
mannequin n woman who
models clothes
manner ⊙ n **1** way, style
2 bearing **3** sort, kind **4** pl social
behaviour **mannered** adj affected
mannerism n person's distinctive
habit
manoeuvre ⊙ n **1** complicated,
perhaps deceptive plan or action

m

handle, direct, conduct;
= **organize**, use, handle, regulate;
= **cope**, survive, succeed, carry on,
make do; = **perform**, do, achieve,
carry out, undertake, operate
mandate n = **command**, order,
commission, instruction, decree
manifest adj = **obvious**, apparent,
patent, evident, clear ≠ **concealed**
▷ v = **display**, show, reveal,
express, demonstrate ≠ **conceal**

manipulate v = **influence**,
control, direct, negotiate, exploit;
= **work**, use, operate, handle
manner n = **style**, way, fashion,
method, custom; = **behaviour**, air,
bearing, conduct, aspect; = **type**,
form, sort, kind, variety
manoeuvre v = **scheme**, wangle
(Inf), machinate ▷ n = **stratagem**,
scheme, trick, tactic, intrigue; often
plural = **movement**, operation,

▷ *v* **2** employ stratagems **3** (cause to) perform manoeuvres

manor *n* large country house with land

manse *n* house of minister in some religious denominations

mansion ❶ *n* large house

mantle ❶ *n* **1** loose cloak **2** covering ▷ *v* **3** cover

mantra *n* sacred word or syllable in Hinduism and Buddhism

manual ❶ *adj* **1** done with the hands **2** by human labour, not automatic ▷ *n* **3** handbook

manufacture ❶ *v* **1** make (materials) into finished articles **2** concoct ▷ *n* **3** making of articles, esp. in large quantities **manufacturer** *n*

manure *n* dung or chemical fertilizer used to enrich land

manuscript *n* **1** book etc. written by hand **2** copy for printing

many *adj* **more, most** **1** numerous ▷ *n* **2** large number

map *n* **1** flat representation of the earth ▷ *v* **2** make map of **3** (with *out*) plan

maple *n* tree of sycamore family

maple sugar *n* (*US & Canad*) sugar made from the sap of the sugar maple

mar ❶ *v* **marring, marred** spoil

Mar. March

maraca *n* shaken percussion instrument

marathon *n* **1** long-distance race **2** endurance contest

marble *n* **1** kind of limestone **2** small ball used in children's game

march ❶ *v* **1** walk with military step **2** go, progress ▷ *n* **3** action of marching **4** distance marched **5** marching tune

March *n* third month

marchioness *n* wife, widow of marquis

mare *n* female horse

margarine *n* butter substitute made from vegetable fats

margin ❶ *n* **1** border, edge **2** space round printed page **3** amount allowed beyond what is necessary **marginal** *adj*

——————— THESAURUS ———————

exercise, war game

mansion *n* = **residence**, manor, hall, villa, seat

mantle *n* = **covering**, screen, curtain, blanket, veil; = **cloak**, wrap, cape, hood, shawl

manual *adj* = **physical**, human; = **hand-operated**, hand, non-automatic ▷ *n* = **handbook**, guide, instructions, bible

manufacture *v* = **make**, build, produce, construct, create; = **concoct**, make up, invent, devise,

fabricate ▷ *n* = **making**, production, construction, assembly, creation

mar *v* = **ruin**, spoil, scar, flaw, impair ≠ **improve**

march *v* = **parade**, walk, file, pace, stride; = **walk**, strut, storm, sweep, stride ▷ *n* = **walk**, trek, slog, yomp (*Brit Inf*), routemarch; = **progress**, development, advance, evolution, progression

margin *n* = **edge**, side, border, boundary, verge

marigold n plant with yellow flowers

marijuana ● n dried flowers and leaves of hemp plant, used as narcotic

marina n mooring facility for pleasure boats

marinade n liquid in which food is soaked before cooking **marinate** v soak in marinade

marine ● adj 1 of the sea or shipping ▷ n 2 soldier trained for land or sea combat 3 fleet **mariner** n sailor

marionette n puppet

marital ● adj of marriage

maritime ● adj 1 of seafaring 2 near the sea

mark ● n 1 dot, scar etc. 2 sign, token 3 letter, number showing evaluation of schoolwork etc. 4 indication 5 target ▷ v 6 make mark on 7 distinguish 8 notice 9 assess 10 stay close to sporting opponent **marked** adj noticeable **marker** n **marksman** n person

skilled in shooting

market ● n 1 place for buying and selling 2 demand for goods ▷ v 3 offer for sale **marketable** adj **market garden** place where fruit and vegetables are grown for sale

marmalade n preserve made of oranges, lemons etc.

marmoset n small bushy-tailed monkey

maroon¹ ● v 1 leave on deserted island etc. 2 isolate

maroon² adj/n (of) brownish-crimson colour

marquee n large tent

marquetry n inlaid work, wood mosaic

marquis n nobleman of rank below duke

marrow n 1 fatty substance inside bones 2 vital part 3 plant with long, green-striped fruit, eaten as vegetable

marry ● v -rying, -ried 1 join as husband and wife 2 unite closely **marriage** n 1 being married

m

marijuana n = **cannabis**, pot (Sl), dope (Sl), grass (Sl), hemp

marine adj = **nautical**, maritime, naval, seafaring, seagoing

marital adj = **matrimonial**, nuptial, conjugal, connubial

maritime adj = **nautical**, marine, naval, oceanic, seafaring; = **coastal**, seaside, littoral

mark n = **spot**, stain, streak, smudge, line; = **characteristic**, feature, standard, quality, measure; = **brand**, impression, label, device, flag; = **target**, goal, aim, purpose,

object ▷ v = **scar**, scratch, stain, streak, blot; = **label**, identify, brand, flag, stamp; = **grade**, correct, assess, evaluate, appraise; = **distinguish**, show, illustrate, exemplify, denote; = **observe**, mind, note, notice, attend to

market n = **fair**, mart, bazaar, souk (Arabic) ▷ v = **sell**, promote, retail, peddle, vend

maroon¹ v = **abandon**, leave, desert, strand, leave high and dry (Inf)

marry v = **tie the knot** (Inf), wed,

2 wedding ceremony

marsh ⊕ *n* low-lying wet land
marshy *adj*

marshal ⊕ *n* **1** high officer of
state **2** (*US*) law enforcement
officer **3** high-ranking officer in the
army, air force ▷ *v* **4** arrange
5 conduct with ceremony

marshmallow *n* spongy pink or
white sweet

marsupial *n* animal that carries
its young in pouch

marten *n* weasel-like animal

martial ⊕ *adj* **1** of war **2** warlike

martin *n* species of swallow

martinet *n* strict disciplinarian

martyr *n* **1** one who suffers or dies
for his beliefs ▷ *v* **2** make martyr of

marvel ⊕ *v* **-velling, -velled**
1 wonder ▷ *n* **2** wonderful thing
marvellous *adj*

marzipan *n* paste of almonds,
sugar etc.

mascara *n* cosmetic for darkening
eyelashes

mascot *n* person, animal or thing

supposed to bring luck

masculine ⊕ *adj* **1** relating to
males **2** manly

mash *n/v* (crush into) soft mass or
pulp

mask ⊕ *n* **1** covering for face
2 disguise, pretence ▷ *v* **3** disguise

masochism *n* abnormal condition
where pleasure (esp. sexual) is
derived from pain **masochist** *n*

mason *n* worker in stone
masonry *n* stonework

masquerade *n* **1** masked ball ▷ *v*
2 appear in disguise

mass ⊕ *n* **1** quantity of matter
2 (*Physics*) amount of matter in body
3 large quantity ▷ *v* **4** form into
mass **massive** *adj* large and heavy
mass-market *adj* appealing to
many people **mass-produce** *v*
produce standardized articles in
large quantities

Mass *n* service in R.C. Church

massacre ⊕ *n* **1** indiscriminate,
large-scale killing ▷ *v* **2** kill
indiscriminately

———————— THESAURUS ————————

get hitched (*Sl*); = **unite**, join, link,
bond, ally

marsh *n* = **swamp**, bog, slough,
fen, quagmire

marshal *v* = **conduct**, take, lead,
guide, steer; = **arrange**, group,
order, line up, organize

martial *adj* = **military**, belligerent,
warlike, bellicose

marvel *v* = **be amazed**, wonder,
gape, be awed ▷ *n* = **wonder**,
phenomenon, miracle, portent

masculine *adj* = **male**, manly,
mannish, manlike, virile

mask *n* = **façade**, disguise, front,
cover, screen ▷ *v* = **disguise**, hide,
conceal, obscure, cover (up)

mass *n* = **lot**, collection, load, pile,
quantity; = **piece**, block, lump,
chunk, hunk; = **size**, matter,
weight, extent, bulk ▷ *adj*
= **large-scale**, general, widespread,
extensive, universal ▷ *v* = **gather**,
assemble, accumulate, collect, rally

massacre *n* = **slaughter**, murder,
holocaust, carnage, extermination
▷ *v* = **slaughter**, kill, murder,
butcher, wipe out

m

massage ❶ n 1 rubbing and
 kneading of muscles etc. as curative
 treatment ▷ v 2 perform massage
masseur n one who practises
 massage
mast n 1 pole for supporting ship's
 sails 2 tall support for aerial etc.
mastectomy n/pl -mies
 surgical removal of breast
master ❶ n 1 one in control
 2 employer 3 owner 4 document
 etc. from which copies are made
 5 expert 6 teacher ▷ adj 7 expert,
 skilled ▷ v 8 overcome 9 acquire
 skill in **masterful** adj 1 expert,
 skilled 2 domineering **masterly**
 adj showing great skill **mastery** n
 1 understanding (of) 2 expertise
 3 victory **mastermind** v 1 plan,
 direct ▷ n 2 one who directs
 complex operation **masterpiece**
 n outstanding work
masticate v chew
mastiff n large dog
masturbate v fondle genital

organs **masturbation** n
mat¹ n 1 small rug 2 piece of fabric
 to protect another surface 3 thick
 tangled mass ▷ v 4 form into such
 mass
mat² adj dull, lustreless
matador n man who kills bull in
 bullfights
match¹ ❶ n 1 contest, game
 2 equal 3 person, thing
 corresponding to another
 4 marriage ▷ v 5 get something
 corresponding to 6 oppose, put in
 competition (with) 7 correspond
 matchmaker n person who
 schemes to bring about marriage
match² n small stick with head
 which ignites when rubbed
 matchbox n **matchstick** n
mate ❶ n 1 comrade 2 husband,
 wife 3 one of pair 4 officer in
 merchant ship ▷ v 5 marry 6 pair
 matey adj (Inf) friendly
material ❶ n 1 substance from
 which thing is made 2 cloth

m

——————— THESAURUS ———————

massage n = **rub-down**,
 manipulation ▷ v = **rub down**,
 manipulate, knead
master n = **lord**, ruler,
 commander, chief, director
 ≠ **servant**; = **expert**, maestro, ace
 (Inf), genius, wizard ≠ **amateur**;
 = **teacher**, tutor, instructor
 ≠ **student** ▷ adj = **main**, principal,
 chief, prime, foremost ≠ **lesser** ▷ v
 = **learn**, understand, pick up, grasp,
 get the hang of (Inf); = **overcome**,
 defeat, conquer, tame, triumph
 over ≠ **give in to**
match² n = **game**, test,

competition, trial, tie; = **marriage**,
 pairing, alliance, partnership;
 = **equal**, rival, peer, counterpart
 ▷ v = **correspond with**, go with, fit
 with, harmonize with;
 = **correspond**, agree, accord,
 square, coincide
mate n (Inf) = **friend**, pal (Inf),
 companion, buddy (Inf), comrade;
 = **partner**, lover, companion,
 spouse, consort; = **assistant**,
 subordinate, apprentice, helper,
 accomplice ▷ v = **pair**, couple,
 breed
material n = **substance**, matter,

3 information on which piece of work is based ▷ *adj* **4** of body **5** affecting physical wellbeing **6** important **materialism** *n* **1** excessive interest in money and possessions **2** doctrine that nothing but matter exists **materialistic** *adj* **materialize** *v* come into existence or view **materially** *adv* appreciably
maternal ❶ *adj* of mother **maternity** *n* motherhood
math *n* (US & Canad) mathematics
mathematics *pl n* science of number, quantity, shape and space **mathematical** *adj* **mathematician** *n*
maths *n* (Inf) mathematics
matinée *n* afternoon performance in theatre
matins *pl n* morning service
matriarch *n* mother as head of family **matriarchal** *adj*
matriculate *v* enrol, be enrolled in college or university
matrimony *n* marriage

matrimonial *adj*
matrix *n/pl* **matrices** **1** substance, situation in which something originates, is enclosed **2** mould
matron *n* **1** married woman **2** woman who superintends domestic arrangements of public institution: former name for NURSING OFFICER
matter ❶ *n* **1** substance of which thing is made **2** affair **3** business **4** trouble **5** pus ▷ *v* **6** be of importance
mattress *n* stuffed flat (sprung) case used as part of bed
mature ❶ *adj* **1** ripe, completely developed **2** grown-up ▷ *v* **3** bring, come to maturity **maturity** *n*
maudlin *adj* weakly sentimental
maul ❶ *v* handle roughly
mausoleum *n* stately building as a tomb
mauve *adj/n* pale purple
maverick ❶ *n* independent,

———————— THESAURUS ————————

stuff; **= cloth**, fabric, textile; **= information**, details, facts, notes, evidence ▷ *adj* **= physical**, solid, substantial, concrete, bodily; **= relevant**, important, significant, essential, vital
maternal *adj* **= motherly**, protective, nurturing, maternalistic
matter *n* **= situation**, concern, business, question, event; **= substance**, material, body, stuff ▷ *v* **= be important**, make a difference, count, be relevant, make any difference

mature *v* **= develop**, grow up, bloom, blossom, come of age ▷ *adj* **= matured**, seasoned, ripe, mellow; **= grown-up**, adult, of age, fully fledged, full-grown **≠ immature**
maul *v* **= mangle**, claw, lacerate, tear; **= ill-treat**, abuse, batter, molest, manhandle
maverick *n* **= rebel**, radical, dissenter, individualist, protester **≠ traditionalist** ▷ *adj* **= rebel**, radical, dissenting, individualistic, eccentric

unorthodox person

maw n stomach

mawkish adj 1 maudlin 2 sickly

maxim n 1 general truth 2 rule of conduct

maximum ❶ adj/n, pl **-mums, -ma** greatest (size or number)
  maximize v increase to maximum

may v, past tense **might** expresses possibility, permission, opportunity etc. **maybe** adv 1 perhaps 2 possibly

May n 1 fifth month 2 (without cap.) hawthorn or its flowers
  mayfly n short-lived aquatic insect

Mayday n international distress signal

mayhem ❶ n violent destruction

mayonnaise n creamy sauce, esp. for salads

mayor n head of municipality
  mayoress n 1 mayor's wife 2 lady mayor

maze ❶ n 1 labyrinth 2 network of paths, lines 3 state of confusion

MBE Member of the Order of the British Empire

MD Doctor of Medicine

me pron object of I

mead n alcoholic drink made from honey

meadow ❶ n piece of grassland

meagre adj lean, scanty

meal¹ n 1 occasion when food is served and eaten 2 the food

meal² n grain ground to powder
  mealy-mouthed adj not outspoken enough

mean¹ ❶ v **meaning, meant** 1 intend 2 signify 3 have a meaning 4 have the intention of behaving **meaning** n
  meaningful adj of great significance

mean² ❶ adj 1 ungenerous, petty 2 miserly 3 callous 4 shabby

mean³ ❶ n 1 middle point ▷ pl 2 that by which thing is done 3 money 4 resources ▷ adj 5 intermediate 6 average
  meantime, meanwhile adv/n (during) time between one happening and another

meander v 1 flow windingly 2 wander aimlessly ▷ n

m

—————— THESAURUS ——————

maximum adj = **greatest**, highest, supreme, paramount, utmost ≠ **minimal** ▷ n = **top**, peak, ceiling, utmost, upper limit ≠ **minimum**

mayhem n = **chaos**, trouble, violence, disorder, destruction

maze n = **web**, confusion, tangle, labyrinth, imbroglio

meadow n = **field**, pasture, grassland, lea (Poet)

mean¹ v = **signify**, indicate,

represent, express, stand for; = **intend**, want, plan, expect, design

mean² adj = **miserly**, stingy, parsimonious, niggardly, mercenary ≠ **generous**; = **dishonourable**, petty, shameful, shabby, vile ≠ **honourable**

mean³ n = **average**, middle, balance, norm, midpoint ▷ adj = **average**, middle, standard

3 wandering course
measles *n* infectious disease producing rash of red spots
measly *adj* (*Inf*) meagre
measure ❶ *n* **1** size, quantity **2** unit, system of measuring **3** course of action **4** law ▷ *v* **5** ascertain size, quantity of **6** be (so much) in size or quantity **7** indicate measurement of **measurable** *adj* **measured** *adj* **1** slow and steady **2** carefully considered **measurement** *n* **1** measuring **2** size
meat ❶ *n* **1** animal flesh as food **2** food **meaty** *adj*
mechanic *n* **1** one who works with machinery ▷ *pl* **2** scientific theory of motion **mechanical** *adj* **1** of, by machine **2** acting without thought
mechanism ❶ *n* **1** structure of machine **2** piece of machinery **3** process, technique **mechanization** *n* **mechanize** *v* **1** equip with machinery **2** make automatic
medal *n* piece of metal with inscription etc. used as reward or

memento **medallion** *n* (design like) large medal
meddle *v* interfere
media *n* pl of MEDIUM used esp. of the mass media, radio, television etc.
median *adj/n* middle (point or line)
mediate ❶ *v* intervene to reconcile **mediation** *n* **mediator** *n*
medic *n* (*Inf*) doctor or medical student
medicine ❶ *n* **1** drug or remedy for treating disease **2** science of preventing, curing disease **medical** *adj* **medicate** *v* impregnate with medicinal substances **medication** *n* (treatment with) medicinal substance **medicinal** *adj* curative
medieval *adj* of Middle Ages
mediocre ❶ *adj* **1** ordinary, middling **2** second-rate **mediocrity** *n* **1** state of being mediocre **2** mediocre person
meditate *v* **1** reflect deeply, esp. on spiritual matters **2** think about, plan **meditation** *n*
medium ❶ *adj* **1** between two qualities, degrees etc. ▷ *n* **2** middle

—————— THESAURUS ——————

measure *v* = **quantify**, determine, assess, weigh, calculate ▷ *n* = **quantity**, share, amount, allowance, portion; = **action**, act, step, procedure, means; = **gauge**, rule, scale, metre, ruler; = **law**, act, bill, legislation, resolution
meat *n* = **food**, flesh
mechanism *n* = **process**, way, means, system, operation; = **machine**, device, tool,

instrument, appliance
mediate *v* = **intervene**, step in (*Inf*), intercede, referee, umpire
medicine *n* = **remedy**, drug, cure, prescription, medication
mediocre *adj* = **second-rate**, average, ordinary, indifferent, middling ≠ **excellent**
medium *adj* = **average**, mean, middle, middling, fair ≠ **extraordinary** ▷ *n*

m

quality **3** means **4** agency of
communicating news etc. to public
5 surroundings
medley n mixture
meek adj submissive, humble
meet ❶ v **meeting, met 1** come
face to face (with) **2** satisfy **3** pay
4 converge **5** assemble **6** come
into contact **meeting** n
megabyte n (Comp) 1 048 576
bytes
megalith n great stone
megalomania n desire for,
delusions of grandeur, power etc.
megalomaniac adj/n
megaphone n cone-shaped
instrument to amplify voice
megaton n explosive power of
1 000 000 tons of TNT
melancholy ❶ n **1** sadness,
dejection ▷ adj **2** gloomy,
dejected
melanin n dark pigment found in
hair, skin etc.
mêlée n confused fight
mellifluous adj (of sound)

smooth, sweet
mellow ❶ adj **1** ripe **2** softened
by age, experience **3** not harsh
4 genial ▷ v **5** make, become
mellow
melodrama n play full of
sensational situations
melodramatic adj
melody ❶ n, pl **-dies 1** series of
musical notes which make tune
2 sweet sound **melodic** adj
melodious adj
melon n large, fleshy, juicy fruit
melt ❶ v **1** (cause to) become
liquid by heat **2** dissolve **3** soften
4 disappear
member ❶ n **1** individual making
up body or society **2** limb **3** any
part of complex whole
membership n
membrane n thin flexible tissue in
plant or animal body
memento n, pl **-tos, -toes**
reminder, souvenir
memo n, pl **memos** short for
MEMORANDUM

m

——————— THESAURUS ———————

= **spiritualist**, seer, clairvoyant,
fortune teller, channeller; = **middle**,
mean, centre, average, compromise
meet v = **encounter**, come across,
run into, happen on, find ≠ **avoid**;
= **gather**, collect, assemble, get
together, come together
≠ **disperse**; = **fulfil**, match (up to),
answer, satisfy, discharge ≠ **fall
short of**; = **experience**, face,
suffer, bear, go through
melancholy adj = **sad**, depressed,
miserable, gloomy, glum ≠ **happy**
▷ n = **sadness**, depression, misery,

gloom, sorrow ≠ **happiness**
mellow adj = **full-flavoured**, rich,
sweet, delicate; = **ripe**, mature,
ripened ≠ **unripe** ▷ v = **relax**,
improve, settle, calm, mature
melody n = **tune**, song, theme, air,
music; = **tunefulness**, harmony,
musicality, euphony,
melodiousness
melt v = **dissolve**, run, soften, fuse,
thaw; often with **away** = **disappear**,
fade, vanish, dissolve, disperse;
= **soften**, relax, disarm, mollify
member n = **representative**,

memoir ❶ *n* autobiography, personal history

memory ❶ *n*, *pl* **-ries** 1 faculty of recalling to mind 2 recollection 3 thing remembered 4 commemoration **memorable** *adj* worthy of remembrance **memorandum** *n* 1 note to help the memory etc. 2 informal letter **memorial** *n* 1 thing which serves to keep in memory ▷ *adj* 2 serving as a memorial **memorize** *v* commit to memory **memory card** small removable data storage device, used in mobile phones, digital cameras, etc. **memory stick, USB memory stick** (*Comp*) same as USB DRIVE

men *n* pl of MAN

menace ❶ *n* 1 threat ▷ *v* 2 threaten

menagerie *n* collection of wild animals

mend ❶ *v* 1 repair 2 correct, put right 3 improve ▷ *n* 4 repaired breakage

menial *adj* 1 requiring little skill 2 servile ▷ *n* 3 servant

meningitis *n* inflammation of the membranes of the brain

menopause *n* final cessation of menstruation

menstruation *n* monthly discharge of blood from womb **menstrual** *adj* **menstruate** *v*

mensuration *n* measuring

mental ❶ *adj* 1 of, by the mind 2 (*Inf*) mad **mentality** *n* way of thinking

menthol *n* substance found in peppermint

mention ❶ *v* 1 refer to briefly ▷ *n* 2 acknowledgment 3 reference to

mentor ❶ *n* wise adviser

menu ❶ *n* list of dishes served

— THESAURUS —

associate, supporter, fellow, subscriber

memoir *n* = **account**, life, record, journal, essay

memory *n* = **recall**, mind, retention, ability to remember, powers of recall; = **recollection**, reminder, reminiscence, impression, echo; = **commemoration**, respect, honour, recognition, tribute

menace *n* (*Inf*) = **nuisance**, plague, pest, annoyance, troublemaker; = **threat**, warning, intimidation, ill-omen, ominousness ▷ *v* = **bully**, threaten, intimidate, terrorize, frighten

mend *v* = **repair**, fix, restore,

renew, patch up; = **darn**, repair, patch, stitch, sew; = **heal**, improve, recover, get better, be all right

mental *adj* = **intellectual**, rational, theoretical, cognitive, brain; (*Inf*) = **insane**, mad, disturbed, unstable, mentally ill

mention *v* = **refer to**, point out, bring up, state, reveal ▷ *n often with* **of** = **reference to**, observation, indication, remark on, allusion to; = **acknowledgment**, recognition, tribute, citation, honourable mention

mentor *n* = **guide**, teacher, coach, adviser, tutor

menu *n* = **bill of fare**, tariff (*chiefly Brit*), set menu, table d'hôte, carte

mercantile *adj* of trade

mercenary *adj* **1** influenced by greed **2** working merely for reward ▷ *n* **3** hired soldier

merchant ❶ *n* **1** one engaged in trade **2** wholesale trader
 merchandise *n* trader's wares
 merchant navy ships engaged in a nation's commerce

mercury *n* silvery metal, liquid at ordinary temperature **mercurial** *adj* lively, changeable

mercy ❶ *n, pl* **-cies 1** refraining from infliction of suffering by one who has right, power to inflict it **2** fortunate occurrence **merciful** *adj*

mere ❶ *adj* **1** only **2** nothing but **merely** *adv*

merge ❶ *v* (cause to) lose identity or be absorbed **merger** *n* combination esp. of business firms

meridian *n* **1** circle of the earth passing through poles **2** highest point

meringue *n* baked mixture of white of eggs and sugar

merit ❶ *n* **1** excellence, worth **2** quality of deserving reward ▷ *v* **3** deserve

mermaid *n* imaginary sea creature half woman, half fish

merry ❶ *adj* **-rier, -riest** joyous, cheerful **merriment** *n*
 merry-go-round *n* roundabout

mesh ❶ *n* **1** (one of the open spaces of, or wires etc. forming) network, net ▷ *v* **2** (cause to) entangle, engage

mesmerize *v* hypnotize

mess ❶ *n* **1** untidy confusion **2** trouble **3** (place where) group regularly eat together ▷ *v* **4** potter (about) **5** muddle **messy** *adj*

message ❶ *n* **1** communication sent **2** meaning, moral
 messenger *n*

Messiah *n* **1** promised saviour **2** Christ

met past tense past participle of MEET

metabolism *n* chemical process

m

--- THESAURUS ---

du jour (*Fr*)

merchant *n* = **tradesman**, dealer, trader, broker, retailer

mercy *n* = **compassion**, pity, forgiveness, grace, kindness ≠ **cruelty**; = **blessing**, boon, godsend

mere *adj* = **simple**, nothing more than, common, plain, pure

merge *v* = **combine**, blend, fuse, amalgamate, unite ≠ **separate**

merit *n* = **advantage**, value, quality, worth, strength ▷ *v* = **deserve**, warrant, be entitled to, earn, have a right to

merry *adj* = **cheerful**, happy, carefree, jolly, festive ≠ **gloomy**; (*Brit Inf*) = **tipsy**, happy, mellow, tiddly (*Sl, chiefly Brit*), squiffy (*Brit Inf*)

mesh *n* = **net**, netting, network, web, tracery ▷ *v* = **engage**, combine, connect, knit, coordinate

mess *n* = **untidiness**, disorder, confusion, chaos, litter

message *n* = **communication**, note, bulletin, word, letter; = **point**, meaning, idea, moral, theme

of living body **metabolic** adj
metal n mineral substance,
malleable and capable of
conducting heat and electricity
metallic adj **metallurgist** n
metallurgy n scientific study of
metals
metamorphosis n, pl -phoses
change of shape, character etc.
metaphor ❶ n figure of speech in
which term is transferred to
something it does not literally apply
to **metaphorical** adj
mete v mete out 1 distribute
2 allot
meteor n small, fast-moving
celestial body, visible as streak of
incandescence if it enters earth's
atmosphere **meteoric** adj 1 of
meteor 2 brilliant but short-lived
meteorite n fallen meteor
meteorology n study of climate,
weather **meteorological** adj
meteorologist n
meter n instrument for recording,
measuring
methane n flammable gas,
compound of carbon and hydrogen
method ❶ n 1 way, manner
2 technique 3 orderliness
methodical adj orderly
meths n (Inf) methylated spirits
methylated spirits alcoholic
mixture used as fuel etc.
meticulous adj particular about
details
metre n 1 unit of length in decimal

system 2 SI unit of length
3 rhythm of poem **metric** adj of
system of weights and measures in
which metre is a unit **metrical** adj
1 of measurement 2 of poetic
metre
metronome n instrument which
marks musical time by means of
ticking pendulum
metropolis n chief city of a region
metropolitan adj
mettle n courage, spirit
mew n/v (utter) cry of cat
mews pl n (with sing or pl v) yard,
street orig. of stables, now oft.
converted to houses
mezzanine n intermediate storey,
balcony between two main storeys
mezzo-soprano n voice, singer
between soprano and contralto
mg milligram
miasma n unwholesome
atmosphere
mica n mineral found as glittering
scales, plates
microbe n 1 minute organism
2 disease germ
microchip n small wafer of silicon
containing electronic circuits
microcosm n miniature
representation of larger system
microfiche n microfilm in sheet
form
microfilm n miniaturized
recording of manuscript, book on
roll of film
microphone n instrument for

———————— THESAURUS ————————

metaphor n = **figure of speech**,
image, symbol, analogy, conceit
(Lit)

method n = **manner**, process,
approach, technique, way;
= **orderliness**, planning, order,

amplifying, transmitting sounds

microprocessor n integrated circuit acting as central processing unit in small computer

microscope n instrument by which very small body is magnified **microscopic** adj very small

microwave n **1** electromagnetic wave with wavelength of a few centimetres, used in radar, cooking etc. **2** oven using microwaves

mid adj intermediate **midday** n noon **midnight** n twelve o'clock at night **midway** adj/adv halfway

middle ● adj **1** equidistant from two extremes ▷ n **2** middle point or part **middling** adj **1** mediocre **2** moderate **middle age** period of life between youth and old age **middle class** social class of businessmen, professional people etc. **middleman** n trader between producer and consumer **middle-of-the-road** adj moderate

midge n gnat or similar insect

midget n **1** (Offens) very small person **2** very small thing

midriff n middle part of body

midst n **in the midst of 1** surrounded by **2** at a point during

midtown n (US & Canad) the centre of a town

midwife n trained person who assists at childbirth **midwifery** n

mien n person's manner or appearance

might¹ ● n power, strength **mightily** adv **mighty** adj

might² past tense of MAY

migraine n severe headache

migrate ● v move from one place to another **migrant** n/adj **migration** n

mike n (Inf) microphone

mild ● adj **1** not strongly flavoured **2** gentle **3** temperate **mildly** adv

mildew n destructive fungus on plants or things exposed to damp

mile n measure of length, 1760 yards, 1.609 km **mileage** n **1** travelling expenses per mile **2** miles travelled (per gallon of petrol) **mileometer** n device that records miles travelled by vehicle **milestone** n significant event

milieu n, pl **milieux, milieus** environment

militant ● adj **1** aggressive, vigorous in support of cause **2** prepared to fight **militancy** n

m

system, purpose

middle n = **centre**, heart, midst, halfway point, midpoint ▷ adj = **central**, medium, mid, intervening, halfway; = **intermediate**, intervening

might¹ n = **power**, force, energy, strength, vigour

migrate v = **move**, travel, journey,

wander, trek

mild adj = **gentle**, calm, easy-going, meek, placid ≠ **harsh**; = **temperate**, warm, calm, moderate, tranquil ≠ **cold**; = **bland**, thin, smooth, tasteless, insipid

militant adj = **aggressive**, active, vigorous, assertive, combative ≠ **peaceful**

military ❶ *adj* **1** of, for, soldiers, armies or war ▷ *n* **2** armed forces **militarism** *n* enthusiasm for military force and methods **militia** *n* military force of citizens for home service

militate *v* (esp. with *against* or *for*) have strong influence, effect on

milk ❶ *n* **1** white fluid with which mammals feed their young **2** fluid in some plants ▷ *v* **3** draw milk from **milky** *adj*

mill ❶ *n* **1** factory **2** machine for grinding, pulverizing corn, paper etc. ▷ *v* **3** put through mill **4** cut fine grooves across edges of (e.g. coins) **5** move in confused manner **miller** *n* **millstone** *n* flat circular stone for grinding

millennium *n/pl* **-nia, -niums 1** period of a thousand years **2** period of peace, happiness

millet *n* cereal grass

milli- *comb. form* thousandth part of, as in *milligram, millilitre; millimetre*

milliner *n* maker of women's hats

million *n* 1000 thousands **millionaire** *n* owner of a million pounds, dollars etc. **millionth** *adj/n*

millipede *n* small animal with many pairs of legs

mime *n* **1** acting without words ▷ *v* **2** perform mime

mimic ❶ *v* **-icking, -icked 1** imitate, esp. for satirical effect ▷ *n* **2** one who does this **mimicry** *n*

mimosa *n* plant with fluffy, yellow flowers

minaret *n* tall slender tower of mosque

mince ❶ *v* **1** cut, chop small **2** soften (words etc.) ▷ *n* **3** minced meat **mincer** *n* **mincing** *adj* affected in manner **mincemeat** *n* mixture of currants, spices, suet etc. **mince pie** pie containing mincemeat

mind ❶ *n* **1** intellectual faculties **2** memory **3** intention **4** taste

_____ THESAURUS _____

military *adj* = **warlike**, armed, soldierly, martial ▷ *n* = **armed forces**, forces, services, army

milk *v* = **exploit**, pump, take advantage of

mill *n* = **grinder**, crusher, quern; = **factory**, works, plant, workshop, foundry ▷ *v* = **grind**, pound, crush, powder, grate

mimic *v* = **imitate**, do (Inf), take off (Inf), ape, parody ▷ *n* = **imitator**, impressionist, copycat (Inf), impersonator, caricaturist

mince *v* = **cut**, grind, crumble, dice,

hash; = **tone down**, spare, moderate, weaken, soften

mind *n* = **memory**, recollection, remembrance, powers of recollection; = **intelligence**, reason, reasoning, understanding, sense; = **intention**, wish, desire, urge, fancy; = **sanity**, reason, senses, judgment, wits ▷ *v* = **take offence at**, dislike, care about, object to, resent; = **be careful**, watch, take care, be wary, be cautious; = **look after**, watch, protect, tend, guard; = **pay**

5 sanity ▷ v **6** take offence at
7 care for **8** attend to **9** heed
minder n (Sl) bodyguard **mindful**
adj heedful **mindless** adj **1** stupid
2 requiring no thought **3** careless
mine¹ ❶ n **1** deep hole for digging
out coal, metals etc. **2** hidden
deposit of explosive to blow up ship
etc. **3** profitable source ▷ v **4** dig
from mine **5** place explosive mines
in, on **miner** n **minefield** n area
of land or sea containing mines
minesweeper n ship for clearing
mines
mine² pron belonging to me
mineral n/adj (of) naturally
occurring inorganic substance
mineralogy n science of minerals
mineral water water containing
dissolved mineral salts
minestrone n soup containing
vegetables and pasta
mingle ❶ v **1** mix, blend **2** mix
socially
mini n **1** something small or
miniature **2** short skirt ▷ adj
3 small
miniature ❶ n **1** small painted

portrait **2** anything on small scale
▷ adj **3** on small scale **miniaturize**
v make to very small scale
minim n (Mus) note half the length
of semibreve
minimum ❶ n/pl **-mums, -ma**
1 lowest size or quantity ▷ adj
2 least possible **minimal** adj
minimize v reduce to minimum
minion n servile dependant
minister ❶ n **1** person in charge
of department of State
2 diplomatic representative
3 clergyman ▷ v **4** take care of
ministerial adj **ministration** n
rendering help **ministry** n/pl
-tries 1 office of clergyman
2 government department
mink n **1** variety of weasel **2** its
fur
minnow n small freshwater fish
minor ❶ adj **1** lesser **2** under age
▷ n **3** person below age of legal
majority **4** scale in music
minority n **1** lesser number, group
2 state of being a minor
minster n cathedral, large church
minstrel n medieval singer,

m

THESAURUS

attention to, mark, note, listen to,
observe
mine¹ n = **pit**, deposit, shaft,
colliery, excavation; = **source**,
store, fund, stock, supply ▷ v = **dig
up**, extract, quarry, unearth,
excavate
mingle v = **mix**, combine, blend,
merge, unite ≠ **separate**;
= **associate**, consort, socialize, rub
shoulders (Inf), hobnob
≠ **dissociate**

miniature adj = **small**, little,
minute, tiny, toy ≠ **giant**
minimum adj = **lowest**, smallest,
least, slightest, minimal
≠ **maximum** ▷ n = **lowest**, least,
lowest level, nadir
minister n = **clergyman**, priest,
vicar, parson, preacher ▷ v often
with **to** = **attend**, serve, tend, take
care of, cater to
minor adj = **small**, lesser, slight,
petty, trivial ≠ **major**

musician, poet

mint¹ ❶ n 1 place where money is coined ▷ adj 2 brand-new ▷ v 3 coin, invent

mint² n aromatic plant

minuet n stately dance

minus prep/adj 1 less 2 lacking 3 negative ▷ n 4 the sign of subtraction (-)

minuscule adj very small

minute¹ ❶ n 1 60th part of hour or degree ▷ pl 2 record of proceedings of meeting etc.

minute² ❶ adj 1 very small 2 precise

minx n bold, flirtatious woman

miracle ❶ n 1 supernatural event 2 marvel **miraculous** adj

mirage n deceptive image in atmosphere

mire n swampy ground, mud

mirror ❶ n 1 glass or polished surface reflecting images ▷ v 2 reflect in or as if in mirror

mirth n merriment, gaiety

mis- comb. form wrong, bad

misadventure n unlucky chance

misanthrope n hater of mankind

misapprehension n misunderstanding

misappropriate v 1 put to dishonest use 2 embezzle

miscellaneous adj mixed **miscellany** n medley

mischief n 1 annoying behaviour 2 inclination to tease 3 harm, annoyance **mischievous** adj

misconception n wrong idea

misconduct ❶ n unethical behaviour

miscreant n evildoer

misdemeanour n minor offence

miser n hoarder of money

miserable ❶ adj 1 very unhappy 2 causing misery 3 worthless 4 squalid **misery** n, pl -eries

misfire v fail to fire, start etc.

misfit n person not suited to environment

misfortune ❶ n (piece of) bad luck

misgiving n (oft. pl) feeling of fear, doubt etc.

THESAURUS

mint¹ v = make, produce, strike, cast, stamp

minute¹ n = moment, second, bit, flash, instant

minute² adj = small, little, tiny, miniature, microscopic ≠ huge; = precise, close, detailed, critical, exact ≠ imprecise

miracle n = wonder, phenomenon, sensation, marvel, amazing achievement

mirror n = looking-glass, glass

(Brit), reflector ▷ v = reflect, follow, copy, echo, emulate

misconduct n = immorality, wrongdoing, mismanagement, malpractice, impropriety

miserable adj ≠ happy; = pathetic, sorry, shameful, despicable, deplorable ≠ respectable

misfortune n often plural = bad luck, adversity, hard luck, ill luck, infelicity

misguided ❶ adj foolish
mishap n minor accident
misjudge v judge wrongly
mislay v put in place which cannot later be remembered
mislead ❶ v give false information to
mismanage v organize badly
misnomer n wrong name or term
misogyny n hatred of women
  misogynist n
misprint n printing error
miss v 1 fail to hit, reach, catch etc. 2 not be in time for 3 notice or regret absence of 4 avoid 5 omit ▷ n 6 fact, instance of missing
  missing adj lost, absent
Miss n 1 title of unmarried woman 2 (without cap.) girl
missal n book containing prayers, rites etc.
missile ❶ n that which may be thrown, shot etc. to damage or destroy
mission ❶ n 1 specific duty 2 delegation 3 those sent
  missionary n/pl **-aries** one sent to a place, society to spread religion

missive n letter
mist ❶ n water vapour in fine drops
  misty adj
mistake ❶ n 1 error ▷ v 2 fail to understand 3 take (person or thing) for another **mistaken** adj
mistletoe n evergreen parasitic plant
mistress ❶ n 1 illicit lover of married man 2 woman with mastery or control 3 title formerly given to married woman
mistrust v 1 not trust ▷ n 2 lack of trust
misunderstand ❶ v fail to understand properly
  misunderstanding n
misuse ❶ n 1 incorrect use ▷ v 2 use wrongly 3 treat badly
mite n 1 very small insect 2 anything very small
mitigate v make less severe
  mitigation n
mitre n 1 bishop's headdress 2 right-angled joint
mitt n covering for hand
mitten n glove with one compartment for thumb and

m

misguided adj = **unwise**, mistaken, misplaced, deluded, ill-advised
mislead v = **deceive**, fool, delude, take someone in (Inf), misdirect
missile n = **projectile**, weapon, shell, rocket
mission n = **task**, job, commission, duty, undertaking
mist n = **fog**, cloud, steam, spray, film
mistake n = **error**, blunder,

oversight, slip, gaffe ▷ v = **confuse with**, take for, mix up with;
= **misunderstand**, misinterpret, misjudge, misread, misconstrue
mistress n = **lover**, girlfriend, concubine, kept woman, paramour
misunderstand v
= **misinterpret**, misread, mistake, misjudge, misconstrue
misuse n = **waste**, squandering, desecration ▷ v = **abuse**, misapply, prostitute

another for fingers

mix ❶ v **1** put together, combine, blend **2** be mixed **3** associate **mixed** adj of different elements, races etc. **mixer** n **mixture** n

mix-up n confused situation

mm millimetre

mnemonic n something to help the memory

moan ❶ v/n (utter) low murmur, usually of pain

moat n deep wide ditch, esp. round castle

mob ❶ n **1** disorderly crowd ▷ v **2** attack in mob, hustle

mobile ❶ adj **1** capable of movement **2** easily changed ▷ n **3** hanging structure designed to move in air currents **mobility** n

mobilize ❶ v prepare, esp. for military service **mobilization** n

moccasin n Amer. Indian soft shoe, usu. of deerskin

mocha n **1** strong dark coffee **2** flavouring of coffee and chocolate

mock ❶ v **1** ridicule **2** mimic ▷ adj **3** sham **mockery** n **1** derision **2** travesty

mode ❶ n **1** manner **2** prevailing fashion **modish** adj fashionable

model ❶ n **1** miniature representation **2** pattern **3** one worthy of imitation **4** person employed to pose, or display clothing ▷ adj **5** made as (miniature) copy **6** exemplary ▷ v **7** make model of **8** mould **9** display (clothing)

modem n device for connecting two computers by telephone line

moderate ❶ adj **1** not going to extremes ▷ n **2** person of

———— THESAURUS ————

mix v = **combine**, blend, merge, join, cross; = **socialize**, associate, hang out (Inf), mingle, circulate ▷ n = **mixture**, combination, blend, fusion, compound

moan v = **groan**, sigh, sob, whine, lament; (Inf) = **grumble**, complain, groan, whine, carp ▷ n = **groan**, sigh, sob, lament, wail; (Inf) = **complaint**, protest, grumble, whine, grouse

mob n = **crowd**, pack, mass, host, drove; (Sl) = **gang**, group, set, lot, crew (Inf) ▷ v = **surround**, besiege, jostle, fall on, set upon

mobile adj = **movable**, moving, travelling, wandering, portable

mobilize v = **rally**, organize, stimulate, excite, prompt;

= **deploy**, prepare, ready, rally, assemble

mock v = **laugh at**, tease, ridicule, taunt, scorn ≠ **respect** ▷ adj = **imitation**, pretended, artificial, fake, false ≠ **genuine**

mode n = **method**, way, system, form, process; = **fashion**, style, trend, rage, vogue

model n = **representation**, image, copy, miniature, dummy; = **pattern**, example, standard, original, ideal; = **sitter**, subject, poser, wear, display, sport ▷ v = **shape**, form, design, fashion, carve

moderate adj = **mild**, reasonable, controlled, limited, steady ≠ **extreme**; = **average**, middling, fair, ordinary, indifferent ▷ v

moderate views ▷ v **3** make, become less excessive **4** preside over **moderation** n **moderator** n arbitrator

modern ❶ adj **1** of present or recent times **2** in, of current fashion **modernity** n **modernize** v bring up to date

modest ❶ adj **1** not overrating one's qualities or achievements **2** moderate, decent **modesty** n

modicum n small quantity

modify ❶ v **-fying, -fied** change slightly **modification** n

modulate v **1** regulate **2** vary in tone **modulation** n

module n (detachable) component with specific function

mogul ❶ n powerful person

mohair n cloth of goat's hair

moist ❶ adj slightly wet **moisten** v **moisture** n liquid, esp. diffused or in drops

molar n/adj (tooth) for grinding

molasses n syrup, by-product of sugar refining

mole¹ n small dark spot on skin

mole² n small burrowing animal

molecule ❶ n simplest freely existing chemical unit **molecular** adj

molest v pester, interfere with so as to annoy or injure

moll n (Sl) gangster's female accomplice

mollify v **-fying, -fied** calm down, placate **mollification** n

mollusc n soft-bodied, usu. hard-shelled animal, e.g. snail

mollycoddle v pamper

molten see MELT

mom n (chiefly US and Canad) an informal word for MOTHER

moment ❶ n short space of, (present) point in, time **momentarily** adv **momentary** adj lasting only a moment

momentous ❶ adj of great importance

momentum ❶ n **1** force of a moving body **2** impetus gained from motion

m

—— THESAURUS ——

= **soften**, control, temper, regulate, curb

modern adj = **current**, contemporary, recent, present-day, latter-day; = **up-to-date**, fresh, new, novel, newfangled ≠ **old-fashioned**

modest adj = **moderate**, small, limited, fair, ordinary; = **unpretentious**, reserved, retiring, shy, coy

modify v = **change**, reform, convert, alter, adjust; = **tone down**, lower, qualify, ease, moderate

mogul n = **tycoon**, baron, magnate, big shot (Inf), big noise (Inf)

moist adj = **damp**, wet, soggy, humid, clammy

molecule n = **particle**, jot, speck

moment n = **instant**, second, flash, twinkling, split second; = **time**, point, stage, juncture

momentous adj = **significant**, important, vital, critical, crucial ≠ **unimportant**

momentum n = **impetus**, force, power, drive, push

monarch ❶ n sovereign ruler **monarchist** n supporter of monarchy **monarchy** n 1 state ruled by sovereign 2 government by sovereign

monastery ❶ n, pl -teries house occupied by religious order **monastic** adj

Monday n second day of the week

money ❶ n banknotes, coins etc., used as medium of exchange **monetary** adj **moneyed, monied** adj rich

mongoose n, pl -gooses small animal of Asia and Africa

mongrel n/adj 1 (animal) of mixed breed 2 hybrid

monitor ❶ n 1 person or device which checks, controls, warns, records 2 pupil assisting teacher with odd jobs 3 type of large lizard ▷ v 4 watch, check on

monk ❶ n one of a religious community of men living apart under vows

monkey ❶ n 1 long-tailed primate 2 mischievous child ▷ v 3 meddle with

mono- comb. form single, as in monosyllabic

monochrome adj of one colour

monocle n single eyeglass

monogamy n custom of being married to one person at a time

monogram n design of letters interwoven

monograph n short book on single subject

monolith n large upright block of stone **monolithic** adj

monologue n long speech by one person

monopoly n exclusive possession of trade, privilege etc. **monopolize** v claim, take exclusive possession of

monotone n speech on one note **monotonous** adj lacking variety, dull **monotony** n

monsoon n 1 seasonal wind of SE Asia 2 very heavy rainfall season

monster ❶ n 1 fantastic imaginary beast 2 huge or misshapen person, animal or thing ▷ adj 3 huge **monstrosity** n 1 monstrous being 2 deformity **monstrous** adj 1 horrible 2 shocking 3 enormous

month n one of twelve periods into which the year is divided **monthly** adj/adv once a month

──────── THESAURUS ────────

monarch n = **ruler**, king or queen, sovereign, tsar, potentate

monastery n = **abbey**, convent, priory, cloister, nunnery

money n = **cash**, capital, currency, hard cash, readies (Inf)

monitor v = **check**, follow, watch, survey, observe ▷ n = **guide**, observer, supervisor, invigilator;

= **prefect** (Brit), head girl, head boy, senior boy, senior girl

monk n = **friar**, brother

monkey n = **simian**, ape, primate; = **rascal**, horror, devil, rogue, imp

monster n = **giant**, mammoth, titan, colossus, monstrosity; = **brute**, devil, beast, demon/villain ▷ adj = **huge**, massive, enormous,

monument ❶ n anything that commemorates, esp. a building or statue **monumental** adj

mooch v (Sl) loaf, slouch

mood¹ ❶ n 1 state of mind and feelings 2 sulk **moody** adj 1 gloomy 2 changeable in mood

mood² n (Grammar) form indicating function of verb

moon ❶ n 1 satellite which revolves round earth 2 any secondary planet ▷ v 3 go about dreamily **moonlight** n

moor¹ ❶ n tract of open uncultivated land **moorhen** n small black water bird

moor² ❶ v secure (ship) with chains or ropes **moorings** pl n ropes etc. for mooring

moose n N Amer. deer

moot adj debatable

mop ❶ n 1 yarn, cloth etc. on end of stick, used for cleaning 2 tangle (of hair etc.) ▷ v 3 clean, wipe as with mop

mope v be gloomy, apathetic

moped n light motorized bicycle

moral ❶ adj 1 pert. to right and wrong conduct 2 of good conduct ▷ n 3 practical lesson, e.g. of fable ▷ pl 4 habits with respect to right and wrong **morality** n 1 good moral conduct 2 moral goodness or badness **moralize** v write, think about moral aspect of things

morale ❶ n degree of confidence, hope

morass n 1 marsh 2 mess

moratorium ❶ n, pl -ria, -riums authorized postponement of payments etc.

morbid adj 1 unduly interested in death 2 gruesome 3 diseased

mordant adj 1 biting 2 corrosive

more ❶ adj, pron 1 greater or additional (amount or number): comparative of MANY and MUCH adv 2 to a greater extent 3 in addition **moreover** adv besides

mores pl n customs and conventions of society

morgue n mortuary

moribund adj 1 dying 2 without force or vitality

————— THESAURUS —————

tremendous, immense

monument n = **memorial**, cairn, marker, shrine, tombstone

mood¹ n = **state of mind**, spirit, humour, temper, disposition

moon v = **idle**, drift, loaf, languish, waste time

moor¹ n = **moorland**, fell (Brit), heath

moor² v = **tie up**, secure, anchor, dock, lash

mop n = **squeegee**, sponge, swab; = **mane**, shock, mass, tangle, mat

moral adj = **good**, just, right, principled, decent ≠ **immoral** ▷ n = **lesson**, meaning, point, message, teaching

morale n = **confidence**, heart, spirit, self-esteem, team spirit

moratorium n = **postponement**, freeze, halt, suspension, standstill

more adj = **extra**, additional, new, other, added ▷ adv = **to a greater extent**, longer, better, further, some more

morning ❶ n early part of day until noon **morn** n (Poet) morning

moron n (Offens) mentally deficient person

morose adj sullen, moody

morphine, morphia n extract of opium used to relieve pain

morrow n (Poet) next day

Morse n telegraphic signalling in which letters are represented by dots and dashes

morsel n small piece

mortal ❶ adj 1 subject to death 2 causing death ▷ n 3 mortal creature **mortality** n 1 state of being mortal 2 death rate 3 great loss of life

mortar n 1 mixture of lime, sand and water for holding bricks together 2 small cannon 3 vessel in which substances are pounded **mortarboard** n square academic cap

mortgage n 1 conveyance of property as security for debt ▷ v 2 pledge as security

mortify v -fying, -fied 1 humiliate 2 subdue by self-denial 3 (of flesh) be affected with gangrene **mortification** n

mortuary n/pl -aries building where corpses are kept before burial or cremation

mosaic n picture or pattern of small bits of coloured stone, glass etc.

mosque n Muslim temple

mosquito n/pl -toes, -tos flying, biting insect

moss n small plant growing in masses on moist surfaces **mossy** adj

most adj/n 1 (of) greatest number, amount or degree: superlative of MUCH and MANY adv 2 in the greatest degree **mostly** adv generally

motel n roadside hotel for motorists

moth n usu. nocturnal insect like butterfly **mothball** n 1 small ball of chemical to repel moths from stored clothing etc. ▷ v 2 store, postpone **moth-eaten** adj 1 damaged by grub of moth 2 scruffy

mother ❶ n 1 female parent 2 head of religious community of women ▷ adj 3 inborn ▷ v 4 act as mother to **motherhood** n **motherly** adj **mother-in-law** n mother of one's wife or husband **mother of pearl** iridescent lining of certain shells

motif ❶ n dominating theme

— THESAURUS —

morning n = **before noon**, forenoon, morn (Poet), a.m.

mortal adj = **human**, worldly, passing, fleshly, temporal; = **fatal**, killing, terminal, deadly, destructive ▷ n = **human being**, being, man, woman, person

mother n = **female parent**, mum (Brit Inf), ma (Inf), mater, dam ▷ v = **nurture**, raise, protect, tend, nurse ▷ adj = **native**, natural, innate, inborn

motif n = **design**, shape, decoration, ornament; = **theme**,

motion ❶ n **1** process or action or way of moving **2** proposal in meeting ▷ v **3** direct by sign

motive ❶ n that which makes person act in particular way **motivate** v incite **motivation** n

motley adj **1** varied **2** multicoloured

motocross n motorcycle race over rough course

motor n **1** that which imparts movement **2** machine to supply power to move ▷ v **3** travel by car **motorist** n **motorhome** n large motor vehicle designed for living in while travelling **motorize** v equip with a motor or motor transport **motorbike, motorcycle** n **motorcar** n **motorway** n main road for fast-moving traffic

mottled adj marked with blotches

motto ❶ n, pl **-toes, -tos** saying adopted as rule of conduct

mould¹ ❶ n **1** hollow object in which metal etc. is cast **2** character **3** shape ▷ v **4** shape **moulding** n ornamental edging

mould² ❶ n fungoid growth caused by dampness **mouldy** adj

mould³ n loose or surface earth **moulder** v decay

moult v **1** cast or shed fur, feathers etc. ▷ n **2** moulting

mound ❶ n **1** heap **2** small hill

mount ❶ v **1** rise **2** increase **3** get on (horse) **4** frame (picture) **5** set up ▷ n **6** support **7** horse **8** hill

mountain ❶ n hill of great size **mountaineer** n one who lives among or climbs mountains **mountainous** adj **mountain bike** bicycle with straight handlebars and heavy-duty tyres

mountebank n charlatan, fake

Mountie n (Inf) a member of the Royal Canadian Mounted Police

mourn ❶ v feel, show sorrow (for)

m

THESAURUS

idea, subject, concept, leitmotif

motion n = **movement**, mobility, travel, progress, flow; = **proposal**, suggestion, recommendation, proposition, submission ▷ v = **gesture**, direct, wave, signal, nod

motive n = **reason**, ground(s), purpose, object, incentive

motto n = **saying**, slogan, maxim, rule, adage

mould¹ n = **cast**, shape, pattern; = **design**, style, fashion, build, form; = **nature**, character, sort, kind, quality ▷ v = **shape**, make, work, form, create; = **influence**, make, form, control, direct

mould² n = **fungus**, blight, mildew

mound n = **heap**, pile, drift, stack, rick; = **hill**, bank, rise, dune, embankment

mount v = **increase**, build, grow, swell, intensify ≠ **decrease**; = **accumulate**, increase, collect, gather, build up; = **ascend**, scale, climb (up), go up, clamber up ≠ **descend** ▷ n = **horse**, steed (Lit); = **backing**, setting, support, stand, base

mountain n = **peak**, mount, horn, ridge, fell (Brit); = **heap**, mass, masses, pile, a great deal

mourn v often with **for** = **grieve for**,

mourner n **mournful** adj **1** sad
2 dismal **mourning** n **1** grieving
2 clothes of mourner
mouse n, pl **mice** small rodent
mousy adj like mouse, esp. in
colour
mousse n dish of flavoured cream
moustache n hair on upper lip
mouth ❶ n **1** opening in head for
eating, speaking etc. **2** opening,
entrance ▷ v **3** form (words) with
lips without speaking **mouth
organ** small musical instrument
mouthpiece n end of anything
placed between lips
move ❶ v **1** change position, place
2 (cause to) be in motion **3** stir
emotions of **4** incite **5** propose
6 change one's dwelling etc. ▷ n
7 a moving **8** motion **movement**
n **1** moving **2** moving parts
3 group with common aim
4 division of piece of music **movie**
n (Inf) film
mow ❶ v **mowing, mowed** cut
(grass etc.) **mower** n

MP 1 Member of Parliament
2 Military Police
mph miles per hour
much ❶ adj **more, most**
1 existing in quantity ▷ n **2** large
amount **3** important matter ▷ adv
4 in a great degree **5** nearly
muck ❶ n **1** dung **2** dirt **mucky**
adj
mucus n fluid secreted by mucous
membranes
mud ❶ n wet and soft earth
muddy adj **mudguard** n cover
over wheel **mudpack** n cosmetic
paste to improve complexion
muddle ❶ v **1** (esp. with up)
confuse **2** bewilder **3** mismanage
▷ n **4** confusion
muesli n mixture of grain, nuts,
dried fruit etc.
muff¹ n tube-shaped covering to
keep hands warm
muff² v bungle, fail in
muffin n light round yeast cake
muffle v wrap up, esp. to deaden
sound **muffler** n scarf

——————————— THESAURUS ———————————

lament, weep for, wail for
mouth n = **lips**, jaws, gob (Sl, esp.
Brit), maw, cakehole (Brit Sl);
= **entrance**, opening, gateway,
door, aperture; = **inlet**, outlet,
estuary, firth, outfall
move v = **transfer**, change, switch,
shift, transpose; = **go**, advance,
progress, shift, proceed; = **relocate**,
leave, remove, quit, migrate;
= **drive**, cause, influence, persuade,
shift ≠ **discourage**; = **touch**, affect,
excite, impress, stir; = **propose**,
suggest, urge, recommend, request

▷ n = **action**, step, manoeuvre;
= **ploy**, action, measure, step,
initiative
mow v = **cut**, crop, trim, shear,
scythe
much adv = **greatly**, a lot,
considerably, decidedly, exceedingly
≠ **hardly**
muck n = **dirt**, mud, filth, ooze,
sludge; = **manure**, dung, ordure
mud n = **dirt**, clay, ooze, silt,
sludge
muddle n = **confusion**, mess,
disorder, chaos, tangle ▷ v

mug¹ ❶ n drinking cup

mug² ❷ n (Sl) **1** face **2** (Sl) fool, simpleton ▷ v **3** rob violently **mugger** n

mug³ v **mugging, mugged** (Inf) (esp. with up) study hard

muggy adj **-gier, -giest** damp and stifling

mulberry n tree whose leaves are used to feed silkworms

mulch n **1** straw, leaves etc. spread as protection for roots of plants ▷ v **2** protect thus

mule n **1** cross between horse and ass **2** hybrid **mulish** adj obstinate

mull v **1** heat (wine) with sugar and spices **2** think (over)

multi- comb. form many, as in multistorey

multifarious adj of various kinds or parts

multiple ❶ adj **1** having many parts ▷ n **2** quantity which contains another an exact number of times **multiplication** n **multiplicity** n variety, greatness in number **multiply** v **1** (cause to) increase **2** combine (two numbers) by multiplication **3** increase by reproduction

multitude ❶ n great number

mum n (Inf) mother

mumble v speak indistinctly

mummy¹ n, pl **-mies** embalmed body **mummify** v

mummy² n (Inf) mother

mumps pl n infectious disease marked by swelling in neck

munch v chew vigorously

mundane ❶ adj **1** ordinary, everyday **2** earthly

municipal ❶ adj belonging to affairs of city or town **municipality** n city or town with local self-government

munificent adj very generous **munificence** n

munted adj (NZ Sl) **1** destroyed or ruined **2** abnormal or peculiar

mural n painting on wall

murder ❶ n **1** unlawful premeditated killing of human being ▷ v **2** kill thus **murderer** n **murderous** adj

murk n darkness **murky** adj

m

--- THESAURUS ---

= **jumble**, disorder, scramble, tangle, mix up; = **confuse**, bewilder, daze, confound, perplex

mug¹ n = **cup**, pot, beaker, tankard

mug² n = **face**, features, countenance, visage; = **fool**, sucker (Sl), chump (Inf), simpleton, easy or soft touch (Sl)

multiple adj = **many**, several, various, numerous, sundry

multitude n = **great number**, host, army, mass, horde

mundane adj = **ordinary**, routine, commonplace, banal, everyday ≠ **extraordinary**; = **earthly**, worldly, secular, mortal, terrestrial ≠ **spiritual**

municipal adj = **civic**, public, local, council, district

murder n = **killing**, homicide, massacre, assassination, slaying ▷ v = **kill**, massacre, slaughter, assassinate, eliminate (Sl)

murmur ⊕ n **-muring, -mured**
1 low, indistinct sound ▷ v **2** make,
utter such a sound **3** complain

muscle ⊕ n **1** part of body which
produces movement by contracting
2 system of muscles **muscular** adj
1 strong **2** of muscle

muse ⊕ v **1** ponder **2** be lost in
thought ▷ n **3** musing **4** reverie
5 goddess inspiring creative artist

museum n (place housing)
collection of historical etc. objects

mush¹ n soft pulpy mass **mushy**
adj

mush² interj order to dogs in sled
team to advance

mushroom n **1** fungoid growth,
typically with stem and cap ▷ v
2 shoot up rapidly

music n **1** art form using
harmonious combination of notes
2 composition in this art **musical**
adj **1** of, like, interested in music
▷ n **2** show, film in which music
plays essential part **musician** n

musk n scent obtained from gland
of deer **musky** adj **muskrat** n
1 N Amer. rodent found near water
2 its fur

muskeg n (Canad) bog or swamp
musket n (Hist) infantryman's gun
Muslim, Moslem n **1** follower of

religion of Islam ▷ adj **2** of Islam

muslin n fine cotton fabric

muss v (US & Canad, Inf) to make
untidy

mussel n bivalve shellfish

must ⊕ v **1** be obliged to, or
certain to ▷ n **2** necessity

mustang n wild horse

mustard n powder made from the
seeds of a plant, used in paste as a
condiment

muster ⊕ v **1** assemble ▷ n
2 assembly, esp. for exercise,
inspection

musty adj **mustier, mustiest**
mouldy, stale

mute ⊕ adj **1** (Offens) unable to
speak **2** silent ▷ n **3** (Mus)
contrivance to soften tone of
instruments **muted** adj **1** muffled
2 subdued

mutilate v **1** deprive of a limb etc.
2 damage

mutiny n, pl **-nies 1** rebellion
against authority, esp. against
officers of disciplined body ▷ v
2 commit mutiny **mutineer** n
mutinous adj

mutter ⊕ v **1** speak, utter
indistinctly **2** grumble ▷ n
3 muttered sound

mutton n flesh of sheep used as food

— THESAURUS —

murmur v = **mumble**, whisper,
mutter ▷ n = **whisper**, drone, purr

muscle n = **tendon**, sinew;
= **strength**, might, power, weight,
stamina

muse v = **ponder**, consider, reflect,
contemplate, deliberate

must n = **necessity**, essential,

requirement, fundamental,
imperative

muster v = **summon up**, marshal
▷ n = **assembly**, meeting,
collection, gathering, rally

mute adj = **silent**, dumb,
unspoken, tacit, wordless

mutter v = **grumble**, complain,

m

mutual ❶ *adj* 1 done, possessed etc. by each of two with respect to the other 2 (*Inf*) common
muzzle *n* 1 mouth and nose of animal 2 cover for these to prevent biting 3 open end of gun ▷ *v* 4 put muzzle on
muzzy *adj* **-zier, -ziest** indistinct, confused
my *adj* belonging to me **myself** *pron* emphatic or reflexive form of ɪ
mynah *n* Indian bird related to starling
myopia *n* short-sightedness **myopic** *adj*
myriad ❶ *adj* 1 innumerable ▷ *n* 2 large number
myrrh *n* aromatic gum, formerly used as incense

myrtle *n* flowering evergreen shrub
myself see MY
mystery ❶ *n, pl* **-teries** 1 obscure or secret thing 2 anything strange or inexplicable **mysterious** *adj*
mystic ❶ *n* one who seeks divine, spiritual knowledge, esp. by prayer, contemplation etc. **mystical** *adj*
mystify *v* **-fying, -fied** bewilder, puzzle
mystique *n* aura of mystery, power etc.
myth ❶ *n* 1 tale with supernatural characters or events 2 imaginary person or object **mythical** *adj* **mythology** *n* myths collectively
myxomatosis *n* contagious, fatal disease of rabbits

―――――― THESAURUS ――――――

murmur, rumble, whine
mutual *adj* = **shared**, common, joint, returned, reciprocal
myriad *n* = **multitude**, host, army, swarm, horde ▷ *adj*
= **innumerable**, countless, untold, incalculable, immeasurable

mystery *n* = **puzzle**, problem, question, secret, riddle
mystical *adj* = **supernatural**, mysterious, transcendental, occult, metaphysical
myth *n* = **legend**, story, fiction, saga, fable; = **illusion**, story, fancy, fantasy, imagination

m

n

nadir n lowest point
naff adj (Sl) inferior or useless
nag¹ ❶ v **nagging, nagged**
1 scold or trouble constantly ▷ n
2 nagging **3** one who nags
nag² ❶ n (Inf) horse
nail ❶ n **1** horny shield at ends of
fingers, toes **2** small metal spike for
fixing wood etc. ▷ v **3** fix with nails
naive, naïve ❶ adj simple,
unaffected, ingenuous **naiveté,
naivety** n
naked ❶ adj **1** without clothes
2 exposed, bare **3** undisguised

name ❶ n **1** word by which
person, thing etc. is denoted
2 reputation ▷ v **3** give name to
4 call by name **5** appoint
6 mention **nameless** adj
1 without a name **2** unknown
3 indescribable **namely** adv that
is to say **namesake** n person with
same name as another
nanny n, pl **-nies** child's nurse
nanny goat she-goat
nap¹ ❶ v **1** take short sleep ▷ n
2 short sleep
nap² ❶ n downy surface on cloth
made by projecting fibres
nape n back of neck
napkin ❶ n **1** cloth, paper for
wiping fingers or lips at table
2 nappy
nappy n, pl **-pies** towelling cloth
to absorb baby's excrement
narcissism n abnormal
admiration for oneself
narcissus n, pl **-cissi** genus
of bulbous plants including
daffodil, esp. one with white
flowers

───── THESAURUS ─────

nab v = **catch**, arrest, apprehend,
seize, grab
nag¹ v = **scold**, harass, badger,
pester, worry ▷ n = **scold**,
complainer, grumbler, virago,
shrew
nag² n = **horse** (US), hack
nail v = **fasten**, fix, secure, attach,
pin
naive, naïve adj = **gullible**,
trusting, credulous, unsuspicious,
green ≠ **worldly**
naked adj = **nude**, stripped,

exposed, bare, undressed
≠ **dressed**
name n = **title**, nickname,
designation, term, handle (Sl) ▷ v
= **call**, christen, baptize, dub, term;
= **nominate**, choose, select,
appoint, specify
nap¹ n = **sleep**, rest, kip (Brit Sl),
siesta, catnap ▷ v = **sleep**, rest,
drop off (Inf), doze, kip (Brit Sl)
nap² n = **pile**, down, fibre, weave,
grain
napkin n = **serviette**, cloth

narcotic ❶ n/adj (drug) producing numbness and stupor

nark v (Sl) annoy, irritate

narrate v tell (story) **narration** n **narrative** n account, story **narrator** n

narrow ❶ adj **1** of little breadth **2** limited ▷ v **3** make, become narrow **narrow-minded** adj **1** illiberal **2** bigoted

nasal adj **1** of nose ▷ n **2** sound partly produced in nose

nasturtium n garden plant with red or orange flowers

nasty ❶ adj -tier, -tiest **1** foul, unpleasant **2** spiteful

nation ❶ n people or race organized as a state **national** adj **1** of, characteristic of, a nation ▷ n **2** citizen **nationalism** n **1** devotion to one's country **2** movement for independence **nationalist** n/adj **nationality** n fact of belonging to a particular nation **nationalization** n acquisition and management of industries by the state **nationalize** v **National Health Service** system of medical services financed mainly by taxation **national service** compulsory military service

native ❶ adj **1** inborn **2** born in particular place ▷ n **3** native person, animal or plant

NATO North Atlantic Treaty Organization

natter (Inf) ▷ v **1** talk idly ▷ n **2** idle talk

natty adj -tier, -tiest neat and smart

nature ❶ n **1** innate qualities of person or thing **2** class, sort **3** (oft. with cap.) power underlying all phenomena **4** natural unspoilt scenery **natural** adj **1** of nature **2** inborn **3** normal **4** unaffected ▷ n **5** something, somebody well suited for something **6** (Mus) character used to remove effect of sharp or flat preceding it **naturalist** n one who studies

n

— THESAURUS —

narcotic adj = **sedative**, calming, hypnotic, analgesic, soporific

narrow adj = **thin**, fine, slim, slender, tapering ≠ **broad**; = **limited**, restricted, confined, tight, close ≠ **wide**; = **insular**, prejudiced, partial, dogmatic, intolerant ≠ **broad-minded** ▷ v = **restrict**, limit, reduce, constrict

nasty adj = **unpleasant**, ugly, disagreeable ≠ **pleasant**; = **spiteful**, mean, offensive, vicious, unpleasant ≠ **pleasant**; = **disgusting**, unpleasant, offensive, vile, distasteful

nation n = **country**, state, realm

native adj = **mother**, indigenous, vernacular = **domestic**, local, indigenous, home ▷ n = **inhabitant**, national, resident, citizen, countryman

nature n = **creation**, world, earth, environment, universe; = **quality**, character, make-up, constitution, essence; = **temperament**, character, personality, disposition, outlook

animals and plants **naturalize** v admit to citizenship **naturally** adv

naturism n nudism

naughty ⊕ adj **-tier, -tiest 1** disobedient **2** (Inf) mildly indecent

nausea ⊕ n feeling that precedes vomiting **nauseate** v sicken **nauseous** adj

nautical adj of seamen or ships **nautical mile** 1852 metres

nave n main part of church

navel n small depression in abdomen where umbilical cord was attached

navigate v **1** direct, plot path of ship etc. **2** travel **navigable** adj **navigation** n **navigator** n

navvy n, pl **-vies** labourer employed on roads, railways etc.

navy ⊕ n, pl **-vies** fleet **2** warships of country with their crews ▷ adj **3** navy-blue **naval** adj of the navy **navy-blue** adj very dark blue

nay adv (Obs) no

NB note well

near ⊕ prep **1** close to ▷ adv **2** at

or to a short distance ▷ adj **3** close at hand **4** closely related **5** stingy ▷ v **6** approach **nearby** adj adjacent **nearly** adv **1** closely **2** almost **nearside** n side of vehicle nearer kerb

neat ⊕ adj **1** tidy, orderly **2** deft **3** undiluted **4** (US & Canad) good or pleasing

nebulous adj vague

necessary ⊕ adj **1** that must be done **2** inevitable ▷ n **3** what is needed **necessarily** adv **necessitate** v make necessary **necessity** n **1** something needed **2** constraining power **3** compulsion **4** poverty

neck n **1** part of body joining head to shoulders **2** narrow part of anything **neckerchief** n cloth tied round the neck **necklace** n ornament round the neck

nectar n honey of flowers

nectarine n variety of peach

née adj indicating maiden name of married woman

need ⊕ v **1** want, require ▷ n

naughty adj = **disobedient**, bad, mischievous, badly behaved, wayward ≠ **good**; = **obscene**, vulgar, improper, lewd, risqué ≠ **clean**

nausea n = **sickness**, vomiting, retching, squeamishness, queasiness

navy n = **fleet**, flotilla, armada

near adj = **close**, neighbouring, nearby, adjacent, adjoining ≠ **far**; = **imminent**, forthcoming, approaching, looming, impending

≠ **far-off**

neat adj = **tidy**, trim, orderly, spruce, shipshape ≠ **untidy**; = **methodical**, tidy, systematic, fastidious ≠ **disorganized**; = **smart**, trim, tidy, spruce, dapper

necessary adj = **needed**, required, essential, vital, compulsory ≠ **unnecessary**; = **inevitable**, certain, unavoidable, inescapable ≠ **avoidable**

need v = **want**, miss, require, lack, have to have ▷ n = **requirement**,

2 (state, instance of) want
3 requirement **4** necessity
5 poverty **needful** *adj* necessary
needless *adj* unnecessary **needy**
adj poor, in want
needle ❶ *n* **1** thin pointed piece of
metal for sewing, knitting **2** stylus
for record player **3** leaf of fir tree
▷ *v* **4** (*Inf*) goad, provoke
needlework *n* sewing, embroidery
nefarious *adj* wicked
negate *v* deny, nullify **negation** *n*
negative ❶ *adj* **1** expressing
denial or refusal **2** lacking
enthusiasm **3** not positive **4** (*of
electrical charge*) having the same
polarity as the charge of an electron
▷ *n* **5** negative word or statement
6 (*Photog*) picture in which lights
and shades are reversed
neglect ❶ *v* **1** take no care of
2 fail to do ▷ *n* **3** fact of neglecting
or being neglected
negligee *v* woman's light dressing
gown
negligence ❶ *n* carelessness
negligent *adj* **negligible** *adj* very

small or unimportant
negotiate ❶ *v* **1** discuss with
view to mutual settlement
2 arrange by conference **3** transfer
(bill, cheque etc.) **4** get over
(obstacle) **negotiable** *adj*
negotiation *n* **negotiator** *n*
neigh *n/v* (utter) cry of horse
neighbour *n* one who lives near
another **neighbourhood** *n*
1 district **2** people of district
neighbouring *adj* nearby
neighbourly *adj* **1** friendly
2 helpful
neither *adj, pron* **1** not the one or
the other ▷ *adv* **2** not on the one
hand **3** not either ▷ *conj* **4** nor yet
nemesis *n, pl* **-ses** retribution/
vengeance
neologism *n* newly-coined word
or phrase
neon *n* inert gas in the atmosphere,
used to illuminate signs and lights
nephew *n* brother's or sister's son
nepotism *n* undue favouritism
towards one's relations
nerve ❶ *n* **1** bundle of fibres

demand, essential, necessity,
requisite; = **necessity**, call,
demand, obligation; = **emergency**,
want, necessity, urgency, exigency
needle *v* = **irritate**, provoke,
annoy, harass, taunt
negative *adj* = **pessimistic**,
cynical, unwilling, gloomy,
jaundiced ≠ **optimistic**;
= **dissenting**, contradictory,
refusing, denying, rejecting
≠ **assenting** ▷ *n* = **denial**, no,
refusal, rejection, contradiction

neglect *v* = **disregard**, ignore, fail
to look after ≠ **look after**; = **shirk**,
forget, overlook, omit, evade ▷ *n*
= **negligence**, inattention ≠ **care**
negligence *n* = **carelessness**,
neglect, disregard, dereliction,
slackness
negotiate *v* = **bargain**, deal,
discuss, debate, mediate;
= **arrange**, work out, bring about,
transact
nerve *n* = **bravery**, courage, bottle
(*Brit Sl*), resolution, daring; (*Inf*)

carrying feeling, impulses to
motion etc. to and from brain
2 assurance **3** coolness in danger
4 audacity ▷ *pl* **5** sensitiveness to
fear, annoyance etc. ▷ *v* **6** give
courage to **nervous** *adj*
1 excitable **2** apprehensive **nervy**
adj nervous, jumpy **nerve-racking**
adj very distressing
nestle ❶ *v* settle comfortably close
to something
net¹ ❶ *n* **1** openwork fabric of
meshes of cord etc. ▷ *v* **2** cover
with, or catch in, net **netting** *n*
string or wire net **netball** *n* game
in which ball has to be thrown
through high net
net², nett ❶ *adj* **1** left after all
deductions ▷ *v* **2** gain, yield as
clear profit
nether *adj* lower
nettle *n* **1** plant with stinging hairs
▷ *v* **2** irritate
network ❶ *n* **1** system of
intersecting lines, roads etc.
2 interconnecting group **3** linked
broadcasting stations

neural *adj* of the nerves
neuralgia *n* pain in, along nerves
neurosis *n, pl* **-ses** relatively mild
mental disorder **neurotic** *adj/n*
neuter *adj* **1** neither masculine nor
feminine ▷ *v* **2** castrate (animals)
neutral ❶ *adj* **1** taking neither
side in war, dispute etc. **2** without
marked qualities ▷ *n* **3** neutral
nation or subject of one **4** position
of disengaged gears **neutrality** *n*
neutralize *v* make ineffective
neutron *n* electrically neutral
particle of nucleus of an atom
never ❶ *adv* at no time
nevertheless *adv* for all that
new ❶ *adj* **1** not existing before,
fresh **2** unfamiliar ▷ *adv* **3** newly
newly *adv* recently, freshly
newcomer *n* recent arrival
newfangled *adj* objectionably or
unnecessarily modern
news ❶ *n* **1** report of recent
happenings **2** interesting fact not
previously known **newsagent** *n*
shopkeeper selling newspapers,
magazines etc. **newsflash** *n* brief

—————————————— THESAURUS ——————————————

= **impudence**, cheek (*Inf*),
audacity, boldness, temerity
nestle *v* = **snuggle**, cuddle, huddle,
curl up, nuzzle
net¹ *n* = **mesh**, netting, network,
web, lattice ▷ *v* = **catch**, bag,
capture, trap, entangle
net², nett *adj* = **after taxes**, final,
clear, take-home, ultimate ▷ *v*
= **earn**, make, clear, gain, realize
network *n* = **web**, system,
arrangement, grid, lattice; = **maze**,
warren, labyrinth

neutral *adj* = **unbiased**, impartial,
disinterested, even-handed,
uninvolved ≠ **biased**;
= **expressionless**, dull
never *adv* = **at no time**, not once,
not ever ≠ **always**
new *adj* = **modern**, recent,
contemporary, up-to-date,
latest ≠ **old-fashioned**; = **extra**,
more, added, new-found,
supplementary
news *n* = **information**, latest (*Inf*),
report, story, exposé

news item, oft. interrupting programme **newspaper** n periodical publication containing news **newsprint** n inexpensive paper **newsreel** n film giving news

newt n small, tailed amphibian

newton n unit of force

next ❶ adj/adv 1 nearest 2 immediately following **next-of-kin** n closest relative

NF Newfoundland

NHS National Health Service

nib n (split) pen point

nibble v 1 take little bites of ▷ n 2 little bite

nice ❶ adj 1 pleasant 2 friendly 3 kind 4 subtle, fine 5 careful, exact **nicely** adv **nicety** n minute distinction or detail

niche ❶ n recess in wall

nick ❶ v 1 make notch in, indent 2 (Sl) steal ▷ n 3 notch 4 (Inf) condition 5 (Sl) prison

nickel n 1 silver-white metal much used in alloys and plating 2 (US & Canad) five cent piece

nickname ❶ n familiar name

nicotine n poisonous oily liquid in tobacco

niece n brother's or sister's daughter

nifty adj -tier, -tiest (Inf) 1 smart 2 quick

niggard n mean, stingy person **niggardly** adj/adv

niggle v 1 find fault continually 2 annoy

nigh adj/adv/prep (Obs) near

night ❶ n time of darkness between sunset and sunrise **nightie, nighty** n nightdress **nightly** adj/adv (happening, done) every night **nightcap** n drink taken before bedtime **nightclub** n place for dancing, music etc., open late at night **nightdress** n woman's loose robe worn in bed **nightingale** n small bird which sings at night **nightmare** n 1 very bad dream 2 terrifying experience **nightshade** n various plants of potato family, some with very poisonous berries **night-time** n

n

THESAURUS

---

next adj = **following**, later, succeeding, subsequent; = **adjacent**, closest, nearest, neighbouring, adjoining ▷ adv = **afterwards**, then, later, following, subsequently

nice adj = **pleasant**, delightful, agreeable, good, attractive ≠ **unpleasant**; = **kind**, helpful, obliging, considerate ≠ **unkind**; = **likable** or **likeable**, friendly, engaging, charming, pleasant;

= **polite**, courteous, well-mannered ≠ **vulgar**

niche n = **recess**, opening, corner, hollow, nook; = **position**, calling, place, slot (Inf), vocation

nick v (Sl) = **steal**, pinch (Inf), swipe (Sl), pilfer; = **cut**, mark, score, chip, scratch ▷ n = **cut**, mark, scratch, chip, scar

nickname n = **pet name**, label, diminutive, epithet, sobriquet

night n = **darkness**, dark,

nil ❶ n nothing, zero

nimble adj agile, quick, dexterous

nimbus n, pl **-bi, -buses 1** rain or storm cloud **2** halo

nincompoop n (Inf) stupid person

nine adj/n cardinal number next above eight **ninth** adj ordinal number **nineteen** adj/n nine more than ten **nineteenth** adj **ninetieth** adj **ninety** adj/n nine tens

nip ❶ v **nipping, nipped 1** pinch sharply **2** detach by pinching, bite **3** check growth (of plants) thus **4** (Inf) hurry ▷ n **5** pinch **6** sharp coldness of weather **7** short drink **nipper** n **1** thing that nips **2** (Inf) small child **nippy** adj **-pier, -piest 1** (Inf) cold **2** quick

nipple n **1** point of breast, teat **2** anything like this

nit n **1** egg of louse or other parasite **2** (Inf) nitwit **nit-picking** adj (Inf) overconcerned with insignificant detail **nitwit** n (Inf) fool

nitrogen n one of the gases making up air **nitrate** n compound of nitric acid and an alkali **nitric** adj **nitroglycerine** n explosive liquid

no ❶ adj **1** not any, not a **2** not at all ▷ adv **3** expresses negative reply ▷ n **4** refusal **5** denial **6** negative vote or voter **no-one, no one** nobody

no. number

noble ❶ adj **1** of the nobility **2** having high moral qualities **3** impressive ▷ n **4** member of the nobility **nobility** n **1** class holding special rank **2** being noble **nobleman** n **nobly** adv

nobody ❶ n **1** no person **2** person of no importance

no-brainer n (Sl) something that requires little or no mental effort

nocturnal adj of, in, by, night

nod ❶ v **nodding, nodded 1** bow head slightly and quickly in assent, command etc. **2** let head droop with sleep ▷ n **3** act of nodding

node n knot or knob

nodule n **1** little knot **2** rounded irregular mineral mass

noise ❶ n **1** any sound, esp. disturbing one ▷ v **2** rumour

——————————— THESAURUS ———————————

night-time

nil n = **nothing**, love, zero

nip v = **pop**, go, run, rush, dash

no interj = **not at all**, certainly not, of course not, absolutely not, never ≠ **yes** ▷ n = **refusal**, rejection, denial, negation ≠ **consent**

noble adj = **worthy**, generous, upright, honourable, virtuous ≠ **despicable**; = **dignified**, great, imposing, impressive, distinguished ≠ **lowly**; = **aristocratic**, lordly,

titled, patrician, blue-blooded ≠ **humble** ▷ n = **lord**, peer, aristocrat, nobleman ≠ **commoner**

nobody n = **nonentity**, lightweight (Inf), zero, cipher ≠ **celebrity**

nod v = **signal**, indicate, motion, gesture; = **salute**, acknowledge ▷ n = **signal**, sign, motion, gesture, indication

noise n = **sound**, row, racket, clamour, din ≠ **silence**

noisy adj

nomad n **1** member of wandering tribe **2** wanderer **nomadic** adj

nomenclature n system of names

nominal ❶ adj **1** in name only **2** (of fee etc.) small

nominate ❶ v **1** propose as candidate **2** appoint to office **nomination** n **nominee** n candidate

non- comb. form indicates the negative of a word

nonchalant adj casually unconcerned, indifferent

noncommissioned officer (Mil) subordinate officer, risen from the ranks

noncommittal adj avoiding definite preference or pledge

nonconformist n dissenter, esp. from Established Church

nondescript adj lacking distinctive characteristics

none ❶ pron **1** no-one, not any ▷ adv **2** in no way **nonetheless** adv despite that, however

nonentity n/pl **-ties** insignificant person, thing

nonevent n disappointing or insignificant occurrence

nonflammable adj not easily set on fire

nonpareil n/adj (person or thing) unequalled or unrivalled

nonplussed adj disconcerted

nonsense ❶ n **1** absurd language **2** absurdity **3** silly conduct

non sequitur statement with little relation to what preceded it

nook n sheltered corner

noon ❶ n midday, twelve o'clock

noose n **1** loop on end of rope **2** snare

nor conj and not

norm ❶ n **1** average level **2** standard **normal** adj **1** ordinary **2** usual **3** conforming to type **normality** n **normally** adv

north ❶ n **1** direction to the right of person facing the sunset ▷ adv/ adj **2** from, towards or in the north **northerly** adj/n wind from the north **northern** adj **northwards** adv

nose ❶ n **1** organ of smell, used also in breathing **2** any projection resembling a nose ▷ v **3** (cause to)

n

───────── THESAURUS ─────────

nominal adj = **titular**, formal, purported, in name only, supposed; = **token**, small, symbolic, minimal, trivial

nominate v = **propose**, suggest, recommend, put forward; = **appoint**, name, choose, select, elect

none pron = **not any**, nothing, zero, not one, nil

nonsense n = **rubbish**, hot air

(Inf), twaddle, drivel, tripe (Inf) ≠ **sense**

noon n = **midday**, high noon, noonday, twelve noon, noontide

norm n = **standard**, rule, pattern, average, par

north adj = **northern**, polar, arctic, boreal, northerly ▷ adv = **northward(s)**, in a northerly direction

nose n = **snout**, bill, beak, hooter (Sl),

move forward slowly and carefully
4 touch with nose **5** smell, sniff
6 pry **nosy** adj (Inf) inquisitive
nose dive sudden drop
nosh (Sl) ▷ n **1** food ▷ v **2** eat
nostalgia ❶ n longing for past
events **nostalgic** adj
nostril n one of the two external
openings of the nose
not adv expressing negation,
refusal, denial
notable ❶ adj/n remarkable
(person) **notably** adv
notary n, pl -ries person
authorized to draw up deeds,
contracts
notation n representation of
numbers, quantities by symbols
notch ❶ n/v (make) V-shaped cut
note ❶ n **1** brief comment or
record **2** short letter **3** banknote
4 symbol for musical sound

5 single tone **6** fame **7** notice ▷ v
8 observe, record **9** heed **noted**
adj well-known **notebook** n small
book with blank pages for writing
nothing n **1** no thing **2** not
anything, nought ▷ adv **3** not at
all, in no way
notice ❶ n **1** observation
2 attention **3** warning,
announcement ▷ v **4** observe,
mention **5** give attention to
notify ❶ v -fying, -fied give
notice of or to
notion ❶ n **1** concept **2** opinion
3 whim
notorious ❶ adj known for
something bad **notoriety** n
notwithstanding ❶ prep **1** in
spite of ▷ adv **2** all the same ▷ conj
3 although
nougat n chewy sweet containing
nuts, fruit etc.

————————————— THESAURUS —————————————

proboscis ▷ v = **ease forward**,
push, edge, shove, nudge
nostalgia n = **reminiscence**,
longing, pining, yearning,
remembrance
notable adj = **remarkable**,
striking, unusual, extraordinary,
outstanding ≠ **imperceptible** ▷ n
= **celebrity**, big name, dignitary,
luminary, personage
notch n = **level** (Inf), step, degree,
grade; = **cut**, nick, incision,
indentation, mark ▷ v = **cut**, mark,
score, nick, scratch
note n = **message**, letter,
communication, memo,
memorandum ▷ v = **notice**, see,
observe, perceive; = **bear in mind**,

be aware, take into account;
= **mention**, record, mark, indicate,
register
notice v = **observe**, see, note,
spot, distinguish ≠ **overlook** ▷ n
= **notification**, warning, advice,
intimation, news; = **attention**,
interest, note, regard,
consideration ≠ **oversight**
notify v = **inform**, tell, advise, alert
to, announce
notion n = **idea**, view, opinion,
belief, concept; = **whim**, wish,
desire, fancy, impulse
notorious adj = **infamous**,
disreputable, opprobrious
notwithstanding prep
= **despite**, in spite of, regardless of

nought n 1 nothing 2 figure o

noun n word used as name of person, idea or thing

nourish ⊕ v 1 feed 2 nurture **nourishment** n

Nov. November

novel¹ ⊕ n fictitious tale in book form **novelist** n

novel² ⊕ adj 1 new, recent 2 strange **novelty** n 1 newness 2 something new 3 small trinket

November n eleventh month

novice ⊕ n beginner

now ⊕ adv 1 at the present time 2 immediately 3 recently ▷ conj 4 seeing that, since **nowadays** adv in these times

nowhere adv not in any place or state

noxious adj poisonous, harmful

nozzle n pointed spout, esp. at end of hose

NS Nova Scotia

nuance n delicate shade of difference

NSW New South Wales

nub n 1 small lump 2 main point

nubile adj 1 sexually attractive 2 marriageable

nucleus ⊕ n, pl -clei 1 centre, kernel 2 core of atom **nuclear** adj of, pert. to atomic nucleus **nuclear energy** energy released by nuclear fission **nuclear fission** disintegration of atom

nude ⊕ n/adj naked (person) **nudism** n practice of nudity **nudist** n **nudity** n

nudge ⊕ v 1 touch slightly with elbow ▷ n 2 such touch

nugget n lump of gold

nuisance ⊕ n something or someone annoying

nuke v (Sl) attack or destroy with nuclear weapons

null adj of no effect, void **nullify** v 1 cancel 2 make useless

numb ⊕ adj 1 deprived of feeling ▷ v 2 make numb

number ⊕ n 1 sum or aggregate 2 word or symbol saying how many 3 single issue of a paper etc.

n

nourish v = **feed**, supply, sustain, nurture; = **encourage**, support, maintain, promote, sustain

novel¹ n = **story**, tale, fiction, romance, narrative

novel² adj = **new**, different, original, fresh, unusual ≠ **ordinary**

novice n = **beginner**, pupil, amateur, newcomer, trainee ≠ **expert**

now adv = **nowadays**, at the moment; = **immediately**, promptly, instantly, at once, straightaway

nucleus n = **centre**, heart, focus, basis, core

nude adj = **naked**, stripped, bare, undressed, stark-naked ≠ **dressed**

nudge n = **push**, touch, dig, elbow, bump

nuisance n = **trouble**, problem, trial, drag (Inf), bother (Inf) ≠ **benefit**

numb adj = **unfeeling**, dead, frozen, paralysed, insensitive ≠ **sensitive** knock out, paralyse ▷ v = **deaden**, freeze, dull, paralyse, immobilize

number n = **numeral**, figure,

4 company, collection
5 identifying number ▷ v **6** count
7 class, reckon **8** give a number to
numberless adj countless
numeral n sign or word denoting a
number **numeracy** n ability to
use numbers in calculations
numerate adj **numerator** n top
part of fraction **numerical** adj of
numbers **numerous** adj many
numskull n dolt, dunce
nun n woman living (in convent)
under religious vows **nunnery** n
convent of nuns
nuptial adj of marriage **nuptials**
pl n wedding
nurse ❶ n **1** person trained for
care of sick or injured ▷ v **2** act as
nurse to **3** suckle **nursery** n
1 room for children **2** rearing place
for plants **nursing home** private
hospital or home for old people
nursing officer administrative
head of nursing staff of hospital

nurture ❶ n **1** bringing up
2 rearing ▷ v **3** bring up **4** educate
5 nourish
nut ❶ n **1** fruit consisting of hard
shell and kernel **2** hollow metal
collar into which a screw fits **3** (Inf)
head **4** (Sl) crank, maniac **nutty**
adj **nutmeg** n aromatic seed of
Indian tree
nutrient adj **1** nourishing ▷ n
2 something nutritious
nutrition ❶ n **1** receiving foods
2 act of nourishing **nutritional,
nutritious, nutritive** adj
nuzzle v **1** burrow, press with nose
2 nestle
NWT Northwest Territories
nylon n **1** synthetic material used
for fabrics etc. ▷ pl **2** stockings of
this
nymph n legendary spirit of sea,
woods etc.
nymphomaniac n woman with
abnormally intense sexual desire

──────── THESAURUS ────────

character, digit, integer; = **amount**,
quantity, collection, aggregate
≠ **shortage**; = **crowd**, horde,
multitude, throng; = **group**, set,
band, crowd, gang ▷ v = **amount
to**, come to, total, add up to
nurse v = **look after**, treat, tend,
care for, take care of; = **harbour**,
have, maintain, preserve, entertain;
= **breast-feed**, feed, nurture,

nourish, suckle
nurture v = **bring up**, raise, look
after, rear, care for ≠ **neglect** ▷ n
= **upbringing**, training, education,
instruction, rearing
nut n (Sl) = **madman**, psycho (Sl),
crank (Inf), lunatic, maniac; (Sl)
= **head**, skull
nutrition n = **food**, nourishment,
sustenance, nutriment

stone column

obese *adj* very fat **obesity** *n*

obey ❶ *v* **1** do the bidding of **2** do as ordered

obituary *n, pl* **-aries 1** notice, record of death **2** biographical sketch of deceased person

object¹ ❶ *n* **1** material thing **2** that to which feeling or action is directed **3** end or aim **4** (*Grammar*) word dependent on verb or preposition

object² ❶ *v* express or feel dislike or reluctance to something **objection** *n* **objectionable** *adj*

objective ❶ *adj* **1** external to the mind **2** impartial ▷ *n* **3** thing or place aimed at

oblige ❶ *v* **1** compel **2** do favour for (someone) **obligate** *v* bind, esp. by legal contract **obligation** *n* **1** binding duty, promise **2** debt of gratitude **obligatory** *adj* **1** required **2** binding **obliging** *adj* ready to serve others, helpful

oblique *adj* **1** slanting **2** indirect

obliterate *v* **1** blot out, efface **2** destroy completely

oblong *adj* **1** rectangular, with adjacent sides unequal ▷ *n*

oaf *n* **1** lout **2** dolt

oak *n* common deciduous tree

OAP old age pensioner

oar *n* wooden lever with broad blade worked by the hands to propel boat

oasis *n, pl* **-ses** fertile spot in desert

oat *n* **1** (*usu. pl*) grain of cereal plant **2** the plant **oatmeal** *n*

oath ❶ *n* **1** confirmation of truth of statement by naming something sacred **2** curse

obdurate *adj* stubborn, unyielding

OBE Officer of the Order of the British Empire

obelisk *n* tapering rectangular

O

THESAURUS

oath *n* = **promise**, bond, pledge, vow, word; = **swear word**, curse, obscenity, blasphemy, expletive

obey *v* = **carry out**, follow, implement, act upon, carry through ≠ **disregard**

object¹ *n* = **thing**, article, body, item, entity; = **purpose**, aim, end, point, plan; = **target**, victim, focus, recipient

object² *v with* **to** = **protest against**, oppose, argue against, draw the line at, take exception to ≠ **accept**

objective *n* = **purpose**, aim, goal, end, plan ▷ *adj* = **factual**, real

oblige *v* = **compel**, make, force, require, bind; = **help**, assist, benefit, please, humour ≠ **bother**

2 oblong figure

obnoxious adj offensive, odious

oboe n woodwind instrument

obscene ❶ adj indecent, repulsive
obscenity n

obscure ❶ adj 1 unclear, indistinct
▷ v 2 make unintelligible 3 dim
4 conceal **obscurity** n
1 indistinctness 2 lack of
intelligibility 3 obscure place or
position

obsequious adj servile, fawning

observe ❶ v 1 notice, remark
2 watch 3 note systematically
4 keep, follow **observance** n
1 keeping of custom 2 ritual,
ceremony **observant** adj quick to
notice **observation** n
observatory n place for watching
stars etc. **observer** n

obsess v haunt, fill the mind
obsession n

obsolete ❶ adj not current;
disused, out of date **obsolescent**

adj going out of use

obstacle ❶ n obstruction

obstetrics pl n branch of medicine
concerned with childbirth
obstetrician n

obstinate adj 1 stubborn 2 hard
to overcome or cure **obstinacy** n

obstreperous adj unruly, noisy

obstruct ❶ v 1 block up 2 hinder
3 impede **obstruction** n
obstructive adj

obtain ❶ v 1 get 2 acquire 3 be
customary **obtainable** adj

obtrude v thrust forward unduly
obtrusive adj

obtuse adj 1 dull of perception
2 stupid 3 greater than right angle
4 not pointed

obverse n 1 complement
2 principal side of coin, medal etc.

obviate v remove, make
unnecessary

obvious ❶ adj clear, evident
obviously adv

——————— THESAURUS ———————

obscene adj = **indecent**, dirty,
offensive, filthy, improper
≠ **decent**; = **offensive**, shocking,
evil, disgusting, outrageous

obscure adj = **unknown**,
little-known, humble, unfamiliar,
out-of-the-way ≠ **famous**;
= **abstruse**, complex, confusing,
mysterious, vague
≠ **straightforward**; = **unclear**,
uncertain, confused, mysterious,
doubtful ≠ **well-known** ▷ v
= **obstruct**, hinder

observe v = **watch**, study, view,
look at, check; = **notice**, see, note,
discover, spot; = **remark**, say,

comment, state, note; = **comply
with**, keep, follow, respect, carry
out ≠ **disregard**

obsolete adj = **outdated**, old,
passé, old-fashioned, discarded
≠ **up-to-date**

obstacle n = **obstruction**, block,
barrier, hurdle, snag

obstruct v = **block**, close, bar,
plug, barricade; = **hold up**, stop,
check, block, restrict

obtain v = **get**, gain, acquire, land,
net ≠ **lose**; = **achieve**, get, gain,
accomplish, attain

obvious adj = **clear**, plain,
apparent, evident, distinct

occasion ❶ *n* **1** time when thing happens **2** reason, need **3** opportunity **4** special event ▷ *v* **5** cause **occasional** *adj* happening, found now and then **occasionally** *adv*

Occident *n* the West **Occidental** *adj*

occult *adj* **1** secret, mysterious **2** supernatural

occupy ❶ *v* **-pying, -pied** **1** inhabit, fill **2** employ **3** take possession of **occupancy** *n* fact of occupying **occupant** *n* **occupation** *n* **1** employment, pursuit **2** tenancy **3** military control of country by foreign power **occupational** *adj* **occupier** *n*

occur ❶ *v* **-curring, -curred** **1** happen **2** come to mind **occurrence** *n* happening

ocean *n* **1** great body of water **2** large division of this **3** the sea

ochre *n* earth used as yellow or brown pigment

o'clock *adv* by the clock

Oct. October

octagon *n* figure with eight angles **octagonal** *adj*

octane *n* chemical found in petrol

octave *n* (*Mus*) **1** eighth note above or below given note **2** this space

octet *n* (music for) group of eight

October *n* tenth month

octopus *n, pl* **-puses** mollusc with eight arms covered with suckers

odd ❶ *adj* **1** strange, queer **2** incidental, random **3** left over or additional **4** not even **5** not part of a set **oddity** *n* **1** odd person or thing **2** quality of being odd **oddments** *pl n* things left over **odds** *pl n* **1** advantage conceded in betting **2** likelihood **odds and ends** odd fragments or scraps

ode *n* lyric poem

≠ unclear
occasion *n* = **time**, moment, point, stage, instance; = **function**, event, affair, do (*Inf*), happening; = **opportunity**, chance, time, opening, window; = **reason**, cause, call, ground(s), excuse ▷ *v* (*Formal*) = **cause**, produce, lead to, inspire, result in

occupy *v* = **inhabit**, own, live in, dwell in, reside in ≠ **vacate**; = **invade**, take over, capture, seize, conquer ≠ **withdraw**; = **hold**, control, dominate, possess; = **take**

up, consume, tie up, use up, monopolize

occur *v* = **happen**, take place, come about, turn up (*Inf*), crop up (*Inf*); = **exist**, appear, be found, develop, turn up

odd *adj* = **peculiar**, strange, unusual, extraordinary, bizarre; = **unusual**, strange, rare, extraordinary, remarkable ≠ **normal**; = **occasional**, various, random, casual, irregular ≠ **regular**; = **spare**, remaining, extra, surplus, solitary ≠ **matched**

odium n hatred, widespread dislike
  odious adj
odour ❶ n smell **odorous** adj
  1 fragrant 2 scented
odyssey ❶ n long eventful journey
oesophagus n, pl **-gi** passage
  between mouth and stomach
of prep denotes removal, separation,
  ownership, attribute, material,
  quality
off ❶ adv 1 away ▷ prep 2 away
  from ▷ adj 3 not operative
  4 cancelled or postponed 5 bad,
  sour etc. **offhand** adj/adv
  1 without previous thought 2 curt
  off-licence n place where alcoholic
  drinks are sold for consumption
  elsewhere **offline** adj/adv not
  connected to the internet **offset** v
  counterbalance, compensate
  offspring n children, issue
offal n 1 edible entrails of animal
  2 refuse
offend ❶ v 1 hurt feelings of,
  displease 2 do wrong 3 disgust

offence n 1 wrong 2 crime
  3 insult **offender** n **offensive** adj
  1 causing displeasure 2 aggressive
  ▷ n 3 position or movement of attack
offer ❶ v 1 present for acceptance
  or refusal 2 tender 3 propose
  4 attempt ▷ n 5 offering, bid
office ❶ n 1 room(s), building, in
  which business, clerical work etc. is
  done 2 commercial or professional
  organization 3 official position
  4 service 5 duty 6 form of
  worship ▷ pl 7 task 8 service
  officer n 1 one in command in
  army, navy, ship etc. 2 official
official ❶ adj 1 with, by, authority
  ▷ n 2 one holding office
  officiate v perform duties of office,
  ceremony
officious adj 1 importunate in
  offering service 2 interfering
offside adj/adv (Sport) illegally
  forward
often ❶ adv many times
ogle v 1 stare, look (at) amorously

━━━━━━━━━━━━━━ THESAURUS ━━━━━━━━━━━━━━

odour n = **smell**, scent, perfume,
  fragrance, stink
odyssey n = **journey**, tour, trip,
  quest, trek
off adv = **away**, out, apart,
  elsewhere, aside ▷ adj = **absent**,
  gone, unavailable; = **cancelled**,
  abandoned, postponed, shelved
offend v = **distress**, upset,
  outrage, wound, slight ≠ **please**
offer v = **provide**, present, furnish,
  afford ≠ **withhold**; = **volunteer**,
  come forward, offer your services;
  = **propose**, suggest, advance,
  submit; = **give**, show, bring,

provide, render ▷ n = **proposal**,
  suggestion, proposition,
  submission; = **bid**, tender, bidding
  price
office n = **place of work**,
  workplace, base, workroom, place
  of business
official adj = **authorized**, formal,
  sanctioned, licensed, proper
  ≠ **unofficial**; = **formal**,
  bureaucratic, ceremonial, solemn,
  ritualistic ▷ n = **officer**, executive,
  agent, representative, bureaucrat
often adv = **frequently**, generally,
  commonly, repeatedly, time and

▷ n **2** this look

ogre n **1** man-eating giant **2** monster

oh interj exclamation of surprise, pain etc.

ohm n unit of electrical resistance

oil ❶ n **1** any viscous liquid with smooth, sticky feel **2** petroleum ▷ v **3** lubricate with oil **oily** adj **oilskin** n cloth treated with oil to make it waterproof

ointment n greasy preparation for healing or beautifying the skin

O.K., okay (Inf) ▷ adj/adv, interj **1** all right ▷ v **2** agree to, endorse

old ❶ adj **1** aged, having lived or existed long **2** belonging to earlier period **olden** adj old **old-fashioned** adj **1** in style of earlier period, out of date **2** fond of old ways

olfactory adj of smelling

oligarchy n, pl **-chies** government by small group

olive n **1** evergreen tree **2** its oil-yielding fruit **3** its wood ▷ adj **4** greyish-green

ombudsman n official who investigates complaints against government organizations

omelette n dish of eggs beaten and fried

omen n prophetic happening **ominous** adj boding evil, threatening

omit ❶ v **omitting, omitted** leave out, leave undone **omission** n

omnibus n **1** book etc. containing several works **2** bus ▷ adj **3** serving, containing several objects

omnipotent adj all-powerful

omniscient adj knowing everything

omnivorous adj eating both animals and plants **omnivore** n

on prep **1** above and touching, at, near, towards etc. **2** attached to **3** concerning **4** performed upon **5** during **6** taking regularly ▷ adj **7** operating **8** taking place ▷ adv **9** so as to be on **10** forwards **11** continuously etc. **12** in progress

oncoming adj approaching from the front **ongoing** adj in progress, continuing **online** adj/adv connected to the internet

once ❶ adv **1** one time **2** formerly **3** ever **at once 1** immediately **2** simultaneously **once-over** n (Inf) quick examination

one adj **1** lowest cardinal number **2** single **3** united **4** only, without others **5** identical ▷ n **6** number or figure 1 **7** unity **8** single specimen ▷ pron **9** particular but not stated person **10** any person **oneself** pron **one-sided** adj

again ≠ **never**

oil v = **lubricate**, grease

old adj = **aged**, elderly, ancient, mature, venerable ≠ **young**; = **out of date**, dated, antique, obsolete, archaic ≠ **up-to-date**

omit v = **leave out**, drop, exclude, eliminate, skip ≠ **include**; = **forget**, overlook, neglect, pass over, lose sight of

once adv = **on one occasion**, one time, one single time; = **at one**

1 partial **2** uneven

onerous *adj* burdensome

onion *n* edible bulb of pungent flavour

onlooker ❶ *n* person who watches without taking part

only ❶ *adj* **1** being the one specimen ▷ *adv* **2** solely, merely, exclusively ▷ *conj* **3** but then **4** excepting that

onset ❶ *n* beginning

onslaught ❶ *n* attack

onto *prep* on top of

onus *n, pl* **onuses** responsibility, burden

onward ❶ *adj* **1** advanced or advancing ▷ *adv* **2** in advance, ahead, forward **onwards** *adv*

onyx *n* variety of quartz

ooze ❶ *v* **1** pass slowly out, exude ▷ *n* **2** sluggish flow **3** wet mud

opal *n* glassy gemstone displaying variegated colours

opaque *adj* not transparent

open ❶ *adj* **1** not shut or blocked up **2** without lid or door **3** bare **4** undisguised **5** not enclosed, covered or exclusive **6** spread out, accessible **7** frank ▷ *v* **8** make or become open **9** begin ▷ *n* **10** clear space, unenclosed country

opening *n* **1** hole, gap **2** beginning **3** opportunity ▷ *adj* **4** first **5** initial **openly** *adv* without concealment

open-minded *adj* unprejudiced

opera *n* musical drama **operatic** *adj* **operetta** *n* light opera

operation *n* **1** the act or method of operating **2** the condition of being in action **3** a surgical procedure carried out to remove, replace or repair a diseased or damaged part of the body

ophthalmic *adj* of eyes

opinion ❶ *n* **1** what one thinks about something **2** belief, judgment **opinionated** *adj*

————————— THESAURUS

time, previously, formerly, long ago, once upon a time

onlooker *n* = **spectator**, witness, observer, viewer, looker-on

only *adj* = **sole**, one, single, individual, exclusive ▷ *adv* = **just**, simply, purely, merely

onset *n* = **beginning**, start, birth, outbreak, inception ≠ **end**

onslaught *n* = **attack**, charge, campaign, strike, assault ≠ **retreat**

onward, onwards *adv* = **forward**, on, forwards, ahead, beyond

ooze *v* = **seep**, well, escape, leak, drain

open *v* = **unfasten**, unlock ≠ **close**; = **unwrap**, uncover, undo, unravel, untie ≠ **wrap** ▷ *adj* = **unclosed**, unlocked, ajar, unfastened, yawning ≠ **closed**; = **unsealed**, unstoppered ≠ **unopened**; = **extended**, unfolded, stretched out, unfurled, straightened out ≠ **shut**; = **frank**, direct, straightforward, sincere, transparent ≠ **sly**; = **receptive**, sympathetic, responsive, amenable, subject; = **unresolved**, unsettled, undecided, debatable, moot

opinion *n* = **belief**, feeling, view,

stubborn in one's opinions

opium *n* narcotic drug made from poppy **opiate** *n* drug containing opium

opossum *n* small Amer. and Aust. marsupial

opponent ❶ *n* adversary, antagonist

opportunity ❶ *n* **1** favourable time or condition **2** good chance **opportunity shop** (Aust & NZ) shop selling second-hand clothes, sometimes for charity

oppose ❶ *v* resist, set against **opposite** *adj* **1** contrary **2** facing ▷ *n* **3** the contrary ▷ *prep, adv* **4** facing **5** on the other side **opposition** *n* **1** resistance **2** hostility **3** group opposing another

oppress ❶ *v* **1** govern by tyranny **2** weigh down **oppression** *n* **oppressive** *adj* **1** tyrannical **2** hard to bear **3** (of weather) hot and tiring

opt ❶ *v* make a choice

optic *adj* of eye or sight **optical** *adj* **optician** *n* maker of, dealer in

spectacles, optical instruments

optimism *n* disposition to look on the bright side **optimist** *n* **optimistic** *adj*

optimum ❶ *adj/n, pl* **-ma, -mums** the best, the most favourable

option ❶ *n* **1** choice **2** thing chosen **optional** *adj* leaving to choice

optometrist *n* person testing eyesight, prescribing corrective lenses

opulent *adj* **1** rich **2** copious **opulence** *n*

opus ❶ *n, pl* **opuses, opera** **1** work **2** musical composition

or *conj* **1** introducing alternatives **2** if not

oracle *n* **1** divine utterance, prophecy given at shrine of god **2** the shrine **3** wise adviser

oral ❶ *adj* **1** spoken **2** by mouth ▷ *n* **3** spoken examination

orange *adj* **1** reddish-yellow ▷ *n* **2** reddish-yellow citrus fruit

orang-utan, orang-utang *n* large reddish-brown ape

O

—————— THESAURUS ——————

idea, theory

opponent *n* = **adversary**, rival, enemy, competitor, challenger ≠ **ally**

opportunity *n* = **chance**, opening, time, turn, moment

oppose *v* = **be against**, fight (against), block, take on, counter ≠ **support**

oppress *v* = **subjugate**, abuse, suppress, wrong, master ≠ **liberate**; = **depress**, burden,

discourage, torment, harass

opt *v* = **choose**, decide, prefer, select, elect ≠ **reject**

optimum *adj* = **ideal**, best, highest, finest, optimal, perfect ≠ **worst**

option *n* = **choice**, alternative, selection, preference, freedom of choice

opus *n* = **work**, piece, production, creation, composition

oral *adj* = **spoken/vocal**, verbal,

orator n 1 maker of speech
2 skilful speaker **oration** n formal
speech **oratory** n 1 speeches
2 eloquence
orb n globe
orbit ❶ n 1 track of planet,
satellite, comet etc. around
another heavenly body 2 field of
influence ▷ v 3 move in, or put
into, an orbit
orchard n (area for) fruit trees
orchestra n 1 band of musicians
2 place for such band in theatre etc.
orchestral adj **orchestrate** v
1 arrange (music) for orchestra
2 organize (something) to
particular effect
orchid n genus of various flowering
plants
ordain ❶ v 1 confer holy orders
upon 2 decree, enact
ordeal ❶ n severe, trying
experience
order n 1 regular, proper or
peaceful arrangement or condition
2 command
ordinal number number

showing position in series
ordinance n decree, rule
ordinary ❶ adj 1 usual, normal
2 commonplace **ordinarily** adv
ordnance n 1 artillery 2 military
stores **ordnance survey** official
geographical survey of Britain
ore n mineral which yields metal
oregano n aromatic herb
organ ❶ n 1 musical wind
instrument of pipes and stops,
played with keys 2 member of
animal or plant with particular
function 3 medium of information
organist n organ player
organism ❶ n plant, animal
organic adj 1 of, derived from,
living organisms 2 of bodily organs
3 (Chem) of compounds formed
from carbon 4 organized,
systematic
organize ❶ v 1 give definite
structure 2 arrange 3 unite in a
society **organization** n 1 act of
organizing 2 structure
3 association, group **organizer** n
orgasm n sexual climax

— THESAURUS —

unwritten
orbit n = **path**, course, cycle, circle,
revolution; = **sphere of influence**,
reach, range, influence, province
▷ v = **circle**, ring, go round, revolve
around, encircle
ordain v = **appoint**, name,
commission, select, invest; (Formal)
= **order**, will, rule, demand, require
ordeal n = **hardship**, trial,
difficulty, test, suffering
≠ **pleasure**
ordinary adj = **usual**, standard,

normal, common, regular;
= **commonplace**, plain, modest,
humble, mundane
organ n = **body part**, part of the
body, element, biological structure;
= **newspaper**, medium, voice,
vehicle, gazette
organism n = **creature**, being,
thing, body, animal
organize v = **arrange**, run, plan,
prepare, set up ≠ **disrupt**; = **put in
order**, arrange, group, list, file
≠ **muddle**

orgy n/pl **-gies 1** drunken or licentious revel **2** unrestrained bout

orient, orientate ❶ n **1** (with cap.) East ▷ v **2** determine (one's) position (also) **oriental** adj/n **orientation** n

orifice n opening, mouth

origami n art of paper folding

origin ❶ n **1** beginning **2** source **3** parentage **original** adj **1** earliest **2** new, not copied **3** thinking or acting for oneself ▷ n **4** thing from which another is copied **originality** n **originally** adv **originate** v **1** come or bring into existence, begin **2** create, pioneer

ornament ❶ n **1** any object used to adorn or decorate ▷ v **2** adorn **ornamental** adj

ornate adj highly decorated or elaborate

ornithology n science of birds

orphan n child whose parents are dead **orphanage** n institution for care of orphans

orthodox ❶ adj **1** holding accepted views **2** conventional

orthodoxy n

oscillate v **1** swing to and fro **2** waver

osmosis n movement of liquid through membrane from higher to lower concentration

osprey n fishing hawk

ossify v **-fying, -fied 1** turn into bone **2** grow rigid

ostensible adj **1** apparent **2** professed

ostentation n show, pretentious display **ostentatious** adj

osteopathy n art of treating disease by manipulation of bones **osteopath** n

ostracize n exclude, banish from society **ostracism** n

ostrich n large flightless bird

other ❶ adj **1** not this **2** not the same **3** alternative ▷ pron **4** other person or thing **otherwise** adv **1** differently ▷ conj **2** or else, if not

otter n furry aquatic fish-eating mammal

ouch interj exclamation of sudden pain

ought v expressing obligation or advisability or probability

O

——— THESAURUS ———

orient, orientate v **= adjust**, adapt, alter, accustom, align; **= get your bearings**, establish your location

origin n **= beginning**, start, birth, launch, foundation ≠ **end**; **= root**, source, basis, base, seed

ornament n **= decoration**, trimming, accessory, festoon, trinket; **= embellishment**,

decoration, embroidery, elaboration, adornment ▷ v **= decorate**, adorn, array, do up (Inf), embellish

orthodox adj **= established**, official, accepted, received, common ≠ **unorthodox**

other adj **= additional**, more, further, new, added; **= different**, alternative, contrasting, distinct, diverse

ounce ⊕ *n* unit of weight, sixteenth of pound (28.4 grams)

our *adj* belonging to us **ours** *pron* **ourselves** *pron* emphatic or reflexive form of WE

oust ⊕ *v* put out, expel

out ⊕ *adv/adj* 1 from within, away 2 wrong 3 not burning 4 not allowed 5 (*Sport*) dismissed **outer** *adj* away from the inside **outermost, outmost** *adj* on extreme outside **outing** *n* pleasure excursion **outward** *adj/adv*

outbreak ⊕ *n* sudden occurrence

outburst ⊕ *n* sudden expression of emotion

outcast *n* rejected person

outcome ⊕ *n* result

outcry ⊕ *n, pl* **-cries** expression of widespread protest

outdoors *adv* in the open air **outdoor** *adj*

outfit ⊕ *n* 1 equipment 2 clothes and accessories 3 (*Inf*) group or association regarded as a unit

outgoing ⊕ *adj* 1 leaving 2 sociable **outgoings** *pl n* expenses

outlandish *adj* queer, extravagantly strange

outlaw ⊕ *n* 1 one beyond protection of the law ▷ *v* 2 make (someone) an outlaw 3 ban

outlay *n* expenditure

outline ⊕ *n* 1 rough sketch 2 general plan 3 lines enclosing visible figure ▷ *v* 4 sketch 5 summarize

outlook ⊕ *n* 1 point of view 2 probable outcome

outlying *adj* remote

outmoded *adj* no longer fashionable or accepted

outpatient *n* patient who does

———————— THESAURUS ————————

O

ounce *n* = **shred**, bit, drop, trace, scrap

oust *v* = **expel**, turn out, dismiss, exclude, exile

out *adj* = **not in**, away, elsewhere, outside, gone; = **extinguished**, ended, finished, dead, exhausted

outbreak *n* = **eruption**, burst, explosion, epidemic, rash

outburst *n* = **explosion**, fit, surge, outbreak, flare-up

outcome *n* = **result**, end, consequence, conclusion, payoff (*Inf*)

outcry *n* = **protest**, complaint, objection, dissent, outburst

outfit *n* = **costume**, dress, clothes, clothing, suit; (*Inf*) = **group**,

company, team, party, unit

outgoing *adj* = **leaving**, former, previous, retiring, withdrawing ≠ **incoming**; = **sociable**, open, social, warm, friendly ≠ **reserved**

outlaw *v* = **ban**, bar, veto, forbid, exclude ≠ **legalise**; = **banish**, put a price on (someone's) head ▷ *n* (*Hist*) = **bandit**, criminal, thief, robber, fugitive

outline *v* = **summarize**, draft, plan, trace, sketch (in); = **silhouette**, etch ▷ *n* = **summary**, review, résumé, rundown, synopsis; = **shape**, lines, form, figure, profile

outlook *n* = **attitude**, opinion, position, approach, mood;

not stay in hospital overnight

outport n (Canad) isolated fishing village, esp. in Newfoundland

outpost n outlying settlement

output ⊙ n 1 quantity produced 2 (Comp) information produced

outrage ⊙ n 1 violation of others' rights 2 shocking act 3 anger arising from this ▷ v 4 commit outrage **outrageous** adj 1 shocking 2 offensive

outright ⊙ adj 1 complete 2 definite ▷ adv 3 completely

outset ⊙ n beginning

outside ⊙ n 1 exterior ▷ adv 2 not inside ▷ adj 3 on exterior 4 unlikely 5 greatest possible **outsider** n 1 person outside specific group 2 contestant thought unlikely to win

outsize, outsized adj larger than normal

outskirts ⊙ pl n outer areas, districts, esp. of city

outspan v (S Afr) relax

outspoken ⊙ adj frank, candid

outstanding ⊙ adj 1 excellent 2 remarkable 3 unsettled, unpaid

outweigh ⊙ v be more important than

outwit v -witting, -witted get the better of by cunning

oval ⊙ adj/n egg-shaped, elliptical (thing)

ovary n, pl -ries female egg-producing organ **ovarian** adj

ovation ⊙ n enthusiastic burst of applause

oven n heated chamber for baking

over ⊙ adv 1 above 2 beyond 3 in

= **prospect(s)**, future, expectations, forecast, prediction

output n = **production**, manufacture, manufacturing, yield, productivity

outrage v = **offend**, shock, upset, wound, insult ▷ n = **indignation**, shock, anger, rage, fury

outright adj = **absolute**, complete, total, perfect, sheer; = **definite**, clear, certain, flat, absolute ▷ adv = **openly**, frankly, plainly, overtly, candidly; = **absolutely**, completely, totally, fully, entirely

outset n = **beginning**, start, opening, onset, inauguration ≠ **finish**

outside n = **exterior**, face, front, covering, skin ▷ adj = **external**,

outer, exterior, outward, extraneous ≠ **inner**; = **remote**, small, unlikely, slight, slim

outskirts pl n = **edge**, boundary, suburbs, fringe, perimeter

outspoken adj = **forthright**, open, frank, straightforward, blunt ≠ **reserved**

outstanding adj = **excellent**, good, great, important, special ≠ **mediocre**; = **unpaid**, remaining, due, pending, payable

outweigh v = **override**, cancel (out), eclipse, offset, compensate for

oval adj = **elliptical**, egg-shaped, ovoid

ovation n = **applause**, hand, cheers, praise, tribute ≠ **derision**

over prep = **above**, on top of; = **on**

excess **4** finished **5** in repetition
6 across **7** downwards ▷ *prep*
8 above **9** upon **10** more than
11 along ▷ *n* **12** (*Cricket*) delivery of
six balls from one end

over- *comb. form* too, too much, in
excess, above

overall ⊕ *n* **1** (*also pl*) loose
garment worn as protection
against dirt etc. ▷ *adj* **2** total

overbearing *adj* domineering

overboard *adv* from a boat into
water **go overboard** go to
extremes

overcast *adj* cloudy

overcome ⊕ *v* **1** conquer
2 surmount **3** make incapable or
powerless

overdose *n/v* (take) excessive
dose of drug

overdraft *n* withdrawal of more
money than is in bank account

overdrive *n* very high gear in
motor vehicle

overgrown *adj* thickly covered
with plants

overhaul ⊕ *v* **1** examine and set
in order ▷ *n* **2** examination and
repair

overhead ⊕ *adj/adv* over one's
head, above

overland *adj/adv* by land

overlap *v* **1** share part of same
space or period of time ▷ *n* **2** area
overlapping

overlook ⊕ *v* **1** fail to notice
2 disregard

overseas *adj/adv* **1** foreign
2 from or to a place over the sea

overshadow ⊕ *v* reduce
significance of

oversight *n* **1** failure to notice
2 mistake

overt ⊕ *adj* open, unconcealed

THESAURUS

top of, on, across, upon ▷ *adv*
= above, overhead, in the sky, on
high, aloft; **= extra**, more, further,
beyond, additional ▷ *adj*
= finished, done (with), through,
ended, closed

overall *adj* **= total**, full, whole,
general, complete ▷ *adv* **= in
general**, generally, mostly, all
things considered, on average

overcome *v* **= defeat**, beat,
conquer, master, overwhelm;
= conquer, beat, master, subdue,
triumph over ▷ *adj*
= overwhelmed, moved, affected,
emotional, choked

overhaul *v* **= check**, service,
maintain, examine, restore;

= overtake, pass, leave behind,
catch up with, get past ▷ *n*
= check, service, examination,
going-over (*Inf*), inspection

overhead *adj* **= raised**,
suspended, elevated, aerial,
overhanging ▷ *adv* **= above**, in the
sky, on high, aloft, up above
≠ underneath

overlook *v* **= look over** *or* **out on**,
have a view of; **= miss**, forget,
neglect, omit, disregard **≠ notice**;
= ignore, excuse, forgive, pardon,
disregard

overshadow *v* **= spoil**, ruin, mar,
wreck, blight; **= outshine**, eclipse,
surpass, dwarf, tower above

overt *adj* **= open**, obvious, plain,

o

overtake ⓘ v 1 move past
2 catch up
overthrow ⓘ v 1 overturn
2 defeat ▷ n 3 ruin 4 fall
overtime n 1 time at work,
outside normal working hours
2 payment for this time 3 (US &
Canad) period of extra time in a
contest or game
overtone n additional meaning
overture n (Mus) 1 orchestral
introduction 2 opening of
negotiations
overwhelm ⓘ v 1 crush
2 submerge **overwhelming** adj
irresistible
overwrought adj overexcited
owe ⓘ v be bound to repay, be

indebted for **owing** adj owed,
due **owing to** caused by, as
result of
owl n night bird of prey
own ⓘ adj 1 emphasizes
possession ▷ v 2 possess
3 acknowledge 4 confess **owner**
n **ownership** n possession
ox n, pl **oxen** castrated bull
oxide n compound of oxygen and
one other element
oxygen n gas in atmosphere
essential to life
oyster n edible mollusc
Oz n (Sl) Australia
oz. ounce
ozone n form of oxygen with
pungent odour

━━━━ THESAURUS ━━━━

public, manifest ≠ hidden
overtake v = **pass**, leave behind,
overhaul, catch up with, get past;
= **outdo**, top, exceed, eclipse,
surpass
overthrow v = **defeat**, overcome,
conquer, bring down, oust
≠ **uphold** ▷ n = **downfall**, fall,
defeat, collapse, destruction
≠ **preservation**
overwhelm v = **overcome**,

devastate, stagger, bowl over (Inf),
knock (someone) for six (Inf);
= **destroy**, defeat, overcome,
crush, massacre
owe v = **be in debt (to)**, be in
arrears (to), be overdrawn (by), be
obligated or indebted (to)
own adj = **personal**, special,
private, individual, particular
▷ v = **possess**, have, keep, hold,
enjoy

O

p 1 page **2** pence **3** penny **4** (*Mus*) piano (softly)

pace ❶ *n* **1** step **2** rate of movement ▷ *v* **3** step **4** set speed for **5** measure **pacemaker** *n* **1** electronic device to regulate heartbeat **2** person who sets speed for race

pacifier *n* (*US & Canad*) a baby's dummy or teething ring

pacify *v* **-fying, -fied** calm **pacifism** *n* **pacifist** *n* **1** advocate of abolition of war **2** one who refuses to help in war

pack ❶ *n* **1** bundle **2** band of animals **3** large set of people or things ▷ *v* **4** put together in suitcase etc. **5** make into a bundle **6** cram **7** fill **package** *n* **1** parcel **2** set of items offered together ▷ *v* **3** put into packages **packet** *n* **1** small parcel **2** small container (and contents)

packsack *n* a US and Canadian word for HAVERSACK

pact ❶ *n* covenant, agreement

pad ❶ *n* **1** soft stuff used as a cushion, protection etc. **2** block of sheets of paper **3** foot or sole of various animals ▷ *v* **4** make soft, fill in, protect etc., with pad **5** walk with soft step

paddle¹ ❶ *n* **1** short oar with broad blade ▷ *v* **2** move by, as with, paddles

paddle² ❶ *v* walk with bare feet in shallow water

paddock *n* small grass enclosure

paddy field field where rice is grown

pademelon, paddymelon [pad]-ee-mel-an *n* small Australian wallaby

padlock *n/v* (fasten with) detachable lock with hinged hoop

—————————————————— THESAURUS ——————————————————

pace *n* = **speed**, rate, tempo, velocity; = **step**, walk, stride, tread, gait ▷ *v* = **stride**, walk, pound, patrol, march up and down

pack *v* = **package**, load, store, bundle, stow; = **cram**, crowd, press, fill, stuff ▷ *n* = **packet**, box, package, carton; = **bundle**, parcel, load, burden, rucksack

pact *n* = **agreement**, alliance, treaty, deal, understanding

pad *n* = **wad**, dressing, pack, padding, compress; = **cushion**, filling, stuffing, pillow, bolster; = **notepad**, block, notebook, jotter, writing pad; (*Sl*) = **home**, flat, apartment, place ▷ *v* = **pack**, fill, protect, stuff, cushion = **lengthen**, stretch, elaborate, fill out, spin out

paddle¹ *n* = **oar**, scull ▷ *v* = **row**, pull, scull

paddle² *v* = **wade**, splash (about),

paediatrics *pl n* branch of medicine dealing with diseases of children **paediatrician** *n*

paella *n* Spanish dish of rice, chicken, shellfish etc.

pagan ❶ *adj/n* heathen

page¹ ❶ *n* one side of leaf of book etc.

page² ❶ *n* **1** boy attendant ▷ *v* **2** summon by loudspeaker announcement or electronic device **pager** *n* small portable electronic signalling device

pageant *n* show of persons in costume in procession, dramatic scenes etc.

pagoda *n* pyramidal temple of Chinese or Indian type

pail *n* bucket

pain ❶ *n* **1** bodily or mental suffering ▷ *pl* **2** trouble ▷ *v* **3** inflict pain upon **painful** *adj* **painkiller** *n* drug that reduces pain **painstaking** *adj* careful

paint ❶ *n* **1** colouring matter spread on a surface ▷ *v* **2** colour, coat, or make picture of, with paint **painter** *n* **painting** *n*

pair ❶ *n* **1** set of two ▷ *v* **2** arrange in twos

pal ❶ *n* (*Inf*) friend

palace *n* **1** residence of king, bishop etc. **2** stately mansion **palatial** *adj*

palate *n* **1** roof of mouth **2** sense of taste **palatable** *adj* agreeable to eat

palaver *n* fuss

pale ❶ *adj* **1** wan, whitish ▷ *v* **2** whiten **3** lose superiority

palette *n* artist's flat board for mixing colours on

palindrome *n* word etc., that is the same when read backwards or forwards

paling *n* upright plank in fence

pall¹ *n* cloth spread over a coffin **pallbearer** *n* one carrying coffin at funeral

pall² *v* **1** become tiresome **2** cloy

pallet *n* portable platform for storing and moving goods

P

THESAURUS

slop

pagan *adj* = **heathen**, infidel, polytheistic, idolatrous ▷ *n* = **heathen**, infidel, polytheist, idolater

page¹ *n* = **folio**, side, leaf, sheet

page² *v* = **call**, summon, send for ▷ *n* = **attendant**, pageboy; = **servant**, attendant, squire, pageboy

pain *n* = **suffering**, discomfort, hurt, irritation, tenderness; = **ache**, stinging, aching, cramp, throb ▷ *v* = **distress**, hurt, torture, grieve,

torment

paint *n* = **colouring**, colour, stain, dye, tint ▷ *v* = **colour**, cover, coat, stain, whitewash; = **depict**, draw, portray, picture, represent

pair *v* = **team**, match (up), join, couple, twin

pal *n* (*Inf*) = **friend**, companion, mate (*Inf*), buddy (*Inf*), comrade

pale *adj* = **light**, soft, faded, subtle, muted; = **dim**, weak, faint, feeble, thin ▷ *v* = **become pale**, blanch, whiten, go white, lose colour

palliate v 1 relieve without curing 2 excuse **palliative** adj/n

pallid adj pale **pallor** n

palm n 1 inner surface of hand 2 tropical tree 3 its leaf as symbol of victory **palmistry** n fortune-telling from lines on palm of hand

palomino n, pl **-nos** golden horse with white mane and tail

palpable adj obvious

palpitate v throb

palsy n paralysis

paltry adj **-trier, -triest** worthless

pamper ❶ v overindulge, spoil

pamphlet ❶ n thin unbound book

pan¹ ❶ n 1 broad, shallow vessel 2 bowl of lavatory 3 depression in ground ▷ v 4 (Inf) criticize harshly

pan² ❶ v **panning, panned** move film camera slowly while filming

pan- comb. form all, as in pan-American

panacea n universal remedy

panache n dashing style

pancake n thin cake of batter fried in pan

pancreas n digestive gland behind stomach

panda n large black and white bearlike mammal of China

pandemonium n din and uproar

pander v 1 (esp. with to) give gratification to ▷ n 2 pimp

pane n sheet of glass

panegyric n speech of praise

panel n 1 compartment of surface, usu. raised or sunk, e.g. in door 2 team in quiz game etc. 3 list of jurors, doctors etc. ▷ v 4 adorn with panels

pang n sudden pain

panic ❶ n 1 sudden and infectious fear ▷ v 2 (cause to) feel panic **panicky** adj

pannier n basket carried by beast of burden, bicycle etc.

panoply n magnificent array

panorama ❶ n wide view

pansy n, pl **-sies** 1 flower, species of violet 2 (Offens) effeminate man

pant ❶ v/n gasp

pantechnicon n large van, esp. for carrying furniture

panther n variety of leopard

pantomime n theatrical show, usu. at Christmas time, often founded on a fairy tale

pantry n, pl **-tries** room for storing food or utensils

pants ❶ pl n 1 undergarment for

pamper v = **spoil**, indulge, pet, cosset, coddle

pamphlet n = **booklet**, leaflet, brochure, circular, tract

pan¹ n = **pot**, container, saucepan ▷ v (Inf) = **criticize**, knock, slam (Sl), censure, tear into (Inf); = **sift out**, look for, search for

pan² v = **move along** or **across**, follow, track, sweep

panic n = **fear**, alarm, terror, anxiety, hysteria ▷ v = **go to pieces**, become hysterical, lose your nerve

panorama n = **view**, prospect, vista

pant v = **puff**, blow, breathe, gasp, wheeze

pants pl n (Brit) = **underpants**, briefs, drawers, knickers, panties;

lower trunk **2** (US & Canad) trousers
pap n soft food
papacy n, pl **-cies** office of Pope
papal adj of the Pope
paper ❶ n **1** material made by
pressing pulp of rags, wood etc.,
into thin sheets **2** sheet of paper
3 newspaper **4** essay ▷ pl
5 documents etc. ▷ v **6** cover with
paper **paperback** n book with
flexible covers
papier-mâché n paper pulp
mixed with paste, shaped and dried
hard
paprika n red pepper
papyrus n, pl **-ri, -ruses 1** species
of reed **2** paper made from this
par n **1** equality of value or standing
2 face value **3** (Golf) estimated
standard score **parity** n
1 equality **2** analogy
parable n allegory, story with
moral lesson
parachute n **1** apparatus
extending like umbrella used to
slow the descent of falling body ▷ v
2 drop by parachute

parade ❶ n **1** display **2** muster of
troops ▷ v **3** march **4** display
paradise ❶ n **1** Heaven **2** state of
bliss **3** Garden of Eden
paradox ❶ n statement that
seems self-contradictory
paradoxical adj
paraffin n waxlike or liquid
hydrocarbon mixture used as fuel,
solvent, etc.
paragon n pattern or model of
excellence
paragraph ❶ n **1** section of
chapter or book ▷ v **2** arrange in
paragraphs
parakeet n small parrot
parallel ❶ adj/n **1** (line or lines)
continuously at equal distances
2 (thing) precisely corresponding
▷ v **3** represent as similar
parallelogram n four-sided figure
with opposite sides parallel
paralysis ❶ n incapacity to move
or feel **paralyse** v **1** affect with
paralysis **2** make immobile
paralytic adj/n
paramedic n person working in

P

(US) = **trousers**, slacks
paper n = **newspaper**, daily,
journal, gazette; = **essay**, article,
treatise, dissertation ▷ v
= **wallpaper**, hang
parade n = **procession**, march,
pageant, cavalcade ▷ v = **march**,
process, promenade; = **flaunt**,
display, exhibit, show off (Inf)
paradise n = **heaven**, Promised
Land, Happy Valley (Islam), Elysian
fields; = **bliss**, delight, heaven,
felicity, utopia

paradox n = **contradiction**,
puzzle, anomaly, enigma,
oddity
paragraph n = **section**, part,
item, passage, clause
parallel n = **equivalent**,
counterpart, match, equal, twin
≠ **opposite** ▷ adj = **matching**,
corresponding, like, similar,
resembling ≠ **different**;
= **equidistant**, alongside, side by
side ≠ **divergent**
paralysis n = **immobility**, palsy

support of medical profession

parameter ❶ n limiting factor

paramilitary adj organized on military lines

paramount ❶ adj supreme

paranoia n mental disease with delusions of persecution etc. **paranoid** adj/n

parapet n low wall along edge of bridge etc.

paraphernalia pl n **1** (used as sing) belongings **2** equipment

paraphrase v express in other words

paraplegia n paralysis of lower body **paraplegic** n/adj

parasite ❶ n animal or plant living in or on another **parasitic** adj

parasol n sunshade

paratroops pl n troops trained to descend by parachute

parboil v boil until partly cooked

parcel ❶ n **1** packet ▷ v **2** wrap up **3** divide into parts

parch v make, become hot and dry

parchment n sheep, goat, calf skin prepared for writing

pardon ❶ v **1** forgive, excuse ▷ n

2 forgiveness **3** release from punishment

pare v **1** peel, trim **2** decrease

parent ❶ n father or mother **parentage** n descent, extraction **parental** adj **parenthood** n

parenthesis n, pl **-ses** word(s) inserted in passage **parentheses** pl n round brackets, (), used to mark this

pariah n social outcast

parish ❶ n district under one clergyman **parishioner** n inhabitant of parish

parity see PAR

park ❶ n **1** large area of land in natural state for recreational use ▷ v **2** leave for short time **3** manoeuvre (car) into suitable space

parka n warm waterproof coat

parkade n (Canad) a building used as a car park

parkette n (Canad) a small public park

parking lot n (US & Canad) area or building where vehicles may be left for a time

━━━━━━━━━ THESAURUS ━━━━━━━━━

parameter n (Inf) usually plural = **limit**, restriction, framework, limitation, specification

paramount adj = **principal**, prime, first, chief, main ≠ **secondary**

parasite n = **sponger** (Inf), leech, hanger-on, scrounger (Inf), bloodsucker (Inf)

parcel n = **package**, case, box, pack, bundle ▷ v often with **up** = **wrap**, pack, package, tie up, do up

pardon v = **forgive**, excuse ≠ **condemn** ▷ n = **forgiveness**, absolution ≠ **condemnation**; = **acquittal**, amnesty, exoneration ≠ **punishment**

parent n = **father** or **mother**, sire, progenitor, procreator, old (Aust & NZ Inf)

parish n = **district**, community

park n = **recreation ground**, garden, playground, pleasure

parlance n particular way of speaking

parley v/n (hold) discussion about terms

parliament ❶ n law-making assembly of country
parliamentary adj

parlor, US **parlour** ❶ n sitting room

parochial adj 1 narrow, provincial 2 of a parish

parody ❶ n/v, pl **-dies** (write) satirical, amusing imitation of a work

parole n 1 release of prisoner on condition of good behaviour ▷ v 2 release on parole

paroxysm n sudden attack of pain, rage, laughter

parquet n flooring of wooden blocks

parrot ❶ n 1 brightly coloured bird which can imitate speaking ▷ v 2 repeat words without thinking

parry ❶ v **-rying, -ried** ward off, turn aside

parsimony n stinginess
parsimonious adj

parsley n herb used for seasoning, garnish etc.

parsnip n root vegetable

parson ❶ n clergyman

part ❶ n 1 portion 2 role 3 duty 4 region 5 component ▷ v 6 divide 7 separate **parting** n 1 division of hair on head 2 separation 3 leave-taking **partly** adv in part

partake v **-taking, -took, -taken** 1 take or have share in 2 take food or drink

partial ❶ adj 1 not complete 2 prejudiced 3 fond of **partially** adv partly

THESAURUS

garden, playpark
parliament n = **assembly**, council, congress, senate, convention

parlour, US **parlor** n (Old-fashioned) = **sitting room**, lounge, living room, drawing room, front room

parody n = **takeoff** (Inf), satire, caricature, send-up (Brit Inf), spoof (Inf) ▷ v = **take off** (Inf), caricature, send up (Brit Inf), burlesque, satirize

parrot v = **repeat**, echo, imitate, copy, mimic

parry v = **evade**, avoid, dodge, sidestep; = **ward off**, block, deflect, repel, rebuff

parson n = **clergyman**, minister, priest, vicar, preacher

part n = **piece**, share, proportion, percentage, bit ≠ **entirety**; often plural = **region**, area, district, neighbourhood, quarter; = **component**, bit, unit, constituent; = **branch**, division, office, section, wing ▷ v = **divide**, separate, break, tear, split ≠ **join**; = **part company**, separate, split up ≠ **meet**

partial adj = **incomplete**, unfinished, imperfect, uncompleted ≠ **complete**; = **biased**, prejudiced, discriminatory, partisan, unfair ≠ **unbiased**

P

participate ❶ v 1 share in 2 take part **participant** n **participation** n

participle n (Grammar) verbal adjective

particle ❶ n minute portion

particular ❶ adj 1 relating to one 2 distinct 3 fussy ▷ n 4 detail, item ▷ pl 5 items of information **particularly** adv

partisan ❶ n 1 adherent of a party 2 guerilla ▷ adj 3 adhering to faction 4 prejudiced

partition ❶ n 1 division 2 interior dividing wall ▷ v 3 divide into sections

partner ❶ n 1 ally or companion 2 spouse **partnership** n

partridge n game bird

party ❶ n, pl **-ties** 1 social assembly 2 group of persons organized together, esp. with common political aim 3 person

pashmina pash-[mee]-na n shawl or scarf made from fine soft goat's wool

pass ❶ v 1 go by, beyond, through etc. 2 exceed 3 transfer 4 spend 5 elapse 6 undergo examination successfully 7 bring a law into force ▷ n 8 way, esp. through mountains 9 permit 10 successful result **passable** adj (just) acceptable **passing** adj 1 transitory 2 casual **pass away** die **pass out** faint

— THESAURUS —

participate v = **take part**, be involved, perform, join, partake ≠ **refrain from**

particle n = **bit**, piece, scrap, grain, shred

particular adj = **specific**, special, exact, precise, distinct ≠ **general**; = **special**, exceptional, notable, uncommon, marked; = **fussy**, demanding, fastidious, choosy (Inf), picky (Inf) ≠ **indiscriminate** ▷ n usually plural = **detail**, fact, feature, item, circumstance

partisan adj = **prejudiced**, one-sided, biased, partial, sectarian ≠ **unbiased** ▷ n = **supporter**, devotee, adherent, upholder ≠ **opponent**; = **underground fighter**, guerrilla, freedom fighter, resistance fighter

partition n = **screen**, wall, barrier; = **division**, separation, segregation

▷ v = **separate**, screen, divide

partner n = **spouse**, consort, significant other (US Inf), mate, husband or wife; = **companion**, ally, colleague, associate, mate

party n = **faction**, set, side, league, camp; = **get-together** (Inf), celebration, do (Inf), gathering, function; = **group**, team, band, company, unit

pass v = **go by** or **past**, overtake, drive past, lap, leave behind ≠ **stop**; = **go**, move, travel, progress, flow; = **run**, move, stroke; = **give**, hand, send, transfer, deliver; = **be left**, come, be bequeathed, be inherited by; = **kick**, hit, loft, head, lob; = **elapse**, progress, go by, lapse, wear on ▷ n = **licence**, ticket, permit, passport, warrant; = **gap**, route, canyon, gorge, ravine

passage ❶ n 1 opening
2 corridor 3 part of book etc.
4 voyage, fare
passé adj out-of-date
passenger ❶ n traveller, esp. by
public conveyance
passion ❶ n 1 ardent desire 2 any
strong emotion 3 great
enthusiasm **passionate** adj
passive ❶ adj 1 submissive
2 inactive
passport n official document
granting permission to travel
abroad etc.
password n secret word to ensure
admission etc.
past ❶ adj 1 ended 2 gone by
3 elapsed ▷ n 4 bygone times
▷ adv 5 by 6 along ▷ prep
7 beyond 8 after
pasta n any of several preparations

of dough, e.g. spaghetti
paste ❶ n 1 soft mixture
2 adhesive ▷ v 3 fasten with paste
pasting n 1 (Sl) defeat 2 strong
criticism **pasty** adj 1 like paste
2 white 3 sickly
pastel ❶ n 1 coloured crayon
2 drawing with crayons 3 pale,
delicate colour ▷ adj 4 (of colour)
pale
pasteurize v sterilize by heat
pastiche n work of art that mixes
or copies styles
pastille n lozenge
pastime ❶ n recreation
pastor ❶ n clergyman **pastoral**
adj 1 of rural life 2 of pastor
pastry n, pl -ries article of food
made chiefly of flour, fat and water
pasture ❶ n 1 ground on which
cattle graze ▷ v 2 (cause to) graze

— THESAURUS —

passage n = **corridor**, hall, lobby,
vestibule; = **alley**, way, close (Brit),
course, road; = **extract**, reading,
piece, section, text; = **journey**,
crossing, trip, trek, voyage;
= **safe-conduct**, right to travel,
freedom to travel, permission to
travel
passenger n = **traveller**, rider,
fare, commuter, fare payer
passion n = **love**, desire, lust,
infatuation, ardour; = **emotion**,
feeling, fire, heat, excitement
≠ **indifference**; = **mania**,
enthusiasm, obsession, bug (Inf),
craving
passive adj = **submissive**,
compliant, receptive, docile,
quiescent ≠ **spirited**

past n = **former times**, long ago,
days gone by, the olden days
≠ **future**; = **background**, life,
history, past life, life story ▷ adj
= **former**, early, previous, ancient,
bygone ≠ **future**; = **previous**,
former, one-time, ex- ▷ prep
= **after**, beyond, later than
paste n = **adhesive**, glue, cement,
gum ▷ v = **stick**, glue, cement,
gum
pastel adj = **pale**, light, soft,
delicate, muted ≠ **bright**
pastime n = **activity**, game,
entertainment, hobby, recreation
pastor n = **clergyman**, minister,
priest, vicar, parson
pasture n = **grassland**, grass,
meadow, grazing

P

pasty n, pl **pasties** small pie of meat and crust, baked without a dish

pat¹ ❶ v **patting, patted 1** tap ▷ n **2** tap **3** small mass, as of butter

pat² adv **1** exactly **2** fluently

patch ❶ n **1** piece of cloth sewed on garment **2** spot **3** plot of ground ▷ v **4** mend **5** repair clumsily **patchy** adj of uneven quality **patchwork** n needlework of different pieces sewn together

pate n **1** head **2** top of head

pâté n spread of finely minced liver etc.

patent ❶ n **1** exclusive right to invention ▷ adj **2** open **3** evident ▷ v **4** secure a patent **patently** adv obviously

paternal adj **1** fatherly **2** of a father **paternity** n fatherhood

path ❶ n **1** way, track **2** course of action

pathetic ❶ adj moving to pity

pathology n science of diseases **pathological** adj **pathologist** n

pathos n power of exciting tender emotions

patient ❶ adj **1** bearing troubles calmly ▷ n **2** person under medical treatment **patience** n

patio n, pl **-tios** paved area adjoining house

patriarch n father and ruler of family

patrician n/adj (one) of noble birth

patriot ❶ n person that loves his or her country **patriotic** adj **patriotism** n

patrol ❶ n **1** regular circuit by guard **2** person, small group patrolling ▷ v **3** go round on guard

patron ❶ n **1** one who aids artists, charities etc. **2** regular customer **3** guardian saint **patronage** n support given by patron **patronize** v **1** assume air of superiority towards **2** be regular customer

———— THESAURUS ————

pat¹ v = **stroke**, touch, tap, pet, caress ▷ n = **tap**, stroke, clap

patch n = **spot**, bit, scrap, shred, small piece; = **plot**, area, ground, land, tract; = **reinforcement**, piece of fabric, piece of cloth, piece of material, piece sewn on ▷ v often with **up** = **mend**, cover, repair, reinforce, stitch (up)

patent n = **copyright**, licence, franchise, registered trademark ▷ adj = **obvious**, apparent, evident, clear, glaring

path n = **way**, road, walk, track, trail; = **route**, way, course, direction

pathetic adj = **sad**, moving, touching, affecting, distressing ≠ **funny**

patient n = **sick person**, case, sufferer, invalid ▷ adj = **forbearing**, understanding, forgiving, mild, tolerant ≠ **impatient**

patriot n = **nationalist**, loyalist, chauvinist

patrol v = **police**, guard, keep watch (on), inspect, safeguard ▷ n = **guard**, watch, watchman, sentinel, patrolman

patron n = **supporter**, friend,

patter n 1 quick succession of taps 2 (Inf) glib, rapid speech ▷ v 3 make quick tapping noise

pattern ❶ n 1 arrangement of repeated parts 2 design 3 plan for cutting cloth etc. 4 model ▷ v 5 model

paunch n belly

pauper n very poor person

pause ❶ v/n stop, rest

pave ❶ v form surface with stone **pavement** n paved footpath

pavilion n 1 clubhouse on playing field etc. 2 building for exhibition etc. 3 large tent

paw ❶ n 1 foot of animal ▷ v 2 scrape with forefoot 3 maul

pawn¹ v deposit (article) as security for money borrowed **pawnbroker** n lender of money on goods deposited

pawn² n 1 piece in chess 2 person used as mere tool

pay ❶ v **paying, paid** 1 give money etc., for goods or services 2 give 3 be profitable to 4 spend ▷ n 5 wages **payable** adj justly due **payee** n person to whom money is paid or due **payment** n **payday** n day when wages are paid

PC 1 personal computer 2 Police Constable 3 Privy Councillor

PE physical education

pea n 1 edible seed, growing in pods, of climbing plant 2 the plant

peace ❶ n 1 freedom from war 2 harmony 3 calm **peaceable** adj disposed to peace **peaceful** adj

peach n fruit of delicate flavour

peacock n male bird with fanlike tail

peak ❶ n 1 pointed end of anything, esp. hilltop 2 highest point

peal n 1 (succession of) loud sound(s) ▷ v 2 sound loudly

peanut n 1 pea-shaped nut ▷ pl 2 (Inf) trifling amount of money

— THESAURUS —

P

champion, sponsor, backer; = **customer**, client, buyer, frequenter, shopper

pattern n = **order**, plan, system, method, sequence; = **design**, arrangement, motif, figure, device; = **plan**, design, original, guide, diagram

pause v = **stop briefly**, delay, break, wait, rest ≠ **continue** ▷ n = **stop**, break, interval, rest, gap ≠ **continuance**

pave v = **cover**, floor, surface, concrete, tile

paw v (Inf) = **manhandle**, grab, maul, molest, handle roughly

pay v = **reward**, compensate, reimburse, recompense, requite; = **spend**, give, fork out (Inf), remit, shell out (Inf); = **bring in**, earn, return, net, yield ▷ n = **wages**, income, payment, earnings, fee

peace n = **truce**, ceasefire, treaty, armistice ≠ **war**; = **stillness**, rest, quiet, silence, calm; = **serenity**, calm, composure, contentment, repose; = **harmony**, accord, agreement, concord

peak n = **high point**, crown, climax, culmination, zenith; = **point**, top, tip, summit, brow ▷ v = **culminate**, climax, come to a

pear n 1 tree yielding sweet, juicy fruit 2 the fruit **pear-shaped** adj shaped like a pear, heavier at the bottom than the top

pearl n hard, lustrous structure found esp. in oyster and used as jewel

peasant ❶ n member of low social class, esp. in rural district

peat n decomposed vegetable substance

pebble n small roundish stone

peccadillo n, pl **-loes, -los** 1 slight offence 2 petty crime

peck ❶ v 1 strike with or as with beak 2 nibble at 3 (Inf) kiss quickly ▷ n 4 pecking movement **peckish** adj (Inf) hungry

pectoral adj of the breast

peculiar ❶ adj 1 strange 2 particular 3 belonging to **peculiarity** n, pl **-ties** 1 oddity 2 characteristic 3 distinguishing feature

pedal n 1 foot lever ▷ v 2 propel bicycle by using its pedals 3 use pedal

pedant n one who insists on petty details of book-learning,

grammatical rules etc. **pedantic** adj

peddle v go round selling goods

pedestal n base of column

pedestrian ❶ n 1 one who walks on foot ▷ adj 2 going on foot 3 commonplace 4 dull

pedestrian crossing place marked where pedestrians may cross road

pedigree ❶ n 1 register of ancestors 2 genealogy

pedlar n 1 one who sells 2 hawker

peek v/n peep, glance

peel ❶ v 1 strip off skin, rind or covering 2 flake off, as skin, rind ▷ n 3 rind, skin

peep ❶ v 1 look slyly or quickly ▷ n 2 such a look

peer¹ ❶ v look closely

peer² ❶ n 1 nobleman 2 one of the same rank **peerage** n **peerless** adj without match or equal **peer group** group of people of similar age, status etc. **peer pressure** influence from one's peer group

peeved adj (Inf) sulky, irritated

peevish adj 1 fretful 2 irritable

──────── THESAURUS ────────

head

peasant n = **rustic**, countryman

peck v = **pick**, hit, strike, tap, poke

peculiar adj = **odd**, strange, unusual, bizarre, funny ≠ **ordinary**; = **special**, particular, unique, characteristic ≠ **common**

pedestrian n = **walker**, foot-traveller ≠ **driver** ▷ adj = **dull**, ordinary, boring, commonplace, mundane ≠ **exciting**

pedigree n = **lineage**, family, line, race, stock

peel n = **rind**, skin, peeling ▷ v = **skin**, scale, strip, pare, shuck

peep v = **peek**, look, eyeball (Sl), sneak a look, steal a look ▷ n = **look**, glimpse, peek, look-see (Sl)

peer¹ v = **squint**, look, spy, gaze, scan

peer² n = **noble**, lord, aristocrat, nobleman; = **equal**, like, fellow,

peewit *n* lapwing

peg ❶ *n* **1** pin for joining, fastening, marking etc. **2** (mark of) level, standard etc. ▷ *v* **3** fasten with pegs **4** stabilize (prices) **5** (with *away*) persevere

pejorative *adj* (of words etc.) with disparaging connotation

pelican *n* waterfowl with large pouch beneath its bill **pelican crossing** road crossing with pedestrian-operated traffic lights

pellet *n* little ball

pelmet *n* ornamental drapery or board, concealing curtain rail

pelt¹ *v* **1** throw missiles **2** rain persistently **3** rush

pelt² *n* raw hide or skin

pelvis *n* bony cavity at base of human trunk **pelvic** *adj*

pen¹ ❶ *n* **1** instrument for writing ▷ *v* **2** compose **3** write **pen friend** friend with whom one corresponds without meeting **penknife** *n* small knife with folding blade

pen² ❶ *n/v* (put in) enclosure

penal *adj* of punishment **penalize** *v* impose penalty on **penalty** *n, pl* **-ties 1** punishment **2** forfeit **3** (*Sport*) handicap

penance *n* suffering submitted to as expression of penitence

pence *n* pl of PENNY

penchant *n* inclination, decided taste

pencil *n* **1** instrument, esp. of graphite, for writing etc. ▷ *v* **2** draw **3** mark with pencil

pendant *n* hanging ornament

pendent *adj* hanging

pending ❶ *prep* **1** during, until ▷ *adj* **2** awaiting settlement **3** imminent

pendulous *adj* hanging, swinging **pendulum** *n* suspended weight swinging to and fro

penetrate ❶ *v* **1** enter into **2** pierce **3** arrive at meaning of **penetrating** *adj* **1** sharp **2** easily heard **3** quick to understand **penetration** *n*

penguin *n* flightless bird

penicillin *n* antibiotic drug

peninsula *n* portion of land nearly surrounded by water **peninsular** *adj*

penis *n* male organ of copulation and urination

penitent *adj* **1** affected by sense of guilt ▷ *n* **2** one that repents **penitence** *n* sorrow for sin **penitentiary** *adj, pl* **-ries** ▷ *n* (*US*) prison

pennant *n* long narrow flag

penny *n, pl* **pence, pennies** Brit.

contemporary, compeer

peg *v* = **fasten**, join, fix, secure, attach

pen¹ *v* = **write (down)**, draft, compose, pencil, draw up

pen² *n* = **enclosure**, pound, fold, cage, coop ▷ *v* = **enclose**, confine,

cage, fence in, coop up

pending *adj* = **undecided**, unsettled, in the balance, undetermined

penetrate *v* = **pierce**, enter, go through, bore, stab (*Inf*); = **grasp**, work out, figure out (*Inf*),

bronze coin, 100th part of pound
penniless adj having no money
pension ❶ n 1 regular payment to old people, soldiers etc. ▷ v 2 grant pension to **pensioner** n
pensive adj thoughtful
pentagon n figure with five angles
penthouse n apartment, flat on top of building
penultimate adj next before the last
penury n extreme poverty
peony n, pl **-nies** plant with showy red, pink, or white flowers
people ❶ pl n 1 persons generally, nation 2 race 3 family ▷ v 4 populate
pep n (Inf) 1 vigour 2 energy ▷ v 3 give energy, enthusiasm **pep talk** (Inf) talk designed to increase confidence, enthusiasm etc.
pepper ❶ n 1 pungent aromatic spice 2 slightly pungent vegetable ▷ v 3 season with pepper 4 sprinkle 5 pelt with missiles **peppermint** n 1 plant noted for aromatic pungent liquor distilled from it 2 sweet flavoured with this **pepper spray** aerosol spray causing temporary blindness and

breathing difficulty, used esp. for self-defence
per prep 1 for each 2 by 3 in manner of
perambulate v 1 walk through or over 2 walk about **perambulator** n pram
per annum (Lat) by the year
per capita (Lat) for each person
perceive ❶ v 1 obtain knowledge of through senses 2 understand **perceptible** adj **perception** n **perceptive** adj
percentage n proportion or rate per hundred **per cent** in each hundred
perch[1] ❶ n 1 resting place, as for bird ▷ v 2 place, as on perch 3 alight on branch etc. 4 balance on
perch[2] n freshwater fish
perchance adv (Obs) perhaps
percolate v 1 pass through fine mesh as liquor 2 filter **percolator** n coffeepot with filter
percussion n striking of one thing against another
peremptory adj imperious
perennial ❶ adj 1 lasting through the years 2 perpetual ▷ n 3 plant

comprehend, fathom
pension n = **allowance**, benefit, welfare, annuity, superannuation
people pl n = **persons**, individuals, folk (Inf), men and women, humanity; = **nation**, public, community, subjects, population; = **race**, tribe ▷ v = **inhabit**, occupy, settle, populate, colonize
pepper n = **seasoning**, flavour,

spice ▷ v = **pelt**, hit, shower, blitz, rake; = **sprinkle**, spot, scatter, dot, fleck
perceive v = **see**, notice, note, identify, discover; = **understand**, gather, see, learn, realize
perch[1] v = **sit**, rest, balance, settle ▷ n = **resting place**, post, branch, pole
perennial adj = **continual**,

lasting more than two years
perfect ❶ *adj* 1 complete
2 unspoilt 3 correct, precise
4 excellent ▷ *v* 5 improve 6 make
skilful **perfection** *n*
perfectionist *n* one who demands
highest standards **perfectly** *adv*
perforate *v* make holes in,
penetrate **perforation** *n*
perform ❶ *v* 1 fulfil 2 function
3 act part 4 play, as on musical
instrument **performance** *n*
perfume ❶ *n* 1 agreeable scent
▷ *v* 2 imbue with an agreeable
odour
perfunctory *adj* done
indifferently
perhaps ❶ *adv* possibly
peril ❶ *n* 1 danger 2 exposure to
injury **perilous** *adj*
perimeter ❶ *n* 1 outer boundary
of area 2 length of this
period ❶ *n* 1 particular portion of

time 2 series of years 3 single
occurrence of menstruation 4 full
stop ▷ *adj* 5 (of furniture, dress
etc.) belonging to a particular time
in history **periodic** *adj* recurring
at regular intervals **periodical** *adj*
1 periodic ▷ *n* 2 publication issued
at regular intervals **periodic table**
(*Chem*) chart showing relationship
of elements to each other
peripatetic *adj* travelling about
periphery *n, pl* **-eries**
1 circumference 2 outside
peripheral *adj* unimportant
periscope *n* instrument used for
giving view of objects on different
level
perish ❶ *v* 1 die 2 rot **perishable**
adj that will not last long
perishing *adj* (*Inf*) very cold
perk ❶ *n* incidental benefit from
employment
perm *n* 1 long-lasting curly

—————— THESAURUS ——————

lasting, constant, enduring,
persistent
perfect *adj* = **faultless**, correct,
pure, impeccable, exemplary
≠ deficient; = **excellent**, ideal,
supreme, superb, splendid;
= **immaculate**, impeccable,
flawless, spotless, unblemished
≠ flawed; = **complete**, absolute,
sheer, utter, consummate **≠ partial**
▷ *v* = **improve**, develop, polish,
refine **≠ mar**
perform *v* = **do**, achieve, carry out,
complete, fulfil; = **fulfil**, carry out,
execute, discharge
perfume *n* = **fragrance**, scent
perhaps *adv* = **maybe**, possibly, it

may be, it is possible (that),
conceivably
peril *n* = **danger**, risk, threat,
hazard, menace
perimeter *n* = **boundary**,
edge, border, bounds, limit
≠ centre
period *n* = **time**, term, season,
space, run
perish *v* = **die**, be killed, expire,
pass away, lose your life; = **be
destroyed**, fall, decline,
collapse, disappear; = **rot**,
waste away, decay, disintegrate,
decompose
perk *n* (*Brit Inf*) = **bonus**, benefit,
extra, plus, fringe benefit

hairstyle ▷ v **2** give a perm

permanent ❶ adj **1** continuing in same state **2** lasting **permanence** n

permeate v **1** pervade **2** pass through pores of **permeable** adj

permit ❶ v **-mitting, -mitted 1** allow **2** give leave to ▷ n **3** warrant or licence to do something **permissible** adj **permission** n **permissive** adj (too) tolerant, esp. sexually

permutation n (Maths) arrangement of a number of quantities in every possible order

pernicious adj **1** wicked **2** harmful

pernickety adj (Inf) fussy

peroxide n short for HYDROGEN PEROXIDE

perpendicular adj/n **1** (line) at right angles to another **2** (something) exactly upright

perpetrate v perform or be responsible for (something bad)

perpetual ❶ adj **1** continuous **2** lasting forever **perpetuate** v **1** make perpetual **2** not to allow to be forgotten **perpetuity** n

perplex v **1** puzzle **2** bewilder **perplexity** n/pl **-ties**

persecute ❶ v oppress because of race, religion etc. **persecution** n

persevere v persist, maintain effort **perseverance** n

persist ❶ v continue in spite of obstacles or objections **persistence** n **persistent** adj

person ❶ n **1** individual (human) being **2** body of human being **3** (Grammar) classification of pronouns and verb forms according to the person speaking, spoken to, or of **personable** adj pleasant in looks and personality **personal** adj **1** individual, private **2** of grammatical person **personality** n **1** distinctive character **2** celebrity **personally** adv **1** independently **2** in one's own opinion **personal computer** small computer for word processing or computer games **personal stereo** portable cassette player with headphones

persona n, pl **-nae** someone's personality as presented to others

————— THESAURUS —————

permanent adj = **lasting**, constant, enduring, persistent, eternal ≠ **temporary**

permit v = **allow**, grant, sanction, let, entitle ≠ **forbid** ▷ n = **licence**, pass, document, certificate, passport ≠ **prohibition**

perpetual adj = **everlasting**, permanent, endless, eternal, lasting ≠ **temporary**; = **continual**, repeated, constant, endless,

continuous ≠ **brief**

persecute v = **victimize**, torture, torment, oppress, pick on ≠ **mollycoddle**; = **harass**, bother, annoy, tease, hassle (Inf) ≠ **leave alone**

persist v = **continue**, last, remain, carry on, keep up; = **persevere**, continue, go on, carry on, keep on

person n = **individual**, being, body, human, soul

personify v -fying, -fied
1 represent as person **2** typify
personification n
personnel ❶ n staff employed in
organization
perspective ❶ n **1** mental view
2 method of drawing on flat surface
to give effect of relative distances
and sizes
Perspex® n transparent acrylic
substitute for glass
perspicacious adj having quick
mental insight
perspire v sweat **perspiration** n
persuade ❶ v **1** make (one) do
something by argument, charm
etc. **2** convince **persuasion** n
1 art, act of persuading **2** belief
persuasive adj
pert adj forward, saucy
pertain v belong, relate, have
reference (to)
pertinacious adj persistent
pertinent adj to the point
pertinence n relevance
perturb v **1** disturb **2** alarm
peruse v read in careful or leisurely

manner **perusal** n
pervade v spread through
pervasive adj
pervert ❶ v **1** turn to wrong use
2 lead astray ▷ n **3** one who
practises sexual perversion
perverse adj **1** obstinately or
unreasonably wrong **2** wayward
perversion n **1** sexual act
considered abnormal **2** corruption
perversity n
peseta n Spanish monetary unit
pessimism n tendency to see
worst side of things **pessimist** n
pessimistic adj
pest ❶ n troublesome or harmful
thing, person or insect **pesticide** n
chemical for killing pests, esp. insects
pester v **1** vex **2** harass
pestilence n epidemic disease
pestle n instrument with which
things are pounded
pet ❶ n **1** animal or person kept or
regarded with affection ▷ adj
2 favourite ▷ v **3** make pet of
4 (Inf) fondle
petal n white or coloured leaflike

P

THESAURUS

---

personnel n = **employees**,
people, staff, workers, workforce
perspective n = **outlook**,
attitude, context, angle, frame of
reference
persuade v = **talk (someone)
into**, urge, influence, win
(someone) over, induce
≠ **dissuade**; = **cause**, lead, move,
influence, motivate
pervert v = **distort**, abuse, twist,
misuse, warp; = **corrupt**, degrade,
deprave, debase, debauch ▷ n

= **deviant**, degenerate, sicko (Inf),
weirdo or weirdie (Inf)
pest n = **infection**, bug, insect,
plague, epidemic; = **nuisance**, trial,
pain (Inf), drag (Inf), bother
pet adj = **favourite**, favoured,
dearest, cherished, fave (Inf) ▷ n
= **favourite**, treasure, darling,
jewel, idol ▷ v = **fondle**, pat,
stroke, caress; = **pamper**, spoil,
indulge, cosset, baby; (Inf)
= **cuddle**, kiss, snog (Brit Sl),
smooch (Inf), neck (Inf)

part of flower

petite adj small, dainty

petition ❶ n 1 request, esp. to sovereign or parliament ▷ v 2 present petition to

petrel n sea bird

petrify v -fying, -fied 1 turn to stone 2 make motionless with fear

petroleum n mineral oil **petrol** n refined petroleum as used in motorcars etc.

petticoat n woman's underskirt

pettifogging adj overconcerned with unimportant detail

petty ❶ adj -tier, -tiest 1 unimportant 2 small-minded **petty cash** cash kept to pay minor expenses **petty officer** noncommissioned officer in navy

petulant adj 1 irritable 2 peevish

petunia n garden plant

pew n fixed seat in church

pewter n greyish alloy of tin and lead

phallus n, pl -luses, -li 1 penis 2 symbol of it used in primitive rites **phallic** adj

phantom ❶ n 1 apparition 2 ghost

Pharaoh n title of ancient Egyptian kings

pharmaceutical adj of drugs or pharmacy **pharmacist** n person qualified to dispense drugs **pharmacology** n study of drugs **pharmacy** n 1 preparation and dispensing of drugs 2 dispensary

phase ❶ n distinct stage in development **phase in, out** introduce or discontinue gradually

PhD Doctor of Philosophy

pheasant n game bird

phenomenon ❶ n, pl -ena 1 anything observed 2 remarkable person or thing **phenomenal** adj

phial n small bottle

philanthropy n practice of doing good to one's fellow men **philanthropic** adj **philanthropist** n

philately n stamp collecting **philatelist** n

philistine n/adj ignorant (person)

philosophy ❶ n, pl -phies 1 study of realities and general principles 2 system of theories on nature of things or on conduct **philosopher** n **philosophical** adj 1 of, like philosophy 2 wise, learned 3 calm, stoical

— THESAURUS —

petition n = appeal, round robin, list of signatures ▷ v = appeal, plead, ask, pray, beg

petty adj = trivial, insignificant, little, small, slight ≠ important; = small-minded, mean, shabby, spiteful, ungenerous ≠ broad-minded

phantom n = spectre, ghost, spirit, shade (Lit), spook (Inf)

phase n = stage, time, point, position, step

phenomenon n = occurrence, happening, fact, event, incident; = wonder, sensation, exception, miracle, marvel

philosophy n = thought, knowledge, thinking, reasoning, wisdom; = outlook, values, principles, convictions, thinking

phlegm n thick yellowish substance formed in throat **phlegmatic** adj not easily agitated

phobia n fear or aversion

phoenix n legendary bird

phone ① n **1** telephone **2** telephone call ▷ v **3** telephone **phonecard** n card used to operate some public telephones

phonetic adj of vocal sounds **phonetics** pl n science of vocal sounds

phoney, phony (Inf) ▷ adj **1** sham **2** suspect ▷ n **3** phoney person or thing

phosphorus n nonmetallic element which appears luminous in the dark **phosphate** n compound of phosphorus **phosphorescence** n faint glow in the dark

photo n, pl **photos** (Inf) photograph **photo finish** finish of a race in which the contestants are so close that a photograph is needed to decide the result

Photoshop® n **1** software application for managing and editing digital images ▷ v **2** (Inf) alter (a digital image) using Photoshop or a similar application

photocopy n, pl **-copies** **1** photographic reproduction ▷ v **2** make photocopy of

photogenic adj tending to look attractive when photographed

photograph ① n **1** picture made by chemical action of light on sensitive film ▷ v **2** take photograph of **photographer** n **photographic** adj **photography** n

photosynthesis n process by which green plant uses sun's energy to make carbohydrates

phrase ① n **1** group of words **2** expression ▷ v **3** express in words **phraseology** n choice of words

physical ① adj **1** of the body, as contrasted with the mind or spirit **2** of material things or nature

physics pl n science of properties of matter and energy **physical** adj **1** bodily, as opposed to mental **2** material **physician** n qualified medical practitioner **physicist** n one skilled in, or student of, physics

physiognomy n face

physiology n science of living things

physiotherapy n therapeutic use of physical means, as massage etc. **physiotherapist** n

physique n bodily structure, constitution

— THESAURUS —

phone n = **telephone**, blower (Inf), mobile, landline ▷ v = **call**, telephone, ring (up) (Inf, chiefly Brit), give someone a call, give someone a ring (Inf, chiefly Brit), give someone a buzz (Inf)

photograph n = **picture**, photo (Inf), shot, print, snap (Inf), selfie (Inf) ▷ v = **take a picture of**, record,

film, shoot, snap (Inf)

phrase n = **expression**, saying, remark, construction, quotation ▷ v = **express**, say, word, put, voice

physical adj = **corporal**, fleshly, bodily, corporeal; = **earthly**, fleshly, mortal, incarnate

physician n = **doctor**, doc (Inf), medic (Inf), general practitioner,

pi n (Maths) ratio of circumference of circle to its diameter

piano n, pl **pianos** 1 musical instrument with keyboard ▷ adj/adv 2 (Mus) softly **pianist** n performer on piano

picador n mounted bullfighter with lance

piccalilli n pickle of vegetables in mustard sauce

piccolo n, pl **-los** small flute

pick¹ ❶ v 1 choose, select carefully 2 pluck, gather 3 find occasion for ▷ n 4 act of picking 5 choicest part **pick on** find fault with **pickpocket** n thief who steals from someone's pocket **pick up** 1 lift 2 obtain 3 collect 4 get better 5 accelerate **pick-up** n 1 small truck 2 device for conversion of mechanical energy into electric signals

pick² tool with curved iron crossbar **pickaxe** n pick

picket ❶ n 1 pointed stake

2 party of trade unionists posted to deter would-be workers during strike ▷ v 3 post as picket

pickle ❶ n 1 food preserved in brine, vinegar etc. 2 awkward situation ▷ v 3 preserve in pickle

picnic ❶ n 1 pleasure excursion including meal out of doors ▷ v 2 take part in picnic

picture ❶ n 1 drawing or painting 2 mental image 3 film, movie ▷ pl 4 cinema ▷ v 5 represent in, or as in, a picture **pictorial** adj 1 of, in, with pictures ▷ n 2 newspaper with pictures **picturesque** adj visually striking, vivid

pidgin n language made up of two or more other languages

pie n baked dish of meat, fruit etc. usu. with pastry crust

piebald adj irregularly marked with black and white **pied** adj 1 piebald 2 variegated

piece ❶ n 1 bit, part, fragment 2 single object 3 literary or musical

medical practitioner

pick¹ v = **select**, choose, identify, elect, nominate ≠ **reject**; = **gather**, pull, collect, take in, harvest; = **provoke**, start, cause, stir up, incite; = **open**, force, crack (Inf), break into, break open ▷ n = **choice**, decision, option, selection, preference; = **best**, prime, finest, elect, elite

picket v = **blockade**, boycott, demonstrate outside ▷ n = **demonstration**, strike, blockade; = **protester**, demonstrator, picketer; = **lookout**, watch, guard,

patrol, sentry

pickle v = **preserve**, marinade, steep ▷ n = **chutney**, relish, piccalilli

picnic n = **excursion**, barbecue, barbie (Inf), cookout (US & Canad), alfresco meal

picture n = **representation**, drawing, painting, portrait, image; = **photograph**, photo, still, shot, selfie (Inf), image ▷ v = **imagine**, see, envision, visualize, conceive of; = **represent**, show, draw, paint, illustrate

piece n = **bit**, slice, part, block,

composition etc. ▷ v **4** mend, put together **piecemeal** adv by, in, or into pieces, a bit at a time

pier ❶ n **1** structure running into sea **2** piece of solid upright masonry

pierce ❶ v **1** make hole in **2** make a way through **piercing** adj **1** shrill **2** alert, probing

piety n, pl **-ties 1** godliness **2** devoutness

pig ❶ n **1** wild or domesticated mammal killed for pork, ham, bacon **2** (Inf) greedy, dirty person **piggish, piggy** adj **pig-headed** adj obstinate

pigeon n bird of wild and domesticated varieties **pigeonhole** n **1** compartment for papers in desk etc. ▷ v **2** defer **3** classify

piggyback n ride on the back

pigment ❶ n colouring matter, paint or dye

pigtail n plait of hair on either side of head

pike¹ n predatory freshwater fish

pike² n long-handled spear

pikelet n (Aust & NZ) small thick pancake

pilau, pilaf, pilaff n Oriental dish of meat or fowl boiled with rice, spices etc.

piker n (Aust & NZ, Sl) shirker

pilchard n small sea fish like herring

pile¹ ❶ **1** heap ▷ v **2** heap (up) **3** (with in or out) crowd ▷ n **4** heap **pile-up** n (Inf) traffic accident with several vehicles

pile² ❶ n beam driven into the ground, esp. as foundation

pile³ ❶ n nap of cloth

piles pl n haemorrhoids

pilfer v steal small items

pilgrim ❶ n one who journeys to sacred place **pilgrimage** n

pill ❶ n small ball of medicine swallowed whole **the pill** oral contraceptive

pillage v/n plunder

pillar ❶ n **1** upright support

P

quantity; = **component**, part, section, bit, unit

pier n = **jetty**, wharf, quay, promenade, landing place; = **pillar**, support, post, column, pile

pierce v = **penetrate**, stab, spike, enter, bore

pig n = **hog**, sow, boar, swine, porker; (Inf) = **slob** (Sl), glutton

pigment n = **colour**, colouring, paint, stain, dye

pile¹ n = **heap**, collection, mountain, mass, stack; (Inf) often plural = **lot(s)**, mountain(s), load(s)

(Inf), oceans, wealth; = **mansion**, building, residence, manor, country house ▷ v = **load**, stuff, pack, stack, charge; = **crowd**, pack, rush, climb, flood

pile² n = **foundation**, support, post, column, beam

pile³ n = **nap**, fibre, down, hair, fur

pilgrim n = **traveller**, wanderer, devotee, wayfarer

pill n = **tablet**, capsule, pellet

pillar n = **support**, post, column, prop, shaft; = **supporter**, leader, mainstay, leading light (Inf),

2 strong supporter **pillar box** red pillar-shaped letter box

pillion n seat behind rider of motorcycle or horse

pillory n, pl **-ries** 1 frame with holes for head and hands in which offender was confined ▷ v 2 expose to ridicule and abuse

pillow n cushion for the head, esp. in bed **pillowcase** n removable cover for pillow

pilot ❶ n 1 person qualified to fly an aircraft or spacecraft 2 one qualified to take charge of ship entering or leaving harbour etc. 3 guide ▷ adj 4 experimental and preliminary ▷ v 5 act as pilot to 6 steer **pilot light** small flame lighting main one in gas appliance

pimento, pimiento n, pl **-tos** 1 allspice 2 sweet red pepper

pimp n 1 one who solicits for prostitute ▷ v 2 act as pimp

pimpernel n plant with small scarlet, blue, or white flowers

pimple n small pus-filled spot on skin **pimply** adj

pin ❶ n 1 piece of stiff wire with point and head, for fastening

2 wooden or metal peg or rivet ▷ v 3 fasten with pin 4 seize and hold fast **pinpoint** v identify exactly

pinstripe n very narrow stripe in fabric **pin-up** n picture of sexually attractive person

pinafore n 1 apron 2 dress with bib top

pincers pl n 1 tool for gripping 2 claws of lobster etc.

pinch ❶ v 1 nip, squeeze 2 stint 3 (Inf) steal 4 (Inf) arrest ▷ n 5 nip 6 small amount 7 emergency

pine¹ ❶ v 1 yearn 2 waste away with grief etc.

pine² ❶ n 1 evergreen coniferous tree 2 its wood

pineapple n tropical plant bearing large edible fruit

pinion n 1 bird's wing ▷ v 2 confine by binding wings, arms etc.

pink ❶ n 1 pale red colour 2 garden plant 3 best condition ▷ adj 4 of the colour pink ▷ v 5 pierce 6 cut indented edge 7 (of engine) knock

pinnacle ❶ n 1 highest point 2 mountain peak 3 pointed turret

---

THESAURUS

---

upholder

pilot n = **airman**, flyer, aviator, aeronaut; = **helmsman**, navigator, steersman ▷ v = **fly**, operate, be at the controls of ▷ adj = **trial**, test, model, sample, experimental

pin v = **fasten**, stick, attach, join, fix; = **hold fast**, hold down, constrain, immobilize, pinion

pinch v = **nip**, press, squeeze,

grasp, compress; = **hurt**, crush, squeeze, pain, cramp; (Brit Inf) = **steal**, lift (Inf), nick (Sl, chiefly Brit), swipe (Sl), knock off (Sl) ▷ n = **nip**, squeeze

pine¹ v = **waste**, decline, sicken, fade, languish

pink adj = **rosy**, rose, salmon, flushed, reddish

pinnacle n = **summit**, top, height, peak

pint n 1 liquid measure 2 1/8 gallon (.568 litre)

pioneer ❶ n 1 explorer 2 early settler 3 originator ▷ v 4 act as pioneer

pious adj 1 devout 2 self-righteous

pip¹ n seed in fruit

pip² n 1 high-pitched sound as time signal on radio 2 spot on cards, dice etc. 3 (Inf) star on junior officer's shoulder showing rank

pipe ❶ n 1 tube of metal or other material 2 tube with small bowl at end for smoking tobacco 3 musical instrument ▷ pl 4 bagpipes ▷ v 5 play on pipe 6 utter in shrill tone 7 convey by pipe 8 ornament with piping **piper** n **piping** n 1 system of pipes 2 decoration of icing on cake 3 fancy edging on clothes **pipeline** n long pipe for transporting oil, water etc.

piquant adj pungent

pique n 1 feeling of injury ▷ v 2 hurt pride of 3 irritate

piranha n fierce tropical Amer. fish

pirate ❶ n 1 sea robber

2 publisher etc. who infringes copyright 3 person broadcasting illegally ▷ v 4 use or reproduce (artistic work etc.) illicitly **piracy** n

pirouette n/v (perform) act of spinning round on toe

pistachio n, pl **-chios** small hard-shelled, sweet-tasting nut

piste n ski slope

pistol n small firearm for one hand

piston n in engine, cylindrical part propelled to and fro in hollow cylinder

pit ❶ n 1 deep hole in ground 2 mine or its shaft 3 depression 4 part of theatre occupied by orchestra 5 servicing area on motor-racing track ▷ v 6 set to fight, match 7 mark with small dents **pitfall** n hidden danger

pitch¹ ❶ v 1 throw 2 set up 3 set the key of (a tune) 4 fall headlong ▷ n 5 act of pitching 6 degree, height, intensity 7 slope 8 degree of highness or lowness of sound 9 (Sport) field of play **pitchfork** n 1 fork for lifting hay etc. ▷ v 2 throw with, as with, pitchfork

pioneer n = **founder**, leader, developer, innovator, trailblazer; = **settler**, explorer, colonist ▷ v = **develop**, create, establish, start, discover

pipe n = **tube**, drain, canal, pipeline, line ▷ v = **convey**, channel, conduct

pirate n = **buccaneer**, raider, marauder, corsair, freebooter ▷ v = **copy**, steal, reproduce, bootleg, appropriate

pit n = **coal mine**, mine, shaft, colliery, mine shaft ▷ v = **scar**, mark, dent, indent, pockmark

pitch¹ n = **sports field**, ground, stadium, arena, park; = **tone**, sound, key, frequency, timbre; = **level**, point, degree, summit, extent; = **talk**, patter, spiel (Inf) ▷ v = **throw**, cast, toss, hurl, fling; = **fall**, drop, plunge, dive, tumble; = **set up**, raise, settle, put up, erect; = **toss (about)**, roll, plunge, lurch

pitch² n dark sticky substance obtained from tar or turpentine

pitcher n large jug

pith n 1 tissue in stems and branches of certain plants 2 essential part **pithy** adj 1 terse, concise 2 consisting of pith

pittance n small amount of money

pituitary adj, pl **-taries** of, pert. to, endocrine gland at base of brain

pity ⊕ n, pl **pities** 1 sympathy for others' suffering 2 regrettable fact ▷ v 3 feel pity for **piteous** adj **pitiful** adj 1 woeful 2 contemptible **pitiless** adj 1 feeling no pity 2 hard, merciless

pivot n 1 shaft or pin on which thing turns ▷ v 2 furnish with pivot 3 hinge on one

pixel n smallest constituent unit of an image, as on a computer screen

pixie n fairy

pizza n baked disc of dough covered with savoury topping

pizzicato adv/adj (Mus) played by plucking strings with finger

placard n notice for posting up or carrying poster

placate v pacify, appease

place ⊕ n 1 locality, spot 2 position 3 duty 4 town, village, residence, buildings 5 employment 6 seat, space ▷ v 7 put in particular place 8 identify 9 make (order, bet etc.)

placebo n, pl **-bos, -boes** inactive substance given to patient in place of active drug

placenta n, pl **-tas, -tae** 1 organ formed in uterus during pregnancy, providing nutrients for fetus 2 afterbirth

placid adj calm

plague ⊕ n 1 highly contagious disease 2 (Inf) nuisance ▷ v 3 trouble, annoy

plaice n flat fish

plaid n 1 long Highland cloak or shawl 2 tartan pattern

plain ⊕ adj 1 flat, level 2 not intricate 3 clear, simple 4 candid, forthright 5 ordinary 6 without

———————————————— THESAURUS ————————————————

pity n = **compassion**, charity, sympathy, kindness, fellow feeling ≠ **mercilessness**; = **shame**, sin (Inf), misfortune, bummer (Sl), crying shame ▷ v = **feel sorry for**, feel for, sympathize with, grieve for, weep for

place n = **spot**, point, position, site, area; = **region**, quarter, district, neighbourhood, vicinity; = **position**, point, spot, location; = **space**, position, seat, chair ▷ v = **lay (down)**, put (down), set (down), stand, position; = **put**, lay,

set, invest, pin; = **classify**, class, group, put, order, go down (US & Canad)

plague n = **disease**, infection, epidemic, pestilence; = **infestation**, invasion, epidemic, influx, host ▷ v = **torment**, trouble, torture (Inf)

plain adj = **unadorned**, simple, basic, severe, bare ≠ **ornate**; = **clear**, obvious, patent, evident, visible ≠ **hidden**; = **straightforward**, open, direct, frank, blunt ≠ **roundabout**; = **ugly**,

decoration **7** not beautiful ▷ *n*
8 tract of level country ▷ *adv*
9 clearly
plaintiff *n (Law)* one who sues in
court
plaintive *adj* sad, mournful
plait *n* **1** braid of hair, straw etc. ▷ *v*
2 weave into plaits
plan ❶ *n* **1** scheme **2** way of
proceeding **3** project **4** drawing
5 map ▷ *v* **6** make plan of
7 arrange beforehand
plane¹ ❶ *n* aeroplane
plane² ❶ *n* **1** smooth surface
2 level **3** tool for smoothing wood
▷ *v* **4** make smooth with plane
▷ *adj* **5** perfectly flat or level
plane³ *n* tree with broad leaves
planet *n* heavenly body revolving
round sun **planetary** *adj*
planetarium *n/pl* **-iums, -ia**
apparatus that shows movement
of sun, moon, stars and planets
by projecting lights on inside of
dome

plank *n* long flat piece of timber
plankton *n* minute animal and
vegetable organisms floating in
ocean
plant ❶ *n* **1** living organism
without power of locomotion
2 building and equipment for
manufacturing purposes ▷ *v* **3** set
in ground to grow **4** establish
5 *(Sl)* hide
plantation *n* **1** estate for
cultivation of tea, tobacco etc.
2 wood of planted trees
plaque *n* **1** ornamental tablet
2 plate of brooch **3** deposit on
teeth
plasma *n* clear, fluid portion of
blood
plaster ❶ *n* **1** mixture of lime,
sand etc. for coating walls etc.
2 adhesive dressing for cut, wound
etc. ▷ *v* **3** apply plaster to **4** apply
like plaster **plastered** *adj (Sl)*
drunk
plastic ❶ *n* **1** synthetic substance,

P

THESAURUS

unattractive, homely *(US & Canad)*,
unlovely, unprepossessing
≠ attractive; **= ordinary**, common,
simple, everyday, commonplace
≠ sophisticated ▷ *n* **= flatland**,
plateau, prairie, grassland, steppe
plan *n* **= scheme**, system, design,
programme, proposal; **= diagram**,
map, drawing, chart,
representation ▷ *v* **= devise**,
arrange, scheme, plot, draft
plane¹ *n* **= aeroplane**, aircraft, jet,
airliner, jumbo jet
plane² *n* **= flat surface**, the flat,
horizontal, level surface; **= level**,

position, stage, condition, standard
▷ *adj* **= level**, even, flat, regular,
smooth
plant *n* **= flower**, bush, vegetable,
herb, weed ▷ *v* **= sow**, scatter,
transplant, implant, put in the
ground; **= seed**, sow, implant
plaster *n* **= mortar**, stucco,
gypsum, plaster of Paris;
= bandage, dressing, sticking
plaster, Elastoplast *(Trademark)*,
adhesive plaster ▷ *v* **= cover**,
spread, coat, smear, overlay
plastic *adj* **= pliant**, soft, flexible,
supple, pliable **≠ rigid**

easily moulded and extremely
durable ▷ *adj* **2** made of plastic
3 easily moulded **plastic surgery**
repair, reconstruction of part of
body for medical or cosmetic
reasons
Plasticine® *n* modelling material
like clay
plate ❶ *n* **1** shallow round dish
2 flat thin sheet of metal, glass etc.
3 utensils of gold or silver **4** device
for printing illustration in book
5 device to straighten children's
teeth **6** (*Inf*) denture ▷ *v* **7** cover
with thin coating of metal
plateau ❶ *n, pl* **-teaus, -teaux**
1 tract of level high land **2** period of
stability
platform ❶ *n* **1** raised level
surface, stage **2** raised area in
station from which passengers
board trains
platinum *n* white heavy malleable
metal
platitude *n* commonplace
remark

platonic *adj* (of love) purely
spiritual, friendly
platoon *n* body of soldiers
employed as unit
platter *n* flat dish
**platypus, duck-billed
platypus** *n* Aust. egg-laying
amphibious mammal
plausible ❶ *adj* **1** apparently
reasonable **2** persuasive
play ❶ *v* **1** amuse oneself
2 contend with in game **3** take
part in (game) **4** trifle **5** act the
part of **6** perform (music)
7 perform on (instrument) ▷ *n*
8 dramatic piece or performance
9 sport **10** amusement **11** activity
12 free movement **13** gambling
player *n* **playful** *adj* lively
playboy *n* rich man who lives for
pleasure **playing card** one of set
of 52 cards **playing fields**
extensive piece of ground for
open-air games **playwright** *n*
author of plays
plaza *n* open space or square

— THESAURUS —

plate *n* = **platter**, dish, dinner
plate, salver, trencher (*Archaic*);
= **helping**, course, serving, dish,
portion; = **layer**, panel, sheet, slab
▷ *v* = **coat**, gild, laminate, cover,
overlay
plateau *n* = **upland**, table,
highland, tableland; = **levelling off**,
level, stage, stability
platform *n* = **stage**, stand,
podium, rostrum, dais; = **policy**,
programme, principle, objective(s),
manifesto
plausible *adj* = **believable**,

possible, likely, reasonable, credible
≠ **unbelievable**; = **glib**, smooth,
specious, smooth-talking,
smooth-tongued
play *v* = **amuse yourself**, have
fun, sport, fool, romp; = **take
part in**, be involved in, engage
in, participate in, compete in;
= **compete against**, challenge,
take on, oppose, contend
against ▷ *n* = **amusement**,
pleasure, leisure, games,
sport; = **drama**, show, piece,
comedy, tragedy

P

plea ❶ n 1 entreaty 2 statement of prisoner or defendant 3 excuse
plead v 1 make earnest appeal 2 address court of law 3 bring forward as excuse or plea
please ❶ v 1 be agreeable to 2 gratify 3 delight 4 be willing ▷ adv 5 word of request **pleasant** adj pleasing, agreeable
pleasantry n joke, humour
pleased adj **pleasing** adj
pleasurable adj giving pleasure
pleasure n 1 enjoyment 2 satisfaction
pleat n 1 fold made by doubling material ▷ v 2 make into pleats
plebeian adj/n (one) of the common people
plectrum n, pl **-trums, -tra** small implement for plucking strings of guitar etc.
pledge ❶ n 1 solemn promise 2 thing given as security ▷ v 3 promise, swear
plenary adj complete
plenipotentiary adj/n (envoy) having full powers
plenitude n abundance

plenty ❶ n 1 abundance 2 quite enough **plenteous** adj ample **plentiful** adj
plethora n oversupply
pleurisy n inflammation of membrane lining chest and covering lungs
pliable adj easily bent or influenced **pliant** adj pliable
pliers pl n tool with hinged arms and jaws for gripping
plight[1] ❶ n distressing state
plight[2] v promise
plimsolls pl n rubber-soled canvas shoes
plinth n slab as base of column etc.
plod v **plodding, plodded** walk or work doggedly
plonk[1] v put down heavily and carelessly
plonk[2] n (Inf) cheap inferior wine
plop n 1 sound of object falling into water without splash ▷ v 2 fall with this sound
plot[1] ❶ n 1 secret plan, conspiracy 2 essence of story, play etc. ▷ v 3 plan secretly 4 mark position of 5 make map of
plot[2] ❶ n small piece of land

P

plea n = **appeal**, request, suit, prayer, petition; = **excuse**, defence, explanation, justification
please v = **delight**, entertain, humour, amuse, suit ≠ **annoy**
pledge n = **promise**, vow, assurance, word, undertaking; = **guarantee**, security, deposit, bail, collateral ▷ v = **promise**, vow, swear, contract, engage
plenty n = **abundance**, wealth,

prosperity, fertility, profusion
plight[1] n = **difficulty**, condition, state, situation, trouble
plot[1] n = **plan**, scheme, intrigue, conspiracy, cabal; = **story**, action, subject, theme, outline ▷ v = **plan**, scheme, conspire, intrigue, manoeuvre; = **devise**, design, lay, conceive, hatch
plot[2] n = **patch**, lot, area, ground, parcel

plough ❶ n 1 implement for turning up soil ▷ v 2 turn up with plough, furrow 3 work at slowly **ploughman** n

plover n shore bird with straight bill and long pointed wings

ploy ❶ n manoeuvre designed to gain advantage

pluck ❶ v 1 pull, pick off 2 strip from 3 sound strings of (guitar etc.) with fingers, plectrum ▷ n 4 courage 5 sudden pull or tug **plucky** adj brave

plug ❶ n 1 thing fitting into and filling hole 2 (Electricity) device connecting appliance to electricity supply 3 (Inf) favourable mention of product etc. intended to promote it ▷ v 4 stop with plug 5 (Inf) advertise product etc. by frequently mentioning it

plum ❶ n 1 fruit with stone 2 tree bearing it 3 choicest part, piece, position etc. ▷ adj 4 choice

plumb ❶ n 1 ball of lead attached to string used for sounding, finding the perpendicular etc. ▷ adj 2 perpendicular ▷ adv 3 exactly 4 perpendicularly ▷ v 5 find depth of 6 equip with, connect to plumbing system **plumber** n worker who attends to water and sewage systems **plumbing** n 1 trade of plumber 2 system of water and sewage pipes **plumb line** cord with plumb attached

plume n 1 feather 2 ornament of feathers etc. ▷ v 3 furnish with plumes 4 pride oneself **plumage** n bird's feathers

plummet ❶ v -meting, -meted 1 plunge headlong ▷ n 2 plumb line

plump¹ ❶ adj 1 fat, rounded ▷ v 2 make, become plump

plump² v 1 drop, fall abruptly 2 choose

plunder ❶ v 1 take by force 2 rob ▷ n 3 booty, spoils

plunge ❶ v 1 put forcibly, throw (into) 2 descend suddenly ▷ n 3 dive **plunger** n suction cap to

───────────── THESAURUS ─────────────

plough v = **turn over**, dig, till, cultivate

ploy n = **tactic**, move, trick, device, scheme

pluck v = **pull out** or **off**, pick, draw, collect, gather; = **tug**, catch, snatch, clutch, jerk ▷ n = **courage**, nerve, bottle (Brit Sl), guts (Inf), grit

plug n = **stopper**, cork, bung, spigot; (Inf) = **mention**, advertisement, advert (Brit Inf), push, publicity ▷ v = **seal**, close, stop, fill, block; (Inf) = **mention**, push, promote, publicize, advertise

plum adj = **choice**, prize, first-class

plumb v = **delve into**, explore, probe, go into, penetrate ▷ adv = **exactly**, precisely, bang, slap, spot-on (Brit Inf)

plummet v = **drop**, fall, crash, nose-dive, descend rapidly

plump¹ adj = **chubby**, fat, stout, round, tubby ≠ **scrawny**

plunder v = **loot**, strip, sack, rob, raid

plunge v = **descend**, fall, drop, crash, pitch; = **hurtle**, charge, career, jump, tear ▷ n = **dive**,

unblock drains **plunging** adj (of neckline) cut low

plural adj 1 of, denoting more than one ▷ n 2 word in its plural form **plurality** n majority

plus ❶ prep 1 with addition of (usu. indicated by the sign +) ▷ adj 2 positive

plush ❶ n 1 fabric with long nap ▷ adj 2 luxurious

ply¹ ❶ v **plying, plied** 1 wield 2 work at 3 supply insistently 4 go to and fro regularly

ply² n 1 fold or thickness 2 strand of yarn **plywood** n board of thin layers of wood glued together

PM prime minister

p.m. after noon

pneumatic adj of, worked by, inflated with wind or air

pneumonia n inflammation of the lungs

PO Post Office

poach¹ v 1 take (game) illegally 2 encroach **poacher** n

poach² v simmer (eggs, fish etc.) gently in water etc.

pocket ❶ n 1 small bag inserted in garment 2 cavity, pouch or hollow 3 isolated group or area ▷ v 4 put into one's pocket 5 appropriate ▷ adj 6 small **pocket money** small allowance, esp. for children

pod ❶ n long seed vessel, as of peas, beans etc.

podgy adj **podgier, podgiest** short and fat

podium ❶ n, pl **-diums, -dia** small raised platform

poem ❶ n imaginative composition in rhythmic lines **poet** n writer of poems **poetic** adj **poetry** n art or work of poet, verse

poep n (Aust & NZ, Sl) emission of gas from the anus

poet ❶ n writer of poems

pogey n (Canad, Sl) money received from the state while out of work

poignant ❶ adj 1 moving 2 keen **poignancy** n

point ❶ n 1 dot 2 punctuation mark 3 detail 4 unit of value, scoring 5 degree, stage

— THESAURUS —

jump, duck, descent

plus prep = **and**, with, added to, coupled with ▷ n (Inf) = **advantage**, benefit, asset, gain, extra

plush adj = **luxurious**, luxury, lavish, rich, sumptuous ≠ **cheap**

ply¹ v = **work at**, follow, exercise, pursue, carry on

pocket n = **pouch**, bag, sack, compartment, receptacle ▷ adj = **small**, compact, miniature,

portable, little ▷ v = **steal**, take, lift (Inf), appropriate, pilfer

pod n = **shell**, case, hull, husk, shuck

podium n = **platform**, stand, stage, rostrum, dais

poem n = **verse**, song, lyric, rhyme, sonnet

poet n = **bard**, rhymer, lyricist, lyric poet, versifier

poignant adj = **moving**, touching, sad, bitter, intense

point n = **essence**, meaning,

6 moment **7** gist **8** purpose **9** special quality **10** sharp end **11** headland **12** direction mark on compass **13** movable rail changing train to other rails **14** power point ▷ *v* **15** show direction or position by extending finger **16** direct **17** sharpen **18** fill up joints with mortar **pointed** *adj* **1** sharp **2** direct **pointer** *n* **1** indicating rod etc. used for pointing **2** indication **3** breed of gun dog **pointless** *adj* futile **point-blank** *adj* **1** at short range **2** blunt, direct ▷ *adv* **3** bluntly

poise *n* **1** composure **2** self-possession **3** balance **poised** *adj* **1** ready **2** showing poise

poison ❶ *n* **1** substance harmful or fatal to living organism ▷ *v* **2** give poison to **3** infect **poisonous** *adj*

poke ❶ *v* **1** push, thrust with finger, stick etc. **2** thrust forward **3** pry ▷ *n* **4** act of poking **poker** *n*

metal rod for poking fire **poky** *adj* small, confined, cramped

poker *n* card game

pole¹ ❶ *n* long, rounded piece of wood etc.

pole² *n* **1** each of the ends of axis of earth or celestial sphere **2** each of opposite ends of magnet, electric cell etc. **polar** *adj* **polarize** *v* (cause to) form into groups with opposite views **polar bear** white bear that lives around North Pole

poleaxe *v* stun with heavy blow

polecat *n* small animal of weasel family

police ❶ *n* **1** civil force which maintains public order ▷ *v* **2** keep in order **policeman** *n* member of police force

policy¹ ❶ *n* course of action adopted, esp. in state affairs

policy² *n* insurance contract

polio, poliomyelitis *n* disease affecting spinal cord, often causing paralysis

subject, question, heart; **= purpose**, aim, object, end, reason; **= aspect**, detail, feature, quality, particular; **= place**, area, position, site, spot; **= moment**, time, stage, period, phase; **= stage**, level, position, condition, degree; **= end**, tip, sharp end, top, spur; **= score**, tally, mark **= headland**, head, cape, promontory ▷ *v* **= aim**, level, train, direct; **= indicate**, show, signal, point to, gesture towards

poison *n* **= toxin**, venom, bane

(Archaic) ▷ *v* **= murder**, kill, give someone poison, administer poison to; **= contaminate**, foul, infect, spoil, pollute

poke *v* **= jab**, push, stick, dig, stab ▷ *n* **= jab**, dig, thrust, nudge, prod

pole¹ *n* **= rod**, post, support, staff, bar

police *n* **= the law** *(Inf)*, police force, constabulary, fuzz *(Sl)*, boys in blue *(Inf)* ▷ *v* **= control**, patrol, guard, watch, protect

policy¹ *n* **= procedure**, plan, action, practice, scheme

polish v 1 make smooth and glossy 2 refine ▷ n 3 shine 4 polishing 5 substance for polishing 6 refinement

polite adj 1 showing regard for others in manners, speech etc. 2 refined, cultured

politics pl n 1 art of government 2 political affairs **politic** adj wise, shrewd **political** adj of the state or its affairs **politician** n one engaged in politics

polka n 1 lively dance 2 music for it **polka dot** one of pattern of bold spots on fabric etc.

poll n 1 voting 2 counting of votes 3 number of votes recorded 4 survey of opinion ▷ v 5 receive (votes) 6 take votes of 7 vote **polling booth** voting place

pollen n fertilizing dust of flower **pollinate** v

pollute v 1 make foul 2 corrupt **pollution** n

polo n game like hockey played on horseback **polo neck** (sweater with) tight turned-over collar

poltergeist n spirit believed to move furniture, throw objects around etc.

polyester n synthetic material

polygamy n custom of being married to several persons at a time **polygamist** n

polygon n figure with many angles or sides

polystyrene n synthetic material used esp. as rigid foam for packing etc.

polythene n tough light plastic material

polyunsaturated adj pert. to fats that do not form cholesterol in blood

polyurethane n synthetic material used esp. in paints

pom n (Aust & NZ, Sl) person from England (also **pommy**)

pomegranate n 1 tree 2 its fruit with thick rind containing many seeds in red pulp

pommel n 1 front of saddle 2 knob of sword hilt

pomp n splendid display or ceremony

pompom n decorative tuft of ribbon, wool, feathers etc.

pompous adj 1 self-important 2 ostentatious 3 (of language)

P

THESAURUS
---

polish n = **varnish**, wax, glaze, lacquer, japan; = **sheen**, finish, glaze, gloss, brightness; = **style**, class (Inf), finish, breeding, grace ▷ v = **shine**, wax, smooth, rub, buff; often with **up** = **perfect**, improve, enhance, refine, finish

polite adj = **mannerly**, civil, courteous, gracious, respectful ≠ **rude**; = **refined**, cultured,

civilized, polished, sophisticated ≠ **uncultured**

politics n = **affairs of state**, government, public affairs, civics

poll n = **survey**, figures, count, sampling, returns; = **election**, vote, voting, referendum, ballot ▷ v = **question**, interview, survey, sample, ballot; = **gain**, return, record, register, tally

inflated, stilted, lofty

pond ❶ *n* small body of still water

ponder ❶ *v* muse, think over

ponderous *adj* **1** heavy, unwieldy **2** boring

pong *n/v (Inf)* (give off) strong unpleasant smell

pontiff *n* **1** Pope **2** bishop **pontificate** *v* speak dogmatically

pontoon¹ *n* flat-bottomed boat or metal drum for use in supporting temporary bridge

pontoon² *n* gambling card game

pony *n, pl* **ponies** horse of small breed **ponytail** *n* long hair tied at back of head

poodle *n* pet dog with long curly hair

pool¹ ❶ *n* **1** small body of still water **2** deep place in river or stream **3** puddle **4** swimming pool

pool² ❶ *n* **1** common fund or resources **2** group of people, e.g. typists, shared by several employers **3** collective stakes in various games

▷ *v* **4** put in common fund

poop *n* ship's stern

poor ❶ *adj* **1** having little money **2** unproductive **3** inadequate **4** inferior **5** miserable, pitiful

poorly *adj* **1** not in good health ▷ *adv* **2** in poor manner

pop ❶ *v* **popping, popped** **1** (cause to) make small explosive sound **2** put or place suddenly ▷ *n* **3** small explosive sound **popcorn** *n* maize that puffs up when roasted

Pope *n* bishop of Rome and head of R.C. Church

poplar *n* tall slender tree

poplin *n* corded fabric, usu. of cotton

poppadom *n* thin round crisp Indian bread

poppy *n, pl* **-pies** bright-flowered plant yielding opium

Popsicle *n (US & Canad)* an ice lolly

populace *n* the common people

popular ❶ *adj* **1** finding general favour **2** of, by the people **popularity** *n* **popularize** *v*

—————————— THESAURUS ——————————

pond *n* = **pool**, tarn, small lake, fish pond, duck pond

ponder *v* = **think about**, consider, reflect on, contemplate, deliberate about

pool¹ *n* = **swimming pool**, lido, swimming bath(s) *(Brit)*, bathing pool *(Archaic)*; = **pond**, lake, mere, tarn; = **puddle**, drop, patch

pool² *n* = **supply**, reserve, fall-back ▷ *v* = **combine**, share, merge, put together, amalgamate

poor *adj* = **impoverished**, broke *(Inf)*, hard up *(Inf)*, short, needy

≠ **rich**; = **unfortunate**, unlucky, hapless, pitiful, luckless

≠ **fortunate**; = **inferior**, unsatisfactory, mediocre, second-rate, rotten *(Inf)*

≠ **excellent**; = **meagre**, inadequate, insufficient, lacking, incomplete ≠ **ample**

pop *(US & Canad)* ▷ *n* = **bang**, report, crack, noise, burst ▷ *v* = **burst**, crack, snap, bang, explode

popular *adj* = **well-liked**, liked, in, accepted, favourite ≠ **unpopular**; = **common**, general, prevailing,

populate ❶ v fill with inhabitants **population** n (number of) inhabitants **populous** adj thickly populated

porcelain n fine earthenware, china

porch n covered approach to entrance of building

porcupine n rodent covered with long, pointed quills

pore¹ ❶ n minute opening, esp. in skin **porous** adj 1 allowing liquid to soak through 2 full of pores

pore² v study closely

pork n pig's flesh as food

pornography ❶ n indecent literature, films etc. **pornographic** adj

porpoise n blunt-nosed sea mammal like dolphin

porridge n soft food of oatmeal etc. boiled in water

port¹ ❶ n (town with) harbour

port² n left side of ship

port³ n strong red wine

port⁴ n opening in side of ship **porthole** n small opening or window in side of ship

portable ❶ adj easily carried

portcullis n grating above gateway that can be lowered to block entrance

portend v 1 foretell 2 be an omen of **portent** n omen

porter ❶ n 1 person employed to carry luggage etc. 2 doorkeeper

portfolio n, pl **-os** 1 flat portable case for loose papers 2 collection of work, shares etc.

portico n, pl **-coes, -cos** porch, covered walkway

portion ❶ n 1 part, share, helping 2 destiny, lot ▷ v 3 divide into shares

portly adj **-lier, -liest** bulky, stout

portmanteau n, pl **-teaus, -teaux** leather suitcase, esp. one opening into two compartments

portray ❶ v make pictures of, describe **portrait** n likeness of (face of) individual **portraiture** n **portrayal** n act of portraying

pose ❶ v 1 place in attitude 2 put forward 3 assume attitude

P

——— THESAURUS ———

current, conventional ≠ **rare**
populate v = **inhabit**, people, live in, occupy, reside in
pore¹ n = **opening**, hole, outlet, orifice
pornography n = **obscenity**, porn (Inf), dirt, filth, indecency
port¹ n = **harbour**, haven, anchorage, seaport
portable adj = **light**, compact, convenient, handy, manageable
porter n (chiefly Brit) = **doorman**, caretaker, janitor, concierge,

gatekeeper
portion n = **part**, bit, piece, section, scrap; = **helping**, serving, piece, plateful; = **share**, allowance, lot, measure, quantity
portray v = **play**, take the role of, act the part of, represent, personate (rare); = **describe**, present, depict, evoke, delineate; = **represent**, draw, paint, illustrate, sketch
pose v = **position yourself**, sit, model, arrange yourself; = **put on**

4 affect or pretend to be a certain character ▷ *n* 5 attitude, esp. one assumed for effect

posh ❶ *adj* 1 luxurious 2 upper-class

position ❶ *n* 1 place 2 situation 3 attitude 4 status 5 employment ▷ *v* 6 place in position

positive ❶ *adj* 1 sure 2 definite 3 assertive 4 constructive 5 not negative ▷ *n* 6 something positive

possess ❶ *v* 1 own 2 have mastery of **possession** *n* 1 act of possessing 2 ownership ▷ *pl* 3 things a person possesses **possessive** *adj* 1 of, indicating possession 2 with excessive desire to possess, control

possible ❶ *adj* 1 that can, or may, be, exist, happen or be done 2 worthy of consideration

possibility *n, pl* **-ties** 1 feasibility 2 chance **possibly** *adv* perhaps

possum see OPOSSUM

post¹ ❶ *n* 1 upright pole to support or mark something ▷ *v* 2 display 3 stick up (on notice board etc.) **poster** *n* large advertisement

post² ❶ *n* 1 official carrying of letters or parcels 2 collection or delivery of these 3 office 4 situation 5 place of duty 6 fort ▷ *v* 7 put into official box for carriage by post 8 station (soldiers etc.) in particular spot **postage** *n* charge for carrying letter **postal** *adj* **postal order** written order for payment of sum of money **postcard** *n* stamped card sent by post **postman** *n* person who collects and delivers post **postmark** *n* official mark stamped

—————————— THESAURUS ——————————

airs, posture, show off (*Inf*) ▷ *n* = **posture**, position, bearing, attitude, stance; = **act**, façade, air, front, posturing

posh *adj* (*Inf, chiefly Brit*); = **smart**, grand, stylish, luxurious, classy (*Sl*); = **upper-class**, high-class

position *n* = **location**, place, point, area, post; = **posture**, attitude, arrangement, pose, stance; = **status**, place, standing, footing, station; = **job**, place, post, opening, office; = **place**, standing, rank, status ▷ *v* = **place**, put, set, stand, arrange

positive *adj* = **beneficial**, useful, practical, helpful, progressive ≠ **harmful**; = **certain**, sure, convinced, confident, satisfied

≠ **uncertain**; = **definite**, real, clear, firm, certain ≠ **inconclusive**; (*Inf*) = **absolute**, complete, perfect, right (*Brit Inf*), real

possess *v* = **own**, have, hold, be in possession of, be the owner of; = **be endowed with**, have, enjoy, benefit from, be possessed of

possible *adj* = **feasible**, viable, workable, achievable, practicable ≠ **unfeasible**; = **likely**, potential, anticipated, probable, odds-on ≠ **improbable**; = **conceivable**, likely, credible, plausible, hypothetical ≠ **inconceivable**

post¹ *v* = **put something up**, display, affix, pin something up

post² *n* = **mail**, collection, delivery, postal service, snail mail (*Inf*);

P

on letters **post office** place where postal business is conducted

post- *comb. form* after, later than, as in *postwar*

posterior *adj* **1** later, hind ▷ *n* **2** buttocks

posterity *n* **1** later generations **2** descendants

posthaste *adv* with great speed

posthumous *adj* occurring after death

postmortem *n* medical examination of dead body

postpone ❶ *v* put off to later time, defer

postscript *n* addition to letter, book

postulate *v* **1** take for granted ▷ *n* **2** something postulated

posture ❶ *n* **1** attitude, position of body ▷ *v* **2** pose

posy *n, pl* **-sies** bunch of flowers

pot ❶ *n* **1** round vessel **2** cooking vessel ▷ *v* **3** put into, preserve in pot **potluck** *n* whatever is available

potassium *n* white metallic element

potato *n/pl* **-toes** **1** plant with tubers grown for food **2** one of these tubers

potato chip *n* the US and Canadian term for CRISP

potent ❶ *adj* powerful, influential **potency** *n*

potentate *n* ruler

potential ❶ *adj* **1** that might exist or act but does not now ▷ *n* **2** possibility

pothole *n* **1** hole in surface of road **2** underground cave

potion *n* dose of medicine or poison

potpourri *n* **1** fragrant mixture of dried flower petals **2** medley

potter¹ ❶ *v* work, act in unsystematic way

potter² *n* maker of earthenware vessel **pottery** *n* **1** earthenware **2** where it is made **3** art of making it

potty¹ *adj* (*Inf*) crazy, silly

potty² *n* bowl used by small child as toilet

pouch *n* **1** small bag **2** pocket ▷ *v* **3** put into pouch

poultice *n* soft composition of mustard, kaolin etc., applied hot to

P

THESAURUS

= **correspondence**, letters, cards, mail ▷ *v* = **send (off)**, forward, mail, get off, transmit

postpone *v* = **put off**, delay, suspend, adjourn, shelve ≠ **go ahead with**

posture *n* = **bearing**, set, attitude, stance, carriage ▷ *v* = **show off** (*Inf*), pose, affect, put on airs

pot *n* = **container**, bowl, pan,

vessel, basin

potent *adj* = **powerful**, commanding, dynamic, dominant, influential

potential *adj* = **possible**, future, likely, promising, probable ▷ *n* = **ability**, possibilities, capacity, capability, aptitude

potter¹ *v* usually with **around** or **about** = **mess about**, tinker, dabble, footle (*Inf*)

sore or inflamed parts of body

poultry n domestic fowls

pounce ❶ v 1 spring (upon) suddenly, swoop (upon) ▷ n 2 swoop, sudden descent

pound¹ ❶ n enclosure for stray animals or officially removed vehicles

pound² ❶ v 1 beat, thump 2 crush to pieces or powder 3 walk, run heavily

pound³ n 1 British monetary unit 2 unit of weight equal to 0.454 kg

pour ❶ v 1 come out in a stream, crowd etc. 2 flow freely 3 rain heavily ▷ v 4 give out thus

pout ❶ v 1 thrust out lips to look sulky ▷ n 2 act of pouting

poverty ❶ n 1 state of being poor 2 lack of, scarcity

powder ❶ n 1 solid matter in fine dry particles 2 medicine in this

form 3 gunpowder 4 face powder etc. ▷ v 5 apply powder to 6 reduce to powder

powdery adj

power ❶ n 1 ability to do or act 2 strength 3 authority 4 control 5 person or thing having authority 6 mechanical energy 7 electricity supply **powerful** adj **powerless** adj

pp pages

PQ Quebec

PR 1 proportional representation 2 public relations

practical ❶ adj 1 given to action rather than theory 2 sensible, realistic 3 skilled **practicable** adj that can be done, used etc. **practically** adv 1 all but 2 sensibly **practical joke** trick intended to make someone look foolish

──────── THESAURUS ────────

pounce v = **attack**, strike, jump, leap, swoop

pound¹ n = **enclosure**, yard, pen, compound, kennels

pound² v sometimes with on = **beat**, strike, hammer, batter, thrash; = **crush**, powder, pulverize; = **pulsate**, beat, pulse, throb, palpitate; = **stomp**, tramp, march, thunder (Inf)

pour v = **let flow**, spill, splash, dribble, drizzle; = **flow**, stream, run, course, rush; = **rain**, pelt (down), teem, bucket down (Inf)

pout v = **sulk**, glower, look petulant, pull a long face ▷ n = **sullen look**, glower, long face

poverty n = **pennilessness**, want, need, hardship, insolvency ≠ **wealth**; = **scarcity**, lack, absence, want, deficit ≠ **abundance**

powder n = **dust**, talc, fine grains, loose particles ▷ v = **dust**, cover, scatter, sprinkle, strew

power n = **control**, authority, influence, command, dominance; = **ability**, capacity, faculty, property, potential ≠ **inability**; = **authority**, right, licence, privilege, warrant

practical adj = **functional**, realistic, pragmatic ≠ **impractical**; = **empirical**, real, applied, actual, hands-on ≠ **theoretical**;

p

practise ❶ v 1 do repeatedly, work at to gain skill 2 do habitually 3 put into action 4 exercise profession **practice** n 1 habit 2 exercise of art or profession 3 action, not theory

pragmatic ❶ adj concerned with practical consequences

prairie n a treeless grassy plain of the central US and S Canada

praise ❶ n 1 commendation 2 fact of praising 3 expression of thanks to God ▷ v 4 express approval, admiration of 5 express thanks to God **praiseworthy** adj

pram n carriage for baby

prance v/n 1 swagger 2 caper

prank n mischievous trick

prattle v talk like child

prawn n edible sea shellfish like shrimp

pray ❶ v 1 ask earnestly 2 entreat

3 offer prayers, esp. to God **prayer** n 1 action, practice of praying to God 2 earnest entreaty

pre- comb. form before, as in prerecord, preshrunk

preach ❶ v 1 deliver sermon 2 give moral, religious advice 3 advocate **preacher** n

preamble n introductory part of story etc.

precarious ❶ adj insecure, unstable, perilous

precaution ❶ n previous care to prevent evil or secure good

precede ❶ v go, come before in rank, order, time etc. **precedence** n priority in position, rank, time etc. **precedent** n previous case or occurrence taken as rule

precept n rule for conduct

precinct ❶ n 1 enclosed, limited area ▷ pl 2 environs

———— THESAURUS ————

= **sensible**, ordinary, realistic, down-to-earth, matter-of-fact ≠ **impractical**; = **feasible**, possible, viable, workable, practicable ≠ **impractical**

practise v = **rehearse**, study, prepare, perfect, repeat; = **do**, train, exercise, drill; = **carry out**, follow, apply, perform, observe

pragmatic adj = **practical**, sensible, realistic, down-to-earth, utilitarian ≠ **idealistic**

praise v = **acclaim**, approve of, honour, cheer, admire ≠ **criticize**; = **give thanks to**, bless, worship, adore, glorify ▷ n = **approval**, acclaim, tribute, compliment, congratulations ≠ **criticism**;

= **thanks**, glory, worship, homage, adoration

pray v = **say your prayers**, offer a prayer, recite the rosary; = **beg**, ask, plead, petition, request

preach v often with **to** = **deliver a sermon**, address, evangelize, preach a sermon; = **urge**, teach, champion, recommend, advise

precarious adj = **insecure**, dangerous, tricky, risky, dodgy (Brit, Aust, & NZ Inf) ≠ **secure**

precaution n = **safeguard**, insurance, protection, provision, safety measure

precede v = **go before**, antedate

precinct n = **area**, quarter, section, sector, district

p

precious ❶ *adj* 1 beloved, cherished 2 of great value
precipice *n* very steep cliff or rock face
precipitate ❶ *v* 1 hasten happening of 2 throw headlong 3 (*Chem*) cause to be deposited in solid form from solution ▷ *adj* 4 too sudden 5 rash ▷ *n* 6 substance chemically precipitated **precipitation** *n* rain, snow etc.
précis *n/pl* précis 1 summary ▷ *v* 2 summarize
precise ❶ *adj* 1 definite 2 exact 3 careful in observance **precisely** *adv* **precision** *n*
preclude *v* prevent
precocious *adj* developed, matured early or too soon
precursor *n* forerunner
predatory *adj* preying on other animals **predator** *n*
predecessor ❶ *n* one who precedes another in office or position
predicament ❶ *n* difficult or

perplexing situation
predict ❶ *v* foretell, prophesy **predictable** *adj* **prediction** *n*
predispose *v* 1 incline, influence 2 make susceptible
predominate *v* be main or controlling element **predominance** *n* **predominant** *adj*
pre-eminent *adj* excelling all others **pre-eminence** *n*
pre-empt *v* do in advance of or to exclusion of others
preen *v* 1 trim (feather) with beak 2 smarten oneself
prefabricated *adj* (of building) manufactured in shaped sections for rapid assembly
preface *n* 1 introduction to book etc. ▷ *v* 2 introduce
prefect *n* 1 person put in authority 2 schoolchild in position of limited authority over others
prefer ❶ *v* -ferring, -ferred 1 like better 2 promote **preferable** *adj* more desirable **preference** *n* **preferential** *adj* special, privileged

———————— THESAURUS ————————

precious *adj* = **valuable**, expensive, fine, prized, dear ≠ **worthless**; = **loved**, prized, dear, treasured, darling; = **affected**, artificial, twee (*Brit Inf*), overrefined, overnice
precipitate *v* = **quicken**, trigger, accelerate, advance, hurry; = **throw**, launch, cast, hurl, fling ▷ *adj* = **hasty**, rash, reckless, impulsive, precipitous
precise *adj* = **exact**, specific,

particular, express, correct ≠ **vague**; = **strict**, particular, exact, formal, careful ≠ **inexact**
predecessor *n* = **previous job holder**, precursor, forerunner, antecedent; = **ancestor**, forebear, antecedent, forefather
predicament *n* = **fix** (*Inf*), situation, spot (*Inf*), hole (*Sl*), mess
predict *v* = **foretell**, forecast, divine, prophesy, augur
prefer *v* = **like better**, favour, go for, pick, fancy

preferment n promotion
prefix n 1 group of letters put at beginning of word ▷ v 2 put as introduction 3 put as prefix
pregnant 𝕠 adj 1 carrying fetus in womb 2 full of meaning, significant **pregnancy** n, pl -cies
prehistoric adj before period in which written history begins
prejudice 𝕠 n 1 preconceived opinion 2 unreasonable or unfair dislike ▷ v 3 influence 4 bias 5 injure **prejudicial** adj
preliminary 𝕠 adj/n preparatory, introductory (action, statement)
prelude 𝕠 n (Mus) 1 introductory movement 2 performance, event etc. serving as introduction
premature 𝕠 adj happening, done before proper time
premeditated adj planned

beforehand
premier 𝕠 n 1 prime minister ▷ adj 2 chief, foremost 3 first
première n first performance of play etc.
premise, premiss 𝕠 n (Logic) proposition from which inference is drawn
premises 𝕠 pl n house, building with its belongings
premium 𝕠 n 1 bonus 2 sum paid for insurance 3 excess over nominal value 4 great value or regard
premonition n presentiment
preoccupy v -pying, -pied occupy to exclusion of other things **preoccupation** n
preordained adj determined in advance

—————— THESAURUS ——————

pregnant adj = **expectant**, expecting (Inf), with child, in the club (Brit Sl), big or heavy with child; = **meaningful**, pointed, charged, significant, telling
prejudice n = **discrimination**, injustice, intolerance, bigotry, unfairness; = **bias**, preconception, partiality, preconceived notion, prejudgment ▷ v = **bias**, influence, colour, poison, distort; = **harm**, damage, hurt, injure, mar
preliminary adj = **first**, opening, trial, initial, test ▷ n = **introduction**, opening, beginning, start, prelude
prelude n = **introduction**, beginning, start; = **overture**, opening, introduction, introductory

movement
premature adj = **early**, untimely, before time, unseasonable; = **hasty**, rash, too soon, untimely, ill-timed
premier n = **head of government**, prime minister, chancellor, chief minister, P.M. ▷ adj = **chief**, leading, first, highest, head
premise n = **assumption**, proposition, argument, hypothesis, assertion
premises pl n = **building(s)**, place, office, property, site
premium n = **fee**, charge, payment, instalment; = **surcharge**, extra charge, additional fee or charge

P

prepare ❶ v 1 make, get ready
2 concoct, make **preparation** n
1 making ready beforehand
2 something prepared, as a
medicine **preparatory** adj
1 serving to prepare 2 introductory
prepared adj 1 ready 2 willing
preposition n word marking
relation between noun or pronoun
and other words
prepossessing v impressive
preposterous adj utterly absurd,
foolish
prerequisite n/adj (something)
required as prior condition
prerogative n peculiar power or
right, esp. as vested in sovereign
prescribe ❶ v 1 set out rules for
2 order use of (medicine)
prescription n 1 prescribing
2 thing prescribed 3 written
statement of it
present¹ ❶ adj 1 that is here
2 now existing or happening ▷ n
3 present time or tense **presence**
n 1 being present 2 appearance,

bearing **presently** adv 1 soon
2 (US) at present
present² ❶ v 1 introduce formally
2 show 3 give ▷ n 4 gift
presentable adj fit to be seen
presentation n **presenter** n
presentiment n sense of
something about to happen
preserve ❶ v 1 keep from harm,
injury or decay ▷ n 2 special area
3 fruit preserved by cooking in
sugar 4 place where game is kept
for private fishing, shooting
preservation n **preservative** n
1 preserving agent ▷ adj
2 preserving
preside ❶ v be in charge
presidency n **president** n head
of society, company, republic etc.
presidential adj
press ❶ v 1 subject to push or
squeeze 2 smooth 3 urge
4 throng 5 hasten ▷ n 6 machine
for pressing, esp. printing machine
7 printing house 8 newspapers
and journalists collectively

———————————— THESAURUS ————————————

prepare v = **make** or **get ready**,
arrange, adapt, adjust
prescribe v = **specify**, order,
direct, stipulate, write a
prescription for
present¹ adj = **current**, existing,
immediate, contemporary,
present-day; = **here**, there, near,
ready, nearby ≠ **absent**
present² n = **gift**, offering, grant,
donation, hand-out ▷ v = **give**,
award, hand over, grant, hand out;
= **put on**, stage, perform, give,
show; = **launch**, display, parade,

exhibit, unveil
preserve v = **maintain**, keep,
continue, sustain, keep up ≠ **end**;
= **protect**, keep, save, maintain,
defend ≠ **attack** ▷ n = **area**,
department, field, territory,
province
preside v = **officiate**, chair,
moderate, be chairperson
press v = **push (down)**, depress,
lean on, press down, force down;
= **push**, squeeze, jam, thrust, ram;
= **hug**, squeeze, embrace, clasp,
crush; = **urge**, beg, petition, exhort,

9 crowd **pressing** *adj* **1** urgent
2 persistent

pressure ❶ *n* **1** act of pressing
2 compelling force **3** (*Physics*)
thrust per unit area

prestige ❶ *n* **1** reputation
2 influence depending on it
prestigious *adj*

presto *adv* (*Mus*) very quickly

presume ❶ *v* **1** take for granted
2 take liberties **presumably** *adv*
presumption *n* **1** forward,
arrogant opinion or conduct
2 strong probability **presumptive**
adj that may be assumed is true or
valid until contrary is proved
presumptuous *adj* forward,
impudent

presuppose *v* assume or take for
granted beforehand
presupposition *n*

pretend ❶ *v* **1** claim or allege
(something untrue) **2** make believe

3 lay claim (to) **pretence** *n*
simulation **pretender** *n* claimant
(to throne) **pretension** *n*
pretentious *adj* **1** making claim to
special merit or importance
2 given to outward show

pretext *n* **1** excuse
2 pretence

pretty ❶ *adj* **-tier, -tiest**
1 appealing in a delicate way ▷ *adv*
2 moderately

prevail ❶ *v* **1** gain mastery
2 be generally established
prevalent *adj* **1** widespread
2 predominant

prevaricate *v* tell lies or speak
evasively **prevaricator** *n*

prevent ❶ *v* stop, hinder
prevention *n* **preventive** *adj/n*

preview ❶ *n* advance showing

previous ❶ *adj* **1** preceding
2 happening before **previously**
adv

—— THESAURUS ——

implore; **= plead**, present, lodge,
submit, tender; **= compress**, grind,
reduce, mill, crush; **= crowd**, push,
gather, surge, flock

pressure *n* **= force**, crushing,
squeezing, compressing, weight;
= power, influence, force,
constraint, sway; **= stress**,
demands, strain, heat, load

prestige *n* **= status**, standing,
credit, reputation, honour

presume *v* **= believe**, think,
suppose, assume, guess (*Inf, chiefly
US & Canad*); **= dare**, venture, go so
far as, take the liberty, make so bold
as

pretend *v* **= feign**, affect, assume,

allege, fake; **= make believe**,
suppose, imagine, act, make up

pretty *adj* **= attractive**, beautiful,
lovely, charming, fair ≠ **plain** ▷ *adv*
(*Inf*) **= fairly**, rather, quite, kind of
(*Inf*), somewhat

prevail *v* **= win**, succeed, triumph,
overcome, overrule; **= be
widespread**, abound,
predominate, be current, be
prevalent

prevent *v* **= stop**, avoid, frustrate,
hamper, foil ≠ **help**

preview *n* **= sample**, sneak
preview, trailer, taster, foretaste

previous *adj* **= earlier**, former,
past, prior, preceding ≠ **later**

P

prey ❶ n 1 animal hunted by another for food 2 victim ▷ v 3 (with on) treat as prey 4 worry, obsess

price ❶ n 1 that for which thing is bought or sold 2 cost ▷ v 3 fix, ask price for **priceless** adj invaluable **pricey** adj **pricier, priciest** (Inf) expensive

prick ❶ v 1 pierce slightly 2 cause to feel sharp pain ▷ n 3 slight hole made by pricking 4 sting **prickle** n 1 thorn, spike ▷ v 2 feel pricking sensation **prickly** adj 1 thorny 2 stinging 3 touchy

pride ❶ n 1 too high an opinion of oneself 2 worthy self-esteem 3 great satisfaction 4 something causing this 5 best part of something **pride oneself** take pride

priest ❶ n official minister of religion **priesthood** n

prig n smug self-righteous person **priggish** adj

prim adj **primmer, primmest** formal and prudish

primacy n, pl **-cies** supremacy

prima donna female opera singer

primary ❶ adj 1 chief 2 earliest 3 elementary

primate¹ n one of order of mammals including monkeys and man

primate² n archbishop

prime ❶ adj 1 fundamental 2 original 3 chief 4 best ▷ n 5 first, best part of anything ▷ v 6 prepare for use **primer** n paint for preliminary coating **Prime Minister** leader of government

primeval adj of earliest age of the world

primitive ❶ adj 1 of an early undeveloped kind 2 crude

primrose n 1 pale yellow spring flower 2 this colour ▷ adj 3 of this colour

prince ❶ n 1 male member of royal family 2 ruler, chief **princely**

prey n = **quarry**, game, kill; = **victim**, target, mug (Brit Sl), dupe, fall guy (Inf)

price n = **cost**, value, rate, charge, figure; = **consequences**, penalty, cost, result, toll ▷ v = **evaluate**, value, estimate, rate, cost

prick v = **pierce**, stab, puncture, punch, lance ▷ n = **puncture**, hole, wound, perforation, pinhole

pride n = **satisfaction**, achievement, fulfilment, delight, content; = **self-respect**, honour, ego, dignity, self-esteem; = **conceit**, vanity, arrogance,

pretension, hubris ≠ **humility**

priest n = **clergyman**, minister, father, divine, vicar

primary adj = **chief**, main, first, highest, greatest ≠ **subordinate**

prime adj = **main**, leading, chief, central, major; = **best**, top, select, highest, quality ▷ n = **peak**, flower, bloom, height, heyday ▷ v = **inform**, tell, train, coach, brief

primitive adj = **early**, first, earliest, original, primary ≠ **modern**; = **crude**, simple, rough, rudimentary, unrefined ≠ **elaborate**

prince n = **ruler**, lord, monarch,

adj **1** generous **2** magnificent
princess *n* female member of royal family

principal ❶ *adj* **1** chief in importance ▷ *n* **2** person for whom another is agent **3** head of institution, esp. school or college **4** sum of money lent and yielding interest **principality** *n* territory of prince

principle ❶ *n* **1** moral rule **2** settled reason of action **3** uprightness **4** fundamental truth

print ❶ *v* **1** reproduce (words, pictures etc.) by pressing inked types on blocks of paper etc. **2** write in imitation of this **3** (*Photog*) produce pictures from negatives **4** stamp (fabric) with design ▷ *n* **5** printed matter **6** photograph **7** impression left by something pressing **8** printed cotton fabric **printer** *n*

prior ❶ *adj* **1** earlier ▷ *n* **2** leader of religious house or order **priority**

n precedence, something given special attention **priory** *n, pl* **-ries** monastery, nunnery under prior, prioress **prior to** before

prise *v* force open by levering

prism *n* transparent solid, usu. with triangular ends and rectangular sides, used to disperse light into spectrum

prison ❶ *n* jail **prisoner** *n* **1** one kept in prison **2** captive

pristine *adj* completely new and pure

private ❶ *adj* **1** secret, not public **2** not general, individual **3** personal **4** secluded **5** denoting soldier of lowest rank ▷ *n* **6** private soldier **privacy** *n* **privatize** *v* transfer (service etc.) from public to private ownership

privation *n* lack of comforts or necessities

privet *n* bushy evergreen shrub used for hedges

privilege *n* right, advantage granted or belonging only to few

P

sovereign, crown prince
principal *adj* = **main**, leading, chief, prime, first ≠ **minor** ▷ *n* = **headmaster** *or* **headmistress**, head (*Inf*), dean, head teacher, rector; = **star**, lead, leader, prima ballerina, leading man *or* lady; = **capital**, money, assets, working capital

principle *n* = **morals**, standards, ideals, honour, virtue; = **rule**, law, truth, precept

print *v* = **run off**, publish, copy, reproduce, issue; = **publish**,

release, circulate, issue, disseminate ▷ *n* = **photograph**, photo, snap; = **picture**, plate, etching, engraving, lithograph; = **copy**, photo (*Inf*), picture, reproduction, replica

prior *adj* = **earlier**, previous, former, preceding, foregoing

prison *n* = **jail**, confinement, nick (*Brit Sl*), cooler (*Sl*), jug (*Sl*)

private *adj* = **exclusive**, individual, privately owned, own, special ≠ **public**; = **secret**, confidential, covert, unofficial, clandestine

privileged *adj* enjoying privilege

privy *adj* **1** admitted to knowledge of secret ▷ *n* **2** lavatory

prize ❶ *n* **1** reward given for success in competition **2** thing striven for **3** thing won, e.g. in lottery etc. ▷ *adj* **4** winning or likely to win prize ▷ *v* **5** value highly

pro¹ *adj/adv* in favour of **pros and cons** arguments for and against

pro² *n* professional

pro- *comb. form* **1** in favour of **2** instead of

probable ❶ *adj* likely **probability** *n, pl* **-ties 1** likelihood **2** anything probable **probably** *adv*

probate *n* **1** proving of authenticity of will **2** certificate of this

probation ❶ *n* **1** system of dealing with lawbreakers by placing them under supervision **2** trial period **probationer** *n* person on probation

probe ❶ *v* **1** search into, examine, question closely ▷ *n* **2** that which probes, or is used to probe **3** thorough inquiry

probity *n* honesty, integrity

problem ❶ *n* **1** matter etc. difficult to deal with or solve **2** question set for solution **problematical** *adj*

proceed ❶ *v* **1** go forward, continue **2** be carried on **3** arise from **4** go to law **procedure** *n* act, manner of proceeding **proceeding** *n* **1** act or course of action ▷ *pl* **2** minutes of meeting **3** legal action **proceeds** *pl n* profit

process ❶ *n* **1** series of actions or changes **2** method of operation **3** state of going on **4** action of law ▷ *v* **5** handle, treat, prepare by special method of manufacture etc. **procession** *n* train of persons in formal order

proclaim ❶ *v* announce publicly, declare **proclamation** *n*

──────── THESAURUS ────────

≠ **public**; = **personal**, individual, secret, intimate, undisclosed

prize *n* = **reward**, cup, award, honour, medal ▷ *adj* = **champion**, best, winning, top, outstanding

probable *adj* = **likely**, possible, apparent, reasonable to think, credible ≠ **unlikely**

probation *n* = **trial period**, trial, apprenticeship

probe *v often with* **into** = **examine**, go into, investigate, explore, search; = **explore**, examine, poke, prod, feel around ▷ *n* = **investigation**, study, inquiry, analysis, examination

problem *n* = **difficulty**, trouble, dispute, plight, obstacle; = **puzzle**, question, riddle, enigma, conundrum

proceed *v* = **begin**, go ahead; = **continue**, go on, progress, carry on, go ahead ≠ **discontinue**

process *n* = **procedure**, means, course, system, action; = **development**, growth, progress, movement, advance ▷ *v* = **handle**, manage, action, deal with, fulfil

proclaim *v* = **announce**, declare, advertise, publish, indicate ≠ **keep**

P

procrastinate v put off, delay
procrastination n

procreate v produce offspring
procreation n

procure v 1 obtain, acquire
2 bring about 3 act as pimp
procurement n **procurer** n
1 one who procures 2 pimp

prod ⊙ v **prodding, prodded**
1 poke ▷ n 2 prodding 3 pointed
instrument

prodigal adj 1 wasteful ▷ n
2 spendthrift

prodigy ⊙ n, pl **-gies** 1 person
with some marvellous gift 2 thing
causing wonder **prodigious** adj
1 very great 2 extraordinary

produce ⊙ v 1 bring into
existence 2 yield 3 bring forward
4 manufacture 5 present on stage,
film, television ▷ n 6 that which is
yielded or made **producer** n
product n 1 thing produced
2 consequence **production** n
1 producing 2 staging of play etc.
productive adj 1 fertile 2 creative

productivity n

profane adj 1 irreverent,
blasphemous 2 not sacred ▷ v
3 treat irreverently **profanity** n/pl
-ties profane talk

profess ⊙ v 1 affirm belief in
2 claim, pretend **profession** n
1 calling or occupation, esp.
learned, scientific or artistic
2 professing **professional** adj
1 engaged in a profession 2 taking
part in sport, music etc. for money
3 skilled ▷ n 4 paid player
professor n teacher of highest
rank in university

proffer v offer

proficient adj 1 skilled 2 expert
proficiency n

profile ⊙ n 1 outline, esp. of face,
as seen from side 2 brief
biographical sketch **profiling** n
practice of categorizing and
predicting the behaviour of people
according to certain characteristics
racial profiling

profit ⊙ n 1 money gained

P

—————— THESAURUS ——————

secret
prod v = **poke**, push, dig, shove,
nudge; = **prompt**, move, urge,
motivate, spur ▷ n = **poke**, push,
dig, shove, nudge; = **prompt**,
signal, cue, reminder, stimulus
prodigy n = **genius**, talent, wizard,
mastermind, whizz (Inf)
produce v = **cause**, effect,
generate, bring about, give rise to;
= **make**, create, develop,
manufacture, construct; = **create**,
develop, write, turn out, compose;
= **yield**, provide, grow, bear, give

▷ n = **fruit and vegetables**, goods,
food, products, crops
profess v = **claim**, allege, pretend,
fake, make out; = **state**, admit,
announce, declare, confess
profile n = **outline**, lines, form,
figure, silhouette; = **biography**,
sketch, vignette, characterization,
thumbnail sketch
profit n often plural = **earnings**,
return, revenue, gain, yield ≠ **loss**;
= **benefit**, good, use, value, gain
≠ **disadvantage** ▷ v = **make
money**, gain, earn; = **benefit**, help,

2 benefit obtained ▷ v 3 benefit
4 earn **profitable** adj **profiteer** n
1 one who makes excessive profits
at public's expense ▷ v 2 profit
thus
profligate adj 1 recklessly
extravagant 2 depraved, immoral
profound ❶ adj 1 very learned
2 deep 3 heartfelt **profundity** n,
pl **-ties**
profuse adj abundant **profusion**
n
progeny n, pl **-nies** children
progenitor n ancestor
prognosis n, pl **-noses** forecast
programme ❶ n 1 plan of
intended proceedings 2 broadcast
on radio or television **program** n
1 instructions for computer ▷ v
2 feed program into (computer)
3 arrange program
progress ❶ n 1 onward
movement 2 sequence ▷ v 3 go
forward 4 improve **progression**
n 1 moving forward

2 improvement **progressive** adj
1 progressing by degrees
2 favouring political or social
reform
prohibit ❶ v forbid **prohibition**
n 1 act of forbidding 2 ban on sale
or drinking of alcohol **prohibitive**
adj 1 tending to forbid or exclude
2 (of cost) too high to be afforded
project ❶ n 1 plan, scheme ▷ v
2 plan 3 throw 4 cause to appear
on distant background 5 stick out
projectile n heavy missile
projection n 1 bulge 2 forecast
projector n apparatus for
projecting photographic images
proletariat n working class
proletarian adj/n
proliferate v grow or reproduce
rapidly **proliferation** n
prolific ❶ adj 1 fruitful
2 producing much
prologue n preface
prolong ❶ v lengthen
promenade n 1 leisurely walk

——————— THESAURUS ———————

serve, gain, promote
profound adj = **sincere**, acute,
intense, great, keen ≠ **insincere**;
= **wise**, learned, deep, penetrating,
philosophical ≠ **uninformed**
programme n = **schedule**, plan,
agenda, timetable, listing;
= **course**, curriculum, syllabus
progress n = **development**,
growth, advance, gain,
improvement ≠ **regression**;
= **movement forward**, passage,
advancement, course, advance
≠ **movement backward** ▷ v
= **move on**, continue, travel,

advance, proceed ≠ **move back**;
= **develop**, improve, advance,
grow, gain ≠ **get behind**
prohibit v = **forbid**, ban, veto,
outlaw, disallow ≠ **permit**;
= **prevent**, restrict, stop, hamper,
hinder ≠ **allow**
project n = **scheme**, plan, job,
idea, campaign ▷ v = **forecast**,
expect, estimate, predict, reckon;
= **stick out**, extend, stand out,
bulge, protrude
prolific adj = **productive**, creative,
fertile, inventive, copious
prolong v = **lengthen**, continue,

2 place made or used for this ▷ *v*
3 take leisurely walk
prominent ❶ *adj* 1 sticking out
2 conspicuous 3 distinguished
prominence *n*
promiscuous *adj* indiscriminate,
esp. in sexual relations
promiscuity *n*
promise ❶ *v* 1 give undertaking
or assurance 2 be likely to ▷ *n*
3 undertaking to do or not to do
something 4 potential **promising**
adj 1 showing good signs, hopeful
2 likely to succeed
promontory *n*, *pl* **-ries** high land
jutting out into sea
promote ❶ *v* 1 help forward
2 move up to higher rank or
position 3 encourage sale of
promoter *n* **promotion** *n*
prompt ❶ *adj* 1 done at once
2 punctual ▷ *adv* 3 punctually ▷ *v*

4 urge, suggest 5 help (actor or
speaker) by suggesting next words
▷ *n* 6 cue, reminder
promulgate *v* proclaim, publish
prone ❶ *adj* 1 lying face
downwards 2 inclined (to)
prong *n* one spike of fork or similar
instrument
pronoun *n* word used to replace
noun
pronounce ❶ *v* 1 utter (formally)
2 give opinion **pronounced** *adj*
strongly marked **pronouncement**
n declaration **pronunciation** *n*
way word etc. is pronounced
proof ❶ *n* 1 evidence 2 thing
which proves 3 test,
demonstration 4 trial impression
from type or engraved plate
5 standard of strength of alcoholic
drink ▷ *adj* 6 giving impenetrable
defence against

THESAURUS
---

perpetuate, draw out, extend
≠ **shorten**
prominent *adj* = **famous**, leading,
top, important, main ≠ **unknown**;
= **noticeable**, obvious,
outstanding, pronounced,
conspicuous ≠ **inconspicuous**
promise *v* = **guarantee**, pledge,
vow, swear, contract; = **seem
likely**, look like, show signs of,
augur, betoken ▷ *n* = **guarantee**,
word, bond, vow, commitment;
= **potential**, ability, talent,
capacity, capability
promote *v* = **help**, back, support,
aid, forward ≠ **impede**;
= **advertise**, sell, hype, publicize,
push; = **raise**, upgrade, elevate,

exalt ≠ **demote**
prompt *v* = **cause**, occasion,
provoke, give rise to, elicit;
= **remind**, assist, cue, help out
▷ *adj* = **immediate**, quick, rapid,
instant, timely ≠ **slow** ▷ *adv* (*Inf*)
= **exactly**, sharp, promptly, on the
dot, punctually
prone *adj* = **liable**, given, subject,
inclined, tending ≠ **disinclined**;
= **face down**, flat, horizontal,
prostrate, recumbent ≠ **face up**
pronounce *v* = **say**, speak, sound,
articulate, enunciate; = **declare**,
announce, deliver, proclaim, decree
proof *n* = **evidence**,
demonstration, testimony,
confirmation, verification ▷ *adj*

P

prop¹ ❶ *n/v* support

prop² *n* object used on set of film, play etc.

propaganda ❶ *n* organized dissemination of information to assist or damage political cause etc.

propagate *v* 1 reproduce, breed 2 spread **propagation** *n*

propel *v* **-pelling, -pelled** cause to move forward **propeller** *n* revolving shaft with blades for driving ship or aircraft **propulsion** *n* act of driving forward

propensity *n, pl* **-ties** 1 inclination 2 tendency

proper ❶ *adj* 1 appropriate 2 correct 3 conforming to etiquette 4 strict 5 (of noun) denoting individual person or place **properly** *adv*

property ❶ *n, pl* **-ties** 1 that which is owned 2 land, real estate 3 quality, attribute

prophet, prophetess ❶ *n* 1 inspired teacher or revealer of God's word 2 foreteller of future **prophecy** *n, pl* **-cies** prediction, prophetic utterance **prophesy** *v* **-sying, -sied** foretell **prophetic** *adj*

proponent *n* one who argues in favour of something

proportion ❶ *n* 1 relative size or number 2 due relation between connected things or parts 3 share ▷ *pl* 4 dimensions ▷ *v* 5 arrange proportions of **proportional, proportionate** *adj* in due proportion

propose ❶ *v* 1 put forward for consideration 2 intend 3 offer marriage **proposal** *n* **proposition** *n* 1 offer 2 statement

propound *v* put forward for consideration

proprietor *n* owner

— THESAURUS —

P

= **impervious**, strong, resistant, impenetrable, repellent

prop¹ *v* = **lean**, place, set, stand, position ▷ *n* = **support**, stay, brace, mainstay, buttress

propaganda *n* = **information**, advertising, promotion, publicity, hype

proper *adj* = **real**, actual, genuine, true, bona fide; = **correct**, accepted, established, appropriate, right ≠ **improper**; = **polite**, right, becoming, seemly, fitting ≠ **unseemly**

property *n* = **possessions**, goods, effects, holdings, capital; = **land**, holding, estate, real estate, freehold; = **quality**, feature, characteristic, attribute, trait

prophet, prophetess *n* = **soothsayer**, forecaster, diviner, oracle, seer

proportion *n* = **part**, share, amount, division, percentage; = **relative amount**, relationship, ratio; = **balance**, harmony, correspondence, symmetry, concord ▷ *pl n* = **dimensions**, size, volume, capacity, extent

propose *v* = **put forward**, present, suggest, advance, submit; = **intend**, mean, plan, aim, design; = **nominate**, name, present,

propriety n, pl **-ties** properness, correct conduct

propulsion see PROPEL

prosaic adj commonplace, unromantic

proscribe v outlaw, condemn

prose n speech or writing not in verse

prosecute ❶ v carry on, bring legal proceedings against
prosecution n **prosecutor** n

prospect ❶ n 1 expectation, chance for success 2 view
prospective adj 1 anticipated 2 future **prospector** n
prospectus n booklet giving details of university, company etc.

prosper ❶ v be successful
prosperity n **prosperous** adj 1 successful 2 well-off

prostate n gland around neck of male bladder

prostitute ❶ n 1 one who offers sexual intercourse in return for payment ▷ v 2 make a prostitute of 3 put to unworthy use
prostitution n

prostrate adj 1 lying flat 2 overcome ▷ v 3 throw flat on ground 4 reduce to exhaustion

protagonist ❶ n 1 leading character in story 2 proponent

protect ❶ v keep from harm
protection n **protective** adj
protector n

protégé n one under another's patronage

protein n any of group of organic compounds which form essential part of food of living creatures

protest ❶ n 1 declaration or demonstration of objection ▷ v 2 object 3 make declaration against 4 assert formally
protestation n strong declaration

Protestant adj 1 relating to Christian church split from R.C. church ▷ n 2 member of Protestant church

protocol ❶ n 1 diplomatic

P

—— THESAURUS ——

recommend; **= offer marriage**, pop the question (Inf), ask for someone's hand (in marriage)

prosecute v (Law) **= take someone to court**, try, sue, indict, arraign

prospect n **= likelihood**, chance, possibility, hope, promise; **= idea**, outlook ▷ pl n **= possibilities**, chances, future, potential, expectations ▷ v **= look**, search, seek, dowse

prosper v **= succeed**, advance, progress, thrive, get on

prostitute n **= whore**, hooker (US

Sl), pro (Sl), tart (Inf), call girl ▷ v **= cheapen**, sell out, pervert, degrade, devalue

protagonist n **= supporter**, champion, advocate, exponent; **= leading character**, principal, central character, hero or heroine

protect v **= keep someone safe**, defend, support, save, guard ≠ endanger

protest v **= object**, demonstrate, oppose, complain, disagree; **= assert**, insist, maintain, declare, affirm ▷ n **= demonstration**, march, rally, sit-in, demo (Inf)

etiquette **2** (*Comp*) set of rules for transfer of data, esp. between different systems

proton *n* positively charged particle in nucleus of atom

prototype ❶ *n* original, model, after which thing is copied

protract *v* **1** lengthen **2** prolong **protractor** *n* instrument for measuring angles

protrude *v* stick out, project **protrusion** *n*

protuberant *adj* bulging out

proud ❶ *adj* **1** pleased, satisfied **2** arrogant, haughty

prove ❶ *v* **proving, proved 1** establish validity of **2** demonstrate, test **3** turn out to be **proven** *adj* proved

proverb *n* short, pithy saying in common use **proverbial** *adj*

provide ❶ *v* **1** make preparation **2** supply, equip **provided that** on

condition that

province ❶ *n* **1** division of country **2** sphere of action ▷ *pl* **3** any part of country outside capital **provincial** *adj* **1** of a province **2** narrow in outlook ▷ *n* **3** unsophisticated person **4** inhabitant of province

provision ❶ *n* **1** providing, esp. for the future **2** thing provided ▷ *pl* **3** food ▷ *v* **4** supply with food **provisional** *adj* temporary

proviso *n, pl* **-sos, -soes** condition

provoke ❶ *v* **1** anger **2** arouse **3** cause **provocation** *n* **provocative** *adj*

prow *n* bow of vessel

prowess ❶ *n* **1** bravery **2** skill

prowl *v* **1** roam stealthily, esp. in search of prey or booty ▷ *n* **2** prowling **prowler** *n*

proximity ❶ *n* nearness

———————————— THESAURUS ————————————

p

protocol *n* = **code of behaviour**, manners, conventions, customs, etiquette

prototype *n* = **original**, model, first, example, standard

proud *adj* = **satisfied**, pleased, content, thrilled, glad ≠ **dissatisfied**; = **conceited**, arrogant, lordly, imperious, overbearing ≠ **humble**

prove *v* = **turn out**, come out, end up; = **verify**, establish, determine, show, confirm ≠ **disprove**

provide *v* = **supply**, give, distribute, outfit, equip ≠ **withhold**; = **give**, bring, add, produce, present

province *n* = **region**, section, district, zone, patch; = **area**, business, concern, responsibility, line

provision *n* = **supplying**, giving, providing, supply, delivery; = **condition**, term, requirement, demand, rider

provoke *v* = **anger**, annoy, irritate, infuriate, hassle (*Inf*) ≠ **pacify**; = **rouse**, cause, produce, promote, occasion ≠ **curb**

prowess *n* = **skill**, ability, talent, expertise, genius ≠ **inability**; = **bravery**, daring, courage, heroism, mettle ≠ **cowardice**

proximity *n* = **nearness**,

proxy ❶ *n, pl* **proxies**
  1 authorized agent or substitute
  2 writing authorizing one to act as
  this
prude *n* one who is excessively
  modest or proper **prudish** *adj*
prudent ❶ *adj* **1** careful, discreet
  2 sensible **3** thrifty **prudence** *n*
prune¹ *n* dried plum
prune² ❶ *v* **1** cut out dead parts,
  excessive branches etc. **2** shorten,
  reduce
pry *v* **prying, pried** make furtive
  or impertinent inquiries
PS postscript
psalm *n* sacred song
pseudo- *comb. form* false
pseudonym *n* **1** false, fictitious
  name **2** pen name
psychic ❶ *adj* **1** of soul or mind
  2 sensitive to phenomena lying
  outside range of normal experience
  psychiatric *adj* of psychiatry
  psychiatrist *n* **psychiatry** *n*
  medical treatment of mental
  diseases **psychoanalysis** *n*
  method of studying and treating
  mental disorders **psychoanalyse**

v **psychoanalyst** *n*
psychological *adj* **1** of psychology
  2 of the mind **psychologist** *n*
psychology *n* **1** study of mind
  2 (*Inf*) person's mental make-up
psychopath *n* person afflicted
  with severe mental disorder
psychopathic *adj* **psychosis** *n*
  severe mental disorder
psychosomatic *adj* (of a physical
  disorder) thought to have
  psychological causes
psychotherapy *n* treatment of
  disease by psychological, not
  physical, means
PTO please turn over
pub ❶ *n* public house, building with
  bar and licence to sell alcoholic
  drinks
puberty *n* sexual maturity
pubic *adj* of the lower abdomen
public ❶ *adj* **1** of or concerning the
  community as a whole **2** not
  private ▷ *n* **3** the community or its
  members **publican** *n* keeper of
  public house **public house** see
  PUB **public school** (*Brit*) private
  fee-paying school

P

——————— THESAURUS ———————

closeness
proxy *n* = **representative**, agent,
  deputy, substitute, factor
prudent *adj* = **cautious**, careful,
  wary, discreet, vigilant ≠ **careless**;
  = **wise**, politic, sensible, shrewd,
  discerning ≠ **unwise**; = **thrifty**,
  economical, sparing, careful, canny
  ≠ **extravagant**
prune² *v* = **cut**, trim, clip, dock,
  shape; = **reduce**, cut, cut back,
  trim, cut down

psychic *adj* = **supernatural**,
  mystic, occult; = **mystical**,
  spiritual, magical, other-worldly,
  paranormal
pub, public house *n* = **tavern**,
  bar, inn, saloon
public *n* = **people**, society,
  community, nation, everyone ▷ *adj*
  = **civic**, government, state,
  national, local; = **general**, popular,
  national, shared, common; = **open**,
  accessible, communal, unrestricted

publicity ❶ *n* **1** process of attracting public attention **2** attention thus gained **publicize** *v* advertise

publish ❶ *v* **1** prepare and issue for sale (books, music etc.) **2** make generally known **3** proclaim **publication** *n* **publisher** *n*

puck *n* rubber disc used instead of ball in ice hockey

pucker *v* **1** gather into wrinkles ▷ *n* **2** crease, fold

pudding ❶ *n* **1** sweet, cooked dessert, often made from suet, flour etc. **2** sweet course of meal **3** soft savoury dish with pastry or batter **4** kind of sausage

puddle *n* small muddy pool

puerile *adj* childish

puff ❶ *n* **1** short blast of breath, wind etc. **2** type of pastry **3** laudatory notice or advertisement ▷ *v* **4** blow abruptly **5** breathe hard **6** send out in a puff **7** inflate **8** advertise **9** smoke hard **puffy** *adj* swollen

puffin *n* sea bird with large brightly-coloured beak

pug *n* small snub-nosed dog

pugnacious *adj* given to fighting **pugnacity** *n*

pull ❶ *v* **1** exert force on object to move it towards source of force **2** remove **3** strain or stretch **4** attract ▷ *n* **5** act of pulling **6** force exerted by this **7** (*Inf*) influence

pulley *n* wheel with groove in rim for cord, used to raise weights

pullover *n* jersey, sweater without fastening, to be pulled over head

pulmonary *adj* of lungs

pulp ❶ *n* **1** soft, moist, vegetable or animal matter **2** flesh of fruit **3** any soft soggy mass ▷ *v* **4** reduce to pulp

pulpit *n* (enclosed) platform for preacher

pulse¹ ❶ *n* **1** movement of blood in arteries corresponding to heartbeat, discernible to touch, e.g. in wrist **2** any regular beat or vibration **pulsate** *v* throb, quiver,

───────── THESAURUS ─────────

≠ **private**; = **well-known**, leading, important, respected, famous

publicity *n* = **advertising**, press, promotion, hype, boost

publish *v* = **put out**, issue, produce, print; = **announce**, reveal, spread, advertise, broadcast

pudding *n* = **dessert**, afters (*Brit Inf*), sweet, pud (*Inf*)

puff *v* = **smoke**, draw, drag (*Sl*), suck, inhale; = **breathe heavily**, pant, exhale, blow, gasp ▷ *n* = **drag**, pull (*Sl*), smoke; = **blast**, breath, whiff, draught, gust

pull *v* = **draw**, haul, drag, trail, tow ≠ **push**; = **extract**, pick, remove, gather, take out ≠ **insert**; (*Inf*) = **attract**, draw, bring in, tempt, lure ≠ **repel**; = **strain**, tear, stretch, rip, wrench ▷ *n* = **tug**, jerk, yank, twitch, heave ≠ **shove**; = **puff**, drag (*Sl*), inhalation; (*Inf*) = **influence**, power, weight, muscle, clout (*Inf*)

pulp *n* = **paste**, mash, mush; = **flesh**, meat, soft part ▷ *v* = **crush**, squash, mash, pulverize

pulse¹ *n* = **beat**, rhythm, vibration, beating, throb

vibrate **pulsation** n

pulse² n edible seed of pod-bearing plant

pulverize v reduce to powder

puma n large Amer. feline carnivore, cougar

pumice n light porous variety of lava

pummel v **-melling, -melled** strike repeatedly

pump¹ ❶ n **1** appliance for raising water, or putting in or taking out air or liquid etc. ▷ v **2** raise, put in, take out etc. with pump **3** work like pump

pump² n light shoe

pumpkin n edible gourd

pun n **1** play on words ▷ v **2** make pun

punch¹ ❶ n **1** tool for perforating or stamping **2** blow with fists **3** (Inf) vigour ▷ v **4** stamp, perforate with punch **5** strike with fist

punch² n drink of spirits or wine with fruit juice etc.

punctilious adj **1** making much of details of etiquette **2** very exact, particular

punctual adj in good time, not late **punctuality** n

punctuate ❶ v **1** put in punctuation marks **2** interrupt at intervals **punctuation** n marks put in writing to assist in making sense clear

puncture ❶ n **1** small hole made by sharp object, esp. in tyre ▷ v **2** prick hole in, perforate

pundit n expert who speaks publicly on subject

pungent adj acrid, bitter

punish ❶ v **1** cause to suffer for offence **2** inflict penalty on **3** use or treat roughly **punishable** adj **punishing** adj harsh, difficult **punishment** n **punitive** adj inflicting or intending to inflict punishment

punnet n small basket for fruit

punter ❶ n **1** person who bets **2** member of public

puny adj **-nier, -niest** small and feeble

pup n young of certain animals, e.g. dog, seal

pupa n, pl **-pae, -pas** stage

pump¹ v = **supply**, send, pour, inject; = **interrogate**, probe, quiz, cross-examine; = **fire**, shoot, discharge, let off

punch¹ v = **hit**, strike, box, smash, belt (Inf) ▷ n = **blow**, hit, sock (Sl), jab, swipe (Inf); (Inf); = **effectiveness**, bite, impact, drive, vigour

punctuate v = **interrupt**, break, pepper, sprinkle, intersperse

puncture n = **flat tyre**, flat; = **hole**, opening, break, cut, nick ▷ v = **pierce**, cut, nick, penetrate, prick

punish v = **discipline**, correct, castigate, chastise, sentence

punitive adj = **retaliatory**, in reprisal, retaliative

punter n = **gambler**, better, backer; (Inf) = **person**, man in the street

between larva and adult in
metamorphosis of insect

pupil ❶ n **1** person being taught
2 opening in iris of eye

puppet ❶ n **1** small doll controlled
by operator's hand **2** (Fig) stooge,
pawn

puppy n, pl **-pies** young dog

purchase ❶ v **1** buy ▷ n **2** buying
3 what is bought **4** leverage, grip

pure ❶ adj **1** unmixed, untainted
2 simple **3** faultless **4** innocent
5 concerned with theory only
purely adv **purification** n **purify**
v **-fying, -fied** make, become
pure, clear or clean **purist** n
person obsessed with strict
obedience to tradition **purity** n
state of being pure

purée n **1** pulp of cooked fruit or
vegetables ▷ v **2** reduce to pulp

purgatory n place or state of
torment, pain or distress, esp. one

that is temporary

purge ❶ v **1** make clean, purify
2 remove, get rid of **3** clear out ▷ n
4 act, process of purging
purgative adj/n

purl n **1** stitch that forms ridge in
knitting ▷ v **2** knit in purl

purloin v **1** steal **2** pilfer

purple n/adj (of) colour between
crimson and violet

purport ❶ v **1** claim to be (true
etc.) **2** signify, imply ▷ n
3 meaning **4** apparent meaning

purpose ❶ n **1** reason, object
2 design **3** aim, intention
4 determination ▷ v **5** intend **on
purpose** intentionally **purposely**
adv

purr n **1** pleased noise which cat
makes ▷ v **2** utter this

purse ❶ n **1** small bag for money
2 resources **3** money as prize
4 (US & Canad) handbag ▷ v

— THESAURUS —

P

pupil n = **student**, schoolboy or
schoolgirl, schoolchild ≠ **teacher**

puppet n = **marionette**, doll,
glove puppet, finger puppet;
= **pawn**, tool, instrument,
mouthpiece, stooge

purchase v = **buy**, pay for, obtain,
get, score (Sl) ≠ **sell** ▷ n
= **acquisition**, buy, investment,
property, gain; = **grip**, hold,
support, leverage, foothold

pure adj = **unmixed**, real, simple,
natural, straight ≠ **adulterated**;
= **clean**, wholesome, sanitary,
spotless, sterilized
≠ **contaminated**; = **complete**,
total, perfect, absolute, sheer

≠ **qualified**; = **innocent**, modest,
good, moral, impeccable
≠ **corrupt**

purge v = **rid**, clear, cleanse, strip,
empty ▷ n = **removal**, elimination,
expulsion, eradication, ejection

purport v = **claim**, allege, assert,
profess

purpose n = **reason**, point, idea,
aim, object; = **aim**, end, plan, hope,
goal; = **determination**, resolve,
will, resolution, ambition

purse n = **pouch**, wallet,
money-bag; (US) = **handbag**, bag,
shoulder bag, pocket book, clutch
bag ▷ v = **pucker**, contract,
tighten, pout, press together

5 pucker **purser** *n* ship's officer who keeps accounts

pursue ① *v* 1 chase 2 engage in 3 continue **pursuer** *n* **pursuit** *n* 1 pursuing 2 occupation

purvey *v* supply (provisions)

pus *n* yellowish matter produced by suppuration

push ① *v* 1 move, try to move away by pressure 2 drive or impel 3 make thrust 4 advance with steady effort ▷ *n* 5 thrust 6 persevering self-assertion 7 big military advance **pusher** *n* seller of illegal drugs **pushy** *adj* assertive, ambitious **pushchair** *n* collapsible chair-shaped carriage for baby

puss, pussy *n, pl* **pusses, pussies pussy** cat

pustule *n* pimple containing pus

put ① *v* **putting, put** 1 place 2 set 3 express 4 throw (esp. shot) ▷ *n* 5 throw **put off** 1 postpone 2 disconcert 3 repel **put up** 1 erect 2 accommodate

putrid *adj* 1 decomposed 2 rotten **putrefy** *v* **-fying, -fied** make or become rotten

putt *v* strike (golf ball) along ground **putter** *n* golf club for putting

putty *n* paste used by glaziers

puzzle ① *v* 1 perplex or be perplexed ▷ *n* 2 bewildering, perplexing question, problem or toy

PVC polyvinyl chloride

pygmy *n* 1 abnormally undersized person 2 *(with cap.)* member of one of dwarf peoples of Equatorial Africa ▷ *adj* 3 very small

pyjamas *pl n* sleeping suit of trousers and jacket

pylon *n* tower-like erection, esp. to carry electric cables

pyramid *n* solid figure or structure with sloping sides meeting at apex, esp. in ancient Egypt

pyre *n* pile of wood for burning dead body

pyromania *n* urge to set things on fire **pyromaniac** *n*

pyrotechnics *n* manufacture, display of fireworks

python *n* large nonpoisonous snake that crushes its prey

P

—————— THESAURUS ——————

pursue *v* = **engage in**, perform, conduct, carry on, practise; = **try for**, seek, desire, search for, aim for; = **continue**, maintain, carry on, keep on, persist in; = **follow**, track, hunt, chase, dog ≠ **flee**

push *v* = **shove**, force, press, thrust, drive ≠ **pull**; = **press**, operate, depress, squeeze, activate

▷ *n* = **shove**, thrust, butt, elbow, nudge ≠ **pull**; *(Inf)* = **drive**, go *(Inf)*, energy, initiative, enterprise

put *v* = **place**, leave, set, position, rest; = **express**, state, word, phrase, utter

puzzle *v* = **perplex**, confuse, baffle, stump, bewilder ▷ *n* = **problem**, riddle, question, conundrum, poser

q

QC (Brit) Queen's Counsel
QLD Queensland
quack n 1 harsh cry of duck
2 pretender to medical or other skill
▷ v 3 (of duck) utter cry
quadrangle n 1 four-sided figure
2 four-sided courtyard in a building
quadrant n quarter of circle
quadrilateral adj/n four-sided
(figure)
quadruped n four-footed animal
quadruple adj 1 fourfold ▷ v
2 make, become four times as
much
quadruplet n one of four
offspring born at one birth
quaff v drink heartily or in one
draught
quagmire n bog, swamp
quail¹ n small bird belonging to
partridge family
quail² v 1 flinch 2 cower
quaint adj 1 interestingly
old-fashioned or odd
2 curious
quake ❶ v shake, tremble
qualify ❶ v -fying, -fied 1 make
(oneself) competent 2 moderate
3 ascribe quality to **qualification**
n 1 skill needed for activity
2 modifying or limiting condition
qualified adj 1 fully trained
2 conditional, restricted
quality ❶ n, pl -ties 1 attribute
2 (degree of) excellence
qualm n 1 misgiving 2 sudden
feeling of sickness
quandary n, pl -ries state of
perplexity, dilemma
quango n, pl -gos partly
independent official body, set up by
government
quantify v -fying, -fied discover
or express the quantity of
quantity ❶ n, pl -ties (specified
or considerable) amount
quantitative easing n practice
of increasing the supply of money in
order to stimulate economic
activity
quarantine n/v (place in)
isolation to prevent spreading of
infection

— THESAURUS —

quake v = **shake**, tremble, quiver,
move, rock
qualify v = **certify**, equip,
empower, train, prepare
≠ **disqualify**; = **restrict**, limit,
reduce, ease, moderate
quality n = **standard**, standing,
class, condition, rank;
= **excellence**, status, merit,
position, value; = **characteristic**,
feature, attribute, point, side
quantity n = **amount**, lot, total,
sum, part; = **size**, measure, mass,
volume, length

quarrel ⊕ n 1 angry dispute 2 argument ▷ v 3 argue 4 find fault with **quarrelsome** adj

quarry¹ ⊕ n 1 object of hunt or pursuit 2 prey

quarry² n 1 excavation where stone etc. is dug for building etc. ▷ v 2 get from quarry

quart n liquid measure, quarter of gallon

quarter ⊕ n 1 fourth part 2 region, district 3 mercy ▷ pl 4 lodgings ▷ v 5 divide into quarters 6 lodge **quarterly** adj happening, due etc. each quarter of year **quartermaster** n officer responsible for stores

quartet n (music for) group of four musicians

quartz n hard glossy mineral

quash ⊕ v 1 annul 2 reject

quasi- comb. form not really, as in quasi-religious

quaver v 1 say or sing in quavering tones 2 tremble, shake, vibrate

▷ n 3 musical note half length of crotchet

quay n 1 solid, fixed landing stage 2 wharf

queasy adj -sier, -siest inclined to, or causing, sickness

queen ⊕ n 1 female sovereign 2 king's wife 3 piece in chess 4 fertile female bee, wasp etc. 5 court card

queer ⊕ adj odd, strange

quell v 1 crush, put down 2 allay

quench v 1 slake 2 extinguish

querulous adj peevish, whining

query ⊕ n/v, pl -ries question

quest ⊕ n/v search

question ⊕ n 1 sentence seeking for answer 2 problem 3 point at issue 4 doubt ▷ v 5 ask questions of 6 dispute 7 doubt **questionable** adj doubtful **questionnaire** n formal list of questions **question mark** punctuation mark (?) written at end of questions

---

THESAURUS

quarrel n = **disagreement**, fight, row, argument, dispute ≠ **accord** ▷ v = **disagree**, fight, argue, row, clash ≠ **get on** or **along (with)**

quarry¹ n = **prey**, victim, game, goal, aim

quarter n = **district**, region, neighbourhood, place, part; = **mercy**, pity, compassion, charity, sympathy ▷ v = **accommodate**, house, lodge, place, board

quash v = **annul**, overturn, reverse, cancel, overthrow; = **suppress**, crush, put down, beat, overthrow

queen n = **sovereign**, ruler,

monarch, leader, Crown; = **leading light**, star, favourite, celebrity, darling

queer adj = **strange**, odd, funny, unusual, extraordinary ≠ **normal**; = **faint**, dizzy, giddy, queasy, light-headed

query n = **question**, inquiry, problem ▷ v = **question**, challenge, doubt, suspect, dispute

quest n = **search**, hunt, mission, enterprise, crusade

question n = **inquiry**, enquiry, query, investigation, examination ≠ **answer**; = **difficulty**, problem,

q

queue ❶ n **1** line of waiting persons, vehicles ▷ v **2** wait in queue

quibble n/v (make) trivial objection

quiche n savoury flan

quick ❶ adj **1** fast **2** lively **3** hasty ▷ n **4** sensitive flesh ▷ adv **5** rapidly **quicken** v make, become faster or more lively **quickly** adj **quicksand** n loose wet sand that engulfs heavy objects **quicksilver** n mercury **quickstep** n fast ballroom dance

quiet ❶ adj **1** with little noise **2** undisturbed **3** not showy or obtrusive ▷ n **4** quietness ▷ v **5** make, become quiet **quieten** v

quiff n tuft of brushed-up hair

quill n **1** large feather **2** pen made from feather **3** spine of porcupine

quilt ❶ n **1** padded coverlet ▷ v **2** stitch (two pieces of cloth) with pad between

quinine n drug used to treat fever and as tonic

quintessence n most perfect representation of a quality **quintessential** adj

quintet n (music for) group of five musicians

quintuplet n one of five offspring born at one birth

quip ❶ n/v (utter) witty saying

quirk n **1** individual peculiarity of character **2** unexpected twist

quit ❶ v **quitting, quit 1** stop doing (something) **2** leave **3** give up

quite ❶ adv **1** completely **2** somewhat ▷ interj **3** expression of agreement

quiver¹ v/n shake, tremble

quiver² n case for arrows

——————— THESAURUS ———————

doubt, argument, dispute ▷ v = **interrogate**, cross-examine, interview, examine, probe; = **dispute**, challenge, doubt, suspect, oppose ≠ **accept**

queue n = **line**, row, file, train, series

quick adj = **fast**, swift, speedy, express, cracking (Brit Inf) ≠ **slow**; = **brief**, passing, hurried, flying, fleeting ≠ **long**; = **immediate**, instant, prompt, sudden, abrupt; = **excitable**, passionate, irritable, touchy, irascible ≠ **calm**

quiet adj = **soft**, low, muted, lowered, whispered ≠ **loud**; = **peaceful**, silent, hushed, soundless, noiseless ≠ **noisy**;

= **calm**, peaceful, tranquil, mild, serene ≠ **exciting** ▷ n = **peace**, rest, tranquillity, ease, silence ≠ **noise**

quilt n = **bedspread**, duvet, coverlet, eiderdown, counterpane

quip n = **joke**, sally, jest, riposte, wisecrack (Inf)

quit v = **resign (from)**, leave, retire (from), pull out (of), step down (from) (Inf); = **stop**, give up, cease, end, drop ≠ **continue**; = **leave**, depart from, go out of, go away from, pull out from

quite adv = **somewhat**, rather, fairly, reasonably, relatively; = **absolutely**, perfectly, completely, totally, fully

q

quiz ❶ *n, pl* **quizzes**
  1 entertainment in which
  knowledge of players is tested by
  questions **2** examination,
  interrogation ▷ *v* **3** question,
  interrogate **quizzical** *adj*
  1 questioning **2** mocking
quoit *n* **1** ring for throwing at peg
  as a game ▷ *pl* **2** this game

quorum *n* least number that must
  be present to make meeting valid
  quorate *adj*
quota ❶ *n* share to be contributed
  or received
quote ❶ *v* **1** repeat passages from
  2 state price for **quotation** *n*
quotient *n* number resulting from
  dividing one number by another

—————— THESAURUS ——————

quiz *n* = **examination**,
questioning, interrogation,
interview, investigation ▷ *v*
= **question**, ask, interrogate,

examine, investigate
quota *n* = **share**, allowance,
ration, part, limit
quote *v* = **repeat**, recite, recall

q

r

R 1 King 2 Queen 3 river

rabbi *n, pl* **-bis** Jewish learned man, spiritual leader

rabbit *n* small burrowing mammal

rabble *n* crowd of vulgar, noisy people

rabid *adj* 1 of, having rabies 2 fanatical

rabies *n* infectious disease transmitted by dogs etc.

raccoon *n* small N Amer. mammal

race¹ ❶ *n* 1 contest of speed 2 rivalry 3 strong current ▷ *pl* 4 meeting for horse racing ▷ *v* 5 (cause to) run, move swiftly **racer** *n*

race² *n* 1 group of people of common ancestry with distinguishing physical features 2 species **racial** *adj* **racism, racialism** *n* 1 belief in superiority of particular race 2 antagonism towards members of different race based on this **racist, racialist** *adj/n*

rack ❶ *n* 1 framework for displaying or holding things 2 instrument of torture ▷ *v* 3 torture

racket¹ ❶ *n* 1 uproar 2 occupation by which money is made illegally **racketeer** *n*

racket², racquet *n* 1 bat used in tennis etc. ▷ *pl* 2 ball game

raconteur *n* skilled storyteller

racy *adj* **racier, raciest** 1 lively 2 piquant

radar *n* device for locating objects by radio waves, which reflect back to their source

radial see RADIUS

radiate ❶ *v* 1 emit, be emitted in rays 2 spread out from centre **radiance** *n* 1 brightness 2 splendour **radiation** *n* 1 transmission of heat, light etc. from one body to another 2 particles, rays emitted in nuclear decay **radiator** *n* 1 heating apparatus for rooms 2 cooling

— THESAURUS —

race¹ *n* = **competition**, contest, chase, dash, pursuit; = **contest**, competition, rivalry ▷ *v* = **compete against**, run against; = **compete**, run, contend, take part in a race

rack *n* = **frame**, stand, structure, framework ▷ *v* = **torture**, torment, afflict, oppress, harrow

racket¹ *n* = **noise**, row, fuss, disturbance, outcry; = **fraud**, scheme

radiate *v* = **emit**, spread, send out, pour, shed; = **show**, display, demonstrate, exhibit, emanate

apparatus of car engine

radical ❶ adj **1** fundamental **2** extreme **3** of root ▷ n **4** person of extreme (political) views

radio n, pl **-dios 1** use of electromagnetic waves for broadcasting, communication etc. **2** device for receiving, amplifying radio signals **3** broadcasting of radio programmes ▷ v **4** transmit message etc. by radio

radioactive adj emitting invisible rays that penetrate matter **radioactivity** n

radiography n production of image on film by radiation

radiology n science of use of rays in medicine

radiotherapy n diagnosis and treatment of disease by X-rays

radish n pungent root vegetable

radium n radioactive metallic element

radius n, pl **radii, radiuses** straight line from centre to circumference of circle **radial** adj

RAF Royal Air Force

raffia n prepared palm fibre for making mats etc.

raffle n **1** lottery in which article is won by one of those buying tickets ▷ v **2** dispose of by raffle

raft n floating structure of logs, planks etc.

rafter n main beam of roof

rag n **1** fragment of cloth **2** torn piece ▷ pl **3** tattered clothing **ragged** adj **ragtime** n style of jazz piano music

ragamuffin n ragged, dirty person, esp. child

rage ❶ n **1** violent anger **2** fury ▷ v **3** speak, act with fury **4** proceed violently, as storm

raglan adj (of sleeve) continuing in one piece to the neck

raid ❶ n **1** attack **2** foray ▷ v **3** make raid on

rail¹ n horizontal bar **railing** n fence, barrier made of rails supported by posts **railway** n track of iron rails on which trains run

rail² v **1** utter abuse **2** scold

rain ❶ n **1** moisture falling in drops from clouds ▷ v **2** pour down as, like rain **rainy** adj

rainbow n arch of colours in sky

rainforest n dense forest in tropics

r

radical adj = **extreme**, complete, entire, sweeping, severe; = **revolutionary**, extremist, fanatical; = **fundamental**, natural, basic, profound, innate ≠ **superficial** ▷ n = **extremist**, revolutionary, militant, fanatic ≠ **conservative**

rage n = **fury**, temper, frenzy, rampage, tantrum ≠ **calmness** ▷ v

= **be furious**, blow up (Inf), fume, lose it (Inf), seethe ≠ **stay calm**

raid v = **steal from**, plunder, pillage, sack ▷ n = **attack**, invasion, foray, sortie, incursion

rain n = **rainfall**, fall, showers, deluge, drizzle ▷ v = **pour**, pelt (down), teem, bucket down (Inf), drizzle; = **fall**, shower, be dropped, sprinkle, be deposited

raise ❶ v 1 lift up 2 set up 3 build 4 increase 5 heighten, as voice 6 breed 7 collect 8 propose, suggest ▷ n (US & Canad) pay rise

raisin n dried grape

rake¹ ❶ n 1 tool with long handle and teeth for gathering leaves etc. ▷ v 2 gather, smooth with rake 3 search over 4 sweep with shot

rake² ❶ n dissolute man

rakish adj 1 dashing 2 speedy

rally ❶ v, pl **-lies** 1 bring together, esp. what has been scattered 2 come together 3 regain health or strength ▷ n 4 assembly, esp. outdoor 5 (Tennis) lively exchange of strokes

ram ❶ n 1 male sheep 2 hydraulic machine 3 battering engine ▷ v 4 force, drive 5 strike against with force 6 stuff

ramble ❶ v 1 walk without definite route 2 talk incoherently ▷ n 3 rambling walk

ramp ❶ n gradual slope joining two level surfaces

rampage ❶ v 1 dash about violently ▷ n 2 angry or destructive behaviour

rampant ❶ adj 1 violent 2 rife 3 rearing

rampart n wall for defence

ramshackle adj rickety

ran past tense of RUN

ranch n Amer. cattle farm

rancid adj smelling or tasting offensively, like stale fat

rancour n bitter hate

random ❶ adj by chance, without plan

——————————— THESAURUS ———————————

raise v = **lift**, elevate, uplift, heave; = **set upright**, lift, elevate; = **increase**, intensify, heighten, advance, boost ≠ **reduce**; = **make louder**, heighten, amplify, louden; = **collect**, gather, obtain, form, mass; = **cause**, start, produce, create, occasion; = **put forward**, suggest, introduce, advance, broach

rake¹ v = **gather**, collect, remove; = **search**, comb, scour, scrutinize

rake² n = **libertine**, playboy, swinger (Sl), lecher, roué ≠ **puritan**

rally n = **gathering**, convention, meeting, congress, assembly; = **recovery**, improvement, revival, recuperation ≠ **relapse** unite ▷ v = **recover**, improve, revive, get

better, recuperate ≠ **get worse**

ram v = **hit**, force, drive into, crash, impact; = **cram**, force, stuff, jam, thrust

ramble n = **walk**, tour, stroll, hike, roaming ▷ v = **walk**, range, wander, stroll, stray; often with **on** = **babble**, rabbit (on) (Brit Inf), waffle (Inf, chiefly Brit), witter on (Inf)

ramp n = **slope**, incline, gradient, rise

rampage v = **go berserk**, storm, rage, run riot, run amok

rampant adj = **widespread**, prevalent, rife, uncontrolled, unchecked; (Heraldry) = **upright**, standing, rearing, erect

random adj = **chance**, casual,

DICTIONARY

randy 🟊 *adj* **randier, randiest**
(*Sl*) sexually aroused

rang past tense of RING²

range 🟊 *n* **1** limits **2** row **3** scope,
distance missile can travel **4** place
for shooting practice **5** kitchen
stove ▷ *v* **6** set in row **7** extend
8 roam **9** fluctuate **ranger** *n*
official patrolling park etc. **rangy**
adj with long, slender limbs

rank¹ 🟊 *n* **1** row, line **2** place
where taxis wait **3** order **4** status
5 relative position ▷ *pl* **6** (also *pl*)
common soldiers **7** great mass of
people ▷ *v* **8** draw up in rank
9 have rank, place

rank² 🟊 *adj* **1** growing too thickly
2 rancid **3** flagrant

rankle *v* continue to cause anger or
bitterness

ransack *v* **1** search thoroughly
2 pillage

ransom 🟊 *n* **1** release from
captivity by payment **2** amount
paid ▷ *v* **3** pay ransom for

rant 🟊 *v* rave in violent language

rap 🟊 *v* **rapping, rapped 1** give
smart slight blow to **2** utter
abruptly **3** perform monologue to
music ▷ *n* **4** smart slight blow
5 punishment **6** monologue set to
music

rapacious *adj* **1** greedy **2** grasping

rape¹ 🟊 *v* **1** force (woman) to
submit to sexual intercourse ▷ *n*
2 act of raping **rapist** *n*

rape² *n* plant with oil-yielding
seeds

rapid 🟊 *adj* **1** quick, swift ▷ *n*
2 (*esp. pl*) part of river with fast,
turbulent current

rapier *n* fine-bladed sword

rapport *n* harmony, agreement

rapt *adj* engrossed **rapture** *n*
ecstasy

rare¹ 🟊 *adj* **1** uncommon **2** of

THESAURUS

accidental, incidental, haphazard
≠ planned

randy *adj* (*Inf*) **= lustful**, hot,
turned-on (*Sl*), aroused, horny (*Sl*)

range *n* **= series**, variety, selection,
assortment, lot; **= limits**, reach ▷ *v*
= vary, run, reach, extend, stretch;
= roam, wander, rove, ramble,
traverse

rank¹ *n* **= status**, level, position,
grade, order; **= class**, caste; **= row**,
line, file, column, group ▷ *v*
= order, dispose; **= arrange**, sort,
line up, array, align

rank² *adj* **= absolute**, complete,
total, gross, sheer; **= foul**, bad,
offensive, disgusting, revolting;

= abundant, lush, luxuriant, dense,
profuse

ransom *n* **= payment**, money,
price, payoff

rant *v* **= shout**, roar, yell, rave, cry

rap *v* **= hit**, strike, knock, crack, tap
▷ *n* **= blow**, knock, crack, tap, clout
(*Inf*); (*Sl*) **= rebuke**, blame,
responsibility, punishment

rape¹ *v* **= sexually assault**, violate,
abuse, ravish, force ▷ *n* **= sexual
assault**, violation, ravishment,
outrage

rapid *adj* **= sudden**, prompt,
speedy, express, swift **≠ gradual**

rare¹ *adj* **= uncommon**, unusual,
few, strange, scarce **≠ common**;

r

exceptionally high quality **rarely** adv seldom **rarity** n

rare² adj (of meat) lightly cooked

raring ⊙ adj **raring to** enthusiastically willing, ready

rascal n 1 rogue 2 naughty (young) person

rash¹ ⊙ adj hasty, reckless

rash² ⊙ n 1 skin eruption 2 outbreak

rasher n slice of bacon

rasp n 1 harsh, grating noise 2 coarse file ▷ v 3 scrape with rasp 4 make scraping noise 5 irritate

raspberry n 1 red, edible berry 2 plant which bears it

Rastafarian n 1 (oft. shortened to **Rasta**) member of Jamaican cult ▷ adj 2 of this cult

rat n 1 small rodent ▷ v 2 inform (on) 3 betray 4 desert **ratty** adj (Inf) irritable **rat race** continual hectic competitive activity

ratchet n set of teeth on bar or wheel allowing motion in one direction only

rate ⊙ n 1 proportion between two things 2 charge 3 degree of speed etc. ▷ pl 4 local tax on business property ▷ v 5 value

rather ⊙ adv 1 to some extent 2 preferably 3 more willingly

ratify ⊙ v **-fying, -fied** confirm **ratification** n

rating ⊙ n 1 valuing 2 classification 3 sailor

ratio ⊙ n, pl **-tios** 1 proportion 2 relation

ration ⊙ n 1 fixed allowance of food etc. ▷ v 2 supply with, limit to certain amount

rational ⊙ adj reasonable, capable of reasoning **rationale** n reason for decision **rationalize** v 1 justify by plausible reasoning 2 reorganize to improve efficiency etc.

━━━━━━━━ THESAURUS ━━━━━━━━

r

= **superb**, great, fine, excellent, superlative

raring adj (in construction raring to do something) = **eager**, impatient, longing, ready, keen

rash¹ adj = **reckless**, hasty, impulsive, imprudent, careless ≠ **cautious**

rash² n = **outbreak of spots**, (skin) eruption; = **spate**, series, wave, flood, plague

rate n = **speed**, pace, tempo, velocity, frequency; = **degree**, standard, scale, proportion, ratio; = **charge**, price, cost, fee, figure ▷ v = **evaluate**, consider, rank, reckon, value; = **deserve**, merit, be entitled

to, be worthy of

rather adv = **preferably**, sooner, more readily, more willingly; = **to some extent**, quite, a little, fairly, relatively

ratify v = **approve**, establish, confirm, sanction, endorse ≠ **annul**

rating n = **position**, placing, rate, order, class

ratio n = **proportion**, rate, relation, percentage, fraction

ration n = **allowance**, quota, allotment, helping, part ▷ v = **limit**, control, restrict, budget

rational adj = **sensible**, sound, wise, reasonable, intelligent

rattle ❶ v 1 (cause to) give out succession of short sharp sounds ▷ n 2 such sound 3 instrument for making it 4 set of horny rings in rattlesnake's tail **rattlesnake** n poisonous snake

raucous adj hoarse

raunchy adj **-chier, -chiest** (Sl) earthy, sexy

ravage ❶ v 1 plunder ▷ n 2 destruction

rave ❶ v 1 talk wildly in delirium or enthusiasm ▷ n 2 wild talk 3 large-scale party with electronic music **raving** adj 1 delirious 2 (Inf) exceptional

raven n 1 black bird ▷ adj 2 jet-black

ravenous adj very hungry

ravine n narrow steep-sided valley

ravioli pl n small squares of pasta with filling

ravish v 1 enrapture 2 rape **ravishing** adj lovely

raw ❶ adj 1 uncooked 2 not

manufactured or refined 3 skinned 4 inexperienced 5 chilly

ray¹ ❶ n 1 narrow beam of light, heat etc. 2 any of set of radiating lines

ray² n marine flatfish

rayon n synthetic fibre

raze v destroy completely

razor n sharp instrument for shaving

razzle-dazzle, razzmatazz n showy activity

RC Roman Catholic

re ❶ prep concerning

RE religious education

re- comb. form again

reach ❶ v 1 arrive at 2 extend 3 touch ▷ n 4 act of reaching 5 grasp 6 range

react ❶ v act in return, opposition or towards former state **reaction** n 1 counter or backward tendency 2 response 3 chemical or nuclear change **reactionary** n/adj (person) opposed to change, esp. in

---

THESAURUS

rattle v = **clatter**, bang, jangle; = **shake**, jolt, vibrate, bounce, jar; (Inf) = **fluster**, shake, upset, disturb, disconcert

ravage v = **destroy**, ruin, devastate, spoil, demolish

rave v = **rant**, rage, roar, go mad (Inf), babble; (Inf) = **enthuse**, praise, gush, be mad about (Inf), be wild about (Inf)

raw adj = **unrefined**, natural, crude, unprocessed, basic ≠ **refined**; = **uncooked**, natural, fresh ≠ **cooked**; = **inexperienced**, new, green, immature, callow

≠ **experienced**; = **chilly**, biting, cold, freezing, bitter

ray¹ n = **beam**, bar, flash, shaft, gleam

re prep = **concerning**, about, regarding, with regard to, with reference to

reach v = **arrive at**, get to, make, attain; = **attain**, get to; = **touch**, grasp, extend to, stretch to, contact ▷ n = **grasp**, range, distance, stretch, capacity; = **jurisdiction**, power, influence

react v = **respond**, act, proceed, behave

r

politics etc. **reactive** *adj*
chemically active **reactor** *n*
apparatus to produce nuclear
energy

read ❶ *v* **reading, read**
1 understand written matter
2 learn by reading **3** read and utter
4 study **5** understand any
indicating instrument **reader** *n*
1 one who reads **2** university
lecturer **3** school textbook
reading *n*

ready ❶ *adj* **readier, readiest**
1 prepared for action **2** willing
readiness *n*

real ❶ *adj* **1** happening **2** actual
3 genuine **realism** *n* regarding
things as they are **realist** *n*
realistic *adj* **reality** *n* real
existence **really** *adv* **real estate**
landed property

realize ❶ *v* **1** grasp significance of

2 make real **3** convert into money

realm ❶ *n* kingdom

realtor *n* *(US & Canad)* agent, esp.
accredited one who sells houses,
etc. for others

ream *n* **1** twenty quires of paper
▷ *pl* **2** *(Inf)* large quantity of written
matter

reap ❶ *v* cut and gather harvest

rear¹ ❶ *n* back part **rear admiral**
high-ranking naval officer

rear² ❶ *v* **1** care for and educate
(children) **2** breed **3** rise on hind
feet

reason ❶ *n* **1** motive **2** ability to
think **3** sanity **4** sensible thought
▷ *v* **5** think logically **6** persuade by
logical argument **reasonable** *adj*
1 sensible **2** suitable **3** logical

reassure ❶ *v* restore confidence to

rebate ❶ *n* discount, refund

rebel ❶ *v* **-belling, -belled 1** resist

————————————— THESAURUS —————————————

read *v* = **scan**, study, look at, pore
over, peruse; = **understand**,
interpret, comprehend, construe,
decipher; = **register**, show, record,
display, indicate

ready *adj* = **prepared**, set, primed,
organized ≠ **unprepared**;
= **completed**, arranged

real *adj* = **true**, genuine, sincere,
factual, unfeigned

realize *v* = **become aware of**,
understand, take in, grasp,
comprehend; = **fulfil**, achieve,
accomplish, make real

realm *n* = **field**, world, area,
province, sphere; = **kingdom**,
country, empire, land, domain

reap *v* = **get**, gain, obtain, acquire,

derive; = **collect**, gather, bring in,
harvest, garner

rear¹ *n* = **back part**, back ≠ **front**

rear² *v* = **bring up**, raise, educate,
train, foster; = **breed**, keep; = **rise**,
tower, soar, loom

reason *n* = **cause**, grounds,
purpose, motive, goal; = **sense**,
mind, understanding, judgment,
logic ≠ **emotion** ▷ *v* = **deduce**,
conclude, work out, make out, infer

reassure *v* = **encourage**, comfort,
hearten, gee up, restore confidence
to

rebate *n* = **refund**, discount,
reduction, bonus, allowance

rebel *n* = **revolutionary**, insurgent,
secessionist, revolutionist ▷ *v*

r

lawful authority ▷ n **2** one who rebels ▷ adj **3** rebelling **rebellion** n organized open resistance to authority **rebellious** adj

rebound ❶ v **1** spring back **2** misfire, esp. so as to hurt perpetrator ▷ n **3** recoiling

rebuff ❶ n/v repulse, snub

rebuke ❶ n/v reprimand

rebut v -butting, -butted refute, disprove **rebuttal** n

recalcitrant adj wilfully disobedient

recall ❶ v **1** remember **2** call back **3** restore ▷ n **4** summons **5** ability to remember

recant v withdraw statement, opinion etc.

recap v **1** recapitulate ▷ n **2** recapitulation

recapitulate v state again briefly

recapitulation n

recede ❶ v **1** go back **2** slope backward

receipt ❶ n **1** written acknowledgment of money received **2** receiving

receive ❶ v **1** accept, experience **2** greet (guests) **receiver** n **1** officer appointed to take public money **2** one who knowingly takes stolen goods **3** equipment in telephone etc. to convert electrical signals into sound etc.

recent ❶ adj **1** lately happened **2** new **recently** adv

receptacle n vessel to contain anything

reception ❶ n **1** receiving **2** formal party **3** area for receiving guests etc. **4** in broadcasting, quality of signals received

---

THESAURUS

= **revolt**, resist, rise up, mutiny; = **defy**, dissent, disobey

rebound v = **bounce**, ricochet, recoil; = **misfire**, backfire, recoil, boomerang

rebuff v = **reject**, refuse, turn down, cut, slight ≠ **encourage** ▷ n = **rejection**, snub, knock-back, slight, refusal (Sl) ≠ **encouragement**

rebuke v = **scold**, censure, reprimand, castigate, chide ≠ **praise** ▷ n = **scolding**, censure, reprimand, row, dressing down (Inf) ≠ **praise**

recall v = **recollect**, remember, evoke, call to mind ▷ n = **recollection**, memory, remembrance; = **annulment**,

withdrawal, repeal, cancellation, retraction

recede v = **fall back**, withdraw, retreat, return, retire

receipt n = **sales slip**, proof of purchase, counterfoil; = **receiving**, delivery, reception, acceptance

receive v = **get**, accept, be given, pick up, collect; = **experience**, suffer, bear, encounter, sustain; = **greet**, meet, admit, welcome, entertain

recent adj = **new**, modern, up-to-date, late, current ≠ **old**

reception n = **party**, gathering, get-together, social gathering, function (Inf); = **response**, reaction, acknowledgment, treatment, welcome

r

receptionist n person who receives clients etc.

receptive adj quick, willing to receive new ideas

recess ❶ n 1 alcove 2 hollow 3 suspension of business

recession ❶ n 1 period of reduction in trade 2 act of receding **recessive** adj receding

recipe ❶ n directions for cooking food

recipient n one that receives

reciprocal adj 1 complementary 2 mutual 3 moving backwards and forwards **reciprocate** v give and receive mutually

recite ❶ v repeat aloud, esp. to audience **recital** n 1 musical performance, usu. by one person 2 narration **recitation** n

reckless ❶ adj incautious

reckon ❶ v 1 count 2 include 3 think

reclaim ❶ v 1 make fit for

cultivation 2 bring back 3 reform 4 demand the return of

recline v sit, lie back

recluse n hermit

recognize ❶ v 1 identify again 2 treat as valid 3 notice **recognition** n

recoil v 1 draw back in horror 2 rebound ▷ n 3 recoiling

recollect v remember **recollection** n

recommend ❶ v 1 advise 2 praise 3 make acceptable **recommendation** n

recompense v 1 reward 2 compensate ▷ n 3 reward 4 compensation

reconcile ❶ v 1 bring back into friendship 2 adjust, harmonize **reconciliation** n

reconnoitre v make survey of **reconnaissance** n survey, esp. for military purposes

reconstitute v restore (food) to

— THESAURUS —

recess n = **break**, rest, holiday, interval, vacation; = **alcove**, corner, bay, hollow, niche

recession n = **depression**, drop, decline, slump ≠ **boom**

recipe n = **directions**, instructions, ingredients

recite v = **perform**, deliver, repeat, declaim

reckless adj = **careless**, wild, rash, precipitate, hasty ≠ **cautious**

reckon v (Inf) = **think**, believe, suppose, imagine, assume; = **consider**, rate, account, judge, regard

reclaim v = **retrieve**, regain;

= **regain**, salvage, recapture, reform, redeem

recognize v = **identify**, know, place, remember, spot; = **acknowledge**, allow, accept, admit, grant ≠ **ignore**; = **appreciate**, respect, notice

recommend v = **advocate**, suggest, propose, approve, endorse ≠ **disapprove of**; = **put forward**, approve, endorse, commend, praise

reconcile v = **resolve**, settle, square, adjust, compose; = **reunite**, bring back together, conciliate; = **make peace between**, reunite, propitiate

former state, esp. by addition of water

record ❶ n 1 document that records 2 disc with indentations which can be transformed into sound 3 best achievement 4 known facts ▷ v 5 put in writing 6 preserve (sound etc.) for reproduction on playback device **recorder** n 1 one that records 2 type of flute 3 judge in certain courts **record player** instrument for reproducing sound on records

recount ❶ v tell in detail

recoup v recover what has been expended or lost

recourse n (resorting to) source of help

recover ❶ v 1 get back 2 become healthy again **recovery** n

recreation ❶ n agreeable relaxation, amusement

recrimination n mutual abuse and blame

recruit ❶ n 1 newly-enlisted soldier 2 one newly joining ▷ v 3 enlist **recruitment** n

rectangle n oblong four-sided figure with four right angles **rectangular** adj

rectify v **-fying, -fied** correct

rectitude n honesty

rector n 1 clergyman with care of parish 2 head of academic institution **rectory** n rector's house

rectum n, pl **-tums, -ta** final section of large intestine

recumbent adj lying down

recuperate v restore, be restored from illness etc.

recur ❶ v **-curring, -curred** 1 happen again 2 go or come back in mind **recurrence** n **recurrent** adj

recycle ❶ v reprocess substance for use again

red ❶ adj/n **redder, reddest** 1 (of) colour of blood 2 (Inf) communist **redden** v **reddish** adj

— THESAURUS —

record n = **document**, file, register, log, report; = **evidence**, trace, documentation, testimony, witness; = **disc**, single, album, LP, vinyl ▷ v = **set down**, minute, note, enter, document; = **make a recording of**, video, tape, video-tape, tape-record; = **register**, show, indicate, give evidence of; = **confidential**, private, unofficial, not for publication

recount v = **tell**, report, describe, relate, repeat

recover v = **get better**, improve, get well, recuperate, heal ≠ **relapse**

recreation n = **leisure**, play, sport, fun, entertainment

recruit v = **assemble**, raise, levy, muster, mobilize ▷ n = **beginner**, trainee, apprentice, novice, convert

recur v = **happen again**, return, repeat, persist, revert

recycle v = **reprocess**, reuse, salvage, reclaim, save

red adj = **crimson**, scarlet, ruby, vermilion, cherry; = **flushed**, embarrassed, blushing, florid, shamefaced; (of hair) = **chestnut**, reddish, flame-coloured, sandy, Titian

r

red-blooded adj 1 (Inf) vigorous 2 virile **red carpet** special welcome for important guest **red-handed** adj (Inf) (caught) in the act **red herring** topic introduced to divert attention **red-hot** adj 1 extremely hot 2 very keen **red tape** excessive adherence to rules **redwood** n giant coniferous tree of California

redeem ❶ v 1 buy back 2 set free 3 free from sin 4 make up for **redemption** n

redolent adj 1 smelling strongly 2 reminiscent (of)

redouble v increase, intensify

redoubtable adj dreaded, formidable

redress ❶ v 1 make amends for ▷ n 2 compensation

reduce ❶ v 1 lower 2 lessen 3 bring by necessity to some state 4 slim 5 simplify **reduction** n

redundant ❶ adj 1 superfluous 2 (of worker) deprived of job because no longer needed

redundancy n

reed n 1 various water plants 2 tall straight stem of one 3 (Mus) vibrating strip of certain wind instruments

reef n 1 ridge of rock or coral near surface of sea 2 part of sail which can be rolled up to reduce area

reek v/n (emit) strong unpleasant smell

reel ❶ n 1 spool on which film, thread etc. is wound 2 (Cinema) portion of film 3 lively dance ▷ v 4 wind on reel 5 draw (in) by means of reel 6 stagger

refectory n, pl **-tories** room for meals in college etc.

refer ❶ v **-ferring, -ferred** 1 relate (to) 2 send to for information 3 ascribe to 4 submit for decision **reference** n 1 act of referring 2 citation 3 appeal to judgment of another 4 testimonial 5 one to whom inquiries as to character etc. may be made

referee ❶ n 1 arbitrator 2 umpire ▷ v 3 act as referee

redeem v = **reinstate**, absolve, restore to favour; = **make up for**, compensate for, atone for, make amends for; = **buy back**, recover, regain, retrieve, reclaim; = **save**, free, deliver, liberate, ransom

redress v = **make amends for**, make up for, compensate for ▷ n = **amends**, payment, compensation, reparation, atonement

reduce v = **lessen**, cut, lower, moderate, weaken ≠ **increase**; = **degrade**, downgrade, break,

humble, bring low ≠ **promote** (Inf, Brit Sl)

redundant adj = **superfluous**, extra, surplus, unnecessary, unwanted ≠ **essential**

reel v = **stagger**, rock, roll, pitch, sway

refer v = **direct**, point, send, guide

referee n = **umpire**, judge, ref (Inf), arbiter, arbitrator ▷ v = **umpire**, judge, mediate, adjudicate, arbitrate

referendum n = **public vote**, popular vote, plebiscite

referendum ❶ *n, pl* **-dums, -da**
submitting of question to
electorate

refill *v* **1** fill again ▷ *n*
2 subsequent filling **3** replacement
supply

refine ❶ *v* purify **refined** *adj*
1 cultured, polite **2** purified
refinement *n* **1** subtlety
2 elaboration **3** fineness of taste or
manners **refinery** *n* place where
sugar, oil etc. is refined

reflect ❶ *v* **1** throw back, esp. light
2 cast (discredit etc.) upon
3 meditate **reflection** *n*
1 reflecting **2** image of object given
back by mirror etc. **3** thought
4 expression of thought **reflective**
adj **reflector** *n*

reflex *n* **1** involuntary action ▷ *adj*
2 (of muscular action) involuntary
3 bent back **reflexive** *adj*
(*Grammar*) describes verb denoting
agent's action on himself

reform ❶ *v* **1** improve **2** abandon

evil practices ▷ *n* **3** improvement
reformation *n*

refract *v* change course of light
etc. passing from one medium to
another **refraction** *n*

refractory *adj* unmanageable

refrain¹ ❶ *v* **refrain from** abstain
(from)

refrain² ❶ *n* chorus

refresh ❶ *v* **1** revive **2** renew
3 brighten **refreshment** *n* that
which refreshes, esp. food, drink

refrigerate *v* **1** freeze **2** cool
refrigerant *n/adj* **refrigeration**
n **refrigerator** *n* apparatus in
which foods, drinks are kept cool

refuge ❶ *n* shelter, sanctuary
refugee *n* one who seeks refuge,
esp. in foreign country

refund ❶ *v* **1** pay back ▷ *n*
2 repayment

refurbish ❶ *v* renovate and
brighten up

refuse¹ ❶ *v* decline, deny, reject
refusal *n*

— THESAURUS —

refine *v* = **purify**, process, filter,
cleanse, clarify; = **improve**, perfect,
polish, hone

reflect *v* = **show**, reveal, display,
indicate, demonstrate; = **throw
back**, return, mirror, echo,
reproduce; = **consider**, think,
muse, ponder, meditate

reform *n* = **improvement**,
amendment, rehabilitation,
betterment ▷ *v* = **improve**,
correct, restore, amend, mend;
= **mend your ways**, go straight
(*Inf*), shape up (*Inf*), turn over a new
leaf, clean up your act (*Inf*)

refrain¹ *v* = **stop**, avoid, cease,
renounce, abstain

refrain² *n* = **chorus**, tune, melody

refresh *v* = **revive**, freshen,
revitalize, stimulate, brace;
= **stimulate**, prompt, renew, jog

refuge *n* = **protection**, shelter,
asylum

refund *n* = **repayment**,
reimbursement, return ▷ *v*
= **repay**, return, restore, pay back,
reimburse

refurbish *v* = **renovate**, restore,
repair, clean up, overhaul

refuse¹ *v* = **decline**, reject, turn

r

refuse² ❶ n rubbish
refute v disprove **refutation** n
regain ❶ v 1 get back, recover
2 reach again
regal ❶ adj of, like a king **regalia**
pl n 1 insignia of royalty
2 emblems of high office
regale v 1 give pleasure to 2 feast
regard ❶ v 1 look at 2 consider
3 relate to ▷ n 4 look 5 attention
6 particular respect 7 esteem ▷ pl
8 expression of good will
regardless adj 1 heedless ▷ adv
2 in spite of everything
regatta n meeting for boat races
regenerate v 1 reform 2 re-create
3 reorganize **regeneration** n
regent n ruler of kingdom during
absence, minority etc. of its
monarch **regency** n
reggae n popular music with
strong beat
regime ❶ n system of government
regiment n 1 organized body of

troops ▷ v 2 discipline (too) strictly
regimental adj
region ❶ n 1 area, district 2 part
3 sphere **regional** adj
register ❶ n 1 list 2 catalogue
3 device for registering 4 range of
voice or instrument ▷ v 5 show, be
shown on meter, face etc. 6 enter
in register 7 record **registrar** n
1 keeper of a register 2 senior
hospital doctor **registration** n
registry n 1 registering 2 place
where registers are kept
regress v revert to former place,
condition etc. **regression** n
regret ❶ v -gretting, -gretted
1 feel sorry, distressed for loss of or
on account of ▷ n 2 feeling of
sorrow **regretful** adj **regrettable**
adj
regular ❶ adj 1 normal 2 habitual
3 according to rule 4 periodical
5 straight ▷ n 6 soldier in standing
army **regularity** n

——————— THESAURUS ———————

down, say no to
refuse² n = **rubbish**, waste, junk
(Inf), litter, garbage
regain v = **recover**, get back,
retrieve, recapture, win back; = **get
back to**, return to, reach again
regal adj = **royal**, majestic, kingly or
queenly, noble, princely
regard v = **consider**, see, rate,
view, judge; = **look at**, view, eye,
watch, observe ▷ n = **respect**,
esteem, thought, concern, care;
= **look**, gaze, scrutiny, stare,
glance
regime n = **government**, rule,
management, leadership, reign

region n = **area**, place, part,
quarter, section
register n = **list**, record, roll, file,
diary ▷ v = **enrol**, enlist, list, note,
enter; = **record**, catalogue,
chronicle, mark, indicate,
manifest
regret v = **be or feel sorry about**,
rue, deplore, bemoan, repent (of)
≠ **be satisfied with**; = **mourn**,
miss, grieve for or over ▷ n
= **remorse**, compunction,
bitterness, repentance, contrition
regular adj = **normal**, common,
usual, ordinary, typical
≠ **infrequent**; = **steady**, consistent

regulate ⊕ v **1** adjust **2** arrange **3** govern **regulation** n

regurgitate v **1** vomit **2** bring back (swallowed food) into mouth

rehabilitate v **1** help (person) to readjust to society after illness, imprisonment etc. **2** restore to former position **rehabilitation** n

rehash n **1** old materials presented in new form ▷ v **2** rework

rehearse ⊕ v **1** practise (play etc.) **2** repeat **3** train **rehearsal** n

reign ⊕ n **1** period of sovereign's rule ▷ v **2** rule

reimburse v pay back

rein n **1** strap attached to bit to guide horse **2** instrument for governing

reincarnation n rebirth of soul in successive bodies

reindeer n, pl **-deer, -deers** deer of cold regions

reinforce ⊕ v strengthen with new support, material, force **reinforcement** n

reinstate ⊕ v replace, restore

reiterate ⊕ v repeat again

reject ⊕ v **1** refuse to accept **2** put aside **3** discard **4** renounce ▷ n **5** person or thing rejected **rejection** n

rejig v **-jigging, -jigged 1** re-equip **2** rearrange

rejoice ⊕ v make or be joyful

rejoin ⊕ v reply **rejoinder** n

rejuvenate v restore to youth

relapse v **1** fall back into evil, illness etc. ▷ n **2** relapsing

relate ⊕ v **1** narrate **2** establish relation between **3** have reference to **4** form sympathetic relationship

relation ⊕ n **1** relative condition **2** connection by blood or marriage **3** connection between things **4** narrative **relationship** n

relative adj **1** dependent on

THESAURUS

regulate v = **control**, run, rule, manage, direct; = **moderate**, control, modulate, fit, balance

rehearse v = **practise**, prepare, run through, go over, train

reign v = **be supreme**, prevail, predominate, hold sway; = **rule**, govern, be in power, influence, command ▷ n = **rule**, power, control, command, monarchy

reinforce v = **support**, strengthen, fortify, toughen, stress

reinstate v = **restore**, recall, re-establish, return

reiterate v (Formal) = **repeat**, restate, say again, do again

reject v = **rebuff**, jilt, turn down, spurn, refuse ≠ **accept**; = **deny**, exclude, veto, relinquish, renounce ≠ **approve**; = **discard**, decline, eliminate, scrap, jettison ≠ **accept** ▷ n = **castoff**, second, discard ≠ **treasure**

rejoice v = **be glad**, celebrate, be happy, glory, be overjoyed ≠ **lament**

rejoin v = **reply**, answer, respond, retort, riposte

relate v = **tell**, recount, report, detail, describe

relation n = **similarity**, link, bearing, bond, comparison; = **relative**, kin, kinsman or kinswoman

r

relation to something else
2 having reference (to) ▷ *n* **3** one
connected by blood or marriage
relax ❶ *v* **1** make, become loose or
slack **2** ease up **3** make, become
less strict **relaxation** *n*
1 recreation **2** abatement
relay ❶ *n* **1** fresh set of people or
animals relieving others **2** *(Radio,
TV)* broadcasting station receiving
programmes from another station
▷ *v* **3** pass on, as message **relay
race** race between teams of which
each runner races part of distance
release ❶ *v* **1** set free **2** permit
showing of (film etc.) ▷ *n*
3 releasing **4** permission to show
publicly **5** film, record etc. newly
issued
relegate ❶ *v* **1** put in less
important position **2** demote
relegation *n*

relent *v* become less severe
relentless *adj*
relevant ❶ *adj* having to do with
the matter in hand **relevance** *n*
reliable ❶ see RELY
relic ❶ *n* thing remaining
relief ❶ *n* **1** alleviation of pain etc.
2 money, food given to victims of
disaster **3** release from duty **4** one
who relieves another **5** bus, plane
etc. operating when a scheduled
service is full **6** freeing of besieged
city **7** projection of carved design
from surface **8** prominence
relieve *v*
religion *n* system of belief in,
worship of a supernatural power or
god **religious** *adj* **1** of religion
2 pious **3** scrupulous
relinquish ❶ *v* give up
relish ❶ *v* **1** enjoy ▷ *n* **2** liking
3 savoury taste **4** sauce **5** pickle

— THESAURUS —

relax *v* = **be** *or* **feel at ease**, chill
out *(Sl, chiefly US)*, take it easy,
lighten up *(Sl)* ≠ **be alarmed**;
= **calm down**, calm, unwind;
= **make less tense**, rest
relay *v* = **broadcast**, carry, spread,
communicate, transmit
release *v* = **set free**, free,
discharge, liberate, drop
≠ **imprison**; = **acquit**, let go, let off,
exonerate, absolve ▷ *n*
= **liberation**, freedom, liberty,
discharge, emancipation
≠ **imprisonment**; = **acquittal**,
exemption, absolution,
exoneration; = **issue**, publication,
proclamation
relegate *v* = **demote**, degrade,

downgrade
relevant *adj* = **significant**,
appropriate, related, fitting, to the
point ≠ **irrelevant**
reliable *adj* = **dependable**,
trustworthy, sure, sound, true
≠ **unreliable**
relic *n* = **remnant**, vestige,
memento, trace, fragment
relief *n* = **ease**, release, comfort,
cure, remedy; = **rest**, respite,
relaxation, break, breather *(Inf)*;
= **aid**, help, support, assistance,
succour
relinquish *v (Formal)* = **give up**,
leave, drop, abandon, surrender
relish *v* = **enjoy**, like, savour, revel
in ≠ **dislike** fancy ▷ *n*

relocate v move to new place, esp. to work

reluctant ⊕ adj unwilling **reluctance** n

rely v -lying, -lied 1 depend (on) 2 trust **reliability** n **reliable** adj **reliance** n 1 trust 2 confidence

remain ⊕ v 1 be left behind 2 continue 3 last **remainder** n **remains** pl n 1 relics 2 dead body

remand v send back, esp. into custody **on remand** in custody

remark ⊕ v/n (make) casual comment (on) **remarkable** adj unusual

remedy ⊕ n, pl -edies 1 means of curing ▷ v 2 put right **remedial** adj

remember ⊕ v retain in, recall to memory **remembrance** n

remind ⊕ v cause to remember **reminder** n

reminisce v talk, write of past

times, experiences etc. **reminiscence** n **reminiscent** adj

remiss adj careless

remit v -mitting, -mitted 1 send money for goods etc. 2 refrain from exacting 3 give up 4 return 5 slacken ▷ n 6 area of authority **remission** n 1 abatement 2 reduction of prison term 3 pardon **remittance** n 1 sending of money 2 money sent

remnant ⊕ n fragment

remonstrate v protest

remorse ⊕ n regret and repentance **remorseful** adj **remorseless** adj pitiless

remote ⊕ adj 1 distant 2 aloof 3 slight **remote control** control of apparatus from distance by electrical device

remove ⊕ v 1 take, go away 2 transfer 3 withdraw **removal** n

remunerate v reward, pay

THESAURUS

= **enjoyment**, liking, love, taste, fancy ≠ **distaste**; = **condiment**, seasoning, sauce

reluctant adj = **unwilling**, hesitant, loath, disinclined, unenthusiastic ≠ **willing**

remain v = **stay**, continue, go on, stand, dwell; = **stay behind**, wait, delay ≠ **go** be left, linger

remark v = **comment**, say, state, reflect, mention; = **notice**, note, observe, perceive, see ▷ n = **comment**, observation, reflection, statement, utterance

remedy n = **cure**, treatment, medicine, nostrum ▷ v = **put right**, rectify, fix, correct, set to

rights

remember v = **recall**, think back to, recollect, reminisce about, call to mind ≠ **forget**; = **bear in mind**, keep in mind

remind v = **jog your memory**, prompt, make you remember

remnant n = **remainder**, remains, trace, fragment, end

remorse n = **regret**, shame, guilt, grief, sorrow

remote adj = **distant**, far, isolated, out-of-the-way, secluded ≠ **nearby**; = **far**, distant; = **slight**, small, outside, unlikely, slim ≠ **strong**

remove v = **take out**, withdraw,

remuneration n **remunerative** adj

renaissance, renascence ❶ n revival, rebirth

renal adj of the kidneys

rend ❶ v **rending, rent 1** tear apart **2** burst

render ❶ v **1** submit **2** give in return **3** cause to become **4** represent **5** melt down **6** plaster

rendezvous n, pl **-vous 1** meeting place **2** appointment

rendition n **1** performance **2** translation

renegade n deserter

renege v go back on (promise etc.)

renew ❶ v **1** begin again **2** make valid again **3** make new **4** restore **5** replenish **renewable** adj **1** able to be renewed **2** (of energy or an energy source) inexhaustible or capable of being perpetually replenished **renewables** pl n

renewable energy sources **renewal** n

renounce ❶ v **1** give up, disown **2** resign, as claim **renunciation** n

renovate ❶ v restore, repair **renovation** n

renown n fame

rent¹ ❶ n **1** payment for use of land, buildings etc. ▷ v **2** hire

rent² ❶ n tear

reorganize v organize in new, more efficient way

repair¹ ❶ v **1** make whole again **2** mend ▷ n **3** repaired part **reparation** n compensation

repair² v go (to)

repartee n **1** witty retort **2** interchange of them

repatriate v send (someone) back to his or her own country **repatriation** n

repay ❶ v **repaying, repaid 1** pay back **2** make return for **repayment** n

extract ≠ **insert**

renaissance, renascence n = **rebirth**, revival, restoration, renewal, resurgence

rend v (Lit) = **tear**, rip, separate, wrench, rupture

render v = **make**, cause to become, leave; = **provide**, give, pay, present, supply; = **represent**, portray, depict, do, give

renew v = **recommence**, continue, extend, repeat, resume; = **reaffirm**, resume, recommence; = **replace**, refresh, replenish, restock; = **restore**, repair, overhaul, mend, refurbish

renounce v = **disown**, quit, forsake, recant, forswear

renovate v = **restore**, repair, refurbish, do up (Inf), renew

rent¹ v = **hire**, lease ▷ n = **hire**, rental, lease, fee, payment

rent² n = **tear**, split, rip, slash, slit

repair¹ v = **mend**, fix, restore, heal, patch ≠ **damage**; = **put right**, make up for, compensate for, rectify, redress ▷ n = **mend**, restoration, overhaul; = **darn**, mend, patch

repay v = **pay back**, refund, settle up, return, square

repeal ❶ v 1 revoke, cancel ▷ n
2 cancellation
repeat ❶ v 1 say, do again 2 recur
▷ n 3 act, instance of repeating
repetition n 1 act of repeating
2 thing repeated **repetitive** adj
repel ❶ v -pelling, -pelled 1 drive
back 2 be repulsive to **repellent**
adj/n
repent v feel regret for deed or
omission **repentance** v
repentant adj
repertoire ❶ n stock of plays,
songs etc. that player or company
can give **repertory** n repertoire
repetition ❶ see REPEAT
replace ❶ v 1 substitute for 2 put
back **replacement** n
replay n 1 reshowing on TV of
sporting incident, esp. in slow
motion 2 second sports match,
esp. following earlier draw ▷ v
3 play (match, recording etc.) again

replenish v fill up again
replete adj filled, gorged
replica ❶ n exact copy **replicate**
v make or be copy of
reply ❶ n/v -plying, -plied
answer
report ❶ n 1 account 2 written
statement of child's progress at
school 3 rumour 4 repute 5 bang
▷ v 6 announce 7 give account of
8 complain about 9 make report
10 present oneself (to) **reporter** n
repose 1 n 2 peace 3 composure
4 sleep ▷ v 5 rest **repository** n
place where valuables are
deposited for safekeeping
repossess v take back property
from one who is behind with
payments
reprehensible adj 1 deserving
censure 2 unworthy
represent ❶ v 1 stand for
2 deputize for 3 act 4 symbolize

— THESAURUS —

repeal v = **abolish**, reverse, revoke,
annul, recall ≠ **pass** ▷ n
= **abolition**, cancellation,
annulment, invalidation,
rescindment ≠ **passing**
repeat v = **reiterate**, restate ▷ n
= **repetition**, echo, reiteration
repel v = **drive off**, fight, resist,
parry, hold off ≠ **submit to**;
= **disgust**, offend, revolt, sicken,
nauseate ≠ **delight**
repertoire n = **range**, list, stock,
supply, store
repetition n = **recurrence**,
repeating, echo
replace v = **take the place of**,
follow, succeed, oust, take over

from; = **substitute**, change,
exchange, switch, swap
replica n = **reproduction**, model,
copy, imitation, facsimile
≠ **original**
reply v = **answer**, respond, retort,
counter, rejoin ▷ n = **answer**,
response, reaction, counter, retort
report v = **inform of**,
communicate, recount; often with
on = **communicate**, tell, state,
detail, describe, post, tweet ▷ n
= **article**, story, piece, write-up;
= **account**, record, statement,
communication, description;
often plural = **news**, word
represent v = **act for**, speak for;

r

5 make out to be **6** describe
representation n
representative n **1** one chosen to stand for group **2** salesman ▷ adj **3** typical
repress ❶ v keep down or under **repression** n **repressive** adj
reprieve ❶ v **1** suspend execution of (condemned person) ▷ n **2** postponement or cancellation of punishment **3** respite
reprimand n/v rebuke
reprisal n retaliation
reproach v **1** blame, rebuke ▷ n **2** scolding **3** thing bringing discredit **reproachful** adj
reprobate adj/n depraved (person)
reproduce ❶ v **1** produce copy of **2** bring new individuals into existence **reproduction** n **reproductive** adj
reprove v censure, rebuke **reproof** n
reptile n cold-blooded, air breathing vertebrate with scales or

plates, as snake
republic n state without monarch governed by elected representatives **republican** adj/n
repudiate v reject authority or validity of
repugnant adj **1** offensive **2** distasteful **3** contrary
repulse v **1** drive back **2** rebuff **3** repel **repulsion** n **repulsive** adj disgusting
reputation ❶ n estimation in which a person is held
request ❶ n **1** asking **2** thing asked for ▷ v **3** ask
Requiem n Mass for the dead
require ❶ v **1** need **2** demand **requirement** n
requisite adj/n essential
requisition n **1** formal demand, e.g. for materials ▷ v **2** demand (supplies) **3** press into service
requite v repay
rescind v cancel
rescue ❶ v -cuing, -cued **1** save, extricate ▷ n **2** rescuing

————————— THESAURUS —————————

r

= **stand for**, serve as, symbolize, mean, betoken; = **exemplify**, embody, symbolize, typify, personify
repress v = **control**, suppress, hold back, bottle up, check ≠ **release**; = **hold back**, suppress, stifle
reprieve v = **grant a stay of execution to**, pardon, let off the hook (Sl) ▷ n = **stay of execution**, amnesty, pardon, remission, deferment
reproduce v = **copy**, recreate, replicate, duplicate, match; = **print**,

copy
reputation n = **name**, standing, character, esteem, stature
request v = **ask for**, appeal for, put in for, demand, desire ▷ n = **appeal**, call, demand, plea, desire
require v = **need**, crave, want, miss, lack; = **order**, demand, command, compel, exact
rescue v = **save**, get out, release, deliver, recover ≠ **desert** ▷ n = **saving**, salvage, deliverance, release, recovery

research ❶ n 1 investigation to gather or discover facts ▷ v 2 investigate

resemble ❶ v 1 be like 2 look like **resemblance** n

resent ❶ v show, feel indignation at **resentful** adj **resentment** n

reserve ❶ v 1 hold back, set aside ▷ n 2 (also pl) something, esp. troops, kept for emergencies 3 area of land reserved for particular purpose or group 4 reticence ▷ adj 5 auxiliary, substitute **reservation** n 1 reserving 2 thing reserved 3 doubt 4 limitation **reserved** adj 1 booked 2 not showing one's feelings

reservoir ❶ n 1 enclosed area for storage of water 2 receptacle for liquid, gas etc.

reshuffle n 1 reorganization ▷ v 2 reorganize

reside ❶ v dwell permanently **residence** n home **resident** adj/n **residential** adj

residue ❶ n remainder **residual** adj

resign ❶ v 1 give up (esp. office, job) 2 reconcile (oneself) to **resignation** n

resilient adj 1 elastic 2 (of person) recovering quickly from shock etc. **resilience** n

resin n sticky substance from plants, esp. firs and pines

resist ❶ v withstand, oppose **resistance** n 1 resisting 2 opposition **resistant** adj **resistor** n component of electrical circuit producing resistance to current

resit v 1 retake (exam) ▷ n 2 exam to be retaken

resolute adj determined **resolution** n 1 resolving

—————— THESAURUS ——————

research n = **investigation**, study, analysis, examination, probe ▷ v = **investigate**, study, examine, explore, probe

resemble v = **be like**, look like, mirror, parallel, be similar to

resent v = **be bitter about**, object to, grudge, begrudge, take exception to ≠ **be content with**

reserve v = **book**, prearrange, engage; = **put by**, secure ▷ n = **store**, fund, savings, stock, supply; = **park**, reservation, preserve, sanctuary, tract; = **shyness**, silence, restraint, constraint, reticence; = **reservation**, doubt, delay,

uncertainty, indecision

reservoir n = **lake**, pond, basin; = **store**, stock, source, supply, reserves

reside v (Formal) = **live**, lodge, dwell, stay, abide ≠ **visit**

residue n = **remainder**, remains, remnant, leftovers, rest

resign v = **quit**, leave, step down (Inf), vacate, abdicate; = **give up**, abandon, yield, surrender, relinquish

resist v = **oppose**, battle against, combat, defy, stand up to ≠ **accept**; = **refrain from**, avoid, keep from, forgo, abstain from ≠ **indulge in**; = **withstand**, be

r

2 firmness **3** thing resolved
4 decision **5** vote
resolve ❶ v **1** decide **2** vote
3 separate component parts of
4 make clear ▷ n **5** absolute
determination
resonance n echoing, esp. in deep
tone **resonant** adj **resonate** v
resort ❶ v **1** have recourse ▷ n
2 place of recreation, e.g. beach
3 recourse
resound ❶ v echo, go on sounding
resource ❶ n **1** ingenuity **2** that
to which one resorts for support
3 expedient ▷ pl **4** stock that can
be drawn on **5** funds **resourceful**
adj
respect ❶ n **1** esteem **2** aspect
3 reference ▷ v **4** treat with
esteem **5** show consideration for
respectability n **respectable** adj

1 worthy of respect **2** fairly good
respectful adj **respecting** prep
concerning **respective** adj
1 relating separately to each
2 separate **respectively** adv
respiration n breathing
respirator n apparatus worn over
mouth and breathed through
respiratory adj
respite ❶ n **1** pause, interval
2 reprieve
resplendent adj brilliant, shining
respond ❶ v **1** answer **2** react
respondent adj **1** replying ▷ n
2 one who answers **3** defendant
response n **responsive** adj
readily reacting
responsible ❶ adj **1** in charge
2 liable to answer for **3** dependable
4 involving responsibility
responsibility n, pl **-ties**

— THESAURUS —

proof against
resolve v **= work out**, answer,
clear up, crack, fathom; **= decide**,
determine, agree, purpose, intend
▷ n **= determination**, resolution,
willpower, firmness, steadfastness
≠ indecision
resort n **= holiday centre**, spot,
retreat, haunt, tourist centre;
= recourse to, reference to
resound v **= echo**, resonate,
reverberate, re-echo
resource n **= means**, course,
resort, device, expedient
respect v **= think highly of**, value,
honour, admire, esteem; **= show
consideration for**, honour,
observe, heed ▷ n **= regard**,
honour, recognition, esteem,

admiration **≠ contempt**;
= consideration, kindness,
deference, tact, thoughtfulness;
= particular, way, point, matter,
sense
respite n **= pause**, break, rest,
relief, halt
respond v **= answer**, return,
reply, counter, retort **≠ remain
silent**; *often with* **to** = **reply to**,
answer
responsible adj **= to blame**,
guilty, at fault, culpable; **= in
charge**, in control, in authority;
= accountable, liable,
answerable **≠ unaccountable**;
= sensible, reliable, rational,
dependable, trustworthy
≠ unreliable

rest¹ ● *n* **1** repose **2** freedom from exertion etc. **3** pause **4** support ▷ *v* **5** take, give rest **6** support, be supported **restful** *adj* **restless** *adj* unable to rest or be still

rest² *n* **1** remainder ▷ *v* **2** remain

restaurant ● *n* commercial establishment serving food

restitution *n* **1** giving back **2** compensation

restive *adj* restless

restore ● *v* **1** repair, renew **2** give back **restoration** *n* **restorative** *adj/n*

restrain ● *v* **1** hold back **2** prevent **restraint** *n* **1** self-control **2** anything that restrains

restrict ● *v* limit **restriction** *n* **restrictive** *adj*

result ● *v* **1** follow as consequence **2** happen **3** end ▷ *n* **4** outcome **resultant** *adj*

resume ● *v* begin again **résumé** *n* summary **resumption** *n*

resurgence ● *n* rising again **resurgent** *adj*

resurrect ● *v* restore to life, use **resurrection** *n*

resuscitate *v* restore to consciousness **resuscitation** *n*

retail *n* **1** sale in small quantities ▷ *adv* **2** by retail ▷ *v* **3** sell, be sold, retail **4** recount **retailer** *n*

retain ● *v* **1** keep **2** engage services of **retainer** *n* **1** fee to

— THESAURUS —

rest¹ *v* = **relax**, take it easy, sit down, be at ease, put your feet up ≠ **work**; = **stop**, have a break, break off, take a breather (*Inf*), halt ≠ **keep going**; = **place**, repose, sit, lean, prop; = **be placed**, sit, lie, be supported, recline ▷ *n* = **relaxation**, repose, leisure ≠ **work**; = **pause**, break, stop, halt, interval; = **refreshment**, release, relief, ease, comfort; = **support**, stand, base, holder, prop; = **calm**, tranquillity, stillness, still, quiet

restaurant *n* = **café**, diner (*chiefly US & Canad*), bistro, cafeteria, tearoom

restore *v* = **reinstate**, re-establish, reintroduce ≠ **abolish**; = **revive**, build up, strengthen, refresh, revitalize ≠ **make worse**; = **re-establish**, replace, reinstate, give back; = **repair**, refurbish,

renovate, reconstruct, fix (up) ≠ **demolish**

restrain *v* = **hold back**, control, check, contain, restrict ≠ **encourage**

restrict *v* = **limit**, regulate, curb, ration ≠ **widen**

result *n* = **consequence**, effect, outcome, end result, product ≠ **cause** ▷ *v* = **arise**, follow, issue, happen, appear = **end in**, bring about, cause, lead to, finish with

resume *v* = **begin again**, continue, go on with, proceed with, carry on ≠ **discontinue**

resurgence *n* = **revival**, return, renaissance, resurrection, resumption

resurrect *v* = **revive**, renew, bring back, reintroduce; = **restore to life**, raise from the dead

retain *v* = **maintain**, reserve, preserve, keep up, continue to

r

retain esp. barrister **2** (Hist) follower of nobleman etc.
retention n **retentive** adj
retaliate ⊕ v repay in kind **retaliation** n
retard ⊕ v **1** make slow **2** impede development of **retarded** adj
retch v try to vomit
reticent adj **1** reserved **2** uncommunicative **reticence** n
retina n, pl **-nas, -nae** light-sensitive membrane at back of eye
retinue n band of followers
retire ⊕ v **1** give up office or work **2** go away **3** go to bed **retirement** n **retiring** adj unobtrusive, shy
retort ⊕ v **1** reply **2** retaliate ▷ n **3** vigorous reply **4** vessel with bent neck used for distilling
retrace v go back over
retract v **1** draw in or back **2** withdraw statement **retraction** n

retreat ⊕ v **1** move back ▷ n **2** withdrawal **3** place to which anyone retires **4** refuge
retrench v reduce expenditure
retribution n recompense, esp. for evil
retrieve ⊕ v **1** fetch back again **2** regain **retrieval** n **retriever** n dog trained to retrieve game
retroactive adj applying to the past
retrograde adj going backwards, reverting
retrospect n survey of past **retrospective** adj
return ⊕ v **1** go, come back **2** give, send back **3** report officially **4** elect ▷ n **5** returning **6** profit **7** report **returning officer** one conducting election
reunion n gathering of people who have been apart **reunite** v bring, come together again

— THESAURUS —

have; = **keep**, save ≠ **let go**
retaliate v = **pay someone back**, hit back, strike back, reciprocate, take revenge ≠ **turn the other cheek**
retard v = **slow down**, check, arrest, delay, handicap ≠ **speed up**
retire v = **stop working**, give up work; = **withdraw**, leave, exit, go away, depart; = **go to bed**, turn in (Inf), hit the sack (SI), hit the hay (SI)
retort v = **reply**, return, answer, respond, counter ▷ n = **reply**, answer, response (Inf), comeback, riposte
retreat v = **withdraw**, back off, draw back, leave, go back

≠ **advance** ▷ n = **flight**, retirement, departure, withdrawal, evacuation ≠ **advance**; = **refuge**, haven, shelter, sanctuary, hideaway
retrieve v = **get back**, regain, recover, restore, recapture
return v = **come back**, go back, retreat, turn back, revert ≠ **depart**; = **put back**, replace, restore, reinstate ≠ **keep**; = **give back**, repay, refund, pay back, reimburse ≠ **keep**; = **recur**, repeat, persist, revert, happen again; = **elect**, choose, vote in ▷ n = **restoration**, reinstatement, re-establishment ≠ **removal**

Rev., Revd. Reverend
rev n (Inf) revolution (of engine)
revalue v adjust exchange value of currency upwards
revamp ⓘ v renovate, restore
reveal ⓘ v 1 make known 2 show **revelation** n
reveille n morning bugle call etc. to waken soldiers
revel ⓘ v -elling, -elled 1 take pleasure (in) 2 make merry ▷ n 3 (usu. pl) merrymaking **revelry** n
revenge ⓘ n 1 retaliation for wrong done ▷ v 2 avenge 3 make retaliation for
revenue ⓘ n income, esp. of state
reverberate v echo, resound **reverberation** n
revere ⓘ v hold in great regard or

religious respect **reverence** n
reverend adj (esp. as prefix to clergyman's name) worthy of reverence **reverent** adj
reverie n daydream
reverse ⓘ v 1 move (vehicle) backwards 2 turn other way round 3 change completely ▷ n 4 opposite 5 side opposite 6 defeat ▷ adj 7 opposite **reversal** n
revert ⓘ v return to former state, subject **reversion** n
review ⓘ v 1 examine 2 reconsider 3 hold, make, write review of ▷ n 4 survey 5 critical notice of book etc. 6 periodical with critical articles 7 (Mil) inspection of troops
revile v abuse viciously

———————— THESAURUS ————————

revamp v = **renovate**, restore, overhaul, refurbish, do up (Inf)
reveal v = **make known**, disclose, give away, make public, tell ≠ **keep secret**; = **show**, display, exhibit, unveil, uncover ≠ **hide**
revel v = **celebrate**, carouse, live it up (Inf), make merry
revenge n = **retaliation**, vengeance, reprisal, retribution, an eye for an eye ▷ v = **avenge**, repay, take revenge for, get your own back for (Inf)
revenue n = **income**, returns, profits, gain, yield ≠ **expenditure**
revere v = **be in awe of**, respect, honour, worship, reverence ≠ **despise**
reverse v (Law) = **change**, cancel, overturn, overthrow, undo ≠ **implement**; = **turn round**, turn

over, turn upside down, upend; = **transpose**, change, move, exchange, transfer ▷ n = **opposite**, contrary, converse, inverse; = **misfortune**, blow, failure, disappointment, setback; = **back**, rear, other side, wrong side, underside ≠ **front** ▷ adj = **opposite**, contrary, converse
revert v = **go back**, return, come back, resume
review n = **survey**, study, analysis, examination, scrutiny; = **critique**, commentary, evaluation, notice, criticism; = **inspection**, parade, march past; = **magazine**, journal, periodical, zine (Inf) ▷ v = **reconsider**, revise, rethink, reassess, re-examine; = **assess**, study, judge, evaluate, criticize

r

revise | 466

333 DICTIONARY

revise ❶ v **1** look over and correct **2** study again (work done previously) **3** change **revision** n

revive ❶ v bring, come back to life, vigour, use etc. **revival** n

revoke v **1** withdraw **2** cancel **revocation** n

revolt ❶ n **1** rebellion ▷ v **2** rise in rebellion **3** feel disgust **4** affect with disgust **revolting** adj disgusting

revolve ❶ v **1** turn round **2** be centred on **3** rotate **revolution** n **1** violent overthrow of government **2** great change **3** complete rotation **revolutionary** adj/n **revolutionize** v

revue n entertainment with sketches and songs

revulsion n repugnance or abhorrence

reward ❶ n **1** thing given in return for service, conduct etc. ▷ v **2** give reward **rewarding** adj

rewind v run (tape, film etc.) back to earlier point

rewire v provide (house, engine etc.) with new wiring

rhapsody n, pl **-dies 1** freely

structured, emotional musical piece **2** expression of enthusiasm **rhapsodic** adj **rhapsodize** v

rhesus n small, long-tailed monkey **rhesus factor** feature distinguishing different types of human blood

rhetoric ❶ n **1** art of effective speaking or writing **2** exaggerated language **rhetorical** adj (of question) not requiring an answer

rheumatism n painful inflammation of joints or muscles **rheumatic** adj/n

rhinoceros n, pl **-oses, -os** large animal with one or two horns on nose

rhododendron n evergreen flowering shrub

rhombus n, pl **-buses, -bi** diamond-shaped figure

rhubarb n garden plant with edible fleshy stalks

rhyme ❶ n **1** identity of final sounds in words **2** word or syllable identical in final sound to another **3** verse marked by rhyme ▷ v **4** (of words) have identical final sounds

THESAURUS

revise v = **change**, review; = **edit**, correct, alter, update, amend

revive v = **revitalize**, restore, renew, rekindle, invigorate

revolt n = **uprising**, rising, revolution, rebellion, mutiny ▷ v = **rebel**, rise up, resist, mutiny; = **disgust**, sicken, repel, repulse, nauseate

revolve v = **go round**, circle, orbit

reward n = **punishment**,

retribution, comeuppance (Sl), just deserts ▷ v = **compensate**, pay, repay, recompense, remunerate ≠ **penalize**

rhetoric n = **hyperbole**, bombast, wordiness, verbosity, grandiloquence; = **oratory**, eloquence, public speaking, speech-making, elocution

rhyme n = **poem**, song, verse, ode, planning

rhythm ● n measured beat of words, music etc. **rhythmic, -ical** adj

rib n 1 one of curved bones springing from spine and forming framework of upper part of body 2 raised series of rows in knitting etc. ▷ v 3 mark with ribs 4 knit to form a rib pattern

ribald adj irreverent, scurrilous

ribbon n 1 narrow band of fabric 2 long strip of anything

rice n 1 Eastern cereal plant 2 its seeds as food

rich ● adj 1 wealthy 2 fertile 3 abounding 4 valuable 5 containing much fat or sugar 6 mellow 7 amusing **riches** pl n wealth **richly** adv 1 elaborately 2 fully

rick¹ n stack of hay etc.

rick² v/n sprain, wrench

rickets n disease of children marked by softening of bones **rickety** adj shaky, unstable

rickshaw n two-wheeled man-drawn Asian vehicle

ricochet v 1 (of bullet) rebound or be deflected ▷ n 2 rebound

rid ● v ridding, rid 1 relieve of 2 free **riddance** n

ridden past participle of RIDE adj afflicted, as in disease-ridden

riddle¹ ● n 1 question made puzzling to test one's ingenuity 2 puzzling thing, person

riddle² ● v 1 pierce with many holes ▷ n 2 coarse sieve

ride ● v riding, rode, ridden 1 sit on and control or propel 2 be carried on or across 3 go on horseback or in vehicle 4 lie at anchor ▷ n 5 journey on horse, in vehicle **rider** n 1 one who rides 2 supplementary clause 3 addition to document

ridge n 1 long narrow hill 2 line of meeting of two sloping surfaces ▷ v 3 form into ridges

ridiculous ● adj deserving to be laughed at, absurd **ridicule** v 1 laugh at, deride ▷ n 2 derision

rife ● adj prevalent, common

riff n short repeated musical phrase

rhythm n = **beat**, swing, accent, pulse, tempo

rich adj = **wealthy**, affluent, well-off, loaded (Sl), prosperous ≠ **poor**; = **well-stocked**, full, productive, ample, abundant ≠ **scarce**; = **full-bodied**, sweet, fatty, tasty, creamy ≠ **bland**; = **fruitful**, productive, fertile, prolific ≠ **barren**

rid v = **free**, clear, deliver, relieve, purge

riddle¹ n = **puzzle**, problem,

conundrum, poser; = **enigma**, question, secret, mystery, puzzle

riddle² v = **pierce**, pepper, puncture, perforate, honeycomb

ride v = **control**, handle, manage; = **travel**, be carried, go, move ▷ n = **journey**, drive, trip, lift, outing

ridiculous adj = **laughable**, stupid, silly, absurd, ludicrous ≠ **sensible**

rife adj = **widespread**, rampant, general, common, universal

r

riffraff *n* rabble
rifle ❶ *v* **1** search and rob ▷ *n*
2 firearm with long barrel
rift ❶ *n* crack, split
rig ❶ *v* **rigging, rigged 1** provide
(ship) with ropes etc. **2** equip
3 arrange in dishonest way ▷ *n*
4 apparatus for drilling for oil
rigging *n* ship's spars and ropes
right ❶ *adj* **1** just **2** in accordance
with truth and duty **3** true
4 correct **5** proper **6** of side that
faces east when front is turned to
north **7** (*Politics*) conservative
8 straight ▷ *v* **9** make, become
right ▷ *n* **10** claim, title etc.
allowed or due **11** what is right
12 conservative political party
▷ *adv* **13** straight **14** properly
15 very **16** on or to right side
rightful *adj* **right angle** angle of

90 degrees **right-hand man** most
valuable assistant
righteous ❶ *adj* **1** virtuous
2 good **righteousness** *n*
rigid ❶ *adj* **1** inflexible **2** stiff
rigidity *n*
rigmarole *n* **1** long, complicated
procedure **2** nonsense
rigor mortis stiffening of body
after death
rigour *n* **1** severity **2** hardship
rigorous *adj*
rile *v* anger
rim ❶ *n* edge
rind *n* outer coating of fruits etc.
ring¹ ❶ *v* **ringing, rang, rung**
1 (cause to) give out resonant
sound like bell **2** telephone ▷ *n*
3 resonant sound
ring² ❶ *n* **1** circular band, esp. for
finger **2** circle of persons

─────── THESAURUS ───────

rifle *v* = **ransack**, rob, burgle, loot,
strip
rift *n* = **breach**, division, split,
separation, falling out (*Inf*); = **split**,
opening, crack, gap, break
rig *v* = **fix**, engineer (*Inf*), arrange,
manipulate, tamper with; (*Naut*)
= **equip**, fit out, kit out, outfit,
supply
right *adj* = **correct**, true, genuine,
accurate, exact ≠ **wrong**; = **proper**,
done, becoming, seemly, fitting
≠ **inappropriate**; = **just**, good, fair,
moral, proper ≠ **unfair** ▷ *adv*
= **correctly**, truly, precisely, exactly,
genuinely ≠ **wrongly**; = **suitably**,
fittingly, appropriately, properly,
aptly ≠ **improperly**; = **exactly**,
squarely, precisely; = **directly**,

straight, precisely, exactly,
unswervingly ▷ *n* = **prerogative**,
business, power, claim, authority;
= **justice**, truth, fairness, legality,
righteousness ≠ **injustice** ▷ *v*
= **rectify**, settle, fix, correct, sort
out
righteous *adj* = **virtuous**, good,
just, fair, moral ≠ **wicked**
rigid *adj* = **strict**, set, fixed, exact,
rigorous ≠ **flexible**; = **inflexible**,
uncompromising, unbending
rim *n* = **edge**, lip, brim
ring¹ *v* = **phone**, call, telephone,
buzz (*Inf, chiefly Brit*); = **chime**,
sound, toll, reverberate, clang ▷ *n*
= **call**, phone call, buzz (*Inf, chiefly
Brit*); = **chime**, knell, peal
ring² *n* = **circle**, round, band,

3 enclosed area ▷ *v* **4** put ring round **ringer** *n* (*Inf*) identical thing or person **ringleader** *n* instigator of mutiny, riot etc. **ringlet** *n* curly lock of hair **ring road** main road that bypasses a town (centre) **ringworm** *n* skin disease

rink *n* sheet of ice for skating

rinse ❶ *v* **1** remove soap from by applying water **2** wash lightly ▷ *n* **3** rinsing **4** liquid to tint hair

riot ❶ *n/v* (engage in) tumult, disorder **riotous** *adj*

RIP rest in peace

rip ❶ *v/n* ripping, ripped cut, slash **ripcord** *n* cord pulled to open parachute **rip off** (*Sl*) cheat by overcharging

ripe ❶ *adj* ready to be harvested, eaten etc. **ripen** *v*

riposte *n* **1** verbal retort **2** counterattack ▷ *v* **3** make riposte

ripple *n* **1** slight wave **2** soft sound ▷ *v* **3** form into little waves **4** (of sounds) rise and fall gently

rise ❶ *v* rising, rose, risen **1** get up **2** move upwards **3** reach higher level **4** increase **5** rebel **6** have its source ▷ *n* **7** rising **8** upslope **9** increase **rising** *n* revolt

risk ❶ *n* **1** chance of disaster or loss ▷ *v* **2** put in jeopardy **3** take chance of **risky** *adj*

risotto *n, pl* **-tos** dish of rice with vegetables, meat etc.

risqué *adj* suggestive of indecency

rissole *n* cake of minced meat coated with breadcrumbs

rite ❶ *n* formal practice or custom, esp. religious **ritual** *n* **1** prescribed order of rites **2** stereotyped behaviour ▷ *adj* **3** concerning rites

---

THESAURUS

circuit, loop; **= arena**, enclosure, circus, rink; **= gang**, group, association, band, circle

rinse *v* **= wash**, clean, dip, splash, cleanse ▷ *n* **= wash**, dip, splash, bath

riot *n* **= disturbance**, disorder, confusion, turmoil, upheaval; **= display**, show, splash, extravaganza, profusion; **= laugh**, joke, scream (*Inf*), hoot (*Inf*), lark ▷ *v* **= rampage**, run riot, go on the rampage

rip *v* **= tear**, cut, split, burst, rend ▷ *n* **= tear**, cut, hole, split, rent

ripe *adj* **= ripened**, seasoned, ready, mature, mellow ≠ **unripe**; **= right**, suitable

rise *v* **= get up**, stand up, get to your feet; **= go up**, climb, ascend ≠ **descend**; **= loom**, tower; **= get steeper**, ascend, go uphill, slope upwards ≠ **drop**; **= increase**, mount ≠ **decrease** ▷ *n* **= upward slope**, incline, elevation, ascent, kopje or koppie (*S Afr*); **= increase**, upturn, upswing, upsurge ≠ **decrease**; **= pay increase**, raise (*US*), increment; **= advancement**, progress, climb, promotion

risk *n* **= danger**, chance, possibility, hazard

rite *n* **= ceremony**, custom, ritual, practice, procedure

r

rival ① n 1 one that competes with another ▷ adj 2 in position of rival ▷ v 3 vie with **rivalry** n

river ① n large natural stream of water

rivet n 1 bolt for fastening metal plates, the end being put through holes and then beaten flat ▷ v 2 fasten firmly **riveting** adj very interesting

rivulet n small stream

RN Royal Navy

road ① n 1 track, way prepared for passengers, vehicles etc. 2 direction, way 3 street **roadblock** n barricade across road to stop traffic for inspection **roadworks** pl n repairs to road

roam ① v wander about, rove

roar ① v/n (utter) loud deep hoarse sound

roast v 1 cook in oven or over open fire 2 make, be very hot ▷ n 3 roasted joint ▷ adj 4 roasted

rob ① v **robbing, robbed** steal

from **robber** n **robbery** n

robe ① n 1 long outer garment ▷ v 2 dress 3 put on robes

robin n small brown bird with red breast

robot ① n automated machine, esp. performing functions in human manner

robust ① adj 1 sturdy 2 strong

rock¹ ① n 1 stone 2 mass of stone 3 hard sweet in sticks **rockery** n mound of stones in garden **rocky** **rocky** adj

rock² ① v 1 (cause to) sway to and fro ▷ n 2 popular music with heavy beat **rocker** n 1 curved piece of wood etc. on which thing may rock 2 rocking chair **rock and roll** style of popular music

rock melon n (Aust, NZ & US) type of melon with sweet orange flesh

rocket n 1 self-propelling device powered by burning of explosive contents ▷ v 2 move fast, esp. upwards, as rocket

──────────── THESAURUS ────────────

rival n = **opponent**, competitor, contender, contestant, adversary ≠ **supporter** ▷ v = **compete with**, match, equal, compare with, come up to ▷ adj = **competing**, conflicting, opposing

river n = **stream**, brook, creek, waterway, tributary; = **flow**, rush, flood, spate, torrent

road n = **roadway**, highway, motorway, track, route

roam v = **wander**, walk, range, travel, stray

roar v = **guffaw**, laugh heartily, hoot, split your sides (Inf); = **cry**,

shout, yell, howl, bellow ▷ n = **guffaw**, hoot

rob v = **steal from**, hold up, mug (Inf); = **raid**, hold up, loot, plunder, burgle

robe n = **gown**, costume, habit

robot n = **machine**, automaton, android, mechanical man

robust adj = **strong**, tough, powerful, fit, healthy ≠ **weak**

rock¹ n = **stone**, boulder

rock² v = **sway**, pitch, swing, reel, toss; = **shock**, surprise, shake, stun, astonish

rod 🛈 n 1 slender straight bar, stick 2 cane

rodent n gnawing animal

rodeo n, pl **-deos** (US & Canad) display of bareback riding, cattle handling etc.

roe¹ n small species of deer

roe² n mass of eggs in fish

rogue 🛈 n 1 scoundrel 2 mischief-loving person or child

role, rôle 🛈 n 1 actor's part 2 specific task or function

roll 🛈 v 1 move by turning over and over 2 wind round 3 smooth out with roller 4 move, sweep along 5 undulate ▷ n 6 act of rolling 7 anything rolled up 8 list 9 small round piece of baked bread 10 continuous sound, as of drums, thunder etc. **roller** n 1 cylinder of wood, stone, metal etc. 2 long wave of sea **roller coaster** narrow undulating railway at funfair **roller skate** skate with wheels instead of runner **rolling pin** cylindrical roller for pastry **rolling stock** locomotives, carriages etc. of railway

rollicking adj boisterously jovial and merry

roly-poly n 1 pudding of suet pastry ▷ adj 2 round, plump

ROM (Comp) read only memory

Roman adj of Rome or Church of Rome **Roman Catholic** member of that section of Christian Church which acknowledges supremacy of the Pope **Roman numerals** letters used to represent numbers

romance 🛈 n 1 love affair 2 mysterious or exciting quality 3 tale of chivalry 4 tale remote from ordinary life ▷ v 5 exaggerate, fantasize **romantic** adj 1 characterized by romance 2 of love 3 (of literature etc.) displaying passion and imagination ▷ n 4 romantic person

Romany adj/n, pl **-nies** Gypsy

romp 🛈 v 1 run, play wildly ▷ n 2 spell of romping **rompers** pl n child's overalls

---

THESAURUS

rod n = **stick**, bar, pole, shaft, cane

rogue n = **scoundrel**, crook (Inf), villain, fraud, blackguard; = **scamp**, rascal, scally (Northwest English dialect)

role n = **job**, part, position, post, task; = **part**, character, representation, portrayal

roll v = **turn**, wheel, spin, go round, revolve; = **trundle**, go, move; = **flow**, run, course; often with **up** = **wind**, bind, wrap, swathe, envelop; = **level**, even, press, smooth, flatten ▷ n = **rumble**,

boom, roar, thunder, reverberation; = **register**, record, list, index, census; = **turn**, spin, rotation, cycle, wheel

romance n = **love affair**, relationship, affair, attachment, liaison; = **excitement**, colour, charm, mystery, glamour; = **story**, tale, fantasy, legend, fairy tale

romp v = **frolic**, sport, have fun, caper, cavort ▷ n = **frolic**, lark (Inf), caper = **win easily**, walk it (Inf), win hands down, win by a mile (Inf)

r

roof n, pl **roofs** 1 outside upper covering of building ▷ v 2 put roof on, over

rooibos n (S Afr) tea prepared from the dried leaves of an African plant

rook n bird of crow family

rookie n (Inf) new recruit

room ❶ n 1 space 2 division of house 3 scope ▷ pl 4 lodgings **roomy** adj spacious

roost n/v perch

rooster n (US & Canad) domestic cock

root, rootle ❶ n 1 underground part of plant 2 source, origin 3 (Anat) embedded portion of tooth, hair etc. ▷ pl 4 person's sense of belonging ▷ v 5 (cause to) take root 6 pull by roots 7 dig, burrow

rope ❶ n 1 thick cord ▷ v 2 secure, mark off with rope

rort n (Aust, Inf) dishonest scheme

rosary n, pl **-saries** 1 series of prayers 2 string of beads for counting these prayers

rose n 1 shrub usu. with prickly stems and fragrant flowers 2 the flower 3 pink colour **rosette** n rose-shaped bunch of ribbon **rosy** adj 1 flushed 2 promising **rose-coloured** adj 1 having colour of rose 2 unjustifiably optimistic **rosehip** n

berry-like fruit of rose plant

rosé n pink wine

rosemary n evergreen fragrant flowering shrub

roster n list of turns of duty

rostrum n/pl **-trums, -tra** platform, stage

rot ❶ v **rotting, rotted** 1 decompose, decay 2 deteriorate physically or mentally ▷ n 3 decay 4 any disease producing decomposition of tissue 5 (Inf) nonsense **rotten** adj 1 decomposed 2 very bad 3 corrupt **rotter** n (Inf) despicable person

rota n roster, list

rotary adj (of movement) circular **rotate** v 1 (cause to) move round centre 2 (cause to) follow set sequence **rotation** n

rote n mechanical repetition

rotor n revolving portion of dynamo motor or turbine

rotund adj 1 round 2 plump

rouge n red powder, cream used to colour cheeks

rough ❶ adj 1 not smooth 2 violent, stormy 3 rude 4 approximate 5 in preliminary form ▷ v 6 make rough 7 plan ▷ n 8 rough state or area 9 sketch

─────────────── THESAURUS ───────────────

room n = **chamber**, office, apartment; = **space**, area, capacity, extent, expanse; = **opportunity**, scope, leeway, chance, range

root n = **stem**, tuber, rhizome; = **source**, cause, heart, bottom, base

rope n = **cord**, line, cable, strand, hawser

rot v = **decay**, spoil, deteriorate,

perish, decompose ▷ n = **decay**, decomposition, corruption, mould, blight; (Inf) = **nonsense**, rubbish, drivel, twaddle, garbage (chiefly US)

rough adj = **uneven**, broken, rocky, irregular, jagged ≠ **even**; = **boisterous**, hard, tough, arduous; = **ungracious**, blunt, rude,

roughen v **roughage** n
unassimilated portion of food **rough
it** live without usual comforts etc.
roulette n gambling game played
with revolving wheel
round ❶ adj **1** spherical, circular,
curved **2** plump **3** complete
4 roughly correct **5** considerable
▷ adv **6** with circular course ▷ n
7 thing round in shape **8** recurrent
duties **9** stage in competition
10 customary course **11** game (of
golf) **12** period in boxing match
etc. **13** cartridge for firearm ▷ prep
14 about **15** on all sides of ▷ v
16 make, become round **17** move
round **rounders** pl n ball game
roundly adv thoroughly
roundabout n **1** revolving circular
platform on which people ride for
amusement **2** road junction at
which traffic passes round central

island ▷ adj **3** not straightforward
round trip journey out and back
again **round up** drive (cattle)
together
rouse ❶ v **1** wake up, stir up,
excite **2** waken
rout ❶ n **1** overwhelming defeat,
disorderly retreat ▷ v **2** put to flight
route ❶ n road, chosen way
routine ❶ n **1** regularity of
procedure ▷ adj **2** ordinary, regular
rove v wander, roam
row¹ ❶ n number of things in a
straight line
row² ❶ (Inf) ▷ n **1** dispute
2 disturbance ▷ v **3** quarrel noisily
rowan n tree producing bright red
berries, mountain ash
rowdy adj/n **-dier, -diest**
disorderly, noisy (person)
rowlock n device to hold oar on
gunwale of boat

——— THESAURUS ———

coarse, brusque ≠ **refined**;
= **unpleasant**, hard, difficult,
tough, uncomfortable ≠ **easy**;
= **approximate**, estimated
≠ **exact**; = **vague**, general, sketchy,
imprecise, inexact; = **basic**, crude,
unfinished, incomplete, imperfect
≠ **complete** ▷ n = **outline**, draft,
mock-up, preliminary sketch
round n = **series**, session, cycle,
sequence, succession; = **stage**,
turn, level, period, division;
= **sphere**, ball, band, ring, circle
▷ adj = **spherical**, rounded, curved,
circular, cylindrical ▷ v = **go round**,
circle, skirt, flank, bypass
rouse v = **wake up**, call, wake,
awaken; = **excite**, move, stir,

provoke, anger
rout v = **defeat**, beat, overthrow,
thrash, destroy ▷ n = **defeat**,
beating, overthrow, thrashing,
pasting (Sl)
route n = **way**, course, road,
direction, path
routine n = **procedure**,
programme, order, practice,
method ▷ adj = **usual**, standard,
normal, customary, ordinary
≠ **unusual**
row¹ n = **line**, bank, range, series, file
row² n (Inf); = **quarrel**, dispute,
argument, squabble, tiff;
= **disturbance**, noise, racket,
uproar, commotion ▷ v = **quarrel**,
fight, argue, dispute, squabble

r

royal ❶ adj of king or queen
royalist n supporter of monarchy
royalty n **1** royal power **2** royal
persons **3** payment for right, use of
invention or copyright
rpm revolutions per minute
RSVP please reply
rub ❶ v **rubbing, rubbed 1** apply
pressure to with circular or
backwards-and-forwards
movement **2** clean, polish, dry
thus **3** abrade, chafe **4** remove by
friction **5** become frayed or worn
by friction ▷ n **6** rubbing
rubber n **1** elastic dried sap of
certain tropical trees **2** synthetic
material resembling this
3 piece of rubber etc. used for
erasing ▷ adj **4** made of rubber
rubbery adj
rubbish ❶ n **1** refuse **2** anything
worthless **3** nonsense ▷ v **4** (Inf)
criticize
rubble n fragments of stone
rubella n mild contagious viral
disease, German measles
ruby n, pl **-bies 1** precious red gem

2 its colour ▷ adj **3** of this colour
ruck¹ n **1** crowd **2** common herd
ruck² n/v crease
rucksack n pack carried on back,
knapsack
rudder n steering device for boat,
aircraft
ruddy adj **-dier, -diest** of healthy
red colour
rude ❶ adj **1** impolite **2** coarse
3 vulgar **4** roughly made
rudiments pl n elements, first
principles **rudimentary** adj
rue ❶ v **ruing, rued 1** grieve for
2 regret **rueful** adj
ruff n **1** frilled collar **2** natural
collar of feathers, fur etc. on some
birds and animals **ruffle** v
1 rumple, annoy, frill ▷ n **2** frilled
trimming
ruffian n violent, lawless person
rug n **1** small floor mat **2** woollen
coverlet
rugby n form of football in which
the ball may be carried
rugged ❶ adj **1** rough
2 strong-featured

—————————————— THESAURUS ——————————————

royal adj = **regal**, kingly, queenly,
princely, imperial; = **splendid**,
grand, impressive, magnificent,
majestic
rub v = **stroke**, massage, caress;
= **polish**, clean, shine, wipe, scour;
= **chafe**, scrape, grate, abrade ▷ n
= **massage**, caress, kneading
rubbish n = **waste**, refuse, scrap,
junk (Inf), litter; = **nonsense**,
garbage (chiefly US), twaddle, rot,
trash
rude adj = **impolite**, insulting,

cheeky, abusive, disrespectful
≠ **polite**; = **uncivilized**, rough,
coarse, brutish, boorish;
= **unpleasant**, sharp, sudden,
harsh, startling
rue v (Lit) = **regret**, mourn, lament,
repent, be sorry for
rugged adj = **rocky**, broken, rough,
craggy, difficult ≠ **even**;
= **strong-featured**, rough-hewn,
weather-beaten ≠ **delicate**;
= **well-built**, strong, tough, robust,
sturdy; = **tough**, strong, robust,

ruin ⊕ n 1 destruction 2 downfall 3 fallen or broken state 4 loss of wealth etc. ▷ pl 5 ruined buildings etc. ▷ v 6 bring or come to ruin **ruinous** adj

rule ⊕ n 1 principle 2 government 3 what is usual 4 measuring stick ▷ v 5 govern 6 decide 7 mark with straight lines **ruler** n 1 one who governs 2 stick for measuring or ruling lines **ruling** n formal decision

rum n spirit distilled from sugar cane

rumba n lively ballroom dance

rumble v/n (make) noise as of distant thunder

ruminate v 1 chew cud 2 ponder over **ruminant** adj/n cud-chewing (animal)

rummage v search thoroughly

rummy n card game

rumour ⊕ n 1 hearsay, unproved statement ▷ v 2 put around as rumour

rump n 1 tail end 2 buttocks

rumple v make untidy, dishevelled

rumpus n, pl -puses disturbance

run ⊕ v running, ran, run 1 move with more rapid gait than walking 2 go quickly 3 flow 4 flee 5 compete in race, contest, election 6 cross by running 7 expose oneself (to risk etc.) 8 cause to run 9 manage 10 operate ▷ n 11 act, spell of running 12 rush 13 tendency, course 14 enclosure for domestic fowls 15 ride in car 16 unravelled stitches 17 score of one at cricket **runner** n 1 racer 2 messenger 3 curved piece of wood on which sleigh slides 4 stem of plant forming new roots 5 strip of cloth, carpet **running** adj 1 continuous 2 consecutive 3 flowing ▷ n 4 act of moving or flowing quickly 5 ride in car 6 continuous period or sequence **runny** adj **rundown** n summary **run-down** adj 1 exhausted 2 decrepit, broken-down **run**

muscular, sturdy ≠ **delicate**

ruin v = **destroy**, devastate, wreck, defeat, smash ≠ **create**; = **bankrupt**, break, impoverish, beggar, pauperize ▷ n = **bankruptcy**, insolvency, destitution; = **disrepair**, decay, disintegration, ruination, wreckage; = **destruction**, fall, breakdown, defeat, collapse ≠ **preservation**

rule n = **regulation**, law, direction, guideline, decree; = **precept**, principle, canon, maxim, tenet; = **custom**, procedure, practice,

routine, tradition ▷ v = **govern**, control, direct, have power over, command over; = **reign**, govern, be in power, be in authority = **control**, monopolize, tyrannize

rumour n = **story**, news, report, talk, word

run v = **race**, rush, dash, hurry, sprint ≠ **dawdle**; = **flee**, escape, take off (Inf), bolt, beat it (Sl) ≠ **stay**; = **take part**, compete; = **continue**, go, stretch, reach, extend ≠ **stop**; (chiefly US & Canad) = **compete**, stand, contend, be a candidate, put yourself up for;

r

down 1 stop working **2** reduce
3 exhaust **4** denigrate
run-of-the-mill adj ordinary **run
out** be completely used up
runway n level stretch where
aircraft take off and land
rune n character of old Germanic
alphabet
rung n crossbar in ladder
runt n unusually small animal
rupture ⊕ n **1** breaking, breach
2 hernia ▷ v **3** break **4** burst, sever
rural ⊕ adj **1** of the country **2** rustic
ruse n stratagem, trick
rush¹ ⊕ v **1** hurry or cause to hurry
2 move violently or rapidly ▷ n
3 rushing ▷ adj **4** done with speed
rush hour period when many
people travel to or from work
rush² n marsh plant with slender
pithy stem

rusk n kind of biscuit
russet n/adj reddish-brown
(colour)
rust ⊕ n **1** reddish-brown coating
formed on iron **2** disease of plants
▷ v **3** affect with rust **rusty** adj
1 corroded **2** reddish-brown **3** out
of practice
rustic adj **1** simple, homespun
2 rural **3** uncouth. boorish ▷ n
4 countryman
rustle¹ v/n (make) sound as of
blown dead leaves etc.
rustle² v (US) steal (cattle) **rustler**
n
rut n **1** furrow made by wheel
2 settled habit
rutabaga n the US and Canadian
name for SWEDE
ruthless ⊕ adj merciless
rye n grain plant bearing it

———————— THESAURUS ————————

= **manage**, lead, direct, be in charge
of, head; = **go**, work, operate,
perform, function; = **perform**, carry
out; = **work**, go, operate, function;
= **pass**, go, move, roll, glide ▷ n
= **race**, rush, dash, sprint, gallop;
= **ride**, drive, trip, spin (Inf), outing;
= **sequence**, period, stretch, spell,
course; = **enclosure**, pen, coop
rupture n = **break**, tear, split,
crack, rent ▷ v = **break**, separate,
tear, split, crack
rural adj = **agricultural**, country

rush¹ v = **hurry**, run, race, shoot, fly
≠ **dawdle**; = **push**, hurry, press,
hustle; = **attack**, storm, charge at
▷ n = **dash**, charge, race, scramble,
stampede; = **hurry**, haste, hustle
▷ adj = **hasty**, fast, quick, hurried,
rapid ≠ **leisurely**
rust n = **corrosion**, oxidation;
= **mildew**, must, mould, rot, blight
▷ v = **corrode**, oxidize
ruthless adj = **merciless**, harsh,
cruel, brutal, relentless
≠ **merciful**

Sabbath *n* day of worship and rest, observed on Saturday in Judaism, on Sunday by Christians
  sabbatical *adj/n* (pert. to) leave for study
sabotage ❶ *n* **1** intentional damage done to roads, machines etc., esp. secretly in war ▷ *v* **2** damage intentionally **saboteur** *n*
sabre *n* curved cavalry sword
sac *n* pouchlike structure in animal or plant
saccharin *n* artificial sweetener
sachet *n* small envelope or bag,

esp. one holding liquid
sack ❶ *n* **1** large bag, esp. of coarse material **2** pillaging **3** (*Inf*) dismissal ▷ *v* **4** pillage (captured town) **5** (*Inf*) dismiss **sackcloth** *n* coarse fabric used for sacks
sacrament *n* one of certain ceremonies of Christian Church
sacred ❶ *adj* **1** dedicated, regarded as holy **2** revered **3** inviolable
sacrifice ❶ *n* **1** giving something up for sake of something else **2** thing so given up **3** making of offering to a god **4** thing offered ▷ *v* **5** offer as sacrifice **6** give up **sacrificial** *adj*
sacrilege *n* misuse, desecration of something sacred **sacrilegious** *adj*
sacrosanct *adj* preserved by religious fear against desecration or violence
sad ❶ *adj* **sadder, saddest** **1** sorrowful **2** unsatisfactory, deplorable **sadden** *v* make sad **sadness** *n*
saddle ❶ *n* **1** rider's seat on horse,

——— THESAURUS ———

sabotage *v* = **damage**, destroy, wreck, disable, disrupt ▷ *n* = **damage**, destruction, wrecking
sack *n* = **bag**, pocket, sac, pouch, receptacle; = **dismissal**, discharge, the boot (*Sl*), the axe (*Inf*), the push (*Sl*) ▷ *v* (*Inf*) = **dismiss**, fire (*Inf*), axe (*Inf*), discharge, give (someone) the push (*Inf*)
sacred *adj* = **holy**, hallowed, blessed, divine, revered ≠ **secular**; = **religious**, holy, ecclesiastical, hallowed ≠ **unconsecrated**;

= **inviolable**, protected, sacrosanct, hallowed, inalienable
sacrifice *v* = **offer**, offer up, immolate; = **give up**, abandon, relinquish, lose, surrender ▷ *n* = **offering**, oblation; = **surrender**, loss, giving up, rejection, abdication
sad *adj* = **unhappy**, down, low, blue, depressed ≠ **happy**; = **tragic**, moving, upsetting, depressing, dismal; = **deplorable**, bad, sorry, terrible, unfortunate ≠ **good**
saddle *v* = **burden**, load,

S

bicycle etc. **2** joint of meat
▷ v **3** put saddle on **4** lay burden on
sadism n love of inflicting pain
sadist n **sadistic** adj
safari n, pl **-ris** expedition to hunt
or observe wild animals, esp. in
Africa
safe ❶ adj **1** secure, protected
2 uninjured, out of danger **3** not
involving risk **4** trustworthy
5 sure ▷ n **6** strong lockable
container **safely** adv **safety** n
safeguard n **1** protection ▷ v
2 protect **safety pin** pin with
guard over the point when closed
saffron n **1** crocus **2** orange-
coloured flavouring obtained from
it **3** orange colour ▷ adj **4** orange
sag ❶ v **sagging, sagged 1** sink in
middle **2** curve downwards under
pressure **3** hang loosely ▷ n
4 droop
saga ❶ n **1** legend of Norse heroes
2 any long (heroic) story
sage ❶ n **1** very wise man ▷ adj
2 wise

sago n starchy cereal from
powdered pith of palm tree
said past tense and past participle
of SAY
sail ❶ n **1** piece of fabric stretched
to catch wind for propelling ship
etc. **2** act of sailing **3** arm of
windmill ▷ v **4** travel by water
5 move smoothly **6** begin voyage
sailor n **1** seaman **2** one who sails
saint n **1** person recognized as
having gained a special place in
heaven **2** exceptionally good
person
sake ❶ n **1** cause, account **2** end,
purpose **for the sake of 1** on
behalf of **2** to please or benefit
salad n mixed raw vegetables or
fruit used as food
salami n variety of highly-spiced
sausage
salary ❶ n, pl **-ries** fixed regular
payment to persons employed usu.
in nonmanual work
sale ❶ n **1** selling **2** selling of
goods at unusually low prices

— THESAURUS —

lumber (Brit Inf), encumber
safe adj = **protected**, secure,
impregnable, out of danger, safe
and sound ≠ **endangered**; = **all
right**, intact, unscathed, unhurt,
unharmed; = **risk-free**, sound,
secure, certain, impregnable ▷ n
= **strongbox**, vault, coffer,
repository, deposit box
sag v = **sink**, bag, droop, fall, slump;
= **drop**, sink, slump, flop, droop
saga n = **carry-on** (Inf, chiefly Brit),
performance (Inf), pantomime
(Inf)

sage n = **wise man**, philosopher,
guru, master, elder ▷ adj = **wise**,
sensible, judicious, sagacious,
sapient
sail v = **go by water**, cruise,
voyage, ride the waves, go by sea;
= **set sail**, embark, get under way,
put to sea, put off; = **pilot**, steer
sake n = **purpose**, interest, reason,
end, aim
salary n = **pay**, income, wage, fee,
payment
sale n = **selling**, marketing,
dealing, transaction, disposal

3 auction **salesman** n **1** shop assistant **2** one travelling to sell goods

salient adj **1** prominent, noticeable **2** jutting out

saline adj **1** containing, consisting of a chemical salt, esp. common salt **2** salty

saliva n liquid which forms in mouth, spittle

sallow adj of unhealthy pale or yellowish colour

sally n, pl **-lies 1** rushing out, esp. by troops **2** witty remark ▷ v **3** rush **4** set out

salmon n **1** large silvery fish with orange-pink flesh valued as food **2** colour of its flesh ▷ adj **3** of this colour

salmonella n, pl **-lae** bacterium causing food poisoning

salon n **1** (reception room for) guests in fashionable household **2** commercial premises of hairdressers, beauticians etc.

saloon n **1** public room, esp. on passenger ship **2** car with fixed roof **saloon bar** first-class bar in hotel etc.

salt 𝟙 n **1** white powdery or crystalline substance consisting mainly of sodium chloride, used to season or preserve food **2** chemical compound of acid and metal ▷ v **3** season, sprinkle with, preserve with salt ▷ adj **4** preserved in salt

salty adj of, like salt **saltcellar** n small vessel for salt at table

salubrious adj favourable to health, beneficial

salutary adj producing beneficial result

salute 𝟙 v **1** greet with words or sign **2** acknowledge with praise **3** perform military salute ▷ n **4** word, sign by which one greets another **5** motion of arm as mark of respect to military superior **6** firing of guns as military greeting of honour

salvation 𝟙 n fact or state of being saved, esp. of soul

salve n **1** healing ointment ▷ v **2** anoint with such, soothe

salver n (silver) tray for presentation of food, letters etc.

salvo n, pl **-vos, -voes** simultaneous discharge of guns etc.

same 𝟙 adj **1** identical, not different, unchanged **2** uniform **3** just mentioned previously

sample 𝟙 n **1** specimen ▷ v **2** take, give sample of **3** try **sampler** n beginner's exercise in

S

—— THESAURUS ——

salt marine, seafarer

salute v = **greet**, welcome, acknowledge, address, hail; = **honour**, acknowledge, recognize, pay tribute or homage to ▷ n = **greeting**, recognition, salutation, address

salvation n = **saving**, rescue,

recovery, salvage, redemption ≠ **ruin**

same adj = **identical**, similar, alike, equal, twin ≠ **different**; = **the very same**, one and the same, selfsame; = **aforementioned**, aforesaid

sample n = **specimen**, example, model, pattern, instance ▷ v

embroidery
sanatorium *n/pl* **-riums, -ria**
1 hospital, esp. for chronically ill
2 health resort
sanctify *v* **-fying, -fied 1** set
apart as holy **2** free from sin
sanctity *n* sacredness **sanctuary**
n **1** holy place **2** place of refuge
3 nature reserve
sanctimonious *adj* making
affected show of piety
sanction ❶ *n* **1** permission,
authorization **2** penalty for
breaking law ▷ *pl* **3** boycott or
other coercive measure, esp. by one
state against another ▷ *v* **4** allow,
authorize
sand *n* **1** substance consisting of
small grains of rock or mineral, esp.
on beach or in desert ▷ *pl*
2 stretches or banks of this ▷ *v*
3 polish, smooth with sandpaper
4 cover, mix with sand **sandy** *adj*
1 like sand **2** sand-coloured
3 consisting of, covered with sand
sandbag *n* **1** bag filled with sand
or earth as protection against
gunfire, floodwater etc. and as
weapon ▷ *v* **2** beat, hit with
sandbag **sandpaper** *n* paper with
sand stuck on it for scraping or

polishing **sandpiper** *n* shore bird
with long bill **sandstone** *n* rock
composed of sand
sandal *n* shoe consisting of sole
attached by straps
sandwich *n* **1** two slices of bread
with meat or other substance
between ▷ *v* **2** insert between two
other things
sane ❶ *adj* **1** of sound mind
2 sensible, rational **sanity** *n*
sang past tense of SING
sanguine *adj* **1** cheerful, confident
2 ruddy in complexion
sanitary *adj* helping protection of
health against dirt etc. **sanitation**
n measures, apparatus for
preservation of public health
sap¹ ❶ *n* **1** moisture which
circulates in plants **2** (*Inf*) foolish
person **sapling** *n* young tree
sap² ❶ *v* **sapping, sapped**
1 undermine **2** weaken
sapphire *n* **1** (usu. blue) precious
stone **2** deep blue ▷ *adj* **3** of deep
blue colour
sarcasm *n* **1** bitter or wounding
ironic remark **2** (use of) such
remarks **sarcastic** *adj*
sarcophagus *n, pl* **-gi, -guses**
stone coffin

──── THESAURUS ────

= **test**, try, experience, taste,
inspect
sanction *v* **= permit**, allow,
approve, endorse, authorize
≠ forbid ▷ *n often plural* **= ban**,
boycott, embargo, exclusion,
penalty **≠ permission**;
= permission, backing, authority,
approval, authorization **≠ ban**

sane *adj* **= rational**, all there (*Inf*),
of sound mind, compos mentis
(*Lat*), in your right mind **≠ insane**;
= sensible, sound, reasonable,
balanced, judicious **≠ foolish**
sap¹ *n* **= juice**, essence, vital fluid,
lifeblood; (*Sl*) **= fool**, jerk (*Sl, chiefly
US & Canad*), idiot, wally (*Sl*), twit (*Inf*)
sap² *v* **= weaken**, drain, undermine,

S

sardine n small fish of herring family

sardonic adj characterized by irony, mockery or derision

sari, saree n long garment worn by Hindu women

sarmie n (S Afr, Sl) sandwich

sartorial adj of tailor, tailoring, or men's clothes

sash n decorative belt, ribbon, wound around the body

Satan n the devil **satanic** adj devilish

satchel n small bag, esp. for school books

satellite n 1 celestial body or man-made projectile orbiting planet 2 person, country etc. dependent on another

satin n fabric (of silk, rayon etc.) with glossy surface on one side

satire ❶ n use of ridicule or sarcasm to expose vice and folly **satirical** adj **satirize** v make object of satire

satisfy ❶ v -fying, -fied 1 please, meet wishes of 2 fulfil, supply adequately 3 convince **satisfaction** n **satisfactory** adj

satsuma n kind of small orange

saturate ❶ v soak thoroughly **saturation** n act, result of saturating

Saturday n seventh day of the week

satyr n 1 woodland deity, part man, part goat 2 lustful man

sauce n 1 liquid added to food to enhance flavour ▷ v 2 add sauce to **saucy** adj impudent **saucepan** n cooking pot with long handle

saucer n 1 curved plate put under cup 2 shallow depression

sauerkraut n dish of shredded cabbage fermented in brine

sauna n steam bath

saunter v 1 walk in leisurely manner, stroll ▷ n 2 leisurely walk or stroll

sausage n minced meat enclosed in thin tube of animal intestine or synthetic material **sausage roll** pastry cylinder filled with sausage

sauté v -téing fry quickly

savage ❶ adj 1 wild 2 ferocious 3 brutal 4 uncivilized, primitive ▷ n 5 member of savage tribe, barbarian ▷ v 6 attack ferociously

S

———— THESAURUS ————

exhaust, deplete

satire n = **mockery**, irony, ridicule; = **parody**, mockery, caricature, lampoon, burlesque

satisfy v = **content**, please, indulge, gratify, pander to ≠ **dissatisfy**; = **convince**, persuade, assure, reassure ≠ **dissuade**; = **comply with**, meet, fulfil, answer, serve ≠ **fail to meet**

saturate v = **flood**, overwhelm, swamp, overrun

savage adj = **cruel**, brutal, vicious, fierce, harsh ≠ **gentle**; = **wild**, fierce, ferocious, unbroken, feral ≠ **tame**; = **primitive**, undeveloped, uncultivated, uncivilized ▷ n = **lout**, yob (Brit Sl), barbarian, yahoo, boor ▷ v = **maul**, tear, claw, attack, mangle (Inf)

save ➊ v 1 rescue, preserve 2 keep
for future 3 prevent need of 4 lay
by money ▷ n 5 (Sport) act of
preventing goal etc. ▷ prep
6 except **saving** adj 1 redeeming
▷ prep 2 excepting ▷ n 3 economy
▷ pl 4 money put by for future use
saviour ➊ n 1 person who rescues
another 2 (with cap.) Christ
savour ➊ n 1 characteristic taste
or smell ▷ v 2 have particular taste
or smell 3 give flavour to 4 have
flavour of 5 enjoy **savoury** adj
1 attractive to taste or smell 2 not
sweet
saw¹ n 1 tool with toothed edge for
cutting wood etc. ▷ v 2 cut with
saw 3 make movements of sawing
sawdust n fine wood fragments
made in sawing
saw² past tense of SEE
saxophone n keyed wind
instrument
say ➊ v **saying, said** 1 speak
2 pronounce 3 state 4 express
5 take as example or as near

enough 6 form and deliver opinion
▷ n 7 what one has to say
8 chance of saying it 9 share in
decision **saying** n maxim, proverb
scab n 1 crust formed over wound
2 skin disease 3 disease of plants
scabbard n sheath for sword or
dagger
scaffold n 1 temporary platform
for workmen 2 gallows
scaffolding n (material for
building) scaffold
scald v 1 burn with hot liquid or
steam 2 heat (liquid) almost to
boiling point ▷ n 3 injury by
scalding
scale¹ ➊ n 1 one of the thin,
overlapping plates covering fishes
and reptiles 2 thin flake 3 crust
which forms in kettles etc. ▷ v
4 remove scales from 5 come off in
scales
scale² ➊ n 1 graduated table or
sequence of marks at regular
intervals used as reference in
making measurements 2 series of

— THESAURUS —

save v = **rescue**, free, release,
deliver, recover ≠ **endanger**;
= **keep**, reserve, set aside, store,
collect ≠ **spend**; = **protect**, keep,
guard, preserve, look after
saviour n = **rescuer**, deliverer,
defender, protector, liberator
savour v = **relish**, delight in, revel
in, luxuriate in; = **enjoy**, appreciate,
relish, delight in, revel in ▷ n
= **flavour**, taste, smell, relish,
smack
say v = **state**, declare, remark,
announce, maintain; = **speak**,

utter, voice, express, pronounce;
= **suggest**, express, imply,
communicate, disclose; = **suppose**,
supposing, imagine, assume,
presume ▷ n = **influence**, power,
control, authority, weight;
= **chance to speak**, vote, voice
scale¹ n = **flake**, plate, layer, lamina
scale² n = **degree**, size, range,
extent, dimensions, measuring
system; = **ranking**, ladder,
hierarchy, series, sequence ▷ v
= **climb up**, mount, ascend,
surmount, clamber up

musical notes **3** ratio of size between a thing and a model or map of it **4** (relative) degree, extent ▷ v **5** climb ▷ adj **6** proportionate

scale³ n (usu. pl) weighing instrument

scallop n **1** edible shellfish **2** edging in small curves like scallop shell ▷ v **3** shape like scallop shell

scalp n **1** skin and hair of top of head ▷ v **2** cut off scalp of

scalpel n small surgical knife

scamp n mischievous person

scamper v **1** run about **2** run hastily ▷ n **3** scampering

scampi pl n large prawns

scan ⊙ v **scanning, scanned** **1** look at carefully **2** examine, search using radar or sonar beam **3** glance over quickly **4** (of verse) conform to metrical rules ▷ n **5** scanning **scanner** n device, esp. electronic, which scans

scandal ⊙ n **1** something disgraceful **2** malicious gossip **scandalize** v shock **scandalous** adj

scant ⊙ adj barely sufficient or not sufficient **scanty** adj

scapegoat ⊙ n person bearing blame due to others

scar ⊙ n **1** mark left by healed wound, burn or sore **2** change resulting from emotional distress ▷ v **3** mark, heal with scar

scarce ⊙ adj **1** hard to find **2** existing or available in insufficient quantity **3** uncommon **scarcely** adv **1** only just **2** not quite **3** definitely or probably not **scarcity, scarceness** n

scare ⊙ v **1** frighten ▷ n **2** fright, sudden panic **scary** adj **scarecrow** n **1** thing set up to frighten birds from crops **2** badly dressed person

scarf n, pl **scarves, scarfs** long narrow strip of material to put round neck, head etc.

scarlet n **1** brilliant red colour ▷ adj **2** of this colour **3** immoral, esp. unchaste **scarlet fever** infectious fever with scarlet rash

scathing adj harshly critical

scatter ⊙ v **1** throw in various

scan v = **glance over**, skim, look over, eye, check; = **survey**, search, investigate, sweep, scour

scandal n = **disgrace**, crime, offence, sin, embarrassment; = **gossip**, talk, rumours, dirt, slander; = **shame**, disgrace, stigma, infamy, opprobrium

scant adj = **inadequate**, meagre, sparse, little, minimal ≠ **adequate**

scapegoat n = **fall guy** (Inf), whipping boy

scar n = **mark**, injury, wound, blemish ▷ v = **mark**, disfigure, damage, mar, mutilate

scarce adj = **in short supply**, insufficient ≠ **plentiful**; = **rare**, few, uncommon, few and far between, infrequent ≠ **common**

scare v = **frighten**, alarm, terrify, panic, shock ▷ n = **fright**, shock, start

scatter v = **throw about**, spread, sprinkle, strew, shower ≠ **gather**;

S

directions **2** put here and there
3 sprinkle **4** disperse
scatterbrain *n* empty-headed
person
scavenge *v* search for (anything
usable), esp. among discarded
material **scavenger** *n* **1** person
who scavenges **2** animal, bird
which feeds on refuse
scenario *n, pl* **-rios 1** summary of
plot of play or film **2** imagined
sequence of future events
scene ⊕ *n* **1** place of action of
novel, play etc. **2** place of any
action **3** subdivision of play **4** view
5 episode **6** display of strong
emotion **scenery** *n* **1** natural
features of district **2** constructions
used on stage to represent scene of
action **scenic** *adj* picturesque
scent ⊕ *n* **1** distinctive smell, esp.
pleasant one **2** trail **3** perfume ▷ *v*
4 detect or track (by smell) **5** sense
6 fill with fragrance
sceptic ⊕ *n* one who maintains
doubt or disbelief **sceptical** *adj*

scepticism *n*
sceptre *n* ornamental staff as
symbol of royal power
schedule ⊕ *n* **1** plan of procedure
for project **2** list **3** timetable ▷ *v*
4 enter into schedule **5** plan to
occur at certain time
scheme ⊕ *n* **1** plan, design
2 project **3** outline ▷ *v* **4** devise,
plan, esp. in underhand manner
scheming *adj*
schism *n* (group resulting from)
division in political party, church etc.
schizophrenia *n* mental disorder
involving deterioration of,
confusion about personality
schizophrenic *adj/n*
school[1] ⊕ *n* **1** institution for
teaching children or for giving
instruction in any subject
2 buildings of such institution
3 group of thinkers, writers, artists
etc. with principles or methods in
common ▷ *v* **4** educate **5** bring
under control, train **scholar** *n*
1 learned person **2** one taught in

——————— THESAURUS ———————

= **disperse**, dispel, disband,
dissipate ≠ **assemble**
scene *n* = **act**, part, division,
episode; = **setting**, set,
background, location, backdrop;
= **site**, place, setting, area, position;
(*Inf*) = **world**, business,
environment, arena; = **view**,
prospect, panorama, vista,
landscape; = **fuss**, to-do, row,
performance, exhibition
scent *n* = **fragrance**, smell,
perfume, bouquet, aroma; = **trail**,
track, spoor ▷ *v* = **smell**, sense,

detect, sniff, discern
sceptic *n* = **doubter**, cynic,
disbeliever
schedule *n* = **plan**, programme,
agenda, calendar, timetable ▷ *v*
= **plan**, set up, book, programme,
arrange
scheme *n* = **plan**, programme,
strategy, system, project; = **plot**,
ploy, ruse, intrigue, conspiracy ▷ *v*
= **plot**, plan, intrigue, manoeuvre,
conspire
school[1] *n* = **academy**, college,
institution, institute, seminary;

school **scholarly** adj learned
scholarship n 1 learning 2 prize, grant to student for payment of school or college fees **scholastic** adj of schools or scholars

school² n shoal (of fish, whales etc.)

schooner n 1 fore-and-aft rigged vessel with two or more masts 2 tall glass

science ⊕ n 1 systematic study and knowledge of natural or physical phenomena 2 any branch of study concerned with observed material facts 3 skill, technique **scientific** adj 1 of the principles of science 2 systematic **scientist** n **science fiction** stories making imaginative use of scientific knowledge

scimitar n curved oriental sword

scintillating adj 1 sparkling 2 animated, witty, clever

scissors pl n cutting instrument of two blades pivoted together

scoff¹ ⊕ v express derision for

scoff² ⊕ v (Sl) eat rapidly

scold v 1 find fault 2 reprimand

scone n small plain cake baked on griddle or in oven

scope ⊕ n 1 range of activity or application 2 room, opportunity

scorch ⊕ v 1 burn, be burnt, on surface ▷ n 2 slight burn

score ⊕ n 1 points gained in game, competition 2 group of 20 3 (esp. pl) a lot 4 musical notation 5 mark or notch, esp. to keep tally 6 reason, account 7 grievance ▷ v 8 gain points in game 9 mark 10 cross out 11 arrange music (for) 12 keep tally of points

scorn ⊕ n 1 contempt, derision ▷ v 2 despise **scornful** adj

scorpion n small lobster-shaped animal with sting at end of jointed tail

scotch v put an end to

scot-free adj without harm or loss

scoundrel n villain, blackguard

scour¹ ⊕ v 1 clean, polish by rubbing 2 clean or flush out

= **group**, set, circle, faction, followers ▷ v = **train**, coach, discipline, educate, drill

science n = **discipline**, body of knowledge, branch of knowledge

scoff¹ v = **scorn**, mock, laugh at, ridicule, knock (Inf)

scoff² v = **gobble (up)**, wolf, devour, bolt, guzzle

scope n = **opportunity**, room, freedom, space, liberty; = **range**, capacity, reach, area, outlook

scorch v = **burn**, sear, roast, wither, shrivel

score v = **gain**, win, achieve, make, get; (Mus) = **arrange**, set, orchestrate, adapt; = **cut**, scratch, mark, slash, scrape ▷ n = **rating**, mark, grade, percentage; = **points**, result, total, outcome; = **composition**, soundtrack, arrangement, orchestration

scorn n = **contempt**, disdain, mockery, derision, sarcasm ≠ **respect** ▷ v = **despise**, reject, disdain, slight, be above ≠ **respect**

scour¹ v = **scrub**, clean, polish, rub, buff

S

scourer n rough pad for cleaning pots and pans

scour² ❶ v move rapidly along or over (territory) in search of something

scourge n 1 whip, lash 2 severe affliction ▷ v 3 flog 4 punish severely

scout ❶ n 1 one sent out to reconnoitre ▷ v 2 act as scout

scowl v/n (make) gloomy or sullen frown

scrabble v scrape at with hands, claws in disorderly manner

scrag n 1 lean person or animal 2 lean end of a neck of mutton **scraggy** adj thin, bony

scram v **scramming, scrammed** (Inf) go away hastily

scramble ❶ v 1 move along or up by crawling, climbing etc. 2 struggle with others (for) 3 mix up 4 cook (eggs) beaten up with milk ▷ n 5 scrambling 6 rough climb 7 disorderly proceeding

scrap ❶ n **scrapping, scrapped**

1 small piece or fragment 2 leftover material 3 (Inf) fight ▷ pl 4 leftover food ▷ v 5 break up, discard as useless 6 (Inf) fight **scrappy** adj 1 unequal in quality 2 badly finished **scrapbook** n book in which newspaper cuttings or pictures are stuck

scrape ❶ v 1 rub with something sharp 2 clean, smooth thus 3 grate 4 scratch 5 rub with harsh noise ▷ n 6 act, sound of scraping **scraper** n instrument for scraping

scratch ❶ v 1 score, make narrow surface mark or wound with something sharp 2 scrape (skin) with nails to relieve itching 3 remove, withdraw from list, race etc. ▷ n 4 wound, mark or sound made by scratching

scrawl v 1 write, draw untidily ▷ n 2 thing scrawled

scrawny adj **scrawnier, scrawniest** thin, bony

scream ❶ v 1 utter piercing cry, esp. of fear, pain etc. 2 utter in a

THESAURUS

scour² v = **search**, hunt, comb, ransack

scout n = **vanguard**, lookout, precursor, outrider, reconnoitrer ▷ v = **reconnoitre**, investigate, watch, survey, observe

scramble v = **struggle**, climb, crawl, swarm, scrabble; = **strive**, rush, contend, vie, run ▷ n = **clamber**, ascent; = **race**, competition, struggle, rush, confusion

scrap n = **piece**, fragment, bit, grain, particle; = **waste**, junk, off

cuts ▷ v = **get rid of**, drop, abandon, ditch (Sl), discard ≠ **bring back**

scrape v = **rake**, sweep, drag, brush; = **grate**, grind, scratch, squeak, rasp; = **graze**, skin, scratch, bark, scuff; = **clean**, remove, scour ▷ n (Inf) = **predicament**, difficulty, fix (Inf), mess, dilemma

scratch v = **rub**, scrape, claw at; = **mark**, cut, score, damage, grate ▷ n = **mark**, scrape, graze, blemish, gash

scream v = **cry**, yell, shriek,

scream ▷ *n* **3** shrill, piercing cry

screech *v/n* scream

screed *n* long (tedious) letter, passage or speech

screen ❶ *n* **1** device to shelter from heat, light, draught, observation etc. **2** blank surface on which photographic images are projected **3** windscreen ▷ *v* **4** shelter, hide **5** show (film) **6** examine (group of people) for political motives or for presence of disease, weapons etc.

screw ❶ *n* **1** metal pin with spiral thread, twisted into materials to pin or fasten **2** anything resembling a screw in shape ▷ *v* **3** fasten with screw **4** twist around **screwdriver** *n* tool for turning screws

scribble ❶ *v* **1** write, draw carelessly **2** make meaningless marks with pen or pencil ▷ *n* **3** something scribbled

scribe *n* **1** writer **2** copyist ▷ *v* **3** scratch a line with pointed instrument

scrimp *v* **1** make too small or short **2** treat meanly

script ❶ *n* **1** (system or style of) handwriting **2** written text of film, play, radio or television programme

scripture *n* **1** sacred writings **2** the Bible

scroll *n* **1** roll of parchment or paper **2** ornament shaped thus

scrotum *n, pl* **-ta, -tums** pouch of skin containing testicles

scrounge *v* (*Inf*) get without cost, by begging **scrounger** *n*

scrub¹ ❶ *v* **scrubbing, scrubbed** **1** clean with hard brush and water **2** scour **3** (*Inf*) delete, cancel

scrub² *n* **scrubbing, scrubbed** **1** stunted trees **2** brushwood

scruff *n* nape of neck

scrum, scrummage *n* (*Rugby*) **1** restarting of play in which opposing packs of forwards push against each other to gain possession of the ball **2** disorderly struggle

scruple *n* **1** doubt or hesitation about what is morally right ▷ *v* **2** hesitate **scrupulous** *adj* **1** extremely conscientious **2** thorough

scrutiny ❶ *n, pl* **-nies 1** close examination **2** critical

screech, bawl ▷ *n* = **cry**, yell, howl, shriek, screech

screen *n* = **cover**, guard, shade, shelter, shield ▷ *v* = **broadcast**, show, put on, present, air; = **cover**, hide, conceal, shade, mask; = **investigate**, test, check, examine, scan; = **process**, sort, examine, filter, scan

screw *v* = **fasten**, fix, attach, bolt, clamp; = **turn**, twist, tighten; (*Inf*)

= **cheat**, do (*Sl*), rip (someone) off (*Sl*), skin (*Sl*), trick (*Inf*)

scribble *v* = **scrawl**, write, jot, dash off

script *n* = **text**, lines, words, book, copy; = **handwriting**, writing, calligraphy, penmanship

scrub¹ *v* = **scour**, clean, polish, rub, wash; (*Inf*) = **cancel**, drop, give up, abolish, forget about

scrutiny *n* = **examination**, study,

S

investigation **scrutinize** v
examine closely

scuba diving sport of swimming
under water using self-contained
breathing apparatus

scud v **scudding, scudded** 1 run
fast 2 run before wind

scuff v 1 drag, scrape with feet in
walking 2 graze ▷ n 3 act, sound
of scuffing

scuffle v 1 fight in disorderly
manner 2 shuffle ▷ n 3 scuffling

scull n 1 oar used in stern of boat
2 short oar used in pairs ▷ v
3 propel, move by means of sculls

scullery n, pl **-leries** place for
washing dishes etc.

sculpture ❶ n 1 art of forming
solid figures 2 product of this art
▷ v 3 represent by sculpture
sculptor n

scum n 1 froth or other floating
matter on liquid 2 waste part of
anything 3 vile people **scummy**
adj

scungy adj **-ier, -iest** (Aust & NZ,
Inf) sordid or dirty

scurrilous adj coarse, indecently
abusive

scurry v **-rying, -ried** 1 run hastily
▷ n 2 bustling haste 3 flurry

scurvy n disease caused by lack of
vitamin C

scuttle¹ n fireside container for coal

scuttle² v 1 rush away 2 run

hurriedly ▷ n 3 hurried run

scuttle³ v make hole in ship to sink
it

scythe n 1 manual implement
with long curved blade for cutting
grass ▷ v 2 cut with scythe

sea ❶ n 1 mass of salt water
covering greater part of earth
2 broad tract of this 3 waves
4 vast expanse ▷ adj 5 of the sea
seagull n gull **sea horse** fish
with bony-plated body and
horselike head **sea lion** kind of
large seal **seaman** n sailor
seasick adj **seasickness** n
nausea caused by motion of ship
seaweed n plant growing in sea
seaworthy adj in fit condition to
put to sea

seal¹ ❶ n 1 piece of metal or stone
engraved with device for
impression on wax etc.
2 impression thus made (on letters
etc.) 3 device, material preventing
passage of water, air, oil etc. ▷ v
4 affix seal to ratify, authorize
5 mark with stamp as evidence of
some quality 6 keep close or secret
7 settle 8 make watertight,
airtight etc.

seal² n amphibious furred
carnivorous mammal with flippers
as limbs

seam ❶ n 1 line of junction of two
edges, e.g. of two pieces of cloth

———————— THESAURUS ————————

investigation, search, analysis
sculpture v = **carve**, form, model,
fashion, shape
sea n = **ocean**, the deep, the waves,
main; = **mass**, army, host, crowd,

mob
seal¹ v = **settle**, clinch, conclude,
consummate, finalize ▷ n
= **sealant**, sealer, adhesive
seam n = **joint**, closure; = **layer**,

2 thin layer, stratum ▷ v **3** mark with furrows or wrinkles **seamless** adj **seamy** adj sordid

seance n meeting at which people attempt to communicate with the dead

sear ❶ v scorch

search ❶ v **1** look over or through to find something ▷ n **2** act of searching **3** quest **searching** adj thorough

season ❶ n **1** one of four divisions of year **2** period during which thing happens etc. ▷ v **3** flavour with salt, herbs etc. **4** make reliable or ready for use **5** make experienced **seasonable** adj **1** appropriate for the season **2** opportune **seasonal** adj varying with seasons **seasoning** n flavouring

seat ❶ n **1** thing for sitting on **2** buttocks **3** base **4** right to sit (e.g. in council etc.) **5** place where something is located, centred **6** locality of disease, trouble etc. **7** country house ▷ v **8** make to sit

9 provide sitting accommodation for **seat belt** belt worn in vehicle to prevent injury in crash

secateurs pl n small pruning shears

secede v withdraw formally from federation, Church etc. **secession** n

seclude v guard from, remove from sight, view, contact with others **secluded** adj **1** remote **2** private **seclusion** n

second¹ ❶ adj **1** next after first **2** alternate, additional **3** of lower quality ▷ n **4** person or thing coming second **5** attendant **6** sixtieth part of minute ▷ v **7** support **second-class** adj inferior **second-hand** adj **1** bought after use by another **2** not original **second sight** supposed ability to predict events

second² v transfer (employee, officer) temporarily

secondary ❶ adj **1** of less importance **2** developed from

vein, stratum, lode

sear v = **wither**, burn, scorch, sizzle

search v = **examine**, investigate, explore, inspect, comb ▷ n = **hunt**, look, investigation, examination, pursuit

season n = **period**, time, term, spell ▷ v = **flavour**, salt, spice, enliven, pep up

seat n = **chair**, bench, stall, stool, pew; = **membership**, place, constituency, chair, incumbency; = **centre**, place, site, heart, capital; = **mansion**, house, residence,

abode, ancestral hall ▷ v = **sit**, place, settle, set, fix; = **hold**, take, accommodate, sit, contain

second¹ adj = **next**, following, succeeding, subsequent; = **additional**, other, further, extra, alternative; = **inferior**, secondary, subordinate, lower, lesser ▷ n = **supporter**, assistant, aide, colleague, backer ▷ v = **support**, back, endorse, approve, go along with

secondary adj = **subordinate**, minor, lesser, lower, inferior

S

something else **3** (*Education*) after primary stage

secret ⊕ *adj* **1** kept, meant to be kept from knowledge of others **2** hidden ▷ *n* **3** thing kept secret **secrecy** *n* keeping or being kept secret **secretive** *adj* given to having secrets

secretary *n, pl* **-ries 1** one employed to deal with papers and correspondence, keep records etc. **2** head of a state department **secretariat** *n* body of secretaries

secrete *v* **1** hide **2** conceal **3** (of gland etc.) collect and supply particular substance in body **secretion** *n*

sect ⊕ *n* **1** group of people (within religious body etc.) with common interest **2** faction **sectarian** *adj*

section ⊕ *n* **1** division **2** portion **3** distinct part **4** cutting **5** drawing of anything as if cut through

sector ⊕ *n* part or subdivision

secular ⊕ *adj* **1** worldly **2** lay, not religious

secure ⊕ *adj* **1** safe **2** firmly fixed **3** certain ▷ *v* **4** gain possession of **5** make safe **6** make firm **security** *n, pl* **-ties 1** state of safety **2** protection **3** anything given as bond or pledge

sedate¹ *adj* calm, serious

sedate² *v* make calm by sedative **sedation** *n* **sedative** *adj* **1** having soothing or calming effect ▷ *n* **2** sedative drug

sediment ⊕ *n* matter which settles to the bottom of liquid

sedition *n* stirring up of rebellion

seduce ⊕ *v* persuade to commit some (wrong) deed, esp. sexual intercourse **seducer** *n* **seduction** *n* **seductive** *adj* alluring

see¹ ⊕ *v* **seeing, saw, seen 1** perceive with eyes or mentally **2** watch **3** find out **4** interview

———————— THESAURUS ————————

≠ **main**; = **resultant**, contingent, derived, indirect ≠ **original**

secret *adj* = **undisclosed**, unknown, confidential, underground, undercover; = **concealed**, hidden, disguised ≠ **unconcealed**

sect *n* = **group**, division, faction, party, camp

section *n* = **part**, piece, portion, division, slice; = **district**, area, region, sector, zone

sector *n* = **part**, division; = **area**, part, region, district, zone

secular *adj* = **worldly**, lay, earthly, civil, temporal ≠ **religious**

secure *v* = **obtain**, get, acquire, score (*Sl*), gain ≠ **lose**; = **attach**, stick, fix, bind, fasten ≠ **detach** ▷ *adj* = **safe**, protected, immune, unassailable ≠ **unprotected**; = **fast**, firm, fixed, stable, steady ≠ **insecure**; = **confident**, sure, easy, certain, assured ≠ **uneasy**

sediment *n* = **dregs**, grounds, residue, lees, deposit

seduce *v* = **tempt**, lure, entice, mislead, deceive; = **corrupt**, deprave, dishonour, debauch, deflower

see¹ *v* = **perceive**, spot, notice, sight, witness; = **understand**, get,

S

5 make sure **6** accompany **7** consider **seeing** *conj* in view of the fact that

see² *n* diocese, office of bishop

seed ❶ *n* **1** reproductive germs of plants **2** one grain of this **3** such grains saved or used for sowing **4** sperm **5** origin ▷ *v* **6** sow with seed **7** produce seed **seedling** *n* young plant raised from seed **seedy** *adj* **1** shabby **2** full of seed

seek ❶ *v* **seeking, sought** make search or enquiry (for)

seem ❶ *v* appear (to be or to do) **seemly** *adj* becoming and proper

seep ❶ *v* trickle through slowly

seesaw *n* **1** plank on which children sit at opposite ends and swing up and down ▷ *v* **2** move up and down

seethe ❶ *v* **seething, seethed** **1** boil, foam **2** be very agitated **3** be in constant movement (as large crowd etc.)

segment ❶ *n* **1** piece cut off **2** section ▷ *v* **3** divide into segments

segregate ❶ *v* set apart from rest **segregation** *n*

seize ❶ *v* **1** grasp **2** lay hold of **3** capture **4** (of machine part) stick tightly through overheating **seizure** *n* **1** act of taking **2** sudden onset of disease

seldom ❶ *adv* not often, rarely

select ❶ *v* **1** pick out, choose ▷ *adj* **2** choice, picked **3** exclusive **selection** *n* **1** option

follow, realize, appreciate; = **find out**, learn, discover, determine, verify; = **consider**, decide, reflect, deliberate, think over; = **make sure**, ensure, guarantee, make certain, see to it; = **accompany**, show, escort, lead, walk; = **speak to**, receive, interview, consult, confer with; = **meet**, come across, happen on, bump into, run across; = **go out with**, court, date (*Inf*, *chiefly US*), go steady with (*Inf*)

seed *n* = **grain**, pip, germ, kernel, egg; = **beginning**, start, germ; = **origin**, source, nucleus; (*chiefly Bible*) = **offspring**, children, descendants, issue, progeny

seek *v* = **look for**, pursue, search for, be after, hunt; = **try**, attempt, aim, strive, endeavour

seem *v* = **appear**, give the impression of being, look

seep *v* = **ooze**, well, leak, soak, trickle

seethe *v* = **be furious**, rage, fume, simmer, see red (*Inf*); = **boil**, bubble, foam, fizz, froth

segment *n* = **section**, part, piece, division, slice

segregate *v* = **set apart**, divide, separate, isolate, discriminate against ≠ **unite**

seize *v* = **grab**, grip, grasp, take, snatch ≠ **let go**; = **take by storm**, take over, acquire, occupy, conquer

seldom *adv* = **rarely**, not often, infrequently, hardly ever ≠ **often**

select *v* = **choose**, take, pick, opt for, decide on ≠ **reject** ▷ *adj* = **choice**, special, excellent, superior, first-class ≠ **ordinary**; = **exclusive**, elite, privileged,

S

2 assortment **selective** *adj* **selector** *n*

self *n, pl* **selves** one's own person or individuality **selfie** *n* (*Inf*) photograph taken by pointing camera at oneself **selfish** *adj* **1** unduly concerned with personal profit or pleasure **2** greedy **selfless** *adj* unselfish

self- *comb. form* of oneself or itself

sell ❶ *v* **selling, sold 1** hand over for a price **2** stock, have for sale **3** make someone accept **4** (*Inf*) betray, cheat **5** find purchasers **seller** *n*

Sellotape *n* **1** type of adhesive tape ▷ *v* **2** (*without cap.*) stick with Sellotape

semaphore *n* system of signalling by human or mechanical arms

semblance *n* **1** (false) appearance **2** image, likeness

semen *n* **1** fluid carrying sperm of male animals **2** sperm

semi- *comb. form* half, partly, not completely, as in *semicircle*

semibreve *n* musical note equal to four crotchets

semicolon *n* punctuation mark (;)

semiconductor *n* substance whose electrical conductivity increases with temperature, used in

transistors, circuits etc.

semidetached *adj* (of house) joined to another by one side only

semifinal *n* match, round etc. before final

seminal *adj* **1** capable of developing **2** influential **3** of semen or seed

seminar *n* meeting of group (of students) for discussion

semiprecious *adj* (of gemstones) having less value than precious stones

semolina *n* hard grains left after sifting of flour, used for puddings etc.

send ❶ *v* **sending, sent 1** cause to go or be conveyed **2** despatch **3** transmit (by radio)

senile *adj* showing weakness of old age **senility** *n*

senior ❶ *adj* **1** superior in rank or standing **2** older ▷ *n* **3** superior **4** elder person **seniority** *n*

sensation ❶ *n* **1** operation of sense, feeling, awareness **2** excited feeling, state of excitement **3** exciting event **sensational** *adj* producing great excitement **sensationalism** *n* deliberate use of sensational material

sense ❶ *n* **1** any of bodily faculties of perception or feeling **2** ability to perceive **3** consciousness

——————————————— THESAURUS ———————————————

cliquish ≠ **indiscriminate**

sell *v* = **trade**, exchange, barter ≠ **buy**; = **deal in**, market, trade in, stock, handle ≠ **buy**

send *v* = **dispatch**, forward, direct, convey, remit = **transmit**, broadcast, communicate

senior *adj* = **higher ranking**,

superior ≠ **subordinate**; = **the elder**, major (*Brit*) ≠ **junior**

sensation *n* = **feeling**, sense, impression, perception, awareness; = **excitement**, thrill, stir, furore, commotion

sense *n* = **feeling**, impression, perception, awareness,

4 meaning **5** coherence **6** sound practical judgment ▷ v **7** perceive **senseless** adj

sensible ❶ adj **1** reasonable, wise **2** aware **sensibility** n ability to feel, esp. emotional or moral feelings

sensitive ❶ adj **1** open to, acutely affected by, external impressions **2** easily affected or altered **3** easily upset by criticism **4** responsive to slight changes **sensitivity, sensitiveness** n **sensitize** v make sensitive

sensor n device that detects or measures the presence of something

sensory adj relating to senses

sensual ❶ adj **1** of senses only and not of mind **2** given to pursuit of pleasures of sense

sensuous adj stimulating, or apprehended by, senses, esp. in aesthetic manner

sentence ❶ n **1** combination of words expressing a thought **2** judgment passed on criminal by court or judge ▷ v **3** pass sentence on, condemn

sentient adj capable of feeling

sentiment ❶ n **1** tendency to be moved by feeling rather than reason **2** mental feeling **3** opinion **sentimental** adj given to indulgence in sentiment and in its expression **sentimentality** n

sentinel n sentry

sentry n, pl **-tries** soldier on watch

separate ❶ v **1** part **2** divide ▷ adj **3** disconnected, distinct, individual **separable** adj **separation** n **1** disconnection **2** living apart of married couple

---

THESAURUS

---

consciousness; **= understanding**, awareness; *sometimes plural*
= intelligence, reason, understanding, brains (*Inf*), judgment ≠ **foolishness**;
= meaning, significance, import, implication, drift ▷ v **= perceive**, feel, understand, pick up, realize ≠ **be unaware of**

sensible adj **= wise**, practical, prudent, shrewd, judicious ≠ **foolish**; **= intelligent**, practical, rational, sound, realistic ≠ **senseless**

sensitive adj **= thoughtful**, kindly, concerned, patient, attentive;
= susceptible to, responsive to, easily affected by; **= touchy**, oversensitive, easily upset, easily offended, easily hurt ≠ **insensitive**

sensual adj **= sexual**, erotic, raunchy (*Sl*), lewd, lascivious;
= physical, bodily, voluptuous, animal, luxurious

sentence n **= punishment**, condemnation ▷ v **= condemn**, doom

sentiment n **= feeling**, idea, view, opinion, attitude;
= sentimentality, emotion, tenderness, romanticism, sensibility

separate adj **= unconnected**, individual, particular, divided, divorced ≠ **connected**;
= individual, independent, apart, distinct ≠ **joined** ▷ v **= divide**, detach, disconnect, disjoin

S

sepia *n* **1** reddish-brown pigment
▷ *adj* **2** of this colour

Sept. September

September *n* ninth month

septet *n* (music for) group of seven
musicians

septic *adj* **1** (of wound) infected
2 of, caused by pus-forming
bacteria

septicaemia *n* blood poisoning

sepulchre *n* **1** tomb **2** burial vault

sequel ❶ *n* **1** consequence
2 continuation, e.g. of story

sequence ❶ *n* arrangement of
things in successive order

sequin *n* small ornamental metal
disc on dresses etc.

seraph *n, pl* **-aphs, -aphim** angel

serenade *n* **1** sentimental song
addressed to woman by lover, esp.
at evening ▷ *v* **2** sing serenade (to
someone)

serendipity *n* gift of making
fortunate discoveries by accident

serene *adj* **1** calm, tranquil
2 unclouded **serenity** *n*

serf *n* one of class of medieval

labourers bound to, and transferred
with, land

sergeant *n* **1** noncommissioned
officer in army **2** police officer
above constable **sergeant major**
highest noncommissioned officer in
regiment

series ❶ *n, pl* **-ries 1** sequence
2 succession, set (e.g. of radio, TV
programmes) **serial** *n* story or
play produced in successive
episodes **serialize** *v*

serious ❶ *adj* **1** thoughtful,
solemn **2** earnest, sincere **3** of
importance **4** giving cause for
concern

sermon ❶ *n* **1** discourse of
religious instruction or exhortation
2 any similar discourse

serpent *n* snake **serpentine** *adj*
twisting, winding like a snake

serrated *adj* having notched,
sawlike edge

serum *n* watery animal fluid, esp.
thin part of blood as used for
inoculation or vaccination

serve ❶ *v* **1** work for, under

THESAURUS

≠ **combine**; = **come apart**, split,
come away ≠ **connect**; = **sever**,
break apart, split in two, divide in
two ≠ **join**; = **split up**, part,
divorce, break up, part company

sequel *n* = **follow-up**,
continuation, development;
= **consequence**, result, outcome,
conclusion, end

sequence *n* = **succession**, course,
series, order, chain

series *n* = **sequence**, course, chain,
succession, run, soapie (Aust Sl)

serious *adj* = **grave**, bad, critical,
dangerous, acute; = **important**,
crucial, urgent, pressing, worrying
≠ **unimportant**; = **thoughtful**,
detailed, careful, deep, profound;
= **deep**, sophisticated

sermon *n* = **homily**, address

serve *v* = **work for**, help, aid,
assist, be in the service of;
= **perform**, do, complete, fulfil,
discharge; = **be adequate**, do,
suffice, suit, satisfy; = **present**,
provide, supply, deliver, set out

another **2** attend (to customers) in shop etc. **3** provide **4** help to (food etc.) **5** present (food etc.) in particular way **6** be member of military unit **7** spend time doing **8** be useful, suitable enough **servant** n personal or domestic attendant **service** n **1** act of serving **2** system organized to provide for needs of public **3** maintenance of vehicle **4** use **5** department of State employment **6** set of dishes etc. **7** form, session of public worship ▷ pl **8** armed forces ▷ v **9** overhaul **serviceable** adj **1** in working order, usable **2** durable **serviceman** n member of armed forced **service station** place supplying fuel, oil, maintenance for motor vehicles

serviette n table napkin

servile adj **1** slavish, without independence **2** fawning

servitude n bondage, slavery

sesame n plant whose seeds and oil are used in cooking

session ❶ n **1** meeting of court etc. **2** continuous series of such meetings **3** any period devoted to an activity

set ❶ v **setting, set 1** put or place in specified position or condition **2** make ready **3** become firm or fixed **4** establish **5** prescribe, allot **6** put to music **7** (of sun) go down ▷ adj **8** fixed, established **9** deliberate **10** unvarying ▷ n **11** act or state of being set **12** bearing, posture **13** (Radio, TV) complete apparatus for reception or transmission **14** (Theatre, Cinema) organized settings and equipment to form ensemble of scene **15** number of associated things, persons **setback** n anything that hinders or impedes **set up** establish

sett, set n badger's burrow

settee n couch

setting ❶ n **1** background **2** surroundings **3** scenery and other stage accessories

---

THESAURUS

---

service n = **facility**, system, resource, utility, amenity; = **ceremony**, worship, rite, observance; = **work**, labour, employment, business, office; = **check**, maintenance check ▷ v = **overhaul**, check, maintain, tune (up), go over

session n = **meeting**, hearing, sitting, period, conference

set v = **put**, place, lay, position, rest; = **arrange**, decide (upon), settle, establish, determine; = **assign**, give, allot, prescribe; = **harden**, stiffen, solidify, cake, thicken; = **go down**, sink, dip, decline, disappear; = **prepare**, lay, spread, arrange, make ready ▷ adj = **established**, planned, decided, agreed, arranged; = **strict**, rigid, stubborn, inflexible ≠ **flexible**; = **conventional**, traditional, stereotyped, unspontaneous ▷ n = **scenery**, setting, scene, stage set; = **position**, bearing, attitude, carriage, posture

setting n = **surroundings**, site, location, set, scene

4 decorative metalwork holding precious stone etc. in position **5** tableware and cutlery for (single place at) table **6** music for song
settle ❶ v **1** arrange **2** establish **3** decide upon **4** end (®dispute etc.) **5** pay **6** make calm or stable **7** come to rest **8** subside **9** become clear **10** take up residence **settlement** n **1** act of settling **2** place newly inhabited **3** money bestowed legally **settler** n colonist
seven adj/n cardinal number next after six **seventh** adj ordinal number **seventeen** adj/n ten plus seven **seventeenth** adj **seventieth** adj **seventy** adj/n ten times seven
sever ❶ v **1** separate, divide **2** cut off **severance** n
several ❶ adj **1** some, a few **2** separate **3** individual ▷ pron **4** indefinite small number
severe ❶ adj **1** strict **2** harsh

3 austere **4** extreme **severity** n
sew v **sewing, sewed, sewn 1** join with needle and thread **2** make by sewing **sewing** n
sewage n refuse, waste matter, excrement conveyed in sewer **sewer** n underground drain
sex ❶ n **1** state of being male or female **2** males or females collectively **3** sexual intercourse ▷ adj **4** concerning sex ▷ v **5** ascertain sex of **sexism** n discrimination on basis of sex **sexist** n/adj **sexual** adj **sexy** adj **sexual intercourse** act of procreation in which male's penis is inserted into female's vagina
sextet n (composition for) six musicians
shabby ❶ adj **-bier, -biest 1** faded, worn **2** poorly dressed **3** mean, dishonourable
shack ❶ n rough hut
shackle n **1** metal ring or fastening for prisoner's wrist or

settle v = **resolve**, work out, put an end to, straighten out; = **pay**, clear, square (up), discharge; = **move to**, take up residence in, live in, dwell in, inhabit; = **colonize**, populate, people, pioneer; = **land**, alight, descend, light, come to rest; = **calm**, quiet, relax, relieve, reassure ≠ **disturb**
sever v = **cut**, separate, split, part, divide ≠ **join**; = **discontinue**, terminate, break off, put an end to, dissociate ≠ **continue**
several adj = **some**, a few, a number of, a handful of

severe adj = **serious**, critical, terrible, desperate, extreme; = **acute**, intense, violent, piercing, harrowing; = **strict**, hard, harsh, cruel, rigid ≠ **lenient**; = **grim**, serious, grave, forbidding, stern ≠ **genial**
sex n (Inf) = **lovemaking**, sexual relations, copulation, fornication, coitus
shabby adj = **tatty**, worn, ragged, scruffy, tattered ≠ **smart**; = **run-down**, seedy, mean, dilapidated
shack n = **hut**, cabin, shanty

S

ankle ▷ v 2 fasten with shackles
3 hamper

shade ❶ n 1 partial darkness
2 shelter, place sheltered from light,
heat etc. 3 darker part of anything
4 depth of colour 5 screen 6 (US)
window blind ▷ v 7 screen from
light, darken 8 represent shades in
drawing **shady** adj 1 shielded
from sun 2 (Inf) dishonest

shadow ❶ n 1 dark figure
projected by anything that
intercepts rays of light 2 patch of
shade 3 slight trace ▷ v 4 cast
shadow over 5 follow and watch
closely **shadowy** adj

shaft ❶ n 1 straight rod, stem,
handle 2 arrow 3 ray, beam (of
light) 4 revolving rod for
transmitting power

shag n 1 long-napped cloth
2 coarse shredded tobacco
shaggy adj 1 covered with rough
hair 2 unkempt

shake ❶ v shaking, shook,
shaken 1 (cause to) move with
quick vibrations 2 tremble 3 grasp
the hand (of another) in greeting
4 upset 5 wave, brandish ▷ n
6 act of shaking 7 vibration 8 jolt
9 (Inf) short period of time **shaky**
adj 1 unsteady, insecure
2 questionable

shale n flaky fine-grained rock

shall v, past tense **should** makes
compound tenses or moods to
express obligation, command,
condition or intention

shallow ❶ adj 1 not deep
2 superficial ▷ n 3 shallow place

sham ❶ adj/n 1 imitation,
counterfeit ▷ v 2 pretend, feign

shamble v walk in shuffling,
awkward way

shambles ❶ pl n messy, disorderly
thing or place

shame ❶ n 1 emotion caused by
consciousness of guilt or dishonour

─────── THESAURUS ───────

shade n = **hue**, tone, colour, tint;
= **dash**, trace, hint, suggestion;
= **screen**, covering, cover, blind,
curtain; (Lit) = **ghost**, spirit,
phantom, spectre, apparition ▷ v
= **darken**, shadow, cloud, dim;
= **cover**, protect, screen, hide,
shield

shadow n = **silhouette**, shape,
outline, profile; = **shade**, dimness,
darkness, gloom, cover ▷ v
= **shade**, screen, shield, darken,
overhang; = **follow**, tail (Inf), trail,
stalk

shaft n = **tunnel**, hole, passage,
burrow, passageway; = **handle**,

staff, pole, rod, stem

shake v = **jiggle**, agitate;
= **tremble**, shiver, quake, quiver;
= **rock**, totter; = **wave**, wield,
flourish, brandish ▷ n = **vibration**,
trembling, quaking, jerk, shiver

shallow adj = **superficial**, surface,
empty, slight, foolish ≠ **deep**

sham n = **fraud**, imitation, hoax,
pretence, forgery ≠ **the real thing**
▷ adj = **false**, artificial, bogus,
pretended, mock ≠ **real**

shambles n = **chaos**, mess,
disorder, confusion, muddle

shame n = **embarrassment**,
humiliation, ignominy,

in one's conduct or state **2** cause of
disgrace **3** pity, hard luck ▷ v
4 cause to feel shame **5** disgrace
6 force by shame (into) **shameful**
adj **shameless** adj **1** with no
sense of shame **2** indecent
shamefaced adj ashamed

shampoo n **1** preparation of liquid
soap for washing hair, carpets etc.
2 this process ▷ v **3** use shampoo
to wash

shamrock n clover leaf, esp. as
Irish emblem

shandy n, pl **-dies** drink of beer
and lemonade

shanty[1] n **1** temporary wooden
building **2** crude dwelling

shanty[2] n sailor's song

shape ❶ n **1** external form or
appearance **2** mould, pattern
3 (Inf) condition ▷ v **4** form, mould
5 develop **shapeless** adj **shapely**

adj well-proportioned

shard n broken piece of pottery

share ❶ n **1** portion **2** quota **3** lot
4 unit of ownership in public
company ▷ v **5** give, take a share
6 join with others in doing, using,
something **shareholder** n

shark n **1** large usu. predatory
sea fish **2** person who cheats
others

sharp ❶ adj **1** having keen cutting
edge or fine point **2** not gradual or
gentle **3** brisk **4** clever **5** harsh
6 dealing cleverly but unfairly
7 shrill **8** strongly marked, esp. in
outline **9** sour ▷ adv **10** promptly
sharpen v make sharp
sharpshooter n marksman

shatter ❶ v **1** break in pieces
2 ruin (plans etc.) **3** disturb
(person) greatly **shattered** adj
(Inf) completely exhausted

——————— THESAURUS

mortification, abashment
≠ shamelessness; **= disgrace**,
scandal, discredit, smear,
disrepute **≠ honour** ▷ v
= embarrass, disgrace,
humiliate, humble, mortify
≠ make proud; **= dishonour**,
degrade, stain, smear, blot
≠ honour

shape n **= appearance**, form,
aspect, guise, likeness; **= form**,
profile, outline, lines, build;
= pattern, model, frame, mould;
= condition, state, health, trim,
fettle ▷ v **= form**, make, produce,
create, model; **= mould**, form,
make, fashion, model

share n **= part**, portion, quota,

ration, lot ▷ v **= divide**, split,
distribute, assign; **= go halves on**,
go fifty-fifty on (Inf)

sharp adj **= keen**, jagged, serrated
≠ blunt; **= quick-witted**, clever,
astute, knowing, quick **≠ dim**;
= cutting, biting, bitter, harsh,
barbed **≠ gentle**; **= sudden**,
marked, abrupt, extreme, distinct
≠ gradual; **= clear**, distinct,
well-defined, crisp **≠ indistinct**;
= sour, tart, pungent, hot, acid
≠ bland ▷ adv **= promptly**,
precisely, exactly, on time, on the
dot **≠ approximately**

shatter v **= smash**, break, burst,
crack, crush; **= destroy**, ruin,
wreck, demolish, torpedo

shave ❶ v **shaving, shaved**
1 cut close, esp. hair of face or
head 2 pare away 3 graze
4 reduce ▷ n 5 shaving **shavings**
pl n parings

shawl n piece of fabric to cover
woman's shoulders or wrap baby

she pron 1 female person, animal
already referred to ▷ comb. form
2 female, as in she-wolf

sheaf n, pl **sheaves** 1 bundle, esp.
of corn 2 loose leaves of paper

shear v **shearing, sheared** 1 clip
hair, wool from 2 cut through
3 fracture **shears** pl n large pair of
scissors

sheath n close-fitting cover, esp.
for knife or sword **sheathe** v put
into sheath

shebeen n (Irish, S Afr & Scot) place
where alcohol is sold illegally

shed¹ ❶ n **shedding, shed** roofed
shelter used as store or workshop

shed² ❶ v **shedding, shed**
1 (cause to) pour forth (e.g. tears,
blood) 2 cast off

sheen ❶ n gloss

sheep n, pl **sheep** ruminant
animal bred for wool or meat
sheepish adj embarrassed, shy
sheepdog n dog used for herding
sheep

sheer ❶ adj 1 perpendicular 2 (of
material) very fine, transparent
3 absolute, unmitigated

sheet ❶ n 1 large piece of cotton
etc. to cover bed 2 broad piece of
any thin material 3 large expanse

sheikh, sheik n Arab chief

shelf n, pl **shelves** 1 board fixed
horizontally (on wall etc.) for
holding things 2 ledge

shell ❶ n 1 hard outer case (esp. of
egg, nut etc.) 2 explosive projectile
3 outer part of structure left when
interior is removed ▷ v 4 take shell
from 5 take out of shell 6 fire at
with shells **shellfish** n 1 mollusc
2 crustacean

shelter ❶ n 1 place, structure
giving protection 2 refuge ▷ v
3 give protection to 4 take shelter

shelve ❶ v 1 put on a shelf 2 put
off 3 slope gradually

shave v = **trim**, crop

shed¹ n = **hut**, shack, outhouse

shed² v = **drop**, spill, scatter; = **cast
off**, discard, moult, slough off;
= **give out**, cast, emit, give, radiate

sheen n = **shine**, gleam, gloss,
polish, brightness

sheer adj = **total**, complete,
absolute, utter, pure ≠ **moderate**;
= **steep**, abrupt, precipitous
≠ **gradual**; = **fine**, thin,
transparent, see-through,
gossamer ≠ **thick**

sheet n = **page**, leaf, folio, piece of
paper; = **plate**, piece, panel, slab

shell n = **husk**, case, pod ▷ v
= **bomb**, bombard, attack, blitz,
strafe

shelter n = **cover**, screen;
= **protection**, safety, refuge, cover
▷ v = **take shelter**, hide, seek
refuge, take cover; = **protect**,
shield, harbour, safeguard, cover
≠ **endanger**

shelve v = **postpone**, defer, freeze,
suspend, put aside

S

shepherd ❶ n **1** one who tends
sheep ▷ v **2** guide, watch over
shepherd's pie dish of minced
meat and potato
sherbet n fruit-flavoured
effervescent powder
sheriff n (US) **1** law enforcement
officer **2** in England and Wales,
chief executive officer of the crown
in a county **3** in Scotland, chief
judge of a district **4** (Canad)
municipal officer who enforces
court orders etc.
sherry n, pl **-ries** fortified wine
shield ❶ n **1** piece of armour
carried on arm **2** any protection
used to stop blows, missiles etc. ▷ v
3 cover, protect
shift ❶ v **1** (cause to) move,
change position ▷ n **2** move,
change of position **3** relay of
workers **4** time of their working
5 woman's underskirt or dress
shiftless adj lacking in resource or
character **shifty** adj evasive, of
dubious character
shilling n former Brit. coin, now 5p
shimmer ❶ v **1** shine with
quivering light ▷ n **2** such light

shin n **1** front of lower leg ▷ v
2 climb with arms and legs
shine ❶ v **shining, shone 1** give
out, reflect light **2** excel **3** polish
▷ n **4** brightness, lustre
5 polishing **shiny** adj
shingle n mass of pebbles
shingles n disease causing rash of
small blisters
ship ❶ n **1** large seagoing vessel
▷ v **2** put on or send (esp. by ship)
shipment n **1** act of shipping
2 goods shipped **shipping** n
1 freight transport business
2 ships collectively **shipshape** adj
orderly, neat **shipwreck** n
1 destruction of ship ▷ v **2** cause
shipwreck of **shipyard** n place for
building and repair of ships
shire n county **shire horse** large
powerful breed of horse
shirk v evade, try to avoid (duty etc.)
shirt n garment with sleeves and
collar for upper part of body
shirty adj **-tier, -tiest** (Inf)
annoyed
shiver¹ ❶ v **1** tremble, usu. with
cold or fear ▷ n **2** act, state of
shivering

shepherd n = **drover**, stockman,
herdsman, grazier ▷ v = **guide**,
conduct, steer, herd, usher
shield n = **protection**, cover,
defence, screen, guard ▷ v
= **protect**, cover, screen, guard,
defend
shift v = **move**, move around,
budge ▷ n = **change**, shifting,
displacement
shimmer v = **gleam**, twinkle,

glisten, scintillate ▷ n = **gleam**,
iridescence
shine v = **gleam**, flash, beam, glow,
sparkle; = **polish**, buff, burnish,
brush; = **be outstanding**, stand
out, excel, be conspicuous ▷ n
= **polish**, gloss, sheen, lustre
ship n = **vessel**, boat, craft
shiver¹ v = **shudder**, shake,
tremble, quake, quiver ▷ n
= **tremble**, shudder, quiver,

shiver² v/n splinter
shoal¹ n large number of fish swimming together
shoal² n 1 stretch of shallow water 2 sandbank
shock¹ ❶ v 1 horrify, scandalize ▷ n 2 violent or damaging blow 3 emotional disturbance 4 state of weakness, illness, caused by physical or mental shock 5 paralytic stroke 6 collision 7 effect on sensory nerves of electric discharge **shocking** adj 1 causing horror, disgust or astonishment 2 (Inf) very bad
shock² n mass of hair
shoddy adj -dier, -diest worthless, trashy
shoe n 1 covering for foot, not enclosing ankle 2 metal rim put on horse's hoof 3 various protective plates or undercoverings ▷ v 4 protect, furnish with shoe(s)
shonky adj -kier, -kiest (Aust & NZ, Inf) unreliable or unsound
shoo interj go away!

shoot ❶ v shooting, shot 1 wound, kill with missile fired from weapon 2 discharge weapon 3 send, slide, push rapidly 4 photograph, film 5 hunt 6 sprout ▷ n 7 young branch, sprout 8 hunting expedition
shop ❶ n 1 place for retail sale of goods and services 2 workshop, works building ▷ v 3 visit shops to buy **shoplifter** n one who steals from shop **shopsoiled** adj damaged from being displayed in shop
shore¹ ❶ n edge of sea or lake
shore² v prop (up)
short ❶ adj 1 not long 2 not tall 3 brief 4 not enough 5 lacking 6 abrupt ▷ adv 7 abruptly 8 without reaching end ▷ n 9 drink of spirits 10 short film ▷ pl 11 short trousers **shortage** n deficiency **shorten** v **shortly** adv 1 soon 2 briefly **shortbread, shortcake** n crumbly biscuit made with butter

trembling, flutter
shock¹ n = **upset**, blow, trauma, bombshell, turn (Inf); = **impact**, blow, clash, collision ▷ v = **shake**, stun, stagger, jolt, stupefy; = **horrify**, appal, disgust, revolt, sicken
shoot v = **open fire on**, blast (Sl), hit, kill, plug (Sl); = **fire**, launch, discharge, project, hurl; = **speed**, race, rush, charge, fly ▷ n = **sprout**, branch, bud, sprig, offshoot
shop n = **store**, supermarket,

boutique, emporium, hypermarket
shore¹ n = **beach**, coast, sands, strand (Poet), seashore
short adj = **brief**, fleeting, momentary ≠ long; = **concise**, brief, succinct, summary, compressed ≠ lengthy; = **small**, little, squat, diminutive, petite ≠ tall; = **abrupt**, sharp, terse, curt, brusque ≠ polite; = **scarce**, wanting, low, limited, lacking ≠ plentiful ▷ adv = **abruptly**, suddenly, without warning ≠ gradually

S

short circuit (*Electricity*) connection, often accidental, of low resistance between two parts of circuit **shortcoming** *n* failing **short cut** quicker route or method **shorthand** *n* method of rapid writing **short list** list of candidates from which final choice will be made **short-sighted** *adj* 1 unable to see faraway things clearly 2 lacking in foresight

shot ❶ *n* 1 act of shooting 2 small lead pellets 3 marksman 4 (*Inf*) attempt 5 photograph 6 dose 7 (*Inf*) injection **shotgun** *n* gun for firing shot at short range **shot put** contest in which athletes throw heavy metal ball

should past tense of SHALL

shoulder ❶ *n* 1 part of body to which arm or foreleg is attached 2 anything resembling shoulder 3 side of road ▷ *v* 4 undertake 5 put on one's shoulder 6 make way by pushing

shout ❶ *n/v* (utter) loud cry

shove ❶ *v/n* push

shovel ❶ *n* 1 instrument for scooping earth etc. ▷ *v* 2 lift, move (as) with shovel

show ❶ *v* **showing, showed, shown** 1 expose to view 2 point out 3 explain 4 prove 5 guide 6 appear 7 be noticeable ▷ *n* 8 display 9 entertainment 10 ostentation 11 pretence **showy** *adj* 1 gaudy 2 ostentatious **show business** the entertainment industry **showcase** *n* 1 glass case to display objects 2 situation in which thing is displayed to best advantage **showdown** *n* confrontation **showman** *n* one skilled at presenting anything effectively **show off** 1 exhibit to invite admiration 2 behave in this way **show-off** *n* **showroom** *n* room in which goods for sale are displayed

shower ❶ *n* 1 short fall of rain 2 anything falling like rain 3 kind of

—————————— THESAURUS ——————————

shot *n* = **discharge**, gunfire, crack, blast, explosion; = **ammunition**, bullet, slug, pellet, projectile; = **marksman**, shooter, markswoman; (*Inf*) = **strike**, throw, lob

shoulder *v* = **bear**, carry, take on, accept, assume; = **push**, elbow, shove, jostle, press

shout *v* = **cry (out)**, call (out), yell, scream, roar ▷ *n* = **cry**, call, yell, scream, roar

shove *v* = **push**, thrust, elbow, drive, press

shovel *v* = **move**, scoop, dredge, load, heap

show *v* = **indicate**, demonstrate, prove, reveal, display ≠ **disprove**; = **display**, exhibit; = **guide**, lead, conduct, accompany, direct; = **demonstrate**, describe, explain, teach, illustrate; = **express**, display, reveal, indicate, register ≠ **hide** ▷ *n* = **display**, sight, spectacle, array; = **exhibition**, fair, display, parade, pageant; = **appearance**, display, pose, parade

shower *v* = **cover**, dust, spray,

bath in which person stands under water spray ▷ v **4** bestow liberally **5** take bath in shower

shrapnel n shell splinters

shred ❶ n **1** fragment, torn strip ▷ v **2** cut, tear to shreds

shrew n **1** animal like mouse **2** bad-tempered woman

shrewd ❶ adj **1** astute **2** crafty

shriek ❶ n/v (utter) piercing cry

shrill adj piercing, sharp in tone

shrimp n **1** small edible crustacean **2** (Inf) undersized person

shrine n place of worship, usu. associated with saint

shrink ❶ v shrinking, shrank **1** become smaller **2** recoil **3** make smaller **shrinkage** n

shrivel v -elling, -elled shrink and wither

shroud ❶ n **1** wrapping for corpse **2** anything which envelops like a shroud ▷ v **3** put shroud on **4** veil

shrub n bush, woody plant

shrubbery n/pl -beries

shrug v shrugging, shrugged **1** raise (shoulders) as sign of indifference, ignorance etc. ▷ n **2** shrugging

shudder ❶ v **1** shake, tremble violently ▷ n **2** shuddering

shuffle ❶ v **1** move feet without lifting them **2** mix (cards) ▷ n **3** shuffling **4** rearrangement

shun ❶ v shunning, shunned keep away from

shunt v **1** push aside **2** move (train) from one line to another

shut ❶ v shutting, shut **1** close **2** forbid entrance to **shutter** n **1** movable window screen **2** device in camera admitting light as required

shuttle ❶ n **1** bobbin-like device to hold thread in weaving, sewing etc. **2** plane, bus etc. travelling to and fro

shuttlecock n cone with feathers, struck to and fro in badminton

---

THESAURUS

---

sprinkle

shred n = **strip**, bit, piece, scrap, fragment; = **particle**, trace, scrap, grain, atom

shrewd adj = **astute**, clever, sharp, keen, smart ≠ **naive**

shriek n = **scream**, cry, yell, screech, squeal

shrink v = **decrease**, dwindle, lessen, grow or get smaller, contract ≠ **grow**

shroud n = **winding sheet**, grave clothes; = **covering**, veil, mantle, screen, pall ▷ v = **conceal**, cover, screen, hide, blanket

shudder v = **shiver**, shake, tremble, quake, quiver ▷ n = **shiver**, tremor, quiver, spasm

shuffle v = **shamble**, stagger, stumble, dodder; = **scuffle**, drag, scrape; = **rearrange**, jumble, mix, disorder, disarrange

shun v = **avoid**, steer clear of, keep away from

shut v = **close**, secure, fasten, seal, slam ≠ **open**

shuttle v = **go back and forth**, commute, go to and fro, alternate

S

shy¹ ⊙ *adj* **1** timid, bashful
2 lacking ▷ *v* **3** start back in fear
4 show sudden reluctance ▷ *n*
5 start of fear by horse
shy² *n/v* throw
sibilant *adj/n* hissing (sound)
sibling *n* brother or sister
sick ⊙ *adj* **1** inclined to vomit
2 not well or healthy **3** (*Inf*)
macabre **4** (*Inf*) bored **5** (*Inf*)
disgusted **sicken** *v* **1** make,
become sick **2** disgust **sickly** *adj*
1 unhealthy **2** inducing nausea
sickness *n*
sickle *n* reaping hook
side ⊙ *n* **1** one of the surfaces of
object that is to right or left
2 aspect **3** faction ▷ *adj* **4** at, in
the side **5** subordinate ▷ *v* **6** (usu.
with *with*) take up cause of **siding**
n short line of rails from main line
sideboard *n* piece of dining room
furniture **sideburns** *pl n* man's
side whiskers **side effect**

additional undesirable effect
sidekick *n* (*Inf*) close associate
sidelong *adj* **1** not directly
forward ▷ *adv* **2** obliquely
sidestep *v* avoid **sidetrack** *v*
divert from main topic **sideways**
adv to or from the side
sidewalk *n* (*US & Canad*) paved
path for pedestrians
sidle *v* **1** move in furtive or stealthy
manner **2** move sideways
siege *n* besieging of town
siesta *n* rest, sleep in afternoon
sieve *n* **1** device with perforated
bottom ▷ *v* **2** sift **3** strain
sift ⊙ *v* separate coarser portion
from finer
sigh *v/n* (utter) long audible
breath
sight ⊙ *n* **1** faculty of seeing
2 thing seen **3** glimpse **4** device
for guiding eye **5** spectacle ▷ *v*
6 catch sight of **7** adjust sights on
gun etc. **sightseeing** *n* visiting

— THESAURUS —

shy¹ *adj* = **timid**, self-conscious,
bashful, retiring, shrinking
≠ **confident**; = **cautious**, wary,
hesitant, suspicious, distrustful
≠ **reckless** ▷ *v* sometimes with **off**
or **away** = **recoil**, flinch, draw back,
start, balk
sick *adj* = **unwell**, ill, poorly (*Inf*),
diseased, ailing ≠ **well**;
= **nauseous**, ill, queasy, nauseated;
= **tired**, bored, fed up, weary, jaded;
(*Inf*) = **morbid**, sadistic, black,
macabre, ghoulish
side *n* = **border**, margin, boundary,
verge, flank ≠ **middle**; = **face**,
surface, facet; = **party**, camp,

faction, cause; = **point of view**,
viewpoint, position, opinion,
angle; = **team**, squad, line-up
▷ *adj* = **subordinate**, minor,
secondary, subsidiary, lesser
≠ **main**
sift *v* = **part**, filter, strain, separate,
sieve; = **examine**, investigate, go
through, research, analyse
sight *n* = **vision**, eyes, eyesight,
seeing, eye; = **spectacle**, show,
scene, display, exhibition; = **view**,
range of vision, visibility; (*Inf*)
= **eyesore**, mess, monstrosity ▷ *v*
= **spot**, see, observe, distinguish,
perceive

sign **❶** n 1 mark, gesture etc. to convey some meaning 2 (board bearing) notice etc. 3 symbol 4 omen ▷ v 5 put one's signature to 6 make sign or gesture

signal **❶** n 1 sign to convey order or information 2 (Radio) sequence of electrical impulses transmitted or received ▷ adj 3 remarkable ▷ v 4 make signals to 5 give orders etc. by signals

signatory n, pl -ries one of those who signs agreements, treaties

signature n person's name written by himself signature tune tune used to introduce television or radio programme

signet n small seal

significant **❶** adj 1 revealing 2 designed to make something known 3 important significance n

signify **❶** v -fying, -fied 1 mean 2 indicate 3 imply 4 be of importance

silage n fodder crop stored in state of partial fermentation

silence **❶** n 1 absence of noise 2 refraining from speech ▷ v 3 make silent 4 put a stop to silencer n device to reduce noise of engine exhaust, gun etc. silent adj

silhouette **❶** n 1 outline of object seen against light ▷ v 2 show in silhouette

silica n naturally occurring dioxide of silicon

silicon n brittle metal-like element found in sand, clay, stone silicon chip tiny wafer of silicon used in electronics

silk n 1 fibre made by silkworms 2 thread, fabric made from this silky adj silkworm n larva of certain moth

sill n ledge beneath window

silly **❶** adj -lier, -liest 1 foolish 2 trivial

silo n, pl -los pit, tower for storing fodder

silt n 1 mud deposited by water ▷ v 2 fill, be choked with silt

---

THESAURUS

sign n = **symbol**, mark, device, logo, badge; = **notice**, board, warning, placard; = **indication**, evidence, mark, signal, symptom ▷ v = **gesture**, indicate, signal, beckon, gesticulate; = **autograph**, initial, inscribe

signal n = **flare**, beam, beacon ▷ v = **gesture**, sign, wave, indicate, motion

significant adj = **important**, serious, material, vital, critical ≠ **insignificant**; = **meaningful**, expressive, eloquent, indicative, suggestive ≠ **meaningless**

signify v = **indicate**, mean, suggest, imply, intimate

silence n = **quiet**, peace, calm, hush, lull ≠ **noise**; = **reticence**, dumbness, taciturnity, muteness ≠ **speech** ▷ v = **quieten**, still, quiet, cut off, stifle ≠ **make louder**

silhouette n = **outline**, form, shape, profile ▷ v = **outline**, etch

silly adj = **stupid**, ridiculous, absurd, daft, inane ≠ **clever**

S

silver n 1 white precious metal
2 silver coins 3 cutlery ▷ adj
4 made of silver 5 resembling silver
or its colour **silvery** adj
similar ⓞ adj resembling, like
similarity n likeness
simile n comparison of one thing
with another
simmer ⓞ v 1 keep or be just
below boiling point 2 be in state of
suppressed rage
simper v smile, utter in silly or
affected way
simple ⓞ adj 1 not complicated
2 plain 3 not complex 4 ordinary
5 stupid **simpleton** n foolish
person **simplicity** n **simplify** v
make simple, plain or easy **simply**
adv
simulate ⓞ v 1 make pretence of
2 reproduce **simulation** n
simultaneous ⓞ adj occurring at
the same time
sin ⓞ n 1 breaking of divine or
moral law or principle ▷ v

2 commit sin **sinful** adj **sinner** n
since prep 1 during period of time
after ▷ conj 2 from time when
3 because ▷ adv 4 from that time
sincere ⓞ adj 1 not hypocritical
2 genuine **sincerity** n
sine n in a right-angled triangle,
ratio of opposite side to hypotenuse
sinew n tough, fibrous cord joining
muscle to bone
sing ⓞ v **singing, sang, sung**
1 utter (sounds, words) with
musical modulation 2 hum, ring
3 celebrate in song **singer** n
singe v **singeing, singed** burn
surface of
single ⓞ adj 1 one only
2 unmarried 3 for one 4 denoting
ticket for outward journey only ▷ n
5 single thing ▷ v 6 pick (out)
single file persons in one line
single-handed adj without
assistance **single-minded** adj
having one aim only
singlet n sleeveless undervest

— THESAURUS —

similar adj = **alike**, resembling,
comparable ≠ **different**
simmer v = **fume**, seethe,
smoulder, rage, be angry
simple adj = **uncomplicated**,
clear, plain, understandable, lucid
≠ **complicated**; = **easy**,
straightforward, not difficult,
effortless, painless; = **plain**,
natural, classic, unfussy,
unembellished ≠ **elaborate**;
= **pure**, mere, sheer, unalloyed;
= **artless**, innocent, naive, natural,
sincere ≠ **sophisticated**
simulate v = **pretend**, act, feign,

affect, put on
simultaneous adj = **coinciding**,
concurrent, contemporaneous,
coincident, synchronous
sin n = **wickedness**, evil, crime,
error, transgression ▷ v
= **transgress**, offend, lapse, err, go
astray
sincere adj = **honest**, genuine,
real, true, serious ≠ **false**
sing v = **croon**, carol, chant,
warble, yodel; = **trill**, chirp, warble
single adj = **one**, sole, lone,
solitary, only; = **individual**,
separate, distinct; = **unmarried**,

DICTIONARY

singular ❶ *adj* **1** remarkable **2** unique **3** denoting one person or thing

sinister ❶ *adj* **1** threatening **2** evil-looking **3** wicked

sink ❶ *v* **sinking, sank, sunk 1** become submerged **2** drop **3** decline **4** penetrate (into) **5** cause to sink **6** make by digging out **7** invest ▷ *n* **8** fixed basin with waste pipe

sinuous *adj* curving

sinus *n* cavity in bone, esp. of skull

sip ❶ *v* **sipping, sipped 1** drink in very small portions ▷ *n* **2** amount sipped

siphon *n/v* (device to) draw liquid from container

sir *n* polite term of address for man

sire *n* **1** male parent, esp. of horse or domestic animal ▷ *v* **2** father

siren *n* device making loud wailing noise

sirloin *n* prime cut of beef

sis *interj* (*S Afr, Inf*) exclamation of disgust

sissy *adj/n, pl* **-sies** weak, cowardly (person)

sister *n* **1** daughter of same parents **2** woman fellow-member **3** senior nurse **sister-in-law** *n/pl* **sisters-in-law 1** sister of husband or wife **2** sibling's wife

sit ❶ *v* **sitting, sat 1** rest on buttocks, thighs **2** perch **3** pose for portrait **4** hold session **5** remain **6** take examination **7** keep watch over baby etc.

sitar *n* stringed musical instrument of India

site ❶ *n* **1** place, space for building ▷ *v* **2** provide with site

situate *v* place **situation** *n* **1** position **2** state of affairs **3** employment

six *adj/n* cardinal number one more than five **sixth** *adj* ordinal number **sixteen** *n/adj* six and ten **sixteenth** *adj* **sixtieth** *adj* **sixty** *n/adj* six times ten

size ❶ *n* **1** dimensions **2** one of series of standard measurements

THESAURUS

free, unattached, unwed; = **separate**, individual, exclusive, undivided, unshared

singular *adj* = **single**, individual; = **remarkable**, outstanding, exceptional, notable, eminent ≠ **ordinary**; = **unusual**, odd, strange, extraordinary, curious ≠ **conventional**

sinister *adj* = **threatening**, evil, menacing, dire, ominous ≠ **reassuring**

sink *v* = **go down**, founder, go under, submerge, capsize;

= **slump**, drop; = **fall**, drop, slip, plunge, subside; = **drop**, fall; = **stoop**, be reduced to, lower yourself

sip *v* = **drink**, taste, sample, sup ▷ *n* = **swallow**, drop, taste, thimbleful

sit *v* = **take a seat**, perch, settle down; = **place**, set, put, position, rest; = **be a member of**, serve on, have a seat on, preside on

site *n* = **area**, plot ▷ *v* = **locate**, put, place, set, position

size *n* = **dimensions**, extent, range, amount, mass

S

▷ v **3** arrange according to size
sizable adj quite large **size up** v (Inf) assess

sizzle ❶ v/n (make) hissing, spluttering sound as of frying

skate¹ n **1** steel blade attached to boot ▷ v **2** glide as on skates **skateboard** n small board mounted on roller-skate wheels

skate² n large marine ray

skein n quantity of yarn, wool etc. in loose knot

skeleton ❶ n **1** bones of animal **2** framework ▷ adj **3** reduced to a minimum

sketch ❶ n **1** rough drawing **2** short humorous play ▷ v **3** make sketch (of) **sketchy** adj

skew adj/v (make) slanting or crooked

skewer n pin to fasten meat

ski n **1** long runner fastened to foot for sliding over snow or water ▷ v **2** slide on skis

skid v skidding, skidded **1** slide (sideways) ▷ n **2** instance of this

skill ❶ n practical ability, cleverness, dexterity **skilful** adj **skilled** adj

skim ❶ v skimming, skimmed **1** remove floating matter from surface of liquid **2** glide over lightly and rapidly **3** read quickly

skimp v **1** give short measure **2** do imperfectly **skimpy** adj scanty

skin ❶ n **1** outer covering of body **2** animal hide **3** fruit rind ▷ v **4** remove skin of **skinless** adj **skinny** adj thin **skinflint** n miser

skint adj (Sl) having no money

skip¹ ❶ v skipping, skipped **1** leap lightly **2** jump over rope **3** pass over, omit ▷ n **4** act of skipping

skip² n skipping, skipped large open container for builders' rubbish etc.

skipper n captain of ship

skirmish n **1** small battle ▷ v **2** fight briefly

skirt ❶ n **1** woman's garment hanging from waist **2** lower part of dress, coat etc. ▷ v **3** border **4** go round **skirting board** narrow board round bottom of wall

skit n satire, esp. theatrical

skite v/n (Aust & NZ) boast

skittish adj frisky, frivolous

skive v evade work

S

— THESAURUS —

sizzle v = **hiss**, spit, crackle, fry, frizzle

skeleton n = **bones**, bare bones

sketch n = **drawing**, design, draft, delineation ▷ v = **draw**, outline, represent, draft, depict

skill n = **expertise**, ability, proficiency, art, technique ≠ **clumsiness**

skim v = **remove**, separate, cream;

= **glide**, fly, coast, sail, float; usually with **over** or **through** = **scan**, glance, run your eye over

skin n = **hide**, pelt, fell; = **peel**, rind, husk, casing, outside

skip¹ v = **hop**, dance, bob, trip, bounce; = **miss out**, omit, leave out, overlook, pass over

skirt v = **border**, edge, flank; often with **around** or **round** = **go round**, circumvent

skivvy *n, pl* **-vies** servant who does menial work

skookum *adj (Canad)* powerful or big

skulduggery *n (Inf)* trickery

skulk *v* sneak out of the way

skull *n* bony case enclosing brain

skunk *n* small N Amer. animal which emits evil-smelling fluid

sky ❶ *n, pl* **skies 1** expanse extending upwards from the horizon **2** outer space **skylark** *n* bird that sings while soaring at great height **skylight** *n* window in roof or ceiling **skyscraper** *n* very tall building

slab ❶ *n* thick, broad piece

slack ❶ *adj* **1** loose **2** careless **3** not busy ▷ *n* **4** loose part ▷ *v* **5** be idle or lazy **slacken** *n* **1** become looser **2** become slower

slag *n* refuse of smelted metal

slake *v* satisfy (thirst)

slalom *n* skiing race over winding course

slam ❶ *v* **slamming, slammed 1** shut noisily **2** bang ▷ *n* **3** (noise of) this action

slang *n* colloquial language

slant ❶ *v* **1** slope **2** write, present (news etc.) with bias ▷ *n* **3** slope **4** point of view **slanting** *adj*

slap ❶ *n* **1** blow with open hand or flat instrument ▷ *v* **2** strike thus **3** *(Inf)* put down carelessly **slapdash** *adj* careless, hasty **slapstick** *n* boisterous knockabout comedy

slash ❶ *v/n* **1** gash **2** cut

slat *n* narrow strip

slate ❶ *n* **1** stone which splits easily in flat sheets **2** piece of this for covering roof ▷ *v* **3** cover with slates **4** abuse

slaughter ❶ *n* **1** killing ▷ *v* **2** kill **slaughterhouse** *n* place where animals are killed for food

— THESAURUS —

sky *n* = **heavens**, firmament

slab *n* = **piece**, slice, lump, chunk, wedge

slack *adj* = **limp**, relaxed, loose, lax; = **loose**, baggy ≠ **taut**; = **slow**, quiet, inactive, dull, sluggish ≠ **busy**; = **negligent**, lazy, lax, idle, inactive ≠ **strict** ▷ *v* = **shirk**, idle, dodge, skive *(Brit Sl)* ▷ *n* = **surplus**, excess, glut, surfeit, superabundance

slam *v* = **bang**, crash, smash; = **throw**, dash, hurl, fling

slant *v* = **slope**, incline, tilt, list, bend; = **bias**, colour, twist, angle, distort ▷ *n* = **slope**, incline, tilt, gradient, camber; = **bias**, emphasis, prejudice, angle, point of view

slap *v* = **smack**, beat, clap, cuff, swipe ▷ *n* = **smack**, blow, cuff, swipe, spank

slash *v* = **cut**, slit, gash, lacerate, score; = **reduce**, cut, decrease, drop, lower ▷ *n* = **cut**, slit, gash, rent, rip

slate *v (Inf, chiefly Brit)* = **criticize**, censure, rebuke, scold, tear into *(Inf)*

slaughter *v* = **kill**, murder, massacre, destroy, execute ▷ *n* = **slaying**, killing, murder, massacre, bloodshed

S

slave ● n **1** captive, person without freedom or personal rights ▷ v **2** work like slave **slavery** n **slavish** adj servile

slaver v/n (dribble) saliva from mouth

slay ● v **slaying, slew, slain** kill

sleazy adj **-zier, -ziest** sordid

sledge¹ n **1** carriage on runners for sliding on snow **2** toboggan ▷ v **3** move on sledge

sledge² n heavy hammer with long handle

sleek ● adj glossy, smooth, shiny

sleep ● n **1** unconscious state regularly occurring in man and animals **2** slumber, repose ▷ v **3** take rest in sleep **sleeper** n **1** one who sleeps **2** beam supporting rails **3** railway sleeping car **sleepless** adj **sleepy** adj

sleet n rain and snow falling together

sleeve n part of garment which covers arm

sleigh n sledge

slender ● adj **1** slim, slight **2** small in amount

sleuth n detective

slice ● n **1** thin flat piece cut off **2** share ▷ v **3** cut into slices

slick ● adj **1** smooth **2** glib **3** skilful ▷ v **4** make glossy, smooth ▷ n **5** slippery area **6** patch of oil on water

slide ● v **sliding, slid 1** slip smoothly along **2** glide **3** pass ▷ n **4** sliding **5** track for sliding **6** glass mount for object to be viewed under microscope **7** photographic transparency

slight ● adj **1** small, trifling **2** slim ▷ v **3** disregard ▷ n **4** act of discourtesy **slightly** adv

slim ● adj **slimmer, slimmest 1** thin **2** slight ▷ v **3** reduce weight

———————— THESAURUS ————————

slave n = **servant**, serf, vassal; = **drudge**, skivvy (chiefly Brit) ▷ v = **toil**, drudge, slog

slay v (Archaic or Lit) = **kill**, slaughter, massacre, butcher

sleek adj = **glossy**, shiny, lustrous, smooth ≠ **shaggy**

sleep n = **slumber(s)**, nap, doze, snooze (Inf), hibernation ▷ v = **slumber**, doze, snooze (Inf), hibernate, take a nap

slender adj = **slim**, narrow, slight, lean, willowy ≠ **chubby**; = **faint**, slight, remote, slim, thin ≠ **strong**

slice n = **piece**, segment, portion, wedge, sliver ▷ v = **cut**, divide, carve, sever, dissect

slick adj = **skilful**, deft, adroit, dexterous, professional ≠ **clumsy**; = **glib**, smooth, plausible, polished, specious ▷ v = **smooth**, sleek, plaster down

slide v = **slip**, slither, glide, skim, coast

slight adj = **small**, minor, insignificant, trivial, feeble ≠ **large**; = **slim**, small, delicate, spare, fragile ≠ **sturdy** ▷ n = **insult**, snub, affront, rebuff, slap in the face (Inf) ≠ **compliment**

slim adj = **slender**, slight, trim, thin, narrow ≠ **chubby**; = **slight**, remote, faint, slender ≠ **strong** ▷ v = **lose weight**, diet ≠ **put on**

by diet and exercise

slime *n* thick, liquid mud **slimy** *adj*
1 of, like, covered in slime
2 insincerely pleasant

sling ① *n* **1** loop for hurling stone
2 bandage for supporting wounded
limb **3** rope for hoisting weights
▷ *v* **4** throw

slink *v* **slinking, slunk** move
stealthily, sneak

slip ① *v* **slipping, slipped 1** (cause
to) move smoothly **2** pass out of
(mind etc.) **3** lose balance by
sliding **4** fall from person's grasp
5 (usu. with *up*) make mistake
6 put on or take off easily, quickly
▷ *n* **7** act or occasion of slipping
8 mistake **9** petticoat **10** small
piece of paper **slipshod** *adj*
slovenly, careless **slipstream** *n*
stream of air forced backwards by
fast-moving object

slipper *n* light shoe for indoors

slippery ① *adj* **1** so smooth as to
cause slipping or to be difficult to
hold **2** unreliable

slit ① *v* **1** make long straight cut in
▷ *n* **2** long straight cut

slither *v* slide unsteadily (down
slope etc.)

sliver *n* splinter

slob *n* (*Inf*) lazy, untidy person

slobber *v/n* slaver

slog *v* **slogging, slogged 1** hit
vigorously **2** work doggedly ▷ *n*
3 struggle

slogan ① *n* distinctive phrase

slop *v* **slopping, slopped 1** spill,
splash ▷ *n* **2** liquid spilt **3** liquid
food ▷ *pl* **4** liquid refuse **sloppy**
adj careless, untidy

slope ① *v* **1** be, place at slant ▷ *n*
2 slant

slot ① *n* **1** narrow hole **2** slit for
coins **3** place in series ▷ *v* **4** put in
slot **5** (*Inf*) place in series

sloth *n* **1** S Amer. animal
2 sluggishness **slothful** *adj*

slouch *v* **1** walk, sit etc. in drooping
manner ▷ *n* **2** drooping posture

slovenly *adj* dirty, untidy

slow ① *adj* **1** lasting a long time

weight

sling *v* (*Inf*) **= throw**, cast, toss,
hurl, fling; **= hang**, suspend

slip *v* **= fall**, skid; **= slide**, slither;
= sneak, creep, steal ▷ *n*
= mistake, failure, error, blunder,
lapse

slippery *adj* **= smooth**, icy, greasy,
glassy, slippy (*Inf or dialect*);
= untrustworthy, tricky, cunning,
dishonest, devious

slit *v* **= cut (open)**, rip, slash, knife,
pierce ▷ *n* **= cut**, gash, incision,
tear, rent

slogan *n* **= catch phrase**, motto,
tag-line, catchword

slope *n* **= inclination**, rise, incline,
tilt, slant ▷ *v* **= slant**, incline, drop
away, fall, rise

slot *n* **= opening**, hole, groove,
vent, slit; (*Inf*) **= place**, time, space,
opening, position ▷ *v* **= fit**, insert

slow *adj* **= unhurried**, sluggish,
leisurely, lazy, ponderous
≠ quick; **= prolonged**, protracted,
long-drawn-out, lingering,
gradual; **= late**, behind, tardy ▷ *v*
often with **down = decelerate**,

S

2 moving at low speed **3** dull ▷ v
4 slacken speed (of) **slowly** adv
sludge n thick mud
slug¹ n **1** land snail with no shell
2 bullet **sluggish** adj **1** slow, inert
2 not functioning well
slug² v **1** hit, slog ▷ n **2** heavy blow
3 portion of spirits
sluice n gate, door to control flow
of water
slum ⦿ n squalid street or
neighbourhood
slumber v/n sleep
slump ⦿ v **1** fall heavily **2** relax
ungracefully **3** decline suddenly
▷ n **4** sudden decline
slur ⦿ v **slurring, slurred 1** pass
over lightly **2** run together (words)
3 disparage ▷ n **4** slight
slurp (Inf) ▷ v **1** eat or drink noisily
▷ n **2** slurping sound
slurry n, pl **-ries** muddy liquid

mixture, as in cement
slush n watery, muddy substance
slut n dirty (immoral) woman
sly ⦿ adj **slyer, slyest 1** cunning
2 deceitful
smack¹ ⦿ v **1** slap **2** open and
close (lips) loudly ▷ n **3** slap
4 such sound **5** loud kiss ▷ adv
6 (Inf) squarely
smack² n **1** taste, flavour ▷ v
2 taste (of) **3** suggest
small ⦿ adj **1** little, unimportant
2 short ▷ n **3** small slender part,
esp. of the back **smallholding** n
small area of farmland **smallpox** n
contagious disease
smart ⦿ adj **1** astute **2** clever
3 well-dressed ▷ v **4** feel, cause
pain ▷ n **5** sharp pain **smarten** v
make or become smart
smash ⦿ v **1** break **2** ruin
3 destroy ▷ n **4** heavy blow

────────────── THESAURUS ──────────

brake
slum n = **hovel**, ghetto, shanty
slump v = **fall**, sink, plunge, crash,
collapse ≠ **increase**; = **sag**, hunch,
droop, slouch, loll ▷ n = **fall**, drop,
decline, crash, collapse ≠ **increase**;
= **recession**, depression,
stagnation, inactivity, hard or bad
times
slur n = **insult**, stain, smear,
affront, innuendo
sly adj = **roguish**, knowing, arch,
mischievous, impish; = **cunning**,
scheming, devious, secret, clever
≠ **open** = **secret**, furtive, stealthy,
covert
smack¹ v = **slap**, hit, strike, clap,
cuff ▷ n = **slap**, blow, cuff, swipe,

spank ▷ adv (Inf) = **directly**, right,
straight, squarely, precisely
small adj = **little**, minute, tiny,
mini, miniature ≠ **big**;
= **unimportant**, minor, trivial,
insignificant, little ≠ **important**;
= **modest**, humble, unpretentious
≠ **grand**
smart adj = **chic**, trim, neat,
stylish, elegant ≠ **scruffy**; = **clever**,
bright, intelligent, quick, sharp
≠ **stupid**; = **brisk**, quick, lively,
vigorous ▷ v = **sting**, burn, hurt
smash v = **break**, crush, shatter,
crack, demolish; = **shatter**, break,
disintegrate, crack, splinter;
= **collide**, crash, meet head-on,
clash, come into collision ▷ n

s

5 collision **smashing** *adj* (Inf) excellent

smattering *n* slight superficial knowledge

smear ❶ *v* rub with grease etc. **2** smudge **3** slander ▷ *n* **4** greasy mark **5** slander

smell ❶ *v* **smelling, smelt** **1** perceive by nose **2** give out odour ▷ *n* **3** faculty of perceiving odours **4** anything detected by sense of smell **smelly** *adj* having nasty smell

smelt *v* extract metal from ore

smile *n* **1** curving or parting of lips in pleased or amused expression ▷ *v* **2** give smile

smirk *n* **1** smile expressing scorn, smugness ▷ *v* **2** give smirk

smite *v* **smiting, smote, smitten** **1** strike **2** afflict

smith *n* worker in iron, gold etc. **smithy** *n* blacksmith's workshop

smithereens *pl n* shattered fragments

smock *n* loose, outer garment

smog *n* mixture of smoke and fog

smoke *n* **1** cloudy mass that rises from fire etc. ▷ *v* **2** give off smoke **3** inhale and expel tobacco smoke **4** expose to smoke **smoker** *n* **smoky** *adj* **smoke screen** thing intended to hide truth

smooth ❶ *adj* **1** not rough, even **2** calm **3** unctuous ▷ *v* **4** make smooth

smother ❶ *v* suffocate

smoulder *v* **1** burn slowly **2** (of feelings) be suppressed

smudge *v/n* (make) smear, stain (on)

smug ❶ *adj* **smugger, smuggest** self-satisfied, complacent

smuggle *v* import, export without paying customs duties **smuggler** *n*

smut *n* **1** piece of soot **2** obscene talk etc. **smutty** *adj*

snack ❶ *n* light, hasty meal

snag ❶ *n* **1** difficulty **2** sharp

THESAURUS

= **collision**, crash, accident

smear *v* = **spread over**, daub, rub on, cover, coat; = **slander**, malign, blacken, besmirch; = **smudge**, soil, dirty, stain, sully ▷ *n* = **smudge**, daub, streak, blot, blotch; = **slander**, libel, defamation, calumny

smell *n* = **odour**, scent, fragrance, perfume, bouquet ▷ *v* = **stink**, reek, pong (Brit Inf); = **sniff**, scent

smooth *adj* = **even**, level, flat, plane, flush ≠ **uneven**; = **sleek**, polished, shiny, glossy, silky ≠ **rough**; = **mellow**, pleasant, mild, agreeable; = **flowing**, steady,

regular, uniform, rhythmic; = **easy**, effortless, well-ordered ▷ *v* = **flatten**, level, press, plane, iron; = **ease**, facilitate ≠ **hinder**

smother *v* = **extinguish**, put out, stifle, snuff; = **suffocate**, choke, strangle, stifle; = **suppress**, stifle, repress, hide, conceal

smug *adj* = **self-satisfied**, superior, complacent, conceited

snack *n* = **light meal**, bite, refreshment(s)

snag *n* = **difficulty**, hitch, problem, obstacle, catch ▷ *v* = **catch**, tear, rip

S

protuberance **3** hole, loop in fabric ▷ v **4** catch, damage on snag

snail n slow-moving mollusc with shell

snake n **1** long scaly limbless reptile ▷ v **2** move like snake

snap ❶ v **snapping, snapped 1** break suddenly **2** make cracking sound **3** bite (at) suddenly **4** speak suddenly, angrily ▷ n **5** act of snapping **6** fastener **7** card game **8** (Inf) snapshot ▷ adj **9** sudden, unplanned **snappy** adj **1** irritable **2** (Sl) quick **3** (Sl) fashionable **snapshot** n photograph

snare ❶ n/v trap

snarl n **1** growl of angry dog **2** tangle ▷ v **3** utter snarl

snatch ❶ v **1** make quick grab (at) **2** seize, catch ▷ n **3** grab **4** fragment

sneak ❶ v **1** move about furtively **2** act in underhand manner ▷ n **3** petty informer **sneaking** adj **1** secret **2** slight but persistent

sneakers pl n (US & Canad) canvas shoes with rubber soles

sneer ❶ n **1** scornful, contemptuous expression or

remark ▷ v **2** give sneer

sneeze v **1** emit breath through nose with sudden involuntary spasm and noise ▷ n **2** act of sneezing

snide adj malicious, supercilious

sniff ❶ v **1** inhale through nose with sharp hiss **2** smell **3** (with at) express disapproval etc. ▷ n **4** act of sniffing **sniffle** v sniff noisily, esp. when suffering from a cold

snigger n **1** sly, disrespectful laugh, esp. partly stifled ▷ v **2** produce snigger

snip v **snipping, snipped 1** cut with quick stroke ▷ n **2** quick cut **3** (Inf) bargain **snippet** n small piece

snipe n **1** wading bird ▷ v **2** shoot at enemy from cover **3** (with at) criticize **sniper** n

snivel v **-elling, -elled 1** sniffle to show distress **2** whine

snob n one who pretentiously judges others by social rank etc. **snobbery** n **snobbish** adj

snooker n game played on table with balls and cues

snoop v **1** pry, meddle **2** peer into

snap v = **break**, crack, separate; = **pop**, click, crackle; = **speak sharply**, bark, lash out at, jump down (someone's) throat (Inf); = **bite at**, bite, nip ▷ adj = **instant**, immediate, sudden, spur-of-the-moment

snare n = **trap**, net, wire, gin, noose ▷ v = **trap**, catch, net, wire, seize

snatch v = **grab**, grip, grasp,

clutch; = **steal**, take, nick (Sl, chiefly Brit), pinch (Inf), lift (Inf) ▷ n = **bit**, part, fragment, piece, snippet

sneak v = **slink**, slip, steal, pad, skulk; = **slip**, smuggle, spirit ▷ n = **informer**, betrayer, telltale, Judas, accuser

sneer v = **scorn**, mock, ridicule, laugh, jeer ▷ n = **scorn**, ridicule, mockery, derision, jeer

sniff v = **breathe in**, inhale

snooty adj **snootier, snootiest** (Sl) haughty

snooze v/n (take) nap

snore v **1** breathe noisily when asleep ▷ n **2** sound of snoring

snorkel n tube for breathing underwater

snort v **1** make (contemptuous) noise by driving breath through nostrils ▷ n **2** act of snorting

snout n animal's nose

snow n **1** frozen vapour which falls in flakes ▷ v **2** fall, sprinkle as snow **snowy** adj **snowball** n **1** snow pressed into hard ball for throwing ▷ v **2** increase rapidly **snowdrift** n bank of deep snow **snowdrop** n small, white, bell-shaped spring flower **snowman** n figure shaped out of snow **snowplough** n vehicle for clearing away snow **snowshoes** pl n racket-shaped shoes for travelling on snow

snub ❶ v **snubbing, snubbed 1** insult (esp. by ignoring) intentionally ▷ n **2** snubbing ▷ adj **3** short and blunt **snub-nosed** adj

snuff¹ n powdered tobacco

snuff² v extinguish (esp. candle)

snuffle v breathe noisily

snug adj **snugger, snuggest** warm, comfortable

snuggle v lie close to, nestle

so adv **1** to such an extent **2** in such a manner **3** very ▷ conj **4** therefore **5** in order that **6** with the result that ▷ interj **7** well! **so-and-so** n **1** (Inf) person whose name is not specified **2** unpleasant person **so-called** adj called by but doubtfully deserving that name

soak ❶ v **1** steep **2** absorb **3** drench **soaking** n/adj

soap n **1** compound of alkali and oil used in washing ▷ v **2** apply soap to **soapy** adj **soap opera** television, radio serial dealing with domestic themes

soar ❶ v **1** fly high **2** increase rapidly

sob ❶ v **sobbing, sobbed 1** catch breath, esp. in weeping ▷ n **2** sobbing

sober ❶ adj **1** not drunk **2** temperate **3** subdued **4** dull **5** solemn ▷ v **6** make, become sober **sobriety** n

soccer n game of football, with spherical ball

sociable adj **1** friendly **2** convivial

social ❶ adj **1** living in communities **2** relating to society **3** sociable ▷ n **4** informal gathering **socialize** v **social**

S

snub v = **insult**, slight, put down, humiliate, cut (Inf) ▷ n = **insult**, put-down, affront, slap in the face

soak v = **wet**, damp, saturate, drench, moisten; = **penetrate**, permeate, seep

soar v = **rise**, increase, grow, mount, climb; = **fly**, wing, climb, ascend ≠ **plunge**

sob v = **cry**, weep, howl, shed tears

sober adj = **abstinent**, temperate, abstemious, moderate ≠ **drunk**; = **serious**, cool, grave, reasonable, steady ≠ **frivolous**; = **plain**, dark, sombre, quiet, subdued ≠ **bright**

social adj = **communal**,

networking site website that allows subscribers to interact, esp. by forming online communities based around shared interests, experiences, etc.

socialism n political system which advocates public ownership of means of production **socialist** n/adj

society ❶ n, pl **-ties** 1 living associated with others 2 those so living 3 companionship 4 association 5 fashionable people collectively

sociology n study of societies **sociological** adj

sock¹ n cloth covering for foot

sock² (Sl) ▷ v 1 hit ▷ n 2 blow

socket n hole or recess for something to fit into

sod n lump of earth with grass

soda n 1 compound of sodium 2 soda water **soda water** water charged with carbon dioxide

sodden adj soaked

sodium n metallic alkaline element **sodium bicarbonate** compound

used in baking powder

sodomy n anal intercourse

sofa ❶ n upholstered seat with back and arms

soft ❶ adj 1 yielding easily to pressure 2 not hard 3 mild 4 easy 5 subdued 6 quiet 7 gentle 8 (too) lenient **soften** v make, become soft or softer **softly** adv

soft drink nonalcoholic drink

software n computer programs

soggy adj **-gier, -giest** damp and heavy

soil¹ ❶ n earth, ground

soil² v make, become dirty

solace n/v comfort in distress

solar adj of the sun

solarium n, pl **-lariums, -laria** place with beds and ultraviolet lights for acquiring artificial suntan

solder n 1 easily-melted alloy used for joining metal ▷ v 2 join with it

soldier ❶ n 1 one serving in army ▷ v 2 serve in army 3 (with on) persist doggedly

sole¹ ❶ adj one and only **solely** adv

— THESAURUS —

community, collective, group, public ▷ n = **get-together** (Inf), party, gathering, function, reception

society n = **the community**, people, the public, humanity, civilization; = **culture**, community, population; = **organization**, group, club, union, league; = **upper classes**, gentry, elite, high society, beau monde

sofa n = **couch**, settee, divan, chaise longue

soft adj = **velvety**, smooth, silky,

feathery, downy ≠ **rough**; = **yielding**, elastic ≠ **hard**; = **soggy**, swampy, marshy, boggy; = **squashy**, sloppy, mushy, spongy, gelatinous; = **pliable**, flexible, supple, malleable, plastic

soil¹ n = **earth**, ground, clay, dust, dirt; = **territory**, country, land

soil² v = **dirty**, foul, stain, pollute, tarnish ≠ **clean**

soldier n = **fighter**, serviceman, trooper, warrior, man-at-arms

sole¹ adj = **only**, one, single, individual, alone

S

1 alone **2** only **3** entirely
sole² n **1** underside of foot
2 underpart of boot etc. ▷ v **3** fit
with sole
sole³ n small edible flatfish
solemn 🟊 adj **1** serious **2** formal
solemnity n **solemnize** v
celebrate, perform
solicit v **-iting, -ited 1** request
2 accost **solicitor** n lawyer who
prepares documents, advises
clients **solicitous** adj **1** anxious
2 eager **solicitude** n
solid 🟊 adj **1** not hollow
2 composed of one substance
3 firm **4** reliable ▷ n **5** body of
three dimensions **6** substance not
liquid or gas **solidarity** n unity
solidify v harden
soliloquy n, pl **-quies** (esp. in
drama) thoughts spoken by person
while alone
solitary 🟊 adj alone, single
solitaire n **1** game for one person
2 single precious stone set by itself
solitude n state of being alone
solo n, pl **-los 1** music for one
performer ▷ adj **2** unaccompanied,
alone **soloist** n
solstice n shortest (winter) or
longest (summer) day

solve 🟊 v **1** work out **2** find
answer to **soluble** adj **1** capable
of being dissolved in liquid **2** able
to be solved **solution** n **1** answer
2 dissolving **3** liquid with
something dissolved in it **solvable**
adj **solvency** n **solvent** adj
1 able to meet financial obligations
▷ n **2** liquid with power of
dissolving
sombre 🟊 adj dark, gloomy
sombrero n, pl **-ros** wide-
brimmed hat
some adj **1** denoting an indefinite
number, amount or extent **2** one
or another **3** certain ▷ pron
4 portion, quantity **somebody**
pron **1** some person ▷ n
2 important person **somehow**
adv by some means **someone**
pron somebody **something** pron
thing not clearly defined
sometime adv **1** at some
unspecified time ▷ adj **2** former
sometimes adv occasionally
somewhat adv rather
somewhere adv at some
unspecified place
somersault n tumbling head over
heels
son n male child **son-in-law** n, pl

—————— THESAURUS ——————

solemn adj = **serious**, earnest,
grave, sober, sedate ≠ **cheerful**;
= **formal**, grand, grave, dignified,
ceremonial ≠ **informal**
solid adj = **firm**, hard, compact,
dense, concrete ≠ **unsubstantial**;
= **strong**, stable, sturdy,
substantial, unshakable
≠ **unstable**; = **reliable**,

dependable, upstanding, worthy,
upright ≠ **unreliable**
solitary adj = **unsociable**,
reclusive, unsocial, isolated, lonely
≠ **sociable**; = **lone**, alone
solve v = **answer**, work out,
resolve, crack, clear up
sombre adj = **gloomy**, sad, sober,
grave, dismal ≠ **cheerful**

sons-in-law child's husband
sonar n device for detecting underwater objects
sonata n piece of music in several movements
song ❶ n 1 singing 2 poem etc. for singing
sonic adj pert. to sound waves
sonnet n fourteen-line poem with definite rhyme scheme
sonorous adj giving out (deep) sound, resonant
soon ❶ adv 1 in a short time 2 before long 3 early, quickly
soot n black powdery substance formed by burning of coal etc. **sooty** adj
soothe ❶ v 1 make calm, tranquil 2 relieve (pain etc.)
sop n 1 piece of bread etc. soaked in liquid 2 bribe ▷ v 3 steep in water etc. 4 soak (up) **soppy** adj (Inf) oversentimental
soporific adj causing sleep

soprano n, pl **-pranos** highest voice in women and boys
sorbet n (fruit-flavoured) water ice
sorcerer n magician **sorcery** n
sordid adj 1 mean, squalid 2 base
sore ❶ adj 1 painful 2 causing annoyance ▷ n 3 sore place **sorely** adv greatly
sorrow ❶ n/v (feel) grief, sadness **sorrowful** adj
sorry ❶ adj **-rier, -riest** 1 feeling pity or regret 2 miserable, wretched
sort ❶ n 1 kind, class ▷ v 2 classify
sortie n sally by besieged forces
SOS n 1 international code signal of distress 2 call for help
so-so adj (Inf) mediocre
soufflé n dish of eggs beaten to froth, flavoured and baked
soul ❶ n 1 spiritual and immortal part of human being 2 person 3 sensitivity 4 type of Black music **soulful** adj

— THESAURUS —

song n = **ballad**, air, tune, carol, chant
soon adv = **before long**, shortly, in the near future
soothe v = **calm**, still, quiet, hush, appease ≠ upset; = **relieve**, ease, alleviate, assuage ≠ irritate
sore adj = **painful**, smarting, raw, tender, burning; = **annoyed**, cross, angry, pained, hurt; = **annoying**, troublesome; (Lit) = **urgent**, desperate, extreme, dire, pressing
sorrow n = **grief**, sadness, woe, regret, distress ≠ joy; = **hardship**, trial, tribulation, affliction, trouble ≠ good fortune ▷ v = **grieve**,

mourn, lament, be sad, bemoan ≠ rejoice
sorry adj = **regretful**, apologetic, contrite, repentant, remorseful ≠ unapologetic; = **sympathetic**, moved, full of pity, compassionate, commiserative ≠ unsympathetic; = **wretched**, miserable, pathetic, mean, poor
sort n = **kind**, type, class, make, order ▷ v = **arrange**, group, order, rank, divide
soul n = **spirit**, essence, life, vital force; = **embodiment**, essence, epitome, personification, quintessence; = **person**, being,

sound¹ ❶ n **1** what is heard **2** noise ▷ v **3** make sound **4** give impression of **5** utter **soundproof** adj

sound² ❶ adj **1** in good condition **2** solid **3** of good judgment **4** thorough **5** deep **soundly** adv thoroughly

sound³ v **1** find depth of, as water **2** ascertain views of **3** probe

sound⁴ ❶ n **1** channel **2** strait

soup n liquid food made by boiling meat, vegetables etc.

sour adj **1** acid **2** gone bad **3** peevish **4** disagreeable ▷ v **5** make, become sour

source ❶ n **1** origin, starting point **2** spring

south n **1** point opposite north **2** region, part of country etc. lying to that side ▷ adj/adv **3** from, towards or in the south **southerly** adj/n wind from the south

southern adj **southward** adj **southwards** adv

souvenir ❶ n keepsake, memento

sou'wester n seaman's waterproof headgear

sovereign ❶ n **1** king, queen **2** former gold coin worth 20 shillings ▷ adj **3** supreme **4** efficacious **sovereignty** n

sow¹ ❶ v sowing, sowed, sown scatter, plant seed

sow² n female adult pig

soya n plant yielding edible beans **soya bean** edible bean used for food and oil **soy sauce** sauce made from fermented soya beans

spa n **1** medicinal spring **2** place, resort with one

space ❶ n **1** extent **2** room **3** period **4** empty place **5** area **6** expanse **7** region beyond earth's atmosphere ▷ v **8** place at

— THESAURUS —

individual, body, creature

sound¹ n = **noise**, din, report, tone, reverberation; = **idea**, impression, drift ▷ v = **toll**, set off; = **resound**, echo, go off, toll, set off; = **seem**, seem to be, appear to be

sound² adj = **fit**, healthy, perfect, intact, unhurt ≠ **frail**; = **sturdy**, strong, solid, stable; = **sensible**, wise, reasonable, right, correct ≠ **irresponsible**

sour adj = **sharp**, acid, tart, bitter, pungent ≠ **sweet**; = **rancid**, turned, gone off, curdled, gone bad ≠ **fresh**; = **bitter**, tart, acrimonious, embittered, disagreeable ≠ **good-natured**

source n = **cause**, origin, derivation, beginning, author; = **informant**, authority

souvenir n = **keepsake**, reminder, memento

sovereign adj = **supreme**, ruling, absolute, royal, principal; = **excellent**, efficient, effectual ▷ n = **monarch**, ruler, king or queen, chief, potentate

sow¹ v = **scatter**, plant, seed, implant

space n = **room**, capacity, extent, margin, scope; = **period**, interval, time, while, span; = **outer space**, the universe, the galaxy, the solar system, the cosmos

S

intervals **spacious** adj roomy, extensive **spacecraft, spaceship** n vehicle for travel beyond earth's atmosphere **spaceman** n astronaut

spade¹ n tool for digging

spade² n suit at cards

spaghetti n pasta in long strings

span ❶ n 1 extent, space 2 stretch of arch etc. 3 space from thumb to little finger ▷ v 4 stretch over 5 measure with hand

spangle n 1 small shiny metallic ornament ▷ v 2 decorate with spangles

spaniel n breed of dog with long ears and silky hair

spank v 1 slap with flat of hand, esp. on buttocks ▷ n 2 spanking

spanner n tool for gripping nut or bolt head

spar ❶ v **sparring, sparred** 1 box 2 dispute, esp. in fun ▷ n 3 sparring

spare ❶ v 1 leave unhurt 2 show mercy 3 do without 4 give away ▷ adj 5 additional 6 in reserve

7 thin 8 lean ▷ n 9 reserve copy **sparing** adj economical, careful

spark ❶ n 1 small glowing or burning particle 2 flash of light produced by electrical discharge 3 trace ▷ v 4 emit sparks 5 kindle

sparkle ❶ v 1 glitter 2 effervesce ▷ n 3 glitter 4 vitality **sparkling** adj 1 glittering 2 (of wines) effervescent

sparrow n small brownish bird **sparrowhawk** n hawk that hunts small birds

sparse adj thinly scattered

spartan adj strict, austere

spasm n 1 sudden convulsive (muscular) contraction 2 sudden burst of activity etc. **spasmodic** adj

spastic adj 1 affected by spasms 2 (*Offens*) suffering cerebral palsy

spate ❶ n 1 rush, outpouring 2 flood

spatial adj of, in space

spatter v 1 splash, cast drops over 2 be scattered in drops

———————— THESAURUS ————————

s **spacious** adj = **roomy**, large, huge, broad, extensive ≠ **limited**

span n = **period**, term, duration, spell; = **extent**, reach, spread, length, distance ▷ v = **extend across**, cross, bridge, cover, link

spar v = **argue**, row, squabble, scrap (*Inf*), wrangle

spare adj = **back-up**, reserve, second, extra, additional; = **extra**, surplus, leftover, over, free ≠ **necessary** ▷ v = **afford**, give, grant, do without, part with;

= **have mercy on**, pardon, leave, let off (*Inf*), go easy on (*Inf*) ≠ **show no mercy to**

spark n = **flicker**, flash, gleam, glint, flare; = **trace**, hint, scrap, atom, jot ▷ v often with **off** = **start**, stimulate, provoke, inspire, trigger (off)

sparkle v = **glitter**, flash, shine, gleam, shimmer ▷ n = **glitter**, flash, gleam, flicker, brilliance; = **vivacity**, life, spirit, dash, vitality

spate n = **flood**, flow, torrent, rush, deluge

▷ *n* **3** spattering

spatula *n* utensil with broad, flat blade for various purposes

spawn *n* **1** eggs of fish or frog ▷ *v* **2** (of fish or frog) cast eggs

spay *v* remove ovaries from (female animal)

speak ❶ *v* **speaking, spoke, spoken 1** utter words **2** converse **3** express **4** communicate in **5** give speech **speaker** *n* **1** one who speaks **2** speech maker **3** loudspeaker

spear *n* **1** long pointed weapon ▷ *v* **2** pierce with spear **spearhead** *n* **1** leading force in attack ▷ *v* **2** lead attack

spearmint *n* type of mint

special ❶ *adj* **1** beyond the usual **2** particular **specialist** *n* one who devotes himself to special subject **speciality** *n* special product, skill, characteristic etc. **specialization** *n* **specialize** *v* **1** be specialist **2** make special

species ❶ *n, pl* **-cies** group of plants or animals that are closely related

specific ❶ *adj* **1** exact in detail **2** characteristic **specification** *n* detailed description of something **specify** *v* state definitely or in detail

specimen ❶ *n* **1** part typifying whole **2** individual example

specious *adj* deceptively plausible, but false

speck *n* **1** small spot, particle ▷ *v* **2** mark with spots **speckle** *n/v* speck

spectacle ❶ *n* **1** show **2** thing exhibited **3** strange, interesting, or ridiculous sight ▷ *pl* **4** pair of lenses for correcting defective sight **spectacular** *adj* **1** impressive **2** showy **spectate** *v* **spectator** *n* one who looks on

spectre ❶ *n* **1** ghost **2** image of something unpleasant

spectrum *n, pl* **-tra** band of colours into which light can be decomposed, e.g. by prism

speculate ❶ *v* **1** guess, conjecture **2** engage in (risky) commercial transactions **speculation** *n* **speculative** *adj*

──── THESAURUS ────

speak *v* = **talk**, say something; = **articulate**, say, pronounce, utter, tell

special *adj* = **exceptional**, important, significant, particular, unique ≠ **ordinary**; = **specific**, particular, distinctive, individual, appropriate ≠ **general**

species *n* = **kind**, sort, type, group, class

specific *adj* = **particular**, special, characteristic, distinguishing

≠ **general**

specimen *n* = **sample**, example, model, type, pattern; = **example**, model, type

spectacle *n* = **show**, display, exhibition, event, performance; = **sight**, wonder, scene, phenomenon, curiosity

spectre *n* = **ghost**, spirit, phantom, vision, apparition

speculate *v* = **conjecture**, consider, wonder, guess, surmise;

S

speculator *n*

speech ❶ *n* **1** act, faculty of speaking **2** words, language **3** (formal) talk given before audience **speechless** *adj* **1** dumb **2** at a loss for words

speed ❶ *n* **1** swiftness **2** rate of progress ▷ *v* **3** move quickly **4** drive vehicle at high speed **5** further **speeding** *n* driving at high speed, esp. over legal limit **speedy** *adj* **speedometer** *n* instrument to show speed of vehicle **speedwell** *n* plant with small blue flowers

spell¹ ❶ *v* **spelling, spelt 1** give letters of in order **2** indicate, result in **spelling** *n*

spell² ❶ *n* **1** magic formula **2** enchantment **spellbound** *adj* **1** enchanted **2** entranced

spell³ ❶ *n* (short) period of time, work

spend ❶ *v* **spending, spent 1** pay out **2** pass (time) **3** use up

completely **spendthrift** *n* wasteful person

sperm *n* **sperms 1** male reproductive cell **2** semen

spew *v* vomit

sphere ❶ *n* **1** ball, globe **2** field of action **spherical** *adj*

spice ❶ *n* **1** aromatic or pungent vegetable substance **2** spices collectively **3** anything that adds relish, interest etc. ▷ *v* **4** season with spices **spicy** *adj*

spick-and-span *adj* neat, smart, new-looking

spider *n* small eight-legged creature which spins web to catch prey **spidery** *adj* thin and angular

spike ❶ *n* **1** sharp point **2** long cluster with flowers attached directly to stalk ▷ *v* **3** pierce, fasten with spike **4** render ineffective **spiky** *adj*

spill ❶ *v* **spilling, spilt 1** (cause to) pour from, flow over, fall out, esp. unintentionally ▷ *n* **2** fall

———————— THESAURUS ————————

= **gamble**, risk, venture, hazard
speech *n* = **communication**, talk, conversation, discussion, dialogue; = **diction**, pronunciation, articulation, delivery, fluency; = **language**, tongue, jargon, dialect, idiom
speed *n* = **rate**, pace ▷ *v* = **race**, rush, hurry, zoom, career ≠ **crawl**
spell¹ *v* = **indicate**, mean, signify, point to, imply
spell² *n* = **incantation**, charm; = **enchantment**, magic, fascination, glamour, allure
spell³ *n* = **period**, time, term,

stretch, course
spend *v* = **pay out**, fork out (*Sl*), expend, disburse ≠ **save**; = **pass**, fill, occupy, while away; = **use up**, waste, squander, empty, drain ≠ **save**
sphere *n* = **ball**, globe, orb, globule, circle; = **field**, department, function, territory, capacity
spice *n* = **excitement**, zest, colour, pep, zing (*Inf*)
spike *n* = **point**, stake, spine, barb, prong ▷ *v* = **impale**, spit, spear, stick
spill *v* = **tip over**, overturn, capsize,

S

3 amount spilt **spillage** n

spin ❶ v **spinning, spun 1** (cause to) revolve rapidly **2** twist into thread **3** prolong ▷ n **4** spinning
spinning n act, process of drawing out and twisting into threads
spin-dryer n machine in which clothes are spun to remove excess water **spin-off** n incidental benefit

spinach n dark green leafy vegetable

spindle n rod, axis for spinning
spindly adj long and slender

spine ❶ n **1** backbone **2** thin spike, esp. on fish etc. **3** ridge **4** back of book **spinal** adj
spineless adj **1** lacking in spine **2** cowardly

spinster n unmarried woman

spiral ❶ n **1** continuous curve drawn at ever increasing distance from fixed point **2** anything resembling this ▷ adj **3** shaped like spiral

spire n pointed part of steeple

spirit ❶ n **1** life principle animating body **2** disposition **3** liveliness **4** courage **5** essential character or meaning **6** soul **7** ghost ▷ pl **8** emotional state **9** strong alcoholic drink ▷ v **10** carry away mysteriously **spirited** adj lively
spiritual adj **1** given to, interested in things of the spirit ▷ n **2** sacred song orig. sung by Black slaves in America **spiritualism** n belief that spirits of the dead communicate with the living
spiritualist n **spirituality** n

spit¹ ❶ v **spitting, spat 1** eject saliva (from mouth) ▷ n **2** spitting, saliva **spittle** n saliva

spit² n **1** sharp rod to put through meat for roasting **2** sandy point projecting into the sea ▷ v **3** thrust through

spite ❶ n **1** malice ▷ v **2** thwart spitefully **spiteful** adj **in spite of** prep **1** regardless of **2** notwithstanding

splash ❶ v **1** scatter liquid about or

knock over, discharge
spin v = **revolve**, turn, rotate, reel, whirl; = **reel**, swim, whirl ▷ n (Inf) = **drive**, ride, joy ride (Inf); = **revolution**, roll, whirl, gyration

spine n = **backbone**, vertebrae, spinal column, vertebral column; = **barb**, spur, needle, spike, ray

spiral adj = **coiled**, winding, whorled, helical ▷ n = **coil**, helix, corkscrew, whorl

spirit n = **soul**, life; = **life force**, vital spark; = **ghost**, phantom, spectre, apparition; = **courage**,

guts (Inf), grit, backbone, spunk (Inf); = **liveliness**, energy, vigour, life, force; = **attitude**, character, temper, outlook, temperament; = **heart**, sense, nature, soul, core

spit¹ v = **eject**, throw out ▷ n = **saliva**, dribble, spittle, drool, slaver

spite n = **malice**, malevolence, ill will, hatred, animosity ≠ **kindness** ▷ v = **annoy**, hurt, injure, harm, vex ≠ **benefit**

splash v = **paddle**, plunge, bathe, dabble, wade; = **scatter**, shower,

S

on, over something **2** print (story, photo) prominently in newspaper ▷ *n* **3** sound of splashing liquid **4** patch, esp. of colour **5** (effect of) extravagant display

splatter *v/n* spatter

splay *adj* **1** spread out **2** turned outwards ▷ *v* **3** spread out **4** twist outwards

spleen *n* organ in the abdomen **splenetic** *adj* spiteful, irritable

splendid ❶ *adj* magnificent, excellent **splendour** *n*

splice *v* **1** join by interweaving strands ▷ *n* **2** spliced joint

splint *n* rigid support for broken limb etc.

splinter ❶ *n* **1** thin fragment ▷ *v* **2** break into fragments

split ❶ *v* **splitting, split 1** break asunder **2** separate **3** divide ▷ *n* **4** crack **5** division **split second** very short period of time

splutter *v* **1** make hissing, spitting sounds **2** utter incoherently with spitting sounds ▷ *n* **3** spluttering

spoil ❶ *v* **spoiling, spoilt 1** damage, injure **2** damage manners or behaviour of (esp. child) by indulgence **3** go bad **spoils** *pl n* booty **spoilsport** *n* person who spoils others' enjoyment

spoke *n* radial bar of a wheel

spokesman, spokeswoman, spokesperson *n* one deputed to speak for others

sponge *n* **1** marine animal **2** its skeleton, or a synthetic substance like it, used to absorb liquids **3** type of light cake ▷ *v* **4** wipe with sponge **5** live at the expense of others **spongy** *adj* **1** spongelike **2** wet and soft

sponsor ❶ *n* **1** one promoting something **2** one who agrees to give money to charity on completion of a specified activity by another **3** godparent ▷ *v* **4** act as sponsor **sponsorship** *n*

spontaneous ❶ *adj* **1** voluntary

────────── THESAURUS ──────────

spray, sprinkle, wet ▷ *n* = **dash**, touch, spattering; = **spot**, burst, patch, spurt

splendid *adj* = **excellent**, wonderful, marvellous, great *(Inf)*, cracking *(Brit Inf)* ≠ **poor**; = **magnificent**, grand, impressive, rich, superb ≠ **squalid**

splinter *n* = **sliver**, fragment, chip, flake ▷ *v* = **shatter**, split, fracture, disintegrate

split *v* = **break**, crack, burst, open, give way; = **cut**, break, crack, snap, chop; = **divide**, separate, disunite, disband, cleave; = **diverge**, separate, branch, fork, part ▷ *n* = **division**, breach, rift, rupture, discord; = **separation**, break-up, split-up

spoil *v* = **ruin**, destroy, wreck, damage, injure ≠ **improve**; = **overindulge**, indulge, pamper, cosset, coddle ≠ **deprive**; = **indulge**, pamper, satisfy, gratify, pander to

sponsor *v* = **back**, fund, finance, promote, subsidize ▷ *n* = **backer**, patron, promoter

spontaneous *adj* = **unplanned**, impromptu, unprompted, willing,

2 natural **spontaneity** n

spoof n mildly satirical parody

spook n (Inf) ghost **spooky** adj

spool n reel, bobbin

spoon n 1 implement with shallow bowl at end of handle for carrying food to mouth etc. ▷ v 2 lift with spoon **spoonful** n **spoon-feed** v give (someone) too much help

sporadic adj 1 intermittent 2 scattered

spore n minute reproductive body of some plants

sporran n pouch worn in front of kilt

sport ❶ n 1 game, activity for pleasure, competition, exercise 2 enjoyment 3 cheerful person, good loser ▷ v 4 wear (esp. ostentatiously) 5 frolic 6 play (sport) **sporting** adj 1 of sport 2 behaving with fairness, generosity **sports car** fast low-built car **sportsman** n 1 one who engages in sport 2 good loser

spot ❶ n 1 small mark, stain 2 blemish 3 pimple 4 place

5 (difficult) situation 6 (Inf) small quantity ▷ v 7 mark with spots 8 detect 9 observe **spotless** adj 1 unblemished 2 pure **spotty** adj 1 with spots 2 uneven **spotlight** n 1 powerful light illuminating small area 2 centre of attention

spouse ❶ n husband or wife

spout v 1 pour out ▷ n 2 projecting tube or lip for pouring liquids 3 copious discharge

sprain v/n wrench, twist

sprat n small sea fish

sprawl ❶ v 1 lie or sit about awkwardly 2 spread in rambling, unplanned way ▷ n 3 sprawling

spray¹ ❶ n 1 (device for producing) fine drops of liquid ▷ v 2 sprinkle with shower of fine drops

spray² ❶ n 1 branch, twig with buds, flowers etc. 2 ornament like this

spread ❶ v **spreading, spread** 1 extend 2 stretch out 3 open out 4 scatter 5 distribute 6 unfold 7 cover ▷ n 8 extent 9 increase 10 ample meal 11 food which can

———— THESAURUS ————

natural ≠ **planned**

sport n = **game**, exercise, recreation, play, amusement; = **fun**, joking, teasing, banter, jest ▷ v (Inf) = **wear**, display, flaunt, exhibit, flourish

spot n = **mark**, stain, speck, scar, blot; = **pimple**, pustule, zit (Sl); = **place**, site, point, position, scene; (Inf) = **predicament**, trouble, difficulty, mess, plight ▷ v = **see**, observe, catch sight of, sight, recognize; = **mark**, stain, soil, dirty,

fleck

spouse n = **partner**, mate, husband or wife, consort, significant other (US Inf)

sprawl v = **loll**, slump, lounge, flop, slouch

spray¹ n = **droplets**, fine mist, drizzle; = **aerosol**, sprinkler, atomizer ▷ v = **scatter**, shower, sprinkle, diffuse

spray² n = **sprig**, floral arrangement, branch, corsage

spread v = **open (out)**, extend,

S

be spread on bread etc.
spread-eagled *adj* with arms and legs outstretched
spree ❶ *n* **1** session of overindulgence **2** romp
sprig *n* small twig
sprightly *adj* **-lier, -liest** lively, brisk
spring ❶ *v* **springing, sprang** **1** leap **2** shoot up or forth **3** come into being **4** appear **5** grow **6** become bent or spilt **7** produce unexpectedly **8** set off (trap) ▷ *n* **9** leap **10** recoil **11** piece of coiled or bent metal with much resilience **12** flow of water from earth **13** first season of year **springy** *adj* elastic
spring-clean *v* clean (house) thoroughly
springbok *n* S Afr. antelope
sprinkle ❶ *v* scatter small drops on, strew **sprinkler** *n* **sprinkling** *n* small quantity or number
sprint ❶ *v* **1** run short distance at great speed ▷ *n* **2** such run, race **sprinter** *n*

sprite *n* elf
sprocket *n* toothed wheel, attached to chain
sprout ❶ *v* **1** put forth shoots, spring up ▷ *n* **2** shoot
spruce¹ *n* variety of fir
spruce² *adj* neat in dress **spruce up** make neat and smart
spry *adj* **spryer, spryest** nimble, vigorous
spur ❶ *n* **1** pricking instrument attached to horseman's heel **2** incitement **3** stimulus ▷ *v* **4** urge on
spurious *adj* not genuine
spurn ❶ *v* reject with scorn
spurt *v* **1** send, come out in jet **2** rush suddenly ▷ *n* **3** jet **4** short sudden effort
spy ❶ *n, pl* **spies 1** one who watches (esp. in rival countries, companies etc.) and reports secretly ▷ *v* **2** act as spy **3** catch sight of
squabble ❶ *v/n* (engage in) petty,

— THESAURUS —

stretch, unfold, sprawl; **= extend**, open, stretch ▷ *n* **= increase**, development, advance, expansion, proliferation; **= extent**, span, stretch, sweep
spree *n* **= fling**, binge (*Inf*), orgy
spring *n* **= flexibility**, bounce, resilience, elasticity, buoyancy ▷ *v* **= jump**, bound, leap, bounce, vault; *often with* **from = originate**, come, derive, start, issue
sprinkle *v* **= scatter**, dust, strew, pepper, shower
sprint *v* **= run**, race, shoot, tear, dash

sprout *v* **= germinate**, bud, shoot, spring
spur *v* **= incite**, drive, prompt, urge, stimulate ▷ *n* **= stimulus**, incentive, impetus, motive, impulse
spurn *v* **= reject**, slight, scorn, rebuff, snub ≠ **accept**
spy *n* **= undercover agent**, mole, nark (*Brit, Aust, & NZ Sl*) ▷ *v* **= catch sight of**, spot, notice, observe, glimpse
squabble *v* **= quarrel**, fight, argue, row, dispute ▷ *n* **= quarrel**, fight, row, argument, dispute

noisy quarrel

squad n small party, esp. of soldiers **squadron** n division of cavalry regiment, fleet or air force

squalid adj mean and dirty **squalor** n

squall n 1 harsh cry 2 sudden gust of wind 3 short storm ▷ v 4 yell

squander v spend wastefully

square n 1 equilateral rectangle 2 area of this shape 3 in town, open space (of this shape) 4 product of a number multiplied by itself 5 instrument for drawing right angles ▷ adj 6 square in form 7 honest 8 straight, even 9 level, equal ▷ v 10 make square 11 find square of 12 pay 13 fit, suit

squash v 1 crush flat 2 pulp 3 suppress ▷ n 4 juice of crushed fruit 5 crowd 6 game played with rackets and ball in walled court

squat v squatting, squatted 1 sit on heels 2 occupy unused premises illegally ▷ adj 3 short and thick **squatter** n

squawk n 1 short harsh cry, esp. of bird ▷ v 2 utter this

squeak v/n (make) short shrill sound or cry

squeal n 1 long piercing squeak ▷ v 2 make one

squeamish adj 1 easily made sick 2 easily shocked

squeeze v 1 press 2 wring 3 force 4 hug ▷ n 5 act of squeezing

squelch v/n (make) wet sucking sound

squid n type of cuttlefish

squiggle n wavy line

squint v 1 have the eyes turn in different directions 2 glance sideways ▷ n 3 this eye disorder 4 glance

squire n country gentleman

squirm v 1 wriggle 2 be embarrassed ▷ n 3 squirming

squirrel n small graceful bushy-tailed tree animal

squirt v 1 (of liquid) force, be forced through narrow opening ▷ n 2 jet of liquid

st. stone (weight)

stab v stabbing, stabbed 1 pierce, strike (at) with pointed weapon ▷ n 2 blow, wound so inflicted 3 sudden sensation, e.g.

squad n = team, group, band, company, force

squander v = waste, spend, fritter away, blow (SI), misuse ≠ save

square adj = fair, straight, genuine, ethical, honest ▷ v often with with = agree, match, fit, correspond, tally

squash v = crush, press, flatten, mash, smash; = suppress, quell, silence, crush, annihilate

squeeze v = press, crush, squash, pinch; = clutch, press, grip, crush, pinch; = cram, press, crowd, force, stuff; = hug, embrace, cuddle, clasp, enfold ▷ n = press, grip, clasp, crush, pinch; = crush, jam, squash, press, crowd

stab v = pierce, stick, wound, knife, thrust ▷ n (Inf) = attempt, go, try, endeavour; = twinge, prick, pang, ache

of fear **4** attempt
stabilize v make or become stable
stabilizer n device to maintain
stability of ship, aircraft etc.
stable¹ n **1** building for horses
2 racehorses of particular owner,
establishment **3** such
establishment ▷ v **4** put into
stable
stable² ● adj **1** firmly fixed
2 steadfast, resolute **stability** n
1 steadiness **2** ability to resist
change
staccato adj/adv (Mus) with the
notes sharply separated
stack ● n **1** ordered pile, heap
2 chimney ▷ v **3** pile in stack
stadium n, pl **-diums, -dia**
open-air arena for athletics etc.
staff ● n **1** body of officers or
workers **2** pole ▷ v **3** supply with
personnel
stag n male deer
stage ● n **1** period, division of
development **2** (platform of)
theatre **3** stopping-place on road,
distance between two of them ▷ v

4 put (play) on stage **5** arrange,
bring about
stagger ● v **1** walk unsteadily
2 astound **3** arrange in overlapping
or alternating positions, times
4 distribute over a period
staid adj of sober and quiet
character, sedate
stain ● v **1** spot, mark **2** apply
liquid colouring to (wood etc.) ▷ n
3 discoloration or mark **4** moral
blemish **stainless** adj **stainless
steel** rustless steel alloy
stairs pl n set of steps, esp. as part
of house **staircase, stairway** n
1 structure enclosing stairs **2** stairs
stake ● n **1** sharpened stick or
post **2** bet **3** investment ▷ v
4 secure, mark out with stakes
5 wager, risk
stalactite n lime deposit hanging
from roof of cave
stalagmite n lime deposit
sticking up from floor of cave
stale ● adj **1** old, lacking freshness
2 lacking energy, interest through
monotony **stalemate** n deadlock

———————— THESAURUS ————————

S **stable²** adj = **secure**, lasting,
strong, sound, fast ≠ **insecure**;
= **well-balanced**, balanced,
sensible, reasonable,
rational
stack n = **pile**, heap, mountain,
mass, load ▷ v = **pile**, heap up,
load, assemble, accumulate
staff n = **workers**, employees,
personnel, workforce, team;
= **stick**, pole, rod, crook, cane
stage n = **step**, leg, phase, point,
level

stagger v = **totter**, reel, sway,
lurch, wobble; = **astound**, amaze,
stun, shock, shake
stain n = **mark**, spot, blot, blemish,
discoloration; = **stigma**, shame,
disgrace, slur, dishonour; = **dye**,
colour, tint ▷ v = **mark**, soil,
discolour, dirty, tinge; = **dye**, colour,
tint
stake n = **pole**, post, stick, pale,
paling
stale adj = **old**, hard, dry, decayed
≠ **fresh**; = **musty**, fusty

stalk¹ ❶ v 1 follow stealthily
2 walk in stiff and stately manner

stalk² n 1 plant's stem 2 anything
like this

stall ❶ n 1 compartment in stable
etc. 2 erection for display and sale
of goods 3 front seat in theatre etc.
▷ v 4 (of motor engine)
unintentionally stop 5 delay

stallion n uncastrated male horse,
esp. for breeding

stalwart ❶ adj 1 strong, brave
2 staunch ▷ n 3 stalwart person

stamina ❶ n power of endurance

stammer ❶ v 1 speak, say with
repetition of syllables ▷ n 2 habit
of so speaking

stamp ❶ v 1 put down foot with
force 2 impress mark on 3 affix
postage stamp ▷ n 4 stamping
with foot 5 imprinted mark
6 appliance for marking 7 piece of
gummed paper printed with device
as evidence of postage etc.

stampede n 1 sudden frightened
rush, esp. of herd of cattle, crowd
▷ v 2 rush

stance ❶ n 1 manner, position of
standing 2 attitude

stanch see STAUNCH

stanchion n upright bar used as
support

stand ❶ v **standing, stood**
1 have, take, set in upright position
2 be situated 3 remain firm or
stationary 4 endure 5 offer
oneself as a candidate 6 be symbol
etc. of 7 (Inf) provide free, treat to
▷ n 8 holding firm 9 position
10 something on which thing may
be placed 11 structure from which
spectators can watch sport etc.
standing n 1 reputation, status
2 duration ▷ adj 3 erect 4 lasting
5 stagnant **standoffish** adj
reserved or haughty

standard ❶ n 1 accepted
example of something against

stalk¹ v = **pursue**, follow, track,
hunt, shadow

stall v = **play for time**, delay,
hedge, temporize

stalwart adj = **loyal**, faithful, firm,
true, dependable; = **strong**,
strapping, sturdy, stout ≠ **puny**

stamina n = **staying power**,
endurance, resilience, force, power

stammer v = **stutter**, falter,
pause, hesitate, stumble over your
words

stamp n = **imprint**, mark, brand,
signature, earmark ▷ v = **print**,
mark, impress; = **trample**, step,
tread, crush; = **identify**, mark,

brand, label, reveal

stance n = **attitude**, stand,
position, viewpoint, standpoint;
= **posture**, carriage, bearing,
deportment

stand v = **be upright**, be erect, be
vertical; = **get to your feet**, rise,
stand up, straighten up; = **be
located**, be, sit, be positioned, be
situated or located; = **be valid**,
continue, exist, prevail, remain valid
▷ n = **position**, attitude, stance,
opinion, determination; = **stall**,
booth, kiosk, table = **support**, base,
platform, stage, rack

standard n = **level**, grade;

S

which others are judged **2** degree, quality **3** flag ▷ *adj* **4** usual **5** of recognized authority, accepted as correct **standardize** *v* regulate by a standard

standpipe *n* tap attached to water main to provide public water supply

standpoint *n* point of view

standstill *n* complete halt

stanza *n* group of lines of verse

staple *n* **1** U-shaped piece of metal used to fasten **2** main product ▷ *adj* **3** principal ▷ *v* **4** fasten with staple **stapler** *n*

star ❶ *n* **1** celestial body, seen as twinkling point of light **2** asterisk (*) **3** celebrated player, actor ▷ *v* **4** adorn with stars **5** mark (with asterisk) **6** feature as star performer ▷ *adj* **7** most important **stardom** *n* **starry** *adj* covered with stars

starfish *n* small star-shaped sea creature

starboard *n* right-hand side of

ship or aeroplane

starch *n* **1** substance forming the main food element in bread, potatoes etc., and used mixed with water, for stiffening linen etc. ▷ *v* **2** stiffen thus **starchy** *adj* **1** containing starch **2** stiff

stare ❶ *v* **1** look fixedly (at) ▷ *n* **2** staring gaze

stark ❶ *adj* **1** blunt, bare **2** desolate **3** absolute ▷ *adv* **4** completely

starling *n* glossy black speckled songbird

start ❶ *v* **1** begin **2** set going **3** make sudden movement ▷ *n* **4** beginning **5** abrupt movement **6** advantage of a lead in a race **starter** *n* **1** first course of meal **2** electric motor starting car engine **3** competitor in race **4** supervisor of start of race

startle ❶ *v* give a fright to

starve *v* (cause to) suffer or die from hunger **starvation** *n*

stash *v* (*Inf*) store in secret place

——————— THESAURUS ———————

= **criterion**, measure, guideline, example, model; *often plural*
= **principles**, ideals, morals, ethics;
= **flag**, banner, ensign ▷ *adj*
= **usual**, normal, customary, average, basic ≠ **unusual**
= **accepted**, official, established, approved, recognized ≠ **unofficial**

star *n* = **heavenly body**, celestial body; = **celebrity**, big name, megastar (*Inf*), name, luminary ▷ *adj* = **leading**, major, celebrated, brilliant, well-known

stare *v* = **gaze**, look, goggle,

watch, gape

stark *adj* = **plain**, harsh, basic, grim, straightforward; = **sharp**, clear, striking, distinct, clear-cut ▷ *adv* = **absolutely**, quite, completely, entirely, altogether

start *v* = **set about**, begin, proceed, embark upon, take the first step ≠ **stop**; = **begin**, arise, originate, issue, appear ≠ **end**; = **set in motion**, initiate, instigate, open, trigger ≠ **stop**; = **establish**, begin, found, create, launch ≠ **terminate** ▷ *n* = **beginning**,

S

state ❶ n **1** condition **2** politically organized people **3** government **4** pomp ▷ v **5** express in words
stately adj dignified, lofty
statement n **1** expression in words **2** account **statesman** n respected political leader
statesmanship n
static ❶ adj **1** motionless, inactive ▷ n **2** electrical interference in radio reception
station ❶ n **1** place where thing stops or is placed **2** stopping place for railway trains **3** local office for police force, fire brigade etc. **4** place equipped for radio or television transmission **5** bus garage **6** post **7** position in life ▷ v **8** put in position **stationary** adj **1** not moving **2** not changing
station wagon n (US & Canad) automobile with a rear door and luggage space behind the rear seats

statue n solid carved or cast image
statuesque adj **1** like statue **2** dignified **statuette** n small statue
stature ❶ n **1** bodily height **2** greatness
status ❶ n **1** position, rank **2** prestige **3** relation to others
status quo existing state of affairs
statute n law **statutory** adj
staunch, stanch ❶ adj trustworthy, loyal
stave n **1** strip of wood in barrel ▷ v **2** break hole in **3** ward (off)
stay¹ ❶ v **1** remain **2** reside **3** endure **4** stop **5** postpone ▷ n **6** remaining, residing **7** postponement
stay² n support, prop
stead n place **in stead** in place (of)
steady ❶ adj **steadier, steadiest 1** firm **2** regular **3** temperate ▷ v

——— THESAURUS ———

outset, opening, birth, foundation ≠ **end**; = **jump**, spasm, convulsion
startle v = **surprise**, shock, frighten, scare, make (someone) jump
state n = **country**, nation, land, republic, territory; = **government**, ministry, administration, executive, regime; = **condition**, shape ▷ v = **say**, declare, specify, present, voice
static adj = **stationary**, still, motionless, fixed, immobile ≠ **moving**
station n = **railway station**, stop, stage, halt, terminal;

= **headquarters**, base, depot;
= **position**, rank, status, standing, post ▷ v = **assign**, post, locate, set, establish
stature n = **height**, build, size
status n = **position**, rank, grade
staunch adj = **loyal**, faithful, stalwart, firm, sound
stay¹ v = **remain**, continue to be, linger, stop, wait ≠ **go** ▷ n = **visit**, stop, holiday, stopover, sojourn; = **postponement**, delay, suspension, stopping, halt
steady adj = **continuous**, regular, constant, consistent, persistent ≠ **irregular**; = **stable**, fixed, secure,

4 make steady **steadily** adv
steadfast adj firm, unyielding
steak n thick slice of meat
steal ⊕ v **stealing, stole, stolen**
1 take without right or permission
2 move silently
stealth ⊕ n secret or underhand
procedure, behaviour **stealthy** adj
steam n **1** vapour of boiling water
▷ v **2** give off steam **3** move by
steam power **4** cook or treat with
steam **steamer** n steam-
propelled ship **steam engine**
engine worked by steam
steamroller n steam-powered
vehicle with heavy rollers, used to
level road surfaces
steed n (Lit) horse
steel n **1** hard and malleable metal
made by mixing carbon in iron ▷ v
2 harden
steep¹ ⊕ adj **1** sloping abruptly
2 (of prices) very high
steep² v soak, saturate
steeple n church tower with spire
steeplechase n race with obstacles
to jump **steeplejack** n one who
builds, repairs chimneys etc.
steer¹ ⊕ v **1** guide, direct course of

vessel, motor vehicle etc. **2** direct
one's course
steer² n castrated male ox
stellar adj of stars
stem¹ ⊕ n **1** stalk, trunk **2** part of
word to which inflections are added
stem² ⊕ v **stemming, stemmed**
check, dam up
stench n foul smell
stencil n **1** thin sheet pierced with
pattern which is brushed over with
paint or ink, leaving pattern on
surface under it **2** the pattern ▷ v
3 make pattern thus
step ⊕ v **stepping, stepped**
1 move and set down foot
2 proceed (in this way) **3** measure
in paces ▷ n **4** stepping **5** series of
foot movements forming part of
dance **6** measure, act, stage in
proceeding **7** board, rung etc. to
put foot on **8** degree in scale
stepladder n folding portable
ladder with supporting frame
stereophonic adj (of sound)
giving effect of coming from many
directions **stereo** n
1 stereophonic sound, record player
etc. ▷ adj **2** stereophonic

firm, safe ≠ **unstable**; = **regular**,
established
steal v = **take**, nick (Sl, chiefly Brit),
pinch (Inf), lift (Inf), embezzle;
= **copy**, take, appropriate, pinch
(Inf)
stealth n = **secrecy**, furtiveness,
slyness, sneakiness,
unobtrusiveness
steep¹ adj = **sheer**, precipitous,
abrupt, vertical ≠ **gradual**;

= **sharp**, sudden, abrupt, marked,
extreme
steer¹ v = **drive**, control, direct,
handle, pilot
stem¹ n = **stalk**, branch, trunk,
shoot, axis
stem² v = **stop**, hold back, staunch,
check, dam
step n = **pace**, stride, footstep;
= **move**, measure, action, means,
act ▷ v = **walk**, pace, tread, move

S

stereotype ❶ n 1 something (monotonously) familiar, conventional ▷ v 2 form stereotype of

sterile ❶ adj 1 unable to produce fruit, crops, young etc. 2 free from (harmful) germs **sterility** n **sterilize** v render sterile

sterling ❶ adj 1 genuine, true 2 of solid worth 3 in British money ▷ n 4 British money

stern¹ adj severe, strict

stern² n rear part of ship

sternum n, pl **-na, -nums** breast bone

steroid n organic compound, oft. used to increase body strength

stethoscope n instrument for listening to action of heart, lungs etc.

stew n 1 food cooked slowly in closed vessel ▷ v 2 cook slowly

steward n 1 one who manages another's property 2 official managing race meeting, assembly etc. 3 attendant on ship or aircraft

stick ❶ n **sticking, stuck** 1 long, thin piece of wood 2 anything shaped like a stick ▷ v 3 pierce, stab 4 place, fasten, as by pins, glue 5 protrude 6 adhere 7 come to stop 8 jam 9 remain **sticker** n adhesive label, poster **sticky** adj 1 covered with, like adhesive substance 2 (of weather) warm, humid 3 (Inf) awkward, tricky

stickleback n small fish with sharp spines on back

stickler n person who insists on something

stiff ❶ adj 1 not easily bent or moved 2 difficult 3 thick, not fluid 4 formal 5 strong or fresh, as breeze **stiffen** v **stiffness** n

stifle ❶ v smother, suppress

stigma ❶ n, pl **-mas, -mata** mark of disgrace **stigmatize** v

stile n arrangement of steps for climbing a fence

still¹ ❶ adj 1 motionless, noiseless

stereotype n = **formula**, pattern ▷ v = **categorize**, typecast, pigeonhole, standardize

sterile adj = **germ-free**, sterilized, disinfected, aseptic ≠ **unhygienic**; = **barren**, infertile, unproductive, childless ≠ **fertile**

sterling adj = **excellent**, sound, fine, superlative

stick n = **twig**, branch; = **cane**, staff, pole, rod, crook ▷ v (Inf) = **put**, place, set, lay, deposit; = **poke**, dig, stab, thrust, pierce; = **fasten**, fix, bind, hold, bond; = **adhere**, cling, become joined, become welded; = **stay**, remain, linger, persist; (Sl) = **tolerate**, take, stand, stomach, abide

stiff adj = **inflexible**, rigid, unyielding, hard, firm ≠ **flexible**; = **formal**, constrained, forced, unnatural, stilted ≠ **informal**; = **vigorous**, great, strong; = **severe**, strict, harsh, hard, heavy

stifle v = **suppress**, repress, stop, check, silence; = **restrain**, suppress, repress, smother

stigma n = **disgrace**, shame, dishonour, stain, slur

still¹ adj = **motionless**, stationary,

▷ *v* **2** quiet ▷ *adv* **3** to this time
4 yet **5** even ▷ *n* **6** photograph,
esp. of film scene **stillness** *n*
stillborn *adj* born dead

still² *n* apparatus for distilling

stimulus ❶ *n, pl* **-li 1** something
that rouses to activity **2** incentive
stimulant *n* drug etc. acting as
stimulus **stimulate** *v* rouse up,
spur **stimulation** *n*

sting ❶ *v* **stinging, stung**
1 thrust sting into **2** cause sharp
pain to **3** feel sharp pain ▷ *n*
4 (wound, pain, caused by) sharp
pointed organ, often poisonous, of
certain creatures

stingy *adj* **-gier, -giest 1** mean
2 niggardly

stink ❶ *v* **1** give out strongly
offensive smell **2** *(Sl)* be abhorrent

stint ❶ *v* **1** be frugal, miserly ▷ *n*
2 allotted amount of work or time
3 limitation, restriction

stipulate ❶ *v* specify in making a

bargain **stipulation** *n* **1** proviso
2 condition

stir ❶ *v* **stirring, stirred 1** (begin
to) move **2** rouse **3** excite ▷ *n*
4 commotion, disturbance

stirrup *n* loop for supporting foot
of rider on horse

stitch *n* **1** movement of needle in
sewing etc. **2** its result in the work
3 sharp pain in side **4** least
fragment (of clothing) ▷ *v* **5** sew

stoat *n* small mammal with brown
coat and black-tipped tail

stock ❶ *n* **1** goods, material
stored, esp. for sale or later use
2 financial shares in, or capital of,
company etc. **3** standing,
reputation **4** farm animals,
livestock **5** plant, stem from which
cuttings are taken **6** handle of gun,
tool etc. **7** liquid broth produced by
boiling meat etc. **8** flowering plant
9 lineage ▷ *adj* **10** kept in stock
11 standard **12** hackneyed ▷ *v*

——————————————— THESAURUS ———————————————

calm, peaceful, serene ≠ **moving**;
= **silent**, quiet, hushed ≠ **noisy** ▷ *v*
= **quieten**, calm, settle, quiet,
silence ≠ **get louder**

stimulus *n* = **incentive**, spur,
encouragement, impetus,
inducement

sting *v* = **hurt**, burn, wound;
= **smart**, burn, pain, hurt, tingle

stink *v* = **reek**, pong *(Brit Inf)* ▷ *n*
= **stench**, pong *(Brit Inf)*, foul smell,
fetor

stint *n* = **term**, time, turn, period,
share ▷ *v* = **be mean**, hold back, be
sparing, skimp on, be frugal

stipulate *v* = **specify**, agree,

require, contract, settle

stir *v* = **mix**, beat, agitate;
= **stimulate**, move, excite, spur,
provoke ≠ **inhibit** ▷ *n*
= **commotion**, excitement, activity,
disorder, fuss

stock *n* = **shares**, holdings,
securities, investments, bonds;
= **property**, capital, assets, funds;
= **goods**, merchandise, wares,
range, choice; = **supply**, store,
reserve, fund, stockpile ▷ *v* = **sell**,
supply, handle, keep, trade in; = **fill**,
supply, provide with, equip, furnish
▷ *adj* = **hackneyed**, routine, banal,
trite, overused; = **regular**, usual,

S

13 keep, store **14** supply with livestock, fish etc. **stockist** *n* dealer who stocks a particular product **stocky** *adj* thickset **stockbroker** *n* agent for buying, selling shares in companies **stock exchange** institution for buying and selling shares **stockpile** *v* acquire and store large quantity of (something) **stocktaking** *n* examination, counting and valuing of goods in a shop etc.

stockade *n* enclosure of stakes, barrier

stocking *n* close-fitting covering for leg and foot

stodgy *adj* **stodgier, stodgiest** heavy, dull

stoep [stoop] *n (S Afr)* verandah

stoic *adj* **1** capable of much self-control, great endurance without complaint ▷ *n* **2** stoical person **stoical** *adj* **stoicism** *n*

stoke *v* feed, tend fire or furnace **stoker** *n*

stole *n* long scarf or shawl

stolid *adj* hard to excite

stomach ❶ *n* **1** sac forming chief digestive organ in any animal **2** appetite ▷ *v* **3** put up with

stomp *v* tread heavily

stone *n* **1** (piece of) rock **2** gem **3** hard seed of fruit **4** hard deposit formed in kidneys, bladder **5** unit of weight, 14 pounds ▷ *v* **6** throw stones at **7** free (fruit) from stones **stony** *adj* **1** of, like stone **2** hard **3** cold **stone-deaf** *adj* completely deaf

stooge *n* person taken advantage of

stool *n* backless chair

stoop ❶ *v* **1** lean forward or down **2** abase, degrade oneself ▷ *n* **3** stooping posture

stop ❶ *v* **stopping, stopped** **1** bring, come to halt **2** prevent **3** desist from **4** fill up an opening **5** cease **6** stay ▷ *n* **7** place where something stops **8** stopping or becoming stopped **9** punctuation mark, esp. full stop **10** set of pipes in organ having tones of a distinct quality **stoppage** *n* **stopper** *n* plug for closing bottle etc.

stopcock *n* valve to control flow of fluid in pipe **stopwatch** *n* watch which can be stopped for exact timing of race

store ❶ *v* **1** stock, keep ▷ *n*

S

ordinary, conventional, customary

stomach *n* = **belly**, gut *(Inf)*, abdomen, tummy *(Inf)*, puku *(NZ)*; = **tummy**, pot ▷ *v* = **bear**, take, tolerate, endure, swallow

stoop *v* = **bend**, lean, bow, duck, crouch ▷ *n* = **slouch**, bad posture, round-shoulderedness, sink to, descend to

stop *v* = **quit**, cease, refrain, put an

end to, discontinue ≠ **start**; = **prevent**, cut short, arrest, restrain, hold back ≠ **facilitate**; = **end**, conclude, finish, terminate ≠ **continue**; = **cease**, shut down, discontinue, desist ≠ **continue** ▷ *n* = **halt**, standstill; = **station**, stage, depot, terminus

store *n* = **shop**, outlet, market, mart; = **supply**, stock, reserve,

2 shop **3** abundance **4** stock
5 place for keeping goods
6 warehouse ▷ *pl* **7** stocks of
goods, provisions **storage** *n*
storey *n* horizontal division of a
building
stork *n* large wading bird
storm ❶ *n* **1** violent weather with
wind, rain etc. **2** assault on fortress
3 violent outbreak ▷ *v* **4** assault
5 take by storm **6** rage **stormy**
adj like storm
story ❶ *n, pl* **-ries** **1** account, tale
2 newspaper report
stout ❶ *adj* **1** fat **2** sturdy,
resolute ▷ *n* **3** strong dark beer
stove *n* apparatus for cooking,
heating etc.
stow *v* pack away **stowaway** *n*
person who hides in ship to obtain
free passage

straddle *v* **1** bestride **2** spread
legs wide
straggle *v* stray, get dispersed,
linger **straggler** *n*
straight ❶ *adj* **1** without bend
2 honest **3** level **4** in order **5** in
continuous succession **6** (of
spirits) undiluted **7** (of face)
expressionless ▷ *n* **8** straight state
or part ▷ *adv* **9** direct **straighten**
v **straightaway** *adv* immediately
straightforward *adj* **1** open, frank
2 simple
strain¹ ❶ *v* **1** stretch tightly
2 stretch to excess **3** filter **4** make
great effort ▷ *n* **5** stretching force
6 violent effort **7** injury from being
strained **8** great demand
9 (condition caused by) overwork,
worry etc. **strained** *adj* **strainer**
n filter, sieve

THESAURUS

fund, quantity; **= repository**,
warehouse, depository, storeroom
▷ *v often with* **away** *or* **up = put by**,
save, hoard, keep, reserve
storm *n* **= tempest**, hurricane,
gale, blizzard, squall; **= outburst**,
row, outcry, furore, outbreak ▷ *v*
= rush, stamp, flounce, fly; **= rage**,
rant, thunder, rave, bluster;
= attack, charge, rush, assault,
assail
story *n* **= tale**, romance, narrative,
history, legend; **= anecdote**,
account, tale, report
stout *adj* **= fat**, big, heavy,
overweight, plump **≠ slim**;
= strong, strapping, muscular,
robust, sturdy **≠ puny**; **= brave**,
bold, courageous, fearless, resolute

≠ timid
straight *adj* **= level**, even, right,
square, true **≠ crooked**; **= frank**,
plain, straightforward, blunt,
outright **≠ evasive**; **= successive**,
consecutive, continuous, running,
solid **≠ discontinuous**; *(Sl)*
= conventional, conservative,
bourgeois **≠ fashionable**;
= honest, just, fair, reliable,
respectable **≠ dishonest**;
= undiluted, pure, neat,
unadulterated, unmixed; **= in
order**, organized, arranged, neat,
tidy **≠ untidy** ▷ *adv* **= directly**,
precisely, exactly, unswervingly, by
the shortest route
strain¹ *v* **= stretch**, tax, overtax;
= strive, struggle, endeavour,

strain² n 1 breed or race 2 trace

strait ❶ n 1 channel of water connecting two larger areas of water ▷ pl 2 position of difficulty or distress **straitjacket** n jacket to confine arms of violent person **strait-laced** adj prudish

strand¹ v 1 run aground 2 leave, be left in difficulties

strand² ❶ n single thread of string, wire etc.

strange ❶ adj 1 odd 2 unaccustomed 3 foreign **strangeness** n **stranger** n 1 unknown person 2 foreigner 3 one unaccustomed (to)

strangle ❶ v 1 kill by squeezing windpipe 2 suppress **strangulation** n strangling **stranglehold** n

strap ❶ n 1 strip, esp. of leather ▷ v 2 fasten, beat with strap **strapping** adj tall and well-made

strategy ❶ n, pl **-gies** 1 overall plan 2 art of war **stratagem** n plan, trick **strategic** adj **strategist** n

stratosphere n layer of atmosphere high above the earth

stratum n, pl **strata** 1 layer, esp. of rock 2 class in society **stratification** n **stratify** v form, deposit in layers

straw n 1 stalks of grain 2 long, narrow tube used to suck up liquid **strawberry** n 1 creeping plant producing red, juicy fruit 2 the fruit

stray ❶ v 1 wander 2 digress 3 get lost ▷ adj 4 strayed 5 occasional 6 scattered ▷ n 7 stray animal

streak ❶ n 1 long line or band 2 element ▷ v 3 mark with streaks 4 move fast 5 run naked in public **streaker** n **streaky** adj

stream ❶ n 1 flowing body of

THESAURUS

labour, go for it (Inf) ≠ **relax**; = **sieve**, filter, sift, purify ▷ n = **pressure**, stress, demands, burden; = **stress**, anxiety; = **worry**, effort, struggle ≠ **ease**; = **burden**, tension; = **injury**, wrench, sprain, pull

strait n often plural = **channel**, sound, narrows

strand² n = **filament**, fibre, thread, string

strange adj = **odd**, curious, weird, wonderful, extraordinary ≠ **ordinary**; = **unfamiliar**, new, unknown, foreign, novel ≠ **familiar**

strangle v = **throttle**, choke, asphyxiate, strangulate; = **suppress**, inhibit, subdue, stifle, repress

strap n = **tie**, thong, belt ▷ v = **fasten**, tie, secure, bind, lash

strategy n = **policy**, procedure, approach, scheme

stray v = **wander**, go astray, drift; = **drift**, wander, roam, meander, rove ▷ adj = **lost**, abandoned, homeless, roaming, vagrant; = **random**, chance, accidental

streak n = **band**, line, strip, stroke, layer; = **trace**, touch, element, strain, dash ▷ v = **speed**, fly, tear, flash, sprint

stream n = **river**, brook, burn

S

water or other liquid **2** steady flow
▷ v **3** flow **4** run with liquid **5** (*Comp*)
send video or audio material over
the internet so that the receiving
system can play it almost
simultaneously **streamer** n
(paper) ribbon, narrow flag
streaming n

street ❶ n road in town or village,
usu. lined with houses **streetwise**
adj adept at surviving in dangerous
environment

streetcar n (*US & Canad*) public
transport vehicle powered by an
overhead wire and running on rails
laid in the road

strength ❶ n **1** quality of being
strong **2** power **strengthen** v

strenuous *adj* **1** energetic
2 earnest

stress ❶ n **1** emphasis **2** tension
▷ v **3** emphasize

stretch ❶ v **1** extend **2** exert to
utmost **3** tighten, pull out **4** reach
5 have elasticity ▷ n **6** stretching,

being stretched **7** expanse **8** spell
stretcher n **1** person, thing that
stretches **2** appliance on which
disabled person is carried

strew v **strewing, strewed**
scatter over surface, spread

stricken *adj* seriously affected by
disease, grief etc.

strict *adj* **1** stern, not lax or
indulgent **2** precisely defined

stricture n critical remark

stride v **striding, strode,
stridden 1** walk with long steps
▷ n **2** single step **3** length of step

strident *adj* harsh, loud
stridently *adv* **stridency** n

strife ❶ n **1** conflict **2** quarrelling

strike ❶ v **striking, struck 1** hit
(against) **2** ignite **3** attack
4 sound (time), as bell in clock etc.
5 affect **6** enter mind of **7** cease
work as protest or to make
demands ▷ n **8** act of striking
striker n **striking** *adj*
noteworthy, impressive

—————————— THESAURUS ——————————

(*Scot*), beck, tributary; **= flow**,
current, rush, run, course ▷ v
= flow, run, pour, issue, flood
street n **= road**, lane, avenue,
terrace, row
strength n **= might**, muscle,
brawn ≠ **weakness**; **= will**,
resolution, courage, character,
nerve; **= health**, fitness, vigour
stress v **= emphasize**, underline,
dwell on ▷ n **= emphasis**,
significance, force, weight;
= strain, pressure, worry, tension,
burden; **= accent**, beat, emphasis,
accentuation

stretch v **= extend**, cover, spread,
reach, put forth; **= last**, continue,
go on, carry on, reach; **= pull**,
distend, strain, tighten, draw out
▷ n **= expanse**, area, tract, spread,
distance; **= period**, time, spell,
stint, term
strife n **= conflict**, battle, clash,
quarrel, friction
strike v **= walk out**, down tools,
revolt, mutiny; **= hit**, smack,
thump, beat, knock; **= drive**, hit,
smack, wallop (*Inf*); **= collide with**,
hit, run into, bump into; **= knock**,
smack, thump, beat

S

string ❶ n 1 (length of) thin cord or other material 2 series 3 fibre in plants ▷ pl 4 conditions ▷ v 5 provide with, thread on string 6 form in line, series **stringed** adj (of musical instruments) furnished with strings **stringy** adj 1 like string 2 fibrous

stringent ❶ adj strict, binding **stringency** n

strip ❶ v **stripping, stripped** 1 lay bare, take covering off 2 undress ▷ n 3 long, narrow piece **stripper** n **striptease** n cabaret or theatre in which person undresses

stripe n narrow mark, band **striped, stripy** adj marked with stripes

strive ❶ v **striving, strove, striven** try hard, struggle

stroke ❶ n 1 blow 2 sudden action, occurrence 3 apoplexy 4 chime of clock 5 mark made by pen, brush etc. 6 style, method of swimming 7 act of stroking ▷ v 8 pass hand lightly over

stroll ❶ v 1 walk in leisurely or idle manner ▷ n 2 leisurely walk

stroller n (US & Canad) chair-shaped carriage for a baby

strong ❶ adj 1 powerful, robust, healthy 2 difficult to break 3 noticeable 4 intense 5 emphatic 6 not diluted 7 having a certain number **strongly** adv

stronghold n fortress

strongroom n room for keeping valuables

stroppy adj **-pier, -piest** (Sl) angry or awkward

structure ❶ n 1 (arrangement of parts in) construction, building etc. 2 form ▷ v 3 give structure to **structural** adj

struggle ❶ v 1 contend 2 fight

string n = **cord**, twine, fibre; = **series**, line, row, file, sequence

stringent adj = **strict**, tough, rigorous, tight, severe ≠ **lax**

strip v = **undress**, disrobe, unclothe; = **plunder**, rob, loot, empty, sack

strive v = **try**, labour, struggle, attempt, toil

stroke v = **caress**, rub, fondle, pet ▷ n = **apoplexy**, fit, seizure, attack, collapse; = **blow**, hit, knock, pat, rap

stroll v = **walk**, ramble, amble, promenade, saunter ▷ n = **walk**, promenade, constitutional, ramble, breath of air

strong adj = **powerful**, muscular, tough, athletic, strapping ≠ **weak**; = **fit**, robust, lusty; = **durable**, substantial, sturdy, heavy-duty, well-built ≠ **flimsy**; = **extreme**, radical, drastic, strict, harsh; = **decisive**, firm, forceful, decided, determined

structure n = **arrangement**, form, make-up, design, organization; = **building**, construction, erection, edifice ▷ v = **arrange**, organize, design, shape, build up

struggle v = **strive**, labour, toil, work, strain; = **fight**, battle, wrestle, grapple, compete ▷ n

S

3 proceed, work, move with difficulty and effort ▷ *n* **4** struggling

strum *v* **strumming, strummed** strike notes of guitar etc.

strut ❶ *v* **strutting, strutted** **1** walk affectedly or pompously ▷ *n* **2** rigid support **3** strutting walk

strychnine *n* poisonous drug

stub *n* **1** remnant of anything, e.g. pencil **2** counterfoil ▷ *v* **3** strike (toes) against fixed object **4** extinguish by pressing against surface **stubby** *adj* short, broad

stubble *n* **1** stumps of cut grain after reaping **2** short growth of beard

stubborn ❶ *adj* unyielding, obstinate

stucco *n* plaster

stud¹ *n* **1** nail with large head **2** removable double-headed button ▷ *v* **3** set with studs

stud² *n* set of horses kept for breeding

studio ❶ *n, pl* **-dios 1** workroom of artist, photographer etc.

2 building, room where film, television or radio shows are made, broadcast

study ❶ *v* **studying, studied** **1** be engaged in learning **2** make study of **3** scrutinize ▷ *n* **4** effort to acquire knowledge **5** subject of this **6** room to study in **7** book, report etc. produced as result of study **8** sketch **student** *n* one who studies **studied** *adj* carefully designed, premeditated **studious** *adj* **1** fond of study **2** painstaking **3** deliberate

stuff ❶ *v* **1** pack, cram, fill (completely) **2** eat large amount **3** fill with seasoned mixture **4** fill (animal's skin) with material to preserve lifelike form ▷ *n* **5** material **6** any substance **7** belongings **stuffing** *n* material for stuffing **stuffy** *adj* **1** lacking fresh air **2** (*Inf*) dull, conventional

stumble ❶ *v* **1** trip and nearly fall **2** falter ▷ *n* **3** stumbling

stump ❶ *n* **1** remnant of tree,

———————— THESAURUS ————————

= effort, labour, toil, work, pains; **= fight**, battle, conflict, clash, contest

strut *v* **= swagger**, parade, peacock, prance

stubborn *adj* **= obstinate**, dogged, inflexible, persistent, intractable ≠ **compliant**

studio *n* **= workshop**, workroom, atelier

study *v* **= learn**, cram (*Inf*), swot (up) (*Brit Inf*), read up, mug up (*Brit Sl*); **= examine**, survey, look at, scrutinize; **= contemplate**, read,

examine, consider, go into ▷ *n* **= examination**, investigation, analysis, consideration, inspection; **= piece of research**, survey, report, paper, review

stuff *n* **= things**, gear, possessions, effects, equipment; **= substance**, material, essence, matter ▷ *v* **= shove**, force, push, squeeze, jam

stumble *v* **= trip**, fall, slip, reel, stagger; **= totter**, reel, lurch, wobble

stump *v* **= baffle**, confuse, puzzle, bewilder, perplex

S

tooth etc., when main part has been cut away **2** one of uprights of wicket in cricket ▷ v **3** confuse, puzzle **4** walk heavily, noisily **stumpy** adj short and thickset

stun ❶ v **stunning, stunned 1** knock senseless **2** amaze **stunning** adj

stunt¹ ❶ n feat of dexterity or daring

stunt² v stop growth of

stupefy v **-fying, -fied 1** make insensitive, lethargic **2** astound **stupefaction** n

stupendous adj **1** astonishing **2** amazing **3** huge

stupid ❶ adj **1** slow-witted **2** silly **stupidity** n

stupor n dazed state

sturdy ❶ adj **-dier, -diest 1** robust, strongly built **2** vigorous

sturgeon n fish yielding caviare

stutter v **1** speak with difficulty **2** stammer ▷ n **3** tendency to stutter

sty n, pl **sties** place to keep pigs in

stye, sty n, pl **styes, sties** inflammation on eyelid

style ❶ n **1** design **2** manner of writing, doing etc. **3** fashion **4** elegance ▷ v **5** design **stylish** adj fashionable **stylist** n **1** one cultivating style **2** designer

stylus n (in record player) tiny point running in groove of record

suave adj smoothly polite

sub n short for SUBMARINE, SUBSCRIPTION, SUBSTITUTE

subconscious adj **1** acting, existing without one's awareness ▷ n **2** (Psychology) part of human mind unknown, or only partly known, to possessor

subdivide v divide again **subdivision** n

subdue ❶ v **-duing, -dued** overcome **subdued** adj **1** cowed, quiet **2** not bright

subject ❶ n **1** person or thing being dealt with or studied **2** person

---
THESAURUS
---

stun v = **overcome**, shock, confuse, astonish, stagger; = **daze**, knock out, stupefy, numb, benumb

stunt¹ n = **feat**, act, trick, exploit, deed

stupid adj = **unintelligent**, thick, simple, slow, dim ≠ **intelligent**; = **silly**, foolish, daft (Inf), rash, pointless ≠ **sensible**; = **senseless**, dazed, groggy, insensate, semiconscious

sturdy adj = **robust**, hardy, powerful, athletic, muscular ≠ **puny**; = **substantial**, solid, durable, well-made, well-built

≠ **flimsy**

style n = **manner**, way, method, approach, technique; = **elegance**, taste, chic, flair, polish; = **design**, form, cut; = **type**, sort, kind, variety, category ▷ v = **design**, cut, tailor, fashion, shape; = **call**, name, term, label, entitle

subdue v = **overcome**, defeat, master, break, control; = **moderate**, suppress, soften, mellow, tone down ≠ **arouse**

subject n = **topic**, question, issue, matter, point; = **citizen**, resident, native, inhabitant, national ▷ adj

S

under rule of government or monarch ▷ adj **3** owing allegiance **4** dependent **5** liable (to) ▷ v **6** cause to undergo **7** subdue **subjection** n act of bringing, or state of being, under control **subjective** adj **1** based on personal feelings, not impartial **2** existing in the mind **subjectivity** n

subjugate v **1** force to submit **2** conquer **subjugation** n

sublet v -letting, -let rent out property rented from someone else

sublime ❶ adj **1** elevated **2** inspiring awe **3** exalted

subliminal adj relating to mental processes of which the individual is not aware

submarine n **1** craft which can travel below surface of sea and remain submerged for long periods ▷ adj **2** below surface of sea

submerge ❶ v place, go under water **submersion** n

subordinate ❶ n/adj **1** (one) of lower rank or less importance ▷ v

2 make, treat as subordinate **subordination** n

subprime adj **1** (of a loan) made to a borrower with a poor credit rating *subprime mortgage* ▷ n **2** such a loan

subscribe ❶ v **1** pay, promise to pay (contribution) **2** give support, approval **subscription** n money paid

subsequent ❶ adj later, following or coming after in time

subservient adj submissive, servile

subside ❶ v **1** abate **2** sink **subsidence** n

subsidiary ❶ adj/n secondary (person or thing)

subsidize v **1** help financially **2** pay grant to **subsidy** n, pl -dies money granted

subsist v exist, sustain life **subsistence** n the means by which one supports life

substance ❶ n **1** (particular kind of) matter **2** essence **3** wealth **substantial** adj **1** considerable

——————— THESAURUS ———————

= **subordinate**, dependent, satellite, inferior, obedient ▷ v = **put through**, expose, submit, lay open

sublime adj = **noble**, glorious, high, great, grand ≠ **lowly**

submerge v = **flood**, swamp, engulf, overflow, inundate

subordinate n = **inferior**, junior, assistant, aide, second ≠ **superior** ▷ adj = **inferior**, lesser, lower, junior, subject ≠ **superior**

subscribe v = **support**, advocate, endorse; = **contribute**, give,

donate

subsequent adj = **following**, later, succeeding, after, successive ≠ **previous**

subside v = **decrease**, diminish, lessen, ease, wane ≠ **increase**; = **collapse**, sink, cave in, drop, lower

subsidiary adj = **secondary**, lesser, subordinate, minor, supplementary ≠ **main**

substance n = **material**, body, stuff, fabric; = **importance**, significance, concreteness;

2 of real value 3 really existing
substantiate v bring evidence for, prove

substitute ❶ v 1 put, serve in place of ▷ n 2 thing, person put in place of another ▷ adj 3 serving as a substitute **substitution** n

subsume v incorporate in larger group

subterfuge n trick, lying excuse used to evade something

subterranean adj underground

subtitle n 1 secondary title of book ▷ pl 2 translation superimposed on foreign film ▷ v 3 provide with subtitle or subtitles

subtle ❶ adj 1 not immediately obvious 2 ingenious 3 crafty 4 making fine distinctions **subtlety** n **subtly** adv

subtract v take away, deduct **subtraction** n

suburb n residential area on outskirts of city **suburban** adj **suburbia** n suburbs and their inhabitants

subvert v 1 overthrow 2 corrupt **subversion** n **subversive** adj

subway n 1 underground passage

2 (US & Canad) underground railway

succeed ❶ v 1 accomplish purpose 2 turn out satisfactorily 3 follow 4 take place of **success** n 1 favourable accomplishment, attainment, issue or outcome 2 successful person or thing **successful** adj **succession** n 1 following 2 series 3 succeeding **successive** adj 1 following in order 2 consecutive **successor** n

succinct adj brief and clear

succour v/n help in distress

succulent adj 1 juicy 2 (of plant) having thick, fleshy leaves ▷ n 3 such plant **succulence** n

succumb ❶ v give way

such adj 1 of the kind or degree mentioned 2 so great, so much

suck v 1 draw into mouth 2 hold in mouth 3 draw in ▷ n 4 sucking **sucker** n 1 person, thing that sucks 2 shoot coming from root or base of stem of plant 3 (Inf) one who is easily deceived

suckle v feed from the breast **suckling** n unweaned infant

suction n 1 drawing or sucking of air or fluid 2 force produced by

S

= **meaning**, main point, gist, import, significance; = **wealth**, means, property, assets, resources

substitute v = **replace**, exchange, swap, change, switch ▷ n = **replacement**, reserve, surrogate, deputy, sub

subtle adj = **faint**, slight, implied, delicate, understated ≠ **obvious**; = **crafty**, cunning, sly, shrewd, ingenious ≠ **straightforward**;

= **muted**, soft, subdued, low-key, toned down

succeed v = **triumph**, win, prevail; = **work out**, work, be successful; = **make it** (Inf), do well, be successful, triumph, thrive ≠ **fail**

succumb v often with **to** = **surrender**, yield, submit, give in, cave in (Inf) ≠ **beat**; with **to** = **catch**, fall ill with

difference in pressure

sudden ① *adj* 1 done, occurring unexpectedly 2 abrupt **suddenly** *adv*

suds *pl n* froth of soap and water

sue ① *v* **suing, sued** 1 prosecute 2 seek justice from 3 make application or entreaty

suede *n* leather with soft, velvety finish

suet *n* hard animal fat

suffer ① *v* 1 undergo 2 tolerate **suffering** *n*

suffice ① *v* be adequate, satisfactory (for) **sufficiency** *n* adequate amount **sufficient** *adj* enough, adequate

suffix *n* group of letters added to end of word

suffocate *v* 1 kill, be killed by deprivation of oxygen 2 smother **suffocation** *n*

suffrage *n* vote or right of voting

suffuse *v* well up and spread over

sugar *n* 1 sweet crystalline substance ▷ *v* 2 sweeten, make pleasant (with sugar) **sugary** *adj*

suggest ① *v* 1 propose 2 call up the idea of **suggestible** *adj* easily

influenced **suggestion** *n* 1 hint 2 proposal 3 insinuation of impression, belief etc. into mind

suggestive *adj* containing suggestions, esp. of something indecent

suicide *n* 1 act of killing oneself 2 one who does this **suicidal** *adj*

suit ① *n* 1 set of clothing 2 garment worn for particular event, purpose 3 one of four sets in pack of cards 4 action at law ▷ *v* 5 make, be fit or appropriate for 6 be acceptable to (someone) **suitability** *n* **suitable** *adj* fitting, convenient **suitcase** *n* flat rectangular travelling case

suite ① *n* 1 matched set of furniture 2 set of rooms 3 retinue

suitor *n* 1 wooer 2 one who sues

sulk *v* 1 be silent, resentful ▷ *n* 2 this mood **sulky** *adj*

sullen *adj* unwilling to talk or be sociable, morose

sully *v* **-lying, -lied** stain, tarnish

sulphur *n* pale yellow nonmetallic element **sulphuric** *adj* **sulphurous** *adj*

sudden *adj* = **quick**, rapid, unexpected, swift, hurried ≠ **gradual**

sue *v* (*Law*) = **take (someone) to court**, prosecute, charge, summon, indict

suffer *v* = **be in pain**, hurt, ache; = **be affected**, have trouble with, be afflicted, be troubled with

suffice *v* = **be enough**, do, be sufficient, be adequate, serve

suggest *v* = **recommend**, propose, advise, advocate, prescribe; = **hint at**, imply, intimate

suit *n* = **outfit**, costume, ensemble, dress, clothing; = **lawsuit**, case, trial, proceeding, cause ▷ *v* = **be acceptable to**, please, satisfy, do, gratify; = **agree with**, become, match, go with, harmonize with

suite *n* = **rooms**, apartment

sultan *n* ruler of Muslim country

sultry *adj* **-trier, -triest 1** (of weather) hot, humid **2** (of person) looking sensual

sum ❶ *n* **1** amount, total **2** problem in arithmetic ▷ *v* **3** add up **4** make summary of main parts

summary ❶ *n, pl* **-ries 1** brief statement of chief points of something ▷ *adj* **2** done quickly **summarily** *adv* **1** speedily **2** abruptly **summarize** *v* make summary of

summer *n* second, warmest season

summit ❶ *n* top, peak

summon ❶ *v* **1** demand attendance of **2** bid witness appear in court **3** gather up (energies etc.) **summons** *n* **1** call **2** authoritative demand

sumo *n* Japanese style of wrestling

sumptuous ❶ *adj* lavish, magnificent **sumptuousness** *n*

sun *n* **1** luminous body round which earth and other planets revolve **2** its rays ▷ *v* **3** expose to sun's rays **sunless** *adj* **sunny** *adj* **1** like the sun **2** warm **3** cheerful **sunbathe** *n* lie in sunshine **sunbeam** *n* ray of sun **sunburn** *n* inflammation of skin due to excessive exposure to

sun **sundown** *n* sunset

sunflower *n* plant with large golden flowers **sunrise** *n* appearance of sun above the horizon **sunset** *n* disappearance of sun below the horizon **sunshine** *n* light and warmth from sun **sunstroke** *n* illness caused by prolonged exposure to hot sun

sundae *n* ice cream topped with fruit etc.

Sunday *n* first day of the week **Sunday school** school for religious instruction of children

sundry *adj* several, various **sundries** *pl n* odd items, not mentioned in detail

sup *v* **supping, supped 1** take by sips **2** take supper ▷ *n* **3** mouthful of liquid

super *adj* (*Inf*) very good

super- *comb. form* above, greater, exceedingly, as in *superhuman, supertanker*

superannuation *n* **1** pension given on retirement **2** contribution by employee to pension

superb ❶ *adj* extremely good or impressive

supercilious *adj* displaying arrogant pride, scorn

superficial ❶ *adj* **1** of or on

s

sum *n* **= amount**, quantity, volume

summary *n* **= synopsis**, résumé, précis, review, outline

summit *n* **= peak**, top, tip, pinnacle, apex ≠ **base**

summon *v* **= send for**, call, bid, invite; *often with* **up = gather**, muster, draw on

sumptuous *adj* **= luxurious**, grand, superb, splendid, gorgeous ≠ **plain**

superb *adj* **= splendid**, excellent, magnificent, fine, grand ≠ **inferior**

superficial *adj* **= shallow**, frivolous, empty-headed, silly, trivial ≠ **serious**; **= hasty**, cursory, surface **2** not careful or thorough **3** without depth, shallow

superfluous *adj* extra, unnecessary **superfluity** *n*

superhuman *adj* beyond normal human ability or experience

superimpose *v* place on or over something else

superintend *v* **1** have charge of **2** overlook **3** supervise **superintendent** *n* senior police officer

superior ❶ *adj* **1** greater in quality or quantity **2** upper, higher in position, rank or quality **3** showing consciousness of being so ▷ *n* **4** supervisor, manager **superiority** *n*

superlative *adj* **1** of, in highest degree or quality **2** surpassing **3** (*Grammar*) denoting form of adjective, adverb meaning *most*

supermarket *n* large self-service store

supernatural ❶ *adj* **1** being beyond the powers or laws of nature **2** miraculous

supernumerary *adj* exceeding

the required or regular number

superpower *n* extremely powerful nation

supersede *v* take the place of

supersonic *adj* denoting speed greater than that of sound

superstition *n* religion, opinion or practice based on belief in luck or magic **superstitious** *adj*

superstructure *n* **1** structure above foundations **2** part of ship above deck

supervise ❶ *v* **1** oversee **2** direct **3** inspect and control **supervision** *n* **supervisor** *n* **supervisory** *adj*

supine *adj* lying on back with face upwards

supper *n* (light) evening meal

supplant *v* take the place of

supple *adj* **1** pliable **2** flexible **supply** *adv*

supplement ❶ *n* **1** thing added to fill up, supply deficiency, esp. extra part added to book etc. ▷ *v* **2** add to **3** supply deficiency **supplementary** *adj*

supply ❶ *v* **-plying, -plied** **1** furnish **2** make available

———————————— THESAURUS ————————————

perfunctory, hurried, casual ≠ **thorough**; = **slight**, surface, external, on the surface, exterior ≠ **profound**

superior *adj* = **better**, higher, greater, grander, surpassing ≠ **inferior**; = **first-class**, excellent, first-rate, choice, exclusive ≠ **average**; = **supercilious**, patronizing, condescending, haughty, disdainful ▷ *n* = **boss**, senior, director, manager, chief (*Inf*)

≠ **subordinate**

supernatural *adj* = **paranormal**, unearthly, uncanny, ghostly, psychic

supervise *v* = **observe**, guide, monitor, oversee, keep an eye on

supplement *v* = **add to**, reinforce, augment, extend ▷ *n* = **pull-out**, insert; = **appendix**, add-on, postscript; = **addition**, extra

supply *v* = **provide**, give, furnish, produce, stock ▷ *n* = **store**, fund, stock, source, reserve

S

3 provide ▷ *n* **4** stock, store **5** food, materials needed for journey etc.

support ⊕ *v* **1** hold up **2** sustain **3** assist ▷ *n* **4** supporting, being supported **5** means of support **supporter** *n* adherent **supporting** *adj* (of role in film etc.) less important **supportive** *adj*

suppose ⊕ *v* **1** assume as theory **2** take for granted **3** accept as likely **supposed** *adj* **1** assumed **2** expected, obliged **3** permitted **supposedly** *adv* **supposition** *n* **1** assumption **2** belief without proof **3** conjecture

suppress ⊕ *v* **1** put down, restrain **2** keep or withdraw from publication **suppression** *n*

suppurate *v* fester, form pus

supreme *adj* **1** highest in authority or rank **2** utmost **supremacy** *n* position of being supreme **supremo** *n* person in overall authority

surcharge *v/n* (make) additional charge

sure ⊕ *adj* **1** certain **2** trustworthy **3** without doubt ▷ *adv* **4** (*Inf*) certainly **surely** *adv* **surety** *n* person, thing acting as guarantee for another's obligations

surf *n* **1** waves breaking on shore ▷ *v* **2** ride surf **surfer** *n* **surfing** *n* sport of riding over surf **surfboard** *n* board used in surfing

surface ⊕ *n* **1** outside face of object **2** plane **3** top **4** superficial appearance ▷ *adj* **5** involving the surface only ▷ *v* **6** come to surface

surfeit *n* **1** excess **2** disgust caused by excess ▷ *v* **3** feed to excess

surge ⊕ *n* **1** wave **2** sudden increase ▷ *v* **3** move in large waves **4** swell

surgeon *n* medical expert who performs operations **surgery** *n*

——————— THESAURUS ———————

support *v* = **help**, back, champion, second, aid ≠ **oppose**; = **provide for**, maintain, look after, keep, fund ≠ **live off**; = **bear out**, confirm, verify, substantiate, corroborate ≠ **refute**; = **bear**, carry, sustain, prop (up), reinforce ▷ *n* = **furtherance**, backing, promotion, assistance, encouragement; = **help**, loyalty ≠ **opposition**

suppose *v* = **imagine**, consider, conjecture, postulate, hypothesize; = **think**, imagine, expect, assume, guess (*Inf, chiefly US & Canad*)

suppress *v* = **stamp out**, stop, check, crush, conquer ≠ **encourage**; = **check**, inhibit, subdue, stop, quell

sure *adj* = **certain**, positive, decided, convinced, confident ≠ **uncertain**; = **inevitable**, guaranteed, bound, assured, inescapable ≠ **unsure**; = **reliable**, accurate, dependable, undoubted, undeniable ≠ **unreliable**

surface *n* = **covering**, face, exterior, side, top ▷ *v* = **emerge**, come up, come to the surface

surge *n* = **rush**, flood; = **flow**, wave, rush, roller, gush ▷ *v* = **rush**, pour, rise, gush; = **roll**, rush, heave

S

1 medical treatment by operation **2** doctor's, dentist's consulting room **surgical** adj

surly adj **-lier, -liest** cross and rude

surmise v/n guess, conjecture

surmount v get over, overcome

surname n family name

surpass ❶ v **1** go beyond **2** excel **3** outstrip **surpassing** adj excellent

surplus ❶ n **1** what remains over in excess ▷ adj **2** spare, superfluous

surprise ❶ n **1** something unexpected **2** emotion aroused by being taken unawares ▷ v **3** cause surprise to **4** astonish **5** take, come upon unexpectedly

surrealism n incongruous combination of images **surreal** adj

surrender ❶ v **1** hand over, give up **2** yield **3** cease resistance ▷ n **4** act of surrendering

surreptitious adj **1** done secretly or stealthily **2** furtive

surrogate n substitute **surrogate mother** woman who bears child on behalf of childless couple

surround ❶ v **1** be, come all round, encompass **2** encircle ▷ n **3** border, edging **surroundings** pl n conditions, scenery etc. around a person, place, environment

surveillance ❶ n close watch, supervision

survey ❶ v **1** view, scrutinize **2** inspect, examine **3** measure, map (land) ▷ n **4** act of surveying **5** inspection **6** report incorporating results of survey **surveyor** n

survive ❶ v **1** continue to live or exist **2** outlive **survival** n continuation of existence **survivor** n one who survives

— THESAURUS —

surpass v = **outdo**, beat, exceed, eclipse, excel

surplus n = **excess**, surfeit ≠ **shortage** ▷ adj = **extra**, spare, excess, remaining, odd ≠ **insufficient**

surprise n = **shock**, revelation, jolt, bombshell, eye-opener (Inf); = **amazement**, astonishment, wonder, incredulity ▷ v = **amaze**, astonish, stun, startle, stagger; = **catch unawares** or **off-guard**, spring upon

surrender v = **give in**, yield, submit, give way, succumb ≠ **resist**; = **give up**, abandon, relinquish, yield, concede ▷ n = **submission**,

cave-in (Inf), capitulation, resignation, renunciation

surround v = **enclose**, ring, encircle, encompass, envelop

surveillance n = **observation**, watch, scrutiny, supervision, inspection

survey n = **poll**, study, research, review, inquiry; = **examination**, inspection, scrutiny ▷ v = **interview**, question, poll, research, investigate; = **look over**, view, examine, observe, contemplate; = **measure**, estimate, assess, appraise

survive v = **remain alive**, last, live on, endure

S

susceptible ⊙ *adj* **1** yielding readily (to) **2** capable (of) **3** impressionable **susceptibility** *n*

suspect ⊙ *v* **1** doubt innocence of **2** have impression of existence or presence of **3** be inclined to believe that ▷ *adj* **4** of suspicious character ▷ *n* **5** suspected person

suspend ⊙ *v* **1** hang up **2** cause to cease for a time **3** keep inoperative **4** sustain in fluid **suspenders** *pl n* straps for supporting stockings

suspense *n* **1** state of uncertainty, esp. while awaiting news, an event etc. **2** anxiety, worry **suspension** *n* **1** state of being suspended **2** springs on axle of body of vehicle

suspicion ⊙ *n* **1** suspecting, being suspected **2** slight trace **suspicious** *adj*

sustain ⊙ *v* **1** keep, hold up **2** endure **3** keep alive **4** confirm **sustenance** *n* food

SUV sport (or sports) utility vehicle: a powerful car with four-wheel drive, designed for road and off-road use

svelte *adj* gracefully slim

swab *n* **1** mop **2** pad of surgical wool etc. for cleaning **3** taking specimen etc. ▷ *v* **4** clean with swab

swag *n* (*Sl*) stolen property

swagger *v* **1** strut **2** boast ▷ *n* **3** strutting gait **4** boastful manner

swallow¹ ⊙ *v* **1** cause, allow to pass down gullet **2** suppress ▷ *n* **3** act of swallowing

swallow² *n* migratory bird with forked tail

swamp ⊙ *n* **1** bog ▷ *v* **2** entangle in swamp **3** overwhelm **4** flood

swan *n* large, web-footed water bird with curved neck

swap, swop ⊙ *v* swapping, swapped **1** exchange **2** barter ▷ *n* **3** exchange

---

THESAURUS

susceptible *adj* = **responsive**, sensitive, receptive, impressionable, suggestible ≠ **unresponsive**

suspect *v* = **believe**, feel, guess, consider, suppose ≠ **know**; = **distrust**, doubt, mistrust ≠ **trust** ▷ *adj* = **dubious**, doubtful, questionable, iffy (*Inf*) ≠ **innocent**

suspend *v* = **postpone**, put off, cease, interrupt, shelve ≠ **continue**; = **hang**, attach, dangle

suspicion *n* = **distrust**, scepticism, mistrust, doubt, misgiving; = **idea**, notion, hunch,

guess, impression; = **trace**, touch, hint, suggestion, shade

sustain *v* = **maintain**, continue, keep up, prolong, protract; = **suffer**, experience, undergo, feel, bear; = **help**, aid, assist; = **keep alive**, nourish, provide for

swallow¹ *v* = **eat**, consume, devour, swig (*Inf*)

swamp *n* = **bog**, marsh, quagmire, slough, fen ▷ *v* = **flood**, engulf, submerge, inundate; = **overload**, overwhelm, inundate

swap, swop *v* = **exchange**, trade, switch, interchange, barter

S

swarm ❶ n **1** large cluster of insects **2** vast crowd ▷ v **3** (of bees) be on the move in swarm **4** gather in large numbers

swarthy adj **-thier, -thiest** dark-complexioned

swastika n symbol of cross with arms bent at right angles

swat v **swatting, swatted 1** hit smartly **2** kill, esp. insects

swathe ❶ v cover with wraps or bandages

sway ❶ v **1** swing unsteadily **2** (cause to) vacillate in opinion etc. ▷ n **3** control **4** power **5** swaying motion

swear ❶ v **swearing, swore, sworn 1** promise on oath **2** cause to take an oath **3** declare **4** curse **swearword** n word considered obscene or blasphemous

sweat ❶ n **1** moisture oozing from, forming on skin **2** (Inf) state of anxiety ▷ v **3** (cause to) exude sweat **4** toil **sweaty** adj

sweatshirt n long-sleeved cotton jersey

sweater n woollen jersey

swede n variety of turnip

sweep ❶ v **sweeping, swept 1** clean with broom **2** pass quickly or magnificently **3** extend in continuous curve **4** carry away suddenly ▷ n **5** act of cleaning with broom **6** sweeping motion **7** wide curve **8** one who cleans chimneys **sweeping** adj **1** wide-ranging **2** without limitations **sweepstake** n lottery with stakes of participants as prize

sweet ❶ adj **1** tasting like sugar **2** agreeable **3** kind, charming **4** fragrant **5** tuneful **6** dear, beloved ▷ n **7** small piece of sweet food **8** sweet course served at end of meal **sweeten** v **sweetener** n **1** sweetening agent **2** (Sl) bribe **sweetness** n **sweet corn** type of maize with sweet yellow kernels **sweetheart** n lover **sweet pea**

THESAURUS

---

swarm n = **multitude**, crowd, mass, army, host ▷ v = **crowd**, flock, throng, mass, stream; = **teem**, crawl, abound, bristle

swathe v = **wrap**, drape, envelop, cloak, shroud

sway v = **move from side to side**, rock, roll, swing, bend; = **influence**, affect, guide, persuade, induce ▷ n = **power**, control, influence, authority, clout (Inf)

swear v = **curse**, blaspheme, be foul-mouthed; = **vow**, promise, testify, attest; = **declare**, assert, affirm

sweat n (Inf) = **panic**, anxiety, worry, distress, agitation ▷ v = **perspire**, glow; (Inf) = **worry**, fret, agonize, torture yourself

sweep v = **brush**, clean; = **clear**, remove, brush, clean ▷ n = **movement**, move, swing, stroke; = **extent**, range, stretch, scope

sweet adj = **sugary**, cloying, saccharine, icky (Inf) ≠ **sour**; = **fragrant**, aromatic ≠ **stinking**; = **fresh**, clean, pure ▷ n usually plural = **confectionery**, candy (US), lolly (Aust & NZ), bonbon; (Brit) = **dessert**, pudding

S

plant of pea family with bright flowers **sweet-talk** v (Inf) coax, flatter

swell ⊕ v swelling, swelled, swollen 1 expand 2 be greatly filled with pride, emotion ▷ n 3 act of swelling or being swollen 4 wave of sea **swelling** n enlargement of part of body, caused by injury or infection

swerve v 1 swing round, change direction during motion 2 turn aside (from duty etc.) ▷ n 3 swerving

swift ⊕ adj 1 rapid, quick ▷ n 2 bird like a swallow

swig n 1 large swallow of drink ▷ v 2 drink thus

swill v 1 drink greedily 2 pour water over or through ▷ n 3 liquid pig food 4 rinsing

swim v swimming, swam, swum 1 support and move oneself in water 2 float 3 be flooded 4 have feeling of dizziness ▷ n 5 spell of swimming **swimmer** n **swimmingly** adv successfully

swindle n/v cheat **swindler** n

swine n 1 pig 2 contemptible person

swing ⊕ v swinging, swung 1 (cause to) move to and fro 2 (cause to) pivot, turn 3 hang 4 be hanged 5 hit out (at) ▷ n 6 act, instance of swinging 7 seat hung to swing on 8 fluctuation (esp. in voting pattern)

swingeing adj punishing, severe

swipe v strike with wide, sweeping or glancing blow

swirl ⊕ v 1 (cause to) move with eddying motion ▷ n 2 such motion

swish v 1 (cause to) move with hissing sound ▷ n 2 the sound

switch ⊕ n 1 mechanism to complete or interrupt electric circuit etc. 2 abrupt change 3 flexible stick or twig 4 tress of false hair ▷ v 5 change abruptly 6 exchange 7 affect (current etc.) with switch **switchboard** n installation for connecting telephone calls

swivel n -elling, -elled 1 mechanism of two parts which can revolve the one on the other ▷ v 2 turn (on swivel)

swoop ⊕ v 1 dive, as hawk ▷ n 2 act of swooping

S

swell v = **increase**, rise, grow, mount, expand ≠ **decrease**; = **expand**, increase, grow, rise, balloon ≠ **shrink** ▷ n = **wave**, surge, billow

swift adj = **quick**, prompt, rapid

swing v = **brandish**, wave, shake, flourish, wield; = **sway**, rock, wave, veer, oscillate; usually with **round** = **turn**, swivel, curve, rotate, pivot; = **hit out**, strike,

swipe, lash out at, slap ▷ n = **swaying**, sway

swirl v = **whirl**, churn, spin, twist, eddy

switch n = **control**, button, lever, on/off device; = **change**, shift, reversal ▷ v = **change**, shift, divert, deviate; = **exchange**, swap, substitute

swoop v = **pounce**, attack, charge, rush, descend

sword n weapon with long blade
  swordfish n fish with elongated
  sharp upper jaw
swot (Inf) ▷ v 1 study hard ▷ n
  2 one who works hard at lessons
sycamore n tree related to maple
sycophant n one using flattery to
  gain favours **sycophantic** adj
syllable n division of word as unit
  for pronunciation
syllabus n, pl -buses, -bi outline
  of course of study
syllogism n form of logical
  reasoning consisting of two
  premises and conclusion
symbol ❶ n 1 sign 2 thing
  representing or typifying
  something **symbolic** adj
  symbolism n **symbolize** v
symmetry n proportion between
  parts **symmetrical** adj
sympathy ❶ n, pl -thies
  1 feeling for another in pain etc.
  2 compassion, pity 3 sharing of
  emotion etc. **sympathetic** adj
  sympathize v
symphony n, pl -nies
  composition for full orchestra
symposium n, pl -siums, -sia
  conference
symptom ❶ n 1 change in body
  indicating disease 2 sign
  symptomatic adj
synagogue n Jewish place of
  worship

sync, synch n (Inf)
  synchronization
synchromesh adj (of gearbox)
  having device that synchronizes
  speeds of gears before they engage
synchronize v 1 make agree in
  time 2 happen at same time
  synchronization n
syncopate v accentuate weak beat
  in bar of music **syncopation** n
syndicate n 1 body of persons
  associated for some enterprise ▷ v
  2 form syndicate 3 publish in many
  newspapers at the same time
syndrome n combination of
  several symptoms in disease
synod n church council
synonym n word with same
  meaning as another **synonymous**
  adj
synopsis n, pl -ses summary,
  outline
syntax n arrangement of words in
  sentence
synthesis n, pl -ses putting
  together, combination **synthesize**
  v make artificially **synthesizer** n
  electronic keyboard instrument
  reproducing wide range of musical
  sounds **synthetic** adj 1 artificial
  2 of synthesis
syphilis n contagious venereal
  disease
syringe n 1 instrument for
  drawing in liquid and forcing it out

——————————— THESAURUS ———————————

symbol n = **metaphor**, image,
  sign, representation,
  token
sympathy n = **compassion**,
  understanding, pity,

commiseration ≠ **indifference**;
= **affinity**, agreement, rapport,
fellow feeling ≠ **opposition**
symptom n = **sign**, mark,
  indication, warning

in fine spray ▷ v **2** spray, cleanse with syringe

syrup n **1** thick solution obtained in process of refining sugar **2** any liquid like this

system ❶ n **1** complex whole **2** method **3** classification

systematic adj methodical

——————— THESAURUS ———————

system n = **arrangement**, structure, organization, scheme, classification; = **method**, practice, technique, procedure, routine

S

ta *interj* (*Inf*) thank you

tab *n* tag, label, short strap

Tabasco® *n* hot red pepper sauce

tabby *adj/n, pl* **-bies** (cat) with stripes on lighter background

table ❶ *n* 1 flat board supported by legs 2 facts, figures arranged in lines or columns ▷ *v* 3 submit (motion etc.) for discussion
tablespoon *n* spoon for serving food

tableau *n, pl* **-leaux** group of persons representing some scene

tablet *n* 1 pill of compressed powdered medicine 2 cake of soap etc. 3 inscribed slab of stone, wood etc. 4 hand-held computer

tabloid *n* small-sized newspaper with many photographs and usu. sensational style

taboo ❶ *adj, pl* **-boos** 1 forbidden ▷ *n* 2 prohibition resulting from social conventions etc.

tacit *adj* implied but not spoken

taciturn *adj* habitually silent

tack¹ ❶ *n* 1 small nail 2 long loose stitch 3 (*Naut*) course of ship obliquely to windward 4 approach, method ▷ *v* 5 nail with tacks 6 stitch lightly 7 append 8 sail to windward

tack² *n* riding harness for horses

tackies, takkies *pl n, sing* **tacky** (*S Afr, Inf*) tennis shoes or plimsolls

tackle ❶ *n* 1 equipment, esp. for lifting 2 (*Sport*) physical challenge of opponent ▷ *v* 3 undertake 4 challenge

tacky¹ *adj* **tackier, tackiest** 1 sticky 2 not quite dry

tacky² *adj* **tackier, tackiest** vulgar, tasteless

tact *n* skill in dealing with people or situations **tactful** *adj* **tactless** *adj*

tactics *pl n* 1 art of handling troops, ships in battle 2 methods, plans **tactical** *adj* **tactician** *n*

tactile *adj* of sense of touch

— THESAURUS —

table *n* = **counter**, bench, stand, board, surface; = **list**, chart, tabulation, record, roll ▷ *v* (*Brit*) = **submit**, propose, put forward, move, suggest

taboo *n* = **prohibition**, ban, restriction, anathema, interdict ▷ *adj* = **forbidden**, banned, prohibited, unacceptable, outlawed

≠ **permitted**

tack¹ *n* = **nail**, pin, drawing pin ▷ *v* = **fasten**, fix, attach, pin, nail; (*Brit*) = **stitch**, sew, hem, bind, baste

tackle *v* = **deal with**, set about, get stuck into (*Inf*), come *or* get to grips with; = **undertake**, attempt, embark upon, get stuck into (*Inf*), have a go *or* stab at (*Inf*) ▷ *n*

tadpole n immature frog

taffeta n stiff silk fabric

tag¹ ❶ n **1** label identifying or showing price of (something) **2** hanging end ▷ v **3** add (on)

tag² n **1** children's game where one chased becomes the chaser upon being touched ▷ v **2** touch

tail ❶ n **1** flexible appendage at animal's rear **2** hindmost, lower or inferior part of anything ▷ pl **3** reverse side of coin ▷ v **4** remove tail of **5** (Inf) follow closely **tailback** n queue of traffic stretching back from obstruction **tailboard** n hinged rear board on lorry etc. **tail coat** man's evening dress jacket **tail off** diminish gradually **tailspin** n spinning dive of aircraft **tailwind** n wind coming from rear

tailor ❶ n maker of clothing, esp. for men **tailor-made** adj well-fitting

taint ❶ v **1** affect or be affected by pollution etc. ▷ n **2** defect **3** contamination

take ❶ v **taking, took, taken** **1** grasp **2** get **3** receive **4** understand **5** consider **6** use **7** capture **8** steal **9** accept **10** bear **11** consume **12** assume **13** carry **14** accompany **15** subtract **16** require **17** contain, hold **18** be effective **19** please ▷ n **20** (recording of) scene filmed without break **takings** pl n earnings, receipts **take after** resemble in face or character **takeaway** n **1** shop, restaurant selling meals for eating elsewhere **2** meal bought at this place **take in** **1** understand **2** include **3** make (garment etc.) smaller **4** deceive **take off** **1** remove **2** (of aircraft) leave ground **3** (Inf) go away **4** (Inf) mimic **take-off** n **takeover** n act of taking control of company by buying large number of its shares

talc, talcum powder n powder, usu. scented, to absorb body moisture

tale ❶ n story, narrative

—————— THESAURUS ——————

= **block**, challenge, apparatus

tag¹ n = **label**, tab, note, ticket, slip ▷ v = **label**, mark

tail n = **extremity**, appendage, brush, rear end, hindquarters ▷ v (Inf) = **follow**, track, shadow, trail, stalk

tailor n = **outfitter**, couturier, dressmaker, seamstress, clothier ▷ v = **adapt**, adjust, modify, style, fashion

taint v = **spoil**, ruin, contaminate, damage, stain ≠ **purify**

take v = **grip**, grab, seize, catch, grasp; = **carry**, bring, bear, transport, ferry ≠ **send**; = **accompany**, lead, bring, guide, conduct; = **remove**, draw, pull, fish, withdraw; = **steal**, appropriate, pocket, pinch (Inf), misappropriate ≠ **return**; = **capture**, seize, take into custody, lay hold of ≠ **release**; = **tolerate**, stand, bear, stomach, endure ≠ **avoid**

tale n = **story**, narrative, anecdote, account, legend

talent ❶ n natural ability
 talented adj gifted
talisman n, pl **-mans** object
 supposed to have magic power
talk ❶ v 1 express, exchange ideas
 etc. in words 2 discuss ▷ n
 3 lecture 4 conversation
 5 rumour 6 discussion **talkative**
 adj
tall ❶ adj 1 high 2 of great stature
tally ❶ v **-lying, -lied**
 1 correspond one with the other
 2 count ▷ n 3 record, account
talon n claw
tambourine n flat half-drum with
 jingling discs of metal attached
tame ❶ adj 1 not wild,
 domesticated 2 uninteresting ▷ v
 3 make tame
tamper v interfere (with)
tampon n plug of cotton wool
 inserted into vagina during
 menstruation

tan adj/n 1 (of) brown colour of
 skin after exposure to sun etc. ▷ v
 2 (cause to) go brown 3 (of animal
 hide) convert to leather **tannin** n
 vegetable substance used as
 tanning agent
tandem n bicycle for two
tandoori adj (of Indian food)
 cooked in a clay oven
tang n strong pungent taste or
 smell **tangy** adj
tangent n line that touches a
 curve **tangential** adj
tangerine n (fruit of) Asian citrus
 tree
tangible ❶ adj 1 that can be
 touched 2 real **tangibility** n
tangle ❶ n 1 confused mass or
 situation ▷ v 2 confuse
tango n, pl **-gos** dance of S Amer.
 origin
tank n 1 storage vessel for liquids
 or gases 2 armoured motor vehicle

━━━━━━━━━━━━━━━━ THESAURUS ━━━━━━━━━━━━━━━━

talent n = **ability**, gift, aptitude,
 capacity, genius
talk v = **speak**, chat, chatter,
 converse, communicate; = **discuss**,
 confer, negotiate, parley,
 confabulate; = **inform**, grass (Brit
 Sl), tell all, give the game away, blab
 ▷ n = **speech**, lecture,
 presentation, report, address
tall adj = **lofty**, big, giant,
 long-legged, lanky; = **high**,
 towering, soaring, steep, elevated
 ≠ **short**; (Inf) = **implausible**,
 incredible, far-fetched,
 exaggerated, absurd ≠ **plausible**
tally n = **record**, score, total, count,
 reckoning ▷ v = **agree**, match,

accord, fit, square ≠ **disagree**
tame adj = **domesticated**, docile,
 broken, gentle, obedient ≠ **wild**;
 = **submissive**, meek, compliant,
 subdued, manageable ≠ **stubborn**;
 = **unexciting**, boring, dull, bland,
 uninspiring ≠ **exciting** ▷ v
 = **domesticate**, train, break in,
 house-train ≠ **make fiercer**;
 = **subdue**, suppress, master,
 discipline, humble ≠ **arouse**
tangible adj = **definite**, real,
 positive, material, actual
 ≠ **intangible**
tangle n = **knot**, twist, web,
 jungle, coil; = **mess**, jam, fix (Inf),
 confusion, complication ▷ v

t

on tracks **tanker** *n* ship, lorry for
carrying liquid

tankard *n* large drinking cup

Tannoy® *n* type of public-address
system

tantalize *v* torment by appearing
to offer something

tantamount *adj* **tantamount to**
equivalent to effect to

tantrum ❶ *n* outburst of temper

tap¹ ❶ *v* **tapping, tapped 1** strike
lightly but with some noise ▷ *n*
2 tapping **tap dance** dance in
which the feet beat out elaborate
rhythms

tap² ❶ *n* **1** valve with handle, plug
etc. to regulate or stop flow of fluid
▷ *v* **2** draw off with tap **3** use,
draw on **4** make secret connection
to telephone wire to overhear
conversation on it

tape ❶ *n* **1** narrow strip of fabric,
paper etc. **2** magnetic recording
▷ *v* **3** record (speech, music etc.)
tape measure tape marked off in
centimetres, inches etc. **tape
recorder** apparatus for recording
sound on magnetized tape

tapeworm *n* long flat parasitic
worm

taper *v* **1** become gradually thinner
▷ *n* **2** thin candle

tapestry *n, pl* **-tries** fabric
decorated with woven designs

tapioca *n* beadlike starch made
from cassava root

tar *n* **1** thick black liquid distilled
from coal etc. ▷ *v* **2** coat, treat
with tar

tarantula *n* large (poisonous)
hairy spider

tardy *adj* **tardier, tardiest** slow,
late

target ❶ *n* **1** thing aimed at
2 victim

tariff ❶ *n* **1** tax levied on imports
etc. **2** list of charges

Tarmac *n* mixture of tar etc.
giving hard, smooth surface to road

tarn *n* small mountain lake

tarnish ❶ *v* **1** (cause to) become
stained or sullied ▷ *n*
2 discoloration, blemish

tarot *n* pack of cards used in
fortune-telling

tarpaulin *n* (sheet of) heavy

= **twist**, knot, mat, coil, mesh
≠ **disentangle**

tantrum *n* = **outburst**, temper,
hysterics, fit, flare-up

tap¹ *v* = **knock**, strike, pat, rap, beat
▷ *n* = **knock**, pat, rap, touch,
drumming

tap² *n* = **valve**, stopcock ▷ *v*
= **listen in on**, monitor, bug (*Inf*),
spy on, eavesdrop on

tape *n* = **binding**, strip, band,
string, ribbon ▷ *v* = **record**, video,

tape-record, make a recording of;
sometimes with **up** = **bind**, secure,
stick, seal, wrap

target *n* = **mark**, goal; = **goal**, aim,
objective, end, mark

tariff *n* = **tax**, duty, toll, levy, excise;
= **price list**, schedule

tarnish *v* = **damage**, taint,
blacken, sully, smirch ≠ **enhance**;
= **stain**, discolour, darken, blot,
blemish ≠ **brighten** ▷ *n* = **stain**,
taint, discoloration, spot, blot

hard-wearing waterproof fabric
tarragon n aromatic herb
tarry v -rying, -ried 1 linger, delay
2 stay behind
tart¹ ❶ n 1 small pie or flan filled
with fruit, jam etc. 2 loose woman
tart² ❶ adj 1 sour 2 sharp 3 bitter
tartan n woollen cloth woven in
pattern of coloured checks
tartar n crust deposited on teeth
task ❶ n piece of work (esp.
unpleasant or difficult) set or
undertaken **taskmaster** n
overseer
tassel n 1 ornament of fringed
knot of threads etc. 2 tuft
taste ❶ n 1 sense by which flavour,
quality of substance is detected by
the tongue 2 (brief) experience of
something 3 small amount
4 liking 5 power of discerning,
judging ▷ v 6 observe or
distinguish the taste of a substance
7 take small amount into mouth
8 experience 9 have specific
flavour **tasteful** adj with,
showing good taste **tasteless** adj

1 bland, insipid 2 showing bad
taste **tasty** adj pleasantly
flavoured **taste bud** small organ
of taste on tongue
tattered adj ragged **tatters** pl n
ragged pieces
tattle v/n gossip, chatter
tattletale (chiefly US and Canad) n a
scandalmonger or gossip
tattoo¹ n 1 beat of drum and bugle
call 2 military spectacle
tattoo² v 1 mark skin in coloured
patterns etc. by pricking ▷ n
2 pattern made thus
tatty adj -tier, -tiest shabby,
worn out
taunt ❶ v 1 provoke with insults
etc. ▷ n 2 scornful remark
taupe adj brownish-grey
taut adj 1 drawn tight 2 under
strain
tavern ❶ n inn, public house
tawdry adj -drier, -driest showy,
but cheap
tawny n/adj -nier, -niest (of)
light yellowish-brown colour
tax ❶ n 1 compulsory payments

————————— THESAURUS —————————

tart¹ n = **pie**, pastry, pasty, tartlet,
patty
tart² adj = **sharp**, acid, sour, bitter,
pungent ≠ **sweet**
task n = **job**, duty, assignment,
exercise, mission
taste n = **flavour**, savour, relish,
smack, tang ≠ **blandness**; = **bit**,
bite, mouthful, sample, dash;
= **liking**, preference, penchant,
fondness, partiality ≠ **dislike**;
= **refinement**, style, judgment,
discrimination, appreciation

≠ **lack of judgment** ▷ v = **have a
flavour of**, smack of, savour of;
= **sample**, try, test, sip, savour;
= **distinguish**, perceive, discern,
differentiate; = **experience**, know,
undergo, partake of, encounter
≠ **miss**
taunt v = **jeer**, mock, tease,
ridicule, provoke ▷ n = **jeer**, dig,
insult, ridicule, teasing
tavern n = **inn**, bar, pub (Inf, chiefly
Brit), public house, hostelry
tax n = **charge**, duty, toll, levy, tariff

imposed by government to raise revenue **2** heavy demand on something ▷ v **3** impose tax on **4** strain **taxation** n levying of taxes **tax return** statement of income for tax purposes

taxi, taxicab n **1** motor vehicle for hire with driver ▷ v **2** (of aircraft) run along ground

taxidermy n art of stuffing animal skins **taxidermist** n

TB tuberculosis

tbc to be confirmed

tea n **1** dried leaves of plant cultivated esp. in Asia **2** infusion of it as beverage **3** meal eaten in afternoon or early evening **tea bag** small porous bag of tea leaves **teapot** n container for making and serving tea **teaspoon** n small spoon for stirring tea etc. **tea towel** towel for drying dishes

teach ❶ v **teaching, taught** **1** instruct **2** educate **3** train **teacher** n

teak n (hard wood from) E Indian tree

team ❶ n **1** set of animals, players of game etc. ▷ v **2** (usu. with *up*) (cause to) make a team **teamwork** n cooperative work by team

tear¹ ❶ v **tearing, tore, torn** **1** pull apart **2** become torn **3** rush ▷ n **4** hole or split **tearaway** n wild or unruly person

tear² n drop of fluid falling from eye **tearful** adj **1** inclined to weep **2** involving tears **teardrop** n **tear gas** irritant gas causing temporary blindness

tease ❶ v **1** tantalize, torment, irritate ▷ n **2** one who teases

teat n **1** nipple of breast **2** rubber nipple of baby's bottle

technical ❶ adj **1** of, specializing in industrial, practical or mechanical arts **2** belonging to particular art or science **3** according to letter of the law **technicality** n point of procedure **technician** n one skilled in technique of an art **technique** n **1** method of performance in an art **2** skill required for mastery of subject

Technicolor® n colour photography, esp. in cinema

technology n **1** application of practical, mechanical sciences **2** technical skills, knowledge **technological** adj

tedious ❶ adj causing fatigue or boredom **tedium** n monotony

t

▷ v = **charge**, rate, assess; = **strain**, stretch, try, test, load

teach v = **instruct**, train, coach, inform, educate

team n = **side**, squad; = **group**, company, set, body, band

tear¹ v = **rip**, split, rend, shred, rupture; = **scratch**, cut (open), gash, lacerate, injure; = **pull**

apart, claw, lacerate, mutilate, mangle ▷ n = **hole**, split, rip, rent, snag

tease v = **mock**, provoke, torment, taunt, goad

technical adj = **scientific**, technological, skilled, specialist, specialized

tedious adj = **boring**, dull, dreary,

tee n (Golf) **1** place from which first stroke of hole is made **2** small peg supporting ball for first stroke

teem v **1** abound with **2** swarm **3** rain heavily

teens pl n years of life from 13 to 19 **teenage** adj **teenager** n young person between 13 and 19

teeter v seesaw, wobble

teeth n pl of TOOTH

teethe v (of baby) grow first teeth **teething troubles** problems, difficulties at first stage of something

teetotal adj pledged to abstain from alcohol **teetotaller** n

Teflon® n substance used for nonstick coatings on saucepans etc.

telecommunications pl n communications by telephone, television etc.

telegram n formerly, message sent by telegraph

telegraph n **1** formerly, electrical apparatus for transmitting messages over distance ▷ v **2** send by telegraph

telepathy n action of one mind on another at a distance **telepathic** adj

telephone ❶ n **1** apparatus for communicating sound to hearer at a distance ▷ v **2** communicate, speak by telephone **telephonist** n person operating telephone switchboard

teleprinter n apparatus for sending and receiving typed messages by wire

telescope ❶ n **1** optical instrument for magnifying distant objects ▷ v **2** slide together **telescopic** adj

television ❶ n **1** system of producing on screen images of distant objects, events etc. by electromagnetic radiation **2** device for receiving this **3** programmes etc. viewed on television set **televise** v **1** transmit by television **2** make, produce as television programme

telex n **1** international communication service ▷ v **2** send by telex

tell ❶ v **telling, told 1** let know **2** order **3** narrate, make known **4** discern **5** distinguish **6** give account **7** be of weight, importance **teller** n **1** narrator

monotonous, drab **≠ exciting**

telephone n = **phone**, mobile (phone), handset, landline, dog and bone (Sl) ▷ v = **call**, phone, ring (chiefly Brit), dial

telescope n = **glass**, scope (Inf), spyglass ▷ v = **shorten**, contract, compress, shrink, condense **≠ lengthen**

television n = **TV**, telly (Brit Inf),

small screen (Inf), the box (Brit Inf), the tube (Sl)

tell v = **inform**, notify, state to, reveal to, express to; = **describe**, relate, recount, report, portray; = **instruct**, order, command, direct, bid; = **distinguish**, discriminate, discern, differentiate, identify; = **have** or **take effect**, register, weigh, count, take its toll

2 bank cashier **telling** *adj*
effective, striking **tell off**
reprimand **telltale** *n* 1 sneak
▷ *adj* 2 revealing

telly *n, pl* **-lies** (*Inf*) television (set)

temerity *n* boldness, audacity

temp *n* (*Inf*) one employed on
temporary basis

temper ❶ *n* 1 frame of mind
2 angry state 3 calmness,
composure ▷ *v* 4 restrain,
moderate 5 harden (metal)

temperament ❶ *n* 1 natural
disposition 2 emotional mood
temperamental *adj* 1 moody
2 erratic

temperate *adj* 1 (of climate) mild
2 not extreme 3 showing
moderation **temperance** *n*
1 moderation 2 abstinence, esp.
from alcohol

temperature *n* 1 degree of heat
or coldness 2 (*Inf*) high body
temperature

tempest *n* violent storm
tempestuous *adj* 1 stormy
2 violent

template *n* pattern used to cut
out shapes accurately

temple ❶ *n* building for worship

tempo *n, pl* **-pi, -pos** rate, rhythm

temporal *adj* 1 of time 2 of this
life or world

temporary ❶ *adj* lasting only a
short time

tempt ❶ *v* try to persuade, entice,
esp. to something wrong or unwise
temptation *n* **tempter** *n*
tempting *adj* attractive, inviting

ten *n/adj* cardinal number after
nine **tenth** *adj* ordinal number

tenable *adj* able to be held,
defended, maintained

tenacious *adj* 1 holding fast
2 retentive 3 stubborn **tenacity**
n

tenant ❶ *n* one who holds lands,
house etc. on rent or lease
tenancy *n*

tench *n, pl* **tench** freshwater fish

tend¹ ❶ *v* 1 be inclined 2 be
conducive 3 make in direction of
tendency *n* inclination
tendentious *adj* controversial

——— THESAURUS ———

temper *n* = **irritability**, irascibility,
passion, resentment, petulance
≠ **good humour**; = **frame of mind**,
nature, mind, mood, constitution;
= **rage**, fury, bad mood, passion,
tantrum; = **self-control**,
composure, cool (*Sl*), calmness,
equanimity ≠ **anger** ▷ *v*
= **moderate**, restrain, tone down,
soften, soothe ≠ **intensify**;
= **strengthen**, harden, toughen,
anneal ≠ **soften**

temperament *n* = **nature**,

character, personality, make-up,
constitution

temple *n* = **shrine**, church,
sanctuary, house of God

temporary *adj* = **impermanent**,
transitory, brief, fleeting, interim
≠ **permanent**

tempt *v* = **attract**, allure

tenant *n* = **leaseholder**, resident,
renter, occupant, inhabitant

tend¹ *v* = **be inclined**, be liable,
have a tendency, be apt, be
prone

t

tend² ⊙ v take care of

tender¹ ⊙ adj 1 not tough 2 easily injured 3 gentle, loving 4 delicate

tender² ⊙ v 1 offer 2 make offer or estimate ▷ n 3 offer or estimate for contract to undertake specific work **legal tender** currency that must, by law, be accepted as payment

tendon n sinew attaching muscle to bone etc.

tendril n slender curling stem by which climbing plant clings

tenement n building divided into separate flats

tenet n belief

tennis n game in which ball is struck with racket by players on opposite sides of net

tenor n 1 male voice between alto and bass 2 general course, meaning

tenpin bowling game in which players try to knock over ten skittles with ball

tense ⊙ adj 1 stretched tight 2 taut 3 emotionally strained ▷ v

4 make, become tense **tensile** adj of, relating to tension **tension** n 1 stretching 2 strain when stretched 3 emotional strain 4 suspense 5 (Electricity) voltage

tent n portable shelter of canvas

tentacle n flexible organ of some animals (e.g. octopus) used for grasping, feeding etc.

tentative ⊙ adj 1 experimental 2 cautious

tenterhooks pl n **on tenterhooks** in anxious suspense

tenuous adj 1 flimsy 2 thin

tenure n (length of time of) possession of office etc.

tepee n N Amer. Indian cone-shaped tent

tepid adj moderately warm

tequila n Mexican alcoholic drink

term ⊙ n 1 word, expression 2 limited period of time 3 period during which schools are open ▷ pl 4 conditions 5 relationship ▷ v 6 name

terminal ⊙ adj 1 at, forming an end 2 (of disease) ending in death

---

THESAURUS

tend² v = **take care of**, look after, keep, attend, nurture ≠ **neglect**; = **maintain**, take care of, nurture, cultivate, manage ≠ **neglect**

tender¹ adj = **gentle**, loving, kind, caring, sympathetic ≠ **harsh**; = **vulnerable**, young, sensitive, raw, youthful ≠ **experienced**

tender² n = **offer**, bid, estimate, proposal, submission ▷ v = **offer**, present, submit, give, propose

tense adj = **strained**, uneasy, stressful, fraught, charged;

= **nervous**, edgy, strained, anxious, apprehensive ≠ **calm** ▷ v = **tighten**, strain, brace, stretch, flex ≠ **relax**

tentative adj = **unconfirmed**, provisional, indefinite, test, trial ≠ **confirmed**; = **hesitant**, cautious, uncertain, doubtful, faltering ≠ **confident**

term n = **word**, name, expression, title, label; = **period**, time, spell, while, season ▷ v = **call**, name, label, style, entitle

▷ *n* **3** terminal part or structure **4** point where current enters, leaves battery etc. **5** device permitting operation of computer at distance

terminate ❶ *v* bring, come to an end **termination** *n*

terminology *n* set of technical terms or vocabulary

terminus *n, pl* **-ni, -nuses** **1** finishing point **2** railway station etc. at end of line

termite *n* wood-eating insect

tern *n* sea bird like gull

terrace *n* **1** raised level place **2** row of houses built as one block **3** (*oft. pl*) unroofed tiers for spectators at sports stadium ▷ *v* **4** form into terrace

terracotta *n/adj* **1** (made of) hard unglazed pottery **2** (of) brownish-red colour

terrain ❶ *n* area of ground, esp. with reference to its physical character

terrapin *n* type of aquatic tortoise

terrestrial ❶ *adj* **1** of the earth **2** of, living on land

terrible ❶ *adj* **1** serious **2** (*Inf*) very bad **3** causing fear **terribly** *adv*

terrier *n* small dog of various breeds

terrific ❶ *adj* **1** very great **2** (*Inf*) good **3** awe-inspiring

terrify ❶ *v* **-fying, -fied** frighten greatly **terrifying** *adj*

territory ❶ *n, pl* **-ries** **1** region **2** geographical area, esp. a sovereign state **territorial** *adj* **Territorial Army** reserve army

terror ❶ *n* **1** great fear **2** (*Inf*) troublesome person or thing **terrorism** *n* use of violence to achieve ends **terrorist** *n/adj* **terrorize** *v* **1** oppress by violence **2** terrify

terse *adj* **1** concise **2** abrupt

tertiary *adj* third in degree, order etc.

Terylene® *n* **1** synthetic yarn **2** fabric made of it

— THESAURUS —

terminal *adj* = **fatal**, deadly, lethal, killing, mortal; = **final**, last, closing, finishing, concluding ≠ **initial** ▷ *n* = **terminus**, station, depot, end of the line

terminate *v* = **end**, stop, conclude, finish, complete ≠ **begin**

terrain *n* = **ground**, country, land, landscape, topography

terrestrial *adj* = **earthly**, worldly, global

terrible *adj* = **awful**, shocking, terrifying, horrible, dreadful; (*Inf*) = **bad**, awful, dreadful, dire,

abysmal ≠ **wonderful**; = **serious**, desperate, severe, extreme, dangerous ≠ **mild**

terrific *adj* (*Inf*) = **excellent**, wonderful, brilliant, amazing, outstanding ≠ **awful**; = **intense**, great, huge, enormous, tremendous

terrify *v* = **frighten**, scare, alarm, terrorize, make your hair stand on end

territory *n* = **district**, area, land, region, country

terror *n* = **fear**, alarm, dread,

test ❶ v 1 try, put to the proof
2 carry out examination on ▷ n
3 examination 4 means of trial
testing adj difficult **test case**
lawsuit viewed as means of
establishing precedent **test
match** international sports
contest, esp. one of series **test
tube** tubelike glass vessel
testament ❶ n (Law) 1 will
2 (with cap.) one of the two main
divisions of the Bible
testate adj (of dead person) having
left a valid will
testicle, testis n either of two
male reproductive glands
testify ❶ v **-fying, -fied** 1 declare
2 bear witness (to)
testimony ❶ n, pl **-nies**
1 affirmation 2 evidence
testimonial n 1 certificate of
character etc. 2 gift expressing
regard for recipient
testy adj **-tier, -tiest** irritable
tetanus n (also called **lockjaw**)
acute infectious disease
tête-à-tête n, pl **-têtes, -tête**
private conversation
tether n 1 rope for fastening

(grazing) animal ▷ v 2 tie up with
rope
tetrahedron n, pl **-drons, -dra**
solid contained by four plane
faces
text ❶ n 1 (actual words of) book,
passage etc. 2 passage of Bible
textual adj **textbook** n book of
instruction on particular subject
textile n any fabric or cloth, esp.
woven
texture ❶ n 1 structure,
appearance 2 consistency
than conj introduces second part of
comparison
thank ❶ v 1 express gratitude to
2 say thanks **thankful** adj
grateful **thankless** adj
unrewarding or unappreciated
thanks pl n words of gratitude
that adj 1 refers to thing already
mentioned 2 refers to thing further
away ▷ pron 3 refers to particular
thing 4 introduces relative clause
▷ conj 5 introduces noun or
adverbial clause
thatch n 1 reeds, straw etc. used
as roofing material ▷ v 2 build roof
with this

— THESAURUS —

fright, panic; = **nightmare**,
monster, bogeyman, devil, fiend
test v = **check**, investigate, assess,
research, analyse; = **examine**, put
someone to the test ▷ n = **trial**,
research, check, investigation,
analysis
testament n = **proof**, evidence,
testimony, witness, demonstration;
= **will**, last wishes
testify v = **bear witness**, state,

swear, certify, assert ≠ **disprove**
testimony n = **evidence**,
statement, submission, affidavit,
deposition; = **proof**, evidence,
demonstration, indication, support
text n = **contents**, words, content,
wording, body; = **words**, wording
texture n = **feel**, consistency,
structure, surface, tissue
thank v = **say thank you to**, show
your appreciation to

thaw ❶ v **1** melt **2** (cause to) unfreeze ▷ n **3** melting (of frost etc.)

the adj the definite article

theatre n **1** place where plays etc. are performed **2** dramatic works generally **3** hospital operating room **theatrical** adj **1** of, for the theatre **2** exaggerated

thee pron (Obs) object of THOU

theft ❶ n stealing

their adj of, belonging to them **theirs** pron belonging to them

them pron object of THEY **themselves** pron emphatic or reflexive form of THEY

theme ❶ n **1** main topic of book etc. **2** subject of composition **3** recurring melody **thematic** adj **theme park** leisure area designed round one subject

then adv **1** at that time **2** next **3** that being so

thence adv (Obs) from that place or time

theology n, pl **-gies** systematic study of religion and religious beliefs **theologian** n **theological** adj

theorem n proposition which can be demonstrated

theory ❶ n, pl **-ries 1** supposition to account for something **2** system of rules and principles, esp. distinguished from practice **theoretical** adj **1** based on theory **2** speculative

therapy ❶ n, pl **-pies** healing treatment **therapeutic** adj **1** of healing **2** serving to improve health **therapist** n

there adv **1** in that place **2** to that point **thereby** adv by that means **therefore** adv that being so **thereupon** adv immediately

therm n unit of measurement of heat **thermal** adj

thermodynamics pl n science that deals with interrelationship of different forms of energy

thermometer n instrument to measure temperature

Thermos® n vacuum flask

thermostat n apparatus for regulating temperature

thesaurus n, pl **-ruses** book containing lists of synonyms

these pron pl of THIS

thesis ❶ n, pl **theses 1** written work submitted for degree, diploma **2** theory maintained in argument

thespian adj **1** of the theatre ▷ n **2** actor, actress

t

thaw v = **melt**, dissolve, soften, defrost, warm ≠ **freeze**

theft n = **stealing**, robbery, thieving, fraud, embezzlement

theme n = **motif**, leitmotif; = **subject**, idea, topic, essence, subject matter

theory n = **belief**, feeling, speculation, assumption, hunch

therapy n = **remedy**, treatment, cure, healing, method of healing

thesis n = **proposition**, theory, hypothesis, idea, view; = **dissertation**, paper, treatise, essay, monograph

they *pron* pronoun of the third person plural

thick ⊙ *adj* 1 fat, broad, not thin 2 dense 3 crowded 4 viscous 5 (of voice) throaty 6 (*Inf*) stupid ▷ *n* 7 busiest part **thicken** *v* 1 make, become thick 2 become complicated **thickness** *n* 1 dimension through an object 2 layer **thickset** *adj* sturdy, stocky

thicket *n* thick growth of trees

thief ⊙ *n, pl* **thieves** one who steals **thieve** *v* steal

thigh *n* upper part of leg

thimble *n* cap protecting end of finger when sewing

thin ⊙ *adj* **thinner, thinnest** 1 of little thickness 2 slim 3 of little density 4 sparse 5 fine 6 not close-packed ▷ *v* 7 make, become thin

thing ⊙ *n* 1 (material) object 2 fact, idea

think ⊙ *v* **thinking, thought** 1 have one's mind at work 2 reflect,

meditate 3 reason 4 deliberate 5 believe

third *adj* 1 of number three in a series ▷ *n* 2 third part **third degree** violent interrogation **third party** (*Law*) person involved by chance in legal proceedings etc.

thirst ⊙ *n* 1 desire to drink 2 feeling caused by lack of drink 3 craving ▷ *v* 4 have thirst **thirsty** *adj*

thirteen *adj/n* three plus ten **thirteenth** *adj*

thirty *adj/n* three times ten **thirtieth** *adj*

this *adj/pron* denotes thing, person near or just mentioned

thistle *n* prickly plant

thither *adv* (*Obs*) to or towards that place

thong *n* narrow strip of leather, strap

thorax *n, pl* **thoraxes, thoraces** part of body between neck and belly

thorn ⊙ *n* 1 prickle on plant 2 bush noted for its thorns **thorny** *adj*

——————— THESAURUS ———————

thick *adj* = **bulky**, broad, big, large, fat ≠ **thin**; = **wide**, across, deep, broad, in extent *or* diameter; = **dense**, close, heavy, compact, impenetrable; = **heavy**, heavyweight, dense, chunky, bulky; = **opaque**, heavy, dense, impenetrable

thief *n* = **robber**, burglar, stealer, plunderer, shoplifter

thin *adj* = **narrow**, fine, attenuated ≠ **thick**; = **slim**, spare, lean, slight, slender ≠ **fat**; = **meagre**, sparse, scanty, poor, scattered ≠ **plentiful**; = **fine**, delicate, flimsy, sheer,

skimpy ≠ **thick**; = **unconvincing**, inadequate, feeble, poor, weak ≠ **convincing**

thing *n* = **substance**, stuff, being, body, material ▷ *pl n* = **possessions**, stuff, gear, belongings, effects

think *v* = **believe**, be of the opinion, be of the view; = **judge**, consider, estimate, reckon, deem

thirst *n* = **dryness**, thirstiness, drought; = **craving**, appetite, longing, desire, passion ≠ **aversion**

thorn *n* = **prickle**, spike, spine, barb

thorough ⊙ *adj* **1** careful, methodical **2** complete
thoroughly *adv* **thoroughbred** *n* pure-bred animal, esp. horse
thoroughfare *n* **1** road or passage **2** right of way

those *pron* pl of THAT

thou *pron* (*Obs*) the second person singular pronoun

though ⊙ *conj* **1** even if ▷ *adv* **2** nevertheless

thought ⊙ *n* **1** process, product of thinking **2** what one thinks **3** meditation **thoughtful** *adj* **1** considerate **2** showing careful thought **3** reflective **thoughtless** *adj* **1** inconsiderate **2** careless

thousand *n/adj* ten hundred **thousandth** *adj*

thrash ⊙ *v* **1** beat **2** defeat soundly **3** move in wild manner

thread ⊙ *n* **1** yarn **2** ridge cut on screw **3** theme ▷ *v* **4** put thread into **5** fit film etc. into machine **6** put on thread **7** pick (one's way etc.) **threadbare** *adj* **1** worn, shabby **2** hackneyed

threat ⊙ *n* **1** declaration of intention to harm, injure etc. **2** dangerous person or thing **threaten** *v* make or be threat to

three *adj/n* one more than two **three-dimensional** *adj* having height, width and depth **three-ply** *adj* having three layers or strands **threesome** *n* group of three

thresh *v* **1** beat to separate grain from husks **2** thrash

threshold ⊙ *n* **1** bar of stone forming bottom of doorway **2** entrance **3** starting point

thrice *adv* three times

——— THESAURUS ———

thorough *adj* = **comprehensive**, full, complete, sweeping, intensive ≠ **cursory**; = **careful**, conscientious, painstaking, efficient, meticulous ≠ **careless**

though *conj* = **although**, while, even if, even though, notwithstanding ▷ *adv* = **nevertheless**, still, however, yet, nonetheless

thought *n* = **thinking**, consideration, reflection, deliberation, musing; = **opinion**, view, idea, concept, notion; = **consideration**, study, attention, care, regard; = **intention**, plan, idea, design, aim; = **hope**, expectation, prospect, aspiration, anticipation

thrash *v* = **defeat**, beat, crush, slaughter (*Inf*), rout; = **beat**, wallop, whip, belt (*Inf*), cane; = **thresh**, flail, jerk, writhe, toss and turn

thread *n* = **strand**, fibre, yarn, filament, line; = **theme**, train of thought, direction, plot, drift ▷ *v* = **move**, pass, ease, thrust, squeeze through

threat *n* = **danger**, risk, hazard, menace, peril; = **threatening remark**, menace; = **warning**, foreshadowing, foreboding

threshold *n* = **entrance**, doorway, door, doorstep; = **start**, beginning, opening, dawn, verge ≠ **end**; = **limit**, margin, starting point, minimum

thrift ❶ n saving, economy **thrifty** adj economical

thrill ❶ n 1 sudden sensation of excitement and pleasure ▷ v 2 (cause to) feel a thrill 3 tremble **thriller** n suspenseful book, film etc. **thrilling** adj

thrive ❶ v **thriving, thrived** 1 grow well 2 prosper

throat n 1 front of neck 2 passage from mouth to stomach **throaty** adj 1 hoarse 2 deep, guttural

throb ❶ v **throbbing, throbbed** 1 quiver strongly, pulsate ▷ n 2 pulsation

throes pl n violent pangs, pain etc. **in the throes of** in the process of

thrombosis n, pl **-ses** clot in blood vessel or heart

throne n 1 ceremonial seat 2 power of sovereign

throng ❶ n/v crowd

throttle ❶ n 1 device controlling amount of fuel entering engine ▷ v 2 strangle 3 restrict

through ❶ prep 1 from end to end 2 in consequence of 3 by means of ▷ adv 4 from end to end 5 to the end ▷ adj 6 completed 7 (Inf) finished 8 continuous 9 (of transport, traffic) not stopping **throughout** adv/prep in every part (of) **throughput** n quantity of material processed

throw ❶ v **throwing, threw, thrown** 1 fling, cast 2 move, put abruptly, carelessly 3 cause to fall ▷ n 4 act or distance of throwing **throwaway** adj 1 designed to be discarded after use 2 done, said casually **throwback** n person, thing that reverts to earlier type

thrush n songbird

thrust ❶ v **thrusting, thrust** 1 push, drive 2 stab ▷ n 3 lunge, stab 4 propulsive force or power

thrift n = **economy**, prudence, frugality, saving, parsimony ≠ **extravagance**

thrill n = **pleasure**, kick (Inf), buzz (Sl), high, stimulation ≠ **tedium** ▷ v = **excite**, stimulate, arouse, move, stir

thrive v = **prosper**, do well, flourish, increase, grow ≠ **decline**

throb v = **pulsate**, pound, beat, pulse, thump; = **vibrate**, pulsate, reverberate, shake, judder (Inf) ▷ n = **pulse**, pounding, beat, thump, thumping

throng v = **crowd**, flock, congregate, converge, mill around ≠ **disperse**

throttle v = **strangle**, choke, garrotte, strangulate

through prep = **via**, by way of, by, between, past; = **because of**, by way of, by means of; = **using**, via, by way of, by means of, by virtue of ▷ adj = **completed**, done, finished, ended

throw v = **hurl**, toss, fling, send, launch; = **toss**, fling, chuck (Inf), cast, hurl ▷ n = **toss**, pitch, fling, sling, lob (Inf)

thrust v = **push**, force, shove, drive, plunge ▷ n = **stab**, pierce, lunge; = **push**, shove, poke, prod

thud *n* **1** dull heavy sound ▷ *v* **2** make thud

thug ⊕ *n* violent person

thumb *n* **1** shortest, thickest finger of hand ▷ *v* **2** handle with thumb **3** signal for lift in vehicle

thumbtack *n* the US and Canadian name for DRAWING PIN

thump ⊕ *n* **1** (sound of) dull heavy blow ▷ *v* **2** strike heavily

thunder ⊕ *n* **1** loud noise accompanying lightning ▷ *v* **2** make noise of or like thunder **thunderbolt, thunderclap** *n* **1** lightning followed by thunder **2** anything unexpected

Thursday *n* fifth day of the week

thus ⊕ *adv* **1** in this way **2** therefore

thwart ⊕ *v* foil, frustrate

thy *adj (Obs)* of or associated with you **thyself** *pron* emphatic or reflexive form of THOU

thyme *n* aromatic herb

tiara *n* coronet

tibia *n, pl* **tibiae, tibias** shinbone

tic *n* spasmodic twitch in muscles, esp. of face

tick¹ ⊕ *n* **1** slight tapping sound, as of watch movement **2** small mark (/) **3** *(Inf)* moment ▷ *v* **4** mark with tick **5** make slight tapping sound

tick² *n* small insect-like parasite living on blood

ticket ⊕ *n* **1** card, paper entitling holder to admission, travel etc. **2** label ▷ *v* **3** attach label to

tickle *v* **1** touch, stroke (person etc.) to produce laughter etc. **2** amuse **3** itch ▷ *n* **4** act, instance of this **ticklish** *adj* **1** sensitive to tickling **2** requiring care

tiddlywinks *pl n* game of trying to flip small plastic discs into cup

tide ⊕ *n* rise and fall of sea happening twice each day **tidal** *adj* **tidal wave** great wave, esp. produced by earthquake **tide over** help someone for a while

tidings *pl n* news

tidy ⊕ *adj* **-dier, -diest 1** orderly, neat ▷ *v* **2** put in order

thug *n* = **ruffian**, hooligan, tough, heavy *(Sl)*, gangster

thump *v* = **strike**, hit, punch, pound, beat ▷ *n* = **blow**, knock, punch, rap, smack; = **thud**, crash, bang, clunk, thwack

thunder *n* = **rumble**, crash, boom, explosion ▷ *v* = **rumble**, crash, boom, roar, resound; = **shout**, roar, yell, bark, bellow

thus *adv* = **therefore**, so, hence, consequently, accordingly; = **in this way**, so, like this, as follows

thwart *v* = **frustrate**, foil, prevent, snooker, hinder ≠ **assist**

tick¹ *n* = **check mark**, mark, line, stroke, dash; *(Brit Inf)* = **moment**, second, minute, flash, instant ▷ *v* = **mark**, indicate, check off; = **click**, tap, ticktock

ticket *n* = **voucher**, pass, coupon, card, slip; = **label**, tag, marker, sticker, card

tide *n* = **current**, flow, stream, ebb, undertow

tidy *adj* = **neat**, orderly, clean, spruce, well-kept ≠ **untidy**; *(Inf)* = **considerable**, large, substantial,

tie ❶ *v* **tying, tied 1** fasten, bind **2** restrict **3** equal (score of) ▷ *n* **4** that with which anything is bound **5** restraint **6** piece of material worn knotted round neck **7** connecting link **8** contest with equal scores **9** match, game in eliminating competition **tied** *adj* **1** (of public house) selling beer etc. of only one brewer **2** (of cottage etc.) rented to tenant employed by owner

tier ❶ *n* row, rank, layer

tiff *n* petty quarrel

tiger *n* large carnivorous feline animal

tight ❶ *adj* **1** taut, tense **2** closely fitting **3** secure, firm **4** not allowing passage of water etc. **5** cramped **6** (*Inf*) mean **7** (*Inf*) drunk **tighten** *v* **tights** *pl n* one-piece clinging garment

covering body from waist to feet **tightrope** *n* taut rope on which acrobats perform

tile *n* **1** flat piece of ceramic, plastic etc. used for roofs, floors etc. ▷ *v* **2** cover with tiles

till¹ ❶ *v* cultivate

till² ❶ *n* **1** drawer for money in shop counter **2** cash register

tiller *n* lever to move rudder of boat

tilt ❶ *v* **1** slope, slant **2** take part in medieval combat with lances **3** thrust (at) ▷ *n* **4** slope **5** (*Hist*) combat for mounted men with lances

timber ❶ *n* **1** wood for building etc. **2** trees

timbre *n* distinctive quality of voice or sound

time ❶ *n* **1** past, present and future as continuous whole **2** hour

---

THESAURUS

goodly, healthy **≠ small** ▷ *v* = **neaten**, straighten, order, clean, groom **≠ disorder**

tie *v* = **fasten**, bind, join, link, connect **≠ unfasten**; = **tether**, secure; = **restrict**, limit, confine, bind, restrain **≠ free** ▷ *n* = **fastening**, binding, link, bond, knot; = **bond**, relationship, connection, commitment, liaison; = **draw**, dead heat, deadlock, stalemate

tier *n* = **row**, bank, layer, line, level

tight *adj* = **close-fitting**, narrow, cramped, snug, constricted **≠ loose**; = **secure**, firm, fast, fixed; = **taut**, stretched, rigid **≠ slack**; = **close**, even, well-matched,

hard-fought, evenly-balanced **≠ uneven**; (*Inf*) = **miserly**, mean, stingy, grasping, parsimonious **≠ generous**; (*Inf*) = **drunk**, intoxicated, plastered (*Sl*), under the influence (*Inf*), tipsy **≠ sober**

till¹ *v* = **cultivate**, dig, plough, work

till² *n* = **cash register**, cash box

tilt *v* = **slant**, tip, slope, list, lean ▷ *n* = **slope**, angle, inclination, list, pitch; (*Medieval history*) = **joust**, fight, tournament, lists, combat

timber *n* = **beams**, boards, planks; = **wood**, logs

time *n* = **period**, term, space, stretch, spell; = **occasion**, point, moment, stage, instance; = **tempo**,

3 duration **4** period **5** point in duration **6** opportunity **7** occasion **8** leisure ▷ *v* **9** choose time for **10** note time taken by **timeless** *adj* changeless, everlasting **timely** *adj* at appropriate time **timer** *n* person, device for recording or indicating time **time bomb** bomb designed to explode at prearranged time **time-lag** *n* period between cause and effect **timetable** *n* plan showing times of arrival and departure etc.

timid *adj* **1** easily frightened **2** shy **timorous** *adj* **1** timid **2** indicating fear

timpani *pl n* set of kettledrums

tin *n* **1** malleable metal **2** container made of tin ▷ *v* **3** put in tin, esp. for preserving **tinny** *adj* (of sound) thin, metallic **tinpot** *adj* (*Inf*) worthless

tinder *n* dry easily-burning material used to start fire

tinge ❶ *n* **1** slight trace ▷ *v* **2** colour, flavour slightly

tingle *v/n* (feel) thrill or pricking sensation

tinker ❶ *n* **1** formerly, travelling mender of pots and pans ▷ *v* **2** fiddle, meddle (with)

tinkle *v* **1** (cause to) give out sounds like small bell ▷ *n* **2** this sound or action

tinsel *n* glittering decorative metallic substance

tint ❶ *n* **1** (shade of) colour **2** tinge ▷ *v* **3** give tint to

tiny ❶ *adj* **tinier, tiniest** very small, minute

tip¹ ❶ *n* **1** slender or pointed end of anything **2** small piece forming an extremity ▷ *v* **3** put a tip on

tip² ❶ *n* **1** small present of money given for service rendered **2** helpful piece of information **tip-off 3** warning, hint ▷ *v* **4** reward with money **tip off 5** give tip to

tip³ ❶ *v* **tipping, tipped 1** tilt, upset **2** touch lightly **3** topple over ▷ *n* **4** place where rubbish is dumped

tipple *v* **1** drink (alcohol) habitually

THESAURUS

beat, rhythm, measure ▷ *v* = **schedule**, set, plan, book, programme

tinge *n* = **tint**, colour, shade; = **trace**, bit, drop, touch, suggestion ▷ *v* = **tint**, colour

tinker *v* = **meddle**, play, potter, fiddle (*Inf*), dabble

tint *n* = **shade**, colour, tone, hue; = **dye**, wash, rinse, tinge, tincture ▷ *v* = **dye**, colour

tiny *adj* = **small**, little, minute, slight, miniature ≠ **huge**

tip¹ *n* = **end**, point, head, extremity, sharp end; = **peak**, top, summit, pinnacle, zenith ▷ *v* = **cap**, top, crown, surmount, finish

tip² *v* = **reward**, remunerate, give a tip to, sweeten (*Inf*); = **predict**, back, recommend, think of ▷ *n* = **gratuity**, gift, reward, present, sweetener (*Inf*); = **hint**, suggestion, piece of advice, pointer

tip³ *v* = **pour**, drop, empty, dump, drain; (*Brit*) = **dump**, empty, unload, pour out

t

▷ *n* **2** drink

tipsy *adj* **-sier, -siest** (slightly) drunk

tiptoe *v* **-toeing, -toed 1** walk on ball of foot and toes **2** walk softly

tiptop *adj* of the best quality or condition

tirade *n* long angry speech or denunciation

tire ❶ *v* **1** reduce energy of, weary **2** bore **3** become tired, bored **tired** *adj* **1** weary **2** hackneyed **tireless** *adj* not tiring easily **tiresome** *adj* irritating, tedious **tiring** *adj*

tissue *n* **1** substance of animal body, plant **2** soft paper handkerchief

tit *n* small bird

titanic *adj* huge, epic

titanium *n* light metallic element

titbit *n* **1** tasty morsel of food **2** scrap (of scandal etc.)

tithe *n* **1** (esp. formerly) tenth part of income, paid to church as tax ▷ *v* **2** exact tithes from

titillate *v* stimulate agreeably

title ❶ *n* **1** name of book **2** heading **3** name, esp. denoting rank **4** legal right or document proving it **5** (*Sport*) championship

titter *v/n* snigger, giggle

titular *adj* **1** pert. to title **2** nominal

TNT SEE TRINITROTOLUENE

to *prep* **1** denoting direction, destination **2** introducing comparison **3** indirect object, infinitive etc. ▷ *adv* **3** to fixed position **to and fro** back and forth

toad *n* animal like large frog **toady** *n* **1** servile flatterer ▷ *v* **2** be ingratiating **toadstool** *n* fungus like mushroom

toast ❶ *n* **1** slice of bread browned on both sides by heat **2** tribute, proposal of health etc. marked by people drinking together **3** person or thing so toasted ▷ *v* **4** make (bread etc.) crisp and brown **5** drink toast to **6** warm at fire **toaster** *n* electrical device for toasting bread

tobacco *n, pl* **-cos, -coes** plant with leaves used for smoking **tobacconist** *n* one who sells tobacco products

toboggan *n* sledge for sliding down slope of snow

today *n* **1** this day ▷ *adv* **2** on this day **3** nowadays

toddle *v* walk with unsteady short steps **toddler** *n* young child beginning to walk

— THESAURUS —

tire *v* = **exhaust**, drain, fatigue, weary, wear out ≠ **refresh**; = **flag**, become tired, fail

title *n* = **name**, designation, term, handle (*Sl*), moniker *or* monicker (*Sl*); (*Sport*); = **championship**, trophy, bays, crown, honour; (*Law*) = **ownership**, right, claim, privilege, entitlement

toast *v* = **brown**, grill, crisp, roast; = **warm (up)**, heat (up), thaw, bring back to life ▷ *n* = **tribute**, compliment, salute, health, pledge; = **favourite**, celebrity, darling, talk, pet ▷ *v* = **drink to**, honour, salute, drink (to) the health of

to-do *n, pl* **-dos** (*Inf*) fuss, commotion

toe *n* **1** digit of foot **2** anything resembling this **toe the line** conform

toffee *n* chewy sweet made of boiled sugar etc.

toga *n* garment worn in ancient Rome

together ❶ *adv* **1** in company **2** simultaneously

toggle *n* small peg fixed crosswise on cord etc. and used for fastening

toil ❶ *n* **1** heavy work or task ▷ *v* **2** labour

toilet ❶ *n* **1** lavatory **2** process of washing, dressing **3** articles used for this **toiletries** *pl n* objects, cosmetics used for cleaning or grooming

token ❶ *n* **1** sign, symbol **2** disc used as money **3** gift card, voucher exchangeable for goods ▷ *adj* **4** nominal

tolerate ❶ *v* **1** put up with

2 permit **tolerable** *adj* **1** bearable **2** fair **tolerance** *n* **tolerant** *adj* **1** forbearing **2** broad-minded **toleration** *n*

toll¹ ❶ *v* **1** ring (bell) slowly at regular intervals ▷ *n* **2** ringing

toll² ❶ *n* **1** tax, esp. for use of bridge or road **2** loss, damage

tom *n* male cat

tomahawk *n* fighting axe of N Amer. Indians

tomato *n, pl* **-toes 1** plant with red fruit **2** the fruit

tomb ❶ *n* **1** grave **2** monument over one **tombstone** *n*

tombola *n* lottery with tickets drawn from revolving drum

tomboy *n* girl who acts, dresses like boy

tome *n* large book

tomfoolery *n* foolish behaviour

tomorrow *adv/n* (on) the day after today

tom-tom *n* drum beaten with hands

—— THESAURUS ——

together *adv* = **collectively**, jointly, as one, with each other, in conjunction ≠ **separately**; = **at the same time**, simultaneously, concurrently, contemporaneously, at one fell swoop ▷ *adj* (*Inf*) = **self-possessed**, composed, well-balanced, well-adjusted

toil *v* = **labour**, work, struggle, strive, sweat (*Inf*) ▷ *n* = **hard work**, effort, application, sweat, graft (*Inf*) ≠ **idleness**

toilet *n* = **lavatory**, bathroom, loo (*Brit Inf*), privy, cloakroom (*Brit*)

token *n* = **symbol**, mark, sign,

note, expression ▷ *adj* = **nominal**, symbolic, minimal, hollow, superficial

tolerate *v* = **endure**, stand, take, stomach, put up with (*Inf*); = **allow**, accept, permit, take, brook ≠ **forbid**

toll¹ *v* = **ring**, sound, strike, chime, knell ▷ *n* = **ringing**, chime, knell, clang, peal

toll² *n* = **charge**, tax, fee, duty, payment; = **damage**, cost, loss, roll, penalty

tomb *n* = **grave**, vault, crypt, mausoleum, sarcophagus

ton n **1** measure of weight, 1016 kg (2240 lbs.) (US) **2** measure of weight, 907 kg (2000 lbs.) **tonnage** n carrying capacity of ship

tone ❶ n **1** quality of musical sound, voice, colour etc. **2** general character ▷ v **3** blend, harmonize (with) **tone-deaf** adj unable to perceive subtle differences in pitch

tongs pl n apparatus for handling coal, sugar etc.

tongue ❶ n **1** organ inside mouth, used for speech, taste etc. **2** language, speech

tonic ❶ n **1** medicine etc. with invigorating effect **2** (Mus) first note of scale ▷ adj **3** invigorating, restorative **tonic water** mineral water oft. containing quinine

tonight n **1** this (coming) night ▷ adv **2** on this night

tonne n metric ton, 1000 kg

tonsil n gland in throat **tonsillitis** n inflammation of tonsils

tonsure n **1** shaving of part of head as religious practice **2** part shaved

too ❶ adv **1** also, in addition

2 overmuch

tool ❶ n **1** implement or appliance for mechanical operations **2** means to an end ▷ v **3** work on with tool **toolbar** n (Comp) row or column of selectable buttons on a computer screen, each allowing the user to access a particular function

toonie, twonie n (Inf) Canadian two-dollar coin

toot n short sound of horn, trumpet etc.

tooth n, pl **teeth 1** bonelike projection in gums of upper and lower jaws of vertebrates **2** prong, cog **toothless** adj **toothpaste** n paste used to clean teeth **toothpick** n small stick for removing food from between teeth

top ❶ n **1** highest part, summit **2** highest rank **3** first in merit **4** garment for upper part of body **5** lid, stopper of bottle etc. ▷ adj **6** highest in position, rank ▷ v **7** cut off, pass, reach, surpass top **8** provide top for **topmost** adj highest **topping** n sauce or garnish for food **top brass**

─────────── THESAURUS ───────────

tone n = **pitch**, inflection, intonation, timbre, modulation; = **volume**, timbre; = **character**, style, feel, air, spirit ▷ v = **harmonize**, match, blend, suit, go well with

tongue n = **language**, speech, dialect, parlance

tonic n = **stimulant**, boost, pick-me-up (Inf), fillip, shot in the arm (Inf)

too adv = **also**, as well, further, in

addition, moreover; = **excessively**, very, extremely, overly, unduly

tool n = **implement**, device, appliance, machine, instrument; = **puppet**, creature, pawn, stooge (Sl), minion

top n = **peak**, summit, head, crown, height ≠ **bottom**; = **lid**, cover, cap, plug, stopper; = **first place**, head, peak, lead, high point ▷ adj = **highest**, loftiest, furthest up, uppermost ▷ v

important officials **top hat** man's tall cylindrical hat **top-heavy** adj unbalanced **top-notch** adj excellent, first-class **topsoil** n surface layer of soil

topaz n precious stone of various colours

topiary n trimming trees, bushes into decorative shapes

topic ❶ n subject of discourse, conversation etc. **topical** adj up-to-date, having news value

topography n, pl **-phies** (description of) surface features of a place **topographic** adj

topple ❶ v (cause to) fall over

topsy-turvy adj in confusion

tor n high rocky hill

torch n 1 portable hand light containing electric battery 2 burning wooden shaft 3 any apparatus burning with hot flame

toreador n bullfighter

torment ❶ v 1 torture in body or mind 2 afflict 3 tease ▷ n 4 suffering, agony of body or mind 5 pest **tormentor, -er** n

tornado ❶ n, pl **-dos, -does** 1 whirlwind 2 violent storm

torpedo n, pl **-does** 1 self-propelled underwater missile with explosive warhead ▷ v 2 strike with torpedo

torpid adj sluggish, apathetic **torpor** n torpid state

torrent n 1 rushing stream 2 downpour **torrential** adj

torrid adj 1 parched 2 highly emotional

torsion n twist, twisting

torso n, pl **-sos** (statue of) body without head or limbs

tortilla n thin Mexican pancake

tortoise n four-footed reptile covered with shell of horny plates **tortoiseshell** n mottled brown shell of turtle

tortuous adj 1 winding, twisting 2 involved, not straightforward

torture ❶ n 1 infliction of severe pain ▷ v 2 inflict severe pain

Tory n, pl **Tories** member of conservative political party

toss ❶ v 1 throw up, about 2 be thrown, fling oneself about

——— THESAURUS ———

= **lead**, head, be at the top of, be first in; = **cover**, garnish, finish, crown, cap; = **surpass**, better, beat, improve on, cap ≠ **not be as good as**

topic n = **subject**, point, question, issue, matter

topple v = **fall over**, fall, collapse, tumble, overturn

torment n = **suffering**, distress, misery, pain, hell ≠ **bliss** ▷ v = **torture**, distress, rack, crucify

≠ **comfort**; = **tease**, annoy, bother, irritate, harass

tornado n = **whirlwind**, storm, hurricane, gale, cyclone

torture v = **torment**, abuse, persecute, afflict, scourge ≠ **comfort** ▷ n = **ill-treatment**, abuse, torment, persecution, maltreatment

toss v = **throw**, pitch, hurl, fling, launch, rock ▷ n = **throw**, pitch, lob (Inf)

t

▷ *n* **3** the act of tossing

tot¹ ❶ *n* **1** very small child **2** small quantity, esp. of drink

tot² *v* **totting, totted 1** add (up) **2** amount to

total ❶ *n* **1** whole amount **2** sum ▷ *adj* **3** complete, absolute ▷ *v* **4** amount to **5** add up **totality** *n* **totally** *adv*

totalitarian *adj* of dictatorial, one-party government

totem *n* tribal badge or emblem **totem pole** carved post of Amer. Indians

totter *v* **1** walk unsteadily **2** begin to fall

toucan *n* large-billed tropical Amer. bird

touch ❶ *v* **1** come into contact with **2** put hand on **3** reach **4** affect emotions of **5** deal with **6** (with *or*) refer to ▷ *n* **7** sense by which qualities of object etc. are

perceived by touching **8** touching **9** characteristic manner or ability **10** slight contact, amount etc. **touching** *adj* **1** emotionally moving ▷ *prep* **2** concerning **touchy** *adj* easily offended **touch down** (of aircraft) land **touchline** *n* side line of pitch in some games **touchstone** *n* criterion

touché *interj* acknowledgment that remark or blow has struck target

tough ❶ *adj* **1** strong **2** able to bear hardship, strain **3** strict **4** difficult **5** needing effort to chew **6** violent ▷ *n* **7** (*Inf*) rough, violent person **toughen** *v*

toupee *n* wig

tour ❶ *n* **1** travelling round **2** journey to one place after another ▷ *v* **3** make tour **tourism** *n* **tourist** *n*

tournament ❶ *n* competition,

tot¹ *n* = **infant**, child, baby, toddler, mite; = **measure**, shot (*Inf*), finger, nip, slug

total *n* = **sum**, entirety, grand total, whole, aggregate ≠ **part** ▷ *adj* = **complete**, absolute, utter, whole, entire ≠ **partial** ▷ *v* = **amount to**, make, come to, reach, equal; = **add up**, work out, compute, reckon, tot up ≠ **subtract**

touch *v* = **feel**, handle, finger, stroke, brush; = **come into contact**, meet, contact, border, graze; = **affect**, influence, inspire, impress; = **consume**, take, drink, eat, partake of; = **move**, stir, disturb ▷ *n* = **contact**, push,

stroke, brush, press; = **feeling**, handling, physical contact; = **bit**, spot, trace, drop, dash; = **style**, method, technique, way, manner

tough *adj* = **hardy**, strong, seasoned, strapping, vigorous; = **violent**, rough, ruthless, pugnacious, hard-bitten; = **strict**, severe, stern, hard, firm ≠ **lenient**; = **hard**, difficult, troublesome, uphill, strenuous ▷ *n* = **ruffian**, bully, thug, hooligan, bruiser (*Inf*)

tour *n* = **journey**, expedition, excursion, trip, outing ▷ *v* = **visit**, explore, go round, inspect, walk round

tournament *n* = **competition**,

contest usu. with several stages

tourniquet *n* bandage, surgical instrument to stop bleeding

tousled *adj* ruffled

tout *v* **1** solicit custom ▷ *n* **2** person who sells tickets at inflated prices

tow ⓣ *v* **1** drag along behind, esp. at end of rope ▷ *n* **2** towing or being towed **towpath** *n* path beside canal or river

towards, toward ⓣ *prep* **1** in direction of **2** with regard to **3** as contribution to

towel *n* cloth for wiping off moisture after washing

tower ⓣ *n* **1** tall strong structure, esp. part of church etc. **2** fortress ▷ *v* **3** stand very high **4** loom (over)

town *n* collection of dwellings etc. larger than village and smaller than city **township** *n* small town

toxic ⓣ *adj* **1** poisonous **2** due to poison **toxicity** *n* strength of a poison **toxin** *n* poison

toy ⓣ *n* **1** something designed to be played with ▷ *adj* **2** very small ▷ *v* **3** trifle **toy boy** much younger lover of older woman

toy-toy *(SAfr)* *n* **1** dance of political protest ▷ *v* **2** perform this dance

trace ⓣ *n* **1** track left by anything **2** indication **3** minute quantity ▷ *v* **4** follow course of **5** find out **6** make plan of **7** draw or copy exactly **tracing paper** transparent paper placed over drawing, map etc. to enable exact copy to be taken

trachea *n, pl* **tracheae** windpipe

track ⓣ *n* **1** mark left by passage of anything **2** path **3** rough road **4** course **5** railway line **6** jointed metal band as on tank etc. **7** separate song, piece on record ▷ *v* **8** follow trail or path of **track events** athletic sports held on running track **track record** past accomplishments **tracksuit** *n* loose-fitting suit worn by athletes etc.

—————— THESAURUS ——————

meeting, event, series, contest

tow *v* = **drag**, draw, pull, haul, tug

towards *prep* = **in the direction of**, to, for, on the way to, en route for; = **regarding**, about, concerning, respecting, in relation to

tower *n* = **column**, pillar, turret, belfry, steeple

toxic *adj* = **poisonous**, deadly, lethal, harmful, pernicious ≠ **harmless**

toy *n* = **plaything**, game, doll

trace *v* = **find**, track (down), discover, detect, unearth; = **outline**, sketch, draw; = **copy**, map, draft, outline, sketch ▷ *n* = **bit**, drop, touch, shadow, suggestion; = **remnant**, sign, record, mark, evidence; = **track**, trail, footstep, path, footprint

track *n* = **path**, way, road, route, trail; = **course**, line, path, orbit, trajectory; = **line**, tramline, marks, traces ▷ *v* = **follow**, pursue, chase, trace, tail *(Inf)*

t

tract¹ ❶ *n* wide expanse, area
tract² ❶ *n* pamphlet, esp. religious one
traction *n* action of pulling
tractor *n* motor vehicle for hauling, pulling etc.
trade ❶ *n* **1** commerce, business **2** skilled craft **3** exchange ▷ *v* **4** engage in trade **trader** *n*
trade-in *n* used article given in part payment for new **trademark, trade name** *n* distinctive legal mark on maker's goods **trade-off** *n* exchange made as compromise **tradesman** *n* **1** dealer **2** skilled worker **trade union** society of workers for protection of their interests
tradition ❶ *n* **1** unwritten body of beliefs, facts etc. handed down from generation to generation **2** custom, practice of long standing **traditional** *adj*
traffic ❶ *n* **1** vehicles passing to

and fro in street, town etc. **2** (illicit) trade ▷ *v* **3** trade **traffic lights** set of coloured lights at road junctions etc.
tragedy ❶ *n, pl* **-dies 1** sad event **2** dramatic, literary work dealing with serious, sad topic **tragedian** *n* actor in, writer of tragedies **tragic** *adj* **1** of, in manner of tragedy **2** disastrous **3** appalling
trail ❶ *v* **1** drag behind one **2** lag behind **3** track, pursue ▷ *n* **4** track or trace **5** rough path **trailer** *n* vehicle towed by another vehicle
train ❶ *v* **1** educate, instruct, cause to grow in particular way **2** follow course of training **3** aim (gun etc.) ▷ *n* **4** line of railway vehicles joined to locomotive **5** succession, esp. of thoughts etc. **6** procession **7** trailing part of dress **trainee** *n* one training to be skilled worker **trainer** *n* **training** *n*

— THESAURUS —

tract¹ *n* = **area**, region, district, stretch, territory
tract² *n* = **treatise**, essay, booklet, pamphlet, dissertation
trade *n* = **commerce**, business, transactions, dealing, exchange; = **job**, employment, business, craft, profession ▷ *v* = **deal**, do business, traffic, truck, bargain; = **exchange**, switch, swap, barter
tradition institution ▷ *n* = **established practice**, custom, convention, habit, ritual
traffic *n* = **transport**, vehicles, transportation, freight; = **trade**, commerce, business, exchange,

truck ▷ *v* = **trade**, deal, exchange, bargain, do business
tragedy *n* = **disaster**, catastrophe, misfortune, adversity, calamity ≠ **fortune**
trail *n* = **path**, track, route, way, course; = **tracks**, path, marks, wake, trace ▷ *v* = **follow**, track, chase, pursue, dog; = **drag**, draw, pull, sweep, haul; = **lag**, follow, drift, wander, linger
train *v* = **instruct**, school, prepare, coach, teach; = **exercise**, prepare, work out, practise, do exercise; = **aim**, point, level, position, direct ▷ *n* = **sequence**, series, chain,

traipse v walk wearily

trait ⊕ n characteristic feature

traitor ⊕ n one who is guilty of treason **traitorous** adj

trajectory n, pl **-ries** line of flight

tram n vehicle running on rails laid on roadway

tramp ⊕ v 1 travel on foot 2 walk heavily ▷ n 3 (homeless) person who travels about on foot 4 walk 5 cargo ship without fixed route

trample ⊕ v tread on and crush under foot

trampoline n tough canvas sheet stretched horizontally with elastic cords etc. to frame

trance ⊕ n 1 unconscious or dazed state 2 state of ecstasy or total absorption

tranche n portion

tranquil adj 1 calm, quiet 2 serene **tranquillity** n **tranquillize** v make calm **tranquillizer** n drug which induces calm state

trans- comb. form across, through, beyond

transact v 1 carry through 2 negotiate **transaction** n 1 performing of business 2 single sale or purchase ▷ pl 3 proceedings

transcend ⊕ v 1 rise above 2 surpass **transcendence** n **transcendent** adj **transcendental** adj 1 surpassing experience 2 supernatural 3 abstruse **transcendentalism** n

transcribe v 1 copy out 2 record for later broadcast **transcript** n copy

transfer ⊕ v **-ferring, -ferred** 1 move, send from one person, place etc. to another ▷ n 2 removal of person or thing from one place to another **transference** n transfer

transfigure v alter appearance of

transfix v 1 astound, stun 2 pierce through

transform ⊕ v change shape, character of **transformation** n **transformer** n (Electricity) apparatus for changing voltage

transgress v 1 break (law) 2 sin

string, set

trait n = **characteristic**, feature, quality, attribute, quirk

traitor n = **betrayer**, deserter, turncoat, renegade, defector ≠ **loyalist**

tramp v = **trudge**, stump, toil, plod, traipse (Inf); = **hike**, walk, trek, roam, march ▷ n = **vagrant**, derelict, drifter, down-and-out; = **tread**, stamp, footstep, footfall; = **hike**, march, trek, ramble, slog

trample v often with **on** = **stamp**, crush, squash, tread, flatten

trance n = **daze**, dream, abstraction, rapture, reverie

transcend v = **surpass**, exceed, go beyond, rise above, eclipse

transfer v = **move**, transport, shift, relocate, transpose ▷ n = **transference**, move, handover, change, shift

transform v = **change**, convert, alter, transmute, remodel

t

transgression n
transient adj fleeting, not permanent
transistor n (Electronics) 1 small, semiconducting device used to amplify electric currents 2 portable radio using transistors
transit ❶ n passage, crossing **transition** n change from one state to another **transitive** adj (of verb) requiring direct object **transitory** adj not lasting long
translate ❶ v 1 turn from one language into another 2 interpret **translation** n **translator** n
translucent adj letting light pass through, semitransparent
transmit ❶ v -mitting, -mitted 1 send, cause to pass to another place, person etc. 2 send out (signals) by means of radio waves **transmission** n 1 transmitting 2 gears by which power is communicated from engine to road wheels
transmute v change in form, properties or nature

transparent ❶ adj 1 letting light pass without distortion 2 that can be seen through **transparency** n 1 quality of being transparent 2 photographic slide
transpire v 1 become known 2 (Inf) happen 3 (of plants) give off water vapour through leaves
transplant ❶ v 1 move and plant again in another place 2 transfer organ surgically ▷ n 3 surgical transplanting of organ
transport ❶ v 1 convey from one place to another 2 deport ▷ n 3 system of conveyance 4 vehicle used for this **transportation** n 1 transporting 2 (Hist) deportation to penal colony
transpose v 1 change order of 2 put music into different key
transverse adj 1 lying across 2 at right angles
transvestite n person who wears clothes of opposite sex
trap ❶ n 1 device for catching game etc. 2 anything planned to deceive, betray etc. 3 arrangement

THESAURUS

transit n = **movement**, transfer, transport, passage, crossing
translate v = **render**, put, change, convert, interpret
transmit v = **broadcast**, televise, relay, air, radio, stream; = **pass on**, carry, spread, send, bear
transparent adj = **clear**, sheer, see-through, lucid, translucent ≠ **opaque**; = **obvious**, plain, patent, evident, explicit ≠ **uncertain**
transplant v = **implant**, transfer,

graft
transport n = **vehicle**, transportation, conveyance; = **transference**, carrying, delivery, distribution, transportation; often plural = **ecstasy**, delight, heaven, bliss, euphoria ≠ **despondency** ▷ v = **convey**, take, move, bring, send; = **enrapture**, move, delight, entrance, enchant; (Hist) = **exile**, banish, deport
trap n = **snare**, net, gin, pitfall, noose; = **ambush**, set-up (Inf) ▷ v

of pipes to prevent escape of gas
4 movable opening ▷ v **5** catch
6 trick **trapper** n one who traps
animals for their fur **trapdoor** n
door in floor or roof

trapeze n horizontal bar
suspended from two ropes for
acrobatics etc.

trapezium n, pl **-ziums, -zia**
four-sided figure with two parallel
sides of unequal length

trappings pl n equipment,
ornaments

trash ❶ n **1** rubbish **2** nonsense
3 (US & Canad) anything worthless

trauma ❶ n **1** emotional shock
2 injury, wound **traumatic** adj
traumatize v

travail v/n labour, toil

travel ❶ v **-elling, -elled 1** go,
move from one place to another
▷ n **2** act of travelling ▷ pl
3 (account of) travelling **traveller**
n **travelogue** n film etc. about
travels

traverse v **1** cross, go through or
over ▷ n **2** traversing **3** path
across

travesty n, pl **-ties 1** grotesque
imitation ▷ v **2** make, be a travesty
of

trawl v fish at deep levels with net
dragged behind boat **trawler** n
trawling boat

tray n flat board, usu. with rim, for
carrying things

treachery n, pl **-eries** deceit,
betrayal **treacherous** adj
1 disloyal **2** unsafe

treacle n thick syrup produced
when sugar is refined

tread ❶ v **treading, trod,
trodden 1** walk **2** trample (on)
▷ n **3** treading **4** fashion of
walking **5** upper surface of step
6 part of tyre which makes contact
with ground **treadmill** n dreary
routine

treadle n lever worked by foot to
turn wheel

treason ❶ n **1** violation by subject
of allegiance to sovereign or state
2 treachery

treasure ❶ n **1** riches **2** valued
person or thing ▷ v **3** prize, cherish
treasurer n official in charge of
funds **treasury** n **1** place for
treasure **2** government
department in charge of finance
treasure-trove n treasure found

= **catch**, snare, ensnare, entrap,
take; = **trick**, fool, cheat, lure, seduce

trash n = **nonsense**, rubbish, rot,
drivel, twaddle ≠ **sense**; (chiefly US
& Canad) = **litter**, refuse, waste,
rubbish, junk (Inf)

trauma n = **shock**, suffering, pain,
torture, ordeal; = **injury**, damage,
hurt, wound, agony

travel v = **go**, journey, move, tour,
progress

tread v = **step**, walk, march, pace,
stamp ▷ n = **step**, walk, pace,
stride, footstep

treason n = **disloyalty**, mutiny,
treachery, duplicity, sedition
≠ **loyalty**

treasure n = **riches**, money, gold,
fortune, wealth; (Inf) = **angel**,
darling, jewel, gem, paragon ▷ v

t

with no evidence of ownership
treat ❶ *n* **1** pleasure, entertainment given ▷ *v* **2** deal with, act towards **3** give medical treatment to **4** provide with treat **treatment** *n* **1** method of counteracting disease **2** act or mode of treating
treatise *n* formal essay
treaty ❶ *n, pl* **-ties** signed contract between states etc.
treble *adj* **1** threefold **2** (*Mus*) high-pitched ▷ *n* **3** soprano voice ▷ *v* **4** increase threefold
tree *n* large perennial plant with woody trunk
trek ❶ *n* **1** long difficult journey ▷ *v* **2** make trek
trellis *n* lattice or grating of light bars
tremble ❶ *v* **1** quiver, shake **2** feel fear ▷ *n* **3** involuntary shaking
tremendous ❶ *adj* **1** vast, immense **2** (*Inf*) exciting **3** (*Inf*) excellent

tremor *n* **1** quiver **2** shaking
tremulous *adj* quivering slightly
trench ❶ *n* long narrow ditch **trench coat** double-breasted waterproof coat
trenchant *adj* cutting, incisive
trend ❶ *n* **1** direction, tendency **2** fashion **trendy** *adj* (*Inf*) consciously fashionable
trepidation *n* fear, anxiety
trespass *v* **1** intrude on property etc. of another ▷ *n* **2** wrongful entering on another's land **3** wrongdoing **trespasser** *n*
trestle *n* board fixed on pairs of spreading legs
trevally *n, pl* **-lies** (*Aust & NZ*) any of various food and game fishes
trews *pl n* close-fitting tartan trousers
tri- *comb. form* three
trial ❶ *n* **1** test, examination **2** (*Law*) investigation of case before judge **3** thing, person that strains endurance or patience

━━━━━━━━━━ THESAURUS ━━━━━━━━━━

= **prize**, value, esteem, adore, cherish
treat *v* = **behave towards**, deal with, handle, act towards, use; = **take care of**, minister to, attend to, give medical treatment to, doctor (*Inf*); = **provide**, stand (*Inf*), entertain, lay on, regale ▷ *n* = **entertainment**, party, surprise, gift, celebration; = **pleasure**, delight, joy, thrill, satisfaction
treaty *n* = **agreement**, pact, contract, alliance, convention
trek *v* = **journey**, march, hike, tramp, rove ▷ *n* = **slog**, tramp

tremble *v* = **shake**, shiver, quake, shudder, quiver ▷ *n* = **shake**, shiver, quake, shudder, wobble
tremendous *adj* = **huge**, great, enormous, terrific, formidable ≠ **tiny**; = **excellent**, great, wonderful, brilliant, amazing ≠ **terrible**
trench *n* = **ditch**, channel, drain, gutter, trough
trend *n* = **tendency**, swing, drift, inclination, current; = **fashion**, craze, fad (*Inf*), mode, thing
trial *n* (*Law*) = **hearing**, case, court case, inquiry, tribunal; = **test**,

triangle *n* figure with three angles **triangular** *adj*

tribe ❶ *n* **1** race **2** subdivision of race of people **tribal** *adj*

tribulation *n* trouble, affliction

tribunal ❶ *n* **1** lawcourt **2** body appointed to inquire into specific matter

tributary *n, pl* **-taries** stream flowing into another

tribute ❶ *n* **1** sign of honour **2** tax paid by one state to another

trice *n* moment, instant

trick ❶ *n* **1** deception **2** prank **3** feat of skill or cunning **4** knack **5** cards played in one round ▷ *v* **6** deceive, cheat **trickery** *n* **trickster** *n* **tricky** *adj* difficult

trickle ❶ *v* **1** (cause to) run, flow, move in thin stream or drops ▷ *n* **2** trickling flow

tricolour *n* three-coloured striped flag

tricycle *n* three-wheeled cycle

trident *n* three-pronged spear

trifle ❶ *n* **1** insignificant thing or matter **2** small amount **3** pudding of sponge cake, whipped cream etc. ▷ *v* **4** toy (with)

trigger ❶ *n* **1** catch which releases spring, esp. to fire gun ▷ *v* **2** (oft. with *off*) set in action etc. **trigger-happy** *adj* tending to be irresponsible

trigonometry *n* branch of mathematics dealing with relations of sides and angles of triangles

trilby *n, pl* **-bies** man's soft felt hat

trill *v/n* (sing, play with) rapid alternation between two close notes

trillion *n* **1** one million million, 10^{12} **2** (*Obs*) one million million million, 10^{18}

trilogy *n, pl* **-gies** series of three related (literary) works

trim ❶ *adj* **trimmer, trimmest 1** neat, smart **2** slender **3** in good order ▷ *v* **4** shorten slightly by cutting **5** prune **6** decorate **7** adjust ▷ *n* **8** decoration **9** order,

——— THESAURUS ———

experiment, evaluation, audition, dry run (*Inf*); = **hardship**, suffering, trouble, distress, ordeal

tribe *n* = **race**, people, family, clan

tribunal *n* = **hearing**, court, trial

tribute *n* = **accolade**, testimonial, eulogy, recognition, compliment ≠ **criticism**

trick *n* = **joke**, stunt, spoof (*Inf*), prank, practical joke; = **deception**, trap, fraud, manoeuvre, ploy; = **sleight of hand**, stunt, legerdemain; = **secret**, skill, knack, hang (*Inf*), technique;

= **mannerism**, habit, characteristic, trait, quirk ▷ *v* = **deceive**, trap, take someone in (*Inf*), fool, cheat

trickle *v* = **dribble**, run, drop, stream, drip ▷ *n* = **dribble**, drip, seepage, thin stream

trifle *n* = **knick-knack**, toy, plaything, bauble, bagatelle

trigger *v* = **bring about**, start, cause, produce, generate ≠ **prevent**

trim *adj* = **neat**, smart, tidy, spruce, dapper ≠ **untidy**; = **slender**, fit,

state of being trim **trimming** *n*
(oft. pl) decoration, addition
trinitrotoluene *n* powerful
explosive
trinity *n, pl* **-ties 1** the state of
being threefold **2** *(with cap.)* state
of God as three persons, Father, Son
and Holy Spirit
trinket *n* small ornament
trio ❶ *n, pl* **trios 1** group of three
2 music for three parts
trip ❶ *n* **1** (short) journey for
pleasure **2** stumble **3** *(Inf)*
hallucinatory experience caused by
drug ▷ *v* **4** (cause to) stumble
5 (cause to) make mistake **6** run
lightly
tripe *n* **1** stomach of cow as food
2 *(Inf)* nonsense
triple ❶ *adj* **1** threefold ▷ *v*
2 treble **triplet** *n* one of three
offspring born at one birth
triplicate *adj* **1** threefold ▷ *n*
2 state of being triplicate **3** one of
set of three copies

tripod *n* stool, stand etc. with
three feet
trite *adj* hackneyed, banal
triumph ❶ *n* **1** great success
2 victory **3** exultation ▷ *v*
4 achieve great success or victory
5 rejoice over victory **triumphal**
adj **triumphant** *adj*
troll *n* giant or dwarf in
Scandinavian mythology and
folklore
trolley *n* **1** small wheeled table for
food and drink **2** wheeled cart for
moving goods etc. **3** *(US)* tram
trollop *n* promiscuous woman
trombone *n* deep-toned brass
instrument **trombonist** *n*
troop ❶ *n* **1** group of persons ▷ *pl*
2 soldiers ▷ *v* **3** move in troop
trooper *n* cavalry soldier
trophy ❶ *n, pl* **-phies** prize,
award
tropic *n* **1** either of two lines of
latitude N and S of equator ▷ *pl*
2 area of earth's surface between

——— THESAURUS ———

slim, sleek, streamlined ▷ *v* = **cut**,
crop, clip, shave, tidy; = **decorate**,
dress, array, adorn, ornament ▷ *n*
= **decoration**, edging, border,
piping, trimming; = **condition**,
health, shape *(Inf)*, fitness,
wellness; = **cut**, crop, clipping,
shave, pruning
trio *n* = **threesome**, trinity, trilogy,
triad, triumvirate
trip *n* = **journey**, outing, excursion,
day out, run; = **stumble**, fall, slip,
misstep ▷ *v* = **stumble**, fall, fall
over, slip, tumble; = **skip**, dance,
hop, gambol

triple *adj* = **treble**, three times ▷ *v*
= **treble**, increase threefold
triumph *n* = **success**, victory,
accomplishment, achievement,
coup ≠ **failure**; = **joy**, pride,
happiness, rejoicing, elation ▷ *v*
often with **over** = **succeed**, win,
overcome, prevail, prosper ≠ **fail**;
= **rejoice**, celebrate, glory, revel,
gloat
troop *n* = **group**, company, team,
body, unit ▷ *v* = **flock**, march,
stream, swarm, throng
trophy *n* = **prize**, cup, award,
laurels; = **souvenir**, spoils, relic,

these lines **tropical** adj **1** pert. to, within tropics **2** (of climate) very hot

trot ❶ v **trotting, trotted 1** (of horse) move at medium pace **2** (of person) run easily with short strides ▷ n **3** trotting, jog **trotter** n **1** horse trained to trot in race **2** foot of pig etc.

troubadour n medieval travelling poet and singer

trouble ❶ n **1** state or cause of mental distress, pain, inconvenience etc. **2** care ▷ v **3** be trouble to **4** be inconvenienced, be agitated **5** take pains **troublesome** adj **troubleshooter** n person employed to deal with problems

trough ❶ n **1** long open vessel, esp. for animals' food or water **2** hollow between waves

trounce v beat thoroughly, thrash

troupe n company of performers **trouper** n

trousers pl n garment covering legs

trousseau n, pl **-seaux, -seaus**

bride's outfit of clothing

trout n freshwater fish

trowel n small tool like spade

truant n one absent without leave **truancy** n

truce ❶ n temporary cessation of fighting

truck¹ n wheeled (motor) vehicle for moving goods

truck² n dealing, esp. in have no truck with

trucker n (US & Canad) truck driver

truculent adj aggressive, defiant

trudge v **1** walk laboriously ▷ n **2** tiring walk

true ❶ adj **truer, truest 1** in accordance with facts **2** faithful **3** correct **4** genuine **truism** n self-evident truth **truly** adv **truth** n **1** state of being true **2** something that is true **truthful** adj **1** accustomed to speak the truth **2** accurate

truffle n **1** edible underground fungus **2** sweet flavoured with chocolate

trump n **1** card of suit ranking above others ▷ v **2** play trump

memento, booty

trot v = **run**, jog, scamper, lope, canter ▷ n = **run**, jog, lope, canter

trouble n = **bother**, problems, concern, worry, stress; usually plural = **distress**, problem, worry, pain, anxiety ≠ **pleasure**; = **ailment**, disease, failure, complaint, illness; = **disorder**, fighting, conflict, bother, unrest ≠ **peace** ▷ v = **bother**, worry, upset, disturb, distress ≠ **please**; = **afflict**, hurt,

bother, cause discomfort to, pain; = **inconvenience**, disturb, burden, put out, impose upon ≠ **relieve**

trough n = **manger**, water trough

truce n = **ceasefire**, peace, moratorium, respite, lull

true adj = **correct**, right, accurate, precise, factual ≠ **false**; = **faithful**, loyal, devoted, dedicated, steady ≠ **unfaithful**; = **exact**, perfect, accurate, precise, spot-on (Brit Inf) ≠ **inaccurate**

trump up invent, concoct

trumpet n 1 metal wind instrument like horn ▷ v 2 blow trumpet 3 make sound like one 4 proclaim **trumpeter** n

truncate v cut short

truncheon n short thick club

trundle v move heavily, as on small wheels

trunk ❶ n 1 main stem of tree 2 person's body excluding head and limbs 3 box for clothes etc. 4 elephant's snout ▷ pl 5 man's swimming costume **trunk call** long-distance telephone call **trunk road** main road

truss v 1 fasten up, tie up ▷ n 2 support 3 medical supporting device

trust ❶ n 1 confidence 2 firm belief 3 reliance 4 combination of business firms 5 care 6 property held for another ▷ v 7 rely on 8 believe in 9 expect, hope 10 consign for care **trustee** n one legally holding property for another **trustful, trusting** adj **trustworthy** adj **trusty** adj

try ❶ v **trying, tried** 1 attempt 2 test, sample 3 afflict 4 examine

in court of law ▷ n 5 attempt, effort 6 (Rugby) score gained by touching ball down over opponent's goal line **tried** adj proved **trying** adj troublesome

tryst n arrangement to meet, esp. secretly

T-shirt n informal (short-sleeved) sweater

tub n 1 open wooden vessel like bottom half of barrel 2 small round container 3 bath **tubby** adj short and fat

tuba n valved brass wind instrument of low pitch

tube n 1 long, narrow hollow cylinder 2 flexible cylinder with cap to hold pastes 3 underground electric railway **tubular** adj

tuber n fleshy underground stem of some plants

tuberculosis n communicable disease, esp. of lung **tubercular** adj **tuberculin** n bacillus used to treat tuberculosis

tuck ❶ v 1 push, fold into small space 2 gather, stitch in folds ▷ n 3 stitched fold 4 (Inf) food

tucker n (Aust & NZ, Inf) food

Tuesday n third day of the week

——————— THESAURUS ———————

trunk n = **stem**, stalk, bole; = **chest**, case, box, crate, coffer; = **body**, torso

trust v = **believe in**, have faith in, depend on, count on, bank on ≠ **distrust**; = **entrust**, commit, assign, confide, consign; = **expect**, hope, suppose, assume, presume ▷ n = **confidence**, credit, belief, faith, expectation

≠ **distrust**

try v = **attempt**, seek, aim, strive, struggle; = **experiment with**, try out, put to the test, test, taste ▷ n = **attempt**, go (Inf), shot (Inf), effort, crack (Inf)

tuck v = **push**, stick, stuff, slip, ease ▷ n (Brit Inf) = **food**, grub (Sl), nosh (Sl); = **fold**, gather, pleat, pinch

tuft n bunch of feathers etc.

tug ❶ v **tugging, tugged** **1** pull hard or violently ▷ n **2** violent pull **3** ship used to tow other vessels **tug-of-war** n contest in which two teams pull against one another on rope

tuition ❶ n teaching, esp. private

tulip n plant with bright cup-shaped flowers

tumble ❶ v **1** (cause to) fall or roll, twist etc. **2** rumple ▷ n **3** fall **tumbler** n **1** stemless drinking glass **2** acrobat **tumbledown** adj dilapidated **tumble dryer** machine that dries laundry by rotating it in warm air

tummy n, pl **-mies** (Inf) stomach

tumour ❶ n abnormal growth in or on body

tumult n violent uproar, commotion **tumultuous** adj

tuna n large marine food and game fish

tundra n vast treeless zone between ice cap and timber line

tune ❶ n **1** melody **2** quality of being in pitch **3** adjustment of musical instrument ▷ v **4** put in tune **5** adjust machine to obtain efficient running **6** adjust radio to

receive broadcast **tuneful** adj **tuner** n

tungsten n greyish-white metal

tunic n **1** close-fitting jacket forming part of uniform **2** loose hip-length garment

tunnel ❶ n **1** underground passage, esp. as track for railway line ▷ v **2** make tunnel (through)

tupik, tupek n (Canad) (esp. in the Arctic) a tent of animal skins, a traditional type of Inuit dwelling

turban n headdress made by coiling length of cloth round head

turbine n rotary engine driven by steam, gas, water or air playing on blades

turbot n large flatfish

tureen n serving dish for soup

turf ❶ n, pl **turfs, turves** **1** short grass with earth bound to it by matted roots ▷ v **2** lay with turf **turf accountant** bookmaker **turf out** (Inf) throw out

turgid adj **1** swollen, inflated **2** bombastic

turkey n large bird reared for food

Turkish adj of Turkey **Turkish bath** steam bath **Turkish delight** jelly-like sweet coated with icing sugar

tug v = **pull**, pluck, jerk, yank, wrench ▷ n = **pull**, jerk, yank

tuition n = **training**, schooling, education, teaching, lessons

tumble v = **fall**, drop, topple, plummet, stumble ▷ n = **fall**, drop, trip, plunge, spill

tumour n = **growth**, cancer, swelling, lump, carcinoma

(Pathology)

tune n = **melody**, air, song, theme, strain(s); = **harmony**, pitch, euphony ▷ v = **tune up**, adjust

tunnel n = **passage**, underpass, passageway, subway, channel ▷ v = **dig**, burrow, mine, bore, drill

turf n = **grass**, sward

t

turmoil ❶ *n* confusion, commotion

turn ❶ *v* **1** move around, rotate **2** change, alter position or direction (of) **3** (oft. with *into*) change in nature **4** make, shape on lathe ▷ *n* **5** turning **6** inclination etc. **7** period **8** short walk **9** (part of) rotation **10** performance **turning** *n* road, path leading off main rout **turncoat** *n* person who deserts party, cause etc. to join another **turn down 1** reduce volume or brightness of **2** refuse **turnout** *n* number of people appearing for some purpose **turnover** *n* **1** total sales made by business **2** rate at which staff leave and are replaced **turnstile** *n* revolving gate for controlling admission of people **turntable** *n* revolving platform **turn up** *v* appear

turnip *n* plant with edible root

turpentine *n* oil from certain trees used in paints etc. **turps** *n* (*Inf*) turpentine

turquoise *n* **1** bluish-green precious stone **2** this colour

turret *n* **1** small tower **2** revolving armoured tower on tank etc.

turtle *n* sea tortoise

tusk *n* long pointed side tooth of elephant etc.

tussle *n/v* fight, wrestle, struggle

tutor ❶ *n* **1** one teaching individuals or small groups ▷ *v* **2** teach **tutorial** *n* period of instruction

tutu *n* skirt worn by ballerinas

tuxedo *n* (*US & Canad*) dinner jacket

TV television

twang *n* **1** vibrating metallic sound **2** nasal speech ▷ *v* **3** (cause to) make such sounds

tweak *v* **1** pinch and twist or pull ▷ *n* **2** tweaking

twee *adj* (*Inf*) oversentimental

tweed *n* rough-surfaced cloth used for clothing

tweet *n* **1** chirp **2** message on Twitter website ▷ *v* **3** chirp **4** post message on Twitter website

tweezers *pl n* small forceps or tongs

twelve *adj/n* two more than ten **twelfth** *adj* ordinal number

twenty *adj/n* twice ten **twentieth** *adj* ordinal number

twerp *n* (*Inf*) stupid person

twice *adv* two times

twiddle *v* **1** fiddle **2** twist

THESAURUS

turmoil *n* = **confusion**, disorder, chaos, upheaval, disarray ≠ **peace**

turn *v* = **change course**, swing round, wheel round, veer, move; = **rotate**, spin, go round (and round), revolve, roll; = **change**, transform, shape, convert, alter; = **shape**, form, fashion, cast, frame; = **go bad**, go off (*Brit Inf*),

curdle, spoil, sour ▷ *n* = **rotation**, cycle, circle, revolution, spin; = **change of direction**, shift, departure, deviation; = **direction**, course, tack, tendency, drift

tutor *n* = **teacher**, coach, instructor, educator, guide ▷ *v* = **teach**, educate, school, train, coach

twig ⓣ *n* small branch, shoot

twilight ⓣ *n* soft light after sunset

twill *n* fabric with surface of parallel ridges

twin ⓣ *n* **1** one of two children born together ▷ *v* **2** pair, be paired

twine *v* **1** twist, coil round ▷ *n* **2** string, cord

twinge *n* **1** momentary sharp pain **2** qualm

twinkle ⓣ *v* **1** shine with dancing light, sparkle ▷ *n* **2** twinkling **3** flash

twirl *v* **1** turn or twist round quickly **2** whirl **3** twiddle

twist ⓣ *v* **1** make, become spiral, by turning with one end fast **2** distort, change **3** wind ▷ *n* **4** twisting

twit *n* **twitting, twitted** (*Inf*) **1** foolish person ▷ *v* **2** taunt

twitch ⓣ *v* **1** give momentary sharp pull or jerk (to) ▷ *n* **2** such pull **3** spasmodic jerk

twitter *v* **1** (of birds) utter tremulous sounds **2** *with capital T* website where people can post short messages about their current activities ▷ *n* **3** tremulous sound **4** *sometimes with capital T* write a short message on the Twitter website

two *n/adj* one more than one

two-faced *adj* deceitful

tycoon ⓣ *n* powerful, influential businessman

type ⓣ *n* **1** class **2** sort **3** model **4** pattern **5** characteristic build **6** specimen **7** block bearing letter used for printing ▷ *v* **8** print with typewriter **typecast** *v* repeatedly cast (actor, actress) in similar roles **typescript** *n* typewritten document **typewriter** *n* keyed writing machine **typist** *n* one who operates typewriter

typhoid fever acute infectious disease, esp. of intestines

typhoon *n* violent tropical storm

typhus *n* infectious feverish disease

THESAURUS
---

twig *n* = **branch**, stick, sprig, shoot, spray

twilight *n* = **dusk**, evening, sunset, early evening, nightfall ≠ **dawn**

twin *n* = **double**, counterpart, mate, match, fellow ▷ *v* = **pair**, match, join, couple, link

twinkle *v* = **sparkle**, flash, shine, glitter, gleam ▷ *n* = **sparkle**, flash, spark, gleam, flicker

twist *v* = **coil**, curl, wind, wrap, screw; = **distort**, screw up, contort, mangle ≠ **straighten** ▷ *n*

= **surprise**, change, turn, development, revelation; = **development**, emphasis, variation, slant; = **wind**, turn, spin, swivel, twirl; = **curve**, turn, bend, loop, arc

twitch *v* = **jerk**, flutter, jump, squirm; = **pull (at)**, tug (at), pluck (at), yank (at) ▷ *n* = **jerk**, tic, spasm, jump, flutter

tycoon *n* = **magnate**, capitalist, baron, industrialist, financier

type *n* = **kind**, sort, class, variety, group

t

typical ⊙ *adj* **1** true to type
2 characteristic **typically** *adv*
typography *n* **1** art of printing
2 style of printing
tyrant *n* oppressive or cruel ruler
tyrannical *adj* **1** despotic

2 ruthless **tyrannize** *v* exert
ruthless or tyrannical authority
(over) **tyrannous** *adj* **tyranny** *n*
despotism
tyre *n* (inflated) rubber ring over
rim of wheel of road vehicle

— THESAURUS —

typical *adj* = **archetypal**,
standard, model, normal, stock

≠ **unusual**

t

ultimatum *n* final terms
ultra- *comb. form* beyond, excessively, as in *ultramodern*
ultraviolet *adj* (of electromagnetic radiation) beyond limit of visibility at violet end of spectrum
umbrage *n* offence, resentment
umbrella *n* folding circular cover of nylon etc. on stick, carried in hand to protect against rain
umpire ❶ *n* **1** person chosen to decide question, or to enforce rules in game ▷ *v* **2** act as umpire
umpteen *adj* (*Inf*) very many
un- *comb. form* indicating not, reversal of an action
unaccountable *adj* that cannot be explained
unanimous ❶ *adj* in complete agreement **unanimity** *n*
unassuming *adj* modest
unaware ❶ *adj* not aware **unawares** *adv* unexpectedly
uncanny *adj* weird, mysterious
unceremonious *adj* **1** without ceremony **2** abrupt, rude

ubiquitous ❶ *adj* everywhere at once
udder *n* milk-secreting organ of cow etc.
UFO unidentified flying object
ugly ❶ *adj* **uglier, ugliest** **1** unpleasant to see, hideous **2** threatening
ukulele, ukelele *n* small four-stringed guitar
ulcer ❶ *n* open sore on skin
ulterior *adj* lying beneath, beyond what is revealed
ultimate ❶ *adj* **1** last, conclusive **2** highest **3** fundamental

——— THESAURUS ———

ubiquitous *adj* = **ever-present**, pervasive, omnipresent, everywhere, universal
ugly *adj* = **unattractive**, homely (*chiefly US*), plain, unsightly, unlovely ≠ **beautiful**; = **unpleasant**, shocking, terrible, nasty, distasteful ≠ **pleasant**
ulcer *n* = **sore**, abscess, peptic ulcer, gumboil
ultimate *adj* = **final**, last, end; = **supreme**, highest, greatest, paramount, superlative
umpire *n* = **referee**, judge, arbiter, arbitrator ▷ *v* = **referee**, judge, adjudicate, arbitrate
unanimous *adj* = **agreed**, united, in agreement, harmonious, like-minded ≠ **divided**
unaware *adj* = **ignorant**, unconscious, oblivious, uninformed, unknowing ≠ **aware**

u

uncertain ⊙ *adj* 1 not able to be known 2 changeable
uncertainty *n*
uncle *n* 1 brother of father or mother 2 husband of parent's sibling
unconscious ⊙ *adj* 1 insensible 2 not aware ▷ *n* 3 set of thoughts, memories etc. of which one is not normally aware
uncouth *adj* clumsy, boorish
unction *n* anointing **unctuous** *adj* excessively polite
under ⊙ *prep* 1 below, beneath 2 included in 3 less than 4 subjected to ▷ *adv* 5 in lower place or condition ▷ *adj* 6 lower
under- *comb. form* beneath, below, lower, as in *underground*
underarm *adj* 1 from armpit to wrist 2 (*Sport*) with hand swung below shoulder level
undercarriage *n* 1 aircraft's landing gear 2 framework supporting body of vehicle
undercurrent *n* 1 current that is not apparent at surface

2 underlying opinion, emotion
undercut *v* charge less than (another trader)
underdog ⊙ *n* person, team unlikely to win
undergo ⊙ *v* experience, endure, sustain
undergraduate *n* student member of university
underground ⊙ *adj* 1 under the ground 2 secret ▷ *adv* 3 secretly ▷ *n* 4 secret but organized resistance to government in power 5 railway system under the ground
undergrowth *n* small trees, bushes growing beneath taller trees
underhand *adj* secret, sly
underlie *v* 1 lie, be placed under 2 be the foundation, cause, or basis of
underline ⊙ *v* 1 put line under 2 emphasize
underling *n* subordinate

—————— THESAURUS ——————

uncertain *adj* = **unsure**, undecided, vague, unclear, dubious ≠ **sure** = **doubtful**, questionable, indefinite, unconfirmed, conjectural ≠ **decided**
unconscious *adj* = **senseless**, knocked out, out cold (*Inf*), out, stunned ≠ **awake**; = **unaware**, ignorant, oblivious, unknowing ≠ **aware**; = **unintentional**, unwitting, inadvertent, accidental ≠ **intentional**
under *prep* = **below**, beneath, underneath ≠ **over**; = **subordinate**

to, subject to, governed by, secondary to ▷ *adv* = **below**, down, beneath ≠ **up**
underdog *n* = **weaker party**, little fellow (*Inf*), outsider
undergo *v* = **experience**, go through, stand, suffer, bear
underground *adj* = **subterranean**, basement, lower-level, sunken, covered; = **secret**, covert, hidden, guerrilla, revolutionary
underline *v* = **emphasize**, stress, highlight, accentuate ≠ **minimize**;

undermine ❶ v 1 wear away base, support of 2 weaken insidiously

underneath adv 1 below ▷ prep 2 under ▷ adj 3 lower ▷ n 4 lower surface

underpants pl n man's underwear for lower part of body

underpass n road that passes under another road or railway line

underpin v give strength, support to

understand ❶ v 1 know and comprehend 2 realize 3 infer 4 take for granted

understudy n 1 one prepared to take over theatrical part ▷ v 2 act as understudy

undertake ❶ v 1 make oneself responsible for 2 enter upon 3 promise **undertaker** n one who arranges funerals **undertaking** n

undertone n 1 dropped tone of voice 2 underlying suggestion

underwear ❶ n garments worn next to skin

underworld ❶ n 1 criminals and their associates 2 (Myth) abode of the dead

underwrite ❶ v 1 agree to pay 2 accept liability in insurance policy **underwriter** n

undo ❶ v 1 untie, unfasten 2 reverse 3 cause downfall of

undulate v move up and down like waves

unearth ❶ v 1 dig up 2 discover

uneasy ❶ adj 1 anxious 2 uncomfortable

unemployed ❶ adj having no paid employment, out of work **unemployment** n

unexceptionable adj beyond criticism

unfold ❶ v 1 open, spread out 2 reveal

——————— THESAURUS ———————

= **underscore**, mark

undermine v = **weaken**, sabotage, subvert, compromise, disable ≠ **reinforce**

understand v = **comprehend**, get, take in, perceive, grasp (Inf); = **believe**, gather, think, see, suppose

undertake v = **agree**, promise, contract, guarantee, engage

underwear n = **underclothes**, lingerie, undies (Inf), undergarments, underthings

underworld n = **criminals**, gangsters, organized crime, gangland (Inf); = **nether world**, Hades, nether regions

underwrite v = **finance**, back, fund, guarantee, sponsor

undo v = **open**, unfasten, loose, untie, unbutton; = **reverse**, cancel, offset, neutralize, invalidate; = **ruin**, defeat, destroy, wreck, shatter

unearth v = **discover**, find, reveal, expose, uncover; = **dig up**, excavate, exhume, dredge up

uneasy adj = **anxious**, worried, troubled, nervous, disturbed ≠ **relaxed**; = **precarious**, strained, uncomfortable, tense, awkward

unemployed adj = **out of work**, redundant, laid off, jobless, idle ≠ **working**

unfold v = **reveal**, tell, present,

u

ungainly *adj* **-lier, -liest**
awkward, clumsy

uni- *comb. form* one, as in *unicycle*

unicorn *n* mythical horselike
animal with single long horn

uniform ❶ *n* **1** identifying clothes
worn by members of same group,
e.g. soldiers, nurses etc. ▷ *adj*
2 not changing **3** regular
uniformity *n*

unify ❶ *v* **-fying, -fied** make or
become one **unification** *n*

unilateral *adj* **1** one-sided **2** (of
contract) binding one party only

union ❶ *n* **1** joining into one
2 state, result of being joined
3 federation **4** trade union
unionize *v* organize (workers) into
trade union

unique ❶ *adj* **1** being only one of
its kind **2** unparalleled

unison *n* (*Mus*) **1** singing etc. of
same notes as others **2** agreement

unit ❶ *n* **1** single thing or person
2 group or individual being part of
larger whole **3** standard quantity

unite ❶ *v* **1** join into one
2 associate **3** become one
4 combine **unity** *n* **1** state of
being one **2** harmony **3** agreement

universe ❶ *n* **1** all existing things
considered as constituting
systematic whole **2** the world
universal *adj* relating to all things
or all people

university *n, pl* **-ties** educational
institution that awards degrees

unkempt *adj* untidy

unless *conj* if not, except

unlike *adj* **1** dissimilar, different
▷ *prep* **2** not typical of **unlikely**
adj improbable

unravel ❶ *v* **-elling, -elled** undo,
untangle

unrest ❶ *n* discontent

unruly *adj* **-lier, -liest** badly

— THESAURUS —

show, disclose; **= open**, spread out,
undo, expand, unfurl

uniform *n* **= regalia**, suit, livery,
colours, habit ▷ *adj* **= consistent**,
unvarying, similar, even, same
≠ varying; **= alike**, similar, like,
same, equal

unify *v* **= unite**, join, combine,
merge, consolidate **≠ divide**

union *n* **= joining**, uniting,
unification, combination, coalition;
= alliance, league, association,
coalition, federation

unique *adj* **= distinct**, special,
exclusive, peculiar, only;
= unparalleled, unmatched,
unequalled, matchless, without

equal

unit *n* **= entity**, whole, item,
feature; **= section**, company,
group, force, detail; **= measure**,
quantity, measurement

unite *v* **= join**, link, combine,
couple, blend **≠ separate**;
= cooperate, ally, join forces, band,
pool **≠ split**

universe *n* **= cosmos**, space,
creation, nature, heavens

unravel *v* **= solve**, explain, work
out, resolve, figure out (*Inf*);
= undo, separate, disentangle, free,
unwind

unrest *n* **= discontent**, rebellion,
protest, strife, agitation **≠ peace**

u

behaved, disorderly
unsavoury *adj* distasteful
unscathed *adj* not harmed
unsightly *adj* ugly
unthinkable ❶ *adj* **1** out of the
question **2** inconceivable
3 unreasonable
until *conj* **1** to the time that
2 (with a negative) before ▷ *prep*
3 up to the time of
unto *prep* (*Obs*) to
untoward *adj* awkward,
inconvenient
unwieldy *adj* **1** awkward
2 bulky
unwind *v* **1** slacken, undo, unravel
2 become relaxed
unwitting *adj* **1** not knowing
2 not intentional
up *prep* **1** from lower to higher
position **2** along ▷ *adv* **3** in or to
higher position, source, activity etc.
4 indicating completion **upward**
adj/adv **upwards** *adv* **upbeat** *adj*
(*Inf*) cheerful **up-to-date** *adj*
modern, fashionable
upbringing ❶ *n* rearing and
education of children

update ❶ *v* bring up to date
upfront *adj* (*Inf*) open, frank
upgrade ❶ *v* **1** promote to higher
position **2** improve
upheaval ❶ *n* sudden or violent
disturbance
uphold ❶ *v* maintain, support
etc.
upholster *v* fit springs, coverings
on chairs etc. **upholstery** *n*
upkeep *n* act, cost of keeping
something in good repair
upon *prep* on
uptown (*US & Canad*) *adj/adv*
towards, in, or relating to some
part of a town that is away from the
centre ▷ *n* such a part of a town,
esp. a residential part
upper ❶ *adj* **1** situated above **2** of
superior quality, status etc. ▷ *n*
3 upper part of boot or shoe **upper
case** capital letters **upper hand**
position of control
upright ❶ *adj* **1** erect **2** honest,
just ▷ *adv* **3** vertically ▷ *n* **4** thing
standing upright, e.g. post in
framework
uprising ❶ *n* rebellion, revolt

unthinkable *adj* = **impossible**,
out of the question, inconceivable,
absurd, unreasonable;
= **inconceivable**, incredible,
unimaginable
upbringing *n* = **education**,
training, breeding, rearing, raising
update *v* = **bring up to date**,
improve, correct, renew, revise
upgrade *v* = **improve**, better,
update, reform, add to
upheaval *n* = **disturbance**,

revolution, disorder, turmoil,
disruption
uphold *v* = **support**, back, defend,
aid, champion
upper *adj* = **topmost**, top
≠ **bottom**; = **higher**, high ≠ **lower**
upright *adj* = **vertical**, straight,
standing up, erect, perpendicular
≠ **horizontal**; = **honest**, good,
principled, just, ethical
≠ **dishonourable**
uprising *n* = **rebellion**, rising,

u

uproar ❶ n tumult, disturbance
uproot v 1 pull up, as by roots
2 displace from usual surroundings
upset ❶ v 1 overturn 2 distress
3 disrupt ▷ n 4 unexpected defeat
5 confusion ▷ adj 6 disturbed
7 emotionally troubled
upshot n outcome, end
upside down, upside-down ❶
1 turned over completely 2 (Inf)
confused
upstage v overshadow
upstart n one suddenly raised to
wealth, power etc.
uptight adj (Inf) 1 tense
2 repressed
uranium n white radioactive
metallic element
urban ❶ adj relating to town or
city
urbane adj elegant, sophisticated
urchin n mischievous, unkempt
child
urge ❶ v 1 exhort earnestly

2 entreat 3 drive on ▷ n 4 strong
desire **urgency** n **urgent** adj
needing attention at once
urine n fluid excreted by kidneys to
bladder and passed as waste from
body **urinal** n place for urinating
urinate v discharge urine
urn v 1 vessel like vase 2 large
container with tap
us pron object of WE
USB Universal Serial Bus: standard
for connecting sockets on
computers **USB drive** n (Comp)
small portable data storage device
with a USB connection
use ❶ v 1 employ 2 exercise
3 exploit 4 consume ▷ n
5 employment 6 need to employ
7 serviceableness 8 profit 9 habit
usable adj fit for use **usage** n
1 act of using 2 custom **used** adj
1 second-hand 2 accustomed
useful adj **useless** adj 1 having
no practical use 2 (Inf) inept

THESAURUS

revolution, revolt, disturbance
uproar n = **commotion**, noise,
racket, riot, turmoil
upset adj = **distressed**, shaken,
disturbed, worried, troubled;
= **sick**, queasy, bad, ill ▷ v
= **distress**, trouble, disturb, worry,
alarm; = **tip over**, overturn,
capsize, knock over, spill; = **mess
up**, spoil, disturb, change, confuse
▷ n = **distress**, worry, trouble,
shock, bother; = **reversal**, shake-up
(Inf), defeat; = **illness**, complaint,
disorder, bug (Inf), sickness
upside down, upside-down
adj = **inverted**, overturned,

upturned; (Inf) = **confused**,
disordered, chaotic, muddled,
topsy-turvy
urban adj = **civic**, city, town,
metropolitan, municipal
urge v = **beg**, exhort, plead,
implore, beseech; = **advocate**,
recommend, advise, support,
counsel ≠ **discourage** ▷ n
= **impulse**, longing, wish, desire,
drive ≠ **reluctance**
use v = **employ**, utilize, work, apply,
operate; sometimes with up
= **consume**, exhaust, spend, run
through, expend; = **take
advantage of**, exploit, manipulate

u

usher ❶ *n* **1** doorkeeper, one showing people to seats etc. ▷ *v* **2** introduce, announce

usual ❶ *adj* habitual, ordinary
usually *adv* as a rule

usurp *v* seize wrongfully

utensil *n* vessel, implement, esp. in domestic use

uterus *n* womb

utility ❶ *n* **1** usefulness **2** benefit **3** useful thing ▷ *adj* **4** made for practical purposes **utilitarian** *adj* useful rather than beautiful

utilize *v*

utmost ❶ *adj* **1** to the highest degree **2** extreme, furthest ▷ *n* **3** greatest possible amount

Utopia *n* imaginary ideal state

utter¹ ❶ *v* express, say
utterance *n*

utter² ❶ *adj* complete, total
utterly *adv*

▷ *n* = **usage**, employment, operation, application **= service**, handling, practice, exercise; **= purpose**, end, reason, object

usher *v* = **escort**, lead, direct, guide, conduct ▷ *n* = **attendant**, guide, doorman, escort, doorkeeper

usual *adj* = **normal**, customary, regular, general, common
≠ **unusual**

utility *n* = **usefulness**, benefit, convenience, practicality, efficacy

utmost *adj* = **greatest**, highest, maximum, supreme, paramount; = **farthest**, extreme, last, final ▷ *n* = **best**, greatest, maximum, highest, hardest

utter¹ *v* = **say**, state, speak, voice, express

utter² *adj* = **absolute**, complete, total, sheer, outright

u

air, gas has been removed
vacuum cleaner apparatus
for removing dust by suction
vacuum flask double-walled
flask with vacuum between
walls, for keeping contents hot
or cold
vagabond n 1 person with no
fixed home 2 wandering beggar or
thief
vagina n passage from womb to
exterior
vagrant n vagabond, tramp
vagrancy n
vague ❶ adj 1 indefinite or
uncertain 2 indistinct 3 not
clearly expressed
vain ❶ adj 1 conceited
2 worthless 3 unavailing
vale n (Poet) valley
valentine n (one receiving) card,
gift, expressing affection, on Saint
Valentine's day
valet n gentleman's personal
servant
valiant adj brave, courageous
valid ❶ adj 1 sound 2 of binding
force in law **validate** v make valid
validity n
Valium® n drug used as
tranquillizer

vacant ❶ adj empty, unoccupied
vacancy n, pl **-cies** untaken job,
room etc.
vacate v quit, leave empty
vacation n 1 time when
universities and law courts are
closed 2 (US & Canad) holidays
vaccinate v inoculate with
vaccine **vaccination** n **vaccine**
n any substance used for
inoculation against disease
vacillate v 1 waver 2 move to
and fro **vacillation** n
vacuous adj not expressing
intelligent thought
vacuum ❶ n, pl **vacuums,
vacua** place, region containing no
matter and from which all or most

—————— THESAURUS ——————

vacant adj = **empty**, free,
available, abandoned, deserted
≠ **occupied**; = **unfilled**,
unoccupied ≠ **taken**
vacuum n = **gap**, lack, absence,
space, deficiency
vague adj = **unclear**, indefinite,
hazy, confused, loose ≠ **clear**;
= **imprecise**, unspecified,

generalized, rough, loose
vain adj = **futile**, useless, pointless,
unsuccessful, idle ≠ **successful**;
= **conceited**, narcissistic, proud,
arrogant, swaggering
≠ **modest**
valid adj = **sound**, good,
reasonable, telling, convincing
≠ **unfounded**; = **legal**, official,

valley ❶ *n* **1** low area between hills **2** river basin

valour *n* bravery

value ❶ *n* **1** cost **2** worth **3** usefulness **4** importance ▷ *pl* **5** principles, standards ▷ *v* **6** estimate value of **7** prize

valuable *adj* **1** precious **2** worthy ▷ *n* **3** (*usu. pl*) valuable thing

valuation *n* estimated worth

value-added tax tax on difference between cost of basic materials and cost of article made from them

valve *n* **1** device to control passage of fluid etc. through pipe **2** (*Anat*) part of body allowing one-way passage of fluids

vampire *n* (in folklore) corpse that rises from dead to drink blood of the living **vampire bat** bat that sucks blood of animals

van¹ *n* **1** covered vehicle, esp. for goods **2** railway carriage for goods and use of guard

van² *n* short for VANGUARD

vandal *n* one who wantonly and deliberately damages or destroys

vandalism *n* **vandalize** *v*

vane *n* **1** weathercock **2** blade of propeller

vanguard *n* leading, foremost group, position etc.

vanilla *n* **1** tropical climbing orchid **2** its seed pod **3** essence of this for flavouring

vanish ❶ *v* disappear

vanity ❶ *n, pl* **-ties** excessive pride or conceit

vanquish *v* conquer, overcome

vantage *n* advantage **vantage point** position that gives overall view

vapid *adj* flat, dull, insipid

vapour *n* **1** gaseous form of a substance **2** steam, mist

vaporize *v* convert into, pass off in, vapour **vaporizer** *n*

variable ❶ see VARY

variegated *adj* having patches of different colours

variety ❶ *n, pl* **-ties** **1** state of being varied or various **2** diversity **3** varied assortment **4** sort or kind

—— THESAURUS ——

legitimate, genuine, authentic ≠ **invalid**

valley *n* = **hollow**, dale, glen, vale, depression

value *n* = **importance**, benefit, worth, merit, point ≠ **worthlessness**; = **cost**, price, worth, rate, market price ▷ *v* = **appreciate**, rate, prize, regard highly, respect ≠ **undervalue**; = **evaluate**, price, estimate, rate, cost

vanish *v* = **disappear**, dissolve,

evaporate, fade away, melt away ≠ **appear**

vanity *n* = **pride**, arrogance, conceit, narcissism, egotism ≠ **modesty**

variable *adj* = **changeable**, unstable, fluctuating, shifting, flexible ≠ **constant**

variety *n* = **diversity**, change, variation, difference, diversification ≠ **uniformity**; = **range**, selection, assortment, mix, collection; = **type**, sort, kind, class, brand

V

various ❶ *adj* diverse, of several kinds

varnish ❶ *n* 1 resinous solution put on surface to make it hard and shiny ▷ *v* 2 apply varnish to

vary ❶ *v* **varying, varied** (cause to) change, diversify, differ **variability** *n* **variable** *adj* 1 changeable 2 unsteady or fickle ▷ *n* 3 something subject to variation **variance** *n* state of discord, discrepancy **variant** *adj* 1 different ▷ *n* 2 alternative form **variation** *n* 1 alteration 2 extent to which thing varies 3 modification **varied** *adj* 1 diverse 2 modified

vase *n* vessel, jar as ornament or for holding flowers

Vaseline® *n* jelly-like petroleum product

vast ❶ *adj* very large

VAT value-added tax

vat *n* large tub, tank

vault¹ ❶ *n* 1 arched roof 2 cellar 3 burial chamber 4 secure room for storing valuables

vault² ❶ *v* 1 spring, jump over with the hands resting on something ▷ *n* 2 such jump

veal *n* calf flesh as food

vector *n* (*Maths*) quantity that has size and direction

veer ❶ *v* 1 change direction 2 change one's mind

vegan *n* one who eats no meat, eggs, or dairy products

vegetable *n* 1 plant, esp. edible one ▷ *adj* 2 of, from, concerned with plants

vegetarian *n* 1 one who does not eat meat or fish ▷ *adj* 2 suitable for vegetarians

vegetate *v* 1 (of plants) grow, develop 2 (of people) live dull, unproductive life **vegetation** *n* plants collectively

vehement *adj* marked by intensity of feeling

vehicle ❶ *n* means of conveying

veil ❶ *n* 1 light material to cover face or head ▷ *v* 2 cover with, as with, veil

vein ❶ *n* 1 tube in body taking

         THESAURUS

various *adj* = **different**, assorted, miscellaneous, varied, distinct ≠ **similar**

varnish *v* = **lacquer**, polish, glaze, gloss

vary *v* = **differ**, be different, be dissimilar, disagree, diverge; = **change**, shift, swing, alter, fluctuate

vast *adj* = **huge**, massive, enormous, great, wide ≠ **tiny**

vault¹ *n* = **strongroom**, repository, depository; = **crypt**, tomb,

catacomb, cellar, mausoleum

vault² *v* = **jump**, spring, leap, clear, bound

veer *v* = **change direction**, turn, swerve, shift, sheer

vehicle *n* = **conveyance**, machine, motor vehicle

veil *n* = **mask**, cover, shroud, film, curtain ▷ *v* = **cover**, screen, hide, mask, shield ≠ **reveal**

vein *n* = **mood**, style, note, tone, mode; = **seam**, layer, stratum, course, current

blood to heart **2** fissure in rock filled with ore **veined** adj

Velcro® n fabric with tiny hooked threads that adheres to coarse surface

velocity ❶ n, pl **-ties 1** rate of motion in given direction **2** speed

velvet n silk or cotton fabric with thick, short pile **velvety** adj **1** of, like velvet **2** soft and smooth

vend v sell **vendor** n **vending machine** machine that dispenses goods automatically

vendetta n prolonged quarrel

veneer n **1** thin layer of fine wood **2** superficial appearance ▷ v **3** cover with veneer

venerable adj worthy of reverence **venerate** v look up to, respect, revere **veneration** n

vengeance ❶ n revenge **vengeful** adj

venison n flesh of deer as food

venom n **1** poison **2** spite **venomous** adj

vent ❶ n **1** small hole or outlet ▷ v **2** give outlet to **3** utter

ventilate v supply with fresh air **ventilation** n **ventilator** n

ventricle n cavity of heart or brain

ventriloquist n one who can so speak that the sounds seem to come from some other person or place **ventriloquism** n

venture ❶ v **1** expose to hazard **2** risk **3** dare **4** have courage to do something or go somewhere ▷ n **5** risky undertaking

venture capitalist provider of capital for new commercial enterprises

venue n **1** meeting place **2** location

veracious adj truthful **veracity** n

verandah, veranda n open or partly enclosed porch on outside of house

verb n part of speech used to express action or being **verbal** adj of, by, or relating to words spoken rather than written **verbatim** adj/ adv word for word

verbose adj long-winded

verdant adj green and fresh

verdict ❶ n **1** decision of jury **2** opinion reached after examination of facts

verge ❶ n **1** edge **2** brink **3** grass border along road ▷ v **4** come close to **5** be on the border of

verger n church caretaker

velocity n = **speed**, pace, rapidity, quickness, swiftness

vengeance n = **revenge**, retaliation, reprisal, retribution, requital ≠ **forgiveness**

vent n = **outlet**, opening, aperture, duct, orifice ▷ v = **express**, release, voice, air, discharge ≠ **hold back**

venture n = **undertaking**, project, enterprise, campaign, risk ▷ v = **go**, travel, journey, set out, wander; = **dare**, presume, have the courage to, be brave enough to, hazard; = **put forward**, volunteer

verdict n = **decision**, finding, judgment, opinion, sentence

verge n = **brink**, point, edge, threshold

V

verify ❶ v **-ifying, -ified 1** prove, confirm truth of **2** test accuracy of **verification** n

veritable adj actual, true

vermilion adj/n (of) bright red colour

vermin pl n harmful animals, parasites etc.

vernacular n **1** commonly spoken language or dialect of particular country or place ▷ adj **2** of vernacular **3** native

verruca n wart, esp. on the foot

versatile ❶ adj capable of, adapted to many different uses, skills etc. **versatility** n

verse n **1** stanza or short subdivision of poem or the Bible **2** poetry **versed in** skilled in

version ❶ n **1** description from certain point of view **2** translation **3** adaptation

versus prep against

vertebra n, pl **vertebrae** single section of backbone **vertebrate** n/adj (animal) with backbone

vertical ❶ adj **1** at right angles to the horizon **2** upright **3** overhead

vertigo n giddiness

verve n **1** enthusiasm **2** vigour

very ❶ adv **1** extremely, to great extent ▷ adj **2** exact, ideal **3** absolute

vespers pl n evening church service

vessel ❶ n **1** any object used as a container, esp. for liquids **2** ship, large boat **3** tubular structure conveying liquids (e.g. blood) in body

vest n **1** undergarment for upper body ▷ v **2** place **3** confer

vestment n robe or official garment

vestibule n entrance hall, lobby

vestige n small trace, amount

vestry n, pl **-tries** room in church for keeping vestments, holding meetings etc.

vet ❶ n short for VETERINARY SURGEON v check suitability of

veteran ❶ n **1** one who has served a long time, esp. in fighting services ▷ adj **2** long-serving

─────────── THESAURUS ───────────

verify v = **check**, make sure, examine, monitor, inspect

versatile adj = **adaptable**, flexible, all-round, resourceful, multifaceted ≠ **unadaptable**

version n = **form**, variety, variant, sort, class; = **adaptation**, edition, interpretation, form, copy; = **account**, report, description, record, reading

vertical adj = sheer, perpendicular, straight (up and down), erect ≠ **horizontal**

very adv = **extremely**, highly, greatly, really, deeply ▷ adj = **exact**, precise, selfsame

vessel n = **ship**, boat, craft; = **container**, receptacle, can, bowl, tank

vet v = **check**, examine, investigate, review, appraise

veteran n = **old hand**, past master, warhorse (Inf), old stager ≠ **novice** ▷ adj = **long-serving**, seasoned, experienced, old, established

v

veterinary adj of, concerning the health of animals **veterinary surgeon** one qualified to treat animal ailments

veto ❶ n, pl **-toes** 1 power of rejecting piece of legislation 2 any prohibition ▷ v 3 enforce veto against

vex v 1 annoy 2 distress **vexation** n 1 cause of irritation 2 state of distress

VHF very high frequency

VI Vancouver Island

via prep by way of

viable ❶ adj 1 practicable 2 able to live and grow independently

viaduct n bridge over valley for road or railway

vibrate v 1 (cause to) move to and fro rapidly and continuously 2 give off (light or sound) by vibration 3 oscillate 4 quiver **vibrant** adj 1 throbbing 2 vibrating 3 appearing vigorous **vibration** n

VIC Victoria (Australian state)

vicar n clergyman in charge of parish **vicarage** n vicar's house

vicarious adj obtained, enjoyed or undergone by imagining another's experiences

vice¹ ❶ n 1 evil or immoral habit or practice 2 criminal immorality, esp. prostitution 3 fault, imperfection

vice² n appliance with screw mechanism for holding things while working on them

vice³ adj serving in place of

viceroy n ruler acting for king in province or dependency

vice versa ❶ (Lat) conversely, the other way round

vicinity n neighbourhood

vicious ❶ adj 1 wicked, cruel 2 ferocious, dangerous **vicious circle** sequence of problems and solutions which always leads back to original problem

victim ❶ n 1 person or thing killed, injured etc. as result of another's deed, or accident, circumstances etc. 2 person cheated 3 sacrifice **victimization** n **victimize** v 1 punish unfairly 2 make victim of

victor ❶ n 1 conqueror 2 winner

---

veto v = **ban**, block, reject, rule out, turn down ≠ **pass** ▷ n = **ban**, dismissal, rejection, vetoing, boycott ≠ **ratification**

viable adj = **workable**, practical, feasible, suitable, realistic ≠ **unworkable**

vice¹ n = **fault**, failing, weakness, limitation, defect ≠ **good point**; = **wickedness**, evil, corruption, sin, depravity ≠ **virtue**

vice versa adv = **the other way round**, conversely, in reverse, contrariwise

vicious adj = **savage**, brutal, violent, cruel, ferocious ≠ **gentle**; = **malicious**, vindictive, spiteful, mean, cruel

victim n = **casualty**, sufferer, fatality ≠ **survivor**; = **scapegoat**, sacrifice, martyr

victor n = **winner**, champion, conqueror, vanquisher, prizewinner ≠ **loser**

V

victorious *adj* **1** winning
2 triumphant **victory** *n* winning
of battle etc.

video *adj, pl* **-os 1** relating to or
used in transmission or production
of television image ▷ *n* **2** video
cassette recorder **3** cassette
containing video tape ▷ *v* **4** record
on video **video cassette recorder**
tape recorder for recording and
playing back TV programmes and
films on cassette **video tape**
magnetic tape used to record TV
programmes

vie ❶ *v* **vying, vied** (with *with*)
contend, compete against or for
someone, something

view ❶ *n* **1** survey by eyes or mind
2 range of vision **3** picture **4** scene
5 opinion **6** purpose ▷ *v* **7** look at
8 survey **9** consider **viewer** *n*
1 one who views **2** one who
watches television **3** optical device
to assist viewing of photographic
slides **viewfinder** *n* window on
camera showing what will appear
in photograph **viewpoint** *n* **1** way
of regarding subject **2** position
commanding view of landscape

vigil *n* keeping awake, watch
vigilance *n* **vigilant** *adj*
watchful, alert

vigilante *n* person who takes it
upon himself or herself to enforce
the law

vignette *n* concise description of
typical features

vigour, *US* **vigor ❶** *n* **1** force,
strength **2** energy, activity
vigorous *adj* **1** strong **2** energetic
3 flourishing

vile ❶ *adj* **1** very wicked, shameful
2 disgusting **3** despicable

vilify *v* **-ifying, -ified** unjustly
attack the character of

villa *n* **1** large, luxurious country
house **2** detached or semidetached
suburban house

village *n* small group of houses in
country area

villain ❶ *n* wicked person
villainous *adj*

vindicate ❶ *v* **1** clear of charges
2 justify **vindication** *n*

vindictive *adj* **1** revengeful
2 inspired by resentment

vine *n* long-stemmed climbing
plant bearing grapes **vineyard** *n*

— THESAURUS —

vie *v* = **compete**, struggle, contend,
strive

view *n sometimes plural* = **opinion**,
belief, feeling, attitude, impression;
= **scene**, picture, sight, prospect,
perspective; = **vision**, sight, visibility,
perspective, eyeshot ▷ *v* = **regard**,
see, consider, perceive, treat

vigour, *US* **vigor** *n* = **energy**,
vitality, power, spirit, strength
≠ **weakness**

vile *adj* = **wicked**, evil, corrupt,
perverted, degenerate
≠ **honourable**; = **disgusting**, foul,
revolting, nasty
≠ **pleasant**

villain *n* = **evildoer**, criminal,
rogue, scoundrel, wretch; = **baddy**
(Inf), antihero ≠ **hero**

vindicate *v* = **clear**, acquit,
exonerate, absolve, let off the hook
≠ **condemn**

v

plantation of vines

vinegar n acid liquid obtained from wine and other alcoholic liquors

vintage ⊙ n **1** gathering of the grapes **2** the yield **3** wine of particular year **4** time of origin ▷ adj **5** best and most typical **vintner** n dealer in wine

vinyl n **1** plastic material with variety of domestic and industrial uses **2** record made of vinyl

viola n see VIOLIN

violate ⊙ v **1** break (law, agreement etc.) **2** rape **3** outrage, desecrate **violation** n

violence ⊙ n **1** use of physical force, usu. intended to cause injury or destruction **2** great force or strength in action, feeling or expression **violent** adj

violet n **1** plant with small bluish-purple or white flowers **2** bluish-purple colour ▷ adj **3** of this colour

violin n small four-stringed musical instrument **viola** n large violin with lower range **violinist** n

VIP ⊙ very important person

viper n poisonous snake

viral adj **1** pert. to a virus **2** spreading rapidly via the internet

virgin ⊙ n **1** one who has not had sexual intercourse ▷ adj **2** without experience of sexual intercourse **3** uncorrupted **4** (of land) untilled **virginal** adj **virginity** n

virile adj **1** (of male) capable of copulation or procreation **2** strong, forceful **virility** n

virtual adj so in effect, though not in appearance or name

virtue ⊙ n **1** moral goodness **2** good quality **3** merit **virtuous** adj morally good

virtuoso n, pl **-sos, -si 1** one with special skill, esp. in music ▷ adj **2** showing special skill **virtuosity** n

virulent adj **1** very infectious, poisonous etc. **2** malicious

virus n infecting agent that causes disease

visa n endorsement on passport permitting bearer to travel into country of issuing government

visage n face

vis-à-vis prep in relation to, regarding

viscount n Brit. nobleman ranking

THESAURUS

---

vintage adj = **high-quality**, best, prime, quality, choice

violate v = **break**, infringe, disobey, transgress, ignore ≠ **obey**; = **invade**, infringe on, disturb, upset, shatter; = **desecrate**, profane, defile, abuse, pollute ≠ **honour**; = **rape**, molest, sexually assault, ravish, abuse

violence n = **brutality**, bloodshed, savagery, fighting, terrorism; = **force**,

power, strength, might, ferocity

VIP n = **celebrity**, big name, star, somebody, luminary

virgin n = **maiden**, girl (Archaic) ▷ adj = **pure**, chaste, immaculate, virginal, vestal ≠ **corrupted**

virtue n = **goodness**, integrity, worth, morality, righteousness ≠ **vice**; = **merit**, strength, asset, plus (Inf), attribute ≠ **failing**

below earl and above baron
viscous adj thick and sticky
visible ⊙ adj that can be seen
visibility n degree of clarity of
vision
vision ⊙ n 1 sight 2 insight
3 dream 4 hallucination
visionary adj 1 marked by vision
2 impractical ▷ n 3 mystic
4 impractical person
visit ⊙ v -iting, -ited 1 go, come
and see 2 stay temporarily with
(someone) ▷ n 3 stay 4 call at
person's home etc. **visitation** n
1 formal visit or inspection
2 affliction or plague **visitor** n
visor n 1 movable front part of
helmet 2 eyeshade, esp. on car
3 peak on cap
vista ⊙ n extensive view
visual ⊙ adj 1 of sight 2 visible
visualize v form mental image of
vital ⊙ adj 1 necessary to,

affecting life 2 lively 3 animated
4 essential **vitality** n life, vigour
vitamin n any of group of
substances occurring in foodstuffs
and essential to health
viva interj long live
vivacious adj lively, sprightly
vivacity n
vivid ⊙ adj 1 bright, intense
2 true to life
vivisection n dissection of, or
operating on, living animals
vixen n female fox
vizor see VISOR
vocabulary ⊙ n, pl -aries 1 list
of words, usu. in alphabetical order
2 stock of words used in particular
language or subject
vocal ⊙ adj 1 of, with, or giving
out voice 2 outspoken, articulate
vocalist n singer **vocals** pl n
singing part
vocation ⊙ n (urge, inclination,

——————— THESAURUS ———————

visible adj = **perceptible**,
observable, clear, apparent, evident
≠ **invisible**
vision n = **image**, idea, dream,
plans, hopes; = **hallucination**,
illusion, apparition, revelation,
delusion; = **sight**, seeing, eyesight,
view, perception; = **foresight**,
imagination, perception, insight,
awareness
visit v = **call on**, drop in on (Inf),
stay at, stay with, stop by ▷ n
= **call**, social call
vista n = **view**, scene, prospect,
landscape, panorama
visual adj = **optical**, optic, ocular;
= **observable**, visible, perceptible,

discernible ≠ **imperceptible**
vital adj = **essential**, important,
necessary, key, basic
≠ **unnecessary**; = **lively**, vigorous,
energetic, spirited, dynamic
≠ **lethargic**
vivid adj = **clear**, detailed, realistic,
telling, moving ≠ **vague**; = **bright**,
brilliant, intense, clear, rich ≠ **dull**
vocabulary n = **language**, words,
lexicon
vocal adj = **outspoken**, frank,
forthright, strident, vociferous
≠ **quiet**; = **spoken**, voiced, uttered,
oral, said
vocation n = **profession**, calling,
job, trade, career

predisposition to) particular career, profession etc. **vocational** adj
vociferous adj shouting, noisy
vodka n spirit distilled from potatoes or grain
vogue ❶ n 1 fashion, style 2 popularity
voice ❶ n 1 sound given out by person in speaking, singing etc. 2 quality of the sound 3 expressed opinion 4 (right to) share in discussion ▷ v 5 give utterance to, express
void ❶ adj 1 empty 2 destitute 3 not legally binding ▷ n 4 empty space ▷ v 5 make ineffectual or invalid 6 empty out
vol. volume
volatile ❶ adj 1 evaporating quickly 2 lively 3 changeable
volcano n, pl **-noes, -nos** 1 hole in earth's crust through which lava, ashes, smoke etc. are discharged 2 mountain so formed **volcanic** adj
vole n small rodent

volition n exercise of will
volley ❶ n 1 simultaneous discharge of weapons or missiles 2 rush of oaths, questions etc. 3 (Sport) kick, stroke etc. at moving ball before it touches ground ▷ v 4 discharge 5 kick, strike etc. in volley **volleyball** n game where ball is hit over high net
volt n unit of electric potential **voltage** n electric potential difference expressed in volts
voluble adj talking easily and at length
volume ❶ n 1 space occupied 2 mass 3 amount 4 power, fullness of voice or sound 5 book 6 part of book bound in one cover **voluminous** adj bulky, copious
voluntary ❶ adj 1 having, done by free will 2 done without payment 3 supported by free-will contributions **volunteer** n 1 one who offers service, joins force etc. of his or her own free will ▷ v 2 offer oneself or one's services

vogue n = **fashion**, trend, craze, style, mode
voice n = **tone**, sound, articulation ▷ v = **express**, declare, air, raise, reveal
void n = **emptiness**, space, vacuum, oblivion, blankness ▷ adj = **invalid**, null and void, inoperative, useless, ineffective ▷ v = **invalidate**, nullify, cancel, withdraw, reverse
volatile adj = **changeable**, shifting, variable, unsettled, unstable ≠ **stable**;

= **temperamental**, erratic, mercurial, up and down (Inf), fickle ≠ **calm**
volley n = **barrage**, blast, burst, shower, hail
volume n = **amount**, quantity, level, body, total; = **capacity**, size, mass, extent, proportions; = **book**, work, title, opus, publication
voluntary adj = **intentional**, deliberate, planned, calculated, wilful ≠ **unintentional**; = **optional**, discretionary, up to the individual, open, unforced

V

voluptuous *adj* **1** of, contributing to pleasures of the senses **2** sexually alluring because of full, shapely figure

vomit ❶ *v* **-iting, -ited 1** eject (contents of stomach) through mouth ▷ *n* **2** matter vomited

voodoo *n* religion involving ancestor worship and witchcraft

voracious *adj* greedy, ravenous **voracity** *n*

vortex *n, pl* **-texes, -tices 1** whirlpool **2** whirling motion

vote ❶ *n* **1** formal expression of choice **2** individual pronouncement **3** right to give it **4** result of voting ▷ *v* **5** express, declare opinion, choice, preference etc. by vote

vouch *v* (usu. with *for*) guarantee **voucher** *n* **1** document to establish facts **2** ticket as substitute for cash

vow ❶ *n* **1** solemn promise, esp. religious one ▷ *v* **2** promise, threaten by vow

vowel *n* **1** any speech sound pronounced without stoppage or friction of the breath **2** letter standing for such sound, as *a, e, i, o, u*

voyage ❶ *n* **1** journey, esp. long one, by sea or air ▷ *v* **2** make voyage

vulcanize *v* treat (rubber) with sulphur at high temperature to increase its durability **vulcanization** *n*

vulgar ❶ *adj* **1** offending against good taste **2** common **vulgarity** *n*

vulnerable ❶ *adj* **1** capable of being physically or emotionally wounded or hurt **2** exposed, open to attack, persuasion etc. **vulnerability** *n*

vulture *n* large bird which feeds on carrion

      THESAURUS

≠ **obligatory**

vomit *v* = **be sick**, throw up (*Inf*), spew, heave, retch

vote *n* = **poll**, election, ballot, referendum, popular vote

vow *v* = **promise**, pledge, swear, commit, engage ▷ *n* = **promise**, commitment, pledge, oath, profession

voyage *n* = **journey**, trip, passage, expedition, crossing

vulgar *adj* = **tasteless**, common ≠ **tasteful**

vulnerable *adj* = **susceptible**, helpless, unprotected, defenceless, exposed ≠ **immune**; = **exposed**, open, unprotected, defenceless, accessible ≠ **well-protected**

V

W

WA 1 2 Washington **3 4** Western Australia

wacky *adj* **wackier, wackiest** (*Inf*) eccentric, funny

wad *n* **1** small pad of fibrous material **2** thick roll of banknotes ▷ *v* **3** pad, stuff etc. with wad

waddle *v* **1** walk like duck ▷ *n* **2** this gait

wade ❶ *v* walk through something that hampers movement, esp. water **wader** *n* person or bird that wades

wafer *n* thin, crisp biscuit

waffle¹ *n/v* (*Inf*) (use) long-winded and meaningless language

waffle² *n* kind of pancake

waft *v* **1** convey smoothly through air or water ▷ *n* **2** breath of wind **3** odour, whiff

wag ❶ *v* **wagging, wagged** **1** (cause to) move rapidly from side to side ▷ *n* **2** instance of wagging **3** (*Inf*) witty person **wagtail** *n* small bird with long tail

wage ❶ *n* **1** (*oft. pl*) payment for work done ▷ *v* **2** carry on

wager *n/v* bet

waggle *v/n* wag

wagon, waggon *n* **1** four-wheeled vehicle for heavy loads **2** railway freight truck

waif *n* homeless person, esp. child

wail ❶ *v/n* cry, lament

waist *n* **1** part of body between hips and ribs **2** various narrow central parts **waistcoat** *n* sleeveless garment worn under jacket or coat

wait ❶ *v* **1** stay in one place, remain inactive in expectation (of something) **2** be prepared (for something) **3** delay **4** serve in restaurant etc. ▷ *n* **5** act or period of waiting **waiter** *n* attendant on guests at hotel, restaurant etc.

waive ❶ *v* **1** forgo **2** not insist on

THESAURUS

waddle *v* = **shuffle**, totter, toddle, sway, wobble

wade *v* = **paddle**, splash, splash about, slop; = **walk through**, cross, ford, travel across, pitch in

wag *v* = **wave**, shake, waggle, stir, quiver ▷ *n* = **wave**, shake, quiver, vibration, wiggle; = **nod**, bob, shake

wage *n often plural* = **payment**, pay, remuneration, fee, reward ▷ *v*

= **engage in**, conduct, pursue, carry on, undertake

wail *v* = **cry**, weep, grieve, lament, howl ▷ *n* = **cry**, moan, howl, lament, yowl

wait *v* = **stay**, remain, stop, pause, rest ≠ **go** ▷ *n* = **delay**, gap, pause, interval, stay

waive *v* = **give up**, relinquish, renounce, forsake, drop ≠ **claim**

W

waiver n (written statement of) this act

wake¹ ❶ v **waking, woke, woken**
1 rouse from sleep 2 stir up ▷ n
3 vigil 4 watch beside corpse
waken v wake

wake² n track or path left by anything that has passed

walk ❶ v 1 (cause, assist to) move, travel on foot at ordinary pace
2 cross, pass through by walking
3 escort, conduct by walking ▷ n
4 act, instance of walking 5 path or other place or route for walking
walking stick stick used as support when walking **Walkman®** n small portable cassette player with headphones **walkover** n (Inf) easy victory

wall ❶ n 1 structure of brick, stone etc. serving as fence, side of building etc. 2 surface of one
3 anything resembling this ▷ v
4 enclose with wall 5 block up with wall **wallflower** n garden plant **wallpaper** n paper, usu. patterned, to cover interior walls
wallaby n, pl **-bies** Aust.

marsupial similar to and smaller than kangaroo

wallet ❶ n small folding case, esp. for paper money, documents etc.

wallop (Inf) ▷ v 1 beat soundly
2 strike hard ▷ n 3 stroke or blow

wallow v 1 roll (in liquid or mud)
2 revel (in) ▷ n 3 wallowing

walnut n 1 large nut with crinkled shell 2 tree it grows on 3 its wood

walrus n, pl **-ruses, -rus** large sea mammal with long tusks

waltz n 1 ballroom dance 2 music for it ▷ v 3 perform waltz

wampum n (US & Canad) shells woven together, formerly used by N American Indians for money and ornament

wan adj **wanner, wannest** pale, pallid

wand n stick, esp. as carried by magician etc.

wander ❶ v 1 roam, ramble 2 go astray, deviate ▷ n 3 wandering

wane ❶ v/n 1 decline 2 (of moon) decrease in size

wangle v (Inf) get by devious methods

───────────────────── THESAURUS ─────────────────────

wake¹ v = **awake**, stir, awaken, come to, arise ≠ **fall asleep**;
= **awaken**, arouse, rouse, waken
▷ n = **vigil**, watch, funeral, deathwatch

walk v = **stride**, stroll, go, move, step; = **escort**, take, see, show, partner ▷ n = **stroll**, hike, ramble, march, trek; = **gait**, step, bearing, carriage, tread; = **path**, footpath, track, way, road

wall n = **partition**, screen, barrier,

enclosure, blockade; = **barrier**, obstacle, barricade, obstruction, check

wallet n = **purse**, pocketbook, pouch, case, holder

wander v = **roam**, walk, drift, stroll, range ▷ n = **excursion**, walk, stroll, cruise, ramble

wane v = **decline**, weaken, diminish, fail, fade ≠ **grow**;
= **diminish**, decrease, dwindle
≠ **wax**

w

want ⓥ v 1 desire 2 lack ▷ n
3 desire 4 need 5 deficiency
wanted adj being sought, esp. by
police **wanting** adj 1 lacking
2 below standard

wanton adj 1 dissolute 2 without
motive 3 unrestrained

war ⓥ n 1 fighting between
nations 2 state of hostility
3 conflict, contest ▷ v 4 make war
warlike adj 1 of, for war 2 fond of
war **warrior** n fighter **warfare** n
hostilities **warhead** n part of
missile etc. containing explosives

warble v sing with trills **warbler**
n any of various kinds of small
songbirds

ward ⓥ n 1 division of city, hospital
etc. 2 minor under care of guardian
warder n jailer **ward off** avert,
repel

warden ⓥ n person in charge of

building, college etc.

wardrobe ⓥ n 1 piece of furniture
for hanging clothes in 2 person's
supply of clothes

ware n 1 goods 2 articles
collectively ▷ pl 3 goods for sale
warehouse n storehouse for
goods

warm ⓥ adj 1 moderately hot
2 serving to maintain heat
3 affectionate 4 enthusiastic ▷ v
5 make, become warm **warmth** n
1 mild heat 2 cordiality 3 intensity
of emotion **warm up** v 1 make or
become warmer 2 do preliminary
exercises

warn ⓥ v 1 put on guard
2 caution 3 give advance
information to **warning** n

warp ⓥ v 1 (cause to) twist (out of
shape) 2 pervert or be perverted

warrant ⓥ n 1 authority

——— THESAURUS ———

want v = **wish for**, desire, long for,
crave, covet ≠ **have**; = **need**,
demand, require, call for ▷ n
= **lack**, need, absence, shortage,
deficiency ≠ **abundance**;
= **poverty**, hardship, privation,
penury, destitution ≠ **wealth**;
= **wish**, will, need, desire,
requirement

war n = **conflict**, drive, attack,
fighting, fight ≠ **peace** ▷ v = **fight**,
battle, clash, wage war, campaign
≠ **make peace**

ward n = **room**, department, unit,
quarter, division; = **district**,
constituency, area, division, zone;
= **dependant**, charge, pupil, minor,
protégé

warden = **jailer**, prison officer,
guard, screw (Sl)

wardrobe n = **clothes cupboard**,
cupboard, closet, cabinet;
= **clothes**, apparel, attire

warm adj = **balmy**, mild,
temperate, pleasant, fine ≠ **cool**;
= **cosy**, snug, toasty (Inf),
comfortable, homely ▷ v = **warm
up**, heat, thaw (out), heat up
≠ **cool down**

warn v = **notify**, tell, remind,
inform, alert; = **advise**, urge,
recommend, counsel, caution

warp v = **distort**, bend, twist,
buckle, deform ▷ n = **twist**, bend,
defect, flaw, distortion

warrant v = **call for**, demand,

w

2 document giving authority ▷ *v*
3 guarantee **4** authorize, justify
warranty *n, pl* **-ties 1** guarantee
of quality of goods **2** security
warren *n* (burrows inhabited by)
colony of rabbits
warrigal *(Aust) n* **1 2** dingo ▷ *adj*
3 4 wild
warrior ⊕ *n* see WAR
wart *n* small hard growth on skin
wart hog kind of Afr. wild pig
wary ⊕ *adj* **warier, wariest**
watchful, cautious, alert
was past tense, first and third
person sing. of BE
wash ⊕ *v* **1** clean (oneself, clothes
etc.) with water, soap etc. **2** be
washable **3** move, be moved by
water **4** flow, sweep over, against
▷ *n* **5** act of washing **6** clothes
washed at one time **7** sweep of
water, esp. set up by moving ship
washable *adj* capable of being

washed without damage **washer**
n **1** one who, that which, washes
2 ring put under nut **washing** *n*
clothes to be washed **washout** *n*
(Inf) complete failure **wash up**
wash dishes and cutlery after meal
wasp *n* striped stinging insect
resembling bee
waste ⊕ *v* **1** expend uselessly
2 fail to take advantage **3** dwindle
4 pine away ▷ *n* **5** act of wasting
6 rubbish **7** desert ▷ *adj*
8 worthless, useless **9** desert
10 wasted **wasteful** *adj*
extravagant
watch ⊕ *v* **1** observe closely
2 guard **3** wait expectantly (for)
4 be on watch ▷ *n* **5** portable
timepiece for wrist, pocket etc.
6 state of being on the lookout
7 spell of duty **watchful** *adj*
watchdog *n* **1** dog kept to guard
property **2** person or group

——————————— THESAURUS ———————————

require, merit, rate; **= guarantee**,
declare, pledge, promise,
ensure ▷ *n* **= authorization**,
permit, licence, permission,
authority
warrior *n* **= soldier**, combatant,
fighter, gladiator, trooper
wary *adj* **= suspicious**, sceptical,
guarded, distrustful, chary
wash *v* **= clean**, scrub, sponge,
rinse, scour; **= launder**, clean, rinse,
dry-clean; **= rinse**, clean, scrub,
lather ▷ *n* **= laundering**, cleaning,
clean, cleansing, dip; **= backwash**,
slipstream, path, trail, train;
= splash, surge, swell, rise and fall,
undulation

waste *v* **= squander**, throw away,
blow *(Sl)*, lavish, misuse **≠ save** ▷ *n*
= squandering, misuse,
extravagance, frittering away,
dissipation **≠ saving**; **= rubbish**,
refuse, debris, scrap, litter ▷ *adj*
= unwanted, useless, worthless,
unused, leftover **≠ necessary**;
= uncultivated, wild, bare, barren,
empty **≠ cultivated**
watch *v* **= look at**, observe, regard,
eye, see; **= spy on**, follow, track,
monitor, keep an eye on ▷ *n*
= wristwatch, timepiece,
chronometer; **= guard**,
surveillance, observation, vigil,
lookout

w

guarding against inefficiency or illegality **watchman** n man guarding building etc., esp. at night **watchword** n 1 password 2 rallying cry

water ❶ n 1 transparent, colourless, odourless, tasteless liquid, substance of rain, river etc. 2 body of water 3 urine ▷ v 4 put water on or into 5 irrigate or provide with water 6 salivate 7 (of eyes) fill with tears **watery** adj 1 wet 2 weak **water closet** sanitary convenience flushed with water **watercolour** n 1 paint thinned with water 2 painting in this **watercress** n plant growing in clear ponds and streams **waterfall** n vertical descent of waters of river **water lily** plant that floats on surface of fresh water **waterlogged** adj saturated, filled with water **watermark** n faint translucent design in sheet of paper **watermelon** n melon with green skin and red flesh **water polo** team game played by swimmers with ball **waterproof** adj 1 not letting water through ▷ v 2 make waterproof ▷ n 3 waterproof garment **watershed** n 1 line

separating two river systems 2 divide **water-skiing** n sport of riding over water on skis towed by speedboat **watertight** adj 1 preventing water from entering or escaping 2 with no weak points **watt** n unit of electric power **wave** ❶ v 1 move to and fro, as hand in greeting or farewell 2 signal by waving 3 give, take shape of waves (as hair etc.) ▷ n 4 ridge and trough on water etc. 5 act, gesture of waving 6 vibration, as in radio waves 7 prolonged spell 8 upsurge 9 wavelike shapes in hair etc. **wavy** adj **wavelength** n distance between the same points of two successive waves **waver** ❶ v 1 hesitate, be irresolute 2 be, become unsteady **wax¹** ❶ v grow, increase **wax²** n 1 yellow, soft, pliable material made by bees 2 this or similar substance used for sealing, making candles etc. 3 waxy secretion of ear ▷ v 4 put wax on **waxy** adj like wax **way** ❶ n 1 manner 2 method 3 direction 4 path 5 passage 6 progress 7 state or condition

water n = **liquid**, H₂O; = **get wet**, cry, weep, become wet, exude water
wave v = **signal**, sign, gesture, gesticulate; = **guide**, point, direct, indicate, signal; = **brandish**, swing, flourish, wag, shake ▷ n = **gesture**, sign, signal, indication, gesticulation; = **ripple**, breaker,

swell, ridge, roller
waver v = **hesitate**, dither (chiefly Brit), vacillate, falter, fluctuate ≠ be decisive; = **flicker**, shake, tremble, wobble, quiver
wax¹ v = **increase**, grow, develop, expand, swell ≠ wane
way n = **method**, means, system, process, technique; = **manner**,

W

8 room for activity **wayfarer** n traveller, esp. on foot **waylay** v lie in wait for and accost, attack **wayside** n/adj (by) side or edge of road **wayward** adj capricious, perverse, wilful

WC water closet

we pron first person plural pronoun

weak ⊕ adj **1** lacking strength **2** irresolute **3** (of sound) faint **4** (of argument) unconvincing **5** unprotected, vulnerable **6** lacking flavour **weaken** v **weakling** n feeble creature **weakly** adj **1** weak **2** sickly ▷ adv **3** in weak manner **weakness** n

weal n streak left on flesh by blow of stick or whip

wealth ⊕ n **1** riches **2** abundance **wealthy** adj

wean v **1** accustom to food other than mother's milk **2** win over, coax away from

weapon n implement to fight with

wear ⊕ v **wearing, wore, worn** **1** have on the body **2** show **3** (cause to) become impaired by use **4** harass or weaken **5** last ▷ n **6** act of wearing **7** things to wear **8** damage caused by use **9** ability to resist effect of constant use

weary ⊕ adj **-rier, -riest 1** tired, exhausted, jaded **2** tiring **3** tedious ▷ v **4** make, become weary **weariness** n

weasel n small carnivorous mammal with long body and short legs

weather ⊕ n **1** day-to-day meteorological conditions, esp. temperature etc. of a place ▷ v **2** affect by weather **3** endure **4** resist **5** come safely through **weathercock** n revolving object

           THESAURUS

style, fashion, mode; *often plural* = **custom**, manner, habit, style, practice; = **route**, direction, course, road, path; = **journey**, approach, passage; = **distance**, length, stretch

weak adj = **feeble**, frail, debilitated, fragile, sickly ≠ **strong**; = **slight**, faint, feeble, pathetic, hollow; = **fragile**, brittle, flimsy, fine, delicate; = **unsafe**, exposed, vulnerable, helpless, unprotected ≠ **secure**

wealth n = **riches**, fortune, prosperity, affluence, money ≠ **poverty**; = **property**, capital, fortune

wear v = **be dressed in**, have on,

sport (Inf), put on; = **show**, present, bear, display, assume; = **deteriorate**, fray, wear thin ▷ n = **clothes**, things, dress, gear (Inf), attire; = **damage**, wear and tear, erosion, deterioration, attrition ≠ **repair**

weary adj = **tired**, exhausted, drained, worn out, done in (Inf) ≠ **energetic**; = **tiring**, arduous, tiresome, laborious, wearisome ≠ **refreshing** ▷ v = **grow tired**, tire, become bored

weather n = **climate**, conditions, temperature, forecast, outlook ▷ v = **withstand**, stand, survive, overcome, resist ≠ **surrender to**

W

to show which way wind blows

weave ❶ v **weaving, wove** 1 form into texture or fabric by interlacing, esp. on loom 2 construct 3 make one's way, esp. with side to side motion

web ❶ n 1 woven fabric 2 net spun by spider 3 membrane between toes of waterfowl, frogs etc.

wed ❶ v **wedding, wedded** 1 marry 2 unite closely **wedding** n marriage ceremony **wedlock** n marriage

wedge ❶ n 1 piece of wood, metal etc. tapering to a thin edge ▷ v 2 fasten, split with wedge 3 stick by compression or crowding

Wednesday n fourth day of the week

wee adj 1 small 2 little

weed n 1 plant growing where undesired ▷ v 2 clear of weeds **weedy** adj 1 full of weeds 2 weak

week n period of seven days

weekly adj/adv happening, done, published etc. once a week

weekday n any day of the week except Saturday or Sunday

weekend n Saturday and Sunday

weep ❶ v **weeping, wept** 1 shed tears (for) 2 grieve

weigh ❶ v 1 find weight of 2 consider 3 have weight 4 be burdensome **weight** n 1 measure of the heaviness of an object 2 quality of heaviness 3 heavy mass 4 object of known mass for weighing 5 importance, influence ▷ v 6 add weight to **weighting** n extra allowance paid in special circumstances

weir n river dam

weird ❶ adj 1 unearthly, uncanny 2 strange, bizarre

welcome ❶ v **-coming, -comed** 1 received gladly 2 freely permitted ▷ n 3 kindly greeting ▷ v 4 greet with pleasure 5 receive gladly

———————— **THESAURUS** ————————

weave v = **knit**, intertwine, plait, braid, entwine; = **zigzag**, wind, crisscross; = **create**, tell, recount, narrate, build

web n = **cobweb**, spider's web; = **mesh**, lattice

wed v = **get married to**, be united to ≠ **divorce**; = **get married**, marry, be united, tie the knot (Inf), take the plunge (Inf) ≠ **divorce**

wedge v = **squeeze**, force, lodge, jam, crowd ▷ n = **block**, lump, chunk

weep v = **cry**, shed tears, sob, whimper, mourn ≠ **rejoice**

weigh v = **have a weight of**, tip the scales at (Inf); often with **up** = **consider**, examine, contemplate, evaluate, ponder; = **compare**, balance, contrast, juxtapose, place side by side

weird adj = **strange**, odd, unusual, bizarre, mysterious ≠ **normal**; = **bizarre**, odd, strange, unusual, queer ≠ **ordinary**

welcome v = **greet**, meet, receive, embrace, hail ≠ **reject**; = **accept gladly**, appreciate, embrace, approve of, be pleased by ▷ n = **greeting**, welcoming, reception,

W

weld ❶ *v* **1** unite metal by softening with heat **2** unite closely ▷ *n* **3** welded joint **welder** *n*

welfare ❶ *n* wellbeing **welfare state** system in which government takes responsibility for wellbeing of citizens

well¹ ❶ *adv* **better, best 1** in good manner or degree **2** suitably **3** intimately **4** fully **5** favourably **6** kindly **7** to a considerable degree ▷ *adj* **8** in good health **9** satisfactory ▷ *interj* **10** exclamation of surprise, interrogation etc. **wellbeing** *n* state of being well, happy, or prosperous **well-disposed** *adj* inclined to be friendly **well-mannered** *adj* having good manners **well-off** *adj* fairly rich **well-read** *adj* having read much

well² ❶ *n* **1** hole sunk into the earth to reach water, gas, oil etc. **2** spring ▷ *v* **3** spring, gush

wellies *pl n* (*Inf*) wellingtons
wellingtons *pl n* high waterproof boots

welter *v* **1** roll or tumble ▷ *n* **2** turmoil, disorder

wench *n* young woman

wend *v* go, travel

went past tense of GO

were past tense of BE

werewolf *n* in folklore, person who can turn into a wolf

west *n* **1** part of sky where sun sets **2** part of country etc. lying to this side ▷ *adj* **3** that is toward or in this region ▷ *adv* **4** to the west **westerly** *adj/adv* **western** *adj* **westernize** *v* adapt to customs and culture of the West **westward** *adj/adv* **westwards** *adv*

wet ❶ *adj* **wetter, wettest 1** having water or other liquid on a surface or being soaked in it **2** rainy **3** (of paint, ink etc.) not yet dry ▷ *v* **4** make wet ▷ *n* **5** moisture, rain

---

                     THESAURUS

acceptance, hail ≠ **rejection**
weld *v* = **join**, link, bond, bind, connect; = **unite**, combine, blend, unify, fuse

welfare *n* = **wellbeing**, good, interest, health, security

well¹ *adv* = **skilfully**, expertly, adeptly, professionally, correctly ≠ **badly**; = **satisfactorily**, nicely, smoothly, successfully, pleasantly ≠ **badly**; = **thoroughly**, completely, fully, carefully, effectively; = **intimately**, deeply, fully, profoundly ≠ **slightly**; = **favourably**, highly, kindly, warmly,

enthusiastically ≠ **unfavourably**; = **considerably**, easily, very much, significantly, substantially; = **fully**, highly, greatly, amply, very much; = **possibly**, probably, certainly, reasonably, conceivably ▷ *adj* = **healthy**, sound, fit, blooming, in fine fettle ≠ **ill**; = **satisfactory**, right, fine, pleasing, proper ≠ **unsatisfactory**

well² *n* = **hole**, bore, pit, shaft ▷ *v* = **flow**, spring, pour, jet, surge

wet *adj* = **damp**, soaking, saturated, moist, watery ≠ **dry**;

w

wet suit close-fitting rubber suit worn by divers etc.

whack ❶ v 1 strike with sharp resounding sound ▷ n 2 such blow

wharf ❶ n, pl **wharves, wharfs** platform at harbour, on river etc. for loading and unloading ships

what pron 1 which thing 2 that which 3 request for statement to be repeated ▷ adj 4 which 5 as much as 6 how great, surprising etc. ▷ adv 7 in which way

whatever pron 1 anything which 2 of what kind it may be

whatsoever adj at all

wheat n cereal plant yielding grain from which bread is chiefly made

wheedle v coax, cajole

wheel ❶ n 1 circular frame or disc revolving on axle 2 anything like a wheel in shape or function 3 act of turning ▷ v 4 (cause to) turn as if on axis 5 (cause to) move on or as if on wheels 6 (cause to) change course, esp. in opposite direction

wheelbarrow n barrow with one wheel **wheelchair** n chair mounted on large wheels, used by invalids

wheeze v 1 breathe with whistling noise ▷ n 2 this sound

whelk n edible shellfish

when adv 1 at what time ▷ conj 2 at the time that 3 although 4 since ▷ pron 5 at which time

whenever adj/conj at whatever time

where adv/conj 1 at what place 2 at or to the place in which

whereabouts adv/conj 1 in what, which place ▷ n 2 present position

whereas conj 1 considering that 2 while, on the contrary **whereby** conj by which **whereupon** conj at which point **wherever** adv at whatever place **wherewithal** n necessary funds, resources etc.

whet v **whetting, whetted** 1 sharpen 2 stimulate

whether conj introduces the first of two alternatives

whey n watery part of milk left after cheese making

which adj 1 used in requests for a selection from alternatives ▷ pron 2 person or thing referred to

whichever pron

whiff ❼ n 1 brief smell or suggestion of 2 puff of air

while conj 1 in the time that 2 in

= **rainy**, damp, drizzly, showery, raining ≠ **sunny**; (Inf) = **feeble**, soft, weak, ineffectual, weedy (Inf) ▷ v = **moisten**, spray, dampen, water, soak ≠ **dry** ▷ n = **rain**, drizzle ≠ **fine weather**; = **moisture**, water, liquid, damp, humidity ≠ **dryness**

whack (Inf) v = **strike**, hit, belt (Inf), bang, smack ▷ n = **blow**, hit,

stroke, belt (Inf), bang; (Inf) = **share**, part, cut (Inf), bit, portion; (Inf) = **attempt**, go (Inf), try, turn, shot (Inf)

wharf n = **dock**, pier, berth, quay, jetty

wheel n = **disc**, ring, hoop ▷ v = **push**, trundle, roll

whiff n = **smell**, hint, scent, sniff, aroma

W

spite of the fact that, although
3 whereas ▷ v **4** pass (time) idly
▷ n **5** period of time

whim ❶ n sudden, passing fancy
whimsy, whimsey n fanciful
mood **whimsical** adj **1** fanciful
2 full of whims

whimper v **1** cry or whine softly
2 complain in this way ▷ n **3** such
cry or complaint

whine ❶ n **1** high-pitched
plaintive cry **2** peevish complaint
▷ v **3** utter this

whinge v **1** complain ▷ n
2 complaint

whinny v **-nying, -nied 1** neigh
softly ▷ n **2** soft neigh

whip ❶ n **1** lash attached to
handle for urging or punishing ▷ v
2 strike with whip **3** beat (cream,
eggs) to a froth **4** pull, move
quickly

whippet n dog like small
greyhound

whirl ❶ v **1** swing rapidly round
2 move rapidly in a circular course

3 drive at high speed ▷ n
4 whirling movement **5** confusion,
bustle, giddiness **whirlpool** n
circular current, eddy **whirlwind** n
1 wind whirling round while
moving forwards ▷ adj **2** very
quick

whirr, whir v **1** (cause to) fly, spin
etc. with buzzing sound ▷ n **2** this
sound

whisk ❶ v **1** brush, sweep, beat
lightly **2** move, remove quickly
3 beat to a froth ▷ n **4** light brush
5 egg-beating implement

whisker n **1** any of the long stiff
hairs at side of mouth of cat or
other animal ▷ pl **2** hair on a man's
face

whisky n, pl **-kies** (Irish, Canad, US
whiskey) spirit distilled from
fermented cereals

whisper ❶ v **1** speak in soft,
hushed tones, without vibration of
vocal cords **2** rustle ▷ n **3** such
speech **4** trace or suspicion
5 rustle

— THESAURUS —

whim n = **impulse**, caprice, fancy,
urge, notion

whine v = **cry**, sob, wail, whimper,
sniffle ▷ n = **cry**, moan, sob,
wail, whimper; = **drone**, note,
hum

whip n = **lash**, cane, birch, crop,
scourge ▷ v = **lash**, cane, flog,
beat, strap; (Inf) = **dash**, shoot, fly,
tear, rush; = **whisk**, beat, mix
vigorously, stir vigorously; = **incite**,
drive, stir, spur, work up

whirl v = **spin**, turn, twist, rotate,
twirl; = **rotate**, roll, twist, revolve,

swirl ▷ n = **revolution**, turn, roll,
spin, twist; = **bustle**, round, series,
succession, flurry; = **confusion**,
daze, dither (chiefly Brit), giddiness,
spin

whisk v = **flick**, whip, sweep,
brush; = **beat**, mix vigorously, stir
vigorously, whip, fluff up ▷ n
= **flick**, sweep, brush, whip;
= **beater**, mixer, blender

whisper v = **murmur**, breathe
≠ **shout**; = **rustle**, sigh, hiss, swish
▷ n = **murmur**, mutter, mumble,
undertone; (Inf) = **rumour**, report,

w

whist n card game

whistle v 1 produce shrill sound by forcing breath through rounded, nearly closed lips 2 make similar sound 3 utter, summon etc. by whistle ▷ n 4 such sound 5 any similar sound 6 instrument to make it

white ❶ adj 1 of the colour of snow 2 pale 3 light in colour 4 having a light-coloured skin ▷ n 5 colour of snow 6 white pigment 7 white part 8 clear fluid round yolk of egg 9 (with cap.) white person **whiten** v **whitewash** n 1 substance for whitening walls etc. ▷ v 2 apply this 3 cover up, gloss over

whither adv (Obs) 1 to what place 2 to which

whittle ❶ v 1 cut, carve with knife 2 pare away

whizz, whiz n **whizzing, whizzed** 1 loud hissing sound ▷ v 2 move with such sound, or make it

who pron 1 what or which person or persons 2 that **whoever** pron who, any one or every one that

whodunnit, whodunit n (Inf) detective story

whole ❶ adj 1 containing all

elements or parts 2 not defective or imperfect 3 healthy ▷ n 4 complete thing or system

wholly adv **wholehearted** adj 1 sincere 2 enthusiastic

wholesale n 1 sale of goods in large quantities to retailers ▷ adj 2 dealing by wholesale 3 extensive

wholesome adj producing good effect, physically or morally

whom pron objective form of WHO

whoop n/v (make) shout or cry expressing excitement etc.

whooping cough infectious disease marked by convulsive coughing with loud whoop or drawing in of breath

whopper n (Inf) unusually large thing **whopping** adj

whore ❶ n prostitute

whose pron of whom or which

why adv for what cause or reason

wick n strip of thread feeding flame of lamp or candle with oil, grease etc.

wicked adj 1 evil, sinful 2 very bad

wicker adj made of woven cane

wicket n 1 set of cricket stumps 2 small gate

wide ❶ adj 1 having a great extent from side to side, broad 2 having

——————— THESAURUS ———————

gossip, innuendo, insinuation; = **rustle**, sigh, hiss, swish

white adj = **pale**, wan, pasty, pallid, ashen

whittle v = **carve**, cut, hew, shape, trim

whole adj = **complete**, full, total, entire, uncut ≠ **partial**; = **undamaged**, intact, unscathed,

unbroken, untouched ≠ **damaged**

whore n = **prostitute**, tart (Inf), streetwalker, call girl

wide adj = **spacious**, broad, extensive, roomy, commodious ≠ **confined**; = **baggy**, full, loose, ample, billowing; = **expanded**, dilated, distended ≠ **shut**; = **broad**, extensive, wide-ranging, large,

considerable distance between
3 spacious **4** vast **5** far from the
mark **6** opened fully ▷ *adv* **7** to the
full extent **8** far from the intended
target **widen** *v* **width** *n* breadth
widespread *adj* extending over a
wide area

widow *n* **1** woman whose spouse
is dead and who has not married
again ▷ *v* **2** make a widow of

widower *n* man whose spouse is
dead and who has not married
again

wield ❶ *v* hold and use

wife ❶ *n, pl* **wives** female partner
in marriage

wig *n* artificial hair for the head

wiggle *v* **1** (cause to) move jerkily
from side to side ▷ *n* **2** wiggling

wild ❶ *adj* **1** not tamed or
domesticated **2** not cultivated
3 savage **4** stormy **5** uncontrolled
6 random **7** excited **8** rash

wildcat *n* any of various
undomesticated feline animals

wild-goose chase search that has

little chance of success **wildlife** *n*
wild animals and plants collectively

wildebeest *n* gnu

wilderness ❶ *n* desert, waste
place

wildfire *n* **1** raging, uncontrollable
fire **2** anything spreading, moving
fast

wilful *adj* **1** obstinate **2** self-willed
3 intentional

will¹ ❶ *n, past* **would 1** faculty of
deciding what one will do
2 purpose **3** volition
4 determination **5** wish
6 directions written for disposal of
property after death ▷ *v* **7** wish
8 intend **9** leave as legacy **willing**
adj **1** ready **2** given cheerfully

willingly *adv* **willingness** *n*

willpower *n* ability to control
oneself, one's actions, impulses

will² *v, past* **would** forms future
tense and indicates intention or
conditional result

will-o'-the-wisp *n* elusive
person or thing

⸻ THESAURUS ⸻

sweeping ≠ **restricted** ▷ *adv*
= **fully**, completely ≠ **partly**; = **off
target**, astray, off course, off the
mark

wield *v* = **brandish**, flourish,
manipulate, swing, use; = **exert**,
maintain, exercise, have, possess

wife *n* = **spouse**, partner, mate,
bride, better half (*humorous*)

wild *adj* = **untamed**, fierce,
savage, ferocious, unbroken
≠ **tame**; = **uncultivated**,
natural ≠ **cultivated**; = **stormy**,
violent, rough, raging, choppy;

= **excited**, crazy (*Inf*), enthusiastic,
raving, hysterical
≠ **unenthusiastic**;
= **uncontrolled**, disorderly,
turbulent, wayward, unruly
≠ **calm**; = **mad** (*Inf*), furious,
fuming, infuriated, incensed

wilderness *n* = **wilds**, desert,
wasteland, uncultivated region

will¹ *n* = **determination**, drive,
purpose, commitment, resolution;
= **wish**, mind, desire, intention,
fancy; = **choice**, prerogative,
volition ▷ *v* = **wish**, want, prefer,

w

willow n **1** tree with long thin flexible branches **2** its wood **willowy** adj slender, supple

willy-nilly adv/adj (occurring) whether desired or not

wilt ⊕ v (cause to) become limp, lose strength etc.

wimp n (Inf) feeble person

wimple n garment framing face, worn by nuns

win ⊕ v **winning, won 1** be successful, victorious **2** get by labour or effort ▷ n **3** victory, esp. in games **winner** n **winning** adj charming **winnings** pl n sum won in game, betting etc. **win-win** adj guaranteeing a favourable outcome for all involved a win-win situation

wince ⊕ v **1** flinch, draw back, as from pain etc. ▷ n **2** this act

winch n **1** machine for hoisting or hauling using cable wound round drum ▷ v **2** move (something) by using a winch

wind¹ ⊕ n **1** air in motion **2** breath **3** flatulence ▷ v **4** render short of breath, esp. by blow etc. **windward** n side against which wind is blowing **windy** adj **1** exposed to wind **2** flatulent **windfall** n

1 unexpected good luck **2** fallen fruit **wind farm** collection of wind-driven turbines for generating electricity **wind instrument** musical instrument played by blowing or air pressure **windmill** n wind-driven apparatus with fanlike sails for raising water, crushing grain etc. **windpipe** n passage from throat to lungs **windscreen** n protective sheet of glass etc. in front of driver or pilot **windsurfing** n sport of sailing standing up on board with single sail

wind² ⊕ v **1** twine **2** meander **3** twist round, coil **4** wrap **5** make ready for working by tightening spring ▷ n **6** act of winding **7** single turn of something wound

window n **1** hole in wall (with glass) to admit light, air etc. **2** anything similar in appearance or function **3** area for display of goods behind glass of shop front **window-shopping** n looking at goods without intending to buy

windshield n the US and Canadian name for WINDSCREEN

wine n **1** fermented juice of grape etc. **2** purplish-red colour

---

THESAURUS

desire, see fit; **= bequeath**, give, leave, transfer, gift

wilt v **= droop**, wither, sag, shrivel; **= weaken**, languish, droop

win v **= be victorious in**, succeed in, prevail in, come first in, be the victor in ≠ **lose**; **= be victorious**, succeed, triumph, overcome, prevail ≠ **lose** ▷ n **= victory**, success, triumph, conquest

≠ **defeat**

wince v **= flinch**, start, shrink, cringe, quail ▷ n **= flinch**, start, cringe

wind¹ n **= air**, blast, hurricane, breeze, draught; **= flatulence**, gas; **= breath**, puff, respiration;

wind² v **= meander**, turn, bend, twist, curve; **= wrap**, twist, reel, curl, loop

W

wing ❶ n 1 feathered limb used by bird in flying 2 organ of flight of insect or some animals 3 main lifting surface of aircraft 4 side area of building, stage etc. 5 group within political party etc. ▷ v 6 fly 7 move, go very fast 8 disable, wound slightly **winger** n (Sport) player positioned at side of pitch

wink ❶ v 1 close and open (one eye) rapidly, esp. to indicate friendliness or as signal 2 twinkle ▷ n 3 act of winking

winkle n edible sea snail **winkle out** extract, prise out

winsome adj charming

winter n 1 coldest season ▷ v 2 pass, spend the winter **wintry** adj 1 of, like winter 2 cold

wipe ❶ v 1 rub so as to clean ▷ n 2 wiping **wiper** n 1 one that wipes 2 automatic wiping apparatus 1 **wipe out** erase 2 annihilate 3 (Sl) kill

wire n 1 metal drawn into thin, flexible strand 2 something made of wire, e.g. fence 3 telegram ▷ v 4 provide, fasten with wire 5 send by telegraph **wiring** n system of

wires **wiry** adj 1 like wire 2 lean and tough **wire-haired** adj (of various breeds of dog) with short stiff hair

wise adj 1 having intelligence and knowledge 2 sensible **wisdom** n (accumulated) knowledge, learning **wisdom tooth** large tooth cut usu. after age of twenty

wish ❶ v 1 desire ▷ n 2 expression of desire 3 thing desired **wishful** adj too optimistic

wishy-washy adj (Inf) insipid, bland

wisp n 1 light, delicate streak, as of smoke 2 twisted handful, usu. of straw etc. 3 stray lock of hair **wispy** adj

wistful adj 1 longing, yearning 2 sadly pensive

wit ❶ n 1 ability to use words, ideas in clever, amusing way 2 person with this ability 3 intellect 4 understanding 5 humour **witticism** n witty remark **wittingly** adv 1 on purpose 2 knowingly **witty** adj

witch ❶ n 1 person, usu. female, who practises magic 2 ugly,

wing n = **faction**, group, arm, section, branch ▷ v = **fly**, soar, glide, take wing; = **wound**, hit, clip

wink v = **blink**, bat, flutter; = **twinkle**, flash, shine, sparkle, gleam ▷ n = **blink**, flutter, blink, glimmer

wipe v = **clean**, polish, brush, rub, sponge; = **erase**, remove ▷ n = **rub**, brush

wish n = **desire**, want, hope, urge,

intention ≠ **aversion** ▷ v = **want**, feel, choose, please, desire

wit n = **humour**, quips, banter, puns, repartee ≠ **seriousness**; = **humorist**, card (Inf), comedian, wag, joker; often plural = **cleverness**, sense, brains, wisdom, common sense ≠ **stupidity**

witch n = **enchantress**, magician, hag, crone, sorceress

W

wicked woman **3** fascinating woman **witchcraft** n **witch doctor** in certain societies, man appearing to cure or cause injury, disease by magic

with prep **1** in company or possession of **2** against **3** in relation to **4** through **5** by means of **within** prep/adv in, inside

without prep **1** lacking **2** (Obs) outside

withdraw ⊕ v -drawing, -drew, -drawn draw back or out **withdrawal** n **withdrawn** adj reserved, unsociable

wither ⊕ v (cause to) wilt, dry up, decline **withering** adj (of glance etc.) scornful

withhold ⊕ v -holding, -held **1** restrain **2** refrain from giving

withstand ⊕ v -standing, -stood oppose, resist, esp. successfully

witness ⊕ n **1** one who sees something **2** testimony **3** one who gives testimony ▷ v **4** give testimony **5** see **6** attest **7** sign

(document) as genuine

wizard ⊕ n **1** sorcerer, magician **2** (Inf) virtuoso **wizardry** n

wizened adj shrivelled, wrinkled

wobble ⊕ v **1** move unsteadily **2** sway ▷ n **3** unsteady movement **wobbly** adj

woe ⊕ n grief **woebegone** adj looking sorrowful **woeful** adj **1** sorrowful **2** pitiful **3** wretched

wok n bowl-shaped Chinese cooking pan

wolf n, pl **wolves 1** wild predatory doglike animal ▷ v **2** eat ravenously

wolverine n carnivorous mammal inhabiting Arctic regions

woman ⊕ n, pl **women 1** adult human female **2** women collectively **womanish** adj effeminate **womanize** v (of man) indulge in many casual affairs **womanly** adj of, proper to woman

womb n female organ in which young develop before birth

wombat n Aust. burrowing marsupial with heavy body, short

withdraw v = **remove**, take off, pull out, extract, take away

wither v = **wilt**, decline, decay, disintegrate, perish ≠ **flourish**; = **waste**, decline, shrivel

withhold v = **keep secret**, refuse, hide, reserve, retain ≠ **reveal**

withstand v = **resist**, suffer, bear, oppose, cope with ≠ **give in to**

witness n = **observer**, viewer, spectator, looker-on, watcher ▷ v = **see**, view, watch, note, notice;

= **countersign**, sign, endorse, validate

wizard n = **magician**, witch, shaman, sorcerer, occultist

wobble v = **shake**, rock, sway, tremble, teeter; = **tremble**, shake ▷ n = **unsteadiness**, shake, tremble

woe n = **misery**, distress, grief, agony, gloom ≠ **happiness**

woman n = **lady**, girl, female, sheila (Aust & NZ Inf), vrou (S Afr) ≠ **man**

W

legs and dense fur

won past tense and past participle of WIN

wonder ❶ n 1 emotion excited by amazing or unusual thing 2 marvel, miracle ▷ v 3 be curious about 4 feel amazement **wonderful** adj 1 remarkable 2 very fine **wondrous** adj 1 inspiring wonder 2 strange

wont n 1 custom ▷ adj 2 accustomed

woo ❶ v court, seek to marry

wood ❶ n substance of trees, timber **firewood** tract of land with growing trees **wooded** adj having many trees **wooden** adj 1 made of wood 2 without expression **woody** adj **woodland** n woods, forest **woodpecker** n bird which searches tree trunks for insects **wood pigeon** large pigeon of Europe and Asia **woodwind** adj/n (of) wind instruments of orchestra **woodworm** n insect larva that bores into wood

woof n barking noise

wool ❶ n 1 soft hair of sheep, goat etc. 2 yarn spun from this **woollen** adj **woolly** adj 1 of wool 2 vague, muddled ▷ n 3 woollen garment

wop-wops pl n (NZ, Inf) remote rural areas

word ❶ n 1 smallest separate meaningful unit of speech or writing 2 term 3 message 4 brief remark 5 information 6 promise 7 command ▷ v 8 express in words, esp. in particular way **wordy** adj using too many words **word processor** keyboard, computer and VDU for electronic organization and storage of text

wore past tense of WEAR

work ❶ n 1 labour 2 employment 3 occupation 4 something made or accomplished 5 production of art or science ▷ pl 6 factory 7 total of person's deeds, writings etc. 8 mechanism of clock etc. ▷ v 9 (cause to)

— THESAURUS —

wonder v = **think**, question, puzzle, speculate, query; = **be amazed**, stare, marvel, be astonished, gape ▷ n = **amazement**, surprise, admiration, awe, fascination; = **phenomenon**, sight, miracle, spectacle, curiosity

woo cultivate; = **court**, pursue

wood n = **timber**, planks, planking, lumber (US); **woods = woodland**, forest, grove, thicket, copse

wool n = **fleece**, hair, coat

word n = **term**, name, expression;

= **chat**, tête-à-tête, talk, discussion, consultation; = **comment**, remark, utterance; = **message**, news, report, information, notice; = **promise**, guarantee, pledge, vow, assurance; = **command**, order, decree, bidding, mandate ▷ v = **express**, say, state, put, phrase

work v = **be employed**, be in work; = **labour**, sweat, slave, toil, slog (away) ≠ **relax**; = **function**, go, run, operate, be in working order ≠ **be out of order**; = **succeed**, operate **10** make, shape **11** apply effort **12** labour **13** be employed **14** turn out successfully **15** ferment **workable** adj **worker** n **workaholic** n person addicted to work **working class** social class consisting of wage earners, esp. manual **working-class** adj **workman** n **manual worker workmanship** n **1** skill of workman **2** way thing is finished **workshop** n place where things are made

world ⊕ n **1** the universe **2** the planet earth **3** sphere of existence **4** mankind **5** any planet **6** society **worldly** adj **1** earthly **2** absorbed in pursuit of material gain

worm n **1** small limbless creeping snakelike creature **2** anything resembling worm in shape or movement ▷ pl **3** (disorder caused by) infestation of worms, esp. in intestines ▷ v **4** crawl **5** insinuate (oneself) **6** extract (secret) craftily

7 rid of worms

worn ⊕ past participle of WEAR

worry ⊕ v **-rying, -ried 1** be (unduly) concerned **2** trouble, pester, harass **3** (of dog) seize, shake with teeth ▷ n **4** (cause of) anxiety, concern **worried** adj

worse adj/adv comparative of BAD or BADLY **worsen** v make, grow worse **worst** adj/adv superlative of BAD or BADLY

worship ⊕ v **-shipping, -shipped 1** show religious devotion to **2** adore **3** love and admire ▷ n **4** act of worshipping **worshipful** adj **worshipper** n

worsted n **1** woollen yarn ▷ adj **2** made of woollen yarn

worth ⊕ adj **1** having or deserving to have value specified **2** meriting ▷ n **3** excellence **4** merit, value **5** usefulness **6** quantity to be had for given sum **worthless** adj **worthwhile** adj worth the time, effort etc. involved **worthy** adj

— THESAURUS —

work out, pay off (Inf), be successful, be effective; **= handle**, move, excite, manipulate, rouse ▷ n **= employment**, business, job, trade, duty ≠ **play**; **= effort**, industry, labour, sweat, toil ≠ **leisure**; **= task**, jobs, projects, commissions, duties; **= handiwork**, doing, act, feat, deed

world n **= earth**, planet, globe; **= mankind**, man, everyone, the public, everybody; **= sphere**, area, field, environment, realm

worn adj **= ragged**, frayed, shabby, tattered, tatty

worry v **= be anxious**, be concerned, be worried, obsess, brood ≠ **be unconcerned**; **= trouble**, upset, bother, disturb, annoy ≠ **soothe** ▷ n **= anxiety**, concern, fear, trouble, unease ≠ **peace of mind**; **= problem**, care, trouble, bother, hassle (Inf)

worship v **= revere**, praise, honour, adore, glorify ≠ **dishonour**; **= love**, adore, idolize, put on a pedestal ≠ **despise** ▷ n **= reverence**, praise, regard, respect, honour

worth n **= value**, price, rate, cost,

W

1 virtuous **2** meriting

would *v* expressing wish, intention, probability: past tense of WILL **would-be** *adj* wishing, pretending to be

wound[1] ❶ *n* **1** injury, hurt from cut, stab etc. ▷ *v* **2** inflict wound on, injure **3** pain

wound[2] past tense and past participle of WIND[2]

wove past tense of WEAVE **woven** past participle of WEAVE

wow *interj* exclamation of astonishment

wowser *n* (*Aust & NZ, sl*) **1** puritanical person **2** teetotaller

wraith *n* apparition

wrangle ❶ *v* **1** quarrel (noisily) **2** dispute ▷ *n* **3** noisy quarrel **4** dispute

wrap ❶ *v* **wrapping, wrapped** **1** cover, esp. by putting something round **2** put round ▷ *n* **3** loose garment **wrapper** *n* covering **wrapping** *n* material used to wrap

wrath ❶ *n* anger

wreak *v* **1** inflict (vengeance) **2** cause

wreath *n* something twisted into ring form, esp. band of flowers etc. as memorial or tribute on grave etc. **wreathe** *v* **1** form into wreath **2** surround **3** wind round

wreck ❶ *n* **1** destruction of ship **2** wrecked ship **3** ruin ▷ *v* **4** cause wreck of **wreckage** *n*

wren *n* kind of small songbird

wrench ❶ *v* **1** twist **2** distort **3** seize forcibly **4** sprain ▷ *n* **5** violent twist **6** tool for twisting or screwing **7** spanner

wrest *v* **1** take by force **2** twist violently

wrestle ❶ *v* **1** fight (esp. as sport) by grappling and trying to throw down **2** strive (with) **3** struggle ▷ *n* **4** wrestling **wrestler** *n* **wrestling** *n*

wretch *n* **1** despicable person **2** miserable creature **wretched** *adj* **1** miserable, unhappy

--- THESAURUS ---

estimate ≠ **worthlessness**; = **merit**, value, quality, importance, excellence ≠ **unworthiness**

wound[1] *n* = **injury**, cut, hurt, trauma (*Pathology*), gash ▷ *v* = **injure**, cut, wing, hurt, pierce; = **offend**, hurt, annoy, sting, mortify

wrangle *v* = **argue**, fight, row, dispute, disagree ▷ *n* = **argument**, row, dispute, quarrel, squabble

wrap *v* = **cover**, enclose, shroud, swathe, encase ▷ *n* = **cloak**, cape, stole, mantle, shawl

wrath *n* = **anger**, rage, temper, fury, resentment ≠ **satisfaction**

wreck *v* = **destroy**, break, smash, ruin, devastate ≠ **build** ▷ *n* = **shipwreck**, hulk

wrench *v* = **twist**, force, pull, tear, rip; = **sprain**, strain, rick ▷ *n* = **twist**, pull, rip, tug, jerk; = **sprain**, strain, twist; = **blow**, shock, upheaval, pang; = **spanner**, adjustable spanner

wrestle *v* = **fight**, battle, struggle, combat, grapple

2 worthless

wriggle v **1** move with twisting action, squirm ▷ n **2** this action

wring v **wringing, wrung 1** twist **2** extort **3** squeeze out

wrinkle ❶ n **1** slight ridge or furrow on skin etc. ▷ v **2** make, become wrinkled **wrinkly** adj

wrist n joint between hand and arm

writ ❶ n written command from law court or other authority

write ❶ v **writing, wrote, written 1** mark paper etc. with symbols or words **2** compose **3** send a letter **4** set down in words **5** communicate in writing **writer** n **1** one who writes **2** author

writing n **write-off** n (Inf) something damaged beyond repair

writhe v twist, squirm in or as in pain etc.

wrong ❶ adj **1** not right or good **2** not suitable **3** incorrect **4** mistaken **5** not functioning properly ▷ n **6** that which is wrong **7** harm ▷ v **8** do wrong to **9** think badly of without justification **wrongful** adj **wrongly** adv

wrote past tense of WRITE

wrought adj (of metals) shaped by hammering or beating

wrung past tense and past participle of WRING

wry adj **wrier, wriest** turned to one side, contorted dryly humorous

——— THESAURUS ———

wrinkle n = **line**, fold, crease, furrow, crow's-foot ▷ v = **crease**, gather, fold, crumple, furrow ≠ **smooth**

writ n = **summons**, document, decree, indictment, court order

write v = **record**, scribble, inscribe, set down, jot down

wrong adj = **amiss**, faulty, unsatisfactory, not right, defective; = **incorrect**, mistaken, false,

inaccurate, untrue; = **inappropriate**, incorrect, unsuitable, unacceptable, undesirable ≠ **correct**; = **bad**, criminal, illegal, evil, unlawful ≠ **moral** ▷ adv = **incorrectly**, badly, wrongly, mistakenly, erroneously ≠ **correctly** ▷ n = **offence**, injury, crime, error, sin ≠ **good deed** ▷ v = **mistreat**, abuse, hurt, harm, cheat ≠ **treat well**

W

xenophobia *n* hatred, fear, of strangers or aliens

Xerox *n* **1** machine for copying printed material ▷ *v* **2** copy with Xerox

Xmas *n* short for CHRISTMAS

X-ray, x-ray *n* **1** stream of radiation capable of penetrating solid bodies ▷ *v* **2** photograph by X-rays

xylophone *n* musical instrument of wooden bars which sound when struck

ya *interj* (S Afr) yes

yacht *n* vessel propelled by sail or power

yak *n* ox of Central Asia

yakka *n* (Aust & NZ, Inf) work

yam *n* sweet potato

yank ❶ *v* 1 jerk, tug 2 pull quickly ▷ *n* 3 quick tug

yap *v* **yapping, yapped** 1 bark (as small dog) 2 talk idly

yard¹ *n* unit of length, .915 metre
yardstick *n* standard of measurement or comparison

yard² *n* piece of enclosed ground, oft. adjoining building and used for some specific purpose

yarn ❶ *n* 1 spun thread 2 tale

yawn *v* 1 open mouth wide, esp. in sleepiness 2 gape ▷ *n* 3 act of yawning

ye *pron* (Obs) you

year *n* 1 time taken by one revolution of earth round sun, about 365 days 2 twelve months
yearling *n* animal one year old
yearly *adv* 1 every year, once a year ▷ *adj* 2 happening once a year

yearn ❶ *v* feel longing, desire

yeast *n* substance used as fermenting agent, esp. in raising bread

yebo *interj* (S Afr, Inf) yes

yell ❶ *v/n* 1 shout 2 scream

yellow *adj* 1 of the colour of lemons, gold etc. 2 (Inf) cowardly ▷ *n* 3 this colour **yellow fever** acute infectious tropical disease

yelp *v/n* (produce) quick, shrill cry

yen ❶ *n* (Inf) longing, craving

yeoman *n, pl* **-men** (Hist) farmer cultivating his own land

yes *interj* expresses consent, agreement, or approval

yesterday *n, adv* 1 (on) day before today 2 (in) recent past

yet ❶ *adv* 1 now 2 still 3 besides 4 hitherto ▷ *conj* 5 but, at the

yank *n* = **pull**, tug, jerk, snatch, hitch

yarn *n* = **thread**, fibre, cotton, wool; (Inf) = **story**, tale, anecdote, account, narrative

yearn *v often with* **for** = **long**, desire, hunger, ache, crave

yell *v* = **scream**, shout, cry out, howl, call out ≠ **whisper** ▷ *n* = **scream**, cry, shout, roar, howl

≠ **whisper**

yen *n* = **longing**, desire, craving, yearning, passion

yet *adv* = **so far**, until now, up to now, still, as yet; = **now**, right now, just now, so soon; = **still**, in addition, besides, to boot, into the bargain ▷ *conj* = **nevertheless**, still, however, for all that, notwithstanding

same time, nevertheless

yeti n apelike creature said to inhabit Himalayas

yew n **1** evergreen tree with dark leaves **2** its wood

yield ❶ v **1** give or return **2** produce **3** give up, surrender ▷ n **4** amount produced

yob, yobbo, yobbo ❶ n (Inf) bad-mannered aggressive youth

yodel v **-delling, -delled** warble in falsetto tone

yoga n Hindu system of certain physical and mental exercises

yogurt, yoghurt n thick, custard-like preparation of curdled milk

yoke n **1** wooden bar put across the necks of two animals to hold them together **2** various objects like a yoke in shape or use **3** fitted part of garment, esp. round neck, shoulders **4** bond or tie **5** domination ▷ v **6** put yoke on **7** couple, unite

yokel n (old-fashioned) country dweller

yolk n yellow central part of egg

Yorkshire pudding baked batter made from flour, milk and eggs

you pron **1** refers to person or persons addressed **2** refers to unspecified person or persons

young ❶ adj **1** not far advanced in growth, life or existence **2** not yet old ▷ n **3** offspring **youngster** n child

your adj of, belonging to you **yours** pron **yourself** pron emphatic or reflexive form of you

youth ❶ n **1** state or time of being young **2** young man **3** young people **youthful** adj

YT Yukon Territory

Yule n Christmas season

yuppie n young highly-paid professional person ▷ adj of, like yuppies

——————————————— THESAURUS ———————————————

yield v = **bow**, submit, give in, surrender, succumb; = **relinquish**, resign, hand over, surrender, turn over ≠ **retain** ▷ n = **produce**, crop, harvest, output

yob, yobbo n = **thug**, hooligan, lout, hoon (Aust & NZ Sl), ruffian

young adj = **immature**, juvenile, youthful, little, green ≠ **old** ▷ pl n = **offspring**, babies, litter, family, issue ≠ **parents**

youth n = **immaturity**, adolescence, boyhood or girlhood, salad days ≠ **old age**; = **boy**, lad, youngster, kid (Inf), teenager ≠ **adult**

zany *adj* **zanier, zaniest** comical, funny in unusual way

zap *v* **zapping, zapped** (*Sl*) attack, kill or destroy

zeal ⊕ *n* **1** fervour **2** keenness, enthusiasm **zealot** *n* **1** fanatic **2** enthusiast **zealous** *adj*

zebra *n* striped Afr. animal like a horse

zenith *n* **1** point of the heavens directly above an observer **2** summit **3** climax

zephyr *n* soft, gentle breeze

zero ⊕ *n, pl* **-ros, -roes 1** nothing **2** figure o **3** point on graduated instrument from which positive and negative quantities are reckoned **4** the lowest point

zest *n* **1** enjoyment **2** excitement, interest, flavour **3** peel of orange or lemon

zigzag *n* **1** line or course with sharp turns in alternating directions ▷ *v* **2** move along in zigzag course

zinc *n* bluish-white metallic element

zip, zipper ⊕ *n* **1** fastener with two rows of teeth that are closed and opened by a sliding clip **2** short whizzing sound **3** (*Inf*) energy, vigour ▷ *v* **4** fasten with zip **5** move with zip

zither *n* flat stringed instrument

zodiac *n* imaginary belt of the heavens along which the sun, moon and chief planets appear to move

zombie, zombi *n* person appearing lifeless

zone ⊕ *n* region with particular characteristics or use

zoo *n, pl* **zoos** place where live animals are kept for show

zoology *n* study of animals **zoological** *adj* **zoologist** *n*

zoom ⊕ *v* move, rise very rapidly move with buzzing or humming sound

zucchini *n* the US and Canadian name for COURGETTE

—— THESAURUS ——

zeal *n* = **enthusiasm**, passion, zest, spirit, verve ≠ **apathy**

zero *n* = **nought**, nothing, nil; = **rock bottom**, the bottom, an all-time low, a nadir, as low as you can get

zip *n* (*Inf*) = **energy**, drive, vigour, verve, zest ≠ **lethargy**

zone *n* = **area**, region, section, sector, district

zoom *v* = **speed**, shoot, fly, rush, flash

Z